W9-CPR-191

THE OLD TESTAMENT STUDY BIBLE

---

1 & 2 KINGS

WORLD LIBRARY PRESS INC.
Springfield, Missouri, U.S.A.

Contributors

VERSE-BY-VERSE COMMENTARY

1 Kings—F. W. Farrar, D.D.
Gregory A. Lint, M.Div.
W. E. Nunnally, Ph.D.
2 Kings—William H. Barnes, Th.D.
Stanley M. Horton, Th.D.

VARIOUS VERSIONS

Todd C. Harder, B.A. Craig M. Froman, M.A.

REVIEW BOARD

Gleason L. Archer, Jr., Ph.D.
Roger D. Cotton, Th.D.
Stanley M. Horton, Th.D.
W. E. Nunnally, Ph.D.
Samuel J. Schultz, Th.D.

ASSISTANT EDITOR

Brian D. Rogers, M.Div.

TECHNICAL ASSISTANCE

Editorial Team: Faye Faucett (editorial assistant); Jess L. Leeper, B.A., James E. Talkington, B.A., Dennis E. Waldrop, M.Div., James R. Wright (Hebrew assistance); Pamela S. Behling, B.S., Sherri L. Campbell, B.S., Jill M. Canaday, B.A., Chuck J. Goldberg, M.Div., Rachel L. Hammar, Kim Kelley, Sheila R. Mixer, B.S., Wade W. Pettenger, B.S.

Computer Consultant: Martin D. Crossland, Ph.D.

Art Director: Terry Van Someren, B.F.A.

Table of Contents

Introduction

This volume of the *Old Testament Study Bible* is part of a set entitled *The Complete Biblical Library: Old Testament.* It is designed to provide the information needed for a basic understanding of the Old Testament—useful for scholars but also for students and laypeople.

The Complete Biblical Library: Old Testament series consists of a fifteen-volume *Study Bible* and a seven-volume *Hebrew-English Dictionary,* which are closely linked. Information about the *Study Bible's* features are found below. The *Hebrew-English Dictionary* (HED) lists all the Hebrew words of the Old Testament in alphabetical order, with an article explaining the background, significance and meaning of the words. The HED also provides a concordance showing each place the words appear in the Old Testament, a list of synonyms and related words, and many other features for a full understanding of each word.

FEATURES OF THE STUDY BIBLE

The *Study Bible* is a combination of study materials which will help both scholar and layperson achieve a better understanding of the Old Testament and its language. Most of these helps are available in various forms elsewhere, but bringing them together in combination will save many hours of research. Many scholars do not have in their personal libraries all the volumes necessary to provide the information so readily available here.

The Complete Biblical Library accomplishes an unusual task: to help scholars in their research and to make available to laypersons the tools to acquire knowledge which, up to this time, has been available only to scholars. Following are the major divisions of the *Study Bible:*

Overview

Each volume contains an encyclopedic survey of the Old Testament Book. It provides a general outline, discusses matters about which there may be a difference of opinion and provides background information regarding the history, cultures, literature and philosophy of the era covered by the Book.

Interlinear

Following the principle of providing help for both the scholar and layperson, a unique interlinear has been supplied. Most interlinears, if not all, give the Hebrew text and meanings of the words. This interlinear contains five parts:

1. *Hebrew Text.* This is the original language of the Old Testament as we have it today.

2. *Grammatical Forms.* These are shown above each Hebrew word, beneath its assigned number. Each word's part of speech is identified (constructs being italicized). This information is repeated, along with the Hebrew word, in the *Hebrew-English Dictionary* where more details may be found.

3. *Transliteration.* No other interlinears provide this. Its purpose is to familiarize laypersons with the proper pronunciation of Hebrew words so they will feel comfortable when using them in teaching situations. Information on pronunciation is found on page 10, which shows the Hebrew alphabet.

4. *Translation.* The basic meaning of each Hebrew word is found beneath it. Rather than merely compiling past interlinears, a fresh translation has been made.

5. *Assigned Numbers.* The unique numbering system of *The Complete Biblical Library* makes cross-reference study between the *Study Bible* and the *Hebrew-English Dictionary* the ultimate in simplicity. Each Hebrew word has been assigned a number.

The *Hebrew-English Dictionary* then follows the same cross-referencing plan with each word listed in alphabetical sequence and labeled with the proper number. If further study on a certain word is desired, information can be found by locating its number in the *Dictionary.*

Various Versions

The various versions section contains a vast comparison of the Old Testament versions. The King James Version is shown in boldface type; then from more than thirty other versions, various ways the Hebrew phrase may be translated can be found. The Hebrew language of ancient times is such a rich language that, to obtain the full meaning of words, several synonyms may be needed.

Verse-by-Verse Commentary

Many scholars have combined their knowledge and skills to provide a reliable commentary. Providing a basic understanding of every verse in the Old Testament, the commentary opens up the nuances of the Hebrew Old Testament.

HEBREW TRANSLATION

No word-for-word translation can be fully "literal" and still express all the nuances of the original language. Rather, the purpose is to help the reader find the English word which most correctly expresses the original Hebrew word in that particular context. The Hebrew language is so rich in meaning that the same word may have a slightly different meaning in another context.

Language idioms offer a special translation problem. Idioms are expressions that have a meaning which cannot be derived from the conjoined meanings of its elements. The Hebrew language abounds in such phrases which, when translated literally, provide insight, and even humor, to the English reader of the pictorial nature of Hebrew.

LITERARY AND BIBLICAL STANDARDS

Hundreds of qualified scholars and specialists in particular fields have participated in producing *The Complete Biblical Library*. Great care has been taken to maintain high standards of scholarship and ethics, involving scholars in Review Boards for the *Study Bible* and the *Hebrew-English Dictionary*. There has been particular concern about giving proper credit for citations from other works, and writers have been instructed to show care in this regard. Any deviation from this principle has been inadvertent and unintentional.

Obviously, with writers coming from widely differing backgrounds, there are differences of opinion as to how to interpret certain passages. But, the focus of *The Complete Biblical Library* is always from a conservative and evangelical standpoint, upholding Scripture as the inspired Word of God. When there are strong differences in the interpretations of a particular passage, we have felt it best to present the contrasting viewpoints.

STUDY HELPS

As you come to the Scripture section of this volume, you will find correlated pages for your study. The facing pages are designed to complement each other, so you will have a better understanding of the Word of God. Each two-page spread will deal with a group of verses.

First is the interlinear with its fivefold helps: (1) the Hebrew text in which the Old Testament was written; (2) the transliteration, showing how to pronounce each word; (3) the translation of each word; (4) an assigned number (you will need this number to learn more about the word in the *Hebrew-English Dictionary*, companion to the *Study Bible*); and (5) the grammatical form.

The second part of each two-page spread contains two features. The various versions section provides an expanded understanding of the various ways Hebrew words or phrases can be translated. The phrase from the King James Version appears in boldface print, then other meaningful ways the Hebrew language has been translated follow. This feature will bring you the riches of the language of the Old Testament.

The verse-by-verse commentary refers to each verse giving a sufficient basic explanation. Significant viewpoints are discussed in addition to the author's.

THE HEBREW ALPHABET

א	aleph	’ (glottal stop)
ב	beth	b, v
ג	gimel	g, gh
ד	daleth	d, dh
ה	he	h
ו	waw	w, v
ז	zayin	z
ח	heth	ch
ט	teth	t̲ (hardened)
י	yodh	y
כ, ךְ, ך	kaph	k, kh
ל	lamedh	l
מ, ם	mem	m
נ, ן	nun	n
ס	samekh	s̲ (hardened)
ע	ayin	‘ (aspiration)
פ, ף	pe	p, ph
צ, ץ	tsade	ts
ק	qoph	q
ר	resh	r
שׂ	sin	s
שׁ	shin	sh
ת	taw	t, th

INTERLINEAR COMPONENTS

A & B: Number

The first line of each record of the interlinear is a numeral which refers to the *Hebrew-English Dictionary*. The numbers should be referenced *only* by the digits before the decimal. Most words have an ordinary numeral. Only the verbs have the extended system.

The digits after the decimal refer to the standard verb chart found in Hebrew grammars. The first digit after the decimal refers to the “mood” of the verb (simple, passive, causative, intensive, reflexive); the second refers to the “tense” (perfect, imperfect, jussive, imperative, infinitive or participle); the third refers to the person, gender and number (such as 3rd masculine singular).

C: Location or Grammar

The second line of the interlinear is the description of the grammatical construction of the Hebrew word. Describing a Hebrew word in this manner is called locating the word. You will notice there is often more than one word written as a single Hebrew word. This is because related words are often joined. A full listing of abbreviations and a brief explanation may be found at the end of the book.

D: Hebrew

This is the original language of the Old Testament as we have it today. The Hebrew text of the interlinear is a comparative text, provided by The Original Word Publishers of Roswell, Georgia.

E: Transliteration

This is the key to pronouncing the word. The transliteration matches that which is found in the Septuagint research of the *New Testament Greek-English Dictionary* of *The Complete Biblical Library.*

F: Translation

This is a fresh translation prepared by the executive editor and the commentary writer.

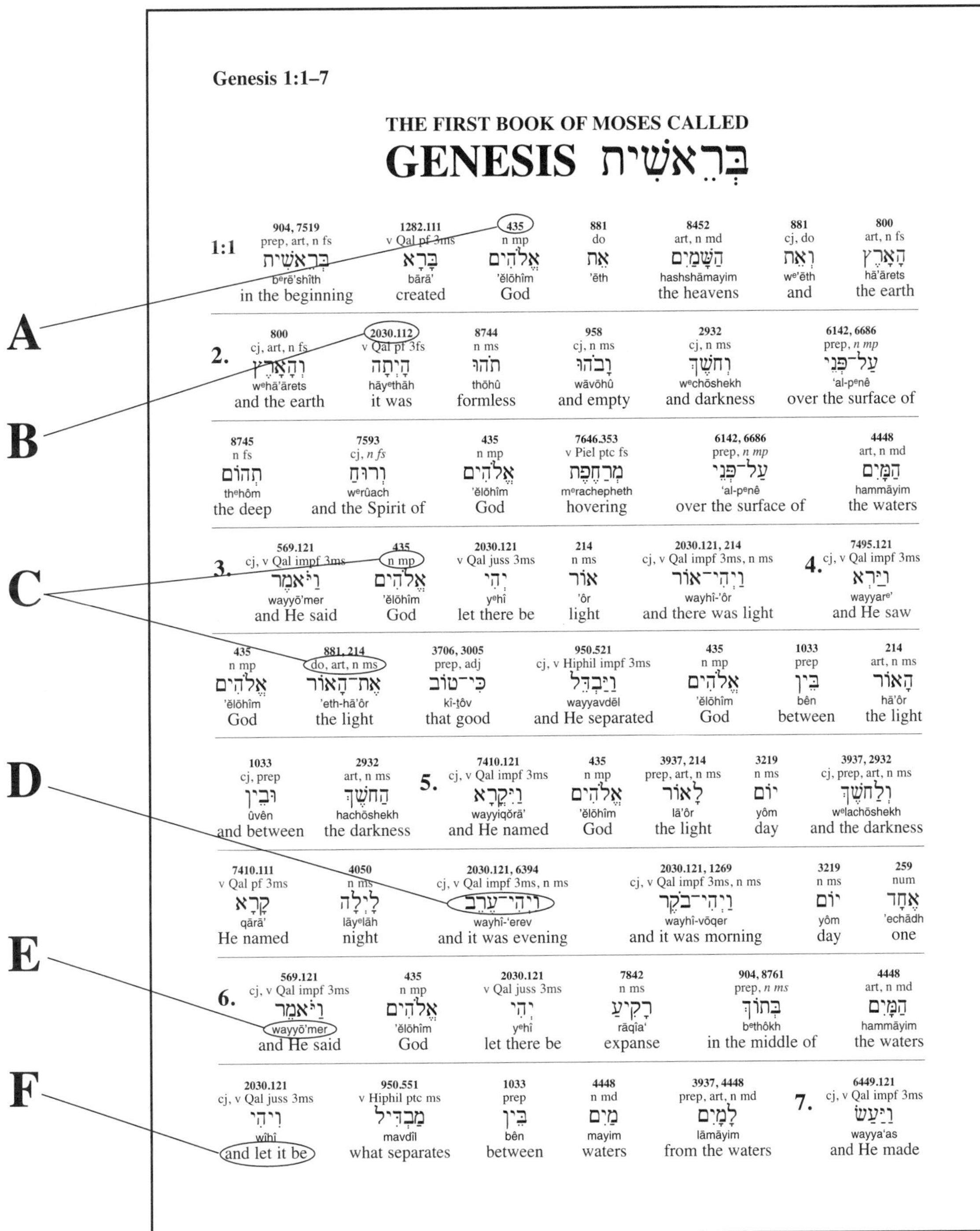

Genesis 1:1–7

THE FIRST BOOK OF MOSES CALLED

GENESIS בְּרֵאשִׁית

1:1	904, 7519	1282.111	435	881	8452	881	800
	prep, art, n fs	v Qal pf 3ms	n mp	do	art, n md	cj, do	art, n fs
	בְּרֵאשִׁית	בָּרָא	אֱלֹהִים	אֵת	הַשָּׁמַיִם	וְאֵת	הָאָרֶץ
	berē'shîth	bārā'	'ĕlōhîm	'ēth	hashshāmayim	we'ēth	hā'ārets
	in the beginning	created	God		the heavens	and	the earth

2.	800	2030.112	8744	958	2932	6142, 6686
	cj, art, n fs	v Qal pf 3fs	n ms	cj, n ms	cj, n ms	prep, *n mp*
	וְהָאָרֶץ	הָיְתָה	תֹהוּ	וָבֹהוּ	וְחֹשֶׁךְ	עַל־פְּנֵי
	wehā'ārets	hāyethāh	thōhû	wāvōhû	wechōshekh	'al-penê
	and the earth	it was	formless	and empty	and darkness	over the surface of

8745	7593	435	7646.353	6142, 6686	4448
n fs	cj, *n fs*	n mp	v Piel ptc fs	prep, *n mp*	art, n md
תְהוֹם	וְרוּחַ	אֱלֹהִים	מְרַחֶפֶת	עַל־פְּנֵי	הַמָּיִם
thehôm	werûach	'ĕlōhîm	merachepheth	'al-penê	hammāyim
the deep	and the Spirit of	God	hovering	over the surface of	the waters

3.	569.121	435	2030.121	214	2030.121, 214	4.	7495.121
	cj, v Qal impf 3ms	n mp	v Qal juss 3ms	n ms	cj, v Qal impf 3ms, n ms		cj, v Qal impf 3ms
	וַיֹּאמֶר	אֱלֹהִים	יְהִי	אוֹר	וַיְהִי־אוֹר		וַיַּרְא
	wayyō'mer	'ĕlōhîm	yehî	'ôr	wayhî-'ôr		wayyare'
	and He said	God	let there be	light	and there was light		and He saw

435	881, 214	3706, 3005	950.521	435	1033	214
n mp	do, art, n ms	prep, adj	cj, v Hiphil impf 3ms	n mp	prep	art, n ms
אֱלֹהִים	אֶת־הָאוֹר	כִּי־טוֹב	וַיַּבְדֵּל	אֱלֹהִים	בֵּין	הָאוֹר
'ĕlōhîm	'eth-hā'ôr	kî-ṭôv	wayyavdēl	'ĕlōhîm	bên	hā'ôr
God	the light	that good	and He separated	God	between	the light

1033	2932	5.	7410.121	435	3937, 214	3219	3937, 2932
cj, prep	art, n ms		cj, v Qal impf 3ms	n mp	prep, art, n ms	n ms	cj, prep, art, n ms
וּבֵין	הַחֹשֶׁךְ		וַיִּקְרָא	אֱלֹהִים	לָאוֹר	יוֹם	וְלַחֹשֶׁךְ
ûvên	hachōshekh		wayyiqrā'	'ĕlōhîm	lā'ôr	yôm	welachōshekh
and between	the darkness		and He named	God	the light	day	and the darkness

7410.111	4050	2030.121, 6394	2030.121, 1269	3219	259
v Qal pf 3ms	n ms	cj, v Qal impf 3ms, n ms	cj, v Qal impf 3ms, n ms	n ms	num
קָרָא	לָיְלָה	וַיְהִי־עֶרֶב	וַיְהִי־בֹקֶר	יוֹם	אֶחָד
qārā'	lāyelāh	wayhî-'erev	wayhî-vōqer	yôm	'echādh
He named	night	and it was evening	and it was morning	day	one

6.	569.121	435	2030.121	7842	904, 8761	4448
	cj, v Qal impf 3ms	n mp	v Qal juss 3ms	n ms	prep, *n ms*	art, n md
	וַיֹּאמֶר	אֱלֹהִים	יְהִי	רָקִיעַ	בְּתוֹךְ	הַמָּיִם
	wayyō'mer	'ĕlōhîm	yehî	rāqîa'	bethôkh	hammāyim
	and He said	God	let there be	expanse	in the middle of	the waters

2030.121	950.551	1033	4448	3937, 4448	7.	6449.121
cj, v Qal juss 3ms	v Hiphil ptc ms	prep	n md	prep, art, n md		cj, v Qal impf 3ms
וִיהִי	מַבְדִּיל	בֵּין	מַיִם	לַמָּיִם		וַיַּעַשׂ
wîhî	mavdîl	bên	mayim	lāmāyim		wayya'as
and let it be	what separates	between	waters	from the waters		and He made

THE BOOK OF

1 KINGS

Expanded Interlinear
Various Versions
Verse-by-Verse Commentary

THE BOOK OF

1 KINGS מְלָכִים א

1:1	4567	1784	2290.111	971.111	904, 3219	3803.326
	cj, art, n ms	pn	v Qal pf 3ms	v Qal pf 3ms	prep, art, n mp	cj, v Piel impf 3mp, ps 3ms
	וְהַמֶּלֶךְ	דָּוִד	זָקֵן	בָּא	בַּיָּמִים	וַיְכַסֻּהוּ
	wehammelekh	dāwidh	zāqēn	bā'	bayyāmîm	waykhassuhû
	now the king	David	he was old	he had gone	in the days	and they covered him

904, 933	3940	3285.121	3937		569.126	3937
prep, art, n mp	cj, neg part	v Qal impf 3ms	prep, ps 3ms	2.	cj, v Qal impf 3mp	prep, ps 3ms
בַּבְּגָדִים	וְלֹא	יִחַם	לוֹ		וַיֹּאמְרוּ	לוֹ
babbeghādhîm	welō'	yicham	lô		wayyō'merû	lô
with the clothing	but not	he was warm	for himself		and they said	to him

5860	1272.326	3937, 112	4567	5472	1359	6198.112
n mp, ps 3ms	v Piel juss 3mp	prep, n ms, ps 1cs	art, n ms	n fs	n fs	cj, v Qal pf 3fs
עֲבָדָיו	יְבַקְשׁוּ	לַאדֹנִי	הַמֶּלֶךְ	נַעֲרָה	בְתוּלָה	וְעָמְדָה
'ăvādhâv	yevaqŏshû	la'dhōnî	hammelekh	na'ărāh	vethûlāh	we'āmedhāh
his servants	let them seek	for my lord	the king	a young woman	a virgin	and she will stand

3937, 6686	4567	2030.122, 3937	5725.153	8311.112	904, 2536
prep, *n mp*	art, n ms	cj, v Qal juss 3fs, prep, ps 3ms	v Qal act ptc fs	cj, v Qal pf 3fs	prep, n ms, ps 2ms
לִפְנֵי	הַמֶּלֶךְ	וּתְהִי־לוֹ	סֹכֶנֶת	וְשָׁכְבָה	בְחֵיקֶךָ
liphnê	hammelekh	ûthehî-lô	sōkheneth	weshākhevāh	vechêqekhā
before	the king	and may she be to him	an attendant	and she will lie down	in your bosom

2657.111	3937, 112	4567		1272.326	5472	3413
cj, v Qal pf 3ms	prep, n ms, ps 1cs	art, n ms	3.	cj, v Piel impf 3mp	n fs	adj
וְחַם	לַאדֹנִי	הַמֶּלֶךְ		וַיְבַקְשׁוּ	נַעֲרָה	יָפָה
wecham	la'dhōnî	hammelekh		wayvaqŏshû	na'ărāh	yāphāh
and he will be warm	for my lord	the king		and they searched for	a young woman	beautiful

904, 3725	1397	3547	4834.126	881, 50	8208
prep, *n ms*	*n ms*	pn	cj, v Qal impf 3mp	do, pn	art, pn
בְּכֹל	גְּבוּל	יִשְׂרָאֵל	וַיִּמְצְאוּ	אֶת־אֲבִישַׁג	הַשּׁוּנַמִּית
bekhōl	gevûl	yisrā'ēl	wayyimtse'û	'eth-'ăvîshagh	hashshûnammîth
over the entirety of	the territory of	Israel	and they found	Abishag	the Shunammite

971.526	881	3937, 4567		5472	3413	5912, 4108
cj, v Hiphil impf 3mp	do, ps 3fs	prep, art, n ms	4.	cj, art, n fs	adj	adv, adv
וַיָּבִאוּ	אֹתָהּ	לַמֶּלֶךְ		וְהַנַּעֲרָה	יָפָה	עַד־מְאֹד
wayyāvi'û	'ōthāhh	lammelekh		wehanna'ărāh	yāphāh	'adh-me'ōdh
and they brought	her	to the king		and the young woman	beautiful	until very

2030.122	3937, 4567	5725.153	8664.322	4567	3940
cj, v Qal impf 3fs	prep, art, n ms	v Qal act ptc fs	cj, v Piel impf 3fs, ps 3ms	cj, art, n ms	neg part
וַתְּהִי	לַמֶּלֶךְ	סֹכֶנֶת	וַתְּשָׁרְתֵהוּ	וְהַמֶּלֶךְ	לֹא
wattehî	lammelekh	sōkheneth	watteshārethēhû	wehammelekh	lō'
and she became	to the king	an attendant	and she ministered to him	and the king	not

3156.111		135	1158, 2389	5558.751	3937, 569.141
v Qal pf 3ms, ps 3fs	5.	cj, pn	*n ms*, pn	v Hithpael ptc ms	prep, v Qal inf con
יְדָעָהּ		וַאֲדֹנִיָּה	בֶן־חַגִּית	מִתְנַשֵּׂא	לֵאמֹר
yedhā'āhh		wa'ădhōnîyāh	ven-chaggîth	mithnassē'	lē'mōr
he had relations with her		and Adonijah	the son of Haggith	exalting himself	saying

1:1. Now king David was old and stricken in years; and they covered him with clothes, but he gat no heat: ... far along in years, *KJVII* ... advanced in years, *Berkeley* ... though they put covers over him, his body was cold, *BB* ... Although he was covered with blankets, he couldn't keep warm, *Beck* ... he obtained no warmth, *Darby*.

2. Wherefore his servants said unto him, Let there be sought for my lord the king a young virgin: ... Let us seek for your Majesty a young maiden, *Fenton* ... a young girl, *JB* ... a young woman, *NCV* ... His attendants said to him, Let us find a young virgin, *REB*.

and let her stand before the king, and let her cherish him, and let her lie in thy bosom, that my lord the king may get heat: ... attend the king, and be a nurse and lie at your breast, and warm your Majesty, *Fenton* ... to wait on the king and look after him; she will lie close beside you and this will keep my lord the king warm, *JB* ... be a companion unto him, *MAST* ... take care of him, *Moffatt* ... If she sleeps with your royal majesty, you will be kept warm, *NAB*.

3. So they sought for a fair damsel throughout all the coasts of Israel, and found Abishag a Shunammite, and brought her to the king: ... beautiful maiden throughout all the territory of Israel, *RSV* ... they looked for a fair girl throughout all the borders of Israel, *KJVII* ... for a fair young girl, they saw Abishag, *BB* ... they looked for a beautiful girl in the whole country of Israel, *Beck* ... After searching everywhere, *NCV*.

4. And the damsel was very fair, and cherished the king, and ministered to him: ... the girl was very beautiful, and she cared for the king and served him, *NCV* ... she took care of the king and waited on him, *NEB* ... the young woman was very lovely, *NKJV* ... She became the king's attendant and served him, *NRSV* ... she became the king's nurse, *RSV*.

but the king knew her not: ... had no intimate relations with her, *NIV* ... did not have sexual relations with her, *NCV* ... had no intercourse with her, *NEB*.

5. Then Adonijah the son of Haggith exalted himself, saying, I will be king: ... lifting himself up in pride, said, I will become king, *BB* ... kept promoting himself and say-

---

The hearts of kings are in Thy rule and governance, and Thou dost dispose and turn them as it seemeth best to thy godly wisdom.

1:1–4. Apparently he could not rise. There was something startling to see: a chasm cleft between David the warrior and David the invalid king in his last days. Even by the partner of his guilt, who had become his favorite queen (1:15), David could only be addressed with periphrases and in the third person. His servants advised, "Let there be sought for my lord the king a young virgin: and let her stand before the king, and let her cherish him and let her lie in thy bosom, that my lord the king may get heat." Bathsheba could only speak to him in such terms as, "Didst not thou, my lord, O king, swear unto thy handmaid?" and even she, when she entered the sick-chamber of his decrepitude, prostrated herself and did obeisance (1:16). Every other word of her speech was interladen with "my lord the king" and "my lord, O king"; and when she left "the presence," she again bowed herself with her face to the earth and did reverence to the king (Ps. 45:11; cf. 2 Sam. 9:6; Est. 3:2–5; 1 Chr. 29:20) with the words, "May my lord, King David, live for ever." The anointed dignity of the prophet who had once so boldly rebuked David's worst crime did not exempt him from the same ceremony, and he too went into the inner chamber bowing before the king.

The darkest elements of a polygamous household would show themselves in the unhappy family of David. David's eldest son was Amnon, the son of Ahinoam of Jezreel; his second, Daniel or Chileab, son of Abigail (2 Sam. 3:3), the wife of Nebal of Carmel; the third, Absalom, son of Maacah, daughter of Talmai, King of Geshur; the fourth, Adonijah, the son of Haggith. Shephatiah and Ithream were the sons of two other wives, and these six sons were born to David in Hebron. When he became king in Jerusalem, he had four sons by Bathsheba, born after the one who died in infancy, and at least nine other sons by various wives, besides his daughter Tamar, sister of Absalom. He had other sons by his concubines. Most of these sons are unknown. Some of them probably died in childhood. David provided for others by making them priests. His line, down to the days of Jeconiah, was continued in the descendants of Solomon, and afterwards in those of the otherwise unknown Nathan. The elder sons, born to him in the days of his more fervent youth, became the authors of the tragedies which laid waste his house. They were youths of splendid beauty, and, as they bore the proud title of "the king's sons," they were from their earliest years encircled by luxury and adulation.

The consequences which followed the onset of David's illness were frightful beyond precedent. David must have learned by experience the truth of

603	4566.125	6449.121	3937	7681	6821	2675
pers pron	v Qal impf 1cs	cj, v Qal impf 3ms	prep, ps 3ms	n ms	cj, n mp	cj, num
אֲנִי	אֶמְלֹךְ	וַיַּעַשׂ	לוֹ	רֶכֶב	וּפָרָשִׁים	וַחֲמִשִּׁים
'ănî	'emlōkh	wayya'as	lô	rekhev	ûphārāshîm	wachmishshîm
I	I will become king	and he made	for himself	chariots	and horsemen	and fifty

382	7608.152	3937, 6686		3940, 6321.111	1	4623, 3219
n ms	v Qal act ptc mp	prep, n mp, ps 3ms	6.	cj, neg part, v Qal pf 3ms, ps 3ms	n ms, ps 3ms	prep, n mp, ps 3ms
אִישׁ	רָצִים	לְפָנָיו		וְלֹא־עֲצָבוֹ	אָבִיו	מִיָּמָיו
'îsh	rātsîm	lephānâv		welō'-'ătsāvô	'āvîw	mîyāmâv
men	running	before him		and he did not displease him	his father	since his days

3937, 569.141	4211	3722	6449.113	1612, 2000	3005, 8717	4108
prep, v Qal inf con	intrg	adv	v Qal pf 2ms	cj, cj, pers pron	*adj*, n ms	adv
לֵאמֹר	מַדּוּעַ	כָּכָה	עָשִׂיתָ	וְגַם־הוּא	טוֹב־תֹּאַר	מְאֹד
lē'mōr	maddûa'	kākhāh	'āsîthā	wegham-hû'	ṭôv-tō'ar	me'ōdh
saying	why	thus	have you done	and also he	beautiful of form	very

881	3314.112	313	54		2030.126	1745	6196	3200
cj, do, ps 3ms	v Qal pf 3fs	adv	pn	7.	cj, v Qal impf 3mp	n mp, ps 3ms	prep	pn
וְאֹתוֹ	יָלְדָה	אַחֲרֵי	אַבְשָׁלוֹם		וַיִּהְיוּ	דְבָרָיו	עִם	יוֹאָב
we'ōthô	yāledhāh	'achrê	'avshālôm		wayyihyû	dhevārâv	'im	yô'āv
and him	she had borne	after	Absalom		and they were	his matters	with	Joab

1158, 7152	6196	55	3669	6038.126	313	135
n ms, pn	cj, prep	pn	art, n ms	cj, v Qal impf 3mp	adv	pn
בֶּן־צְרוּיָה	וְעִם	אֶבְיָתָר	הַכֹּהֵן	וַיַּעְזְרוּ	אַחֲרֵי	אֲדֹנִיָּה
ben-tserûyāh	we'im	'evyāthār	hakkōhēn	wayya'ăzrû	'achrê	'ădhōnîyāh
the son of Zeruiah	and with	Abiathar	the priest	and they helped	after	Adonijah

	6923	3669	1172	1158, 3179	5600	5204	8483
8.	cj, pn	art, n ms	cj, pn	*n ms*, pn	cj, pn	art, n ms	cj, pn
	וְצָדוֹק	הַכֹּהֵן	וּבְנָיָהוּ	בֶּן־יְהוֹיָדָע	וְנָתָן	הַנָּבִיא	וְשִׁמְעִי
	wetsādhôq	hakkōhēn	ûvenāyāhû	ven-yehôyādhā'	wenāthān	hannāvî'	weshim'î
	but Zadok	the priest	and Benaiah	the son of Jehoiada	and Nathan	the prophet	and Shimei

7760	1399	866	3937, 1784	3940	2030.116	6196, 135
pn	cj, art, n mp	rel pron	prep, pn	neg part	v Qal pf 3cp	prep, pn
וְרֵעִי	וְהַגִּבּוֹרִים	אֲשֶׁר	לְדָוִד	לֹא	הָיוּ	עִם־אֲדֹנִיָּהוּ
werē'î	wehaggibbôrîm	'ăsher	ledhāwidh	lō'	hāyû	'im-'ădhōnîyāhû
and Rei	and the mighty men	who	to David	not	they were	with Adonijah

	2159.121	135	6887	1267	4968	6196	63	2201
9.	cj, v Qal impf 3ms	pn	n fs	cj, n ms	cj, n ms	prep	*n fs*	art, pn
	וַיִּזְבַּח	אֲדֹנִיָּהוּ	צֹאן	וּבָקָר	וּמְרִיא	עִם	אֶבֶן	הַזֹּחֶלֶת
	wayyizbach	'ădhōnîyāhû	tsō'n	ûvāqār	ûmerî'	'im	'even	hazzōcheleth
	and he slaughtered	Adonijah	sheep	and oxen	and fatlings	beside	the stone of	the Zoheleth

866, 703	6100	6100	7410.121	881, 3725, 250	1158	4567
rel part, prep	pn	pn	cj, v Qal impf 3ms	do, *adj*, n mp, ps 3ms	*n mp*	art, n ms
אֲשֶׁר־אֵצֶל	עֵין	רֹגֵל	וַיִּקְרָא	אֶת־כָּל־אֶחָיו	בְּנֵי	הַמֶּלֶךְ
'ăsher-'ētsel	'ên	rōghēl	wayyiqrā'	'eth-kol-'echâv	benê	hammelekh
which beside	En	Rogel	and he called	all his brothers	the sons of	the king

3937, 3725, 596	3171	5860	4567		881, 5600	5204	1172
cj, prep, *adj*, *n mp*	pn	*n mp*	art, n ms	10.	cj, do, pn	art, n ms	cj, pn
וּלְכָל־אַנְשֵׁי	יְהוּדָה	עַבְדֵי	הַמֶּלֶךְ		וְאֶת־נָתָן	הַנָּבִיא	וּבְנָיָהוּ
ûlăkhol-'anshê	yehûdhāh	'avdhê	hammelekh		we'eth-nāthān	hannāvî'	ûvenāyāhû
and all the men of	Judah	the servants of	the king		but Nathan	the prophet	and Benaiah

ing, I'm going to be king, *Beck* ... raised himself, *Fenton* ... began making his boast, *Goodspeed* ... was growing pretentious and saying, I shall become king!, *JB*.

and he prepared him chariots and horsemen, and fifty men to run before him: ... made ready his carriages of war and his horsemen, with fifty runners to go, *BB* ... He provided himself with a chariot and horses and 50 men who ran ahead of him, *Beck* ... himself a carriage and horses, *Fenton* ... procured a chariot and team with fifty guards, *JB*.

6. And his father had not displeased him at any time in saying, Why hast thou done so?: ... Never once in his life had his father crossed him by saying, Why are you behaving like that?, *JB* ... had not grieved him all his life, *MAST* ... checked him all his life, by asking what he meant by his conduct, *Moffatt* ... rebuked him or asked why he was doing this, *NAB* ... crossed him at any time, *NASB*.

and he also was a very goodly man; and his mother bare him after Absalom: ... handsome too; his mother had given birth to, *JB* ... he was born, *MAST* ... and next in age to Absalom by the same mother, *NAB*.

7. And he conferred with Joab the son of Zeruiah, and with Abiathar the priest: and they following Adonijah helped him: ... Adonijah spoke with Joab son of Zeruiah and Abiathar the priest, and they agreed to help him, *NCV* ... He talked with Joab son of Zeruiah and with Abiathar the priest, and they gave him their strong support, *NEB* ... took counsel with Joab son of Zeruiah and with Abiathar the priest, and they assured him, *REB*.

8. But Zadok the priest, and Benaiah the son of Jehoiada, and Nathan the prophet, and Shimei, and Rei, and the mighty men which belonged to David, were not with Adonijah: ... and David's bodyguard of heroes did not take his side, *REB* ... men of war, did not take the side of Adonijah, *BB* ... warriors were not with Adonijah, *Beck* ... the Heroes who were with David, *Fenton*.

9. And Adonijah slew sheep and oxen and fat cattle by the stone of Zoheleth, which is by En-rogel: ... sacrificed sheep and oxen, and fat calves, *Fenton* ... fattened calves at the Sliding Stone which is beside Fuller's Spring, *JB* ... he slaughtered sheep, oxen, and fatlings, *NAB* ... the Serpent's Stone, which is beside, *Goodspeed*.

and called all his brethren the king's sons, and all the men of Judah the king's servants: ... invited all his brothers, the king's sons, and all the nobles of Judah in the king's service, *Fenton* ... together with all the royal officials of Judah, *Goodspeed* ... the royal princes, *JB*.

10. But Nathan the prophet, and Benaiah, and the mighty men, and Solomon his brother, he called not: ... he did not invite the prophet Nathan, or Benaiah, or the pick of the army, or his brother, *NAB* ... Adonijah did not invite

---

the exhortation, "Desire not a multitude of unprofitable children, neither delight in ungodly sons. Though they multiply, rejoice not in them, except the fear of the LORD be with them: for one that is just is better than a thousand; and better it is to die without children, than to have those that are ungodly" (2 Sam. 3:1–5; 1 Chr. 3:1–9; 14:3–7). The days which followed were thickly strewn with calamities for the rapidly aging and heartbroken king. His helpless decline would be shaken by attempted usurpation.

1:5–10. The fate of Amnon and of Absalom might have warned the son who was now the eldest, and who had succeeded to their claims.

Adonijah was the son of Haggith, "the dancer." His father had piously given him the name, which means "Yahweh is my LORD." He, too, was "a very goodly man," treated by David with foolish indulgence and humored in all his wishes. Although the rights of primogeniture were ill-defined, a king's eldest son, endowed as Adonijah was, would naturally be looked on as the heir, and Adonijah was impatient for the great prize. Following the example of Absalom, "he exalted himself, saying, 'I will be king,'" and, as an unmistakable sign of his intentions, prepared for himself fifty runners with chariots and horses (or horsemen).

David, unwarned by the past, or perhaps too ill and secluded to be aware of what was going on, put no obstacle in his way. Adonijah's cause seemed safe when he had won over Joab, the commander of the forces, and Abiathar, the chief priest. But the young man's precipitancy spoiled everything. David lingered on. It was perhaps a palace secret that a strong court-party was in favor of Solomon and that David was inclined to leave his kingdom to this younger son by his favorite wife.

So Adonijah, once more imitating the tactics of Absalom, prepared a great feast at the "Dragon stone" by the Fullers' Well, in the valley below Jerusalem. He sacrificed sheep and fat oxen and cattle and invited all the king's fifteen sons, omitting Solomon, his sole rival whom he feared. To this feast he also invited Joab and Abiathar, and all the men of Judah, the king's servants, by which are probably intended "all the captains of the host" who formed the nucleus of the militia forces (1 Ki. 1:9–25).

Verse	Number	Parsing	Hebrew	Transliteration	English
	881, 1399	cj, do, art, n mp	וְאֶת־הַגִּבּוֹרִים	we'eth-haggibbôrîm	and the mighty men
	881, 8406	cj, do, pn	וְאֶת־שְׁלֹמֹה	we'eth-shelōmōh	and Solomon
	250	n ms, ps 3ms	אָחִיו	'āchîw	his brother
	3940	neg part	לֹא	lō'	not
	7410.111	v Qal pf 3ms	קָרָא	qārā'	he called
11.	569.121	cj, v Qal impf 3ms	וַיֹּאמֶר	wayyō'mer	then he said
	5600	pn	נָתָן	nāthān	Nathan
	420, 1368	prep, pn	אֶל־בַּת־שֶׁבַע	'el-bath-sheva'	to Bathsheba
	525, 8406	*n fs*, pn	אֵם־שְׁלֹמֹה	'ēm-shelōmōh	the mother of Solomon
	3937, 569.141	prep, v Qal inf con	לֵאמֹר	lē'mōr	saying
	1950B, 3940	intrg part, neg part	הֲלוֹא	hălō'	have not
	8471.114	v Qal pf 2fs	שָׁמַעַתְּ	shāma'at	you heard
	3706	cj	כִּי	kî	that
	4566.111	v Qal pf 3ms	מָלַךְ	mālakh	he became king
	135	pn	אֲדֹנִיָּהוּ	'ădhōnîyāhû	Adonijah
	1158, 2389	*n ms*, pn	בֶן־חַגִּית	ven-chaggîth	the son of Haggith
	112	cj, n mp, ps 1cp	וַאדֹנֵינוּ	wa'ădhōnênû	and our lord
	1784	pn	דָוִד	dhāwidh	David
	3940	neg part	לֹא	lō'	not
	3156.111	v Qal pf 3ms	יָדָע	yādhā'	he knows
12.	6498	cj, adv	וְעַתָּה	we'attāh	and now
	2050.132	v Qal impv 2fs	לְכִי	lekhî	come
	3398.125	v Qal juss 1cs, ps 2fs	אִיעָצֵךְ	'î'ātsēkh	let me advise you
	5167	part	נָא	nā'	please
	6332	n fs	עֵצָה	'ētsāh	counsel
	4561.332	cj, v Piel impv 2fs	וּמַלְּטִי	ûmalletî	and save
	881, 5497	do, n fs, ps 2fs	אֶת־נַפְשֵׁךְ	'eth-naphshēkh	your life
	881, 5497	cj, do, *n fs*	וְאֶת־נֶפֶשׁ	we'eth-nephesh	and the life of
	1158	n ms, ps 2fs	בְּנֵךְ	benēkh	your son
	8406	pn	שְׁלֹמֹה	shelōmōh	Solomon
13.	2050.132	v Qal impv 2fs	לְכִי	lekhî	go
	971.132	v Qal impv 2fs	וּבֹאִי	ûvō'î	and enter
	420, 4567	prep, art, n ms	אֶל־הַמֶּלֶךְ	'el-hammelekh	to the king
	1784	pn	דָּוִד	dāwidh	David
	569.112	cj, v Qal pf 2fs	וְאָמַרְתְּ	we'āmart	then you will say
	420	prep, ps 3ms	אֵלָיו	'ēlâv	to him
	1950B, 3940, 887	intrg part, neg part, pers pron	הֲלֹא־אַתָּה	hălō'-'attāh	have you not
	112	n ms, ps 1cs	אֲדֹנִי	'ădhōnî	my lord
	4567	art, n ms	הַמֶּלֶךְ	hammelekh	the king
	8123.213	v Niphal pf 2ms	נִשְׁבַּעְתָּ	nishba'ttā	you have sworn
	3937, 526	prep, n fs, ps 2ms	לַאֲמָתְךָ	la'ămāthekhā	to your female servant
	3937, 569.141	prep, v Qal inf con	לֵאמֹר	lē'mōr	saying
	3706, 8406	cj, pn	כִּי־שְׁלֹמֹה	kî-shelōmōh	surely Solomon
	1158	n ms, ps 2fs	בְּנֵךְ	venēkh	your son
	4566.121	v Qal impf 3ms	יִמְלֹךְ	yimlōkh	he will become king
	313	adv, ps 1cs	אַחֲרָי	'achray	after me
	2000	cj, pers pron	וְהוּא	wehû'	and he
	3553.121	v Qal impf 3ms	יֵשֵׁב	yēshēv	he will sit
	6142, 3802	prep, n ms, ps 1cs	עַל־כִּסְאִי	'al-kis'î	on my throne
	4211	cj, intrg	וּמַדּוּעַ	ûmaddûa'	so why
	4566.111	v Qal pf 3ms	מָלַךְ	mālakh	has he become king
	135	pn	אֲדֹנִיָהוּ	'ădhōnîāhû	Adonijah
14.	2079	intrj	הִנֵּה	hinnēh	behold
	5968	adv, ps 2fs	עוֹדָךְ	'ôdhākh	still you
	1744.353	v Piel ptc fs	מְדַבֶּרֶת	medhabbereth	speaking
	8427	adv	שָׁם	shām	there
	6196, 4567	prep, art, n ms	עִם־הַמֶּלֶךְ	'im-hammelekh	with the king
	603	cj, pers pron	וַאֲנִי	wa'ănî	then I
	971.125	v Qal impf 1cs	אָבוֹא	'āvô'	I will enter
	313	adv, ps 2fs	אַחֲרַיִךְ	'achrayikh	after you
	4527.315	cj, v Piel pf 1cs	וּמִלֵּאתִי	ûmillē'thî	and I will make complete
	881, 1745	do, n mp, ps 2fs	אֶת־דְּבָרָיִךְ	'eth-devārāyikh	your words
15.	971.122	cj, v Qal impf 3fs	וַתָּבֹא	wattāvō'	so she entered
	1368	pn	בַת־שֶׁבַע	vath-sheve'	Bathsheba
	420, 4567	prep, art, n ms	אֶל־הַמֶּלֶךְ	'el-hammelekh	to the king

Nathan the prophet, Benaiah, his father's special guard, *NCV* ... or the warriors, *NRSV* ... send for Nathan the prophet and Benaiah and the other men of war, *BB*.

11. Wherefore Nathan spake unto Bath-sheba the mother of Solomon, saying, Hast thou not heard that Adonijah the son of Haggith doth reign, and David our lord knoweth it not?: ... Then Nathan said to Bathsheba, Solomon's mother: Have you not heard, *NAB* ... Has it not come to our ears that Adonijah, the son of Haggith, has made himself king without the knowledge, *BB* ... is becoming king, and our lord David doesn't know about it, *Beck* ... Haven't you heard that Haggith's son Adonijah has made himself king? And King David doesn't know anything about it!, *Good News* ... unknown to our lord David, Adonijah son of Haggith has become king?, *JB*.

12. Now therefore come, let me, I pray thee, give thee counsel, that thou mayest save thine own life, and the life of thy son Solomon: ... let me advise you so that you may save your life and that of your, *NAB* ... I strongly advise you to save yourself and your sons, *NCV* ... what to do for your own safety and for the safety of, *NEB* ... I beg you, come, let me give you counsel, *KJVII*.

13. Go and get thee in unto king David, and say unto him, Didst not thou, my lord, O king, swear unto thine handmaid, saying: ... go to King David and say to him, Did you not, O my lord, take an oath to me, your servant, *BB* ... Leave and go to King David and ask him, Didn't you, my lord the king, swear to your maid, *Beck* ... my master O king, swear to your maidservant, *Berkeley* ... proceed to King David, *Fenton*.

Assuredly Solomon thy son shall reign after me, and he shall sit upon my throne? why then doth Adonijah reign?: ... Truly Solomon your son will be king after me, seated on the seat of my kingdom, *BB* ... shall occupy my throne?, *Berkeley* ... Then why is Adoniah reigning?, *Fenton* ... How does it happen that Adonijah is becoming king?, *Beck*.

14. Behold, while thou yet talkest there with the king, I also will come in after thee, and confirm thy words: ... while you are still there talking to the king, I shall come in after you and confirm what you say, *JB* ... I will come in behind you, *Moffatt* ... speaking to the king, *NAB* ... will fill up thy words, *Douay* ... tell him that what you have said about Adonijah is true, *NCV* ... follow you in and tell the whole story, *NEB*.

15. And Bath-sheba went in unto the king into the chamber: and the king was very old; and Abishag the Shunammite ministered unto the king: ... in his private chamber; he was now very old, and Abishag the Shunammite was waiting on him, *NEB* ... to see the aged king in his room, where Abishag the Shunammite was attending him, *NIV* ... was serving the king, *NKJV* ... to the king in the bedroom, *Beck* ... into his own apartment, for the king was very old, and Abishag the Shunammite was caring for him, *Berkeley*.

At this feast, Adonijah threw off the mask. The watchful eye of one man, Nathan, the old prophet, saw the danger. Adonijah was thirty-five; Solomon was comparatively a child. "Solomon, my son, is young and tender," says David (1 Chr. 29:1). We do not know what his age was at the date of Adonijah's rebellion. Josephus presumes that he was between twelve and fifteen, and this approximate age would agree with the fact that he seems to have taken no step on his own behalf, while Nathan and Bathsheba acted for him.

1:11–14. The crisis was one of extreme peril. Nathan was now old, and David was older, but he rose to the occasion and promptly caused the instant collapse of Adonijah's conspiracy.

Adonijah had counted on the jealousy of the tribe of Judah, on the king's seclusion and walling popularity, on the support of "all the captains of the host," on the acquiescence of all the other princes, and above all on the favor of the ecclesiastical and military power of the kingdom as represented by Abiathar and Joab. To Solomon himself, as yet a shadowy figure and so much younger, he attached no importance. He treated his aged father as a cipher, and Nathan as of no particular account. He overlooked the influence of Bathsheba, the prestige which attached to the nomination of a reigning king, and above all the resistance of the mercenaries and their captain Benaiah.

Nathan had no sooner received tidings of what was going on at Adonijah's feast than he hurried to Bathsheba. "Had she heard," asked Nathan, "that Adonijah's coronation was going on at that moment? Let her hurry to King David, and inquire whether he had given any sanction to proceedings which contravened the oath which he had given her that her son Solomon should be his heir." As soon as she had broken the intelligence to the king, Nathan would come and confirm her words.

1:15–21. Bathsheba did not lose a moment. She knew that if Adonijah's conspiracy succeeded, her own life and that of her son would be in grave danger. The helplessness of David's condition is shown by the fact that Bathsheba had to make her

2410	4567	2290.111	4108	50	8208	8664.353
art, n ms	cj, art, n ms	v Qal pf 3ms	adv	cj, pn	art, pn	v Piel ptc fs
הַחַדְרָה	וְהַמֶּלֶךְ	זָקֵן	מְאֹד	וַאֲבִישַׁג	הַשּׁוּנַמִּית	מְשָׁרַת
hachadhrāh	wehammelekh	zāqēn	me'ōdh	wa'ăvîshagh	hashshûnammîth	meshārath
to the inner room	and the king	he was old	very	and Abishag	the Shunammite	ministering to

881, 4567		7199.122	1368	8246.722	3937, 4567
do, art, n ms	**16.**	cj, v Qal impf 3fs	pn	cj, v Hithpael impf 3fs	prep, art, n ms
אֶת־הַמֶּלֶךְ		וַתִּקֹּד	בַּת־שֶׁבַע	וַתִּשְׁתַּחוּ	לַמֶּלֶךְ
'eth-hammelekh		wattiqqōdh	bath-sheva'	wattishtachû	lammelekh
the king		and she bowed down	Bathsheba	and she prostrated herself	to the king

569.121	4567	4242, 3937		569.122	3937	112	887
cj, v Qal impf 3ms	art, n ms	intrg, prep, ps 2fs	**17.**	cj, v Qal impf 3fs	prep, ps 3ms	n ms, ps 1cs	pers pron
וַיֹּאמֶר	הַמֶּלֶךְ	מַה־לָּךְ		וַתֹּאמֶר	לוֹ	אֲדֹנִי	אַתָּה
wayyō'mer	hammelekh	mah-lākh		wattō'mer	lô	'ădhōnî	'attāh
and he said	the king	what to you		and she said	to him	my lord	you

8123.213	904, 3176	435	3937, 526	3706, 8406	1158
v Niphal pf 2ms	prep, pn	n mp, ps 2ms	prep, n fs, ps 2ms	cj, pn	n ms, ps 2ms
נִשְׁבַּעְתָּ	בַּיהוָה	אֱלֹהֶיךָ	לַאֲמָתֶךָ	כִּי־שְׁלֹמֹה	בְנֵךְ
nishba'ttā	bayhwāh	'ĕlōhêkhā	la'ămāthekhā	kî-shelōmōh	venēkh
you have sworn	by Yahweh	your God	to your female servant	that Solomon	your son

4566.121	313	2000	3553.121	6142, 3802		6498	2079
v Qal impf 3ms	adv, ps 1cs	cj, pers pron	v Qal impf 3ms	prep, n ms, ps 1cs	**18.**	cj, adv	intrj
יִמְלֹךְ	אַחֲרָי	וְהוּא	יֵשֵׁב	עַל־כִּסְאִי		וְעַתָּה	הִנֵּה
yimlōkh	'achrāy	wehû'	yēshēv	'al-kis'î		we'attāh	hinnēh
he will become king	after me	and he	he will sit	on my throne		but now	behold

135	4566.111	6498	112	4567	3940	3156.113
pn	v Qal pf 3ms	cj, adv	n ms, ps 1cs	art, n ms	neg part	v Qal pf 2ms
אֲדֹנִיָּה	מָלָךְ	וְעַתָּה	אֲדֹנִי	הַמֶּלֶךְ	לֹא	יָדָעְתָּ
'ădhōnîyāh	mālākh	we'attāh	'ădhōnî	hammelekh	lō'	yādhā'ttā
Adonijah	he has become king	but now	my lord	the king	not	you know

	2159.121	8228	4968, 6887	3937, 7524	7410.121
19.	cj, v Qal impf 3ms	n ms	cj, n ms, cj, n fs	prep, art, n ms	cj, v Qal impf 3ms
	וַיִּזְבַּח	שׁוֹר	וּמְרִיא־וְצֹאן	לָרֹב	וַיִּקְרָא
	wayyizbach	shôr	ûmerî'-wetsō'n	lārōv	wayyiqrā'
	and he slaughtered	oxen	and fatlings and sheep	for the multitude	and he called

3937, 3725, 1158	4567	420, 55	3669	420, 3200	8015	6893
prep, *adj, n mp*	art, n ms	cj, prep, pn	art, n ms	cj, prep, pn	*n ms*	art, n ms
לְכָל־בְּנֵי	הַמֶּלֶךְ	וּלְאֶבְיָתָר	הַכֹּהֵן	וּלְיֹאָב	שַׂר	הַצָּבָא
lekhol-benê	hammelekh	ûlā'evyāthār	hakkōhēn	ûlāyō'āv	sar	hatstsāvā'
to all the sons of	the king	and to Abiathar	the priest	and to Joab	the commander of	the army

420, 8406	5860	3940	7410.111		887	112	4567
cj, prep, pn	n ms, ps 2ms	neg part	v Qal pf 3ms	**20.**	cj, pers pron	n ms, ps 1cs	art, n ms
וְלִשְׁלֹמֹה	עַבְדְּךָ	לֹא	קָרָא		וְאַתָּה	אֲדֹנִי	הַמֶּלֶךְ
welishlōmōh	'avdekhā	lō'	qārā'		we'attāh	'ădhōnî	hammelekh
but to Solomon	your servant	not	he called		and you	my lord	the king

6084	3725, 3547	6142	3937, 5222.541	3937	4449	3553.121
n fd	*adj*, pn	prep, ps 2ms	prep, v Hiphil inf con	prep, ps 3mp	intrg	v Qal impf 3ms
עֵינֵי	כָל־יִשְׂרָאֵל	עָלֶיךָ	לְהַגִּיד	לָהֶם	מִי	יֵשֵׁב
'ênê	khol-yisrā'ēl	'ālêkhā	lehaggîdh	lāhem	mî	yēshēv
the eyes of	all Israel	on you	to tell	to them	who	he will sit

6142, 3802	112, 4567	313		2030.111	3626, 8311.141
prep, *n ms*	n ms, ps 1cs, art, n ms	adv, ps 3ms	**21.**	cj, v Qal pf 3ms	prep, v Qal inf con
עַל־כִּסֵּא	אֲדֹנִי־הַמֶּלֶךְ	אַחֲרָיו		וְהָיָה	כִּשְׁכַּב
'al-kissē'	'ădhōnî-hammelekh	'achrâv		wehāyāh	kishkhav
on the throne of	my lord the king	after him		or it will be	when sleeping

112, 4567	6196, 1	2030.115	603	1158	8406	2492
n ms, ps 1cs, art, n ms	prep, n mp, ps 3ms	cj, v Qal pf 1cs	pers pron	cj, n ms, ps 1cs	pn	n mp
אֲדֹנִי־הַמֶּלֶךְ	עִם־אֲבֹתָיו	וְהָיִיתִי	אֲנִי	וּבְנִי	שְׁלֹמֹה	חַטָּאִים
'ădhōnî-hammelekh	'im-'ăvōthâv	wehāyîthî	'ănî	ûvenî	shelōmōh	chattā'îm
my lord the king	with his ancestors	then I will be	I	and my son	Solomon	offenders

16. And Bath-sheba bowed, and did obeisance unto the king. And the king said, What wouldest thou?: ... fell upon her knees and paid homage to the king, the king asked, What do you wish, *Berkeley* ... approached and bowed to the king, and the king asked, What is the matter, *Fenton* ... knelt, prostrated herself before the king, *JB* ... bowed herself and worshipped the king. And the king said to her: What is thy will, *Douay* ... bowed low before the king, and he asked, "What do you want?," *Good News*.

17. And she said unto him, My lord, thou swarest by the LORD thy God unto thine handmaid, saying: ... She answered, My master, you made a promise to me in the name of the LORD your God, *NCV* ... you swore to me your servant, *NEB* ... to your slave-girl, *KJVII* ... you took an oath by the LORD your God and gave your word, *BB*.

Assuredly Solomon thy son shall reign after me, and he shall sit upon my throne: ... Your son Solomon will become king after me, and he will rule on my throne, *NCV* ... should succeed you as king, and that he should sit, *NEB* ... seated on the seat of my kingdom, *BB* ... occupy my throne, *Berkeley*.

18. And now, behold, Adonijah reigneth; and now, my lord the king, thou knowest it not: ... Adonijah has become king, and you, my master, O king, do not know about it, *Berkeley* ... here is Adonijah become king, all unknown to your majesty, *NEB* ... has already become king, and you don't know anything, *Good News* ... unknown to you, *NCV*.

19. And he hath slain oxen and fat cattle and sheep in abundance, and hath called all the sons of the king, and Abiathar the priest, and Joab the captain of the host: but Solomon thy servant hath he not called: ... He has sacrificed great numbers of oxen, buffaloes, and sheep, and has invited to the feast all the king's sons, *NEB* ... all the children of the king, *NRSV* ... has put to death oxen and fat beasts and sheep in great numbers, *BB* ... but he hasn't invited your servant Solomon, *Beck*.

20. And thou, my lord, O king, the eyes of all Israel are upon thee, that thou shouldest tell them who shall sit on the throne of my lord the king after him: ... All Israel is looking to you, my lord the king, to tell them who should succed my lord the king in sitting on his throne, *Beck* ... to inform them as to who is to occupy the throne of my master, *Berkeley* ... you are the man, my lord king, to whom all Israel looks, *JB* ... waiting for you to make known to them who is to sit on the throne after your royal majesty, *NAB* ... to decide for them who is to succeed, *Moffatt*.

21. Otherwise it shall come to pass, when my lord the king shall sleep with his fathers, that I and my son Solomon shall be counted offenders: ... If this is not done, when my lord the king sleeps with his fathers, I and my son Solomon will be considered criminals, *NAB* ... As soon as you die, Solomon and I will be treated as criminals, *NCV* ... when you, sir, rest with your forefathers, *NEB* ... laid to rest with his fathers, *NIV* ... will be made outlaws, *BB*.

22. And, lo, while she yet talked with the king, Nathan the prophet also came in: ... Nathan the reciter came, *Fenton* ... Bathsheba was still addressing the king when Nathan the prophet arrived, *REB* ... She was still

way into "the inner chamber" to visit him. In violation of the immemorial etiquette of an Eastern household, she spoke to him without being summoned, and in the presence of another woman, Abishag, his fair young nurse. With profound obeisances she entered and told the poor old hero that Adonijah had practically usurped the throne, but that the eyes of all Israel were awaiting his decision as to who should be his successor. She asked whether he were really indifferent to the peril of herself and of Solomon, for Adonijah's success would mean their doom.

1:22–27. While she yet spoke, Nathan was announced, as had been concerted between them, and he repeated the story of what was going on at Adonijah's feast. It is remarkable that he says nothing to David either about consulting the Urim, or in any way ascertaining the will of God. He and

22.	2079	5968	1744.353	6196, 4567	5600	5204	971.111
	cj, intrj	adv, ps 3fs	v Piel ptc fs	prep, art, n ms	cj, pn	art, n ms	v Qal pf 3ms
	וְהִנֵּה	עוֹדֶנָּה	מְדַבֶּרֶת	עִם־הַמֶּלֶךְ	וְנָתָן	הַנָּבִיא	בָּא
	w^{e}hinnēh	ʻôdhennāh	m^{e}dhabbereth	ʻim-hammelekh	w^{e}nāthān	hannāvî'	bā'
	and behold	still she	speaking	with the king	then Nathan	the prophet	he entered

23.	5222.526	3937, 4567	3937, 569.141	2079	5600	5204	971.121
	cj, v Hiphil impf 3mp	prep, art, n ms	prep, v Qal inf con	intrj	pn	art, n ms	cj, v Qal impf 3ms
	וַיַּגִּידוּ	לַמֶּלֶךְ	לֵאמֹר	הִנֵּה	נָתָן	הַנָּבִיא	וַיָּבֹא
	wayyaggîdhû	lammelekh	lē'mōr	hinnēh	nāthān	hannāvî'	wayyāvō'
	and they reported	to the king	saying	behold	Nathan	the prophet	and he entered

3937, 6686	4567	8246.721	3937, 4567	6142, 653	800
prep, *n mp*	art, n ms	cj, v Hithpael impf 3ms	prep, art, n ms	prep, n md, ps 3ms	n fs
לִפְנֵי	הַמֶּלֶךְ	וַיִּשְׁתַּחוּ	לַמֶּלֶךְ	עַל־אַפָּיו	אַרְצָה
liphnê	hammelekh	wayyishtachû	lammelekh	ʻal-'appâv	'ār^{e}tsāh
before	the king	and he prostrated himself	to the king	on his nostrils	to the ground

24.	569.121	5600	112	4567	887	569.113	135
	cj, v Qal impf 3ms	pn	n ms, ps 1cs	art, n ms	pers pron	v Qal pf 2ms	pn
	וַיֹּאמֶר	נָתָן	אֲדֹנִי	הַמֶּלֶךְ	אַתָּה	אָמַרְתָּ	אֲדֹנִיָּהוּ
	wayyō'mer	nāthān	'ădhōnî	hammelekh	'attāh	'āmartā	'ădhōnîyāhû
	and he said	Nathan	my lord	the king	you	you have said	Adonijah

4566.121	313	2000	3553.121	6142, 3802	25.	3706
v Qal impf 3ms	adv, ps 1cs	cj, pers pron	v Qal impf 3ms	prep, n ms, ps 1cs		cj
יִמְלֹךְ	אַחֲרָי	וְהוּא	יֵשֵׁב	עַל־כִּסְאִי		כִּי
yimlōkh	'achrāy	w^{e}hû'	yēshēv	ʻal-kis'î		kî
he will become king	after me	and he	he will sit	on my throne		because

3495.111	3219	2159.121	8228	4968, 6887	3937, 7524
v Qal pf 3ms	art, n ms	cj, v Qal impf 3ms	n ms	cj, n ms, cj, n fs	prep, art, n ms
יָרַד	הַיּוֹם	וַיִּזְבַּח	שׁוֹר	וּמְרִיא־וְצֹאן	לָרֹב
yāradh	hayyôm	wayyizbach	shôr	ûm^{e}rî'-w^{e}tsō'n	lārōv
he has gone down	today	and he slaughtered	oxen	and fatlings and sheep	for the multitude

7410.121	3937, 3725, 1158	4567	3937, 8015	6893	420, 55
cj, v Qal impf 3ms	prep, *adj*, *n mp*	art, n ms	cj, prep, *n mp*	art, n ms	cj, prep, pn
וַיִּקְרָא	לְכָל־בְּנֵי	הַמֶּלֶךְ	וּלְשָׂרֵי	הַצָּבָא	וּלְאֶבְיָתָר
wayyiqrā'	l^{e}khol-b^{e}nê	hammelekh	ûlăsārê	hatstsāvā'	ûlă'evyāthār
and he called	to all the sons of	the king	and to the commanders of	the army	and to Abiathar

3669	2079	404.152	8685.152	3937, 6686	569.126
art, n ms	cj, intrj, ps 3mp	v Qal act ptc mp	cj, v Qal act ptc mp	prep, n mp, ps 3ms	cj, v Qal impf 3mp
הַכֹּהֵן	וְהִנָּם	אֹכְלִים	וְשֹׁתִים	לְפָנָיו	וַיֹּאמְרוּ
hakkōhēn	w^{e}hinnām	'ōkh^{e}lîm	w^{e}shōthîm	l^{e}phānâv	wayyō'm^{e}rû
the priest	and behold they	eating	and drinking	before him	and they are saying

2513.121	4567	135	26.	3937	603, 5860	3937, 6923	3669
v Qal juss 3ms	art, n ms	pn		cj, prep, ps 1cs	pers pron, n ms, ps 2ms	cj, prep, pn	art, n ms
יְחִי	הַמֶּלֶךְ	אֲדֹנִיָּהוּ		וְלִי	אֲנִי־עַבְדֶּךָ	וּלְצָדֹק	הַכֹּהֵן
y^{e}chî	hammelekh	'ădhōnîyāhû		w^{e}lî	'ănî-ʻavdekhā	ûlătsādhōq	hakkōhēn
may he live	the king	Adonijah		yet to me	I your servant	and to Zadok	the priest

3937, 1172	1158, 3179	420, 8406	5860	3940	7410.111	27.	524
cj, prep, pn	*n ms*, pn	cj, prep, pn	n ms, ps 2ms	neg part	v Qal pf 3ms		cj
וְלִבְנָיָהוּ	בֶן־יְהוֹיָדָע	וְלִשְׁלֹמֹה	עַבְדְּךָ	לֹא	קָרָא		אִם
w^{e}livnāyāhû	ven-y^{e}hôyādhāʻ	w^{e}lishlōmōh	ʻavd^{e}khā	lō'	qārā'		'im
and to Benaiah	the son of Jehoiada	and to Solomon	your servant	not	he called		if

4623, 881	112	4567	2030.211	1745	2172	3940	3156.513
prep, do	n ms, ps 1cs	art, n ms	v Niphal pf 3ms	art, n ms	art, dem pron	cj, neg part	v Hiphil pf 2ms
מֵאֵת	אֲדֹנִי	הַמֶּלֶךְ	נִהְיָה	הַדָּבָר	הַזֶּה	וְלֹא	הוֹדַעְתָּ
mē'ēth	'ădhōnî	hammelekh	nihyāh	haddāvār	hazzeh	wᵉlō'	hôdha'ättā
from	my lord	the king	it has been	the matter	the this	or not	you made known to

881, 5860	4449	3553.121	6142, 3802	112, 4567	313
do, n mp, ps 2ms	intrg	v Qal impf 3ms	prep, *n ms*	n ms, ps 1cs, art, n ms	adv, ps 3ms
אֶת־עַבְדֶּיךָ	מִי	יֵשֵׁב	עַל־כִּסֵּא	אֲדֹנִי־הַמֶּלֶךְ	אַחֲרָיו
'eth-'avdêkhā	mî	yēshēv	'al-kissē'	'ădhōnî-hammelekh	'achrâv
your servants	who	he will sit	on the throne of	my lord the king	after him

28.

6257.121	4567	1784	569.121	7410.133, 3937	3937, 1368
cj, v Qal impf 3ms	art, n ms	pn	cj, v Qal impf 3ms	v Qal impv 2mp, prep, ps 1cs	prep, pn
וַיַּעַן	הַמֶּלֶךְ	דָּוִד	וַיֹּאמֶר	קִרְאוּ־לִי	לְבַת־שָׁבַע
wayya'an	hammelekh	dāwidh	wayyō'mer	qir'û-lî	lᵉvath-shāva'
and he answered	the king	David	and he said	call for me	to Bathsheba

speaking, when Nathan arrived at the palace, *Good News*.

23. And they told the king, saying, Behold Nathan the prophet. And when he was come in before the king, he bowed himself before the king with his face to the ground: ... The king was informed that Nathan was there; he came into the king's presence and prostrated himself, *REB* ... they reported to the king, saying, Nathan the Reciter is here, *Fenton* ... did obeisance to the king with his face to the earth, *Goodspeed* ... he went down on his face on the earth, *BB*.

24. And Nathan said, My lord, O king, hast thou said, Adonijah shall reign after me, and he shall sit upon my throne?: ... My lord king, said Nathan, is this, then, your decree, Adonijah is to be king after me, *JB* ... have you given orders that Adonijah is to reign after you, *Moffatt* ... Have you decided, my lord king, *NAB* ... your majesty must, I suppose, have declared that Adonijah should succeed you, *NEB*.

25. For he is gone down this day, and hath slain oxen and fat cattle and sheep in abundance, and hath called all the king's sons, and the captains of the host, and Abiathar the priest: ... He has today gone down and sacrificed great numbers of oxen, buffaloes, and sheep, and has invited to the feast, *NEB* ... has sacrificed oxen, fatlings, *RSV* ... has killed a great many of oxen, *KJVII* ... has put to death oxen and fat beasts and sheep in great numbers, and has sent for all the king's sons to come to him, *BB*.

and, behold, they eat and drink before him, and say, God save king Adonijah: ... at this very moment they are eating and drinking in his presence and shouting, Long live King Adonijah, *NEB* ... feasting before him and crying, Long life to King Adonijah!, *BB* ... Even now they are, *Berkeley*.

26. But me, even me thy servant, and Zadok the priest, and Benaiah the son of Jehoiada, and thy servant Solomon, hath he not called: ... he did not invite, *Berkeley* ... he has not sent for, *BB* ... there is no invitation, *Fenton* ... your own servant, or Zadok the priest, *NCV*.

27. Is this thing done by my lord the king, and thou hast not showed it unto thy servant: ... Did you do this? Since we are your servants, why didn't you tell us, *NCV* ... Has this been done by your majesty's authority, while we your servants have not been told, *NEB* ... Is this something my lord the king has done without letting his servants know, *NIV* ... Has this thing been brought about by my lord the king and you have not, *NRSV* ... been done by my lord the king, without giving word, *BB*.

who should sit on the throne of my lord the king after him?: ... who should be king after you?, *NCV* ... sit on the throne of my lord the king after him?, *NIV* ... occupy the throne of my master, *Berkeley* ... placed on my lord the king's seat after him, *BB*.

28. Then king David answered and said, Call me Bath-sheba. And she

---

Bathsheba rely exclusively on four motives—David's rights of nomination, his promise, the danger to Solomon and the contempt shown in Adonijah's proceedings.

1:28–35. The news woke in David a flash of his old energy. With instant decision he summoned Bathsheba, who, as custom required, had left the chamber when Nathan entered. Using his strong and favorite adjuration, "As the LORD liveth, that hath redeemed my soul out of all adversity" (2 Sam. 4:9; Ps. 34:6), he pledged himself to carry out that very day the oath that Solomon should be his heir. She bowed her face to the earth in adoration with the words, "Let my lord, King David, live for ever." He

971.122	3937, 6686	4567	6198.122	3937, 6686	4567		8123.221
cj, v Qal impf 3fs	prep, *n mp*	art, n ms	cj, v Qal impf 3fs	prep, *n mp*	art, n ms	**29.**	cj, v Niphal impf 3ms
וַתָּבֹא	לִפְנֵי	הַמֶּלֶךְ	וַתַּעֲמֹד	לִפְנֵי	הַמֶּלֶךְ		וַיִּשָּׁבַע
wattāvō'	liphnê	hammelekh	watta'ămōdh	liphnê	hammelekh		wayyishshāva'
and she entered	before	the king	and she stood	before	the king		and he swore

4567	569.121	2508, 3176	866, 6540.111	881, 5497	4623, 3725, 7150
art, n ms	cj, v Qal impf 3ms	*adj*, pn	rel pron, v Qal pf 3ms	do, n fs, ps 1cs	prep, *adj*, n fs
הַמֶּלֶךְ	וַיֹּאמַר	חַי־יְהוָה	אֲשֶׁר־פָּדָה	אֶת־נַפְשִׁי	מִכָּל־צָרָה
hammelekh	wayyō'mar	chay-yehwāh	'ăsher-pādhāh	'eth-naphshî	mikkol-tsārāh
the king	and he said	Yahweh living	Who has redeemed	my life	from all adversity

	3706	3626, 866	8123.215	3937	904, 3176	435	3547
30.	cj	prep, rel part	v Niphal pf 1cs	prep, ps 2fs	prep, pn	*n mp*	pn
	כִּי	כַּאֲשֶׁר	נִשְׁבַּעְתִּי	לָךְ	בַּיהוָה	אֱלֹהֵי	יִשְׂרָאֵל
	kî	ka'ăsher	nishba'ăttî	lākh	bayhwāh	'ĕlōhê	yisrā'ēl
	that	just as	I swore	to you	by Yahweh	the God of	Israel

3937, 569.141	3706, 8406	1158	4566.121	313	2000
prep, v Qal inf con	cj, pn	n ms, ps 2fs	v Qal impf 3ms	adv, ps 1cs	cj, pers pron
לֵאמֹר	כִּי־שְׁלֹמֹה	בְּנֵךְ	יִמְלֹךְ	אַחֲרַי	וְהוּא
lē'mōr	kî-shelōmōh	venēkh	yimlōkh	'achray	wehû'
saying	surely Solomon	your son	he will become king	after me	and he

3553.121	6142, 3802	8809	3706	3772	6449.125	3219	2172
v Qal impf 3ms	prep, n ms, ps 1cs	prep, ps 1cs	cj	adv	v Qal impf 1cs	art, n ms	art, dem pron
יֵשֵׁב	עַל־כִּסְאִי	תַּחְתָּי	כִּי	כֵּן	אֶעֱשֶׂה	הַיּוֹם	הַזֶּה
yēshēv	'al-kis'î	tachtāy	kî	kēn	'e'ĕseh	hayyôm	hazzeh
he will sit	on my throne	instead of me	even	so	I will do	the day	the this

	7199.122	1368	653	800	8246.722	3937, 4567
31.	cj, v Qal impf 3fs	pn	n md	n fs	cj, v Hithpael impf 3fs	prep, art, n ms
	וַתִּקֹּד	בַּת־שֶׁבַע	אַפַּיִם	אֶרֶץ	וַתִּשְׁתַּחוּ	לַמֶּלֶךְ
	wattiqqōdh	bath-sheva'	'appayim	'erets	wattishtachû	lammelekh
	and she bowed down	Bathsheba	nostrils	the ground	and she prostrated herself	to the king

569.122	2513.121	112	4567	1784	3937, 5986		569.121
cj, v Qal impf 3fs	v Qal juss 3ms	n ms, ps 1cs	art, n ms	pn	prep, n ms	**32.**	cj, v Qal impf 3ms
וַתֹּאמֶר	יְחִי	אֲדֹנִי	הַמֶּלֶךְ	דָּוִד	לְעֹלָם		וַיֹּאמֶר
wattō'mer	yechî	'ădhōnî	hammelekh	dāwidh	le'ōlām		wayyō'mer
and she said	may he live	my lord	the king	David	for ever		and he said

4567	1784	7410.133, 3937	3937, 6923	3669	3937, 5600	5204
art, n ms	pn	v Qal impv 2mp, prep, ps 1cs	prep, pn	art, n ms	cj, prep, pn	art, n ms
הַמֶּלֶךְ	דָּוִד	קִרְאוּ־לִי	לְצָדוֹק	הַכֹּהֵן	וּלְנָתָן	הַנָּבִיא
hammelekh	dāwidh	qir'û-lî	letsādhôq	hakkōhēn	ûlănāthān	hannāvî'
the king	David	call for me	to Zadok	the priest	and to Nathan	the prophet

3937, 1172	1158, 3179	971.126	3937, 6686	4567		569.121
cj, prep, pn	*n ms*, pn	cj, v Qal impf 3mp	prep, *n mp*	art, n ms	**33.**	cj, v Qal impf 3ms
וְלִבְנָיָהוּ	בֶּן־יְהוֹיָדָע	וַיָּבֹאוּ	לִפְנֵי	הַמֶּלֶךְ		וַיֹּאמֶר
welivnāyāhû	ben-yehôyādhā'	wayyāvō'û	liphnê	hammelekh		wayyō'mer
and to Benaiah	the son of Jehoiada	and they entered	before	the king		and he said

4567	3937	4089.133	6196	881, 5860	112
art, n ms	prep, ps 3mp	v Qal impv 2mp	prep, ps 2mp	do, *n mp*	n mp, ps 2mp
הַמֶּלֶךְ	לָהֶם	קְחוּ	עִמָּכֶם	אֶת־עַבְדֵי	אֲדֹנֵיכֶם
hammelekh	lāhem	qōchû	'immākhem	'eth-'avdhê	'ădhōnêkhem
the king	to them	take	with you	the servants of	your lord

7680.517	881, 8406	1158	6142, 6756	866, 3937
cj, v Hiphil pf 2mp	do, pn	n ms, ps 1cs	prep, art, n fs	rel part, prep, ps 1cs
וְהִרְכַּבְתֶּם	אֶת־שְׁלֹמֹה	בְּנִי	עַל־הַפִּרְדָּה	אֲשֶׁר־לִי
wehirkavtem	'eth-shelōmōh	venî	'al-happirdāh	'ăsher-lî
and you must cause to ride	Solomon	my son	on the female mule	which to me

3495.517	881	420, 1556		5066.111	881	8427	6923
cj, v Hiphil pf 2mp	do, ps 3ms	prep, pn	**34.**	cj, v Qal pf 3ms	do, ps 3ms	adv	pn
וְהוֹרַדְתֶּם	אֹתוֹ	אֶל־גִּחוֹן		וּמָשַׁח	אֹתוֹ	שָׁם	צָדוֹק
wehôradhtem	'ōthô	'el-gichôn		ûmāshach	'ōthô	shām	tsādhôq
and you must bring down	him	to Gihon		and he must anoint	him	there	Zadok

3669	5600	5204	3937, 4567	6142, 3547	8965.117
art, n ms	cj, pn	art, n ms	prep, n ms	prep, pn	cj, v Qal pf 2mp
הַכֹּהֵן	וְנָתָן	הַנָּבִיא	לְמֶלֶךְ	עַל־יִשְׂרָאֵל	וּתְקַעְתֶּם
hakkōhēn	wenāthān	hannāvî'	lemelekh	'al-yisrā'ēl	ûtheqa'ăttem
the priest	and Nathan	the prophet	as king	over Israel	then you will blow

came into the king's presence, and stood before the king: ... Call Bathsheba for me, *Berkeley* ... Tell Bathsheba to come in! So she came in and stood before the king, *NCV* ... Ask Bathsheba to come back in, *Good News* ... king David ordered Bathsheba to be recalled, *Moffatt* ... Call Bathsheba here, *NAB*.

29. And the king sware, and said, As the LORD liveth, that hath redeemed my soul out of all distress: ... made this promise, The LORD has saved me from all trouble, *NCV* ... swore an oath to her: As the LORD lives, who has delivered me from all my troubles, *NEB* ... saved my life from every adversity, *NRSV* ... affirmed, By the life of the LORD who has redeemed me, *Berkeley*.

30. Even as I sware unto thee by the LORD God of Israel, saying, Assuredly Solomon thy son shall reign after me: ... since I have sworn to you by the Lord, the God of Israel, Solomon your son shall be king after me, *Berkeley* ... As I took an oath to you by the Lord, the God of Israel, saying, Certainly Solomon your son will become, *BB* ... I will fulfill the oath, *NAB*.

and he shall sit upon my throne in my stead: ... occupy my throne in my place, *Berkeley* ... seated on my seat, *BB* ... should sit upon my throne, *NAB*.

even so will I certainly do this day: ... I will perform it this very day, *Berkeley* ... that is what I will do today, *Beck* ... I shall bring it about this very day, *JB*.

31. Then Bath-sheba bowed with her face to the earth, and did reverence to the king, and said, Let my lord king David live for ever: ... honored the king, *KJVII* ... bowed down to the ground, *Beck* ... fell upon her knees with her face to the ground and paid homage, *Berkeley* ... did obeisance, *Goodspeed* ... knelt down, prostrated herself on her face, *JB*.

32. And king David said, Call me Zadok the priest, and Nathan the prophet, and Benaiah the son of Jehoiada. And they came before the king: ... they came into the king's presence, *JB* ... Tell Zadok the priest, Nathan the prophet and Benaiah son of Jehoiada to come in, *NCV* ... he gave them these orders, *NEB* ... Summon to me the priest Zadok, *NRSV* ... Send for Zadok the priest, *BB*.

33. The king also said unto them, Take with you the servants of your lord: ... officers of your Prince, *Fenton* ... Take the royal guard, *JB* ... Take your lord's personal troops, *Moffatt* ... Take my court officials, *Good News*.

and cause Solomon my son to ride upon mine own mule, and bring him down to Gihon: ... put ... on my beast, *BB* ... on my own horse, *Fenton* ... mount my son Solomon upon ... and convey him, *Moffatt* ... have my son Solomon ride ... and escort him down, *Good News*.

34. And let Zadok the priest and Nathan the prophet anoint him there king over Israel: and blow ye with the trumpet, and say, God save king Solomon: ... blow a trumpet blast and proclaim, Long live king Solomon, *Moffatt* ... you shall blow the horn and cry, *NAB* ... should pour olive oil on him and make him king, *NCV* ... Let king Solomon live!, *KJVII* ... put the holy oil on him to make him king over Israel; and sounding the horn say, Long life to King Solomon!, *BB*.

35. Then ye shall come up after him, that he may come and sit upon my throne; for he shall be king in my stead: ... Follow him up there as he comes and sits on my throne and succeeds me as king, *Beck* ... come up again after him, so that he may enter and occupy, *Berkeley* ... proceed with him and bring him and set him on my throne, and he shall be my Deputy-vice-King, *Fenton* ... you are to escort him back, and he is then to assume my throne and be king in place of me, *JB*.

and I have appointed him to be ruler over Israel and over Judah:

904, 8223	569.117	2513.121	4567	8406	35.	6148.117
prep, art, n ms	cj, v Qal pf 2mp	v Qal juss 3ms	art, n ms	pn		cj, v Qal pf 2mp
בַּשּׁוֹפָר	וַאֲמַרְתֶּם	יְחִי	הַמֶּלֶךְ	שְׁלֹמֹה		וַעֲלִיתֶם
bashshôphār	wa'ămartem	y^{e}chî	hammelekh	sh^{e}lōmōh		wa'ălîthem
into the ram's horn	and you will say	may he live	the king	Solomon		then you must come up

313	971.111	3553.111	6142, 3802	2000	4566.121
prep, ps 3ms	cj, v Qal pf 3ms	cj, v Qal pf 3ms	prep, n ms, ps 1cs	cj, pers pron	v Qal impf 3ms
אַחֲרָיו	וּבָא	וְיָשַׁב	עַל־כִּסְאִי	וְהוּא	יִמְלֹךְ
'achrâv	ûvā'	w^{e}yāshav	'al-kis̱'î	w^{e}hû'	yimlōkh
after him	and he must come	and he must sit	on my throne	and he	he will become king

8809	881	6943.315	3937, 2030.141	5233	6142, 3547
prep, ps 1cs	cj, do, ps 3ms	v Piel pf 1cs	prep, v Qal inf con	n ms	prep, pn
תַּחְתָּי	וְאֹתוֹ	צִוִּיתִי	לִהְיוֹת	נָגִיד	עַל־יִשְׂרָאֵל
tachtāy	w^{e}'ōthô	tsiwwîthî	lihyôth	nāghîdh	'al-yisrā'ēl
instead of me	and him	I have commanded	to be	leader	over Israel

6142, 3171	36.	6257.121	1172	1158, 3179	881, 4567	569.121
cj, prep, pn		cj, v Qal impf 3ms	pn	*n ms*, pn	do, art, n ms	cj, v Qal impf 3ms
וְעַל־יְהוּדָה		וַיַּעַן	בְּנָיָהוּ	בֶּן־יְהוֹיָדָע	אֶת־הַמֶּלֶךְ	וַיֹּאמֶר
w^{e}'al-y^{e}hûdhāh		wayya'an	b^{e}nāyāhû	ven-y^{e}hôyādhā'	'eth-hammelekh	wayyō'mer
and over Judah		and he answered	Benaiah	the son of Jehoiada	the king	and he said

549	3772	569.121	3176	435	112	4567	37.	3626, 866	2030.111
intrj	adv	v Qal juss 3ms	pn	*n mp*	n ms, ps 1cs	art, n ms		prep, rel part	v Qal pf 3ms
אָמֵן	כֵּן	יֹאמַר	יְהוָה	אֱלֹהֵי	אֲדֹנִי	הַמֶּלֶךְ		כַּאֲשֶׁר	הָיָה
'āmēn	kēn	yō'mar	y^{e}hwāh	'ĕlōhê	'ădhōnî	hammelekh		ka'ăsher	hāyāh
amen	so	may He say	Yahweh	the God of	my lord	the king		just as	He has been

3176	6196, 112	4567	3772	2030.121	6196, 8406	1461.321
pn	prep, n ms, ps 1cs	art, n ms	adv	v Qal juss 3ms	prep, pn	cj, v Piel juss 3ms
יְהוָה	עִם־אֲדֹנִי	הַמֶּלֶךְ	כֵּן	יְהִי	עִם־שְׁלֹמֹה	וִיגַדֵּל
y^{e}hwāh	'im-'ădhōnî	hammelekh	kēn	y^{e}hî	'im-sh^{e}lōmōh	wîghaddēl
Yahweh	with my lord	the king	so	may He be	with Solomon	and may He make greater

881, 3802	4623, 3802	112	4567	1784	38.	3495.121	6923
do, n ms, ps 3ms	prep, *n ms*	n ms, ps 1cs	art, n ms	pn		cj, v Qal impf 3ms	pn
אֶת־כִּסְאוֹ	מִכִּסֵּא	אֲדֹנִי	הַמֶּלֶךְ	דָּוִד		וַיֵּרֶד	צָדוֹק
'eth-kis̱'ô	mikkis̱s̱ē'	'ădhōnî	hammelekh	dāwidh		wayyēredh	tsādhôq
his throne	than the throne of	my lord	the king	David		so he went down	Zadok

3669	5600	5204	1172	1158, 3179	3903
art, n ms	cj, pn	art, n ms	cj, pn	*n ms*, pn	cj, art, pn
הַכֹּהֵן	וְנָתָן	הַנָּבִיא	וּבְנָיָהוּ	בֶּן־יְהוֹיָדָע	וְהַכְּרֵתִי
hakkōhēn	w^{e}nāthān	hannāvî'	ûv^{e}nāyāhû	ven-y^{e}hôyādhā'	w^{e}hakk^{e}rēthî
the priest	and Nathan	the prophet	and Benaiah	the son of Jehoiada	and the Cherethites

6676	7680.526	881, 8406	6142, 6756	4567	1784
cj, art, pn	cj, v Hiphil impf 3mp	do, pn	prep, *n fs*	art, n ms	pn
וְהַפְּלֵתִי	וַיַּרְכִּבוּ	אֶת־שְׁלֹמֹה	עַל־פִּרְדַּת	הַמֶּלֶךְ	דָּוִד
w^{e}happ^{e}lēthî	wayyarkivû	'eth-sh^{e}lōmōh	'al-pirdath	hammelekh	dāwidh
and the Pelethites	and they caused to ride	Solomon	on the female mule of	the king	David

2050.526	881	6142, 1556	39.	4089.121	6923	3669	881, 7451
cj, v Hiphil impf 3mp	do, ps 3ms	prep, pn		cj, v Qal impf 3ms	pn	art, n ms	do, *n fs*
וַיֹּלִכוּ	אֹתוֹ	עַל־גִּחוֹן		וַיִּקַּח	צָדוֹק	הַכֹּהֵן	אֶת־קֶרֶן
wayyōlikhû	'ōthô	'al-gichôn		wayyiqqach	tsādhôq	hakkōhēn	'eth-qeren
and they brought	him	beside Gihon		and he took	Zadok	the priest	the horn of

8467	4623, 164	5066.121	881, 8406	8965.126	904, 8223
art, n ms	prep, art, n ms	cj, v Qal impf 3ms	do, pn	cj, v Qal impf 3mp	prep, art, n ms
הַשֶּׁמֶן	מִן־הָאֹהֶל	וַיִּמְשַׁח	אֶת־שְׁלֹמֹה	וַיִּתְקְעוּ	בַּשּׁוֹפָר
hashshemen	min-hā'ōhel	wayyimshach	'eth-sh^{e}lōmōh	wayyithqŏ'û	bashshôphār
the olive oil	from the tent	and he anointed	Solomon	and they blew	into the ram's horn

569.126	3725, 6194	2513.121	4567	8406		6148.126
cj, v Qal impf 3mp	*adj*, art, n ms	v Qal juss 3ms	art, n ms	pn	**40.**	cj, v Qal impf 3mp
וַיֹּאמְרוּ	כָּל־הָעָם	יְחִי	הַמֶּלֶךְ	שְׁלֹמֹה		וַיַּעֲלוּ
wayyō'm^{e}rû	kol-hā'ām	y^{e}chî	hammelekh	sh^{e}lōmōh		wayya'ălû
and they said	all the people	may he live	the king	Solomon		and they went up

... for I have made him the leader of Israel, *Beck* ... he shall be king in my place, *Berkeley* ... I will instruct him in his administration over Israel, *Fenton* ... him have I commanded to be leader over Israel, *Goodspeed* ... he is the man whom I have appointed as ruler, *JB*.

36. And Benaiah the son of Jehoiada answered the king, and said, Amen: the LORD God of my lord the king say so too: ... May the LORD, the God of my lord the king, so decree, *NAB* ... LORD, the God of my master, has declared, *NCV* ... It shall be done, *NEB* ... may Yahweh, God of my lord the king, confirm it, *JB* ... So be it, said Benaiah the son of Jehoiada to the king. May the Eternal confirm this order of my lord king!, *Moffatt*.

37. As the LORD hath been with my lord the king, even so be he with Solomon, and make his throne greater than the throne of my lord king David: ... may the LORD be with Solomon as he has been with you, and may he make Solomon's reign even greater than yours, *NLT* ... the seat of his authority, *BB* ... was with my master the king, so may He be, *Berkeley* ... extend his throne more than your Majesty David's, *Fenton* ... make his reign even more prosperous than yours, *Good News*.

38. So Zadok the priest, and Nathan the prophet, and Benaiah the son of Jehoiada, and the Cherethites, and the Pelethites, went down, and caused Solomon to ride upon king David's mule, and brought him to Gihon: ... they mounted Solomon on King David's mule and escorted him, *JB* ... the foreign bodyguard marched down; ... and conveyed him to Gihon, *Moffatt* ... royal bodyguards put Solomon on King David's mule and escorted him to Gihon Spring, *Good News*.

39. And Zadok the priest took an horn of oil out of the tabernacle, and anointed Solomon: ... the horn, *NKJV* ... from the tent, *NRSV* ... took the vessel of oil out of the Tent, and put the holy oil on Solomon, *BB* ... from the Hall and consecrated Solomon, *Fenton* ... took the container of olive oil which he had brought from the Tent of the LORD's presence, *Good News*.

And they blew the trumpet; and all the people said, God save king Solomon: ... when the horn was sounded, all the people said, Long life to King Solomon, *BB* ... sounded a trumpet, and all the forces cried, Long life, *Fenton*

40. And all the people came up after him, and the people piped

then summoned Zadok, the second priest, Nathan and Benaiah, and told them what to do. They were to take the bodyguard which was under Benaiah's command, to place Solomon on the king's own mule (which was regarded as the highest honor of all honors; cf. Gen. 41:43; Est. 6:8) to conduct him down the Valley of Jehoshaphat to Gihon (2 Chr. 32:30; 33:14), where the pool would furnish the water for the customary ablutions, to anoint him king, and then to blow the consecrated ram's horn, or shophar (2 Ki. 9:13), with the shout, "God save King Solomon!" After this, the boy was to be seated on the throne and proclaimed ruler over Israel and Judah.

1:36–40. Benaiah was one of David's twelve chosen captains, who was placed at the head of one of the monthly courses of 24,000 soldiers in the third month. The chronicler calls him a priest (1 Chr. 27:5). His available forces made him master of the situation, and he joyfully accepted the commission with, "Amen! So may Yahweh say," and with the prayer that the throne of Solomon might be even greater than the throne of David. Joab was commander-in-chief of the army, but his forces had not been summoned or mobilized. Accustomed to a bygone state of things, he had failed to observe that Benaiah's palace regiment of 600 picked men could strike a blow long before he was ready for action. These guards were "executioners and runners" (1 Sam. 30:14); perhaps an alien body of faithful mercenaries originally composed partly of Philistines. They formed a compact body of defenders, always prepared for action. Their one duty was to be ready at a moment's notice to carry out the king's commands. Such a picked

3725, 6194	313	6194	2591.352	904, 2592	7976	7977	1448
adj, art, n ms	prep, ps 3ms	cj, art, n ms	v Piel ptc mp	prep, art, n mp	cj, adj	n fs	adj
כָּל־הָעָם	אַחֲרָיו	וְהָעָם	מְחַלְּלִים	בַּחֲלִלִים	וּשְׂמֵחִים	שִׂמְחָה	גְדוֹלָה
khol-hā'ām	'achrâv	wehā'ām	mechallelîm	bachlilîm	ûsemēchîm	simchāh	ghedhôlāh
all the people	after him	and the people	piping	on the flutes	and joyful	joy	great

1260.222	800	904, 7249		8471.121	135
cj, v Niphal impf 3fs	art, n fs	prep, n ms, ps 3mp	**41.**	cj, v Qal impf 3ms	pn
וַתִּבָּקַע	הָאָרֶץ	בְּקוֹלָם		וַיִּשְׁמַע	אֲדֹנִיָּהוּ
wattibbāqa'	hā'ārets	beqôlām		wayyishma'	'ădhōnîyāhû
and it was split	the ground	by their sound		and he heard	Adonijah

3725, 7410.156	866	882	2062	3735.316	3937, 404.141
cj, *adj*, art, v Qal pass ptc mp	rel pron	prep, ps 3ms	cj, pers pron	v Piel pf 3cp	prep, v Qal inf con
וְכָל־הַקְּרֻאִים	אֲשֶׁר	אִתּוֹ	וְהֵם	כִּלּוּ	לֶאֱכֹל
wekhol-haqqeru'îm	'ăsher	'ittô	wehēm	killû	le'ěkhōl
and all those called	who	with him	and they	they finished	eating

8471.121	3200	881, 7249	8223	569.121	4211	7249, 7439
cj, v Qal impf 3ms	pn	do, *n ms*	art, n ms	cj, v Qal impf 3ms	intrg	*n ms*, art, n fs
וַיִּשְׁמַע	יוֹאָב	אֶת־קוֹל	הַשּׁוֹפָר	וַיֹּאמֶר	מַדּוּעַ	קוֹל־הַקִּרְיָה
wayyishma'	yô'āv	'eth-qôl	hashshôphār	wayyō'mer	maddûa'	qôl-haqqiryāh
and he heard	Joab	the sound of	the ram's horn	and he said	why	the sound of the city

2064.153		5968	1744.351	2079	3230	1158, 55	3669
v Qal act ptc fs	**42.**	adv, ps 3ms	v Piel ptc ms	cj, intrj	pn	*n ms*, pn	art, n ms
הוֹמָה		עוֹדֶנּוּ	מְדַבֵּר	וְהִנֵּה	יוֹנָתָן	בֶּן־אֶבְיָתָר	הַכֹּהֵן
hômāh		'ôdhennû	medhabbēr	wehinnēh	yônāthān	ben-'evyāthār	hakkōhēn
making an uproar		still he	speaking	and behold	Jonathan	the son of Abiathar	the priest

971.111	569.121	135	971.131	3706	382	2524	887
v Qal pf 3ms	cj, v Qal impf 3ms	pn	v Qal impv 2ms	cj	*n ms*	n ms	pers pron
בָּא	וַיֹּאמֶר	אֲדֹנִיָּהוּ	בֹּא	כִּי	אִישׁ	חַיִל	אַתָּה
bā'	wayyō'mer	'ădhōnîyāhû	bō'	kî	'îsh	chayil	'attāh
he came	and he said	Adonijah	enter	because	a man of	strength	you

3008	1339.323		6257.121	3230	569.121
cj, n ms	v Piel impf 2ms	**43.**	cj, v Qal impf 3ms	pn	cj, v Qal impf 3ms
וְטוֹב	תְּבַשֵּׂר		וַיַּעַן	יוֹנָתָן	וַיֹּאמֶר
wetôv	tevassēr		wayya'an	yônāthān	wayyō'mer
and something good	you are reporting		and he answered	Jonathan	and he said

3937, 135	61	112	4567, 1784	4566.511	881, 8406
prep, pn	adv	n mp, ps 1cp	art, n ms, pn	v Hiphil pf 3ms	do, pn
לַאֲדֹנִיָּהוּ	אֲבָל	אֲדֹנֵינוּ	הַמֶּלֶךְ־דָּוִד	הִמְלִיךְ	אֶת־שְׁלֹמֹה
la'ădhōnîyāhû	'ăvāl	'ădhōnênû	hammelekh-dāwidh	himlîkh	'eth-shelōmōh
to Adonijah	truly	our lord	the king David	he has made king	Solomon

	8365.121	882, 4567	881, 6923	3669	881, 5600	5204
44.	cj, v Qal impf 3ms	prep, ps 3ms, art, n ms	do, pn	art, n ms	cj, do, pn	art, n ms
	וַיִּשְׁלַח	אִתּוֹ־הַמֶּלֶךְ	אֶת־צָדוֹק	הַכֹּהֵן	וְאֶת־נָתָן	הַנָּבִיא
	wayyishlach	'ittô-hammelekh	'eth-tsādhôq	hakkōhēn	we'eth-nāthān	hannāvî'
	and he sent	with him the king	Zadok	the priest	and Nathan	the prophet

1172	1158, 3179	3903	6676	7680.526
cj, pn	*n ms*, pn	cj, art, pn	cj, art, pn	cj, v Hiphil impf 3mp
וּבְנָיָהוּ	בֶּן־יְהוֹיָדָע	וְהַכְּרֵתִי	וְהַפְּלֵתִי	וַיַּרְכִּבוּ
ûvenāyāhû	ben-yehôyādhā'	wehakkerēthî	wehappelēthî	wayyarkivû
and Benaiah	the son of Jehoiada	and the Cherethites	and the Pelethites	and they caused to ride

with pipes: ... went up after him playing upon flutes, *Goodspeed* ... people all escorted him back, with pipes playing, *JB* ... The troops all marched up behind him, *Moffatt.*

and rejoiced with great joy, so that the earth rent with the sound of them: ... rejoicing with such great outburst that the earth was rent with their noise, *Goodspeed* ... loud rejoicing and shouts to split the earth, *JB* ... dancing and cheering in their delight so loudly that the earth seemed to be splitting, *Moffatt* ... the earth shook, *NASB* ... the earth rang with the noise of their cry, *Douay.*

41. And Adonijah and all the guests that were with him heard it as they had made an end of eating: ... it came to the ears of Adonijah and all the guests who were with him, when their meal was ended, *BB* ... When Adonijah and all his guests heard this, they stopped eating, *Beck* ... heard it just as they had finished, *Berkeley* ... as they were all at dinner, *Fenton* ... ended their banquet, *NAB* ... were finishing the feast, *Good News.*

And when Joab heard the sound of the trumpet, he said, Wherefore is this noise of the city being in an uproar?: ... hearing the sound of the horn, said, What is the reason of this noise as if the town was worked up, *BB* ... What does this uproar in the city mean, *Moffatt* ... Why is the city in such a noisy uproar, *NKJV* ... What's going on?, *NLT.*

42. And while he yet spake, behold, Jonathan the son of Abiathar the priest came: and Adonijah said unto him, Come in; for thou art a valiant man, and bringest good tidings: ... you are a mighty man and you bring good news, *KJVII* ... thou art a worthy man, *ASV* ... while the words were on his lips ... man of good faith and the news which you have for us will be good, *BB* ... man of standing and surely, *Berkeley* ... powerful man, and one of good luck, *Fenton* ... honest man, so you must be bringing good news, *JB.*

43. And Jonathan answered and said to Adonijah, Verily our lord king David hath made Solomon king: ... No! Our master King David has made Solomon the new king, *NCV* ... The truth is, *JB* ... On the contrary!, *NAB* ... Not so, for our lord king David hath appointed, *Douay*... Far otherwise, *NEB.*

44. And the king hath sent with him Zadok the priest, and Nathan the prophet, and Benaiah the son of Jehoiada, and the Cherethites, and the Pelethites, and they have caused him to ride upon the king's

---

regiment has often held in its hands the prerogative of an empire. They were originally, at any rate, identical with the gibbôrîm (HED #1399; 2 Sam. 23:8–39; 1 Chr. 11:10–47; 1 Ki. 1:8) and had been at first commanded by men who had earned rank by personal prowess. But for their intervention on this occasion, Adonijah would have become king.

While Adonijah's followers were wasting time over their turbulent banquet, the younger court party was carrying out the unexpectedly vigorous suggestions of the aged king. While the eastern hills echoed with "Long live King Adonijah," the western hills resounded with shouts of "Long live King Solomon!" The young Solomon had been ceremoniously mounted on the king's mule, and the procession had gone down to Gihon. There, with the solemnity which is only mentioned in cases of disputed succession, Nathan the prophet and Zadok the priest anointed the son of Bathsheba with the horn of perfumed oil which the latter had taken from the sacred tent at Zion.

These measures had been neglected by Adonijah's party in the precipitation of their plot, and they were regarded as being of the utmost importance, as they are in Persia to this day. Then the trumpets blew, and the vast crowd which had assembled shouted, "God save King Solomon!" The people broke into acclamations and danced and played on pipes, and the earth rang again with the mighty sound. Adonijah had fancied, and he subsequently asserted, that "all Israel set their faces on me that I should reign." But his vanity had misled him. Many of the people may have seen through his shallow character and may have dreaded the rule of such a king. Others were still attached to David and were prepared to accept his choice, while others were struck with the grave bearing and the youthful beauty of the son of Bathsheba. The multitude probably consisted of opportunists ready to shout with the winner whoever he might be.

1:41–48. The old warrior Joab, perhaps less dazed with wine and enthusiasm than the other guests of Adonijah, was the first to catch the sound of the trumpet blasts and of the general rejoicing, and to understand its significance. As he started up in surprise, the guests caught sight of Jonathan, son of Abiathar, a swift-footed priest who had acted as a spy for David in Jerusalem at Absalom's rebellion (2 Sam. 15:27; 17:17), but who now, like his father Abiathar and so many of his betters, had gone over to Adonijah. The prince welcomed him as a "man of worth," one who was sure to bring tidings of good omen (2 Sam. 18:27); but Jonathan burst out with, "Nay, but our lord, King David, hath made Solomon king." He does not seem to have been in

881	6142	6756	4567		5066.126	881	6923	3669
do, ps 3ms	prep	*n fs*	art, n ms	**45.**	cj, v Qal impf 3mp	do, ps 3ms	pn	art, n ms
אֹתוֹ	עַל	פִּרְדַּת	הַמֶּלֶךְ		וַיִּמְשְׁחוּ	אֹתוֹ	צָדוֹק	הַכֹּהֵן
'ōthô	'al	pirdath	hammelekh		wayyimshᵉchû	'ōthô	tsādhôq	hakkōhēn
him	on	the female mule of	the king		and they anointed	him	Zadok	the priest

5600	5204	3937, 4567	904, 1556	6148.126	4623, 8427	7976
cj, pn	art, n ms	prep, n ms	prep, pn	cj, v Qal impf 3mp	prep, adv	adj
וְנָתָן	הַנָּבִיא	לְמֶלֶךְ	בְּגִחוֹן	וַיַּעֲלוּ	מִשָּׁם	שְׂמֵחִים
wᵉnāthān	hannāvî'	lᵉmelekh	bᵉghichôn	wayya'ălû	mishshām	sᵉmēchîm
and Nathan	the prophet	as king	in Gihon	and they went up	from there	joyful

2016.222	7439	2000	7249	866	8471.117		1612
cj, v Niphal impf 3fs	art, n fs	pers pron	art, n ms	rel part	v Qal pf 2mp	**46.**	cj, cj
וַתֵּהֹם	הַקִּרְיָה	הוּא	הַקּוֹל	אֲשֶׁר	שְׁמַעְתֶּם		וְגַם
wattēhōm	haqqiryāh	hû'	haqqôl	'ăsher	shᵉma'ăttem		wᵉgham
and it is in an uproar	the city	it	the sound	which	you have heard		and also

3553.111	8406	6142	3802	4548		1612, 971.116	5860
v Qal pf 3ms	pn	prep	*n ms*	art, n fs	**47.**	cj, cj, v Qal pf 3cp	*n mp*
יָשַׁב	שְׁלֹמֹה	עַל	כִּסֵּא	הַמְּלוּכָה		וְגַם־בָּאוּ	עַבְדֵי
yāshav	shᵉlōmōh	'al	kissē'	hammᵉlûkhāh		wᵉgham-bā'û	'avdhê
he has sat	Solomon	on	the throne of	the kingship		and also they came	the servants of

4567	3937, 1313.341	881, 112	4567	1784	3937, 569.141
art, n ms	prep, v Piel inf con	do, n mp, ps 1cp	art, n ms	pn	prep, v Qal inf con
הַמֶּלֶךְ	לְבָרֵךְ	אֶת־אֲדֹנֵינוּ	הַמֶּלֶךְ	דָּוִד	לֵאמֹר
hammelekh	lᵉvārēkh	'eth-'ădhōnênû	hammelekh	dāwidh	lē'mōr
the king	to bless	our lord	the king	David	saying

3296.521	435	8428	8406	4623, 8428
v Hiphil juss 3ms	n mp, ps 2ms	*n ms*	pn	prep, n ms, ps 2ms
יֵיטֵב	אֱלֹהֶיךָ	אֶת־שֵׁם	שְׁלֹמֹה	מִשְּׁמֶךָ
yêtēv	'ĕlōhêkhā	'eth-shēm	shᵉlōmōh	mishshᵉmekhā
may He cause to be better	your God	the name of	Solomon	than your name

1461.321	881, 3802	4623, 3802	8246.721	4567
cj, v Piel juss 3ms	do, n ms, ps 3ms	prep, n ms, ps 2ms	cj, v Hithpael impf 3ms	art, n ms
וִיגַדֵּל	אֶת־כִּסְאוֹ	מִכִּסְאֶךָ	וַיִּשְׁתַּחוּ	הַמֶּלֶךְ
wîghaddēl	'eth-kis'ô	mikkis'ekhā	wayyishtachû	hammelekh
and may He make greater	his throne	than your throne	and he prostrated himself	the king

6142, 5085		1612, 3722	569.111	4567	1313.155	3176	435
prep, art, n ms	**48.**	cj, cj, adv	v Qal pf 3ms	art, n ms	v Qal pass ptc ms	pn	*n mp*
עַל־הַמִּשְׁכָּב		וְגַם־כָּכָה	אָמַר	הַמֶּלֶךְ	בָּרוּךְ	יְהוָה	אֱלֹהֵי
'al-hammishkāv		wᵉgham-kākhāh	'āmar	hammelekh	bārûkh	yᵉhwāh	'ĕlōhê
on the bed		and also thus	he said	the king	blessed	Yahweh	the God of

3547	866	5598.111	3219	3553.151	6142, 3802	6084	7495.154
pn	rel pron	v Qal pf 3ms	art, n ms	v Qal act ptc ms	prep, n ms, ps 1cs	cj, n fd, ps 1cs	v Qal act ptc fp
יִשְׂרָאֵל	אֲשֶׁר	נָתַן	הַיּוֹם	יֹשֵׁב	עַל־כִּסְאִי	וְעֵינַי	רֹאוֹת
yisrā'ēl	'ăsher	nāthan	hayyôm	yōshēv	'al-kis'î	wᵉ'ênay	rō'ôth
Israel	Who	He has given	today	one who sits	on my throne	and my eyes	seeing

	2829.126	7251.126	3725, 7410.156	866	3937, 135
49.	cj, v Qal impf 3mp	cj, v Qal impf 3mp	*adj*, art, v Qal pass ptc mp	rel pron	prep, pn
	וַיֶּחֶרְדוּ	וַיָּקֻמוּ	כָּל־הַקְּרֻאִים	אֲשֶׁר	לַאֲדֹנִיָּהוּ
	wayyecherdhû	wayyāqumû	kol-haqqᵉru'îm	'ăsher	la'ădhōnîyāhû
	then they trembled	and they arose	all those called	who	to Adonijah

mule: ... mounted him on the king's mule, *NEB* ... made him ride upon, *Berkeley* ... king's beast, *BB*.

45. And Zadok the priest and Nathan the prophet have anointed him king in Gihon: and they are come up from thence rejoicing, so that the city rang again: ... have consecrated him King at Ghikhon, and have gone up from there cheering, *Fenton* ... town is in uproar, *Goodspeed* ... come back rejoicing till the city resounds, *Mofatt* ... Now the whole city is excited, *NCV* ... put the holy oil on him ... came back from there with joy, and the town was all worked up, *BB*.

This is the noise that ye have heard: ... and that sudden roar which you have heard is the sound of them, *Fenton* ... That was the noise, *Goodspeed* ... That is the noise you heard, *Moffatt* ... has come to your ears, *BB*.

46. And also Solomon sitteth on the throne of the kingdom: ... More than that, Solomon has taken his seat on the royal throne, *NEB* ... now sits on, *NRSV* ... has occupied, *Berkeley*.

47. And moreover the king's servants came to bless our lord king David, saying: ... the seat of his authority greater than your seat, *BB* ... king's men also have come to congratulate, *Beck* ... have already gone to compliment our master King David, *Berkeley* ... ministers of King David have also come to thank our King David, *Fenton*.

God make the name of Solomon better than thy name, and make his throne greater than thy throne: ... May your God make Solomon more famous than you, *Beck* ... more renowned than you and magnify his throne above yours, *Berkeley* ... Thy God make the name of Solomon more excellent than thy name, *Darby* ... May it please your God to make the name of Solomon more than your name, and may He extend his throne more than He extended yours, *Fenton*.

And the king bowed himself upon the bed: ... and the king was bent low in worship on his bed, *BB* ... Then the king did homage upon his bed, *Berkeley* ... And they have bowed to the king who was on his couch, *Fenton*.

48. And also thus said the king, Blessed be the LORD God of Israel: ... Blessed be Yahweh, *JB* ... Blessed be the Eternal, *Moffatt* ... May the God of Israel be praised, *BB* ... Let us praise the LORD, *Good News*.

which hath given one to sit on my throne this day: ... who has today granted one of my offspring, *Goodspeed* ... for setting one of my own sons on the throne, *JB* ... given one of my seed to be king in my place this day, *BB* ... made one of my descendants succeed me as king, *Good News*.

mine eyes even seeing it: ... my own eyes beholding it, *Goodspeed* ... while I am still alive to see it, *JB* ... actually allowed me this day to see a son of mine, *Moffatt* ... has let my eyes, *BB* ... and has let me live to see it, *Good News*.

49. And all the guests that were with Adonijah were afraid, and rose up, and went every man his way: ... were frightened. They got up and left, *Beck* ... got up in fear and went away, *BB* ... were terrified and arose, and everyone went to his carriage, *Fenton* ... taking fright, got

---

a hurry to bring this fatal intelligence; for he had not only waited until the entire ceremony at Gihon was over, but to the close of the enthronement of Solomon in Jerusalem. He had seen the young king seated on the throne of state in the midst of the jubilant people. David had been carried out upon his couch and, bowing his head in worship before the multitude, had said, "Blessed be the LORD God of Israel, which hath given one to sit on my throne this day, mine eyes even seeing it."

1:49–53. The report fell like a thunderbolt among Adonijah's unprepared adherents. A general flight took place, each man being only eager to save himself. The straw fire of their enthusiasm had already flared itself away. Deserted by everyone and fearing to pay the forfeit of his life, Adonijah fled to the nearest sanctuary, where the Ark stood on Mount Zion under the care of his supporter, the high priest Abiathar (1 Ki. 1:50). There he caught hold of the horns of the altar—wooden projections at each of its corners, overlaid with brass. When sacrifices were offered, the animals were tied to these horns of the altar (Exo. 27:2ff; 29:12; 30:10; Ps. 118:27; cf. Exo. 21:14), and they were smeared with the victim's blood, just as in after days the propitiatory was sprinkled with the blood of the bull and the goat on the Great Day of Atonement. The mercy seat thus became a symbol of atonement and an appeal to God that He would forgive the sinful priest and the sinful nation who came before Him with the blood of expiation. The mercy seat would have furnished an inviolable sanctuary had it not been enclosed in the Holiest Place, unapproachable by any feet but that of the high priest once a year. The horns of the altar were, however, available for refuge to any offender, and their protection involved an appeal to the mercy of man as to the mercy of God (Exo. 21:14).

There in wretched plight clung the fallen prince, hurled down in one day from the summit of his ambition. He refused to leave the spot unless King

2050.126	382	3937, 1932	50.	135	3486.111	4623, 6686	8406
cj, v Qal impf 3mp	n ms	prep, n ms, ps 3ms		cj, pn	v Qal pf 3ms	prep, *n mp*	pn
וַיֵּלְכוּ	אִישׁ	לְדַרְכּוֹ		וַאֲדֹנִיָּהוּ	יָרֵא	מִפְּנֵי	שְׁלֹמֹה
wayyēlᵉkhû	'îsh	lᵉdharkô		wa'ădhōnîyāhû	yārē'	mippᵉnê	shᵉlōmōh
and they went	each	to his way		and Adonijah	he was afraid	from before	Solomon

7251.121	2050.121	2480.521	904, 7451	4326
cj, v Qal impf 3ms	cj, v Qal impf 3ms	cj, v Hiphil impf 3ms	prep, *n fp*	art, n ms
וַיָּקָם	וַיֵּלֶךְ	וַיַּחֲזֵק	בְּקַרְנוֹת	הַמִּזְבֵּחַ
wayyāqām	wayyēlekh	wayyachzēq	bᵉqarnôth	hammizbēach
and he rose up	and he went	and he siezed	onto the horns of	the altar

51.	5222.621	3937, 8406	3937, 569.141	2079	135	3486.111
	cj, v Hophal impf 3ms	prep, pn	prep, v Qal inf con	intrj	pn	v Qal pf 3ms
	וַיֻּגַּד	לִשְׁלֹמֹה	לֵאמֹר	הִנֵּה	אֲדֹנִיָּהוּ	יָרֵא
	wayyuggadh	lishlōmōh	lē'mōr	hinnēh	'ădhōnîyāhû	yārē'
	and it was reported	to Solomon	saying	behold	Adonijah	he feared

881, 4567	8406	2079	270.111	904, 7451	4326	3937, 569.141
do, art, n ms	pn	cj, intrj	v Qal pf 3ms	prep, *n fp*	art, n ms	prep, v Qal inf con
אֶת־הַמֶּלֶךְ	שְׁלֹמֹה	וְהִנֵּה	אָחַז	בְּקַרְנוֹת	הַמִּזְבֵּחַ	לֵאמֹר
'eth-hammelekh	shᵉlōmōh	wᵉhinnēh	'āchaz	bᵉqarnôth	hammizbēach	lē'mōr
the king	Solomon	and behold	he has siezed	onto the horns of	the altar	saying

8123.221, 3937	3626, 3219	4567	8406	524, 4322.521	881, 5860
v Niphal juss 3ms, prep, ps 1cs	prep, art, n ms	art, n ms	pn	cj, v Hiphil impf 3ms	do, n ms, ps 3ms
יִשָּׁבַע־לִי	כַיּוֹם	הַמֶּלֶךְ	שְׁלֹמֹה	אִם־יָמִית	אֶת־עַבְדּוֹ
yishshāva‘-lî	khayyôm	hammelekh	shᵉlōmōh	'im-yāmîth	'eth-‘avdô
may he swear to me	like the day	the king	Solomon	whether he will execute	his servant

904, 2820	52.	569.121	8406	524	2030.121	3937, 1158, 2524
prep, art, n fs		cj, v Qal impf 3ms	pn	cj	v Qal impf 3ms	prep, *n ms*, n ms
בֶּחָרֶב		וַיֹּאמֶר	שְׁלֹמֹה	אִם	יִהְיֶה	לְבֶן־חַיִל
bechārev		wayyō'mer	shᵉlōmōh	'im	yihyeh	lᵉven-chayil
with the sword		and he said	Solomon	if	he is	a son of wealth

3940, 5489.121	4623, 8000	800	524, 7750	4834.222, 904
neg part, v Qal impf 3ms	prep, n fs, ps 3ms	n fs	cj, cj, n fs	v Niphal impf 3fs, prep, ps 3ms
לֹא־יִפֹּל	מִשַּׂעֲרָתוֹ	אַרְצָה	וְאִם־רָעָה	תִּמָּצֵא־בוֹ
lō'-yippōl	missa‘ărāthô	'ārᵉtsāh	wᵉ'im-rā‘āh	thimmātsē'-vô
it will not fall	from one of his hairs	to the ground	but if evil	it is found in him

4322.111	53.	8365.121	4567	8406	3495.526	4623, 6142
cj, v Qal pf 3ms		cj, v Qal impf 3ms	art, n ms	pn	cj, v Hiphil impf 3mp, ps 3ms	prep, prep
וָמֵת		וַיִּשְׁלַח	הַמֶּלֶךְ	שְׁלֹמֹה	וַיֹּרִדֻהוּ	מֵעַל
wāmēth		wayyishlach	hammelekh	shᵉlōmōh	wayyōridhuhû	mē‘al
then he must die		and he sent	the king	Solomon	and they brought him down	from on

4326	971.121	8246.721	3937, 4567	8406
art, n ms	cj, v Qal impf 3ms	cj, v Hithpael impf 3ms	prep, art, n ms	pn
הַמִּזְבֵּחַ	וַיָּבֹא	וַיִּשְׁתַּחוּ	לַמֶּלֶךְ	שְׁלֹמֹה
hammizbēach	wayyāvō'	wayyishtachû	lammelekh	shᵉlōmōh
the altar	and he entered	and he prostrated himself	to the king	Solomon

569.121, 3937	8406	2050.131	3937, 1041	2:1	7414.126
cj, v Qal impf 3ms, prep, ps 3ms	pn	v Qal impv 2ms	prep, n ms, ps 2ms		cj, v Qal impf 3mp
וַיֹּאמֶר־לוֹ	שְׁלֹמֹה	לֵךְ	לְבֵיתֶךָ		וַיִּקְרְבוּ
wayyō'mer-lô	shᵉlōmōh	lēkh	lᵉvêthekhā		wayyiqrᵉvû
and he said to him	Solomon	go	to your house		and they drew near

3219, 1784	3937, 4322.141	6943.321	881, 8406	1158	3937, 569.141
n mp, pn	prep, v Qal inf con	cj, v Piel impf 3ms	do, pn	n ms, ps 3ms	prep, v Qal inf con
יְמֵי־דָוִד	לָמוּת	וַיְצַו	אֶת־שְׁלֹמֹה	בְנוֹ	לֵאמֹר
yemê-dhāwidh	lāmûth	waytsaw	'eth-shelōmōh	venô	lē'mōr
the days of David	to die	and he commanded	Solomon	his son	saying

2. 609	2050.151	904, 1932	3725, 800	2480.113
pers pron	v Qal act ptc ms	prep, *n ms*	*adj*, art, n fs	cj, v Qal pf 2ms
אָנֹכִי	הֹלֵךְ	בְּדֶרֶךְ	כָּל־הָאָרֶץ	וְחָזַקְתָּ
'ānōkhî	hōlēkh	bedherekh	kol-hā'ārets	wechāzaqōttā
I	going	on the way of	all the earth	now you must be strong

up and made off in their several directions, *JB* ... rose in panic and scattered, *NEB* ... trembled, and rose, *RSV* ... every man of them got up and went home, *Moffatt*.

50. And Adonijah feared because of Solomon, and arose, and went, and caught hold on the horns of the altar: ... was also afraid of Solomon, so he went and took hold of the corners, *NCV* ... was so fearful of Solomon, *Berkeley* ... in terror of Solomon, got up and ran to catch hold of the knobs, *Moffatt*.

51. And it was told Solomon, saying, Behold, Adonijah feareth king Solomon: for, lo, he hath caught hold on the horns of the altar, saying, Let king Solomon swear unto me today that he will not slay his servant with the sword: ... received this report: Look, Adonijah is so fearful of, *Berkeley* ... kill his servant, *Fenton* ... his servant murdered, *Moffatt* ... Adonijah is terrified of King Solomon and is now clinging to ... his servant executed, *JB*.

52. And Solomon said, If he will show himself a worthy man, there shall not an hair of him fall to the earth: ... is seen to be a man of good faith, ... will be touched, *BB* ... Should he bear himself honourably ... not one hair of his shall fall to the ground, *JB* ... proves himself an honest man, not a hair of him shall fall to the ground, *Moffatt* ... If he is loyal, not even a hair on his head will be touched, *Good News*.

but if wickedness shall be found in him, he shall die: ... wrongdoing is seen in him, he is to be put to death, *BB* ... evil be found, *Berkeley* ... he proves difficult, *JB* ... he is convicted of crime, then die he must, *Moffatt* ... but if he is not, he will die, *Good News*.

53. So king Solomon sent, and they brought him down from the altar. And he came and bowed himself to king Solomon: and Solomon said unto him, Go to thine house: ... he came and did homage ... told him to go home, *Moffatt* ... prostrated himself before the king, and Solomon ordered him, *NEB* ... gave honour, *BB* ... going in he worshipped, *Douay*.

2:1. Now the days of David drew nigh that he should die; and he charged Solomon his son, saying: ... the time of David's death came near; and he gave orders, *BB* ... was about to die, *Good News* ... he gave his last instructions, *Beck* ... he advised, *Berkeley* ... he enjoined, *Darby*.

2. I go the way of all the earth: be thou strong therefore, and show thyself a man: ... of all mankind. Take courage and be a man, *NAB* ... of all flesh, *Douay* ... My time to die is near. Be a good and strong leacer, *NCV* ... Be strong, be courageous, *NRSV*.

3. And keep the charge of the LORD thy God, to walk in his ways: ... Fulfil your duty to, *NEB* ... observe what the LORD your God requires, *NIV* ... Do everything the LORD your God ordered you to do, *Beck*.

to keep his statutes, and his commandments, and his judgments, and his testimonies: ... conform to

Solomon would first of all swear that he would not slay his servant with the sword (1 Ki. 1:51). Adonijah saw that all was over with his cause. "God," says the Portuguese proverb, "can write straight on crooked lines"; and as is so often the case, the crisis which brought about his will was the immediate result of an endeavor to defeat it.

2:1–4. In the Book of Samuel, we have the last words of David in the form of a brief and vivid psalm, of which the leading principle is, "He that ruleth over men must be just, ruling in the fear of God." A king's justice must be shown alike in his gracious influence upon the good and his stern justice to the wicked. The worthless sons of Belial are, he says, "to be beaten down like thorns with spear-shafts and iron" (2 Sam. 23:1–7).

The same principle dominates in the charge which he gave to Solomon, perhaps after the magnificent public inauguration of his reign described in 1 Chr. 28–29. He bade his young son to show himself a man and be rigidly faithful to the law of Moses, earning thereby the prosperity that would never fail to attend true righteousness (Deut. 17:18ff). Thus the promise to David: "There shall

2030.113	3937, 382		8490.113	881, 5111	3176	435
cj, v Qal pf 2ms	prep, n ms	3.	cj, v Qal pf 2ms	do, n fs	pn	n mp, ps 2ms
וְהָיִיתָ	לְאִישׁ		וְשָׁמַרְתָּ	אֶת־מִשְׁמֶרֶת	יְהוָה	אֱלֹהֶיךָ
wehāyîthā	le'îsh		weshāmartā	'eth-mishmereth	yehwāh	'ĕlōhêkhā
and you must become	a man		and you must observe	the commission of	Yahweh	your God

3937, 2050.141	904, 1932	3937, 8490.141	2807	4851
prep, v Qal inf con	prep, n mp, ps 3ms	prep, v Qal inf con	n fp, ps 3ms	n fp, ps 3ms
לָלֶכֶת	בִּדְרָכָיו	לִשְׁמֹר	חֻקֹּתָיו	מִצְוֹתָיו
lālekheth	bidhrākhâv	lishmōr	chuqqōthâv	mitswōthâv
to walk	in his ways	to observe	his statutes	his commandments

5122	5925	3626, 3918.155	904, 8784	5057	3937, 4775
cj, n mp, ps 3ms	cj, n fp, ps 3ms	prep, art, v Qal pass ptc ms	prep, n fs	pn	prep, prep
וּמִשְׁפָּטָיו	וְעֵדְוֹתָיו	כַּכָּתוּב	בְּתוֹרַת	מֹשֶׁה	לְמַעַן
ûmishpāṭâv	we'ēdhewōthâv	kakkāthûv	bethôrath	mōsheh	lema'an
and his ordinances	and his testimonies	like what was written	in the Law of	Moses	so that

7959.523	881	3725, 866	6449.123	881	3725, 866	6680.123	8427		3937, 4775
v Hiphil impf 2ms	do	adj, rel part	v Qal impf 2ms	cj, do	adj, rel part	v Qal impf 2ms	adv	4.	prep, prep
תַּשְׂכִּיל	אֵת	כָּל־אֲשֶׁר	תַּעֲשֶׂה	וְאֵת	כָּל־אֲשֶׁר	תִּפְנֶה	שָׁם		לְמַעַן
taskîl	'ēth	kol-'ăsher	ta'ăseh	we'ēth	kol-'ăsher	tiphneh	shām		lema'an
you will succeed		all that	you will do	and	all where	you will turn	there		so that

7251.521	3176	881, 1745	866	1744.311	6142	3937, 569.141
v Hiphil impf 3ms	pn	do, n ms, ps 3ms	rel part	v Piel pf 3ms	prep, ps 1cs	prep, v Qal inf con
יָקִים	יְהוָה	אֶת־דְּבָרוֹ	אֲשֶׁר	דִּבֶּר	עָלַי	לֵאמֹר
yāqîm	yehwāh	'eth-devārô	'ăsher	dibber	'ālay	lē'mōr
He will establish	Yahweh	his word	which	he has spoken	concerning me	saying

524, 8490.126	1158	881, 1932	3937, 2050.141	3937, 6686	904, 583
cj, v Qal impf 3mp	n mp, ps 2ms	do, n ms, ps 3mp	prep, v Qal inf con	prep, n mp, ps 1cs	prep, n fs
אִם־יִשְׁמְרוּ	בָנֶיךָ	אֶת־דַּרְכָּם	לָלֶכֶת	לְפָנַי	בֶּאֱמֶת
'im-yishmerû	vānêkhā	'eth-darkām	lālekheth	lephānay	be'ĕmeth
if they are careful	your sons	their way	to walk	before Me	with reliability

904, 3725, 3949	904, 3725, 5497	3937, 569.141	3940, 3901.221	3937
prep, adj, n ms, ps 3mp	cj, prep, adj, n fs, ps 3mp	prep, v Qal inf con	neg part, v Niphal impf 3ms	prep, ps 2ms
בְּכָל־לְבָבָם	וּבְכָל־נַפְשָׁם	לֵאמֹר	לֹא־יִכָּרֵת	לְךָ
bekhol-levāvām	ûvekhol-naphshām	lē'mōr	lō'-yikkārēth	lekhā
with all their heart	and with all their soul	saying	he will not be cut off	of you

382	4623, 6142	3802	3547		1612	887	3156.113	881	866, 6449.111
n ms	prep, prep	n ms	pn	5.	cj, cj	pers pron	v Qal pf 2ms	do	rel part, v Qal pf 3ms
אִישׁ	מֵעַל	כִּסֵּא	יִשְׂרָאֵל		וְגַם	אַתָּה	יָדַעְתָּ	אֵת	אֲשֶׁר־עָשָׂה
'îsh	mē'al	kissē'	yisrā'ēl		wegham	'attāh	yādha'ttā	'ēth	'ăsher-'āsāh
a man	from on	the throne of	Israel		and also	you	you know		what he did

3937	3200	1158, 7152	866	6449.111	3937, 8530, 8015
prep, ps 1cs	pn	n ms, pn	rel part	v Qal pf 3ms	prep, num, n mp
לִי	יוֹאָב	בֶּן־צְרוּיָה	אֲשֶׁר	עָשָׂה	לִשְׁנֵי־שָׂרֵי
lî	yô'āv	ben-tserûyāh	'ăsher	'āsāh	lishnê-sārê
to me	Joab	the son of Zeruiah	what	he did	to the two of the commanders of

6893	3547	3937, 69	1158, 5553	3937, 6248	1158, 3616
n fp	pn	prep, pn	n ms, pn	cj, prep, pn	n ms, pn
צִבְאוֹת	יִשְׂרָאֵל	לְאַבְנֵר	בֶּן־נֵר	וְלַעֲמָשָׂא	בֶּן־יֶתֶר
tsiv'ôth	yisrā'ēl	le'avnēr	ben-nēr	wela'ămāsā'	ven-yether
the armies of	Israel	to Abner	the son of Ner	and to Amasa	the son of Jether

2103.121	7947.121	1879, 4560	904, 8361	5598.121
cj, v Qal impf 3ms, ps 3mp	cj, v Qal impf 3ms	*n mp*, n fs	prep, n ms	cj, v Qal impf 3ms
וַיַּהַרְגֵם	וַיָּשֶׂם	דְּמֵי־מִלְחָמָה	בְּשָׁלֹם	וַיִּתֵּן
wayyaharghēm	wayyāsem	d^e^mê-milchāmāh	b^e^shālōm	wayyittēn
since he killed them	and he set	bloodshed of war	during peace	and he put

1879	4560	904, 2383	866	904, 5158	904, 5458	866
n mp	n fs	prep, n fs, ps 3ms	rel part	prep, n md, ps 3ms	cj, prep, n fs, ps 3ms	rel part
דְּמֵי	מִלְחָמָה	בַּחֲגֹרָתוֹ	אֲשֶׁר	בְּמָתְנָיו	וּבְנַעֲלוֹ	אֲשֶׁר
d^e^mê	milchāmāh	bachghōrāthô	'ăsher	b^e^māth^e^nâv	ûv^e^na'ălô	'ăsher
bloodshed of	war	on his belt	which	around his waist	and on his sandals	which

his ways, observe ... his solemn precepts, *NEB* ... his decrees and commands, his laws and requirements, *NIV* ... carry out his rules, commandments, decrees, and solemn instructions, *Beck* ... keeping his laws and his orders and his rules and his words, *BB* ... his ordinances, *NRSV*.

as it is written in the law of Moses: ... as they are written, *NEB* ... as written, *NIV* ... recorded in the law of Moses, *BB*.

that thou mayest prosper in all that thou doest, and whithersoever thou turnest thyself: ... you may prosper in whatever you do and whichever way you turn, *NEB* ... do well in all you do and wherever you go, *BB* ... will succeed in everything you do and everywhere you go, *Beck*.

4. That the LORD may continue his word which he spake concerning me, saying: ... will carry out what He promised me, *Beck* ... confirm the word which He spoke to me, *Berkeley* ... may establish his word that he spoke, *Goodspeed* ... If you obey him, the LORD will keep the promise he made when he told me, *Good News*.

If thy children take heed to their way, to walk before me in truth with all their heart and with all their soul: ... descendants will be careful to live before Me sincerely with all their hearts and lives, *Beck* ... your sons watch their steps, so as to walk before Me devotedly, with their whole heart, *Berkeley* ... keep My path, *Fenton* ... guard their steps by walking before me in truth with all their mind and with all their heart, *Goodspeed* ... as long as they were careful to obey his commands faithfully, *Good News*.

there shall not fail thee (said he) a man on the throne of Israel: ... you will never fail to have a descendant, *Beck* ... there shall never be wanting for you a man, *Berkeley* ... a man from you upon the throne, *Fenton* ... fail you a man, *Goodspeed* ... that my descendants would rule Israel, *Good News*.

5. Moreover thou knowest also what Joab the son of Zeruiah did to me, and what he did to the two captains of the hosts of Israel, unto Abner the son of Ner, and unto Amasa the son of Jether: ... you remember ... He killed the two commanders of Israel's armies ... He did this as if he and they were at war, although it was a time of peace, *NCV*.

whom he slew, and shed the blood of war in peace: ... how he murdered them, JB ... He took revenge ... bloodshed without provocation, *NAB*

---

not fail thee a man on the throne of Israel," would be continued in the time of Solomon.

2:5–7. The character of Joab furnishes us with a singular study. He, Abishai and Asahel were the brave, impetuous sons of Zeruiah, the sister or half-sister of David. They were about his own age, and it is not impossible that they were the grandsons of Nahash, king of Ammon (2 Sam. 17:25; 1 Chr. 2:16). In the days of Saul, they had embraced the cause of David, heart and soul. They had endured all the hardships and fought through all the struggles of his freebooting days. Joab had been David's chief military commander for forty years. It was Joab who had conquered the Ammonites and Moabites and stormed the City of Waters. It was Joab who, at David's unqualified request, had brought about the murder of Uriah. It was Joab who, after wise but fruitless remonstrance, had been forced to number the people. His murder of the princely Abner, the son of Ner, might have been excused as the duty of an avenger of blood, for Abner, with one thrust of his mighty spear, had killed the young Asahel after the vain warning for Ashahel to break off his pursuit. At that early period of his reign, David was either unable or unwilling to punish the outrage, though he ostentatiously deplored it.

Doubtless in slaying Absalom, in spite of the king's entreaty, Joab had inflicted an agonizing wound on the pride and tenderness of his master. But Absalom was in open rebellion, and Joab may have held that David's probable pardon of the handsome rebel would be both weak and fatal. This death was inflicted in a manner needlessly

904, 7559		6449.113	3626, 2551	3940, 3495.523
prep, n fd, ps 3ms	6.	cj, v Qal pf 2ms	prep, n fs, ps 2ms	cj, neg part, v Hiphil juss 2ms
בְּרַגְלָיו		וְעָשִׂיתָ	כְּחָכְמָתֶךָ	וְלֹא־תוֹרֵד
beraghlâv		we'āsîthā	kechokhmāthekhā	welō'-thôrēdh
on his feet		then you must do	according to your wisdom	and do not allow to go down to

7939	904, 8361	8061		3937, 1158	1299	1610
n fs, ps 3ms	prep, n ms	n fs	7.	cj, prep, *n mp*	pn	art, pn
שֵׂיבָתוֹ	בְּשָׁלֹם	שְׁאֹל		וְלִבְנֵי	בַּרְזִלַּי	הַגִּלְעָדִי
sêvāthô	beshālōm	she'ōl		welivnê	varzillay	haggil'ādhî
his gray hair	in peace	the grave		but with the sons of	Barzillai	the Gileadite

6449.123, 2721	2030.116	904, 404.152	8374	3706, 3772
v Qal impf 2ms, n ms	cj, v Qal pf 3cp	prep, *v Qal act ptc mp*	n ms, ps 2ms	cj, adv
תַּעֲשֶׂה־חֶסֶד	וְהָיוּ	בְּאֹכְלֵי	שֻׁלְחָנֶךָ	כִּי־כֵן
ta'ăseh-chesedh	wehāyû	be'ōkhelê	shulchānekhā	kî-khēn
you will act with kindness	and they will be	among those eating from	your table	because so

7414.116	420	904, 1300.141	4623, 6686	54	250
v Qal pf 3cp	prep, ps 1cs	prep, v Qal inf con, ps 1cs	prep, *n mp*	pn	n ms, ps 2ms
קָרְבוּ	אֵלַי	בְּבָרְחִי	מִפְּנֵי	אַבְשָׁלוֹם	אָחִיךָ
qārvû	'ēlay	bevārechî	mippenê	'avshālôm	'āchîkhā
they came near	to me	when my fleeing	from before	Absalom	your brother

	2079	6196	8483	1158, 1660	1158, 3336	4623, 1016
8.	cj, intrj	prep, ps 2ms	pn	*n ms*, pn	*n ms*, art, pn	prep, pn
	וְהִנֵּה	עִמְּךָ	שִׁמְעִי	בֶן־גֵּרָא	בֶן־הַיְמִינִי	מִבַּחֻרִים
	wehinnēh	'immekhā	shim'î	ven-gērā'	ven-haymînî	mibbachurîm
	and behold	with you	Shimei	the son of Gera	a son of the Benjamites	from Bahurim

2000	7327.311	7329	4998.257	904, 3219	2050.141
cj, pers pron	v Piel pf 3ms, ps 1cs	n fs	v Niphal ptc fs	prep, *n ms*	v Qal inf con, ps 1cs
וְהוּא	קִלְלַנִי	קְלָלָה	נִמְרֶצֶת	בְּיוֹם	לֶכְתִּי
wehû'	qilelanî	qŏlālāh	nimretseth	beyôm	lekhtî
and he	he cursed me	a curse	something grievous	on the day of	my going to

4404	2000, 3495.111	3937, 7410.141	3497	8123.225	3937
pn	cj, pers pron, v Qal pf 3ms	prep, v Qal inf con, ps 1cs	art, pn	cj, v Niphal impf 1cs	prep, ps 3ms
מַחֲנָיִם	וְהוּא־יָרַד	לִקְרָאתִי	הַיַּרְדֵּן	וָאֶשָּׁבַע	לוֹ
machnāyim	wehû'-yāradh	liqŏrā'thî	hayyardēn	wā'eshshāva'	lô
Mahanaim	and he he came down	to meet me	the Jordan	and I swore	to him

904, 3176	3937, 569.141	524, 4322.525	904, 2820		6498
prep, pn	prep, v Qal inf con	cj, v Hiphil impf 1cs, ps 2ms	prep, art, n fs	9.	cj, adv
בַּיהוָה	לֵאמֹר	אִם־אֲמִיתְךָ	בֶּחָרֶב		וְעַתָּה
vayhwāh	lē'mōr	'im-'ămîthekhā	bechārev		we'attāh
by Yahweh	saying	if I execute you	with the sword		and now

414, 5536.323	3706	382	2550	887	3156.113	881	866
adv, v Piel juss 2ms, ps 3ms	cj	n ms	adj	pers pron	cj, v Qal pf 2ms	do	rel part
אַל־תְּנַקֵּהוּ	כִּי	אִישׁ	חָכָם	אָתָּה	וְיָדַעְתָּ	אֵת	אֲשֶׁר
'al-tenaqqēhû	kî	'îsh	chākhām	'āttāh	weyādha'ttā	'ēth	'ăsher
do not consider him exempt	because	a man	wise	you	and you know		what

6449.123, 3937	3495.513	881, 7939	904, 1879	8061
v Qal impf 2ms, prep, ps 3ms	cj, v Hiphil pf 2ms	do, n fs, ps 3ms	prep, n ms	n fs
תַּעֲשֶׂה־לּוֹ	וְהוֹרַדְתָּ	אֶת־שֵׂיבָתוֹ	בְּדָם	שְׁאוֹל
ta'ăseh-lô	wehôradhtā	'eth-sêvāthô	bedhām	she'ôl
you should do to him	that you must bring down to	his gray hair	with blood	the grave

... He killed them both, breaking the peace by bloody acts of war, *NEB* ... taking vengeance during peace for blood shed during war, *Moffatt*.

and put the blood of war upon his girdle that was about his loins, and in his shoes that were on his feet: ... staining the belt round my waist and the sandals on my feet with the blood of war, *JB* ... on the belt about my waist and the sandal on my foot, *NAB* ... He put their blood on the belt around his waist and on his sandals on his feet, *NCV* ... staining the very girdle round his waist and the shoes on his feet with innocent blood, *Moffatt*.

6. Do therefore according to thy wisdom: ... Deal with him, *NIV* ... as your wisdom prompts you, *NEB* ... be guided by your wisdom, *BB* ... Act wisely, *Beck* ... do to him as your skill dictates, *Fenton* ... Do with him what you think best, *NLT*.

and let not his hoar head go down to the grave in peace: ... do not let his grey hairs, *NEB* ... white head go down to the underworld, *BB* ... go down peacefully into the grave, *Beck* ... don't let him die, *NLT*.

7. But show kindness unto the sons of Barzillai the Gileadite, and let them be of those that eat at thy table: ... act kindly, and let them be guests, *Fenton* ... treat them with faithful love, let them be among those, *JB* ... Be kind to the family ... let them be among the guests, *Moffatt* ... show kindness ... and take care of them, *Good News*.

for so they came to me when I fled because of Absalom thy brother: ... for they entertained me, *Fenton* ... were as kind to me when I was fleeing from your brother, *JB* ... fed me when I fled from, *Moffatt* ... assisted me when I fled from Absalom, *NASB*.

8. And, behold, thou hast with thee Shimei the son of Gera, a Benjamite of Bahurim, which cursed me with a grievous curse in the day when I went to Mahanaim: ... who put a bitter curse on me on the day, *BB* ... spoke insulting curses against me, *Beck* ... cursed me with foul curses, *Fenton* ... He called down a terrible curse, *JB* ... cursed me violently, *Berkeley*.

but he came down to meet me at Jordan, and I sware to him by the LORD, saying, I will not put thee to death with the sword: ... Jordan River, I gave him my solemn promise in the name of the LORD that I would not have him killed, *Good News* ... gave him my oath, *BB* ... I promised him, swearing ... I will not kill you, *Beck* ... I will not slay you, *Goodspeed*.

9. Now therefore hold him not guiltless: for thou art a wise man, and knowest what thou oughtest to do unto him: ... you must not let him go unpunished ... will know how to deal with him, *JB* ... have your wits about you, you know what to do with him, *Moffatt* ... You are a prudent man, *NAB* ... You are a wise man, *NCV* ... do not consider him innocent. You are a man of wisdom, *NIV*.

but his hoar head bring thou down to the grave with blood: ... his grey head down, *JB* ... down his grey head

---

cruel, but might have been excused as an opportune death on the battlefield, though probably Joab had many an old grudge to pay off besides the burning of his barley field. After Absalom's rebellion, David foolishly and unjustly offered the commandership of the army to his nephew Amasa. Amasa was the son of his sister Abigail by an Ishmaelite father, named Jether (2 Sam. 17:25; 19:13; 1 Chr. 2:17). Joab simply would not tolerate being superseded in the command which he had earned by lifelong and perilous services. With deadly treachery, Joab invited his kinsman to embrace him, then drove a sword into Amasa's bowels. David had heard about, or perhaps had seen, the revolting spectacle which Joab presented, with the blood of war shed in peace, dyeing his girdle and streaming down to his shoes with its horrible crimson. Yet, even by that act, Joab had once more saved David's tottering throne. The historian faithfully records that David, on his deathbed, neither forgot nor forgave. But neither did he forget those who helped him, and he now commanded Solomon to provide for the sons of Barzillai, who had helped David's cause in a peaceful manner.

2:8–10. The other victim whose doom was bequeathed to the new king was Shimei, the son of Gera. He had cursed David at Bahurim on the day of his flight and in the hour of his extremest humiliation. He had walked on the opposite side of the valley, flinging stones and dust at David, cursing him with a grievous curse as a man of Belial and a man of blood, and telling him that the loss of his kingdom was the retribution which had fallen upon him for the blood of the house of Saul which he had shed. So grievous was the trial of these insults that the place where the king and his people rested that night received the pathetic name of Ayephim, "the place of the weary" (2 Sam. 16:5, 14; 17:18).

David slept with his fathers and passed before that bar where all is judged of truly. His life is an April day, half sunshine and half gloom. His sins were great, but his penitence was deep, lifelong and sincere. He gave occasion for the enemies of God to blas-

10.	8311.121	1784	6196, 1	7196.221	904, 6111	1784
	cj, v Qal impf 3ms	pn	prep, n mp, ps 3ms	cj, v Niphil impf 3ms	prep, *n fs*	pn
	וַיִּשְׁכַּב	דָּוִד	עִם־אֲבֹתָיו	וַיִּקָּבֵר	בְּעִיר	דָּוִד
	wayyishkav	dāwidh	‘im-’ăvōthâv	wayyiqqāvēr	be‘îr	dāwidh
	then he lay	David	with his ancestors	and he was buried	in the city of	David

11.	3219	866	4566.111	1784	6142, 3547	727	8523	904, 2367
	cj, art, n mp	rel part	v Qal pf 3ms	pn	prep, pn	num	n fs	prep, pn
	וְהַיָּמִים	אֲשֶׁר	מָלַךְ	דָּוִד	עַל־יִשְׂרָאֵל	אַרְבָּעִים	שָׁנָה	בְּחֶבְרוֹן
	wehayyāmîm	’ăsher	mālakh	dāwidh	‘al-yisrā’ēl	’arbā‘îm	shānāh	bechevrôn
	and the days	that	he reigned	David	over Israel	forty	years	in Hebron

4566.111	8124	8523	904, 3503	4566.111	8421	8421	8523
v Qal pf 3ms	num	n fp	conj, prep, pn	v Qal pf 3ms	num	cj, num	n fp
מָלַךְ	שֶׁבַע	שָׁנִים	וּבִירוּשָׁלַםִ	מָלַךְ	שְׁלֹשִׁים	וְשָׁלֹשׁ	שָׁנִים
mālakh	sheva‘	shānîm	ûvîrûshālam	mālakh	shelōshîm	weshālōsh	shānîm
he reigned	seven	years	and in Jerusalem	he reigned	thirty	and three	years

12.	8406	3553.111	6142, 3802	1784	1	3679.222
	cj, pn	v Qal pf 3ms	prep, *n ms*	pn	n ms, ps 3ms	cj, v Niphal impf 3fs
	וּשְׁלֹמֹה	יָשַׁב	עַל־כִּסֵּא	דָּוִד	אָבִיו	וַתִּכֹּן
	ûshelōmōh	yāshav	‘al-kissē’	dāwidh	’āvîw	wattikkōn
	and Solomon	he sat	on the throne of	David	his father	and it was established

4577	4108	13.	971.121	135	1158, 2389	420, 1368
n fs, ps 3ms	adv		cj, v Qal impf 3ms	pn	*n ms*, pn	prep, pn
מַלְכֻתוֹ	מְאֹד		וַיָּבֹא	אֲדֹנִיָּהוּ	בֶּן־חַגִּית	אֶל־בַּת־שֶׁבַע
malkhuthô	me’ōdh		wayyāvō’	’ădhōnîyāhû	ven-chaggêth	’el-bath-sheva‘
his kingship	very		and he came	Adonijah	the son of Haggith	to Bathsheba

525, 8406	569.122	1950B, 8361	971.141	569.121	8361
n fs, pn	cj, v Qal impf 3fs	intrg part, n ms	v Qal inf con, ps 2ms	cj, v Qal impf 3ms	n ms
אֵם־שְׁלֹמֹה	וַתֹּאמֶר	הֲשָׁלוֹם	בֹּאֶךָ	וַיֹּאמֶר	שָׁלוֹם
’ēm-shelōmōh	wattō’mer	hăshālôm	bō’ekhā	wayyō’mer	shālôm
the mother of Solomon	and she said	is peace	your coming	and he said	peace

14.	569.121	1745	3937	420	569.122	1744.331
	cj, v Qal impf 3ms	n ms	prep, ps 1cs	prep, ps 2fs	cj, v Qal impf 3fs	v Piel impv 2ms
	וַיֹּאמֶר	דָּבָר	לִי	אֵלָיִךְ	וַתֹּאמֶר	דַּבֵּר
	wayyō’mer	dāvār	lî	’ēlāyikh	wattō’mer	dabbēr
	and he said	a word	to me	to you	and she said	speak

15.	569.121	879	3156.114	3706, 3937	2030.112	4548	6142
	cj, v Qal impf 3ms	pers pron	v Qal pf 2fs	cj, prep, ps 1cs	v Qal pf 3fs	art, n fs	cj, prep, ps 1cs
	וַיֹּאמֶר	אַתְּ	יָדַעַתְּ	כִּי־לִי	הָיְתָה	הַמְּלוּכָה	וְעָלַי
	wayyō’mer	’atte	yādha‘atte	kî-lî	hāyethāh	hammelûkhāh	we‘ālay
	and he said	you	you know	that to me	it was	the kingship	and on me

7947.116	3725, 3547	6686	3937, 4566.141	5621.122	4548
v Qal pf 3cp	*adj*, pn	n mp, ps 3mp	prep, v Qal inf con	cj, v Qal impf 3fs	art, n fs
שָׂמוּ	כָל־יִשְׂרָאֵל	פְּנֵיהֶם	לִמְלֹךְ	וַתִּסֹּב	הַמְּלוּכָה
sāmû	khol-yisrā’ēl	penêhem	limlōkh	wattissōv	hammelûkhāh
they had set	all Israel	their faces	to reign	but it turned away	the kingship

2030.122	3937, 250	3706	4623, 3176	2030.112	3937	16.	6498
cj, v Qal impf 3fs	prep, n ms, ps 1cs	cj	prep, pn	v Qal pf 3fs	prep, ps 3ms		cj, adv
וַתְּהִי	לְאָחִי	כִּי	מֵיְהוָה	הָיְתָה	לוֹ		וְעַתָּה
wattehî	le’āchî	kî	mēyehwāh	hāyethāh	lô		we‘attāh
and it became	to my brother	because	from Yahweh	it was	to him		and now

to death, *Moffatt* ... to send down his hoary head in blood, *NAB* ... you must be sure he is killed, *NCV*.

10. So David slept with his fathers, and was buried in the city of David: ... rested with, *NKJV* ... slept with his ancestors, *NRSV* ... David went to rest ... his body was put into the earth in the town of, *BB* ... afterwards lay down with his fathers, and they buried him, *Fenton* ... died and was buried, *Good News*.

11. And the days that David reigned over Israel were forty years: seven years reigned he in Hebron, and thirty and three years reigned he in Jerusalem: ... he was king ... he was king, *Goodspeed* ... The length of David's reign, *NAB* ... He had ruled over Israel forty years, *NCV*.

12. Then sat Solomon upon the throne of David his father: ... became king after, *NCV* ... succeeded his father David as king, *NEB* ... occupied the throne of his father, *Berkeley* ... took his place on the seat of David, *BB*.

and his kingdom was established greatly: ... and he was in firm control of his kingdom, *NCV* ... was firmly established on the throne, *NEB* ... was made safe and strong, *BB* ... became very firmly established, *Beck*.

13. And Adonijah the son of Haggith came to Bath-sheba the mother of Solomon. And she said, Comest thou peaceably? And he said, Peaceably: ... Does peace come with you?, *Fenton* ... Is your coming friendly? ... Friendly, *Goodspeed* ... "Do you come as a friend?" she asked. "Yes, he answered," *Moffatt* ... "Do you come in peace?" Bathsheba asked. "This is a peaceful visit," *NCV* ... "Is this a friendly visit?" she asked. "It is," *Good News*.

14. He said moreover, I have somewhat to say unto thee. And she said, Say on: ... and added, "I have something to tell you." "Speak," she said, *Beck* ... and continued, "May I have a word with you?" "Speak," she responded, *Berkeley* ... I would have a word with you," he went on to say, *Goodspeed* ... "I have something to say to you." "Say it," *Moffatt*.

15. And he said, Thou knowest that the kingdom was mine, and that all Israel set their faces on me, that I should reign: ... You remember that at one time ... All the people of Israel recognized me as their king, *NCV* ... and all Israel expected me to be king, *NAB* ... had the idea that I would be their king, *BB* ... preferred me, *Douay*.

howbeit the kingdom is turned about, and is become my brother's: for it was his from the Lord: ... kingdom escaped me ... for the Lord gave it to him, *NAB* ... but the kingdom is transferred ... for it was appointed him, *Douay* ... things have changed. Now my brother is the king, because the Lord chose him, *NCV* ... for that was what the Lord wanted, *Beck*.

16. And now I ask one petition of thee, deny me not. And she said unto him, Say on: ... asking you one favour:, *Moffatt* ... I want to ask you to do one thing for me. Don't refuse me, *Beck* ... ask one request ... Do

---

pheme, but he also taught all who love God to praise and pray. If his record contains some dark passages, and his character shows many inconsistencies, we can never forget his courage, his flashes of nobleness, his intense spirituality whenever he was true. His name is a beacon-light of warning against the glamor and strength of evil passions. But he showed us also what repentance can do, and we are sure that his sins were forgiven him because he turned away from his wickedness. David was buried in his own city—the stronghold of Zion, and his tomb was pointed out a thousand years later in the days of Christ (Acts 2:29).

2:11–12. The reign of Solomon began with a threefold deed of blood. An Eastern king, surrounded by the many princes of a polygamous family and liable to endless jealousies and plots is always in a condition of unstable equilibrium. The death of a rival is regarded as his only safe imprisonment. On the other hand, it must be remembered that Solomon allowed his other brethren and kinsmen to live; and, in point of fact, his younger brother Nathan became the ancestor of the divine Messiah of his race (Luke 3:31).

2:13–18. It was the restless ambition of Adonijah which again brought down an avalanche of ruin. He and his adherents were necessarily under the cold shadow of royal disfavor, and they must have known that they had sinned too deeply to be forgiven. They felt the position intolerable.

Perhaps one of those followers—the experienced Joab or Jonathan, son of Abiathar—whispered to him that he need not yet acquiesce in the ruin of his hopes and suggested a subtle method of strengthening his cause and keeping his claim before the eyes of the people.

Alarmed at his visit she asked, "Comest thou peaceably?" He came, he humbly assured her, to ask a favor. Might she not think of his case with a little pity? He was the elder son; the kingdom by right of primogeniture was his; all Israel, so he flattered himself, had wished for his accession. But it had all been in vain; Yahweh had given the kingdom to his brother. Might he not be allowed some small consolation, some little accession to his dignity?

8072	259	609	8068.151	4623, 882	414, 8178.524	881, 6686
n fs	num	pers pron	v Qal act ptc ms	prep, prep, ps 2fs	adv, v Hiphil juss 2fs	do, n mp, ps 1cs
שְׁאֵלָה	אַחַת	אָנֹכִי	שֹׁאֵל	מֵאִתָּךְ	אַל־תָּשִׁבִי	אֶת־פָּנָי
she'ēlāh	'achath	'ānōkhî	shō'ēl	mē'ittākh	'al-tāshivî	'eth-pānāy
a request	one	I	asking	from with you	do not turn away	my face

569.122	420	1744.331		569.121	569.132, 5167	3937, 8406
cj, v Qal impf 3fs	prep, ps 3ms	v Piel impv 2ms	**17.**	cj, v Qal impf 3ms	v Qal impv 2fs, part	prep, pn
וַתֹּאמֶר	אֵלָיו	דַּבֵּר		וַיֹּאמֶר	אִמְרִי־נָא	לִשְׁלֹמֹה
wattō'mer	'ēlâv	dabbēr		wayyō'mer	'imrî-nā'	lishlōmōh
and she said	to him	speak		and he said	say please	to Solomon

4567	3706	3940, 8178.521	881, 6686	5598.121, 3937	881, 50
art, n ms	cj	neg part, v Hiphil impf 3ms	do, n mp, ps 2fs	cj, v Qal juss 3ms, prep, ps 1cs	do, pn
הַמֶּלֶךְ	כִּי	לֹא־יָשִׁיב	אֶת־פָּנָיִךְ	וְיִתֶּן־לִי	אֶת־אֲבִישַׁג
hammelekh	kî	lō'-yāshîv	'eth-pānāyikh	weyitten-lî	'eth-'ăvîshagh
the king	because	he will not turn away	your face	that he may give to me	Abishag

8208	3937, 828		569.122	1368	3005	609	1744.325
art, pn	prep, n fs	**18.**	cj, v Qal impf 3fs	pn	adj	pers pron	v Piel impf 1cs
הַשּׁוּנַמִּית	לְאִשָּׁה		וַתֹּאמֶר	בַּת־שֶׁבַע	טוֹב	אָנֹכִי	אֲדַבֵּר
hashshûnammîth	le'ishshāh		wattō'mer	bath-sheva'	ṯôv	'ānōkhî	'ădhabbēr
the Shunammite	for a wife		and she said	Bathsheba	good	I	I will speak

6142	420, 4567		971.122	1368	420, 4567	8406
prep, ps 2ms	prep, art, n ms	**19.**	cj, v Qal impf 3fs	pn	prep, art, n ms	pn
עָלֶיךָ	אֶל־הַמֶּלֶךְ		וַתָּבֹא	בַּת־שֶׁבַע	אֶל־הַמֶּלֶךְ	שְׁלֹמֹה
'ālêkhā	'el-hammelekh		wattāvō'	vath-sheva'	'el-hammelekh	shelōmōh
concerning you	to the king		and she entered	Bathsheba	to the king	Solomon

3937, 1744.341, 3937	6142, 135	7251.121	4567	3937, 7410.141
prep, v Piel inf con, prep, ps 3ms	prep, pn	cj, v Qal impf 3ms	art, n ms	prep, v Qal inf con, ps 3fs
לְדַבֶּר־לוֹ	עַל־אֲדֹנִיָּהוּ	וַיָּקָם	הַמֶּלֶךְ	לִקְרָאתָהּ
ledhabber-lô	'al-'ădhōnîyāhû	wayyāqām	hammelekh	liqŏrā'thāhh
to speak to him	concerning Adonijah	and he rose up	the king	to meet her

8246.721	3937	3553.121	6142, 3802	7947.121	3802
cj, v Hithpael impf 3ms	prep, ps 3fs	cj, v Qal impf 3ms	prep, n ms, ps 3ms	cj, v Qal impf 3ms	n ms
וַיִּשְׁתַּחוּ	לָהּ	וַיֵּשֶׁב	עַל־כִּסְאוֹ	וַיָּשֶׂם	כִּסֵּא
wayyishtachû	lāhh	wayyēshev	'al-kis'ô	wayyāsem	kissē'
and he prostrated himself	to her	then he sat	on his throne	and he set up	a throne

3937, 525	4567	3553.122	3937, 3332		569.122	8072	259
prep, *n fs*	art, n ms	cj, v Qal impf 3fs	prep, n fs, ps 3ms	**20.**	cj, v Qal impf 3fs	n fs	num
לְאֵם	הַמֶּלֶךְ	וַתֵּשֶׁב	לִימִינוֹ		וַתֹּאמֶר	שְׁאֵלָה	אַחַת
le'ēm	hammelekh	wattēshev	lîmînô		wattō'mer	she'ēlāh	'achath
for the mother of	the king	and she sat	to his right side		and she said	a request	one

7278	609	8068.153	4623, 882	414, 8178.523	881, 6686
adj	pers pron	v Qal act ptc fs	prep, prep, ps 2ms	adv, v Hiphil juss 2ms	do, n mp, ps 1cs
קְטַנָּה	אָנֹכִי	שֹׁאֶלֶת	מֵאִתָּךְ	אַל־תָּשֶׁב	אֶת־פָּנָי
qŏṯannāh	'ānōkhî	shō'eleth	mē'ittākh	'al-tāshev	'eth-pānāy
small	I	asking	from with you	do not turn away	my face

569.121, 3937	4567	8068.132	525	3706	3940, 8178.525
cj, v Qal impf 3ms, prep, ps 3fs	art, n ms	v Qal impv 2fs	n fs, ps 1cs	cj	neg part, v Hiphil impf 1cs
וַיֹּאמֶר־לָהּ	הַמֶּלֶךְ	שַׁאֲלִי	אִמִּי	כִּי	לֹא־אָשִׁיב
wayyō'mer-lāhh	hammelekh	sha'ălî	'immî	kî	lō'-'āshîv
and he said to her	the king	ask	my mother	because	I will not turn away

881, 6686	21.	569.122	5598.621	881, 50	8208	3937, 135
do, n mp, ps 2fs		cj, v Qal impf 3fs	v Hophal juss 3ms	do, pn	art, pn	prep, pn
אֶת־פָּנָיִךְ׃		וַתֹּאמֶר	יֻתַּן	אֶת־אֲבִישַׁג	הַשֻּׁנַמִּית	לַאֲדֹנִיָּהוּ
'eth-pānāyikh		wattō'mer	yuttan	'eth-'ăvîshagh	hashshunammîth	la'ădhōnîyāhû
your face		and she said	may it be allowed	Abishag	the Shunammite	to Adonijah

250	3937, 828	22.	6257.121	4567	8406	569.121	3937, 525
n ms, ps 2ms	prep, n fs		cj, v Qal impf 3ms	art, n ms	pn	cj, v Qal impf 3ms	prep, n fs, ps 3ms
אָחִיךָ	לְאִשָּׁה		וַיַּעַן	הַמֶּלֶךְ	שְׁלֹמֹה	וַיֹּאמֶר	לְאִמּוֹ
'āchîkhā	le'ishshāh		wayya'an	hammelekh	shelōmōh	wayyō'mer	le'immô
your brother	for a wife		and he answered	the king	Solomon	and he said	to his mother

not turn your face from me, *Fenton* ... Go on, she said, *JB*.

17. And he said, Speak, I pray thee, unto Solomon the king, (for he will not say thee nay,): ... Please ask King Solomon, who will not refuse you, *NAB* ... "I know king Solomon will do anything you ask him, Adonijah continued, *NCV* ... cannot deny thee anything), *Douay* ... Will you go to Solomon the king (for I know he will not say, No, to you) and put before him my request, *BB*.

that he give me Abishag the Shunammite to wife: ... to give me Abishag the Shunammite to be my wife, *NCV* ... put before him my request that he will give me Abishag, *BB*.

18. And Bath-sheba said, Well; I will speak for thee unto the king: ... "Very well" ... "I will talk to the king for you," *Beck* ... to the king on your behalf, *Berkeley*.

19. Bath-sheba therefore went unto king Solomon, to speak unto him for Adonijah: ... Bathsheba went to King Solomon to have talk with him on Adonijah's account, *BB*.

And the king rose up to meet her, and bowed himself unto her, and sat down on his throne: ... When Solomon saw her, he stood up to meet her, *NCV* ... king rose to meet her and kissed her, and seated himself, *NEB* ... And the king got up to come to her, and went down low to the earth before her; then he took his place on the king's seat, *BB* ... did obeisance to her, *Goodspeed* ... stood to greet his mother and bowed to her, *Good News*.

and caused a seat to be set for the king's mother; and she sat on his right hand: ... they placed a cushion for the mother of the king, *Fenton* ... He told some servants to bring another throne for his mother. Then she sat down at his right side, *NCV* ... another throne was provided for the mother of the king who sat at his right, *Berkeley*.

20. Then she said, I desire one small petition of thee; I pray thee, say me not nay: ... one small favor of you. Do not deny me, *KJVII* ... "I'm asking you one little thing" ... "don't refuse me," *Beck* ... I have one small request to make of you ... I hope you won't turn me down, *NLT*.

And the king said unto her, Ask on, my mother: for I will not say thee nay: ... I will not deny you, *KJVII* ... Ask it, my mother, the king told her, for I won't refuse you, *Beck* ... What is it, my mother? ... You know I won't refuse you, *NLT*.

21. And she said, Let Abishag the Shunammite be given to Adonijah thy brother to wife: ... Permit Abishag the Shunammite to become the wife of Adonijah, *Berkeley* ... Will you give Abishag the Shunamite to Adoniah for a wife, *Fenton* ... Let Abishag of Shunem ... be given in marriage to your brother, *JB*.

22. And king Solomon answered and said unto his mother, And why dost thou ask Abishag the Shunammite for Adonijah?: ... why do you request Abishag of

Flattered by his humility and his appeal, Bathsheha encouraged him to proceed, and he begged that, as Solomon would refuse no request of his mother, would she ask that Abishag might be his wife? With extraordinary lack of insight, Bathsheba, ambitious as she was, failed to see the subtle significance of the request and promised to present his petition (Ps. 45:9).

2:19–25. She went to Solomon, who immediately rose to meet her and seated her with all honor on a throne at his right hand. She had only come, she said, to ask a small petition.

"Ask on, my mother," said the king tenderly, "for I will not refuse your request."

But no sooner had she mentioned the "small petition" than Solomon burst into a flame of fury. Why did she not ask for the kingdom for Adonijah at once? He was the elder. He had the chief priest and the chief captain with him. They must be privy to this new plot. But by the God who had given him his father's kingdom and established him a house, Adonijah had made the request to his own cost and should die that day.

The command was instantly given to Benaiah, who, as captain of the bodyguard, was also chief

4066	879	8068.153	881, 50	8208	3937, 135
cj, intrg	pers pron	v Qal act ptc fs	do, pn	art, pn	prep, pn
וְלָמָה	אַתְּ	שֹׁאֶלֶת	אֶת־אֲבִישַׁג	הַשֻּׁנַמִּית	לַאֲדֹנִיָּהוּ
wᵉlāmāh	'attᵉ	shō'eleth	'eth-'ăvîshagh	hashshunammîth	la'ădhōnîyāhû
and why	you	asking	Abishag	the Shunammite	to Adonijah

8068.132, 3937	881, 4548	3706	2000	250	1448	4623
cj, v Qal impv 2fs, prep, ps 3ms	do, art, n fs	cj	pers pron	n ms, ps 1cs	art, adj	prep, ps 1cs
וְשַׁאֲלִי־לוֹ	אֶת־הַמְּלוּכָה	כִּי	הוּא	אָחִי	הַגָּדוֹל	מִמֶּנִּי
wᵉsha'ălî-lô	'eth-hammᵉlûkhāh	kî	hû'	'āchî	haggādhôl	mimmenî
then ask for him	the kingship	because	he	my brother	the greater	than me

3937	3937, 55	3669	3937, 3200	1158, 7152		8123.221
cj, prep, ps 3ms	cj, prep, pn	art, n ms	cj, prep, pn	*n ms*, pn	23.	cj, v Niphal impf 3ms
וְלוֹ	וּלְאֶבְיָתָר	הַכֹּהֵן	וּלְיוֹאָב	בֶּן־צְרוּיָה		וַיִּשָּׁבַע
wᵉlô	ûlă'evyāthār	hakkōhēn	ûlᵉyô'āv	ben-tsᵉrûyāh		wayyishshāva'
and to him	and to Abiathar	the priest	and to Joab	the son of Zeruiah		and he swore

4567	8406	904, 3176	3937, 569.141	3662	6449.121, 3937	435	3662
art, n ms	pn	prep, pn	prep, v Qal inf con	adv	v Qal juss 3ms, prep, ps 1cs	n mp	cj, adv
הַמֶּלֶךְ	שְׁלֹמֹה	בַּיהוָה	לֵאמֹר	כֹּה	יַעֲשֶׂה־לִּי	אֱלֹהִים	וְכֹה
hammelekh	shᵉlōmōh	bayhwāh	lē'mōr	kōh	ya'ăseh-lî	'ĕlōhîm	wᵉkhōh
the king	Solomon	by Yahweh	saying	thus	may He do to me	God	and thus

3362.521	3706	904, 5497	1744.311	135	881, 1745	2172
v Hiphil juss 3ms	cj	prep, n fs, ps 3ms	v Piel pf 3ms	pn	do, art, n ms	art, dem pron
יוֹסִיף	כִּי	בְנַפְשׁוֹ	דִּבֶּר	אֲדֹנִיָּהוּ	אֶת־הַדָּבָר	הַזֶּה
yôsîph	kî	vᵉnaphshô	dibber	'ădhōnîyāhû	'eth-haddāvār	hazzeh
may He add	because	with his life	he has spoken	Adonijah	the word	the this

	6498	2508, 3176	866	3679.511	3553.521
24.	cj, adv	*adj*, pn	rel pron	v Hiphil pf 3ms, ps 1cs	cj, v Hiphil impf 3ms, ps 1cs
	וְעַתָּה	חַי־יְהוָה	אֲשֶׁר	הֱכִינַנִי	וַיּוֹשִׁיבִינִי
	wᵉ'attāh	chay-yᵉhwāh	'ăsher	hĕkhînanî	wayyôshîvaynî
	and now	Yahweh living	Who	He has established me	and He caused me to sit

6142, 3802	1784	1	866	6449.111, 3937	1041	3626, 866
prep, *n ms*	pn	n ms, ps 1cs	cj, rel pron	v Qal pf 3ms, prep, ps 1cs	n ms	prep, rel part
עַל־כִּסֵּא	דָּוִד	אָבִי	וַאֲשֶׁר	עָשָׂה־לִי	בַּיִת	כַּאֲשֶׁר
'al-kissē'	dāwidh	'āvî	wa'ăsher	'āsāh-lî	bayith	ka'ăsher
on the throne of	David	my father	and Who	He made for me	a household	just as

1744.311	3706	3219	4322.621	135		8365.121	4567
v Piel pf 3ms	cj	art, n ms	v Hophal impf 3ms	pn	25.	cj, v Qal impf 3ms	art, n ms
דִּבֵּר	כִּי	הַיּוֹם	יוּמַת	אֲדֹנִיָּהוּ		וַיִּשְׁלַח	הַמֶּלֶךְ
dibbēr	kî	hayyôm	yûmath	'ădhōnîyāhû		wayyishlach	hammelekh
He spoke	that	today	he will be executed	Adonijah		and he sent	the king

8406	904, 3135	1172	1158, 3179	6534.121, 904	4322.121
pn	prep, *n fs*	pn	*n ms*, pn	cj, v Qal impf 3ms, prep, ps 3ms	cj, v Qal impf 3ms
שְׁלֹמֹה	בְּיַד	בְּנָיָהוּ	בֶּן־יְהוֹיָדָע	וַיִּפְגַּע־בּוֹ	וַיָּמֹת
shᵉlōmōh	bᵉyadh	bᵉnāyāhû	ven-yᵉhôyādhā'	wayyiphga'-bô	wayyāmōth
Solomon	by the hand of	Benaiah	the son of Jehoiada	and he attacked on him	and he died

	420, 55	3669	569.111	4567	6300	2050.131	6142, 7898
26.	cj, prep, pn	art, n ms	v Qal pf 3ms	art, n ms	pn	v Qal impv 2ms	prep, n mp, ps 2ms
	וּלְאֶבְיָתָר	הַכֹּהֵן	אָמַר	הַמֶּלֶךְ	עֲנָתֹת	לֵךְ	עַל־שָׂדֶיךָ
	ûlă'evyāthār	hakkōhēn	'āmar	hammelekh	'ănāthōth	lēkh	'al-sādhêkhā
	and to Abiathar	the priest	he said	the king	Anathoth	go	onto your field

Shunem for Adonijah?, *JB* ... Why do you ask me to give him Abishag?, *NCV* ... How can you possibly be asking me to give Abishag to Adonijah? Solomon demanded, *NLT*.

ask for him the kingdom also: ... You might as well request the kingdom for him, *JB* ... Why don't you also ask for him to become the king, *NCV* ... asking me to give him the kingdom!, *NLT* ... ask for the throne, *NEB*.

for he is mine elder brother; even for him, and for Abiathar the priest, and for Joab the son of Zeruiah: ... Abiathar the priest and Joab son of Zeruiah are on his side, *JB*.

23. Then king Solomon sware by the LORD: ... took an oath by the Lord, *BB* ... Solomon made a solemn promise in the LORD's name, *Good News*.

saying, God do so to me, and more also, if Adonijah have not spoken this word against his own life: ... Saying, May God's punishment be on me if Adonijah does not give payment for these words with his life, *BB* ... punish me more and more if Adonijah doesn't pay with his life for what he said, *Beck* ... requite me and worse, if Adonijah has not spoken this word, *Goodspeed* ... may God bring unnameable ills on me, and worse ills, too, *JB* ... God kill me and worse, if this plea of Adonijah does not cost him his life!, *Moffatt* ... God strike me dead if I don't make Adonijah pay, *Good News*.

24. Now therefore, as the LORD liveth: ... now, as the LORD lives, *NAB* ... Now by the living LORD, *BB*.

which hath established me, and set me on the throne of David my father, and who hath made me an house, as he promised: ... who has seated me firmly ... and made of me a dynasty, *NAB* ... By the LORD who has given me the throne ... and who has kept his promise and given the kingdom to me and my people, *NCV* ... who has given me my place on the seat ... and made me one of a line of kings, as he gave me his word, *BB* ... who has confirmed me ... and who has made me a house, *Berkeley*.

Adonijah shall be put to death this day: ... this day shall Adonijah be put to death, *NAB* ... Adonijah will die today, *NCV* ... truly Adonijah will be put to death this day, *BB*.

25. And king Solomon sent by the hand of Benaiah the son of Jehoiada; and he fell upon him that he died: ... and he made an attack on him and put him to death, *BB* ... ordered Benaiah, Jehoiada's son, to do it. And he struck him, *Beck* ... commissioned Benaiah son of Jehoiada to strike him down, and that was how he died, *JB* ... who slew him, *Douay* ... he went and killed Adonijah, *NCV*.

26. And unto Abiathar the priest said the king, Get thee to Anathoth, unto thine own fields; for thou art worthy of death: but I will not at this time put thee to death: ... for death would be your right reward; but I will not put you to death now, *BB* ... Go to your home in Anathoth, for you deserve to die, but I will not kill you now, *Beck* ... your property at Anathoth. You deserve to die, but I will not now put you to death, *Berkeley* ... Anathoth your estate, for you are a dead man, but I will not kill you to-day, *Fenton* ... Go to your country home in Anathoth. You deserve to die, but I will not have you put to death now, *Good News*.

because thou barest the ark of the LORD GOD before David my father: ... because you took up the ark of the Lord God, *BB* ... because you carried the sacred ark of the LORD God ahead, *Beck* ... bore the ark of the LORD God, *Berkeley* ... because you served the altar of the High LORD, *Fenton* ... for you were in charge of the LORD's Covenant Box while you were with my father David, *Good News*.

and because thou hast been afflicted in all wherein my father was afflicted: ... you were with him

---

executioner. He slew Adonijah that same hour, and so the third of David's splendid sons died a death of violence in his youth.

2:26–27. The fall of Adonijah involved his chief votaries in ruin. Abiathar had been a friend and follower of David from his youthful days. When Doeg, the treacherous Edomite, had informed Saul that the priests of Nob had shown kindness to David in his hunger and distress, the diabolic king had not shrunk from employing the Edomite herdsman to massacre all on whom he could lay his hands. From this slaughter of eighty-five priests who wore linen ephods, Abiathar had fled to David, who alone could protect him from the king's pursuit (1 Sam. 22:23). Assuming his complicity in Adonijah's request, Solomon sent for him, and sternly told him that he was "a man of death," i.e., that death was his dessert. But it would have been outrageous to slay an aged priest, the sole survivor of a family slaughtered for David's sake, and one who had so long stood at the head of the whole religious organization, wearing the Urim and carrying the Ark. He was therefore summarily deposed from his functions and dismissed to his paternal fields at Anathoth, a priestly town about six miles from Jerusalem. We hear no more of him; but Solomon's warning, "I will not at this time put thee to death," was sufficient to show him that, if he mixed himself with court intrigues again, he would ultimately pay the forfeit with his life.

3706	382	4323	887	904, 3219	2172	3940	4322.525
cj	*n ms*	n ms	pers pron	cj, prep, art, n ms	art, dem pron	neg part	v Hiphil impf 1cs, ps 2ms
כִּי	אִישׁ	מָוֶת	אַתָּה	וּבַיּוֹם	הַזֶּה	לֹא	אֲמִיתֶךָ
kî	'îsh	māweth	'attāh	ûvayyôm	hazzeh	lō'	'ămîthekhā
because	a man of	death	you	but on the day	the this	not	I will execute you

3706, 5558.113	881, 751	112	3176	3937, 6686	1784	1	3706
cj, v Qal pf 2ms	do, *n ms*	n mp, ps 1cs	pn	prep, *n mp*	pn	n ms, ps 1cs	cj, cj
כִּי־נָשָׂאתָ	אֶת־אֲרוֹן	אֲדֹנָי	יְהוִֹה	לִפְנֵי	דָּוִד	אָבִי	וְכִי
kî-nāsā'thā	'eth-'ărôn	'ădhōnāy	yᵉhōwih	liphnê	dāwidh	'āvî	wᵉkhî
because you carried	the Ark of	my Lord	Yahweh	before	David	my father	and because

6257.713	904, 3725	866, 6257.711	1		1691.321
v Hithpael pf 2ms	prep, n ms	rel part, v Hithpael pf 3ms	n ms, ps 1cs	**27.**	cj, v Piel impf 3ms
הִתְעַנִּיתָ	בְּכֹל	אֲשֶׁר־הִתְעַנָּה	אָבִי		וַיְגָרֶשׁ
hith'anîthā	bᵉkhōl	'ăsher-hith'annāh	'āvî		wayghāresh
you were afflicted	with everything	which he was afflicted	my father		and he drove out

8406	881, 55	4623, 2030.141	3669	3937, 3176	3937, 4527.341	881, 1745	3176
pn	do, pn	prep, v Qal inf con	n ms	prep, pn	prep, v Piel inf con	do, *n ms*	pn
שְׁלֹמֹה	אֶת־אֶבְיָתָר	מִהְיוֹת	כֹּהֵן	לַיהוָה	לְמַלֵּא	אֶת־דְּבַר	יְהוָה
shᵉlōmōh	'eth-'evyāthār	mihyôth	kōhēn	layhwāh	lᵉmallē'	'eth-dᵉvar	yᵉhwāh
Solomon	Abiathar	from being	a priest	to Yahweh	to fulfill	the word of	Yahweh

866	1744.311	6142, 1041	6165	904, 8350		8444	971.112
rel part	v Piel pf 3ms	prep, *n ms*	pn	prep, pn	**28.**	cj, art, n fs	v Qal pf 3fs
אֲשֶׁר	דִּבֶּר	עַל־בֵּית	עֵלִי	בְּשִׁלֹה		וְהַשְּׁמֻעָה	בָּאָה
'ăsher	dibber	'al-bêth	'ēlî	bᵉshilōh		wᵉhashshᵉmu'āh	bā'āh
which	He had spoken	against the household of	Eli	in Shiloh		and the report	it came

5912, 3200	3706	3200	5371.111	313	135	313	54	3940
prep, pn	cj	pn	v Qal pf 3ms	adv	pn	cj, prep	pn	neg part
עַד־יוֹאָב	כִּי	יוֹאָב	נָטָה	אַחֲרֵי	אֲדֹנִיָּה	וְאַחֲרֵי	אַבְשָׁלוֹם	לֹא
'adh-yô'āv	kî	yô'āv	nāṭāh	'achrê	'ădhōnîyāh	wᵉ'achrê	'avshālôm	lō'
unto Joab	because	Joab	he had stretched out	after	Adonijah	but after	Absalom	not

5371.111	5308.121	3200	420, 164	3176	2480.521
v Qal pf 3ms	cj, v Qal impf 3ms	pn	prep, *n ms*	pn	cj, v Hiphil impf 3ms
נָטָה	וַיָּנָס	יוֹאָב	אֶל־אֹהֶל	יְהוָה	וַיַּחֲזֵק
nāṭāh	wayyānās̱	yô'āv	'el-'ōhel	yᵉhwāh	wayyachzēq
he had stretched out	and he fled	Joab	to the Tent of	Yahweh	and he seized

904, 7451	4326		5222.621	3937, 4567	8406	3706	5308.111
prep, *n fp*	art, n ms	**29.**	cj, v Hophal impf 3ms	prep, art, n ms	pn	cj	v Qal pf 3ms
בְּקַרְנוֹת	הַמִּזְבֵּחַ		וַיֻּגַּד	לַמֶּלֶךְ	שְׁלֹמֹה	כִּי	נָס
bᵉqarnôth	hammizbēach		wayyuggadh	lammelekh	shᵉlōmōh	kî	nās̱
onto the horns of	the altar		and it was reported	to the king	Solomon	that	he had fled

3200	420, 164	3176	2079	703	4326	8365.121	8406
pn	prep, *n ms*	pn	cj, intrj	prep	art, n ms	cj, v Qal impf 3ms	pn
יוֹאָב	אֶל־אֹהֶל	יְהוָה	וְהִנֵּה	אֵצֶל	הַמִּזְבֵּחַ	וַיִּשְׁלַח	שְׁלֹמֹה
yô'āv	'el-'ōhel	yᵉhwāh	wᵉhinnēh	'ētsel	hammizbēach	wayyishlach	shᵉlōmōh
Joab	to the Tent of	Yahweh	and behold	beside	the altar	so he sent	Solomon

881, 1172	1158, 3179	3937, 569.141	2050.131	6534.131, 904
do, pn	*n ms*, pn	prep, v Qal inf con	v Qal impv 2ms	v Qal impv 2ms, prep, ps 3ms
אֶת־בְּנָיָהוּ	בֶּן־יְהוֹיָדָע	לֵאמֹר	לֵךְ	פְּגַע־בּוֹ
'eth-bᵉnāyāhû	ven-yᵉhôyādhā'	lē'mōr	lēkh	pᵉgha'-bô
Benaiah	the son of Jehoiada	saying	go	attack on him

30.							
	971.121	1172	420, 164	3176	569.121	420	3662, 569.111
	cj, v Qal impf 3ms	pn	prep, *n ms*	pn	cj, v Qal impf 3ms	prep, ps 3ms	adv, v Qal pf 3ms
	וַיָּבֹא	בְּנָיָהוּ	אֶל־אֹהֶל	יְהוָה	וַיֹּאמֶר	אֵלָיו	כֹּה־אָמַר
	wayyāvō'	venāyāhû	'el-'ōhel	yehwāh	wayyō'mer	'ēlâv	kōh-'āmar
	and he came	Benaiah	to the Tent of	Yahweh	and he said	to him	thus he has said

4567	3428.131	569.121	3940	3706	6553	4322.125	8178.521
art, n ms	v Qal impv 2ms	cj, v Qal impf 3ms	neg part	cj	adv	v Qal impf 1cs	cj, v Hiphil impf 3ms
הַמֶּלֶךְ	צֵא	וַיֹּאמֶר	לֹא	כִּי	פֹּה	אָמוּת	וַיָּשֶׁב
hammelekh	tsē'	wayyō'mer	lō'	kî	phōh	'āmûth	wayyāshev
the king	come out	and he said	no	rather	here	I will die	and he brought back to

in all his troubles, *BB* ... because you shared all my father's sufferings, *Beck* ... endured all the afflictions my father suffered, *Berkeley* ... suffered in all my father suffered, *Fenton*.

27. So Solomon thrust out Abiathar from being priest unto the Lord: ... excluded Abiathar, *Goodspeed* ... deposed Abiathar from his office of priest, *NAB* ... deprived Abiathar of the priesthood, *JB* ... dismissed Abiathar, *NASB* ... cast out Abiathar, *Douay*.

that he might fulfil the word of the Lord, which he spake concerning the house of Eli in Shiloh: ... thus fulfilling the prophecy which the Lord had made in Shiloh about the house of Eli, *NAB*.

28. Then tidings came to Joab: When the report reached Joab, *Berkeley* ... When Joab heard about what had happened, he was afraid, *NCV* ... When the news reached Joab, *NIV*.

for Joab had turned after Adonijah, though he turned not after Absalom: ... had supported Adonijah, though he had not supported Absalom, *Berkeley* ... He had supported Adonijah but not Absalom, *NCV* ... had been one of Adonijah's supporters, though he had not been on Absalom's side, *BB* ... had defected to Adonijah, though he had not defected to Absalom, *NKJV* ... who had conspired with Adonijah, though not with Absalom, *NIV*.

And Joab fled unto the tabernacle of the Lord, and caught hold on the horns of the altar: ... ran to the Tent of the Lord and took hold of the corners, *NCV* ... went in flight to the Tent of the Lord, and put his hands on, *BB* ... he fled to the Hall of the Ever-living, and seized the horns, *Fenton*.

29. And it was told king Solomon that Joab was fled unto the tabernacle of the Lord; and, behold, he is by the altar. Then Solomon sent Benaiah the son of Jehoiada, saying, Go, fall upon him: ... was informed, *Berkeley* ... with the order, Go, strike him down, *NAB* ... Go execute him, *Fenton* ... Go, make an attack on him, *BB* ... sent Benaiah to kill Joab, *Good News*.

30. And Benaiah came to the tabernacle of the Lord, and said unto him, Thus saith the king, Come forth: ... into the tent of the Lord and said to him, Come out, *Goodspeed* ... went to the Tent of Yahweh. 'By order of the king,' he said, 'come out!', *JB* ... went to the Eternal's Tent and gave him the king's order to come away, *Moffatt*.

And he said, Nay; but I will die here. And Benaiah brought the king word again, saying, Thus said Joab, and thus he answered me: ... No, for I prefer to die here, *Goodspeed* ... No; but let death come to me here. And Benaiah went back to the king and gave him word of the answer which Joab had given, *BB* ... took back his message to the king, telling him what Joab had said in reply to him, *Moffatt*.

2:28–35. The doom fell next on the arch-offender Joab, the hero of a hundred fights. He had, if the reading of some of the Greek, Syriac and Vulgate versions be correct, "turned after Adonijah, and had not turned after Solomon" (rather than Absalom). Solomon could hardly have felt at ease when a commander so powerful and so popular was disaffected to his rule, and Joab read his own sentence in the execution of Adonijah. On hearing the news the old hero fled up Mount Zion and clung to the horns of the altar. But Abiathar, who might have asserted the sacredness of the asylum, was in disgrace, and Joab was not to escape.

The Levite-soldier had no hesitation about acting as executioner, but he did not like to slay any man, and above all such a man, in a place so sacred (2 Ki. 11:15)—in a place where his blood would be mingled with that of the sacrifices with which the horns of the altar were besmeared.

"The king bids thee come forth," he said.

"Nay," said Joab, "but I will die here."

Perhaps he thought that he might be protected by the asylum, as Adonijah had been; perhaps he hoped that in any case his blood might cry to God for vengeance, if he was slain in the sanctuary of Mount Zion and on the very altar of burnt offering.

3662	3200	3662, 1744.311	3937, 569.141	1745	881, 4567	1172
cj, adv	pn	adv, v Piel pf 3ms	prep, v Qal inf con	n ms	do, art, n ms	pn
וְכֹה	יוֹאָב	כֹּה־דִבֶּר	לֵאמֹר	דָּבָר	אֶת־הַמֶּלֶךְ	בְּנָיָהוּ
wekhōh	yô'āv	kōh-dhibber	lē'mōr	dāvār	'eth-hammelekh	benāyāhû
and thus	Joab	thus he has said	saying	a word	the king	Benaiah

3626, 866	6449.131	4567	3937	569.121		6257.111
prep, rel part	v Qal impv 2ms	art, n ms	prep, ps 3ms	cj, v Qal impf 3ms	**31.**	v Qal pf 3ms, ps 1cs
כַּאֲשֶׁר	עֲשֵׂה	הַמֶּלֶךְ	לוֹ	וַיֹּאמֶר		עָנָנִי
ka'ăsher	'ăsēh	hammelekh	lô	wayyō'mer		'ānānî
just as	do	the king	to him	so he said		he has answered me

5681.513	7196.113	6534.131, 904	1744.311
cj, v Hiphil pf 2ms	cj, v Qal pf 2ms, ps 3ms	cj, v Qal impv 2ms, prep, ps 3ms	v Piel pf 3ms
וַהֲסִירֹתָ	וּקְבַרְתּוֹ	וּפְגַע־בּוֹ	דִּבֵּר
wahs̲îrōthā	ûqŏvartô	ûphegha'-bô	dibber
and you must remove	for you must bury him	and attack on him	he has spoken

4623, 6142	4623, 6142	3200	8581.111	866	2703	1879
cj, prep, prep	prep, prep, ps 1cs	pn	v Qal pf 3ms	rel part	sub	*n mp*
וּמֵעַל	מֵעָלַי	יוֹאָב	שָׁפַךְ	אֲשֶׁר	חִנָּם	דְּמֵי
ûmē'al	mē'ālay	yô'āv	shāphakh	'ăsher	chinnām	demê
and from beside	from beside me	Joab	he shed	which	without cause	the bloodshed

881, 1879	3176	8178.511		1	1041
do, n ms, ps 3ms	pn	cj, v Hiphil pf 3ms	**32.**	n ms, ps 1cs	*n ms*
אֶת־דָּמוֹ	יְהוָה	וְהֵשִׁיב		אָבִי	בֵּית
'eth-dāmô	yehwāh	wehēshîv		'āvî	bêth
his blood	Yahweh	and He will cause to return		my father	the household of

4623	3005	6926	904, 8530, 596	6534.111	866	6142, 7513
prep, ps 3ms	cj, adj	adj	prep, num, n mp	v Qal pf 3ms	cj	prep, n ms, ps 3ms
מִמֶּנּוּ	וְטֹבִים	צַדִּקִים	בִּשְׁנֵי־אֲנָשִׁים	פָּגַע	אֲשֶׁר	עַל־רֹאשׁוֹ
mimmennû	weṭōvîm	tsaddiqîm	bishnê-'ănāshîm	pāgha'	'ăsher	'al-rō'shô
than he	and better	more righteous	on two men	he attacked	because	on his head

881, 69	3156.111	3940	1784	1	904, 2820	2103.121
do, pn	v Qal pf 3ms	neg part	pn	cj, n ms, ps 1cs	prep, art, n fs	cj, v Qal impf 3ms, ps 3mp
אֶת־אַבְנֵר	יָדָע	לֹא	דָוִד	וְאָבִי	בַּחֶרֶב	וַיַּהַרְגֵם
'eth-'avnēr	yādhā'	lō'	dhāwidh	we'āvî	bacherev	wayyahargēm
Abner	he knew	not	David	and my father	with the sword	and he killed them

1158, 3616	881, 6248	3547	8015, 6893	1158, 5553
n ms, pn	cj, do, pn	pn	*n ms*, *n ms*	*n ms*, pn
בֶּן־יֶתֶר	וְאֶת־עֲמָשָׂא	יִשְׂרָאֵל	שַׂר־צְבָא	בֶּן־נֵר
ven-yether	we'eth-'ămāsā'	yisrā'ēl	sar-tsevā'	ben-nēr
the son of Jether	and Amasa	Israel	the commander of the army of	the son of Ner

904, 7513	1879	8178.116		3171	8015, 6893
prep, *n ms*	n mp, ps 3mp	cj, v Qal pf 3cp	**33.**	pn	*n ms*, *n ms*
בְּרֹאשׁ	דְמֵיהֶם	וְשָׁבוּ		יְהוּדָה	שַׂר־צְבָא
berō'sh	dhemêhem	weshāvû		yehûdhāh	sar-tsevā'
on the head of	their bloodshed	and it will return		Judah	the commander of the army of

3937, 2320	3937, 1784	3937, 5986	2320	904, 7513	3200
cj, prep, n ms, ps 3ms	cj, prep, n ms	prep, n ms	n ms, ps 3ms	cj, prep, *n ms*	pn
וּלְזַרְעוֹ	וּלְדָוִד	לְעֹלָם	זַרְעוֹ	וּבְרֹאשׁ	יוֹאָב
ûlăzar'ô	ûlădhāwidh	le'ōlām	zar'ô	ûverō'sh	yô'āv
and to his descendants	but to David	for ever	his descendants	and on the head of	Joab

3937, 1041 cj, prep, n ms, ps 3ms וּלְבֵיתוֹ ûlăvêthô and to his household	3937, 3802 cj, prep, n ms, ps 3ms וּלְכִסְאוֹ ûlăkhis'ô and to his throne	2030.121 v Qal impf 3ms יִהְיֶה yihyeh it will be	8361 n ms שָׁלוֹם shālôm peace	5912, 5986 adv, adv עַד־עוֹלָם 'adh-'ôlām until forever	4623, 6196 prep, prep מֵעִם mē'im from with	3176 pn יְהוָה y^{e}hwāh Yahweh

34.	6148.121 cj, v Qal impf 3ms וַיַּעַל wayya'al so he went up	1172 pn בְּנָיָהוּ b^{e}nāyāhû Benaiah	1158, 3179 *n ms*, pn בֶּן־יְהוֹיָדָע ben-y^{e}hôyādhā' the son of Jehoiada	6534.121, 904 cj, v Qal impf 3ms, prep, ps 3ms וַיִּפְגַּע־בּוֹ wayyiphga'-bô and he attacked on him

4322.521 cj, v Hiphil impf 3ms, ps 3ms וַיְמִתֵהוּ waymithēhû and he executed him	7196.221 cj, v Niphil impf 3ms וַיִּקָּבֵר wayyiqqāvēr and he was buried	904, 1041 prep, n ms, ps 3ms בְּבֵיתוֹ b^{e}vêthô in his house	904, 4198 prep, art, n ms בַּמִּדְבָּר bammidhbār in the wilderness

31. And the king said unto him, Do as he hath said, and fall upon him, and bury him: ... make an attack on him there, and put his body into the earth, *BB* ... strike him down and bury him, *Beck* ... Do as I have ordered! and execute him, and bury him, *Fenton* ... strike him down and bury him, *JB* ... Kill him, *Good News.*

that thou mayest take away the innocent blood, which Joab shed, from me, and from the house of my father: ... take away from me and from my family the blood of one put to death by Joab without cause, *BB* ... the blood of innocent people Joab poured out, *Beck* ... take away the innocent blood J'oab shed, *Fenton* ... so rid me and my family today, *JB* ... Then neither I nor any other of David's descendants will any longer be held responsible for what Joab did when he killed innocent men, *Good News.*

32. And the LORD shall return his blood upon his own head: ... The Eternal will make his murders fall on his own head, *Moffatt* ... The LORD will hold him responsible for his own blood, *NAB* ... will repay him for the blood he shed, *NIV* ... will punish him for his bloody deed, *Beck.*

who fell upon two men more righteous and better than he, and slew them with the sword: ... for he struck down two men higher and better than himself, *Moffatt* ... better and more just, *NAB* ... he killed two men, *NCV.*

my father David not knowing thereof, to wit, Abner the son of Ner, captain of the host of Israel, and Amasa the son of Jether, captain of the host of Judah: ... without my father David's knowledge, *NAB* ... Without my father knowing it, *NCV.*

33. Their blood shall therefore return upon the head of Joab, and upon the head of his seed for ever: ... may their bloody deeds be brought back on the heads of Joab and his descendants, *Beck* ... and the head of his race, *Fenton* ... The guilt of their blood shall recoil, *NEB* ... The punishment for their murders will fall, *Good News.*

but upon David, and upon his seed, and upon his house, and upon his throne, shall there be peace for ever from the LORD: ... his family and the seat of his kingdom, *BB* ... his descendants and his family, and his throne have peace, *Beck* ... to David and his race, and house, and throne, may there be peace for ever, *Fenton* ... will enjoy perpetual prosperity from the LORD, *NEB* ... the LORD will always give success to David's descendants who sit on his throne, *Good News.*

34. So Benaiah the son of Jehoiada went up, and fell upon him, and slew him: ... struck him down, killing him, *Moffatt* ... went back, *NAB* ... went up to the altar and struck Joab down and killed him, *NEB.*

and he was buried in his own house in the wilderness: ... in the desert, *Goodspeed* ... in the open country of Judah, *Moffatt* ... his body was put to rest in his house in the waste land, *BB* ... on the edge of the wilderness, *NEB.*

Benaiah naturally scrupled under such circumstances to carry out Solomon's order and went back to him for instruction. Solomon had no such scruples and perhaps held that this act was meritorious (cf. Deut. 19:13). "Slay him," he said, "where he stands! He is a twofold murderer; let his blood be on his head." Then Benaiah went back and killed him, and was promoted to his vacant office. Such was the dismal end of so much valor and so much glory! He had taken the sword, and he perished by the sword. And the Jews believed that the curse of David clung to his house forever, and that among his descendants there never lacked one that was a leper or a lame man or a suicide or a pauper (2 Sam. 3:28f).

35.	5598.121	4567	881, 1172	1158, 3179	8809	6142, 6893
	cj, v Qal impf 3ms	art, n ms	do, pn	*n ms*, pn	prep, ps 3ms	prep, art, n ms
	וַיִּתֵּן	הַמֶּלֶךְ	אֶת־בְּנָיָהוּ	בֶּן־יְהוֹיָדָע	תַּחְתָּיו	עַל־הַצָּבָא
	wayyittēn	hammelekh	'eth-bᵉnāyāhû	ven-yᵉhôyādhā'	tachtâv	'al-hatstsāvā'
	and he appointed	the king	Benaiah	the son of Jehoiada	instead of him	over the army

881, 6923	3669	5598.111	4567	8809	55	36.	8365.121
cj, do, pn	art, n ms	v Qal pf 3ms	art, n ms	prep	pn		cj, v Qal impf 3ms
וְאֶת־צָדוֹק	הַכֹּהֵן	נָתַן	הַמֶּלֶךְ	תַּחַת	אֶבְיָתָר		וַיִּשְׁלַח
wᵉ'eth-tsādhôq	hakkōhēn	nāthan	hammelekh	tachath	'evyāthār		wayyishlach
and Zadok	the priest	he appointed	the king	instead of	Abiathar		and he sent

4567	7410.121	3937, 8483	569.121	3937	1161.131, 3937	1041
art, n ms	cj, v Qal impf 3ms	prep, pn	cj, v Qal impf 3ms	prep, ps 3ms	v Qal impv 2ms, prep, ps 2ms	n ms
הַמֶּלֶךְ	וַיִּקְרָא	לְשִׁמְעִי	וַיֹּאמֶר	לוֹ	בְּנֵה־לְךָ	בַיִת
hammelekh	wayyiqrā'	lᵉshim'î	wayyō'mer	lô	bᵉnēh-lᵉkhā	vayith
the king	and he called	to Shimei	and he said	to him	build for yourself	a house

904, 3503	3553.113	8427	3940, 3428.123	4623, 8427	590	590
prep, pn	cj, v Qal pf 2ms	adv	cj, neg part, v Qal impf 2ms	prep, adv	adv	cj, adv
בִּירוּשָׁלִַם	וְיָשַׁבְתָּ	שָׁם	וְלֹא־תֵצֵא	מִשָּׁם	אָנֶה	וָאָנָה
bîrûshālam	wᵉyāshavtā	shām	wᵉlō'-thētsē'	mishshām	'āneh	wā'ānāh
in Jerusalem	and you must dwell	there	and you must not go out	from there	where	and where

37.	2030.111	904, 3219	3428.141	5882.113	881, 5337	7224
	cj, v Qal pf 3ms	prep, *n ms*	v Qal inf con, ps 2ms	cj, v Qal pf 2ms	do, *n ms*	pn
	וְהָיָה	בְּיוֹם	צֵאתְךָ	וְעָבַרְתָּ	אֶת־נַחַל	קִדְרוֹן
	wᵉhāyāh	bᵉyôm	tsē'thᵉkhā	wᵉ'āvartā	'eth-nachal	qidhrôn
	and it will be	on the day of	your going out	and you pass over	the stream of	Kidron

3156.142	3156.123	3706	4322.142	4322.123	1879	2030.121
v Qal inf abs	v Qal impf 2ms	cj	v Qal inf abs	v Qal impf 2ms	n ms, ps 2ms	v Qal impf 3ms
יָדֹעַ	תֵּדַע	כִּי	מוֹת	תָּמוּת	דָּמְךָ	יִהְיֶה
yādhōa'	tēdha'	kî	môth	tāmûth	dāmᵉkhā	yihyeh
knowing	you certainly know	that	dying	you will certainly die	your blood	it will be

904, 7513	38.	569.121	8483	3937, 4567	3005	1745	3626, 866
prep, n ms, ps 2ms		cj, v Qal impf 3ms	pn	prep, art, n ms	adj	art, n ms	prep, rel part
בְרֹאשֶׁךָ		וַיֹּאמֶר	שִׁמְעִי	לַמֶּלֶךְ	טוֹב	הַדָּבָר	כַּאֲשֶׁר
vᵉrō'shekhā		wayyō'mer	shim'î	lammelekh	tôv	haddāvār	ka'ăsher
on your head		and he said	Shimei	to the king	good	the word	just as

1744.311	112	4567	3772	6449.121	5860	3553.121	8483
v Piel pf 3ms	n ms, ps 1cs	art, n ms	adv	v Qal impf 3ms	n ms, ps 2ms	cj, v Qal impf 3ms	pn
דִּבֶּר	אֲדֹנִי	הַמֶּלֶךְ	כֵּן	יַעֲשֶׂה	עַבְדֶּךָ	וַיֵּשֶׁב	שִׁמְעִי
dibber	'ădhōnî	hammelekh	kēn	ya'ăseh	'avdekhā	wayyēshev	shim'î
he has spoken	my lord	the king	so	he will do	your servant	and he dwelled	Shimei

904, 3503	3219	7521	39.	2030.121	4623, 7377	8421	8523
prep, pn	n mp	adj		cj, v Qal impf 3ms	prep, *n ms*	num	n fp
בִּירוּשָׁלִַם	יָמִים	רַבִּים		וַיְהִי	מִקֵּץ	שָׁלֹשׁ	שָׁנִים
bîrûshālam	yāmîm	rabbîm		wayhî	miqqēts	shālōsh	shānîm
in Jerusalem	days	many		but it happened	from the end of	three	years

1300.126	8530, 5860	3937, 8483	420, 403	1158, 4757	4567
cj, v Qal impf 3mp	num, n mp	prep, pn	prep, pn	*n ms*, pn	*n ms*
וַיִּבְרְחוּ	שְׁנֵי־עֲבָדִים	לְשִׁמְעִי	אֶל־אָכִישׁ	בֶּן־מַעֲכָה	מֶלֶךְ
wayyivrᵉchû	shᵉnê-'ăvādhîm	lᵉshim'î	'el-'ākhîsh	ben-ma'ăkhāh	melekh
that they were fleeing	two of the slaves	to Shimei	to Achish	the son of Maacah	the king of

35. And the king put Benaiah the son of Jehoiada in his room over the host: ... in his place over the army, *BB* ... In his place as head of the army, *JB* ... king then made Benaiah ... commander of the army in Joab's place, *NCV* ... into his post as commander-in-chief, *Moffatt*.

and Zadok the priest did the king put in the room of Abiathar: ... he put in the place of Abiathar, *BB* ... the king made Zadok priest instead of Abiathar, *Beck* ... the new high priest in Abiathar's place, *NCV*.

36. And the king sent and called for Shimei, and said unto him, Build thee an house in Jerusalem, and dwell there, and go not forth thence any whither: ... the king summoned Shimei, *Berkeley* ... Build a house for yourself in Jerusalem and live there. Don't leave the city, *NCV* ... keep there and go to no other place, *BB* ... abide there, and go not forth, *Darby* ... reside there, and do not go out from there whatever happens, *Fenton*.

37. For it shall be, that on the day thou goest out, and passest over the brook Kidron: ... go over to the stream of Kidron, *BB* ... If you ever leave and so much as cross the brook Kidron, *Beck* ... the ravine of Kidron, *JB* ... cross the Kidron Valley, *NAB*.

thou shalt know for certain that thou shalt surely die: thy blood shall be upon thine own head: ... death will overtake you: and your blood will be on your head, *BB* ... you will certainly die, and you will be responsible for your own death, *Beck* ... be certain you shall die without fail, *NAB* ... you yourself will be to blame, *Good News*.

38. And Shimei said unto the king, The saying is good: ... Shimei answered the king, I agree with what you say, *NCV* ... The offer is good, *Berkeley* ... I accept your sentence, *NEB* ... The stipulation is fair, *Goodspeed* ... That is a fair demand, *JB*.

as my lord the king hath said, so will thy servant do: ... I will do what you say, my Master and king, *NCV* ... Your servant will do as my master the king has ordered, *Berkeley* ... as your majesty commands, *NEB*.

And Shimei dwelt in Jerusalem many days: ... lived in Jerusalem for a long time, *NCV* ... resided in Jerusalem some years, *Fenton*.

39. And it came to pass at the end of three years, that two of the servants of Shimei ran away unto Achish son of Maachah king of Gath: ... two of his slaves ran away, *Fenton* ... two of the servants of Shimei went in flight, *BB* ... slaves escaped, *Beck*.

And they told Shimei, saying, Behold, thy servants be in Gath: ... informed that his servants, *NAB* ... Shimei heard, *NCV*.

40. And Shimei arose, and saddled his ass, and went to Gath to Achish

---

2:36–46. Shimei's turn came next. A watchful eye was fixed implacably on this last indignant representative of the ruined house of Saul. Solomon had sent and ordered him to leave his estate at Bahurim and build a house at Jerusalem, forbidding him to go "any whither" (1 Ki. 2:36), and telling him that if on any pretense he passed the wadi of Kidron, he should be put to death. As he could not visit Bahurim, or any of his Benjamite connections, without passing the Kidron, all danger of further intrigues seemed to be obviated. To these terms the dangerous man had sworn, and for three years he kept them faithfully. At the end of that time, two of his slaves fled from him to Achish, son of Maachah, King of Gath (1 Sam. 21:10; 27:2). When informed of their whereabouts, Shimei, apparently with no thought of evil, saddled his mule and went to demand their restoration. As he had not crossed the Kidron and had merely gone to Gath on private business, he thought that Solomon would never hear of it, or would at any rate treat the matter as harmless. Solomon, however, regarded his conduct as a proof of retributive dementation. He sent for him, bitterly upbraided him and ordered Benaiah to slay him. So perished the last of Solomon's enemies, but Shimei had two illustrious descendants, Mordecai and Queen Esther (Est. 2:5).

Solomon perhaps conceived himself to be only acting up to the true kingly ideal. "A king that sitteth in the throne of judgment scattereth away all evil with his eyes" (Prov. 20:8); "A wise king scattereth the wicked, and bringeth the wheel over them" (v. 26); "An evil man seeketh only rebellion: therefore a cruel messenger shall be sent against him" (17:11); "The fear of a king is as the roaring of a lion; whoso provoketh him to anger sinneth against his own soul" (20:2). On the other hand, he continued hereditary kindness to Chimham, son of the old chief Barzillai the Gileadite, who became the founder of the Khan at Bethlehem in which, a thousand years later, Christ was born (1 Ki. 2:7; Jer. 41:17).

The elevation of Zadok to the high priesthood vacated by the disgrace of Abiathar restored the priestly succession to the elder line of the House of Aaron. Aaron had been the father of four sons: Nadab, Abihu, Eleazar and Ithamar. The two eldest had perished childless in the wilderness, apparently for the profanation of serving the Tabernacle while

1709	5222.526	3937, 8483	3937, 569.141	2079	5860	904, 1709
pn	cj, v Hiphil impf 3mp	prep, pn	prep, v Qal inf con	intrj	n mp, ps 2ms	prep, pn
גַּת	וַיַּגִּידוּ	לְשִׁמְעִי	לֵאמֹר	הִנֵּה	עֲבָדֶיךָ	בְּגַת
gath	wayyaggîdhû	lᵉshimʿî	lē'mōr	hinnēh	ʿăvādhêkhā	bᵉghath
Gath	and they reported	to Shimei	saying	behold	your servants	in Gath

40.	7251.121	8483	2372.121	881, 2645	2050.121	1709	420, 403
	cj, v Qal impf 3ms	pn	cj, v Qal impf 3ms	do, n ms, ps 3ms	cj, v Qal impf 3ms	pn	prep, pn
	וַיָּקָם	שִׁמְעִי	וַיַּחֲבֹשׁ	אֶת־חֲמֹרוֹ	וַיֵּלֶךְ	גַּתָה	אֶל־אָכִישׁ
	wayyāqām	shimʿî	wayyachvōsh	'eth-chămōrô	wayyēlekh	gathāh	'el-'ākhîsh
	and he rose up	Shimei	and he saddled	his donkey	and he went	to Gath	to Achish

3937, 1272.341	881, 5860	2050.121	8483	971.521	881, 5860
prep, v Piel inf con	do, n mp, ps 3ms	cj, v Qal impf 3ms	pn	cj, v Hiphil impf 3ms	do, n mp, ps 3ms
לְבַקֵּשׁ	אֶת־עֲבָדָיו	וַיֵּלֶךְ	שִׁמְעִי	וַיָּבֵא	אֶת־עֲבָדָיו
lᵉvaqqēsh	'eth-ʿăvādhâv	wayyēlekh	shimʿî	wayyāvē'	'eth-ʿăvādhâv
to search for	his slaves	and he went	Shimei	and he brought	his slaves

4623, 1709	41.	5222.621	3937, 8406	3706, 2050.111	8483	4623, 3503	1709
prep, pn		cj, v Hophal impf 3ms	prep, pn	cj, v Qal pf 3ms	pn	prep, pn	pn
מִגַּת		וַיֻּגַּד	לִשְׁלֹמֹה	כִּי־הָלַךְ	שִׁמְעִי	מִירוּשָׁלַם	גַּת
miggath		wayyuggadh	lishlōmōh	kî-hālakh	shimʿî	mîrûshālam	gath
from Gath		and it was reported	to Solomon	that he had gone	Shimei	from Jerusalem	Gath

8178.121	42.	8365.121	4567	7410.121	3937, 8483	569.121
cj, v Qal impf 3ms		cj, v Qal impf 3ms	art, n ms	cj, v Qal impf 3ms	prep, pn	cj, v Qal impf 3ms
וַיָּשָׁב		וַיִּשְׁלַח	הַמֶּלֶךְ	וַיִּקְרָא	לְשִׁמְעִי	וַיֹּאמֶר
wayyāshōv		wayyishlach	hammelekh	wayyiqŏrā'	lᵉshimʿî	wayyō'mer
and he returned		and he sent	the king	and he called	to Shimei	and he said

420	1950B, 3940	8123.515	904, 3176	5967.525	904
prep, ps 3ms	intrg part, neg part	v Hiphil pf 1cs, ps 2ms	prep, pn	cj, v Hiphil impf 1cs	prep, ps 2ms
אֵלָיו	הֲלוֹא	הִשְׁבַּעְתִּיךָ	בַּיהוָה	וָאָעִד	בְּךָ
'ēlâv	hălô'	hishbaʿăttîkhā	vayhwāh	wā'āʿidh	bᵉkhā
to him	did not	I cause you to swear	by Yahweh	and I testified	against you

3937, 569.141	904, 3219	3428.141	2050.113	590	590	3156.142
prep, v Qal inf con	prep, *n ms*	v Qal inf con, ps 2ms	cj, v Qal pf 2ms	adv	cj, adv	v Qal inf abs
לֵאמֹר	בְּיוֹם	צֵאתְךָ	וְהָלַכְתָּ	אָנֶה	וָאָנָה	יָדֹעַ
lē'mōr	bᵉyôm	tsē'thᵉkhā	wᵉhālakhtā	'āneh	wā'ānāh	yādhōaʿ
saying	on the day of	your going out	and you will go	where	and where	knowing

3156.123	3706	4322.142	4322.123	569.123	420	3005
v Qal impf 2ms	cj	v Qal inf abs	v Qal impf 2ms	cj, v Qal impf 2ms	prep, ps 1cs	adj
תֵּדַע	כִּי	מוֹת	תָּמוּת	וַתֹּאמֶר	אֵלַי	טוֹב
tēdhaʿ	kî	môth	tāmûth	wattō'mer	'ēlay	ṭôv
you certainly know	that	dying	you will certainly die	and you said	to me	good

1745	8471.115	43.	4211	3940	8490.113	881	8095	3176
art, n ms	v Qal pf 1cs		cj, intrg	neg part	v Qal pf 2ms	do	*n fs*	pn
הַדָּבָר	שָׁמָעְתִּי		וּמַדּוּעַ	לֹא	שָׁמַרְתָּ	אֵת	שְׁבֻעַת	יְהוָה
haddāvār	shāmāʿättî		ûmaddûaʿ	lō'	shāmartā	'ēth	shᵉvuʿath	yᵉhwāh
the word	I have heard		now why	not	you have observed		the oath of	Yahweh

881, 4851	866, 6943.315	6142	44.	569.121	4567
cj, do, art, n fs	rel part, v Piel pf 1cs	prep, ps 2ms		cj, v Qal impf 3ms	art, n ms
וְאֶת־הַמִּצְוָה	אֲשֶׁר־צִוִּיתִי	עָלֶיךָ		וַיֹּאמֶר	הַמֶּלֶךְ
wᵉ'eth-hammitswāh	'ăsher-tsiwwîthî	ʿālêkhā		wayyō'mer	hammelekh
and the commandment	which I commanded	concerning you		and he said	the king

420, 8483	887	3156.113	881	3725, 7750	866	3156.111	3949	866
prep, pn	pers pron	v Qal pf 2ms	do	*adj*, art, n fs	rel part	v Qal pf 3ms	n ms, ps 2ms	rel part
אֶל־שִׁמְעִי	אַתָּה	יָדַעְתָּ	אֵת	כָּל־הָרָעָה	אֲשֶׁר	יָדַע	לְבָבְךָ	אֲשֶׁר
'el-shim'î	'attāh	yādha'ättā	'ēth	kol-hārā'āh	'ăsher	yādha'	levāvekhā	'ăsher
to Shimei	you	you know		all the evil	which	it knows	your heart	which

6449.113	3937, 1784	1	8178.511	3176	881, 7750
v Qal pf 2ms	prep, pn	n ms, ps 1cs	cj, v Hiphil pf 3ms	pn	do, n fs, ps 2ms
עָשִׂיתָ	לְדָוִד	אָבִי	וְהֵשִׁיב	יְהוָה	אֶת־רָעָתְךָ
'āsîthā	ledhāwidh	'āvî	wehēshîv	yehwāh	'eth-rā'āthekhā
you did	to David	my father	now He will cause to return	Yahweh	your evil

to seek his servants: ... Shimei got up, saddled his donkey, *Beck* ... to find his slaves, *JB* ... went to Achish at Gath to find them, *NCV* ... in search of his slaves, *NEB*.

and Shimei went, and brought his servants from Gath: ... He found them and brought them back home, *Good News* ... went off and brought his slaves back, *JB* ... brought them back, *NCV* ... returned with them, *NEB*.

41. And it was told Solomon that Shimei had gone from Jerusalem to Gath, and was come again: ... news was given, *BB* ... it was reported to Solomon, *Fenton* ... Someone told Solomon, *NCV* ... Solomon was informed that Shimei ... returned, *Berkeley*.

42. And the king sent and called for Shimei, and said unto him, Did I not make thee to swear by the LORD, and protested unto thee: ... I made you a promise in the name of the LORD, *NCV* ... Did I not require you ... Did I not give you this solemn warning, *NEB* ... solemnly adjure you, *NRSV* ... Did I not make you take an oath by the LORD, protesting to you, *BB* ... didn't I warn you, *Beck*.

saying, Know for a certain, on the day thou goest out, and walkest abroad any whither, that thou shalt surely die?: ... not to leave Jerusalem. I warned you if you went out anywhere you would die, *NCV* ... If ever you leave this city for any other place, you shall die; make no mistake about it?, *NEB* ... Be certain that on the day when you go out from here, wherever you go, death will overtake you?, *BB*.

and thou saidst unto me, The word that I have heard is good: ... and you agreed to what I said, *NCV* ... I accept your sentence; I obey, *NEB* ... The sentence is fair; I accept, *NRSV* ... Very well!, *BB* ... and you told me, What you say is good. I will obey?, *Beck*.

43. Why then hast thou not kept the oath of the LORD, and the commandment that I have charged thee with?: ... why did you not keep ... the command which I laid upon you?, *Berkeley* ... Why didn't you keep what you promised the LORD ... and do what I ordered you to do, *Beck* ... to Yahweh and the order which I imposed on you?, *JB* ... to the Eternal and the orders I enjoined upon you?, *Moffatt* ... why did you break your promise to the LORD and disobey my command?, *NCV*.

44. The king said moreover to Shimei, Thou knowest all the wickedness which thine heart is privy to, that thou didst to David my father: ... You have knowledge of all the evil which you did, *BB* ... know all the evil that is on your conscience, *Beck* ... You are aware of all the evil which you knowingly did, *Berkeley* ... all the wrong which your heart desired should be done to David, *Fenton* ... which you acknowledge in your heart, *NASB*.

therefore the LORD shall return thy wickedness upon thine own head: ... now the LORD has sent back your evil on yourself, *BB* ... holds you responsible for the evil you did, *Beck* ... is bringing your iniquity, *Goodspeed* ... requites you for your own wickedness, *NAB* ... will punish you for it, *Good News*.

in a state of intoxication and offering "strange fire" upon the altar (Lev. 10:1–20; Num. 3:4; 26:61). The son of Eleazar was the fierce priestly avenger Phinehas. The order of succession known is as follows: Aaron, Eleazar, Ithamar, Phinehas, (gap), Abishua, Eli, Bukk, Phinehas, Uzzi, Ahitub, Zerahiah, Ahiah (1 Sam. 14:3), Meraioth, Ahimelech, Amariah, Abiathar, Ahitub and Zadok.

The question naturally arises how the line of succession came to be disturbed, since Eleazar, and his seed after him, had been promised "the covenant of an everlasting priesthood" (Num. 25:13). As the elder line continued unbroken, how was it that, for five generations at least, from Eli to Abiathar, we find the younger line of Ithamar in secure and lineal possession of the high priesthood? Jewish tradition has perhaps revealed the secret, and a very curious one it is. We are told that Phinehas was high priest when Jephthah made his rash vow and that his was the hand which carried out the human sacrifice of Jephthah's

904, 7513	45.	4567	8406	1313.155	3802	1784	2030.121
prep, n ms, ps 2ms		cj, art, n ms	pn	v Qal pass ptc ms	cj, n ms	pn	v Qal impf 3ms
בְרֹאשֶׁךָ		וְהַמֶּלֶךְ	שְׁלֹמֹה	בָּרוּךְ	וְכִסֵּא	דָוִד	יִהְיֶה
berō'shekhā		wehammelekh	shelōmōh	bārûkh	wekhissē'	dhāwidh	yihyeh
on your head		but the king	Solomon	blessed	and the throne of	David	it will be

3679.255	3937, 6686	3176	5912, 5986	46.	6943.321	4567	881, 1172
v Niphal ptc ms	prep, n mp	pn	adv, adv		cj, v Piel impf 3ms	art, n ms	do, pn
נָכוֹן	לִפְנֵי	יְהוָה	עַד־עוֹלָם		וַיְצַו	הַמֶּלֶךְ	אֶת־בְּנָיָהוּ
nākhôn	liphnê	yehwāh	'adh-'ôlām		waytsaw	hammelekh	'eth-benāyāhû
established	before	Yahweh	until forever		and he commanded	the king	Benaiah

1158, 3179	3428.121	6534.121, 904	4322.121	4608
n ms, pn	cj, v Qal impf 3ms	cj, v Qal impf 3ms, prep, ps 3ms	cj, v Qal impf 3ms	cj, art, n fs
בֶּן־יְהוֹיָדָע	וַיֵּצֵא	וַיִּפְגַּע־בּוֹ	וַיָּמֹת	וְהַמַּמְלָכָה
ben-yehôyādhā'	wayyētsē'	wayyiphga'-bô	wayyāmōth	wehammamlākhāh
the son of Jehoiada	and he went out	and he attacked on him	and he died	and the kingdom

3679.212	904, 3135, 8406	3:1	2967.721	8406
v Niphal pf 3fs	prep, n ms, pn		cj, v Hithpael impf 3ms	pn
נָכוֹנָה	בְּיַד־שְׁלֹמֹה		וַיִּתְחַתֵּן	שְׁלֹמֹה
nākhônāh	beyadh-shelōmōh		wayyithchattēn	shelōmōh
it was established	in the hand of Solomon		and he became related by marriage to	Solomon

881, 6799	4567	4875	4089.121	881, 1351, 6799	971.521
do, pn	n ms	pn	cj, v Qal impf 3ms	do, n fs, pn	cj, v Hiphil impf 3ms, ps 3fs
אֶת־פַּרְעֹה	מֶלֶךְ	מִצְרָיִם	וַיִּקַּח	אֶת־בַּת־פַּרְעֹה	וַיְבִיאֶהָ
'eth-par'ōh	melekh	mitsrāyim	wayyiqqach	'eth-bath-par'ōh	wayvî'eāh
Pharaoh	the king of	Egypt	and he took	the daughter of Pharaoh	and he brought her

420, 6111	1784	5912	3735.341	3937, 1161.141	881, 1041	881, 1041
prep, n fs	pn	adv	v Piel inf con, ps 3ms	prep, v Qal inf con	do, n ms, ps 3ms	cj, do, n ms
אֶל־עִיר	דָּוִד	עַד	כַּלֹּתוֹ	לִבְנוֹת	אֶת־בֵּיתוֹ	וְאֶת־בֵּית
'el-'îr	dāwidh	'adh	kallōthô	livnôth	'eth-bêthô	we'eth-bêth
to the city of	David	until	his finishing	to build	his house	and the house of

3176	881, 2440	3503	5623	2.	7828	6194	2159.352
pn	cj, do, n fs	pn	adv		adv	art, n ms	v Piel ptc mp
יְהוָה	וְאֶת־חוֹמַת	יְרוּשָׁלַם	סָבִיב		רַק	הָעָם	מְזַבְּחִים
yehwāh	we'eth-chômath	yerûshālam	sāvîv		raq	hā'ām	mezabbechîm
Yahweh	and the wall of	Jerusalem	all around		however	the people	sacrificing

904, 1154	3706	3940, 1161.211	1041	3937, 8428	3176	5912
prep, art, n fp	cj	neg part, v Niphal pf 3ms	n ms	prep, n ms	pn	adv
בַּבָּמוֹת	כִּי	לֹא־נִבְנָה	בַיִת	לְשֵׁם	יְהוָה	עַד
babbāmôth	kî	lō'-nivnāh	vayith	leshēm	yehwāh	'adh
on the high places	because	it had not been built	a temple	to the name of	Yahweh	up to

3219	2062	3.	154.121	8406	881, 3176	3937, 2050.141	904, 2807
art, n mp	art, dem pron		cj, v Qal impf 3ms	pn	do, pn	prep, v Qal inf con	prep, n fs
הַיָּמִים	הָהֵם		וַיֶּאֱהַב	שְׁלֹמֹה	אֶת־יְהוָה	לָלֶכֶת	בְּחֻקּוֹת
hayyāmîm	hāhēm		wayye'ĕhav	shelōmōh	'eth-yehwāh	lālekheth	bechuqqôth
the days	the those		and he loved	Solomon	Yahweh	to walk	in the statutes of

1784	1	7828	904, 1154	2000	2159.351	7281.551
pn	n ms, ps 3ms	adv	prep, art, n fp	pers pron	v Piel ptc ms	cj, v Hiphil ptc ms
דָּוִד	אָבִיו	רַק	בַּבָּמוֹת	הוּא	מְזַבֵּחַ	וּמַקְטִיר
dāwidh	'āvîw	raq	babbāmôth	hû'	mezabbēach	ûmaqtîr
David	his father	only	on the high places	he	sacrificing	and burning incense

45. And king Solomon shall be blessed, and the throne of David shall be established before the LORD for ever: ... the LORD will bless me and make the rule of David safe, *NCV* ... throne of David will be secure ... for all time, *NEB* ... a blessing will be on King Solomon, and the kingdom of David will keep its place, *BB* ... David's throne shall endure, *NAB*.

46. So the king commanded Benaiah the son of Jehoiada; which went out, and fell upon him, that he died: ... king gave orders to Benaiah, *BB* ... went out and struck him, *Beck* ... he went and assailed him, *Fenton* ... took Shimei outside and killed him, *NLT* ... he went out and struck him down, *RSV*.

And the kingdom was established in the hand of Solomon: ... Solomon's authority over the kingdom was complete, *BB* ... firmly established, *Beck* ... completely established, *Goodspeed* ... kingship was secured to the hand of Solomon, *Fenton* ... Solomon had complete control of the kingdom, *Moffatt*.

3:1. And Solomon made affinity with Pharaoh king of Egypt, and took Pharaoh's daughter, and brought her into the city of David, until he had made an end of building his own house, and the house of the LORD, and the wall of Jerusalem round about: ... Solomon became son-in-law of Pharaoh, king of Egypt, and took Pharaoh's daughter as his wife, keeping her in the town of David, *BB* ... by marrying Pharaoh's daughter, *Beck* ... Solomon entered into a marriage alliance, *Berkeley* ... Solomon afterwards contracted a treaty of marriage with Pharoh king of the Mitzeraim, and married Pharoh's daughter, *Fenton*.

2. Only the people sacrificed in high places: ... people also sacrificed at the shrines, *Moffatt* ... people were still sacrificing at altars in many places of worship, *NCV* ... the people had altars on the hills, *Fenton* ... the people of Israel sacrificed their offerings at local altars, *NLT*.

because there was no house built unto the name of the LORD, until those days: ... at that time a dwelling-place for the name of Yahweh had not yet been built, *JB* ... no temple had yet been built in honour of the Eternal, *Moffatt* ... The Temple for the worship of the LORD had not yet been finished, *NCV* ... a House had not been built to the name of the EVER-LIVING, *Fenton* ... a temple honoring the name of the LORD, *NLT*.

3. And Solomon loved the LORD, walking in the statutes of David his father: ... Solomon, in his love for the LORD, kept the laws, *BB* ... lived according to the rules, *Beck* ... walking in all the Institutions, *Fenton* ... he followed the precepts, *JB* ... followed the instructions, *Good News*.

only he sacrificed and burnt incense in high places: ... made offerings and let them go up in smoke on the hight places, *BB* ... sacrificed and burnt incense on the hills, *Fenton* ... slaughtered animals and offered them as sacrifices on various altars, *Good News*.

---

daughter. But the inborn feelings of humanity in the hearts of the people were stronger than the terrors of superstition, and arising in indignation against the high priest who could thus imbrue his hands in an innocent maiden's blood, they drove him from his office and appointed a son of Ithamar in his place.

But whether this legend about Phinehas be tenable or not, it is certain that the House of Ithamar fell into deadly disrepute and abject misery. In this the people saw the fulfillment of an old traditional curse, pronounced by some unknown "man of God" on the House of Eli, that there should be no old man in his house forever; that his descendants should die in the flower of their age; and that they should come cringing to the descendants of the priest whom God would raise up in his stead, to get some humble place about the priesthood for a piece of silver and a morsel of bread (1 Sam. 2:27–36).

3:1–4. It would have thrown an interesting light on the character and development of Solomon, if we had been able to conjecture with any certainty his age when the request of Bathsheba caused David to make him the unquestioned king. The pagan historian Eupolemos, quoted by Eusebius, says that he was twelve; Josephus asserts that he was fifteen. If Rehoboam was indeed as old as forty-one when he came to the throne (1 Ki. 14:21), Solomon can hardly have been less than twenty at his accession, for in that case he must have been married before David's death (1 Ki. 11:42). But the reading "forty-one" in 1 Ki. 14:21 is altered by some into "twenty-one," and we are left in complete uncertainty. Solomon is called "a child" (1 Ki. 3:7), "young and tender" (1 Chr. 29:1), but his acts show the full vigor and decision of a man (cf. 1 Chr. 16:39f; 2 Chr. 1:3).

The composite character of the Books of Kings leads to some disturbance of the order of events, and 1 Ki. 3:1–4 is perhaps inserted to explain Solomon's sacrifice at the high place of Gibeon (Josh. 18:21–25), where stood the brazen altar of the old Tabernacle (1 Chr. 16:39f; 21:29; 2 Chr. 1:3). But no apology is needed for that act (Exo. 20:24; see Judg. 6:24; 13:19; 1 Sam. 9:12). The use

4.	2050.121	4567	1423	3937, 2159.141	8427	3706	2026	1154
	cj, v Qal impf 3ms	art, n ms	pn	prep, v Qal inf con	adv	cj	pers pron	art, n fs
	וַיֵּלֶךְ	הַמֶּלֶךְ	גִּבְעֹנָה	לִזְבֹּחַ	שָׁם	כִּי	הִיא	הַבָּמָה
	wayyēlekh	hammelekh	giv'ōnāh	lizbbōach	shām	kî	hî'	habbāmāh
	and he went	the king	to Gibeon	to sacrifice	there	because	it	the high place

1448	512	6150	6148.521	8406	6142	4326
art, adj	num	n fp	v Hiphil impf 3ms	pn	prep	art, n ms
הַגְּדוֹלָה	אֶלֶף	עֹלוֹת	יַעֲלֶה	שְׁלֹמֹה	עַל	הַמִּזְבֵּחַ
haggᵉdhôlāh	'eleph	'ōlōth	ya'ăleh	shᵉlōmōh	'al	hammizbēach
the great	one thousand	burnt offerings	he caused to go up	Solomon	on	the altar

2000	5.	904, 1423	7495.211	3176	420, 8406	904, 2573	4050
art, dem pron		prep, pn	v Niphal pf 3ms	pn	prep, pn	prep, n ms	art, n ms
הַהוּא		בְּגִבְעוֹן	נִרְאָה	יְהוָה	אֶל־שְׁלֹמֹה	בַּחֲלוֹם	הַלָּיְלָה
hahû'		bᵉghiv'ôn	nir'āh	yᵉhōwāh	'el-shᵉlōmōh	bachlôm	hallāyᵉlāh
the that		at Gibeon	He appeared	Yahweh	to Solomon	in a dream	at night

569.121	435	8068.131	4242	5598.125, 3937	6.	569.121	8406
cj, v Qal impf 3ms	n mp	v Qal impv 2ms	intrg	v Qal impf 1cs, prep, ps 2ms		cj, v Qal impf 3ms	pn
וַיֹּאמֶר	אֱלֹהִים	שְׁאַל	מָה	אֶתֶּן־לָךְ		וַיֹּאמֶר	שְׁלֹמֹה
wayyō'mer	'ĕlōhîm	shᵉ'al	māh	'etten-lākh		wayyō'mer	shᵉlōmōh
and He said	God	ask	what	will I give to you		and he said	Solomon

887	6449.113	6196, 5860	1784	1	2721	1448	3626, 866
pers pron	v Qal pf 2ms	prep, n ms, ps 2ms	pn	n ms, ps 1cs	n ms	adj	prep, rel part
אַתָּה	עָשִׂיתָ	עִם־עַבְדְּךָ	דָוִד	אָבִי	חֶסֶד	גָּדוֹל	כַּאֲשֶׁר
'attāh	'āsîthā	'im-'avdᵉkhā	dhāwidh	'āvî	chesedh	gādhôl	ka'ăsher
You	You have acted	with your servant	David	my father	kindness	great	when

2050.111	3937, 6686	904, 583	904, 6930	904, 3599	3949
v Qal pf 3ms	prep, n mp, ps 2ms	prep, n fs	cj, prep, n fs	cj, prep, *n fs*	n ms
הָלַךְ	לְפָנֶיךָ	בֶּאֱמֶת	וּבִצְדָקָה	וּבְיִשְׁרַת	לֵבָב
hālakh	lᵉphānêkhā	be'ĕmeth	ûvitsdhāqāh	ûvᵉyishrath	lēvāv
he walked	before you	with reliability	and with righteousness	and with uprightness of	heart

6196	8490.123, 3937	881, 2721	1448	2172
prep, ps 2ms	cj, v Qal impf 2ms, prep, ps 3ms	do, art, n ms	art, adj	art, dem pron
עִמָּךְ	וַתִּשְׁמָר־לוֹ	אֶת־הַחֶסֶד	הַגָּדוֹל	הַזֶּה
'immākh	wattishmār-lô	'eth-hachesedh	haggādhôl	hazzeh
with You	and you kept for him	the steadfast love	the great	the this

5598.123, 3937	1158	3553.151	6142, 3802	3626, 3219	2172
cj, v Qal impf 2ms, prep, ps 3ms	n ms	v Qal act ptc ms	prep, n ms, ps 3ms	prep, art, n ms	art, dem pron
וַתִּתֶּן־לוֹ	בֵן	יֹשֵׁב	עַל־כִּסְאוֹ	כַּיּוֹם	הַזֶּה
wattitten-lô	vēn	yōshēv	'al-kis'ô	kayyôm	hazzeh
and You gave to him	a son	one who sits	on his throne	like the day	the this

7.	6498	3176	435	887	4566.513	881, 5860
	cj, adv	pn	n mp, ps 1cs	pers pron	v Hiphil pf 2ms	do, n ms, ps 2ms
	וְעַתָּה	יְהוָה	אֱלֹהָי	אַתָּה	הִמְלַכְתָּ	אֶת־עַבְדְּךָ
	wᵉ'attāh	yᵉhwāh	'ĕlōhāy	'attāh	himlakhtā	'eth-'avdᵉkhā
	and now	O Yahweh	my God	You	You have caused me to reign	your servant

8809	1784	1	609	5470	7275	3940	3156.125	3428.141
prep	pn	n ms, ps 1cs	cj, pers pron	n ms	adj	neg part	v Qal impf 1cs	v Qal inf con
תַּחַת	דָּוִד	אָבִי	וְאָנֹכִי	נַעַר	קָטֹן	לֹא	אֵדַע	צֵאת
tachath	dāwidh	'āvî	wᵉ'ānōkhî	na'ar	qātōn	lō'	'ēdha'	tsē'th
instead of	David	my father	but I	a boy	small	not	I know	going out

971.141		5860	904, 8761	6194	866	1013.113
cj, v Qal inf con		cj, n ms, ps 2ms	prep, *n ms*	n ms, ps 2ms	rel pron	v Qal pf 2ms
וָבֹא	**8.**	וְעַבְדְּךָ	בְּתוֹךְ	עַמְּךָ	אֲשֶׁר	בָּחָרְתָּ
wāvō'		we'avdekhā	bethôkh	'ammekhā	'ăsher	bāchārettā
or coming in		and your servant	in the midst of	your people	whom	You chose

6194, 7521	866	3940, 4630.221	3940	5807.221
n ms, adj	rel pron	neg part, v Niphal impf 3ms	cj, neg part	v Niphal impf 3ms
עַם־רָב	אֲשֶׁר	לֹא־יִמָּנֶה	וְלֹא	יִסָּפֵר
'am-rāv	'ăsher	lō'-yimmāneh	welō'	yissāphēr
a numerous people	who	they cannot be counted	indeed not	they can be written

4. And the king went to Gibeon to sacrifice there; for that was the great high place: ... since that was the principal high place, *JB* ... as that was the chief shrine, *Moffatt* ... the most renowned, *NAB* ... most important place of worship, *NCV* ... the chief hill-shrine, *NEB*.

a thousand burnt offerings did Solomon offer upon that altar: ... a thousand victims Solomon used to sacrifice, *Moffatt* ... Upon its altar Solomon offered a thousand holocausts, *NAB* ... he used to offer a thousand whole-offerings on its altar, *NEB*.

5. In Gibeon the LORD appeared to Solomon in a dream by night: and God said, Ask what I shall give thee: ... had a vision of the LORD ... Say what I am to give you, *BB* ... during the night, *JB* ... Ask for whatever you want me to give you, *NIV* ... What would you like me to give you?, *Good News*.

6. And Solomon said, Thou hast shown unto thy servant David my father great mercy: ... You showed most faithful love, *JB* ... proved thyself most generous, *Moffatt* ... shown great favor, *NAB* ... were very kind, *NCV* ... Great was your mercy, *BB*.

according as he walked before thee in truth, and in righteousness, and in uprightness of heart with thee: ... when he lived his life before you in faithfulness and uprightness and integrity of heart, *JB* ... a loyal and honest life with upright mind, *Moffatt* ... because he behaved faithfully toward you, with justice, *NAB* ... He obeyed you, and he was honest and lived right, *NCV* ... as his life before you was true and upright and his heart was true to you, *BB*.

and thou hast kept for him this great kindness, that thou hast given him a son to sit on his throne, as it is this day: ... you have continued this most faithful love to him, *JB* ... this great favor toward him, even today, *NAB* ... you allowed his son to be king after him, *NCV* ... maintained this great and constant love towards him, *NEB* ... you have kept for him this greatest mercy, a son to take his place, *BB*.

7. And now, O LORD my God, thou hast made thy servant king instead of David my father: ... reign in place of David my father, *Fenton* ... king in succession to, *JB*.

and I am but a little child: I know not how to go out or come in: ... although I am a young man and don't know how to be a ruler, *Beck* ... I am very young; I may not know how to conduct myself, *Fenton* ... unskilled in leadership, *JB* ... do not know how to carry out my duties, *NIV* ... a little child in comparison, *Goodspeed*.

8. And thy servant is in the midst of thy people which thou hast chosen: ... surrounded by thine own, *Moffatt* ... here is your servant, surrounded, *JB* ... your servant has round him the people of your selection, *Beck*.

a great people, that cannot be numbered nor counted for multitude: ... a vast host, too great, *Moffatt* ... its number cannot be counted or reckoned, *JB* ... no account of them may be given, *BB* ... too many to be counted or recorded, *Beck*.

---

of high places, even when they were consecrated to the worship of Yahweh, was regarded in later days as involving principles of danger and became a grave offense in the eyes of all who took the Deuteronomic standpoint. But high places to Yahweh, as distinct from those dedicated to idols, were not condemned by the earlier prophets, and the resort to them was never regarded as blameworthy before the establishment of the central sanctuary.

3:5–9. The Jews recognized three modes of divine communication—by dreams, by Urim and by prophets. The highest and most immediate illumination was the prophetic. The revelation by means of the primitive Urim and Thummin was the direct method.

Full of the thoughts inspired by an intense devotion and a yearning desire to rule aright, the sleeping soul of Solomon became bright with eyes, and in his dream he made a worthy answer to the appeal of God.

Solomon made the wise choice. In his dream he thanked God for his mercifully fulfilled promise to David his father, and with a touching humble confession. He begged for an understanding heart to judge between right and wrong.

4623, 7524		5598.113	3937, 5860	3949	8471.151
prep, *n ms*	**9.**	cj, v Qal pf 2ms	prep, n ms, ps 2ms	n ms	v Qal act ptc ms
מֵרֹב		וְנָתַתָּ	לְעַבְדְּךָ	לֵב	שֹׁמֵעַ
mērōv		wenāthattā	le'avdekhā	lēv	shōmēa'
because a multitude		so You must give	to your servant	a heart	one which listens

3937, 8570.141	881, 6194	3937, 1032.541	1033, 3005	3937, 7737	3706	4449
prep, v Qal inf con	do, n ms, ps 2ms	prep, v Hiphil inf con	prep, adj	prep, adj	cj	intrg
לִשְׁפֹּט	אֶת־עַמְּךָ	לְהָבִין	בֵּין־טוֹב	לְרָע	כִּי	מִי
lishpōṯ	'eth-'ammekhā	lehāvîn	bên-ṭôv	lerā'	kî	mî
to judge	your people	to discern	between good	with evil	because	who

3310.121	3937, 8570.141	881, 6194	3633	2172		3296.121
v Qal impf 3ms	prep, v Qal inf con	do, n ms, ps 2ms	art, adj	art, dem pron	**10.**	cj, v Qal impf 3ms
יוּכַל	לִשְׁפֹּט	אֶת־עַמְּךָ	הַכָּבֵד	הַזֶּה		וַיִּיטַב
yûkhal	lishpōṯ	'eth-'ammekhā	hakkāvēdh	hazzeh		wayyîṭav
he is able	to judge	your people	the heavy	the this		and it seemed good

1745	904, 6084	112	3706	8068.111	8406	881, 1745	2172
art, n ms	prep, *n fd*	n mp, ps 1cs	cj	v Qal pf 3ms	pn	do, art, n ms	art, dem pron
הַדָּבָר	בְּעֵינֵי	אֲדֹנָי	כִּי	שָׁאַל	שְׁלֹמֹה	אֶת־הַדָּבָר	הַזֶּה
haddāvār	be'ênê	'ădhōnāy	kî	shā'al	shelōmōh	'eth-haddāvār	hazzeh
the word	in the eyes of	the Lord	that	he requested	Solomon	the thing	the this

	569.121	435	420	3391	866	8068.113	881, 1745
11.	cj, v Qal impf 3ms	n mp	prep, ps 3ms	cj	rel part	v Qal pf 2ms	do, art, n ms
	וַיֹּאמֶר	אֱלֹהִים	אֵלָיו	יַעַן	אֲשֶׁר	שָׁאַלְתָּ	אֶת־הַדָּבָר
	wayyō'mer	'ĕlōhîm	'ēlāv	ya'an	'ăsher	shā'altā	'eth-haddāvār
	and he said	God	to him	because	that	you have asked	the thing

2172	3940, 8068.113	3937	3219	7521	3940, 8068.113
art, dem pron	cj, neg part, v Qal pf 2ms	prep, ps 2ms	n mp	adj	cj, neg part, v Qal pf 2ms
הַזֶּה	וְלֹא־שָׁאַלְתָּ	לְּךָ	יָמִים	רַבִּים	וְלֹא־שָׁאַלְתָּ
hazzeh	welō'-shā'altā	lekhā	yāmîm	rabbîm	welō'-shā'altā
the this	and you have not asked	for yourself	days	many	and you have not asked

3937	6484	3940	8068.113	5497	342.152
prep, ps 2ms	n ms	cj, neg part	v Qal pf 2ms	*n fs*	v Qal act ptc mp, ps 2ms
לְּךָ	עֹשֶׁר	וְלֹא	שָׁאַלְתָּ	נֶפֶשׁ	אֹיְבֶיךָ
lekhā	'ōsher	welō'	shā'altā	nephesh	'ōyevêkhā
for yourself	riches	and not	you have asked for	the life of	your enemies

8068.113	3937	1032.541	3937, 8471.141	5122		2079
cj, v Qal impf 2ms	prep, ps 2ms	v Hiphil inf con	prep, v Qal inf con	n ms	**12.**	intrj
וְשָׁאַלְתָּ	לְּךָ	הָבִין	לִשְׁמֹעַ	מִשְׁפָּט		הִנֵּה
weshā'altā	lekhā	hāvîn	lishmōa'	mishpāṭ		hinnēh
but you have asked for	for yourself	discerning	to listen to	justice		behold

6449.115	3626, 1745	2079	5598.115	3937	3949	2550
v Qal pf 1cs	prep, n mp, ps 2ms	intrj	v Qal pf 1cs	prep, ps 2ms	n ms	adj
עָשִׂיתִי	כִּדְבָרֶךָ	הִנֵּה	נָתַתִּי	לְךָ	לֵב	חָכָם
'āsîthî	kidhvārêkhā	hinnēh	nāthattî	lekhā	lēv	chākhām
I will do	according to your words	behold	I will give	to you	a heart	wise

1032.255	866	3765	3940, 2030.111	3937, 6686	313
cj, v Niphal ptc ms	rel part	prep, ps 2ms	neg part, v Qal pf 3ms	prep, n mp, ps 2ms	cj, adv, ps 2ms
וְנָבוֹן	אֲשֶׁר	כָּמוֹךָ	לֹא־הָיָה	לְפָנֶיךָ	וְאַחֲרֶיךָ
wenāvôn	'ăsher	kāmôkhā	lō'-hāyāh	lephānêkhā	we'achrêkhā
and discerning	which	like you	he has not been	before you	and after you

3940, 7251.121 neg part, v Qal impf 3ms לֹא־יָקוּם lō'-yāqûm he will not arise	3765 prep, ps 2ms כָּמוֹךָ kāmôkhā like you	**13.**	1612 cj, cj וְגַם wegham and also	866 rel part אֲשֶׁר 'ăsher what	3940, 8068.113 neg part, v Qal pf 2ms לֹא־שָׁאַלְתָּ lō'-shā'altā you have not asked for	5598.115 v Qal pf 1cs נָתַתִּי nāthattî I will give

3937 prep, ps 2ms לָךְ lākh to you	1612, 6484 cj, n ms גַּם־עֹשֶׁר gam-'ōsher both riches	1612, 3638 cj, n ms גַּם־כָּבוֹד gam-kāvôdh and honor	866 cj אֲשֶׁר 'ăsher that	3940, 2030.111 neg part, v Qal pf 3ms לֹא־הָיָה lō'-hāyāh he will not be	3765 prep, ps 2ms כָּמוֹךָ khāmôkhā like you	382 n ms אִישׁ 'îsh a man	904, 4567 prep, art, n mp בַּמְּלָכִים bammelākhîm among the kings

3725, 3219 *adj*, n mp, ps 2ms כָּל־יָמֶיךָ kol-yāmêkhā all your days	**14.**	524 cj, cj וְאִם we'im and if	2050.123 v Qal impf 2ms תֵּלֵךְ tēlēkh you will walk	904, 1932 prep, n mp, ps 1cs בִּדְרָכַי bidhrākhay in my ways	3937, 8490.141 prep, v Qal inf con לִשְׁמֹר lishmōr to observe	2807 n mp, ps 1cs חֻקַּי chuqqay my statutes

9. Give therefore thy servant an understanding heart to judge thy people, that I may discern between good and bad: ... to listen justly to Your People, and to distinguish between right or wrong, *Fenton* ... an attentive mind to judge thy people in righteousness, *Goodspeed* ... to understand how to govern your people, *JB* ... give me an obedient heart so I can rule the people in the right way, *NCV*.

for who is able to judge this thy so great a people?: ... to administer justice to this splendid People of Yours, *Fenton* ... how could one otherwise govern, *JB* ... who can bear the weight of this government, *Moffatt* ... Otherwise, it is impossible to rule, *NCV*.

10. And the speech pleased the Lord, that Solomon had asked this thing: ... The LORD was well pleased, *NEB* ... pleasing in the sight of the LORD, *Berkeley* ... acceptable in the sight of the EVER-LIVING, *Fenton* ... in the eyes of the LORD, *Goodspeed*.

11. And God said unto him, Because thou hast asked this thing, and hast not asked for thyself long life; neither hast asked riches for thyself, nor hast asked the life of thine enemies; but hast asked for thyself understanding to discern judgment: ... not for long life for yourself or for wealth or for the destruction of your haters, but for wisdom to be a judge of causes, *BB* ... how to be just in giving judgment, *Beck* ... asked intelligence for yourself to listen to justice, *Fenton* ... to perceive justice, *Goodspeed* ... so that you may know what is right, *NAB*.

12. Behold, I have done according to thy words: lo, I have given thee a wise and an understanding heart: ... I do as you requested, *NAB* ... discerning mind, *NRSV* ... wise and far-seeing heart, *BB* ... I'm giving you such intelligence , *Beck* ... I will do what you asked, *NCV*.

so that there was none like thee before thee, neither after thee shall any arise like unto thee: ... there has never been anyone like you up to now, and after you there will come no one to equal you, *NAB* ... nobody before you or after you will be like you, *Beck* ... greater than anyone has had in the past or will have in the future, *NCV*.

13. And I have also given thee that which thou hast not asked, both riches, and honour: so that there shall not be any among the kings like unto thee all thy days: ... no other king will be like you as long as you live, *Beck* ... wealth and splendour such as no man of the kings of all your time possesses, *Fenton* ... glory as no other king can match, *JB* ... no king shall ever be your equal, *Moffatt* ... no other ... as great as you, *NCV* ... shall compare with you, *NRSV*.

14. And if thou wilt walk in my ways, to keep my statutes and my commandments, as thy father David did walk, then I will lengthen thy days: ... observe my ordinances ... I will also give you long life, *REB* ... keeping my laws and orders, *BB* ... keep my precepts,

3:10–14. God was pleased with the noble, unselfish request. The youthful king might have besought the boon of a long life, which was so highly valued for executing political plans. Instead of this, he had asked for "understanding to discern judgment," and the lesser gifts were freely accorded him. God promised him that he would be a king of unprecedented greatness. He freely gave him riches and honor, and, contingent on his continued faithfulness, a long life. The condition was broken, and Solomon was not more than sixty years old when he was called before the God whom he forsook (Neh. 13:26).

3:15. When Solomon awoke, he realized it was a dream. But he also knew well that it was more than a dream. In reverential gratitude he

4851	3626, 866	2050.111	1784	1	773.515
cj, n fp, ps 1cs	prep, rel part	v Qal pf 3ms	pn	n ms, ps 2ms	cj, v Hiphil pf 1cs
וּמִצְוֺתַי	כַּאֲשֶׁר	הָלַךְ	דָּוִיד	אָבִיךָ	וְהַאֲרַכְתִּי
ûmitswōthay	ka'ăsher	hālakh	dāwîdh	'āvîkhā	weha'arakhtî
and my commandments	just as	he walked	David	your father	and I will lengthen

881, 3219		3477.121	8406	2079	2573	971.121	3503
do, n mp, ps 2ms	**15.**	cj, v Qal impf 3ms	pn	cj, intrj	n ms	cj, v Qal impf 3ms	pn
אֶת־יָמֶיךָ		וַיִּקַץ	שְׁלֹמֹה	וְהִנֵּה	חֲלוֹם	וַיָּבוֹא	יְרוּשָׁלַם
'eth-yāmêkhā		wayyiqats	shelōmōh	wehinnēh	chălôm	wayyāvô'	yerûshālam
your days		and he awoke	Solomon	and behold	a dream	and he came to	Jerusalem

6198.121	3937, 6686	751	1311, 112	6148.521
cj, v Qal impf 3ms	prep, *n mp*	*n ms*	*n fs*, n mp, ps 1cs	cj, v Hiphil impf 3ms
וַיַּעֲמֹד	לִפְנֵי	אֲרוֹן	בְּרִית־אֲדֹנָי	וַיַּעַל
wayya'ămōdh	liphnê	'ărôn	berîth-'ădhōnāy	wayya'al
and he stood	before	the Ark of	the Covenant of the Lord	and he caused to go up

6150	6449.121	8399	6449.121	5136	3937, 3725, 5860
n fp	cj, v Qal impf 3ms	n mp	cj, v Qal impf 3ms	n ms	prep, *adj*, n mp, ps 3ms
עֹלוֹת	וַיַּעַשׂ	שְׁלָמִים	וַיַּעַשׂ	מִשְׁתֶּה	לְכָל־עֲבָדָיו
'ōlôth	wayya'as	shelāmîm	wayya'as	mishteh	lekhol-'ăvādhâv
burnt offerings	and he made	peace offerings	and he made	a feast	for all his servants

	226	971.127	8692	5571	2193	420, 4567	6198.127	3937, 6686
16.	adv	v Qal impf 3fp	num	n fp	n fp	prep, art, n ms	v Qal impf 3fp	prep, n mp, ps 3ms
	אָז	תָּבֹאנָה	שְׁתַּיִם	נָשִׁים	זֹנוֹת	אֶל־הַמֶּלֶךְ	וַתַּעֲמֹדְנָה	לְפָנָיו
	'āz	tāvō'nāh	shettayim	nāshîm	zōnôth	'el-hammelekh	watta'ămōdhenāh	lephānâv
	then	they came	two	women	prostitutes	to the king	and they stood	before him

	569.122	828	259	1031	112	603	828	2148
17.	cj, v Qal impf 3fs	art, n fs	art, num	part	n ms, ps 1cs	pers pron	cj, art, n fs	art, dem pron
	וַתֹּאמֶר	הָאִשָּׁה	הָאַחַת	בִּי	אֲדֹנִי	אֲנִי	וְהָאִשָּׁה	הַזֹּאת
	wattō'mer	hā'ishshāh	hā'achath	bî	'ădhōnî	'ănî	wehā'ishshāh	hazzō'th
	and she said	the woman	the first	oh	my lord	I	and the woman	the this

3553.154	904, 1041	259	3314.125	6196	904, 1041		2030.121
v Qal act ptc fp	prep, n ms	num	cj, v Qal impf 1cs	prep, ps 3fs	prep, art, n ms	**18.**	cj, v Qal impf 3ms
יֹשְׁבֹת	בְּבַיִת	אֶחָד	וָאֵלֵד	עִמָּהּ	בַּבָּיִת		וַיְהִי
yōshevōth	bevayith	'echādh	wā'ēlēdh	'immāhh	babbāyith		wayhî
dwelling	in a house	one	and I gave birth	with her	in the house		and it was

904, 3219	8389	3937, 3314.141	3314.122	1612, 828	2148
prep, art, n ms	art, num	prep, v Qal inf con, ps 1cs	cj, v Qal impf 3fs	cj, art, n fs	art, dem pron
בַּיּוֹם	הַשְּׁלִישִׁי	לְלִדְתִּי	וַתֵּלֶד	גַּם־הָאִשָּׁה	הַזֹּאת
bayyôm	hashshelîshî	lelidhtî	wattēledh	gam-hā'ishshāh	hazzō'th
on the day	the third	of my giving birth	then she bore	also the woman	the this

601	3267	375, 2299	882	904, 1041	2190	8692, 601
cj, pers pron	adv	*sub*, n ms	prep, ps 1cp	prep, art, n ms	prep	num, pers pron
וַאֲנַחְנוּ	יַחְדָּו	אֵין־זָר	אִתָּנוּ	בַּבַּיִת	זוּלָתִי	שְׁתַּיִם־אֲנַחְנוּ
wa'ănachnû	yachdāw	'ên-zār	'ittānû	babbayith	zûlāthî	shettayim-'ănachnû
and we	together	there was not a stranger	with us	in the house	except	we two

904, 1041		4322.121	1158, 828	2148	4050	866	8311.112
prep, art, n ms	**19.**	cj, v Qal impf 3ms	*n ms*, art, n fs	art, dem pron	n ms	cj	v Qal pf 3fs
בַּבָּיִת		וַיָּמָת	בֶּן־הָאִשָּׁה	הַזֹּאת	לָיְלָה	אֲשֶׁר	שָׁכְבָה
babbāyith		wayyāmāth	ben-hā'ishshāh	hazzō'th	lāyelāh	'ăsher	shākhevāh
in the house		then he died	the son of the woman	the this	at night	because	she lay

6142 prep, ps 3ms עָלָיו 'ālâv on him	**20.**	7251.122 cj, v Qal impf 3fs וַתָּקָם wattāqām then she rose up	904, 8761 prep, *n ms* בְּתוֹךְ bethôkh in the middle of	4050 art, n ms הַלַּיְלָה hallaylāh the night	4089.122 cj, v Qal impf 3fs וַתִּקַּח wattiqqach and she took	881, 1158 do, n ms, ps 1cs אֶת־בְּנִי 'eth-benî my son

4623, 703 prep, prep, ps 1cs מֵאֶצְלִי mē'etslî from beside me	526 cj, n fs, ps 2ms וַאֲמָתְךָ wa'ămāthekhā and your female servant	3585 adj יְשֵׁנָה yeshēnāh sleeping	8311.522 cj, v Hiphil impf 3fs, ps 3ms וַתַּשְׁכִּיבֵהוּ wattashkîvēhû and she laid him	904, 2536 prep, n ms, ps 3fs בְּחֵיקָהּ bechêqāhh in her bosom

Douay ... keep my rules, *Beck* ... walk in My paths, to guard My Institutions, and commands, *Fenton*.

15. And Solomon awoke; and, behold, it was a dream. And he came to Jerusalem, and stood before the ark of the covenant of the LORD, and offered up burnt offerings, and offered peace offerings: ... Ark of the Agreement with the LORD, where he made burnt offerings and fellowship offerings, *NCV* ... sacrificed whole-offerings and brought shared-offerings, *NEB* ... communion sacrifices, *JB* ... offered sacrifices and thank-offerings and drink-offerings, *Fenton*.

and made a feast to all his servants: ... for all his leaders and officers, *NCV* ... to all his household, *NEB* ... for all his court, *NIV* ... held a banquet for all those in his service, *JB* ... with all his ministers, *Fenton*.

16. Then came there two women, that were harlots, unto the king, and stood before him: ... prostitutes came, *NRSV* ... two loose women of the town came and took their places before the king, *BB* ... two women of ill repute, *Berkeley* ... two women of ill fame, *Goodspeed* ... appealed to him, *Fenton*.

17. And the one woman said, O my lord, I and this woman dwell in one house; and I was delivered of a child with her in the house: ... live in the same house, and while she was in the house I gave birth to a child, *JB* ... I bore a child in the house beside her, *Moffatt* ... I was delivered of a child with her in the chamber, *Douay* ... lived in a single house, and I bore a child there in the house, *Fenton*.

18. And it came to pass the third day after that I was delivered, that this woman was delivered also: and we were together: ... Three days later this woman also gave birth to a baby, *NCV*.

there was no stranger with us in the house, save we two in the house: ... No one else was in the house with us; it was just the two of us, *NCV* ... We were alone together, *JB* ... there was no one there but us two, *NAB* ... no other person was with us, *Douay* ... We were quite alone; no one else was with us, *NEB*.

19. And this woman's child died in the night; because she overlaid it: ... son died because she lay on him, *NIV* ... sleeping on her child, was the cause of its death, *BB* ... she smothered him by lying on him, *NAB* ... one night she accidentally rolled over on her baby and smothered it, *Good News*.

20. And she arose at midnight, and took my son from beside me, while thine handmaid slept, and laid it in her bosom: ... in the middle of the night ... and laid him in, *NASB* ... from my bed during the night while I was asleep, and she carried him to her bed, *NCV* ... put him by her breast, *NIV* ... from my side while

offered a second sacrifice of burnt offerings before the Ark on Mount Zion and added to them peace offerings, with which he made a great feast to all his servants. Twice again did God appear to Solomon, but the second time it was to warn and the third time to condemn.

3:16–28. The reality of the gift which Solomon had received from God was speedily to be tested. Two harlots came before him. One had lain on her child in the night, and, stealing the living child of the other, she put her dead child in its place. There was no evidence to be had. It was simply the bare word of one disreputable woman against the bare word of the other. With instant decision, and a flash of insight into the springs of human actions, Solomon gave the apparently feigned order to cut the children in two and divide them between the claimants. The delinquent accepted the horrible decision, but the mother of the living child wished more for the child's well-being than for her own rights. She intervened, reacting to the horrible thought, and cried out, "O my lord, give her the living child, and in no wise slay it." Observing the opposing attitudes, Solomon burst out with the triumphant verdict, "Give her the living child! she is the mother thereof!" The true mother acted with preservation, seeing more value in the child than that of mere property.

881, 1158	4322.151	8311.512	904, 2536		7251.125	904, 1269
cj, do, n ms, ps 3fs	art, v Qal act ptc ms	v Hiphil pf 3fs	prep, n ms, ps 1cs		cj, v Qal impf 1cs	prep, art, n ms
וְאֶת־בְּנָהּ	הַמֵּת	הִשְׁכִּיבָה	בְּחֵיקִי	**21.**	וָאָקֻם	בַבֹּקֶר
we'eth-benāhh	hammēth	hishkîvāh	vechêqî		wā'āqum	babbōqer
and her son	the dead one	she laid	in my bosom		and I arose	in the morning

3937, 3352.541	881, 1158	2079, 4322.111	1032.725	420
prep, v Hiphil inf con	do, n ms, ps 1cs	cj, intrj, v Qal pf 3ms	cj, v Hithpolel impf 1cs	prep, ps 3ms
לְהֵינִיק	אֶת־בְּנִי	וְהִנֵּה־מֵת	וָאֶתְבּוֹנֵן	אֵלָיו
lehênîq	'eth-benî	wehinnēh-mēth	wā'ethbōnēn	'ēlāv
to nurse	my son	but behold he was dead	and I considered carefully	toward him

904, 1269	2079	3940, 2030.111	1158	866	3314.115		569.122
prep, art, n ms	cj, intrj	neg part, v Qal pf 3ms	n ms, ps 1cs	rel pron	v Qal pf 1cs		cj, v Qal impf 3fs
בַבֹּקֶר	וְהִנֵּה	לֹא־הָיָה	בְנִי	אֲשֶׁר	יָלָדְתִּי	**22.**	וַתֹּאמֶר
babbōqer	wehinnēh	lō'-hāyāh	venî	'ăsher	yālādhettî		wattō'mer
in the morning	and behold	he was not	my son	whom	I had borne		but she said

828	311	3940	3706	1158	2508	1158	4322.151
art, n fs	art, adj	neg part	cj	n ms, ps 1cs	art, adj	cj, n ms, ps 2fs	art, v Qal act ptc ms
הָאִשָּׁה	הָאַחֶרֶת	לֹא	כִּי	בְּנִי	הַחַי	וּבְנֵךְ	הַמֵּת
hā'ishshāh	hā'achereth	lō'	khî	benî	hachay	ûvenēkh	hammēth
the woman	the other	no	rather	my son	the living	and your son	the dead one

2148	569.151	3940	3706	1158	4322.151	1158	2508
cj, dem pron	v Qal act ptc fs	neg part	cj	n ms, ps 2fs	art, v Qal act ptc ms	cj, n ms, ps 1cs	art, adj
וְזֹאת	אֹמֶרֶת	לֹא	כִּי	בְּנֵךְ	הַמֵּת	וּבְנִי	הֶחָי
wezō'th	'ōmereth	lō'	khî	benēkh	hammēth	ûvenî	hechāy
and this one	saying	no	rather	your son	the dead one	and my son	the one living

1744.327	3937, 6686	4567		569.121	4567	2148	569.151
cj, v Piel impf 3fp	prep, *n mp*	art, n ms		cj, v Qal impf 3ms	art, n ms	dem pron	v Qal act ptc fs
וַתְּדַבֵּרְנָה	לִפְנֵי	הַמֶּלֶךְ	**23.**	וַיֹּאמֶר	הַמֶּלֶךְ	זֹאת	אֹמֶרֶת
wattedhabbērenāh	liphnê	hammelekh		wayyō'mer	hammelekh	zō'th	'ōmereth
and they spoke	before	the king		and he said	the king	this one	saying

2172, 1158	2508	1158	4322.151	2148	569.151	3940
dem pron, n ms, ps 1cs	art, adj	cj, n ms, ps 2fs	art, v Qal act ptc ms	cj, dem pron	v Qal act ptc fs	neg part
זֶה־בְּנִי	הַחַי	וּבְנֵךְ	הַמֵּת	וְזֹאת	אֹמֶרֶת	לֹא
zeh-benî	hachay	ûvenēkh	hammēth	wezō'th	'ōmereth	lō'
this my son	the one living	and your son	the dead one	and that one	saying	no

3706	1158	4322.151	1158	2508		569.121	4567
cj	n ms, ps 2fs	art, v Qal act ptc ms	cj, n ms, ps 1cs	art, adj		cj, v Qal impf 3ms	art, n ms
כִּי	בְּנֵךְ	הַמֵּת	וּבְנִי	הֶחָי	**24.**	וַיֹּאמֶר	הַמֶּלֶךְ
khî	benēkh	hammēth	ûvenî	hechāy		wayyō'mer	hammelekh
rather	your son	the dead one	and my son	the one living		and he said	the king

4089.133	3937, 2820	971.526	2820	3937, 6686	4567
v Qal impv 2mp	prep, ps 1cs, n fs	cj, v Hiphil impf 3mp	art, n fs	prep, *n mp*	art, n ms
קְחוּ	לִי־חָרֶב	וַיָּבִאוּ	הַחֶרֶב	לִפְנֵי	הַמֶּלֶךְ
qōchû	lî-chārev	wayyāvi'û	hacherev	liphnê	hammelekh
take	for me a sword	and they brought	the sword	before	the king

	569.121	4567	1535.133	881, 3315	2508	3937, 8530	5598.133
	cj, v Qal impf 3ms	art, n ms	v Qal impv 2mp	do, art, n ms	art, adj	prep, num	cj, v Qal impv 2mp
25.	וַיֹּאמֶר	הַמֶּלֶךְ	גִּזְרוּ	אֶת־הַיֶּלֶד	הַחַי	לִשְׁנָיִם	וּתְנוּ
	wayyō'mer	hammelekh	gizrû	'eth-hayyeledh	hachay	lishnāyim	ûthenû
	and he said	the king	divide	the child	the one living	into two	and give

881, 2783	3937, 259	881, 2783	3937, 259		569.122	828	866, 1158
do, art, n ms	prep, num	cj, do, art, n ms	prep, num	**26.**	cj, v Qal impf 3fs	art, n fs	rel pron, n ms, ps 3fs
אֶת־הַחֲצִי	לְאַחַת	וְאֶת־הַחֲצִי	לְאֶחָת		וַתֹּאמֶר	הָאִשָּׁה	אֲשֶׁר־בְּנָהּ
'eth-hachtsî	le'achath	we'eth-hachtsî	le'echāth		wattō'mer	hā'ishshāh	'ăsher-benāhh
the half	to one	and the half	to one		but she said	the woman	who her son

2508	420, 4567	3706, 3770.216	7641	6142, 1158
art, adj	prep, art, n ms	cj, v Niphal pf 3cp	n mp, ps 3fs	prep, n ms, ps 3fs
הַחַי	אֶל־הַמֶּלֶךְ	כִּי־נִכְמְרוּ	רַחֲמֶיהָ	עַל־בְּנָהּ
hachay	'el-hammelekh	kî-nikhmerû	rachmêāh	'al-benāhh
the one living	to the king	because they came to fruition	her compassions	concerning her son

569.122	1031	112	5598.133, 3937	881, 3314.155	2508
cj, v Qal impf 3fs	part	n ms, ps 1cs	v Qal impv 2mp, prep, ps 3fs	do, art, v Qal pass ptc ms	art, adj
וַתֹּאמֶר	בִּי	אֲדֹנִי	תְּנוּ־לָהּ	אֶת־הַיָּלוּד	הַחַי
wattō'mer	bî	'ădhōnî	tenû-lāhh	'eth-hayyālûdh	hachay
and she said	oh	my lord	give to her	the one born	the one living

4322.542	414, 4322.528	2148	569.151	1612, 3937	1612, 3937
cj, v Hiphil inf abs	adv, v Hiphil juss 2mp, ps 3ms	cj, dem pron	v Qal act ptc fs	cj, prep, ps 1cs	cj, prep, ps 2fs
וְהָמֵת	אַל־תְּמִיתֻהוּ	וְזֹאת	אֹמֶרֶת	גַּם־לִי	גַּם־לָךְ
wehāmēth	'al-temîthuhû	wezō'th	'ōmereth	gam-lî	gham-lākh
but killing	do not slay him	but that one	saying	both to me	and to you

your servant was sleeping and she took it in her arms, *BB*.

and laid her dead child in my bosom: ... she put the dead baby in my bed, *NCV* ... dead son by my breast, *NIV* ... in my arms, *BB*.

21. And when I rose in the morning to give my child suck, behold, it was dead: ... got up to suckle my child, there he was, dead, *JB* ... to nurse my child, and I found him dead, *NAB* ... give my child the breast, *BB* ... to feed my baby, *NCV*.

but when I had considered it in the morning, behold, it was not my son, which I did bear: ... I looked at him carefully, and he was not the child I had borne at all, *JB* ... looked well at it in the morning, *MAST* ... in the morning light, I saw it was not the son, *NAB* ... looking at it with care, I saw that it was not my son, *BB* ... looked at him more closely, *NCV*.

22. And the other woman said, Nay; but the living is my son, and the dead is thy son. And this said, No; but the dead is thy son, and the living is my son: ... But the first said, No; the dead child is your son and the living one mine, *BB* ... the first retorted, That is not true!, *JB*.

Thus they spake before the king: ... So they kept on talking, *BB* ... they argued, *Beck* ... And so they wrangled, *JB* ... And in this manner they strove, *Douay* ... they argued back and forth, *NLT*.

23. Then said the king, The one saith, This is my son that liveth, and thy son is the dead: and the other saith, Nay; but thy son is the dead, and my son is the living: ... This is my son that is alive, and your son is dead ... Not so! Your son is dead, and my son is the living one, *NRSV* ... This woman asserts, *Berkeley* ... Each of you claims that the living child is hers and that the dead child belongs to the other one, *Good News*.

24. And the king said, Bring me a sword. And they brought a sword before the king: ... Fetch me a sword, *MAST* ... king sent his servants to get a sword, *NCV* ... he ordered, Get me a sword, *Berkeley* ... a sword was brought into the king's presence, *JB*.

25. And the king said, Divide the living child in two, and give half to the one, and half to the other: ... the king gave the order: Cut the living child in two, *NEB* ... Split the living child into two, *Fenton* ... give each woman half of it, *Good News*.

26. Then spake the woman whose the living child was unto the king: ... woman to whom the living child belonged spoke to the king, *Goodspeed* ... the mother of the living child addressed the king, *JB* ... whose son it was, *NAB* ... The real mother, *NCV*.

for her bowels yearned upon her son: ... motherly tenderness was aroused for her son, *Goodspeed* ... felt acutely for her son, *JB* ... in the anguish she felt for it, *NAB* ... she was deeply stirred over her son, *NASB* ... full of love for her son, *NCV* ... yearning with a mother's love, *Beck*.

and she said, O my lord, give her the living child, and in no wise slay it: ... Give her the living child, and by no means slay it, *Goodspeed* ... I beg you ... let them give her the live child; on no account let them kill him!, *JB* ... Please, my master, don't kill him! Give the baby to her!, *NCV* ... whatever you do, do not kill it, *NEB*.

3940	2030.121	1535.133		6257.121	4567	569.121
neg part	v Qal impf 3ms	v Qal impv 2mp		cj, v Qal impf 3ms	art, n ms	cj, v Qal impf 3ms
לֹא	יִהְיֶה	גְּזֹרוּ	27.	וַיַּעַן	הַמֶּלֶךְ	וַיֹּאמֶר
lō'	yihyeh	gezōrû		wayya'an	hammelekh	wayyō'mer
not	he will be	divide		then he answered	the king	and he said

5598.133, 3937	881, 3314.155	2508	4322.542	3940
v Qal impv 2mp, prep, ps 3fs	do, art, v Qal pass ptc ms	art, adj	cj, v Hiphil inf abs	neg part
תְּנוּ־לָהּ	אֶת־הַיָּלוּד	הַחַי	וְהָמֵת	לֹא
tenû-lāhh	'eth-hayyālûdh	hachay	wehāmēth	lō'
give to her	the one born	the one living	but killing	not

4322.528	2026	525		8471.126	3725, 3547	881, 5122
v Hiphil impf 2mp, ps 3ms	pers pron	n fs, ps 3ms		cj, v Qal impf 3mp	*adj*, pn	do, art, n ms
תְמִיתֻהוּ	הִיא	אִמּוֹ	28.	וַיִּשְׁמְעוּ	כָל־יִשְׂרָאֵל	אֶת־הַמִּשְׁפָּט
themîthuhû	hî'	'immô		wayyishme'û	khol-yisrā'ēl	'eth-hammishpāṭ
you will slay him	she	his mother		and they heard	all Israel	the judgment

866	8570.111	4567	7495.126	4623, 6686	4567	3706	7495.116
rel part	v Qal pf 3ms	art, n ms	cj, v Qal impf 3mp	prep, *n mp*	art, n ms	cj	v Qal pf 3cp
אֲשֶׁר	שָׁפַט	הַמֶּלֶךְ	וַיִּרְאוּ	מִפְּנֵי	הַמֶּלֶךְ	כִּי	רָאוּ
'ăsher	shāphaṭ	hammelekh	wayyir'û	mippenê	hammelekh	kî	rā'û
which	he judged	the king	and they looked	from before	the king	because	they saw

3706, 2551	435	904, 7419	3937, 6449.141	5122		2030.121
cj, *n fs*	n mp	prep, n ms, ps 3ms	prep, v Qal inf con	n ms		cj, v Qal impf 3ms
כִּי־חָכְמַת	אֱלֹהִים	בְּקִרְבּוֹ	לַעֲשׂוֹת	מִשְׁפָּט	4:1	וַיְהִי
kî-chokhmath	'ĕlōhîm	beqirbô	la'ăsôth	mishpāṭ		wayhî
that the wisdom of	God	within him	to do	justice		and it was

4567	8406	4567	6142, 3725, 3547		431	8015	866, 3937
art, n ms	pn	n ms	prep, *adj*, pn		cj, dem pron	art, n mp	rel pron, prep, ps 3ms
הַמֶּלֶךְ	שְׁלֹמֹה	מֶלֶךְ	עַל־כָּל־יִשְׂרָאֵל	2.	וְאֵלֶּה	הַשָּׂרִים	אֲשֶׁר־לוֹ
hammelekh	shelōmōh	melekh	'al-kol-yisrā'ēl		we'ēlleh	hassārîm	'ăsher-lô
the king	Solomon	king	over all Israel		and these	the officials	who to him

6051	1158, 6923	3669		461	282	1158	8306	5810
pn	*n ms*, pn	art, n ms		pn	cj, pn	*n mp*	pn	n mp
עֲזַרְיָהוּ	בֶּן־צָדוֹק	הַכֹּהֵן	3.	אֱלִיחֹרֶף	וַאֲחִיָּה	בְּנֵי	שִׁישָׁא	סֹפְרִים
'ăzaryāhû	ven-tsādhôq	hakkōhēn		'ĕlîchōreph	wa'ăchîyāh	benê	shîshā'	sōpherîm
Azariah	the son of Zadok	the priest		Elihoreph	and Ahiah	the sons of	Shisha	scribes

3194	1158, 287	2226.551		1172	1158, 3179
pn	*n ms*, pn	art, v Hiphil ptc ms		cj, pn	*n ms*, pn
יְהוֹשָׁפָט	בֶּן־אֲחִילוּד	הַמַּזְכִּיר	4.	וּבְנָיָהוּ	בֶּן־יְהוֹיָדָע
yehôshāphāṭ	ben-'ăchîlûdh	hammazkîr		ûvenāyāhû	ven-yehôyādhā'
Jehoshaphat	the son of Ahilud	the recorder		and Benaiah	the son of Jehoiada

6142, 6893	6923	55	3669		6051	1158, 5600
prep, art, n ms	cj, pn	cj, pn	n mp		cj, pn	*n ms*, pn
עַל־הַצָּבָא	וְצָדוֹק	וְאֶבְיָתָר	כֹּהֲנִים	5.	וַעֲזַרְיָהוּ	בֶּן־נָתָן
'al-hatstsāvā'	wetsādhôq	we'evyāthār	kōhenîm		wa'ăzaryāhû	ven-nāthān
over the army	and Zadok	and Abiathar	priests		and Azariah	the son of Nathan

6142, 5507.256	2156	1158, 5600	3669	7751	4567		302
prep, art, v Niphal ptc mp	cj, pn	*n ms*, pn	n ms	*n ms*	art, n ms		cj, pn
עַל־הַנִּצָּבִים	וְזָבוּד	בֶּן־נָתָן	כֹּהֵן	רֵעֶה	הַמֶּלֶךְ	6.	וַאֲחִישָׁר
'al-hanitstsāvîm	wezāvûdh	ben-nāthān	kōhēn	rē'eh	hammelekh		wa'ăchîshār
over the governors	and Zabud	the son of Nathan	a priest	a friend of	the king		and Ahishar

But the other said, Let it be neither mine nor thine, but divide it: ... interrupted, It shall be neither mine nor yours!, *Goodspeed* ... He shall belong to neither of us. Cut him in half!, *JB* ... Neither of us will have him. Cut him into two pieces, *NCV*.

27. Then the king answered and said, Give her the living child, and in no wise slay it: she is the mother thereof: ... Give the first woman the living baby ... and don't kill it. She is his mother, *Beck* ... the king gave his decision. 'Give the live child to the first woman', *JB* ... certainly you must not kill him—for she is his mother, *Berkeley* ... she is the real mother, *NCV*.

28. And all Israel heard of the judgment which the king had judged; and they feared the king: ... they stood in awe of him, *NEB* ... When the people of Israel heard about King Solomon's decision, they respected him very much, *NCV* ... the king had rendered; and they stood in awe, *NRSV* ... the verdict the king had given, *NIV* ... they respected the king very highly, *Beck*.

for they saw that the wisdom of God was in him, to do judgment: ... the wisdom of God within him to administer justice, *NEB* ... to make the right decisions, *NCV* ... because they perceived, *NRSV*.

4:1. So king Solomon was king over all Israel: ... ruled, *Beck* ... reigned over, *Moffatt*.

2. And these were the princes which he had; Azariah the son of Zadok the priest: ... his high officials, *RSV* ... His ministers of state, *Moffatt* ... his leading officers, *NCV* ... chief men, *BB*.

3. Elihoreph and Ahiah, the sons of Shisha, scribes: ... Chancellors, *Fenton* ... recorded what happened in the courts; *NCV* ... Court secretaries, *Good News*.

Jehoshaphat the son of Ahilud, the recorder: ... herald, *JB* ... recorded the history of the people, *NCV* ... In charge of the records, *Good News*.

4. And Benaiah the son of Jehoiada was over the host: and Zadok and Abiathar were the priests: ... commander-in-chief, *Moffatt* ... commander of the army, *NAB* ... the chief priests, *Beck*.

5. And Azariah the son of Nathan was over the officers: ... Superintendent of the regional governers, *NEB* ... over those in authority in the different divisions of the country, *BB* ... head of the prefects, *Moffatt* ... in charge of the district officers, *NIV*.

and Zabud the son of Nathan was principal officer, and the king's friend: ... a priest and the king's friend, *NKJV* ... a priest and personal adviser to the king, *NIV*.

6. And Ahishar was over the household: ... responsible for everything in the palace, *NCV* ... Comptroller, *NEB* ... controller of the king's house, *BB*.

and Adoniram the son of Abda was over the tribute: ... superintendent of the forced labor, *NAB* ... in charge of the labor force, *NCV* ... Superintendent of the forced levy,

---

Modern critics, wise after the event, express themselves very slightingly of the amount of intelligence required for the decision, but the people saw the value of the presence of mind and rapid intuition which settled the question by bringing an individual dilemma under the immediate arbitrariness of a general law. They rejoiced to recognize the practical wisdom which God had given to their young king. The word chokhmāh (HED #2551), which is represented by one large section of Jewish literature, implied the practical intelligence derived from insight or experience, the power to govern oneself and others. Its conclusions were expressed chiefly in a gnomic form, and they pass through various stages, especially in the Books of Proverbs, Job and Ecclesiastes. Solomon's varied intellectual wisdom created deeper astonishment.

4:1–6. The fourth chapter of the Book of Kings gives us the constitution of his court as it was in the middle of his reign, when two of his daughters were already married. The highest officers of the kingdom were called sārîm (HED #8015), "princes," a title which in David's reign had been borne almost alone by Joab, who was sarha-tsāvā' (HED #8015, 6893), or captain of the host." The son of Zadok I is named first as "the priest." The two chief secretaries, sōpherîm (HED #5810), were Elihoreph and Ahiah. They inherited the office of their father Shavsha (1 Chr. 18:16), who had been the secretary of David. It was their duty to record decrees and draw up the documents of state. Jehoshaphat, the son of Ahilud, continued to hold the office of annalist or historiographer, the officer known as the Waka Nuwish in Persian courts (cf. Est. 6:1). Azariah was over the twelve governors. His brother Zabud became "priest" and "king's friend" (2 Sam. 15:37). Ahishar was over the household. That is, he was the chamberlain, vizier, or mayor of the palace, wearing on his shoulder the key which was the symbol of his authority (Isa. 22:21). Adoniram or Adoran, who had been tax collector for David, still held that onerous and invidious office (2 Sam. 20:24), which subsequently, in his advanced old age, cost him his life. Benaiah succeeded to the chief-captaincy of Joab.

6142, 1041	138	1158, 5862	6142, 4671		3937, 8406
prep, art, n ms	cj, pn	*n ms*, pn	prep, art, n ms		cj, prep, pn
עַל־הַבָּיִת	וַאֲדֹנִירָם	בֶּן־עַבְדָּא	עַל־הַמַּס	7.	וְלִשְׁלֹמֹה
‘al-habbāyith	wa’ădhōnîrām	ben-‘avdā’	‘al-hammas̱		welishlōmōh
over the household	and Adoniram	the son of Abda	over the forced labor		and to Solomon

8530, 6461	5507.256	6142, 3725, 3547	3677.316	881, 4567
num, num	v Niphal ptc mp	prep, *adj*, pn	cj, v Pilpel pf 3cp	do, art, n ms
שְׁנֵים־עָשָׂר	נִצָּבִים	עַל־כָּל־יִשְׂרָאֵל	וְכִלְכְּלוּ	אֶת־הַמֶּלֶךְ
shenêm-‘āsār	nitstsāvîm	‘al-kol-yisrā’ēl	wekhilkelû	’eth-hammelekh
twelve	governors	over all Israel	and they provided for	the king

881, 1041	2414	904, 8523	2030.121	6142, 259	3937, 3677.341		431
cj, do, n ms, ps 3ms	n ms	prep, art, n fs	v Qal impf 3ms	prep, num	prep, v Pilpel inf con		cj, dem pron
וְאֶת־בֵּיתוֹ	חֹדֶשׁ	בַּשָּׁנָה	יִהְיֶה	עַל־אֶחָד	לְכַלְכֵּל	8.	וְאֵלֶּה
we’eth-bêthô	chōdhesh	bashshānāh	yihyeh	‘al-’echādh	lekhalkēl		we’ēlleh
and his household	a month	in the year	he was	over one	to provide		and these

8428	1158, 2449	904, 2098	688		1158, 1917	904, 4902
n mp, ps 3mp	*n ms*, pn	prep, *n ms*	pn		*n ms*, pn	prep, pn
שְׁמוֹתָם	בֶּן־חוּר	בְּהַר	אֶפְרָיִם	9.	בֶּן־דֶּקֶר	בְּמָקַץ
shemôthām	ben-chûr	behar	’ephrāyim		ben-deqer	bemāqats
their names	the son of Hur	in the hills of	Ephraim		the son of Dekar	in Makaz

904, 8546	1094	1094	362B	362B	362B		1158, 2723	1158, 725
cj, prep, pn	cj, pn	pn	cj, pn	pn	pn		*n ms*, pn	prep, pn
וּבְשַׁעַלְבִים	וּבֵית	שָׁמֶשׁ	וְאֵילוֹן	בֵּית	חָנָן	10.	בֶּן־חֶסֶד	בָּאֲרֻבּוֹת
ûvesha‘alvîm	ûvêth	shāmesh	we’êlôn	bêth	chānān		ben-ches̱edh	bā’ărubbôth
and in Shaalbim	and Beth	Shemesh	and Elon	Beth	Hanan		the son of Hesed	in Arubboth

3937	7915	3725, 800	2764		1158, 41	3725, 5498	1725
prep, ps 3ms	pn	cj, *adj*, *n fs*	pn		*n ms*, pn	*adj*, *n fs*	pn
לוֹ	שֹׂכֹה	וְכָל־אֶרֶץ	חֵפֶר	11.	בֶּן־אֲבִינָדָב	כָּל־נָפַת	דֹּאר
lô	sōkhōh	wekhol-’erets	chēpher		ben-’ăvînādhāv	kol-nāphath	dō’r
to him	Sochoh	and all the land of	Hepher		the son of Abinadab	all the region of	Dor

3064	1351, 8406	2030.112	3937	3937, 828		1219
pn	*n fs*, pn	v Qal pf 3fs	prep, ps 3ms	prep, n fs		pn
טָפַת	בַּת־שְׁלֹמֹה	הָיְתָה	לּוֹ	לְאִשָּׁה	12.	בַּעֲנָא
ṯāphath	bath-shelōmōh	hāyethāh	lô	le’ishshāh		ba‘ănā’
Taphath	the daughter of Solomon	she was	to him	for a wife		Baanah

1158, 287	8923	4163	3725, 1093	1093	866	703	7177
n ms, pn	pn	cj, pn	cj, *adj*, pn	pn	rel part	prep	pn
בֶּן־אֲחִילוּד	תַּעְנַךְ	וּמְגִדּוֹ	וְכָל־בֵּית	שְׁאָן	אֲשֶׁר	אֵצֶל	צָרְתַנָה
ben-’ăchîlûdh	ta‘ănakh	ûmeghiddô	wekhol-bêth	she’ān	’ăsher	’ētsel	tsārethanāh
the son of Ahilud	Taanach	and Megiddo	and all Beth	Shean	which	beside	Zartanah

4623, 8809	3937, 3262	4623, 1093	1093	5912	62C	62C	5912	4623, 5885
prep, prep	prep, pn	prep, pn	pn	prep	pn	pn	prep	prep, n ms
מִתַּחַת	לְיִזְרְעֶאל	מִבֵּית	שְׁאָן	עַד	אָבֵל	מְחוֹלָה	עַד	מֵעֵבֶר
mittachath	leyizre’e’l	mibbêth	she’ān	‘adh	’āvēl	mechôlāh	‘adh	mē‘ēver
from below	to Jezreel	from Beth	Shean	unto	Abel	Meholah	unto	from the opposite side

3937, 3471		1158, 1430	904, 7721	7721	3937	2459B	2459B
prep, pn		*n ms*, pn	prep, pn	pn	prep, ps 3ms	pn	pn
לְיָקְמְעָם	13.	בֶּן־גֶּבֶר	בְּרָמֹת	גִּלְעָד	לוֹ	חַוֹּת	יָאִיר
leyāqŏm‘ām		ben-gever	berāmōth	gil‘ādh	lô	chawwōth	yā’îr
of Jokmeam		the son of Geber	in Ramoth	Gilead	to him	Havvoth	Jair

1158, 4667	866	904, 1609	3937	2346	732	866	904, 1347
n ms, pn	rel part	prep, pn	prep, ps 3ms	*n ms*	pn	rel part	prep, art, pn
בֶּן־מְנַשֶּׁה	אֲשֶׁר	בַּגִּלְעָד	לוֹ	חֶבֶל	אַרְגֹּב	אֲשֶׁר	בַּבָּשָׁן
ben-m^{e}nashsheh	'ăsher	baggil'ādh	lô	chevel	'argōv	'ăsher	babbāshān
the son of Manasseh	which	in the Gilead	to him	the region of	Argob	which	in the Bashan

8666	6111	1448	2440	1308	5361		293	1158, 5916
num	n fp	adj	n fs	cj, *n ms*	n ms	**14.**	pn	*n ms*, pn
שִׁשִּׁים	עָרִים	גְּדֹלוֹת	חוֹמָה	וּבְרִיחַ	נְחֹשֶׁת		אֲחִינָדָב	בֶּן־עִדֹּא
shishshîm	'ārîm	g^{e}dhōlôth	chômāh	ûv^{e}rîach	n^{e}chōsheth		'ăchînādhāv	ben-'iddō'
sixty	cities	great	walls	and bars of	bronze		Ahinadab	the son of Iddo

NEB ... in charge of conscript labor, *Berkeley*.

7. And Solomon had twelve officers over all Israel, which provided victuals for the king and his household: ... overseers ... who supplied food, *Berkeley* ... administrators ... who saw to the provisioning, *JB* ... governors over the districts of Israel, who gathered food from their districts, *NCV* ... regional governers, *NEB* ... commissaries, *NAB*.

each man his month in a year made provision: ... supplying food for one month in the year, *Berkeley* ... provide for one month in the year, *JB* ... Each governor was responsible, *NCV*.

8. And these are their names: The son of Hur, in mount Ephraim;

9. The son of Dekar, in Makaz, and in Shaalbim, and Beth-shemesh, and Elon-bethhanan;

10. The son of Hesed, in Aruboth; to him pertained Sochoh, and all the land of Hepher: ... to him belonged Sochoh, *NKJV* ... land of Hepher were under his control, *BB* ... his district was Socoh and the whole territory of Hepher, *JB*.

11. The son of Abinadab, in all the region of Dor; which had Taphath the daughter of Solomon to wife: ... Taphath, Solomon's daughter was his wife, *Berkeley* ... all the uplands, *Moffatt* ... all the height, *NASB* ... Ben-Abinadab was governer of Naphoth Dor. He was married to Taphath, Solomon's daughter, *NCV*.

12. Baana the son of Ahilud; to him pertained Taanach and Megiddo, and all Bethshean, which is by Zartanah beneath Jezreel, from Beth-shean to Abel-meholah, even unto the place that is beyond Jokneam: ... Baana son of Ahilud was governor of Tanach, Megiddo, and all, *NCV*.

13. The son of Geber, in Ramoth-gilead; to him pertained the towns of Jair the son of Manasseh, which are in Gilead; to him also pertained the region of Argob, which is in Bashan, threescore great cities with walls and brasen bars: ... Ben-Geber was governor of Ramoth in Gilead, *NCV* ... sixty great towns with walls and locks of brass, *BB* ... 60 large cities with walls and copper gate bars, *Beck* ... he had the tent villages, *Berkeley* ... sixty large towns walled and bolted with bronze, *Moffatt* ... having charge of the villages of Jair, son of Manasseh, in Gilead; and of the district of Argob, *NAB*.

We hear nothing more of him, but the subsequent history shows that when David gathered around him this half-alien and wholly mercenary force in a country which had no standing army, he turned the sovereignty into what the Greeks would have called a tyranny. As the only armed force in the kingdom, the bodyguard overawed opposition and was wholly at the disposal of the king. These troops were to Solomon at Jerusalem what the Praetorians were to Tiberius at Rome.

The mas̱ (HED #4671) means the "levy," "corvee," or "forced labor." In other words, Adoram was overseer of the foremen.

4:7–19. Solomon was an expensive king, and the Jewish kings had no private revenue from which the necessary resources could be supplied. In order to secure contributions for the maintenance of the royal establishment, Solomon appointed twelve governors. The districts entirely and designedly ignored the old tribal limits, which Solomon may have wished to obliterate. Ben-Hur administered the hill country of Ephraim; Ben-Dekar had his headquarters in Dan; Ben-Hesed had the maritime plain; Ben-Abinadab the fertile region of Carmel, and he was wedded to Solomon's daughter Taphath; Baana, son of Ahilud, managed the plain of Esdraelon; Ben-Geber the mountainous country east of Jordan, including Gilead and Argob with its basaltic towns; Ahinadab, son of Iddo, was officer in Mahanaim; Ahimaaz in Naphtali (he was married to Solomon's daughter Basmath and was perhaps the son of Zadok); Baanah, son of David's faithful Hushai, was in Asher; Shimei, son of Elah, in Benjamin; Jehoshaphat in Issachar. Geber adminis-

4404		291	904, 5503	1612, 2000	4089.111	881, 1338
pn	**15.**	pn	prep, pn	cj, pers pron	v Qal pf 3ms	do, pn
מַחֲנָיְמָה		אֲחִימַעַץ	בְּנַפְתָּלִי	גַּם־הוּא	לָקַח	אֶת־בָּשְׂמַת
machnāyᵉmāh		'ăchîma'ats	bᵉnaphtālî	gam-hû'	lāqach	'eth-bāsᵉmath
Mahanaim		Ahimaaz	in Naphtali	also he	he took	Basemath

1351, 8406	3937, 828		1219	1158, 2458	904, 862	1203
n fs, pn	prep, n fs	**16.**	pn	*n ms*, pn	prep, pn	cj, pn
בַּת־שְׁלֹמֹה	לְאִשָּׁה		בַּעֲנָא	בֶּן־חוּשָׁי	בְּאָשֵׁר	וּבְעָלוֹת
bath-shᵉlōmōh	lᵉ'ishshāh		ba'ănā'	ben-chûshāy	bᵉ'āshēr	ûvᵉ'ālôth
the daughter of Solomon	for a wife		Baanah	the son of Hushai	in Asher	and Bealoth

	3194	1158, 6765	904, 3551		8483	1158, 421	904, 1175
17.	pn	*n ms*, pn	prep, pn	**18.**	pn	*n ms*, pn	prep, pn
	יְהוֹשָׁפָט	בֶּן־פָּרוּחַ	בְּיִשָּׂכָר		שִׁמְעִי	בֶן־אֵלָא	בְּבִנְיָמִן
	yᵉhôshāphāṯ	ben-pārûach	bᵉyisākhār		shim'î	ven-'ēlā'	bᵉvinyāmin
	Jehoshaphat	the son of Paruah	in Issachar		Shimei	the son of Elah	in Benjamin

	1430	1158, 220	904, 800	1609	800	5700	4567	578
19.	pn	*n ms*, pn	prep, *n fs*	pn	*n fs*	pn	*n ms*	art, pn
	גֶּבֶר	בֶּן־אֻרִי	בְּאֶרֶץ	גִּלְעָד	אֶרֶץ	סִיחוֹן	מֶלֶךְ	הָאֱמֹרִי
	gever	ben-'urî	bᵉ'erets	gil'ādh	'erets	s̱îchôn	melekh	hā'ĕmōrî
	Geber	the son of Uri	in the land of	Gilead	the land of	Sihon	the king of	the Amorites

5965	4567	1347	5518	259	866	904, 800		3171
cj, pn	*n ms*	art, pn	cj, n ms	num	rel pron	prep, art, n fs	**20.**	pn
וְעֹג	מֶלֶךְ	הַבָּשָׁן	וּנְצִיב	אֶחָד	אֲשֶׁר	בָּאָרֶץ		יְהוּדָה
wᵉ'ōgh	melekh	habbāshān	ûnᵉtsîv	'echādh	'ăsher	bā'ārets		yᵉhûdhāh
and Og	the king of	the Bashan	and a governor	one	who	in the land		Judah

3547	7521	3626, 2437	866, 6142, 3328	3937, 7524	404.152
cj, pn	adj	prep, art, n ms	rel part, prep, art, n ms	prep, art, n ms	v Qal act ptc mp
וְיִשְׂרָאֵל	רַבִּים	כַּחוֹל	אֲשֶׁר־עַל־הַיָּם	לָרֹב	אֹכְלִים
wᵉyisrā'ēl	rabbîm	kachôl	'ăsher-'al-hayyām	lārōv	'ōkhᵉlîm
and Israel	many	like the sand	which beside the sea	for a multitude	eating

8685.152	7976		8406	2030.111	5090.151	904, 3725, 4608
cj, v Qal act ptc mp	cj, adj	**21.**	cj, pn	v Qal pf 3ms	v Qal act ptc ms	prep, *adj*, art, n fp
וְשֹׁתִים	וּשְׂמֵחִים		וּשְׁלֹמֹה	הָיָה	מוֹשֵׁל	בְּכָל־הַמַּמְלָכוֹת
wᵉshōthîm	ûsᵉmēchîm		ûshᵉlōmōh	hāyāh	môshēl	bᵉkhol-hammamᵉlākhôth
and drinking	and joyful		and Solomon	he was	a ruler	over all the kingdoms

4623, 5282	800	6674	5912	1397	4875	5242.552
prep, art, pn	*n fs*	pn	cj, prep	*n ms*	pn	v Hiphil ptc mp
מִן־הַנָּהָר	אֶרֶץ	פְּלִשְׁתִּים	וְעַד	גְּבוּל	מִצְרָיִם	מַגִּשִׁים
min-hannāhār	'erets	pᵉlishtîm	wᵉ'adh	gᵉvûl	mitsrāyim	maggishîm
from the Euphrates	the land of	Philistines	even unto	the territory of	Egypt	offering

4647	5856.152	881, 8406	3725, 3219	2522		2030.121
n fs	cj, v Qal act ptc mp	do, pn	*adj, n mp*	n mp, ps 3ms	**22.**	cj, v Qal impf 3ms
מִנְחָה	וְעֹבְדִים	אֶת־שְׁלֹמֹה	כָּל־יְמֵי	חַיָּיו		וַיְהִי
minchāh	wᵉ'ōvᵉdhîm	'eth-shᵉlōmōh	kol-yᵉmê	chayyâv		wayhî
a tribute	and serving	Solomon	all the days of	his life		and it was

4035, 8406	3937, 3219	259	8421	3864	5755	8666	3864
n ms, pn	prep, n ms	num	num	*n ms*	n fs	cj, num	*n ms*
לֶחֶם־שְׁלֹמֹה	לְיוֹם	אֶחָד	שְׁלֹשִׁים	כֹּר	סֹלֶת	וְשִׁשִּׁים	כֹּר
lechem-shᵉlōmōh	lᵉyôm	'echādh	shᵉlōshîm	kōr	s̱ōleth	wᵉshishshîm	kōr
the food of Solomon	for a day	one	thirty	measures of	fine flour	and sixty	measures of

14. Ahinadab the son of Iddo had Mahanaim;

15. Ahimaaz was in Naphtali; he also took Basmath the daughter of Solomon to wife: ... governor of Naphtali. (He was married to Basemath, Solomon's daughter), *NCV* ... Solomon's daughter, as his wife, *NRSV* ... Ahimaaz, who was married to Basemath, *NAB*.

16. Baanah the son of Hushai was in Asher and in Aloth;

17. Jehoshaphat the son of Paruah, in Issachar;

18. Shimei the son of Elah, in Benjamin;

19. Geber the son of Uri was in the country of Gilead, in the country of Sihon king of the Amorites, and of Og king of Bashan; and he was the only officer which was in the land: ... In addition, one governor over all the governors in the land, *REB* ... one overseer had authority over all the overseers who were in the land, *BB* ... which district was a single government, *Fenton* ... one officer was over all the officials, *Goodspeed* ... All these prefects were under a single chief, *Moffatt*.

20. Judah and Israel were many, as the sand which is by the sea in multitude, eating and drinking, and making merry: ... were as numerous as the sand that is on the seashore in abundance, *NASB* ... as grains of sand on the seashore. The people ate, drank, and were happy, *NCV* ... countless as the sands of the sea; they ... enjoyed life, *NEB* ... they took their food and drink with joy in their hearts, *BB* ... increased like the sand which is by the sea, *Fenton*.

21. And Solomon reigned over all kingdoms from the river unto the land of the Philistines, and unto the border of Egypt: they brought presents, and served Solomon all the days of his life: ... brought tribute and continued to serve, *Goodspeed* ... countries brought Solomon the payments he demanded, and they were under his control, *NCV* ... and were subject to him, *NEB* ... men gave him offerings and were his servants, *BB* ... They paid him taxes, *Good News*.

22. And Solomon's provision for one day was thirty measures of fine flour, and threescore measures of meal: ... Solomon needed much food each day to feed himself and all the people who ate at his table, *NCV* ... thirty cors of choice flour, and sixty cors of meal, *NRSV* ... the amount of Solomon's food, *BB* ... Solomon's food supply, *Berkeley* ... The daily food requirements for Solomon's palace, *NLT*.

23. Ten fat oxen, and twenty oxen out of the pastures, and an hundred sheep, beside harts, and roebucks,

---

tered alone the ancient dominions of Sihon and Og. We see with surprise that Judah seems to have been exempted from the burdens imposed on the other districts, and if so, the impolitic exemption was a main cause of the subsequent jealousies.

The chief function of these officers was to furnish provisions for the immense numbers who were connected with the court. The curious list is given of the provision required for one day: thirty measures of fine flour, sixty of bread, ten fat oxen, twenty pasture oxen and one hundred sheep, besides the delicacies of harts, gazelles, fallow-deer and fatted birds; perhaps capons or geese, but the exact type of bird cannot be determined (1 Ki. 4:23). Some speculate that this would provide for about 15,000 persons. In this there is nothing extraordinary, though the number is disproportionate by our standards, to the smallness of the kingdom. About the same number were daily supported by the kings of the great empire of Persia. We see how rapidly the state of royalty had developed when we compare Solomon's superb surroundings with the humble palace of Ishbosheth less than fifty years earlier—a palace of which the only guard was one sleepy woman who had been sifting wheat in the noontide and had fallen asleep over her task in the porch.

4:20–28. Yet in the earlier years of the reign, while the people, dazzled by the novel sense of national importance, felt the stimulus given to trade and industry, the burden was not painfully felt. They multiplied in numbers and lived under their vines and fig trees in peace and festivity. But much of their prosperity was hollow and short-lived. Wealth led to vice and corruption, and in place of the old mountain breezes of freedom which purified the air, the nation, like Issachar, became like a donkey crouching between two burdens and bowing its shoulders to the yoke in the hot valley.

It is impossible to overlook the general drift of Jewish royalty toward pure materialism in the days of Solomon. We search in vain for the lofty spirituality which survived even in the rough epoch of the Judges and the rude simplicity of David's earlier reign. The noble aspirations which throb in one Davidic Psalm are worth all the gorgeous formalism of the temple service. Amid the luxuries of plenty and the feasts of wine on the lees there seems to have been an ever-deepening famine of the Word of God.

There was one innovation, which struck the imagination of Solomon's contemporaries, but was looked on with entire disfavor by those who had been trained in the old pious ways. Solomon had

6887	4109	7759	1267	6465	1304	1267	6463	23.	7343
n fs	cj, num	n ms	*n ms*	cj, num	adj	n ms	num		n ms
צֹאן	וּמֵאָה	רְעִי	בָּקָר	וְעֶשְׂרִים	בְּרִאִים	בָקָר	עֲשָׂרָה		קָמַח
tsō'n	ûmē'āh	re'î	bāqār	we'esrîm	berî'îm	vāqār	'ăsārāh		qāmach
sheep	and one hundred	the pasture	oxen of	and twenty	fattened	oxen	ten		flour

70.156	1285	3286	6906	4623, 358	3937, 940
v Qal pass ptc mp	cj, n mp	cj, n ms	cj, n ms	prep, n ms	prep, n ms
אֲבוּסִים	וּבַרְבֻּרִים	וְיַחְמוּר	וּצְבִי	מֵאַיָּל	לְבַד
'ăvûsîm	ûvarburîm	weyachmûr	ûtsevî	mē'ayyāl	levadh
fattened	and fowl	and roebuck	and gazelle	from the male deer	besides

4623, 8942	5282	904, 3725, 5885	7575.151	3706, 2000	24.
prep, pn	art, pn	prep, *adj, n ms*	v Qal act ptc ms	cj, pers pron	
מִתִּפְסַח	הַנָּהָר	בְּכָל־עֵבֶר	רֹדֶה	כִּי־הוּא	
mittiphsach	hannāhār	bekhol-'ēver	rōdheh	kî-hû'	
from Tiphsah	the Euphrates	over all the opposite side of	dominating	because He	

2030.111	8361	5282	5885	904, 3725, 4567	5912, 6017
v Qal pf 3ms	cj, n ms	art, pn	*n ms*	prep, *adj, n mp*	cj, prep, pn
הָיָה	וְשָׁלוֹם	הַנָּהָר	עֵבֶר	בְּכָל־מַלְכֵי	וְעַד־עַזָּה
hāyāh	weshālôm	hannāhār	'ēver	bekhol-malkhê	we'adh-'azzāh
it was	and peace	the Euphrates	the opposite side of	over all the kings of	even unto Gaza

3937, 1020	3547	3171	3553.121	25.	4623, 5623	4623, 3725, 5885	3937
prep, n ms	cj, pn	pn	cj, v Qal impf 3ms		prep, adv	prep, *adj*, n mp, ps 3ms	prep, ps 3ms
לָבֶטַח	וְיִשְׂרָאֵל	יְהוּדָה	וַיֵּשֶׁב		מִסָּבִיב	מִכָּל־עֲבָרָיו	לוֹ
lāvetach	weyisrā'ēl	yehûdhāh	wayyēshev		missāvîv	mikkol-'ăvārâv	lô
with safety	and Israel	Judah	and they dwelled		all around	from all his sides	to him

3725	916	5912, 916	4623, 1896	8711	8809	1655	8809	382
adj	pn	cj, prep, pn	prep, pn	n fs, ps 3ms	cj, prep	n fs, ps 3ms	prep	n ms
כֹּל	שָׁבַע	וְעַד־בְּאֵר	מִדָּן	תְּאֵנָתוֹ	וְתַחַת	גַּפְנוֹ	תַּחַת	אִישׁ
kōl	shāva'	we'adh-be'ēr	middān	te'ēnāthô	wethachath	gaphnô	tachath	'îsh
all	Sheba	even unto Beer	from Dan	his fig tree	and beneath	his vine	beneath	a man

5670	747	512	727	3937, 8406	2030.121	26.	8406	3219
n mp	*n fp*	num	num	prep, pn	cj, v Qal impf 3ms		pn	*n mp*
סוּסִים	אֻרְוֹת	אֶלֶף	אַרְבָּעִים	לִשְׁלֹמֹה	וַיְהִי		שְׁלֹמֹה	יְמֵי
sûsîm	'urwōth	'eleph	'arbā'îm	lishlōmōh	wayhî		shelōmōh	yemê
horses	stalls for	thousands	forty	to Solomon	and they were		Solomon	the days of

5507.256	3677.316	27.	6821	512	8530, 6461	3937, 4980
art, v Niphal ptc mp	cj, v Pilpel pf 3cp		n mp	num	cj, num, num	prep, n ms, ps 3ms
הַנִּצָּבִים	וְכִלְכְּלוּ		פָּרָשִׁים	אֶלֶף	וּשְׁנֵים־עָשָׂר	לְמֶרְכָּבוֹ
hanitstsāvîm	wekhilkelû		pārāshîm	'eleph	ûshenêm-'āsār	lemerkāvô
the governors	and they provided for		horsemen	thousands	and twelve	for his chariots

4567, 8406	420, 8374	3725, 7416	881	8406	881, 4567	431
art, n ms, pn	prep, *n ms*	*adj*, art, adj	cj, do	pn	do, art, n ms	art, dem pron
הַמֶּלֶךְ־שְׁלֹמֹה	אֶל־שֻׁלְחַן	כָּל־הַקָּרֵב	וְאֵת	שְׁלֹמֹה	אֶת־הַמֶּלֶךְ	הָאֵלֶּה
hammelekh-shelōmōh	'el-shulchan	kol-haqqārēv	we'ēth	shelōmōh	'eth-hammelekh	hā'ēlleh
King Solomon	to the table of	all those approaching	and	Solomon	the king	the these

8730	8002	28.	1745	5952.326	3940	2414	382
cj, art, n ms	cj, art, n fp		n ms	v Piel impf 3mp	neg part	n ms, ps 3ms	n ms
וְהַתֶּבֶן	וְהַשְּׂעֹרִים		דָּבָר	יְעַדְּרוּ	לֹא	חָדְשׁוֹ	אִישׁ
wehatteven	wehasse'ōrîm		dāvār	ye'adderû	lō'	chādheshô	'îsh
and the straw	and the barley		a thing	they allowed to be missing	not	his month	a man

3937, 5670	3937, 7698	971.526	420, 4887	866	2030.121, 8427
prep, art, n mp	cj, prep, art, n ms	v Hiphil impf 3mp	prep, art, n ms	rel part	v Qal impf 3ms, adv
לַסּוּסִים	וְלָרֶכֶשׁ	יָבִאוּ	אֶל־הַמָּקוֹם	אֲשֶׁר	יִהְיֶה־שָּׁם
lassûsîm	w^{e}lārākhesh	yāvi'û	'el-hammāqôm	'ăsher	yihyeh-shām
for the horses	and for the workhorses	they brought	to the place	where	he was there

382	3626, 5122		5598.121	435	2551	3937, 8406	8722
n ms	prep, n ms, ps 3ms	29.	cj, v Qal impf 3ms	n mp	n fs	prep, pn	cj, n fs
אִישׁ	כְּמִשְׁפָּטוֹ		וַיִּתֵּן	אֱלֹהִים	חָכְמָה	לִשְׁלֹמֹה	וּתְבוּנָה
'îsh	k^{e}mishpāṯô		wayyittēn	'ĕlōhîm	chokhmāh	lishlōmōh	ûth^{e}vûnāh
a man	according to his duty		and He gave	God	wisdom	to Solomon	and insight

and fallowdeer, and fatted fowl: ... twenty pasture-fed cattle, one hundred sheep, besides deer, gazelles, roebucks, *NRSV* ... oxen from the fields, *BB* ... twenty meadow-fed oxen ... and guinea-fowl, *Moffatt* ... a hundred rams, besides ... roes, and buffles, *Douay* ... ten cows that were fed on good grain, twenty cows that were raised in the fields, *NCV* ... 10 stall-fed cattle, 20 pasture-fed cattle, *Good News*.

24. For he had dominion over all the region on this side the river, from Tiphsah even to Azzah, over all the kings on this side the river: ... Solomon controlled all the countries west of the Euphrates River, the land from Tiphsah to Gaza, *NCV* ... he was paramount over all the land west of the Euphrates from Tiphsah to Gaza, ruling all the kings west of the river, *REB* ... he had the rule over all, *KJVII* ... he had authority over all the country, *BB* ... he had dominion over everything, *Berkeley*.

and he had peace on all sides round about him: ... on all sides of his kingdom, *NCV* ... he enjoyed peace, *REB* ... he was at peace with all the neighboring countries, *Good News*.

25. And Judah and Israel dwelt safely, every man under his vine and under his fig tree, from Dan even to Beer-sheba, all the days of Solomon: ... lived in safety, *NASB* ... without any fear, *Douay* ... lived in peace; all of his people were able to sit, *NCV* ... securely, *Beck* ... All through his reign, *REB*.

26. And Solomon had forty thousand stalls of horses for his chariots, and twelve thousand horsemen: ... boxed-off spaces for horses for his carriages, *BB* ... twelve thousand for the saddle, *Douay* ... cavalry horses, *NEB*.

27. And those officers provided victual for king Solomon, and for all that came unto king Solomon's table, every man in his month: ... supplied provisions, *Goodspeed* ... deputies, *NASB* ... the foresaid governors of the king fed them; and they furnished the necessaries also ... with great care in their time, *Douay* ... those overseers, ... food was produced for Solomon and all his guests, *BB* ... Each month one of the district governors gave, *NCV*.

they lacked nothing: ... fell short in nothing, *Goodspeed* ... nothing was overlooked, *BB* ... never fell short in their deliveries, *NEB* ... he had everything he needed, *NCV*.

28. Barley also and straw for the horses and dromedaries brought they unto the place where the officers were, every man according to his charge: ... grain and dry grass for the horses and the carriage-horses, to the right place, every man as he was ordered, *BB* ... As they were assigned, *Beck* ... and the camels, each according to his allot-

immense stables for his chariot horses and the swift riding horses of his couriers. It seems to have been Solomon's ambition to equal or outshine "the chariots of Pharaoh," with which his Egyptian queen had been familiar at Tanis. This feature of his reign is dwelt upon in the Arabian legends, as well as in all the historical records of his greatness (1 Ki. 5:6; 9:19; 10:26, 28). But the maintenance of a cavalry force had always been discouraged by the religious teachers of Israel. The use of horses in war is forbidden in Deuteronomy (Deut. 17:16). Joshua had hamstrung the horses of the Canaanites and burned their chariots at Misrephoth-Maim. David had followed his example. Barak had defeated the iron chariots of Sisera, and David the splendid cavalry of Hadadezer with the simple infantry of Israel (16:9; 1 Sam. 8:11f; 2 Sam. 8:4). The spirit of faithfulness spoke in such words as, "Some trust in chariots, and some in horses: but we will remember the name of the LORD our God" (Ps. 20:7). Solomon's successors discovered that they had not gained in strength by adopting this branch of military service in their hilly and rocky land. They found that "an horse is a vain thing for safety: neither shall he deliver any by his great strength" (Pss. 33:17; 76:6; 147:10). Those entrusted to provide the needs of the kingdom did not fail to do so. Neither did God fail to provide what He had promised.

4:29–34. According to God's word in the dream, given to Solomon (3:3–14), Yahweh granted Solomon

7528.542	4108	7621	3949	3626, 2437	866	6142, 8004	3328
v Hiphil inf abs	adv	cj, *n ms*	n ms	prep, art, n ms	rel part	prep, *n fs*	art, n ms
הַרְבֵּה	מְאֹד	וְרֹחַב	לֵב	כַּחוֹל	אֲשֶׁר	עַל־שְׂפַת	הַיָּם
harbēh	m^{e}'ōdh	w^{e}rōchav	lēv	kachôl	'ăsher	'al-s^{e}phath	hayyām
making great	very	and breadth of	heart	like the sand	which	on the shore of	the sea

30.	7528.122	2551	8406	4623, 2551	3725, 1158, 7208
	cj, v Qal impf 3fs	*n fs*	pn	prep, *n fs*	*adj, n mp*, n ms
	וַתֵּרֶב	חָכְמַת	שְׁלֹמֹה	מֵחָכְמַת	כָּל־בְּנֵי־קֶדֶם
	watterev	chokhmath	sh^{e}lōmōh	mēchokhmath	kol-b^{e}nê-qedhem
	and it became greater	the wisdom of	Solomon	than the wisdom of	all the sons of the east

4623, 3725	2551	4875	31.	2549.121	4623, 3725, 119
cj, prep, *n ms*	*n fs*	pn		cj, v Qal impf 3ms	prep, *adj*, art, n ms
וּמִכֹּל	חָכְמַת	מִצְרָיִם		וַיֶּחְכַּם	מִכָּל־הָאָדָם
ûmikkōl	chokhmath	mitsrāyim		wayyechăkkam	mikkol-hā'ādhām
and than the entirety of	the wisdom of	Egypt		and he was wiser	than all humankind

4623, 394	249	2037	3753	1922	1158	4370
prep, pn	art, pn	cj, pn	cj, pn	cj, pn	*n mp*	pn
מֵאֵיתָן	הָאֶזְרָחִי	וְהֵימָן	וְכַלְכֹּל	וְדַרְדַּע	בְּנֵי	מָחוֹל
mē'êthān	hā'ezrāchî	w^{e}hêmān	w^{e}khalkōl	w^{e}dharda'	b^{e}nê	māchôl
than Ethan	the Ezrahite	and Heman	and Calcol	and Darda	the sons of	Mahol

2030.121, 8428	904, 3725, 1504	5623	32.	1744.321	8421
cj, v Qal impf 3ms, n ms, ps 3ms	prep, *adj*, art, n mp	adv		cj, v Piel impf 3ms	num
וַיְהִי־שְׁמוֹ	בְכָל־הַגּוֹיִם	סָבִיב		וַיְדַבֵּר	שְׁלֹשֶׁת
wayhî-sh^{e}mô	v^{e}khol-haggôyim	sāvîv		waydhabbēr	sh^{e}lōsheth
and his name was	among all the nations	all around		and he spoke	thirty

512	5091	2030.121	8302	2675	512
num	n ms	cj, v Qal impf 3ms	n ms, ps 3ms	num	cj, num
אֲלָפִים	מָשָׁל	וַיְהִי	שִׁירוֹ	חֲמִשָּׁה	וָאָלֶף
'ălāphîm	māshāl	wayhî	shîrô	chămishshāh	wā'āleph
thousands	proverbs	and they were	his songs	five	and one thousand

33.	1744.321	6142, 6320	4623, 753	866	904, 3976	5912
	cj, v Piel impf 3ms	prep, art, n mp	prep, art, n ms	rel part	prep, art, pn	cj, prep
	וַיְדַבֵּר	עַל־הָעֵצִים	מִן־הָאֶרֶז	אֲשֶׁר	בַּלְּבָנוֹן	וְעַד
	waydhabbēr	'al-hā'ētsîm	min-hā'erez	'ăsher	ball^{e}vānôn	w^{e}'adh
	and he spoke	concerning the trees	from the cedars	which	in the Lebanon	even unto

230	866	3428.151	904, 7306	1744.321	6142, 966
art, n ms	rel part	v Qal act ptc ms	prep, art, n ms	cj, v Piel impf 3ms	prep, art, n fs
הָאֵזוֹב	אֲשֶׁר	יֹצֵא	בַּקִּיר	וַיְדַבֵּר	עַל־הַבְּהֵמָה
hā'ēzôv	'ăsher	yōtsē'	baqqîr	waydhabbēr	'al-habb^{e}hēmāh
the hyssop	which	sprouting	on the wall	then he spoke	concerning the animals

6142, 5991	6142, 7719	6142, 1759
cj, prep, art, n ms	cj, prep, art, n ms	cj, prep, art, n mp
וְעַל־הָעוֹף	וְעַל־הָרֶמֶשׂ	וְעַל־הַדָּגִים
w^{e}'al-hā'ôph	w^{e}'al-hāremes	w^{e}'al-haddāghîm
and concerning the birds	and concerning the creeping things	and concerning the fish

34.	971.126	4623, 3725, 6194	3937, 8471.141	881	2551	8406	4623, 881
	cj, v Qal impf 3mp	prep, *adj*, art, n mp	prep, v Qal inf con	do	*n fs*	pn	prep, do
	וַיָּבֹאוּ	מִכָּל־הָעַמִּים	לִשְׁמֹעַ	אֵת	חָכְמַת	שְׁלֹמֹה	מֵאֵת
	wayyāvō'û	mikkol-hā'ammîm	lishmōa'	'ēth	chokhmath	sh^{e}lōmōh	mē'ēth
	and they came	from all the peoples	to hear		the wisdom of	Solomon	from

3725, 4567	800	866	8471.116	881, 2551		8365.121	2538
adj, n mp	art, n fs	rel pron	v Qal pf 3cp	do, n fs, ps 3ms		cj, v Qal impf 3ms	pn
כָּל־מַלְכֵי	הָאָרֶץ	אֲשֶׁר	שָׁמְעוּ	אֶת־חָכְמָתוֹ	5:1	וַיִּשְׁלַח	חִירָם
kol-malkhê	hā'ārets	'ăsher	shāmeʻû	'eth-chokhmāthô		wayyishlach	chîrām
all the kings of	the earth	who	they had heard	his wisdom		and he sent	Hiram

4567, 7145	881, 5860	420, 8406	3706	8471.111	3706	881
n ms, pn	do, n mp, ps 3ms	prep, pn	cj	v Qal pf 3ms	cj	do, ps 3ms
מֶלֶךְ־צוֹר	אֶת־עֲבָדָיו	אֶל־שְׁלֹמֹה	כִּי	שָׁמַע	כִּי	אֹתוֹ
melekh-tsôr	'eth-'ăvādhâv	'el-shelōmōh	kî	shāma'	kî	'ōthô
the king of Tyre	his slaves	unto Solomon	because	he had heard	that	him

ment, *Berkeley* ... and swift steeds to the place where it should be, *NASB* ... each person brought this grain to the right place, *NCV* ... brought to the proper place their quotas, *NIV*.

29. And God gave Solomon wisdom and understanding exceeding much, and largeness of heart, even as the sand that is on the sea shore: ... a great store of wisdom and good sense, and a mind of wide range, as wide as the sand by the seaside, *BB* ... a wide range of knowledge, *Beck* ... in very exceptional measure, and breadth of mind, *Goodspeed* ... very great discernment, *NASB* ... unusual wisdom and insight, and knowledge too great to be measured, *Good News*.

30. And Solomon's wisdom excelled the wisdom of all the children of the east country, and all the wisdom of Egypt: ... surpassed the wisdom of all the Orientals, and of the Egyptians, *Douay* ... greater than the wisdom of all the men of the East, *NIV* ... superior to the wisdom of the Easterners, *Berkeley* ... was wiser than, *Good News* ... exceeded that of all, *NLT*.

31. For he was wiser than all men; than Ethan the Ezrahite, and Heman, and Chalcol, and Darda, the sons of Mahol: and his fame was in all nations round about: ... became famous in all the surrounding countries, *NCV* ... in all neighboring nations, *Goodspeed* ... known in all the surrounding nations, *NASB* ... renowned, *Douay* ... wiser than anyone on earth ... he had a great name among all, *BB*.

32. And he spake three thousand proverbs: ... was the originator of 3,000 proverbs, *Berkeley* ... maker of three thousand wise sayings, *BB* ... He composed three thousand aphorisms, *Moffatt* ... parables, *Douay* ... wise sayings, *NCV*.

and his songs were a thousand and five: ... author of 1,005 songs, *Berkeley* ... songs numbered, *Moffatt* ... poems, *Douay* ... wrote, *NCV*.

33. And he spake of trees, from the cedar tree that is in Lebanon even unto the hyssop that springeth out of the wall: ... down to the marjoram that grows out of the wall, *NEB* ... many kinds of plants—everything from the great cedar trees of Lebanon to the weeds, *NCV*.

he spake also of beasts, and of fowl, and of creeping things, and of fishes: ... reptiles, *NEB* ... animals, birds, crawling things, *NCV* ... the small things of the earth, *BB*.

34. And there came of all people to hear the wisdom of Solomon, from all kings of the earth, which had heard of his wisdom: ... People came from every nation, deputed by all the kings in the world, *Moffatt* ... The kings of all nations sent them to him, because they had heard of, *NCV* ... Men of all races came to listen, *NEB* ... sent by, *NIV* ... to give ear to, *BB* ... Kings all over the world heard, *Good News*.

great wisdom (chokhmāh, HED #2551). Due to Solomon's steadfast obedience to Yahweh's statutes, as David had instructed Solomon to do, the LORD granted him a request. Because the LORD was pleased with the request for wisdom, He granted Solomon riches and a long life as well. The new king was a good steward of the blessings God bestowed on him.

The wisdom Yahweh granted was characterized by discernment (4:29), as evidenced by the correct decision regarding the two women claiming the same child. Further evidence of the fruition of God's gift to Solomon was exhibited in the writing of proverbs and songs totaling more that 4000; understanding of trees, plants, animals and birds; and his surpassing fame of wise men, both domestic and foreign. Solomon's wisdom became greater than Ethan, the Ezrahite (author of Ps. 89), Henan (author of Ps. 88), and Calcol and Darda (or Dara; cf. 1 Chr. 2:6), of whom no writing of Scripture can be proven.

5:1–6. Into the work of the Temple Solomon threw himself with hearty zeal in the month Zif of the fourth year of his reign, when his kingdom was consolidated (1 Ki. 6:1). It commanded all his sympathies as an artist, a lover of magnificence and a ruler bent on the work of centralization. It was a task to which he was bound by the solemn exhortation of his father, and he felt, doubtless, its political as well as its religious importance. With

5066.116	3937, 4567	8809	1	3706	154.151	2030.111	2538
v Qal pf 3cp	prep, n ms	prep	n ms, ps 3ms	cj	v Qal act ptc ms	v Qal pf 3ms	pn
מָשְׁחוּ	לְמֶלֶךְ	תַּחַת	אָבִיהוּ	כִּי	אֹהֵב	הָיָה	חִירָם
māshechû	lemelekh	tachath	'āvîhû	kî	'ōhēv	hāyāh	chîrām
they had anointed	as king	instead of	his father	because	one who loves	he was	Hiram

3937, 1784	3725, 3219		8365.121	8406	420, 2538	3937, 569.141		887
prep, pn	*adj*, art, n mp	**2.**	cj, v Qal impf 3ms	pn	prep, pn	prep, v Qal inf con	**3.**	pers pron
לְדָוִד	כָּל־הַיָּמִים		וַיִּשְׁלַח	שְׁלֹמֹה	אֶל־חִירָם	לֵאמֹר		אַתָּה
ledhāwidh	kol-hayyāmîm		wayyishlach	shelōmōh	'el-chîrām	lē'mōr		'attāh
David	all the days		and he sent	Solomon	to Hiram	saying		you

3156.113	881, 1784	1	3706	3940	3310.111	3937, 1161.141	1041
v Qal pf 2ms	do, pn	n ms, ps 1cs	cj	neg part	v Qal pf 3ms	prep, v Qal inf con	n ms
יָדַעְתָּ	אֶת־דָּוִד	אָבִי	כִּי	לֹא	יָכֹל	לִבְנוֹת	בַּיִת
yādha'ättā	'eth-dāwidh	'āvî	kî	lō'	yākhōl	livnôth	bayith
you know	David	my father	that	not	he was able	to build	a temple

3937, 8428	3176	435	4623, 6686	4560	866	5621.116	5912
prep, *n ms*	pn	n ms, ps 3 ms	prep, *n mp*	art, n fs	rel part	v Qal pf 3cp, ps 3ms	adv
לְשֵׁם	יְהוָה	אֱלֹהָיו	מִפְּנֵי	הַמִּלְחָמָה	אֲשֶׁר	סְבָבֻהוּ	עַד
leshēm	yehwāh	'ĕlōhâv	mippenê	hammilchāmāh	'ăsher	sevāvuhû	'adh
to the name of	Yahweh	his God	from before	the warfare	which	they surrounded him	until

5598.141, 3176	881	8809	3834	7559		6498	5299.511
v Qal inf con, pn	do, ps 3mp	prep	*n fp*	n fs, ps 3ms	**4.**	cj, adv	v Hiphil pf 3ms
תֵּת־יְהוָה	אֹתָם	תַּחַת	כַּפּוֹת	רַגְלוֹ		וְעַתָּה	הֵנִיחַ
tēth-yehwāh	'ōthām	tachath	kappôth	raghlô		we'attāh	hēnîach
Yahweh putting	them	beneath	the soles of	his feet		and now	He has caused to rest

3176	435	3937	4623, 5623	375	7931	375	6535	7737
pn	pn, ps 1 cs	prep, ps 1cs	prep, adv	*sub*	n ms	cj, *sub*	n ms	adj
יְהוָה	אֱלֹהָי	לִי	מִסָּבִיב	אֵין	שָׂטָן	וְאֵין	פֶּגַע	רָע
yehwāh	'ĕlōhay	lî	missāvîv	'ên	sātān	we'ên	pegha'	rā'
Yahweh	my God	to me	all around	there is not	an adversary	and there is not	incidents	evil

	2079	569.151	3937, 1161.141	1041	3937, 8428	3176	435
5.	cj, intrj, ps 1cs	v Qal act ptc ms	prep, v Qal inf con	n ms	prep, *n ms*	pn	n mp, ps 1cs
	וְהִנְנִי	אֹמֵר	לִבְנוֹת	בַּיִת	לְשֵׁם	יְהוָה	אֱלֹהָי
	wehinenî	'ōmēr	livnôth	bayith	leshēm	yehwāh	'ĕlōhāy
	now behold I	saying	to build	a temple	to the name of	Yahweh	my God

3626, 866	1744.311	3176	420, 1784	1	3937, 569.141	1158	866
prep, rel part	v Piel pf 3ms	pn	prep, pn	n ms, ps 1cs	prep, v Qal inf con	n ms, ps 2ms	rel pron
כַּאֲשֶׁר	דִּבֶּר	יְהוָה	אֶל־דָּוִד	אָבִי	לֵאמֹר	בִּנְךָ	אֲשֶׁר
ka'ăsher	dibber	yehwāh	'el-dāwidh	'āvî	lē'mōr	binkhā	'ăsher
just as	He has spoken	Yahweh	to David	my father	saying	your son	whom

5598.125	8809	6142, 3802	2000, 1161.121	1041	3937, 8428
v Qal impf 1cs	prep, ps 2ms	prep, n ms, ps 2ms	pers pron, v Qal impf 3ms	art, n ms	prep, n ms, ps 1cs
אֶתֵּן	תַּחְתֶּיךָ	עַל־כִּסְאֶךָ	הוּא־יִבְנֶה	הַבַּיִת	לִשְׁמִי
'ettēn	tachtêkhā	'al-kis'ekhā	hû'-yivneh	habbayith	lishmî
I will put	instead of you	on your throne	he he will build	the Temple	to my name

	6498	6943.331	3901.126, 3937	753	4623, 3976	5860
6.	cj, adv	v Piel impv 2ms	cj, v Qal juss 3mp, prep, ps 1cs	n mp	prep, art, pn	cj, n mp, ps 1cs
	וְעַתָּה	צַוֵּה	וְיִכְרְתוּ־לִי	אֲרָזִים	מִן־הַלְּבָנוֹן	וַעֲבָדַי
	we'attāh	tsawwēh	weyikhrethû-lî	'ărāzîm	min-hallevānôn	wa'ăvādhay
	and now	command	that they may cut down for me	cedars	from the Lebanon	and my slaves

2030.126	6196, 5860	7964	5860	5598.125	3937
v Qal impf 3mp	prep, n mp, ps 2ms	cj, *n ms*	n mp, ps 2ms	v Qal impf 1cs	prep, ps 2ms
יִהְיוּ	עִם־עֲבָדֶיךָ	וּשְׂכַר	עֲבָדֶיךָ	אֶתֵּן	לְךָ
yihyû	‘im-‘ǎvādhêkhā	ûsekhar	‘ǎvādhêkhā	’ettēn	lekhā
they will be	with your slaves	and the wage of	your servants	I will pay	to you

3626, 3725	866	569.123	3706	887	3156.113	3706	375	904
prep, adj	rel part	v Qal impf 2ms	cj	pers pron	v Qal pf 2ms	cj	*sub*	prep, ps 1cp
כְּכֹל	אֲשֶׁר	תֹּאמֵר	כִּי	אַתָּה	יָדַעְתָּ	כִּי	אֵין	בָּנוּ
kekhōl	’ǎsher	tō’mēr	kî	’attāh	yādha‘ättā	kî	’ên	bānû
according to all	which	you will say	because	you	you know	that	there is not	among us

382	3156.151	3937, 3901.141, 6320	3626, 6992		2030.121	3626, 8471.141
n ms	v Qal act ptc ms	prep, v Qal inf con, n mp	prep, art, pn		cj, v Qal impf 3ms	prep, v Qal inf con
אִישׁ	יֹדֵעַ	לִכְרָת־עֵצִים	כַּצִּדֹנִים	7.	וַיְהִי	כִּשְׁמֹעַ
’îsh	yōdhēa‘	likhrāth-‘ētsîm	katstsidhōnîm		wayhî	kishmōa‘
a man	knowing	to cut trees	like the Sidonians		and it was	when hearing

5:1. And Hiram king of Tyre sent his servants unto Solomon; for he had heard that they had anointed him king in the room of his father: ... instead of his father, *KJVII* ... had been made king in place of his father, *BB* ... sent an embassy ... having learnt that he had been anointed king in succession to his father, *JB* ... consecrated king ... he sent his officers, *Moffatt* ... sent his envoys, *NIV*.

for Hiram was ever a lover of David: ... had ever been a friend to David, *BB* ... had always been friendly, *Moffatt* ... always been on a friendly terms, *NIV* ... been fond of, *Goodspeed*.

2. And Solomon sent to Hiram, saying: ... answer, *NEB* ... message, *NLT* ... word, *RSV* ... sent men ... to tell him, *Beck*.

3. Thou knowest how that David my father could not build an house unto the name of the LORD his God: ... a temple in honour of the Eternal, *Moffatt* ... a temple for worshiping, *NCV*.

for the wars which were about him on every side: ... had to fight many wars with the countries around him, *NCV* ... because he was surrounded by armed nations, *NEB* ... his enemies surrounded him, *NRSV*.

until the LORD put them under the soles of his feet: ... the Eternal had crushed under him the warlike foes who surrounded him, *Moffatt* ... allowed him to defeat all his enemies, *NCV* ... made them subject to him, *NEB* ... gave him victory over, *NLT*.

4. But now the LORD my God hath given me rest on every side, so that there is neither adversary nor evil occurrent: ... peace on all sides of my country. I have no enemies now, and no danger threatens my people, *NCV* ... evil event, *Darby* ... not one enemy, no calamities, *JB* ... I have neither foe nor misfortune, *Moffatt* ... no one to oppose me, I fear no attack, *NEB* ... disaster, *NIV*.

5. And, behold, I purpose to build an house unto the name of the LORD my God: ... so it is my purpose to make, *BB* ... I'm thinking of building a temple to honor, *Beck* ... I intend, *Berkeley* ... I am planning, *Goodspeed*.

as the LORD spake unto David my father, saying, Thy son, whom I will set upon thy throne in thy room, he shall build an house unto my name: ... in your place, *NIV* ... revealed to David, *Berkeley* ... the temple in my honour, *Moffatt*.

6. Now therefore command thou that they hew me cedar trees out of

---

his sincere desire to build to God's glory was mingled a prophetic conviction that his task would be fraught with immense issues for the future of his people and of all the world. The presence of the Temple left its impress on the very name of Jerusalem. Although it has nothing to do with the Temple or with Solomon, it became known to the heathen world as Hierosolyma, which, as we see from Eupolemos (Eusebius, *Prarp. Evang.*, 9:34), the Gentile world supposed to mean "the temple [hieron] of Solomon."

The materials already provided were of priceless value. David had consecrated to God the spoils which he had won from conquered kings. A king whose court was simple and inexpensive was quite able to amass treasures of gold and silver, brass and iron, precious marbles and onyx stones. Solomon had only to add to these sacred stores (1 Chr. 22:14).

5:7–12. He inherited the friendship which David had enjoyed, with Hiram, King of Tyre, who, according to the strange phrase of the Vatican Septuagint, sent his servants "to anoint" Solomon.

2538	881, 1745	8406	7975.121	4108	569.121	1313.155	3176
pn	do, *n mp*	pn	cj, v Qal impf 3ms	adv	cj, v Qal impf 3ms	v Qal pass ptc ms	pn
חִירָם	אֶת־דִּבְרֵי	שְׁלֹמֹה	וַיִּשְׂמַח	מְאֹד	וַיֹּאמֶר	בָּרוּךְ	יְהוָה
chîrām	'eth-divrê	shᵉlōmōh	wayyismach	mᵉ'ōdh	wayyō'mer	bārûkh	yᵉhwāh
Hiram	his words	Solomon	that he was glad	very	and he said	blessed	Yahweh

3219	866	5598.111	3937, 1784	1158	2550	6142, 6194	7521	2172
art, n ms	rel pron	v Qal pf 3ms	prep, pn	n ms	adj	prep, art, n ms	art, adj	art, dem pron
הַיּוֹם	אֲשֶׁר	נָתַן	לְדָוִד	בֵּן	חָכָם	עַל־הָעָם	הָרָב	הַזֶּה
hayyôm	'ăsher	nāthan	lᵉdhāwidh	bēn	chākhām	'al-hā'ām	hārāv	hazzeh
today	Who	He has given	to David	a son	wise	over the people	the great	the this

	8365.121	2538	420, 8406	3937, 569.141	8471.115	881	866, 8365.113
8.	cj, v Qal impf 3ms	pn	prep, pn	prep, v Qal inf con	v Qal pf 1cs	do	rel part, v Qal pf 2ms
	וַיִּשְׁלַח	חִירָם	אֶל־שְׁלֹמֹה	לֵאמֹר	שָׁמַעְתִּי	אֵת	אֲשֶׁר־שָׁלַחְתָּ
	wayyishlach	chîrām	'el-shᵉlōmōh	lē'mōr	shāma'ttî	'ēth	'ăsher-shālachtā
	and he sent	Hiram	unto Solomon	saying	I have heard		what you sent

420	603	6449.125	881, 3725, 2761	904, 6320	753
prep, ps 1cs	pers pron	v Qal impf 1cs	do, *adj*, n ms, ps 2ms	prep, *n mp*	n mp
אֵלָי	אֲנִי	אֶעֱשֶׂה	אֶת־כָּל־חֶפְצְךָ	בַּעֲצֵי	אֲרָזִים
'ēlāy	'ănî	'e'ĕseh	'eth-kol-chephtsᵉkhā	ba'ătsê	'ărāzîm
to me	I	I will do	all your wishes	with trees of	cedars

904, 6320	1293		5860	3495.526	4623, 3976	3328
cj, prep, art, *n mp*	n mp	**9.**	n mp, ps 1cs	v Hiphil impf 3mp	prep, art, pn	n ms
וּבַעֲצֵי	בְרוֹשִׁים		עֲבָדַי	יֹרִדוּ	מִן־הַלְּבָנוֹן	יָמָּה
ûva'ătsê	vᵉrôshîm		'ăvādhay	yōridhû	min-hallᵉvānôn	yāmmāh
and with trees of	cypresses		my slaves	they will bring down	from the Lebanon	westward

603	7947.125	1752	904, 3328	5912, 4887	866, 8365.123
cj, pers pron	v Qal impf 1cs, ps 3mp	n fp	prep, art, n ms	prep, art, n ms	rel part, v Qal impf 2ms
וַאֲנִי	אֲשִׂימֵם	דֹּבְרוֹת	בַּיָּם	עַד־הַמָּקוֹם	אֲשֶׁר־תִּשְׁלַח
wa'ănî	'ăsîmēm	dōvᵉrôth	bayyām	'adh-hammāqôm	'ăsher-tishlach
and I	I will place them	rafts	by the sea	unto the place	which you sent

420	5492.315	8427	887	5558.123	887	6449.123
prep, ps 1cs	cj, v Piel pf 1cs, ps 3mp	adv	cj, pers pron	v Qal impf 2ms	cj, pers pron	v Qal impf 2ms
אֵלַי	וְנִפַּצְתִּים	שָׁם	וְאַתָּה	תִּשָּׂא	וְאַתָּה	תַּעֲשֶׂה
'ēlay	wᵉnippatstîm	shām	wᵉ'attāh	thissā'	wᵉ'attāh	ta'ăseh
to me	then I will scatter them	there	and you	you will carry	and you	you will do

881, 2761	3937, 5598.141	4035	1041		2030.121	2538
do, n ms, ps 1cs	prep, v Qal inf con	*n ms*	n ms, ps 1cs	**10.**	cj, v Qal impf 3ms	pn
אֶת־חֶפְצִי	לָתֵת	לֶחֶם	בֵּיתִי		וַיְהִי	חִירוֹם
'eth-chephtsî	lāthēth	lechem	bêthî		wayhî	chîrôm
my wishes	to give	the food of	my household		and it was	Hiram

5598.151	3937, 8406	6320	753	6320	1293	3725, 2761
v Qal act ptc ms	prep, pn	*n mp*	n mp	cj, *n mp*	n mp	*adj*, n ms, ps 3ms
נֹתֵן	לִשְׁלֹמֹה	עֲצֵי	אֲרָזִים	וַעֲצֵי	בְרוֹשִׁים	כָּל־חֶפְצוֹ
nōthēn	lishlōmōh	'ătsê	'ărāzîm	wa'ătsê	vᵉrôshîm	kol-chephtsô
giving	to Solomon	trees of	cedars	and trees of	cypresses	all his wishes

	8406	5598.111	3937, 2538	6465	512	3864	2498	4499
11.	cj, pn	v Qal pf 3ms	prep, pn	num	num	*n ms*	n fp	n fs
	וּשְׁלֹמֹה	נָתַן	לְחִירָם	עֶשְׂרִים	אֶלֶף	כֹּר	חִטִּים	מַכֹּלֶת
	ûshᵉlōmōh	nāthan	lᵉchîrām	'esrîm	'eleph	kōr	chittîm	makkōleth
	and Solomon	he gave	to Hiram	twenty	thousands	measures of	wheat	food

Lebanon: ... Give orders, *NAB*... send your men to cut down, *NCV*.

and my servants shall be with thy servants: ... shall accompany, *NAB* ... will work with, *NCV*.

and unto thee will I give hire for thy servants according to all that thou shalt appoint: ... I will pay them whatever wages you decide, *NCV* ... sum you fix, *NEB* ... wages you set, *NRSV* ... will give you payment, *BB*.

for thou knowest that there is not among us any that can skill to hew timber like unto the Sidonians: ... no one is skilled in cutting timber, *NAB* ... We don't have anyone who can cut down trees, *NCV* ... it is common knowledge that we have no such wood-cutters, *BB* ... there is not a single person, *Berkeley*.

7. And it came to pass, when Hiram heard the words of Solomon, that he rejoiced greatly, and said, Blessed be the LORD this day, which hath given unto David a wise son over this great people: ... Khiram heard the demands of Solomon he was greatly pleased, *Fenton* ... received the message ... he was greatly delighted, *Berkeley* ... overjoyed, *Moffatt* ... exceedingly, *Douay* ... Praise the LORD today!, *NCV*.

8. And Hiram sent to Solomon, saying, I have considered the things which thou sentest to me for: ... he sent this reply to Solomon: I have received your message, NEB ... received your communication to me, *Berkeley*.

and I will do all thy desire concerning timber of cedar, and concerning timber of fir: ... all you wish, *NEB* ... all the cedar and pine trees you want, *NCV* ... cedar and cypress logs, *NKJV* ... pine logs, *NIV* ... juniper, *JB* ... I am ready to comply with your request, *Berkeley*.

9. My servants shall bring them down from Lebanon unto the sea: ... My workmen, *Fenton* ... shall bring the timber down, *Moffatt* ... My men, *Good News*.

and I will convey them by sea in floats unto the place that thou shalt appoint me: ... direct in rafts on the sea to whatever place you instruct me, *Fenton* ... conveyed by sea to the place you designate, *Berkeley* ... make the logs into floats to reach any spot you decide upon, *Moffatt* ... tie them together in rafts to float them down the coast, *Good News*.

and will cause them to be discharged there, and thou shalt receive them: ... deliver it there, and you accept it, *Fenton* ... have them taken apart so that you can take them up, *Berkeley* ... broken up for you to take away, *Moffatt* ... take the lumber, *NAB* ... untie them ... will take charge of them, *Good News*.

and thou shalt accomplish my desire, in giving food for my household: ... may pay me by supplying food for my household, *Berkeley* ... by providing the food for my servants, *Moffatt* ... shall furnish the provisions, *NAB* ... for my men, *Good News*.

10. So Hiram gave Solomon cedar trees and fir trees according to all his desire: ... cedar and cypress timber, *NASB* ... as much cedar and pine as he wanted, *NCV* ... all ... he had need of, *BB* ... the cedar wood and juniper he wanted, *JB* ... to his entire satisfaction, *Goodspeed*.

11. And Solomon gave Hiram twenty thousand measures of wheat for food to his household, and twenty measures of pure oil:

The friendliest overtures passed between the two kings in letters, to which Josephus appeals as still extant. A commercial treaty was made by which Solomon engaged to furnish the Tyrian king with annual revenues of wheat, barley and oil (Ezek. 27:17; Acts 12:20), and Hiram put at Solomon's disposal the skilled labor of an army of Sidonian wood-cutters and artisans. The huge trunks of cedar and cypress were sent down the heights of Lebanon and laboriously dragged by road or river to the shore. There they were constructed into immense rafts, which were floated 100 miles along the coast to Joppa, where they were again dragged with enormous toil for 35 miles up the steep and rocky roads to Jerusalem.

For more than twenty years, while Solomon was building the Temple and his various royal constructions, Jerusalem became a hive of ceaseless and varied industry. Its ordinary inhabitants must have been swelled by an army of Canaanite serfs and Phoenician artisans to whom residences were assigned in Ophel. There lived the hewers and bevellers of stone; the cedar cutters of Gebal or Biblos (1 Ki. 5:18); the cunning workmen in gold or brass; the bronze casters who made their molds in the clay ground of the Jordan valley; the carvers and engravers; the dyers who stained wool with the purple of the murex and the scarlet dye of the trumpet fish; the weavers and embroiderers of fine linen. Every class of laborer was put into requisition, from the descendants of the Gibeonite Nethinim (HED #5595), who were rough hewers of wood and drawers of water, to the trained artificers whose beautiful productions were the wonder of the world. The "father," or master-workman, of the whole community was a half caste, who also bore the name of Hiram and was the son of a woman of Naphtali by a Tyrian father (2 Chr. 2:13; 4:16).

3937, 1041	6465	3864	8467	3924	3662, 5598.121	8406	3937, 2538
prep, n ms, ps 3ms	cj, num	*n ms*	n ms	adj	adv, v Qal impf 3ms	pn	prep, pn
לְבֵיתוֹ	וְעֶשְׂרִים	כֹּר	שֶׁמֶן	כָּתִית	כֹּה־יִתֵּן	שְׁלֹמֹה	לְחִירָם
levêthô	we'esrîm	kōr	shemen	kāthîth	kōh-yittēn	shelōmōh	lechîrām
to his household	and twenty	measures of	olive oil	pressed	thus he gave	Solomon	to Hiram

8523	904, 8523		3176	5598.111	2551	3937, 8406	3626, 866
n fs	prep, n fs	**12.**	cj, pn	v Qal pf 3ms	n fs	prep, pn	prep, rel part
שָׁנָה	בְשָׁנָה		וַיהוָה	נָתַן	חָכְמָה	לִשְׁלֹמֹה	כַּאֲשֶׁר
shānāh	veshānāh		wayhwāh	nāthan	chokhmāh	lishlōmōh	ka'ăsher
year	by year		and Yahweh	He gave	wisdom	to Solomon	just as

1744.311, 3937	2030.121	8361	1033	2538	1033	8406
v Piel pf 3ms, prep, ps 3ms	cj, v Qal impf 3ms	n ms	prep	pn	cj, prep	pn
דִּבֶּר־לוֹ	וַיְהִי	שָׁלֹם	בֵּין	חִירָם	וּבֵין	שְׁלֹמֹה
dibber-lô	wayhî	shālōm	bên	chîrām	ûvên	shelōmōh
He had spoken to him	and it was	peace	between	Hiram	and between	Solomon

3901.126	1311	8530		6148.521	4567	8406
cj, v Qal impf 3mp	n fs	num, ps 3mp	**13.**	cj, v Hiphil impf 3ms	art, n ms	pn
וַיִּכְרְתוּ	בְרִית	שְׁנֵיהֶם		וַיַּעַל	הַמֶּלֶךְ	שְׁלֹמֹה
wayyikhrethû	verîth	shenêhem		wayya'al	hammelekh	shelōmōh
and they cut	a covenant	the two of them		and he caused to go up	the king	Solomon

4671	4623, 3725, 3547	2030.121	4671	8421	512	382
n ms	prep, *adj*, pn	cj, v Qal impf 3ms	art, n ms	num	num	n ms
מַס	מִכָּל־יִשְׂרָאֵל	וַיְהִי	הַמַּס	שְׁלֹשִׁים	אֶלֶף	אִישׁ
mas̱	mikkol-yisrā'ēl	wayhî	hammas̱	shelōshîm	'eleph	'îsh
conscription	from all Israel	and it was	the conscription	thirty	thousands	men

	8365.121	3976	6467	512	904, 2414	2588
14.	cj, v Qal impf 3ms, ps 3mp	pn	num	num	prep, art, n ms	*n fp*
	וַיִּשְׁלָחֵם	לְבָנוֹנָה	עֲשֶׂרֶת	אֲלָפִים	בַּחֹדֶשׁ	חֲלִיפוֹת
	wayyishlāchēm	levānônāh	'ăsereth	'ălāphîm	bachōdhesh	chălîphôth
	and he sent them out	to Lebanon	ten	thousands	during the month	replacements of

2414	2030.126	904, 3976	8530	2414	904, 1041	138
n ms	v Qal impf 3mp	prep, art, pn	num	n mp	prep, n ms, ps 3ms	cj, pn
חֹדֶשׁ	יִהְיוּ	בַּלְּבָנוֹן	שְׁנַיִם	חֳדָשִׁים	בְּבֵיתוֹ	וַאֲדֹנִירָם
chōdhesh	yihyû	vallevānôn	shenayim	chădhāshîm	bevêthô	wa'ădhōnîrām
a month	they were	in the Lebanon	two	months	in his house	and Adoniram

6142, 4671		2030.121	3937, 8406	8124	512	5558.151
prep, art, n ms	**15.**	cj, v Qal impf 3ms	prep, pn	num	num	v Qal act ptc ms
עַל־הַמַּס		וַיְהִי	לִשְׁלֹמֹה	שִׁבְעִים	אֶלֶף	נֹשֵׂא
'al-hammas̱		wayhî	lishlōmōh	shiv'îm	'eleph	nōsē'
over the forced labor		and it was	to Solomon	seventy	thousands	those who carry

5632	8470	512	2778.151	904, 2098		3937, 940	4623, 8015
n ms	cj, num	num	v Qal act ptc ms	prep, art, n ms	**16.**	prep, n ms	prep, *n mp*
סַבָּל	וּשְׁמֹנִים	אֶלֶף	חֹצֵב	בָּהָר		לְבַד	מִשָּׂרֵי
s̱abbāl	ûshemōnîm	'eleph	chōtsēv	bāhār		levadh	missārê
loads	and eighty	thousands	hewers	in the hills		besides	of the officials of

5507.256	3937, 8406	866	6142, 4536	8421	512	8421
art, v Niphal ptc mp	prep, pn	rel pron	prep, art, n fs	num	num	cj, num
הַנִּצָּבִים	לִשְׁלֹמֹה	אֲשֶׁר	עַל־הַמְּלָאכָה	שְׁלֹשֶׁת	אֲלָפִים	וּשְׁלֹשׁ
hanitstsāvîm	lishlōmōh	'ăsher	'al-hammelā'khāh	shelōsheth	'ălāphîm	ûshelōsh
the governors	to Solomon	who	over the craftsmanship	thirty	thousands	and three

… bushels of wheat and beaten oil as food for his servant, *Moffatt* … 20,000 kors of wheat … and twenty kors of beaten oil, *NASB* … purest oil, *Douay* … pure olive oil, *NCV* … grain and clear oil, *BB*.

thus gave Solomon to Hiram year by year: … such was Solomon's annual gift to Hiram, *Moffatt*.

12. And the LORD gave Solomon wisdom, as he promised him: and there was peace between Hiram and Solomon; and they two made a league together: … made an agreement together, *BB* … made a treaty with one another, *Beck* … ratified a treaty, *Goodspeed* … good relations persisted between Solomon and Hiram, and the two of them concluded a treaty, *JB* … an alliance, *Moffatt* … a covenant, *NASB*.

13. And king Solomon raised a levy out of all Israel; and the levy was thirty thousand men: … chose workmen, *Douay* … forced thirty thousand men of Israel to help in this work, *NCV* … raised up a labor force, *NKJV* … conscripted laborers, *NIV* … drafted forced labor, *Beck*.

14. And he sent them to Lebanon, ten thousand a month by courses: a month they were in Lebanon, and two months at home: … in relays, *Goodspeed* … Adoniram was in charge of the draft, *NAB* … He divided them into three groups of 10,000 men, *Good News*.

and Adoniram was over the levy: … in charge of the forced labor, *Beck* … the conscript laborers, *Berkeley*.

15. And Solomon had threescore and ten thousand that bare burdens, and fourscore thousand hewers in the mountains: … 70,000 carriers and 80,000 stonecutters, *NAB* … 70,000 transporters, and 80,000 hewers of stone, *NASB* … forced eighty thousand men to work in the hill country, cutting stone, and he had seventy thousand men to carry the stones, *NCV* … hauliers and … quarrymen, *NEB* … for the work of transport, *BB*.

16. Beside the chief of Solomon's officers which were over the work, three thousand and three hundred, which ruled over the people that wrought in the work: … chief overseers … there wre 3,300 foremen directing the people, *Berkeley* … to supervise, *Good News* … as well as the administra-

---

Some writers have tried to minimize Solomon's work as a builder and have spoken of the Temple as an exceedingly insignificant structure which would not stand a moment's comparison with the smallest and humblest of our own cathedrals. Insignificant in comparative size it certainly was, but we must not forget its costly splendor, the remote age in which the work was achieved and the truly stupendous constructions which the design required.

Mount Moriah was selected as a site hallowed by the tradition of Abraham's sacrifice, and more recently by David's vision of the Angel of the pestilence with his drawn sword on the threshing floor of the Jebusite, Araunah. But to utilize this doubly consecrated area involved almost superhuman difficulties, which would have been avoided if the loftier but less suitable height of the Mount of Olives could have been chosen. The rugged summit had to be enlarged to a space of 500 square yards, and this level was supported by Cyclopean walls, which have long been the wonder of the world. The magnificent wall on the east side, known as "the Jews' wailing place," is doubtless the work of Solomon, and after outlasting "the drums and tramplings of a hundred triumphs," it remains to this day in uninjured massiveness.

One of the finely beveled stones is over 38 feet long and 7 feet high, and weighs more than 100 tons. The vast stones were hewn from a quarry above the level of the wall and lowered by rollers down an inclined plane. Part of the old wall rises 30 feet above the present level of the soil, but a far larger part of the height lies hidden 80 feet under the accumulated debris of the often captured city. At the southwest angle, by Robinson's arch, three pavements were discovered, one beneath the other, showing the gradual filling up of the valley, and on the lowest of these the broken voussoirs of the arch were found. In Solomon's day the whole of this mighty wall was visible. On one of the lowest stones have been discovered the Phoenician paint marks which indicated where each of the huge masses, so carefully dressed, edge-drafted, and beveled, was to be placed in the structure. The caverns, quarries, water storages, and subterranean conduits hewn out of the solid rock over which Jerusalem is built could only have been constructed at the cost of immeasurable toil. They would be wonderful even with our infinitely more rapid methods and more powerful agencies, but when we remember that they were made 3000 years ago, we do not wonder that their massiveness has perplexed the imagination of millions of visitors from every nation.

5:13–18. It was perhaps from his Egyptian father-in-law that Solomon, to his own cost, learned the secret of forced labor which alone rendered such undertakings possible. In their Egyptian bondage, the forefathers of Israel had been fatally familiar with the ugly word maṣ (HED #4671), the labor wrung from them by hard

4109	7575.152	904, 6194	6449.152	904, 4536
num	art, v Qal act ptc mp	prep, art, n ms	art, v Qal act ptc mp	prep, art, n fs
מֵאוֹת	הָרֹדִים	בָּעָם	הָעֹשִׂים	בַּמְּלָאכָה
mē'ôth	hārōdhîm	bā'ām	hā'ōsîm	bammelā'khāh
hundreds of	the bosses	among the people	those working	among the craftsmanship

17.	6943.321	4567	5450.526	63	1448	63	3479
	cj, v Piel impf 3ms	art, n ms	cj, v Hiphil impf 3mp	n fp	adj	n fp	adj
	וַיְצַו	הַמֶּלֶךְ	וַיַּסִּעוּ	אֲבָנִים	גְּדֹלוֹת	אֲבָנִים	יְקָרוֹת
	waytsaw	hammelekh	wayyassi'û	'ăvānîm	gedhōlôth	'ăvānîm	yeqārôth
	and he commanded	the king	and they quarried	stones	great	stones	costly

3937, 3354.341	1041	63	1527	18.	6704.126
prep, v Piel inf con	art, n ms	*n fp*	n fs		cj, v Qal impf 3mp
לְיַסֵּד	הַבָּיִת	אַבְנֵי	גָזִית		וַיִּפְסְלוּ
leyassēdh	habbāyith	'avnê	ghāzîth		wayyiphselû
to lay the foundation of	the Temple	stones of	squared stone		and they carved out

1161.152	8406	1161.152	2538	1414	3679.526
v Qal act ptc mp	pn	cj, *v Qal act ptc mp*	pn	cj, art, pn	cj, v Hiphil impf 3mp
בֹּנֵי	שְׁלֹמֹה	וּבֹנֵי	חִירוֹם	וְהַגִּבְלִים	וַיָּכִינוּ
bōnê	shelōmōh	ûvōnê	chîrôm	wehaggivlîm	wayyākhînû
the builders of	Solomon	and the builders of	Hiram	and the Gebalites	so they prepared

6320	63	3937, 1161.141	1041	6:1	2030.121	904, 8470	8523
art, n mp	cj, art, n fp	prep, v Qal inf con	art, n ms		cj, v Qal impf 3ms	prep, num	n fs
הָעֵצִים	וְהָאֲבָנִים	לִבְנוֹת	הַבָּיִת		וַיְהִי	בִשְׁמוֹנִים	שָׁנָה
hā'ētsîm	wehā'ăvānîm	livnôth	habbāyith		wayhî	vishmônîm	shānāh
the trees	and the stones	to build	the Temple		and it was	in the eightieth	year

727	4109	8523	3937, 3428.141	1158, 3547	4623, 800, 4875
cj, num	num	n fs	prep, v Qal inf con	*n mp*, pn	prep, *n fs*, pn
וְאַרְבַּע	מֵאוֹת	שָׁנָה	לְצֵאת	בְנֵי־יִשְׂרָאֵל	מֵאֶרֶץ־מִצְרַיִם
we'arba'	mē'ôth	shānāh	letsē'th	benê-yisrā'ēl	mē'erets-mitsrayim
and four	hundredth of	year	of the going out of	the children of Israel	from the land of Egypt

904, 8523	7536	904, 2414	2180	2000	2414	8529	3937, 4566.141
prep, art, n fs	art, num	prep, *n ms*	pn	pers pron	art, n ms	art, num	prep, v Qal inf con
בַּשָּׁנָה	הָרְבִיעִית	בְּחֹדֶשׁ	זִו	הוּא	הַחֹדֶשׁ	הַשֵּׁנִי	לִמְלֹךְ
bashshānāh	hārevî'îth	bechōdhesh	ziw	hû'	hachōdhesh	hashshēnî	limlōkh
in the year	the fourth	in the month of	Ziv	it	the month	the second	of the reigning of

8406	6142, 3547	1161.121	1041	3937, 3176	2.	1041	866
pn	prep, pn	cj, v Qal impf 3ms	art, n ms	prep, pn		cj, art, n ms	rel part
שְׁלֹמֹה	עַל־יִשְׂרָאֵל	וַיִּבֶן	הַבַּיִת	לַיהוָה		וְהַבַּיִת	אֲשֶׁר
shelōmōh	'al-yisrā'ēl	wayyiven	habbayith	layhwāh		wehabbayith	'ăsher
Solomon	over Israel	that he began to build	the Temple	to Yahweh		and the building	which

1161.111	4567	8406	3937, 3176	8666, 527	775	6465	7621
v Qal pf 3ms	art, n ms	pn	prep, pn	num, n fs	n ms, ps 3ms	cj, num	n ms, ps 3ms
בָּנָה	הַמֶּלֶךְ	שְׁלֹמֹה	לַיהוָה	שִׁשִּׁים־אַמָּה	אָרְכּוֹ	וְעֶשְׂרִים	רָחְבּוֹ
bānāh	hammelekh	shelōmōh	layhwāh	shishshîm-'ammāh	'ārekkô	we'esrîm	rāchăbbô
he built	the king	Solomon	to Yahweh	sixty cubits	its length	and twenty	its width

8421	527	7253	3.	197	6142, 6686	2033	1041	6465
cj, num	n fs	n fs, ps 3ms		cj, art, n ms	prep, *n mp*	*n ms*	art, n ms	num
וּשְׁלֹשִׁים	אַמָּה	קוֹמָתוֹ		וְהָאוּלָם	עַל־פְּנֵי	הֵיכַל	הַבַּיִת	עֶשְׂרִים
ûshelōshîm	'ammāh	qômāthô		wehā'ûlām	'al-penê	hêkhal	habbayith	'esrîm
and thirty	cubits	its height		and the porch	opposite	the Temple of	the building	twenty

527	775	6142, 6686	7621	1041	6460	904, 527	7621
n fs	n ms, ps 3ms	prep, *n mp*	*n ms*	art, n ms	num	prep, art, n fs	n ms, ps 3ms
אַמָּה	אָרְכּוֹ	עַל־פְּנֵי	רֹחַב	הַבָּיִת	עֶשֶׂר	בָּאַמָּה	רָחְבּוֹ
'ammāh	'ārekkô	'al-pene	rōchav	habbāyith	'eser	bā'ammāh	rāchăbbô
cubits	its length	opposite	the width of	the building	ten	with the cubit	its width

6142, 6686	1041		6449.121	3937, 1041	2574	8627	334.156
prep, *n mp*	art, n ms	**4.**	cj, v Qal impf 3ms	prep, art, n ms	*n mp*	n mp	v Qal pass ptc mp
עַל־פְּנֵי	הַבָּיִת		וַיַּעַשׂ	לַבַּיִת	חַלּוֹנֵי	שְׁקֻפִים	אֲטֻמִים
'al-pene	habbāyith		wayya'as	labbāyith	challônê	shequphîm	'ătumîm
opposite	the building		and he made	for the building	windows of	slants	shutters

tors, officials who supervised the work, *JB* ... directing the people engaged in the work, *NAB* ... who controlled the workmen, *Moffatt*.

17. And the king commanded, and they brought great stones, costly stones, and hewed stones: ... By order of the king, fine, large blocks were quarried, *NAB* ... cut large blocks of fine stone, *NCV* ... they quarried huge, massive blocks, *NEB* ... stones of high price, were cut out, *BB* ... rare blocks of stone, *Beck* ... special stones ... dressed stones, *JB*.

to lay the foundation of the house: ... to give the temple a foundation of hewn stone, *NAB* ... so that the base of the house might be made of squared stone, *BB*.

18. And Solomon's builders and Hiram's builders did hew them, and the stonesquarers: so they prepared timber and stones to build the house: ... and the men of Gebal shaped the stones and prepared the lumber, *Beck* ... the people of Solomon, and the people of Khiram carved, and planned, and shaped ... to build the Temple, *Fenton* ... the masons ... the Giblians, *Douay* ... the logs, *NCV* ... shaped the blocks, *NEB* ... dressed the stones and ran grooved edges round them, *Moffatt*.

6:1. And it came to pass in the four hundred and eightieth year after the children of Israel were come out of the land of Egypt, in the fourth year of Solomon's reign over Israel, in the month Zif, which is the second month, that he began to build the house of the Lord: ... the building of the Lord's house was started, *BB* ... the LORD's temple, *Beck* ... after the exodus, *Goodspeed* ... the construction of the temple of the LORD, *NAB*.

2. And the house which king Solomon built for the LORD, the length thereof was threescore cubits, and the breadth thereof twenty cubits, and the height thereof thirty cubits: ... The temple ... was sixty cubits long, twenty wide and thirty high, *NIV* ... 90 feet long, 30 feet wide, and 45 feet hight, *Berkeley* ... and twenty-five high, *NAB*.

3. And the porch before the temple of the house, twenty cubits was the length thereof, according to the breadth of the house; and ten cubits was the breadth thereof before the house: ... The covered way before the Temple, *BB* ... in front of the main structure of the temple was twenty cubits long, equal to the width of the temple, and 10 cubits deep to the front of the temple, *Beck* ... a colonnade ... following the form of the building, and rising ten cubits up the face of the structure, *Fenton* ... along the width of the nave, *NAB* ... was fifteen feet deep and thirty feet wide, *NCV* ... The entrance room was 15 feet deep and 30 feet wide, as wide as the sanctuary itself, *Good News*.

4. And for the house he made windows of narrow lights: ... beveled

---

task-masters (Exo. 1–2). In the reign of Solomon, it once more became only too common on the lips of the burdened people (1 Ki. 4:6; 5:13f, 17f; 9:15, 21; 12:18).

Four classes were subject to it. The lightest labor was required from the native freeborn Israelites, or 'ezrāch (HED #248). They were not regarded as bondsmen, yet 30,000 of these were required to work in relays of 10,000 one month of every three, in the forest of Lebanon. There were the strangers, or resident aliens (gērîm, HED #1658), such as the Phoenicians and Giblites, who were Hiram's subjects and worked for pay. There were three classes of slaves: those taken in war, those sold for debt and those born in Israel. Lowest and most wretched of all, there were the vassal Canaanites or tôshāvîm (HED #8785), from whom were drawn 70,000 burden-bearers, and 80,000 quarrymen.

6:1–7. A most important verse as to dating of Israelite history is found in 1 Ki. 6:1. Four hundred eighty years after the Exodus, the foundation of Solomon's temple was laid. Knowing that King David conquered Jerusalem just before 1000 B.C., archaeology, along with calculations from the historical accounts, has placed the laying of the foundation for the Temple at 960 B.C. Thus, the Exodus surely predates 1440 B.C. and could not have occurred in the 1200s, as some purport.

5. 1161.121	6142, 7306	1041	3436	5623	881, 7306	1041
cj, v Qal impf 3ms	prep, *n ms*	art, n ms	n ms	adv	do, *n mp*	art, n ms
וַיִּבֶן	עַל־קִיר	הַבַּיִת	יָצוּעַ	סָבִיב	אֶת־קִירוֹת	הַבַּיִת
wayyiven	‘al-qîr	habbayith	yātsôa‘	sāvîv	’eth-qîrôth	habbayith
and he built	beside the wall of	the Temple	stories	all around	the walls of	the Temple

5623	3937, 2033	3937, 1735	6449.121	7029	5623
adv	prep, art, n ms	cj, prep, art, n ms	cj, v Qal impf 3ms	n fp	adv
סָבִיב	לַהֵיכָל	וְלַדְּבִיר	וַיַּעַשׂ	צְלָעוֹת	סָבִיב
sāvîv	lahêkhāl	wᵉladdᵉvîr	wayya‘as	tsᵉlā‘ôth	sāvîv
all around	to the Temple	and to the hindermost room	and he made	side chambers	all around

6. 3436	8811	2675	904, 527	7621	8814	8666
art, n ms	art, adj	num	prep, art, n fs	n ms, ps 3fs	cj, art, adj	num
הַיָּצוּעַ	הַתַּחְתֹּנָה	חָמֵשׁ	בָּאַמָּה	רָחֲבָּהּ	וְהַתִּיכֹנָה	שֵׁשׁ
hayyātsôa‘	hattachtōnāh	chāmēsh	bā’ammāh	rāchăbbāhh	wᵉhattîkhōnāh	shēsh
the stories	the lower	five	with the cubit	its width	and the middle one	six

904, 527	7621	8389	8124	904, 527	7621	3706	4192
prep, art, n fs	n ms, ps 3fs	cj, art, num	num	prep, art, n fs	n ms, ps 3fs	cj	n fp
בָּאַמָּה	רָחֲבָּהּ	וְהַשְּׁלִישִׁית	שֶׁבַע	בָּאַמָּה	רָחֲבָּהּ	כִּי	מִגְרָעוֹת
bā’ammāh	rāchăbbāhh	wᵉhashshᵉlîshîth	sheva‘	bā’ammāh	rāchăbbāhh	kî	mighrā‘ôth
with the cubit	its width	and the third	seven	with the cubit	its width	because	niches

5598.111	3937, 1041	5623	2445	3937, 1153	270.141
v Qal pf 3ms	prep, art, n ms	adv	n ms	prep, neg part	v Qal inf con
נָתַן	לַבַּיִת	סָבִיב	חוּצָה	לְבִלְתִּי	אֱחֹז
nāthan	labbayith	sāvîv	chûtsāh	lᵉviltî	’ĕchōz
he put	for the building	all around	to the outside	that not	to fasten

904, 7306, 1041	**7.** 1041	904, 1161.241	63, 8400
prep, n mp, art, n ms	cj, art, n ms	prep, v Niphal inf con, ps 3ms	n fs, adj
בְּקִירוֹת־הַבָּיִת	וְהַבַּיִת	בְּהִבָּנֹתוֹ	אֶבֶן־שְׁלֵמָה
bᵉqîrôth-habbāyith	wᵉhabbayith	bᵉhibbānōthô	’even-shᵉlēmāh
into the walls of the building	and the building	when its being built	a complete stone

4703	1161.211	4879	1676	3725, 3747	1298	3940, 8471.211
n ms	v Niphal pf 3ms	cj, n fp	cj, art, n ms	*adj, n ms*	n ms	neg part, v Niphal pf 3ms
מַסָּע	נִבְנָה	וּמַקָּבוֹת	וְהַגַּרְזֶן	כָּל־כְּלִי	בַרְזֶל	לֹא־נִשְׁמַע
massā‘	nivnāh	ûmaqqāvôth	wᵉhaggarzen	kol-kᵉlî	varzel	lō’-nishma‘
quarrying	it was built	but hammers	and the axe	every tool of	iron	it was not heard

904, 1041	904, 1161.241	**8.** 6860	7029	8814
prep, art, n ms	prep, v Niphal inf con, ps 3ms	*n ms*	art, n fs	art, adj
בַּבַּיִת	בְּהִבָּנֹתוֹ	פֶּתַח	הַצֵּלָע	הַתִּיכֹנָה
babbayith	bᵉhibbānōthô	pethach	hatstsēlā‘	hattîkhōnāh
in the building	when its being built	the entrance of	the side chamber	the middle one

420, 3931	1041	3332	904, 4019	6148.126	6142, 8814
prep, *n fs*	art, n ms	art, adj	cj, prep, n mp	v Qal impf 3mp	prep, art, adj
אֶל־כֶּתֶף	הַבַּיִת	הַיְמָנִית	וּבְלוּלִּים	יַעֲלוּ	עַל־הַתִּיכֹנָה
’el-ketheph	habbayith	haymānîth	ûvᵉlûllîm	ya‘ălû	‘al-hattîkhōnāh
toward the side of	the Temple	the right	and by a stairwell	they went up	onto the middle

4623, 8814	420, 8421	**9.** 1161.121	881, 1041	3735.321
cj, prep, art, adj	prep, art, num	cj, v Qal impf 3ms	do, art, n ms	cj, v Piel impf 3ms, ps 3ms
וּמִן־הַתִּיכֹנָה	אֶל־הַשְּׁלִשִׁים	וַיִּבֶן	אֶת־הַבַּיִת	וַיְכַלֵּהוּ
ûmin-hattîkhōnāh	’el-hashshᵉlishîm	wayyiven	’eth-habbayith	waykhallēhû
and from the middle	to the third	and he built	the building	and he finished it

frames, *NKJV* ... clerestory windows in the temple, *NIV* ... recessed frames, *NRSV* ... embrasures, *REB* ... network across, *BB* ... frames and latticework, *JB*.

5. And against the wall of the house he built chambers round about, against the walls of the house round about, both of the temple and of the oracle: and he made chambers round about: ... he built side rooms; all around the walls both of the temple and the inner room and he made cells all around, *Berkeley* ... next to the walls of the main structure and the inner sanctuary a structure with side rooms, *Beck* ... encircling the whole of the Temple, lodges joined to the wall in regular order, and also made a verandah, *Fenton* ... which enclosed the nave and the sanctuary, an annex of several stories was built, *NAB* ... inclosed galleries against the wall of the house round about in conformity ... and the inner room, *Goodspeed*.

6. The nethermost chamber was five cubits broad, and the middle was six cubits broad, and the third was seven cubits broad: ... The lowest story was five cubits wide, *NASB* ... The floor that was underneath, *Douay* ... The Temple wall that formed the side of each room was thinner than the wall in the room below, *NCV*.

for without in the wall of the house he made narrowed rests round about, that the beams should not be fastened in the walls of the house: ... on the outside he made offsets in the wall of the house all around, *NASB* ... built into this wall, *NCV* ... he made rebates all round the outside of the main wall so that the bearer beams might not be set into the walls, *NEB* ... there was a space all round the outside walls of the house so that the boards supporting the rooms did not have to be fixed, *BB* ... He made ledges, *Beck*.

7. And the house, when it was in building, was built of stone made ready before it was brought thither: so that there was neither hammer nor axe nor any tool of iron heard in the house, while it was in building: ... When the temple was built, it was done with stones that were perfectly shaped when they were quarried, and no hammer, chisel, *Beck* ... Temple was itself built of stone finished at the quarry; the stones cut, carved, and polished, *Fenton* ... with quarry-dressed stone; no sound of hammer or pick, *JB* ... built of stones hewed and made ready, *Douay* ... prepared at the same place ... no noise of, *NCV*.

8. The door for the middle chamber was in the right side of the house: and they went up with winding stairs into the middle chamber, and out of the middle into the third: ... entrance to the lowest arcade was in the right-hand corner ... there was access by a spiral stairway from that to the middle arcade, and from the middle arcade to the highest, *NEB* ... lower rooms beside the Temple was on the south side, *NCV* ... went up by twisting steps, *BB* ... Folding gates with a platform were at the right side, *Fenton* ... lowest story of the annex was on the south side of the Temple, *Good News*.

9. So he built the house, and finished it; and covered the house with beams and boards of cedar: ... he roofed the Temple with a coffered ceiling, *JB* ... with planks of cedar over beams, *MAST* ... was built to its full height, it was roofed in with rafters, *NAB* ... he paneled the temple, *NKJV* ... made the ceiling, *RSV* ... completed it by wainscoting the building with planks, *Fenton*.

Apart from the lavish expense of its materials, the actual Temple was architecturally a poor and commonplace structure. It was quite small—only ninety feet long, thirty-five feet broad and forty-five feet high. It was meant for the symbolic habitation of God, not for the worship of great congregations. It only represented the nascent art and limited resources of a small kingdom, and was totally devoid alike of the pure and stately beauty of the Parthenon and the awe-inspiring grandeur of the great Egyptian temples with their avenues of obelisks and sphinxes and their colossal statues of deities and kings.

"Staring right on with calm, eternal eyes." When Justinian boastfully exclaimed, as he looked at his church, "I have vanquished thee, O Solomon," and when the Khalif Omar, pointing to the Dome of the Rock, murmured, "Behold, a greater than Solomon is here," they forgot the vast differences between them and the Jewish king in the epoch at which they lived and the resources which they could command. The Temple was built in "majestic silence."

"No workman's axe, no ponderous hammer rung. Like some tall palm the noiseless fabric sprung." This was due to religious reverence. It could be easily accomplished, because each stone and beam was carefully prepared to be fitted in its exact place before it was carried up the temple hill.

6:8–13. The elaborate measurements of Solomon's temple are too late in age, too divergent in particulars, too loosely strung together, too much mingled with later reminiscences and altogether too architecturally insufficient to enable us to reconstruct the exact building, or even to form more than a vague conception of its external appearance. Keil says that the descriptions given in Kings and Chronicles are independent extracts

5802.121	881, 1041	1387	7901	904, 753	**10.** 1161.121
cj, v Qal impf 3ms	do, art, n ms	n mp	cj, n fp	prep, art, n mp	cj, v Qal impf 3ms
וַיִּסְפֹּן	אֶת־הַבַּיִת	גֵּבִים	וּשְׂדֵרֹת	בָּאֲרָזִים	וַיִּבֶן
wayyispōn	'eth-habbayith	gēvîm	ûsᵉdhērōth	bā'ărāzîm	wayyiven
and he covered	the building	beams	and joists	with the cedars	and he built

881, 3436	6142, 3725, 1041	2675	527	7253	270.121	881, 1041
do, art, n ms	prep, *adj*, art, n ms	num	n fp	n fs, ps 3ms	cj, v Qal impf 3ms	do, art, n ms
אֶת־הַיָּצוּעַ	עַל־כָּל־הַבַּיִת	חָמֵשׁ	אַמּוֹת	קוֹמָתוֹ	וַיֶּאֱחֹז	אֶת־הַבַּיִת
'eth-hayyātsôa'	'al-kol-habbayith	chāmēsh	'ammôth	qômāthô	wayye'ĕchōz	'eth-habbayith
the story	over all the building	five	cubits	its height	and he joined to	the building

904, 6320	753	**11.** 2030.121	1745, 3176	420, 8406
prep, *n mp*	n mp	cj, v Qal impf 3ms	*n ms*, pn	prep, pn
בַּעֲצֵי	אֲרָזִים	וַיְהִי	דְּבַר־יְהוָה	אֶל־שְׁלֹמֹה
ba'ătsê	'ărāzîm	wayhî	dᵉvar-yᵉhwāh	'el-shᵉlōmōh
with the wood of	cedars	and it was	the word of Yahweh	unto Solomon

3937, 569.141	**12.** 1041	2172	866, 887	1161.151	524, 2050.123
prep, v Qal inf con	art, n ms	art, dem pron	rel part, pers pron	v Qal act ptc ms	cj, v Qal impf 2ms
לֵאמֹר	הַבַּיִת	הַזֶּה	אֲשֶׁר־אַתָּה	בֹנֶה	אִם־תֵּלֵךְ
lē'mōr	habbayith	hazzeh	'ăsher-'attāh	vōneh	'im-tēlēkh
saying	the Temple	the this	which you	building	if you walk

904, 2807	881, 5122	6449.123	8490.113	881, 3725, 4851
prep, n fp, ps 1cs	cj, do, n mp, ps 1cs	v Qal impf 2ms	cj, v Qal pf 2ms	do, *adj*, n fp, ps 1cs
בְּחֻקֹּתַי	וְאֶת־מִשְׁפָּטַי	תַּעֲשֶׂה	וְשָׁמַרְתָּ	אֶת־כָּל־מִצְוֹתַי
bᵉchuqqōthay	wᵉ'eth-mishpāṭay	ta'ăseh	wᵉshāmartā	'eth-kol-mitswōthay
by my statutes	and my ordinances	you do	and you must observe	all my commandments

3937, 2050.141	904	7251.515	881, 1745	882	866	1744.315
prep, v Qal inf con	prep, ps 3mp	cj, v Hiphil pf 1cs	do, n ms, ps 1cs	prep, ps 2ms	rel part	v Piel pf 1cs
לָלֶכֶת	בָּהֶם	וַהֲקִמֹתִי	אֶת־דְּבָרִי	אִתָּךְ	אֲשֶׁר	דִּבַּרְתִּי
lālekheth	bāhem	wahqimōthî	'eth-dᵉvārî	'ittākh	'ăsher	dibbartî
to walk	in them	then I will raise up	my word	with you	which	I spoke

420, 1784	1	**13.** 8331.115	904, 8761	1158	3547	3940
prep, pn	n ms, ps 2ms	cj, v Qal pf 1cs	prep, *n ms*	*n mp*	pn	cj, neg part
אֶל־דָּוִד	אָבִיךָ	וְשָׁכַנְתִּי	בְּתוֹךְ	בְּנֵי	יִשְׂרָאֵל	וְלֹא
'el-dāwidh	'āvîkhā	wᵉshākhantî	bᵉthôkh	bᵉnê	yisrā'ēl	wᵉlō'
to David	your father	and I will remain	in the midst of	the children of	Israel	and not

6013.125	881, 6194	3547	**14.** 1161.121	8406	881, 1041
v Qal impf 1cs	do, n ms, ps 1cs	pn	cj, v Qal impf 3ms	pn	do, art, n ms
אֶעֱזֹב	אֶת־עַמִּי	יִשְׂרָאֵל	וַיִּבֶן	שְׁלֹמֹה	אֶת־הַבַּיִת
'e'ĕzōv	'eth-'ammî	yisrā'ēl	wayyiven	shᵉlōmōh	'eth-habbayith
I will abandon	my people	Israel	and he built	Solomon	the building

3735.321	**15.** 1161.121	881, 7306	1041	4623, 1041
cj, v Piel impf 3ms, ps 3ms	cj, v Qal impf 3ms	do, *n mp*	art, n ms	prep, n ms
וַיְכַלֵּהוּ	וַיִּבֶן	אֶת־קִירוֹת	הַבַּיִת	מִבַּיְתָה
waykhallēhû	wayyiven	'eth-qîrôth	habbayith	mibbaythāh
and he finished it	and he built	the walls of	the Temple	from to the inside

904, 7029	753	4623, 7463	1041	5912, 7306	5803
prep, *n fp*	n mp	prep, *n ms*	art, n ms	prep, *n mp*	art, n ms
בְּצַלְעוֹת	אֲרָזִים	מִקַּרְקַע	הַבַּיִת	עַד־קִירוֹת	הַסִּפֻּן
bᵉtsal'ôth	'ărāzîm	miqqarqa'	habbayith	'adh-qîrôth	hassippun
with beams of	cedars	from the floor of	the Temple	unto the walls of	the ceiling

10. And then he built chambers against all the house, five cubits high: and they rested on the house with timber of cedar: ... cedar beams rested on the temple, *Beck* ... fastened ... with cedar lumber, *Berkeley* ... a floor over all, *Douay* ... constructed the terrace five cubits high against the whole building, braced the house with struts of cedar, *NEB*.

11. And the word of the LORD came to Solomon, saying: ... spoke, *Beck* ... EVER-LIVING, *Fenton* ... gave this message, *NLT*.

12. Concerning this house which thou art in building, if thou wilt walk in my statutes, and execute my judgments, and keep all my commandments to walk in them: ... you have built for Me, if you walk according to my Institutions, and practise my Decrees ... to guide yourself, *Fenton* ... carry out my ordinances, and ... by conforming your conduct to them, *Goodspeed* ... if you are obedient ... and conform to my precepts and loyally observe, *NEB* ... follow my decrees, carry out my regulations, *NIV* ... my laws and give effect to my decisions and be guided by my rules, *BB*.

then will I perform my word with thee, which I spake unto David thy father: ... confirm the promise I gave you, which I promised, *Fenton* ... fulfil my promise, *NEB* ... give effect, *BB*.

13. And I will dwell among the children of Israel: ... be ever among, *BB* ... abide, *Berkeley* ... rest in the midst, *Fenton* ... make my home, *JB*.

and will not forsake my people Israel: ... go away, *BB* ... leave, *Berkeley* ... abandon, *Fenton*.

14. So Solomon built the house, and finished it: ... the Temple, *Fenton* ... the LORD's house, *NEB* ... made the building of the house complete, *BB* ... to completion, *Berkeley*.

15. And he built the walls of the house within with boards of cedar, both the floor of the house, and the walls of the ceiling: ... lined the inner walls, *NEB* ... inside walls of the temple, *NKJV*.

---

and vague in essential details. Critics and architects have attempted to reproduce the Temple on Greek, Egyptian and Phoenician models, so entirely unlike each other as to show that we can arrive at no certainty. It is, however, most probable that, alike in ornamentation and conception, the building was predominantly Phoenician. Severe in outline, gorgeous in detail, it was more like the temple of Venus-Astarte at Paphos than any other. Fortunately the details, apart from such dim symbolism as we may detect in them, have no religious importance, but only a historic and antiquarian interest.

6:14–18. The Temple, called bayith (HED #1041) or hêkhal (HED #2033), was surrounded by the thickly clustered houses of the Levites and by porticoes through which the precincts were entered by numerous gates of wood overlaid with brass. A grove of olives, palms, cedars and cypresses, the home of many birds, probably adorned the outer court. This court was shut from the "higher court," (Jer. 36:10) afterwards known as "the Court of the Priests," by a partition of three rows of hewn stones surmounted by a cornice of cedar beams. In the higher court, which was reached by a flight of steps, was the vast new altar of brass, fifteen feet high and thirty feet long, of which the hollow was filled with earth and stones, and of which the blazing sacrifices were visible in the court below (2 Chr. 4:1; cf. Ezek. 43:17).

The huge molten sea also stood here, borne on the backs of twelve brazen oxen, of which three faced to each quarter of the heavens. It was in the form of a lotus blossom, and its rim was hung with 300 wild gourds in bronze, cast in two rows. Its reservoir of 880 gallons of water was for the priestly ablutions necessary in the butcheries of sacrifice, and its usefulness was supplemented by ten brazen caldrons on wheels, five on each side, adorned like "the sea," with pensile garlands and cherubic emblems. Whether "the brazen serpent of the wilderness," to which the children of Israel burnt incense down to the day of Hezekiah, was in that court or in the Temple we do not know.

On the western side of this court, facing the rising sun, stood the Temple itself, on a platform elevated some sixteen feet from the ground. Its side chambers were "lean-to" annexes (tsēlā'; HED #7029) in three stories, all accessible by one central entrance on the outside. Their beams rested on rebatements in the thickness of the wall, and the highest was the broadest. Above these were windows "skewed and closed," as the margin of the KJV says; or "broad within and narrow without"; or, as it should rather be rendered, "with closed cross beams," i.e., with immovable lattices, which could not be opened and shut, but which allowed the escape of the smoke of lamps and the fumes of incense. These chambers must also have had windows. They were used to store the garments of the priests and other necessary paraphernalia of the temple service, but as to all details we are left completely in the dark.

7099.311	6320	4623, 1041	7099.321	881, 7463	1041
v Piel pf 3ms	n ms	prep, n ms	cj, v Piel impf 3ms	do, *n ms*	art, n ms
צִפָּה	עֵץ	מִבָּיִת	וַיְצַף	אֶת־קַרְקַע	הַבַּיִת
tsippāh	ʿēts	mibbāyith	waytsaph	'eth-qarqa'	habbayith
he overlaid with	wood	from the inside	and he overlaid with	the floor of	the Temple

904, 7029	1293		1161.121	881, 6465	527	4623, 3526
prep, *n fp*	n mp	**16.**	cj, v Qal impf 3ms	do, num	n fs	prep, *n md*
בְּצַלְעוֹת	בְּרוֹשִׁים		וַיִּבֶן	אֶת־עֶשְׂרִים	אַמָּה	מִיַּרְכּוֹתֵי
b^{e}tsal'ôth	b^{e}rôshîm		wayyiven	'eth-'esrîm	'ammāh	mîyarkôthê
with beams of	cypress		and he built	twenty	cubits	from the rear portions of

1041	904, 7029	753	4623, 7463	5912, 7306	1161.121	3937
art, n ms	prep, *n fp*	n mp	prep, art, n ms	prep, art, n mp	cj, v Qal impf 3ms	prep, ps 3ms
הַבַּיִת	בְּצַלְעוֹת	אֲרָזִים	מִן־הַקַּרְקַע	עַד־הַקִּירוֹת	וַיִּבֶן	לוֹ
habbayith	b^{e}tsal'ôth	'ărāzîm	min-haqqarqa'	'adh-haqqîrôth	wayyiven	lô
the Temple	with beams of	cedars	from the floor	unto the walls	and he built	to it

4623, 1041	3937, 1735	3937, 7231	7231		727
prep, n ms	prep, n ms	prep, *n ms*	art, n mp	**17.**	cj, num
מִבַּיִת	לִדְבִיר	לְקֹדֶשׁ	הַקֳּדָשִׁים		וְאַרְבָּעִים
mibbayith	lidhvîr	l^{e}qōdhesh	haqq^{e}dhāshîm		w^{e}'arbā'îm
from inside	to the inmost room	to the Holy Place of	the holy places		and forty

904, 527	2030.111	1041	2000	2033	3937, 6686		753
prep, art, n fs	v Qal pf 3ms	art, n ms	pers pron	art, n ms	prep, n mp, ps 1cs	**18.**	cj, n ms
בָּאַמָּה	הָיָה	הַבָּיִת	הוּא	הַהֵיכָל	לְפָנָי		וְאֶרֶז
bā'ammāh	hāyāh	habbāyith	hû'	hahêkhāl	liphnāy		w^{e}'erez
with the cubit	it was	the building	it	the Temple	before me		and cedar

420, 1041	6687	4897	6747	6604.156	7001	3725
prep, art, n ms	prep	*n fs*	n mp	cj, *v Qal pass ptc mp*	n mp	art, n ms
אֶל־הַבַּיִת	פְּנִימָה	מִקְלַעַת	פְּקָעִים	וּפְטוּרֵי	צִצִּים	הַכֹּל
'el-habbayith	p^{e}nîmāh	miqŏla'ath	p^{e}qā'îm	ûph^{e}ṭûrê	tsitstsîm	hakkōl
to the inside	within	wood carving of	buds	and made elaborate	blossoms	everything

753	375	63	7495.211		1735	904, 8761, 1041
n ms	*sub*	n fs	v Niphal pf 3ms	**19.**	cj, n ms	prep, *n ms*, art, n ms
אֶרֶז	אֵין	אֶבֶן	נִרְאָה		וּדְבִיר	בְּתוֹךְ־הַבַּיִת
'erez	'ên	'even	nir'āh		ûdh^{e}vîr	b^{e}thôkh-habbayith
cedar	there was not	a stone	it was seen		and the inmost room	in the middle of the building

4623, 6687	3679.511	3937, 5598.141	8427	881, 751	1311	3176
prep, prep	v Hiphil pf 3ms	prep, v Qal inf con	adv	do, *n ms*	*n fs*	pn
מִפְּנִימָה	הֵכִין	לְתִתֵּן	שָׁם	אֶת־אֲרוֹן	בְּרִית	יְהוָה
mipp^{e}nîmāh	hēkhîn	l^{e}thittēn	shām	'eth-'ărôn	b^{e}rîth	y^{e}hwāh
from within	he had prepared	to put	there	the Ark of	the Covenant of	Yahweh

	3937, 6686	1735	6465	527	775	6465	527	7621
20.	cj, prep, *n mp*	art, n ms	num	n fs	n ms	cj, num	n fs	n ms
	וְלִפְנֵי	הַדְּבִיר	עֶשְׂרִים	אַמָּה	אֹרֶךְ	וְעֶשְׂרִים	אַמָּה	רֹחַב
	w^{e}liphnê	hadd^{e}vîr	'esrîm	'ammāh	'ōrekh	w^{e}'esrîm	'ammāh	rōchav
	and before	the inmost room	twenty	cubits	length	and twenty	cubits	width

6465	527	7253	7099.321	2174	5646.155	7099.321
cj, num	n fs	n fs, ps 3ms	cj, v Piel impf 3ms, ps 3ms	n ms	v Qal pass ptc ms	cj, v Piel impf 3ms
וְעֶשְׂרִים	אַמָּה	קוֹמָתוֹ	וַיְצַפֵּהוּ	זָהָב	סָגוּר	וַיְצַף
w^{e}'esrîm	'ammāh	qômāthô	waytsappēhû	zāhāv	sāghûr	waytsaph
and twenty	cubits	its height	and he overlaid it with	gold	covered	and he overlaid

and he covered them on the inside with wood: ... covering the interior from floor to rafters, *NEB* ... paneled them, *NKJV* ... paneled with wood, *NLT*.

and covered the floor of the house with planks of fir: ... laid with boards of pine, *NEB* ... cypress, *NKJV*.

16. And he built twenty cubits on the sides of the house, both the floor and the walls with boards of cedar: he even built them for it within, even for the oracle: ... at the back of the house a further space ... was shut in, *BB* ... farthest end of the temple, *Beck* ... in the rear of the Temple. It was 30 feet long and was partitioned of by cedar boards reaching from the floor to the ceiling, *Good News* ... a space of twenty cubits was set off, *NAB*.

even for the most holy place: ... inmost room, *BB* ... inner room, the most holy place, *Beck* ... a sanctuary, *Berkeley* ... the Most Holy Place, *Good News* ... the holy of holies, *NAB* ... most sacred place, *Goodspeed*.

17. And the house, that is, the temple before it, was forty cubits long: ... the nave in front of the inner sanctuary, *NASB* ... before the doors of the oracle, *Douay* ... The main room, the one in front of the Most Holy Place, was sixty feet long, *NCV* ... main hall, *NIV* ... the temple proper, *Goodspeed*.

18. And the cedar of the house within was carved with knobs and open flowers: all was cedar; there was no stone seen: ... ornamented with designs of buds and flowers, *BB* ... inside the temple were carved gourds, *Beck* ... ornamentally carved with gourds and rosettes, *JB* ... pictures of flowers and plants, *NCV* ...

Of the external aspect of the building in Solomon's day we know nothing. We cannot even tell whether it had one level roof, or whether the Holy of Holies was like a lower chancel at the end of it; nor whether the roof was flat or, as the rabbis say, ridged; nor whether the outer surface of the three-storied chambers which surrounded it was of stone, or planked with cedar, or overlaid with plinths of gold and silver; nor whether, in any case, it was ornamented with carvings or left blank; nor whether the cornices only were decorated with open flowers like the Assyrian rosettes. Nor do we know with certainty whether it was supported within by pillars (1 Ki. 10:12) or not.

In front of or just within the porch were two superb pillars, regarded as miracles of Tyrian art, made of fluted bronze, 27 feet high and 18 feet thick. Their capitals of 7 1/2 feet in height resembled an open lotus blossom, surrounded by double wreaths of 200 pensile bronze pomegranates, supporting an abacus, carved with conventional lily work. Both pomegranates and lilies had a symbolic meaning. The pillars were for unknown reasons called Jachin and Boaz. Much about them is obscure. It is not even known whether they stood detached like obelisks, or formed Propylaea; or supported the architraves of the porch itself; or were a sort of gateway, surmounted by a *melathron* with two *epithemas*, like a Japanese or Indian *toran*.

The porch ('ûlām, HED #197), which was of the same height as the house (i.e., forty-five feet high), was hung with the gilded shields of Hadadezer's soldiers which David had taken in battle, and perhaps also with consecrated armor, like the sword of Goliath (2 Sam. 8:7; 1 Chr. 18:7), to show that "unto the LORD is our defence" (Ps. 89:18) and that "the shields of the earth belong unto God" (47:9).

A door of cypress wood, of two leaves, made in four squares, seven and one-half feet broad and high, turning on golden hinges overlaid with gold, and carved with palm branches and festoons of lilies and pomegranates, opened from the porch into the main apartment. This was the Holy Place, or Sanctuary (miqdāsh, HED #4881), and sometimes specially called "the Palace" in Aramaic (hêkhal, HED #A2034 or bîrāh, HED #A21039; Ezra 5:14f, etc.). Before it, as in the Tabernacle, hung an embroidered curtain (māsākh, HED #4689). It was probably supported by four pillars on each side. In the interspaces were five tables on each side, overlaid with gold, and each encircled by a wreath of gold (zēr, HED #2300). On these were placed the cakes of shewbread (1 Ki. 7:48; 2 Chr. 4:8; 13:11; 29:18). At the end of the chamber, on each side the door of the Holiest, were five golden candlesticks with chains of wreathed gold hanging between them. In the center of the room stood the golden altar of incense, and somewhere (we must suppose) the golden candlestick of the Tabernacle, with its seven branches ornamented with lilies, pomegranates and chalices of almond flowers. Nothing which was in the darkness of the Holiest was visible except the projecting golden staves with which the Ark had been carried to its place. The Holy Place itself was lighted by narrow slits.

6:19. The entrance to the Holiest (d[e]vîr, (HED #1735), or oracle, which corresponded to the Greek *adytum*, was through a two-leaved door of olive wood, six feet high and broad, overlaid with gold,

5646.155	2174	4623, 6687	881, 1041	8406	7099.321	21.	753	4326
v Qal pass ptc ms	n ms	prep, prep	do, art, n ms	pn	cj, v Piel impf 3ms		n ms	n ms
סָגוּר	זָהָב	מִפְּנִימָה	אֶת־הַבַּיִת	שְׁלֹמֹה	וַיְצַף		אֶרֶז	מִזְבֵּחַ
sāghûr	zāhāv	mipp^{e}nîmāh	'eth-habbayith	sh^{e}lōmōh	waytsaph		'ārez	mizbēach
covered	gold	from within	the building	Solomon	and he overlaid with		cedar	an altar of

7099.321	1735	3937, 6686	2174	904, 7871	5882.321
cj, v Piel impf 3ms, ps 3ms	art, n ms	prep, n mp	n ms	prep, n fp	v Piel impf 3ms
וַיְצַפֵּהוּ	הַדְּבִיר	לִפְנֵי	זָהָב	בְּרַתִּיקוֹת	וַיְעַבֵּר
waytsappēhû	hadd^{e}vîr	liphnê	zāhāv	b^{e}rattîqôth	way'abbēr
and he overlaid it with	the inmost room	before	gold	by chains of	and he caused to pass by

3725, 1041	5912, 8882.141	2174	7099.311	881, 3725, 1041	22.	2174
adj, art, n ms	adv, v Qal inf con	n ms	v Piel pf 3ms	cj, do, adj, art, n ms		n ms
כָּל־הַבָּיִת	עַד־תֹּם	זָהָב	צִפָּה	וְאֶת־כָּל־הַבַּיִת		זָהָב
kol-habbāyith	'adh-tōm	zāhāv	tsippāh	w^{e}'eth-kol-habbayith		zāhāv
all the building	until the finishing of	gold	he overlaid with	and all the building		gold

6449.121	23.	2174	7099.311	866, 3937, 1735	3725, 4326
cj, v Qal impf 3ms		n ms	v Piel pf 3ms	rel part, prep, n ms	cj, adj, art, n ms
וַיַּעַשׂ		זָהָב	צִפָּה	אֲשֶׁר־לַדְּבִיר	וְכָל־הַמִּזְבֵּחַ
wayya'as		zāhāv	tsippāh	'ăsher-ladd^{e}vîr	w^{e}khol-hammizbēach
and he made		gold	he overlaid with	which to the inmost room	and all the altar

2675	24.	7253	527	6460	6320, 8467	3872	8530	904, 1735
cj, num		n fs, ps 3ms	n fp	num	n mp, n ms	n mp	num	prep, art, n ms
וְחָמֵשׁ		קוֹמָתוֹ	אַמּוֹת	עֶשֶׂר	עֲצֵי־שָׁמֶן	כְרוּבִים	שְׁנֵי	בַּדְּבִיר
w^{e}chāmēsh		qômāthô	'ammôth	'eser	'ătsê-shāmen	kh^{e}rûvîm	sh^{e}nê	badd^{e}vîr
and five		its height	cubits	ten	trees of olive oil	cherubim	two	in the inmost room

8529	3872	3796	527	2675	259	3872	3796	527
art, num	art, n ms	n fs	n fp	cj, num	art, num	art, n ms	n fs	n fp
הַשֵּׁנִית	הַכְּרוּב	כְּנַף	אַמּוֹת	וְחָמֵשׁ	הָאֶחָת	הַכְּרוּב	כְּנַף	אַמּוֹת
hashshēnîth	hakk^{e}rûv	k^{e}naph	'ammôth	w^{e}chāmēsh	hā'echāth	hakk^{e}rûv	k^{e}naph	'ammôth
the second	the cherub	the wing of	cubits	and five	the first	the cherub	the wing of	cubits

6460	25.	3796	5912, 7382	3796	4623, 7382	527	6460
cj, num		n fd, ps 3ms	cj, prep, n fp	n fd, ps 3ms	prep, n fp	n fp	num
וְעֶשֶׂר		כְּנָפָיו	וְעַד־קְצוֹת	כְּנָפָיו	מִקְצוֹת	אַמּוֹת	עֶשֶׂר
w^{e}'eser		k^{e}nāphāv	w^{e}'adh-qǒtsôth	k^{e}nāphâv	miqǒtsôth	'ammôth	'eser
and ten		its wings	even unto the ends of	its wings	from the ends of	cubits	ten

3937, 8530	259	7379	259	4201	8529	3872	904, 527
prep, num	num	cj, n ms	num	n fs	art, num	art, n ms	prep, art, n fs
לִשְׁנֵי	אֶחָד	וְקֶצֶב	אַחַת	מִדָּה	הַשֵּׁנִי	הַכְּרוּב	בָּאַמָּה
lishnê	'echādh	w^{e}qetsev	'achath	middāh	hashshēnî	hakk^{e}rûv	bā'ammāh
to the two of	one	and a figure	one	a measurement	the second	the cherub	with the cubit

3872	3772	904, 527	6460	259	3872	7253	26.	3872
art, n ms	cj, adv	prep, art, n fs	num	art, num	art, n ms	n fs		art, n mp
הַכְּרוּב	וְכֵן	בָּאַמָּה	עֶשֶׂר	הָאֶחָד	הַכְּרוּב	קוֹמַת		הַכְּרֻבִים
hakk^{e}rûv	w^{e}khēn	bā'ammāh	'eser	hā'echādh	hakk^{e}rûv	qômath		hakk^{e}ruvîm
the cherub	and so	with the cubit	ten	the one	the cherub	the height of		the cherubim

6688	1041	904, 8761	881, 3872	5598.121	27.	8529
art, adj	art, n ms	prep, n ms	do, art, n mp	cj, v Qal impf 3ms		art, num
הַפְּנִימִי	הַבַּיִת	בְּתוֹךְ	אֶת־הַכְּרוּבִים	וַיִּתֵּן		הַשֵּׁנִי
happ^{e}nîmî	habbayith	b^{e}thôkh	'eth-hakk^{e}rûvîm	wayyittēn		hashshēnî
the inner	the Temple	in the middle of	the cherubim	and he put		the second

the turnings and the joints thereof artfully wrought and carvings projecting out, *Douay*.

19. And the oracle he prepared in the house within, to set there the ark of the covenant of the LORD: ... an inner shrine in the furthest recesses of the house to receive, *NEB* ... inner room at the back of the Temple to keep the Ark of the Agreement, *NCV* ... inner sanctuary within the temple, *Beck* ... where the LORD's Covenant Box was to be placed, *Good News*.

20. And the oracle in the forepart was twenty cubits in length, and twenty cubits in breadth, and twenty cubits in the height thereof: ... the surface of the Recess, *Fenton* ... inner room, *Goodspeed* ... inner sanctuary, *NASB*.

and he overlaid it with pure gold: ... plated over with clear gold, *BB* ... fine gold, *Beck* ... red gold, *NEB*.

and so covered the altar which was of cedar: ... altar of cedar-wood, plating it with gold, *BB*.

21. So Solomon overlaid the house within with pure gold: and he made a partition by the chains of gold before the oracle; and he overlaid it with gold: ... covered with gold, ... across in front of the inmost room, which itself was covered with gold, *BB* ... solid gold, *Berkeley* ... red gold and drew a Veil with golden chains across the front of the inner shrine, *NEB* ... interior of the temple ... He made in front of the sanctuary a cedar altar, *NAB* ... in front of the inner sanctuary, *NRSV*.

22. And the whole house he overlaid with gold, until he had finished all the house: also the whole altar that was by the oracle he overlaid with gold: ... covered the whole of the Temple with gold to the top. All ... that was opposite the Recess, were plated with gold, *Fenton* ... nothing in the temple that was not covered, *Douay* ... the Most Holy Place, was covered, *NCV* ... the whole altar by the inner shrine, *NEB* ... altar that belonged to the inner sanctuary, *NIV*.

23. And within the oracle he made two cherubims of olive tree, each ten cubits high: ... inner sanctuary, *RSV* ... inmost room he made two winged, *BB* ... inner room he made two angels, *Beck* ... inner shrine, *NEB* ... creatures were made of olive wood and placed in the Most Holy Place, *Good News*.

24. And five cubits was the one wing of the cherub, and five cubits the other wing of the cherub: from the uttermost part of the one wing unto the uttermost part of the other were ten cubits: ... With outstretched wings five cubits wide; the distance from the edge of one wing to the edge of the other was ten cubits, *BB* ... it was ten cubits from the tip of one wing to the tip of the other, *Goodspeed* ... from the extremity of one wing to the extremity of the other wing, *Douay*.

25. And the other cherub was ten cubits: both the cherubims were of one measure and one size: ... The two winged ones were ten cubits high, of the same size and form, *BB* ... Both angels had the same measurements and the same shape, *Beck* ... The shape of both was the same, *Fenton* ... the two cherubim were identical, *NIV* ... the measure, and the work was the same, *Douay*.

26. The height of the one cherub was ten cubits, and so was it of the other cherub: ... two of them were ten cubits high, *BB* ... height of one was the same as the other's, *JB* ... and in like manner the other cherub, *Douay*.

27. And he set the cherubims within the inner house: ... angels in the inner room of the temple, *Beck* ... so one's wings touched the other's wings, *Fenton* ... in the middle of the inner chamber, *JB* ... side by side in the Most Holy Place, *Good News*.

and they stretched forth the wings of the cherubims, so that the wing

---

and carved with palms, cherubim and open flowers. The partition was made of cedarwood. The floor of the whole house was made of cedar overlaid with gold. The interior of this "Oracle," as it was called—for the title "Holy of Holies" is of later origin—was, at any rate in the later temples, concealed by an embroidered veil of blue, purple and crimson, looped up with golden chains.

6:20–36. The Oracle, like the New Jerusalem of the Apocalypse, was a perfect cube, thirty feet broad and long and high, covered with gold, but shrouded in perpetual and unbroken darkness. No light was ever visible in it save such as was shed by the crimson gleam of the thurible of incense which the high priest carried into it once a year on the day of atonement.

In the center of the floor must apparently have risen the mass of rock which is still visible in the Mosque of Omar, from which it is called Al Sakhra, "the Dome of the Rock." Tradition pointed to it as the spot on which Abraham had laid for sacrifice the body of his son Isaac, when the angel restrained the descending knife. It was also the site of Araunah's threshing-floor and had been therefore hallowed by two angelic apparitions (2 Sam. 24:25; 1 Chr. 22:1; 2 Chr. 3:1). On it was deposited, with solemn ceremony the fearsome Ark of the Covenant, which had been preserved through the wanderings and wars of the Exodus and the troublous days of the Judges.

It contained the most sacred possession of the nation, the most priceless treasure which Israel

6816.126	881, 3796	3872	5236.122	3796, 259	904, 7306
cj, v Qal impf 3mp	do, *n fp*	art, n mp	cj, v Qal impf 3fs	*n fs*, art, num	prep, art, n ms
וַיִּפְרְשׂוּ	אֶת־כַּנְפֵי	הַכְּרֻבִים	וַתִּגַּע	כְּנַף־הָאֶחָד	בַּקִּיר
wayyiphr^{e}sû	'eth-kanphê	hakk^{e}ruvîm	wattigga'	k^{e}naph-hā'echādh	baqqîr
and they spread out	the wings of	the cherubim	and it touched	the wing of the one	on the wall

3796	3872	8529	5236.153	904, 7306	8529	3796
cj, *n fs*	art, n ms	art, num	v Qal act ptc fs	prep, art, n ms	art, num	cj, n fp, ps 3mp
וּכְנַף	הַכְּרוּב	הַשֵּׁנִי	נֹגַעַת	בַּקִּיר	הַשֵּׁנִי	וְכַנְפֵיהֶם
ûkh^{e}naph	hakk^{e}rûv	hashshēnî	nōgha'ath	baqqîr	hēshshēnî	w^{e}khanphêhem
and the wing of	the cherub	the second	touching	on the wall	the second	and their wings

420, 8761	1041	5236.154	3796	420, 3796		7099.321
prep, *n ms*	art, n ms	v Qal act ptc fp	n fs	prep, n fs		cj, v Piel impf 3ms
אֶל־תּוֹךְ	הַבַּיִת	נֹגְעֹת	כָּנָף	אֶל־כָּנָף	**28.**	וַיְצַף
'el-tôkh	habbayith	nōgh^{e}'ōth	kānāph	'el-kānāph		waytsaph
to the middle of	the Temple	touching	a wing	to a wing		and he overlaid with

881, 3872	2174		881	3725, 7306	1041	4672	7333.111	6855
do, art, n mp	n ms		cj, do	*adj, n mp*	art, n ms	adv	v Qal pf 3ms	*n mp*
אֶת־הַכְּרוּבִים	זָהָב	**29.**	וְאֵת	כָּל־קִירוֹת	הַבַּיִת	מֵסַב	קָלַע	פִּתּוּחֵי
'eth-hakk^{e}rûvîm	zāhāv		w^{e}'ēth	kol-qîrôth	habbayith	mēsav	qāla'	pittûchê
the cherubim	gold		and	all the walls of	the Temple	all around	he carved	carvings of

4897	3872	8891	6604.156	7001	4623, 3937, 6686
n fp	n mp	cj, n fp	cj, *v Qal pass ptc mp*	n mp	prep, prep, n mp
מִקְלְעוֹת	כְּרוּבִים	וְתִמֹרֹת	וּפְטוּרֵי	צִצִּים	מִלִּפְנִים
miqŏl'ôth	k^{e}rûvîm	w^{e}thimōrōth	ûph^{e}ṭûrê	tsitstsîm	milliphnîm
wood carvings of	cherubim	and palm trees	and made elaborate	blossoms	from to within

3937, 2535		881, 7463	1041	7099.311	2174	3937, 6687
cj, prep, art, adj		cj, do, *n ms*	art, n ms	v Piel pf 3ms	n ms	prep, prep
וְלַחִיצוֹן	**30.**	וְאֶת־קַרְקַע	הַבַּיִת	צִפָּה	זָהָב	לִפְנִימָה
w^{e}lachîtsôn		w^{e}'eth-qarqa'	habbayith	tsippāh	zāhāv	liphnîmāh
and to the outside		and the floor of	the Temple	he overlaid with	gold	to within

3937, 2535		881	6860	1735	6449.111	1878
cj, prep, art, adj		cj, do	*n ms*	art, n ms	v Qal pf 3ms	*n fp*
וְלַחִיצוֹן	**31.**	וְאֵת	פֶּתַח	הַדְּבִיר	עָשָׂה	דַּלְתוֹת
w^{e}lachîtsôn		w^{e}'ēth	pethach	hadd^{e}vîr	'āsāh	dalthôth
and to the outside		and	the entrance of	the inmost room	he made	the doors of

6320, 8467	356	4331	2653		8692	1878	6320, 8467
n mp, n ms	art, n ms	n fp	num		cj, num	*n fp*	*n mp*, n ms
עֲצֵי־שָׁמֶן	הָאַיִל	מְזוּזוֹת	חֲמִשִׁית	**32.**	וּשְׁתֵּי	דַּלְתוֹת	עֲצֵי־שֶׁמֶן
'ătsê-shāmen	hā'ayil	m^{e}zûzôth	chămishîth		ûsh^{e}ttê	dalthôth	'ătsê-shemen
trees of olive oil	the post	doorposts	a fifth		and the two of	the doors of	trees of olive oil

7333.111	6142	4897	3872	8891	6604.156
cj, v Qal pf 3ms	prep, ps 3mp	*n fp*	n mp	cj, n fp	cj, *v Qal pass ptc mp*
וְקָלַע	עֲלֵיהֶם	מִקְלְעוֹת	כְּרוּבִים	וְתִמֹרוֹת	וּפְטוּרֵי
w^{e}qāla'	'ălêhem	miqŏl'ôth	k^{e}rûvîm	w^{e}thimōrôth	ûph^{e}ṭûrê
and he carved	on them	wood carvings of	cherubim	and palm trees	and made elaborate

7001	7099.111	2174	7574.521	6142, 3872	6142, 8891
n mp	cj, v Qal pf 3ms	n ms	cj, v Hiphil impf 3ms	prep, art, n fp	cj, prep, art, n fp
צִצִּים	וְצִפָּה	זָהָב	וַיָּרֶד	עַל־הַכְּרוּבִים	וְעַל־הַתִּמֹּרוֹת
tsitstsîm	w^{e}tsippāh	zāhāv	wayyāredh	'al-hakk^{e}rûvîm	w^{e}'al-hattimōrôth
blossoms	and he overlaid with	gold	and he beat down	on the cherubim	and on the palm trees

882, 2174		3772	6449.111	3937, 6860	2033	4331	6320, 8467
prep, art, n ms	**33.**	cj, adv	v Qal pf 3ms	prep, *n ms*	art, n ms	n fp	*n mp*, n ms
אֶת־הַזָּהָב		וְכֵן	עָשָׂה	לְפֶתַח	הַהֵיכָל	מְזוּזוֹת	עֲצֵי־שָׁמֶן
'eth-hazzāhāv		w^{e}khēn	'āsāh	l^{e}phethach	hahêkhāl	m^{e}zûzôth	'ătsê-shāmen
with the gold		and so	he made	for the entrance of	the Temple	doorposts	trees of olive oil

4623, 881	7536		8692	1878	6320	1293	8530	7029
prep, do	num	**34.**	cj, num	*n fp*	*n mp*	n mp	num	n mp
מֵאֵת	רְבִעִית		וּשְׁתֵּי	דַלְתוֹת	עֲצֵי	בְרוֹשִׁים	שְׁנֵי	צְלָעִים
mē'ēth	r^{e}vi'îth		ûsh^{e}ttê	dhalthôth	'ătsê	v^{e}rôshîm	sh^{e}nê	ts^{e}lā'îm
from	a fourth part		and the two of	the doors of	the trees of	cypresses	two	beams

1878	259	1591	8530	7335	1878	8529	1591		7333.111
art, n fs	art, num	n mp	cj, num	n mp	art, n fs	art, num	n mp	**35.**	cj, v Qal pf 3ms
הַדֶּלֶת	הָאַחַת	גְּלִילִים	וּשְׁנֵי	קְלָעִים	הַדֶּלֶת	הַשֵּׁנִית	גְּלִילִים		וְקָלַע
haddeleth	hā'achath	g^{e}lîlîm	ûsh^{e}nê	qōlā'îm	haddeleth	hashshēnîth	g^{e}lîlîm		w^{e}qāla'
the door	the one	pivots	and two	curtains	the door	the second	pivots		and he carved

of the one touched the one wall, and the wing of the other cherub touched the other wall; and their wings touched one another in the midst of the house: ... wings of the angels extended, *Beck* ... in the center of the house, *Berkeley* ... wings were spread out ... at the middle of the hall, wing touching wing, *Fenton* ... met in the middle of the chamber wing to wing, *JB.*

28. And he overlaid the cherubims with gold: ... winged ones were plated over, *BB* ... covered the angels, *Beck* ... two winged creatures, *Good News.*

29. And he carved all the walls of the house round about with carved figures of cherubims and palm trees and open flowers, within and without: ... All round the Temple ... rosettes, both inside and outside, *JB* ... all sides of both the inner and the outer rooms, *NAB* ... pictures of creatures with wings ... both the main room and the inner room, *NCV* ... inner and outer sanctuaries, *NKJV* ... into the walls, *Beck.*

30. And the floor of the house he overlaid with gold, within and without: ... covered the floors of both the inner and outer rooms of the temple, *NIV* ... both rooms, *NCV* ... the inner chamber and the outer, *NEB* ... sanctuaries, *NKJV.*

31. And for the entering of the oracle he made doors of olive tree: ... For the way into the inmost room, *BB* ... the entrance to the inner sanctuary, *Beck* ... inner room he made folding doors, *Goodspeed* ... door of the Debir with uprights of wild-olive wood, *JB* ... double door ... of the Most Holy Place, *Good News.*

the lintel and side posts were a fifth part of the wall: ... the arch and the door supports forming a five-sided opening, *BB* ... frame and the doorposts had five sides, *Beck* ... pilasters and doorposts formed a pentagonal, *Goodspeed* ... door jambs with five indented sections, *JB* ... top of the doorway was a pointed arch, *Good News.*

32. The two doors also were of olive tree; and he carved upon them carvings of cherubims and palm trees and open flowers: ... carvings very much projecting, *Douay* ... Creatures with wings, *NCV* ... cut designs of winged ones, *BB.*

and overlaid them with gold, and spread gold upon the cherubims, and upon the palm trees: ... overlaid with gold, which was also molded to, *NAB* ... pressing down the gold on the angels, *Beck* ... hammering the gold, *NEB.*

33. So also made he for the door of the temple posts of olive tree, a fourth part of the wall: ... he made square doorposts of olive wood for the entrance to the temple, *Berkeley* ... Similarly, he made uprights of wild-olive wood for the door of the Hekal, and door jambs with four indented sections, *JB* ... entrance to the nave, where the doorposts ... were rectangular, *NAB* ... sanctuary, *NKJV* ... main room a rectangular doorframe, *Good News.*

34. And the two doors were of fir tree: the two leaves of the one door were folding, and the two leaves of the other door were folding: ... of cypress wood, *Goodspeed* ... two leaves of juniper: one leaf had two ribs binding it, *JB* ... two panels comprised one folding door, *NKJV* ... pine, *NCV* ... each leaf having two swivel-pins, *NEB.*

35. And he carved thereon cherubims and palm trees and open flowers: and covered them with gold fitted upon the carved work: ... overlaid them with gold hammered evenly, *NIV* ... ornamented with designs of winged ones ... plated over, *BB* ... angels ... gold, evenly applying, *Beck* ... evenly spread over the engraved work, *Berkeley.*

36. And he built the inner court with three rows of hewed stone, and a row of cedar beams: ... walled off by means of three

3872	8891	6604.156	7001	7099.111	2174	3595.455
n mp	cj, n fp	cj, *v Qal pass ptc mp*	n mp	cj, v Qal pf 3ms	n ms	v Pual ptc ms
כְּרוּבִים	וְתִמֹּרוֹת	וּפְטֻרֵי	צִצִּים	וְצִפָּה	זָהָב	מְיֻשָּׁר
kerûvîm	wethimōrōth	ûpheṯurê	tsitstsîm	wetsippāh	zāhāv	meyushshār
cherubim	and palm trees	and made elaborate	blossoms	and he overlaid with	gold	smoothed

6142, 2806.455	36.	1161.121	881, 2793	6688	8421	3015
prep, art, v Pual ptc ms		cj, v Qal impf 3ms	do, art, n fs	art, adj	num	*n mp*
עַל־הַמְּחֻקֶּה		וַיִּבֶן	אֶת־הֶחָצֵר	הַפְּנִימִית	שְׁלֹשָׁה	טוּרֵי
'al-hammechuqqeh		wayyiven	'eth-hechātsēr	happenîmîth	shelōshāh	ṯûrê
on the engraved work		and he built	the court	the inner	three	rows of

1527	3015	3901.158	753	37.	904, 8523	7536	3354.411
n fs	cj, *n ms*	*v Qal pass ptc fp*	n mp		prep, art, n fs	art, num	v Pual pf 3ms
גָזִית	וְטוּר	כְּרֻתֹת	אֲרָזִים		בַּשָּׁנָה	הָרְבִיעִית	יֻסַּד
ghāzîth	weṯûr	keruthōth	'ărāzîm		bashshānāh	hārevî'îth	yussadh
squared stone	and a row of	cuttings of	cedars		in the year	the fourth	it was laid

1041	3176	904, 3505	2180	38.	904, 8523	259	6462
n ms	pn	prep, *n ms*	pn		cj, prep, n fs	art, num	num
בֵּית	יְהוָה	בְּיֶרַח	זִו		וּבַשָּׁנָה	הָאַחַת	עֶשְׂרֵה
bêth	yehwāh	beyerach	ziw		ûvashshānāh	hā'achath	'esrēh
the Temple of	Yahweh	in the month of	Ziv		and in the year	the one	ten

904, 3505	980	2000	2414	8454	3735.111	1041
prep, *n ms*	pn	pers pron	art, n ms	art, num	v Qal pf 3ms	art, n ms
בְּיֶרַח	בּוּל	הוּא	הַחֹדֶשׁ	הַשְּׁמִינִי	כָּלָה	הַבַּיִת
beyerach	bûl	hû'	hachōdhesh	hashshemînî	kālāh	habbayith
in the month of	Bul	it	the month	the eighth	it was finished	the Temple

3937, 3725, 1745	3937, 3725, 5122	1161.121	8124	8523
prep, *adj*, n mp, ps 3ms	cj, prep, *adj*, n ms, ps 3ms	cj, v Qal impf 3ms, ps 3ms	num	n fp
לְכָל־דְּבָרָיו	וּלְכָל־מִשְׁפָּטוֹ	וַיִּבְנֵהוּ	שֶׁבַע	שָׁנִים
lekhol-devārâv	ûlekhol-mishpāṯô	wayyivnēhû	sheva'	shānîm
with all its objects	and with all its directions	and he built it	seven	years

7:1	881, 1041	1161.111	8406	8421	6462	8523	3735.321
	cj, do, n ms, ps 3ms	v Qal pf 3ms	pn	num	num	n fs	cj, v Piel impf 3ms
	וְאֶת־בֵּיתוֹ	בָּנָה	שְׁלֹמֹה	שְׁלֹשׁ	עֶשְׂרֵה	שָׁנָה	וַיְכַל
	we'eth-bêthô	bānāh	shelōmōh	shelōsh	'esrēh	shānāh	waykhal
	but his house	he built	Solomon	three	ten	years	and he finished

881, 3725, 1041	2.	1161.121	881, 1041	3402	3976	4109
do, *adj*, n ms, ps 3ms		cj, v Qal impf 3ms	do, *n ms*	*n ms*	art, pn	num
אֶת־כָּל־בֵּיתוֹ		וַיִּבֶן	אֶת־בֵּית	יַעַר	הַלְּבָנוֹן	מֵאָה
'eth-kol-bêthô		wayyiven	'eth-bêth	ya'ar	hallevānôn	mē'āh
all his house		and he built	the house of	the forest of	the Lebanon	one hundred

527	775	2675	527	7621	8421	527	7253	6142
n fs	n ms, ps 3ms	cj, num	n fs	n ms, ps 3ms	cj, num	n fs	n fs, ps 3ms	prep
אַמָּה	אָרְכּוֹ	וַחֲמִשִּׁים	אַמָּה	רָחְבּוֹ	וּשְׁלֹשִׁים	אַמָּה	קוֹמָתוֹ	עַל
'ammāh	'ārekkô	wachmishshîm	'ammāh	rāchăbbô	ûshelōshîm	'ammāh	qômāthô	'al
cubits	its length	and fifty	cubits	its width	and thirty	cubits	its height	on

727	3015	6204	753	3901.158	753	6142, 6204
num	*n mp*	*n mp*	n mp	cj, *v Qal pass ptc fp*	n mp	prep, art, n mp
אַרְבָּעָה	טוּרֵי	עַמּוּדֵי	אֲרָזִים	וּכְרֻתוֹת	אֲרָזִים	עַל־הָעַמּוּדִים
'arbā'āh	ṯûrê	'ammûdhê	'ărāzîm	ûkheruthôth	'ărāzîm	'al-hā'ammûdhîm
four	rows of	the pillars of	cedars	and cuttings of	cedars	on the pillars

courses, *NAB* ... polished stones, *Douay* ... dressed stone and one course of lengths of cedar, *NEB* ... enclosed by walls, *NCV* ... one course of trimmed, *NIV* ... finished cedar, *Beck*.

37. In the fourth year was the foundation of the house of the LORD laid, in the month Zif: ... base of the house was put in its place, *BB* ... fourth year of Solomon's reign, *Beck* ... began the structure ... month Ziu, *Fenton* ... Temple was laid in the second month, the month of Ziv, *Good News* ... founded, *Douay*.

38. And in the eleventh year, in the month Bul, which is the eighth month, was the house finished throughout all the parts thereof, and according to all the fashion of it. So was he seven years in building it: ... built exactly as it was planned, *NCV* ... in all its details and according to all its plans, *NKJV* ... specifications, *NIV* ... complete in every detail, as it had been designed, *BB* ... the Temple, *JB*.

7:1. But Solomon was building his own house thirteen years, and he finished all his house: ... it was complete, *BB* ... palace, *Moffatt* ... finished his entire house, *Goodspeed* ... construction, *NAB* ... brought it to perfection, *Douay*.

2. He built also the house of the forest of Lebanon; the length thereof was an hundred cubits, and the breadth thereof fifty cubits, and the height thereof thirty cubits, upon four rows of cedar pillars, with cedar beams upon the pillars: ... columns, over which were laid lengths, *NEB* ... supporting trimmed cedar, *NIV* ... Woods of Lebanon, *BB* ... palace, *Beck* ... constructed of Lebanese lumber, *Berkeley*.

---

guarded for the world. This treasure was the two tables of the Ten Commandments, engraved (in the anthropomorphic language of the ancient record) by the actual finger of God; the tables which Moses had shattered on the rocks of Mount Sinai as he descended to the backsliding people (1 Ki. 8:9).

The Ark was covered with its lid or "mercy seat," overshadowed by the wings of two small cherubim; but Solomon had prepared for its reception a new and far more magnificent covering, in the form of two colossal cherubim, fifteen feet high, of which each expanded wing was seven and one-half feet long. These wings touched the outer walls of the Oracle and also touched each other over the center of the Ark.

Such was the Temple. It was the "forum, fortress, university, and sanctuary" of the Jews and the transitory emblem of the Church of Christ's kingdom. It was destined to occupy a large share in the memory, and even in the religious development, of the world, because it became the central point around which crystallized the entire history of the chosen people. The kings of Judah are henceforth estimated with almost exclusive reference to the relation in which they stood to the centralized worship of Yahweh.

6:37–38. But for all this, Solomon's temple only took seven and a half years to build; but, as we shall see, its objects were wholly different from those of the great shrines today. The wealth lavished upon it needed but little repair. It stood for more than four centuries.

7:1–51. *Chapter seven appears in the narrative as a part of a complex on the glorification of Solomon. This section begins, in 3:1, immediately at the conclusion of the succession narrative (2:46). After describing Solomon's piety (3:3–15), wisdom (3:16–28), and power (4:1–5:18), the writer goes on to record the building of the Temple and palace (chs. 6–7). Chapter eight recounts the elaborate ceremonies performed in dedication of the Temple, and include a portrait of Solomon functioning as priest, offering sacrifice and uttering a priestly prayer of dedication and blessing. Chapters 9 and 10 report the positive responses of God and man to all these activities. Seen in such a context, the building of the Temple and palace complex should be understood as Solomon's crowning glory, the highest expressions of his royal piety, wisdom and power.*

Although the account of the building of Solomon's temple might appear to the modern Christian and the detailed descriptions and long lists of utensils might strike the believer on this side of the cross as irrelevant, yet there are many things which can be learned and applied to the life of faith. Beside the normal explanatory comments expected in a commentary of this sort, it is to these things that we will also direct our attention.

7:1. The verse begins with the Hebrew word wᵉ (HED #2134), which usually means "and." The NASB incorrectly translates this word with the temporal "now." The NIV translates it as a contrastive, and the KJV provides the clearest sense of the author's intentions by using the word "but." What is being contrasted here is the length of time Solomon spent on his own "house" as opposed to the time he spent on the LORD's "house." The author appears to offer a very subtle commentary here on the slowly declining state of Solomon's priorities. This suggestion is further supported by the fact that the same

3.	5802.155	904, 753	4623, 4762	6142, 7029	866	6142, 6204
	cj, v Qal pass ptc ms	prep, art, n ms	prep, prep	prep, art, n fp	rel part	prep, art, n mp
	וְסָפֻן	בָּאָרֶז	מִמַּעַל	עַל־הַצְּלָעֹת	אֲשֶׁר	עַל־הָעַמּוּדִים
	wesāphun	bā'erez	mimma'al	'al-hatstselā'ōth	'āsher	'al-hā'ammûdhîm
	and covered	with the cedar	from above	on the side chambers	which	on the pillars

727	2675	2675	6461	3015	4.	8627	8421	3015
num	cj, num	num	num	art, n ms		cj, n mp	num	n mp
אַרְבָּעִים	וַחֲמִשָּׁה	חֲמִשָּׁה	עָשָׂר	הַטּוּר		וּשְׁקֻפִים	שְׁלֹשָׁה	טוּרִים
'arbā'îm	wachmishshāh	chămishshāh	'āsār	hattûr		ûshequphîm	shelōshāh	ṯûrîm
forty	and five	five	ten	the row		and slants	three	rows

4372	420, 4372	8421	6718	5.	3725, 6860	4331
cj, n fs	prep, n fs	num	n fp		cj, *adj*, art, n mp	cj, art, n fp
וּמֶחֱזָה	אֶל־מֶחֱזָה	שָׁלֹשׁ	פְּעָמִים		וְכָל־הַפְּתָחִים	וְהַמְּזוּזוֹת
ûmechĕzāh	'el-mechĕzāh	shālōsh	pe'āmîm		wekhol-happethāchîm	wehammezûzôth
and a window	to a window	three	times		and all the entrances	and the doorposts

7541.156	8626	4272	4372	420, 4372	8421	6718	6.	881
v Qal pass ptc mp	n ms	cj, prep	n fs	prep, n fs	num	n fp		cj, do
רְבֻעִים	שָׁקֶף	וּמוּל	מֶחֱזָה	אֶל־מֶחֱזָה	שָׁלֹשׁ	פְּעָמִים		וְאֵת
revu'îm	shāqeph	ûmûl	mechĕzāh	'el-mechĕzāh	shālōsh	pe'āmîm		we'ēth
squared	slanting	and at the front of	a window	to a window	three	times		and

197	6204	6449.111	2675	527	775	8421	527
n ms	art, n mp	v Qal pf 3ms	num	n fs	n ms, ps 3ms	cj, num	n fs
אוּלָם	הָעַמּוּדִים	עָשָׂה	חֲמִשִּׁים	אַמָּה	אָרְכּוֹ	וּשְׁלֹשִׁים	אַמָּה
'ûlām	hā'ammûdhîm	'āsāh	chămishshîm	'ammāh	'ārekkô	ûshelōshîm	'ammāh
the porch of	the pillars	he made	fifty	cubits	its length	and thirty	cubits

7621	197	6142, 6686	6204	5853	6142, 6686
n ms, ps 3ms	cj, n ms	prep, n mp, ps 3mp	cj, n mp	cj, n ms	prep, n mp, ps 3mp
רָחְבּוֹ	וְאוּלָם	עַל־פְּנֵיהֶם	וְעַמֻּדִים	וְעָב	עַל־פְּנֵיהֶם
rāchăbbô	we'ûlām	'al-penêhem	we'ammudhîm	we'āv	'al-penêhem
its width	and a porch	opposite their faces	and pillars	and a thicker pillar	opposites their faces

7.	197	3802	866	8570.121, 8427	197	5122
	cj, *n ms*	art, n ms	rel part	v Qal impf 3ms, adv	*n ms*	art, n ms
	וְאוּלָם	הַכִּסֵּא	אֲשֶׁר	יִשְׁפָּט־שָׁם	אֻלָם	הַמִּשְׁפָּט
	we'ûlām	hakkissē'	'āsher	yishpāṯ-shām	'ulām	hammishpāṯ
	and the porch of	the throne	where	he would judge there	the porch of	the judgment

3. And it was covered with cedar above upon the beams, that lay on forty-five pillars, fifteen in a row: … with colonnades of cedar, and cedar beams upon the pillars, with a cedar ceiling over the verandahs, *Fenton* … upper part was panelled with cedar right down to the tie-beams, *JB* … beams resting on, *NAB* … roofed … forty-five rafters, *NRSV*.

4. And there were windows in three rows, and light was against light in three ranks: … window frames … and window opposite window in three tiers, *RSV* … corresponded to each other at three levels, *REB* … window-frames, window facing window in every line, *BB* … in strict alignment, *NAB* … On each of the two side walls there were, *Good News*.

5. And all the doors and posts were square, with the windows: and light was against light in three ranks: … squared artistic frames, and window was opposite window, *NASB* … window corresponded to window at three levels, *NEB* … rectangular frames; … tiers, *NKJV* … squared copings, *Fenton* … faced the opposite rows, *Good News*.

6. And he made a porch of pillars; the length thereof was fifty cubits, and the breadth thereof thirty cubits: and the porch was before them: and the other pillars and the thick beam were before them: … columns and a cornice in front of them, *Goodspeed* … Colonnade, *JB* … extended the width of the columned hall, and there was a canopy in front, *NAB* … Hall of Pillars: … a portico, *NKJV* … an overhanging roof, *NIV*.

7. Then he made a porch for the throne where he might judge, even

author informs us that merely one of the four wings (the "forest of Lebanon," 7:2) of the royal complex is twice as large as the entire Temple (6:2). Further, Solomon furnished his palace, the royal complex, with cedar (7:2f, 7f, 12) in imitation of the grandeur of the Temple (6:9f, 15f, 18, 20). Finally, Solomon made sure that his royal domicile was in no way inferior to the dwelling of the LORD by making them equal in height (6:2; 7:2; this is especially significant in this culture, which emphasized the importance of height in matters involving the deity—"high places," terminology like "high and lifted up" [Isa. 6:1], Assyrian ziggurats, etc.). Even certain aspects of the palace are specifically compared to corresponding elements of the Temple (7:12).

The Hebrew term bāyith (HED #1041) usually means simply "house." There are numerous other nuances of the term, however, including "temple," "pagan shrine," "dynasty" and "palace." Here the word takes on the secondary meaning "palace." The author could have employed more technical terms such as hêkhal (HED #2033) or 'armôn (HED #783), but chose bāyith possibly to draw an even closer connection between the Temple and the palace which rivaled it in splendor and size.

The detail of thirteen years is especially significant, since it informs the reader that Solomon expended almost *twice* the time on his own dwelling as he did on the dwelling of the Most High God.

Untranslated in NIV, but correctly rendered "entire" in NRSV and "all [of]" in KJV, the phrase, "*all of* his house," refers to the four wings of the royal complex. These wings are named in 7:2, 6ff.

Verse 2 begins the passage that describes the palace complex of the king. The reader should note that the chronicler excised this passage in his account of the acts of King Solomon. It is our opinion that the chronicler viewed the opulence of the palace complex and its obvious competition with the glory of the Temple to be unflattering to the persona of Solomon (cf. the previous discussion on the function of the contrastive "but" in v. 1).

The detail which is employed in its description, as well as that of the Temple and its furnishings, is unparalleled in Scripture with the exception of the Tabernacle. In addition, the account is loaded with technical architectural terms. This has led many commentators to suggest that these phenomena are due to the author's access to royal archives which contained billing and inventory lists. We therefore have here an opportunity to make an important observation about the nature of biblical historiography. Although many have come to view the historical reports of the Bible with the same skepticism which is attached to legends like King Arthur or Robin Hood, the evidence consistently argues to the contrary. Often, biblical authors make use of written sources contemporary with the events they describe (the "Book of Jasher," Josh. 10:13 and 2 Sam. 1:18; the "Chronicles of the Kings of Israel," 1 Ki. 14:19 and 15:31, etc.; the "Chronicles of the Kings of Judah," 1 Ki. 14:29 and 15:7, etc.; the "Chronicles of King David," 1 Chr. 27:24; the "Acts of Solomon," 1 Ki. 11:41; the "Book of Samuel the Seer" and the "Book of Nathan the Prophet," 1 Chr. 29:29 and 2 Chr. 9:29; the "Book of Shemiah the Prophet," 2 Chr. 12:15; and the "Midrash of the Prophet Iddo," 2 Chr. 13:22). The historians in the Bible have done their homework. The accounts given are reliable, often based on official archival materials. The discoveries of archeology have also vindicated innumerable historical accounts contained in the Bible. The point is this: the Bible is not a book of make-believe. Nor is it a book of mysterious symbols and hidden knowledge available only to the initiated. Finally, it is not to be written off as vain philosophical or theological speculations divorced from reality. The Bible is the self-revelation of God to man given within the parameters of time and space. The Bible, therefore, is necessarily connected to history, not divorced from it. True biblical faith is faith which rests firmly on God's historic acts of salvation on our behalf (cf. Paul's comments on this very issue in 1 Cor. 15:1–20). We dare not lose this distinctive of the Judeo-Christian heritage, lest we risk assuming the nebulous, relative, world- and reality-denying worldview which characterizes most cults and world religions.

7:2–5. The "House of the Forest of Lebanon." This large hall was so named because of the many cedar pillars (forty-five) which supported the building. Where the modern versions read "four rows," we suggest reading "three rows," in deference to the Greek. This would then give three rows of fifteen pillars, which corresponds to the total number (forty-five) given in the text. The function of this hall is unclear. The Arabic version suggests that its purpose was to serve as an armory (cf. also 1 Ki. 10:17; 2 Chr. 9:16). Some commentators, noting the size and imposing architectural features, have suggested that the "Forest of Lebanon" served as an ante-chamber, or waiting room, intended to impress guests with Solomon's wealth, power and wisdom even before

6449.111	5802.155	904, 753	4623, 7463	5912, 7463		1041
v Qal pf 3ms	cj, v Qal pass ptc ms	prep, art, n ms	prep, art, n ms	prep, art, n ms		cj, n ms, ps 3ms
עָשָׂה	וְסָפוּן	בָּאָרֶז	מֵהַקַּרְקַע	עַד־הַקַּרְקָע	8.	וּבֵיתוֹ
‘āsāh	w^{e}sāphûn	bā'erez	mēhaqqarqa‘	‘adh-haqqarqā‘		ûvêthô
he made	and being covered	with the cedar	from the floor	unto the floor		and his house

866, 3553.121	8427	2793	311	4623, 1041	3937, 197	3626, 4801
rel part, v Qal impf 3ms	adv	n ms	art, adj	prep, *n ms*	prep, art, n ms	prep, art, n ms
אֲשֶׁר־יֵשֶׁב	שָׁם	חָצֵר	הָאַחֶרֶת	מִבֵּית	לָאוּלָם	כַּמַּעֲשֶׂה
'ăsher-yēshev	shām	chātsēr	hā'achereth	mibbêth	lā'ûlām	kamma‘ăseh
where he would dwell	there	the court	the other	from the house of	the porch	like the work

2172	2030.111	1041	6449.121	3937, 1351, 6799	866	4089.111
art, dem pron	v Qal pf 3ms	cj, n ms	v Qal impf 3ms	prep, *n fs*, pn	rel pron	v Qal pf 3ms
הַזֶּה	הָיָה	וּבַיִת	יַעֲשֶׂה	לְבַת־פַּרְעֹה	אֲשֶׁר	לָקַח
hazzeh	hāyāh	ûvayith	ya‘ăseh	l^{e}vath-par‘ōh	'ăsher	lāqach
the this	it was	and a house	he made	for the daughter of Pharaoh	whom	he took

8406	3626, 197	2172		3725, 431	63	3479	3626, 4201
pn	prep, art, n ms	art, dem pron		*adj*, dem pron	n fp	adj	prep, *n fp*
שְׁלֹמֹה	כָּאוּלָם	הַזֶּה	9.	כָּל־אֵלֶּה	אֲבָנִים	יְקָרֹת	כְּמִדֹּת
sh^{e}lōmōh	kā'ûlām	hazzeh		kol-'ēlleh	'ăvānîm	y^{e}qārōth	k^{e}middōth
Solomon	like the porch	the this		all these	stones	costly	like the measurements of

1527	1688.458	904, 4190	4623, 1041	4623, 2445	4623, 4676
n fs	v Poal ptc fp	prep, art, n fs	prep, n ms	cj, prep, n ms	cj, prep, n ms
גָּזִית	מְגֹרָרוֹת	בַּמְּגֵרָה	מִבַּיִת	וּמִחוּץ	וּמִמַּסָּד
gāzîth	m^{e}ghōrārôth	bamm^{e}ghērāh	mibbayith	ûmichûts	ûmimmassādh
a squared stone	being sawed	with the saw	from inside	and from outside	and from the foundation

5912, 3056	4623, 2445	5912, 2793	1448		3354.455
prep, art, n mp	cj, prep, n ms	prep, art, n fs	art, adj		cj, v Pual ptc ms
עַד־הַטְּפָחוֹת	וּמִחוּץ	עַד־הֶחָצֵר	הַגְּדוֹלָה	10.	וּמְיֻסָּד
‘adh-hatt^{e}phāchôth	ûmichûts	‘adh-hechātsēr	hagg^{e}dhôlāh		ûm^{e}yussādh
unto the coping	and from outside	unto the court	the great		and a completely laid foundation

63	3479	63	1448	63	6460	527	63	8470	527
n fp	adj	n fp	adj	*n fp*	num	n fp	cj, *n fp*	num	n fp
אֲבָנִים	יְקָרוֹת	אֲבָנִים	גְּדֹלוֹת	אַבְנֵי	עֶשֶׂר	אַמּוֹת	וְאַבְנֵי	שְׁמֹנֶה	אַמּוֹת
'ăvānîm	y^{e}qārôth	'ăvānîm	g^{e}dhōlôth	'avnê	‘eser	'ammôth	we'avnê	sh^{e}mōneh	'ammôth
stones	costly	stones	great	stones of	ten	cubits	and stones of	eight	cubits

the porch of judgment: and it was covered with cedar from one side of the floor to the other: … throne hall, the Hall of Justice, *NIV* … Hall of the Throne where he was to pronounce, *NRSV* … rafters, *RSV* … Portico of Judgement, *REB* … decide court cases, *Beck* … covered room for his high seat when he gave decisions, *BB*.

8. And his house where he dwelt had another court within the porch, which was of the like work. Solomon made also an house for Pharaoh's daughter, whom he had taken to wife, like unto this porch: … other than that of the porch of judgment but of the same workmanship, *Berkeley* … Beside this palace, where he resided, a court was behind the Palatial-hall, *Fenton* … farther back, *Goodspeed* … living quarters, in the other court and inwards from the Hall, were of the same construction, *JB* … Hall of Judgment … same kind of house for his wife, *Good News*.

9. All these were of costly stones, according to the measures of hewed stones, sawed with saws, within and without, even from the foundation unto the coping, and so on the outside toward the great court: … buildings were of fine stones, hewn to size and trimmed front and back … to the bonding course, *NAB* … structures, from the outside to the great courtyard and from foundation to eaves, were made of blocks of high-grade stone cut to size and trimmed with a saw on their inner and outer faces, *NIV* … were constructed, *Berkeley* … special stones, *JB*.

10. And the foundation was of costly stones, even great stones, stones of ten cubits, and stones of

meeting the great king. On the basis of the wording of 1 Ki. 10:21 and 2 Chr. 9:20, it is possible that this large structure was used at times as a banquet hall.

7:6. The hall of pillars and its porch is the second building of the royal complex. This indeed probably served as a waiting room for individuals awaiting an audience with the king, whether for judgment or to pay a court visit. Therefore, it may have been located directly adjacent to the hall of judgment (cf. v. 7).

7:7. The reading "from floor to ceiling" adopted by the NIV is preferred over that of the KJV, RSV and others, "from floor to floor." The Latin Vulgate and the Peshitto support this correction of the Masoretic text.

The creation of a specific edifice on a grand scale for the purpose of judging would appear to make common sense. Most modern readers of Scripture are acquainted with such court buildings in their own contexts. Nevertheless, for this very reason this passage of Scripture is valuable to us beyond the historical/architectural information it yields. When Solomon built this magnificent court building, it was not for utilitarian purposes alone. The mere building of a specific structure for judgment was a breach of a time-honored tradition. From early times, the Israelite leader held court in accessible, unintimidating surroundings (Moses, Deborah, etc.). The city gate is specifically mentioned as one such spot (2 Sam. 15:2; Amos 5:15). Solomon's example for such a judgment hall came not from his Israelite predecessors, but rather from the pagan nations of the ancient Near East. Therefore, it would appear that Solomon was more interested in impressing his audiences than in making himself accessible to the nation. In this light, it should be noted that this "courtroom" also doubled as a throne room. Indeed, this appears to be the function emphasized by the biblical author, as its title was "the Hall of the Throne." In this manner, the writer gives us yet another indication of the subtle changes taking place in the priorities of Solomon, which culminated in the full-blown sins of ch. 11. From this we must learn to never "give place"—give opportunity to the tempter (cf. Eph. 4:27)—even in the small things.

7:8. The phrase, "His house," refers to the royal residence proper. All the preceding was simply preparatory. The exquisite furnishings of the ancillary buildings and the detail in which they are described make the author's job easy at this point. He is able to supply the shorthand phrase "of the same workmanship" to show that even as no effort or expense was spared on the aforementioned wings of the royal complex, so the royal palace was equally magnificent.

A palace similar in grandeur to his own was constructed for his first wife, the daughter of the king of Egypt. She is first introduced in 3:1, which describes the marriage as part of a political arrangement. Although his relationship was intended to cultivate peace and increase Solomon's power, it eventually proved to be a major part of Solomon's undoing. The precedent this marriage alliance established opened the door to many other such arrangements (11:1). The clear command of God was that the king not multiply wives (Deut. 17:17). Further, such relationships had at their core a self-reliance, a trusting in man for peace and protection. Such a self-centered, thus man-centered, approach eventually fails, as man is not reliable and trustworthy like God. In addition, it displays a lack of faith in and contempt for the LORD, our Protector and Provider. Just as it is for us, it was a short step for Solomon to go deeper in sin (11:2–10) and eventually bring God's wrath and the division of the kingdom (11:11ff). The initial step down this road was taken in 3:1. The building of a house for this woman in such proximity to the very Temple of God and even rivaling it in glory was an ominous sign of bad things to come for Solomon and his kingdom.

7:9–12. Costly stones ... cut according to measure, sawed with saws. Normally in buildings of this nature, stone masons formed stones by use of a hammer and chisel. Such exquisite work was required in this project, however, that the more accurate and aesthetically pleasing method of cutting the soft limestone with saws was employed. Again, it is telling that this procedure is not specifically mentioned in connection with the building of the Temple (cf. 6:7, which suggests that the more conventional method of hammer and chisel was used in the construction of the Temple). The fact that this was a very costly process is repeated three times (vv. 9ff).

The creation of the furnishings for the Temple consumes the remainder of the chapter. It should be noted that the Temple itself had already been built. The work done by Hiram, therefore, had nothing to do with the Temple building itself, but rather with the objects of metal used in decoration and in temple worship.

11.	4623, 3937, 4762	63	3479	3626, 4201	1527	753
	cj, prep, prep, prep	n fp	adj	prep, *n fp*	n fs	cj, n ms
	וּמִלְמַעְלָה	אֲבָנִים	יְקָרוֹת	כְּמִדּוֹת	גָּזִית	וָאָרֶז
	ûmilma‘ălāh	'ăvānîm	yeqārôth	kemiddôth	gāzîth	wā'ārez
	and from above	stones	costly	like the measurements of	a squared stone	and cedar

12.	2793	1448	5623	8421	3015	1527	3015
	cj, n fs	art, adj	adv	num	n mp	n fs	cj, *n ms*
	וְחָצֵר	הַגְּדוֹלָה	סָבִיב	שְׁלֹשָׁה	טוּרִים	גָּזִית	וְטוּר
	wechātsēr	haggedhôlāh	sāvîv	shelōshāh	ṭûrîm	gāzîth	weṭûr
	and the court	the great	all around	three	rows	squared stones	and a row of

3918.158	753	3937, 2793	1041, 3176	6688
v Qal pass ptc fp	n mp	cj, prep, *n fs*	*n ms*, pn	art, adj
כְּרֻתֹת	אֲרָזִים	וְלַחֲצַר	בֵּית־יְהוָה	הַפְּנִימִית
keruthōth	'ărāzîm	welachtsar	bêth-yehwāh	happenîmîth
cuttings of	cedars	and for the court of	the Temple of Yahweh	the inner

3937, 197	1041	**13.**	8365.121	4567	8406	4089.121
cj, prep, *n ms*	art, n ms		cj, v Qal impf 3ms	art, n ms	pn	cj, v Qal impf 3ms
וּלְאֻלָם	הַבָּיִת		וַיִּשְׁלַח	הַמֶּלֶךְ	שְׁלֹמֹה	וַיִּקַּח
ûlā'ulām	habbāyith		wayyishlach	hammelekh	shelōmōh	wayyiqqach
and for the porch of	the building		and he sent	the king	Solomon	and he took

880, 2538	4623, 7145	**14.**	1158, 828	496	2000	4623, 4431	5503
do, pn	prep, pn		*n ms*, n fs	n fs	pers pron	prep, *n ms*	pn
אֶת־חִירָם	מִצֹּר		בֶּן־אִשָּׁה	אַלְמָנָה	הוּא	מִמַּטֵּה	נַפְתָּלִי
'eth-chîrām	mitstsōr		ben-'ishshāh	'almānāh	hû'	mimmaṭṭēh	naphtālî
Hiram	from Tyre		the son of a woman	a widow	he	from the tribe of	Naphtali

1	382, 7158	2896.151	5361	4527.221	882, 2551
cj, n ms, ps 3ms	*n ms*, pn	v Qal act ptc ms	n fs	cj, v Niphal impf 3ms	prep, art, n fs
וְאָבִיו	אִישׁ־צֹרִי	חֹרֵשׁ	נְחֹשֶׁת	וַיִּמָּלֵא	אֶת־הַחָכְמָה
we'āvîw	'îsh-tsōrî	chōrēsh	nechōsheth	wayyimmālē'	'eth-hachokhmāh
and his father	a man of the Tyrians	an engraver	bronze	and he was filled	with the wisdom

882, 8722	882, 1907	3937, 6449.141	3725, 4536	904, 5361
cj, prep, art, n fs	cj, prep, art, n fs	prep, v Qal inf con	*adj*, n fs	prep, art, n fs
וְאֶת־הַתְּבוּנָה	וְאֶת־הַדַּעַת	לַעֲשׂוֹת	כָּל־מְלָאכָה	בַּנְּחֹשֶׁת
we'eth-hattevûnāh	we'eth-hadda‘ath	la‘ăsôth	kol-melā'khāh	bannechōsheth
and with the skill	and with the knowledge	to make	all craftsmanship	with the bronze

971.121	420, 4567	8406	6449.121	881, 3725, 4536	**15.**	6961.121
cj, v Qal impf 3ms	prep, art, n ms	pn	cj, v Qal impf 3ms	do, *adj*, n fs, ps 3ms		cj, v Qal impf 3ms
וַיָּבוֹא	אֶל־הַמֶּלֶךְ	שְׁלֹמֹה	וַיַּעַשׂ	אֶת־כָּל־מְלַאכְתּוֹ		וַיָּצַר
wayyāvô'	'el-hammelekh	shelōmōh	wayya‘as	'eth-kol-mela'khettô		wayyātsar
and he came	to the king	Solomon	and he made	all his craftsmanship		and he molded

881, 8530	6204	5361	8470	6462	527	7253	6204	259
do, num	art, n mp	n fs	num	num	n fs	*n fs*	art, n ms	art, num
אֶת־שְׁנֵי	הָעַמּוּדִים	נְחֹשֶׁת	שְׁמֹנֶה	עֶשְׂרֵה	אַמָּה	קוֹמַת	הָעַמּוּד	הָאֶחָד
'eth-shenê	hā‘ammûdhîm	nechōsheth	shemōneh	‘esrēh	'ammāh	qômath	hā‘ammûdh	hā'echādh
the two of	the pillars	bronze	eight	ten	cubits	the height of	the pillar	the one

2432	8692, 6462	527	5621.121	881, 6204	8529	**16.**	8692
cj, *n ms*	num, num	n fs	v Qal impf 3ms	do, art, n ms	art, num		cj, num
וְחוּט	שְׁתֵּים־עֶשְׂרֵה	אַמָּה	יָסֹב	אֶת־הָעַמּוּד	הַשֵּׁנִי		וּשְׁתֵּי
wechûṭ	shettêm-‘esrēh	'ammāh	yāsōv	'eth-hā‘ammûdh	hashshēnî		ûshettê
and a cord of	twelve	cubits	he put around	the pillar	the second		and two

eight cubits: ... the base was of great masses of highly priced stone, *BB* ... expensive stones, large stones, *Berkeley* ... huge stones, *JB* ... huge blocks, enormous blocks, *Moffatt* ... fine, large blocks, *NAB* ... heavy stones, massive blocks, *NEB*.

11. And above were costly stones, after the measures of hewed stones, and cedars: ... Overhead were highly priced stones cut to measure, *BB* ... expensive stones, *Berkeley* ... special stones, *JB* ... On top of these foundation stones, *NCV* ... above were heavy stones dressed to measure, *NEB* ... high-grade stone cut to size, *NIV*.

12. And the great court round about was with three rows of hewed stones, and a row of cedar beams, both for the inner court of the house of the LORD: ... courses of dressed stone to one layer of cedar beams all around, *NRSV* ... dressed stone and a series of cedar rafters, *Berkeley* ... a bonding course, *NAB* ... great courtyard was surrounded by a wall, *NIV*.

and for the porch of the house: ... vestibule, *NRSV* ... portico, *NIV*.

13. And king Solomon sent and fetched Hiram out of Tyre: ... brought, *NKJV* ... brought from Tyre, *NAB* ... Huram brought to him, *NCV* ... asked for a man named Huram, *NLT* ... invited and received, *NRSV* ... craftsman living in the city, *Good News*.

14. He was a widow's son of the tribe of Naphtali, and his father was a man of Tyre, a worker in brass: ... a native, *Beck* ... Tyrian bronze worker, *Berkeley* ... an artisan in bronze, *NRSV* ... no longer living ... a skilled bronze craftsman, *Good News*.

and he was filled with wisdom, and understanding, and cunning to work all works in brass: ... A craftsman in bronze, wise, adroit and skilful at doing a brazier's work, *Darby* ... knowledge and an expert worker, *BB* ... coppersmith with great intelligence, understanding, and skill for all kinds of craftsmanship, *Beck* ... for making any work in bronze, *RSV* ... talented, and skilled, *Berkeley*.

And he came to king Solomon, and wrought all his work: ... summoned him, *Darby* ... did all his work for him, *BB* ... invitation to be in charge, *Good News*.

15. For he cast two pillars of brass, of eighteen cubits high apiece: and a line of twelve cubits did compass either of them about: ... hollow bronze columns were cast ... in circumference; their metal was of four fingers' thickness, *NAB* ... cast in a mould, *NEB* ... surrounding, *Fenton* ... would encircle it, *NRSV*.

16. And he made two chapiters of molten brass, to set upon the tops of the pillars: the height of the one chapiter was five cubits, and the height of the other chapiter was five cubits: ... two capitals of solid copper, *NEB* ... cast bronze, *NKJV* ... molten bronze, *NRSV* ... melted

---

7:13–14. The Hiram here is called Huram-Abi in 2 Chr. 2:13 and 4:16. He is surely not the Hiram who ruled Tyre (5:1; Tyre was an important Phoenician seaport). Verse 14 describes this Hiram as the son of a widow woman from the tribe of Naphtali who was married to a man of Tyre. Second Chronicles 2:14 intimates that he was a member of the tribe of Dan. By combining these two descriptions, we understand that this Hiram/Huram-Abi was the product of the union of a woman of Dan and a man of Naphtali, and thus Hiram is technically numbered among the tribe of Naphtali. (It should come as no surprise that a Danite would marry a member of the tribe of Naphtali. Such interaction was probably commonplace, for whereas the tribe of Dan had originally been allotted an area much further south, at some time after the death of Samson, the tribe of Dan was forced to migrate [Judg. 18:1]. They eventually settled at the foot of Mt. Hermon, on the northeast corner of the tribal allotment of Naphtali [Judg. 18:7, 27ff]). However, the father died, so the woman remarried a man of Tyre (a Phoenician) and relocated there. Most commentators suggest that this genealogical information is given to explain how an individual from Phoenicia came to be involved in the furnishing of the Temple.

The description of Hiram's professional skills (cf. the expanded version in 2 Chr. 2:14) appears to draw a connection between Hiram and Bezalel (Exo. 31:3), the craftsman who was instrumental in the construction of the Temple's predecessor, the Tabernacle.

7:15–22. The creation of the two bronze pillars. These two pillars were only decorative. They stood alone, supporting no part of the Temple proper. Indeed, according to the Greek account and Jer. 52:21, they were hollow. Although many commentators have sought to attach various symbolic meanings to these pillars (fertility, even phallic symbols), it appears that this was simply the architectural style for temples in the Near East at that time. This phenomenon has been discovered in temples at Shechem, Khorsabad, and throughout Asia and Babylonia. Perhaps more importantly, examples have also been unearthed at the sites of Tyre and Byblos, both in Phoenicia. Nevertheless, it is interesting that in Ezekiel's vision of a purified temple, no such constructions are described. It is therefore

3934	6449.111	3937, 5598.141	6142, 7513	6204	3441.655	5361
n fp	v Qal pf 3ms	prep, v Qal inf con	prep, *n mp*	art, n mp	*v Hophal ptc ms*	n fs
כֹתָרֹת	עָשָׂה	לָתֵת	עַל־רָאשֵׁי	הָעַמּוּדִים	מֻצָק	נְחֹשֶׁת
khōthārōth	‘āsāh	lāthēth	‘al-rā’shê	hā‘ammûdhîm	mutsaq	nechōsheth
capitals	he made	to put	on the tops of	the pillars	being poured	bronze

2675	527	7253	3934	259	2675	527	7253	3934
num	n fp	*n fs*	art, n fs	art, num	cj, num	n fp	*n fs*	art, n fs
חָמֵשׁ	אַמּוֹת	קוֹמַת	הַכֹּתֶרֶת	הָאֶחָת	וְחָמֵשׁ	אַמּוֹת	קוֹמַת	הַכֹּתֶרֶת
chāmēsh	’ammôth	qômath	hakkōthereth	hā’echāth	wechāmēsh	’ammôth	qômath	hakkōthereth
five	cubits	the height of	the capital	the first	and five	cubits	the height of	the capital

8529		7877	4801	7877	1463	4801	8663	3937, 3934	866
art, num	**17.**	n mp	*n ms*	n fs	adj	*n ms*	n fp	prep, art, n fp	rel part
הַשֵּׁנִית		שְׂבָכִים	מַעֲשֵׂה	שְׂבָכָה	גְּדִלִים	מַעֲשֵׂה	שַׁרְשְׁרוֹת	לַכֹּתָרֹת	אֲשֶׁר
hashshēnîth		sevākhîm	ma‘ăsēh	sevākhāh	gedhilîm	ma‘ăsēh	sharsherôth	lakkōthārōth	’ăsher
the second		netting	work of	netting	tassels	work of	chains	for the capitals	that

6142, 7513	6204	8124	3937, 3934	259	8124	3937, 3934
prep, *n ms*	art, n mp	num	prep, art, n fs	art, num	cj, num	prep, art, n fs
עַל־רֹאשׁ	הָעַמּוּדִים	שִׁבְעָה	לַכֹּתֶרֶת	הָאֶחָת	וְשִׁבְעָה	לַכֹּתֶרֶת
‘al-rō’sh	hā‘ammûdhîm	shiv‘āh	lakkōthereth	hā’echāth	weshiv‘āh	lakkōthereth
on the tops of	the pillars	seven	for the capital	the first	and seven	for the capital

8529		6449.121	881, 6204	8530	3015	5623	6142, 7877
art, num	**18.**	cj, v Qal impf 3ms	do, art, n mp	cj, num	n mp	adv	prep, art, n fs
הַשֵּׁנִית		וַיַּעַשׂ	אֶת־הָעַמּוּדִים	וּשְׁנֵי	טוּרִים	סָבִיב	עַל־הַשְּׂבָכָה
hashshēnîth		wayya‘as	’eth-hā‘ammûdhîm	ûshenê	tûrîm	sāvîv	‘al-hassevākhāh
the second		and he made	the pillars	and two	rows	all around	on the netting

259	3937, 3803.341	881, 3934	866	6142, 7513	7705	3772
art, num	prep, v Piel inf con	do, art, n fp	rel part	prep, *n ms*	art, n mp	cj, adv
הָאֶחָת	לְכַסּוֹת	אֶת־הַכֹּתָרֹת	אֲשֶׁר	עַל־רֹאשׁ	הָרִמֹּנִים	וְכֵן
hā’echāth	lekhassôth	’eth-hakkōthārōth	’ăsher	‘al-rō’sh	hārimmōnîm	wekhēn
the first	to cover	the capitals	that	on the tops of	the pomegranates	and so

6449.111	3937, 3934	8529		3934	866	6142, 7513	6204
v Qal pf 3ms	prep, art, n fs	art, num	**19.**	cj, n fp	rel part	prep, *n ms*	art, n mp
עָשָׂה	לַכֹּתֶרֶת	הַשֵּׁנִית		וְכֹתָרֹת	אֲשֶׁר	עַל־רֹאשׁ	הָעַמּוּדִים
‘āsāh	lakkōthereth	hashshēnîth		wekhōthārōth	’ăsher	‘al-rō’sh	hā‘ammûdhîm
he made	for the capital	the second		and the capitals	that	on the tops of	the pillars

4801	8236	904, 197	727	527		3934	6142, 8530
n ms	n ms	prep, art, n ms	num	n fp	**20.**	cj, n fp	prep, num
מַעֲשֵׂה	שׁוּשַׁן	בָּאוּלָם	אַרְבַּע	אַמּוֹת		וְכֹתָרֹת	עַל־שְׁנֵי
ma‘ăsēh	shûshan	bā’ûlām	’arba‘	’ammôth		wekhōthārōth	‘al-shenê
a work of	a lily	on the porch	four	cubits		and the capitals	on the two of

6204	1612, 4623, 4762	4623, 3937, 6202	1027	866	3937, 5885	7877
art, n mp	cj, prep, prep	prep, prep, *n fs*	art, n fs	rel part	prep, *n ms*	art, n fs
הָעַמּוּדִים	גַּם־מִמַּעַל	מִלְּעֻמַּת	הַבֶּטֶן	אֲשֶׁר	לְעֵבֶר	ַשְּׂבָכָה
hā‘ammûdhîm	gam-mimma‘al	mille‘ummath	habbeten	’ăsher	le‘ēver	haassevākhāhh
the pillars	also from above	from to beside	the knob	which	to the side of	the netting

7705	4109	3015	5623	6142	3934	8529
cj, art, n mp	num	n mp	adv	prep	art, n fs	art, num
וְהָרִמּוֹנִים	מָאתַיִם	טֻרִים	סָבִיב	עַל	הַכֹּתֶרֶת	הַשֵּׁנִית
wehārimmônîm	mā’thayim	turîm	sāvîv	‘al	hakkōthereth	hashshēnîth
and the pomegranates	two hundred	rows	all around	on	the capital	the second

21.

7251.521	881, 6204	3937, 197	2033	7251.521
cj, v Hiphil impf 3ms	do, art, n mp	prep, *n ms*	art, n ms	cj, v Hiphil impf 3ms
וַיָּקֶם	אֶת־הָעַמֻּדִים	לְאֻלָם	הַהֵיכָל	וַיָּקֶם
wayyāqem	'eth-hā'ammudhîm	l^{e}'ulām	hahêkhāl	wayyāqem
and he erected	the pillars	at the porch of	the Temple	and he erected

881, 6204	3332	7410.121	881, 8428	3308	7251.521	881, 6204
do, art, n ms	art, adj	cj, v Qal impf 3ms	do, n ms, ps 3ms	pn	cj, v Hiphil impf 3ms	do, art, n ms
אֶת־הָעַמּוּד	הַיְמָנִי	וַיִּקְרָא	אֶת־שְׁמוֹ	יָכִין	וַיָּקֶם	אֶת־הָעַמּוּד
'eth-hā'ammûdh	haymānî	wayyiqŏrā'	'eth-sh^{e}mô	yākhîn	wayyāqem	'eth-hā'ammûdh
the pillar	the right	and he called	its name	Jachin	and he erected	the pillar

copper, *KJVII* ... made two crowns ... of brass made soft in the fire, *BB* ... to place, *Fenton*.

17. And nets of checker work, and wreaths of chain work, for the chapiters which were upon the top of the pillars; seven for the one chapiter, and seven for the other chapiter: ... great woven chains for the crowns that were upon the heads of the columns, *Fenton* ... two sets of filigree to cover the moulding of the two capitals surmounting, *JB* ... network and twisted threads, *NASB* ... made two bands of ornamental network, in festoons of chain-work, *NEB* ... decorated with a design of interwoven chains, *Good News*.

18. And he made the pillars, and two rows round about upon the one network, to cover the chapiters that were upon the top, with pomegranates: ... pomegranates in two rows encircling each network to decorate the capitals on top of the pillars, *NIV* ... columns with two rows around each latticework, *NRSV* ... pomegranates in two rows all round, *REB* ... ornaments of apples; and two lines of apples ... the crowns of the pillars, *BB* ... one trelliswork, *Berkeley*.

and so did he for the other chapiter: ... He did the same for each capital, *NIV* ... two crowns in the same way, *BB*.

19. And the chapiters that were upon the top of the pillars were of lily work in the porch, four cubits: ... tiaras, *Fenton* ... capitals surrounding, *JB* ... shaped like lillies, and they were six feet tall, *NCV* ... vestibule, *NEB* ... hall, *NKJV* ... portico, *NIV*.

20. And the chapiters upon the two pillars had pomegranates also above, over against the belly which was by the network: and the pomegranates were two hundred in rows round about upon the other chapiter: ... capitals of both pillars, above the bowl-shaped part next to, *NIV* ... above the rounded projection that was beside the latticework, *NRSV* ... immediately above the cushion, extending beyond the network upwards, *REB* ... net-work pattern, which went the full round of the pillar, *Knox* ... crowns ... apples in lines round every crown, *BB*.

21. And he set up the pillars in the porch of the temple: and he set up the right pillar, and called the name thereof Jachin: and he set up the left pillar, and called the name thereof Boaz: ... at the portico, *NIV* ... columns were then erected adjacent to, *NAB* ... of the nave, *NASB* ... by the vestibule, *NKJV* ... at the doorway, *BB*.

---

possible that, like today, some ancients attached pagan symbolism to these pillars, and Ezekiel would have none of that.

According to v. 21, these pillars were located "in/at the porch of the nave," a relatively ambiguous description of placement. The Chronicles (2 Chr. 3:15) and Josephus (*Antiquities*, VIII:iii:4), however, help us to understand that this location was to be found directly in front of the front entry to the Temple.

Because of the brevity of the names "Jachin" and "Boaz" their meanings are not as clear as we would like them to be. Literally, they are to be translated, "It/He will establish/uphold" and "In it/him [is] strength," respectively. It is not clear whether the subject is the Temple, God, or Solomon. Most likely, the subject is God, and the names are shorthand for "God will establish the Temple/kingdom" and "God is the strength of the king/his people," respectively.

7:23–26. The creation of the "sea." Although the text does not specifically state it, the "sea" was also probably made of bronze. It was intended to correspond to the "sea" of the Tabernacle, which was also made of bronze. According to the dimensions given in v. 23, this container could hold between 10,000 and 11,000 gallons of water. It appears that its purpose was twofold. First, it served as a reservoir from which ten smaller containers were refilled (cf. vv. 37 and 38). Second, it served as a place for ritual bathing for priests prior to their service at the altar (2 Chr. 4:6; cf. Exo. 30:18–21). In this respect, the washing of the priests foreshadowed developments throughout the Intertestamental Period which culminated in the

7974	7410.121	881, 8428	1191		6142	7513	6204	4801
art, adj	cj, v Qal impf 3ms	do, n ms, ps 3ms	pn	**22.**	cj, prep	*n ms*	art, n mp	*n ms*
הַשְּׂמָאלִי	וַיִּקְרָא	אֶת־שְׁמוֹ	בֹּעַז		וְעַל	רֹאשׁ	הָעַמּוּדִים	מַעֲשֵׂה
hass^{e}mā'lî	wayyiqŏrā'	'eth-sh^{e}mô	bō'az		w^{e}'al	rō'sh	hā'ammûdhîm	ma'ăsēh
the left	and he called	its name	Boaz		and on	the top of	the pillars	work of

8236	8882.122	4536	6204		6449.121	881, 3328
n ms	cj, v Qal impf 3fs	*n fs*	art, n mp	**23.**	cj, v Qal impf 3ms	do, art, n ms
שׁוֹשָׁן	וַתִּתֹּם	מְלֶאכֶת	הָעַמּוּדִים		וַיַּעַשׂ	אֶת־הַיָּם
shôshān	wattittōm	m^{e}le'kheth	hā'ammûdhîm		wayya'as	'eth-hayyām
a lily	and it was finished	the craftsmanship of	the pillars		and he made	the sea

3441.655	6460	904, 527	4623, 8004	5912, 8004	5902	5623	2675
v Hophal ptc ms	num	prep, art, n fs	prep, n fs, ps 3ms	prep, n fs, ps 3ms	adj	adv	cj, num
מוּצָק	עֶשֶׂר	בָּאַמָּה	מִשְּׂפָתוֹ	עַד־שְׂפָתוֹ	עָגֹל	סָבִיב	וְחָמֵשׁ
mûtsāq	'eser	bā'ammāh	miss^{e}phāthô	'adh-s^{e}phāthô	'āghōl	s̱āvîv	w^{e}chāmēsh
being poured	ten	with the cubit	from its shore	unto its shore	round	all around	and five

904, 527	7253	7246	8421	904, 527	5621.121	881
prep, art, n fs	n fs, ps 3ms	cj, *n ms*	num	prep, art, n fs	v Qal impf 3ms	do, ps 3ms
בָּאַמָּה	קוֹמָתוֹ	וּקְוֵה	שְׁלֹשִׁים	בָּאַמָּה	יָסֹב	אֹתוֹ
bā'ammāh	qômāthô	ûqŏwēh	sh^{e}lōshîm	bā'ammāh	yās̱ōv	'ōthô
with the cubit	its height	and a line of	thirty	with the cubit	he put around	it

5623		6747	4623, 8809	3937, 8004	5623	5621.152	881
adv	**24.**	cj, n mp	prep, prep	prep, n fs, ps 3ms	adv	v Qal act ptc mp	do, ps 3ms
סָבִיב		וּפְקָעִים	מִתַּחַת	לִשְׂפָתוֹ	סָבִיב	סֹבְבִים	אֹתוֹ
s̱āvîv		ûph^{e}qā'îm	mittachath	lisphāthô	s̱āvîv	s̱ōv^{e}vîm	'ōthô
all around		and buds	from beneath	to its shore	all around	going around	it

6460	904, 527	5545.552	881, 3328	5623	8530	3015	6747
num	prep, art, n fs	v Hiphil ptc mp	do, art, n ms	adv	num	n mp	art, n mp
עֶשֶׂר	בָּאַמָּה	מַקִּפִים	אֶת־הַיָּם	סָבִיב	שְׁנֵי	טוּרִים	הַפְּקָעִים
'eser	bā'ammāh	maqqiphîm	'eth-hayyām	s̱āvîv	sh^{e}nê	ṯûrîm	happ^{e}qā'îm
ten	with the cubit	encircling	the sea	all around	two	rows	the buds

3441.156	904, 3441.157		6198.151	6142, 8530	6461	1267	8421
v Qal pass ptc mp	prep, v Qal pass ptc fs, ps 3ms	**25.**	v Qal act ptc ms	prep, num	num	n ms	num
יְצֻקִים	בִּיצֻקָתוֹ		עֹמֵד	עַל־שְׁנֵי	עָשָׂר	בָקָר	שְׁלֹשָׁה
y^{e}tsuqîm	bîtsuqāthô		'ōmēdh	'al-sh^{e}nê	'āsār	bāqār	sh^{e}lōshāh
being poured	when its being poured		standing	on two	ten	oxen	three

6680.152	7103	8421	6680.152	3328	8421	6680.152	5221
v Qal act ptc mp	n fs	cj, num	v Qal act ptc mp	n ms	cj, num	v Qal act ptc mp	n ms
פֹּנִים	צָפוֹנָה	וּשְׁלֹשָׁה	פֹּנִים	יָמָּה	וּשְׁלֹשָׁה	פֹּנִים	נֶגְבָּה
phōnîm	tsāphônāh	ûsh^{e}lōshāh	phōnîm	yāmmāh	ûsh^{e}lōshāh	pōnîm	neghbāh
facing	northward	and three	facing	westward	and three	facing	southward

8421	6680.152	4350	3328	6142	4623, 3937, 4767	3725, 268
cj, num	v Qal act ptc mp	n ms	cj, art, n ms	prep, ps 3mp	prep, prep, prep	cj, *adj*, n mp, ps 3mp
וּשְׁלֹשָׁה	פֹּנִים	מִזְרָחָה	וְהַיָּם	עֲלֵיהֶם	מִלְמָעְלָה	וְכָל־אֲחֹרֵיהֶם
ûsh^{e}lōshāh	pōnîm	mizrāchāh	w^{e}hayyām	'ălêhem	milmā'ălāh	w^{e}khol-'ăchōrêhem
and three	facing	eastward	and the sea	on them	from above	and all their backs

1041		5880	3056	8004	3626, 4801
n ms	**26.**	cj, n ms, ps 3ms	n ms	cj, n fs, ps 3ms	prep, *n ms*
בָּיְתָה		וְעָבְיוֹ	טֶפַח	וּשְׂפָתוֹ	כְּמַעֲשֵׂה
bāy^{e}thāh		w^{e}'āv^{e}yô	ṯephach	ûs^{e}phāthô	k^{e}ma'ăsēh
toward the inside		and its thickness	a handbreadth	and its shore	like a work of

8004, 3683	6776	8236	512	1352	3677.521
n fs, n fs	*n ms*	n ms	num	n ms	v Hiphil impf 3ms
שְׂפַת־כּוֹס	פֶּרַח	שׁוֹשָׁן	אַלְפַּיִם	בַּת	יָכִיל
s^{e}phath-kôs	perach	shôshān	'alpayim	bath	yākhîl
a brim of a cup	a blossom of	a lily	two thousand	baths	it had a capacity of

27.

6449.121	881, 4488	6460	5361	727	904, 527	775	4488
cj, v Qal impf 3ms	do, art, n fp	num	n fs	num	prep, art, n fs	n ms	art, n fs
וַיַּעַשׂ	אֶת־הַמְּכֹנוֹת	עֶשֶׂר	נְחֹשֶׁת	אַרְבַּע	בָּאַמָּה	אֹרֶךְ	הַמְּכוֹנָה
wayya'as	'eth-hamm^{e}khōnôth	'eser	n^{e}chōsheth	'arba'	bā'ammāh	'ōrekh	hamm^{e}khônāh
and he made	the bases	ten	bronze	four	with the cubit	length	the base

259	727	904, 527	7621	8421	904, 527	7253	28. 2172
art, num	cj, num	prep, art, n fs	n ms, ps 3fs	cj, num	prep, art, n fs	n fs, ps 3fs	cj, dem pron
הָאֶחָת	וְאַרְבַּע	בָּאַמָּה	רָחְבָּהּ	וְשָׁלֹשׁ	בָּאַמָּה	קוֹמָתָהּ	וְזֶה
hā'echāth	w^{e}'arba'	bā'ammāh	rāchăbbāhh	w^{e}shālōsh	bā'ammāh	qômāthāhh	w^{e}zeh
each one	and four	with the cubit	its width	and three	with the cubit	its height	and this

22. And upon the top of the pillars was lily work: so was the work of the pillars finished: ... a design of flowers, *BB* ... Last over the top of the columns he placed, *Fenton* ... in the shape of lilies, *NKJV* ... in lily pattern, *Knox*.

23. And he made a molten sea, ten cubits from the one brim to the other: it was round all about, and his height was five cubits: and a line of thirty cubits did compass it round about: ... He cast, too, a great round basin of molten work, *Knox* ... great metal water-vessel, ten cubits across from edge to edge, *BB* ... pool of cast metal, *Beck* ... an artificial sea ... circular in form, *Fenton* ... a cord thirty cubits long gave the measurement of its girth, *JB*.

24. And under the brim of it round about there were knobs compassing it, ten in a cubit, compassing the sea round about: the knobs were cast in two rows, when it was cast: ... edge of it, circling it all round for ten cubits, were two lines of flower buds, *BB* ... Rosebud decorations, *Berkeley* ... gourds surrounding the Sea, *JB* ... a graven work, *Douay* ... bronze plants which surrounded the bowl, *NCV* ... below its brim were ornamental buds, *NKJV*.

25. It stood upon twelve oxen, three looking toward the north, and three looking toward the west, and three looking toward the south, and three looking toward the east: and the sea was set above upon them, and all their hinder parts were inward: ... back parts pointed, *NKJV* ... Sea stood on twelve bulls, *NIV* ... mounted on, *REB* ... The basin stood on the figures, *Knox* ... turned to the middle of it, *BB*.

26. And it was an handbreadth thick, and the brim thereof was wrought like the brim of a cup, with flowers of lilies: ... thick as a man's open hand, and was curved like the edge of a cup, like the flower of a lily, *BB* ... Shaped like the bulb of a lily, *Beck* ... curving outward like the petals, *Good News*.

it contained two thousand baths: ... it would take, *BB* ... could hold two thousand measures, *JB*.

27. And he made ten bases of brass; four cubits was the length of one base, and four cubits the breadth thereof, and three cubits the height of it: ... ten wheeled bases, *BB* ... stands of bronze, *Goodspeed* ... pedestals, *Fenton* ... trolleys, *NEB* ... carts, *NKJV*.

28. And the work of the bases was on this manner: ... design of the

New Testament Period in the forms of Jewish ritual immersion and Christian baptism.

Verse 25 describes the base on which the bronze "sea" rested. It was comprised of the figures of twelve oxen, three facing each direction (cf. Num. 2:3–32). The number twelve must surely be representative of the twelve tribes (cf. Num. 7:3, 87). Although the view that these figures were fertility symbols (cf. Exo. 32; 1 Ki. 12:28) should be rejected, it is nevertheless unclear how the prohibitions of Exo. 20:4, Deut. 4:15–18, and 5:8 apply here. In later Judaism, these restrictions came to prohibit all artistic representations of animals and humans. Evidently, in the time of Solomon, these texts were understood to refer exclusively to idolatrous creations.

7:27–39. The creation of the ten bronze watercarts. The watercarts were made up of two parts: a movable "stand" (NIV) or "base" (KJV), and a "laver" (KJV) or "basin" (NIV). The workmanship of the stands is described in vv. 27–37; the description of the basins appears in vv. 38 and 39. Both were made of bronze. The purpose of the stands was for trans-

4801	4488	4675	3937	4675	1033	8343
n ms	art, n fs	n fp	prep, ps 3mp	cj, n fp	prep	art, n mp
מַעֲשֵׂה	הַמְּכוֹנָה	מִסְגְּרֹת	לָהֶם	וּמִסְגְּרֹת	בֵּין	הַשְׁלַבִּים
maʿăsēh	hammᵉkhônāh	mis̱gᵉrōth	lāhem	ûmis̱gᵉrōth	bên	hashlabbîm
the construction of	the base	frames	to them	and frames	between	the joints

	6142, 4675	866	1033	8343	761	1267	3872
29.	cj, prep, art, n fp	rel part	prep	art, n mp	n mp	n ms	cj, n mp
	וְעַל־הַמִּסְגְּרוֹת	אֲשֶׁר	בֵּין	הַשְׁלַבִּים	אֲרָיוֹת	בָּקָר	וּכְרוּבִים
	wᵉʿal-hammis̱gᵉrôth	'ăsher	bên	hashlabbîm	'ărāyôth	bāqār	ûkhᵉrûvîm
	and on the frames	that	between	the joints	the lions	oxen	and cherubim

6142, 8343	3772	4623, 4762	4623. 8809	3937, 761	3937, 1267	4049
cj, prep, art, n mp	adv	prep, prep	cj, prep, prep	prep, n mp	cj, prep, art, n ms	n fp
וְעַל־הַשְׁלַבִּים	כֵּן	מִמַּעַל	וּמִתַּחַת	לָאֲרָיוֹת	וְלַבָּקָר	לֹיוֹת
wᵉʿal-hashlabbîm	kēn	mimmāʿal	ûmittachath	la'ărāyôth	wᵉlabbāqār	lōyôth
and on the joints	so	from above	and from below	to the lions	and to the oxen	adjoinders

4801	4309		727	210	5361	3937, 4488	259
n ms	n ms	**30.**	cj, num	*n mp*	n fs	prep, art, n fs	art, num
מַעֲשֵׂה	מוֹרָד		וְאַרְבָּעָה	אוֹפַנֵּי	נְחֹשֶׁת	לַמְּכוֹנָה	הָאַחַת
maʿăsēh	môrādh		wᵉ'arbāʿāh	'ôphannê	nᵉchōsheth	lammᵉkhônāh	hā'achath
a work of	something beveled		and four	wheels of	bronze	to the base	each one

5837	5361	727	6718	3931	3937	4623, 8809	3937, 3715
cj, *n mp*	n fs	cj, num	n fp, ps 3ms	n fp	prep, ps 3mp	prep, prep	prep, art, n ms
וְסַרְנֵי	נְחֹשֶׁת	וְאַרְבָּעָה	פַּעֲמֹתָיו	כְּתֵפֹת	לָהֶם	מִתַּחַת	לַכִּיֹּר
wᵉs̱arnê	nᵉchōsheth	wᵉ'arbāʿāh	phaʿămōthâv	kᵉthēphōth	lāhem	mittachath	lakkîyōr
and axles of	bronze	and four	its feet	sides	to them	from beneath	to the laver

3931	3441.158	4623, 5885	382	4049		6552
art, n fp	v Qal pass ptc fp	prep, *n ms*	n ms	n fp	**31.**	cj, n ms, ps 3ms
הַכְּתֵפֹת	יְצֻקוֹת	מֵעֵבֶר	אִישׁ	לֹיוֹת		וּפִיהוּ
hakkᵉthēphōth	yᵉtsuqôth	mēʿēver	'îsh	lōyôth		ûphîhû
the sides	being poured	from the opposite side of	each	adjoinders		and its opening

4623, 1041	3937, 3934	4767	904, 527	6552	5902	4801, 3774
prep, n ms	prep, art, n fs	cj, adv	prep, art, n fs	cj, n ms, ps 3fs	adj	*n ms*, n ms
מִבֵּית	לַכֹּתֶרֶת	וָמַעְלָה	בָּאַמָּה	וּפִיהָ	עָגֹל	מַעֲשֵׂה־כֵן
mibbêth	lakkōthereth	wāmaʿălāh	bā'ammāh	ûphîāh	ʿāghōl	maʿăsēh-khēn
from inside	to the capital	and upward	with the cubit	and its opening	round	a work of a pedestal

527	2783	527	1612, 6142, 6552	4897	4675	7541.458
n fs	cj, *n ms*	art, n fs	cj, cj, prep, n ms, ps 3fs	n fp	cj, n fp, ps 3mp	v Pual ptc fp
אַמָּה	וַחֲצִי	הָאַמָּה	וְגַם־עַל־פִּיהָ	מִקְלָעוֹת	וּמִסְגְּרֹתֵיהֶם	מְרֻבָּעוֹת
'ammāh	wachtsî	hā'ammāh	wᵉgham-ʿal-pîāh	miqōlāʿôth	ûmis̱gᵉrōthêhem	mᵉrubbāʿôth
a cubit	and the half of	the cubit	and also on its opening	carvings	and their frames	squared

3940	5902		727	210	3937, 4623, 8809	3937, 4675	3135
neg part	adj	**32.**	cj, num	art, n mp	prep, prep, prep	prep, art, n fp	cj, *n fp*
לֹא	עֲגֻלּוֹת		וְאַרְבַּעַת	הָאוֹפַנִּים	לְמִתַּחַת	לַמִּסְגְּרוֹת	וִידוֹת
lō'	ʿăghullôth		wᵉ'arbaʿath	hā'ôphanîm	lᵉmittachath	lammis̱gᵉrôth	wîdhôth
not	round		and four	the wheels	to from beneath	to the frames	and the holders of

210	904, 4488	7253	210	259	527	2783
art, n mp	prep, art, n fs	cj, *n fs*	art, n fs	art, num	n fs	cj, *n ms*
הָאוֹפַנִּים	בַּמְּכוֹנָה	וְקוֹמַת	הָאוֹפַן	הָאֶחָד	אַמָּה	וַחֲצִי
hā'ôphanîm	bammᵉkhônāh	wᵉqômath	hā'ôphan	hā'echādh	'ammāh	wachtsî
the wheels	with the base	and the height of	the wheel	the one	a cubit	and the half of

527		4801	210	3626, 4801	210	4981
art, n fs	33.	cj, *n ms*	art, n mp	prep, *n ms*	*n ms*	art, n fs
הָאַמָּה		וּמַעֲשֵׂה	הָאוֹפַנִּים	כְּמַעֲשֵׂה	אוֹפַן	הַמֶּרְכָּבָה
hā'ammāh		ûma'ăsēh	hā'ôphanîm	kema'ăsēh	'ôphan	hammerkāvāh
the cubit		and the work of	the wheels	like a work of	the wheel of	the chariot

3135	1384	2947	2948	3725	3441.655
n fp, ps 3mp	cj, n mp, ps 3mp	cj, n mp, ps 3mp	cj, n mp, ps 3mp	art, n ms	v Hophal ptc ms
יְדוֹתָם	וְגַבֵּיהֶם	וְחִשֻּׁקֵיהֶם	וְחִשֻּׁרֵיהֶם	הַכֹּל	מוּצָק
yedhôthām	weghabbêhem	wechishshuqêhem	wechishshurêhem	hakkōl	mûtsāq
their holders	and their rims	and their spokes	and their hubs	everything	being poured

carts, *NKJV* ... stands were made, *NIV* ... stands were of embossed work, *Knox*.

they had borders, and the borders were between the ledges: ... panels were between frames, *NKJV* ... side panels attached to uprights, *NIV* ... moulding between the shafts, *Knox* ... sides were square, fixed in a framework, *BB* ... chassis set in, *Beck*.

29. And on the borders that were between the ledges were lions, oxen, and cherubims: ... crosspieces of the undercarriage were lions and bulls and winged creatures, *JB* ... On the sides were bronze lions, bulls, *NCV* ... moulding, too, between the upper and the lower rims, *Knox* ... with the ... on the panels, *Good News*.

and upon the ledges there was a base above: ... on top of the undercarriage was a support, *JB* ... the shafts above them the same pattern, *Knox*.

and beneath the lions and oxen were certain additions made of thin work: ... wreaths, was bevelled work, *Goodspeed* ... scrolls, *JB* ... in relief, *NAB* ... bands of brass hanging down, *Douay* ... hanging work, *NASB*.

30. And every base had four brasen wheels, and plates of brass: and the four corners thereof had undersetters: under the laver were undersetters molten, at the side of every addition: ... turning on brass rods, and their four angles had angle-plates under them; the angle-plates under the base were of metal, and there were ornaments, *BB* ... stand ... four legs with flanges on them beneath the basis. The flanges were made of cast metal with wreath-work on the sides, *Beck* ... bronze axles ... the supports under the eaves ... with rosettes, *Berkeley* ... corners were supports for a basin, *NRSV* ... Every cart, *NKJV*.

31. And the mouth of it within the chapiter and above was a cubit: ... inside the angle-plate was one cubit across, BB ... an opening from within to the crown on top, *Beck* ... cast each with a wreath and an opening from the inner side of the naves ... circumference of the mouth, *Fenton* ... where the shoulderings met to the top, *JB*.

but the mouth thereof was round after the work of the base, a cubit and an half: ... like a pillar, *BB* ... a pedestal, *Beck* ... a stand for a vessel, *JB* ... circular frame on top, *Good News*.

and also upon the mouth of it were gravings with their borders, foursquare, not round: ... corners round it there were engraved columns, and the space between them was filled by other columns, square, *Knox* ... had designs cut on it, *BB* ... around the opening there were engravings. The chassis, *Beck* ... coverings over the mouth with square indents, *Fenton*.

32. And under the borders were four wheels; and the axletrees of the wheels were joined to the base: and the height of a wheel was a cubit and half a cubit: ... below the paneling ... wheels and the stand were of one piece, *NAB* ... wheelforks were made in one piece with the trolleys, *NEB* ... joined to the cart, *NKJV* ... attached to the stand, *NIV* ... connected under the stand itself, *Knox*.

33. And the work of the wheels was like the work of a chariot wheel: their axletrees, and their naves, and

portation of the basins, which sat in a cradle on top of the stands (vv. 31, 35). The stands were therefore equipped with four large wheels, for the amount of water transported in the basins was far too heavy to be carried by hand. On the basis of the capacity and size given in v. 38, it has been determined that each basin was capable of holding 220 gallons of water.

These watercarts were refilled with water taken from the "sea" (cf. vv. 23–26 and commentary). The watercarts were then wheeled back to their stations, five on the north side of the Temple, and five on the south side of the Temple (v. 39). Although the purpose of these portable water sources is not clear from the account given by the writer of Kings, the chronicler informs us that as the priests had washed themselves in the sea, so they used the watercarts to wash burnt offerings (2 Chr. 4:6).

	727	3931	420	727	6682	4488	259	4623, 4488
34.	cj, num	n fp	prep	num	*n fp*	art, n fs	art, num	prep, art, n fs
	וְאַרְבַּע	כְּתֵפוֹת	אֶל	אַרְבַּע	פִּנּוֹת	הַמְּכֹנָה	הָאֶחָת	מִן־הַמְּכֹנָה
	w^{e}'arba'	k^{e}thēphôth	'el	'arba'	pinnôth	hamm^{e}khōnāh	hā'echāth	min-hamm^{e}khōnāh
	and four	sides	toward	four	corners	the base	each one	from the base

3931		904, 7513	4488	2783	527	7253	5902	5623
n mp, ps 3fs	**35.**	cj, prep, *n ms*	art, n fs	*n ms*	art, n fs	n fs	adj	adv
כְּתֵפֶיהָ		וּבְרֹאשׁ	הַמְּכוֹנָה	חֲצִי	הָאַמָּה	קוֹמָה	עָגֹל	סָבִיב
k^{e}thēphêāh		ûv^{e}rō'sh	hamm^{e}khônāh	chătsî	hā'ammāh	qômāh	'āghōl	sāvîv
its sides		and on the top of	the base	one half of	the cubit	height	round	all around

6142	7513	4488	3135	4675	4623		6858.321
cj, prep	*n ms*	art, n fs	n fp, ps 3fs	cj, n fp, ps 3fs	prep, ps 3fs	**36.**	cj, v Piel impf 3ms
וְעַל	רֹאשׁ	הַמְּכֹנָה	יְדֹתֶיהָ	וּמִסְגְּרֹתֶיהָ	מִמֶּנָּה		וַיְפַתַּח
w^{e}'al	rō'sh	hamm^{e}khōnāh	y^{e}dhōthêāh	ûmisg^{e}rōthêāh	mimmennāh		wayphattach
and on	the top of	the base	its holders	and its frames	from it		and he engraved

6142, 4008	3135	6142	4675	3872	761	8891
prep, art, *n mp*	n fp, ps 3fs	cj, prep	n fp, ps 3fs	n mp	n mp	cj, n fp
עַל־הַלֻּחֹת	יְדֹתֶיהָ	וְעַל	מִסְגְּרֹתֶיהָ	כְּרוּבִים	אֲרָיוֹת	וְתִמֹרֹת
'al-halluchōth	y^{e}dhōthêāh	w^{e}'al	wamisg^{e}rōthêāh	k^{e}rûvîm	'ărāyôth	w^{e}thimōrōth
on the boards	its holders	and on	its frames	cherubim	lions	and palm trees

3626, 4788, 382	4049	5623		3626, 2148	6449.111	881
prep, *n ms*, n ms	cj, n fp	adv	**37.**	prep, dem pron	v Qal pf 3ms	do
כְּמַעַר־אִישׁ	וְלֹיוֹת	סָבִיב		כָּזֹאת	עָשָׂה	אֵת
k^{e}ma'ar-'îsh	w^{e}lōyôth	sāvîv		kāzō'th	'āsāh	'ēth
according to the nakedness of each	and adjoinders	all around		like this	he made	

6460	4488	3441.655	259	4201	259	7379	259
num	art, n fp	v Hophal ptc ms	num	n fs	num	n ms	num
עֶשֶׂר	הַמְּכֹנוֹת	מוּצָק	אֶחָד	מִדָּה	אַחַת	קֶצֶב	אֶחָד
'eser	hamm^{e}khōnôth	mûtsāq	'echādh	middāh	'achath	qetsev	'echādh
ten	the bases	being poured	one	a measurement	one	a figure	one

3937, 3725		6449.121	6463	3715	5361	727	1352
prep, n ms, ps 3fp	**38.**	cj, v Qal impf 3ms	num	*n fp*	n fs	num	n ms
לְכֻלָּהְנָה		וַיַּעַשׂ	עֲשָׂרָה	כִּירוֹת	נְחֹשֶׁת	אַרְבָּעִים	בַּת
l^{e}khullāh^{e}nāh		wayya'as	'ăsārāh	khîyōrôth	n^{e}chōsheth	'arbā'îm	bath
for their entirety		and he made	ten	lavers of	bronze	forty	baths

3677.521	3715	259	727	904, 527	3715	259	3715
v Hiphil impf 3ms	art, n ms	art, num	num	prep, art, n fs	art, n ms	art, num	n ms
יָכִיל	הַכִּיּוֹר	הָאֶחָד	אַרְבַּע	בָּאַמָּה	הַכִּיּוֹר	הָאֶחָד	כִּיּוֹר
yākhîl	hakkîyôr	hā'echādh	'arba'	bā'ammāh	hakkîyôr	hā'echādh	kîyôr
it had a capacity of	the laver	the one	four	with the cubit	the laver	the one	a laver

259	6142, 4488	259	3937, 6460	4488		5598.121	881, 4488
num	prep, art, n fs	art, num	prep, num	art, n fp	**39.**	cj, v Qal impf 3ms	do, art, n fp
אֶחָד	עַל־הַמְּכֹנָה	הָאַחַת	לְעֶשֶׂר	הַמְּכוֹנוֹת		וַיִּתֵּן	אֶת־הַמְּכֹנוֹת
'echādh	'al-hamm^{e}khōnāh	hā'achath	l^{e}'eser	hamm^{e}khônôth		wayyittēn	'eth-hamm^{e}khōnôth
one	on the base	each one	for the ten of	the bases		and he put	the bases

2675	6142, 3931	1041	4623, 3332	2675	6142, 3931	1041
num	prep, *n fs*	art, n ms	prep, adj	cj, num	prep, *n fs*	art, n ms
חָמֵשׁ	עַל־כֶּתֶף	הַבַּיִת	מִיָּמִין	וְחָמֵשׁ	עַל־כֶּתֶף	הַבַּיִת
chāmēsh	'al-ketheph	habbayith	mîyāmîn	w^{e}chāmēsh	'al-ketheph	habbayith
five	on the side of	the Temple	from the right	and five	on the side of	the Temple

4623, 7974	881, 3328	5598.111	4623, 3931	1041	3332	7209
prep, n ms, ps 3ms	cj, do, art, n ms	v Qal pf 3ms	prep, *n fs*	art, n ms	art, adj	adv
מִשְּׂמֹאלוֹ	וְאֶת־הַיָּם	נָתַן	מִכֶּתֶף	הַבַּיִת	הַיְמָנִית	קֵדְמָה
miss^{e}mō'lô	w^{e}'eth-hayyām	nāthan	mikketheph	habbayith	haymānîth	qēdh^{e}māh
from its left	and the sea	he put	from the side of	the Temple	the right	eastward

4623, 4272	5221		6449.121	2538	881, 3715	881, 3381
prep, prep	pn	**40.**	cj, v Qal impf 3ms	pn	do, art, n mp	cj, do, art, n mp
מִמּוּל	נֶגֶב		וַיַּעַשׂ	חִירוֹם	אֶת־הַכִּיֹּרוֹת	וְאֶת־הַיָּעִים
mimmûl	neghev		wayya'as	chîrôm	'eth-hakkîyōrôth	w^{e}'eth-hayyā'îm
from facing	the south		and he made	Hiram	the lavers	and the shovels

their felloes, and their spokes, were all molten: ... made like carriage-wheels; the rods on which they were fixed, the parts forming their edges, their rods and the middle points of them, were all formed out of liquid metal, *BB* ... workmanship, *NASB* ... axles, rims, spokes, and hubs were all cast metal, *Beck* ... made of bronze, *NCV* ... molten bronze, *NLT*.

34. And there were four undersetters to the four corners of one base: ... supports ... of each stand, *RSV* ... handles, *REB* ... brackets, springing ... were of molten work, *Knox* ... angle-plates, *BB*.

and the undersetters were of the very base itself: ... supports were of one piece with the stands, *RSV* ... of one piece with the trolley, *REB* ... bottoms, *Tyndale* ... part of the stand itself, *Knox* ... forming part of the structure of, *BB*.

35. And in the top of the base was there a round compass of half a cubit high: ... stand there was a round band, *Beck* ... a round opening, *Goodspeed* ... circular in shape, *JB* ... a raised collar, *NAB* ... A strip of bronze around the top of each stand was nine inches deep, *NCV* ... cart ... it was perfectly round, *NKJV*.

and on the top of the base the ledges thereof and the borders thereof were of the same: ... supports which were of one piece with the chassis, *Beck* ... border-frames, *Goodspeed* ... lugs, *JB* ... panels which were of one piece, *NAB* ... cart, its flanges and its panels were of the same casting, *NKJV*.

36. For on the plates of the ledges thereof, and on the borders thereof, he graved cherubims, lions, and palm trees, according to the proportion of every one, and additions round about: ... wherever there was a clear space on each, with wreaths all around, *NKJV* ... on the surfaces of the supports and on the panels, in every available space, *NIV* ... blank space, with spiral work, *REB* ... on the surfaces of the handles, *KJVII* ... spaces of the flat sides and on the frames ... with ornamented edges, *BB*.

37. After this manner he made the ten bases: ... stands in the same way, *Beck* ... bronze for each stand was melted and poured into a mold, *NCV*.

all of them had one casting, one measure, and one size: ... cast in the same way with the same measurements and form, *Beck* ... identical in cast, size, and shape, *Berkeley* ... stands were the same, *NCV* ... cast alike, *NEB* ... same mold, *NKJV*.

38. Then made he ten lavers of brass: one laver contained forty baths: and every laver was four cubits: and upon every one of the ten bases one laver: ... bronze, *NKJV* ... basins, *NIV* ... each holding three hundred gallons, *Knox* ... washing-vessels, *BB* ... a capacity of 240 gallons, *Berkeley* ... Huram also made ten basins, one for each cart, *Good News*.

39. And he put five bases on the right side of the house, and five on the left side of the house: ... arranged the stands, *JB* ... trolleys, *NEB* ... carts, *NKJV*.

and he set the sea on the right side of the house eastward over against the south: ... placed off to the southeast from the south of the temple, *NAB* ... large bowl in the southeast corner of the Temple, *NCV*

40. And Hiram made the lavers, and the shovels, and the basins: ... sprinkling bowls, *NIV* ... Pot and shovel and bucket Hiram made, *Knox* ... spades, *BB*.

7:40a. The creation of the bronze altar objects. After the creation of the larger objects, such as the pillars, the sea, and the watercarts, Hiram produced the items needed for divine service at the altar. Although not stated in this text, it is clear from v. 45 that these utensils were also made of bronze. The purpose of the "basins," "shovel," and "bowls" is unclear to most Christian readers due to lack of familiarity with the sacrificial system. It is true that Jesus is the ultimate and final sacrifice, and that the sacrificial system described in the OT is now ineffective. Nevertheless, it remains the Word of God. Therefore, it is profitable to strengthen and inform

881, 4353	3735.321	2538	3937, 6449.141	881, 3725, 4536	866
cj, do, art, n mp	cj, v Piel impf 3ms	pn	prep, v Qal inf con	do, *adj*, art, n fs	rel part
וְאֶת־הַמִּזְרָקוֹת	וַיְכַל	חִירָם	לַעֲשׂוֹת	אֶת־כָּל־הַמְּלָאכָה	אֲשֶׁר
we'eth-hammizrāqôth	waykhal	chîrām	la'ăsôth	'eth-kol-hammelā'khāh	'ăsher
and the basins	and he finished	Hiram	to make	all the craftsmanship	that

6449.111	3937, 4567	8406	1041	3176	**41.**	6204	8530
v Qal pf 3ms	prep, art, n ms	pn	*n ms*	pn		n mp	num
עָשָׂה	לַמֶּלֶךְ	שְׁלֹמֹה	בֵּית	יְהוָה		עַמֻּדִים	שְׁנַיִם
'āsāh	lammelekh	shelōmōh	bêth	yehwāh		'ammudhîm	shenayim
he did	for the king	Solomon	the Temple of	Yahweh		pillars	two

1583	3934	866, 6142, 7513	6204	8692	7877	8692
cj, *n fp*	art, n fp	rel part, prep, *n ms*	art, n mp	num	cj, art, n fp	num
וְגֻלֹּת	הַכֹּתָרֹת	אֲשֶׁר־עַל־רֹאשׁ	הָעַמֻּדִים	שְׁתָּיִם	וְהַשְּׂבָכוֹת	שְׁתַּיִם
weghullōth	hakkōthārōth	'ăsher-'al-rō'sh	hā'ammudhîm	shettāyim	wehassevākhôth	shettayim
and the bowls of	the capitals	that on the tops of	the pillars	two	and the netting	two

3937, 3803.341	881, 8692	1583	3934	866	6142, 7513	6204
prep, v Piel inf con	do, num	*n fp*	art, n fp	rel part	prep, *n ms*	art, n mp
לְכַסּוֹת	אֶת־שְׁתֵּי	גֻּלֹּת	הַכֹּתָרֹת	אֲשֶׁר	עַל־רֹאשׁ	הָעַמּוּדִים
lekhassôth	'eth-shettê	gullōth	hakkōthārōth	'ăsher	'al-rō'sh	hā'ammûdhîm
to cover	the two of	the bowls of	the capitals	that	on the tops of	the pillars

42.	881, 7705	727	4109	3937, 8692	7877	8530, 3015
	cj, do, art, n mp	num	num	prep, num	art, n fp	num, n mp
	וְאֶת־הָרִמֹּנִים	אַרְבַּע	מֵאוֹת	לִשְׁתֵּי	הַשְּׂבָכוֹת	שְׁנֵי־טוּרִים
	we'eth-hārimmōnîm	'arba'	mē'ôth	lishtê	hassevākhôth	shenê-ṯûrîm
	and the pomegranates	four	hundreds	for the two of	the netting	two rows

7705	3937, 7877	259	3937, 3803.341	881, 8692	1583	3934
n mp	prep, art, n fs	art, num	prep, v Piel inf con	do, num	*n fp*	art, n fp
רִמֹּנִים	לַשְּׂבָכָה	הָאֶחָת	לְכַסּוֹת	אֶת־שְׁתֵּי	גֻּלֹּת	הַכֹּתָרֹת
rimmōnîm	lassevākhāh	hā'echāth	lekhassôth	'eth-shettê	gullōth	hakkōthārōth
pomegranates	for the netting	each one	to cover	the two of	the bowls of	the capitals

866	6142, 6686	6204	**43.**	881, 4488	6460	881, 3715	6463
rel part	prep, *n mp*	art, n mp		cj, do, art, n fp	num	cj, do, art, n mp	num
אֲשֶׁר	עַל־פְּנֵי	הָעַמּוּדִים		וְאֶת־הַמְּכֹנוֹת	עֶשֶׂר	וְאֶת־הַכִּירֹת	עֲשָׂרָה
'ăsher	'al-penê	hā'ammûdhîm		we'eth-hammekhōnôth	'eser	we'eth-hakkîyōrōth	'ăsārāh
that	opposite	the pillars		and the bases	ten	and the lavers	ten

6142, 4488	**44.**	881, 3328	259	881, 1267	8530, 6461	8809	3328
prep, art, n fp		cj, do, art, n ms	art, num	cj, do, art, n ms	num, num	prep	art, n ms
עַל־הַמְּכֹנוֹת		וְאֶת־הַיָּם	הָאֶחָד	וְאֶת־הַבָּקָר	שְׁנֵים־עָשָׂר	תַּחַת	הַיָּם
'al-hammekhōnôth		we'eth-hayyām	hā'echādh	we'eth-habbāqār	shenêm-'āsār	tachath	hayyām
on the bases		and the sea	the one	and the oxen	twelve	beneath	the sea

45.	881, 5707	881, 3381	881, 4353	881	3725, 3747	164	866
	cj, do, art, n fp	cj, do, art, n mp	cj, do, art, n mp	cj, do	*adj*, art, n mp	art, n ms	rel part
	וְאֶת־הַסִּירוֹת	וְאֶת־הַיָּעִים	וְאֶת־הַמִּזְרָקוֹת	וְאֵת	כָּל־הַכֵּלִים	הָאֹהֶל	אֲשֶׁר
	we'eth-hassîrôth	we'eth-hayyā'îm	we'eth-hammizrāqôth	we'ēth	kol-hakkēlîm	hā'ōhel	'ăsher
	and the pails	and the shovels	and the basins	and	all the utensils	the Tent	that

6449.111	2538	3937, 4567	8406	1041	3176	5361	4965.455
v Qal pf 3ms	pn	prep, art, n ms	pn	*n ms*	pn	n fs	v Pual ptc ms
עָשָׂה	חִירָם	לַמֶּלֶךְ	שְׁלֹמֹה	בֵּית	יְהוָה	נְחֹשֶׁת	מְמֹרָט
'āsāh	chîrām	lammelekh	shelōmōh	bêth	yehwāh	nechōsheth	memōrāṯ
he made	Hiram	for the king	Solomon	the Temple of	Yahweh	bronze	being burnished

So Hiram made an end of doing all the work that he made king Solomon for the house of the Lord: ... Huram finished all the work he had undertaken for King Solomon in the temple, *NIV* ... he was to do, *NKJV* ... all that king Solomon needed for the service, *Knox* ... had assigned him to make for the Temple, *NLT*.

41. The two pillars, and the two bowls of the chapiters that were on the top of the two pillars: ... two cups of the crowns, BB ... mouldings of the capitals, *Beck* ... bowl-like capitals, *Berkeley* ... two columns and the wreathed crowns, *Fenton* ... surrounding, *JB*.

and the two networks, to cover the two bowls of the chapiters which were upon the top of the pillars: ... two cups of the crowns, *BB* ... mouldings of the capitals, *Beck* ... trellisworks covering the two bowl-like capitals, *Berkeley* ... wreaths of the crowns which were on the tops of the columns, *Fenton* ... sets of filigree, *JB*.

42. And four hundred pomegranates for the two networks, even two rows of pomegranates for one network, to cover the two bowls of the chapiters that were upon the pillars: ... in double rows on both pieces ... two nodes of the capitals where they met the columns, *NAB* ... cords, *Douay* ... latticeworks, *NRSV* ... apples ... cups of the crowns, *BB* ... bronze pomegranates, *Good News*.

43. And the ten bases, and ten lavers on the bases: ... stands and the ten basins, *JB* ... with a bowl on each stand, *NCV* ... trolleys and the ten basins on the trolleys, *NEB* ... carts, and ten lavers on the carts, *NKJV* ... water carts, *NLT*.

44. And one sea, and twelve oxen under the sea: ... single great basin ... twelve oxen that supported it, *Knox* ... great water-vessel, *BB* ... the one pool with the 12 cattle, *Beck* ... large bowl with twelve bulls, *NCV* ... one tank, and the twelve bullocks, *Fenton*.

45. And the pots, and the shovels, and the basins: ... small bowls, and all the utensils for the Temple of the Lord, *NCV* ... bowls, NKJV ... bucket, *Knox* ... spades, *BB* ... ash containers, the scoops, and sprinkling bowls, *JB*.

---

our faith (2 Tim. 3:16). In addition, it gives us the background against which to better understand and appreciate the sacrifice of Christ and the way it fits into the redemptive plan of God. (The writer of Hebrews certainly used it in this way.) Finally, passages such as this, although they may not contain material immediately applicable to the life of the modern Christian, nevertheless usually preserve principles which are eternal and which are very much applicable to us today.

The "basins" here are not the "basins" transported by the watercarts. Rather, this item leads a list of materials connected directly to service on and around the altar. The creation of these utensils was evidently inspired by passages such as Exo. 27:3, 19 and 38:3. These passages show clearly that the "basins" were large pots used for boiling the flesh of thanksgiving/peace offerings (cf. Lev. 7:15); the "shovels" (along with the "shovels" and "braziers," cf. Exo. 27:3; 38:3) were used for tending and removing coals and ash from the altar; and the "bowls" (derived from the Hebrew root zāraq [HED #2323], literally, "to sprinkle," "to splash") were used to contain water and to catch blood for the purpose of sprinkling for purification and consecration (cf. Exo. 12:22; 24:6; Lev. 14:5ff, 50f; and more generally Exo. 29:16–21; Lev. 1:5, 11; 3:2, 8, 13; 4:6, 17; 7:2; 16:14f).

These bronze altar objects no longer exist. Even if they did, they would be of no practical use; especially for the Christian. Nevertheless, these Solomonic corollaries to the vessels used in the Tabernacle remind the Christian of some very important spiritual realities: (1) God makes sure we are properly equipped to do his will (Heb. 13:21, etc.); (2) God makes provision for the smaller or less significant things we need as well as the large things (cf. Phil. 4:19); and (3) the less significant things are indispensable—the whole cannot work without them (1 Cor. 12:22–26).

7:40b–47. The inventory of bronze objects. This material probably derived directly from a billing or inventory list available to the writer from the royal archives. It comprises a summary of items already described in the previous verses. Nevertheless, there are some helpful additional facts mentioned in this "shortlist" which were not included in the longer descriptions. (1) Mention has already been made of the fact that v. 45 helps us to understand that the "sea" and the "altar objects" were made of bronze. (2) Verse 46 informs us that the actual work of casting was not done inside the Temple, or even in Jerusalem. Rather, this work was accomplished near the Jordan River just below the Sea of Galilee. It is at this very location that the closest large clay deposit to Jerusalem lies (Smith, 488). Clay suitable for digging molds as well as a plentiful water source are essential in the type of casting used to create these objects. Amazingly, excavations in this area have uncovered evidence of intense metallurgical activity! When the

46.	904, 3724	3497	3441.111	4567	904, 4721	124
	prep, *n fs*	art, pn	v Qal pf 3ms, ps 3mp	art, n ms	prep, *n ms*	art, n fs
	בְּכִכַּר	הַיַּרְדֵּן	יְצָקָם	הַמֶּלֶךְ	בְּמַעֲבֵה	הָאֲדָמָה
	bekhikkar	hayyardēn	yetsāqām	hammelekh	bema'ăvēh	hā'ădhāmāh
	in the plain of	the Jordan	he poured them	the king	in the clay of	the ground

1033	5713	1033	7177	47.	5299.521	8406	881, 3725, 3747
prep	pn	cj, prep	pn		cj, v Hiphil impf 3ms	pn	do, *adj*, art, n mp
בֵּין	סֻכּוֹת	וּבֵין	צָרְתָן		וַיַּנַּח	שְׁלֹמֹה	אֶת־כָּל־הַכֵּלִים
bên	sukkôth	ûvên	tsārethān		wayyannach	shelōmōh	'eth-kol-hakkēlîm
between	Succoth	and between	Zarethan		and he allowed to rest	Solomon	all the utensils

4623, 7524	4108	4108	3940	2811.211	5129	5361
prep, n ms	adv	adv	neg part	v Niphal pf 3ms	*n ms*	art, n fs
מֵרֹב	מְאֹד	מְאֹד	לֹא	נֶחְקַר	מִשְׁקַל	הַנְּחֹשֶׁת
mērōv	me'ōdh	me'ōdh	lō'	nechqar	mishqal	hannechōsheth
because an abundance	very	very	not	it was searched out	the weight of	the bronze

48.	6449.121	8406	881	3725, 3747	866	1041	3176	881
	cj, v Qal impf 3ms	pn	do	*adj*, art, n mp	rel part	*n ms*	pn	do
	וַיַּעַשׂ	שְׁלֹמֹה	אֵת	כָּל־הַכֵּלִים	אֲשֶׁר	בֵּית	יְהוָה	אֵת
	wayya'as	shelōmōh	'ēth	kol-hakkēlîm	'ăsher	bêth	yehwāh	'ēth
	thus he made	Solomon		all the utensils	that	the Temple of	Yahweh	

4326	2174	881, 8374	866	6142	4035	6686	2174
n ms	art, n ms	cj, do, art, n ms	rel part	prep, ps 3ms	*n ms*	art, n mp	n ms
מִזְבַּח	הַזָּהָב	וְאֶת־הַשֻּׁלְחָן	אֲשֶׁר	עָלָיו	לֶחֶם	הַפָּנִים	זָהָב
mizbach	hazzāhāv	we'eth-hashshulchān	'ăsher	'ālâv	lechem	happānîm	zāhāv
the altar of	the gold	and the table	which	on it	the bread of	the presence	gold

49.	881, 4645	2675	4623, 3332	2675	4623, 7974	3937, 6686
	cj, do, art, n fp	num	prep, adj	cj, num	prep, adj	prep, *n mp*
	וְאֶת־הַמְּנֹרוֹת	חָמֵשׁ	מִיָּמִין	וְחָמֵשׁ	מִשְּׂמֹאול	לִפְנֵי
	we'eth-hammenōrôth	chāmēsh	mîyāmîn	wechāmēsh	missemō'wl	liphnê
	and the lampstands	five	from the right	and five	from the left	before

1735	2174	5646.155	6776	5552	4598	2174
art, n ms	n ms	v Qal pass ptc ms	cj, art, n ms	cj, art, n mp	cj, art, n md	n ms
הַדְּבִיר	זָהָב	סָגוּר	וְהַפֶּרַח	וְהַנֵּרֹת	וְהַמֶּלְקָחַיִם	זָהָב
haddevîr	zāhāv	sāghûr	wehapperach	wehannērōth	wehammelqachayim	zāhāv
the inmost room	gold	covered	and the flowers	and the lamps	and the snuffers	gold

50.	5789	4345	4353	3834	4426	2174	5646.155
	cj, art, n mp	cj, art, n fp	cj, art, n mp	cj, art, n fp	cj, art, n fp	n ms	v Qal pass ptc ms
	וְהַסִּפּוֹת	וְהַמְזַמְּרוֹת	וְהַמִּזְרָקוֹת	וְהַכַּפּוֹת	וְהַמַּחְתּוֹת	זָהָב	סָגוּר
	wehassippôth	wehamzammerôth	wehammizrāqôth	wehakkappôth	wehammachtôth	zāhāv	sāghûr
	and the bowls	and the hooks	and the basins	and the ladles	and the censers	gold	covered

6847	3937, 1878	1041	6688	3937, 7231	7231
cj, art, n fp	prep, *n fp*	art, n ms	art, adj	prep, *n ms*	art, n mp
וְהַפֹּתוֹת	לְדַלְתוֹת	הַבַּיִת	הַפְּנִימִי	לְקֹדֶשׁ	הַקֳּדָשִׁים
wehappōthôth	ledhalthôth	habbayith	happenîmî	leqōdhesh	haqqedhāshîm
and the forefront	for the doors of	the Temple	the inner	to the Holy Place of	the holy places

3937, 1878	1041	3937, 2033	2174	51.	8396.122	3725, 4536
prep, *n fp*	art, n ms	prep, art, n ms	n ms		cj, v Qal impf 3fs	*adj*, art, n fs
לְדַלְתֵי	הַבַּיִת	לַהֵיכָל	זָהָב		וַתִּשְׁלַם	כָּל־הַמְּלָאכָה
ledhalthê	habbayith	lahêkhāl	zāhāv		wattishlam	kol-hammelā'khāh
for the doors of	the Temple	to the Temple	gold		so it was completed	all the craftsmanship

and all these vessels, which Hiram made to king Solomon for the house of the LORD, were of bright brass: ... Huram made everything King Solomon wanted from polished bronze, *NCV* ... burnished bronze, *NKJV* ... appurtenances, *Knox* ... polished brass, *BB* ... Temple of Yahweh, *JB*.

46. In the plain of Jordan did the king cast them, in the clay ground between Succoth and Zarthan: ... soil of the Jordan valley, *Knox* ... made them of liquid metal in the lowland of Jordan, at the way across the river, at Adama, *BB* ... in the clay molds, *Berkeley* ... by process of sand casting, *JB* ... foundry, *REB*.

47. And Solomon left all the vessels unweighed, because they were exceeding many: neither was the weight of the brass found out: ... abundance of brass that was in them, *Tyndale* ... such a great number of them; it was not possible to get the weight, *BB* ... equipment ... nobody tried to find out how much the bronze weighed, *Beck* ... could not be ascertained because it was past counting, *Berkeley* ... could not be determined, *Goodspeed* ... was never known, *NCV*.

48. And Solomon made all the vessels that pertained unto the house of the LORD: ... items for the Temple of the Lord, *NCV* ... He made also all the furnishings, *NEB*.

the altar of gold, and the table of gold, whereupon the showbread was: ... the bread that shows God's people are in his presence, *NCV* ... Bread of the Presence, *NEB* ... hallowed loaves were set out, *Knox* ... holy bread was placed, *BB*.

49. And the candlesticks of pure gold, five on the right side, and five on the left, before the oracle: ... the lampstands, five to the right and five to the left of the sanctuary, were made of solid gold, *Berkeley* ... the lampstands ... in front of the Most Holy Place, *NCV* ... on the left side of the inner shrine, *NEB* ... the wick-trimmers, *NKJV* ... five on the south side and five on the north, before the inner sanctuary, *RSV*.

with the flowers, and the lamps, and the tongs of gold: ... the blossoms, the lights, *Berkeley* ... the lily-work, and the golden lamps that rested in them, *Knox*.

50. And the bowls, and the snuffers, and the basins, and the spoons, and the censers of pure gold: ... cups, snuffers, tossing-bowls, saucers, and firepans of red gold, *REB* ... the

---

Bible displays such reliability on "insignificant" matters of an historical nature, it is all the more easy to trust it when it speaks on spiritual matters (John 3:16; Rom. 3:23, etc.). On the surface, v. 47 might seem to suggest that the number and weight of these objects prevented Solomon from weighing them. This begs the question, however, if Solomon was so wise and powerful, and if Hiram had the skill to make such objects, why could they not devise a means by which to weigh them? In actuality, the statement is a common oriental means of emphasizing the overwhelming nature of the number of vessels and their combined weight (cf. similar statements in Gen. 16:10; 32:12; 41:49; Judg. 6:5; 7:12; 1 Ki. 3:8; 8:5; 2 Ki. 25:16; 1 Chr. 22:3, 16; 2 Chr. 5:6; 12:3; Job 5:9; 9:10; 34:24; Ps. 105:34; S.S. 6:8; Jer. 2:32; 52:20; Isa. 5:14; Joel 1:6; Heb. 11:12; Rev. 7:9).

7:48–51. *The inventory of gold objects. "And Solomon made" (v. 48). It is probably that Solomon did not make these vessels himself, even as he did not build his own palace (7:1f, 6ff) or the Temple (6:2, 9f, 12, 14ff, 19, 20–22, 28–33, 35f, 38). Rather, Solomon probably had the gold objects made. Since the bronze objects were made by Hiram, it is quite likely that Solomon had him make the gold objects as well (2 Chr. 2:14 claims he also had expertise in working with gold). The inclusion of the golden objects along with the bronze objects in Hiram's responsibility may be behind the phrase "so he ... performed all his work" (1 Ki. 7:14).*

7:48a. "The golden altar." This altar was the altar of incense. It was first mentioned in this account in 6:22, and was the successor to the altar of incense in the Tabernacle (Exo. 30:27; 31:8). It was part of the command of David to Solomon (1 Chr. 28:18, cf. 2 Chr. 26:16 and Luke 1:11]). This phrase cannot refer to the altar used for animal sacrifice (usually called by the technical term "the altar of burnt offering"), since its horns were overlaid with bronze (Exo. 38:2) and it had a bronze grate (Exo. 35:16). It is also clear that there was eventually a stationary altar built of stones in the temple precinct (Isa. 27:9; cf. Exo. 20:25).

7:48b–50a. The table of shewbread and the menorah. These articles were also made of gold, and were intended to be replicas of the same articles in the Tabernacle (Exo. 25:23–40). Even the order in which they are mentioned and the utensils needed to service the menorah are reminiscent of the description of the original objects of the Tabernacle.

7:51. The dedicated things. The descriptions of the things dedicated by David are found in 2 Sam. 8:7, 10ff and 1 Chr. 18:7–11. Solomon added to this treasure (1 Chr. 29:3; cf. 22:14), as did the nobility (1 Chr. 29:6f). These gifts were placed under the care of the Levites (1 Chr. 26:20).

866	6449.111	4567	8406	1041	3176	971.521	8406
rel part	v Qal pf 3ms	art, n ms	pn	*n ms*	pn	cj, v Hiphil impf 3ms	pn
אֲשֶׁר	עָשָׂה	הַמֶּלֶךְ	שְׁלֹמֹה	בֵּית	יְהוָה	וַיָּבֵא	שְׁלֹמֹה
’ăsher	‘āsāh	hammelekh	shelōmōh	bêth	yehwāh	wayyāvē’	shelōmōh
that	he made	the king	Solomon	the Temple of	Yahweh	and he brought	Solomon

881, 7231	1784	1	881, 3826B	881, 2174	881, 3747	5598.111
do, *n mp*	pn	n ms, ps 3ms	do, art, n ms	cj, do, art, n ms	cj, do, art, n mp	v Qal pf 3ms
אֶת־קָדְשֵׁי	דָּוִד	אָבִיו	אֶת־הַכֶּסֶף	וְאֶת־הַזָּהָב	וְאֶת־הַכֵּלִים	נָתַן
’eth-qādheshê	dāwidh	’āvîw	’eth-hakkeseph	we’eth-hazzāhāv	we’eth-hakkēlîm	nāthan
the holy things of	David	his father	the silver	and the gold	and the utensils	he put

904, 212	1041	3176		226	7234.521	8406	881, 2292
prep, *n mp*	*n ms*	pn		adv	v Hiphil impf 3ms	pn	do, *n mp*
בְּאֹצְרוֹת	בֵּית	יְהוָה	**8:1**	אָז	יַקְהֵל	שְׁלֹמֹה	אֶת־זִקְנֵי
be’ōtserôth	bêth	yehwāh		’āz	yaqhēl	shelōmōh	’eth-ziqnê
into the treasuries of	the Temple of	Yahweh		then	he assembled	Solomon	the elders of

3547	881, 3725, 7513	4431	5562	1	3937, 1158
pn	do, *adj*, *n mp*	art, n mp	*n mp*	art, n mp	prep, *n mp*
יִשְׂרָאֵל	אֶת־כָּל־רָאשֵׁי	הַמַּטּוֹת	נְשִׂיאֵי	הָאָבוֹת	לִבְנֵי
yisrā’ēl	’eth-kol-rā’shê	hammattôth	nesî’ê	hā’āvôth	livnê
Israel	all the heads of	the tribes	the tribal leaders of	the ancestors	of the descendants of

3547	420, 4567	8406	3503	3937, 6148.541	881, 751
pn	prep, art, n ms	pn	pn	prep, v Hiphil inf con	do, *n ms*
יִשְׂרָאֵל	אֶל־הַמֶּלֶךְ	שְׁלֹמֹה	יְרוּשָׁלִַם	לְהַעֲלוֹת	אֶת־אֲרוֹן
yisrā’ēl	’el-hammelekh	shelōmōh	yerûshālām	leha‘ălôth	’eth-’ărôn
Israel	to the king	Solomon	Jerusalem	to bring up	the Ark of

1311, 3176	4623, 6111	1784	2026	6995		7234.226
n fs, pn	prep, *n fs*	pn	pers pron	pn		cj, v Niphal impf 3mp
בְּרִית־יְהוָה	מֵעִיר	דָּוִד	הִיא	צִיּוֹן	**2.**	וַיִּקָּהֲלוּ
berîth-yehwāh	mē‘îr	dāwidh	hî’	tsîyôn		wayyiqqāhelû
the Covenant of Yahweh	from the city of	David	it	Zion		and they were assembled

420, 4567	8406	3725, 382	3547	904, 3505	393	904, 2374	2000
prep, art, n ms	pn	*adj*, *n ms*	pn	prep, *n ms*	art, pn	prep, art, n ms	pers pron
אֶל־הַמֶּלֶךְ	שְׁלֹמֹה	כָּל־אִישׁ	יִשְׂרָאֵל	בְּיֶרַח	הָאֵתָנִים	בֶּחָג	הוּא
’el-hammelekh	shelōmōh	kol-’îsh	yisrā’ēl	beyerach	hā’ēthānîm	bechāgh	hû’
to the king	Solomon	all the men of	Israel	in the month of	Ethanim	at the feast	it

2414	8113		971.126	3725	2292	3547	5558.126
art, n ms	art, num		cj, v Qal impf 3mp	*n ms*	*n mp*	pn	cj, v Qal impf 3mp
הַחֹדֶשׁ	הַשְּׁבִיעִי	**3.**	וַיָּבֹאוּ	כֹּל	זִקְנֵי	יִשְׂרָאֵל	וַיִּשְׂאוּ
hachōdhesh	hashshevî‘î		wayyāvō’û	kōl	ziqnê	yisrā’ēl	wayyis’û
the month	the seventh		and they came	the entirety of	the elders of	Israel	and they lifted up

3669	881, 751		6148.526	881, 751	3176	881, 164	4287
art, n mp	do, art, n ms		cj, v Hiphil impf 3mp	do, *n ms*	pn	cj, do, *n ms*	n ms
הַכֹּהֲנִים	אֶת־הָאָרוֹן	**4.**	וַיַּעֲלוּ	אֶת־אֲרוֹן	יְהוָה	וְאֶת־אֹהֶל	מוֹעֵד
hakkōhenîm	’eth-hā’ārôn		wayya‘ălû	’eth-’ărôn	yehwāh	we’eth-’ōhel	mô‘ēdh
the priests	the Ark		and they brought up	the Ark of	Yahweh	and the Tent of	Meeting

881, 3725, 3747	7231	866	904, 164	6148.526	881
cj, do, *adj*, *n mp*	art, n ms	rel part	prep, art, n ms	cj, v Hiphil impf 3mp	do, ps 3mp
וְאֶת־כָּל־כְּלֵי	הַקֹּדֶשׁ	אֲשֶׁר	בָּאֹהֶל	וַיַּעֲלוּ	אֹתָם
we’eth-kol-kelê	haqqōdhesh	’ăsher	bā’ōhel	wayya‘ălû	’ōthām
and all the utensils of	the holy place	that	in the Tent	and they brought up	them

3669	4015		4567	8406	3725, 5920	3547
art, n mp	cj, art, n mp		cj, art, n ms	pn	cj, *adj*, *n fs*	pn
הַכֹּהֲנִים	וְהַלְוִיִּם	**5.**	וְהַמֶּלֶךְ	שְׁלֹמֹה	וְכָל־עֲדַת	יִשְׂרָאֵל
hakkōh^{e}nîm	w^{e}halwîyim		w^{e}hammelekh	sh^{e}lōmōh	w^{e}khol-'ădhath	yisrā'ēl
the priests	and the Levites		and the king	Solomon	and all the congregation of	Israel

3366.256	6142	882	3937, 6686	751	2159.352	6887	1267
art, v Niphal ptc mp	prep, ps 3ms	prep, ps 3ms	prep, *n mp*	art, *n ms*	v Piel ptc mp	n fs	cj, n ms
הַנּוֹעָדִים	עָלָיו	אִתּוֹ	לִפְנֵי	הָאָרוֹן	מְזַבְּחִים	צֹאן	וּבָקָר
hannô'ādhîm	'ālâv	'ittô	liphnê	hā'ārôn	m^{e}zabb^{e}chîm	tsō'n	ûvāqār
those meeting together	facing him	with him	before	the Ark	sacrificing	sheep	and oxen

sprinkling bowls, the incense ladles and the pans, of real gold, *JB* ... the cups and the scissors ... fire-trays, *BB* ... the deep bowls, the trimmers, the sprinkling bowls, and the fire pans of fine gold, *Beck* ... wick trimmers, small bowls, pans, and dishes used to carry coals, *NCV* ... for carrying live coals, *Good News*.

and the hinges of gold, both for the doors of the inner house, the most holy place, and for the doors of the house, to wit, of the temple: ... panels for the doors of the inner sanctuary, the Most Holy Place, *REB* ... inner sanctuary and for the temple building, *Knox* ... pins on which the doors were turned, *BB* ... sockets of gold for the doors of the inner building, *Beck* ... the gold hinges, *NCV*.

51. So was ended all the work that king Solomon made for the house of the LORD. And Solomon brought in the things which David his father had dedicated; even the silver, and the gold, and the vessels, did he put among the treasures of the house of the LORD: ... sacred treasures ... deposited them in the storehouses, *NEB* ... completed all the work needed for the service, *Knox* ... holy things, *BB* ... the gifts ... consecrated, *JB* ... had set apart for the Temple, *NCV* ... dedicated offerings, *NAB*.

8:1. Then Solomon assembled the elders of Israel, and all the heads of the tribes, the chief of the fathers of the children of Israel, unto king Solomon in Jerusalem: ... sent for all the responsible men of Israel, and all the chiefs of the tribes, *BB* ... to transfer, *Berkeley* ... leaders of the tribes, the princes in the ancestral houses of the Israelites, *NAB* ... called for the older leaders, *NCV* ... summoned all the leaders of the tribes and clans of Israel to come to him in Jerusalem, *Good News*.

that they might bring up the ark of the covenant of the LORD out of the city of David, which is Zion: ... to come to him in Jerusalem to take the ark of the Lord's agreement, *BB* ... take the Lord's Covenant Box from Zion, *Good News*.

2. And all the men of Israel assembled themselves unto king Solomon at the feast in the month Ethanim, which is the seventh month: ... Solomon's presence at the pilgrim-feast, *NEB* ... time of the festival, *NIV* ... festival day, *Douay* ... annual Festival of Shelters in early autumn, *NLT*.

3. And all the elders of Israel came, and the priests took up the ark: ... older leaders of Israel arrived, the priests lifted up, *NCV* ... carried, *NRSV* ... all the responsible men, *BB* ... Judges of Israel consequently came, *Fenton* ... Covenant Box, *Good News*.

4. And they brought up the ark of the LORD, and the tabernacle of the

According to 2 Ki. 12:18, Joash gave this gold as tribute to Hazael king of Aram (cf., however, 2 Ki. 14:14; 16:8; 18:16; 20:13; 24:13; 25:15; 2 Chr. 12:9; 16:2; 25:24; Jer. 52:19). It is conceivable that some of these objects were brought back during the return from exile (cf. Ezra 1:7–11).

8:1–66. *The dedication ceremony was carried out with the utmost pomp. It required nearly a year to complete the necessary preparations, and the ceremony with its feasts occupied fourteen days, which were partly coincident with the autumn Feast of Tabernacles.*

The dedication falls into three great acts. The first was the removal of the Ark to its new home (1 Ki. 8:1–11); then followed the speech and the prayer of Solomon (vv. 12–61); and, finally, the many sacrifices were offered (vv. 62–66).

The old Tabernacle, or what remained of it, with its precious heirlooms, was carried by priests and Levites from the high place at Gibeon, which was henceforth abandoned. This procession was met by another, far more numerous and splendid, consisting of all the elders and leaders, who brought the Ark from the tent erected for it on Mount Zion by David forty years before the same positions (although, perhaps, not altogether the same individuals).

8:1–5. The Israelites had flocked to Jerusalem in countless multitudes. The king, in his most regal

866	3940, 5807.226	3940	4630.226	4623, 7524
rel part	neg part, v Niphal impf 3mp	cj, neg part	v Niphal impf 3mp	prep, n ms
אֲשֶׁר	לֹא־יִסָּפְרוּ	וְלֹא	יִמָּנוּ	מֵרֹב
'ăsher	lō'-yissāpherû	welō'	yimmānû	mērōv
that	they could not be counted	and not	they could be numbered	because an abundance

	971.526	3669	881, 751	1311, 3176	420, 4887
6.	cj, v Hiphil impf 3mp	art, n mp	do, *n ms*	*n fs*, pn	prep, n ms, ps 3ms
	וַיָּבִאוּ	הַכֹּהֲנִים	אֶת־אֲרוֹן	בְּרִית־יְהוָה	אֶל־מְקוֹמוֹ
	wayyāvi'û	hakkōhenîm	'eth-'ărôn	berîth-yehwāh	'el-meqômô
	and they brought	the priests	the Ark of	the Covenant of Yahweh	to its place

420, 1735	1041	420, 7231	7231	420, 8809	3796
prep, *n ms*	art, n ms	prep, *n ms*	art, n mp	prep, prep	*n fp*
אֶל־דְּבִיר	הַבַּיִת	אֶל־קֹדֶשׁ	הַקֳּדָשִׁים	אֶל־תַּחַת	כַּנְפֵי
'el-devîr	habbayith	'el-qōdhesh	haqqedhāshîm	'el-tachath	kanphê
to the inmost room of	the Temple	to the Holy Place of	the holy places	to beneath	the wings of

3872		3706	3872	6816.152	3796	420, 4887	751
art, n mp	**7.**	cj	art, n mp	v Qal act ptc mp	n fd	prep, *n ms*	art, *n ms*
הַכְּרוּבִים		כִּי	הַכְּרוּבִים	פֹּרְשִׂים	כְּנָפַיִם	אֶל־מְקוֹם	הָאָרוֹן
hakkerûvîm		kî	hakkerûvîm	pōresîm	kenāphayim	'el-meqôm	hā'ārôn
the cherubim		because	the cherubim	spreading out	the wings	toward the place of	the Ark

5718.126	3872	6142, 751	6142, 940	4623, 3937, 4767
cj, v Qal impf 3mp	art, n mp	prep, art, n ms	cj, prep, n mp, ps 3ms	prep, prep, prep
וַיָּסֹכּוּ	הַכְּרֻבִים	עַל־הָאָרוֹן	וְעַל־בַּדָּיו	מִלְמָעְלָה
wayyāsōkû	hakkeruvîm	'al-hā'ārôn	we'al-baddâv	milmā'lāh
and they covered	the cherubim	above the Ark	and over its poles	from upward

	773.526	940	7495.226	7513	940	4623, 7231
8.	cj, v Hiphil impf 3mp	art, n mp	cj, v Niphal impf 3mp	*n mp*	art, n mp	prep, art, n ms
	וַיַּאֲרִכוּ	הַבַּדִּים	וַיֵּרָאוּ	רָאשֵׁי	הַבַּדִּים	מִן־הַקֹּדֶשׁ
	wayya'ărikhû	habbaddîm	wayyērā'û	rā'shê	habbaddîm	min-haqqōdhesh
	and they made long	the poles	and they were seen	the tips of	the poles	from the Holy Place

6142, 6686	1735	3940	7495.226	2445	2030.126	8427	5912
prep, *n mp*	art, n ms	cj, neg part	v Niphal impf 3mp	art, n ms	cj, v Qal impf 3mp	adv	prep
עַל־פְּנֵי	הַדְּבִיר	וְלֹא	יֵרָאוּ	הַחוּצָה	וַיִּהְיוּ	שָׁם	עַד
'al-penê	haddevîr	welō'	yērā'û	hachûtsāh	wayyihyû	shām	'adh
opposite	the inmost room	but not	they were seen	to the outside	and they are	there	unto

3219	2172		375	904, 751	7828	8530	4008	63
art, n ms	art, dem pron	**9.**	*sub*	prep, art, n ms	adv	num	*n mp*	art, n fp
הַיּוֹם	הַזֶּה		אֵין	בָּאָרוֹן	רַק	שְׁנֵי	לֻחוֹת	הָאֲבָנִים
hayyôm	hazzeh		'ên	bā'ārôn	raq	shenê	luchôth	hā'ăvānîm
the day	the this		there was not	in the Ark	except	the two of	the tablets of	the stones

866	5299.511	8427	5057	904, 2822	866	3901.111	3176	6196, 1158
rel part	v Hiphil pf 3ms	adv	pn	prep, pn	rel part	v Qal pf 3ms	pn	prep, *n mp*
אֲשֶׁר	הִנִּחַ	שָׁם	מֹשֶׁה	בְּחֹרֵב	אֲשֶׁר	כָּרַת	יְהוָה	עִם־בְּנֵי
'ăsher	hiniach	shām	mōsheh	bechōrēv	'ăsher	kārath	yehwāh	'im-benê
which	he caused to rest	there	Moses	at Horeb	where	he cut	Yahweh	with the children of

3547	904, 3428.141	4623, 800	4875		2030.121	904, 3428.141
pn	prep, v Qal inf con, ps 3mp	prep, *n fs*	pn	**10.**	cj, v Qal impf 3ms	prep, v Qal inf con
יִשְׂרָאֵל	בְּצֵאתָם	מֵאֶרֶץ	מִצְרָיִם		וַיְהִי	בְּצֵאת
yisrā'ēl	betsē'thām	mē'erets	mitsrāyim		wayhî	betsē'th
Israel	when their coming out	from the land of	Egypt		and it was	when coming out

congregation, and all the holy vessels that were in the tabernacle, even those did the priests and the Levites bring up: ... tent of meeting, *Goodspeed* ... all the sacred vessels, *NAB* ... the Meeting tent, *NCV* ... Tent of the Presence and all the sacred furnishings, *NEB* ... tent where God had met with His people and all the holy utensils in it, *Beck*.

5. And king Solomon, and all the congregation of Israel, that were assembled unto him, were with him before the ark, sacrificing sheep and oxen, that could not be told nor numbered for multitude: ... and the whole community of Israel that had gathered ... couldn't be recorded or counted, *Beck* ... for the occasion, *Berkeley* ... countless, innumerable, *JB* ... no one could count them all, *NCV* ... in numbers past counting or reckoning, *NEB*.

6. And the priests brought in the ark of the covenant of the LORD unto his place, into the oracle of the house, to the most holy place, even under the wings of the cherubims: ... in the inner sanctuary of the temple, *NIV* ... took the ark of the agreement ... in the inner room of the house, in the most holy place, under the wings of the winged ones, *BB* ... angels, *Beck* ... in the Holy of Holies, *Berkeley* ... carried the Covenant Box into the Temple ... beneath the winged creatures, *Good News*.

7. For the cherubims spread forth their two wings over the place of the ark, and the cherubims covered the ark and the staves thereof above: ... made a covering above the ark and its poles, *Goodspeed* ... forming a canopy over the ark and its shafts, *JB* ... sheltering the ark and its poles from above, *NAB* ... formed a screen above the Ark and its poles, *NEB* ... overshadowed, *NKJV*.

8. And they drew out the staves, that the ends of the staves were seen out in the holy place before the oracle, and they were not seen without: and there they are unto this day: ... the poles were so long that the ends of the poles were seen from the holy place before the inner sanctuary; but they could not be seen from outside, *RSV* ... The poles projected and their ends were visible from the Holy Place immediately in front of the inner shrine, *REB* ... rods were so long that their ends were seen from the holy place, in front of the inmost room, *BB* ... by anyone standing before the inner room, *Beck* ... seen by anyone standing directly in front of the Most Holy Place, *Good News*.

9. There was nothing in the ark save the two tables of stone, which Moses put there at Horeb, when the LORD made a covenant with the children of Israel, when they came out of the land of Egypt: ... except two tablets, *Goodspeed* ... with the Israelites at their departure from the land of Egypt, *NAB* ... had put in the Ark at Mount Sinai. That was where the LORD made his agreement with the Israelites, *NCV*.

10. And it came to pass, when the priests were come out of the holy place, that the cloud filled the house of the LORD: ... emerged from the holy place, *Berkeley* ... came out from the Sanctuary, *Fenton* ... withdrew from the Holy Place, the cloud filled the temple, *NIV* ... left

---

state, accompanied the procession, and the Ark passed through myriads of worshipers crowded in the outer court, from the tent on Mount Zion. To indicate that this was to be the resting place for the Ark forever, the staves, contrary to the old law, were drawn out of the golden rings through which they ran, in order that no human hand might touch the sacred emblem itself where it was borne on the shoulders of the Levitical priests. "And there they are unto this day," writes the ancient recorder (1 Ki. 8:8).

8:6. Consider, first, the Ark. Every step towards the Holiest was a step of deepening reverence. The Holy Land was sacred, but Jerusalem was more sacred than all the rest. The Temple was the most sacred part of the city; the oracle was the most sacred part of the Temple; the Ark was the most sacred thing in the Oracle; yet the Ark was only sacred because God had chosen to dwell above it.

8:7–8. Consider, next, the meaning of the cherubim. The infinite sanctity given to the conception of the moral Law was enhanced by the introduction of these overshadowing figures. We are never told in the entire Books of Scripture what was the form of these cherubim; nor is their function anywhere specially defined. That the cherubim over the Ark were not identical with the fourfold-visaged four of Ezekiel's vision (Ezek. 1) we know, because they certainly had but one face. But we now know that among the Assyrians, Persians, Egyptians and other nations nothing was more common than these cherubic emblems, which were introduced into their palaces and temple, under the forms of winged lions, oxen, men and eagle-headed human figures. We see also that in the Tabernacle, and to a still greater extent in the Temple, a tacit paradox to the stringency of the second commandment seems to have been made in favor of the component parts of these cherub figures. Yet the first two commandments have more to do with pluralism than prohibition oficons which are for the purpose of glorifying God and accepting his Presence.

8:9–11. The king is the one predominant figure, and the high priest is not once mentioned. Nathan is only mentioned by the heathen historian

3669	4623, 7231	6281	4527.111	881, 1041	3176
art, n mp	prep, art, n ms	cj, art, n ms	v Qal pf 3ms	do, *n ms*	pn
הַכֹּהֲנִים	מִן־הַקֹּדֶשׁ	וְהֶעָנָן	מָלֵא	אֶת־בֵּית	יְהוָה
hakkōhᵉnîm	min-haqqōdhesh	wᵉheʿānān	mālēʾ	ʾeth-bêth	yᵉhwāh
the priests	from the Holy Place	then the cloud	it filled	the Temple of	Yahweh

11.	3940, 3310.116	3669	3937, 6148.141	3937, 8664.341	4623, 6686
	cj, neg part, v Qal pf 3cp	art, n mp	prep, v Qal inf con	prep, v Piel inf con	prep, *n mp*
	וְלֹא־יָכְלוּ	הַכֹּהֲנִים	לַעֲמֹד	לְשָׁרֵת	מִפְּנֵי
	wᵉlōʾ-yākhᵉlû	hakkōhᵉnîm	laʿămōdh	lᵉshārēth	mippᵉnê
	and they were not able	the priests	to stand	to minister	because of the presence of

6281	3706, 4527.111	3638, 3176	881, 1041	3176	12.	226	569.111
art, n ms	cj, v Qal pf 3ms	*n ms*, pn	do, *n ms*	pn		adv	v Qal pf 3ms
הֶעָנָן	כִּי־מָלֵא	כְבוֹד־יְהוָה	אֶת־בֵּית	יְהוָה		אָז	אָמַר
heʿānān	kî-mālēʾ	khᵉvôdh-yᵉhwāh	ʾeth-bêth	yᵉhwāh		ʾāz	ʾāmar
the cloud	because it had filled	the glory of Yahweh	the Temple of	Yahweh		then	he said

8406	3176	569.111	3937, 8331.141	904, 6441	13.	1161.142
pn	pn	v Qal pf 3ms	prep, v Qal inf con	prep, art, n ms		v Qal inf abs
שְׁלֹמֹה	יְהוָה	אָמַר	לִשְׁכֹּן	בָּעֲרָפֶל		בָּנֹה
shᵉlōmōh	yᵉhwāh	ʾāmar	lishkōn	bāʿărāphel		bānōh
Solomon	Yahweh	He said	to dwell	in the thick cloud		building

1161.115	1041	2166	3937	4487	3937, 3553.141	5986
v Qal pf 1cs	*n ms*	n ms	prep, ps 2fs	n ms	prep, v Qal inf con, ps 2ms	n mp
בָנִיתִי	בֵּית	זְבֻל	לָךְ	מָכוֹן	לְשִׁבְתְּךָ	עוֹלָמִים
vānîthî	bêth	zᵉvul	lākh	mākhôn	lᵉshivtᵉkhā	ʿôlāmîm
I have completely built	a Temple of	dwelling	for You	a place	for your dwelling	the future

14.	5621.521	4567	881, 6686	1313.321	881	3725, 7235
	cj, v Hiphil impf 3ms	art, n ms	do, n mp, ps 3ms	cj, v Piel impf 3ms	do	*adj, n ms*
	וַיַּסֵּב	הַמֶּלֶךְ	אֶת־פָּנָיו	וַיְבָרֶךְ	אֵת	כָּל־קְהַל
	wayyassēv	hammelekh	ʾeth-pānāv	wayvārekh	ʾēth	kol-qᵉhal
	and he turned around	the king	his face	and he blessed		all the assembly of

3547	3725, 7235	3547	6198.151	15.	569.121	1313.155
pn	cj, *adj, n ms*	pn	v Qal act ptc ms		cj, v Qal impf 3ms	v Qal pass ptc ms
יִשְׂרָאֵל	וְכָל־קְהַל	יִשְׂרָאֵל	עֹמֵד		וַיֹּאמֶר	בָּרוּךְ
yisrāʾēl	wᵉkhol-qᵉhal	yisrāʾēl	ʿōmēdh		wayyōʾmer	bārûkh
Israel	and all the assembly of	Israel	standing		and he said	blessed

3176	435	3547	866	1744.311	904, 6552	881	1784	1
pn	*n mp*	pn	rel pron	v Piel pf 3ms	prep, n ms, ps 3ms	do	pn	n ms, ps 1cs
יְהוָה	אֱלֹהֵי	יִשְׂרָאֵל	אֲשֶׁר	דִּבֶּר	בְּפִיו	אֵת	דָּוִד	אָבִי
yᵉhwāh	ʾĕlōhê	yisrāʾēl	ʾăsher	dibber	bᵉphîw	ʾēth	dāwidh	ʾāvî
Yahweh	the God of	Israel	Who	He has spoken	with his mouth		David	my father

904, 3135	4527.311	3937, 569.141	16.	4623, 3219	866	3428.515
cj, prep, n fs, ps 3ms	v Piel pf 3ms	prep, v Qal inf con		prep, art, n ms	rel part	v Hiphil pf 1cs
וּבְיָדוֹ	מִלֵּא	לֵאמֹר		מִן־הַיּוֹם	אֲשֶׁר	הוֹצֵאתִי
ûvᵉyādhô	millēʾ	lēʾmōr		min-hayyôm	ʾăsher	hôtsēʾthî
and with his hand	he has fulfilled	saying		from the day	which	I led out

881, 6194	881, 3547	4623, 4875	3940, 1013.115	904, 6111	4623, 3725
do, n ms, ps 1cs	do, pn	prep, pn	neg part, v Qal pf 1cs	prep, n fs	prep, *adj*
אֶת־עַמִּי	אֶת־יִשְׂרָאֵל	מִמִּצְרַיִם	לֹא־בָחַרְתִּי	בְּעִיר	מִכֹּל
ʾeth-ʿammî	ʾeth-yisrāʾēl	mimmitsrayim	lōʾ-vāchartî	vᵉʿîr	mikkōl
my people	Israel	from Egypt	I did not choose	in a city	among the entirety of

8101 n mp שִׁבְטֵי shivṭê the tribes of	3547 pn יִשְׂרָאֵל yisrā'ēl Israel	3937, 1161.141 prep, v Qal inf con לִבְנוֹת livnôth to build	1041 n ms בַּיִת bayith a house	3937, 2030.141 prep, v Qal inf con לִהְיוֹת lihyôth for being	8428 n ms, ps 1cs שְׁמִי shemî my name	8427 adv שָׁם shām there	1013.125 cj, v Qal impf 1cs וָאֶבְחַר wā'evchar but I chose

904, 1784 prep, pn בְּדָוִד bedhāwidh with David	3937, 2030.141 prep, v Qal inf con לִהְיוֹת lihyôth to be	6142, 6194 prep, n ms, ps 1cs עַל־עַמִּי 'al-'ammî over my people	3547 pn יִשְׂרָאֵל yisrā'ēl Israel	**17.**	2030.121 cj, v Qal impf 3ms וַיְהִי wayhî and it was	6196, 3949 prep, *n ms* עִם־לְבַב 'im-levav with the heart of

the inner sanctuary, the whole of the Lord's house was wreathed in cloud, *Knox* ... were leaving the Temple, it was suddenly filled, *Good News*.

11. So that the priests could not stand to minister because of the cloud: for the glory of the LORD had filled the house of the LORD: ... and serve on account of, *Beck* ... lost in that cloud, the priests could not wait upon the Lord with his accustomed service; his own glory was there, filling his own house, *Knox* ... for the splendour of the EVER-LIVING filled the House of the EVER-LIVING, *Fenton* ... could not continue their work, because the Temple was filled, *NCV* ... could not continue ministering, *NKJV*.

12. Then spake Solomon, The LORD said that he would dwell in the thick darkness: ... in a dark cloud, *NIV* ... in a heavy cloud, *Berkeley* ... you have chosen to live in clouds and darkness, *Good News*.

13. I have surely built thee an house to dwell in, a settled place for thee to abide in for ever: ... an exalted house, And a place for You to dwell in, *NKJV* ... a magnificent temple, *NIV* ... a lofty house, a dwelling-place for you to occupy, *REB* ... a princely dwelling, a residence, *JB* ... thy dwelling, thy throne for ever immovable, *Knox* ... a glorious Temple for you, where you can live forever!, *NLT*.

14. And the king turned his face about, and blessed all the congregation of Israel: (and all the congregation of Israel stood;): ... turned around and blessed the whole community, *Beck* ... all the Assembly of Israel, *Fenton* ... turned and greeted, *NAB*.

15. And he said, Blessed be the LORD God of Israel, which spake with his mouth unto David my father, and hath with his hand fulfilled it, saying: ... who himself gave his word to David my father, and with his strong hand has made his word come true, *BB* ... You promised my father David, and with Your hand You carried it out, *Beck* ... by His hand accomplishes His word, *Fenton* ... by his hand has brought it to fulfillment, *NAB* ... He has done what he promised, *NCV*.

16. Since the day that I brought forth my people Israel out of Egypt, I chose no city out of all the tribes of Israel to build an house, that my name might be therein; but I chose David to be over my people Israel: ... to rule my people, *NIV* ... to lead, *NCV* ... to have charge of, *Berkeley* ... has been marked out by me for the building of a house for the resting-place of my name; but I made selection of David to be king, *BB* ... as the place where a temple should be built to honor my name, *NLT*.

Eupolemos. Visible to the whole vast multitude, Solomon stood in the inner court on a high scaffolding of brass. Then came a burst of music and psalmody from the priests and musicians, robed in white robes, who densely thronged the steps of the great altar. They held in their hands their glittering harps and cymbals, and psalteries in their precious frames of red sandal wood, and twelve of their number rent the air with the blast of their silver trumpets as Solomon, in this supreme hour of his prosperity, shone forth before his people.

But someone greater than Solomon was there. No matter what human achievement can in any wise be attributed to the human king, this only amounts to an understanding seen by the ordinary human eye. Far greater than any human achievement, is God's glory, which the LORD chooses to manifest when people realize that it is Yahweh, the Ever-Living One, Who is able to honor any man above another. It is only in times of our humility, and recognition of God's incomparable majesty, that we seem to amount to more than we are—dust. And so Solomon did understand and did attribute and did receive the blessing of the LORD upon his efforts. So kind and eager is the LORD to dwell among his people and to show himself great.

8:12–21. At the sight of that stately figure in its gorgeous robes the song of praise was swelled by innumerable voices, and, to crown all, a blaze of sudden glory wrapped the Temple and the whole

1784	1	3937, 1161.141	1041	3937, 8428	3176	435	3547
pn	n ms, ps 1cs	prep, v Qal inf con	n ms	prep, *n ms*	pn	*n mp*	pn
דָּוִד	אָבִי	לִבְנוֹת	בַּיִת	לְשֵׁם	יְהוָה	אֱלֹהֵי	יִשְׂרָאֵל
dāwidh	'āvî	livnôth	bayith	leshēm	yehwāh	'ĕlōhê	yisrā'ēl
David	my father	to build	a house	to the name of	Yahweh	the God of	Israel

	569.121	3176	420, 1784	1	3391	866	2030.111	6196, 3949
18.	cj, v Qal impf 3ms	pn	prep, pn	n ms, ps 1cs	cj	rel part	v Qal pf 3ms	prep, n ms, ps 2ms
	וַיֹּאמֶר	יְהוָה	אֶל־דָּוִד	אָבִי	יַעַן	אֲשֶׁר	הָיָה	עִם־לְבָבְךָ
	wayyō'mer	yehwāh	'el-dāwidh	'āvî	ya'an	'ăsher	hāyāh	'im-levāvekhā
	but He said	Yahweh	to David	my father	because	that	it was	with your heart

3937, 1161.141	1041	3937, 8428	3004.513	3706	2030.111	6196, 3949
prep, v Qal inf con	n ms	prep, n ms, ps 1cs	v Hiphil pf 2ms	cj	v Qal pf 3ms	prep, n ms, ps 2ms
לִבְנוֹת	בַּיִת	לִשְׁמִי	הֱטִיבֹתָ	כִּי	הָיָה	עִם־לְבָבֶךָ
livnôth	bayith	lishmî	hĕṯîvōthā	kî	hāyāh	'im-levāvekhā
to build	a house	to my name	you have done well	because	it was	with your heart

	7828	887	3940	1161.123	1041	3706	524, 1158	3428.151
19.	adv	pers pron	neg part	v Qal impf 2ms	art, n ms	cj	cj, n ms, ps 2ms	art, v Qal act ptc ms
	רַק	אַתָּה	לֹא	תִבְנֶה	הַבָּיִת	כִּי	אִם־בִּנְךָ	הַיֹּצֵא
	raq	'attāh	lō'	thivneh	habbāyith	kî	'im-binkhā	hayyōtsē'
	except	you	not	you will build	the house	but	rather your son	one coming out

4623, 2604	2000, 1161.121	1041	3937, 8428		7251.521
prep, n fd, ps 2ms	pers pron, v Qal impf 3ms	art, n ms	prep, n ms, ps 1cs	**20.**	cj, v Hiphil impf 3ms
מֵחֲלָצֶיךָ	הוּא־יִבְנֶה	הַבַּיִת	לִשְׁמִי		וַיָּקֶם
mēchălātsêkhā	hû'-yivneh	habbayith	lishmî		wayyāqem
from your loins	he he will build	the house	to my name		and He caused to stand

3176	881, 1745	866	1744.311	7251.125	8809	1784	1
pn	do, n ms, ps 3ms	rel part	v Piel pf 3ms	cj, v Qal impf 1cs	prep	pn	n ms, ps 1cs
יְהוָה	אֶת־דְּבָרוֹ	אֲשֶׁר	דִּבֵּר	וָאָקֻם	תַּחַת	דָּוִד	אָבִי
yehwāh	'eth-devārô	'ăsher	dibbēr	wā'āqum	tachath	dāwidh	'āvî
Yahweh	his word	which	He spoke	and I arose	instead of	David	my father

3553.125	6142, 3802	3547	3626, 866	1744.311	3176	1161.125
cj, v Qal impf 1cs	prep, *n ms*	pn	prep, rel part	v Piel pf 3ms	pn	cj, v Qal impf 1cs
וָאֵשֵׁב	עַל־כִּסֵּא	יִשְׂרָאֵל	כַּאֲשֶׁר	דִּבֶּר	יְהוָה	וָאֶבְנֶה
wā'ēshēv	'al-kissē'	yisrā'ēl	ka'ăsher	dibbēr	yehwāh	wā'evneh
and I am sitting	on the throne of	Israel	just as	He spoke	Yahweh	and I built

1041	3937, 8428	3176	435	3547		7947.125	8427	4887
art, n ms	prep, *n ms*	pn	*n mp*	pn	**21.**	cj, v Qal impf 1cs	adv	n ms
הַבַּיִת	לְשֵׁם	יְהוָה	אֱלֹהֵי	יִשְׂרָאֵל		וָאָשִׂם	שָׁם	מָקוֹם
habbayith	leshēm	yehwāh	'ĕlōhê	yisrā'ēl		wā'āsim	shām	māqôm
the Temple	to the name of	Yahweh	the God of	Israel		and I have set	there	a place

3937, 751	866, 8427	1311	3176	866	3901.111	6196, 1
prep, art, n ms	rel part, adv	*n fs*	pn	rel part	v Qal pf 3ms	prep, n mp, ps 1cp
לָאָרוֹן	אֲשֶׁר־שָׁם	בְּרִית	יְהוָה	אֲשֶׁר	כָּרַת	עִם־אֲבֹתֵינוּ
lā'ārôn	'ăsher-shām	berîth	yehwāh	'ăsher	kārath	'im-'ăvōthênû
for the Ark	which there	the Covenant of	Yahweh	which	He cut	with our ancestors

904, 3428.541	881	4623, 800	4875		6198.121	8406
prep, v Hiphil inf con, ps 3ms	do, ps 3mp	prep, *n fs*	pn	**22.**	cj, v Qal impf 3ms	pn
בְּהוֹצִיאוֹ	אֹתָם	מֵאֶרֶץ	מִצְרָיִם		וַיַּעֲמֹד	שְׁלֹמֹה
behôtsî'ô	'ōthām	mē'erets	mitsrāyim		wayya'ămōdh	shelōmōh
when his leading out	them	from the land of	Egypt		and he stood	Solomon

17. And it was in the heart of David my father to build an house for the name of the LORD God of Israel: ... in the mind of, *Goodspeed* ... had set his heart on building a temple for, *JB* ... wished to build a temple to the honor of the LORD, *NAB* ... wanted to build a temple, *NCV* ... planned, *Beck*.

18. And the LORD said unto David my father, Whereas it was in thine heart to build an house unto my name, thou didst well that it was in thine heart: ... that he had done well to conceive such a purpose in his heart, *Knox* ... to have in your heart the desire to make a house for my name, *BB* ... It was good, *NCV* ... your purpose was good, *NEB* ... You were right in wanting to build a temple for me, *Good News*.

19. Nevertheless thou shalt not build the house; but thy son that shall come forth out of thy loins, he shall build the house unto my name: ... you are not the one to build the temple, but your son, who is your own flesh and blood, *NIV* ... son who shall be born to you, *NRSV* ... A house shall be built in my honour, but by thy son, the heir of thy body, *Knox* ... you yourself will not be the builder of my house; but your son, the offspring of your body, *BB* ... you are not the man to build the temple, *JB*.

20. And the LORD hath performed his word that he spake, and I am risen up in the room of David my father, and sit on the throne of Israel, as the LORD promised: ... now the LORD has fulfilled the promise that he made: I have succeeded my father David *NAB* ... the LORD has kept his promise. I am the king now in place of David my father. Now I rule Israel, *NCV* ... has upheld the promise, *NRSV* ... the Lord has made his word come true; for I have taken my father David's place on the seat of the kingdom of Israel, *BB* ... and now I stand in my father's place, *Beck*.

and have built an house for the name of the LORD God of Israel: ... I have built this temple to honor the LORD, *NAB* ... made a house, *BB*.

21. And I have set there a place for the ark, wherein is the covenant of the LORD, which he made with our fathers, when he brought them out of the land of Egypt: ... the agreement, *BB* ... in it I've made a place for the sacred ark, *Beck* ... which he made with our ancestors, *JB* ... with our forefathers, *NEB* ... to find a home for this ark, *Knox*.

22. And Solomon stood before the altar of the LORD in the presence of all the congregation of Israel, and spread forth his hands toward heaven: ... in front of the whole community of Israel, faced the LORD's altar, *Beck* ... in the sight of the assembly, *Douay* ... spread out his hands toward the sky, *NCV* ... in full view of all Israel, and lifted his hands, *Knox*.

23. And he said, LORD God of Israel, there is no God like thee, in

---

scene in heaven's own splendor (2 Chr. 5:13f). First, the king, standing with his back to the people, broke out into a few words of prophetic song. Then, turning to the multitude, he blessed them—he, and not the high priest—and briefly told them the history and significance of this house of God, warning them faithfully that the Temple after all was but the emblem of God's Presence in the midst of them, and that the Most High dwelleth not in temples made with hands, neither is worshiped with men's hands as though He needed anything.

8:22–53. Could the whole Covenant of the Law and the gospel have been symbolized more simply, yet with diviner force? The Temple itself, with all its sacrifices, with all its service and ceremonial and all the gorgeous vestments of Aaron's vestry, served but to teach the infinite worth of simple righteousness. The heart of the Mosaic legislation was nothing so poor, so paltry, so material as the promotion of liturgical Levitism, and the pomp of ritual, and the organization of priestly functions—as though these in themselves had any value in the sight of God. It lay in the lesson that "obedience is better than sacrifice, and to hearken than the fat of rams." The law of Moses—the ten words which constituted the inmost preciousness of his legislation—was, alas! a violated law. For the disobedient it had no message but the wrathful menace of death. But to show that God had not abandoned his disobedient children, but would still enable them to keep that Law, and to repent for its transgression, the cherubim were there. Their presence on the propitiatory was meant to reveal the glory of the gospel. The high priest, who alone saw them on the Great Day of Israel, was a type of Him Who, not with the blood of bulls and goats, but in his own blood (i.e., in the glory of the life outpoured for man), entered into God's Presence within the veil.

In the dazzling living creatures before the throne in the Revelation of St. John, we see once more these cherubim of Eden, who, having indicated at the Fall an awful warning, and represented in the Tabernacle a blessed hope, symbolize, in the last Book of the Bible, a divine fulfilment. They are there no longer with fiery swords, in wrathful aspect, in repellent silence; but, gracious and beautiful, they join in the new song of the redeemed multitude under the shadow of the Tree of Life, to which all

3937, 6686	4326	3176	5224	3725, 7235	3547	6816.121
prep, *n mp*	*n ms*	pn	prep	*adj*, *n ms*	pn	cj, v Qal impf 3ms
לִפְנֵי	מִזְבַּח	יְהוָה	נֶגֶד	כָּל־קְהַל	יִשְׂרָאֵל	וַיִּפְרֹשׂ
liphnê	mizbach	yehwāh	neghedh	kol-qōhal	yisrā'ēl	wayyiphrōs
before	the altar of	Yahweh	opposite	all the assembly of	Israel	and he spread out

3834	8452		569.121	3176	435	3547
n fd, ps 3ms	art, n md	**23.**	cj, v Qal impf 3ms	pn	*n mp*	pn
כַּפָּיו	הַשָּׁמָיִם		וַיֹּאמַר	יְהוָה	אֱלֹהֵי	יִשְׂרָאֵל
kappâv	hashshāmāyim		wayyō'mar	yehwāh	'ĕlōhê	yisrā'ēl
his palms	the heavens		and he said	O Yahweh	the God of	Israel

375, 3765	435	904, 8452	4623, 4762	6142, 800	4623, 8809
sub, prep, ps 2ms	n mp	prep, art, n md	prep, prep	cj, prep, art, n fs	prep, prep
אֵין־כָּמוֹךָ	אֱלֹהִים	בַּשָּׁמַיִם	מִמַּעַל	וְעַל־הָאָרֶץ	מִתָּחַת
'ên-kāmôkhā	'ĕlōhîm	bashshāmayim	mimma'al	we'al-hā'ārets	mittāchath
there is none like You	God	in the heavens	from above	and on the earth	from beneath

8490.151	1311	2721	3937, 5860	2050.152
v Qal act ptc ms	art, n fs	cj, art, n ms	prep, n mp, ps 2ms	art, v Qal act ptc mp
שֹׁמֵר	הַבְּרִית	וְהַחֶסֶד	לַעֲבָדֶיךָ	הַהֹלְכִים
shōmēr	habberîth	wehachesedh	la'ăvādhêkhā	hahōlekhîm
One Who keeps	the Covenant	and the steadfast love	with your servants	the ones walking

3937, 6686	904, 3725, 3949		866	8490.113	3937, 5860	1784
prep, n mp, ps 2ms	prep, *adj*, n ms, ps 3mp	**24.**	rel pron	v Qal pf 2ms	prep, n ms, ps 2ms	pn
לְפָנֶיךָ	בְּכָל־לִבָּם		אֲשֶׁר	שָׁמַרְתָּ	לְעַבְדְּךָ	דָּוִד
lephānêkhā	bekhol-libbām		'ăsher	shāmartā	le'avdekhā	dāwidh
before You	with all their heart		Who	You have kept	with your servant	David

1	881	866, 1744.313	3937	1744.323	904, 6552
n ms, ps 1cs	do	rel pron, v Piel pf 2ms	prep, ps 3ms	cj, v Piel impf 2ms	prep, n ms, ps 2ms
אָבִי	אֵת	אֲשֶׁר־דִּבַּרְתָּ	לוֹ	וַתְּדַבֵּר	בְּפִיךָ
'āvî	'ēth	'ăsher-dibbartā	lô	wattedhabbēr	bephîkhā
my father		Who spoke	to him	yes You spoke	with your mouth

904, 3135	4527.313	3626, 3219	2172		6498	3176	435
cj, prep, n fs, ps 2ms	v Piel pf 2ms	prep, art, n ms	art, dem pron	**25.**	cj, adv	pn	*n mp*
וּבְיָדְךָ	מִלֵּאתָ	כַּיּוֹם	הַזֶּה		וְעַתָּה	יְהוָה	אֱלֹהֵי
ûveyādhekhā	millē'thā	kayyôm	hazzeh		we'attāh	yehwāh	'ĕlōhê
and with your hand	you fulfilled	like the day	the this		and now	O Yahweh	the God of

3547	8490.131	3937, 5860	1784	1	881	866	1744.313	3937
pn	v Qal impv 2ms	prep, n ms, ps 2ms	pn	n ms, ps 1cs	do	rel part	v Piel pf 2ms	prep, ps 3ms
יִשְׂרָאֵל	שְׁמֹר	לְעַבְדְּךָ	דָוִד	אָבִי	אֵת	אֲשֶׁר	דִּבַּרְתָּ	לוֹ
yisrā'ēl	shemōr	le'avdekhā	dhāwidh	'āvî	'ēth	'ăsher	dibbartā	lô
Israel	keep	with your servant	David	my father		what	You spoke	to him

3937, 569.141	3940, 3901.221	3937	382	4623, 3937, 6686	3553.151
prep, v Qal inf con	neg part, v Niphal impf 3ms	prep, ps 2ms	n ms	prep, prep, n mp, ps 1cs	v Qal act ptc ms
לֵאמֹר	לֹא־יִכָּרֵת	לְךָ	אִישׁ	מִלְּפָנַי	יֹשֵׁב
lē'mōr	lō'-yikkārēth	lekhā	'îsh	millephānay	yōshēv
saying	he will not be cut off	to you	a man	from before Me	one who sits

6142, 3802	3547	7828	524, 8490.126	1158	881, 1932	3937, 2050.141
prep, *n ms*	pn	adv	cj, v Qal impf 3mp	n mp, ps 2ms	do, n ms, ps 3mp	prep, v Qal inf con
עַל־כִּסֵּא	יִשְׂרָאֵל	רַק	אִם־יִשְׁמְרוּ	בָנֶיךָ	אֶת־דַּרְכָּם	לָלֶכֶת
'al-kissē'	yisrā'ēl	raq	'im-yishmerû	vānêkhā	'eth-darkām	lālekheth
on the throne of	Israel	only	if they are careful	your sons	their way	to walk

heaven above, or on earth beneath, who keepest covenant and mercy with thy servants that walk before thee with all their heart: ... keeping faith and mercy unchanging for your servants, while they go in your ways, *BB* ... when their hearts are altogether loyal to You, *Beck* ... who are faithful to you, *NAB* ... You keep your agreement of love with your servants who truly follow you, *NCV* ... showing them constant love while they continue faithful, *REB* ... show them your love when they live in wholehearted obedience to you, *Good News*.

24. Who hast kept with thy servant David my father that thou promisedst him: thou spakest also with thy mouth, and hast fulfilled it with thine hand, as it is this day: ... you have kept the word which you gave to your servant David, my father; with your mouth you said it and with your hand you have made it come true this day, *BB* ... thou didst speak with thy lips, *Goodspeed* ... Today you have carried it out by your power, *JB* ... You spoke it with your own mouth and finished it with your hands, *NCV* ... as you declared to him; you promised, *NRSV*.

25. Therefore now, LORD God of Israel, keep with thy servant David my father that thou promisedst him, saying, There shall not fail thee a man in my sight to sit on the throne of Israel; so that thy children take heed to their way, that they walk before me as thou hast walked before me: ... You will never want for a man appointed by me to sit on the throne of Israel, if only your sons look, *REB* ... You will never be without a man to take his place on the seat of the kingdom of Israel before me, if only your children give attention, *BB* ... You will always have a man sitting on the throne of Israel before Me if only your descendant will watch their ways to live before Me, *Beck* ... You shall never lack before Me an occupant for the throne of Israel, provided, indeed, *Berkeley* ... provided that your sons are careful how they behave, *JB*.

---

have free access in that recovered Eden. In the Temple—glimmering through the rising fumes of incense, which were the type of accepted prayer, their golden plumage sprinkled with the blood of the atoning sacrifice—they became a type both of all creation, up to its most celestial beings, gazing in adoration on the will of God, and of all creation, in its groaning and travailing, restored through the precious blood that speaketh better things than the blood of Abel. Not all, of course, of these deep meanings were present to the souls of Israel's worshipers; but the best of them might with joy see something of the things which we see when we say that in these glorious figures are summed up the three chief images of all Scripture: first, the primeval dispensation, "In the day that thou eatest thereof, thou shalt surely die"; next, in the wilderness, "This do, and thou shalt live"; last of all! in the gospel dispensation, "Thou wast slain, and wast redeemed us to God by thy blood out of every kindred and tongue and people and nation, and hast made us unto our God kings and priests."

Consider the law of a central sanctuary. It is strongly laid down, and incessantly insisted on, throughout the Book of Deuteronomy (see Deut. 12:5–19). Yet that law does not seem to have been so much as noticed by any of the earlier prophets or judges, or by Saul or by David. The judges and early kings offered sacrifices at any place which they regarded as sacred—Bochim, Ophrah, Mizpeh, Gilgal, Bethel, Bethlehem, etc. (Judg. 2:5; 6:24; 8:27; 20:1; 21:1, 4; 1 Sam. 7:9; 10:8; 11:15; 13:9; 16:5). The rule of one place for sacrifice was not regarded for a moment by the kings of the Northern Kingdom. The transgression of it was not made a subject of complaint by Elijah, Elisha or any of the earlier prophets. Not one of the kings, even of the most pious kings—Asa, Jehoshaphat, Joash, Amaziah, Uzziah, Jothan—rigidly enforced it until the reign of Josiah. The law seems to have remained an absolutely dead letter for hundreds of years. Now this need not be accounted for by saying that the Law only belonged in reality to the days of Josiah and of the exile. In "the Book of the Covenant" (Exo. 24:7), which is the most ancient part of these codes, the rest of the Law being "prescribed" as individual cases were brought to Moses to judge, there is not only no insistence on a central shrine, but many of the regulations would have been rendered impossible had such a shrine existed (e.g., Exo. 21:6, 22:7f, where "the judges" should be "God.") Indeed, so far from insistence on one Temple, we expressly read, "An altar of earth thou shalt make unto me, and shalt sacrifice thereon thy burnt offerings, and thy peace offerings, thy sheep, and thine oxen: in all places where I record my name, and I will come unto thee, and bless thee" (Exo. 20:26).

The Book of Leviticus lays down a singularly developed code of ritual, "extending to the minutest details of worship and of life." Yet there is scarcely the shadow of a trace of the observance of even its most reiterated and important provisions during centuries of Israelite history. It is emphatically a priestly Book; yet from the days of David down to those of

3937, 6686	3626, 866	2050.113	3937, 6686	26.	6498	435	3547
prep, n mp, ps 1cs	prep, rel part	v Qal pf 2ms	prep, n mp, ps 1cs		cj, adv	*n mp*	pn
לְפָנַי	כַּאֲשֶׁר	הָלַכְתָּ	לְפָנָי		וְעַתָּה	אֱלֹהֵי	יִשְׂרָאֵל
lephānay	ka'ăsher	hālakhtā	lephānāy		we'attāh	'ĕlōhê	yisrā'ēl
before Me	just as	you walked	before Me		and now	the God of	Israel

548.221	5167	1745	866	1744.313	3937, 5860	1784	1
v Niphal juss 3ms	part	n mp, ps 2ms	rel part	v Piel pf 2ms	prep, n ms, ps 2ms	pn	n ms, ps 1cs
יֵאָמֶן	נָא	דְּבָרֶיךָ	אֲשֶׁר	דִּבַּרְתָּ	לְעַבְדְּךָ	דָּוִד	אָבִי
yē'āmen	nā'	devāreykhā	'ăsher	dibbartā	le'avdekhā	dāwidh	'āvî
may it become true	please	your words	which	You spoke	to your servant	David	my father

27.	3706	1950B, 562	3553.121	435	6142, 800	2079	8452
	cj	intrg part, adv	v Qal impf 3ms	n mp	prep, art, n fs	intrj	art, n md
	כִּי	הַאֻמְנָם	יֵשֵׁב	אֱלֹהִים	עַל־הָאָרֶץ	הִנֵּה	הַשָּׁמַיִם
	kî	hă'umnām	yēshēv	'ĕlōhîm	'al-hā'ārets	hinnēh	hashshāmayim
	yet	will truly	He dwell	God	on the earth	behold	the heavens

8452	8452	3940	3677.326	652	3706, 1041
cj, *n md*	art, n md	neg part	v Pilpel impf 3mp, ps 2ms	cj	cj, art, n ms
וּשְׁמֵי	הַשָּׁמַיִם	לֹא	יְכַלְכְּלוּךָ	אַף	כִּי־הַבַּיִת
ûshemê	hashshāmayim	lō'	yekhalkelûkhā	'aph	kî-habbayith
even the heavens of	the heavens	not	they can contain You	also	except the building

2172	866	1161.115	28.	6680.113	420, 8940	5860
art, dem pron	rel part	v Qal pf 1cs		cj, v Qal pf 2ms	prep, *n fs*	n ms, ps 2ms
הַזֶּה	אֲשֶׁר	בָּנִיתִי		וּפָנִיתָ	אֶל־תְּפִלַּת	עַבְדְּךָ
hazzeh	'ăsher	bānîthî		ûphānîthā	'el-tephillath	'avdekhā
the this	which	I have built		but You have turned	toward the prayer of	your servant

420, 8798	3176	435	3937, 8471.141	420, 7726
cj, prep, n fs, ps 3ms	pn	n mp, ps 1cs	prep, v Qal inf con	prep, art, n fs
וְאֶל־תְּחִנָּתוֹ	יְהוָה	אֱלֹהָי	לִשְׁמֹעַ	אֶל־הָרִנָּה
we'el-techinnāthô	yehwāh	'ĕlōhāy	lishmōa'	'el-hārinnāh
and toward his supplication	O Yahweh	my God	to listen	to the lamentation

420, 8940	866	5860	6663.751	3937, 6686	3219
cj, prep, art, n fs	rel part	n ms, ps 2ms	v Hithpael ptc ms	prep, n mp, ps 2ms	art, n ms
וְאֶל־הַתְּפִלָּה	אֲשֶׁר	עַבְדְּךָ	מִתְפַּלֵּל	לְפָנֶיךָ	הַיּוֹם
we'el-hattephillāh	'ăsher	'avdekhā	mithpallēl	lephānêkhā	hayyôm
and to the prayer	which	your servant	praying	before You	today

29.	3937, 2030.141	6084	6858.158	420, 1041	2172	4050	3219
	prep, v Qal inf con	n fd, ps 2ms	v Qal pass ptc fp	prep, art, n ms	art, dem pron	n ms	cj, n ms
	לִהְיוֹת	עֵינֶךָ	פְּתֻחוֹת	אֶל־הַבַּיִת	הַזֶּה	לַיְלָה	וָיוֹם
	lihyôth	'ênekhā	phethuchôth	'el-habbayith	hazzeh	laylāh	wāyôm
	for being	your eyes	opened	toward the Temple	the this	night	and day

420, 4887	866	569.113	2030.121	8428	8427	3937, 8471.141
prep, art, n ms	rel part	v Qal pf 2ms	v Qal impf 3ms	n ms, ps 1cs	adv	prep, v Qal inf con
אֶל־הַמָּקוֹם	אֲשֶׁר	אָמַרְתָּ	יִהְיֶה	שְׁמִי	שָׁם	לִשְׁמֹעַ
'el-hammāqôm	'ăsher	'āmartā	yihyeh	shemî	shām	lishmōa'
toward the place	which	You have said	it will be	my name	there	to listen

420, 8940	866	6663.721	5860	420, 4887	2172
prep, art, n fs	rel part	v Hithpael impf 3ms	n ms, ps 2ms	prep, art, n ms	art, dem pron
אֶל־הַתְּפִלָּה	אֲשֶׁר	יִתְפַּלֵּל	עַבְדְּךָ	אֶל־הַמָּקוֹם	הַזֶּה
'el-hattephillāh	'ăsher	yithpallēl	'avdekhā	'el-hammāqôm	hazzeh
to the prayer	which	he is praying	your servant	toward the place	the this

866	3547	6194	5860	420, 8798	8471.113	
rel part	pn	cj, n ms, ps 2ms	n ms, ps 2ms	prep, *n fs*	cj, v Qal pf 2ms	**30.**
אֲשֶׁר	יִשְׂרָאֵל	וְעַמְּךָ	עַבְדְּךָ	אֶל־תְּחִנַּת	וְשָׁמַעְתָּ	
'ăsher	yisrā'ēl	we'ammekhā	'avdekhā	'el-techinnath	weshāma'āttā	
which	Israel	and your people	your servant	to the supplication of	then You will hear	

420, 4887	8471.123	887	2172	420, 4887	6663.726
prep, *n ms*	v Qal impf 2ms	cj, pers pron	art, dem pron	prep, art, n ms	v Hithpael impf 3mp
אֶל־מְקוֹם	תִּשְׁמַע	וְאַתָּה	הַזֶּה	אֶל־הַמָּקוֹם	יִתְפַּלְלוּ
'el-meqôm	tishma'	we'attāh	hazzeh	'el-hammāqôm	yithpalelû
toward the place of	You will listen	and You	the this	toward the place	they are praying

866	881		5739.113	8471.113	420, 8452	3553.141
rel part	do	**31.**	cj, v Qal pf 2ms	cj, v Qal pf 2ms	prep, art, n md	v Qal inf con, ps 2ms
אֲשֶׁר	אֵת		וְסָלַחְתָּ	וְשָׁמַעְתָּ	אֶל־הַשָּׁמַיִם	שִׁבְתְּךָ
'ăsher	'ēth		wesālāchăttā	weshāma'āttā	'el-hashshāmayim	shivtekhā
which			and You will forgive	then You will hear	to the heavens	your dwelling

427	5558.111, 904	3937, 7739	382	2490.121
n fs	cj, v Qal pf 3ms, prep, ps 3ms	prep, n ms, ps 3ms	n ms	v Qal impf 3ms
אָלָה	וְנָשָׁא־בוֹ	לְרֵעֵהוּ	אִישׁ	יֶחֱטָא
'ālāh	wenāshā'-vô	lerē'ēhû	'îsh	yechětā'
an oath	and he has lifted up against him	against his fellow	a man	he sins

26. And now, O God of Israel, let thy word, I pray thee, be verified, which thou spakest unto thy servant David my father: ... may this promise which you made to my father David, your servant, be confirmed, *NAB* ... let thy words be established, *Douay* ... please continue to keep that promise you made, *NCV* ... let Your word come true, *NKJV* ... let thy word be stable, *Tyndale*.

27. But will God indeed dwell on the earth? behold, the heaven and heaven of heavens cannot contain thee; how much less this house that I have builded?: ... does God really live on earth? The heaven, yes, the heaven of heavens, cannot hold You; how much less this temple I built!, *Beck* ... the highest heaven cannot contain thee, *Goodspeed* ... The sky and the highest place in heaven cannot contain you, *NCV* ... Heaven itself, *REB* ... If the very heavens, and the heavens that are above the heavens, cannot contain thee, what welcome can it offer thee, *Knox*.

28. Yet have thou respect unto the prayer of thy servant, and to his supplication, O Lord my God, to hearken unto the cry and to the prayer, which thy servant prayeth before thee today: ... let your heart be turned to the prayer of your servant, O Lord God, and to his prayer for grace; give ear, *BB* ... that Thou mayest be responsive to, *Berkeley* ... listen favourably to the prayer and entreaty of your servant, Yahweh my God, *JB* ... have regard to the prayer of thy servant, and to his supplications, O Lord my God. Hear the hymn, *Douay* ... Look kindly on the prayer and petition of your servant, O Lord, my God, and listen to the cry of supplication, *NAB*.

29. That thine eyes may be open toward this house night and day, even toward the place of which thou hast said, My name shall be there: ... Night and day please watch over this Temple where you have said, I will be worshiped there, *NCV* ... should be ever watching, night and day, over this temple of thine, the chosen sanctuary of thy name, *Knox* ... where you have decreed you shall be honored, *NAB* ... Watch over this Temple day and night, *Good News*.

that thou mayest hearken unto the prayer which thy servant shall make toward this place: ... hearing the prayer which your servant may make, turning to this place, *BB* ... is offering toward this house, *Berkeley* ... Listen to the prayer, *JB* ... May you always hear the prayer I make, *NLT*.

30. And hearken thou to the supplication of thy servant, and of thy people Israel, when they shall pray toward this place: and hear thou in heaven thy dwellingplace: and when thou hearest, forgive: ... Listen to the petitions ... which they offer in this place. Listen from your heavenly dwelling and grant pardon, *NAB* ... show them mercy, *Douay* ... May you hear the humble and earnest requests from me and your people, *NLT* ... hear the pleading, *Beck* ... give ear and forgive, *Berkeley*.

31. If any man trespass against his neighbour, and an oath be laid upon him to cause him to swear, and the oath come before thine altar in this house: ... If anyone wrongs another person and has to take an oath, and so he comes and swears before Your altar in this temple, *Beck* ... he is adjured to take an oath, and the adjuration is made, *NEB* ... If a man sins against his

3937, 426.541	971.111	427	3937, 6686	4326
prep, v Hiphil inf con, ps 3ms	cj, v Qal pf 3ms	n fs	prep, *n mp*	n ms, ps 2ms
לְהַאֲלֹתוֹ	וּבָא	אָלָה	לִפְנֵי	מִזְבַּחֲךָ
lᵉha'ălōthô	ûvā'	'ālāh	liphnê	mizbachkhā
to cause him to swear an oath	and he comes	he swears an oath	before	your altar

904, 1041	2172		887	8471.123	8452	6449.113
prep, art, n ms	art, dem pron	32.	cj, pers pron	v Qal impf 2ms	art, n md	cj, v Qal pf 2ms
בַּבַּיִת	הַזֶּה		וְאַתָּה	תִּשְׁמַע	הַשָּׁמַיִם	וְעָשִׂיתָ
babbayith	hazzeh		wᵉ'attāh	tishma'	hashshāmayim	wᵉ'āsîthā
in the Temple	the this		then You	You will hear	the heavens	and You will execute

8570.113	881, 5860	3937, 7855.541	7857	3937, 5598.141	1932
cj, v Qal pf 2ms	do, n mp, ps 2ms	prep, v Hiphil inf con	n ms	prep, v Qal inf con	n ms, ps 3ms
וְשָׁפַטְתָּ	אֶת־עֲבָדֶיךָ	לְהַרְשִׁיעַ	רָשָׁע	לָתֵת	דַּרְכּוֹ
wᵉshāphaṭṭā	'eth-'ăvādhêkhā	lᵉharshîa'	rāshā'	lāthēth	darkô
and You will judge	your servants	to condemn	the evildoer	to put	his way

904, 7513	3937, 6927.541	6926	3937, 5598.141	3937
prep, n ms, ps 3ms	cj, prep, v Hiphil inf con	n ms	prep, v Qal inf con	prep, ps 3ms
בְּרֹאשׁוֹ	וּלְהַצְדִּיק	צַדִּיק	לָתֶת	לוֹ
bᵉrō'shô	ûlăhatsdîq	tsaddîq	lātheth	lô
on his head	and to vindicate	the righteous	to give	to him

3626, 6930		904, 5238.241	6194	3547	3937, 6686
prep, n fs, ps 3ms	33.	prep, v Niphal inf con	n ms, ps 2ms	pn	prep, *n mp*
כְּצִדְקָתוֹ		בְּהִנָּגֵף	עַמְּךָ	יִשְׂרָאֵל	לִפְנֵי
kᵉtsidhqāthô		bᵉhinnāghēph	'ammᵉkhā	yisrā'ēl	liphnê
according to his righteousness		when being stricken	your people	Israel	before

342.151	866	2490.126, 3937	8178.116	420	3142.516
v Qal act ptc ms	rel part	v Qal impf 3mp, prep, ps 2ms	cj, v Qal pf 3cp	prep, ps 2ms	cj, v Hiphil pf 3cp
אוֹיֵב	אֲשֶׁר	יֶחֶטְאוּ־לָךְ	וְשָׁבוּ	אֵלֶיךָ	וְהוֹדוּ
'ôyēv	'ăsher	yecheṭ'û-lākh	wᵉshāvû	'ēlêkhā	wᵉhôdhû
the enemy	when	they sin against You	but they return	to You	and they praise

881, 8428	6663.716	2706.716	420	904, 1041	2172
do, n ms, ps 2ms	cj, v Hithpael pf 3cp	cj, v Hithpael pf 3cp	prep, ps 2ms	prep, art, n ms	art, dem pron
אֶת־שְׁמֶךָ	וְהִתְפַּלְלוּ	וְהִתְחַנְּנוּ	אֵלֶיךָ	בַּבַּיִת	הַזֶּה
'eth-shᵉmekhā	wᵉhithpalᵉlû	wᵉhithchannᵉnû	'ēlêkhā	babbayith	hazzeh
your name	and they pray	and they make supplication	to You	in the Temple	the this

	887	8471.123	8452	5739.113	3937, 2496	6194	3547
34.	cj, pers pron	v Qal impf 2ms	art, n md	cj, v Qal pf 2ms	prep, *n fs*	n ms, ps 2ms	pn
	וְאַתָּה	תִּשְׁמַע	הַשָּׁמַיִם	וְסָלַחְתָּ	לְחַטַּאת	עַמְּךָ	יִשְׂרָאֵל
	wᵉ'attāh	tishma'	hashshāmayim	wᵉsālachtā	lᵉchaṭṭa'th	'ammᵉkhā	yisrā'ēl
	then You	You will hear	the heavens	and You will forgive	the sin of	your people	Israel

8178.513	420, 124	866	5598.113	3937, 1
cj, v Hiphil pf 2ms, ps 3mp	prep, art, n fs	rel part	v Qal pf 2ms	prep, n mp, ps 3mp
וַהֲשֵׁבֹתָם	אֶל־הָאֲדָמָה	אֲשֶׁר	נָתַתָּ	לַאֲבוֹתָם
wahshēvōthām	'el-hā'ădhāmāh	'ăsher	nāthattā	la'ăvôthām
and You will allow them to return	to the land	which	You gave	to their ancestors

	904, 6352.241	8452	3940, 2030.121	4443	3706
35.	prep, v Niphal inf con	n md	cj, neg part, v Qal impf 3ms	n ms	cj
	בְּהֵעָצֵר	שָׁמַיִם	וְלֹא־יִהְיֶה	מָטָר	כִּי
	bᵉhē'ātsēr	shāmayim	wᵉlō'-yihyeh	māṭār	kî
	when being shut up	the heavens	and there is not	rain	because

2490.126, 3937	6663.716	420, 4887	2172	3142.516
v Qal impf 3mp, prep, ps 2ms	cj, v Hithpael pf 3cp	prep, art, n ms	art, dem pron	cj, v Hiphil pf 3cp
יֶחֶטְאוּ־לָךְ	וְהִתְפַּלְלוּ	אֶל־הַמָּקוֹם	הַזֶּה	וְהוֹדוּ
yecheṯ'û-lākh	wehithpalelû	'el-hammāqôm	hazzeh	wehôdhû
they sin against You	but they pray	toward the place	the this	and they praise

881, 8428	4623, 2496	8178.126	3706	6257.126	36. 887
do, n ms, ps 2ms	cj, prep, n fs, ps 3mp	v Qal impf 3mp	cj	v Qal impf 3mp, ps 3mp	cj, pers pron
אֶת־שְׁמֶךָ	וּמֵחַטָּאתָם	יְשׁוּבוּן	כִּי	תַעֲנֵם	וְאַתָּה
'eth-shemekhā	ûmēchaṯṯā'thām	yeshûvûn	kî	tha'ănēm	we'attāh
your name	and from their sin	they turn away	because	You afflict them	then You

8471.123	8452	5739.113	3937, 2496	5860	6194
v Qal impf 2ms	art, n md	cj, v Qal pf 2ms	prep, *n fs*	n mp, ps 2ms	cj, n ms, ps 2ms
תִּשְׁמַע	הַשָּׁמַיִם	וְסָלַחְתָּ	לְחַטַּאת	עֲבָדֶיךָ	וְעַמְּךָ
tishma'	hashshāmayim	wesālachtā	lechaṯṯa'th	'ăvādhêkhā	we'ammekhā
You will hear	the heavens	and You will forgive	the sin of	your servants	and your people

3547	3706	3498.523	881, 1932	3009B	866	2050.126, 904
pn	cj	v Hiphil impf 2ms, ps 3mp	do, art, n fs	art, adj	rel part	v Qal impf 3mp, prep, ps 3fs
יִשְׂרָאֵל	כִּי	תוֹרֵם	אֶת־הַדֶּרֶךְ	הַטּוֹבָה	אֲשֶׁר	יֵלְכוּ־בָהּ
yisrā'ēl	kî	thôrēm	'eth-hadderekh	haṯṯôvāh	'ăsher	yēlekhû-vāhh
Israel	because	You teach them	the way	the good	which	they should walk in it

5598.113	4443	6142, 800	866, 5598.113	3937, 6194	3937, 5338
cj, v Qal pf 2ms	n ms	prep, n fs, ps 2ms	rel part, v Qal pf 2ms	prep, n ms, ps 2ms	prep, n fs
וְנָתַתָּה	מָטָר	עַל־אַרְצְךָ	אֲשֶׁר־נָתַתָּה	לְעַמְּךָ	לְנַחֲלָה
wenāthattāh	māṯār	'al-'artsekhā	'ăsher-nāthattāh	le'ammekhā	lenachlāh
and You give	rain	on your land	which You have given	to your people	for an inheritance

neighbor and is required to take an oath sanctioned by a curse, *NAB* ... When a person is accused of wronging another and is brought to your altar in this Temple to take an oath that he is innocent, *Good News*.

32. Then hear thou in heaven, and do, and judge thy servants, condemning the wicked, to bring his way upon his head; and justifying the righteous, to give him according to his righteousness: ... and rewarding him according to his justice, *Douay* ... hear in heaven. Judge the case, punish the guilty, but declare that the innocent person is not guilty, *NCV* ... condemning the guilty man and bringing his deeds upon his own head, acquitting the innocent and rewarding him as his innocence may deserve, *NEB* ... and vindicating the righteous, *NRSV*.

33. When thy people Israel be smitten down before the enemy, because they have sinned against thee, and shall turn again to thee, and confess thy name, and pray, and make supplication unto thee in this house: ... are defeated, *RSV* ... if they come here repentant, and acknowledging thy power, pray to thee and plead with thee in this temple, *Knox* ... are overcome in war, *BB* ... but then return to you and acknowledge your name, and pray and seek your favours in this Temple, *JB*.

34. Then hear thou in heaven, and forgive the sin of thy people Israel, and bring them again unto the land which thou gavest unto their fathers: ... you gave to their ancestors, *NCV* ... restore them to the land which, *NEB* ... be merciful unto the sin of thy servants, *Tyndale* ... give ear in heaven, and let the sin of your people have forgiveness, *BB*.

35. When heaven is shut up, and there is no rain, because they have sinned against thee; if they pray toward this place, and confess thy name, and turn from their sin, when thou afflictest them: ... because You made them suffer, *Beck* ... When heaven is sealed up so that it does not rain, *Berkeley* ... If the skies are restrained, *Fenton* ... When you hold back the rain, *Good News*.

36. Then hear thou in heaven, and forgive the sin of thy servants, and of thy people Israel, that thou teach them the good way wherein they should walk, and give rain upon thy land, which thou hast given to thy people for an inheritance: ... for you are constantly showing them the good way which they must follow, *JB* ... teaching them the right way to live and sending rain upon this land of yours, *NAB* ... in possession, *Douay* ... Teach them to do what is right. Then please send rain to this land you have given particularly to them, *NCV*.

37. If there be in the land famine, if there be pestilence, blasting,

	7743	3706, 2030.121	904, 800	1746	3706, 2030.121	8169	3539
37.	n ms	cj, v Qal impf 3ms	prep, art, n fs	n ms	cj, v Qal impf 3ms	n ms	n ms
	רָעָב	כִּי־יִהְיֶה	בָּאָרֶץ	דֶּבֶר	כִּי־יִהְיֶה	שִׁדָּפוֹן	יֵרָקוֹן
	rā'āv	kî-yihyeh	vā'ārets	dever	kî-yihyeh	shiddāphôn	yērāqôn
	famine	when it is	in the land	the plague	when it is	scorching heat	mildew

722	2730	3706	2030.121	3706	7173.111, 3937	342.151
n ms	n ms	cj	v Qal impf 3ms	cj	v Qal pf 3ms, prep, ps 3ms	v Qal act ptc ms, ps 3ms
אַרְבֶּה	חָסִיל	כִּי	יִהְיֶה	כִּי	יָצַר־לוֹ	אֹיְבוֹ
'arbeh	chāsîl	kî	yihyeh	kî	yātsar-lô	'ōyevô
migratory locusts	locusts	when	it is	that	he oppresses them	their enemy

904, 800	8554	3725, 5237	3706, 4382		3725, 8940	3725, 8798	866
prep, *n fs*	n mp, ps 3ms	*adj*, n ms	*adj*, n fs	**38.**	*adj*, n fs	*adj*, n fs	rel part
בְּאֶרֶץ	שְׁעָרָיו	כָּל־נֶגַע	כָּל־מַחֲלָה		כָּל־תְּפִלָּה	כָּל־תְּחִנָּה	אֲשֶׁר
be'erets	she'ārâv	kol-negha'	kol-machlāh		kol-tephillāh	khol-techinnāh	'ăsher
in the land of	his gates	all striking	all sickness		all prayer	all supplication	which

2030.122	3937, 3725, 119	3937, 3725	6194	3547	866	3156.126	382
v Qal impf 3fs	prep, *adj*, art, n ms	prep, adj	n ms, ps 2ms	pn	rel pron	v Qal impf 3mp	n ms
תִהְיֶה	לְכָל־הָאָדָם	לְכֹל	עַמְּךָ	יִשְׂרָאֵל	אֲשֶׁר	יֵדְעוּן	אִישׁ
thihyeh	lekhol-hā'ādhām	lekhōl	'ammekhā	yisrā'ēl	'ăsher	yēdhe'ûn	'îsh
it will be	for all humankind	for all	your people	Israel	who	they know	a man

5237	3949	6816.111	3834	420, 1041	2172
n ms	n ms, ps 3ms	cj, v Qal pf 3ms	n fd, ps 3ms	prep, art, n ms	art, dem pron
נֶגַע	לְבָבוֹ	וּפָרַשׂ	כַּפָּיו	אֶל־הַבַּיִת	הַזֶּה
negha'	levāvô	ûphāras	kappâv	'el-habbayith	hazzeh
the wound of	his heart	and he spreads out	his palms	toward the Temple	the this

	887	8471.123	8452	4487	3553.141	5739.113
39.	cj, pers pron	v Qal impf 2ms	art, n md	*n ms*	v Qal inf con, ps 2ms	cj, v Qal pf 2ms
	וְאַתָּה	תִּשְׁמַע	הַשָּׁמַיִם	מְכוֹן	שִׁבְתֶּךָ	וְסָלַחְתָּ
	we'attāh	tishma'	hashshāmayim	mekhôn	shivtekhā	wesālachtā
	then You	You will hear	the heavens	the abode of	your dwelling	and You will forgive

6449.113	5598.113	3937, 382	3626, 3725, 1932	866
cj, v Qal pf 2ms	cj, v Qal pf 2ms	prep, art, n ms	prep, *adj*, n mp, ps 3ms	rel part
וְעָשִׂיתָ	וְנָתַתָּ	לָאִישׁ	כְּכָל־דְּרָכָיו	אֲשֶׁר
we'āsîthā	wenāthattā	lā'îsh	kekhol-derākhâv	'ăsher
and You will execute	and You will give	to each	according to all his ways	which

3156.123	881, 3949	3706, 887	3156.113	3937, 940	881, 3949
v Qal impf 2ms	do, n ms, ps 3ms	cj, pers pron	v Qal pf 2ms	prep, n ms, ps 2ms	do, *n ms*
תֵּדַע	אֶת־לְבָבוֹ	כִּי־אַתָּה	יָדַעְתָּ	לְבַדְּךָ	אֶת־לְבַב
tēdha'	'eth-levāvô	kî-'attāh	yādha'āttā	levaddekhā	'eth-levav
You know	his heart	because You	You know	only You	the hearts of

3725, 1158	119		3937, 4775	3486.126	3725, 3219	866, 2062
adj, *n mp*	art, n ms	**40.**	prep, prep	v Qal impf 3mp, ps 2ms	*adj*, art, n mp	rel part, pers pron
כָּל־בְּנֵי	הָאָדָם		לְמַעַן	יִרָאוּךָ	כָּל־הַיָּמִים	אֲשֶׁר־הֵם
kol-benê	hā'ādhām		lema'an	yirā'ûkhā	kol-hayyāmîm	'ăsher-hēm
all the children of	humankind		so that	they may fear You	all the days	which they

2552	6142, 6686	124	866	5598.113	3937, 1		1612
adj	prep, *n mp*	art, n fs	rel part	v Qal pf 2ms	prep, n mp, ps 1cp	**41.**	cj, cj
חַיִּים	עַל־פְּנֵי	הָאֲדָמָה	אֲשֶׁר	נָתַתָּה	לַאֲבֹתֵינוּ		וְגַם
chayyîm	'al-penê	hā'ădhāmāh	'ăsher	nāthattāh	la'ăvōthênû		wegham
living	on the surface of	the land	which	You gave	to our ancestors		and also

420, 5425	866	3940, 6194	3547	2000	971.111	4623, 800
prep, art, n ms	rel pron	neg part, prep, n ms, ps 2ms	pn	pers pron	cj, v Qal pf 3ms	prep, n fs
אֶל־הַנָּכְרִי	אֲשֶׁר	לֹא־מֵעַמְּךָ	יִשְׂרָאֵל	הוּא	וּבָא	מֵאֶרֶץ
'el-hannākherî	'ăsher	lō'-mē'ammekhā	yisrā'ēl	hû'	ûvā'	mē'erets
to the foreigner	who	not among your people	Israel	he	and he comes	from a land

7632	3937, 4775	8428		3706	8471.126	881, 8428	1448
adj	prep, prep	n ms, ps 2ms	**42.**	cj	v Qal impf 3mp	do, n ms, ps 2ms	art, adj
רְחוֹקָה	לְמַעַן	שְׁמֶךָ		כִּי	יִשְׁמְעוּן	אֶת־שִׁמְךָ	הַגָּדוֹל
rechôqāh	lema'an	shemekhā		kî	yishme'ûn	'eth-shimkhā	haggādhôl
far away	because of	your name		because	they will hear	your name	the great

881, 3135	2481	2307	5371.157	971.111	6663.711
cj, do, n fs, ps 2ms	art, adj	cj, n fs, ps 2ms	art, v Qal pass ptc fs	cj, v Qal pf 3ms	cj, v Hithpael pf 3ms
וְאֶת־יָדְךָ	הַחֲזָקָה	וּזְרֹעֲךָ	הַנְּטוּיָה	וּבָא	וְהִתְפַּלֵּל
we'eth-yādhekhā	hachzāqāh	ûzărō'ăkhā	hannetûyāh	ûvā'	wehithpallēl
and your hand	the strong	and your arm	the one outstretched	and he comes	and he prays

420, 1041	2172		887	8471.123	8452	4487
prep, art, n ms	art, dem pron	**43.**	pers pron	v Qal impf 2ms	art, n md	*n ms*
אֶל־הַבַּיִת	הַזֶּה		אַתָּה	תִּשְׁמַע	הַשָּׁמַיִם	מְכוֹן
'el-habbayith	hazzeh		'attāh	tishma'	hashshāmayim	mekhôn
toward the Temple	the this		You	You will hear	the heavens	the abode of

mildew, locust, or if there be caterpiller; if their enemy besiege them in the land of their cities; whatsoever plague, whatsoever sickness there be: ... or grasshoppers, *NKJV* ... whatever disaster or disease may come, *NIV* ... or pestilence, or blight either black or red, or locusts developing or fully grown, *REB* ... If there is no food in the land, or if there is disease, or if the fruits of the earth are damaged through heat or water, locust or worm; if their towns are shut in by their attackers; whatever trouble, whatever disease there may be, *BB*.

38. What prayer and supplication soever be made by any man, or by all thy people Israel, which shall know every man the plague of his own heart, and spread forth his hands toward this house: ... whose heart convicts him, who prays or pleads, *Beck* ... who recognizes what his trouble is and stretches out, *Berkeley* ... as each one, prompted by the remorse of his own heart, spreads out, *NEB* ... each one aware of the afflictions of his own heart, *NIV*.

39. Then hear thou in heaven thy dwellingplace, and forgive, and do, and give to every man according to his ways, whose heart thou knowest; (for thou, even thou only, knowest the hearts of all the children of men;): ... forgive, act, and render to all whose hearts you know, *NRSV* ... Give ear in heaven your living-place, acting in mercy; and give to every man whose secret heart is open to you, the reward of all his ways, *BB* ... Give each what he deserves as You know his heart, *Beck* ... pardon, and examine, and grant to each according to his need, as You know his heart, *Fenton*.

40. That they may fear thee all the days that they live in the land which thou gavest unto our fathers: ... they may reverence you throughout their lives in the country which you gave to our ancestors, *JB* ... your people will respect you as long as they live, *NCV* ... they may give you worship all the days of their life, *BB* ... they may revere Thee, *Berkeley*.

41. Moreover concerning a stranger, that is not of thy people Israel, but cometh out of a far country for thy name's sake: ... as for the man from a strange land, who is not of your people Israel; when he comes from a far country because of the glory of your name, *BB* ... comes from a distant land to honor you, *NAB* ... Even the foreigner, not belonging to your people Israel but coming from a distant country, attracted by your name, *Berkeley*.

42. (For they shall hear of thy great name, and of thy strong hand, and of thy stretched out arm;) when he shall come and pray toward this house: ... Your powerful hand and outstretched arm, *Beck* ... Thy mighty hand, *Berkeley* ... when he comes and prays toward this temple, *NAB*.

43. Hear thou in heaven thy dwellingplace, and do according to all that the stranger calleth to thee for: ... listen from your heavenly dwelling. Do all that the foreigner asks of you, *NAB* ... in the firmament of thy dwelling place, and do all those things for which that stranger shall call upon thee, *Douay* ... everything the foreigner requests of Thee, *Berkeley* ... where you reside, and grant all that the foreigner asks, *JB*.

that all people of the earth may know thy name, to fear thee, as do thy people Israel; and that they

3553.141	6449.113	3626, 3725	866, 7410.121	420
v Qal inf con, ps 2ms	cj, v Qal pf 2ms	prep, adj	rel part, v Qal impf 3ms	prep, ps 2ms
שִׁבְתְּךָ	וְעָשִׂיתָ	כְּכֹל	אֲשֶׁר־יִקְרָא	אֵלֶיךָ
shivtekhā	weʿāsîthā	kekhōl	'ăsher-yiqŏrā'	'ēlêkhā
your dwelling	and You will execute	according to all	that he calls	to You

5425	3937, 4775	3156.126	3725, 6194	800	881, 8428	3937, 3486.141
art, n ms	prep, prep	v Qal impf 3mp	*adj, n mp*	art, n fs	do, n ms, ps 2ms	prep, v Qal inf con
הַנָּכְרִי	לְמַעַן	יֵדְעוּן	כָּל־עַמֵּי	הָאָרֶץ	אֶת־שְׁמֶךָ	לְיִרְאָה
hannākherî	lemaʿan	yēdheʿûn	kol-ʿammê	hā'ārets	'eth-shemekhā	leyir'āh
the foreigner	so that	they will know	all the peoples of	the earth	your name	to fear

881	3626, 6194	3547	3937, 3156.141	3706, 8428	7410.211
do, ps 2ms	prep, n ms, ps 2ms	pn	cj, prep, v Qal inf con	cj, n ms, ps 2ms	v Niphal pf 3ms
אֹתְךָ	כְּעַמְּךָ	יִשְׂרָאֵל	וְלָדַעַת	כִּי־שִׁמְךָ	נִקְרָא
'ōthekhā	keʿammekhā	yisrā'ēl	welādhaʿath	kî-shimkhā	niqŏrā'
You	like you people	Israel	and to know	because your name	it is called

6142, 1041	2172	866	1161.115		3706, 3428.121	6194
prep, art, n ms	art, dem pron	rel part	v Qal pf 1cs		cj, v Qal impf 3ms	n ms, ps 2ms
עַל־הַבַּיִת	הַזֶּה	אֲשֶׁר	בָּנִיתִי	**44.**	כִּי־יֵצֵא	עַמְּךָ
ʿal-habbayith	hazzeh	'ăsher	bānîthî		kî-yētsē'	ʿammekhā
onto the Temple	the this	which	I have built		when they go out	your people

3937, 4560	6142, 342.151	904, 1932	866	8365.123
prep, art, n fs	prep, v Qal act ptc ms, ps 3ms	prep, art, n ms	rel part	v Qal impf 2ms, ps 3mp
לַמִּלְחָמָה	עַל־אֹיְבוֹ	בַּדֶּרֶךְ	אֲשֶׁר	תִּשְׁלָחֵם
lammilchāmāh	ʿal-'ōyevô	badderekh	'ăsher	tishlāchēm
into the battle	against their enemy	in the way	which	You will send them out

6663.716	420, 3176	1932	6111	866	1013.113	904
cj, v Hithpael pf 3cp	prep, pn	*n ms*	art, n fs	rel part	v Qal pf 2ms	prep, ps 3fs
וְהִתְפַּלְלוּ	אֶל־יְהוָה	דֶּרֶךְ	הָעִיר	אֲשֶׁר	בָּחַרְתָּ	בָּהּ
wehithpalelû	'el-yehwāh	derekh	hā'îr	'ăsher	bāchartā	bāhh
and they pray	to Yahweh	the way of	the city	which	You have chosen	with it

1041	866, 1161.115	3937, 8428		8471.113	8452
cj, art, n ms	rel part, v Qal pf 1cs	prep, n ms, ps 2ms		cj, v Qal pf 2ms	art, n md
וְהַבַּיִת	אֲשֶׁר־בָּנִתִי	לִשְׁמֶךָ	**45.**	וְשָׁמַעְתָּ	הַשָּׁמַיִם
wehabbayith	'ăsher-bānithî	lishmekhā		weshāmaʿättā	hashshāmayim
and the Temple	which I have built	to your name		then You will hear	the heavens

881, 8940	881, 8798	6449.113	5122		3706
do, n fs, ps 3mp	cj, do, n fs, ps 3mp	cj, v Qal pf 2ms	n ms, ps 3mp		cj
אֶת־תְּפִלָּתָם	וְאֶת־תְּחִנָּתָם	וְעָשִׂיתָ	מִשְׁפָּטָם	**46.**	כִּי
'eth-tephillāthām	we'eth-techinnāthām	weʿāsîthā	mishpāṭām		kî
their prayer	and their supplication	and You will execute	their justice		when

2490.126, 3937	3706	375	119	866	3940, 2490.121
v Qal impf 3mp, prep, ps 2ms	cj	*sub*	n ms	rel pron	neg part, v Qal impf 3ms
יֶחֶטְאוּ־לָךְ	כִּי	אֵין	אָדָם	אֲשֶׁר	לֹא־יֶחֱטָא
yecheṭ'û-lākh	kî	'ên	'ādhām	'ăsher	lō'-yechĕṭā'
they sin against You	because	there is not	humankind	who	he does not sin

613.113	904	5598.113	3937, 6686	342.151
cj, v Qal pf 2ms	prep, ps 3mp	cj, v Qal pf 2ms, ps 3mp	prep, *n mp*	v Qal act ptc ms
וְאָנַפְתָּ	בָם	וּנְתַתָּם	לִפְנֵי	אוֹיֵב
we'ānaphtā	vām	ûnethattām	liphnê	'ōyēv
and You are angry	with them	and You give them	before	the enemy

8091.116	8091.152	420, 800	342.151	7632
cj, v Qal pf 3cp, ps 3mp	v Qal act ptc mp, ps 3mp	prep, *n fs*	art, v Qal act ptc ms	adj
וְשָׁבוּם	שֹׁבֵיהֶם	אֶל־אֶרֶץ	הָאוֹיֵב	רְחוֹקָה
weshāvûm	shōvêhem	'el-'erets	hā'ôyēv	rechôqāh
and they take them captive	their captors	to the land of	the enemy	far away

173	7427		8178.516	420, 3949	904, 800	866
cj	adj	**47.**	cj, v Hiphil pf 3cp	prep, n ms, ps 3mp	prep, art, n fs	rel part
אוֹ	קְרוֹבָה		וְהֵשִׁיבוּ	אֶל־לִבָּם	בָּאָרֶץ	אֲשֶׁר
'ô	qōrôvāh		wehēshîvû	'el-libbām	bā'ārets	'ăsher
or	near		but they cause to return	to their heart	in the land	which

8091.216, 8427	8178.116	2706.716	420
v Niphal pf 3cp, adv	cj, v Qal pf 3cp	cj, v Hithpael pf 3cp	prep, ps 2ms
נִשְׁבּוּ־שָׁם	וְשָׁבוּ	וְהִתְחַנְּנוּ	אֵלֶיךָ
nishbû-shām	weshāvû	wehithchannenû	'ēlêkhā
they have been taken captive there	and they turn back	and they make supplication	to You

904, 800	8091.152	3937, 569.141	2490.119	5971.519
prep, *n fs*	v Qal act ptc mp, ps 3mp	prep, v Qal inf con	v Qal pf 1cp	cj, v Hiphil pf 1cp
בְּאֶרֶץ	שֹׁבֵיהֶם	לֵאמֹר	חָטָאנוּ	וְהֶעֱוִינוּ
be'erets	shōvêhem	lē'mōr	chāṭā'nû	wehe'ĕwînû
in the land of	their captors	saying	we have sinned	and we have acted perversely

7855.119		8178.116	420	904, 3725, 3949
v Qal pf 1cp	**48.**	cj, v Qal pf 3cp	prep, ps 2ms	prep, *adj*, n ms, ps 3mp
רָשָׁעְנוּ		וְשָׁבוּ	אֵלֶיךָ	בְּכָל־לְבָבָם
rāshā'ănû		weshāvû	'ēlêkhā	bekhol-levāvām
we have acted wickedly		and they return	to You	with all their heart

may know that this house, which I have builded, is called by thy name: ... then people everywhere will know you and respect you, just as your people in Israel do. Then everyone will know I built this Temple as a place to worship you, *NCV* ... revere Thee, *Berkeley* ... the peoples of the world may know you and obey you, *Good News* ... may acknowledge your name and, *JB*.

44. If thy people go out to battle against their enemy, whithersoever thou shalt send them, and shall pray unto the LORD toward the city which thou hast chosen, and toward the house that I have built for thy name: ... Whatever the direction in which you may send your people forth to war against their enemies, if they pray to you, O Lord, toward the city you have chosen and the temple I have built in your honor, *NAB* ... along some road on which you send them, *NCV* ... built in honour of thy name, *NEB* ... their attackers, by whatever way you may send them, if they make their prayer to the Lord, turning their faces to this town of yours, *BB*.

45. Then hear thou in heaven their prayer and their supplication, and maintain their cause: ... and plead and do for them what is right, *Beck* ... and support their cause, *Berkeley* ... and grant them their right, *Fenton* ... and uphold their cause, *Goodspeed*.

46. If they sin against thee, (for there is no man that sinneth not,) and thou be angry with them, and deliver them to the enemy, so that they carry them away captives unto the land of the enemy, far or near: ... and abandon them to the enemy, and their captors carry them off to a hostile country, *JB* ... so that their captors deport them to a hostile land, *NAB* ... (and what man is free from sin?), *NEB* ... and give them up into the power of those who are fighting against them, so that they take them away as prisoners into a strange land, *BB*.

47. Yet if they shall bethink themselves in the land whither they were carried captives, and repent, and make supplication unto thee in the land of them that carried them captives, saying, We have sinned, and have done perversely, we have committed wickedness: ... if in the land of exile they come to their senses and repent and plead with You in the land of exile, *Beck* ... done wrong, and transgressed, *Berkeley* ... and have done iniquity, we have dealt perversely, *Darby* ... and have acted perversely and wickedly, *Goodspeed*.

48. And so return unto thee with all their heart, and with all their soul, in the land of their enemies, which led them away captive, and pray unto thee toward their land, which thou gavest unto their fathers, the city which thou hast

881	866, 8091.116	342.152	904, 800	904, 3725, 5497
do, ps 3mp	rel part, v Qal pf 3cp	v Qal act ptc mp, ps 3mp	prep, *n fs*	cj, prep, *adj*, n fs, ps 3mp
אֹתָם	אֲשֶׁר־שָׁבוּ	אֹיְבֵיהֶם	בְּאֶרֶץ	וּבְכָל־נַפְשָׁם
'ōthām	'ăsher-shāvû	'ōyevêhem	be'erets	ûvekhol-naphshām
them	who they took captive	their enemies	in the land of	and with all their soul

6111	3937, 1	5598.113	866	800	1932	420	6663.716
art, n fs	prep, n mp, ps 3mp	v Qal pf 2ms	rel part	n fs, ps 3mp	*n ms*	prep, ps 2ms	cj, v Hithpael pf 3cp
הָעִיר	לַאֲבוֹתָם	נָתַתָּה	אֲשֶׁר	אַרְצָם	דֶּרֶךְ	אֵלֶיךָ	וְהִתְפַּלְלוּ
hā'îr	la'ăvôthām	nāthattāh	'ăsher	'artsām	derekh	'ēlêkhā	wehithpalelû
the city	to their ancestors	You gave	which	their land	the way of	to You	and they pray

3937, 8428	866, 1161.115	1041	1013.113	866
prep, n ms, ps 2ms	rel part, v Qal pf 1cs	cj, art, n ms	v Qal pf 2ms	rel part
לִשְׁמֶךָ	אֲשֶׁר־בָּנִיתָ	וְהַבַּיִת	בָּחַרְתָּ	אֲשֶׁר
lishmekhā	'ăsher-bānîthā	wehabbayith	bāchartā	'ăsher
to your name	which I have built	and the Temple	You have chosen	which

881, 8940	3553.141	4487	8452	8471.113	
do, n fs, ps 3mp	v Qal inf con, ps 2ms	*n ms*	art, n md	cj, v Qal pf 2ms	49.
אֶת־תְּפִלָּתָם	שִׁבְתְּךָ	מְכוֹן	הַשָּׁמַיִם	וְשָׁמַעְתָּ	
'eth-tephillāthām	shivtekhā	mekhôn	hashshāmayim	weshāma'ättā	
their prayer	your dwelling	the abode of	the heavens	then You will hear	

3937, 6194	5739.113		5122	6449.113	881, 8798
prep, n ms, ps 2ms	cj, v Qal pf 2ms	50.	n ms, ps 3mp	cj, v Qal pf 2ms	cj, do, n fs, ps 3mp
לְעַמְּךָ	וְסָלַחְתָּ		מִשְׁפָּטָם	וְעָשִׂיתָ	וְאֶת־תְּחִנָּתָם
le'ammekhā	wesālachtā		mishpātām	we'āsîthā	we'eth-techinnāthām
your people	and You will forgive		their justice	and You will execute	and their supplication

6839.116, 904	866	3937, 3725, 6840	2490.116, 3937	866
v Qal pf 3cp, prep, ps 2ms	rel part	cj, prep, *adj*, n mp, ps 3mp	v Qal pf 3cp, prep, ps 2ms	rel pron
פָּשְׁעוּ־בָךְ	אֲשֶׁר	וּלְכָל־פִּשְׁעֵיהֶם	חָטְאוּ־לָךְ	אֲשֶׁר
pāshe'û-vākh	'ăsher	ûlăkhol-pish'êhem	chāṯe'û-lākh	'ăsher
they have transgressed against You	which	and all their offenses	they sinned against You	who

8091.152	3937, 6686	3937, 7641	5598.113
v Qal act ptc mp, ps 3mp	prep, *n mp*	prep, n mp	cj, v Qal pf 2ms, ps 3mp
שֹׁבֵיהֶם	לִפְנֵי	לְרַחֲמִים	וּנְתַתָּם
shōvêhem	liphnê	lerachmîm	ûnethattām
their captors	before	compassion	and You give them

2062	5338	3706, 6194		7638.316
pers pron	cj, n fs, ps 2ms	cj, n ms, ps 2ms	51.	cj, v Piel pf 3cp, ps 3mp
הֵם	וְנַחֲלָתְךָ	כִּי־עַמְּךָ		וְרִחֲמוּם
hēm	wenachlāthekhā	kî-'ammekhā		werichāmûm
they	and your inheritance	because your people		and they will have compassion on them

1298	3685	4623, 8761	4623, 4875	3428.513	866
art, n ms	*n ms*	prep, *n ms*	prep, pn	v Hiphil pf 2ms	rel pron
הַבַּרְזֶל	כּוּר	מִתּוֹךְ	מִמִּצְרַיִם	הוֹצֵאתָ	אֲשֶׁר
habbarzel	kûr	mittôkh	mimmitsrayim	hôtsē'thā	'ăsher
the iron	the furnace of	from the middle of	from Egypt	You brought out	whom

5860	420, 8798	6858.158	6084	3937, 2030.141	
n ms, ps 2ms	prep, *n fs*	v Qal pass ptc fp	n fd, ps 2ms	prep, v Qal inf con	52.
עַבְדְּךָ	אֶל־תְּחִנַּת	פְּתֻחוֹת	עֵינֶיךָ	לִהְיוֹת	
'avdekhā	'el-techinnath	phethuchôth	'ênêkhā	lihyôth	
your servant	to the supplication of	opened	your eyes	to be	

chosen, and the house which I have built for thy name: ... with all their mind and heart, *Goodspeed* ... turning towards the country which you gave to their ancestors, *JB* ... and the temple I have built in your honor, *NAB* ... if they repent, *NRSV*.

49. Then hear thou their prayer and their supplication in heaven thy dwellingplace, and maintain their cause: ... and their plea, *NRSV* ... and see right done to them, *BB* ... and support their cause, *Berkeley* ... uphold their cause, *Goodspeed*.

50. And forgive thy people that have sinned against thee, and all their transgressions wherein they have transgressed against thee: ... for all the crimes against you of which they have been guilty, *JB* ... the offenses they have committed against you, *NAB* ... and all their iniquities, *Douay* ... Answering with forgiveness the people who have done wrong against you, and overlooking the evil which they have done against you, *BB*.

and give them compassion before them who carried them captive, that they may have compassion on them: ... allow them to arouse the pity of their captors so that these may have pity on them, *JB* ... grant them mercy before their captors, so that these will be merciful to them, *NAB* ... cause their conquerors to show them mercy, *NIV* ... let those who made them prisoners be moved with pity for them, *BB*.

51. For they be thy people, and thine inheritance, which thou broughtest forth out of Egypt, from the midst of the furnace of iron: ... and Your possession whom You brought out of Egypt from the middle of the iron smelter, *Beck* ... Thy people, *Berkeley* ... that Iron foundry, *JB* ... your special possession—whom you brought out of the iron-smeltering furnace of Egypt, *NLT*.

52. That thine eyes may be open unto the supplication of thy servant, and unto the supplication of thy people Israel, to hearken unto them in all that they call for unto thee: ... Let your eyes be open to the plea of your servant, and to the plea of your people Israel, listening to them whenever they call to you, *NRSV* ... open to the entreaty of, *REB* ... let thy eyes be watchful, to look down upon me, thy servant, and upon thy people, when they cry for aid; give all their requests a hearing, *Knox* ... Always give attention when Your servant pleads and Your people Israel ask for mercy, *Beck*.

53. For thou didst separate them from among all the people of the earth, to be thine inheritance, as thou spakest by the hand of Moses thy servant, when thou broughtest our fathers out of Egypt, O Lord GOD: ... to be your heritage, as you said *BB* ... You selected them, *Fenton* ... You chose them from all the peoples to be your own people, *Good News* ... you it was who set them apart, *JB*.

Josiah, the priests, with few exceptions, are almost ignored in the national records. They took the color of their opinions from the reigning kings, even in matters which were contrary to the whole extent and spirit of the Mosaic code. Samuel, who was not a priest, nor even a Levite, performed every function of a priest, and of a high priest, all his life long.

As we have seen, in spite of the positive distinctness of the Second Commandment, not only was the "calf-worship" established, with scarcely a protest, throughout the Northern Kingdom; but Solomon even ventured, without question or reproof, to place twelve oxen under his brazen sea, and to adorn the steps of his throne with golden lions.

No ceremony was more awful, or more strikingly symbolic, in the later religion of Israel, than that of the Great Day of Atonement. It was the only appointed fast in the Jewish year, a day so sacred that it acquired the name of Yoma, "the Day." Yet the Day of Atonement, with its arresting ceremonies and intense significance, is not so much as once mentioned outside the Levitical code by a single prophet, or priest or king. It is not even mentioned—which is exceedingly strange—in the postexilic Books of Chronicles. Between the Book of Leviticus (with its supposed date of 1491 B.C.) down to the days of Philo, Josephus and the New Testament, there is not so much as a hint of the observance of this central ceremony of the whole Levitical Law!

8:54–66. After this he advanced to the altar, and kneeling on his knees (2 Chr. 6:13). He prayed with the palms of his hands upturned to heaven, as though to receive in deep humility the outpoured benefits. The prayer, as here given, consists of an introduction, seven petitions, and a conclusion. It was a passionate entreaty that God would hear, both individually and nationally, both in prosperity and in adversity, the supplications of his people, and even of strangers, who should either pray in the courts of that his house, or should make it the Kibleh of their devotions.

After the dedicatory prayer both the outer and the inner court of the Temple reeked and swam with the blood of countless victims—victims so numerous that the great brazen altar became wholly insufficient for them. At the close of the entire festival they departed to their homes with joy and gladness (1 Ki. 8:66).

420, 8798	6194	3547	3937, 8471.141	420	904, 3725
cj, prep, *n fs*	n ms, ps 2ms	pn	prep, v Qal inf con	prep, ps 3mp	prep, n ms
וְאֶל־תְּחִנַּת	עַמְּךָ	יִשְׂרָאֵל	לִשְׁמֹעַ	אֲלֵיהֶם	בְּכֹל
we'el-techinnath	'ammekhā	yisrā'ēl	lishmōa'	'ălêhem	bekhōl
and to the supplication of	your people	Israel	to listen	to them	in all

7410.141	420		3706, 887	950.513	3937	3937, 5338
v Qal inf con, ps 3mp	prep, ps 2ms	**53.**	cj, pers pron	v Hiphil pf 2ms, ps 3mp	prep, ps 2ms	prep, n fs
קְרָאָם	אֵלֶיךָ		כִּי־אַתָּה	הִבְדַּלְתָּם	לְךָ	לְנַחֲלָה
qāre'ām	'ēlêkhā		kî-'attāh	hivdaltām	lekhā	lenachlāh
their calling	to You		because You	You separated them	to yourself	for an inheritance

4623, 3725	6194	800	3626, 866	1744.313	904, 3135
prep, *adj*	*n mp*	art, n fs	prep, rel part	v Piel pf 2ms	prep, *n fs*
מִכֹּל	עַמֵּי	הָאָרֶץ	כַּאֲשֶׁר	דִּבַּרְתָּ	בְּיַד
mikkōl	'ammê	hā'ārets	ka'ăsher	dibbartā	beyadh
among the entirety of	the peoples of	the earth	just as	You have spoken	by the hand of

5057	5860	904, 3428.541	881, 1	4623, 4875	112	3176
pn	n ms, ps 2ms	prep, v Hiphil inf con, ps 2ms	do, n mp, ps 1cp	prep, pn	n mp, ps 1cs	pn
מֹשֶׁה	עַבְדֶּךָ	בְּהוֹצִיאֲךָ	אֶת־אֲבֹתֵינוּ	מִמִּצְרַיִם	אֲדֹנָי	יְהוִה
mōsheh	'avdekhā	behôtsî'ăkhā	'eth-'ăvōthênû	mimmitsrayim	'ădhōnāy	yehwih
Moses	your servant	when your leading out	our ancestors	from Egypt	O my Lord	Yahweh

	2030.121	3626, 3735.341	8406	3937, 6663.741	420, 3176	881	3725, 8940
54.	cj, v Qal impf 3ms	prep, v Piel inf con	pn	prep, v Hithpael inf con	prep, pn	do	*adj*, art, n fs
	וַיְהִי	כְּכַלּוֹת	שְׁלֹמֹה	לְהִתְפַּלֵּל	אֶל־יְהוָה	אֵת	כָּל־הַתְּפִלָּה
	wayhî	kekhallôth	shelōmōh	lehithpallēl	'el-yehwāh	'ēth	kol-hattephillāh
	and it was	when finishing	Solomon	praying	to Yahweh		all the prayer

8798	2148	7251.111	4623, 3937, 6686	4326	3176	4623, 3895.141
cj, art, n fs	art, dem pron	v Qal pf 3ms	prep, prep, *n mp*	*n ms*	pn	prep, v Qal inf con
וְהַתְּחִנָּה	הַזֹּאת	קָם	מִלִּפְנֵי	מִזְבַּח	יְהוָה	מִכְּרֹעַ
wehattechinnāh	hazzō'th	qām	milliphnê	mizbach	yehwāh	mikkerōa'
and the supplication	the this	he arose	from before	the altar of	Yahweh	from kneeling

6142, 1314	3834	6816.158	8452		6198.121	1313.321
prep, n fp, ps 3ms	cj, n fd, ps 3ms	v Qal pass ptc fp	art, n md	**55.**	cj, v Qal impf 3ms	cj, v Piel impf 3ms
עַל־בִּרְכָּיו	וְכַפָּיו	פְּרֻשׂוֹת	הַשָּׁמָיִם		וַיַּעֲמֹד	וַיְבָרֶךְ
'al-birkâv	wekhappâv	perusôth	hashshāmāyim		wayya'ămōdh	wayvārekh
on his knees	and his palms	being spread	the heavens		and he stood	and he blessed

881	3725, 7235	3547	7249	1448	3937, 569.141		1313.155	3176
do	*adj*, *n ms*	pn	n ms	adj	prep, v Qal inf con	**56.**	v Qal pass ptc ms	pn
אֵת	כָּל־קְהַל	יִשְׂרָאֵל	קוֹל	גָּדוֹל	לֵאמֹר		בָּרוּךְ	יְהוָה
'ēth	kol-qehal	yisrā'ēl	qôl	gādhôl	lē'mōr		bārûkh	yehwāh
	all the assembly of	Israel	a voice	great	saying		blessed	Yahweh

866	5598.111	4640	3937, 6194	3547	3626, 3725	866
rel pron	v Qal pf 3ms	n fs	prep, n ms, ps 3ms	pn	prep, adj	rel part
אֲשֶׁר	נָתַן	מְנוּחָה	לְעַמּוֹ	יִשְׂרָאֵל	כְּכֹל	אֲשֶׁר
'ăsher	nāthan	menûchāh	le'ammô	yisrā'ēl	kekhōl	'ăsher
Who	He has given	a resting place	to his people	Israel	according to all	which

1744.311	3940, 5489.111	1745	259	4623, 3725	1745	3005	866
v Piel pf 3ms	neg part, v Qal pf 3ms	n ms	num	prep, *adj*	n ms, ps 3ms	art, adj	rel part
דִּבֵּר	לֹא־נָפַל	דָּבָר	אֶחָד	מִכֹּל	דְּבָרוֹ	הַטּוֹב	אֲשֶׁר
dibbēr	lō'-nāphal	dāvār	'echādh	mikkōl	devārô	hattôv	'ăsher
He spoke	it has not fallen	a word	one	among the entirety of	his words	the good	which

1744.311	904, 3135	5057	5860		2030.121	3176	435	6196
v Piel pf 3ms	prep, *n fs*	pn	n ms, ps 3ms	**57.**	v Qal juss 3ms	pn	n mp, ps 1cp	prep, ps 1cp
דִּבֶּר	בְּיַד	מֹשֶׁה	עַבְדּוֹ		יְהִי	יְהוָה	אֱלֹהֵינוּ	עִמָּנוּ
dibber	beyadh	mōsheh	ʻavdô		yehî	yehwāh	'ĕlōhênû	ʻimmānû
He spoke	by the hand of	Moses	his servant		may He be	Yahweh	our God	with us

3626, 866	2030.111	6196, 1	414, 6013.121	414, 5389.121
prep, rel part	v Qal pf 3ms	prep, n mp, ps 1cp	adv, v Qal juss 3ms, ps 1cp	cj, adv, v Qal juss 3ms, ps 1cp
כַּאֲשֶׁר	הָיָה	עִם־אֲבֹתֵינוּ	אַל־יַעַזְבֵנוּ	וְאַל־יִטְּשֵׁנוּ
ka'ăsher	hāyāh	ʻim-'ăvōthênû	'al-ya'azvēnû	we'al-yitteshēnû
just as	He was	with our ancestors	may He not forsake us	and may He not abandon us

	3937, 5371.541	3949	420	3937, 2050.141	904, 3725, 1932
58.	prep, v Hiphil inf con	n ms, ps 1cp	prep, ps 3ms	prep, v Qal inf con	prep, *adj*, n mp, ps 3ms
	לְהַטּוֹת	לְבָבֵנוּ	אֵלָיו	לָלֶכֶת	בְּכָל־דְּרָכָיו
	lehattôth	levāvēnû	'ēlâv	lālekheth	bekhol-derākhâv
	to incline	our heart	to Him	to walk	in all his ways

54. And it was so, that when Solomon had made an end of praying all this prayer and supplication unto the LORD, he arose from before the altar of the LORD, from kneeling on his knees with his hands spread up to heaven: ... entire prayer of petition, *NAB* ... finished offering all this prayer and this plea, *NRSV* ... after making all these prayers and requests, *BB* ... where he had been kneeling with uplifted hands, *Good News*.

55. And he stood, and blessed all the congregation of Israel with a loud voice, saying: ... the whole assembly of Israel, *JB* ... all the people, *NCV* ... getting on his feet, he gave a blessing to all the men of Israel, *BB* ... and shouted this blessing over the entire community, *NLT*.

56. Blessed be the LORD, that hath given rest unto his people Israel, according to all that he promised: ... just as He promised, *Beck* ... who has given consolation, *Fenton* ... Praise the LORD who has given his people peace, as he promised he would, *Good News* ... He promised he would give rest to his people Israel, and he has given us rest, *NCV*.

there hath not failed one word of all his good promise, which he promised by the hand of Moses his servant: ... Not one of all the good promises He made by His servant Moses has failed to come true, *Beck* ... not a single detail of His good words spoken through Moses His servant has failed, *Berkeley* ... has gone unfulfilled of the entire generous promise, *NAB*.

57. The LORD our God be with us, as he was with our fathers: let him not leave us, nor forsake us: ... may he not leave us or abandon us, *NRSV* ... never forsaking us, never casting us away, *Knox* ... let him never go away from us or give us up, *BB* ... as he was with our ancestors, *Good News*.

58. That he may incline our hearts unto him, to walk in all his ways,

But whatever the Temple might be to the people, the king used it as his own chapel. Three times a year, we are told, he offered (and by all appearances, offered with his own hand without the intervention of any priest) burnt offerings and peace offerings upon the altar. Not only this, but he actually "burnt incense upon the altar that was before the LORD,"—the very thing which was regarded as so deadly a crime in the case of King Uzziah (1 Ki. 9:25). Throughout the history of the monarchy, the priests, with scarcely any exception, seem to have been passive tools in the hands of the kings. Even under Rehoboam, much more under Ahaz and Manasseh, the sacred precincts were defiled with nameless abominations, to which, so far as we know, the priests offered no resistance.

"The hour cometh, when ye shall neither in this mountain, nor yet at Jerusalem, worship the Father. ... But the hour cometh, and now is, when the true worshippers shall worship the Father in spirit and in truth" (John 4:21, 23).

Five long chapters of the First Book of Kings are devoted to the description of Solomon's temple, which occupies a still larger space in the Books of Chronicles. The Temple was regarded as the permanent form of the ancient Tabernacle, which is described with lengthy and minute detail in Exodus. It might seem, therefore, that there must be some clear explanation of the idea which this sacred building was intended to embody. Yet it is by no means easy to ascertain what this idea was, and those who have deeply studied the ques-

3937, 8490.141	4851	2807	5122	866	6943.311
cj, prep, v Qal inf con	n fp, ps 3ms	cj, n mp, ps 3ms	cj, n mp, ps 3ms	rel part	v Piel pf 3ms
וְלִשְׁמֹר	מִצְוֹתָיו	וְחֻקָּיו	וּמִשְׁפָּטָיו	אֲשֶׁר	צִוָּה
welishmōr	mitswōthâv	wechuqqâv	ûmishpāṭâv	'ăsher	tsiwwāh
and to observe	his commandments	and his statutes	and his ordinances	that	He commanded

881, 1		2030.126	1745	431	866	2706.715
do, n mp, ps 1cp	59.	cj, v Qal juss 3mp	n mp, ps 1cs	dem pron	rel part	v Hithpael pf 1cs
אֶת־אֲבֹתֵינוּ		וְיִהְיוּ	דְבָרַי	אֵלֶּה	אֲשֶׁר	הִתְחַנַּנְתִּי
'eth-'ăvōthênû		weyihyû	dhevāray	'ēlleh	'ăsher	hithchannantî
our ancestors		and may they be	my words	these	which	I have made supplication

3937, 6686	3176	7427	420, 3176	435	3221	4050	3937, 6449.141
prep, *n mp*	pn	adj	prep, pn	n mp, ps 1cp	adv	cj, n ms	prep, v Qal inf con
לִפְנֵי	יְהוָה	קְרֹבִים	אֶל־יְהוָה	אֱלֹהֵינוּ	יוֹמָם	וָלָיְלָה	לַעֲשׂוֹת
liphnê	yehwāh	qōrōvîm	'el-yehwāh	'ĕlōhênû	yômām	wālāyelāh	la'ăsôth
before	Yahweh	near	to Yahweh	our God	by day	and by night	to execute

5122	5860	5122	6194	3547	1745, 3219
n ms	n ms, ps 3ms	cj, *n ms*	n ms, ps 3ms	pn	*n ms*, n ms
מִשְׁפַּט	עַבְדּוֹ	וּמִשְׁפַּט	עַמּוֹ	יִשְׂרָאֵל	דְּבַר־יוֹם
mishpaṭ	'avdô	ûmishpaṭ	'ammô	yisrā'ēl	devar-yôm
the justice of	his servant	and the justice of	his people	Israel	the matter of a day

904, 3219		3937, 4775	3156.141	3725, 6194	800	3706	3176	2000
prep, n ms, ps 3ms	60.	prep, prep	v Qal inf con	*adj*, *n mp*	art, n fs	cj	pn	pers pron
בְּיוֹמוֹ		לְמַעַן	דַּעַת	כָּל־עַמֵּי	הָאָרֶץ	כִּי	יְהוָה	הוּא
beyômô		lema'an	da'ath	kol-'ammê	hā'ārets	kî	yehwāh	hû'
in its day		so that	to know	all the peoples of	the earth	that	Yahweh	He

435	375	5968		2030.111	3949	8400	6196	3176
art, n mp	*sub*	adv	61.	cj, v Qal pf 3ms	n ms, ps 2mp	adj	prep	pn
הָאֱלֹהִים	אֵין	עוֹד		וְהָיָה	לְבַבְכֶם	שָׁלֵם	עִם	יְהוָה
hā'ĕlōhîm	'ên	'ôdh		wehāyāh	levavkhem	shālēm	'im	yehwāh
God	there is not	another		now it must be	your heart	complete	with	Yahweh

435	3937, 2050.141	904, 2807	3937, 8490.141	4851	3626, 3219
n mp, ps 1cp	prep, v Qal inf con	prep, n mp, ps 3ms	cj, prep, v Qal inf con	n fp, ps 3ms	prep, art, n ms
אֱלֹהֵינוּ	לָלֶכֶת	בְּחֻקָּיו	וְלִשְׁמֹר	מִצְוֹתָיו	כַּיּוֹם
'ĕlōhênû	lālekheth	bechuqqâv	welishmōr	mitswōthâv	kayyôm
our God	to walk	in his statutes	and to observe	his commandments	like the day

2172		4567	3725, 3547	6196	2159.152	2160	3937, 6686
art, dem pron	62.	cj, art, n ms	cj, *adj*, pn	prep, ps 3ms	v Qal act ptc mp	n ms	prep, *n mp*
הַזֶּה		וְהַמֶּלֶךְ	וְכָל־יִשְׂרָאֵל	עִמּוֹ	זֹבְחִים	זֶבַח	לִפְנֵי
hazzeh		wehammelekh	wekhol-yisrā'ēl	'immô	zōvechîm	zevach	liphnê
the this		and the king	and all Israel	with him	sacrificing	a sacrifice	before

3176		2159.121	8406	881	2160	8399	866
pn	63.	cj, v Qal impf 3ms	pn	do	*n ms*	art, n mp	rel part
יְהוָה		וַיִּזְבַּח	שְׁלֹמֹה	אֵת	זֶבַח	הַשְּׁלָמִים	אֲשֶׁר
yehwāh		wayyizbach	shelōmōh	'ēth	zevach	hashshelāmîm	'ăsher
Yahweh		and he slaughtered	Solomon		the sacrifice of	the peace offerings	which

2159.111	3937, 3176	1267	6465	8530	512	6887	4109	6465
v Qal pf 3ms	prep, pn	n ms	num	cj, num	num	cj, n ms	num	cj, num
זָבַח	לַיהוָה	בָּקָר	עֶשְׂרִים	וּשְׁנַיִם	אֶלֶף	וְצֹאן	מֵאָה	וְעֶשְׂרִים
zāvach	layhwāh	bāqār	'esrîm	ûshenayim	'eleph	wetsō'n	mē'āh	we'esrîm
he sacrificed	to Yahweh	oxen	twenty	and two	thousands	and sheep	one hundred	and twenty

and to keep his commandments, and his statutes, and his judgments, which he commanded our fathers: ... and his ordinances, *Goodspeed* ... and laws and ordinances which he gave our ancestors, *JB* ... May he draw our hearts to himself, that we may follow him in everything, *NAB* ... that we may conform to all his ways, *NEB*.

59. And let these my words, wherewith I have made supplication before the LORD, be nigh unto the LORD our God day and night, that he maintain the cause of his servant, and the cause of his people Israel at all times, as the matter shall require: ... as each day may require, *NKJV* ... which I have prayed before the LORD, be near to the LORD, *NIV* ... that he might see right done to his servant and to his people Israel, *BB* ... words that I have prayed in the presence of the LORD be before him constantly ... our daily needs, *NLT*.

60. That all the people of the earth may know that the LORD is God, and that there is none else: ... there is no other, *RSV* ... all nations of the earth may know that the Lord, he is God and none but he, *Tyndale* ... the LORD alone is enduring, *Fenton* ... no other besides him, *Douay*.

61. Let your heart therefore be perfect with the LORD our God, to walk in his statutes, and to keep his commandments, as at this day: ... You must fully obey the LORD our God and follow all his laws and commands. Continue to obey in the future as you do now, *NCV* ... you will be perfect in loyalty, *NEB* ... your hearts must be fully committed to the LORD our God, to live by his decrees, *NIV* ... let your hearts be without sin before, *BB*.

62. And the king, and all Israel with him, offered sacrifice before the LORD: ... and all the people with him, sacrificed sacrifices to, *Fenton* ... offered victims, *Douay* ... in the Lord's presence, *Knox*.

63. And Solomon offered a sacrifice of peace offerings, which he offered unto the LORD, two and twenty thousand oxen, and an hundred and twenty thousand sheep. So the king and all the children of Israel dedicated the house of the LORD: ... kept the feast of the opening of the Lord's house, *BB* ... dedicated the LORD's temple, *Beck* ... as the thank-offering, which was sacrificed to, *Fenton* ... a communion sacrifice of, *JB*.

---

tion have in age after age been led to widely different views.

Philo and Josephus, with certain variations of detail, regard it as a symbol of the universe—the world of idea and the world of sense. Thus the seven-branched candlestick represents the seven planets; the twelve cakes of shewbread are the twelve signs of the Zodiac; the court is the earth; the sanctuary the sea; and the oracle the heavens. The theory derives no importance from its authorship. Neither Philo nor Josephus, nor the rabbis, nor the early Church fathers who adopted their views, have the least authority in such matters; and Philo, who led the way in mystical interpretation, abounds in fantasies which are ludicrously impossible, and are now universally rejected.

The Talmudists held that the Tabernacle was the exact copy of one in heaven, and that its services reflected those of the heavenly hierarchy. This view went into the extreme of literalism, as the other did into the extreme of spiritualization. It was based on the text, "Look that thou make them after their pattern, which was shown thee in the mount" (Exo. 25:40; 26:30; Acts 7:44; Heb. 8:5). The Book of Chronicles goes so far in this direction as to say that David received from Yahweh the exact pattern of the Temple down to its minutest details, together with the entire priestly and Levitical organization of its services. "All this," says David to Solomon, "the LORD made me understand in writing, by his hand upon me, even all the works of this pattern."

Christian writers have seen in the Temple an emblem of the visible, the invisible and the triumphant Church. Such symbolic interpretation depends on the most arbitrary combinations, and does not rise higher than an exercise of fancy. It does not have much exegetical importance.

Luther thought that the Tabernacle and Temple were emblems of human nature: the court, the sanctuary; and the oracle corresponding to the body, the soul, and the spirit. Later writers have pushed this opinion, already sufficiently baseless, into the absurdest detail.

The much simpler view of Maimonides, who is followed by Spencer, is that the Temple was simply the palace of Yahweh, with its vestibule, its audience hall, its presence-chamber, its attendant courtiers, its throne, and its offerings of food, wine and sacrifice. The simplicity of this conception seems to agree with what we know about ancient forms of worship, and it is certain that in many heathen temples the offerings of food and wine were supposed to be consumed by the god. The name "palace" is, however, only given to the Temple in one chapter (1 Chr. 29:1, 19); and the Hebrew, or rather the Persian, word so rendered (bîrāh, HED #1038) may also be rendered "fortress."

512	2699.126	881, 1041	3176	4567	3725, 1158	3547
num	cj, v Qal impf 3mp	do, *n ms*	pn	art, n ms	cj, *adj*, *n mp*	pn
אָלֶף	וַיַּחְנְכוּ	אֶת־בֵּית	יְהוָה	הַמֶּלֶךְ	וְכָל־בְּנֵי	יִשְׂרָאֵל
'āleph	wayyachn^{e}khû	'eth-bêth	y^{e}hwāh	hammelekh	w^{e}khol-b^{e}nê	yisrā'ēl
thousands	and they dedicated	the Temple of	Yahweh	the king	and all the children of	Israel

64.

904, 3219	2000	7227.311	4567	881, 8761	2793	866	3937, 6686
prep, art, n ms	art, dem pron	v Piel pf 3ms	art, n ms	do, *n ms*	art, n ms	rel part	prep, *n mp*
בַּיּוֹם	הַהוּא	קִדַּשׁ	הַמֶּלֶךְ	אֶת־תּוֹךְ	הֶחָצֵר	אֲשֶׁר	לִפְנֵי
bayyôm	hahû'	qiddash	hammelekh	'eth-tôkh	hechātsēr	'āsher	liphnê
on the day	the that	he consecrated	the king	the middle of	the court	which	before

1041, 3176	3706, 6449.111	8427	881, 6150	881, 4647	881
n ms, pn	cj, v Qal pf 3ms	adv	do, art, n fs	do, art, n fs	cj, do
בֵית־יְהוָה	כִּי־עָשָׂה	שָׁם	אֶת־הָעֹלָה	וְאֶת־הַמִּנְחָה	וְאֵת
vêth-y^{e}hwāh	kî-'āsāh	shām	'eth-hā'ōlāh	w^{e}'eth-hamminchāh	w^{e}'ēth
the Temple of Yahweh	because he had made	there	the burnt offering	and the offering	and

2561	8399	3706, 4326	5361	866	3937, 6686	3176	7275
n mp	art, n mp	cj, *n ms*	art, n fs	rel part	prep, *n mp*	pn	adj
חֶלְבֵי	הַשְּׁלָמִים	כִּי־מִזְבַּח	הַנְּחֹשֶׁת	אֲשֶׁר	לִפְנֵי	יְהוָה	קָטֹן
chelvê	hashsh^{e}lāmîm	kî-mizbach	hann^{e}chōsheth	'āsher	liphnê	y^{e}hwāh	qāṭōn
the fat of	the peace offerings	because the altar of	the bronze	that	before	Yahweh	smaller

4623, 3310.541	881, 6150	881, 4647	881	2561	8399
prep, v Hiphil inf con	do, art, n fs	do, art, n fs	cj, do	*n mp*	art, n mp
מֵהָכִיל	אֶת־הָעֹלָה	וְאֶת־הַמִּנְחָה	וְאֵת	חֶלְבֵי	הַשְּׁלָמִים
mēhākhîl	'eth-hā'ōlāh	w^{e}'eth-hamminchāh	w^{e}'ēth	chelvê	hashsh^{e}lāmîm
than being able	the burnt offering	and the offering	and	the fat of	the peace offerings

65.

6449.121	8406	904, 6496, 2026	881, 2374	3725, 3547	6196
cj, v Qal impf 3ms	pn	prep, art, n fs, art, pers pron	do, art, n ms	cj, *adj*, pn	prep, ps 3ms
וַיַּעַשׂ	שְׁלֹמֹה	בָּעֵת־הַהִיא	אֶת־הֶחָג	וְכָל־יִשְׂרָאֵל	עִמּוֹ
wayya'as	sh^{e}lōmōh	vā'ēth-hahî'	'eth-hechāgh	w^{e}khol-yisrā'ēl	'immô
so he made	Solomon	when its time	the feast	and all Israel	with him

7235	1448	4623, 3937, 971.141	2679	5912, 5337	4875	3937, 6686	3176
n ms	adj	prep, prep, v Qal inf con	pn	prep, *n ms*	pn	prep, *n mp*	pn
קָהָל	גָּדוֹל	מִלְּבוֹא	חֲמָת	עַד־נַחַל	מִצְרַיִם	לִפְנֵי	יְהוָה
qāhāl	gādhôl	mill^{e}vô'	chămāth	'adh-nachal	mitsrayim	liphnê	y^{e}hwāh
an assembly	great	from to entering	Hamath	unto the wadi of	Egypt	before	Yahweh

435	8124	3219	8124	3219	727	6461	3219		904, 3219
n mp, ps 1cp	num	n mp	cj, num	n mp	num	num	n ms	**66.**	prep, art, n ms
אֱלֹהֵינוּ	שִׁבְעַת	יָמִים	וְשִׁבְעַת	יָמִים	אַרְבָּעָה	עָשָׂר	יוֹם		בַּיּוֹם
'ĕlōhênû	shiv'ath	yāmîm	w^{e}shiv'ath	yāmîm	'arbā'āh	'āsār	yôm		bayyôm
our God	seven	days	and seven	days	four	ten	days		on the day

8454	8365.311	881, 6194	1313.326	881, 4567	2050.126
art, num	v Piel pf 3ms	do, art, n ms	cj, v Piel impf 3mp	do, art, n ms	cj, v Qal impf 3mp
הַשְּׁמִינִי	שִׁלַּח	אֶת־הָעָם	וַיְבָרְכוּ	אֶת־הַמֶּלֶךְ	וַיֵּלְכוּ
hashsh^{e}mînî	shillach	'eth-hā'ām	wayvār^{e}khû	'eth-hammelekh	wayyēl^{e}khû
the eighth	he sent out	the people	and they blessed	the king	and they went

3937, 164	7976	3005	3949	6142	3725, 3008	866	6449.111
prep, n mp, ps 3mp	adj	cj, *adj*	n ms	prep	*adj*, art, n fs	rel part	v Qal pf 3ms
לְאָהֳלֵיהֶם	שְׂמֵחִים	וְטוֹבֵי	לֵב	עַל	כָּל־הַטּוֹבָה	אֲשֶׁר	עָשָׂה
l^{e}'āh^{e}lêhem	s^{e}mēchîm	w^{e}ṭôvê	lēv	'al	kol-haṭṭôvāh	'āsher	'āsāh
to their tents	joyful	and merry of	heart	concerning	all the good	that	He did

64. The same day did the king hallow the middle of the court that was before the house of the Lord: ... the king consecrated, *NAB* ... the king made holy the middle part of the courtyard which is in front of the Temple, *NCV* ... of the open square in front of, *BB* ... the king had set apart the center of, *Berkeley*.

for there he offered burnt offerings, and meat offerings, and the fat of the peace offerings: because the brasen altar that was before the Lord was too little to receive the burnt offerings, and meat offerings, and the fat of the peace offerings: ... the bronze altar before the Lord was too small, *NAB* ... grain offerings, and the fat of the fellowship offerings, *NIV* ... the bronze altar in the Lord's presence, *NLT* ... there was not room on the brass altar, *BB*.

65. And at that time Solomon held a feast, and all Israel with him, a great congregation, from the entering in of Hamath unto the river of Egypt, before the Lord our God, seven days and seven days, even fourteen days: ... a solemn feast, *Douay* ... Solomon observed the festival at that time, and all Israel with him, a vast assembly, *NIV* ... It was a large crowd that had come from the land between Hamath and the river of, *Beck* ... celebrated the pilgrim-feast, *NEB*.

66. On the eighth day he sent the people away: and they blessed the king, and went unto their tents joyful and glad of heart for all the goodness that the Lord had done for David his servant, and for Israel his people: ... when he dismissed them, *Berkeley* ... they went to their homes rejoicing, and gladhearted, *Fenton* ... went home happy and glad at heart for all the prosperity granted, *NEB* ... joyful and in good spirits, *NRSV*.

9:1. And it came to pass, when Solomon had finished the building of the house of the Lord, and the king's house, and all Solomon's desire which he was pleased to do: ... everything Solomon delighted in doing, *Beck* ... and the palace of the king, and all the other things Solomon had wanted to construct, *Berkeley* ... the royal palace, *JB* ... all the plans for building on which he had set his heart, *NEB*.

In truth, we cannot be sure that the idea of the Temple remained single and definite through so many ages. It was probably a composite and varying emblem, of which the original significance had become mingled with many later elements. It is, however, certain that many numbers and details were symbolic, and there was a deep insight and magnificent completeness in the manner in which certain truths were conveyed by its construction and its central service.

The book in which its symbolism is most thoroughly worked out is Bahr's *Symbolik*. He elaborates, in a simpler form, the opinion of Philo, that the Temple represented "the structure which God has erected, the house in which God lives." So far, the fact cannot be disputed. In Exo. 29:45, we are told that the Tabernacle functioned as the house of God because He would dwell in the midst of the children of Israel and be their God. But Bahr takes a great leap when he proceeds to explain the house of God as "the creation of heaven and earth." If his views were true as a whole, it would indeed be strange that they are not indicated in a single passage of either the Old or New Testaments.

The Tabernacle was called "the Tabernacle of the Testimony" because its two tables of stone were a witness of the Covenant between God and man. It was also called "the Tabernacle of Meeting," which does not mean the place where Israel assembled, but the place where God met Moses and the children of Israel (Num. 17:7; 18:2; 2 Chr. 24:6; Acts 7:44; Exo. 29:10; 1 Ki. 8:4; 2 Chr. 8:13). "And there I will meet with thee, and I will commune with thee from above the mercy seat," says Yahweh to Moses (Exo. 25:22); and "at the door of tabernacle of the congregation before the Lord: where I will meet you, to speak there unto thee. And there I will meet with the children of Israel" (Exo. 29:42f). Thus, in its broadest idea, the Temple brought before the soul of every thoughtful Israelite three great beliefs: that God deigned to dwell in the midst of his people; that, in his infinite mercy and condescension, He admitted a reciprocity between himself and his human children; and that the most absolute expression of his will was the moral law, obedience to which was the condition of heavenly favor and earthly happiness.

"In the Porch," says Bishop Hall, "we may see the regenerate soul entering into the blessed society or the Church; in the Holy Place we may see a figure of the Communion of the true visible Church on earth; in the Holy of Holies the glories of Heaven opened to us by our true High Priest Christ Jesus, who entered once for all to make an Atonement betwixt God and man."

9:1–9. When the festival was over, God appeared to Solomon in a vision, as He had done at Gibeon. So far, Solomon had not gravely or consciously deflected from the ideal of a theocratic king. Anything which had been worldly or mistaken in his policy the oppression into which he had been led, the

3176	3937, 1784	5860	3937, 3547	6194		2030.121	3626, 3735.341
pn	prep, pn	n ms, ps 3ms	cj, prep, pn	n ms, ps 3ms	**9:1**	cj, v Qal impf 3ms	prep, v Piel inf con
יְהוָה	לְדָוִד	עַבְדּוֹ	וּלְיִשְׂרָאֵל	עַמּוֹ		וַיְהִי	כְּכַלּוֹת
y^{e}hwāh	l^{e}dhāwidh	'avdô	ûlăyisrā'ēl	'ammô		wayhî	k^{e}khallôth
Yahweh	for David	his servant	and for Israel	his people		and it was	when finishing

8406	3937, 1161.141	881, 1041, 3176	881, 1041	4567	881
pn	prep, v Qal inf con	do, *n ms*, pn	cj, do, *n ms*	art, n ms	cj, do
שְׁלֹמֹה	לִבְנוֹת	אֶת־בֵּית־יְהוָה	וְאֶת־בֵּית	הַמֶּלֶךְ	וְאֵת
sh^{e}lōmōh	livnôth	'eth-bêth-y^{e}hwāh	w^e'eth-bêth	hammelekh	w^e'ēth
Solomon	to build	the house of Yahweh	and the house of	the king	and

3725, 2946	8406	866	2759.111	3937, 6449.141		7495.221	3176
adj, *n ms*	pn	rel part	v Qal pf 3ms	prep, v Qal inf con	**2.**	cj, v Niphal impf 3ms	pn
כָּל־חֵשֶׁק	שְׁלֹמֹה	אֲשֶׁר	חָפֵץ	לַעֲשׂוֹת		וַיֵּרָא	יְהוָה
kol-chēsheq	sh^{e}lōmōh	'ăsher	chāphēts	la'ăsôth		wayyērā'	y^{e}hwāh
all the desire of	Solomon	what	he desired	to do		then He appeared	Yahweh

420, 8406	8529	3626, 866	7495.211	420	904, 1423
prep, pn	num	prep, rel part	v Niphal pf 3ms	prep, ps 3ms	prep, pn
אֶל־שְׁלֹמֹה	שֵׁנִית	כַּאֲשֶׁר	נִרְאָה	אֵלָיו	בְּגִבְעוֹן
'el-sh^{e}lōmōh	shēnîth	ka'ăsher	nir'āh	'ēlâv	b^{e}ghiv'ôn
unto Solomon	a second time	just as	He had appeared	to him	at Gibeon

	569.121	3176	420	8471.115	881, 8940	881, 8798	866
3.	cj, v Qal impf 3ms	pn	prep, ps 3ms	v Qal pf 1cs	do, n fs, ps 2ms	cj, do, n fs, ps 2ms	rel part
	וַיֹּאמֶר	יְהוָה	אֵלָיו	שָׁמַעְתִּי	אֶת־תְּפִלָּתְךָ	וְאֶת־תְּחִנָּתְךָ	אֲשֶׁר
	wayyō'mer	y^{e}hwāh	'ēlâv	shāma'ttî	'eth-t^{e}phillāth^{e}khā	w^e'eth-t^{e}chinnāth^{e}khā	'ăsher
	and He said	Yahweh	to him	I have heard	your prayer	and your supplication	which

2706.713	3937, 6686	7227.515	881, 1041	2172	866
v Hithpael pf 2ms	prep, n mp, ps 1cs	v Hiphil pf 1cs	do, art, n ms	art, dem pron	rel part
הִתְחַנַּנְתָּה	לְפָנָי	הִקְדַּשְׁתִּי	אֶת־הַבַּיִת	הַזֶּה	אֲשֶׁר
hithchannantāh	l^{e}phānay	hiqŏddashtî	'eth-habbayith	hazzeh	'ăsher
You have made supplication	before Me	I have consecrated	the Temple	the this	which

1161.113	3937, 7947.141, 8428	8427	5912, 5986	2030.116	6084
v Qal pf 2ms	prep, v Qal inf con, n ms, ps 1cs	adv	adv, adv	cj, v Qal pf 3cp	n fd, ps 1cs
בָּנִתָה	לָשׂוּם־שְׁמִי	שָׁם	עַד־עוֹלָם	וְהָיוּ	עֵינַי
bānithāh	lāsûm-sh^{e}mî	shām	'adh-'ôlām	w^{e}hāyû	'ênay
You have built	to place my name	there	until forever	and they will be	my eyes

3949	8427	3725, 3219		887	524, 2050.123	3937, 6686	3626, 866
cj, n ms, ps 1cs	adv	*adj*, art, n mp	**4.**	cj, pers pron	cj, v Qal impf 2ms	prep, n mp, ps 1cs	prep, rel part
וְלִבִּי	שָׁם	כָּל־הַיָּמִים		וְאַתָּה	אִם־תֵּלֵךְ	לְפָנַי	כַּאֲשֶׁר
w^{e}libbî	shām	kol-hayyāmîm		w^e'attāh	'im-tēlēkh	l^{e}phānay	ka'ăsher
and my heart	there	all the days		and you	if you walk	before Me	just as

2050.111	1784	1	904, 8866	904, 3598	3937, 6449.141
v Qal pf 3ms	pn	n ms, ps 2ms	prep, *n ms*, n ms	cj, prep, n ms	prep, v Qal inf con
הָלַךְ	דָּוִד	אָבִיךָ	בְּתָם־לֵבָב	וּבְיֹשֶׁר	לַעֲשׂוֹת
hālakh	dāwidh	'āvîkhā	b^{e}thām-lēvāv	ûv^{e}yōsher	la'ăsôth
he walked	David	your father	with integrity of heart	and with uprightness	to do

3626, 3725	866	6943.315	2807	5122	8490.123
prep, adj	rel part	v Piel pf 1cs, ps 2ms	n mp, ps 1cs	cj, n mp, ps 1cs	v Qal impf 2ms
כְּכֹל	אֲשֶׁר	צִוִּיתִיךָ	חֻקַּי	וּמִשְׁפָּטַי	תִּשְׁמֹר
k^{e}khōl	'ăsher	tsiwwîthîkhā	chuqqay	ûmishpāṭay	tishmōr
according to all	that	I commanded you	my statutes	and my ordinances	you observe

5.

7251.515	881, 3802	4608	6142, 3547	3937, 5986	3626, 866
cj, v Hiphil pf 1cs	do, *n ms*	n fs, ps 2ms	prep, pn	prep, n ms	prep, rel part
וַהֲקִמֹתִי	אֶת־כִּסֵּא	מַמְלַכְתְּךָ	עַל־יִשְׂרָאֵל	לְעֹלָם	כַּאֲשֶׁר
wahqimōthî	'eth-kissē'	mamlakhtᵉkhā	'al-yisrā'ēl	lᵉ'ōlām	ka'ăsher
then I will establish	the throne of	your kingship	over Israel	for ever	just as

1744.315	6142, 1784	1	3937, 569.141	3940, 3901.221	3937	382
v Piel pf 1cs	prep, pn	n ms, ps 2ms	prep, v Qal inf con	neg part, v Niphal impf 3ms	prep, ps 2ms	n ms
דִּבַּרְתִּי	עַל־דָּוִד	אָבִיךָ	לֵאמֹר	לֹא־יִכָּרֵת	לְךָ	אִישׁ
dibbartî	'al-dāwidh	'āvîkhā	lē'mōr	lō'-yikkārēth	lᵉkhā	'îsh
I spoke	to David	your father	saying	he will not be cut off	to you	a man

2. That the LORD appeared to Solomon the second time, as he had appeared unto him at Gibeon: ... came to him again in a vision, as he had done at, *BB* ... just as he had done before, *NCV*.

3. And the LORD said unto him, I have heard thy prayer and thy supplication, that thou hast made before me: ... plea you have made, *NIV* ... entreaty which you, *JB* ... of petition which you offered in my presence, *NAB* ... your request, *NLT*.

I have hallowed this house, which thou hast built, to put my name there for ever: ... made holy this house which you have made, *BB* ... consecrated this house which you have built by placing, *Berkeley* ... sanctified, Goodpseed ... set apart this Temple, *NLT*.

and mine eyes and mine heart shall be there perpetually: ... will be there at all times, *BB* ... My eyes and My heart shall be there continually, *Berkeley*

4. And if thou wilt walk before me, as David thy father walked, in integrity of heart, and in uprightness, to do according to all that I have commanded thee, and wilt keep my statutes and my judgments: ... with an undivided heart and steadfastly; do thou fulfil all that I command, hold true to my observances, *Knox* ... serve me in honesty and integrity, *Good News* ... live before Me as your father David lived, with a sincere heart and righteously, and do everything I ordered and keep My rules and My regulations, *Beck* ... endeavouring to do right ... preserving My Institutions and Decrees, *Fenton*.

5. Then I will establish the throne of thy kingdom upon Israel for ever, as I promised to David thy father, saying, There shall not fail thee a man upon the throne of Israel: ... I shall make your royal throne secure, *JB* ... You shall always have someone from your line on, *NAB* ... make your kingdom strong, *NCV* ... You shall not fail to have a man on, *NKJV*.

heathen alliances which he had formed, his crowded harem, his evident fondness for material splendor which carried with it the peril of selfish pride were only signs of partial knowledge and human frailty. His heart was still, on the whole, right with God. He was once more assured in nightly vision that his prayer and supplication were accepted. The promise was renewed that if he would walk in integrity and uprightness his throne should be established forever; but that if he or his children swerved into apostasy Israel should be driven into exile, and, as a warning to all lands, "this house, which I have hallowed for My name, will I cast out of My sight, and Israel shall be a proverb and a byword among all people."

Following the Covenant meant sacrifices—often and many. Sacrifices were of two kinds, bloody, or unbloody. The latter were oblations. Such were the cakes of shewbread, the meal and drink offerings, the first sheaf at Passover and the two loaves at Pentecost. In almost every instance, the minchāh (HED #4647) accompanied the offering of a sacrificial victim.

There were two general rules regarding all sacrifice victims: that they should be without blemish and without spot, as types of perfectness; and that every sacrifice should be salted with salt, as an antiseptic, and therefore a type of incorruption (Mark 9:49).

Sacrificial victims could only be chosen from oxen, sheep, goats, turtle doves and young pigeons—the latter being the offering of the poor who could not afford the costlier victims.

Sacrifices were also generally divided into free, or obligatory; public, or private; and most holy or less holy, of which the latter were slain at the north and the former at the east side of the altar (Lev. 6:17; 7:1; 14:13). The offerer, according to the Rabbis, had to do five things: lay on hands, slay, skin, dissect and wash the entrails. The priest had to also do five things at the altar itself: catch the blood, sprinkle it, light the fire, bring up the pieces and complete the sacrifices.

Sacrifices are chiefly dwelt upon in the priestly regulations; but nowhere in the OT is their signifi-

4623, 6142	3802	3547	6.	524, 8178.142	8178.128	894	1158
prep, prep	*n ms*	pn		cj, v Qal inf abs	v Qal impf 2mp	pers pron	cj, n mp, ps 2mp
מֵעַל	כִּסֵּא	יִשְׂרָאֵל		אִם־שׁוֹב	תְּשֻׁבוּן	אַתֶּם	וּבְנֵיכֶם
mē'al	kissē'	yisrā'ēl		'im-shôv	teshuvûn	'attem	ûvenêkhem
from on	the throne of	Israel		if turning back	you at all turn back	you	or your sons

4623, 313	3940	8490.128	4851	2807	866	5598.115
prep, prep, ps 1cs	cj, neg part	v Qal impf 2mp	n fp, ps 1cs	n fp, ps 1cs	rel part	v Qal pf 1cs
מֵאַחֲרַי	וְלֹא	תִשְׁמְרוּ	מִצְוֹתַי	חֻקֹּתַי	אֲשֶׁר	נָתַתִּי
mē'achray	welō'	thishmerû	mitswōthay	chuqqōthay	'ăsher	nāthattî
from after Me	and not	you observe	my commandments	my statutes	which	I have put

3937, 6686	2050.117	5856.117	435	311	8246.717	3937
prep, n mp, ps 2mp	cj, v Qal pf 2mp	cj, v Qal pf 2mp	n mp	adj	cj, v Hithpael pf 2mp	prep, ps 3mp
לִפְנֵיכֶם	וַהֲלַכְתֶּם	וַעֲבַדְתֶּם	אֱלֹהִים	אֲחֵרִים	וְהִשְׁתַּחֲוִיתֶם	לָהֶם
liphnêkhem	wahlakhtem	wa'ăvadhtem	'ĕlōhîm	'ăchērîm	wehishtachwîthem	lāhem
before you	and you walk	and you serve	gods	others	and you worship	them

7.	3901.515	881, 3547	4623, 6142	6686	124	866	5598.115
	cj, v Hiphil pf 1cs	do, pn	prep, prep	*n mp*	art, n fs	rel part	v Qal pf 1cs
	וְהִכְרַתִּי	אֶת־יִשְׂרָאֵל	מֵעַל	פְּנֵי	הָאֲדָמָה	אֲשֶׁר	נָתַתִּי
	wehikhrattî	'eth-yisrā'ēl	mē'al	penê	hā'ădhāmāh	'ăsher	nāthattî
	then I will cut off	Israel	from on	the surface of	the land	which	I have given

3937	881, 1041	866	7227.515	3937, 8428	8365.325
prep, ps 3mp	cj, do, art, n ms	rel part	v Hiphil pf 1cs	prep, n ms, ps 1cs	v Piel impf 1cs
לָהֶם	וְאֶת־הַבַּיִת	אֲשֶׁר	הִקְדַּשְׁתִּי	לִשְׁמִי	אֲשַׁלַּח
lāhem	we'eth-habbayith	'ăsher	hiqŏddashtî	lishmî	'ăshallach
to them	and the Temple	which	I have consecrated	to my name	I will throw away

4623, 6142	6686	2030.111	3547	3937, 5091	397, 8531
prep, prep	n mp, ps 1cs	cj, v Qal pf 3ms	pn	prep, n ms	cj, prep, n fs
מֵעַל	פָּנָי	וְהָיָה	יִשְׂרָאֵל	לְמָשָׁל	וְלִשְׁנִינָה
mē'al	pānāy	wehāyāh	yisrā'ēl	lemāshāl	welishnînāh
from beside	my presence	and they will become	Israel	for a saying	and for a taunt

904, 3725, 6194	8.	1041	2172	2030.121	6169	3725, 5882.151
prep, *adj*, art, n mp		cj, art, n ms	art, dem pron	v Qal impf 3ms	adj	*adj*, v Qal act ptc ms
בְּכָל־הָעַמִּים		וְהַבַּיִת	הַזֶּה	יִהְיֶה	עֶלְיוֹן	כָּל־עֹבֵר
bekhol-hā'ammîm		wehabbayith	hazzeh	yihyeh	'elyôn	kol-'ōvēr
among all the peoples		and the Temple	the this	it will be	high	all the ones passing

6142	8460.121	8652.111	569.116	6142, 4242
prep, ps 3ms	v Qal impf 3ms	cj, v Qal pf 3ms	cj, v Qal pf 3cp	cj, intrg
עָלָיו	יִשֹּׁם	וְשָׁרַק	וְאָמְרוּ	עַל־מֶה
'ālâv	yishshōm	weshāraq	we'āmerû	'al-meh
beside it	they will be horrified	and they will whistle	and they will say	because of why

6449.111	3176	3722	3937, 800	2148	3937, 1041	2172
v Qal pf 3ms	pn	adv	prep, art, n fs	art, dem pron	cj, prep, art, n ms	art, dem pron
עָשָׂה	יְהוָה	כָּכָה	לָאָרֶץ	הַזֹּאת	וְלַבַּיִת	הַזֶּה
'āsāh	yehwāh	kākhāh	lā'ārets	hazzō'th	welabbayith	hazzeh
has He done	Yahweh	thus	to the land	the this	and to the Temple	the this

9.	569.116	6142	866	6013.116	881, 3176	435	866
	cj, v Qal pf 3cp	cj	rel part	v Qal pf 3cp	do, pn	n mp, ps 3mp	rel pron
	וְאָמְרוּ	עַל	אֲשֶׁר	עָזְבוּ	אֶת־יְהוָה	אֱלֹהֵיהֶם	אֲשֶׁר
	we'āmerû	'al	'ăsher	'āzevû	'eth-yehwāh	'ĕlōhêhem	'ăsher
	and they will say	because	that	they abandoned	Yahweh	their God	Who

6. But if ye shall at all turn from following me, ye or your children, and will not keep my commandments and my statutes which I have set before you, but go and serve other gods, and worship them: ... or your sons turn away from me and do not observe the commands and decrees I have given you, *NIV* ... your decendants abandon me and disobey my commands and laws, *NLT* ... stop following me, *Good News* ... laws which I have laid down for you, *JB*.

7. Then will I cut off Israel out of the land which I have given them; and this house, which I have hallowed for my name, will I cast out of my sight: ... I shall banish Israel from the country ... and shall disown this Temple which I have consecrated, *JB* ... and repudiate the temple I have consecrated to my honor, *NAB* ... I will take away Israel from the face of the land ... which I have sanctified to my name, *Douay* ... I will renounce, *NEB*.

and Israel shall be a proverb and a byword among all people: ... All the nations will make fun of Israel and speak evil about them, *NCV* ... an object of ridicule among, *NIV* ... I will make Israel an objet of mockery and ridicule among the nations, *NLT*.

8. And at this house, which is high, every one that passeth by it shall be astonished, and shall hiss; and they shall say, Why hath the LORD done thus unto this land, and to this house?: ... house will become a heap of ruins, *NRSV* ... every passer-by will be appalled and gasp at the sight of it; and they will ask, *REB* ... which has been famous, everyone who passes by it shall be amazed, *KJVII* ... The passer-by will stand wondering, and hiss in derision, *Knox*.

9. And they shall answer, Because they forsook the LORD their God, who brought forth their fathers out of the land of Egypt, and have taken hold upon other gods, and have worshipped them, and served them: therefore hath the LORD brought upon them all this evil: ... Because they were turned away from the Lord their God, *BB* ... That is why the LORD brought all this calamity on them, *Beck* ... they embraced other gods ... all this misfortune upon them, *Berkeley* ... the EVER-LIVING brought upon them all this suffering, *Fenton*.

10. And it came to pass at the end of twenty years, when Solomon had built the two houses, the house of the LORD, and the king's house: ... years that it took Solomon to erect the two buildings, the Temple of Yahweh and the royal palace, *JB* ... Now it happened, *NKJV* ... had put up the two houses, *BB*.

---

cance formally explained, and for many centuries, the Levitical ritual was not highly regarded (see Judg. 6:19ff; 1 Sam. 2:13; 14:35; 1 Ki. 19:21; 2 Ki. 5:17).

The sacrifices commanded in the Pentateuch fall under four heads. The "burnt offering" ('ōlāh, kālîl, HED #3752), typified complete self-dedication, that which even the heathen might offer; the "sin offering" (chăṯṯā'th, HED #2496), made atonement for the offender; the "trespass offering" ('āshām, HED #844), atoned for some special offense, whether doubtful or certain, committed through ignorance; and was following the other sacrifices, the thank offering, eucharistic "peace offering" (shelem, HED #8399) or "offering of completion" in which the flesh was eaten by the priest and the worshipers.

The central significance of the whole doctrine lies in the ancient opinion that "the blood" of the sacrifice was "its life." This was why an expiatory power was ascribed to the blood. There was certainly no transfer of guilt to the animal, for its blood remained clean and cleansing. Nor was the animal supposed to undergo the transgressor's punishment; first, because this is nowhere stated, and next, because, had that been the case, fine flour would certainly not have been permitted (as it was) as a sin offering (Lev. 5:11ff). Moreover, no willful offense (no offense "with uplifted hand," i.e., with evil premeditation) could be atoned for either by sin or trespass offerings. Although, certainly some latitude was given to the situation in which sin was an involuntary error; but this did not indicate a lack of responsibility for purification. The sin offering was further offered for some purely accidental and ceremonial offenses, which could not involve any real consciousness of guilt. The "blood of the covenant" (Exo. 24:4–8) was not of the sin offering, but of peace and burnt offerings. "The atoning virtue of the blood lies not in its material substance, but in the life of which it is the vehicle," says Bishop Westcott. "The blood always includes the thought of the life preserved and active beyond death. It is not simply the price by which the redeemed were purchased, but the power by which they were quickened so as to be capable of belonging to God." "To drink the blood of Christ," says Clement of Alexandria, "is to partake of the Lord's incorruption."

Yet, following the Covenant also meant offering with a pure heart. "Hath the LORD as great delight in ... sacrifices," asks the indignant Samuel "as in obeying the voice of the LORD? Behold, to obey is better than sacrifice, and to hearken than the fat of rams" (1 Sam. 15:22).

3428.511	881, 1	4623, 800	4875	2480.526	904, 435	311
v Hiphil pf 3ms	do, n mp, ps 3mp	prep, *n fs*	pn	cj, v Hiphil impf 3mp	prep, n mp	adj
הוֹצִיא	אֶת־אֲבֹתָם	מֵאֶרֶץ	מִצְרָיִם	וַיַּחֲזִקוּ	בֵּאלֹהִים	אֲחֵרִים
hôtsî'	'eth-'ăvōthām	mē'erets	mitsrayim	wayyachziqû	bē'lōhîm	'ăchērîm
He led out	their ancestors	from the land of	Egypt	and they took hold	on gods	others

8246.726	3937	5856.126	6142, 3772	971.511	3176
cj, v Hithpael impf 3mp	prep, ps 3mp	cj, v Qal impf 3mp, ps 3mp	prep, adv	v Hiphil pf 3ms	pn
וַיִּשְׁתַּחוּ	לָהֶם	וַיַּעַבְדֻם	עַל־כֵּן	הֵבִיא	יְהוָה
wayyishtachû	lāhem	wayya'avdhum	'al-kēn	hēvî'	yehwāh
and they worshiped	them	and they served them	therefore	He has brought	Yahweh

6142	881	3725, 7750	2148		2030.121	4623, 7381	6465	8523
prep, ps 3mp	do	*adj*, art, n fs	art, dem pron	**10.**	cj, v Qal impf 3ms	prep, *n ms*	num	n fs
עֲלֵיהֶם	אֵת	כָּל־הָרָעָה	הַזֹּאת		וַיְהִי	מִקְצֵה	עֶשְׂרִים	שָׁנָה
'ălêhem	'ēth	kol-hārā'āh	hazzō'th		wayhî	miqōtsēh	'esrîm	shānāh
on them		all the evil	the this		and it was	from the end of	twenty	years

866, 1161.111	8406	881, 8530	1041	881, 1041	3176	881, 1041
rel part, v Qal pf 3ms	pn	do, num	art, n mp	do, *n ms*	pn	cj, do, *n ms*
אֲשֶׁר־בָּנָה	שְׁלֹמֹה	אֶת־שְׁנֵי	הַבָּתִּים	אֶת־בֵּית	יְהוָה	וְאֶת־בֵּית
'ăsher-bānāh	shelōmōh	'eth-shenê	habbāttîm	'eth-bêth	yehwāh	we'eth-bêth
when he had built	Solomon	the two of	the buildings	the Temple of	Yahweh	and the house of

4567		2538	4567, 7145	5558.311	881, 8406	904, 6320	753
art, n ms	**11.**	pn	*n ms*, pn	v Piel pf 3ms	do, pn	prep, *n mp*	n mp
הַמֶּלֶךְ		חִירָם	מֶלֶךְ־צֹר	נִשָּׂא	אֶת־שְׁלֹמֹה	בַּעֲצֵי	אֲרָזִים
hammelekh		chîrām	melekh-tsōr	nissā'	'eth-shelōmōh	ba'ătsê	'ărāzîm
the king		Hiram	the king of Tyre	he delivered to	Solomon	with trees of	cedars

904, 6320	1293	904, 2174	3937, 3725, 2761	226	5598.121
cj, prep, *n mp*	n mp	cj, prep, art, n ms	prep, *adj*, n ms, ps 3ms	adv	v Qal impf 3ms
וּבַעֲצֵי	בְרוֹשִׁים	וּבַזָּהָב	לְכָל־חֶפְצוֹ	אָז	יִתֵּן
ûva'ătsê	verôshîm	ûvazzāhāv	lekhol-chephtsô	'āz	yittēn
and with trees of	cypresses	and with the gold	for all his desire	then	he gave

4567	8406	3937, 2538	6465	6111	904, 800	1592		3428.121
art, n ms	pn	prep, pn	num	n fs	prep, *n fs*	art, pn	**12.**	cj, v Qal impf 3ms
הַמֶּלֶךְ	שְׁלֹמֹה	לְחִירָם	עֶשְׂרִים	עִיר	בְּאֶרֶץ	הַגָּלִיל		וַיֵּצֵא
hammelekh	shelōmōh	lechîrām	'esrîm	'îr	be'erets	haggālîl		wayyētsē'
the king	Solomon	to Hiram	twenty	cities	in the land of	the Galilee		and he went out

2538	4623, 7145	3937, 7495.141	881, 6111	866	5598.111, 3937	8406
pn	prep, pn	prep, v Qal inf con	do, art, n fp	rel part	v Qal pf 3ms, prep, ps 3ms	pn
חִירָם	מִצֹּר	לִרְאוֹת	אֶת־הֶעָרִים	אֲשֶׁר	נָתַן־לוֹ	שְׁלֹמֹה
chîrām	mitstsōr	lir'ôth	'eth-he'ārîm	'ăsher	nāthan-lô	shelōmōh
Hiram	from Tyre	to see	the cities	which	he gave to him	Solomon

3940	3595.116	904, 6084		569.121	4242	6111	431
cj, neg part	v Qal pf 3cp	prep, n fd, ps 3ms	**13.**	cj, v Qal impf 3ms	intrg	art, n fp	art, dem pron
וְלֹא	יָשְׁרוּ	בְּעֵינָיו		וַיֹּאמֶר	מָה	הֶעָרִים	הָאֵלֶּה
welō'	yāsherû	be'ênāv		wayyō'mer	māh	he'ārîm	hā'ēlleh
but not	they were right	in his eyes		and he said	what	the cities	the these

866, 5598.113	3937	250	7410.121	3937	800	3640	5912
rel part, v Qal pf 2ms	prep, ps 1cs	n ms, ps 1cs	cj, v Qal impf 3ms	prep, ps 3mp	*n fs*	pn	prep
אֲשֶׁר־נָתַתָּה	לִי	אָחִי	וַיִּקְרָא	לָהֶם	אֶרֶץ	כָּבוּל	עַד
'ăsher-nāthattāh	lî	'āchî	wayyiqōrā'	lāhem	'erets	kāvûl	'adh
which you have given	to me	O my brother	and he called	them	the land of	Cabul	unto

3219 art, n ms הַיּוֹם hayyôm the day	2172 art, dem pron הַזֶּה hazzeh the this	**14.**	8365.121 cj, v Qal impf 3ms וַיִּשְׁלַח wayyishlach and he sent	2538 pn חִירָם chîrām Hiram	3937, 4567 prep, art, n ms לַמֶּלֶךְ lammelekh to the king	4109 num מֵאָה mē'āh one hundred	6465 cj, num וְעֶשְׂרִים we'esrîm and twenty	3724 *n fs* כִּכַּר kikkar talents of

2174 n ms זָהָב zāhāv gold	**15.**	2172 cj, dem pron וְזֶה wezeh and this	1745, 4671 *n ms*, art, n ms דְבַר־הַמַּס dhevar-hammas the matter of the forced labor	866, 6148.511 rel part, v Hiphil pf 3ms אֲשֶׁר־הֶעֱלָה 'ăsher-he'ĕlāh which he had levied	4567 art, n ms הַמֶּלֶךְ hammelekh the king	8406 pn שְׁלֹמֹה shelōmōh Solomon

11. (Now Hiram the king of Tyre had furnished Solomon with cedar trees and fir trees, and with gold, according to all his desire,) that then king Solomon gave Hiram twenty cities in the land of Galilee: ... had supplied ... and cypress lumber, *Beck* ... and pine wood, and gold, and all that he wished, *Fenton* ... juniper wood, *JB* ... King Solomon transferred twenty cities in Galilee to Hiram, *Berkeley*.

12. And Hiram came out from Tyre to see the cities which Solomon had given him; and they pleased him not: ... but he was not satisfied with them, *NAB* ... Hiram went from Tyre to inspect, *NEB* ... they did not please him, *NKJV* ... they didn't look good to him, *Beck*.

13. And he said, What cities are these which thou hast given me, my brother? And he called them the land of Cabul unto this day: ... and complained, What kind of towns, *Berkeley* ... What good are these towns, *NCV* ... Hiram called that area Cabul, "worthless," as it is still known today, *NLT* ... What sort of towns, *BB*.

14. And Hiram sent to the king sixscore talents of gold: ... one hundred and twenty talents of gold, *Goodspeed* ... 3,500,000 dollars in gold, *Berkeley* ... about nine thousand pounds of gold, *NCV*.

15. And this is the reason of the levy which king Solomon raised; for to build the house of the LORD, and his own house, and Millo, and the wall of Jerusalem, and Hazor, and Megiddo, and Gezer: ... this is the account of the forced labor which King Solomon levied, *RSV* ... the record of the forced labour which King Solomon conscripted, *REB* ... the labor-levy, *KJVII* ... this was the way of Solomon's system of forced work, *BB*.

9:10–14. After twenty years of work, the Temple and the palace were completed. Perhaps to commemorarate the number the years of cooperation between himself and Hiram, the king of Tyre, Solomon gave his fellow king twenty cities. All the wood and gold needed for Solomon's building project had been supplied by Hiram, so Solomon felt the need to give a gift of thanks. Perhaps also the towns being located in the region of Galilee indicated that Solomon was not afraid of the northern king taking control of land closer to Israelite territory.

Despite Solomon's intent, which surely must have been innocent, Hiram considered the towns to be of inferior quality, at least in comparison with the 120 talents of gold he had given to Solomon. Hiram named the towns "the land of Cabul." The name is a play on words, sounding like a Hebrew expression which means "good for nothing." It may be that Hiram was more understanding than it seems at first reading. Solomon's youth could not be blamed for the blunder, but perhaps, even after twenty years of reigning, it was the first time Solomon had given a tribute to any other king. He was more used to receiving because of the noteriety which God had granted him among the nations. Hiram calls Solomon "my brother," a designation of peace often used after an altercation of any degree (cf. 1 Ki. 20:32). Since no mention is made in the Scripture of any retribution being exacted by Hiram, and because he proceeded to name the towns, indicates that he accepted the gift, regardless of the evaluation. The biblical history simply continues with the recapping of the twenty years, moving on to the matter of the forced labor levied by Solomon during the time.

9:15–19. Conscripting forced labor from the former owners of the Promised Land, who were not driven out, Solomon not only built the Temple and the palaces, but the Millo (which some translate, e.g. NIV, "supporting terraces"), the wall of Jerusalem and several towns, including three major ones. Hazor was the city burned by Joshua during the conquest nearly 500 years before. Megiddo was in the territory of Manasseh. The king of Megiddo was

3937, 1161.141	881, 1041	3176	881, 1041	881, 4545	881	2440
prep, v Qal inf con	do, *n ms*	pn	cj, do, n ms, ps 3ms	cj, do, art, pn	cj, do	*n fs*
לִבְנוֹת	אֶת־בֵּית	יְהוָה	וְאֶת־בֵּיתוֹ	וְאֶת־הַמִּלּוֹא	וְאֵת	חוֹמַת
livnôth	'eth-bêth	yehwāh	we'eth-bêthô	we'eth-hammillô'	we'ēth	chômath
to build	the Temple of	Yahweh	and his house	and the Millo	and	the wall of

3503	881, 2780	881, 4163	881, 1537		6799	4567, 4875	6148.111
pn	cj, do, pn	cj, do, pn	cj, do, pn	**16.**	pn	*n ms*, pn	v Qal pf 3ms
יְרוּשָׁלַם	וְאֶת־חָצֹר	וְאֶת־מְגִדּוֹ	וְאֶת־גָּזֶר		פַּרְעֹה	מֶלֶךְ־מִצְרַיִם	עָלָה
yerûshālām	we'eth-chātsōr	we'eth-meghiddô	we'eth-gāzer		par'ōh	melekh-mitsrayim	'ālāh
Jerusalem	and Hazor	and Megiddo	and Gezer		Pharaoh	the king of Egypt	he had gone up

4058.121	881,1537	8041.121	904, 813	881, 3793	3553.151
cj, v Qal impf 3ms	do, pn	cj, v Qal impf 3ms, ps 3fs	prep, art, n fs	cj, do, art, pn	art, v Qal act ptc ms
וַיִּלְכֹּד	אֶת־גֶּזֶר	וַיִּשְׂרְפָהָ	בָּאֵשׁ	וְאֶת־הַכְּנַעֲנִי	הַיֹּשֵׁב
wayyilkōdh	'eth-gezer	wayyisrephāhh	bā'ēsh	we'eth-hakkena'ănî	hayyōshēv
and he captured	Gezer	and he burned it	with the fire	and the Canaanites	those dwelling

904, 6111	2103.111	5598.121	8360	3937, 1351	828	8406
prep, art, n fs	v Qal pf 3ms	cj, v Qal impf 3ms, ps 3fs	n mp	prep, n fs, ps 3ms	*n fs*	pn
בָּעִיר	הָרָג	וַיִּתְּנָהּ	שִׁלֻּחִים	לְבִתּוֹ	אֵשֶׁת	שְׁלֹמֹה
bā'îr	hārāgh	wayyittenāhh	shilluchîm	levittô	'ēsheth	shelōmōh
in the city	he killed	and he gave it	dowry	to his daughter	the wife of	Solomon

	1161.121	8406	881, 1537	881, 1070	1070	8811		881, 1215
17.	cj, v Qal impf 3ms	pn	do, pn	cj, do, pn	pn	adj	**18.**	cj, do, pn
	וַיִּבֶן	שְׁלֹמֹה	אֶת־גָּזֶר	וְאֶת־בֵּית	חֹרֹן	תַּחְתּוֹן		וְאֶת־בַּעֲלָת
	wayyiven	shelōmōh	'eth-gāzer	we'eth-bêth	chōrōn	tachtôn		we'eth-ba'ălāth
	then he built	Solomon	Gezer	and Beth	Horon	lower		and Baalath

881, 8888	904, 4198	904, 800		881	3725, 6111	4694	866
cj, do, pn	prep, art, n ms	prep, art, n fs	**19.**	cj, do	*adj, n fp*	art, n fp	rel part
וְאֶת־תָּמָר	בַּמִּדְבָּר	בָּאָרֶץ		וְאֵת	כָּל־עָרֵי	הַמִּסְכְּנוֹת	אֲשֶׁר
we'eth-tāmār	bammidhbār	bā'ārets		we'ēth	kol-'ārê	hammiskenôth	'ăsher
and Tamar	in the wilderness	in the land		and	all the cities of	the storehouses	which

2030.116	3937, 8406	881	6111	7681	881	6111	6821	881
v Qal pf 3cp	prep, pn	cj, do	*n fp*	art, n ms	cj, do	*n fp*	art, n mp	cj, do
הָיוּ	לִשְׁלֹמֹה	וְאֵת	עָרֵי	הָרֶכֶב	וְאֵת	עָרֵי	הַפָּרָשִׁים	וְאֵת
hāyû	lishlōmōh	we'ēth	'ārê	hārekhev	we'ēth	'ārê	happārāshîm	we'ēth
they were	to Solomon	and	the cities of	the chariots	and	the cities of	the horsemen	and

2946	8406	866	2945.111	3937, 1161.141	904, 3503	904, 3976
n ms	pn	rel part	v Qal pf 3ms	prep, v Qal inf con	prep, pn	cj, prep, art, pn
חֵשֶׁק	שְׁלֹמֹה	אֲשֶׁר	חָשַׁק	לִבְנוֹת	בִּירוּשָׁלַם	וּבַלְּבָנוֹן
chēsheq	shelōmōh	'ăsher	chāshaq	livnôth	bîrûshālam	ûvallevānôn
the desire of	Solomon	which	he desired	to build	in Jerusalem	and in the Lebanon

904, 3725	800	4617		3725, 6194	3613.255	4623, 578
cj, prep, *n ms*	*n fs*	n fs, ps 3ms	**20.**	*adj*, art, n ms	art, v Niphal ptc ms	prep, art, pn
וּבְכֹל	אֶרֶץ	מֶמְשַׁלְתּוֹ		כָּל־הָעָם	הַנּוֹתָר	מִן־הָאֱמֹרִי
ûvekhōl	'erets	memshaltô		kol-hā'ām	hannôthār	min-hā'ĕmōrî
and everywhere in	the land of	his dominion		all the people	those remaining	from the Amorites

2958	6773	2433	3092	866	3940, 4623, 1158	3547
art, pn	art, pn	art, pn	cj, art, pn	rel pron	neg part, prep, *n mp*	pn
הַחִתִּי	הַפְּרִזִּי	הַחִוִּי	וְהַיְבוּסִי	אֲשֶׁר	לֹא־מִבְּנֵי	יִשְׂרָאֵל
hachittî	happerizzî	hachiwwî	wehayvûsî	'ăsher	lō'-mibbenê	yisrā'ēl
the Hittites	the Perizzites	the Hivites	and the Jebusites	who	not from the sons of	Israel

866 rel pron אֲשֶׁר 'ăsher whom	904, 800 prep, art, n fs בָּאָרֶץ bā'ārets in the land	313 adv, ps 3mp אַחֲרֵיהֶם 'achrêhem after them	3613.216 v Niphal pf 3cp נֹתְרוּ nōthᵉrû they remained	866 rel pron אֲשֶׁר 'ăsher who	1158 n mp, ps 3mp בְּנֵיהֶם bᵉnêhem their descendants	21.	2065 pers pron הֵמָּה hēmmāh they

6148.521 cj, v Hiphil impf 3ms, ps 3mp וַיַּעֲלֵם wayya'ălēm so he caused them to go up	3937, 2868.541 prep, v Hiphil inf con, ps 3mp לְהַחֲרִימָם lᵉhachrîmām to destroy them	3547 pn יִשְׂרָאֵל yisrā'ēl Israel	1158 *n mp* בְּנֵי bᵉnê the sons of	3940, 3310.116 neg part, v Qal pf 3cp לֹא־יָכְלוּ lō'-yākhᵉlû they were not able

16. For Pharaoh king of Egypt had gone up, and taken Gezer, and burnt it with fire, and slain the Canaanites that dwelt in the city, and given it for a present unto his daughter, Solomon's wife: ... burning it down and putting to death the Canaanites living in the town, and he gave it for a bride-offering to his daughter, *BB* ... as a wedding present, *Beck* ... had come up and captured Gezer, *Berkeley* ... and slaughtered the Cananites, *Fenton*.

17. And Solomon built Gezer, and Beth-horon the nether: ... rebuilt Gezer, *JB* ... lower Beth-horon, *Goodspeed* ... and Bethhor-on the lower, *KJVII*.

18. And Baalath, and Tadmor in the wilderness, in the land: ... in the desert land, *Berkeley* ... in the waste land, *BB* ... within the country, *Beck*.

19. And all the cities of store that Solomon had, and cities for his chariots, and cities for his horsemen, and that which Solomon desired to build in Jerusalem, and in Lebanon, and in all the land of his dominion: ... storage towns owned by Solomon, all the towns for his chariots and horses, and whatever Solomon was pleased to build, *JB* ... all his cities for supplies, *NAB* ... and cities for his cavalry, *NKJV* ... towns for his chariots and war horses, and that which Solomon took delight to build in, *Beck*.

20. And all the people that were left of the Amorites, Hittites, Perizzites, Hivites, and Jebusites, which were not of the children of Israel: ... all the people who survived, *Berkeley* ... All the non-Israelite people who remained in the land, descendants of, *NAB* ... who did not belong to Israel, *NEB* ... who were not a part of the people of Israel, *Beck*.

among the thirty-one Joshua had conquered (Josh. 12:21). The relative importance of Gezer is given to us here in this passage. Ephraim did not drive out the Canaanites of Gezer (Judg. 1:29), but Pharaoh of Solomon's time killed all of the Canaanite inhabitants and gave the city to his daughter as a wedding present. Solomon rebuilt the city.

Solomon also rebuilt Beth-Horon, Baalath and Tadmor (or Tamar), as well as several cities of storage for grain and military equipment. These domestic improvements were probably nothing to be concerned about with regard to Solomon's spiritual condition. Even Hazor and Megiddo were Canaanite inhabited, but were Israelite cities according to Joshua's allotment to the tribes. But the rebuilding of Gezer showed something further. Gezer should belong to the tribe of Ephraim, not Solomon's foreign wife. Disturbing spiritual factors have begun to enter the picture, indicating that Solomon was no longer relying on God's wisdom, but on the political systems of the world.

Should we be so harsh on Solomon, passing judgment with our limited wisdom? Certainly not on that basis, but we have the progression of history and the principles of the Law as recorded by the Scripture to rely on. "Neither shalt thou make marriages with them; thy daughter thou shalt not give unto his son, nor his daughter shalt thou take unto thy son" (Deut. 7:3). Solomon's marriage to the daughter of Pharaoh and his rebuilding of the dowry city are early indications of his heart turning away. In 1 Ki. 11:1, a few years later, the historian sadly notes, "But king Solomon loved many strange women, together with the daughter of Pharaoh, women of the Moabites, Ammonites, Edomites, Zidonians, and Hittites." "Solomon held fast to them in love" (v. 2, NIV). Such an attachment was no quick decision, but many decisions over the years, eventually leading to irreparable damage to the kingdom (1 Ki. 11:11; 14:14ff). Solomon also built a palace and the Millo for the daughter of Pharaoh (9:24).

9:20–28. The inhabitants of the Promised Land who were not driven out by the Israelites during Joshua's time were made into slaves by Solomon for the purpose of building and transporting of building materials. Solomon did not make slaves of any of the

8406	3937, 4671, 5856.151	5912	3219	2172		4623, 1158	3547
pn	prep, *n ms*, v Qal act ptc ms	adv	art, n ms	art, dem pron	**22.**	cj, prep, *n mp*	pn
שְׁלֹמֹה	לְמַס־עֹבֵד	עַד	הַיּוֹם	הַזֶּה		וּמִבְּנֵי	יִשְׂרָאֵל
shelōmōh	lemas-‘ōvēdh	‘adh	hayyôm	hazzeh		ûmibbenê	yisrā’ēl
Solomon	for forced labor of slaves	until	the day	the this		but from the sons of	Israel

3940, 5598.111	8406	5860	3706, 2062	596	4560	5860
neg part, v Qal pf 3ms	pn	n ms	cj, pers pron	*n mp*	art, n fs	cj, n mp, ps 3ms
לֹא־נָתַן	שְׁלֹמֹה	עֶבֶד	כִּי־הֵם	אַנְשֵׁי	הַמִּלְחָמָה	וַעֲבָדָיו
lō’-nāthan	shelōmōh	‘āvedh	kî-hēm	’anshê	hammilchāmāh	wa‘ăvādhâv
he did not allow	Solomon	slaves	because they	the men of	the war	and his servants

8015	8388	8015	7681
cj, n mp, ps 3ms	cj, n mp, ps 3ms	cj, *n mp*	n ms, ps 3ms
וְשָׂרָיו	וְשָׁלִשָׁיו	וְשָׂרֵי	רִכְבּוֹ
wesārâv	weshālishâv	wesārê	rikhbô
and his commanders	and his adjutant officers	and the commanders of	his chariots

6821		431	8015	5507.256	866
cj, n mp, ps 3ms	**23.**	dem pron	*n mp*	art, v Niphal ptc mp	rel pron
וּפָרָשָׁיו		אֵלֶּה	שָׂרֵי	הַנִּצָּבִים	אֲשֶׁר
ûphārāshâv		’ēlleh	sārê	hanitstsāvîm	’ăsher
and his horsemen		these	the commanders of	the foremen	who

6142, 4536	3937, 8406	2675	2675	4109	7575.152
prep, art, n fs	prep, pn	num	cj, num	num	art, v Qal act ptc mp
עַל־הַמְּלָאכָה	לִשְׁלֹמֹה	חֲמִשִּׁים	וַחֲמֵשׁ	מֵאוֹת	הָרֹדִים
‘al-hammelā’khāh	lishlōmōh	chămishshîm	wachmēsh	mē’ôth	hārōdhîm
over the craftsmanship	to Solomon	fifty	and five	hundreds	bosses

904, 6194	6449.152	904, 4536		395	1351, 6799
prep, art, n ms	art, v Qal act ptc mp	prep, art, n fs	**24.**	adv	*n fs*, pn
בָּעָם	הָעֹשִׂים	בַּמְּלָאכָה		אַךְ	בַּת־פַּרְעֹה
bā‘ām	hā‘ōsîm	bammelā’khāh		’akh	bath-par‘ōh
among the people	those working	among the craftsmanship		only	the daughter of Pharaoh

6148.112	4623, 6111	1784	420, 1041	866	1161.111, 3937	226	1161.111
v Qal pf 3fs	prep, *n fs*	pn	prep, n ms, ps 3fs	rel part	v Qal pf 3ms, prep, ps 3fs	adv	v Qal pf 3ms
עָלְתָה	מֵעִיר	דָּוִד	אֶל־בֵּיתָהּ	אֲשֶׁר	בָּנָה־לָהּ	אָז	בָּנָה
‘ālethāh	mē‘îr	dāwidh	’el-bêthāhh	’ăsher	bānāh-lāhh	’āz	bānāh
she went up	from the city of	David	to her house	which	he had built for her	then	he built

881, 4545		6148.511	8406	8421	6718	904, 8523
do, art, pn	**25.**	cj, v Hiphil pf 3ms	pn	num	n fp	prep, art, n fs
אֶת־הַמִּלּוֹא		וְהֶעֱלָה	שְׁלֹמֹה	שָׁלֹשׁ	פְּעָמִים	בַּשָּׁנָה
’eth-hammillô’		wehe‘ĕlāh	shelōmōh	shālōsh	pe‘āmîm	bashshānāh
the Millo		and he caused to go up	Solomon	three	times	during the year

6150	8399	6142, 4326	866	1161.111	3937, 3176
n fp	cj, n mp	prep, art, n ms	rel part	v Qal pf 3ms	prep, pn
עֹלוֹת	וּשְׁלָמִים	עַל־הַמִּזְבֵּחַ	אֲשֶׁר	בָּנָה	לַיהוָה
‘ōlôth	ûshelāmîm	‘al-hammizbēach	’ăsher	bānāh	layhwāh
burnt offerings	and peace offerings	on the altar	which	he built	to Yahweh

7281.542	882	866	3937, 6686	3176	8396.311	881, 1041
cj, v Hiphil inf abs	prep, ps 3ms	rel part	prep, *n mp*	pn	cj, v Piel pf 3ms	do, art, n ms
וְהַקְטֵיר	אִתּוֹ	אֲשֶׁר	לִפְנֵי	יְהוָה	וְשִׁלַּם	אֶת־הַבָּיִת
wehaqṭēr	’ittô	’ăsher	liphnê	yehwāh	weshillam	’eth-habbāyith
and burning incense	with it	which	before	Yahweh	and he made complete	the Temple

26.						
604	6449.111	4567	8406	904, 6337	866	882, 363
cj, n ms	v Qal pf 3ms	art, n ms	pn	prep, pn	rel part	prep, pn
וָאֳנִי	עָשָׂה	הַמֶּלֶךְ	שְׁלֹמֹה	בְּעֶצְיוֹן־גֶּבֶר	אֲשֶׁר	אֶת־אֵלוֹת
wā'ānî	'āsāh	hammelekh	sh^elōmōh	b^e'etsyôn-gever	'ăsher	'eth-'ēlôth
and ships	he made	the king	Solomon	in Ezion-Geber	which	beside Eloth

				27.	
6142, 8004	3328, 5676	904, 800	110	8365.121	2538
prep, *n fs*	*n ms*, pn	prep, *n fs*	pn	cj, v Qal impf 3ms	pn
עַל־שְׂפַת	יַם־סוּף	בְּאֶרֶץ	אֱדוֹם	וַיִּשְׁלַח	חִירָם
'al-s^ephath	yam-sûph	b^e'erets	'ĕdhôm	wayyishlach	chîrām
on the shore of	the Sea of Reeds	in the land of	Edom	and he sent	Hiram

21. Their children that were left after them in the land, whom the children of Israel also were not able utterly to destroy, upon those did Solomon levy a tribute of bondservice unto this day: ... the descendants of whom remained in the country, *Fenton* ... Solomon forced them to work as slaves, as is still true today, *NCV* ... to destroy completely, *NKJV* ... children of Israel could not exterminate, *NIV*.

22. But of the children of Israel did Solomon make no bondmen: but they were men of war, and his servants, and his princes, and his captains, and rulers of his chariots, and his horsemen: ... of the Israelites Solomon made no slaves, *NRSV* ... they were the soldiers, they were his officials, his commanders, his captains, his chariot commanders, *RSV* ... None of the Israelites were put to forced labour, *REB* ... they served him as fighting men, as his commanders and lieutenants, and as the captains of his chariots and of his cavalry, *Beck*.

23. These were the chief of the officers that were over Solomon's work, five hundred and fifty, which bare rule over the people that wrought in the work: ... chief officials who supervised Solomon's work; 550 of them who directed the people who did the work, *Berkeley* ... Commanders of the Engineers, who were over the works of Solomon, *Fenton* ... who had charge of, *Goodspeed* ... his most important officers, *NCV*.

24. But Pharaoh's daughter came up out of the city of David unto her house which Solomon had built for her: then did he build Millo: ... Solomon brought Pharaoh's daughter up, *NEB* ... to the palace Solomon had built for her, he constructed the supporting terraces, *NIV* ... Pharaoh's daughter moved from David's city to her palace, *Beck* ... Solomon filled the land on the east side of the city, after his wife, the daughter of the king of Egypt, had moved, *Good News*.

25. And three times in a year did Solomon offer burnt offerings and peace offerings upon the altar which he built unto the LORD, and he burnt incense upon the altar that was before the LORD. So he finished the house: ... thank-offerings, *Goodspeed* ... communion sacrifices, *JB* ... fellowship offerings, *NCV* ... making smoke offerings, *NEB*.

26. And king Solomon made a navy of ships in Ezion-geber, which is beside Eloth, on the shore of the Red sea, in the land of Edom: ... built a fleet, *NKJV* ... made a sea-force, *BB* ... equipped a fleet, *JB*.

27. And Hiram sent in the navy his servants, shipmen that had knowledge of the sea, with the servants of

Israelites, but 550 men did have to oversee the work as foremen, being stationed at the building sites. The people were also taxed (probably on their food, cp. 1 Ki. 5:10ff), and they were required to serve in the army, being fully equipped and ready for battle, with chariots and military rank. National defense was needed to back up foreign treaties. Possible curses inflicted by the gods on anyone breaking a treaty was always more respected if military might was available to deliver a convincing blow.

Solomon was not only concerned with national security, but with the affections of the new wife he had acquired. He built a palace for his bride, the daughter of Pharaoh as well as the Millo (either a separate building or perhaps translated as "supporting structures" for her palace). The king still "made complete the temple," however, offering the proper sacrifices. But notice that the text does not say that Solomon kept the Covenant or followed after the Law. Solomon had apparently begun to follow the form, but his heart was drifting.

He also continued his cooperation with Hiram, building ships at Ezion-Geber on the shore of the Red Sea. Hiram sent experienced sailors to man the ships. Sailing to Ophir, they brought back 420 talents of gold. The text does not say that the 420 talents was the total after returning 120 talents to Hiram, nor does it record that Solomon returned 120 talents from the 420. Hiram's continued cooperation further supports the idea that the 20 cities in

904, 604	881, 5860	596	605	3156.152	3328	6196	5860
prep, art, n ms	do, n mp, ps 3ms	*n mp*	n fp	*v Qal act ptc mp*	art, n ms	prep	*n mp*
בָּאֳנִי	אֶת־עֲבָדָיו	אַנְשֵׁי	אֳנִיּוֹת	יֹדְעֵי	הַיָּם	עִם	עַבְדֵי
bā'ănî	'eth-'ăvādhâv	'anshê	'ănîyôth	yōdhᵉ'ê	hayyām	'im	'avdhê
with the ships	his slaves	the men of	ships	those knowing	the sea	with	the servants of

8406		971.126	209	4089.126	4623, 8427	2174	727, 4109
pn	28.	cj, v Qal impf 3mp	pn	cj, v Qal impf 3mp	prep, adv	n ms	num, num
שְׁלֹמֹה		וַיָּבֹאוּ	אוֹפִירָה	וַיִּקְחוּ	מִשָּׁם	זָהָב	אַרְבַּע־מֵאוֹת
shᵉlōmōh		wayyāvō'û	'ôphîrāh	wayyiqŏchû	mishshām	zāhāv	'arba'-mē'ôth
Solomon		and they went	to Ophir	and they took	from there	gold	four hundreds

6465	3724	971.526	420, 4567	8406		4573, 8088
cj, num	n fs	cj, v Hiphil impf 3mp	prep, art, n ms	pn	10:1	cj, *n fs*, pn
וְעֶשְׂרִים	כִּכָּר	וַיָּבִאוּ	אֶל־הַמֶּלֶךְ	שְׁלֹמֹה		וּמַלְכַּת־שְׁבָא
wᵉ'esrîm	kikkār	wayyāvi'û	'el-hammelekh	shᵉlōmōh		ûmalkath-shᵉvā'
and twenty	talents	and they brought	to the king	Solomon		and the queen of Sheba

8471.153	881, 8475	8406	3937, 8428	3176	971.122
v Qal act ptc fs	do, *n ms*	pn	prep, *n ms*	pn	cj, v Qal impf 3fs
שֹׁמַעַת	אֶת־שֵׁמַע	שְׁלֹמֹה	לְשֵׁם	יְהוָה	וַתָּבֹא
shōma'ath	'eth-shēma'	shᵉlōmōh	lᵉshēm	yᵉhwāh	wattāvō'
hearing	the report about	Solomon	of the name of	Yahweh	and she came

3937, 5441.341	904, 2512		971.122	3503	904, 2524	3633
prep, v Piel inf con, ps 3ms	prep, n fp	2.	cj, v Qal impf 3fs	pn	prep, n ms	adj
לְנַסֹּתוֹ	בְּחִידוֹת		וַתָּבֹא	יְרוּשָׁלַמָה	בְּחַיִל	כָּבֵד
lᵉnassōthô	bᵉchîdhôth		wattāvō'	yᵉrûshālamāh	bᵉchayil	kāvēdh
to test him	with difficult sayings		and she came	to Jerusalem	with wealth	heavy

4108	1622	5558.152	1336	2174	7521, 4108	63	3479
adv	n mp	v Qal act ptc mp	n mp	cj, n ms	adj, adv	cj, n fs	adj
מְאֹד	גְּמַלִּים	נֹשְׂאִים	בְּשָׂמִים	וְזָהָב	רַב־מְאֹד	וְאֶבֶן	יְקָרָה
mᵉ'ōdh	gᵉmallîm	nōsᵉ'îm	bᵉsāmîm	wᵉzāhāv	rav-mᵉ'ōdh	wᵉ'even	yᵉqārāh
very	camels	bearing	balsam oils	and gold	very many	and stones	precious

971.122	420, 8406	1744.322	420	881	3725, 866	2030.111
cj, v Qal impf 3fs	prep, pn	cj, v Piel impf 3fs	prep, ps 3ms	do	*adj*, rel part	v Qal pf 3ms
וַתָּבֹא	אֶל־שְׁלֹמֹה	וַתְּדַבֵּר	אֵלָיו	אֵת	כָּל־אֲשֶׁר	הָיָה
wattāvō'	'el-shᵉlōmōh	wattᵉdhabbēr	'ēlâv	'ēth	kol-'ăsher	hāyāh
and she came	unto Solomon	and she spoke	to him		all that	it was

6196, 3949		5222.521, 3937	8406	881, 3725, 1745	3940, 2030.111
prep, n ms, ps 3fs	3.	cj, v Hiphil impf 3ms, prep, ps 3fs	pn	do, *adj*, n mp, ps 3fs	neg part, v Qal pf 3ms
עִם־לְבָבָהּ		וַיַּגֶּד־לָהּ	שְׁלֹמֹה	אֶת־כָּל־דְּבָרֶיהָ	לֹא־הָיָה
'im-lᵉvāvāhh		wayyaggedh-lāhh	shᵉlōmōh	'eth-kol-dᵉvārêâ	lō'-hāyāh
with her heart		and he told her	Solomon	all her words	it was not

1745	6180.255	4623, 4567	866	3940	5222.511	3937		7495.122
n ms	v Niphal ptc ms	prep, art, n ms	rel part	neg part	v Hiphil pf 3ms	prep, ps 3fs	4.	cj, v Qal impf 3fs
דָּבָר	נֶעְלָם	מִן־הַמֶּלֶךְ	אֲשֶׁר	לֹא	הִגִּיד	לָהּ		וַתֵּרֶא
dāvār	ne'ălām	min-hammelekh	'ăsher	lō'	higgîdh	lāhh		wattēre'
a matter	hidden	from the king	which	not	he explained	to her		and she saw

4573, 8088	881	3725, 2551	8406	1041	866	1161.111
n fs, pn	do	*adj*, *n fs*	pn	cj, art, n ms	rel part	v Qal pf 3ms
מַלְכַּת־שְׁבָא	אֵת	כָּל־חָכְמַת	שְׁלֹמֹה	וְהַבַּיִת	אֲשֶׁר	בָּנָה
malkath-shᵉvā'	'ēth	kol-chokhmath	shᵉlōmōh	wᵉhabbayith	'ăsher	bānāh
the queen of Sheba		all the wisdom of	Solomon	and the Temple	which	he had built

Solomon: ... seamen who knew the sea, to work, *NKJV* ... sailors, *NIV* ... sent experienced crews of sailors to sail the ships with Solomon's men, *NLT* ... sent men of his own, mariners that had long experience, *Knox*.

28. And they came to Ophir, and fetched from thence gold, four hundred and twenty talents, and brought it to king Solomon: ... and took it back to, *BB* ... collected from there, *Fenton* ... The ships sailed to Ophir and brought back, *NCV*.

10:1. And when the queen of Sheba heard of the fame of Solomon concerning the name of the LORD, she came to prove him with hard questions: ... to test him with, *KJVII* ... to put his wisdom to the test with, *BB* ... puzzling questions, *Beck* ... perplexing questions, *Berkeley*.

2. And she came to Jerusalem with a very great train, with camels that bare spices, and very much gold, and precious stones: and when she was come to Solomon, she communed with him of all that was in her heart: ... arrived at Jerusalem with a very great troop bringing perfumes, *Fenton* ... she asked him all the questions she could think of, *Good News* ... she discussed with him everything that she had in mind, *JB* ... Arriving at Jerusalem with a very great caravan, *NIV*.

3. And Solomon told her all her questions: there was not any thing hid from the king, which he told her not: ... answered all, *NKJV* ... nothing was too hard for the king to explain to her, *NIV* ... there was no secret which the king did not make clear to her, *BB* ... not one of them was too obscure for the king to answer for her, *JB*.

4. And when the queen of Sheba had seen all Solomon's wisdom, and the house that he had built: ... witnessed Solomon's great wisdom, *NAB* ... learned that Solomon was very wise, *NCV* ... realized how wise Solomon was, *NLT* ... had observed all, *NRSV*.

5. And the meat of his table, and the sitting of his servants, and the attendance of his ministers, and their apparel, and his cupbearers, and his ascent by which he went up unto the house of the LORD; there was no more spirit in her: ... the seating of his officials, and the attendance of his servants, their clothing, his cupbearers, and his burnt offerings, *RSV* ... she was breathless, *Beck* ... the food at his table, and all his servants seated there, and those who were waiting on him in their places, and their robes, and his wine-servants, and the burned offerings which he made, *BB* ... amazed, *Good News*.

---

the region of Galilee were considered acceptable in Hiram's final estimation. If Solomon was required any repayment or reciprocation, the Bible does not record it. Thus, one clear point that the author intends the reader to understand is that Hiram and Solomon carried no ill feelings toward one another, and this was one the most important factors which led to Solomon's ability to expand the territory and influence of his kingdom. Yet Solomon was all too soon to forget that this attitude of good will was precipitated directly by God's actions and was not the earthly king's own doing.

10:1–29. *The history of the Temple is the event which gives supreme religious importance to the reign of one who became in other respects a worldly and irreligious king. Solomon gave an impulse to outward service, not to spiritual life. The other fragments of his story which have been preserved for us are mainly of a political character. They point us to Solomon in his wealth and ostentation, and contain nothing especially edifying. Our LORD thought less of all this splendor than of the flower of the field. "Consider the lilies of the field, how they grow; they toil not, neither do they spin: yet I say unto you! that Solomon in all his glory was not arrayed like one of these."*

Princes who have once begun to build find a certain fascination in the task. After the seven years devoted to the Temple, Solomon occupied thirteen more in building with Lebanon cedar for himself, for his audience-chamber and for Pharaoh's daughter.

10:1–5. *"The queen of the south shall rise up in the judgment with this generation, and shall condemn it: for she came from the uttermost parts of the earth to hear the wisdom of Solomon" (Matt. 12:42).*

This career of magnificence culminated in the visit of the Queen of Sheba, who came to him across the desert with "a very great train of her camels, bearing spices and very much gold and precious stones." She saw his abounding prosperity, his peaceful people, his houses, his vineyards at Beth-Haccerem, his parks and gardens, his pools and fruit trees, his herds of cattle, his horses, chariots, and palanquins and all the delight of the sons of men. She saw his men singers and women singers with their harps of decorative wood and gold. She saw him at the banquet at his golden table covered in boundless profusion with delicacies brought from every land. She saw his hosts of beautiful and richly dressed slaves with lavers, dishes and goblets all

	4120	8374	4319	5860	4771	8664.351
5.	cj, *n ms*	n ms, ps 3ms	cj, *n ms*	n mp, ps 3ms	cj, *n ms*	v Piel ptc ms, ps 3ms
	וּמַאֲכַל	שֻׁלְחָנוֹ	וּמוֹשַׁב	עֲבָדָיו	וּמַעֲמַד	מְשָׁרְתוֹ
	ûma'ăkhal	shulchānô	ûmôshav	'ăvādhâv	ûma'ămadh	meshārethô
	and the food of	his table	and the chairs of	his servants	and the service of	his administrators

4540	5126	6150	866	6148.521
cj, n mp, ps 3mp	cj, n mp, ps 3ms	cj, n fs, ps 3ms	rel part	v Hiphil impf 3ms
וּמַלְבֻּשֵׁיהֶם	וּמַשְׁקָיו	וְעֹלָתוֹ	אֲשֶׁר	יַעֲלֶה
ûmalbushêhem	ûmashqâv	we'ōlāthô	'ăsher	ya'ăleh
and their clothes	and his cupbearers	and his burnt offerings	which	he caused to go up

1041	3176	3940, 2030.111	904	5968	7593		569.122
n ms	pn	cj, neg part, v Qal pf 3ms	prep, ps 3fs	adv	n fs	**6.**	cj, v Qal impf 3fs
בֵּית	יְהוָה	וְלֹא־הָיָה	בָּהּ	עוֹד	רוּחַ		וַתֹּאמֶר
bêth	yehwāh	welō'-hāyāh	vāhh	'ôdh	rûach		wattō'mer
the Temple of	Yahweh	and it was not	in her	anymore	a spirit		and she said

420, 4567	583	2030.111	1745	866	8471.115	904, 800
prep, art, n ms	n fs	v Qal pf 3ms	art, n ms	rel part	v Qal pf 1cs	prep, n fs, ps 1cs
אֶל־הַמֶּלֶךְ	אֱמֶת	הָיָה	הַדָּבָר	אֲשֶׁר	שָׁמַעְתִּי	בְּאַרְצִי
'el-hammelekh	'ĕmeth	hāyāh	haddāvār	'ăsher	shāma'ättî	be'artsî
to the king	a truth	it was	the word	which	I heard	in my land

6142, 1745	6142, 2551		3940, 548.515	3937, 1745	5912
prep, n mp, ps 2ms	cj, prep, n fs, ps 2ms	**7.**	cj, neg part, v Hiphil pf 1cs	prep, art, n mp	adv
עַל־דְּבָרֶיךָ	וְעַל־חָכְמָתֶךָ		וְלֹא־הֶאֱמַנְתִּי	לַדְּבָרִים	עַד
'al-devārêkhā	we'al-chokhmāthekhā		welō'-he'ĕmantî	laddevārîm	'adh
concerning your matters	and concerning your wisdom		and I did not believe	the words	until

866, 971.115	7495.127	6084	2079	3940, 5222.611, 3937	2783
rel part, v Qal pf 1cs	cj, v Qal impf 3fp	n fd, ps 1cs	cj, intrj	neg part, v Hophal pf 3ms, prep, ps 1cs	art, n ms
אֲשֶׁר־בָּאתִי	וַתִּרְאֶינָה	עֵינַי	וְהִנֵּה	לֹא־הֻגַּד־לִי	הַחֵצִי
'ăsher-bā'thî	wattir'ênāh	'ênay	wehinnēh	lō'-huggadh-lî	hachētsî
that I came	and they saw	my eyes	and behold	it was not reported to me	the half

3362.513	2551	3008	420, 8444	866	8471.115		869
v Hiphil pf 2ms	n fs	cj, n ms	prep, art, n fs	rel part	v Qal pf 1cs	**8.**	n mp
הוֹסַפְתָּ	חָכְמָה	וָטוֹב	אֶל־הַשְּׁמוּעָה	אֲשֶׁר	שָׁמַעְתִּי		אַשְׁרֵי
hôsaphtā	chokhmāh	wātôv	'el-hashshemû'āh	'ăsher	shāmā'ättî		'ashrê
you have added	wisdom	and good things	to the report	which	I heard		happy

596	869	5860	431	6198.152	3937, 6686	8878
n mp, ps 2ms	n mp	n mp, ps 2ms	dem pron	art, v Qal act ptc mp	prep, n mp, ps 2ms	adv
אֲנָשֶׁיךָ	אַשְׁרֵי	עֲבָדֶיךָ	אֵלֶּה	הָעֹמְדִים	לְפָנֶיךָ	תָּמִיד
'ănāshêkhā	'ashrê	'ăvādhêkhā	'ēlleh	hā'ōmedhîm	lephānêkhā	tāmîdh
your men	happy	your servants	these	those standing	before you	continually

8471.152	881, 2551		2030.121	3176	435	1313.155	866
art, v Qal act ptc mp	do, n fs, ps 2ms	**9.**	v Qal juss 3ms	pn	n mp, ps 2ms	v Qal pass ptc ms	rel pron
הַשֹּׁמְעִים	אֶת־חָכְמָתֶךָ		יְהִי	יְהוָה	אֱלֹהֶיךָ	בָּרוּךְ	אֲשֶׁר
hashshōme'îm	'eth-chokhmāthekhā		yehî	yehwāh	'ĕlōhêkhā	bārûkh	'ăsher
those hearing	your wisdom		may He be	Yahweh	your God	blessed	Who

2759.111	904	3937, 5598.141	6142, 3802	3547	904, 157	3176
v Qal pf 3ms	prep, ps 2ms	prep, v Qal inf con, ps 2ms	prep, *n ms*	pn	prep, *n fs*	pn
חָפֵץ	בְּךָ	לְתִתְּךָ	עַל־כִּסֵּא	יִשְׂרָאֵל	בְּאַהֲבַת	יְהוָה
chāphēts	bekhā	lethittekhā	'al-kissē'	yisrā'ēl	be'ahvath	yehwāh
He desired	with you	to put you	on the throne of	Israel	with the love of	Yahweh

5122	3937, 6449.141	3937, 4567	7947.121	3937, 5986	881, 3547
n ms	prep, v Qal inf con	prep, n ms	cj, v Qal impf 3ms, ps 2ms	prep, n ms	do, pn
מִשְׁפָּט	לַעֲשׂוֹת	לְמֶלֶךְ	וַיְשִׂימְךָ	לְעֹלָם	אֶת־יִשְׂרָאֵל
mishpāṭ	la'ăsôth	lemelekh	waysîmekhā	le'ōlām	'eth-yisrā'ēl
justice	to execute	as king	and He has appointed you	for ever	Israel

2174	3724	6465	4109	3937, 4567	5598.122		6930
n ms	*n fs*	cj, num	num	prep, art, n ms	cj, v Qal impf 3fs	**10.**	cj, n fs
זָהָב	כִּכַּר	וְעֶשְׂרִים	מֵאָה	לַמֶּלֶךְ	וַתִּתֵּן		וּצְדָקָה
zāhāv	kikkar	we'esrîm	mē'āh	lammelekh	wattittēn		ûtsedhāqāh
gold	talents of	and twenty	one hundred	to the king	and she gave		and righteousness

3626, 1336	3940, 971.111	3479	63	4108	7528.542	1336
prep, art, n ms	neg part, v Qal pf 3ms	adj	cj, n fs	adv	v Hiphil inf abs	cj, n mp
כַּבֹּשֶׂם	לֹא־בָא	יְקָרָה	וְאֶבֶן	מְאֹד	הַרְבֵּה	וּבְשָׂמִים
khabbōsem	lō'-vā'	yeqārāh	we'even	me'ōdh	harbēh	ûvesāmîm
like the balsam oil	it did not come in	precious	and stones	very	making great	and balsam oils

6. And she said to the king, It was a true report that I heard in mine own land of thy acts and of thy wisdom: ... about your wisdom in handling your affairs was true, *JB* ... the word I heard in mine own land, *Tyndale* ... of your accomplishments and, *NRSV* ... The account which was given to me, *BB*.

7. Howbeit I believed not the words, until I came, and mine eyes had seen it: and, behold, the half was not told me: thy wisdom and prosperity exceedeth the fame which I heard: ... I didn't believe what I was told till I came and saw it with my own eyes. Actually I wasn't told half of it. You have more wisdom and prosperity than anything I've heard, *Beck* ... wealth are much greater, *Good News* ... I would not believe the words until I came and saw, *Goodspeed* ... go far beyond the report which I had of them, *NEB*.

8. Happy are thy men, happy are these thy servants, which stand continually before thee, and that hear thy wisdom: ... How happy your men must be! How happy your officials, *NIV* ... What a privilege for your officials, *NLT* ... fortunate these courtiers of yours who are continually present with you, *Berkeley* ... Happy are your wives! Happy are these your servants, who continually attend you, *NRSV*.

9. Blessed be the Lord thy God, which delighted in thee, to set thee on the throne of Israel: because the Lord loved Israel for ever, therefore made he thee king, to do judgment and justice: ... that you may execute justice and righteousness, *RSV* ... because he loves Israel unendingly, he has made you king to maintain law and, *REB* ... be praised, whose pleasure it was to put you on the seat of the kingdom of Israel; because the Lord's love for Israel is eternal, he has made you king, to be their judge in righteousness, *BB* ... who has shown you his favour, *JB*.

10. And she gave the king an hundred and twenty talents of gold, and of spices very great store, and precious stones: there came no more such abundance of spices as these which the queen of Sheba gave to king Solomon: ... Never again did anyone bring, *NAB* ... and jewels, *NCV* ... spices in great abundance, *NKJV* ... large quantities of, *NIV*.

11. And the navy also of Hiram, that brought gold from Ophir, brought in from Ophir great plenty of almug trees, and pre-

made of the gold of Uphaz. She saw him dispensing justice in his pillared hall of cedar, seated on his lion-throne. She saw the golden shields and targets carried before him as he went in state to the Temple over the mount, across the valley, and mounted from the palace to the sacred courts by the gilded staircase with its balustrades of aromatic balsam. Perhaps she was present as a spectator at some great temple festival. And when she had tested his wisdom by communing with him of all that was in her heart, "there was no more spirit in her."

10:6–13. She confessed that the half of his wisdom and glory had not been reported to her. Happy were his servants; happy were the courtiers who stood by him and heard his words! Blessed was the Lord his God Who delighted in him, and who, out of love for Israel, had given them such a king to do justice and judgment among them. The visit ended with an interchange of royal presents. Solomon, we are vaguely told, "gave unto her all her desire, whatsoever she asked," and sent her away glad-hearted to her native land, leaving behind her a trail of legends. Before her departure,

2000	5968	3937, 7524	866, 5598.112	4573, 8088	3937, 4567	8406
art, dem pron	adv	prep, art, n ms	rel part, v Qal pf 3fs	*n fs*, pn	prep, art, n ms	pn
הַהוּא	עוֹד	לָרֹב	אֲשֶׁר־נָתְנָה	מַלְכַּת־שְׁבָא	לַמֶּלֶךְ	שְׁלֹמֹה
hahû'	'ôdh	lārōv	'ăsher-nāthenāh	malkath-shevā'	lammelekh	shelōmōh
the that	again	for the abundance	which she gave	the queen of Sheba	to the king	Solomon

11.	1612	604	2538	866, 5558.111	2174	4623, 209	971.511	4623, 209
	cj, cj	*n ms*	pn	rel part, v Qal pf 3ms	n ms	prep, pn	v Hiphil pf 3ms	prep, pn
	וְגַם	אֳנִי	חִירָם	אֲשֶׁר־נָשָׂא	זָהָב	מֵאוֹפִיר	הֵבִיא	מֵאֹפִיר
	wegham	'ănî	chîrām	'ăsher-nāsā'	zāhāv	mē'ôphîr	hēvî'	mē'ôphîr
	and also	the ships of	Hiram	which they carried	gold	from Ophir	they brought	from Ophir

6320	490	7528.542	4108	63	3479	12.	6449.121	4567
n mp	n mp	v Hiphil inf abs	adv	cj, n fs	adj		cj, v Qal impf 3ms	art, n ms
עֲצֵי	אַלְמֻגִּים	הַרְבֵּה	מְאֹד	וְאֶבֶן	יְקָרָה		וַיַּעַשׂ	הַמֶּלֶךְ
'ätsê	'almuggîm	harbēh	me'ōdh	we'even	yeqārāh		wayya'as	hammelekh
trees of	almug wood	making great	very	and stones	precious		and he made	the king

881, 6320	490	4704	3937, 1041, 3176	3937, 1041	4567
do, *n mp*	art, n mp	n ms	prep, *n ms*, pn	cj, prep, *n ms*	art, n ms
אֶת־עֲצֵי	הָאַלְמֻגִּים	מִסְעָד	לְבֵית־יְהוָה	וּלְבֵית	הַמֶּלֶךְ
'eth-'ätsê	hā'almuggîm	mis'ādh	levêth-yehwāh	ûlāvêth	hammelekh
the trees of	the almug wood	pillars	for the temple of Yahweh	and for the house of	the king

3780	5213	3937, 8301.152	3940	971.111, 3772	6320	490
cj, n mp	cj, n mp	prep, art, v Qal act ptc mp	neg part	v Qal pf 3ms, adv	*n mp*	n mp
וְכִנֹּרוֹת	וּנְבָלִים	לַשָּׁרִים	לֹא	בָא־כֵן	עֲצֵי	אַלְמֻגִּים
wekhinnōrôth	ûnevālîm	lashshārîm	lō'	vā'-khēn	'ätsê	'almuggîm
and zithers	and harps	for the singers	not	it had come in so	trees of	almug wood

3940	7495.211	5912	3219	2172	13.	4567	8406	5598.111
cj, neg part	v Niphal pf 3ms	adv	art, n ms	art, dem pron		cj, art, n ms	pn	v Qal pf 3ms
וְלֹא	נִרְאָה	עַד	הַיּוֹם	הַזֶּה		וְהַמֶּלֶךְ	שְׁלֹמֹה	נָתַן
welō'	nir'āh	'adh	hayyôm	hazzeh		wehammelekh	shelōmōh	nāthan
and not	it had been seen	until	the day	the this		and the king	Solomon	he gave

3937, 4573, 8088	881, 3725, 2761	866	8068.112	4623, 3937, 940	866
prep, *n fs*, pn	do, *adj*, n ms, ps 3fs	rel part	v Qal pf 3fs	prep, prep, n ms	rel part
לְמַלְכַּת־שְׁבָא	אֶת־כָּל־חֶפְצָהּ	אֲשֶׁר	שָׁאָלָה	מִלְּבַד	אֲשֶׁר
lemalkath-shevā'	'eth-kol-chephtsāhh	'ăsher	shā'ālāh	millevadh	'ăsher
to the queen of Sheba	all her desire	that	she asked	besides	what

5598.111, 3937	3626, 3135	4567	8406	6680.122	2050.122
v Qal pf 3ms, prep, ps 3fs	prep, *n fs*	art, n ms	pn	cj, v Qal impf 3fs	cj, v Qal impf 3fs
נָתַן־לָהּ	כְּיַד	הַמֶּלֶךְ	שְׁלֹמֹה	וַתֵּפֶן	וַתֵּלֶךְ
nāthan-lāhh	keyadh	hammelekh	shelōmōh	wattēphen	wattēlekh
he had given to her	according to the hand of	the king	Solomon	then she turned	and she went

3937, 800	2026	5860	14.	2030.121	5129	2174
prep, n fs, ps 3fs	pers pron	cj, n mp, ps 3fs		cj, v Qal impf 3ms	*n ms*	art, n ms
לְאַרְצָהּ	הִיא	וַעֲבָדֶיהָ		וַיְהִי	מִשְׁקַל	הַזָּהָב
le'artsāhh	hî'	wa'ăvādhêāh		wayhî	mishqal	hazzāhāv
to her land	she	and her servants		and it was	the weight of	the gold

866, 971.111	3937, 8406	904, 8523	259	8666	4109	8666	8666	3724
rel pron, v Qal pf 3ms	prep, pn	prep, n fs	num	num	num	num	cj, num	*n fs*
אֲשֶׁר־בָּא	לִשְׁלֹמֹה	בְּשָׁנָה	אֶחָת	שֵׁשׁ	מֵאוֹת	שִׁשִּׁים	וָשֵׁשׁ	כִּכַּר
'ăsher-bā'	lishlōmōh	beshānāh	'echāth	shēsh	mē'ôth	shishshîm	wāshēsh	kikkar
which came in	to Solomon	in a year	one	six	hundreds	sixty	and six	talents of

2174 n ms זָהָב zāhāv gold	15.	3937, 940 prep, n ms לְבַד levadh besides	4623, 596 prep, *n mp* מֵאַנְשֵׁי mē'anshê from the men of	8780.152 art, v Qal act ptc mp הַתָּרִים hattārîm the explorers	4686 cj, *n ms* וּמִסְחַר ûmischar and the trade of	7691.152 art, v Qal act ptc mp הָרֹכְלִים hārōkhelîm the traders

3725, 4567 cj, *adj*, *n mp* וְכָל־מַלְכֵי wekhol-malkhê and all the kings of	6395 art, pn הָעֶרֶב hā'erev the Arabia	6589 cj, *n mp* וּפַחוֹת ûphachôth and the governors of	800 art, n fs הָאָרֶץ hā'ārets the land	16.	6449.121 cj, v Qal impf 3ms וַיַּעַשׂ wayya'as and he made	4567 art, n ms הַמֶּלֶךְ hammelekh the king

8406 pn שְׁלֹמֹה shelōmōh Solomon	4109 num מָאתַיִם mā'thayim two hundred	7065 n fs צִנָּה tsinnāh large shields	2174 n ms זָהָב zāhāv gold	8250.155 v Qal pass ptc ms שָׁחוּט shāchût hammered	8666, 4109 num, num שֵׁשׁ־מֵאוֹת shēsh-mē'ôth six hundred	2174 n ms זָהָב zāhāv gold	6148.521 v Hiphil impf 3ms יַעֲלֶה ya'ăleh he sent up

cious stones: ... the fleet of Hiram, which carried gold, *NRSV* ... Hiram's ships, *NLT* ... the sea-force of Hiram, in addition to gold from Ophir, came back with much sandal-wood and jewels, *BB* ... juniper wood and, *NCV*.

12. And the king made of the almug trees pillars for the house of the Lord, and for the king's house, harps also and psalteries for singers: there came no such almug trees, nor were seen unto this day: ... and lutes for the singers, *NEB* ... king made steps of the almug wood ... and stringed instruments for singers, *NKJV* ... used the almugwood to make supports for the temple of the Lord and for the royal palace, and to make harps and lyres for the musicians, *NIV* ... Accordingly the king made of the sandalwood pilasters, *Goodspeed*.

13. And king Solomon gave unto the queen of Sheba all her desire, whatsoever she asked, beside that which Solomon gave her of his royal bounty. So she turned and went to her own country, she and her servants: ... presented the queen of Sheba with everything that she expressed a wish for, *JB* ... in addition to what he had already given her of his wealth, *NCV* ... besides all the other customary gifts he had so generously given, *NLT* ... in addition to what he gave her freely from the impulse of his heart, *BB*.

14. Now the weight of gold that came to Solomon in one year was six hundred threescore and six talents of gold: ... gold received annually by Solomon amounted to, *JB* ... six hundred and sixty-six talents, *Fenton* ... about fifty thousand pounds, *NCV* ... over twenty-five tons, *Good News*.

15. Beside that he had of the merchantmen, and of the traffic of the spice merchants, and of all the kings of Arabia, and of the governors of the country: ... in addition to the tolls levied by the customs officers and profits on foreign trade, and the tribute of the kings of Arabia and the regional governors, *NEB* ... from the traveling merchants, from the income of traders ... and from the governors of the country, *NKJV* ... beside that produced by taxes on traders, and the import duties, and tribute from all the kingdoms of the west, and the Dependencies of the country, *Fenton* ... what came in from mercantile taxes and the profits from trade, *Berkeley*.

16. And king Solomon made two hundred targets of beaten gold: six hundred shekels of gold went to one target: ... two hundred body-covers of hammered gold, *BB* ... 200 large shields, *Beck* ... two hundred shields of the purest gold, *Douay*.

17. And he made three hundred shields of beaten gold; three pound of gold went to one shield: and the king put them in the house of the forest of Lebanon: ... three hundred smaller body-covers of hammered gold, *BB* ... king put them in the

she opened her treasures and gave him vast stores of spicery and gold (Ps. 72:15).

10:14–15. He further dazzled his people by an extensive system of foreign commerce. His land-traffic with Arabia familiarized them with spicery (necofh), gum tragacanth, frankincense, myrrh, aloes, cassia and precious stones of all kinds. From Egypt he obtained horses and chariots. They were brought from Tekoa, by his merchants, and kept by Solomon, or sold at a profit.

10:16–17. Chief among Solomon's buildings was the house of the forest of Lebanon, a sort of arsenal so called from its triple rows of cedar pillars, on which hung the golden shields for the

6142, 7065	259		8421, 4109	4182	2174	8250.155	8421
prep, art, n fs	art, num	17.	cj, num, num	n mp	n ms	v Qal pass ptc ms	num
עַל־הַצִּנָּה	הָאֶחָת		וּשְׁלֹשׁ־מֵאוֹת	מָגִנִּים	זָהָב	שָׁחוּט	שְׁלֹשֶׁת
'al-hatstsinnāh	hā'echāth		ûshelōsh-mē'ôth	māghinîm	zāhāv	shāchûṯ	shelōsheth
onto the large shield	the one		and three hundreds	shields	gold	hammered	thirty

4632	2174	6148.521	6142, 4182	259	5598.121	4567
n mp	n ms	v Hiphil impf 3ms	prep, art, n fs	art, num	cj, v Qal impf 3ms, ps 3mp	art, n ms
מָנִים	זָהָב	יַעֲלֶה	עַל־הַמָּגֵן	הָאֶחָת	וַיִּתְּנֵם	הַמֶּלֶךְ
mānîm	zāhāv	ya'ăleh	'al-hammāghēn	hā'echāth	wayyittenēm	hammelekh
minas	gold	he sent up	onto the shield	the one	and he put them	the king

1041	3402	3976		6449.121	4567	3802, 8514	1448
n ms	n ms	art, pn	18.	cj, v Qal impf 3ms	art, n ms	*n ms*, n fs	adj
בֵּית	יַעַר	הַלְּבָנוֹן		וַיַּעַשׂ	הַמֶּלֶךְ	כִּסֵּא־שֵׁן	גָּדוֹל
bêth	ya'ar	hallevānôn		wayya'as	hammelekh	kissē'-shēn	gādhôl
the house of	the forest of	the Lebanon		and he made	the king	a throne of ivory	great

7099.321	2174	6581.655		8666	4766	3937, 3802	7513, 5902
cj, v Piel impf 3ms, ps 3ms	n ms	v Hophal ptc ms	19.	num	n fp	prep, art, n ms	cj, n ms, adj
וַיְצַפֵּהוּ	זָהָב	מוּפָז		שֵׁשׁ	מַעֲלוֹת	לַכִּסֵּה	וְרֹאשׁ־עָגֹל
waytsappēhû	zāhāv	mûphāz		shēsh	ma'ălôth	lakkissēh	werō'sh-'āghōl
and he overlaid it with	gold	made pure		six	steps	to the throne	and a round top

3937, 3802	4623, 313	3135	4623, 2172	4623, 2172	420, 4887	8140
prep, art, n ms	prep, prep, ps 3ms	cj, n fp	prep, adv	cj, prep, adv	prep, *n ms*	art, n fs
לַכִּסֵּה	מֵאַחֲרָיו	וְיָדֹת	מִזֶּה	וּמִזֶּה	אֶל־מְקוֹם	הַשָּׁבֶת
lakkissēh	mē'achrâv	weyādhōth	mizzeh	ûmizzeh	'el-meqôm	hashshāveth
to the throne	from behind it	and sides	from here	and from there	toward the place of	the seat

8530	761	6198.152	703	3135		8530	6461	761	6198.152
cj, num	n mp	v Qal act ptc mp	prep	art, n fp	20.	cj, num	num	n mp	v Qal act ptc mp
וּשְׁנַיִם	אֲרָיוֹת	עֹמְדִים	אֵצֶל	הַיָּדוֹת		וּשְׁנֵים	עָשָׂר	אֲרָיִים	עֹמְדִים
ûshenayim	'ărāyôth	'ōmedhîm	'ētsel	hayyādhôth		ûshenêm	'āsār	'ărāyîm	'ōmedhîm
and two	lions	standing	beside	the sides		and two	ten	lions	standing

8427	6142, 8666	4766	4623, 2172	4623, 2172	3940, 6449.211	3772
adv	prep, num	art, n fp	prep, adv	cj, prep, adv	neg part, v Niphal pf 3ms	adv
שָׁם	עַל־שֵׁשׁ	הַמַּעֲלוֹת	מִזֶּה	וּמִזֶּה	לֹא־נַעֲשָׂה	כֵן
shām	'al-shēsh	hamma'ălôth	mizzeh	ûmizzeh	lō'-na'ăsāh	khēn
there	beside six	the steps	from here	and from there	it had not been done	so

3937, 3725, 4608		3725	3747	5126	4567	8406	2174	3725
prep, *adj*, n fp	21.	cj, adj	*n mp*	*n ms*	art, n ms	pn	n ms	cj, nms
לְכָל־מַמְלָכוֹת		וְכֹל	כְּלֵי	מַשְׁקֵה	הַמֶּלֶךְ	שְׁלֹמֹה	זָהָב	וְכֹל
lekhol-mamlākhôth		wekhōl	kelê	mashqēh	hammelekh	shelōmōh	zāhāv	wekhōl
of all kingdoms		and all	vessels of	the cupbearer of	the king	Solomon	gold	and all

3747	1041, 3402	3976	2174	5646.155	375	3826B
n mp	*n ms, n ms*	art, pn	n ms	v Qal pass ptc ms	*sub*	n ms
כְּלֵי	בֵּית־יַעַר	הַלְּבָנוֹן	זָהָב	סָגוּר	אֵין	כֶּסֶף
kelê	bêth-ya'ar	hallevānôn	zāhāv	sāghûr	'ên	keseph
the vessels of	the house of the forest of	the Lebanon	gold	covered	there was not	silver

3940	2913.211	904, 3219	8406	3937, 4114		3706	604	8998
neg part	v Niphal pf 3ms	prep, *n mp*	pn	prep, indef pron	22.	cj	*n fs*	pn
לֹא	נֶחְשָׁב	בִּימֵי	שְׁלֹמֹה	לִמְאוּמָה		כִּי	אֳנִי	תַּרְשִׁישׁ
lō'	nechshāv	bîmê	shelōmōh	lim'ûmāh		kî	'ănî	tharshîsh
not	it was reckoned	in the days of	Solomon	for something		because	the ships of	Tarshish

3937, 4567	904, 3328	6196	604	2538	259	3967, 8421	8523	971.122
prep, art, n ms	prep, art, n ms	prep	*n fs*	pn	num	prep, num	n fp	v Qal impf 3fs
לַמֶּלֶךְ	בַּיָּם	עִם	אֳנִי	חִירָם	אַחַת	לְשָׁלֹשׁ	שָׁנִים	תָּבוֹא
lammelekh	bayyām	'im	'ănî	chîrām	'achath	l^{e}shālōsh	shānîm	tāvô'
to the king	on the sea	with	the ships of	Hiram	one	to three	years	they came

604	8998	5558.153	2174	3826B	8527	7257	8829
n fs	pn	v Qal act ptc fs	n ms	cj, n ms	n mp	cj, n mp	cj, n mp
אֳנִי	תַרְשִׁישׁ	נֹשְׂאֵת	זָהָב	וָכֶסֶף	שֶׁנְהַבִּים	וְקֹפִים	וְתֻכִּיִּים
'ănî	tharshîsh	nōs^{e}'ēth	zāhāv	wākhe<u>s</u>eph	shenhabbîm	w^{e}qōphîm	w^{e}thukkîyîm
ships of	Tarshish	carrying	gold	and silver	ivory	and apes	and baboons

Palace of, *Fenton* ... in the Hall of, *Good News*.

18. Moreover the king made a great throne of ivory, and overlaid it with the best gold: ... and lined it with gold unalloyed, *Knox* ... made a great ivory seat, plated with the best, *BB* ... covered it with pure gold, *Beck* ... plated it with refined gold, *Fenton*.

19. The throne had six steps, and the top of the throne was round behind: and there were stays on either side on the place of the seat, and two lions stood beside the stays: ... six steps going up to it, and the top of it was round at the back; there were arms on the two sides of the seat, and two lions by the side of the arms, *BB* ... armrests on both sides of the chair, *NCV* ... back of the throne was a calf's head, and, *RSV* ... The seat itself had two supporters, *Knox*.

20. And twelve lions stood there on the one side and on the other upon the six steps: there was not the like made in any kingdom: ... on each side of the six stairs. None exactly like this had been made, *Beck* ... No throne like this had ever existed, *Good News* ... Nothing like this was produced, *NAB* ... there was no such work, *Douay*.

21. And all king Solomon's drinking vessels were of gold, and all the vessels of the house of the forest of Lebanon were of pure gold; none were of silver: it was nothing accounted of in the days of Solomon: ... because silver was not valuable in Solomon's time, *NCV* ... and all the household articles in the Palace of the Forest of Lebanon were pure gold, *NIV* ... silver was little thought of, *Knox* ... for in Solomon's time it was considered worthless, *NAB*.

22. For the king had at sea a navy of Tharshish with the navy of Hiram: once in three years came the navy of Tharshish, bringing gold, and silver, ivory, and apes, and peacocks: ... and elephants' teeth, *Douay* ... King Solomon also had many trading ships at sea, along with Hiram's ships, *NCV* ... king had a fleet of merchantmen at sea, *NEB* ... and monkeys, *NKJV*.

king's guards when they attended his great visits to the Temple.

10:18–20. The justice hall of Jerusalem, built of gold and cedar, contained the famous lion throne of gold and ivory, with two lions on each of its six steps. It is not known whether these buildings formed part of the palace and harem of Solomon; it would be impossible to attempt to completely reconstruct them.

Solomon also built the fortification of Jerusalem known as the "Millo," and the wall of Jerusalem. He repaired the breaches of the city of David, as well as the fortresses and treasure cities to which we have already alluded (9:15), and the summer palaces in the region of Lebanon known as "the delights of Solomon" (9:19). Amid these records of palatial architecture, we hear next to nothing of the religious life.

10:21–25. He found a ready market for them among the Hittite and Aramaean kings (v. 29). Emulating the Phoenicians, and apparently invading the monopoly of Tyre, he had (if we may take the chronicler literally) a fleet of "ships of Tarshish" which sailed along the coasts of Spain (2 Chr. 9:21). Above all, he made the daring attempt to establish a fleet of Tarshish-ships at Ezion-Geber, the port of Elath, north of the Gulf of Aqaba. This fleet sailed from the Red Sea to Ophir—perhaps Abhira, at the mouth of the Indus—and amazed the Hebrews with the sight of impressive baboons, wrinkled chattering apes, the red and richly scented wood of India, and the large tusks of elephants from which cunning artificers carved the smooth ivory to inlay furniture, thrones, and ultimately even houses, with lustrous ornamentation. Cinnamon came to him from Ceylon, and "sapphires" (lapis lazuli) from Babylon. Other services which he rendered to his capital and kingdom were more real and permanent.

First, Jerusalem may have been in part indebted to Solomon for its supply of water. The magnificent springs of pure gushing water at Etam are still

23.	1461.121	4567	8406	4623, 3725	4567	800
	cj, v Qal impf 3ms	art, n ms	pn	prep, *nms*	*n mp*	art, n fs
	וַיִּגְדַּל	הַמֶּלֶךְ	שְׁלֹמֹה	מִכֹּל	מַלְכֵי	הָאָרֶץ
	wayyighdal	hammelekh	shelōmōh	mikkōl	malkhê	hā'ārets
	and he became great	the king	Solomon	among the entirety of	the kings of	the earth

3937, 6484	3937, 2551	24.	3725, 800	1272.352	881, 6686	8406
prep, n ms	cj, prep, n fs		cj, *adj*, art, n fs	v Piel ptc mp	do, *n mp*	pn
לְעֹשֶׁר	וּלְחָכְמָה		וְכָל־הָאָרֶץ	מְבַקְשִׁים	אֶת־פְּנֵי	שְׁלֹמֹה
le'ōsher	ûlăchokhmāh		wekhol-hā'ārets	mevaqōshîm	'eth-penê	shelōmōh
of riches	and of wisdom		and all the earth	seeking	the presence of	Solomon

3937, 8471.141	881, 2551	866, 5598.111	435	904, 3949	25.	2065
prep, v Qal inf con	do, n fs, ps 3ms	rel part, v Qal pf 3ms	n mp	prep, n ms, ps 3ms		cj, pers pron
לִשְׁמֹעַ	אֶת־חָכְמָתוֹ	אֲשֶׁר־נָתַן	אֱלֹהִים	בְּלִבּוֹ		וְהֵמָּה
lishmōa'	'eth-chokhmāthô	'ăsher-nāthan	'ĕlōhîm	belibbô		wehēmmāh
to listen to	his wisdom	which He had put	God	within his heart		and they

971.552	382	4647	3747	3826B	3747	2174	7969	5584
v Hiphil ptc mp	n ms	n fs, ps 3ms	*n mp*	n ms	cj, *n mp*	n ms	cj, n fp	cj, n ms
מְבִאִים	אִישׁ	מִנְחָתוֹ	כְּלֵי	כֶסֶף	וּכְלֵי	זָהָב	וּשְׂלָמוֹת	וְנֵשֶׁק
mevi'îm	'îsh	minchāthô	kelê	kheseph	ûkhelê	zāhāv	ûselāmôth	wenēsheq
bringing	each	his gift	vessels of	silver	and vessels of	gold	and cloaks	and weapons

1336	5670	6755	1745, 8523	904, 8523	26.	636.121
cj, n mp	n mp	cj, n mp	*n ms*, n fs	prep, n fs		cj, v Qal impf 3ms
וּבְשָׂמִים	סוּסִים	וּפְרָדִים	דְּבַר־שָׁנָה	בְּשָׁנָה		וַיֶּאֱסֹף
ûvesāmîm	sûsîm	ûpherādhîm	devar-shānāh	beshānāh		wayye'ĕsōph
and balsam oils	horses	and mules	the things of the year	in the year		and he gathered

8406	7681	6821	2030.121, 3937	512	727, 4109
pn	n ms	cj, n mp	cj, v Qal impf 3ms, prep, ps 3ms	num	cj, num, num
שְׁלֹמֹה	רֶכֶב	וּפָרָשִׁים	וַיְהִי־לוֹ	אֶלֶף	וְאַרְבַּע־מֵאוֹת
shelōmōh	rekhev	ûphārāshîm	wayhî-lô	'eleph	we'arba'-mē'ôth
Solomon	chariots	and horsemen	and there were to him	one thousand	and four hundreds

7681	8530, 6461	512	6821	5328.521	904, 6111	7681
n ms	cj, num, num	num	n mp	cj, v Hiphil impf 3ms, ps 3mp	prep, *n fp*	art, n ms
רֶכֶב	וּשְׁנֵים־עָשָׂר	אֶלֶף	פָּרָשִׁים	וַיַּנְחֵם	בְּעָרֵי	הָרֶכֶב
rekhev	ûshenêm-'āsār	'eleph	pārāshîm	wayyanchēm	be'ārê	hārekhev
chariots	and twelve	thousands	horsemen	and he deployed them	in the cities of	the chariots

6196, 4567	904, 3503	27.	5598.121	4567	881, 3826B	904, 3503
cj, prep, art, n ms	prep, pn		cj, v Qal impf 3ms	art, n ms	do, art, n ms	prep, pn
וְעִם־הַמֶּלֶךְ	בִּירוּשָׁלָם		וַיִּתֵּן	הַמֶּלֶךְ	אֶת־הַכֶּסֶף	בִּירוּשָׁלַם
we'im-hammelekh	bîrûshālām		wayyittēn	hammelekh	'eth-hakkeseph	bîrûshālam
and with the king	in Jerusalem		and he put	the king	the silver	in Jerusalem

3626, 63	881	753	5598.111	3626, 8622	904, 8590
prep, art, n fp	cj, do	art, n mp	v Qal pf 3ms	prep, art, n fp	prep, art, pn
כָּאֲבָנִים	וְאֵת	הָאֲרָזִים	נָתַן	כַּשִּׁקְמִים	אֲשֶׁר־בַּשְּׁפֵלָה
kā'ăvānîm	we'ēth	hā'ărāzîm	nāthan	kashshiqōmîm	'ăsher-bashshephēlāh
like the stones	and	the cedars	he put	like the sycamores	which in the Shephelah

3937, 7524	28.	4296	5670	866	3937, 8406	4623, 4875
prep, art, n ms		cj, *n ms*	art, n mp	rel part	prep, pn	prep, pn
לָרֹב		וּמוֹצָא	הַסּוּסִים	אֲשֶׁר	לִשְׁלֹמֹה	מִמִּצְרָיִם
lārōv		ûmôtsā'	hassûsîm	'ăsher	lishlōmōh	mimmitsrāyim
because of the abundance		and the export of	the horses	which	to Solomon	from Egypt

4623, 7247	5692.152	4567	4089.126	4623, 7247	904, 4378B
cj, prep, pn	v Qal act ptc mp	art, n ms	v Qal impf 3mp	prep, pn	prep, n ms
וּמִקְוֵה	סֹחֲרֵי	הַמֶּלֶךְ	יִקְחוּ	מִקְוֵה	בִּמְחִיר
ûmiqōwēh	sōchărê	hammelekh	yiqōchû	miqōwēh	bimchîr
and from Kue	the merchants of	the king	they received	from Kue	with a price

29.

6148.122	3428.122	4981	4623, 4875	904, 8666	4109	3826B	5670
cj, v Qal impf 3fs	cj, v Qal impf 3fs	n fs	prep, pn	prep, num	num	n ms	cj, n ms
וַתַּעֲלֶה	וַתֵּצֵא	מֶרְכָּבָה	מִמִּצְרַיִם	בְּשֵׁשׁ	מֵאוֹת	כֶּסֶף	וְסוּס
watta'ăleh	wattētsē'	merkāvāh	mimmitsrayim	beshēsh	mē'ôth	keseph	wesûs
and it went up	and it went out	a chariot	from Egypt	with six	hundreds	silver	and a horse

23. So king Solomon exceeded all the kings of the earth for riches and for wisdom: ... was greater in, *NIV* ... became richer and wiser than any other king, *NLT* ... excelled all the kings of the earth, *NRSV* ... Solomon outdid all the kings, *REB*.

24. And all the earth sought to Solomon, to hear his wisdom, which God had put in his heart: ... all the world resorted to Solomon, *Tyndale* ... from all over the earth they came to see Solomon and to give ear to, *BB* ... The whole world consulted Solomon to benefit from the wisdom with which God had endowed him, *Berkeley* ... which God had implanted in his heart, *JB*.

25. And they brought every man his present, vessels of silver, and vessels of gold, and garments, and armour, and spices, horses, and mules, a rate year by year: ... Each one brought his yearly tribute, *NAB* ... perfumes and, *NEB* ... a set rate, *NKJV* ... weaponry, *NRSV*.

26. And Solomon gathered together chariots and horsemen: and he had a thousand and four hundred chariots, and twelve thousand horsemen, whom he bestowed in the cities for chariots, and with the king at Jerusalem: ... stationed in the chariot cities, *RSV* ... got together war-carriages and horsemen, *BB* ... also acquired, *Berkeley* ... which he placed in cavalry barracks, *Fenton*.

27. And the king made silver to be in Jerusalem as stones, and cedars made he to be as the sycamore trees that are in the vale, for abundance: ... sycamore trees that are in the lowland, *Goodspeed* ... of the foothills, *NAB* ... be as common as sycamores which grow in the plains, *Douay* ... as plentiful as sycamore-fig trees in the foothills, *NIV*.

28. And Solomon had horses brought out of Egypt, and linen yarn: the king's merchants received the linen yarn at a price: ... at the prevailing price, *Berkeley* ... and the collecting merchants were paid for them by the king according to contract, *Fenton* ... at a set price, *Douay* ... at the current price, *NKJV*.

called "Solomon's fountains," and it is believed that he used their rocky basins as reservoirs from which to irrigate his garden in the Wadi Urtas. Etam is two miles distance from Jerusalem, and if Solomon built the aqueduct which once conveyed its water supply to the city, he proved himself a genuine benefactor (see Gen. 2:4ff). There was an immense need for the continual water, spoken of by Tacitus, for the purifications of the Temple.

Second, maritime allusions now began to appear in Hebrew literature (2 Chr. 9:21). And maritime enterprise produced the marvelous effect it always does on the character and progress of the nation. Along the main roads, including the king's highways, construction was necessitated by the outburst of commercial activity, hundreds of foreign visitors, merchant men and itinerant traffickers, as well as governors of provinces, and vassal or allied princes. The isolated and stationary tribes of Palestine suddenly found themselves face to face with a new and splendid civilization. Admiring visitors flocked to see the great king's magnificence and to admire his foreign curiosities, bringing with them presents of gold and silver, armor and spicery, horses and mules, the broidered garments of Babylon, and robes rich with the crimson, purple and scarlet dyes of Tyre (1 Ki. 10:25).

10:26–29. And to sum up the account, which reads like a page of the most beautiful fantasy, the king made silver to be as stones in Jerusalem, so that it was nothing to be accounted of in the day of Solomon, and the cedars were made to be as the sycamores which are in the Shephelah in multitude.

It is around this epoch of Solomon's career that the legends of the East mainly cluster. They have received a larger development from the allusions to Mohammed in the Koran. They take the place of the personal incidents, of which so few are

904, 2675	4109	3772	3937, 3725, 4567	2958	3937, 4567	782
prep, art, num	cj, num	cj, adv	prep, *adj*, *n mp*	art, pn	cj, prep, *n mp*	pn
בַּחֲמִשִּׁים	וּמֵאָה	וְכֵן	לְכָל־מַלְכֵי	הַחִתִּים	וּלְמַלְכֵי	אֲרָם
bachmishshîm	ûmē'āh	wekhēn	lekhol-malkhê	hachittîm	ûlămalkhê	'ărām
with fifty	and one hundred	and so	to all the kings of	the Hittites	and to all the kings of	Aram

904, 3135	3428.526		4567	8406	154.111	5571	5425
prep, n fs, ps 3mp	v Hiphil impf 3mp	**11:1**	cj, art, n ms	pn	v Qal pf 3ms	n fp	adj
בְּיָדָם	יֹצִאוּ		וְהַמֶּלֶךְ	שְׁלֹמֹה	אָהַב	נָשִׁים	נָכְרִיּוֹת
beyādhām	yōtsi'û		wehammelekh	shelōmōh	'āhav	nāshîm	nākherîyôth
into their hand	they exported		then the king	Solomon	he loved	women	foreign

7521	881, 1351, 6799	4263	6206	111	6992	2958
adj	cj, do, *n fs*, pn	pn	pn	pn	pn	pn
רַבּוֹת	וְאֶת־בַּת־פַּרְעֹה	מוֹאֲבִיּוֹת	עַמֳּנִיּוֹת	אֲדֹמִיֹּת	צֵדְנִיֹּת	חִתִּיֹּת
rabbôth	we'eth-bath-par'ōh	mô'ăvîyôth	'ammenîyôth	'ădhōmîyōth	tsēdhenîyōth	chittîyōth
many	and the daughter of Pharaoh	Moabites	Ammonites	Edomites	Sidonians	Hittites

	4623, 1504	866	569.111, 3176	420, 1158	3547	3940, 971.128
2.	prep, art, n mp	rel pron	v Qal pf 3ms, pn	prep, *n mp*	pn	neg part, v Qal impf 2mp
	מִן־הַגּוֹיִם	אֲשֶׁר	אָמַר־יְהוָה	אֶל־בְּנֵי	יִשְׂרָאֵל	לֹא־תָבֹאוּ
	min-haggôyim	'ăsher	'āmar-yehwāh	'el-benê	yisrā'ēl	lō'-thāvō'û
	from the nations	whom	Yahweh had said	to the children of	Israel	you should not enter

904	2062	3940, 971.126	904	409	5371.526
prep, ps 3mp	cj, pers pron	neg part, v Qal impf 3mp	prep, ps 2mp	adv	v Hiphil impf 3mp
בָהֶם	וְהֵם	לֹא־יָבֹאוּ	בָכֶם	אָכֵן	יַטּוּ
vāhem	wehēm	lō'-yāvō'û	vākhem	'ākhēn	yattû
with them	and they	they should not enter	with you	surely	they will turn aside

881, 3949	313	435	904	1740.111	8406	3937, 154.141
do, n ms, ps 2mp	adv	n mp, ps 3mp	prep, ps 3mp	v Qal pf 3ms	pn	prep, v Qal inf con
אֶת־לְבַבְכֶם	אַחֲרֵי	אֱלֹהֵיהֶם	בָּהֶם	דָּבַק	שְׁלֹמֹה	לְאַהֲבָה
'eth-levavkhem	'achrê	'ĕlōhêhem	bāhem	dāvaq	shelōmōh	le'ahvāh
your hearts	after	their gods	with them	he clung	Solomon	to love

	2030.121, 3937	5571	8022	8124	4109	6637	8421
3.	cj, v Qal impf 3ms, prep, ps 3ms	n fp	n fp	num	num	cj, n fp	num
	וַיְהִי־לוֹ	נָשִׁים	שָׂרוֹת	שְׁבַע	מֵאוֹת	וּפִלַגְשִׁים	שְׁלֹשׁ
	wayhî-lô	nāshîm	sārôth	sheva'	mē'ôth	ûphilaghshîm	shelōsh
	and they were to him	wives	princesses	seven	hundreds	and concubines	three

4109	5371.526	5571	881, 3949		2030.121	3937, 6496
num	cj, v Hiphil impf 3mp	n fp, ps 3ms	do, n ms, ps 3ms	**4.**	cj, v Qal impf 3ms	prep, *n fs*
מֵאוֹת	וַיַּטּוּ	נָשָׁיו	אֶת־לִבּוֹ		וַיְהִי	לְעֵת
mē'ôth	wayyattû	nāshâv	'eth-libbô		wayhî	le'ēth
hundreds	and they turned aside	his wives	his heart		and it was	at the time of

2294	8406	5571	5371.516	881, 3949	313	435	311
n fs	pn	n fp, ps 3ms	v Hiphil pf 3cp	do, n ms, ps 3ms	adv	n mp	adj
זִקְנַת	שְׁלֹמֹה	נָשָׁיו	הִטּוּ	אֶת־לְבָבוֹ	אַחֲרֵי	אֱלֹהִים	אֲחֵרִים
ziqnath	shelōmōh	nāshâv	hittû	'eth-levāvô	'achrê	'ĕlōhîm	'ăchērîm
the old age of	Solomon	his wives	they turned aside	his heart	after	gods	others

3940, 2030.111	3949	8400	6196, 3176	435	3626, 3949	1784
cj, neg part, v Qal pf 3ms	n ms, ps 3ms	adj	prep, pn	pn, ps 3ms	prep, *n ms*	pn
וְלֹא־הָיָה	לְבָבוֹ	שָׁלֵם	עִם־יְהוָה	אֱלֹהָיו	כִּלְבַב	דָּוִיד
welō'-hāyāh	levāvô	shālēm	'im-yehwāh	'ĕlōhâv	kilvav	dāwîdh
and it was not	his heart	complete	with Yahweh	his God	like the heart of	David

29. And a chariot came up and went out of Egypt for six hundred shekels of silver, and an horse for an hundred and fifty: and so for all the kings of the Hittites, and for the kings of Syria, did they bring them out by their means: ... They imported a chariot from Egypt for six hundred shekels of silver, and a horse for a hundred and fifty. They also exported them to all the kings of the Hittites and of the Arameans, *NIV* ... so throught the king's traders they were exported, *NRSV* ... the merchants obtained them for export from, *REB* ... they carried on trade with all the kings of the Hittites and the kings of the Arameans, *Goodspeed*.

11:1. But king Solomon loved many strange women, together with the daughter of Pharaoh, women of the Moabites, Ammonites, Edomites, Zidonians, and Hittites: ... foreign women, *JB* ... women who were not from Israel, *NCV* ... gave his heart to many women of alien birth, *Knox*.

2. Of the nations concerning which the LORD said unto the children of Israel, Ye shall not go in to them, neither shall they come in unto you: ... You are not to go among them nor they among you, *JB* ... not associate with them, neither shall they associate, *NASB* ... You must not marry people of other nations, *NCV* ... not intermarry with them, nor they with you, *NKJV*.

for surely they will turn away your heart after their gods: Solomon clave unto these in love: ... clung to, *Goodspeed* ... will be sure to sway your hearts to their own gods. But Solomon was deeply attached to them, *JB* ... held fast to, *NASB* ... they will entice you to serve their gods. But Solomon was devoted to them and loved them dearly, *NEB*.

3. And he had seven hundred wives, princesses, and three hundred concubines: and his wives turned away his heart: ... wives led him astray, *NIV* ... led his heart away from the Lord, *NLT* ... they influenced him, *REB* ... lured his heart away, *Beck*.

4. For it came to pass, when Solomon was old, that his wives turned away his heart after other gods: and his heart was not perfect with the LORD his God, as was the heart of David his father: ... so that his heart was no longer true to, *Berkeley* ... his heart was not at peace with his EVER-LIVING GOD, *Fenton* ... they had led him into the worship of foreign gods. He was not faithful to, *Good News* ... swayed his heart to other gods; and his heart was not wholly with Yahweh his God, *JB*.

5. For Solomon went after Ashtoreth the goddess of the Zidonians, and after Milcom the abomination of the Ammonites: ... and after Milcom the detestable idol, *NASB* ... worshipped Ashtoreth the goddess of, *Douay* ... and Milcom, the disgusting god, *BB* ... the loathsome god, *NEB*.

---

recorded, although Solomon occupies so large a space in sacred history. That stately and melancholy figure in some respects is the grandest and the saddest in the Sacred Volume. He is in detail little more than a mighty shadow. Yet in later Jewish records he is scarcely mentioned.

11:1–43. "That luxorious king, whose heart, though large, beguiled by fair idolatresses, fell to idols foul."

11:1–13. The polygamy of Solomon sprang naturally from the false position which he had created for himself. A king who puts a space of awful distance between himself and the mass of his subjects—a king whose will is so absolute that life is in his smile and death in his frown—is inevitably punished by the loneliest isolation. He may have favorites, he may have flatterers, but he can have no friends. A thronged harem becomes to him not only a matter of ostentation and luxury, but a necessary resource from a vacuous of a desolate heart. Tiberius was driven to the orgies of Caprex by the intolerableness of his isolation. The weariness of the king who used to take his courtiers by the button-hole and say, "Ennuyons-nous ensemble," drove him to fill up his degraded leisure in the Parc aux Cerfs. Yet even Louis XV had more possibilities of rational intercourse with human beings than a Solomon or a Xerxes. It was in the nature of things that Solomon, when he had imitated all the other surroundings of an Oriental despot, should sink, like other Oriental despots, from sensuousness into sensualism, from sensualism into religious degeneracy and dishonorable enervation.

11:1–4. Two facts, both full of warning, are indicated as the sources of his ruin: the number of his wives and their heathen extraction.

"He had," we are told, "seven hundred wives, princesses, and three hundred concubines."

The numbers make up a thousand, and are almost incredible.

The heathen religion of these strange women from so many nations "turned away the heart of Solomon after other gods." Solomon had most likely read the stern prohibitions against intermarriage with the Canaanite nations which now stand on the page of the Pentateuch. Nonetheless, he broke them, for the Hittites and the Phoenicians were Canaanites. Marriages with Egyptians,

1		2050.121	8406	313	6492	435	6992
n ms, ps 3ms	5.	cj, v Qal impf 3ms	pn	adv	pn	*n mp*	pn
אָבִיו		וַיֵּלֶךְ	שְׁלֹמֹה	אַחֲרֵי	עַשְׁתֹּרֶת	אֱלֹהֵי	צִדֹנִים
'āvîw		wayyēlekh	shᵉlōmōh	'achrê	'ashtōreth	'ĕlōhê	tsidhōnîm
his father		and he went	Solomon	after	Ashtoreth	the goddess of	the Sidonians

313	4585	8617	6206		6449.121	8406	7737
cj, prep	pn	*n ms*	pn	6.	cj, v Qal impf 3ms	pn	art, adj
וְאַחֲרֵי	מִלְכֹּם	שִׁקֻּץ	עַמֹּנִים		וַיַּעַשׂ	שְׁלֹמֹה	הָרַע
wᵉ'achrê	milkōm	shiqquts	'ammōnîm		wayya'as	shᵉlōmōh	hāra'
and after	Milcom	the abomination of	Ammonites		and he did	Solomon	what is evil

904, 6084	3176	3940	4527.311	313	3176	3626, 1784	1
prep, *n fd*	pn	cj, neg part	v Piel pf 3ms	adv	pn	prep, pn	n ms, ps 3ms
בְּעֵינֵי	יְהוָה	וְלֹא	מִלֵּא	אַחֲרֵי	יְהוָה	כְּדָוִד	אָבִיו
bᵉ'ênê	yᵉhwāh	wᵉlō'	millē'	'achrê	yᵉhwāh	kᵉdhāwidh	'āvîw
in the eyes of	Yahweh	and not	he acted completely	after	Yahweh	as David	his father

	226	1161.121	8406	1154	3937, 3767	8617	4262
7.	adv	v Qal impf 3ms	pn	n fs	prep, pn	*n ms*	pn
	אָז	יִבְנֶה	שְׁלֹמֹה	בָּמָה	לִכְמוֹשׁ	שִׁקֻּץ	מוֹאָב
	'āz	yivneh	shᵉlōmōh	bāmāh	likhmôsh	shiqquts	mô'āv
	then	he built	Solomon	a high place	for Chemosh	the abomination of	Moab

904, 2098	866	6142, 6686	3503	3937, 4571	8617	1158
prep, art, n ms	rel part	prep, *n mp*	pn	cj, prep, pn	*n ms*	*n mp*
בָּהָר	אֲשֶׁר	עַל־פְּנֵי	יְרוּשָׁלָם	וּלְמֹלֶךְ	שִׁקֻּץ	בְּנֵי
bāhār	'ăsher	'al-pᵉnê	yᵉrûshālām	ûlămōlekh	shiqquts	bᵉnê
on the mountain	which	opposite	Jerusalem	and for Molech	the abomination of	the sons of

6205		3772	6449.111	3937, 3725, 5571	5425	7281.554	2159.354
pn	8.	cj, adv	v Qal pf 3ms	prep, *adj*, n fp, ps 3ms	art, adj	v Hiphil ptc fp	cj, v Piel ptc fp
עַמּוֹן		וְכֵן	עָשָׂה	לְכָל־נָשָׁיו	הַנָּכְרִיּוֹת	מַקְטִירוֹת	וּמְזַבְּחוֹת
'ammôn		wᵉkhēn	'āsāh	lᵉkhol-nāshâv	hannākhᵉrîyôth	maqṭîrôth	ûmᵉzabbᵉchôth
Ammon		and so	he did	for all his wives	the foreign	burning incense	and sacrificing

3937, 435		613.721	3176	904, 8406	3706, 5371.111
prep, n mp, ps 3fp	9.	cj, v Hithpael impf 3ms	pn	prep, pn	cj, v Qal pf 3ms
לֵאלֹהֵיהֶן		וַיִּתְאַנַּף	יְהוָה	בִּשְׁלֹמֹה	כִּי־נָטָה
lē'lōhêhen		wayyith'annaph	yᵉhwāh	bishlōmōh	kî-nāṭāh
to their gods		and He became angry	Yahweh	with Solomon	because he had turned away

3949	4623, 6196	3176	435	3547	7495.211	420
n ms, ps 3ms	prep, prep	pn	*n mp*	pn	art, v Niphal pf 3ms	prep, ps 3ms
לְבָבוֹ	מֵעִם	יְהוָה	אֱלֹהֵי	יִשְׂרָאֵל	הַנִּרְאָה	אֵלָיו
lᵉvāvô	mē'im	yᵉhwāh	'ĕlōhê	yisrā'ēl	hanir'āh	'ēlâv
his heart	from with	Yahweh	the God of	Israel	the One Who appeared	to him

6718		6943.311	420	6142, 1745	2172
n fd	10.	cj, v Piel pf 3ms	prep, ps 3ms	prep, art, n ms	art, dem pron
פַּעֲמָיִם		וְצִוָּה	אֵלָיו	עַל־הַדָּבָר	הַזֶּה
pa'ămāyim		wᵉtsiwwāh	'ēlâv	'al-haddāvār	hazzeh
twice		and He had commanded	to him	concerning the matter	the this

3937, 1153, 2050.141	313	435	311	3940	8490.111	881
prep, neg part, v Qal inf con	prep	n mp	adj	cj, neg part	v Qal pf 3ms	do
לְבִלְתִּי־לֶכֶת	אַחֲרֵי	אֱלֹהִים	אֲחֵרִים	וְלֹא	שָׁמַר	אֵת
lᵉviltî-lekheth	'achrê	'ĕlōhîm	'ăchērîm	wᵉlō'	shāmar	'ēth
about not going	after	gods	others	and not	he observed	

866, 6943.311	3176		569.121	3176	3937, 8406	3391	866
rel part, v Piel pf 3ms	pn		cj, v Qal impf 3ms	pn	prep, pn	cj	rel part
אֲשֶׁר־צִוָּה	יְהוָה	**11.**	וַיֹּאמֶר	יְהוָה	לִשְׁלֹמֹה	יַעַן	אֲשֶׁר
'ăsher-tsiwwāh	yehwāh		wayyō'mer	yehwāh	lishlōmōh	ya'an	'ăsher
what He had commanded	Yahweh		and He said	Yahweh	to Solomon	because	that

2030.112, 2148	6196	3940	8490.113	1311	2807	866
v Qal pf 3fs, dem pron	prep, ps 2ms	cj, neg part	v Qal pf 2ms	n fs, ps 1cs	cj, n fp, ps 1cs	rel part
הָיְתָה־זֹּאת	עִמָּךְ	וְלֹא	שָׁמַרְתָּ	בְּרִיתִי	וְחֻקֹּתַי	אֲשֶׁר
hāyethāh-zō'th	'immākh	welō'	shāmartā	berîthî	wechuqqōthay	'ăsher
this has been	with you	and not	you have observed	my covenant	and my statutes	which

6. And Solomon did evil in the sight of the LORD, and went not fully after the LORD, as did David his father: ... and did not fully follow, *NKJV* ... did not follow the LORD completely, *NIV* ... did not wholly follow, *RSV* ... not walking in the Lord's ways with all his heart, *BB*.

7. Then did Solomon build an high place for Chemosh, the abomination of Moab, in the hill that is before Jerusalem, and for Molech, the abomination of the children of Ammon: ... the disgusting god of Moab, in the mountain before Jerusalem, and for Molech, the disgusting god worshipped by the children of, *BB* ... the abominable idol of Moab, *Beck* ... Solomon also built towers to the abominable Kemosh of Moab, *Fenton* ... On the mountain east of Jerusalem he built a place to worship Chemosh, *Good News*.

8. And likewise did he for all his strange wives, which burnt incense and sacrificed unto their gods: ... He did the same for all his foreign wives, who offered incense and, *JB* ... with burning of perfumes to their gods, *BB* ... he did in this manner for all his wives that were strangers, *Douay*.

9. And the LORD was angry with Solomon, because his heart was turned from the LORD God of Israel, which had appeared unto him twice: ... The LORD was provoked, *Berkeley* ... was displeased with Solomon, for his heart declined from the, *Fenton* ... who had twice come to him in a vision, *BB* ... because his mind was turned away, *Douay*.

10. And had commanded him concerning this thing, that he should not go after other gods: but he kept not that which the LORD commanded: ... But Solomon did not obey the LORD's command, *NCV* ... had strictly commanded him not to follow other gods; but he disobeyed, *NEB* ... he had forbidden Solomon to follow other gods, *NIV* ... warned him against this very sin of alien worship; a warning that went unremembered, *Knox*.

11. Wherefore the LORD said unto Solomon, Forasmuch as this is done of thee, and thou hast not kept my covenant and my

Moabites and Edomites had not been, in so many words, forbidden, but the feeling of later ages applied the rule analogously to them. The result proved how necessary the law was. When Solomon was old, his heart was no longer proof against feminine wiles. He was not old in years, for this was some time before his death, and when he died, he was little more than sixty. But a polygamous despot gets old before his time.

11:5–13. The attempt made by some to gloss over Solomon's apostasy as a sign of a large-hearted tolerance is an astonishing misreading of history. There should always be tolerance for harmless divergences of opinion though it is only a growth of modern days; but tolerance for iniquity is a wrong to holiness.

The worship of these devils, adored as deities, was stained with the worst passions which degrade human nature. They were themselves the personification of perverted instincts. Milton describes it thus:

"First Moloch, horrid king, besmeared with blood
Of human sacrifice, and parents' tears: ...
Next, Chemos, the obscene dread of Moab's sons,
Peor his other name, when he enticed
Israel in Sittim, on their march from Nile,
To do him wanton rites, which cost them woe.
Yet thence his lustful orgies he enlarged
Even to that hill of scandal, by the Grove
Of Moloch homicide; lust, hard by hate:
Till good Josiah drove them thence to hell.
... With these in troop
Came Ashtoreth, whom the Phoenicians call
Astarte, queen of heaven, with crescent horns;
To whose bright image nightly by the moon
Sidonian virgins paid their vows and songs;
In Sion also not unsung, where stood
Her temple on the offensive mountain, built
By that uxorious king, whose heart, though large,
Beguiled by fair idolatresses, fell
To idols foul."

6943.315	6142	7458.142	7458.125	881, 4608
v Piel pf 1cs	prep, ps 2ms	v Qal inf abs	v Qal impf 1cs	do, art, n fs
צִוִּיתִי	עָלֶיךָ	קָרֹעַ	אֶקְרַע	אֶת־הַמַּמְלָכָה
tsiwwîthî	‘ālêkhā	qārōa‘	'eqŏra‘	'eth-hammamlākhāh
I have commanded	concerning you	tearing away	I will surely tear away	the kingship

4623, 6142	5598.115	3937, 5860		395, 904, 3219	3940
prep, prep, ps 2ms	cj, v Qal pf 1cs, ps 3fs	prep, n ms, ps 2ms	**12.**	adv, prep, n mp, ps 2ms	neg part
מֵעָלֶיךָ	וּנְתַתִּיהָ	לְעַבְדֶּךָ		אַךְ־בְּיָמֶיךָ	לֹא
mē‘ālêkhā	ûnethattîāh	le‘avdekhā		'akh-beyāmêkhā	lō'
from upon you	and I will give it	to your servant		only in your days	not

6449.125	3937, 4775	1784	1	4623, 3135	1158	7458.125
v Qal impf 1cs, ps 3fs	prep, prep	pn	n ms, ps 2ms	prep, *n fs*	n ms, ps 2ms	v Qal impf 1cs, ps 3fs
אֶעֱשֶׂנָּה	לְמַעַן	דָּוִד	אָבִיךָ	מִיַּד	בִּנְךָ	אֶקְרָעֶנָּה
'e‘ĕsennāh	lema‘an	dāwidh	'āvîkhā	mîyadh	binkhā	'eqŏrā‘ennāh
I will do it	because of	David	your father	from the hand of	your son	I will tear it

	7828	881, 3725, 4608	3940	7458.125	8101	259	5598.125
13.	adv	do, *adj*, art, n fs	neg part	v Qal impf 1cs	*n ms*	num	v Qal impf 1cs
	רַק	אֶת־כָּל־הַמַּמְלָכָה	לֹא	אֶקְרָע	שֵׁבֶט	אֶחָד	אֶתֵּן
	raq	'eth-kol-hammamlākhāh	lō'	'eqŏrā‘	shēvet	'echādh	'ettēn
	yet	all the kingdom	not	I will tear away	a tribe	one	I will give

3937, 1158	3937, 4775	1784	5860	3937, 4775	3503	866	1013.115
prep, n ms, ps 2ms	prep, prep	pn	n ms, ps 1cs	cj, prep, prep	pn	rel part	v Qal pf 1cs
לִבְנֶךָ	לְמַעַן	דָּוִד	עַבְדִּי	וּלְמַעַן	יְרוּשָׁלַם	אֲשֶׁר	בָּחַרְתִּי
livnekhā	lema‘an	dāwidh	‘avdî	ûlăma‘an	yerûshālam	'ăsher	bāchāretti
to your son	because of	David	my servant	and because of	Jerusalem	which	I have chosen

	7251.521	3176	7931	3937, 8406	881	108	111
14.	cj, v Hiphil impf 3ms	pn	n ms	prep, pn	do	pn	art, pn
	וַיָּקֶם	יְהוָה	שָׂטָן	לִשְׁלֹמֹה	אֵת	הֲדַד	הָאֲדֹמִי
	wayyāqem	yehwāh	sātān	lishlōmōh	'ēth	hedhadh	hā'ădhōmî
	and He raised up	Yahweh	an adversary	against Solomon		Hadad	the Edomite

4623, 2320	4567	2000	904, 110		2030.121	904, 2030.141	1784
prep, *n ms*	art, n ms	pers pron	prep, pn	**15.**	cj, v Qal impf 3ms	prep, v Qal inf con	pn
מִזֶּרַע	הַמֶּלֶךְ	הוּא	בֶּאֱדוֹם		וַיְהִי	בִּהְיוֹת	דָּוִד
mizzera‘	hammelekh	hû'	be'ĕdhôm		wayhî	bihyôth	dāwidh
from the descendants of	the king	he	in Edom		and it was	when being	David

881, 110	904, 6148.141	3200	8015	6893	3937, 7196.341	881, 2592
do, pn	prep, v Qal inf con	pn	*n ms*	art, n ms	prep, v Piel inf con	do, art, n ms
אֶת־אֱדוֹם	בַּעֲלוֹת	יוֹאָב	שַׂר	הַצָּבָא	לְקַבֵּר	אֶת־הַחֲלָלִים
'eth-'ĕdhôm	ba‘ălôth	yô'āv	sar	hatstsāvā'	leqabbēr	'eth-hachlālîm
Edom	when going up	Joab	the commander of	the army	to bury	the slain

5409.521	3725, 2227	904, 110		3706	8666	2414	3553.111, 8427
cj, v Hiphil impf 3ms	*adj*, n ms	prep, pn	**16.**	cj	num	n mp	v Qal pf 3ms, adv
וַיַּךְ	כָּל־זָכָר	בֶּאֱדוֹם		כִּי	שֵׁשֶׁת	חֳדָשִׁים	יָשַׁב־שָׁם
wayyakh	kol-zākhār	be'ĕdhôm		kî	shēsheth	chădhāshîm	yāshav-shām
and he struck down	every male	in Edom		because	six	months	he stayed there

3200	3725, 3547	5912, 3901.511	3725, 2227	904, 110		1300.121	108
pn	cj, *adj*, pn	adv, v Hiphil pf 3ms	*adj*, n ms	prep, pn	**17.**	cj, v Qal impf 3ms	pn
יוֹאָב	וְכָל־יִשְׂרָאֵל	עַד־הִכְרִית	כָּל־זָכָר	בֶּאֱדוֹם		וַיִּבְרַח	אֲדַד
yô'āv	wekhol-yisrā'ēl	‘adh-hikhrîth	kol-zākhār	be'ĕdhôm		wayyivrach	'ădhadh
Joab	and all Israel	until he had cut off	every male	in Edom		and he fled	Hadad

statutes, which I have commanded thee, I will surely rend the kingdom from thee, and will give it to thy servant: ... Because you have done this, and have not kept my agreement and my laws, which I gave you, I will take the kingdom away from you by force and, *BB* ... I will surely tear the kingdom away from you, *Berkeley* ... Because you have deliberately broken your covenant with me and disobeyed my commands, I promise that, *Good News* ... Since you have behaved like this and have not kept my covenant or the laws which I laid down for you, *JB*.

12. Notwithstanding in thy days I will not do it for David thy father's sake: but I will rend it out of the hand of thy son: ... I will not do this during your lifetime, however, for the sake of your father David; it is your son whom I will deprive, *NAB* ... while you are alive because of my love for your father David. I will tear it away from your son when he becomes king, *NCV* ... I will take it from thy son, *Tyndale* ... it is thy son that shall lose his kingdom, *Knox*.

13. Howbeit I will not rend away all the kingdom; but will give one tribe to thy son for David my servant's sake, and for Jerusalem's sake which I have chosen: ... I shall not tear the whole kingdom from him, *JB* ... I will not take the whole kingdom away, *Good News* ... I will leave him one tribe to rule, *NCV* ... and because of Jerusalem, the town of my selection, *BB*.

14. And the LORD stirred up an adversary unto Solomon, Hadad the Edomite: he was of the king's seed in Edom: ... the LORD raised up, *NKJV* ... from the royal line of Edom, *NIV* ... the Lord sent Hadad the Edomite to make trouble for Solomon, *BB* ... LORD raised a man to oppose, *Beck*.

15. For it came to pass, when David was in Edom, and Joab the captain of the host was gone up to bury the slain, after he had smitten every male in Edom: ... had crushed Edom, *JB* ... of the army had gone to bury the dead and cut down every male in, *Berkeley* ... had conquered Edom, *NAB* ... had defeated Edom, *NCV*.

16. (For six months did Joab remain there with all Israel, until he had cut off every male in Edom:): ... until he had destroyed, *NEB* ... until he had cut down, *NKJV* ... he had eliminated, *NRSV* ... they had killed, *Beck*.

17. That Hadad fled, he and certain Edomites of his father's servants with him, to go into Egypt; Hadad being yet a little child: ... Hadad escaped, *Fenton* ... Hadad was a young boy, *NASB* ... Adad, still in early boyhood, took refuge in Egypt, *Knox* ... went to flight in Egypt, *BB*.

What tolerance should there be for idols whose service was horrible infanticide and shameless lust? What fellowship hath righteousness with unrighteousness? and what communion hath light with darkness? and what concord hath Christ with an infidel? and what agreement hath the Temple of God with idols? How vile was the worship of Chemosh that Israel had already experienced in the wilderness where he was called Peor (Num. 25:3). They were to learn what Molech was thereafter by many horrible experiences. Had Solomon never heard that the LORD God was a zealous God and would not tolerate the rivalries of gods of fire and of lust? At least he was not afraid to desecrate one, if not two, of the summits of the Mount of Olives with shrines to these monstrous images

And, to top it all, Solomon not only showed this guilty complaisance to all his strange wives, but even, sinking into the lowest abyss of apostasy, "burnt incense and sacrificed unto their gods."

He built a Temple in Zion, then he built a temple for Chemosh for his mistresses in the very face of God's house. Because Solomon fed them in their superstition, he drew the sin home to himself, and is branded for what he should have forbidden.

11:14–22. Early in Solomon's reign, two adversaries had declared their existence, but only became of much account in the darker and later days of decline (1 Ki. 11:9–25).

One of these was Hadad, Prince of Edom. The prowess of Joab had inflicted an overwhelming and all but exterminating reverse upon the Edomites in the days of David. Joab had remained six months in the conquered district to bury his comrades who had been slain in the terrible encounter, and to extirpate as far as possible the detested race. But the king's servants had been able to save Hadad, then but a little child, from the indiscriminate massacre, as the sole survivor of his house. The young Edomite prince was conveyed by them through Midian and the desert of Paran into Egypt. There, for political reasons, he had been kindly received by the Pharaoh of the day, whom some speculate to be Pinotem I of the Tanite dynasty, the father of Psinaces, whose alliance Solomon had secured by marriage with his daughter. Pinotem not only welcomed the fugitive Edomite as the last scion of a kingly race, but even deigned to bestow on him the hand of the sister of Tahpenes, his own Gebira or queen-mother. Their son Genubath was brought up

2000	596	111	4623, 5860	1	882	3937, 971.141
pers pron	cj, n mp	pn	prep, *n mp*	n ms, ps 3ms	prep, ps 3ms	prep, v Qal inf con
הוּא	וַאֲנָשִׁים	אֲדֹמִיִּים	מֵעַבְדֵי	אָבִיו	אִתּוֹ	לָבוֹא
hû'	wa'ănāshîm	'ădhōmîyîm	mē'avdhê	'āvîw	'ittô	lāvô'
he	and men	Edomites	from the servants of	his father	with him	to enter

4875	1976	5470	7278		7251.126	4623, 4220	971.126	6531
pn	cj, pn	n ms	adj	**18.**	cj, v Qal impf 3mp	prep, pn	cj, v Qal impf 3mp	pn
מִצְרָיִם	וַהֲדַד	נַעַר	קָטָן		וַיָּקֻמוּ	מִמִּדְיָן	וַיָּבֹאוּ	פָּארָן
mitsrāyim	wahdhadh	na'ar	qāṯān		wayyāqumû	mimmidhyān	wayyāvō'û	pā'rān
Egypt	and Hadad	a boy	small		and they arose	from Midian	and they came	Paran

4089.126	596	6196	4623, 6531	971.126	4875	420, 6799
cj, v Qal impf 3mp	n mp	prep, ps 3mp	prep, pn	cj, v Qal impf 3mp	pn	prep, pn
וַיִּקְחוּ	אֲנָשִׁים	עִמָּם	מִפָּארָן	וַיָּבֹאוּ	מִצְרַיִם	אֶל־פַּרְעֹה
wayyiqŏchû	'ănāshîm	'immām	mippā'rān	wayyāvō'û	mitsrayim	'el-par'ōh
and they took	men	with them	from Paran	and they entered	Egypt	unto Pharaoh

4567, 4875	5598.121, 3937	1041	4035	569.111	3937	800
n ms, pn	cj, v Qal impf 3ms, prep, ps 3ms	n ms	cj, n ms	v Qal pf 3ms	prep, ps 3ms	cj, n fs
מֶלֶךְ־מִצְרַיִם	וַיִּתֶּן־לוֹ	בַּיִת	וְלֶחֶם	אָמַר	לוֹ	וְאֶרֶץ
melekh-mitsrayim	wayyitten-lô	vayith	welechem	'āmar	lô	we'erets
the king of Egypt	and he gave to him	a house	and food	he said	to him	and land

5598.111	3937		4834.121	108	2682	904, 6084	6799	4108
v Qal pf 3ms	prep, ps 3ms	**19.**	cj, v Qal impf 3ms	pn	n ms	prep, *n fd*	pn	adv
נָתַן	לוֹ		וַיִּמְצָא	הֲדַד	חֵן	בְּעֵינֵי	פַּרְעֹה	מְאֹד
nāthan	lô		wayyimtsā'	hedhadh	chēn	be'ênê	phar'ōh	me'ōdh
he gave	to him		and he found	Hadad	favor	in the eyes of	Pharaoh	very

5598.121, 3937	828	881, 269	828	269	8804	1409
cj, v Qal impf 3ms, prep, ps 3ms	n fs	do, *n fs*	n fs, ps 3ms	*n fs*	pn	art, n fs
וַיִּתֶּן־לוֹ	אִשָּׁה	אֶת־אֲחוֹת	אִשְׁתּוֹ	אֲחוֹת	תַּחְפְּנֵיס	הַגְּבִירָה
wayyitten-lô	'ishshāh	'eth-'ăchôth	'ishtô	'ăchôth	tachpenēs	haggevîrāh
and he gave to him	a wife	the sister of	his wife	the sister of	Tahpenes	the queen

	3314.122	3937	269	8804	881	1633	1158
20.	cj, v Qal impf 3fs	prep, ps 3ms	*n fs*	pn	do	pn	n ms, ps 3ms
	וַתֵּלֶד	לוֹ	אֲחוֹת	תַּחְפְּנֵיס	אֵת	גְּנֻבַת	בְּנוֹ
	wattēledh	lô	'ăchôth	tachpenēs	'ēth	genuvath	benô
	and she bore	to him	the sister of	Tahpenes		Genubath	his son

1621.122	8804	904, 8761	1041	6799	2030.121	1633
cj, v Qal impf 3fs, ps 3ms	pn	prep, *n ms*	*n ms*	pn	cj, v Qal impf 3ms	pn
וַתִּגְמְלֵהוּ	תַּחְפְּנֵס	בְּתוֹךְ	בֵּית	פַּרְעֹה	וַיְהִי	גְּנֻבַת
wattighmelēhû	thachpenēs	bethôkh	bêth	par'ōh	wayhî	ghenuvath
and she weaned him	Tahpenes	in the middle of	the house of	Pharaoh	and he was	Genubath

1041	6799	904, 8761	1158	6799		1976	8471.111
n ms	pn	prep, *n ms*	*n mp*	pn	**21.**	cj, pn	v Qal pf 3ms
בֵּית	פַּרְעֹה	בְּתוֹךְ	בְּנֵי	פַּרְעֹה		וַהֲדַד	שָׁמַע
bêth	par'ōh	bethôkh	benê	phar'ōh		wahdhadh	shāma'
the household of	Pharaoh	in the midst of	the sons of	Pharaoh		and Hadad	he heard

904, 4875	3706, 8311.111	1784	6196, 1	3706, 4322.111	3200
prep, pn	cj, v Qal pf 3ms	pn	prep, n mp, ps 3ms	cj, cj, v Qal pf 3ms	pn
בְּמִצְרַיִם	כִּי־שָׁכַב	דָּוִד	עִם־אֲבֹתָיו	וְכִי־מֵת	יוֹאָב
bemitsrayim	kî-shākhav	dāwidh	'im-'ăvōthâv	wekhî-mēth	yô'āv
in Egypt	that he had lain	David	with his ancestors	and that he had died	Joab

8015, 6893	569.121	108	420, 6799	8365.331
n ms, art, n ms	cj, v Qal impf 3ms	pn	prep, pn	v Piel impv 2ms, ps 1cs
שַׂר־הַצָּבָא	וַיֹּאמֶר	הֲדַד	אֶל־פַּרְעֹה	שַׁלְּחֵנִי
sar-hatstsāvā'	wayyō'mer	h^{e}dhadh	'el-par'ōh	shall^{e}chēnî
the commander of the army	and he said	Hadad	unto Pharaoh	send me out

2050.125	420, 800		569.121	3937	6799	3706	4242, 887
cj, v Qal juss 1cs	prep, n fs, ps 1cs	**22.**	cj, v Qal impf 3ms	prep, ps 3ms	pn	cj	intrg, pers pron
וְאֵלֵךְ	אֶל־אַרְצִי		וַיֹּאמֶר	לוֹ	פַּרְעֹה	כִּי	מָה־אַתָּה
w^e'ēlēkh	'el-'artsî		wayyō'mer	lô	phar'ōh	kî	māh-'attāh
that I may go	to my land		but he said	to him	Pharaoh	because	what you

2741.151	6196	2079	1272.351	3937, 2050.141	420, 800
v Qal act ptc ms	prep, ps 1cs	cj, intrj, ps 2ms	v Piel ptc ms	prep, v Qal inf con	prep, n fs, ps 2ms
חָסֵר	עִמִּי	וְהִנְּךָ	מְבַקֵּשׁ	לָלֶכֶת	אֶל־אַרְצְךָ
chāsēr	'immî	w^{e}hinn^{e}khā	m^{e}vaqqēsh	lālekheth	'el-'artsekhā
lacking	with me	now behold you	seeking	to go	to your land

18. And they arose out of Midian, and came to Paran: and they took men with them out of Paran, and they came to Egypt, unto Pharaoh king of Egypt; which gave him an house, and appointed him victuals, and gave him land: ... ordered provisions for him, *Berkeley* ... and appointed him food, *Goodspeed* ... provided him with a house, undertook to maintain him, and assigned him an estate, *JB* ... assigned him an allowance of food, *NRSV*.

19. And Hadad found great favour in the sight of Pharaoh, so that he gave him to wife the sister of his own wife, the sister of Tahpenes the queen: ... Hadad was very pleasing to Pharaoh, *BB* ... Pharaoh liked Hadad very much, *Beck* ... he gave him in marriage the sister of, *RSV* ... gave him his own sister-in-law, *Knox*.

20. And the sister of Tahpenes bare him Genubath his son, whom Tahpenes weaned in Pharaoh's house: and Genubath was in Pharaoh's household among the sons of Pharaoh: ... whom Tahpenes brought up in Pharaoh's palace, Genubath living in Pharaoh's palace with Pharaoh's own children, *JB* ... The sister of Tahpenes gave birth by him to his son Genubath, *NRSV* ... who was raised by the queen in the palace, where he lived with the king's sons, *Good News*.

21. And when Hadad heard in Egypt that David slept with his fathers, and that Joab the captain of the host was dead, Hadad said to Pharaoh, Let me depart, that I may go to mine own country: ... that David had been laid to rest with, *Knox* ... send me back to my country, *BB* ... Let me leave and go to my own country, *Beck* ... that David had died, *Good News*.

22. Then Pharaoh said unto him, But what hast thou lacked with me, that, behold, thou seekest to go to thine own country? And he answered, Nothing: howbeit let me go in any wise: ... Why do you want to go back to your own country? What haven't I given you here, *NCV* ... What is it that you find wanting in my country that you want to go back to your own, *NEB* ... Nothing, but do let me go, anyway, *NKJV* ... Nothing, but please let me go, *JB*.

among the Egyptian princes. But amid the luxurious splendors of Pharaoh's palace, Hadad carried in his heart an undying thirst for vengeance on the destroyer of his family and race. The names of David and Joab inspired a terror which made rebellion impossible for a time; but when Hadad heard, with grim satisfaction, of Joab's judicial murder, and that David had been succeeded by a peaceful son no charm of an Egyptian palace and royal bride could weigh in the balance against the fierce passion of an avenger of blood. Better the wild freedom of Idumea than the sluggish ease of Egypt. He asked the Pharaoh's leave to return to his own country, and, braving the reproach of ingratitude, made his way back to the desolated fields and cities of his unfortunate people. He developed their resources, and nursed their hopes of the coming day of vengeance. If he could do nothing else he could at least act as a desperate marauder and prove himself an adversary to the successor of his foe (1 Ki. 11:14). Solomon was strong enough to keep open the road to Ezion-Gebir, but Hadad was probably master of Sela and Maon.

11:23–25. Another enemy was Rezon, of whom but little is known. David had won a great victory, the most remarkable of all his successes, over Hadadezer, King of Zobah, and had then signalized his conquest by placing garrisons in Syria of

569.121	3940	3706	8365.342	8365.323	23.	7251.521	435
cj, v Qal impf 3ms	neg part	cj	v Piel inf abs	v Piel impf 2ms, ps 1cs		cj, v Hiphil impf 3ms	n mp
וַיֹּ֫אמֶר	לֹא	כִּי	שַׁלֵּחַ	תְּשַׁלְּחֵנִי		וַיָּקֶם	אֱלֹהִים
wayyō'mer	lō'	kî	shallēach	teshallechênî		wayyāqem	'ĕlōhîm
and he said	no	rather	sending out	you must send me out		and He raised up	God

3937	7931	881, 7616	1158, 453	866	1300.111	4623, 881	1977
prep, ps 3ms	n ms	do, pn	*n ms*, pn	rel pron	v Qal pf 3ms	prep, do	pn
לוֹ	שָׂטָן	אֶת־רְזוֹן	בֶּן־אֶלְיָדָע	אֲשֶׁר	בָּרַח	מֵאֵת	הֲדַדְעֶזֶר
lô	sāṭān	'eth-rezôn	ben-'elyādhā'	'ăsher	bārach	mē'ēth	hedhadh'ezer
against him	an adversary	Rezon	the son of Eliada	who	he had fled	from	Hadadezer

4567, 6941	112	24.	7192.121	6142	596	2030.121
n ms, pn	n mp, ps 3ms		cj, v Qal impf 3ms	prep, ps 3ms	n mp	cj, v Qal impf 3ms
מֶלֶךְ־צוֹבָה	אֲדֹנָיו		וַיִּקְבֹּץ	עָלָיו	אֲנָשִׁים	וַיְהִי
melekh-tsôvāh	'ădhōnâv		wayyiqōbbōts	'ālâv	'ănāshîm	wayhî
the king of Zobah	his master		and he gathered	beside him	men	and he was

8015, 1447	904, 2103.141	1784	881	2050.126	1894
n ms, n ms	prep, v Qal inf con	pn	do, ps 3mp	cj, v Qal impf 3mp	pn
שַׂר־גְּדוּד	בַּהֲרֹג	דָּוִד	אֹתָם	וַיֵּלְכוּ	דַּמֶּשֶׂק
sar-gedhûdh	bahrōgh	dāwidh	'ōthām	wayyēlekhû	dhammeseq
a leader of a troop	when killing	David	them	and they went to	Damascus

3553.126	904	4566.126	904, 1894	25.	2030.121	7931
cj, v Qal impf 3mp	prep, ps 3fs	cj, v Qal impf 3mp	prep, pn		cj, v Qal impf 3ms	n ms
וַיֵּשְׁבוּ	בָהּ	וַיִּמְלְכוּ	בְּדַמָּשֶׂק		וַיְהִי	שָׂטָן
wayyēshevû	vāhh	wayyimlekhû	bedhammāseq		wayhî	sāṭān
and they dwelled	in it	and they reigned	in Damascus		and he was	an adversary

3937, 3547	3725, 3219	8406	881, 7750	866	1976	7258.121
prep, pn	*adj, n mp*	pn	cj, do, art, n fs	rel pron	pn	cj, v Qal impf 3ms
לְיִשְׂרָאֵל	כָּל־יְמֵי	שְׁלֹמֹה	וְאֶת־הָרָעָה	אֲשֶׁר	הֲדָד	וַיָּקָץ
leyisrā'ēl	kol-yemê	shelōmōh	we'eth-hārā'āh	'ăsher	hedhādh	wayyāqāts
to Israel	all the days of	Solomon	and the evildoer	who	Hadad	and he loathed

904, 3547	4566.121	6142, 782	26.	3493	1158, 5203	694
prep, pn	cj, v Qal impf 3ms	prep, pn		cj, pn	*n ms*, pn	pn
בְּיִשְׂרָאֵל	וַיִּמְלֹךְ	עַל־אֲרָם		וְיָרָבְעָם	בֶּן־נְבָט	אֶפְרָתִי
beyisrā'ēl	wayyimlōkh	'al-'ărām		weyārov'ām	ben-nevāṭ	'ephrāthî
against Israel	and he reigned	over Aram		and Jeroboam	the son of Nebat	an Ephrathite

4623, 7149	8428	525	7153	828	496	5860	3937, 8406
prep, art, pn	cj, *n ms*	n fs, ps 3ms	pn	n fs	n fs	n ms	prep, pn
מִן־הַצְּרֵדָה	וְשֵׁם	אִמּוֹ	צְרוּעָה	אִשָּׁה	אַלְמָנָה	עֶבֶד	לִשְׁלֹמֹה
min-hatstserēdhāh	weshēm	'immô	tserû'āh	'ishshāh	'almānāh	'evedh	lishlōmōh
from the Zareda	and the name of	his mother	Zeruah	a woman	a widow	a servant	to Solomon

7597.521	3135	904, 4567	27.	2172	1745	866, 7597.511	3135
cj, v Hiphil impf 3ms	n fs	prep, art, n ms		cj, dem pron	art, n ms	rel part, v Hiphil pf 3ms	n fs
וַיָּרֶם	יָד	בַּמֶּלֶךְ		וְזֶה	הַדָּבָר	אֲשֶׁר־הֵרִים	יָד
wayyārem	yādh	bammelekh		wezeh	haddāvār	'ăsher-hērîm	yādh
and he raised	a hand	against the king		and this	the matter	which he raised	a hand

904, 4567	8406	1161.111	881, 4545	5646.111	881, 6806	6111	1784
prep, art, n ms	pn	v Qal pf 3ms	do, art, pn	v Qal pf 3ms	do, *n fs*	*n fs*	pn
בַּמֶּלֶךְ	שְׁלֹמֹה	בָּנָה	אֶת־הַמִּלּוֹא	סָגַר	אֶת־פֶּרֶץ	עִיר	דָּוִד
bammelekh	shelōmōh	bānāh	'eth-hammillô'	sāghar	'eth-perets	'îr	dāwidh
against the king	Solomon	he built	the Millo	he closed	the breach of	the city of	David

1		382	3493	1399	2524	7495.121	8406
n ms, ps 3ms	**28.**	cj, art, n ms	pn	*n ms*	n ms	cj, v Qal impf 3ms	pn
אָבִיו		וְהָאִישׁ	יָרָבְעָם	גִּבּוֹר	חָיִל	וַיַּרְא	שְׁלֹמֹה
'āvîw		w^{e}hā'îsh	yārov'ām	gibbôr	chāyil	wayyar^{e}'	sh^{e}lōmōh
his father		and the man	Jeroboam	a warrior of	the army	and he saw	Solomon

881, 5470	3706, 6449.151	4536	2000	6734.521	881
do, art, n ms	cj, v Qal act ptc ms	n fs	pers pron	cj, v Hiphil impf 3ms	do, ps 3ms
אֶת־הַנַּעַר	כִּי־עֹשֵׂה	מְלָאכָה	הוּא	וַיַּפְקֵד	אֹתוֹ
'eth-hanna'ar	kî-'ōsēh	m^{e}lā'khāh	hû'	wayyaphqēdh	'ōthô
the young man	that doing	work	he	and he commissioned	him

23. And God stirred him up another adversary, Rezon the son of Eliadah, which fled from his lord Hadadezer king of Zobah: ... stirred him up *another* foe, *KJVII* ... God gave Solomon another enemy to contend with, *Knox* ... God sent another trouble-maker, *BB* ... God also raised up Rezon, Eliada's son, to oppose him, *Beck*.

24. And he gathered men unto him, and became captain over a band, when David slew them of Zobah: and they went to Damascus, and dwelt therein, and reigned in Damascus: ... and became leader of a marauding band, and they went to Damascus, *Goodspeed* ... when David defeated them with slaughter, Rezon gathered men about him and became leader of a band, went to Damascus, settled there, and became king in Damascus, *NAB* ... and became the leader of a band of rebels when David destroyed the forces of Zobah; the rebels went to Damascus, where they settled and took control, *NIV* ... and became captain over a band of raiders, when David killed those of Zobah, *NKJV*.

25. And he was an adversary to Israel all the days of Solomon, beside the mischief Hadad did: and he abhorred Israel, and reigned over Syria: ... he was a trouble to Israel all through the days of Solomon. And this is the damage Hadad did: he was cruel to Israel while he was ruler over Edom, *BB* ... He was Israel's opponent throughout the lifetime of Solomon, beside the harm that Hadad did and he loathed Israel when he was king in Edom, *Berkeley* ... he was an enemy to Israel in the time of Solomon ... and he was an annoyance to Israel, *Fenton* ... he despised Israel, *NRSV*.

26. And Jeroboam the son of Nebat, an Ephrathite of Zereda, Solomon's servant, whose mother's name was Zeruah, a widow woman, even he lifted up his hand against the king: ... rebelled against the king, *REB* ... turned against the king, *Good News* ... revolted against the king, *JB*.

27. And this was the cause that he lifted up his hand against the king: Solomon built Millo, and repaired the breaches of the city of David his father: ... this is the reason why he rebelled against, *NASB* ... This is the story of how Jeroboam turned against the king. Solomon was filling in the land and repairing the wall of Jerusalem, *NCV* ... Solomon had built the Millo and repaired the damages to, *NKJV* ... This was the situation when he rebelled, *Beck*.

Damascus. On this occasion Rezon, the son of Eli, who is perhaps identical with Hezion, the grandfather of Ben-Hadad, King of Syria in the days of Asa, fled from the host of Hadadezer with some of the Syrian forces. With these and all whom he could collect about him, he became a guerrilla captain. After a successful period of predatory warfare he found himself strong enough to seize Damascus, where, to all appearance, he founded a powerful hereditary kingdom. Thus with Hadad in the south to plunder his commercial caravans, and Rezon on the north to threaten his communication with Tiphsah, and alarm his excursions to his retreats in Lebanon, Solomon was made keenly to feel that his power was rather an unsubstantial pageant than a solid dominion.

11:26–28. The enmity of these powerful enemies from Edom and Syria was a hereditary legacy from the wars of David and the ruthless savagery of Joab. A third adversary was far more terrible, and he was called into existence by the conduct of Solomon himself. This was Jeroboam, the son of Nebat. In himself he was of no account, being a man of isolated position and obscure origin. He was the son of a widow named Zeruah, who lived at Zarthan in the Jordan valley. The position of a widow in the ancient world was one of feebleness and difficulty; and if we may trust the apocryphal additions to the Septuagint, Zeruah was not only a widow but a harlot. But Jeroboam, whose name perhaps indicates that he was born in the golden days of Solomon's prosperity, was a youth of vigor and capacity. He made his way from

3937, 3725, 5630	1041	3231		2030.121	904, 6496	2026
prep, *adj*, *n ms*	*n ms*	pn		cj, v Qal impf 3ms	prep, art, n fs	art, dem pron
לְכָל־סֵבֶל	בֵּית	יוֹסֵף	**29.**	וַיְהִי	בָּעֵת	הַהִיא
lᵉkhol-s̱ēvel	bêth	yôs̱ēph		wayhî	bā'ēth	hahî'
over all the forced labor of	the household of	Joseph		and it was	at the time	the that

3493	3428.111	4623, 3503	4834.121	881	282	8296
cj, pn	v Qal pf 3ms	prep, pn	cj, v Qal impf 3ms	do, ps 3ms	pn	art, pn
וְיָרָבְעָם	יָצָא	מִירוּשָׁלִַם	וַיִּמְצָא	אֹתוֹ	אֲחִיָּה	הַשִּׁילֹנִי
wᵉyārov'ām	yātsā'	mîrûshālām	wayyimtsā'	'ōthô	'ăchîyāh	hashshîlōnî
that Jeroboam	he went out	from Jerusalem	and he found	him	Ahijah	the Shilonite

5204	904, 1932	2000	3803.751	904, 7969	2413	8530
art, n ms	prep, art, n ms	cj, pers pron	v Hithpael ptc ms	prep, n fs	adj	cj, num, ps 3mp
הַנָּבִיא	בַּדֶּרֶךְ	וְהוּא	מִתְכַּסֶּה	בְּשַׂלְמָה	חֲדָשָׁה	וּשְׁנֵיהֶם
hannāvî'	badderekh	wᵉhû'	mithkas̱s̱eh	bᵉsalmāh	chădhāshāh	ûshᵉnêhem
the prophet	on the road	but he	covered himself	with a cloak	new	and the two of them

3937, 940	904, 7898		8945.121	282	904, 7969	2413	866
prep, n ms, ps 3mp	prep, art, n ms		cj, v Qal impf 3ms	pn	prep, art, n fs	art, adj	rel part
לְבַדָּם	בַּשָּׂדֶה	**30.**	וַיִּתְפֹּשׂ	אֲחִיָּה	בַּשַּׂלְמָה	הַחֲדָשָׁה	אֲשֶׁר
lᵉvaddām	bassādheh		wayyithpōs	'ăchîyāh	bassalmāh	hachdhāshāh	'āsher
by themselves	in the field		and he took hold of	Ahijah	by the cloak	the new	which

6142	7458.121	8530	6461	7459		569.121	3937, 3493
prep, ps 3ms	cj, v Qal impf 3ms, ps 3fs	num	num	n mp		cj, v Qal impf 3ms	prep, pn
עָלָיו	וַיִּקְרָעֶהָ	שְׁנֵים	עָשָׂר	קְרָעִים	**31.**	וַיֹּאמֶר	לְיָרָבְעָם
'ālâv	wayyiqrā'eāh	shᵉnêm	'āsār	qŏrā'îm		wayyō'mer	lᵉyārov'ām
on him	and he tore it apart	two	ten	pieces		and he said	to Jeroboam

4089.131, 3937	6463	7459	3706	3662	569.111	3176	435
v Qal impv 2ms, prep, ps 2ms	num	n mp	cj	adv	v Qal pf 3ms	pn	*n mp*
קַח־לְךָ	עֲשָׂרָה	קְרָעִים	כִּי	כֹּה	אָמַר	יְהוָה	אֱלֹהֵי
qach-lᵉkhā	'ăsārāh	qŏrā'îm	kî	khōh	'āmar	yᵉhwāh	'ĕlōhê
take for yourself	ten	pieces	because	thus	He has said	Yahweh	the God of

3547	2079	7458.151	881, 4608	4623, 3135	8406	5598.115
pn	intrj, ps 1cs	v Qal act ptc ms	do, art, n fs	prep, *n fs*	pn	cj, v Qal pf 1cs
יִשְׂרָאֵל	הִנְנִי	קֹרֵעַ	אֶת־הַמַּמְלָכָה	מִיַּד	שְׁלֹמֹה	וְנָתַתִּי
yisrā'ēl	hinᵉnî	qōrēa'	'eth-hammamlākhāh	mîyadh	shᵉlōmōh	wᵉnāthattî
Israel	behold I	tearing	the kingdom	from the hand of	Solomon	and I will give

3937	881	6463	8101		8101	259	2030.121, 3937
prep, ps 2ms	do	num	art, n mp		cj, art, n ms	art, num	v Qal impf 3ms, prep, ps 3ms
לְךָ	אֵת	עֲשָׂרָה	הַשְּׁבָטִים	**32.**	וְהַשֵּׁבֶט	הָאֶחָד	יִהְיֶה־לּוֹ
lᵉkhā	'ēth	'ăsārāh	hashshᵉvāṯîm		wᵉhashshēveṯ	hā'echādh	yihyeh-lô
to you		ten	the tribes		but the tribe	the one	it will be to him

3937, 4775	5860	1784	3937, 4775	3503	6111	866	1013.115
prep, prep	n ms, ps 1cs	pn	cj, prep, prep	pn	art, n fs	rel part	v Qal pf 1cs
לְמַעַן	עַבְדִּי	דָוִד	וּלְמַעַן	יְרוּשָׁלַם	הָעִיר	אֲשֶׁר	בָּחַרְתִּי
lᵉma'an	'avdî	dhāwidh	ûlăma'an	yᵉrûshālam	hā'îr	'ăsher	bācharttî
because of	my servant	David	and because of	Jerusalem	the city	which	I have chosen

904	4623, 3725	8101	3547		3391	866
prep, ps 3fs	prep, *adj*	*n mp*	pn		cj	rel part
בָהּ	מִכֹּל	שִׁבְטֵי	יִשְׂרָאֵל	**33.**	יַעַן	אֲשֶׁר
vāhh	mikkōl	shivṯê	yisrā'ēl		ya'an	'ăsher
with it	among the entirety of	the tribes of	Israel		because	that

28. And the man Jeroboam was a mighty man of valour: and Solomon seeing the young man that he was industrious, he made him ruler over all the charge of the house of Joseph: ... mighty man of war, *KJVII* ... a man of standing, *NIV* ... Solomon saw that he was a good worker and made him overseer of all the work given to the sons of Joseph, *BB* ... he appointed him over all the builders of the house of, *Fenton*.

29. And it came to pass at that time when Jeroboam went out of Jerusalem, that the prophet Ahijah the Shilonite found him in the way; and he had clad himself with a new garment; and they two were alone in the field: ... met him on the road, wearing a new cloak, *NLT* ... came across him on the road; now Ahijah had put on a new robe; and the two of them were by themselves in, *BB* ... met him and turned him aside, *Berkeley* ... The two of them were alone in the open country, *NRSV*.

30. And Ahijah caught the new garment that was on him, and rent it in twelve pieces: ... seized the new robe which was upon him, and tore it into, *Fenton* ... tore it into twelve strips, *JB* ... divided it into twelve parts, *Douay* ... took his new coat and tore it into, *NCV*.

31. And he said to Jeroboam, Take thee ten pieces: for thus saith the LORD, the God of Israel, Behold, I will rend the kingdom out of the hand of Solomon, and will give ten tribes to thee: ... I am going to tear the kingdom from the hand of Solomon, *NEB* ... Take ten of the parts, for this is what the Lord has said: See, I will take the kingdom away from Solomon by force, and, *BB* ... I will tear the kingship from the hand of, *Fenton* ... the God of Israel has declared that he is about to tear the kingdom from, *REB*.

32. (But he shall have one tribe for my servant David's sake, and for Jerusalem's sake, the city which I have chosen out of all the tribes of Israel:): ... One tribe shall remain his, for the sake of my servant David, and of Jerusalem, among all the cities of Israel the city of my choice, *Knox* ... he shall retain one tribe, *Berkeley* ... the city I have chosen to be my own from the whole land of Israel, *Good News* ... I will allow him to control one tribe, *NCV*.

33. Because that they have forsaken me, and have worshipped Ashtoreth the goddess of the Zidonians, Chemosh the god of the Moabites, and Milcom the god of the children of Ammon, and have not walked in my ways, to do that which is right in mine eyes, and to keep my statutes and my judgments, as did David his father: ... he has prostrated himself before Ashtoreth, *NEB* ... doing what is right in my sight and keeping my statutes and my ordinances, *NRSV* ... he has bowed down before Ashtoreth, *REB* ... to do that pleaseth me, and mine ordinances and customs, *Tyndale*.

---

the wretched clay fields of Zeredah to Jerusalem, and there became one of the vast undistinguished gang who were known as "slaves of Solomon." The conscripted labor from all parts of Palestine was then engaged in building the Millo and the huge walls and causeway in the valley between Zion and Moriah, which was afterwards known as the Valley of the Cheesemakers. Here the unknown youth distinguished himself by his strenuousness, and by the influence which he rapidly acquired. Solomon knew the value of a man "diligent in his business," and therefore worthy to stand before kings. Untrammeled by any rules of seniority, and able to make and unmake as he thought fit, Solomon promoted him while still young, and at one bound, to a position of great rank and influence. Jeroboam was an Ephraimite, and Solomon therefore "gave him charge over all the compulsory levies (mas̱, HED #4671) of the tribe of the house of Joseph"—that is, of the proud and powerful tribes of Ephraim and Manasseh, who practically represented all Israel except Judah, Benjamin and the almost nominal Simeon.

But a yet deeper feeling was at work against Solomon. The men of Ephraim and all the northern tribes had not only begun to ask why Judah was to monopolize the king's partiality, but the much more dangerous question, What right has the king to enforce on us these dreary and interminable labors, in making a city of palaces and an impregnable fortress of a capital which is to overshadow our glory and command our subjection? With consummate astuteness, by a word here and a word there, Jeroboam was able to pose before Solomon as the enforcer of a stern yoke, and before his countrymen as one who hated the hard necessity and would fain be their deliverer from it.

And while he was already in heart a rebel against the household of David, he received what he regarded as a divine sanction to his career of ambition.

11:29–40. But the hour had now struck for a prophet to speak the word of the LORD. If the king, surrounded by formidable guards and a glittering court, was too exalted to be reached by a humble son of the people, it was time for Ahijah to follow the precedent of Samuel. He obeyed a divine intimation in selecting the successor who should punish the great king's rebellion against God, and inaugurate a rule of purer obedience than now

6013.116	8246.726	3937, 6492	435	6992	3937, 3767
v Qal pf 3cp, ps 1cs	cj, v Hithpael impf 3mp	prep, pn	*n fp*	pn	prep, pn
עֲזָבוּנִי	וַיִּשְׁתַּחֲווּ	לְעַשְׁתֹּרֶת	אֱלֹהֵי	צִדֹנִין	לִכְמוֹשׁ
'ăzāvûnî	wayyishtachwû	le'ashtōreth	'ĕlōhê	tsidhōnîn	likhmôsh
they have abandoned Me	and they bowed down	to Ashtoreth	the goddess of	Sidonians	to Chemosh

435	4262	3937, 4585	435	1158, 6205	3940, 2050.116
n mp	pn	cj, prep, pn	*n mp*	*n mp*, pn	cj, neg part, v Qal pf 3cp
אֱלֹהֵי	מוֹאָב	וּלְמִלְכֹּם	אֱלֹהֵי	בְנֵי־עַמּוֹן	וְלֹא־הָלְכוּ
'ĕlōhê	mô'āv	ûlāmilkōm	'ĕlōhê	venê-'ammôn	welō'-hālekhû
the god of	Moab	and Milcom	the god of	the sons of Ammon	and they have not walked

904, 1932	3937, 6449.141	3596	904, 6084	2807	5122
prep, n mp, ps 1cs	prep, v Qal inf con	art, adj	prep, n fd, ps 1cs	cj, n fp, ps 1cs	cj, n mp, ps 1cs
בִדְרָכַי	לַעֲשׂוֹת	הַיָּשָׁר	בְּעֵינַי	וְחֻקֹּתַי	וּמִשְׁפָּטַי
vidhrākhay	la'ăsôth	hayyāshār	be'ênay	wechuqqōthay	ûmishpāṭay
in my ways	to do	what is upright	in my eyes	and my statutes	and my ordinances

3626, 1784	1		3940, 4089.125	881, 3725, 4608	4623, 3135	3706
prep, pn	n ms, ps 3ms	**34.**	cj, neg part, v Qal impf 1cs	do, *adj*, art, n fs	prep, n fs, ps 3ms	cj
כְּדָוִד	אָבִיו		וְלֹא־אֶקַּח	אֶת־כָּל־הַמַּמְלָכָה	מִיָּדוֹ	כִּי
kedhāwidh	'āvîw		welō'-'eqqach	'eth-kol-hammamlākhāh	mîyādhô	kî
like David	his father		but I will not take	all the kingdom	from his hand	rather

5562	8308.125	3725	3219	2522	3937, 4775	1784
n ms	v Qal impf 1cs, ps 3ms	*n ms*	*n mp*	n mp, ps 3ms	prep, prep	pn
נָשִׂיא	אֲשִׁתֶנּוּ	כֹּל	יְמֵי	חַיָּיו	לְמַעַן	דָּוִד
nāsî'	'ăshithennû	kōl	yemê	chayyâv	lema'an	dāwidh
a tribal leader	I will appoint him	the entirety of	the days of	his life	because of	David

5860	866	1013.115	881	866	8490.111	4851
n ms, ps 1cs	rel pron	v Qal pf 1cs	do, ps 3ms	rel pron	v Qal pf 3ms	n fp, ps 1cs
עַבְדִּי	אֲשֶׁר	בָּחַרְתִּי	אֹתוֹ	אֲשֶׁר	שָׁמַר	מִצְוֹתַי
'avdî	'ăsher	bāchartî	'ōthô	'ăsher	shāmar	mitswōthay
my servant	whom	I chose	him	who	he observed	my commandments

2807		4089.115	4548	4623, 3135	1158	5598.115
cj, n fp, ps 1cs	**35.**	cj, v Qal pf 1cs	art, n fs	prep, *n fs*	n ms, ps 3ms	cj, v Qal pf 1cs, ps 3fs
וְחֻקֹּתָי		וְלָקַחְתִּי	הַמְּלוּכָה	מִיַּד	בְּנוֹ	וּנְתַתִּיהָ
wechuqqōthāy		welāqachtî	hammelûkhāh	mîyadh	benô	ûnethattîāh
and my statutes		yet I will take	the kingdom	from the hand of	his son	and I will give it

3937	881	6467	8101		3937, 1158	5598.125	8101, 259	3937, 4775
prep, ps 2ms	do	num	art, n mp	**36.**	cj, prep, n ms, ps 3ms	v Qal impf 1cs	n ms, num	prep, prep
לְךָ	אֵת	עֲשֶׂרֶת	הַשְּׁבָטִים		וְלִבְנוֹ	אֶתֵּן	שֵׁבֶט־אֶחָד	לְמַעַן
lekhā	'ēth	'ăsereth	hashshevāṭîm		welivnô	'ettēn	shēveṭ-'echādh	lema'an
to you		ten	the tribes		yet to his son	I will give	one tribe	so that

2030.141, 5402	3937, 1784, 5860	3725, 3219	3937, 6686	904, 3503	6111	866
v Qal inf con, n ms	prep, pn, n ms, ps 1cs	*adj*, art, n mp	prep, n mp, ps 1cs	prep, pn	art, n fs	rel part
הֱיוֹת־נִיר	לְדָוִיד־עַבְדִּי	כָּל־הַיָּמִים	לְפָנַי	בִּירוּשָׁלַם	הָעִיר	אֲשֶׁר
hĕyôth-nîr	ledhāwîdh-'avdî	kol-hayyāmîm	lephānay	bîrûshālam	hā'îr	'ăsher
a lamp being	for David my servant	all the days	before Me	in Jerusalem	the city	which

1013.115	3937	3937, 7947.141	8428	8427		881	4089.125
v Qal pf 1cs	prep, ps 1cs	prep, v Qal inf con	n ms, ps 1cs	adv	**37.**	cj, do, ps 2ms	v Qal impf 1cs
בָּחַרְתִּי	לִי	לָשׂוּם	שְׁמִי	שָׁם		וְאֹתְךָ	אֶקַּח
bāchartî	lî	lāsûm	shemî	shām		we'ōthekhā	'eqqach
I have chosen	for myself	to put	my name	there		and you	I will take

4566.113	904, 3725	866, 181.322	5497	2030.113	4567
cj, v Qal pf 2ms	prep, n ms	rel part, v Piel impf 3fs	n fs, ps 2ms	cj, v Qal pf 2ms	n ms
וּמָלַכְתָּ	בְּכֹל	אֲשֶׁר־תְּאַוֶּה	נַפְשְׁךָ	וְהָיִיתָ	מֶלֶךְ
ûmālakhtā	bekhōl	'ăsher-te'awweh	naphshekhā	wehāyîthā	melekh
and you will reign	over all	which it desires	your soul	and you will become	a king

6142, 3547		2030.111	524, 8490.123	881, 3725, 866	6943.325
prep, pn	38.	cj, v Qal pf 3ms	cj, v Qal impf 2ms	do, *adj*, rel part	v Piel impf 1cs, ps 2ms
עַל־יִשְׂרָאֵל		וְהָיָה	אִם־תִּשְׁמַע	אֶת־כָּל־אֲשֶׁר	אֲצַוֶּךָ
'al-yisrā'ēl		wehāyāh	'im-tishma'	'eth-kol-'ăsher	'ătsawwekhā
over Israel		and it will be	if you listen to	all that	I command you

34. Howbeit I will not take the whole kingdom out of his hand: but I will make him prince all the days of his life for David my servant's sake, whom I chose, because he kept my commandments and my statutes: ... I will certainly establish him as ruler during his lifetime, for David, *Goodspeed* ... kept my commandments and my laws, *JB* ... commandments and my precepts, *Douay* ... David, the one whom I chose and who obeyed my commands and laws, I will let Solomon reign for the rest of his life, *NLT*.

35. But I will take the kingdom out of his son's hand, and will give it unto thee, even ten tribes: ... I shall take the kingship from his hand, *Fenton* ... and give it to you, that is, ten tribes of it, *Berkeley*.

36. And unto his son will I give one tribe, that David my servant may have a light always before me in Jerusalem, the city which I have chosen me to put my name there: ... may have a light for ever burning before me in, *BB* ... the favoured sanctuary of my name, *Knox* ... in order that there may be a Davidic light before Me continually in, *Berkeley* ... I will always have a descendant of my servant David ruling in Jerusalem, the city I have chosen as the place where I am worshiped, *Good News*.

37. And I will take thee, and thou shalt reign according to all that thy soul desireth, and shalt be king over Israel: ... over all that you yourself desire, *Goodspeed* ... You nonetheless I shall appoint to rule over as much as you wish, *JB* ... I will make you rule over everything you want. You will rule over all of Israel, *NCV* ... you shall reign over all your heart desires, *NKJV*.

38. And it shall be, if thou wilt hearken unto all that I command thee, and wilt walk in my ways, and do that is right in my sight, to keep my statutes and my commandments, as David my servant did; that I will be with thee, and build thee a sure house, as I built for David, and will give Israel unto thee: ... if you give attention to the orders I give you, walking in my ways and doing what is right in my eyes and keeping my laws and my orders as David my servant did; then I will be with you, building up for you a safe house, as I did for, *BB*

existed under the shadow of the throne. He was the annalist or historiographer of Solomon's court (2 Chr. 9:29); but loyalty to a backsliding king had come to mean disloyalty to God. There was but one man who seemed marked out for the perilous honor of a throne. It was the brave, vigorous, ambitious youth of Ephraim who had risen to high promotion and had won the hearts of his people, though Solomon had made him the task-master of their forced labor. On one occasion Jeroboam left Jerusalem, perhaps to visit his native Zeredah and his widowed mother (1 Ki. 11:29). Ahijah intentionally met him on the road. He drew him aside from the public path into a solitary place. There, seen by none, he took off his own shoulders the new stately abba in which he had clad himself, and proceeded to give to Jeroboam one of those object-lessons in the form of an acted parable, which to the Eastern mind are more effective than any words. Rending the new garment into twelve pieces, he gave ten to Jeroboam, telling him that Yahweh would thus rend the kingdom from the hands of Solomon because of his unfaithfulness, leaving his son but one tribe that the lamp of David might not be utterly extinguished. Jeroboam should be king over Israel; to the House of David should be left but an insignificant fragment. God would build a sure house for Jeroboam as He had done for David, if he would keep his commandments, though the House of David "should not be afflicted for ever" (1 Ki. 11:34–39).

A scene so memorable, a prophecy of such grave significance, could hardly remain a secret. Ahijah may have hinted it among his sympathizers. Jeroboam would hardly be able to conceal from his friends the immense hopes which it excited; and as his position probably gave him the command of troops he became dangerous. His designs reached the ears of

2050.113	904, 1932	6449.113	3596	904, 6084	3937, 8490.141
cj, v Qal pf 2ms	prep, n mp, ps 1cs	cj, v Qal pf 2ms	art, adj	prep, n fd, ps 1cs	prep, v Qal inf con
וְהָלַכְתָּ	בִדְרָכַי	וְעָשִׂיתָ	הַיָּשָׁר	בְּעֵינַי	לִשְׁמוֹר
wehālakhtā	vidhrākhay	we'āsîthā	hayyāshār	be'ênay	lishmôr
and you walk	in my ways	and you do	what is upright	in my eyes	to observe

2807	4851	3626, 866	6449.111	1784	5860	2030.115
n fp, ps 1cs	cj, n fp, ps 1cs	prep, rel part	v Qal pf 3ms	pn	n ms, ps 1cs	cj, v Qal pf 1cs
חֻקּוֹתַי	וּמִצְוֹתַי	כַּאֲשֶׁר	עָשָׂה	דָּוִד	עַבְדִּי	וְהָיִיתִי
chuqqôthay	ûmitswōthay	ka'ăsher	'āsāh	dāwidh	'avdî	wehāyîthî
my statutes	and my commandments	just as	he did	David	my servant	and I will be

6196	1161.115	3937	1041, 548.255	3626, 866	1161.115	3937, 1784
prep, ps 2ms	cj, v Qal pf 1cs	prep, ps 2ms	*n ms*, v Niphal ptc ms	prep, rel part	v Qal pf 1cs	prep, pn
עִמָּךְ	וּבָנִיתִי	לְךָ	בַּיִת־נֶאֱמָן	כַּאֲשֶׁר	בָּנִיתִי	לְדָוִד
'immākh	ûvānîthî	lekhā	vayith-ne'ĕmān	ka'ăsher	bānîthî	ledhāwidh
with you	and I will build	you	a reliable household	just as	I built	for David

5598.115	3937	881, 3547		6257.325	881, 2320	1784	3937, 4775
cj, v Qal pf 1cs	prep, ps 2ms	do, pn	39.	cj, v Piel impf 1cs	do, *n ms*	pn	prep, prep
וְנָתַתִּי	לְךָ	אֶת־יִשְׂרָאֵל		וַאֲעַנֶּה	אֶת־זֶרַע	דָּוִד	לְמַעַן
wenāthattî	lekhā	'eth-yisrā'ēl		wa''anneh	'eth-zera'	dāwidh	lema'an
and I will give	to you	Israel		and I will afflict	the seed of	David	because of

2148	395	3940	3725, 3219		1272.321	8406	3937, 4322.541
dem pron	adv	neg part	*adj*, art, n mp	40.	cj, v Piel impf 3ms	pn	prep, v Hiphil inf con
זֹאת	אַךְ	לֹא	כָּל־הַיָּמִים		וַיְבַקֵּשׁ	שְׁלֹמֹה	לְהָמִית
zō'th	'akh	lō'	khol-hayyāmîm		wayvaqqēsh	shelōmōh	lehāmîth
this	only	not	all the days		so he sought	Solomon	to kill

881, 3493	7251.121	3493	1300.121	4875	420, 8307	4567, 4875
do, pn	cj, v Qal impf 3ms	pn	cj, v Qal impf 3ms	pn	prep, pn	*n ms*, pn
אֶת־יָרָבְעָם	וַיָּקָם	יָרָבְעָם	וַיִּבְרַח	מִצְרַיִם	אֶל־שִׁישַׁק	מֶלֶךְ־מִצְרָיִם
'eth-yārov'ām	wayyāqām	yārov'ām	wayyivrach	mitsrayim	'el-shîshaq	melekh-mitsrayim
Jeroboam	but he arose	Jeroboam	and he fled to	Egypt	to Shishak	the king of Egypt

2030.121	904, 4875	5912, 4322.141	8406		3615	1745
cj, v Qal impf 3ms	prep, pn	adv, v Qal inf con	pn	41.	cj, *n ms*	*n mp*
וַיְהִי	בְמִצְרַיִם	עַד־מוֹת	שְׁלֹמֹה		וְיֶתֶר	דִּבְרֵי
wayhî	vemitsrayim	'adh-môth	shelōmōh		weyether	divrê
and he was	in Egypt	until the dying of	Solomon		and the remainder of	the events of

8406	3725, 866	6449.111	2551	1950B, 3940, 2062	3918.156
pn	cj, *adj*, rel part	v Qal pf 3ms	cj, n fs, ps 3ms	intrg part, neg part, pers pron	v Qal pass ptc mp
שְׁלֹמֹה	וְכָל־אֲשֶׁר	עָשָׂה	וְחָכְמָתוֹ	הֲלוֹא־הֵם	כְּתֻבִים
shelōmōh	wekhol-'ăsher	'āsāh	wechokhmāthô	hălô'-hēm	kethuvîm
Solomon	and all that	he did	and his wisdom	are they not	things written

6142, 5809	1745	8406		3219	866	4566.111	8406
prep, *n ms*	*n mp*	pn	42.	cj, art, n mp	rel part	v Qal pf 3ms	pn
עַל־סֵפֶר	דִּבְרֵי	שְׁלֹמֹה		וְהַיָּמִים	אֲשֶׁר	מָלַךְ	שְׁלֹמֹה
'al-sēpher	divrê	shelōmōh		wehayyāmîm	'ăsher	mālakh	shelōmōh
on the scroll of	the events of	Solomon		and the days	which	he reigned	Solomon

904, 3503	6142, 3725, 3547	727	8523		8311.121	8406
prep, pn	prep, *adj*, pn	num	n fs	43.	cj, v Qal impf 3ms	pn
בִירוּשָׁלַםִ	עַל־כָּל־יִשְׂרָאֵל	אַרְבָּעִים	שָׁנָה		וַיִּשְׁכַּב	שְׁלֹמֹה
vîrûshālam	'al-kol-yisrā'ēl	'arbā'îm	shānāh		wayyishkav	shelōmōh
in Jerusalem	over all Israel	forty	years		then he lay	Solomon

6196, 1	7196.221	904, 6111	1784	1	4566.121	7628
prep, n mp, ps 3ms	cj, v Niphil impf 3ms	prep, *n fs*	pn	n ms, ps 3ms	cj, v Qal impf 3ms	pn
עִם־אֲבֹתָיו	וַיִּקָּבֵר	בְּעִיר	דָּוִד	אָבִיו	וַיִּמְלֹךְ	רְחַבְעָם
'im-'ăvōthâv	wayyiqqāvēr	beʻîr	dāwidh	'āvîw	wayyimlōkh	rechav'ām
with his ancestors	and he was buried	in the city of	David	his father	and he reigned	Rehoboam

1158	8809		2050.121	7628	8328	3706	8328
n ms, ps 3ms	prep, ps 3ms	**12:1**	cj, v Qal impf 3ms	pn	pn	cj	pn
בְּנוֹ	תַּחְתָּיו		וַיֵּלֶךְ	רְחַבְעָם	שְׁכֶם	כִּי	שְׁכֶם
benô	tachtâv		wayyēlekh	rechav'ām	shekhem	kî	shekhem
his son	instead of him		and he went to	Rehoboam	Shechem	because	Shechem

... If you will listen to what I tell you and follow my ways and do whatever I consider to be right, *NLT* ... I will be with you. I will build you a dynasty as enduring as the one I built for David, and *NIV* ... and establish your dynasty firmly as I did David's, *Berkeley*.

39. And I will for this afflict the seed of David, but not for ever: ... I will punish David's line for this, *NAB* ... punish David's children because of this, *NCV* ... the descendants of David for this, *Goodspeed* ... I depress the race of David because of this, but not for all time, *Fenton*.

40. Solomon sought therefore to kill Jeroboam. And Jeroboam arose, and fled into Egypt, unto Shishak king of Egypt, and was in Egypt until the death of Solomon: ... Solomon tried to kill Jeroboam, *NIV* ... Jeroboam promptly fled to Egypt, *NRSV* ... but he was up and gone; he took refuge with Sesac king of Egypt, and remained there till Solomon's death, *Knox* ... Solomon was looking for a chance to put Jeroboam to death; but he went in flight to Egypt, *BB*.

41. And the rest of the acts of Solomon, and all that he did, and his wisdom, are they not written in the book of the acts of Solomon? ... The rest of what Solomon said and, *Beck* ... are they not recorded in the book of, *Berkeley* ... the rest of the affairs of Solomon, *Fenton* ... the rest of the records of Solomon, *Goodspeed*.

42. And the time that Solomon reigned in Jerusalem over all Israel was forty years: ... Solomon ruled in Jerusalem over all Israel for, *NCV* ... the period that, *NKJV* ... He was forty years on the throne, with his capital in Jerusalem, *Knox*.

43. And Solomon slept with his fathers, and was buried in the city of David his father: and Rehoboam his son reigned in his stead: ... Solomon rested with his ancestors, *NAB* ... he died and was buried in Jerusalem ... And his son Rehoboam became king in his place, *NCV* ... Rehoboam succeeded him, *JB* ... reigned in his place, *NKJV*.

12:1. And Rehoboam went to Shechem: for all Israel were come to Shechem to make him king: ... had come together to make him king, *BB* ... the whole of Israel had assembled to crown him king, *Knox* ... having come to Shechem to proclaim him king, *JB*.

Solomon, and he sought to put Jeroboam to death. The young man, who had probably betrayed his secret ambition, and may even have attempted some premature and abortive insurrection, escaped from Jerusalem, and took refuge in Egypt. There the Bubastite dynasty had displaced the Tanite, and from Shishak I, the earliest Pharaoh whose individuality eclipsed the common dynastic name, he received so warm a welcome that, according to one story, Shishak gave him in marriage Ano, the elder sister of his Queen Tahpanes (or Thekemina, Septuagint) and of Hadad's wife. He stayed in Egypt till the death of Solomon, and then returned to Zeredah, either in consequence of the summons of his countrymen, or that he might be ready for any turn of events.

11:41–43. So Solomon passed away—the last king of all Palestine till another king arose a thousand years later; like him in his fondness for magnificence, like him in his tamperings with idolatry, like him in being the builder of the Temple, but in all other respects a for more grievous sinner and a far more inexcusable tyrant—Herod, falsely called "The Great."

And in the same age arose another King of Solomon's descendants, whose palace was the shop of the carpenter and his throne the cross, and whose mortal body was the true Temple of the Supreme—that King whose kingdom is an everlasting kingdom, and whose dominion endureth throughout all ages.

12:1–5. *"A foolish son is the calamity of his father"* (Prov. 19:13).

"Solomon ... left behind one of his sons, expansive in folly, limited in sense, Roboam, who by his policy made the people rebel" (Sirach 47:23).

971.111	3725, 3547	4566.541	881	**2.** 2030.121
v Qal pf 3ms	*adj*, pn	prep, v Hiphil inf con	do, ps 3ms	cj, v Qal impf 3ms
בָּא	כָל־יִשְׂרָאֵל	לְהַמְלִיךְ	אֹתוֹ	וַיְהִי
bā'	khol-yisrā'ēl	lehamlîkh	'ōthô	wayhî
they had come to	all Israel	to cause to reign	him	and it was

3626, 8471.141	3493	1158, 5203	2000	5968	904, 4875	866	1300.111
prep, v Qal inf con	pn	*n ms*, pn	cj, pers pron	adv, ps 3ms	prep, pn	rel part	v Qal pf 3ms
כְּשְׁמֹעַ	יָרָבְעָם	בֶּן־נְבָט	וְהוּא	עוֹדֶנּוּ	בְמִצְרַיִם	אֲשֶׁר	בָּרַח
kishmōa'	yārov'ām	ben-nevāṭ	wehû'	'ôdhennû	vemitsrayim	'ăsher	bārach
when hearing	Jeroboam	the son of Nebat	for he	still he	in Egypt	where	he had fled

4623, 6686	4567	8406	3553.121	3493	904, 4875	**3.** 8365.126
prep, *n mp*	art, n ms	pn	cj, v Qal impf 3ms	pn	prep, pn	cj, v Qal impf 3mp
מִפְּנֵי	הַמֶּלֶךְ	שְׁלֹמֹה	וַיֵּשֶׁב	יָרָבְעָם	בְּמִצְרָיִם	וַיִּשְׁלְחוּ
mippenê	hammelekh	shelōmōh	wayyēshev	yārov'ām	bemitsrāyim	wayyishlechû
from before	the king	Solomon	and he dwelled	Jeroboam	in Egypt	and they sent out

7410.126, 3937	971.121	3493	3725, 7235	3547
cj, v Qal impf 3mp, prep, ps 3ms	cj, v Qal impf 3ms	pn	cj, *adj*, *n ms*	pn
וַיִּקְרְאוּ־לוֹ	וַיָּבֹאו	יָרָבְעָם	וְכָל־קְהַל	יִשְׂרָאֵל
wayyiqŏr'û-lô	wayyāvō'û	yārov'ām	wekhol-qŏhal	yisrā'ēl
and they called to him	and he came	Jeroboam	and all the assembly of	Israel

1744.326	420, 7628	3937, 569.141	**4.** 1	7481.511	881, 6144
cj, v Piel impf 3mp	prep, pn	prep, v Qal inf con	n ms, ps 2ms	v Hiphil pf 3ms	do, n ms, ps 1cp
וַיְדַבְּרוּ	אֶל־רְחַבְעָם	לֵאמֹר	אָבִיךָ	הִקְשָׁה	אֶת־עֻלֵּנוּ
waydhabberû	'el-rechav'ām	lē'mōr	'āvîkhā	hiqōshāh	'eth-'ullēnû
and they spoke	to Rehoboam	saying	your father	he made difficult	our yoke

887	6498	7327.531	4623, 5865	1	7482	4623, 6144
cj, pers pron	adv	v Hiphil impv 2ms	prep, *n fs*	n ms, ps 2ms	art, adj	cj, prep, n ms, ps 3ms
וְאַתָּה	עַתָּה	הָקֵל	מֵעֲבֹדַת	אָבִיךָ	הַקָּשָׁה	וּמֵעֻלּוֹ
we'attāh	'attāh	hāqēl	mē'ăvōdhath	'āvîkhā	haqqāshāh	ûmē'ullô
but you	now	lighten	from the work of	your father	the hard	and from his yoke

3633	866, 5598.111	6142	5856.120	**5.** 569.121	420
art, adj	rel part, v Qal pf 3ms	prep, ps 1cp	cj, v Qal juss 1cp, ps 2ms	cj, v Qal impf 3ms	prep, ps 3mp
הַכָּבֵד	אֲשֶׁר־נָתַן	עָלֵינוּ	וְנַעַבְדֶךָּ	וַיֹּאמֶר	אֲלֵיהֶם
hakkāvēdh	'ăsher-nāthan	'ālênû	wena'avdhekkā	wayyō'mer	'ălêhem
the heavy	which he put	on us	that we may serve you	and he said	to them

2050.133	5968	8421	3219	8178.133	420	2050.126	6194
v Qal impv 2mp	adv	num	n mp	cj, v Qal impv 2mp	prep, ps 1cs	cj, v Qal impf 3mp	art, n ms
לְכוּ	עֹד	שְׁלֹשָׁה	יָמִים	וְשׁוּבוּ	אֵלָי	וַיֵּלְכוּ	הָעָם
lekhû	'ōdh	shelōshāh	yāmîm	weshûvû	'ēlāy	wayyēlekhû	hā'ām
go	while	three	days	then return	to me	and they went	the people

6. 3398.221	4567	7628	881, 2292	866, 2030.116	6198.152
cj, v Niphal impf 3ms	art, n ms	pn	do, art, n mp	rel pron, v Qal pf 3cp	v Qal act ptc mp
וַיִּוָּעַץ	הַמֶּלֶךְ	רְחַבְעָם	אֶת־הַזְּקֵנִים	אֲשֶׁר־הָיוּ	עֹמְדִים
wayyiwwā'ats	hammelekh	rechav'ām	'eth-hazzeqēnîm	'ăsher-hāyû	'ōmedhîm
and he counseled with	the king	Rehoboam	the elders	who they were	standing

881, 6686	8406	1	904, 2030.141	2508	3937, 569.141	351
do, *n mp*	pn	n ms, ps 3ms	prep, v Qal inf con, ps 3ms	adj	prep, v Qal inf con	intrg
אֶת־פְּנֵי	שְׁלֹמֹה	אָבִיו	בִּהְיֹתוֹ	חַי	לֵאמֹר	אֵיךְ
'eth-penê	shelōmōh	'āvîw	bihyōthô	chay	lē'mōr	'êkh
the presence of	Solomon	his father	when his being	living	saying	how

2. And it came to pass, when Jeroboam the son of Nebat, who was yet in Egypt, heard of it, (for he was fled from the presence of king Solomon, and Jeroboam dwelt in Egypt;): ... Jerabam-ben-Nebat heard of it while still in Mitzer, *Fenton* ... he returned to his native city of Zeredah in the highlands of Ephraim, *Goodspeed* ... a fugitive from the face of king Solomon, *Douay*.

3. That they sent and called him. And Jeroboam and all the congregation of Israel came, and spake unto Rehoboam, saying: ... the people sent messengers to invite him back, *Beck*.

4. Thy father made our yoke grievous: ... treated us harshly and placed heavy burdens on us, *Good News*.

now therefore make thou the grievous service of thy father, and his heavy yoke which he put upon us, lighter, and we will serve thee: ... lighten the heavy rule he imposed upon us and his crushing service, *Moffatt* ... lighten the unbearable service, *Berkeley* ... make the hard service and the heavy yoke which he put on us lighter, *KJVII* ... don't make us work as hard as he did, *NCV*.

5. And he said unto them, Depart yet for three days, then come again to me. And the people departed: ... Give me two days, *Knox* ... Go till the third day, *Douay* ... Give me three days to think this over, *NLT*.

6. And king Rehoboam consulted with the old men: ... the advisers, *Fenton* ... took counsel with the old men, *MAST* ... asked the older leaders, *NCV*.

that stood before Solomon his father while he yet lived: ... stood before Solomon his father while he was yet alive, *RSV* ... that had been courtiers in the life-time of his father, *Knox*.

and said, How do ye advise that I may answer this people?: ... to reply to this people?, *Goodspeed*.

Rehoboam, succeeded in Jerusalem without opposition, 937 B.C. But the northern tribes were in no mood to regard as final the prerogative acceptance of the son of Solomon by the rival tribe of Judah. David had won them by his vivid personality; Solomon had dazzled them by his royal magnificence. It did not follow that they were blindly to accept a king who emerged for the first time from the shadow of the harem, and was the son of an Ammonitess, who worshiped Chemosh. Instead of going to Rehoboam at Jerusalem as the tribes had gone to David at Hebron, they summoned an assembly at their ancient city of Shechem, on the site of the modern Nablus, between Mount Ebal and Gerizim. In this fortress-sanctuary they determined, as "men of Israel," to bring their grievances under the notice of the new sovereign before they formally ratified his succession. According to one view they summoned Jeroboam, who had already returned to Zeredah, to be their spokesman. When the assembly met they told the king that they would accept him if he would lighten the grievous service which his father had put upon them. Rehoboam, taken by surprise, said that they should receive his answer in "three days."

In the interval he consulted the aged counselors of his father. Their answer was an astute insight into human nature. "Give the people a civil answer," they said; "tell them that you are their servant. Content with this they will be scattered to their homes, and you will bind them to your yoke for ever." In an answer so deceptive, but so immoral, the corrupting influence of the Solomonian autocracy is as conspicuous as in that of the malapert youths who made their appeal to the king's conceit. "Who knoweth whether he shall be a wise man or a fool?" asks the preacher in the Book of Ecclesiastes (Ecc. 2:19). Apparently he had done little or nothing to save his son from being the latter.

If Rehoboam had received the least political training, or had been possessed of the smallest common sense, he would have been able to read the signs of the times sufficiently well to know that everything might be lost by blustering arrogance, and everything gained by temporizing plausibility. Had Rehoboam been a man like David, or even like Saul in his better day, he might have grappled to himself the affections of his people as with hooks of steel by seizing the opportunity of abating their burdens, and offering them a sincere assurance that he would study their peace and welfare above all. Had he been a man of ordinary intelligence, he would have seen that the present was not the moment to exacerbate a discontent which was already dangerous. But the counsel of the elders was utterly distasteful to a man who, after long insignificance, had just begun to feel the vertigo of autocracy. His sense of his right was strong in exact proportion to his own worthlessness. He turned to the young men who had grown up with him.

12:6–11. "Threaten this insolent peasantry," they said, "with your royal severity. Tell them that you do not intend to give up your sacred right to enforced labor, such as your brother or Egypt has

894	3398.256	3937, 8178.541	881, 6194, 2172	1745	7.	1744.321
pers pron	v Niphal ptc mp	prep, v Hiphil inf con	do, art, n ms, art, dem pron	n ms		cj, v Piel impf 3ms
אַתֶּם	נוֹעָצִים	לְהָשִׁיב	אֶת־הָעָם־הַזֶּה	דָּבָר		וַיְדַבֵּר
’attem	nô‘ātsîm	lehāshîv	’eth-hā‘ām-hazzeh	dāvār		waydhabbēr
you	advising	to bring back to	this people	a word		and he spoke

420	3937, 569.141	524, 3219	2030.123, 5860	3937, 6194	2172
prep, ps 3ms	prep, v Qal inf con	cj, art, n ms	v Qal impf 2ms, n ms	prep, art, n ms	art, dem pron
אֵלָיו	לֵאמֹר	אִם־הַיּוֹם	תִּהְיֶה־עֶבֶד	לָעָם	הַזֶּה
’ēlâv	lē’mōr	’im-hayyôm	tihyeh-‘evedh	lā‘ām	hazzeh
to him	saying	if today	you will be a servant	to the people	the this

5856.113	6257.113	1744.313	420	1745	3005
cj, v Qal pf 2ms, ps 3mp	cj, v Qal pf 2ms, ps 3mp	cj, v Piel pf 2ms	prep, ps 3mp	n mp	adj
וַעֲבַדְתָּם	וַעֲנִיתָם	וְדִבַּרְתָּ	אֲלֵיהֶם	דְּבָרִים	טוֹבִים
wa‘ăvadhtām	wa‘ănîthām	wedhibbartā	’ălêhem	devārîm	ṯôvîm
and you serve them	and you answer them	and you speak	to them	words	good

2030.116	3937	5860	3725, 3219	8.	6013.121	881, 6332
cj, v Qal pf 3cp	prep, ps 2ms	n mp	*adj*, art, n mp		cj, v Qal impf 3ms	do, *n fs*
וְהָיוּ	לְךָ	עֲבָדִים	כָּל־הַיָּמִים		וַיַּעֲזֹב	אֶת־עֲצַת
wehāyû	lekhā	‘ăvādhîm	kol-hayyāmîm		wayya‘ăzōv	’eth-‘ătsath
then they will be	to you	servants	all the days		but he abandoned	the advice of

2292	866	3398.116	3398.221	881, 3315	866
art, n mp	rel pron	v Qal pf 3cp, ps 3ms	cj, v Niphal impf 3ms	do, art, n mp	rel pron
הַזְּקֵנִים	אֲשֶׁר	יְעָצֻהוּ	וַיִּוָּעַץ	אֶת־הַיְלָדִים	אֲשֶׁר
hazzeqēnîm	’ăsher	ye‘ātsuhû	wayyiwwā‘ats	’eth-haylādhîm	’ăsher
the elders	who	they counseled with him	and he counseled with	the young men	who

1461.116	882	866	6198.152	3937, 6686	9.	569.121
v Qal pf 3cp	prep, ps 3ms	rel pron	art, v Qal act ptc mp	prep, n mp, ps 3ms		cj, v Qal impf 3ms
גָּדְלוּ	אִתּוֹ	אֲשֶׁר	הָעֹמְדִים	לְפָנָיו		וַיֹּאמֶר
gādhelû	’ittô	’ăsher	hā‘ōmedhîm	lephānâv		wayyō’mer
they had grown up	with him	who	those standing	before him		and he said

420	4242	894	3398.256	8178.520	1745	881, 6194	2172
prep, ps 3mp	intrg	pers pron	v Niphal ptc mp	cj, v Hiphil impf 1cp	n ms	do, art, n ms	art, dem pron
אֲלֵיהֶם	מָה	אַתֶּם	נוֹעָצִים	וְנָשִׁיב	דָּבָר	אֶת־הָעָם	הַזֶּה
’ălêhem	māh	’attem	nô‘ātsîm	wenāshîv	dāvār	’eth-hā‘ām	hazzeh
to them	what	you	advising	and we will bring back to	a word	the people	the this

866	1744.316	420	3937, 569.141	7327.531	4623, 6144	866, 5598.111
rel pron	v Piel pf 3cp	prep, ps 1cs	prep, v Qal inf con	v Hiphil impv 2ms	prep, art, n ms	rel part, v Qal pf 3ms
אֲשֶׁר	דִּבְּרוּ	אֵלַי	לֵאמֹר	הָקֵל	מִן־הָעֹל	אֲשֶׁר־נָתַן
’ăsher	dibberû	’ēlay	lē’mōr	hāqēl	min-hā‘ōl	’ăsher-nāthan
who	they spoke	to me	saying	lighten	from the yoke	which he had put

1	6142	10.	1744.326	420	3315	866	1461.116
n ms, ps 2ms	prep, ps 1cp		cj, v Piel impf 3mp	prep, ps 3ms	art, n mp	rel pron	v Qal pf 3cp
אָבִיךָ	עָלֵינוּ		וַיְדַבְּרוּ	אֵלָיו	הַיְלָדִים	אֲשֶׁר	גָּדְלוּ
’āvîkhā	‘ālênû		waydhabberû	’ēlâv	haylādhîm	’ăsher	gādhelû
your father	on us		and they spoke	to him	the young men	who	they had grown up

882	3937, 569.141	3662, 569.123	3937, 6194	2172	866	1744.316
prep, ps 3ms	prep, v Qal inf con	adv, v Qal impf 2ms	prep, art, n ms	art, dem pron	rel pron	v Piel pf 3cp
אִתּוֹ	לֵאמֹר	כֹּה־תֹאמַר	לָעָם	הַזֶּה	אֲשֶׁר	דִּבְּרוּ
’ittô	lē’mōr	kōh-thō’mar	lā‘ām	hazzeh	’ăsher	dibberû
with him	saying	thus you will speak	to the people	the this	who	they spoke

7. And they spake unto him, saying, If thou wilt be a servant unto this people this day: ... you are willing to serve this people, *REB* ... yield to this people today, and condescend to them, *Douay*.

and wilt serve them, and answer them, and speak good words to them, then they will be thy servants for ever: ... speak good words to them, *Darby* ... grant them their petition, *NASB* ... they will always serve you loyally, *Good News* ... they will always be your loyal subjects, *NLT*.

8. But he forsook the counsel of the old men, which they had given him: ... declined the counsel of the elders, *Rotherham* ... disregarded the advice that the older men gave, *NRSV* ... the advice of the old men, *Fenton*.

and consulted with the young men that were grown up with him, and which stood before him: ... took counsel with the young men, *RSV* ... the young men that were nourished up with him, *Tyndale* ... who had grown up with him and who were his companions, *Goodspeed* ... went to the young men of his generation, *BB*.

9. And he said unto them, What counsel give ye that we may answer this people, who have spoken to me, saying, Make the yoke which thy father did put upon us lighter?: ... which your father imposed on us!, *JB* ... Don't make us work as hard as your father, *NCV*.

10. And the young men that were grown up with him spake unto him, saying, Thus shalt thou speak unto this people that spake unto thee, saying, Thy father made our yoke heavy, but make thou it lighter unto us: ... say to this people who petitioned you, *Berkeley* ... This is what you should tell those complainers, *NLT*.

thus shalt thou say unto them, My little finger shall be thicker than my father's loins: ... than in all the breadth of thy father's back, *Knox* ... than my father's body, *BB* ... than my father's thighs, *Moffatt*.

---

always enjoyed. Tell them that your little finger shall be thicker than your father's loins, and that instead of his whips you will chastise them with leaded thongs. That is the way to show yourself every inch a king."

The insensate advice of these youths proved itself attractive to the empty and infatuated prince. He accepted it in the dementation which is a presage of ruin; for, as the pious historian says, "the cause was from the LORD."

The announcement of this incredibly foolish reply woke in the men of Israel an answering shout of rebellion. In the rhythmic war-cry of Sheba, the son of Bichri, which had become proverbial (2 Sam. 20:1), they cried—

"What portion have we in David? Neither have we inheritance in the son of Jesse. To your tents, O Israel: now see to thine own house, David" (2 Ki. 16). Unable to appease the wild tumult, Rehoboam again showed his want of sense by sending an officer to the people whose position and personality were most sure to be offensive to them. He sent "Adoram, who was over the tribute"—the man who stood, before the Ephraimites especially, as the representative of every thing in monarchical government which was to them most entirely odious. Josephus says that he hoped to mollify the indignant people. But it was too late. They stoned the aged Al-ham-Mas with stones that he died; and when the foolish king witnessed or heard of the fate of a man who had grown gray as the chief agent of despotism he felt that it was high time to look after his own safety. Apparently, he had come with no other escort than that of the men of Judah who formed a part of the national militia. Of Cherethites, Pelethites and Gittites we hear no more. The princeling of a despoiled and humiliated kingdom was perhaps in no condition to provide the pay of these foreign mercenaries. The king found that the name of David was no longer potent, and that royalty had lost its awful glamor. He made an effort to reach his chariot, and, barely succeeding, fled with headlong speed to Jerusalem. From that day for ever the unity of Israel was broken, and "the twelve tribes" became a name for two mutually antagonistic powers. The men of Israel at once chose Jeroboam for their king, and an event was accomplished which had its effect on the history of all succeeding times. The only Israelites over whom the house of David continued to rule were those who, like the scattered remnant of Simeon, dwelt in the cities of Judah (1 Ki. 12:17).

Thus David's grandson found that his kingdom over a people had shrunk to the headship of a tribe, with a sort of nominal suzerainty over Edom and part of Philistia. He was reduced to the comparative insignificance of David's own position during his first seven years, when he was only king in Hebron. This disruption was the beginning of endless material disasters to both kingdoms; but it was the necessary condition of high spiritual blessings, for "it was of the LORD."

Politically it is easy to see that one cause of the revolt lay in the too great rapidity in which

420	3937, 569.141	1	3632.511	881, 6144	887	7327.531
prep, ps 2ms	prep, v Qal inf con	n ms, ps 2ms	v Hiphil pf 3ms	do, n ms, ps 1cp	cj, pers pron	v Hiphil impv 2ms
אֵלֶיךָ	לֵאמֹר	אָבִיךָ	הִכְבִּיד	אֶת־עֻלֵּנוּ	וְאַתָּה	הָקֵל
’ēlêkhā	lē’mōr	’āvîkhā	hikhbîdh	’eth-‘ullēnû	we’attāh	hāqēl
to you	saying	your father	he made heavy	our yoke	but you	lighten

4623, 6142	3662	1744.323	420	7276	5875.111	4623, 5158
prep, prep, ps 1cp	adv	v Piel impf 2ms	prep, ps 3mp	n ms, ps 1cs	v Qal pf 3ms	prep, *n mp*
מֵעָלֵינוּ	כֹּה	תְּדַבֵּר	אֲלֵיהֶם	קָטָנִּי	עָבָה	מִמָּתְנֵי
mē‘ālênû	kōh	tedhabbēr	’ălêhem	qāṭānî	‘āvāh	mimmāthenê
from on us	thus	you will speak	to them	my smallest part	it is thicker	than the loins of

1	**11.**	6498	1	6227.511	6142	6144	3633	603
n ms, ps 1cs		cj, adv	n ms, ps 1cs	v Hiphil pf 3ms	prep, ps 2mp	n ms	adj	cj, pers pron
אָבִי		וְעַתָּה	אָבִי	הֶעֱמִיס	עֲלֵיכֶם	עֹל	כָּבֵד	וַאֲנִי
’āvî		we‘attāh	’āvî	he‘ĕmîs	‘ălêkhem	‘ōl	kāvēdh	wa’ănî
my father		and now	my father	he caused to load	on you	a yoke	heavy	but I

3362.525	6142, 6144	1	3364.311	881	904, 8199	603
v Hiphil impf 1cs	prep, n ms, ps 2mp	n ms, ps 1cs	v Piel pf 3ms	do, ps 2mp	prep, art, n mp	cj, pers pron
אוֹסִיף	עַל־עֻלְּכֶם	אָבִי	יִסַּר	אֶתְכֶם	בַּשּׁוֹטִים	וַאֲנִי
’ôsîph	‘al-‘ullekhem	’āvî	yissar	’ethkhem	bashshôṭîm	wa’ănî
I will add	onto your yoke	my father	he rebuked	you	with the whips	but I

3364.325	881	904, 6375	**12.**	971.121	3493	3725, 6194
v Piel impf 1cs	do, ps 2mp	prep, art, n mp		cj, v Qal impf 3ms	pn	cj, *adj*, art, n ms
אֲיַסֵּר	אֶתְכֶם	בָּעַקְרַבִּים		וַיָּבוֹ	יָרָבְעָם	וְכָל־הָעָם
’ăyassēr	’ethkhem	bā‘aqōrabbîm		wayyāvô	yārov‘ām	wekhol-hā‘ām
I will rebuke	you	with the scorpions		and he entered	Jeroboam	and all the people

420, 7628	904, 3219	8389	3626, 866	1744.311	4567	3937, 569.141
prep, pn	prep, art, n ms	art, num	prep, rel part	v Piel pf 3ms	art, n ms	prep, v Qal inf con
אֶל־רְחַבְעָם	בַּיּוֹם	הַשְּׁלִישִׁי	כַּאֲשֶׁר	דִּבֶּר	הַמֶּלֶךְ	לֵאמֹר
’el-rechav‘ām	bayyôm	hashshelîshî	ka’ăsher	dibber	hammelekh	lē’mōr
to Rehoboam	on the day	the third	just as	he had spoken	the king	saying

8178.133	420	904, 3219	8389	**13.**	6257.121	4567	881, 6194
v Qal impv 2mp	prep, ps 1cs	prep, art, n ms	art, num		cj, v Qal impf 3ms	art, n ms	do, art, n ms
שׁוּבוּ	אֵלָי	בַּיּוֹם	הַשְּׁלִישִׁי		וַיַּעַן	הַמֶּלֶךְ	אֶת־הָעָם
shûvû	’ēlay	bayyôm	hashshelîshî		wayya‘an	hammelekh	’eth-hā‘ām
return	to me	on the day	the third		and he answered	the king	the people

7482	6013.121	881, 6332	2292	866	3398.116
adv	cj, v Qal impf 3ms	do, *n fs*	art, n mp	rel pron	v Qal pf 3cp, ps 3ms
קָשָׁה	וַיַּעֲזֹב	אֶת־עֲצַת	הַזְּקֵנִים	אֲשֶׁר	יְעָצֻהוּ
qāshāh	wayya‘ăzōv	’eth-‘ătsath	hazzeqēnîm	’ăsher	ye‘ātsuhû
severely	for he abandoned	the advice of	the elders	who	they counseled with him

14.	1744.321	420	3626, 6332	3315	3937, 569.141
	cj, v Piel impf 3ms	prep, ps 3mp	prep, *n fs*	art, n mp	prep, v Qal inf con
	וַיְדַבֵּר	אֲלֵיהֶם	כַּעֲצַת	הַיְלָדִים	לֵאמֹר
	waydhabbēr	’ălêhem	ka‘ătsath	haylādhîm	lē’mōr
	and he spoke	to them	according to the advice of	the young men	saying

1	3632.511	881, 6144	603	636.515	6142, 6144	1
n ms, ps 1cs	v Hiphil pf 3ms	do, n ms, ps 2mp	cj, pers pron	v Hiphil pf 1cs	prep, n ms, ps 2mp	n ms, ps 1cs
אָבִי	הִכְבִּיד	אֶת־עֻלְּכֶם	וַאֲנִי	אֹסִיף	עַל־עֻלְּכֶם	אָבִי
’āvî	hikhbîdh	’eth-‘ullekhem	wa’ănî	’ōsîph	‘al-‘ullekhem	’āvî
my father	he made heavy	your yoke	but I	I will add	onto your yoke	my father

3364.311	881	904, 8199	603	3364.325	881	904, 6375
v Piel pf 3ms	do, ps 2mp	prep, art, n mp	cj, pers pron	v Piel impf 1cs	do, ps 2mp	prep, art, n mp
יִסַּר	אֶתְכֶם	בַּשּׁוֹטִים	וַאֲנִי	אֲיַסֵּר	אֶתְכֶם	בָּעַקְרַבִּים
yissar	'ethkhem	bashshôṯîm	wa'ănî	'ăyassēr	'ethkhem	bā'aqōrabbîm
he rebuked	you	with the whips	but I	I will rebuke	you	with the scorpions

15.

3940, 8471.111	4567	420, 6194	3706, 2030.112	5622	4623, 6196	3176
cj, neg part, v Qal pf 3ms	art, n ms	prep, art, n ms	cj, v Qal pf 3fs	n fs	prep, prep	pn
וְלֹא־שָׁמַע	הַמֶּלֶךְ	אֶל־הָעָם	כִּי־הָיְתָה	סִבָּה	מֵעִם	יְהוָה
welō'-shāma'	hammelekh	'el-hā'ām	kî-hāyethāh	sibbāh	mē'im	yehwāh
so he did not listen	the king	to the people	because it was	a changing	from with	Yahweh

3937, 4775	7251.541	881, 1745	866	1744.311	3176	904, 3135	282
prep, prep	v Hiphil inf con	do, n ms, ps 3ms	rel part	v Piel pf 3ms	pn	prep, *n fs*	pn
לְמַעַן	הָקִים	אֶת־דְּבָרוֹ	אֲשֶׁר	דִּבֶּר	יְהוָה	בְּיַד	אֲחִיָּה
lema'an	hāqîm	'eth-devārô	'ăsher	dibber	yehwāh	beyadh	'ăchîyāh
so that	establishing	his word	which	He had spoken	Yahweh	by the hand of	Ahijah

11. And now whereas my father did lade you with a heavy yoke, I will add to your yoke: ... placed heavy burdens on you, *Good News* ... If my father's rule pressed hard on you, *Moffatt* ... He forced you to work hard, but I will make you work even harder, *NCV*.

my father hath chastised you with whips, but I will chastise you with scorpions: ... whipped you, but I shall flay you, *REB* ... will correct you with scourges, *Geneva* ... I shall apply a spiked lash!, *JB*.

12. So Jeroboam and all the people came to Rehoboam the third day, as the king had appointed, saying, Come to me again the third day: ... returned to hear Rehoboam's decision, *NLT*.

13. And the king answered the people roughly, and forsook the old men's counsel that they gave him: ... answered the people roughly, and forsook the advice, *Darby* ... refused the counsels of the old men, *Fenton*.

14. And spake to them after the counsel of the young men, saying, My father made your yoke heavy, and I will add to your yoke: my father also chastised you with whips, but I will chastise you with scorpions: ... I'll flog you with bull-whips!, *Good News* ... but I will give it with snakes, *BB* ... but I will use the lash, *NEB*.

15. Wherefore the king hearkened not unto the people; for the cause was from the LORD: ... it was a turn of affairs brought about by the LORD, *RSV* ... it was a thing brought about by the LORD, *Goodspeed* ... the Lord had left him to his own devices, *Knox*.

that he might perform his saying, which the LORD spake by Ahijah the Shilonite unto Jeroboam the son of Nebat: ... that He might establish His word, *MAST* ... said by Ahiah the Silonite unto Jeroboam, *Tyndale*.

kings, who as it was assumed, were to be elective, or at least to depend on the willing obedience of the people, had transformed themselves into hereditary despots. Judah might still accept the sway of a king of her own tribe; but the powerful and jealous Ephraimites, at the head of the northern confederation, refused to regard themselves as the destined footstool for a single family. As in the case of Saul and of David, they determined once more to accept no king who did not owe his sovereignty to their own free choice.

12:12–15. "It was of the LORD" (v. 15). It is no small proof of the insight and courageous faithfulness of the historian that he accepts without question the verdict of ancient prophecy that the disruption was God's doing; for everything which happened in the four subsequent centuries, alike in Judah and in Israel, seemed to belie this pious conviction. We, in the light of later history, are now able to see that the disseverance of Israel's unity worked out results of eternal advantage to mankind; but in the sixth century before Christ, no event could have seemed to be so absolutely disastrous. It must have worn the aspect of an extinction of the glory of the house of Jacob. It involved the obliteration of the great majority of the descendants of the patriarchs, and the reduction of the rest to national insignificance and apparently hopeless servitude. Throughout those centuries of troubled history, in the struggle for existence which was the lot of both kingdoms alike, it was difficult to say whether their antagonism or their friendship, their

8296 art, pn הַשִּׁילֹנִי hashshîlōnî the Shilonite	420, 3493 prep, pn אֶל־יָרָבְעָם 'el-yārov'ām unto Jeroboam	1158, 5203 *n ms*, pn בֶּן־נְבָט ben-nevāṭ the son of Nebat	**16.**	7495.121 cj, v Qal impf 3ms וַיַּרְא wayyare' and they saw	3725, 3547 *adj*, pn כָּל־יִשְׂרָאֵל kāl-yisrā'ēl all Israel	3706 cj כִּי kî that

3940, 8471.111 neg part, v Qal pf 3ms לֹא־שָׁמַע lō'-shāma' he did not listen	4567 art, n ms הַמֶּלֶךְ hammelekh the king	420 prep, ps 3mp אֲלֵיהֶם 'ălêhem to them	8178.526 cj, v Hiphil impf 3mp וַיָּשִׁבוּ wayyāshivû and they brought back to	6194 art, n ms הָעָם hā'ām the people	881, 4567 do, art, n ms אֶת־הַמֶּלֶךְ 'eth-hammelekh the king

1745 n ms דָּבָר dāvār a word	3937, 569.141 prep, v Qal inf con לֵאמֹר lē'mōr saying	4242, 3937 intrg, prep, ps 1cp מַה־לָּנוּ mah-lānû what to us	2610 n ms חֵלֶק chēleq a portion	904, 1784 prep, pn בְּדָוִד bedhāwidh in David	3940, 5338 cj, neg part, n fs וְלֹא־נַחֲלָה welō'-nachlāh and not an inheritance

904, 1158, 3571 prep, *n ms*, pn בְּבֶן־יִשַׁי beven-yishay with the son of Jesse	3937, 164 prep, n mp, ps 2ms לְאֹהָלֶיךָ le'ōhālêkhā to your tents	3547 pn יִשְׂרָאֵל yisrā'ēl O Israel	6498 adv עַתָּה 'attāh now	7495.131 v Qal impv 2ms רְאֵה re'ēh look at	1041 n ms, ps 2ms בֵּיתְךָ vêthekhā your household	1784 pn דָּוִד dāwidh O David

2050.121 cj, v Qal impf 3ms וַיֵּלֶךְ wayyēlekh and they went	3547 pn יִשְׂרָאֵל yisrā'ēl Israel	3937, 164 prep, n mp, ps 3ms לְאֹהָלָיו le'ōhālâv to their tents	**17.**	1158 cj, *n mp* וּבְנֵי ûvenê and the children of	3547 pn יִשְׂרָאֵל yisrā'ēl Israel	3553.152 art, v Qal act ptc mp הַיֹּשְׁבִים hayyshevîm those dwelling

904, 6111 prep, *n fp* בְּעָרֵי be'ārê in the cities of	3171 pn יְהוּדָה yehûdhāh Judah	4566.121 cj, v Qal impf 3ms וַיִּמְלֹךְ wayyimlōkh and he reigned	6142 prep, ps 3mp עֲלֵיהֶם 'ălêhem over them	7628 pn רְחַבְעָם rechav'ām Rehoboam	**18.**	8365.121 cj, v Qal impf 3ms וַיִּשְׁלַח wayyishlach and he sent out	4567 art, n ms הַמֶּלֶךְ hammelekh the king

7628 pn רְחַבְעָם rechav'ām Rehoboam	881, 148 do, pn אֶת־אֲדֹרָם 'eth-'ădhōrām Adoram	866 rel pron אֲשֶׁר 'ăsher who	6142, 4671 prep, art, n ms עַל־הַמַּס 'al-hammas over the forced labor	7563.126 cj, v Qal impf 3mp וַיִּרְגְּמוּ wayyirgemû and they stoned	3725, 3547 *adj*, pn כָל־יִשְׂרָאֵל khol-yisrā'ēl all Israel	904 prep, ps 3ms בּוֹ bô on him

63 n fs אֶבֶן 'even stones	4322.121 cj, v Qal impf 3ms וַיָּמֹת wayyāmōth and he died	4567 cj, art, n ms וְהַמֶּלֶךְ wehammelekh and the king	7628 pn רְחַבְעָם rechav'ām Rehoboam	563.711 v Hithpael pf 3ms הִתְאַמֵּץ hith'ammēts he took courage	3937, 6148.141 prep, v Qal inf con לַעֲלוֹת la'ălôth to go up	904, 4981 prep, art, n fs בַּמֶּרְכָּבָה bammerkāvāh on the chariot

3937, 5308.141 prep, v Qal inf con לָנוּס lānûs to flee to	3503 pn יְרוּשָׁלָם yerûshālām Jerusalem	**19.**	6839.126 cj, v Qal impf 3mp וַיִּפְשְׁעוּ wayyiphshe'û and they transgressed	3547 pn יִשְׂרָאֵל yisrā'ēl Israel	904, 1041 prep, *n ms* בְּבֵית bevêth against the household of	1784 pn דָּוִד dāwidh David

5912 adv עַד 'adh until	3219 art, n ms הַיּוֹם hayyôm the day	2172 art, dem pron הַזֶּה hazzeh the this	**20.**	2030.121 cj, v Qal impf 3ms וַיְהִי wayhî and it was	3626, 8471.141 prep, v Qal inf con כִּשְׁמֹעַ kishmōa' when hearing	3725, 3547 *adj*, pn כָּל־יִשְׂרָאֵל kol-yisrā'ēl all Israel	3706, 8178.111 cj, v Qal pf 3ms כִּי־שָׁב kî-shāv that he had returned

16. So when all Israel saw that the king hearkened not unto them, the people answered the king, saying: ... realized that the king had rejected their request, they shouted, *NLT* ... would give no attention to them, the people in answer said, *BB*.

What portion have we in David? neither have we inheritance in the son of Jesse: ... Or what inheritance in the son of Isai?, *Douay* ... We have no heritage in the son of Jesse, *NAB*.

to your tents, O Israel: now see to thine own house, David. So Israel departed unto their tents: ... Go Home, Israel! Now look after your own family, David, *Beck* ... Men of Israel, let's go home! Let Rehoboam look out for himself!, *Good News* ... To your homes O Israel! Now see to thine own house O David! And Israel departed to their homes, *Rotherham*.

17. But as for the children of Israel which dwelt in the cities of Judah, Rehoboam reigned over them: ... But Rehoboam reigned over the children of Israel who dwelt in the cities of Judah, *NKJV* ... Rehoboam continued to be king over the Israelites who lived in the cities of Judah, *Berkeley* ... none but the Israelites living in the cities of Juda would acknowledge Roboam as king, *Knox*.

18. Then king Rehoboam sent Adoram, who was over the tribute: ... Then King Rehoboam sent out Adoram, the commander of the forced levies, *NEB* ... Then king Rehoboam sent Adoram, who was over the men subject to taskwork, *ASV*.

and all Israel stoned him with stones, that he died: ... but the Parliament of Israel rose against him and stoned him to death, *Fenton*.

Therefore king Rehoboam made speed to get him up to his chariot, to flee to Jerusalem: ... made haste to mount his chariot, *NASB* ... ran to go and get into, *KJVII*.

19. So Israel rebelled against the house of David unto this day: ... Since then, Israel has been against the family, *NCV* ... against the dynasty of David, as it still does, *Moffatt* ... transgresseth against, *Young* ... departed from, *Tyndale*.

20. And it came to pass, when all Israel heard that Jeroboam was come again, that they sent and called him unto the congregation, and made him king over all Israel:

there was none that followed the house of David, but the tribe of Judah only: ... no one who followed the house of David, except the tribe of Judah alone, *NRSV* ... nobody outside the tribe of Judah who followed David's dynasty, *Beck* ... Only the tribe of Judah remained loyal to David's descendants, *Good News*.

---

open wars or their matrimonial alliances, were productive of the greater ruin. Each section of the nation fatally hampered and counterpoised the other with a perpetual rivalry and menace. Ephraim envied Judah, and Judah vexed Ephraim. In extreme cases the south was ready to purchase the intervention of Syria, or even of Assyria, to check and overwhelm its northern rival, while the north could raise up Egypt or Edom to harass the Southern Kingdom with intolerable raids.

To us the Southern Kingdom, the kingdom of Judah, seems the more important and the more interesting division of the people. It became the heir of all the promises, the nurse of the messianic hope, the mother of the four greater prophets, the continuer of all the subsequent history after the glory of Israel had been stamped out by Assyria forever.

The Northern Kingdom was unhampered by the bad example and erroneous development of the preceding royalty. Jeroboam had not stained his career with crimes like David; nor had he sunk, as Solomon had done, into polygamy and idolatry. It seemed unlikely that he, with so fatal an example before his eyes, could be tempted into oppressive tyranny, futile commerce or luxurious ostentation. He could found a new dynasty, free from the trammels of a bad commencement, and as fully built on divine command as that of the household of Jesse.

Nor was it a small advantage that the new kingdom had an immense superiority over its southern compeer in richness of soil and beauty of scenery. To it belonged the fertile plain of Jezreel, rolling with harvests of golden grain. Its command of Accho gave it access to the treasures of the shore and of the sea. To it belonged the purple heights of Carmel and the silver Lake of Galilee, with its inexhaustible fish; and the fields of Gennesareth, which were a wonder of the world for their tropical luxuriance. Theirs also were the lilied waters and paper-reeds of Merom, and the soft, green, park-like scenery of Gerizim, and the roses of Sharon, and the cedars of Lebanon, and the vines and fig trees and ancient terebinths of all the land of Ephraim, and the forest glades of Zebulun and Naphtali, and the wild uplands beyond the Jordan—which were all far different from the "awful barrenness" of Judah, with its monotony of rounded hills.

12:16–20. Under these favorable conditions three great advantages were exceptionally developed in the Northern Kingdom. It evidently enjoyed a larger freedom as well as a greater prosperity. The Ten Tribes also developed a more bril-

3493	8365.126	7410.126	881	420, 5920	4566.526
pn	cj, v Qal impf 3mp	cj, v Qal impf 3mp	do, ps 3ms	prep, art, n fs	cj, v Hiphil impf 3mp
יָרָבְעָם	וַיִּשְׁלְחוּ	וַיִּקְרְאוּ	אֹתוֹ	אֶל־הָעֵדָה	וַיַּמְלִיכוּ
yārov'ām	wayyishlechû	wayyiqŏr'û	'ōthô	'el-hā'ēdhāh	wayyamlîkhû
Jeroboam	then they sent out	and they called	him	to the assembly	and they caused to rule

881	6142, 3725, 3547	3940	2030.111	313	1041, 1784	2190
do, ps 3ms	prep, *adj*, pn	neg part	v Qal pf 3ms	prep	*n ms*, pn	prep
אֹתוֹ	עַל־כָּל־יִשְׂרָאֵל	לֹא	הָיָה	אַחֲרֵי	בֵּית־דָּוִד	זוּלָתִי
'ōthô	'al-kol-yisrā'ēl	lō'	hāyāh	'achrê	vêth-dāwidh	zûlāthî
him	over all Israel	not	he was	after	the household of David	except

8101, 3171	3937, 940		971.121	7628	3503	7234.521
n ms, pn	prep, n ms, ps 3ms		cj, v Qal impf 3ms	pn	pn	cj, v Hiphil impf 3ms
שֵׁבֶט־יְהוּדָה	לְבַדּוֹ	**21.**	וַיָּבֹא	רְחַבְעָם	יְרוּשָׁלַם	וַיַּקְהֵל
shēveṭ-yehûdhāh	levaddô		wayyāvō'û	rechav'ām	yerûshālam	wayyaqŏhēl
the tribe of Judah	by themselves		and he entered	Rehoboam	Jerusalem	and he assembled

881, 3725, 1041	3171	881, 8101	1175	4109	8470	512
do, *adj*, *n ms*	pn	cj, do, *n ms*	pn	num	cj, num	num
אֶת־כָּל־בֵּית	יְהוּדָה	וְאֶת־שֵׁבֶט	בִּנְיָמִן	מֵאָה	וּשְׁמֹנִים	אֶלֶף
'eth-kol-bêth	yehûdhāh	we'eth-shēveṭ	binyāmin	mē'āh	ûshemōnîm	'eleph
all the household of	Judah	and the tribe of	Benjamin	one hundred	and eighty	thousands

1013.155	6449.151	4560	3937, 4032.241	6196, 1041	3547
v Qal pass ptc ms	*v Qal act ptc ms*	n fs	prep, v Niphal inf con	prep, *n ms*	pn
בָּחוּר	עֹשֵׂה	מִלְחָמָה	לְהִלָּחֵם	עִם־בֵּית	יִשְׂרָאֵל
bāchûr	'ōsēh	milchāmāh	lehillāchēm	'im-bêth	yisrā'ēl
chosen ones	makers of	war	to fight	against the household of	Israel

3937, 8178.541	881, 4548	3937, 7628	1158, 8406		2030.121
prep, v Hiphil inf con	do, art, n fs	prep, pn	*n ms*, pn		cj, v Qal impf 3ms
לְהָשִׁיב	אֶת־הַמְּלוּכָה	לִרְחַבְעָם	בֶּן־שְׁלֹמֹה	**22.**	וַיְהִי
lehāshîv	'eth-hammelûkhāh	lirchav'ām	ben-shelōmōh		wayhî
to cause to return	the kingdom	to Rehoboam	the son of Solomon		and it was

1745	435	420, 8484	382, 435	3937, 569.141		569.131
n ms	art, n mp	prep, pn	*n ms*, art, n mp	prep, v Qal inf con		v Qal impv 2ms
דְּבַר	הָאֱלֹהִים	אֶל־שְׁמַעְיָה	אִישׁ־הָאֱלֹהִים	לֵאמֹר	**23.**	אֱמֹר
devar	hā'ělōhîm	'el-shema'ăyāh	'îsh-hā'ělōhîm	lē'mōr		'ěmōr
the word of	God	to Shemaiah	the man of God	saying		say

420, 7628	1158, 8406	4567	3171	420, 3725, 1041	3171
prep, pn	*n ms*, pn	*n ms*	pn	cj, prep, *adj*, *n ms*	pn
אֶל־רְחַבְעָם	בֶּן־שְׁלֹמֹה	מֶלֶךְ	יְהוּדָה	וְאֶל־כָּל־בֵּית	יְהוּדָה
'el-rechav'ām	ben-shelōmōh	melekh	yehûdhāh	we'el-kol-bêth	yehûdhāh
to Rehoboam	the son of Solomon	the king of	Judah	and to all the household of	Judah

1175	3615	6194	3937, 569.141		3662	569.111	3176
cj, pn	cj, *n ms*	art, n ms	prep, v Qal inf con		adv	v Qal pf 3ms	pn
וּבִנְיָמִין	וְיֶתֶר	הָעָם	לֵאמֹר	**24.**	כֹּה	אָמַר	יְהוָה
ûvinyāmîn	weyether	hā'ām	lē'mōr		kōh	'āmar	yehwāh
and Benjamin	and the remainder of	the people	saying		thus	He has said	Yahweh

3940, 6148.128	3940, 4032.228	6196, 250	1158, 3547
neg part, v Qal impf 2mp	cj, neg part, v Niphal impf 2mp	prep, n mp, ps 2mp	*n mp*, pn
לֹא־תַעֲלוּ	וְלֹא־תִלָּחֲמוּן	עִם־אֲחֵיכֶם	בְּנֵי־יִשְׂרָאֵל
lō'-tha'ălû	welō'-thillāchămûn	'im-'ăchêkhem	benê-yisrā'ēl
you must not go up	and you must not fight	against your brothers	the children of Israel

21. And when Rehoboam was come to Jerusalem, he assembled all the house of Judah, with the tribe of Benjamin, an hundred and fourscore thousand chosen men: ... he gathered all the house of Juda and the tribe of Benjamin an hundred and four score thousands of chosen men and good warriors, *Tyndale* ... he mobilized the armies of Judah and Benjamin, *NLT*.

which were warriors, to fight against the house of Israel, to bring the kingdom again to Rehoboam the son of Solomon: ... to fight against Israel and recover his kingdom, *REB* ... their cry was that Roboam, Solomon's heir, must be restored to his kingdom, *Knox* ... to bring the kingdom back to Rehoboam, *MAST*.

22. But the word of God came unto Shemaiah the man of God, saying: ... Then came the word of God, *Rotherham* ... the word of God is unto, *Young* ... But this message came from the Eternal, *Moffatt* ... But God spoke his word, *NCV*.

23. Speak unto Rehoboam, the son of Solomon, king of Judah, and unto all the house of Judah and Benjamin, and to the remnant of the people, saying: ... and to the remainder of the people, *Darby*.

24. Thus saith the LORD, Ye shall not go up, nor fight against your brethren the children of Israel: ... Yahweh says this: Do not go and make war on your brothers, the Israelites, *JB* ... Do not attack your own brothers, the people, *Good News* ... your kinsmen, *RSV*.

return every man to his house; for this thing is from me: ... Let each return to his home, for this event has come from Me!, *Fenton* ... Let each one of you go home, for I am causing this affair, *Berkeley* ... this thing is of me, *ASV*.

They hearkened therefore to the word of the LORD, and returned to depart, according to the word of the LORD: ... They listened to the word of the LORD and went back, as the LORD had told them, *REB* ... They accepted this message of the LORD and gave up the expedition accordingly, *NAB* ... They hearkened to the word of the Lord, and returned from their journey, as the Lord commanded them, *Douay* ... So they heeded the word of the LORD and went home again, *NRSV*.

---

liant literature. But the main endowment of the new kingdom consisted in the magnificent development and independence of the prophets.

It was not till after the overthrow of the ten tribes that the glory of prophecy migrated southwards, and Jerusalem produced the mighty triad of Isaiah, Jeremiah and Ezekiel. For the two and a half centuries that the Northern Kingdom lasted, scarcely one prophet is heard of in Judah except the scarcely known Hanani, and Eliezer, the son of Mareshah (2 Chr. 20:37). To the north belongs the great herald-prophet, the mighty Elijah; the softer spirit of the statesman-prophet Elisha; the undaunted Micaiah, son of Imlah; the picturesque Micah; the historic Jonah; the plaintive Hosea; and that bold and burning patriot, a fragment of whose prophecy now forms part of the Book of Zechariah. Amos, indeed, belonged by birth to Tekoa, which was in Judah, but his prophetic activity was confined to Bethel and Jezreel. The schools of the prophets at Ramah, Bethel, Jericho and Gilgal were all in Israel. The passages in the third section of the Book of Zechariah are alone sufficient to show how vast was the influence in the affairs of the nation of the prophets of the north, and how fearless their intervention. Even when they were most fiercely persecuted, they were not afraid to lambast the most powerful kings—Ahab and Jeroboam II in all their pride (Zech. 11:4–17; 13:7ff). Samaria and Galilee were rich in prophetic lives; and they, too, were the destined scene of the life of Him of whom all the prophets prophesied, and from whose inspiration they drew their heavenly fire.

Against these advantages, however, must be set two serious and ultimately fatal drawbacks—germs of disease which lay in the very constitution of the kingdom, and from the first doomed it to death. One of these was the image-worship, and the other was the lack of one predominant and continuous dynasty.

12:21–33. *"For from Israel was it also: the workman made it; therefore it is not God: but, the calf of Samaria shall be broken in pieces" (Hos. 8:6).*

The condemnation of the first king of Israel sounds like a melancholy and menacing refrain through the whole history of the Northern Kingdom. Let us consider the extent and nature of his crime. "Calf-worship," as it was contemptuously called in later days, did not present itself as "calf-worship" to Jeroboam or his people. To them it was only the more definite adoration of Yahweh under the guise of the cherubic emblem which Solomon had himself enshrined in the Temple and Moses himself had sanctioned in the Tabernacle. Jeroboam's chief sin was not that as a king he tolerated, or even set up, a sort of idolatry, but that he induced the whole body of his subjects to share in his evil innovations.

The charge brought against him was threefold. First, he set up the golden calves at Dan and Bethel.

8178.133	382	3937, 1041	3706	4623, 882	2030.211	1745	2172
v Qal impv 2mp	n ms	prep, n ms, ps 3ms	cj	prep, prep, ps 1cs	v Niphal pf 3ms	art, n ms	art, dem pron
שׁוּבוּ	אִישׁ	לְבֵיתוֹ	כִּי	מֵאִתִּי	נִהְיָה	הַדָּבָר	הַזֶּה
shûvû	'îsh	levêthô	kî	mē'ittî	nihyāh	haddāvār	hazzeh
return	each	to his house	because	from with Me	it has become	the word	the this

8471.126	881, 1745	3176	8178.126	3937, 2050.141	3626, 1745
cj, v Qal impf 3mp	do, *n ms*	pn	cj, v Qal impf 3mp	prep, v Qal inf con	prep, *n ms*
וַיִּשְׁמְעוּ	אֶת־דְּבַר	יְהוָה	וַיָּשֻׁבוּ	לָלֶכֶת	כִּדְבַר
wayyishme'û	'eth-devar	yehwāh	wayyāshuvû	lālekheth	kidhvar
and they heard	the word of	Yahweh	so they turned	to go	according to the word of

3176		1161.121	3493	881, 8328	904, 2098	688	3553.121
pn	**25.**	cj, v Qal impf 3ms	pn	do, pn	prep, *n ms*	pn	cj, v Qal impf 3ms
יְהוָה		וַיִּבֶן	יָרָבְעָם	אֶת־שְׁכֶם	בְּהַר	אֶפְרָיִם	וַיֵּשֶׁב
yehwāh		wayyiven	yārov'ām	'eth-shekhem	behar	'ephrayim	wayyēshev
Yahweh		and he built	Jeroboam	Shechem	in the hills of	Ephraim	and he dwelled

904	3428.121	4623, 8427	1161.121	881, 6683		569.121
prep, ps 3fs	cj, v Qal impf 3ms	prep, adv	cj, v Qal impf 3ms	do, pn	**26.**	cj, v Qal impf 3ms
בָּהּ	וַיֵּצֵא	מִשָּׁם	וַיִּבֶן	אֶת־פְּנוּאֵל		וַיֹּאמֶר
bāhh	wayyētsē'	mishshām	wayyiven	'eth-penû'ēl		wayyō'mer
in it	and he went out	from there	and he built	Penuel		and he said

3493	904, 3949	6498	8178.122	4608	3937, 1041	1784
pn	prep, n ms, ps 3ms	adv	v Qal impf 3fs	art, n fs	prep, *n ms*	pn
יָרָבְעָם	בְּלִבּוֹ	עַתָּה	תָּשׁוּב	הַמַּמְלָכָה	לְבֵית	דָּוִד
yārov'ām	belibbô	'attāh	tāshûv	hammamlākhāh	levêth	dāwidh
Jeroboam	within his heart	now	it will return	the kingdom	to the household of	David

	524, 6148.121	6194	2172	3937, 6449.141	2160	904, 1041, 3176
27.	cj, v Qal impf 3ms	art, n ms	art, dem pron	prep, v Qal inf con	n mp	prep, *n ms*, pn
	אִם־יַעֲלֶה	הָעָם	הַזֶּה	לַעֲשׂוֹת	זְבָחִים	בְּבֵית־יְהוָה
	'im-ya'ăleh	hā'ām	hazzeh	la'ăsôth	zevāchîm	bevêth-yehwāh
	if they go up	the people	the this	to make	sacrifices	in the Temple of Yahweh

904, 3503	8178.111	3949	6194	2172	420, 112	420, 7628
prep, pn	cj, v Qal pf 3ms	*n ms*	art, n ms	art, dem pron	prep, n mp, ps 3mp	prep, pn
בִּירוּשָׁלַםִ	וְשָׁב	לֵב	הָעָם	הַזֶּה	אֶל־אֲדֹנֵיהֶם	אֶל־רְחַבְעָם
bîrûshālam	weshāv	lēv	hā'ām	hazzeh	'el-'ădhōnêhem	'el-rechav'ām
in Jerusalem	then it will return	the heart of	the people	the this	to their lord	to Rehoboam

4567	3171	2103.116	8178.116	420, 7628	4567, 3171
n ms	pn	cj, v Qal pf 3cp, ps 1cs	cj, v Qal pf 3cp	prep, pn	*n ms*, pn
מֶלֶךְ	יְהוּדָה	וַהֲרָגֻנִי	וְשָׁבוּ	אֶל־רְחַבְעָם	מֶלֶךְ־יְהוּדָה
melekh	yehûdhāh	wahrāghunî	weshāvû	'el-rechav'ām	melekh-yehûdhāh
the king of	Judah	and they will kill me	and they will return	to Rehoboam	the king of Judah

	3398.221	4567	6449.121	8530	5903	2174	569.121
28.	cj, v Niphal impf 3ms	art, n ms	cj, v Qal impf 3ms	num	*n mp*	n ms	cj, v Qal impf 3ms
	וַיִּוָּעַץ	הַמֶּלֶךְ	וַיַּעַשׂ	שְׁנֵי	עֶגְלֵי	זָהָב	וַיֹּאמֶר
	wayyiwwā'ats	hammelekh	wayya'as	shenê	'eghlê	zāhāv	wayyō'mer
	and he took counsel	the king	and he made	the two of	the calves of	gold	and he said

420	7521, 3937	4623, 6148.141	3503	2079	435	3547	866
prep, ps 3mp	adj, prep, ps 2mp	prep, v Qal inf con	pn	intrj	n mp, ps 2ms	pn	rel pron
אֲלֵהֶם	רַב־לָכֶם	מֵעֲלוֹת	יְרוּשָׁלַםִ	הִנֵּה	אֱלֹהֶיךָ	יִשְׂרָאֵל	אֲשֶׁר
'ălēhem	rav-lākhem	mē'ălôth	yerûshālam	hinnēh	'ĕlōhêkhā	yisrā'ēl	'ăsher
to them	much to you	from going up	Jerusalem	behold	your gods	O Israel	who

25. Then Jeroboam built Shechem in mount Ephraim, and dwelt therein: ... lived in it, *KJVII* ... in the highlands of Ephraim, *Goodspeed* ... made the town of Shechem in the hill-country of Ephraim a strong place, and was living there, *BB* ... rebuilt Shechem ... and took up residence, *NEB*.

and went out from thence, and built Penuel: ... Then he left that place and fortified Penuel, *Beck* ... Later he went and built up the town of Peniel, *NLT*.

26. And Jeroboam said in his heart, Now shall the kingdom return to the house of David: ... return to the dynasty of David, *NLT* ... kingdom will return to David's line, *Beck*.

27. If this people go up to do sacrifice in the house of the LORD at Jerusalem, then shall the heart of this people turn again unto their lord, even unto Rehoboam king of Judah: ... their hearts will be turned to their master, *Berkeley* ... they will want to be ruled again by Rehoboam, *NCV* ... it will revive their allegiance, *NEB* ... in the House of the EVER-LIVING at Jerusalem, *Fenton*.

and they shall kill me, and go again to Rehoboam king of Judah: ... go back, *NKJV* ... will put me to death, *JB* ... return to his allegiance, *Knox*.

28. Whereupon the king took counsel, and made two calves of gold, and said unto them, It is too much for you to go up to Jerusalem: ... So he thought the matter over, *Moffatt* ... too long a journey for you, *NCV* ... You have been going up to Jerusalem long enough, *NAB* ... two oxen, *BB*.

behold thy gods, O Israel, which brought thee up out of the land of Egypt: ... that brought you up from, *NASB*.

Secondly, he "made priests from among all the people, which were not of the sons of Levi." Thirdly, he established his "harvest feast" not on the fifteenth day of the seventh month, which was the Feast of Tabernacles, but on the fifteenth day of the eighth month. In estimating these sins, let us endeavor—for it is a sacred duty—to be just.

We read in the Authorized Version that "he made priests of the lowest of the people" (v. 31), and this tends to increase the prejudice against him. But to have done this wilfully would have been entirely against his own interests. The more honorable his priests were, the more was his new worship likely to succeed. The Hebrew only says that "he made priests of all classes of the people," or, as the Revised Version renders it, "from among all the people." No doubt this was a heinous innovation.

In choosing Dan and Bethel as the seats for his new altars, the king was not actuated by purely arbitrary considerations. They were ancient and venerated shrines of pilgrimage and worship (Judg. 18:30; 20:18, 26; 1 Sam. 10:3). He did not create any sacredness which was not already attached to them in the popular imagination. In point of fact he would have served the ends of a worldly policy much better if he had chosen Shechem; for Dan and Bethel were the two farthest parts of his kingdom. Dan was in constant danger from the Syrians, and Bethel, which is only twelve miles from Jerusalem, more than once fell into the hands of the kings of Judah, though they neither retained possession of it, nor disturbed the shrines, nor threw down the calf of the new worship. Jeroboam could not have created the calf-worship if he had not found everything prepared for its acceptance. Dan had been, since the earliest days, the seat of a chapelry and ephod. Bethel was associated with some of the nation's holiest memories since the days of their forefather Israel.

Jeroboam was clearly guilty of unjustifiable willfulness in altering the time for observing the Feast of Tabernacles from the seventh to the eighth month. This, however, was incidental and subordinate compared with the setting up of the golden calves.

Jeroboam felt that if his people flocked to do sacrifice at the new and gorgeous Temple in Jerusalem they would return to their old monarchy and put him to death. He wished to avoid the fate of Ishbosheth (2 Sam. 4:7). He believed that he should be doing both a popular and a politic act if he saved them from the burden of this long journey and again decentralized the cult which Solomon had so recently centralized. He determined, therefore, to furnish the ten tribes with high places, and temples of high places, and objects of worship which might rival the golden cherubim of Zion, and be honored with festal music and royal pomp.

Beyond all question, Jeroboam neither did nor would have dreamed of bidding his whole people to abandon their faith and worship foreign gods. He only encouraged them to worship Yahweh along with other gods. Later prophets and poets, like Hosea and the psalmist, spoke in scorn of his images as mere calves, and spoke of him as likening his Maker to an ox that eateth hay (2 Chr. 11:15). They regarded them as figures of Baal and Astarte, because of the obvious attempt to liken the worship of Yahweh to the practices of other nations. Oddly enough, Jeroboam always regarded

6148.516	4623, 800	4875	29.	7947.121	881, 259	904, 1044
v Hiphil pf 3cp, ps 2ms	prep, *n fs*	pn		cj, v Qal impf 3ms	do, art, num	prep, pn
הֶעֱלוּךָ	מֵאֶרֶץ	מִצְרָיִם		וַיָּשֶׂם	אֶת־הָאֶחָד	בְּבֵית־אֵל
he'ělûkhā	mē'erets	mitsrāyim		wayyāsem	'eth-hā'echādh	bevêth-'ēl
they brought you up	from the land of	Egypt		and he placed	the one	in Bethel

881, 259	5598.111	904, 1896	30.	2030.121	1745	2172	3937, 2496
cj, do, art, num	v Qal pf 3ms	prep, pn		cj, v Qal impf 3ms	art, n ms	art, dem pron	prep, n fs
וְאֶת־הָאֶחָד	נָתַן	בְּדָן		וַיְהִי	הַדָּבָר	הַזֶּה	לְחַטָּאת
we'eth-hā'echādh	nāthan	bedhān		wayhî	haddāvār	hazzeh	lechattā'th
and the other	he put	in Dan		and it was	the thing	the this	a sin

2050.126	6194	3937, 6686	259	5912, 1896	31.	6449.121	881, 1041
cj, v Qal impf 3mp	art, n ms	prep, *n mp*	art, num	prep, pn		cj, v Qal impf 3ms	do, n ms
וַיֵּלְכוּ	הָעָם	לִפְנֵי	הָאֶחָד	עַד־דָּן		וַיַּעַשׂ	אֶת־בֵּית
wayyēlekhû	hā'ām	liphnê	hā'echādh	'adh-dān		wayya'as	'eth-bêth
and they went	the people	before	the one	unto Dan		and he made	temples

1154	6449.121	3669	4623, 7382	6194	866	3940, 2030.116
n fp	cj, v Qal impf 3ms	n mp	prep, *n fp*	art, n ms	rel pron	neg part, v Qal pf 3cp
בָּמוֹת	וַיַּעַשׂ	כֹּהֲנִים	מִקְצוֹת	הָעָם	אֲשֶׁר	לֹא־הָיוּ
bāmôth	wayya'as	kōhenîm	miqōtsôth	hā'ām	'ăsher	lō'-hāyû
high places	and he made	priests	from the ends of	the people	who	they were not

4623, 1158	4015	32.	6449.121	3493	2374	904, 2414
prep, *n mp*	pn		cj, v Qal impf 3ms	pn	n ms	prep, art, n ms
מִבְּנֵי	לֵוִי		וַיַּעַשׂ	יָרָבְעָם	חָג	בַּחֹדֶשׁ
mibbenê	lēwî		wayya'as	yārov'ām	chāgh	bachōdhesh
from the descendants of	Levi		and he made	Jeroboam	a feast	during the month

8454	904, 2675, 6461	3219	3937, 2414	3626, 2374	866	904, 3171
art, num	prep, art, num, num	n ms	prep, art, n ms	prep, art, n ms	rel part	prep, pn
הַשְּׁמִינִי	בַּחֲמִשָּׁה־עָשָׂר	יוֹם	לַחֹדֶשׁ	כֶּחָג	אֲשֶׁר	בִּיהוּדָה
hashshemînî	bachmishshāh-'āsār	yôm	lachōdhesh	kechāgh	'ăsher	bîhûdhāh
the eighth	on the fifteen	day	of the month	like the feast	which	in Judah

6148.521	6142, 4326	3772	6449.111	904, 1044	3937, 2159.341
cj, v Hiphil impf 3ms	prep, art, n ms	adv	v Qal pf 3ms	prep, pn	prep, v Piel inf con
וַיַּעַל	עַל־הַמִּזְבֵּחַ	כֵּן	עָשָׂה	בְּבֵית־אֵל	לְזַבֵּחַ
wayya'al	'al-hammizbēach	kēn	'āsāh	bevêth-'ēl	lezabbēach
and he caused to go up	on the altar	so	he did	in Bethel	to sacrifice

3937, 5903	866, 6449.111	6198.511	904, 1044	1044	881, 3669
prep, art, n mp	rel part, v Qal pf 3ms	cj, v Hiphil pf 3ms	prep, pn	pn	do, *n mp*
לָעֲגָלִים	אֲשֶׁר־עָשָׂה	וְהֶעֱמִיד	בְּבֵית	אֵל	אֶת־כֹּהֲנֵי
lā'ăghālîm	'ăsher-'āsāh	wehe'ĕmîdh	bevêth	'ēl	'eth-kōhenê
to the calves	which he had made	and he caused to stand	in Beth	el	the priests of

1154	866	6449.111	33.	6148.521	6142, 4326
art, n fp	rel part	v Qal pf 3ms		cj, v Hiphil impf 3ms	prep, art, n ms
הַבָּמוֹת	אֲשֶׁר	עָשָׂה		וַיַּעַל	עַל־הַמִּזְבֵּחַ
habbāmôth	'ăsher	'āsāh		wayya'al	'al-hammizbēach
the high places	which	he had made		and he caused to go up	on the altar

866, 6449.111	904, 1044	904, 2675	6461	3219	904, 2414	8454
rel part, v Qal pf 3ms	prep, pn	prep, art, num	num	n ms	prep, art, n ms	art, num
אֲשֶׁר־עָשָׂה	בְּבֵית־אֵל	בַּחֲמִשָּׁה	עָשָׂר	יוֹם	בַּחֹדֶשׁ	הַשְּׁמִינִי
'ăsher-'āsāh	bevêth-'ēl	bachmishshāh	'āsār	yôm	bachōdhesh	hashshemînî
which he had made	in Bethel	on the five	ten	day	during the month	the eighth

29. And he set the one in Beth-el, and the other put he in Dan: ... placed these calf idols at the southern and northern ends of Israel, *NLT*.

30. And this thing became a sin: for the people went to worship before the one, even unto Dan: ... seek the one, *Goodspeed* ... in procession before one of them all the way, *Beck*.

31. And he made an house of high places, and made priests of the lowest of the people, which were not of the sons of Levi: ... who were not, *NASB* ... temples in the high places, *Douay* ... built places of worship on hilltops, *Good News* ... priests from the masses, who were not Levitical, *Moffatt* ... appointed priests from ordinary families, who were not of levitical descent, *JB*.

32. And Jeroboam ordained a feast in the eighth month, on the fifteenth day of the month, like unto the feast that is in Judah, and he offered upon the altar. So did he in Beth-el, sacrificing unto the calves that he had made: ... held on a day in mid-autumn, similar to the annual Festival of Shelters, *NLT* ... appointed a feast-day of his own, *Knox* ... instituted a pilgrim-feast, *REB*.

and he placed in Beth-el the priests of the high places which he had made: ... he put in Bethel the priests of the hill altars, *Tyndale*.

33. So he offered upon the altar which he had made in Beth-el the fifteenth day of the eighth month, even in the month which he had devised of his own heart: ... that he alone had devised, *NRSV* ... Jeroboam ascended the altar he built, *NAB*.

and ordained a feast unto the children of Israel: and he offered upon the altar, and burnt incense: ... and went upon the altar to burn, *Douay* ... offereth on the altar—to make perfume, *Young* ... ordered a feast, *KJVII* ... made the smoke of his offerings go up, *BB*.

---

himself as a worshiper of Yahweh. He named his son and destined successor Abijah ("Yahweh is my Father"). Rehoboam himself was a far worse offender than he was, so far as the sanction of idolatry was concerned.

He sinned, and yet he made Israel to sin. It is true that he did not sin against the full extent of the light and knowledge vouchsafed to men in later days. The sin of which he was guilty was the sin of worldly policy. With professions of religion on his lips he pandered to the rude and sensuous instinct which makes materialism in worship so much more attractive to all weak minds than spirituality. Proclaiming as his motive the rights of the people, he accelerated their religious degeneracy. (Tobit [1:4–7] boasts that "when all the tribes of Naphthali fell from the house of Jerusalem and sacrificed to the heifer Baal, I alone went often to Jerusalem at the feasts," and, in general, observed the provisions of the Levitical law.)

There seems to have been but little religion in Jeroboam's temperament. In every other great national gathering at Shechem and other sacred places we read of religious rites (Josh. 24:1; 1 Sam. 10:19; 2 Sam. 5:1ff; 1 Ki. 8:1–5, 62). No mention is made of them, no allusion occurs respecting them, in the assembly to which Jeroboam owed his throne. He might at least have consulted Ahijah, who had given him, when he was still a subject, the divine promise and sanction of royalty. He might, had he chosen, have followed a higher and purer guidance than that of his own personal misgiving and his own arbitrary will. The error which he committed was this—he trusted in policy, not in the Living God.

The venerable sanctuaries of Dan and Bethel prepared the way for the temples of Ashtaroth and Bethel at Samaria and Jezreel. The religion of the kingdom of Israel at last sank lower than that of the kingdom of Judah against which it had revolted. "The sin of Jeroboam the son of Nebat, who made Israel to sin," is the sin again and again repeated in the policy, half-worldly, half-religious, which has prevailed through large tracts of ecclesiastical history. Many are the forms of worship which, with high pretensions, have been nothing else but so many various and opposite ways of breaking the First Commandment. Many a time has the end been held to justify the means, and the divine character been degraded by the pretense, or even the sincere intention, of upholding his cause, for the sake of secular aggrandizement; for the sake of binding together good systems, which it was feared would otherwise fall to pieces; for the sake of supporting the faith of the multitude for fear they should otherwise fall away to rival sects, or lest the enemy should come and take away their place and nation. False arguments have been used in support of religious truths, false miracles promulgated or tolerated, false readings in the sacred text defended.... And so the faith of mankind has been undermined by the very means intended to preserve it. The whole subsequent history is a record of the mode by which, with the best intentions, a Church and nation may be corrupted.

904, 2414	866, 943.111	4623, 937, 940	6449.121	2374	3937, 1158
prep, art, n ms	rel part, v Qal pf 3ms	prep, prep, n ms	cj, v Qal impf 3ms	n ms	prep, *n mp*
בַּחֹדֶשׁ	אֲשֶׁר־בָּדָא	מִלִּבַּד	וַיַּעַשׂ	חָג	לִבְנֵי
bachōdhesh	'ăsher-bādhā'	millibbadh	wayya'as	chāgh	livnê
during the month	which he had devised	by himself	and he made	a feast	for the children of

3547	6148.521	6142, 4326	3937, 7281.541		2079	382
pn	cj, v Hiphil impf 3ms	prep, art, n ms	prep, v Hiphil inf con	**13:1**	cj, intrj	*n ms*
יִשְׂרָאֵל	וַיַּעַל	עַל־הַמִּזְבֵּחַ	לְהַקְטִיר		וְהִנֵּה	אִישׁ
yisrā'ēl	wayya'al	'al-hammizbēach	lehaqṭîr		wehinnēh	'îsh
Israel	and he caused to go up	on the altar	to burn incense		and behold	a man of

435	971.111	4623, 3171	904, 1745	3176	420, 1044	3493
n mp	v Qal pf 3ms	prep, pn	prep, *n ms*	pn	prep, pn	cj, pn
אֱלֹהִים	בָּא	מִיהוּדָה	בִּדְבַר	יְהוָה	אֶל־בֵּית־אֵל	וְיָרָבְעָם
'ĕlōhîm	bā'	mîhûdhāh	bidhvar	yehwāh	'el-bêth-'ēl	weyārov'ām
God	he came	from Judah	with the word of	Yahweh	unto Bethel	and Jeroboam

6198.151	6142, 4326	3937, 7281.541		7410.121	6142, 4326
v Qal act ptc ms	prep, art, n ms	prep, v Hiphil inf con	**2.**	cj, v Qal impf 3ms	prep, art, n ms
עֹמֵד	עַל־הַמִּזְבֵּחַ	לְהַקְטִיר		וַיִּקְרָא	עַל־הַמִּזְבֵּחַ
'ōmēdh	'al-hammizbēach	lehaqṭîr		wayyiqrā'	'al-hammizbēach
standing	beside the altar	to burn incense		and he called	beside the altar

904, 1745	3176	569.121	4326	4326	3662	569.111	3176
prep, *n ms*	pn	cj, v Qal impf 3ms	n ms	n ms	adv	v Qal pf 3ms	pn
בִּדְבַר	יְהוָה	וַיֹּאמֶר	מִזְבֵּחַ	מִזְבֵּחַ	כֹּה	אָמַר	יְהוָה
bidhvar	yehwāh	wayyō'mer	mizbēach	mizbēach	kōh	'āmar	yehwāh
by the word of	Yahweh	and he said	O altar	O altar	thus	He has said	Yahweh

2079, 1158	3314.255	3937, 1041, 1784	3086	8428	2159.111
intrj, n ms	v Niphal ptc ms	prep, *n ms*, pn	pn	n ms, ps 3ms	cj, v Qal pf 3ms
הִנֵּה־בֵן	נוֹלָד	לְבֵית־דָּוִד	יֹאשִׁיָּהוּ	שְׁמוֹ	וְזָבַח
hinnēh-vēn	nôlādh	levêth-dāwidh	yō'shîyāhû	shemô	wezāvach
behold a son	being born	to the household of David	Josiah	his name	and he will sacrifice

6142	881, 3669	1154	7281.552	6142	6344
prep, ps 2ms	do, *n mp*	art, n fp	art, v Hiphil ptc mp	prep, ps 2ms	cj, *n fp*
עָלֶיךָ	אֶת־כֹּהֲנֵי	הַבָּמוֹת	הַמַּקְטִרִים	עָלֶיךָ	וְעַצְמוֹת
'ālêkhā	'eth-kōhenê	habbāmôth	hammaqṭirîm	'ālêkhā	we'atsmôth
on you	the priests of	the high places	those burning incense	on you	yes the bones of

119	8041.126	6142		5598.111	904, 3219	2000	4295
n ms	v Qal impf 3mp	prep, ps 2ms	**3.**	cj, v Qal pf 3ms	prep, art, n ms	art, dem pron	n ms
אָדָם	יִשְׂרְפוּ	עָלֶיךָ		וְנָתַן	בַּיּוֹם	הַהוּא	מוֹפֵת
'ādhām	yisrephû	'ālêkhā		wenāthan	bayyôm	hahû'	môphēth
humankind	they will burn	on you		and he gave	on the day	the that	a sign

3937, 569.141	2172	4295	866	1744.311	3176	2079	4326
prep, v Qal inf con	dem pron	art, n ms	rel part	v Piel pf 3ms	pn	intrj	art, n ms
לֵאמֹר	זֶה	הַמּוֹפֵת	אֲשֶׁר	דִּבֶּר	יְהוָה	הִנֵּה	הַמִּזְבֵּחַ
lē'mōr	zeh	hammôphēth	'ăsher	dibber	yehwāh	hinnēh	hammizbēach
saying	this	the sign	which	He has spoken	Yahweh	behold	the altar

7458.255	8581.211	1942	866, 6142		2030.121
v Niphal ptc ms	cj, v Niphal pf 3ms	art, n ms	rel part, prep, ps 3ms	**4.**	cj, v Qal impf 3ms
נִקְרָע	וְנִשְׁפַּךְ	הַדֶּשֶׁן	אֲשֶׁר־עָלָיו		וַיְהִי
niqōrā'	wenishpakh	haddeshen	'ăsher-'ālāv		wayhî
being torn down	and they will be poured out	the ashes	that on it		and it was

3626, 8471.141	4567	881, 1745	382, 435	866	7410.111	6142, 4326
prep, v Qal inf con	art, n ms	do, *n ms*	*n ms*, art, n mp	rel part	v Qal pf 3ms	prep, art, n ms
כִּשְׁמֹעַ	הַמֶּלֶךְ	אֶת־דְּבַר	אִישׁ־הָאֱלֹהִים	אֲשֶׁר	קָרָא	עַל־הַמִּזְבֵּחַ
khishmōa'	hammelekh	'eth-d^{e}var	'îsh-hā'ĕlōhîm	'ăsher	qārā'	'al-hammizbēach
when hearing	the king	the words of	the man of God	which	he called	beside the altar

904, 1044	8365.121	3493	881, 3135	4623, 6142	4326	3937, 569.141
prep, pn	cj, v Qal impf 3ms	pn	do, n fs, ps 3ms	prep, prep	art, n ms	prep, v Qal inf con
בְּבֵית־אֵל	וַיִּשְׁלַח	יָרָבְעָם	אֶת־יָדוֹ	מֵעַל	הַמִּזְבֵּחַ	לֵאמֹר
b^{e}vêth-'ēl	wayyishlach	yārov'ām	'eth-yādhô	mē'al	hammizbēach	lē'mōr
in Bethel	then he put out	Jeroboam	his hand	from beside	the altar	saying

13:1. And, behold, there came a man of God out of Judah by the word of the LORD unto Beth-el: and Jeroboam stood by the altar to burn incense: ... standing by the altar to make a perfume, *Rotherham* ... to offer incense, *Geneva* ... he arrived there just as Jeroboam was approaching the altar to offer a sacrifice, *NLT*.

2. And he cried against the altar in the word of the LORD, and said, O altar, altar, thus saith the LORD: ... and at Yahweh's command this man denounced the altar, *JB*.

Behold, a child shall be born unto the house of David, Josiah by name: ... I see a prince that is to come, born of David's race, Josias, *Knox* ... A child by the name of Josiah, *Berkeley* ... There will be a son born in David's line, *Beck*.

and upon thee shall he offer the priests of the high places that burn incense upon thee: ... and he shall offer on you ... who burn incense on you, *KJVII* ... who shall slaughter upon you, *NAB* ... for the places of worship now make their sacrifices on you, but Josiah will sacrifice those priests, *NCV* ... serving at the pagan altars who offer sacrifices, *Good News*.

and men's bones shall be burnt upon thee: ... and human bones will be burned on you, *NIV*.

3. And he gave a sign the same day, saying, This is the sign which the LORD hath spoken: ... This is the sign which the LORD has ordained, *NEB* ... At the same time he announced this miracle predicted by the Eternal, *Moffatt*.

Behold, the altar shall be rent, and the ashes that are upon it shall be poured out: ... See, the altar will be broken and the burned waste on it overturned, *BB* ... is rent, and the ashes poured forth that are on it, *Young* ... torn down, and the ashes that are on it, *NRSV*.

4. And it came to pass, when king Jeroboam heard the saying of the man of God, which had cried against the altar in Beth-el, that he put forth his hand from the altar, saying, Lay hold on him: ... that Jeroboam put forth, *MAST* ... he stretched out ... Arrest him!, *NKJV*.

13:1–10. We are told that Jeroboam, whose position probably made him restless and insecure, first built or fortified Shechem, and then went across the Jordan and established another palace and stronghold at Penuel. After this he shifted his residence once more to the beautiful town of Tirzah, where he built for himself the palace which Zimri afterwards burnt over his own head. Although the prophet Shemaiah forbade Rehoboam's attempt to crush him in a great war, Jeroboam remained at war with him and Abijah all his life, till his reign of two-and-twenty troubled years ended apparently by a sudden death—for the chronicler says that "the LORD struck him, and he died."

Nearly all that we know of Jeroboam apart from these incidental notices is made up of two stories, both of which are believed by critics to date from a long subsequent age, but which the compiler of the Book of Kings introduced into his narrative from their in intrinsic force and religious instructiveness.

The first of these stories tells us of the only spontaneous prophetic protest against his proceedings of which we read. So ancient is this curious narrative that tradition had entirely forgotten the names of the two prophets concerned in it. It probably assumed shape from the dim local reminiscences evoked in the days of Josiah's reformation, when the grave of a forgotten prophet of Judah was discovered among the tombs at Bethel, three hundred and twenty years after the events described.

A nameless man of God—Josephus calls him Jadon, and some have identified him with Iddo—came out of Judah to atone for the silence of Israel, and to protest in God's name against the new worship. His protest, however, is against "the altar." He does not say a word about the golden calves. Jeroboam, perhaps, at his dedication festival of the king's shrine

8945.133	3111.122	3135	866	8365.111	6142	3940
v Qal impv 2mp, ps 3ms	cj, v Qal impf 3fs	n fs, ps 3ms	rel part	v Qal pf 3ms	prep, ps 3ms	cj, neg part
תִּפְשֻׂהוּ	וַתִּיבַשׁ	יָדוֹ	אֲשֶׁר	שָׁלַח	עָלָיו	וְלֹא
tiphsuhû	wattîvash	yādhô	'ăsher	shālach	'ālâv	welō'
take hold of him	but it withered	his hand	which	he had put out	beside him	and not

3310.111	3937, 8178.541	420		4326	7458.211
v Qal pf 3ms	prep, v Hiphil inf con, ps 3fs	prep, ps 3ms	**5.**	cj, art, n ms	v Niphal pf 3ms
יָכֹל	לַהֲשִׁיבָהּ	אֵלָיו		וְהַמִּזְבֵּחַ	נִקְרָע
yākhōl	lahshîvāhh	'ēlāv		wehammizbēach	niqŏrā'
he was able	to bring it back	to himself		and the altar	it was torn down

8581.221	1942	4623, 4326	3626, 4295	866	5598.111
cj, v Niphal impf 3ms	art, n ms	prep, art, n ms	prep, art, n ms	rel part	v Qal pf 3ms
וַיִּשָּׁפֵךְ	הַדֶּשֶׁן	מִן־הַמִּזְבֵּחַ	כַּמּוֹפֵת	אֲשֶׁר	נָתַן
wayyishshāphēkh	haddeshen	min-hammizbēach	kammôphēth	'ăsher	nāthan
and they were poured out	the ashes	from the altar	according to the sign	which	he had given

382	435	904, 1745	3176		6257.121	4567	569.121
n ms	art, n mp	prep, *n ms*	pn	**6.**	cj, v Qal impf 3ms	art, n ms	cj, v Qal impf 3ms
אִישׁ	הָאֱלֹהִים	בִּדְבַר	יְהוָה		וַיַּעַן	הַמֶּלֶךְ	וַיֹּאמֶר
'îsh	hā'ĕlōhîm	bidhvar	yehwāh		wayya'an	hammelekh	wayyō'mer
the man of	God	by the word of	Yahweh		and he answered	the king	and he said

4220, 382	435	2571.331, 5167	881, 6686	3176	435
prep, *n ms*	art, n mp	v Piel impv 2ms, part	do, *n mp*	pn	n mp, ps 2ms
אֶל־אִישׁ	הָאֱלֹהִים	חַל־נָא	אֶת־פְּנֵי	יְהוָה	אֱלֹהֶיךָ
'el-'îsh	hā'ĕlōhîm	chal-nā'	'eth-penê	yehwāh	'ĕlōhêkhā
to the man of	God	entreat please	the presence of	Yahweh	your God

6663.731	1185	8178.122	3135	420	2571.321
cj, v Hithpael impv 2ms	prep, ps 1cs	cj, v Qal juss 3fs	n fs, ps 1cs	prep, ps 1cs	cj, v Piel impf 3ms
וְהִתְפַּלֵּל	בַּעֲדִי	וְתָשֹׁב	יָדִי	אֵלָי	וַיְחַל
wehithpallēl	ba'ădhî	wethāshōv	yādhî	'ēlāy	waychal
and pray	for me	that it may be restored	my hand	to me	and he entreated

382, 435	881, 6686	3176	8178.122	3135, 4567	420
n ms, art, n mp	do, *n mp*	pn	cj, v Qal impf 3fs	*n fs*, art, n ms	prep, ps 3ms
אִישׁ־הָאֱלֹהִים	אֶת־פְּנֵי	יְהוָה	וַתָּשָׁב	יַד־הַמֶּלֶךְ	אֵלָיו
'îsh-hā'ĕlōhîm	'eth-penê	yehwāh	wattāshāv	yadh-hammelekh	'ēlāv
the man of God	the presence of	Yahweh	and it returned	the hand of the king	to him

2030.122	3626, 904, 7518		1744.321	4567	4220, 382	435
cj, v Qal impf 3fs	prep, prep, art, adv	**7.**	cj, v Piel impf 3ms	art, n ms	prep, *n ms*	art, n mp
וַתְּהִי	כְּבָרִאשֹׁנָה		וַיְדַבֵּר	הַמֶּלֶךְ	אֶל־אִישׁ	הָאֱלֹהִים
wattehî	kevāri'shōnāh		waydhabbēr	hammelekh	'el-'îsh	hā'ĕlōhîm
and it became	like previously		and he spoke	the king	to the man of	God

971.131, 882	1041	5777.131	5598.125	3937	5164
v Qal impv 2ms, prep, ps 1cs	art, n ms	v Qal impv 2ms	cj, v Qal juss 1cs	prep, ps 2ms	n fs
בֹּאָה־אִתִּי	הַבַּיְתָה	וּסְעָדָה	וְאֶתְּנָה	לְךָ	מַתָּת
bō'āh-'ittî	habbaythāh	ûse'ādhāh	we'ettenāh	lekhā	mattāth
come with me	to the house	and support	that I may give	to you	a gift

	569.121	382, 435	420, 4567	524, 5598.123, 3937	881, 2783
8.	cj, v Qal impf 3ms	*n ms*, art, n mp	prep, art, n ms	cj, v Qal impf 2ms, prep, ps 1cs	do, *n ms*
	וַיֹּאמֶר	אִישׁ־הָאֱלֹהִים	אֶל־הַמֶּלֶךְ	אִם־תִּתֶּן־לִי	אֶת־חֲצִי
	wayyō'mer	'îsh-hā'ĕlōhîm	'el-hammelekh	'im-titten-lî	'eth-chătsî
	but he said	the man of God	to the king	if you give to me	half of

1041	3940	971.125	6196	3940, 404.125	4035	3940
n ms, ps 2ms	neg part	v Qal impf 1cs	prep, ps 2ms	cj, neg part, v Qal impf 1cs	n ms	cj, neg part
בֵּיתֶךָ	לֹא	אָבֹא	עִמָּךְ	וְלֹא־אֹכַל	לֶחֶם	וְלֹא
vêthekhā	lō'	'āvō'	'immākh	wᵉlō'-'ōkhal	lechem	wᵉlō'
your household	not	I will go	with you	and I will not eat	bread	and not

8685.125, 4448	904, 4887	2172		3706, 3772	6943.311	881
v Qal impf 1cs, n md	prep, art, n ms	art, dem pron		cj, adv	v Piel pf 3ms	do, ps 1cs
אֶשְׁתֶּה־מַּיִם	בַּמָּקוֹם	הַזֶּה	9.	כִּי־כֵן	צִוָּה	אֹתִי
'eshteh-mayim	bammāqôm	hazzeh		kî-khēn	tsiwwāh	'ōthî
I will drink water	in the place	the this		because so	He has commanded	me

904, 1745	3176	3937, 569.141	3940, 404.123	4035	3940
prep, *n ms*	pn	prep, v Qal inf con	neg part, v Qal impf 2ms	n ms	cj, neg part
בִּדְבַר	יְהוָה	לֵאמֹר	לֹא־תֹאכַל	לֶחֶם	וְלֹא
bidhvar	yᵉhwāh	lē'mōr	lō'-thō'khal	lechem	wᵉlō'
by the word of	Yahweh	saying	you must not eat	bread	and not

And his hand, which he put forth against him, dried up, so that he could not pull it in again to him: ... as he extended it from him, that he was not able to return it to himself, *Fenton* ... he had thrust forth against him was dried up, *Rotherham* ... he had pointed at him became paralysed, *REB* ... he put forth against him, withered up, *Goodspeed*.

5. The altar also was rent, and the ashes poured out from the altar: ... and the altar burst apart and the ashes from the altar were spilt, *JB*.

according to the sign which the man of God had given by the word of the LORD: ... token ... at the commandment, *Tyndale* ... the very sign which the Lord had inspired his prophet to fortell, *Knox* ... this was the miracle the man of God did, *Beck*.

6. And the king answered and said unto the man of God, Entreat now the face of the LORD thy God, and pray for me, that my hand may be restored me again: ... the favor of the LORD your God, *NRSV* ... make an appeal ... to be kind, *Beck* ... Do appease the Eternal your God and pray for me, *Moffatt* ... pray ... and make intercession for me, *Tyndale*.

And the man of God besought the LORD, and the king's hand was restored him again, and became as it was before: ... king's hand became normal again, *NLT* ... the man of God besought the face of the Lord, *Douay* ... was restored to its former condition, *Berkeley* ... the king recovered the normal use of his hand, *NAB*.

7. And the king said unto the man of God, Come home with me, and refresh thyself, and I will give thee a reward: ... refresh yourself, and I will give you a reward, *NASB* ... take refreshment, *Goodspeed* ... to my house for food and rest, *BB*.

8. And the man of God said unto the king, If thou wilt give me half thine house, I will not go in with thee, neither will I eat bread nor drink water in this place: ... If you would give me half of your palace, *Beck* ... gave me half of your wealth, *Good News* ... before a crust of bread or a drop of water should pass my lips, *Knox*.

9. For so was it charged me by the word of the LORD, saying, Eat no bread, nor drink water, nor turn again by the same way that thou camest: ... I was directed by, *Berkeley* ... I have had Yahweh's order, *JB* ... so was it charged me by, *MAST* ... the message of the EVER-LIVING commanded me, *Fenton*.

at Bethel, was standing on the altar-slope, as Solomon had done in the Temple, to burn incense. Suddenly, the man of God appeared and threatened to the altar the destruction and desecration which subsequently fell upon it. We cannot be sure that some of the details are not later additions supplied from subsequent events. Josephus rationalizes the story very absurdly in the style of Paulus. The sign of the destruction or rending of the altar, and the outpouring of the ashes, may have been first fulfilled in that memorable earthquake which became a date in Israel (Amos 9:1). The desecration which it received at the hands of Josiah reminded men of the threat of the unknown messenger. Then we are told that Jeroboam raised his hand in anger, with the order to secure the bold offender, but that his arm at once "dried up," and was only restored by the man of God (1 Ki. 13:6) at the king's entreaty. The king invited the prophet to go home and refresh himself and receive a reward; but he replied that not half Jeroboam's house could tempt him to break the command which he had received to eat no bread neither drink water at Bethel.

8685.123, 4448	3940	8178.123	904, 1932	866	2050.113
v Qal impf 2ms, n mp	cj, neg part	v Qal impf 2ms	prep, art, n ms	rel part	v Qal pf 2ms
תִשְׁתֶּה־מָּיִם	וְלֹא	תָשׁוּב	בַּדֶּרֶךְ	אֲשֶׁר	הָלָכְתָּ
thishteh-māyim	welō’	thāshûv	badderekh	’ăsher	hālākhettā
you will drink water	and not	you will return	on the road	which	you walked

10.	2050.121	904, 1932	311	3940, 8178.111	904, 1932	866	971.111
	cj, v Qal impf 3ms	prep, n ms	adj	cj, neg part, v Qal pf 3ms	prep, art, n ms	rel part	v Qal pf 3ms
	וַיֵּלֶךְ	בְּדֶרֶךְ	אַחֵר	וְלֹא־שָׁב	בַּדֶּרֶךְ	אֲשֶׁר	בָּא
	wayyēlekh	bedherekh	’achēr	welō’-shāv	badderekh	’ăsher	bā’
	and he went	on a road	another	and he did not return	on the road	which	he came

904	420, 1044	11.	5204	259	2292	3553.151	904, 1044
prep, ps 3fs	prep, pn		cj, n ms	num	adj	v Qal act ptc ms	prep, pn
בָהּ	אֶל־בֵּית־אֵל		וְנָבִיא	אֶחָד	זָקֵן	יֹשֵׁב	בְּבֵית־אֵל
vāhh	’el-bêth-’ēl		wenāvî’	’echādh	zāqēn	yōshēv	bevêth-’ēl
on it	unto Bethel		and a prophet	one	old	dwelling	in Bethel

971.121	1158	5807.321, 3937	881, 3725, 4801	866, 6449.111
cj, v Qal impf 3ms	n ms, ps 3ms	cj, v Piel impf 3ms, prep, ps 3ms	do, *adj*, art, n ms	rel part, v Qal pf 3ms
וַיָּבוֹא	בְנוֹ	וַיְסַפֶּר־לוֹ	אֶת־כָּל־הַמַּעֲשֶׂה	אֲשֶׁר־עָשָׂה
wayyāvô’	venô	waysapper-lô	’eth-kol-hamma‘ăseh	’ăsher-‘āsāh
and he came	his son	and he recounted to him	all the works	that he had done

382, 435	3219	904, 1044	1745	866	1744.311	420, 4567
n ms, art, n mp	art, n ms	prep, pn	art, n mp	rel part	v Piel pf 3ms	prep, art, n ms
אִישׁ־הָאֱלֹהִים	הַיּוֹם	בְּבֵית־אֵל	אֶת־הַדְּבָרִים	אֲשֶׁר	דִּבֶּר	אֶל־הַמֶּלֶךְ
’îsh-hā’ĕlōhîm	hayyôm	bevêth-’ēl	’eth-haddevārîm	’ăsher	dibber	’el-hammelekh
the man of God	today	in Bethel	the words	which	he had spoken	to the king

5807.326	3937, 1	12.	1744.321	420	1
cj, v Piel impf 3mp, ps 3mp	prep, n ms, ps 3mp		cj, v Piel impf 3ms	prep, ps 3mp	n ms, ps 3mp
וַיְסַפְּרוּם	לַאֲבִיהֶם		וַיְדַבֵּר	אֲלֵהֶם	אֲבִיהֶם
waysapperûm	la’ăvîhem		waydhabbēr	’ălēhem	’ăvîhem
and they recounted to them	to their father		and he spoke	to them	their father

338, 2172	1932	2050.111	7495.126	1158	881, 1932	866	2050.111
intrg, dem pron	art, n ms	v Qal pf 3ms	cj, v Qal impf 3mp	n mp, ps 3ms	do, art, n ms	rel part	v Qal pf 3ms
אֵי־זֶה	הַדֶּרֶךְ	הָלָךְ	וַיִּרְאוּ	בָנָיו	אֶת־הַדֶּרֶךְ	אֲשֶׁר	הָלַךְ
’ê-zeh	hadderekh	hālākh	wayyir’û	vānāv	’eth-hadderekh	’ăsher	hālakh
where this	the road	he went	and they saw	his sons	the road	which	he walked

382	435	866, 971.111	4623, 3171	13.	569.121	420, 1158
n ms	art, n mp	rel pron, v Qal pf 3ms	prep, pn		cj, v Qal impf 3ms	prep, n mp, ps 3ms
אִישׁ	הָאֱלֹהִים	אֲשֶׁר־בָּא	מִיהוּדָה		וַיֹּאמֶר	אֶל־בָּנָיו
’îsh	hā’ĕlōhîm	’ăsher-bā’	mîhûdhāh		wayyō’mer	’el-bānâv
the man of	God	who he had come	from Judah		and he said	to his sons

2372.133, 3937	2645	2372.126, 3937	2645	7680.121
v Qal impv 2mp, prep, ps 3ms	art, n ms	cj, v Qal impf 3mp, prep, ps 3ms	art, n ms	cj, v Qal impf 3ms
חִבְשׁוּ־לִי	הַחֲמוֹר	וַיַּחְבְּשׁוּ־לוֹ	הַחֲמוֹר	וַיִּרְכַּב
chivshû-lî	hachmôr	wayyachbeshû-lô	hachmôr	wayyirkav
saddle for me	the donkey	and they saddled for him	the donkey	and he rode

6142	14.	2050.121	313	382	435	4834.121
prep, ps 3ms		cj, v Qal impf 3ms	prep	*n ms*	art, n mp	cj, v Qal impf 3ms, ps 3ms
עָלָיו		וַיֵּלֶךְ	אַחֲרֵי	אִישׁ	הָאֱלֹהִים	וַיִּמְצָאֵהוּ
‘ālâv		wayyēlekh	’achrê	’îsh	hā’ĕlōhîm	wayyimtsā’ēhû
on it		and he went	after	the man of	God	and he found him

3553.151	**8809**	**428**	**569.121**	**420**	**1950B, 887**	**382, 435**
v Qal act ptc ms	prep	art, n fs	cj, v Qal impf 3ms	prep, ps 3ms	intrg part, pers pron	*n ms*, art, n mp
יֹשֵׁב	תַּחַת	הָאֵלָה	וַיֹּאמֶר	אֵלָיו	הַאַתָּה	אִישׁ־הָאֱלֹהִים
yōshēv	tachath	hā'ēlāh	wayyō'mer	'ēlâv	ha'attāh	'îsh-hā'ělōhîm
sitting	beneath	the great tree	and he said	to him	are you	the man of God

866, 971.113	**4623, 3171**	**569.121**	**603**	**15.** **569.121**	**420**
rel pron, v Qal pf 2ms	prep, pn	cj, v Qal impf 3ms	pers pron	cj, v Qal impf 3ms	prep, ps 3ms
אֲשֶׁר־בָּאתָ	מִיהוּדָה	וַיֹּאמֶר	אָנִי	וַיֹּאמֶר	אֵלָיו
'ăsher-bā'thā	mîhûdhāh	wayyō'mer	'ānî	wayyō'mer	'ēlâv
who you came	from Judah	and he said	I	and he said	to him

2050.131	**882**	**1041**	**404.131**	**1035**	**16.** **569.121**	**3940**
v Qal impv 2ms	prep, ps 1cs	art, n ms	cj, v Qal impv 2ms	n ms	cj, v Qal impf 3ms	neg part
לֵךְ	אִתִּי	הַבָּיְתָה	וֶאֱכֹל	לָחֶם	וַיֹּאמֶר	לֹא
lēkh	'ittî	habbāy^{e}thāh	we'ěkhōl	lāchem	wayyō'mer	lō'
come	with me	to the house	and eat	bread	but he said	not

10. So he went another way, and returned not by the way that he came to Beth-el: ... went home, *NLT* ... did not return by the road he had taken, *NEB* ... he went back, *REB*.

11. Now there dwelt an old prophet in Beth-el: ... At that time there was an aged prophet, *REB* ... living in the city, *NAB* ... old seer dwelling at Bethel, *Knox*.

and his sons came and told him all the works that the man of God had done that day in Beth-el: the words which he had spoken unto the king, them they told also to their father: ... to the king, *KJVII* ... told him all the deeds, *Goodspeed* ... what he had said to King Jeroboam, *Good News* ... he said to the king they relayed to their father, *Berkeley*.

12. And their father said unto them, What way went he? For his sons had seen what way the man of God went, which came from Judah: ... Which road did he take?, *NEB* ... Which road did he use when he left?, *NCV* ... they told their father which road the man of God had taken, *NLT*.

13. And he said unto his sons, Saddle me the ass. So they saddled him the ass: and he rode thereon: ... he rode on it, *NKJV* ... rode thereon, *Darby* ... they saddled the donkey, and he left, *NCV* ... saddled the donkey for him, he rode off on it, *Beck*.

14. And went after the man of God, and found him sitting under an oak: and he said unto him, Art thou the man of God that camest from Judah? And he said, I am: ... He came on him seated under a terebinth, *REB* ... sitting under a turpentine tree, *Douay*.

15. Then he said unto him, Come home with me, and eat bread: ... with me to my house and eat bread, *Fenton* ... back to the house with me and have a meal, *BB* ... take some food, *JB* ... bade him come home and share his meal, *Knox*.

16. And he said, I may not return with thee, nor go in with thee: neither will I eat bread nor drink water with thee in this place: ... I am not allowed to eat any food or drink any water, *NLT* ... accept your hospitality, *Good News*.

13:11–30. An old Israelite prophet was living at Bethel, and his son told Jeroboam how the prophet had done the works of God. Jeroboam rode after him to bring him to his house. He found him seated under "the terebinth"—evidently some aged and famous tree. When he refused the renewed invitation, the old man lyingly said to him that he too was a man of God and had been bidden by an angel to bring him back. Deceived, perhaps too easily, the man of God from Judah went back. It would have been well for him if he had believed that even "an angel of God," or what may seem to wear such a semblance, may preach a false message, and may deserve nothing but an anathema (Gal. 1:8). With terrible swiftness the delusion was dispelled. While he was eating in Bethel, the old prophet, overcome by an impulse of inspiration, told him that for his disobedience he should perish and lie in a strange grave. Accordingly he had not gone far from Bethel when a lion met and killed him, not, however, mangling or devouring him, but standing still with the ass beside the carcase. On hearing this the old prophet of Bethel went and brought back the corpse. He mourned over his victim with the cry, "Alas, my brother," (cf. Jer. 22:18) and bade his sons that when he died they should bury him in the same sepulcher with the man of God, for all that he had prophesied should come to pass.

3310.125	3937, 8178.141	882	3937, 971.141	882	3940, 404.125
v Qal impf 1cs	prep, v Qal inf con	prep, ps 2ms	cj, prep, v Qal inf con	prep, ps 2ms	cj, neg part, v Qal impf 1cs
אוּכַל	לָשׁוּב	אִתָּךְ	וְלָבוֹא	אִתָּךְ	וְלֹא־אֹכַל
'ûkhal	lāshûv	'ittākh	welāvô'	'ittākh	welō'-'ōkhal
I am able	to return	with you	nor to go	with you	and I must not eat

4035	3940, 8685.125	882	4448	904, 4887	2172		3706, 1745
n ms	cj, neg part, v Qal impf 1cs	prep, ps 2ms	n md	prep, art, n ms	art, dem pron	**17.**	cj, n ms
לֶחֶם	וְלֹא־אֶשְׁתֶּה	אִתְּךָ	מַיִם	בַּמָּקוֹם	הַזֶּה		כִּי־דָבָר
lechem	welō'-'eshteh	'ittekhā	mayim	bammāqôm	hazzeh		kî-dhāvār
bread	and I must not drink	with you	water	in the place	the this		because a word

420	904, 1745	3176	3940, 404.123	4035	3940, 8685.123	8427
prep, ps 1cs	prep, *n ms*	pn	neg part, v Qal impf 2ms	n ms	cj, neg part, v Qal impf 2ms	adv
אֵלַי	בִּדְבַר	יְהוָה	לֹא־תֹאכַל	לֶחֶם	וְלֹא־תִשְׁתֶּה	שָׁם
'ēlay	bidhvar	yehwāh	lō'-thō'khal	lechem	welō'-thishteh	shām
to me	by the word of	Yahweh	you must not eat	bread	and you must not drink	there

4448	3940, 8178.123	3937, 2050.141	904, 1932	866, 2050.113	904
n mp	neg part, v Qal impf 2ms	prep, v Qal inf con	prep, art, n ms	rel part, v Qal pf 2ms	prep, ps 3fs
מָיִם	לֹא־תָשׁוּב	לָלֶכֶת	בַּדֶּרֶךְ	אֲשֶׁר־הָלַכְתָּ	בָּהּ
māyim	lō'-thāshûv	lālekheth	badderekh	'ăsher-hālakhtā	bāhh
water	you must not return	to walk	on the road	which you have walked	on it

	569.121	3937	1612, 603	5204	3765	4534	1744.311
18.	cj, v Qal impf 3ms	prep, ps 3ms	cj, pers pron	n ms	prep, ps 2ms	cj, n ms	v Piel pf 3ms
	וַיֹּאמֶר	לוֹ	גַּם־אֲנִי	נָבִיא	כָּמוֹךָ	וּמַלְאָךְ	דִּבֶּר
	wayyō'mer	lô	gam-'ănî	nāvî'	kāmôkhā	ûmal'ākh	dibber
	and he said	to him	also I	a prophet	like you	and an angel	he spoke

420	904, 1745	3176	3937, 569.141	8178.531	882
prep, ps 1cs	prep, *n ms*	pn	prep, v Qal inf con	v Hiphil impv ms, ps 3ms	prep, ps 2ms
אֵלַי	בִּדְבַר	יְהוָה	לֵאמֹר	הֲשִׁבֵהוּ	אִתְּךָ
'ēlay	bidhvar	yehwāh	lē'mōr	heshivēhû	'ittekhā
to me	by the word of	Yahweh	saying	bring him back	with you

420, 1041	404.121	4035	8685.121	4448	3703.311	3937
prep, n ms, ps 2ms	cj, v Qal juss 3ms	n ms	cj, Qal juss 3ms	n mp	v Piel pf 3ms	prep, ps 3ms
אֶל־בֵּיתֶךָ	וְיֹאכַל	לֶחֶם	וְיֵשְׁתְּ	מָיִם	כִּחֵשׁ	לוֹ
'el-bêthekhā	weyō'khal	lechem	weyēsht	māyim	kichēsh	lô
to your house	that he may eat	bread	and he may drink	water	he lied	to him

	8178.121	882	404.121	4035	904, 1041	8685.121	4448
19.	cj, v Qal impf 3ms	prep, ps 3ms	cj, v Qal impf 3ms	n ms	prep, n ms, ps 3ms	cj, v Qal impf 3ms	n mp
	וַיָּשָׁב	אִתּוֹ	וַיֹּאכַל	לֶחֶם	בְּבֵיתוֹ	וַיֵּשְׁתְּ	מָיִם
	wayyāshāv	'ittô	wayyō'khal	lechem	bevêthô	wayyēsht	māyim
	and he returned	with him	and he ate	bread	in his house	and he drank	water

	2030.121	2062	3553.152	420, 8374	2030.121	1745, 3176
20.	cj, v Qal impf 3ms	pers pron	v Qal act ptc mp	prep, art, n ms	cj, v Qal impf 3ms	*n ms*, pn
	וַיְהִי	הֵם	יֹשְׁבִים	אֶל־הַשֻּׁלְחָן	וַיְהִי	דְּבַר־יְהוָה
	wayhî	hēm	yōshevîm	'el-hashshulchān	wayhî	devar-yehwāh
	and it was	they	sitting	to the table	and it was	the word of Yahweh

420, 5204	866	8178.511		7410.121	420, 382	435
prep, art, n ms	rel pron	v Hiphil pf 3ms, ps 3ms	**21.**	cj, v Qal impf 3ms	prep, *n ms*	art, n mp
אֶל־הַנָּבִיא	אֲשֶׁר	הֱשִׁיבוֹ		וַיִּקְרָא	אֶל־אִישׁ	הָאֱלֹהִים
'el-hannāvî'	'ăsher	hĕshîvô		wayyiqōrā'	'el-'îsh	hā'ĕlōhîm
to the prophet	who	he had brought him back		and he called out	to the man of	God

866, 971.111	4623, 3171	3937, 569.141	3662	569.111	3176	3391	3706
rel pron, v Qal pf 3ms	prep, pn	prep, v Qal inf con	adv	v Qal pf 3ms	pn	cj	cj
אֲשֶׁר־בָּא	מִיהוּדָה	לֵאמֹר	כֹּה	אָמַר	יְהוָה	יַעַן	כִּי
'āsher-bā'	mîhûdhāh	lē'mōr	kōh	'āmar	y^{e}hwāh	ya'an	kî
who he had come	from Judah	saying	thus	He has said	Yahweh	because	that

4947.113	6552	3176	3940	8490.113	881, 4851
v Qal pf 2ms	*n ms*	pn	cj, neg part	v Qal pf 2ms	do, art, n fs
מָרִיתָ	פִּי	יְהוָה	וְלֹא	שָׁמַרְתָּ	אֶת־הַמִּצְוָה
mārîthā	pî	y^{e}hwāh	w^{e}lō'	shāmartā	'eth-hammitswāh
you have rebelled against	the mouth of	Yahweh	and not	you have observed	the commandments

866	6943.311	3176	435		8178.123	404.123
rel part	v Piel pf 3ms, ps 2ms	pn	n mp, ps 2ms	**22.**	cj, v Qal impf 2ms	cj, v Qal impf 2ms
אֲשֶׁר	צִוְּךָ	יְהוָה	אֱלֹהֶיךָ		וַתָּשָׁב	וַתֹּאכַל
'ăsher	tsiww^{e}khā	y^{e}hwāh	'ĕlōhêkhā		wattāshāv	wattō'khal
which	He commanded you	Yahweh	your God		but you have returned	and you have eaten

17. For it was said to me by the word of the LORD: ... For a command came to me, *NASB* ... for the LORD's direction to me was, *Berkeley* ... was declared unto me, *Goodspeed* ... have received Yahweh's order, *JB* ... the Message of the EVER-LIVING commanded me, *Fenton*.

Thou shalt eat no bread nor drink water there, nor turn again to go by the way that thou camest: ... Don't eat or drink there, or even go back the way you came, *Beck* ... return on the same road by which, *NCV* ... not drink at Bethel, nor leave it by the way I entered it, *Knox* ... nor return by going the way, *NKJV*.

18. He said unto him, I am a prophet also as thou art; and an angel spake unto me by the word of the LORD, saying: ... an angel commanded, *NEB* ... a messenger, *Young* ... a Preacher like yourself, and a Divine Messenger spoke, *Fenton*.

Bring him back with thee into thine house, that he may eat bread and drink water. But he lied unto him: ... was deceiving, *NRSV* ... This was a lie, *Moffatt* ... He deceived him, *Rotherham* ... said false words, *BB*.

19. So he went back with him, and did eat bread in his house, and drank water: ... eateth bread ... drinketh water, *Young* ... the man of Judah, *REB*.

20. And it came to pass, as they sat at the table, that the word of the LORD came unto the prophet that brought him back: ... the LORD spoke his word, *NCV* ... came to the seer that had detained him, *Knox*.

21. And he cried unto the man of God that came from Judah, saying: ... proclaimed to the man of God, *NRSV* ... addressed the man of God, *JB*.

Thus saith the LORD, Forasmuch as thou hast disobeyed the mouth of the LORD, and hast not kept the commandment which the LORD thy God commanded thee: ... Because you rebelled against the LORD's Word, *Beck* ... have disobeyed the command, *NASB* ... hast been disobedient unto the mouth, *ASV* ... gave thee a strict injunction, *Knox*.

22. But camest back, and hast eaten bread and drunk water in the place, of the which the LORD did say to thee, Eat no bread, and drink no water: ... to eat and drink in the place where he forbade it, *REB* ... where he said you were to take no food or water, *BB* ... you returned and ate a meal in a place he had ordered you not to, *Good News*.

Josephus adds many idle touches to this story. If in a tale which assumed its present form so long after the events imaginative details were introduced, the incident of the lion subserves the moral aim of the narrative (2 Ki. 17:25; Jer. 25:30, 49:19). The significance of the story for us is happily neither historic nor evidential, but it is profoundly moral. It is the lesson not to linger in the neighborhood of temptation, nor to be dilatory in the completion of duty. It is the lesson to be ever on our guard against the tendency to assume inspired sanction for the conduct and opinions which coincide with our own secret wishes. Satan finds it easy to secure our credence when he answers us according to our idols and can quote Scripture for our purpose as well as his own; and God sometimes punishes men by granting them their own desires, and sending leanness withal into their bones. The man of God from Judah had received a distinct injunction from which the invitation of a king had been insufficient to shake him. If the old prophet willfully lied, his victim was

4035	8685.123	4448	904, 4887	866	1744.311	420	414, 404.123
n ms	cj, v Qal impf 2ms	n md	prep, art, n ms	rel part	v Piel pf 3ms	prep, ps 2ms	adv, v Qal juss 2ms
לֶחֶם	וַתֵּשְׁתְּ	מַיִם	בַּמָּקוֹם	אֲשֶׁר	דִּבֶּר	אֵלֶיךָ	אַל־תֹּאכַל
lechem	wattēsht	mayim	bammāqôm	'āsher	dibber	'ēlêkhā	'al-tō'khal
bread	and you have drunk	water	in the place	which	He spoke	to you	do not eat

4035	414, 8685.123	4448	3940, 971.122	5215	420, 7197	1
n ms	cj, adv, v Qal juss 2ms	n mp	neg part, v Qal impf 3fs	n fs, ps 2ms	prep, *n ms*	n mp, ps 2ms
לֶחֶם	וְאַל־תֵּשְׁתְּ	מָיִם	לֹא־תָבוֹא	נִבְלָתְךָ	אֶל־קֶבֶר	אֲבֹתֶיךָ
lechem	we'al-tēsht	māyim	lō'-thāvô'	nivlāthekhā	'el-qever	'ăvōthêkhā
bread	and do not drink	water	it will not enter	your corpse	into the tomb of	your ancestors

	2030.121	313	404.141	4035	313	8685.141
23.	cj, v Qal impf 3ms	prep	v Qal inf con, ps 3ms	n ms	cj, prep	v Qal inf con, ps 3ms
	וַיְהִי	אַחֲרֵי	אָכְלוֹ	לֶחֶם	וְאַחֲרֵי	שְׁתוֹתוֹ
	wayhî	'achrê	'ākhelô	lechem	we'achrê	shethôthô
	and it was	after	his eating	bread	and after	his drinking

2372.121, 3937	2645	3937, 5204	866	8178.511
cj, v Qal impf 3ms, prep, ps 3ms	art, n ms	prep, art, n ms	rel pron	v Hiphil pf 3ms, ps 3ms
וַיַּחֲבָשׁ־לוֹ	הַחֲמוֹר	לַנָּבִיא	אֲשֶׁר	הֱשִׁיבוֹ
wayyachvāsh-lô	hachmôr	lannāvî'	'ăsher	hĕshîvô
that he saddled for him	the donkey	for the prophet	whom	he had brought him back

	2050.121	4834.121	765	904, 1932	4322.521
24.	cj, v Qal impf 3ms	cj, v Qal impf 3ms, ps 3ms	n ms	prep, art, n ms	cj, v Hiphil impf 3ms, ps 3ms
	וַיֵּלֶךְ	וַיִּמְצָאֵהוּ	אַרְיֵה	בַּדֶּרֶךְ	וַיְמִיתֵהוּ
	wayyēlekh	wayyimtsā'ēhû	'aryēh	badderekh	waymîthēhû
	and he went	but it found him	a lion	on the road	and it killed him

2030.122	5215	8390.657	904, 1932	2645	6198.151	703
cj, v Qal impf 3fs	n fs, ps 3ms	v Hophal ptc fs	prep, art, n ms	cj, art, n ms	v Qal act ptc ms	prep, ps 3fs
וַתְּהִי	נִבְלָתוֹ	מֻשְׁלֶכֶת	בַּדֶּרֶךְ	וְהַחֲמוֹר	עֹמֵד	אֶצְלָהּ
wattehî	nivlāthô	mushlekheth	badderekh	wehachmôr	'ōmēdh	'etslāhh
and it was	his corpse	thrown down	on the road	and the donkey	standing	beside it

765	6198.151	703	5215		2079	596	5882.152
cj, art, n ms	v Qal act ptc ms	prep	art, n fs	**25.**	cj, intrj	n mp	v Qal act ptc mp
וְהָאַרְיֵה	עֹמֵד	אֵצֶל	הַנְּבֵלָה		וְהִנֵּה	אֲנָשִׁים	עֹבְרִים
wehā'aryēh	'ōmēdh	'ētsel	hannevēlāh		wehinnēh	'ănāshîm	'ōverîm
and the lion	standing	beside	the corpse		and behold	men	passing by

7495.126	881, 5215	8390.657	904, 1932	881, 765	6198.151	703
cj, v Qal impf 3mp	do, art, n fs	v Hophal ptc fs	prep, art, n ms	cj, do, art, n ms	v Qal act ptc ms	prep
וַיִּרְאוּ	אֶת־הַנְּבֵלָה	מֻשְׁלֶכֶת	בַּדֶּרֶךְ	וְאֶת־הָאַרְיֵה	עֹמֵד	אֵצֶל
wayyir'û	'eth-hannevēlāh	mushlekheth	badderekh	we'eth-hā'aryēh	'ōmēdh	'ētsel
and they looked at	the corpse	thrown down	on the road	and the lion	standing	beside

5215	971.126	1744.326	904, 6111	866	5204	2292
art, n fs	cj, v Qal impf 3mp	cj, v Piel impf 3mp	prep, art, n fs	rel part	art, n ms	art, n ms
הַנְּבֵלָה	וַיָּבֹאוּ	וַיְדַבְּרוּ	בָּעִיר	אֲשֶׁר	הַנָּבִיא	הַזָּקֵן
hannevēlāh	wayyāvō'û	waydhabberû	vā'îr	'āsher	hannāvî'	hazzāqēn
the corpse	and they came	and they spoke	in the city	which	the prophet	the old man

3553.151	904		8471.121	5204	866	8178.511
v Qal act ptc ms	prep, ps 3fs	**26.**	cj, v Qal impf 3ms	art, n ms	rel pron	v Hiphil pf 3ms, ps 3ms
יֹשֵׁב	בָּהּ		וַיִּשְׁמַע	הַנָּבִיא	אֲשֶׁר	הֱשִׁיבוֹ
yōshēv	bāhh		wayyishma'	hannāvî'	'ăsher	hĕshîvô
dwelling	in it		and he heard	the prophet	who	he had brought him back

4623, 1932	569.121	382	435	2000	866	4947.111
prep, art, n ms	cj, v Qal impf 3ms	*n ms*	art, n mp	pers pron	rel pron	v Qal pf 3ms
מִן־הַדֶּרֶךְ	וַיֹּאמֶר	אִישׁ	הָאֱלֹהִים	הוּא	אֲשֶׁר	מָרָה
min-hadderekh	wayyō'mer	'îsh	hā'ělōhîm	hû'	'ăsher	mārāh
from the road	and he said	the man of	God	he	who	he rebelled against

881, 6552	3176	5598.121	3176	3937, 765	8132.121
do, *n ms*	pn	cj, v Qal impf 3ms, ps 3ms	pn	prep, art, n ms	cj, v Qal impf 3ms, ps 3ms
אֶת־פִּי	יְהוָה	וַיִּתְּנֵהוּ	יְהוָה	לָאַרְיֵה	וַיִּשְׁבְּרֵהוּ
'eth-pî	y^ehwāh	wayyitt^enēhû	y^ehwāh	lā'aryēh	wayyishb^erēhû
the mouth of	Yahweh	so he gave him over	Yahweh	to the lion	and he broke him into pieces

4322.521	3626, 1745	3176	866	1744.311, 3937
cj, v Hiphil impf 3ms, ps 3ms	prep, *n ms*	pn	rel part	v Piel pf 3ms, prep, ps 3ms
וַיְמִתֵהוּ	כִּדְבַר	יְהוָה	אֲשֶׁר	דִּבֶּר־לוֹ
waymithēhû	kidhvar	y^ehwāh	'ăsher	dibber-lô
and he killed him	according to the word of	Yahweh	which	He had spoken to him

thy carcase shall not come unto the sepulchre of thy fathers: ... thy dead body shall not be brought into, *Douay* ... into the tomb of your ancestors, *Beck* ... buried in your family grave, *NCV*.

23. And it came to pass, after he had eaten bread, and after he had drunk, that he saddled for him the ass, to wit, for the prophet whom he had brought back: ... they saddled for him a donkey belonging to the prophet, *NRSV*.

24. And when he was gone, a lion met him by the way, and slew him: ... the man of God started off again, *NLT* ... when he was gone, *Geneva* ... a lion came rushing at him and put him to death, *BB* ... once more he departed, *Goodspeed*.

and his carcase was cast in the way, and the ass stood by it, the lion also stood by the carcase: ... his dead body was cast out, *Rotherham* ... thrown in the highway, *KJVII* ... his corpse lay stretched out on the road, *JB*.

25. And, behold, men passed by, and saw the carcase cast in the way, and the lion standing by the carcase: and they came and told it in the city where the old prophet dwelt: ... carried the news to the city where the old prophet lived, *NAB* ... reported it in the Village in which the old Preacher, *Fenton* ... Passers-by told how they had seen it, *Knox* ... told the news at the town-gate where the old prophet was sitting, *Moffatt*.

26. And when the prophet that brought him back from the way heard thereof, he said, It is the man of God, who was disobedient unto the word of the LORD: ... rebelled against the word, *Berkeley* ... disobeyed the LORD's command!, *Good News* ... went against the word, *BB* ... the direction of the EVER-LIVING, *Fenton*.

therefore the LORD hath delivered him unto the lion, which hath torn him, and slain him, according to the word of the LORD, which he spake unto him: ... the LORD sent a lion to kill him, just as he said he would, *NCV* ... which has mangled him and slain him, *Goodspeed* ... it has broken his neck and killed him in fulfillment of the word, *NEB*.

27. And he spake to his sons, saying, Saddle me the ass. And they saddled him: ... And he spoke to his sons, *NKJV* ... He told his sons to saddle the donkey, *REB* ... Put the saddle on the donkey for me, *Beck*.

willingly seduced. We may think his sin venial, his punishment excessive. It will not seem so unless we unduly extenuate his sin and unduly exaggerate the nature of his penalty.

His sin consisted in his ready acceptance of a sham inspiration which came to him from a tainted source, and which he ought to have suspected because it conceded what he desired. God's indisputable intimations to our individual souls are not to be set aside except by intimations no less indisputable. There had been an obvious reason for the command which God had given. The reason still existed; the prohibition had not been withdrawn. The sham revelation furnished him with an excuse; it did not give him a justification. Why did he yield so readily? It was for the same reason which causes so many to sin. "The tempting opportunity 'did but meet, as sooner or later it always will meet,' the susceptible disposition."

Yet his punishment does not justify us in branding him as a weak or a vicious man. We must judge him and all men, at his best, not at his worst; in his

	1744.321	420, 1158	3937, 569.141	2372.133, 3937	881, 2645
27.	cj, v Piel impf 3ms	prep, n mp, ps 3ms	prep, v Qal inf con	v Qal impv 2mp, prep, ps 3ms	do, art, n ms
	וַיְדַבֵּר	אֶל־בָּנָיו	לֵאמֹר	חִבְשׁוּ־לִי	אֶת־הַחֲמוֹר
	waydhabbēr	'el-bānâv	lē'mōr	chivshû-lî	'eth-hachmôr
	and he spoke	to his sons	saying	saddle for me	the donkey

2372.126		2050.121	4834.121	881, 5215	8390.657	904, 1932
cj, v Qal impf 3mp	**28.**	cj, v Qal impf 3ms	cj, v Qal impf 3ms	do, n fs, ps 3ms	v Hophal ptc fs	prep, art, n ms
וַיַּחֲבשׁוּ		וַיֵּלֶךְ	וַיִּמְצָא	אֶת־נִבְלָתוֹ	מֻשְׁלֶכֶת	בַּדֶּרֶךְ
wayyachvōshû		wayyēlekh	wayyimtsā'	'eth-nivlāthô	mushlekheth	badderekh
and they saddled		and he went	and he found	his corpse	thrown down	on the road

2645	765	6198.152	703	5215	3940, 404.111	765
cj, n ms	cj, art, n ms	v Qal act ptc mp	prep	art, n fs	neg part, v Qal pf 3ms	art, n ms
וַחֲמוֹר	וְהָאַרְיֵה	עֹמְדִים	אֵצֶל	הַנְּבֵלָה	לֹא־אָכַל	הָאַרְיֵה
wachmôr	wehā'aryēh	'ōmedhîm	'ētsel	hannevēlāh	lō'-'ākhal	hā'aryēh
and the donkey	and the lion	standing	beside	the corpse	it had not eaten	the lion

881, 5215	3940	8132.111	881, 2645		5558.121	5204
do, art, n fs	cj, neg part	v Qal pf 3ms	do, art, n ms	**29.**	cj, v Qal impf 3ms	art, n ms
אֶת־הַנְּבֵלָה	וְלֹא	שָׁבַר	אֶת־הַחֲמוֹר		וַיִּשָּׂא	הַנָּבִיא
'eth-hannevēlāh	welō'	shāvar	'eth-hachmôr		wayyissā'	hannāvî'
the corpse	and not	he had broken	the donkey		and he lifted up	the prophet

881, 5215	382, 435	5299.521	420, 2645	8178.521
do, *n fs*	*n ms*, art, n mp	cj, v Hiphil impf 3ms, ps 3ms	prep, art, n ms	cj, v Hiphil impf 3ms, ps 3ms
אֶת־נִבְלַת	אִישׁ־הָאֱלֹהִים	וַיַּנִּחֵהוּ	אֶל־הַחֲמוֹר	וַיְשִׁיבֵהוּ
'eth-nivlath	'îsh-hā'ĕlōhîm	wayyanichēhû	'el-hachmôr	wayshîvēhû
the corpse of	the man of God	and he laid it	onto the donkey	and he brought him back

971.121	420, 6111	5204	2292	3937, 5792.141	3937, 7196.141
cj, v Qal impf 3ms	prep, *n fs*	art, n ms	art, n ms	prep, v Qal inf con	cj, prep, v Qal inf con, ps 3ms
וַיָּבֹא	אֶל־עִיר	הַנָּבִיא	הַזָּקֵן	לִסְפֹּד	וּלְקָבְרוֹ
wayyāvō'	'el-'îr	hannāvî'	hazzāqēn	lispōdh	ûlăqāverô
and he came	to the city of	the prophet	the old man	to lament	and to bury him

	5299.521	881, 5215	904, 7197	5792.126	6142	2013
30.	cj, v Hiphil impf 3ms	do, n fs, ps 3ms	prep, n ms, ps 3ms	cj, v Qal impf 3mp	prep, ps 3ms	intrj
	וַיַּנַּח	אֶת־נִבְלָתוֹ	בְּקִבְרוֹ	וַיִּסְפְּדוּ	עָלָיו	הוֹי
	wayyannach	'eth-nivlāthô	beqivrô	wayyispedhû	'ālâv	hôy
	and he laid	his corpse	in his tomb	and they lamented	concerning him	alas

250		2030.121	313	7196.141	881	569.121
n ms, ps 1cs	**31.**	cj, v Qal impf 3ms	prep	v Qal inf con, ps 3ms	do, ps 3ms	cj, v Qal impf 3ms
אָחִי		וַיְהִי	אַחֲרֵי	קָבְרוֹ	אֹתוֹ	וַיֹּאמֶר
'āchî		wayhî	'achrê	qāverô	'ōthô	wayyō'mer
my brother		and it was	after	his burying	him	and he said

420, 1158	3937, 569.141	904, 4322.141	7196.117	881	904, 7197
prep, n mp, ps 3ms	prep, v Qal inf con	prep, v Qal inf con, ps 1cs	cj, v Qal pf 2mp	do, ps 1cs	prep, art, n ms
אֶל־בָּנָיו	לֵאמֹר	בְּמוֹתִי	וּקְבַרְתֶּם	אֹתִי	בַּקֶּבֶר
'el-bānâv	lē'mōr	bemôthî	ûqŏvartem	'ōthî	baqqever
to his sons	saying	when my dying	then you must bury	me	in the tomb

866	382	435	7196.155	904	703	6344	5299.533
rel part	*n ms*	art, n mp	v Qal pass ptc ms	prep, ps 3ms	prep	n fp, ps 3ms	v Hiphil impv 2mp
אֲשֶׁר	אִישׁ	הָאֱלֹהִים	קָבוּר	בּוֹ	אֵצֶל	עַצְמֹתָיו	הַנִּיחוּ
'ăsher	'îsh	hā'ĕlōhîm	qāvûr	bô	'ētsel	'atsmōthâv	hanîchû
which	the man of	God	buried	in it	beside	his bones	lay

881, 6344		3706	2030.142	2030.121	1745	866	7410.111
do, n fp, ps 1cs	**32.**	cj	v Qal inf abs	v Qal impf 3ms	art, n ms	rel part	v Qal pf 3ms
אֶת־עַצְמֹתָי		כִּי	הָיֹה	יִהְיֶה	הַדָּבָר	אֲשֶׁר	קָרָא
'eth-'atsmōthāy		kî	hāyōh	yihyeh	haddāvār	'ăsher	qārā'
my bones		because	being	it will surely be	the event	which	he called out

904, 1745	3176	6142, 4326	866	904, 1044	6142
prep, *n ms*	pn	prep, art, n ms	rel part	prep, pn	cj, prep
בִּדְבַר	יְהוָה	עַל־הַמִּזְבֵּחַ	אֲשֶׁר	בְּבֵית־אֵל	וְעַל
bidhvar	yehwāh	'al-hammizbēach	'ăsher	bevêth-'ēl	we'al
by the word of	Yahweh	concerning the altar	which	in Bethel	and concerning

3725, 1041	1154	866	904, 6111	8497		313	1745
adj, n mp	art, n fp	rel part	prep, *n fp*	pn	**33.**	prep	art, n ms
כָּל־בָּתֵּי	הַבָּמוֹת	אֲשֶׁר	בְּעָרֵי	שֹׁמְרוֹן		אַחַר	הַדָּבָר
kol-bāttê	habbāmôth	'ăsher	be'ārê	shōmerôn		'achar	haddāvār
all the temples of	the high places	which	in the cities of	Samaria		after	the event

28. And he went and found his carcase cast in the way: ... cast along in the way, *Tyndale* ... he found the dead body, *Douay*.

and the ass and the lion standing by the carcase: the lion had not eaten the carcase, nor torn the ass: ... not devoured the corpse nor torn the donkey, *Berkeley* ... neither devoured the body nor broken the back of the donkey, *REB* ... attacked the donkey, *NLT* ... torn the donkey in pieces, *Beck*.

29. And the prophet took up the carcase of the man of God, and laid it upon the ass, and brought it back: and the old prophet came to the city, to mourn and to bury him: ... lifted the corpse, *JB* ... took up the dead body, *KJVII* ... the aged prophet came into the city, to make lamentation, *Rotherham*.

30. And he laid his carcase in his own grave: ... The prophet buried the body in his own family grave, *NCV* ... he put the body in the restingplace made ready for himself, *BB* ... corpse in his own sepulchre, *Darby*.

and they mourned over him, saying, Alas, my brother!: ... Alas, brother, alas the day!, *Knox* ... My brother, my brother!, *NEB* ... mourned over it as if it were his brother, *Fenton* ... crying out in grief, *NLT*.

31. And it came to pass, after he had buried him, that he spake to his sons, saying, When I am dead, then bury me in the sepulchre wherein the man of God is buried; lay my bones beside his bones: ... body by his body, *Beck* ... remains beside his, *NAB* ... put me by his bones so that my bones may be kept safe with his bones, *BB* ... in this tomb where God's prophet rests, *Knox*.

32. For the saying which he cried by the word of the Lord against the altar in Beth-el, and against all the houses of the high places which are in the cities of Samaria, shall surely come to pass: ... the message the Lord told him to proclaim, *NLT* ... become a reality, *KJVII* ... for the sentence which he pronounced at the Lord's command, *NEB* ... What the Lord spoke through him will certainly come true, *NCV*.

33. After this thing Jeroboam returned not from his evil way, but made again of the lowest of the people priests of the high places: ... did not abandon his evil ways, but went on appointing priests for the shrines from all classes of the people, *REB* ... continued to choose priests from ordinary families, *Good News*.

whosoever would, he consecrated him, and he became one of the priests of the high places: ... he filled his hand, and he was made a priest, *Douay* ... he made a priest of anyone desiring it, *BB* ... a priest for the places of worship was allowed to be one, *NCV* ... he consecrated anyone he liked, *Moffatt*.

---

hours of faithfulness and splendid courage, not in his moment of unworthy acquiescence.

13:31–34. And his speedy punishment was his best blessing. Who knows what might not have happened to him if the speck of conventionality and corruption had been allowed to spread? Who can tell whether in due time he might not have sunk into something no better than his miserable tempter? Rather than that we should be in any respect false to our loftiest ideals, or less noble than our better selves, let the lion meet us, let the tower of Siloam fall on us, let our blood be mingled with our sacrifices. Better physical death than spiritual degeneracy.

2172	3940, 8178.111	3493	4623, 1932	7737	8178.121
art, dem pron	neg part, v Qal pf 3ms	pn	prep, n fs, ps 3ms	art, adj	cj, v Qal impf 3ms
הַזֶּה	לֹא־שָׁב	יָרָבְעָם	מִדַּרְכּוֹ	הָרָעָה	וַיָּשָׁב
hazzeh	lō'-shāv	yārov'ām	middarkô	hārā'āh	wayyāshāv
the this	he did not turn back	Jeroboam	from his way	the evil	and he returned

6449.121	4623, 7382	6194	3669	1154	2760	4527.321
cj, v Qal impf 3ms	prep, *n fp*	art, n ms	*n mp*	n fp	art, adj	v Piel impf 3ms
וַיַּעַשׂ	מִקְצוֹת	הָעָם	כֹּהֲנֵי	בָמוֹת	הֶחָפֵץ	יְמַלֵּא
wayya'as	miqōtsôth	hā'ām	kōhᵉnê	vāmôth	hechāphēts	yᵉmallē'
and he made	from the ends of	the people	priests of	high places	those desirous	he filled

881, 3135	2030.121	3669	1154		2030.121	1745
do, n fs, ps 3ms	cj, v Qal juss 3ms	*n mp*	n fp	**34.**	cj, v Qal impf 3ms	prep, art, n ms
אֶת־יָדוֹ	וִיהִי	כֹּהֲנֵי	בָמוֹת		וַיְהִי	בַּדָּבָר
'eth-yādhô	wîhî	kōhᵉnê	vāmôth		wayhî	baddāvār
their hand	that they might be	priests of	high places		and it was	when the thing

2172	3937, 2496	1041	3493	3937, 3701.541	3937, 8436.541
art, dem pron	prep, *n fs*	*n ms*	pn	cj, prep, v Hiphil inf con	cj, prep, v Hiphil inf con
הַזֶּה	לְחַטַּאת	בֵּית	יָרָבְעָם	וּלְהַכְחִיד	וּלְהַשְׁמִיד
hazzeh	lᵉchatta'th	bêth	yārov'ām	ûlăhakhchîdh	ûlăhashmîdh
the this	a sin of	the household of	Jeroboam	and to destroy	and to exterminate

4623, 6142	6686	124		904, 6496	2026	2571.111	27
prep, prep	*n mp*	art, n fs	**14:1**	prep, art, n fs	art, dem pron	v Qal pf 3ms	pn
מֵעַל	פְּנֵי	הָאֲדָמָה		בָּעֵת	הַהִיא	חָלָה	אֲבִיָּה
mē'al	pᵉnê	hā'ădhāmāh		bā'ēth	hahî'	chālāh	'ăvîyāh
from on	the surface of	the land		at the time	the that	he became sick	Abijah

1158, 3493		569.121	3493	3937, 828	7251.132	5167
n ms, pn	**2.**	cj, v Qal impf 3ms	pn	prep, n fs, ps 3ms	v Qal impv 2fs	part
בֶן־יָרָבְעָם		וַיֹּאמֶר	יָרָבְעָם	לְאִשְׁתּוֹ	קוּמִי	נָא
ven-yārov'ām		wayyō'mer	yārov'ām	lᵉ'ishtô	qûmî	nā'
the son of Jeroboam		and he said	Jeroboam	to his wife	arise	please

8521.714	3940	3156.126	3706, 891	828	3493
cj, v Hithpael pf 2fs	cj, neg part	v Qal impf 3mp	cj, pers pron	*n fs*	pn
וְהִשְׁתַּנִּית	וְלֹא	יֵדְעוּ	כִּי־אַתִּי	אֵשֶׁת	יָרָבְעָם
wᵉhishtanîth	wᵉlō'	yēdhᵉ'û	kî-'attî	'ēsheth	yārov'ām
and you will disguise yourself	that not	they will know	that you	the wife of	Jeroboam

2050.114	8350	2079, 8427	282	5204	2000, 1744.311	6142
cj, v Qal pf 2fs	pn	intrj, adv	pn	art, n ms	pers pron, v Piel pf 3ms	prep, ps 1cs
וְהָלַכְתְּ	שִׁלֹה	הִנֵּה־שָׁם	אֲחִיָּה	הַנָּבִיא	הוּא־דִבֶּר	עָלַי
wᵉhālakht	shilōh	hinnēh-shām	'ăchîyāh	hannāvî'	hû'-dhibber	'ālay
and you will go	Shiloh	behold there	Ahijah	the prophet	he he spoke	concerning me

3937, 4567	6142, 6194	2172		4089.114	904, 3135	6463	4035
prep, n ms	prep, art, n ms	art, dem pron	**3.**	cj, v Qal pf 2fs	prep, n fs, ps 2fs	num	n ms
לְמֶלֶךְ	עַל־הָעָם	הַזֶּה		וְלָקַחַתְּ	בְּיָדֵךְ	עֲשָׂרָה	לֶחֶם
lᵉmelekh	'al-hā'ām	hazzeh		wᵉlāqachattᵉ	bᵉyādhēkh	'ăsārāh	lechem
as king	over the people	the this		and you will take	in your hand	ten	bread

5535	1254	1756	971.114	420	2000	5222.521
cj, n mp	cj, *n ms*	n ms	cj, v Qal pf 2fs	prep, ps 3ms	pers pron	v Hiphil impf 3ms
וְנִקֻּדִים	וּבַקְבֻּק	דְּבַשׁ	וּבָאת	אֵלָיו	הוּא	יַגִּיד
wᵉniqqudhîm	ûvaqōbbuq	dᵉvash	ûvā'th	'ēlâv	hû'	yaggîdh
and baked goods	and a jar of	honey	and you will go	to him	he	he will tell

3937	4242, 2030.121	3937, 5470		6449.122	3772	828	3493
prep, ps 2fs	intrg, v Qal impf 3ms	prep, art, n ms	**4.**	cj, v Qal impf 3fs	adv	*n fs*	pn
לָךְ	מַה־יִּהְיֶה	לַנָּעַר		וַתַּעַשׂ	כֵּן	אֵשֶׁת	יָרָבְעָם
lākh	mah-yihyeh	lannā‘ar		watta‘as	kēn	'ēsheth	yārov‘ām
you	what will happen	to the boy		and she did	so	the wife of	Jeroboam

7251.122	2050.122	8350	971.122	1041	282	282
cj, v Qal impf 3fs	cj, v Qal impf 3fs	pn	cj, v Qal impf 3fs	*n ms*	pn	cj, pn
וַתָּקָם	וַתֵּלֶךְ	שִׁלֹה	וַתָּבֹא	בֵּית	אֲחִיָּה	וַאֲחִיָּהוּ
wattāqām	wattēlekh	shilōh	wattāvō'	bêth	'ăchîyāh	wa'ăchîyāhû
and she arose	and she went to	Shiloh	and she came to	the house of	Ahijah	and Ahijah

3940, 3310.111	3937, 7495.141	3706	7251.116	6084
neg part, v Qal pf 3ms	prep, v Qal inf con	cj	v Qal pf 3cp	n fd, ps 3ms
לֹא־יָכֹל	לִרְאוֹת	כִּי	קָמוּ	עֵינָיו
lō'-yākhōl	lir'ôth	kî	qāmû	‘ênāv
he was not able	to see	because	they had become fixed	his eyes

4623, 7938		3176	569.111	420, 282	2079	828
prep, n ms, ps 3ms	**5.**	cj, pn	v Qal pf 3ms	prep, pn	intrj	*n fs*
מִשֵּׂיבוֹ		וַיהוָה	אָמַר	אֶל־אֲחִיָּהוּ	הִנֵּה	אֵשֶׁת
missêvô		wayhwāh	'āmar	'el-'ăchîyāhû	hinnēh	'ēsheth
from his elderly condition		but Yahweh	He said	unto to Ahijah	behold	the wife of

34. And this thing became sin unto the house of Jeroboam, even to cut it off, and to destroy it from off the face of the earth: ... even to blot it out, *NASB* ... the death of all his family, *NLT* ... Such conduct made the House of Jeroboam a sinful House, and caused its ruin and extinction, *JB* ... so as to exterminate, *NKJV*.

14:1. At that time Abijah the son of Jeroboam fell sick: ... King Jeroboam's son Abijah got sick, *Good News* ... Abia fell sick, *Knox* ... became very sick, *NLT*.

2. And Jeroboam said to his wife, Arise, I pray thee, and disguise thyself, that thou be not known to be the wife of Jeroboam; and get thee to Shiloh: ... dress yourself so people won't know you are my wife, *NCV* ... put on different clothing, *BB* ... change thy dress, *Douay*.

behold, there is Ahijah the prophet, which told me that I should be king over this people: ... the man who predicted that I was to reign, *Moffatt*.

3. And take with thee ten loaves, and cracknels, and a cruse of honey, and go to him: he shall tell thee what shall become of the child: ... some cakes for his children, and a jar, *Moffatt* ... some pastry, and a pot, *Knox* ... some raisins, and a flask of syrup, *NEB* ... some savoury food, *JB*.

4. And Jeroboam's wife did so, and arose, and went to Shiloh, and came to the house of Ahijah. But Ahijah could not see; for his eyes were set by reason of his age: ... unable to see, because he was very old, *BB* ... his eyes had become dim because of his age, *Goodspeed* ... his sight was gone, *NIV* ... He was an old man now and could no longer see, *NLT*.

14:1–3. The other story about Jeroboam is full of pathos; and though here, too, there are obvious signs that, in its present form, it could hardly have come from a contemporary source, it doubtless records a historic tradition. It is missing in the Septuagint, though in some copies the blank is supplied from Aquila's version.

Jeroboam was living with his queen at Tirzah when, as a judgment on him for his neglect of the divine warning, his eldest and much loved son, Abijah, fell sick. Torn with anxiety the king asked his wife to disguise herself that she might not be recognized on her journey, and to go to Shiloh, where Ahijah the prophet lived, to inquire about the dear youth's fate. "Take with you," he said, "as a present to the prophet ten loaves, and some little cakes for the prophet's children, and a cruse of honey."

14:4. Jeroboam remembered that Ahijah's former prophecy had been fulfilled, and believed that he would again be able to reveal the future, and say whether the heir to the throne would recover. The queen obeyed; and if she were indeed the Egyptian princess Ano, it must have been for her a strange experience. Through the winding valley, she reached the home of the aged prophet unrecognized.

3493	971.153	3937, 1938.141	1745	4623, 6196	420, 1158	3706, 2571.151
pn	v Qal act ptc fs	prep, v Qal inf con	n ms	prep, prep, ps 2ms	prep, n ms, ps 3fs	cj, v Qal act ptc ms
יָרָבְעָם	בָּאָה	לִדְרֹשׁ	דָּבָר	מֵעִמְּךָ	אֶל־בְּנָהּ	כִּי־חֹלֶה
yārov'ām	bā'āh	lidhrōsh	dāvār	mē'immekhā	'el-benāhh	kî-chōleh
Jeroboam	coming	to inquire	a word	from with you	about her son	because sick

2000	3626, 2173	3626, 2172	1744.323	420	2030.121
pers pron	prep, dem pron	cj, prep, dem pron	v Piel impf 2ms	prep, ps 3fs	cj, v Qal impf 3ms
הוּא	כָּזֹה	וְכָזֶה	תְּדַבֵּר	אֵלֶיהָ	וִיהִי
hû'	kāzōh	wekhāzeh	tedhabbēr	'ēlêāh	wîhî
he	like this	and like that	you will speak	to her	and it was

3626, 971.141	2026	5422.753		2030.121	3626, 8471.141
prep, v Qal inf con, ps 3fs	cj, pers pron	v Hithpael ptc fs	**6.**	cj, v Qal impf 3ms	prep, v Qal inf con
כְּבֹאָהּ	וְהִיא	מִתְנַכֵּרָה		וַיְהִי	כִּשְׁמֹעַ
khevō'āhh	wehî'	mithnakkērāh		wayhî	khishmōa'
when her coming	that she	assuming an identity		and it was	when hearing

282	881, 7249	7559	971.153	904, 6860	569.121	971.132
pn	do, *n ms*	n fd, ps 3fs	v Qal act ptc fs	prep, art, n ms	cj, v Qal impf 3ms	v Qal impv 2fs
אֲחִיָּהוּ	אֶת־קוֹל	רַגְלֶיהָ	בָּאָה	בַּפֶּתַח	וַיֹּאמֶר	בֹּאִי
'ăchîyāhû	'eth-qôl	raghlêāh	bā'āh	vappethach	wayyō'mer	bō'î
Ahijah	the sound of	her feet	coming	in the doorway	and he said	come in

828	3493	4066	2172	879	5422.753	609	8365.155
n fs	pn	intrg	dem pron	pers pron	v Hithpael ptc fs	cj, pers pron	v Qal pass ptc ms
אֵשֶׁת	יָרָבְעָם	לָמָּה	זֶּה	אַתְּ	מִתְנַכֵּרָה	וְאָנֹכִי	שָׁלוּחַ
'ēsheth	yārov'ām	lāmmāh	zeh	'atte	mithnakkērāh	we'ānōkhî	shālûach
the wife of	Jeroboam	why	this	you	assuming an identity	for I	one sent out

420	7482		2050.132	569.132	3937, 3493	569.111	3176	435
prep, ps 2fs	adv	**7.**	v Qal impv 2fs	v Qal impv 2fs	prep, pn	v Qal pf 3ms	pn	*n mp*
אֵלַיִךְ	קָשָׁה		לְכִי	אִמְרִי	לְיָרָבְעָם	כֹּה־אָמַר	יְהוָה	אֱלֹהֵי
'ēlayikh	qāshāh		lekhî	'imrî	leyārov'ām	kōh-'āmar	yehwāh	'ĕlōhê
to you	severely		go	say	to Jeroboam	He has said	Yahweh	the God of

3547	3391	866	7597.515	4623, 8761	6194	5598.125
pn	cj	rel part	v Hiphil pf 1cs, ps 2ms	prep, *n ms*	art, n ms	cj, v Qal impf 1cs, ps 2ms
יִשְׂרָאֵל	יַעַן	אֲשֶׁר	הֲרִימֹתִיךָ	מִתּוֹךְ	הָעָם	וָאֶתֶּנְךָ
yisrā'ēl	ya'an	'ăsher	herîmōthîkhā	mittôkh	hā'ām	wā'ettenkhā
Israel	because	that	I exalted you	from the midst of	the people	and I placed you

5233	6142	6194	3547		7458.125	881, 4608	4623, 1041
n ms	prep	n ms, ps 1cs	pn	**8.**	cj, v Qal impf 1cs	do, art, n fs	prep, *n ms*
נָגִיד	עַל	עַמִּי	יִשְׂרָאֵל		וָאֶקְרַע	אֶת־הַמַּמְלָכָה	מִבֵּית
nāghîdh	'al	'ammî	yisrā'ēl		wā'eqōra'	'eth-hammamlākhāh	mibbêth
a leader	over	my people	Israel		and I tore away	the kingdom	from the household of

1784	5598.125	3937	3940, 2030.113	3626, 5860	1784	866
pn	cj, v Qal impf 1cs, ps 3fs	prep, ps 2ms	cj, neg part, v Qal pf 2ms	prep, n ms, ps 1cs	pn	rel pron
דָּוִד	וָאֶתְּנֶהָ	לָךְ	וְלֹא־הָיִיתָ	כְּעַבְדִּי	דָוִד	אֲשֶׁר
dāwidh	wā'etteneāh	lākh	welō'-hāyîthā	ke'avdî	dhāwidh	'ăsher
David	and I gave it	to you	but you have not been	like my servant	David	who

8490.111	4851	866, 2050.111	313	904, 3725, 3949
v Qal pf 3ms	n fp, ps 1cs	cj, rel pron, v Qal pf 3ms	prep, ps 1cs	prep, *adj*, n ms, ps 3ms
שָׁמַר	מִצְוֹתַי	וַאֲשֶׁר־הָלַךְ	אַחֲרַי	בְּכָל־לְבָבוֹ
shāmar	mitswōthay	wa'ăsher-hālakh	'achray	bekhol-levāvô
he observed	my commandments	and who he walked	after Me	with all his heart

3937, 6449.141 prep, v Qal inf con לַעֲשׂוֹת la‘ăsôth to do	7828 adv רַק raq only	3596 art, adj הַיָּשָׁר hayyāshār what is upright	904, 6084 prep, n fd, ps 1cs בְּעֵינָי be‘ênāy in my eyes	**9.**	7778.523 cj, v Hiphil impf 2ms וַתָּרַע wattāra‘ and you have acted wickedly

3937, 6449.141 prep, v Qal inf con לַעֲשׂוֹת la‘ăsôth to do	4623, 3725 prep, n ms מִכֹּל mikkōl among everyone	866, 2030.116 rel pron, v Qal pf 3cp אֲשֶׁר־הָיוּ 'ăsher-hāyû who they were	3937, 6686 prep, n mp, ps 2ms לְפָנֶיךָ lephānêkhā before you	2050.123 cj, v Qal impf 2ms וַתֵּלֶךְ wattēlekh and you went

6449.123, 3937 cj, v Qal impf 2ms, prep, ps 2ms וַתַּעֲשֶׂה־לְּךָ watta‘ăseh-lekhā and you made for yourself	435 n mp אֱלֹהִים 'ĕlōhîm gods	311 adj אֲחֵרִים 'ăchērîm others	4691 cj, n fp וּמַסֵּכוֹת ûmassēkhôth and cast images	3937, 3832.541 prep, v Hiphil inf con, ps 1cs לְהַכְעִיסֵנִי lehakh‘îsēnî to provoke Me to anger	881 cj, do, ps 1cs וְאֹתִי we'ōthî but Me

5. And the Lord said unto Ahijah, Behold, the wife of Jeroboam cometh to ask a thing of thee for her son; for he is sick: thus and thus shalt thou say unto her: for it shall be, when she cometh in, that she shall feign herself to be another woman: ... is coming to seek an oracle from you, because of the condition of her son, *Berkeley* ... she shall pretend, *KJVII* ... will be in disguise, *NAB* ... concealing who she was, *REB*.

6. And it was so, when Ahijah heard the sound of her feet, as she came in at the door, that he said: ... heard her footsteps, *NLT*.

Come in, thou wife of Jeroboam; why feignest thou thyself to be another?: ... do you pretend to be somebody else?, *Beck* ... conceal who you are?, *REB* ... are you in disguise?, *NAB*.

for I am sent to thee with heavy tidings: ... to you with a harsh message, *NASB* ... with hard news, *KJVII* ... I have bad news for you, *JB*.

7. Go, tell Jeroboam, Thus saith the Lord God of Israel, Forasmuch as I exalted thee from among the people, and made thee prince over my people Israel: ... made you leader over my people, *NRSV* ... made you ruler, *NKJV* ... raised you up, *NIV* ... made you supreme, *Moffatt*.

8. And rent the kingdom away from the house of David, and gave it thee: ... took the kingdom away by force from the seed of David, *BB* ... tore away, *Berkeley* ... away from David's family, *NCV*.

and yet thou hast not been as my servant David, who kept my commandments, and who followed me with all his heart, to do that only which was right in mine eyes: ... doing that which was well pleasing in my sight, *Douay* ... who was completely loyal to me, *Good News*.

9. But hast done evil above all that were before thee: for thou hast gone and made thee other gods, and molten images, to provoke me to anger, and hast cast me behind thy back: ... You have done more evil than all who lived before you, *NLT* ... done worse than all who preceded you, *NAB* ... turned your back on me, *NEB*.

14:5–6. But he had received a divine intimation of her errand; and though his eyes were now blind with the *gutta serena*, he at once addressed her by name when he heard the sound of her approaching footsteps. The message which he was bidden to pronounce was utterly terrible; it was unrelieved by a single gleam of mitigation or a single expression of pity. It reproached and denounced Jeroboam for faithless ingratitude in that he had cast God behind his back; it threatened hopeless and shameful extermination to all his house. His dynasty should be swept away like dung. The corpses of his children should be left unburied and be devoured by vultures and wild dogs. The moment the feet of the queen reached her house the youth should die, and this bereavement, heavy as it was, should be the sole act of mercy in the tragedy, for it should take away Abijah from the dreadful days to come, because in him alone of the House of Jeroboam had God seen something good. The avenger should be a new king, and all this should come to pass "even now" (1 Ki. 14:14).

14:7–16. This speech of the prophet is given in a rhythmic form, and has probably been mingled with later touches. It falls into two strophes (vv. 7–12, 12–16) of 3 + 2 and 2 + 3 verses. The expression "thou hast done above all that were before thee, for thou hast gone and made thee other gods" suits

8390.513	313	1488		3937, 3772	2079	971.551	7750
v Hiphil pf 2ms	prep	n ms, ps 2ms	**10.**	prep, adv	intrj, ps 1cs	v Hiphil ptc ms	adj
הִשְׁלַכְתָּ	אַחֲרֵי	גַוֶּךָ		לָכֵן	הִנְנִי	מֵבִיא	רָעָה
hishlakhtā	'achrê	ghawwekhā		lākhēn	hin^{e}nî	mēvî'	rā'āh
you have thrown down	behind	your back		therefore	behold I	bringing	evil

420, 1041	3493	3901.515	3937, 3493	8697.551	904, 7306
prep, *n ms*	pn	cj, v Hiphil pf 1cs	prep, pn	v Hiphil ptc ms	prep, n ms
אֶל־בֵּית	יָרָבְעָם	וְהִכְרַתִּי	לְיָרָבְעָם	מַשְׁתִּין	בְּקִיר
'el-bêth	yārov'ām	w^{e}hikhrattî	l^{e}yārov'ām	mashtîn	b^{e}qîr
to the household of	Jeroboam	and I will cut off	of Jeroboam	those urinating	on a wall

6352.155	6013.155	904, 3547	1220.315	313	1041, 3493
v Qal pass ptc ms	cj, v Qal pass ptc ms	prep, pn	cj, v Piel pf 1cs	prep	*n ms*, pn
עָצוּר	וְעָזוּב	בְּיִשְׂרָאֵל	וּבִעַרְתִּי	אַחֲרֵי	בֵית־יָרָבְעָם
'ātsûr	w^{e}'āzûv	b^{e}yisrā'ēl	ûvi'artî	'achrê	vêth-yārov'ām
those restrained	and those freed	in Israel	and I will burn	after	the household of Jeroboam

3626, 866	1220.321	1598	5912, 8882.141		4322.151	3937, 3493
prep, rel part	v Piel impf 3ms	art, n ms	adv, v Qal inf con, ps 3ms	**11.**	art, v Qal act ptc ms	prep, pn
כַּאֲשֶׁר	יְבַעֵר	הַגָּלָל	עַד־תֻּמּוֹ		הַמֵּת	לְיָרָבְעָם
ka'ăsher	y^{e}va'ēr	haggālāl	'adh-tummô		hammēth	l^{e}yārov'ām
just as	someone burns	the dung	until its being finished		the dead ones	to Jeroboam

904, 6111	404.126	3732	4322.151	904, 7898	404.126	5991
prep, art, n fs	v Qal impf 3mp	art, n mp	cj, art, v Qal act ptc ms	prep, art, n ms	v Qal impf 3mp	*n ms*
בָּעִיר	יֹאכְלוּ	הַכְּלָבִים	וְהַמֵּת	בַּשָּׂדֶה	יֹאכְלוּ	עוֹף
bā'îr	yō'kh^{e}lû	hakk^{e}lāvîm	w^{e}hammēth	bassādheh	yō'kh^{e}lû	'ôph
in the city	they will eat	the dogs	and the dead ones	in the field	they will eat	the birds of

8452	3706	3176	1744.311		879	7251.132	2050.132
art, n md	cj	pn	v Piel pf 3ms	**12.**	cj, pers pron	v Qal impv 2fs	v Qal impv 2fs
הַשָּׁמָיִם	כִּי	יְהוָה	דִּבֵּר		וְאַתְּ	קוּמִי	לְכִי
hashshāmāyim	kî	y^{e}hwāh	dibbēr		w^{e}'att^{e}	qûmî	l^{e}khî
the heavens	because	Yahweh	He has spoken		now you	arise	go

3937, 1041	904, 971.141	7559	6111	4322.111	3315
prep, n ms, ps 2fs	prep, v Qal inf con	n fd, ps 2fs	art, n fs	cj, v Qal pf 3ms	art, n ms
לְבֵיתֵךְ	בְּבֹאָה	רַגְלַיִךְ	הָעִירָה	וּמֵת	הַיָּלֶד
l^{e}vêthēkh	b^{e}vō'āh	raghlayikh	hā'îrāh	ûmēth	hayyāledh
to your house	when entering	your feet	to the city	then he will die	the boy

	5792.116, 3937	3725, 3547	7196.116	881	3706, 2172
13.	cj, v Qal pf 3cp, prep, ps 3ms	*adj*, pn	cj, v Qal pf 3cp	do, ps 3ms	cj, dem pron
	וְסָפְדוּ־לוֹ	כָל־יִשְׂרָאֵל	וְקָבְרוּ	אֹתוֹ	כִּי־זֶה
	w^{e}sāph^{e}dhû-lô	khol-yisrā'ēl	w^{e}qāv^{e}rû	'ōthô	kî-zeh
	and they will lament for him	all Israel	and they will bury	him	because this one

3937, 940	971.121	3937, 3493	420, 7197	3391	4834.211, 3937	1745
prep, n ms, ps 3ms	v Qal impf 3ms	prep, pn	prep, n ms	cj	v Niphal pf 3ms, prep, ps 3ms	n ms
לְבַדּוֹ	יָבֹא	לְיָרָבְעָם	אֶל־קָבֶר	יַעַן	נִמְצָא־בוֹ	דָּבָר
l^{e}vaddô	yāvō'	l^{e}yārov'ām	'el-qāver	ya'an	nimtsā'-vô	dāvār
by himself	he will come	of Jeroboam	to the tomb	because	it has been found in him	a thing

3005	420, 3176	435	3547	904, 1041	3493
adj	prep, pn	*n mp*	pn	prep, *n ms*	pn
טוֹב	אֶל־יְהוָה	אֱלֹהֵי	יִשְׂרָאֵל	בְּבֵית	יָרָבְעָם
ṯôv	'el-y^{e}hwāh	'ĕlōhê	yisrā'ēl	b^{e}vêth	yārov'ām
good	to Yahweh	the God of	Israel	within the household of	Jeroboam

14.

7251.511	3176	3937	4567	6142, 3547	866	3901.521
cj, v Hiphil pf 3ms	pn	prep, ps 3ms	n ms	prep, pn	rel pron	v Hiphil impf 3ms
וְהֵקִים	יְהוָה	לוֹ	מֶלֶךְ	עַל־יִשְׂרָאֵל	אֲשֶׁר	יַכְרִית
wehēqîm	yehwāh	lô	melekh	'al-yisrā'ēl	'ăsher	yakhrîth
and He will raise up	Yahweh	for himself	a king	over Israel	who	he will cut off

881, 1041	3493	2172	3219	4242	1612, 6498		5409.511
do, *n ms*	pn	dem pron	art, n ms	cj, intrg	cj, adv	**15.**	cj, v Hiphil pf 3ms
אֶת־בֵּית	יָרָבְעָם	זֶה	הַיּוֹם	וּמֶה	גַּם־עַתָּה		וְהִכָּה
'eth-bêth	yārov'ām	zeh	hayyôm	ûmeh	gam-'attāh		wehikkāh
the household of	Jeroboam	this	today	and what	also now		and He will strike down

3176	881, 3547	3626, 866	5290.121	7354	904, 4448	5612.111
pn	do, pn	prep, rel part	v Qal impf 3ms	art, n ms	prep, art, n md	cj, v Qal pf 3ms
יְהוָה	אֶת־יִשְׂרָאֵל	כַּאֲשֶׁר	יָנוּד	הַקָּנֶה	בַּמַּיִם	וְנָתַשׁ
yehwāh	'eth-yisrā'ēl	ka'ăsher	yānûdh	haqqāneh	bammayim	wenāthash
Yahweh	Israel	just as	someone swishes	the reed	in the waters	and He will pluck out

10. Therefore, behold, I will bring evil upon the house of Jeroboam, and will cut off from Jeroboam him that pisseth against the wall, and him that is shut up and left in Israel: ... cutting off every male of his family, *Beck* ... I shall destroy them all, every mother's son, *REB* ... every man-child, *ASV* ... those sitting on the wall, *Young*.

and will take away the remnant of the house of Jeroboam, as a man taketh away dung, till it be all gone: ... as one burns up dung, *NRSV* ... be brushed away like a man brushing away waste till it is all gone, *BB*.

11. Him that dieth of Jeroboam in the city shall the dogs eat: ... who come to death in the town, will become food for the dogs, *BB* ... one of Jeroboam's line dies in the city, dogs will devour him, *NAB*.

and him that dieth in the field shall the fowls of the air eat: for the LORD hath spoken it: ... will be eaten by vultures, *Good News* ... who dies out in the country, the wild birds shall eat, *Moffatt* ... the birds of the sky shall eat them in the fields, *Fenton*.

12. Arise thou therefore, get thee to thine own house: and when thy feet enter into the city, the child shall die: ... As soon as you enter your city, your son will die, *NCV* ... While your feet are approaching, *Berkeley* ... at the moment your feet enter the town, *JB* ... When you step, *Beck*.

13. And all Israel shall mourn for him, and bury him: for he only of Jeroboam shall come to the grave, because in him there is found some good thing toward the LORD God of Israel in the house of Jeroboam: ... He is the only one belonging to Jeroboam who will be buried, *NIV* ... he alone of all Jeroboam's family will have proper burial, because in him alone could ... find anything good, *NEB* ... something pleasing to the LORD, *RSV*.

14. Moreover the LORD shall raise him up a king over Israel, who shall cut off the house of Jeroboam that day: but what? even now: ... this will happen soon, *NCV* ... this is the day, *NKJV* ... today, even now!, *NLT*.

15. For the LORD shall smite Israel, as a reed is shaken in the water: ... till it sways like a reed in water, *Moffatt*.

and he shall root up Israel out of this good land, which he gave to their fathers: ... pull Israel up from this beautiful country, *Fenton* ... uproot Israel from this prosperous land which he gave to their ancestors, *JB*.

---

the case of Jeroboam. (The Septuagint omits the prophecy of Israel's ultimate captivity.) They seem to charge Jeroboam with sanctioning Asherim, or wooden images of the goddess Asherah, of which we read in the history of Judah, but which are never mentioned in the acts of Jeroboam, and do not accord with his vowed policy.

14:17–20. The awful prophecy was fulfilled. As the hapless mother set foot on the threshold of her palace at beautiful Tirzah, the young prince died, and she heard the wail of the mourners for him. He alone was buried in the grave of his fathers, and Israel mourned for him. He was evidently a prince of much hope and promise, and the deaths of such princes have always peculiarly affected the sympathy of nations. It was better that Abijah should die than that he should live to be overwhelmed in the shameful ruin which soon overtook his house. It was better far that he should die than that he should grow up to frustrate the promise of his youth. He was beckoned by the hand of God "because in him was found some good thing towards the LORD God of Israel." We are

3937, 1	5598.111	866	2148	3009B	124	4623, 6142	881, 3547
prep, n mp, ps 3mp	v Qal pf 3ms	rel part	art, dem pron	art, adj	art, n fs	prep, prep	do, pn
לַאֲבוֹתֵיהֶם	נָתַן	אֲשֶׁר	הַזֹּאת	הַטּוֹבָה	הָאֲדָמָה	מֵעַל	אֶת־יִשְׂרָאֵל
la'ăvôthêhem	nāthan	'ăsher	hazzō'th	haṯṯôvāh	hā'ădhāmāh	mē'al	'eth-yisrā'ēl
to their ancestors	He gave	which	the this	the good	the land	from on	Israel

6449.116	866	3391	3937, 5282	4623, 5885	2306.311
v Qal pf 3cp	rel part	cj	prep, art, pn	prep, n ms	cj, v Piel pf 3ms, ps 3mp
עָשׂוּ	אֲשֶׁר	יַעַן	לַנָּהָר	מֵעֵבֶר	וְזֵרָם
'āsû	'ăsher	ya'an	lannāhār	mē'ēver	wᵉzērām
they have made	that	because	of the Euphrates	from the opposite side	and he will scatter them

881, 3547	5598.121		881, 3176	3832.552	881, 867
do, pn	cj, v Qal impf 3ms	**16.**	do, pn	v Hiphil ptc mp	do, n mp, ps 3mp
אֶת־יִשְׂרָאֵל	וְיִתֵּן		אֶת־יְהוָה	מַכְעִיסִים	אֶת־אֲשֵׁרֵיהֶם
'eth-yisrā'ēl	wᵉyittēn		'eth-yᵉhwāh	makh'îsîm	'eth-'ăshērêhem
Israel	and He will give		Yahweh	provoking to anger	their Asherah poles

881, 3547	2490.511	866	2490.111	866	3493	2496	937
do, pn	v Hiphil pf 3ms	cj, rel part	v Qal pf 3ms	rel part	pn	*n fp*	prep
אֶת־יִשְׂרָאֵל	הֶחֱטִיא	וַאֲשֶׁר	חָטָא	אֲשֶׁר	יָרָבְעָם	חַטֹּאות	בִּגְלַל
'eth-yisrā'ēl	hechĕṭî'	wa'ăsher	chāṭā'	'ăsher	yārov'ām	chaṭṭō'wth	bighlal
Israel	he caused to sin	and which	he has sinned	which	Jeroboam	the sins of	because of

2026	8995	971.122	2050.122	3493	828	7251.122	
pers pron	pn	cj, v Qal impf 3fs	cj, v Qal impf 3fs	pn	*n fs*	cj, v Qal impf 3fs	**17.**
הִיא	תִּרְצָתָה	וַתָּבֹא	וַתֵּלֶךְ	יָרָבְעָם	אֵשֶׁת	וַתָּקָם	
hî'	thirtsāthāh	wattāvō'	wattēlekh	yārov'ām	'ēsheth	wattāqām	
she	to Tirzah	and she came	and she went	Jeroboam	the wife of	and she rose up	

7196.126		4322.111	5470	904, 5790, 1041	971.153
cj, v Qal impf 3mp	**18.**	v Qal pf 3ms	cj, art, n ms	prep, *n ms*, art, n ms	v Qal act ptc fs
וַיִּקְבְּרוּ		מֵת	וְהַנַּעַר	בְּסַף־הַבַּיִת	בָּאָה
wayyiqōbbᵉrû		mēth	wᵉhanna'ar	vᵉsaph-habbayith	bā'āh
and they buried		he died	and the child	into the threshold of the house	coming

866	3176	3626, 1745	3725, 3547	5792.126, 3937	881
rel part	pn	prep, *n ms*	*adj*, pn	cj, v Qal impf 3mp, prep, ps 3ms	do, ps 3ms
אֲשֶׁר	יְהוָה	כִּדְבַר	כָּל־יִשְׂרָאֵל	וַיִּסְפְּדוּ־לוֹ	אֹתוֹ
'ăsher	yᵉhwāh	kidhvar	kol-yisrā'ēl	wayyispᵉdhû-lô	'ōthô
which	Yahweh	according to the word of	all Israel	and they lamented for him	him

3615		5204	282	904, 3135, 5860	1744.311
cj, *n ms*	**19.**	art, n ms	pn	prep, *n fs*, n ms, ps 3ms	v Piel pf 3ms
וְיֶתֶר		הַנָּבִיא	אֲחִיָּהוּ	בְּיַד־עַבְדּוֹ	דִּבֶּר
wᵉyether		hannāvî'	'ăchîyāhû	bᵉyadh-'avdô	dibber
and the remainder of		the prophet	Ahijah	by the hand of his servant	He had spoken

3918.156	2079	4566.111	866	4032.211	866	3493	1745
v Qal pass ptc mp	intrj, ps 3mp	v Qal pf 3ms	cj, rel part	v Niphal pf 3ms	rel part	pn	*n mp*
כְּתוּבִים	הִנָּם	מָלָךְ	וַאֲשֶׁר	נִלְחַם	אֲשֶׁר	יָרָבְעָם	דִּבְרֵי
kᵉthûvîm	hinnām	mālākh	wa'ăsher	nilcham	'ăsher	yārov'ām	divrê
things written	behold they	he reigned	and that	he fought	that	Jeroboam	the events of

866	3219		3547	3937, 4567	3219	1745	6142, 5809
rel part	cj, art, n mp	**20.**	pn	prep, *n mp*	art, n mp	*n mp*	prep, *n ms*
אֲשֶׁר	וְהַיָּמִים		יִשְׂרָאֵל	לְמַלְכֵי	הַיָּמִים	דִּבְרֵי	עַל־סֵפֶר
'ăsher	wᵉhayyāmîm		yisrā'ēl	lᵉmalkhê	hayyāmîm	divrê	'al-sēpher
which	and the days		Israel	of the kings of	the days	the events of	on the scroll of

4566.111	3493	6465	8692	8523	8311.121	6196, 1
v Qal pf 3ms	pn	num	cj, num	n fs	cj, v Qal impf 3ms	prep, n mp, ps 3ms
מָלַךְ	יָרָבְעָם	עֶשְׂרִים	וּשְׁתַּיִם	שָׁנָה	וַיִּשְׁכַּב	עִם־אֲבֹתָיו
mālakh	yārov'ām	'esrîm	ûsh^ettayim	shānāh	wayyishkav	'im-'ăvōthâv
he reigned	Jeroboam	twenty	and two	years	then he lay	with his ancestors

4566.121	5247	1158	8809		7628	1158, 8406
cj, v Qal impf 3ms	pn	n ms, ps 3ms	prep, ps 3ms	**21.**	cj, pn	n ms, pn
וַיִּמְלֹךְ	נָדָב	בְּנוֹ	תַּחְתָּיו		וּרְחַבְעָם	בֶּן־שְׁלֹמֹה
wayyimlōkh	nādhāv	b^enô	tachtâv		ûr^echav'ām	ben-sh^elōmōh
and he reigned	Nadab	his son	instead of him		and Rehoboam	the son of Solomon

and shall scatter them beyond the river, because they have made their groves, provoking the LORD to anger: ... by making their Asherim, *Berkeley* ... their wooden images, *NKJV* ... by making Asherah poles, *NIV* ... made them groves to anger the Lord, *Tyndale* ... men that defied the Lord with forest-shrines of their own fashioning, *Knox*.

16. And he shall give Israel up because of the sins of Jeroboam, who did sin, and who made Israel to sin: ... will abandon Israel on account of Jeroboam's sin, *Beck* ... he induced all Israel, *Fenton* ... which Jeroboam has done and made Israel do, *BB* ... then he made the people of Israel sin, *NCV*.

17. And Jeroboam's wife arose, and departed, and came to Tirzah: and when she came to the threshold of the door, the child died: ... just as she walked through the door of her home, *NLT* ... crossed the threshold of the palace, the child was already dead, *JB* ... she was just entering over the threshold, *Goodspeed*.

18. And they buried him; and all Israel mourned for him, according to the word of the LORD, which he spake by the hand of his servant Ahijah the prophet: ... as the LORD had prophesied through his servant, *NAB* ... buried him, and made lamentation, *MAST* ... as the Eternal had predicted, *Moffatt*.

19. And the rest of the acts of Jeroboam, how he warred, and how he reigned: ... other events of Jeroboam's reign, in war and peace, *REB* ... his wars and how he ruled, *NIV*. **behold, they are written in the book of the chronicles of the kings of Israel:** ... the book of the words of the days, *Douay* ... the Book of the Annals of the Kings, *NRSV* ... the records of the events of the times, *Fenton* ... the book of the stories, *Tyndale*.

20. And the days which Jeroboam reigned were two and twenty years: and he slept with his fathers, and Nadab his son reigned in his stead: ... Nadab succeeded him as king, *Beck* ... his son reigned in his place, *NKJV* ... the throne passed to his son Nadab, *Knox* ... he died, and his son Nadab became king, *NCV*.

21. And Rehoboam the son of Solomon reigned in Judah. Rehoboam was forty and one years old when he began to reign: ... forty-one years old when he

not told wherein the goodness consisted, but Rabbinic tradition guessed that in opposition to his father he discountenanced the calf-worship and encouraged and helped the people to continue their visits to Jerusalem. Such a king might indeed have recovered the whole kingdom, and have dispossessed David's degenerate line. But it was not to be.

But the passage about Abijah has a unique preciousness, because it stands alone in Scripture as an expression of the truth that early death is no sign at all of the divine anger, and that the length or brevity of life are matters of little significance to God, seeing that, at the best, the longest life is but as one tick of the clock in the eternal silence. The promise to filial obedience, "that thy days may be long," if the Fifth Commandment is primarily national; and although undoubtedly "length of days" then, as now, was regarded as a blessing (Job 12:12; Ps. 21:4; Prov. 3:2–16), yet the blessing is purely relative, and wholly incommensurate with others which affect the character and the life to come.

14:21–24. The only records of Rehoboam, the son of Solomon, are meager records of disaster and disgrace. He reigned seventeen years, and his mother, the Ammonitess Naamah, occupied the position of queen-mother. She was, doubtless, a worshiper in the shrine which Solomon had built for her national god, Molech of Ammon, who was the same as the Ashtar-Chemosh of the Moabite stone—the male form of Ashtoreth. Whether her son was forty-one when he succeeded to the throne or whether this was time of his sole reign, we do not know (1 Ki. 14:21). His attempted expedition against Jeroboam was forbidden by Shemaiah; but

4566.111	904, 3171	1158, 727	259	8523	7628	904, 4566.141
v Qal pf 3ms	prep, pn	*n ms*, num	cj, num	n fs	pn	prep, v Qal inf con, ps 3ms
מָלַךְ	בִּיהוּדָה	בֶּן־אַרְבָּעִים	וְאַחַת	שָׁנָה	רְחַבְעָם	בְּמָלְכוֹ
mālakh	bîhûdhāh	ben-'arbā'îm	we'achath	shānāh	rechav'ām	bemālekhô
he reigned	in Judah	a son of forty	and one	years	Rehoboam	when his reigning

8124	6462	8523	4566.111	904, 3503	6111	866, 1013.111	3176
cj, num	num	n fs	v Qal pf 3ms	prep, pn	art, n fs	rel part, v Qal pf 3ms	pn
וּשְׁבַע	עֶשְׂרֵה	שָׁנָה	מָלַךְ	בִּירוּשָׁלַם	הָעִיר	אֲשֶׁר־בָּחַר	יְהוָה
ûsheva'	'esrēh	shānāh	mālakh	bîrûshālam	hā'îr	'ăsher-bāchar	yehwāh
and seven	ten	years	he reigned	in Jerusalem	the city	which He had chosen	Yahweh

3937, 7947.141	881, 8428	8427	4623, 3725	8101	3547	8428
prep, v Qal inf con	do, n ms, ps 3ms	adv	prep, n ms	*n mp*	pn	cj, *n ms*
לָשׂוּם	אֶת־שְׁמוֹ	שָׁם	מִכֹּל	שִׁבְטֵי	יִשְׂרָאֵל	וְשֵׁם
lāsûm	'eth-shemô	shām	mikkōl	shivtê	yisrā'ēl	weshēm
to put	his name	there	among the entirety	the tribes of	Israel	and the name of

525	5462	6206		6449.121	3171	7737	904, 6084
n fs, ps 3ms	pn	art, pn	**22.**	cj, v Qal impf 3ms	pn	art, adj	prep, *n fd*
אִמּוֹ	נַעֲמָה	הָעַמֹּנִית		וַיַּעַשׂ	יְהוּדָה	הָרַע	בְּעֵינֵי
'immô	na'ămāh	hā'ammōnîth		wayya'as	yehûdhāh	hāra'	be'ênê
his mother	Naamah	the Ammonite		and they did	Judah	what is evil	in the eyes of

3176	7349.326	881	4623, 3725	866	6449.116
pn	cj, v Piel impf 3mp	do, ps 3ms	prep, n ms	rel part	v Qal pf 3cp
יְהוָה	וַיְקַנְאוּ	אֹתוֹ	מִכֹּל	אֲשֶׁר	עָשׂוּ
yehwāh	wayqan'û	'ōthô	mikkōl	'ăsher	'āsû
Yahweh	and they caused to be zealous	Him	among the entirety	that	they had done

1	904, 2496	866	2490.116		1161.126	1612, 2065	3937
n mp, ps 3mp	prep, n fp, ps 3mp	rel part	v Qal pf 3cp	**23.**	cj, v Qal impf 3mp	cj, pers pron	prep, ps 3mp
אֲבֹתָם	בְּחַטֹּאתָם	אֲשֶׁר	חָטָאוּ		וַיִּבְנוּ	גַּם־הֵמָּה	לָהֶם
'ăvōthām	bechattō'thām	'ăsher	chātā'û		wayyivnû	gham-hēmmāh	lāhem
their fathers	with their sins	that	they sinned		and they built	also they	for themselves

1154	4838	867	6142	3725, 1421	1393	8809	3725, 6320
n fp	cj, n fp	cj, n mp	prep	*adj*, n fs	adj	cj, prep	*adj*, n ms
בָּמוֹת	וּמַצֵּבוֹת	וַאֲשֵׁרִים	עַל	כָּל־גִּבְעָה	גְבֹהָה	וְתַחַת	כָּל־עֵץ
bāmôth	ûmatstsēvôth	wa'ăshērîm	'al	kol-giv'āh	ghevōhāh	wethachath	kol-'ēts
high places	and pillars	and Asherah poles	on	all the hills	high	and beneath	all the trees

7776		1612, 7228	2030.111	904, 800	6449.116	3626, 3725
adj	**24.**	cj, cj, n ms	v Qal pf 3ms	prep, art, n fs	v Qal pf 3cp	prep, n ms
רַעֲנָן		וְגַם־קָדֵשׁ	הָיָה	בָּאָרֶץ	עָשׂוּ	כְּכֹל
ra'ănān		wegham-qādhēsh	hāyāh	vā'ārets	'āsû	kekhōl
luxurious		and also male cult prostitutes	they were	in the land	they did	according to all

8774	1504	866	3542.511	3176	4623, 6686	1158
art, *n fp*	art, n mp	rel part	v Hiphil pf 3ms	pn	prep, *n mp*	*n mp*
הַתּוֹעֲבֹת	הַגּוֹיִם	אֲשֶׁר	הוֹרִישׁ	יְהוָה	מִפְּנֵי	בְּנֵי
hattô'ăvōth	haggôyim	'ăsher	hôrîsh	yehwāh	mippenê	benê
the detestable things of	the nations	which	He had dispossessed	Yahweh	from before	the sons of

3547		2030.121	904, 8523	2653	3937, 4567	7628	6148.111
pn	**25.**	cj, v Qal impf 3ms	prep, art, n fs	art, num	prep, art, n ms	pn	v Qal pf 3ms
יִשְׂרָאֵל		וַיְהִי	בַּשָּׁנָה	הַחֲמִישִׁית	לַמֶּלֶךְ	רְחַבְעָם	עָלָה
yisrā'ēl		wayhî	bashshānāh	hachmîshîth	lammelekh	rechav'ām	'ālāh
Israel		and it was	in the year	the fifth	of the king	Rehoboam	he went up

8239	4567, 4875	6142, 3503	26.	4089.121	881, 212
pn	*n ms*, pn	prep, pn		cj, v Qal impf 3ms	do, *n mp*
שׁוּשַׁק	מֶלֶךְ־מִצְרַיִם	עַל־יְרוּשָׁלָם		וַיִּקַּח	אֶת־אֹצְרוֹת
shûshaq	melekh-mitsrayim	'al-yerûshālām		wayyiqqach	'eth-'ōtserôth
Shishak	the king of Egypt	against Jerusalem		and he took	the treasures of

1041, 3176	881, 212	1041	4567	881, 3725	4089.111
n ms, pn	cj, do, *n mp*	*n ms*	art, n ms	cj, do, art, n ms	v Qal pf 3ms
בֵּית־יְהוָה	וְאֶת־אוֹצְרוֹת	בֵּית	הַמֶּלֶךְ	וְאֶת־הַכֹּל	לָקָח
bêth-yehwāh	we'eth-'ôtsrôth	bêth	hammelekh	we'eth-hakkōl	lāqāch
the Temple of Yahweh	and the treasures of	the house of	the king	and everything	he took

became king, *NCV* ... when elected king, *Fenton*.

and he reigned seventeen years in Jerusalem, the city which the LORD did choose out of all the tribes of Israel, to put his name there. And his mother's name was Naamah an Ammonitess: ... chose out of all the cities of Israel to be the sanctuary of, *Knox* ... tribes of Israel to receive, *NEB* ... as the place to honor, *NLT*.

22. And Judah did evil in the sight of the LORD, and they provoked him to jealousy with their sins which they had committed, above all that their fathers had done: ... arouse his anger against them than all their ancestors, *Good News* ... far more than their fathers did by the sins, *Berkeley* ... beyond anything that their forefathers, *REB*.

23. For they also built them high places, and images, and groves, on every high hill, and under every green tree: ... pillars, and Asherim, *MRB* ... erected shrines, obelisks, and sacred poles, *Moffatt*.

24. And there were also sodomites in the land: ... male devotees of the fertility cult, *Goodspeed* ... There were even male prostitutes, *NCV* ... who were used for sex purposes in the worship of the gods, *BB* ... there were also perverted persons, *NKJV*.

and they did according to all the abominations of the nations which the LORD cast out before the children of Israel: ... people engaged in all the detestable practices of the nations the LORD had driven out, *NIV* ... which the LORD drove out before the people, *RSV* ... He copied all the shameful practices, *JB*.

25. And it came to pass in the fifth year of king Rehoboam, that Shishak king of Egypt came up against Jerusalem: ... Sesac king of Egypt marched on, *Knox* ... attacked Jerusalem, *NEB* ... King of the Mitzeraim, advanced against, *Fenton*.

26. And he took away the treasures of the house of the LORD, and the treasures of the king's house; he even took away all: and he took away all the shields of gold which Solomon had made: ... the stored wealth, *BB* ... He ransacked the Temple of the LORD and the royal palace, *NLT* ... seized everything, *NEB* ... plundering everywhere, *Knox*.

27. And king Rehoboam made in their stead brasen shields: ... made substitute shields of bronze, *Berkeley* ... shields of brass, *MAST*.

and committed them unto the hands of the chief of the guard, which kept the door of the king's

ineffectual and distressing war smoldered on between the Northern and Southern Kingdoms. Jeroboam sinned by the erection in the old sanctuaries of the two golden calves, but Rehoboam surely sinned far more heinously. He not only sanctioned the high places—which to him may have been very venial, since they held their own unchallenged till the days of Hezekiah—but he allowed stone obelisks (matstsevāh, HED #4838) in honor of Baal and pillars (chammān, HED #2658) of the goddess ('ăshērāh, HED #867) to be set up on every high hill and under every green tree. Worse than this, and a proof of the abyss of corruption into which the evil example of Solomon had beguiled the nation, there were found in the land temple prostitutes, the infamous partakers of a most foul fertility worship. In spite of Temple and priesthood, "they did according to all the abominations of the nations which the LORD drave out before the children of Israel." Since Rehoboam thus sinned so much more heinously than his northern compeer we can hardly admire the conduct of the Levites, who, according to the chronicler, fled southward in swarms from the innovations of the son of Nebat.

14:25–28. Such atrocities could not be left unpunished. Where the carcass is the eagles will gather. In the fifth year of Rehoboam, Shishak, king of Egypt, put an end to the short-lived glories of the age of Solomon. Of his reason for invading Palestine we know nothing. It was probably mere

4089.121	881, 3725, 4182	2174	866	6449.111	8406	**27.** 6449.121
cj, v Qal impf 3ms	do, *adj*, *n mp*	art, n ms	rel part	v Qal pf 3ms	pn	cj, v Qal impf 3ms
וַיִּקַּח	אֶת־כָּל־מָגִנֵּי	הַזָּהָב	אֲשֶׁר	עָשָׂה	שְׁלֹמֹה	וַיַּעַשׂ
wayyiqqach	'eth-kol-māghinnê	hazzāhāv	'ăsher	‘āsāh	shelōmōh	wayya‘as
and he took	all the shields of	the gold	which	he had made	Solomon	so he made

4567	7628	8809	4182	5361	6734.511	6142, 3135
art, n ms	pn	prep, ps 3mp	*n mp*	n fs	cj, v Hiphil pf 3ms	prep, *n fs*
הַמֶּלֶךְ	רְחַבְעָם	תַּחְתָּם	מָגִנֵּי	נְחֹשֶׁת	וְהִפְקִיד	עַל־יַד
hammelekh	rechav‘ām	tachtām	māghinnê	nechōsheth	wehiphqîdh	‘al-yadh
the king	Rehoboam	instead of them	shields of	bronze	and he deployed	on the hands of

8015	7608.152	8490.152	6860	1041	4567
n mp	art, v Qal act ptc mp	art, v Qal act ptc mp	*n ms*	*n ms*	art, n ms
שָׂרֵי	הָרָצִים	הַשֹּׁמְרִים	פֶּתַח	בֵּית	הַמֶּלֶךְ
sārê	hārātsîm	hashshōmerîm	pethach	bêth	hammelekh
the commanders of	those running	the lookouts	the entrance of	the house of	the king

28. 2030.121	4623, 1823, 971.141	4567	1041	3176	5558.126
cj, v Qal impf 3ms	prep, *sub*, v Qal inf con	art, n ms	*n ms*	pn	v Qal impf 3mp, ps 3mp
וַיְהִי	מִדֵּי־בֹא	הַמֶּלֶךְ	בֵּית	יְהוָה	יִשָּׂאוּם
wayhî	middê-vō'	hammelekh	bêth	yehwāh	yissā'ûm
and it was	of all of his going to	the king	the Temple of	Yahweh	they carried them

7608.152	8178.516	420, 8702	7608.152
art, v Qal act ptc mp	cj, v Hiphil pf 3cp, ps 3mp	prep, *n ms*	art, v Qal act ptc mp
הָרָצִים	וֶהֱשִׁיבוּם	אֶל־תָּא	הָרָצִים
hārātsîm	wehěshîvûm	'el-tā'	hārātsîm
those running	then they brought them back	to the armory of	those running

29. 3615	1745	7628	3725, 866	6449.111
cj, *n ms*	*n mp*	pn	cj, *adj*, rel part	v Qal pf 3ms
וְיֶתֶר	דִּבְרֵי	רְחַבְעָם	וְכָל־אֲשֶׁר	עָשָׂה
weyether	divrê	rechav‘ām	wekhol-'ăsher	‘āsāh
and the remainder of	the events of	Rehoboam	and all that	he did

1950B, 3940, 2065	3918.156	6142, 5809	1745	3219	3937, 4567
intrg part, neg part, pers pron	v Qal pass ptc mp	prep, *n ms*	*n mp*	art, n mp	prep, *n mp*
הֲלֹא־הֵמָּה	כְּתוּבִים	עַל־סֵפֶר	דִּבְרֵי	הַיָּמִים	לְמַלְכֵי
hălō'-hēmmāh	khethûvîm	‘al-s̱ēpher	divrê	hayyāmîm	lemalkhê
are they not	things written	on the scroll of	the events of	the days	of the kings of

3171	**30.** 4560	2030.112	1033, 7628	1033	3493	3725, 3219
pn	cj, n fs	v Qal pf 3fs	prep, pn	cj, prep	pn	*adj*, art, n mp
יְהוּדָה	וּמִלְחָמָה	הָיְתָה	בֵּין־רְחַבְעָם	וּבֵין	יָרָבְעָם	כָּל־הַיָּמִים
yehûdhāh	ûmilchāmāh	hāyethāh	vên-rechav‘ām	ûvên	yārov‘ām	kol-hayyāmîm
Judah	and war	it was	between Rehoboam	and between	Jeroboam	all the days

31. 8311.121	7628	6196, 1	7196.221	6196, 1
cj, v Qal impf 3ms	pn	prep, n mp, ps 3ms	cj, v Niphil impf 3ms	prep, n mp, ps 3ms
וַיִּשְׁכַּב	רְחַבְעָם	עִם־אֲבֹתָיו	וַיִּקָּבֵר	עִם־אֲבֹתָיו
wayyishkav	rechav‘ām	‘im-'ăvōthâv	wayyiqqāvēr	‘im-'ăvōthâv
then he lay	Rehoboam	with his ancestors	and he was buried	with his ancestors

904, 6111	1784	8428	525	5462	6206	4566.121
prep, *n fs*	pn	cj, *n ms*	n fs, ps 3ms	pn	art, pn	cj, v Qal impf 3ms
בְּעִיר	דָּוִד	וְשֵׁם	אִמּוֹ	נַעֲמָה	הָעַמֹּנִית	וַיִּמְלֹךְ
be‘îr	dāwidh	weshēm	'immô	na‘ămāh	hā‘ammōnîth	wayyimlōkh
in the city of	David	and the name of	his mother	Naamah	the Ammonite	and he reigned

house: ... guard who guarded the entry to the royal palace, *Moffatt* ... escort who guarded the entrance, *REB* ... the king's palace gate, *JB* ... into the hand of the captains of the shieldbearers, *Douay*.

28. And it was so, when the king went into the house of the LORD, that the guard bare them, and brought them back into the guard chamber: ... Temple of the LORD, the guards carried the shields, *NCV* ... to the guardroom, *NRSV* ... the chamber of the runners, *Rotherham*.

29. Now the rest of the acts of Rehoboam, and all that he did, are they not written in the book of the chronicles of the kings of Judah?: ... of the records, *Goodspeed* ... recorded in the record of events in the days, *Fenton* ... of the history, *BB* ... the scroll of the annals of Judah's kings, *Beck*.

30. And there was war between Rehoboam and Jeroboam all their days: ... constant war, *Moffatt* ... continually, *RSV* ... continual fighting, *REB*.

31. And Rehoboam slept with his fathers, and was buried with his fathers in the city of David: ... died and was buried in the royal tombs, *Good News* ... among his ancestors, *NLT*.

And his mother's name was Naamah an Ammonitess. And Abijam his son reigned in his stead: ... became king in his place, *Berkeley* ... succeeded him, *JB* ... the throne passed to his son Abiam, *Knox*.

15:1. Now in the eighteenth year of king Jeroboam the son of Nebat reigned Abijam over Judah: ... Abijah became king of Judah, *NIV* ... began to rule, *NLT* ... Abiam began to reign, *Fenton*.

---

ambition and the love of plunder, stimulated by stories which Jeroboam may have brought to him about the inexhaustible riches of Jerusalem. He is the first Pharaoh in the Bible whose individuality was so marked as to transcend and replace the common title. He was astute enough to seize the opportunity of self-aggrandizement which offered itself when Jeroboam took refuge at his court. The splendid memorial of Shishak's achievements was carved on the great temple of Amon at Karnak. There the most conspicuous figure is the colossal likeness of the king. His right hand holds a sword; his left grasps by the hair a long line which passes round the necks of a troop of 38 mean and diminutive Jewish captives. The smaller figure of the god Amon leads other strings of 133 captives, and the third king from his left hand bears a name which Champollion deciphered Yudeh-Malk, which he took to mean King of Judah. Shishak came, saw,—and plundered. His chief spoil was taken from the poor dishonored Temple and the king's palace. Judah specially grieved for the loss of the shields of gold which hung on the cedar pillars of the house of the forest of Lebanon (1 Ki. 10:17)—apparently both those which Solomon had made, and those which David had consecrated from the spoils of Hadadezer, King of Zobah (2 Sam. 8:7). Perhaps a great soul would hardly have been consoled by putting mean substitutes in their place. Rehoboam, however, made bronze imitations of them in the guard room, and marched in pomp to the Temple preceded by his meanly armed runners, as though everything was the same as before.

14:29–31. Rehoboam was succeeded by his son Abijam. There is a little doubt as to the exact name of this king. The Book of Chronicles calls him Abijah (2 Chr. 12:16), but in 1 Ki. 15:1, 7f, he is called Abijam. As the curious form Abijam seems to be unmeaning, it has been precariously conjectured that dislike to his idolatries led the Jews to alter a name which means "Yahweh is my Father." Some doubt also rests on the name of his mother. She is here called "Maacha, the daughter of Abishalom," but in Chronicles "Michaiah, the daughter of Uriel of Gibeah." Maachah was perhaps the granddaughter of Absalom, whose beautiful daughter Tamar (named after his dishonored sister) may have been the wife of Uriel. In that case her name, Maachah, was a name given her in reminiscence of her royal descent as a great-granddaughter of the princess of Geshur, who was mother of Absalom. All sorts of secrets, however, sometimes lie behind these changes of names. She was the second, but favorite wife of Rehoboam; and Abijam, who was not the eldest son, owed his throne to his father's preference for her (2 Chr. 11:18–23).

15:1–8. All that we are here told of Abijam is that "his heart was not perfect with Yahweh his God," and that "he walked in all the sins of his father"; though "for David's sake his God gave him a lamp in Jerusalem"; and that, after a brief reign of three years—i.e., of one year and parts of two others—he slept with his fathers. For "the rest of his acts and all that he did," the historian refers us to the chronicles of the kings of Judah: he does not trouble himself with military details. The

38	1158	8809		904, 8523	8470	6462	3937, 4567
pn	n ms, ps 3ms	prep, ps 3ms	**15:1**	cj, prep, *n fs*	num	num	prep, art, n ms
אֲבִיָּם	בְּנוֹ	תַּחְתָּיו		וּבִשְׁנַת	שְׁמֹנֶה	עֶשְׂרֵה	לַמֶּלֶךְ
'ăvîyām	b^{e}nô	tachtâv		ûvishnath	sh^{e}mōneh	'esrēh	lammelekh
Abijam	his son	instead of him		and the year of	eight	ten	of the king

3493	1158, 5203	4566.111	38	6142, 3171		8421	8523	4566.111
pn	*n ms*, pn	v Qal pf 3ms	pn	prep, pn	**2.**	num	n fp	v Qal pf 3ms
יָרָבְעָם	בֶּן־נְבָט	מָלַךְ	אֲבִיָּם	עַל־יְהוּדָה		שָׁלֹשׁ	שָׁנִים	מָלַךְ
yārov'ām	ben-n^{e}vāṭ	mālakh	'ăvîyām	'al-y^{e}hûdhāh		shālōsh	shānîm	mālakh
Jeroboam	the son of Nebat	he reigned	Abijam	over Judah		three	years	he reigned

904, 3503	8428	525	4757	1351, 54		2050.121
prep, pn	cj, *n ms*	n fs, ps 3ms	pn	*n fs*, pn	**3.**	cj, v Qal impf 3ms
בִּירוּשָׁלִָם	וְשֵׁם	אִמּוֹ	מַעֲכָה	בַּת־אֲבִישָׁלוֹם		וַיֵּלֶךְ
bîrûshālām	w^{e}shēm	'immô	ma'ăkhāh	vath-'ăvîshālôm		wayyēlekh
in Jerusalem	and the name of	his mother	Maacah	the daughter of Abishalom		and he walked

904, 3725, 2496	1	866, 6449.111	3937, 6686	3940, 2030.111	3949
prep, *adj*, *n fp*	n ms, ps 3ms	rel part, v Qal pf 3ms	prep, n mp, ps 3ms	cj, neg part, v Qal pf 3ms	n ms, ps 3ms
בְּכָל־חַטֹּאות	אָבִיו	אֲשֶׁר־עָשָׂה	לְפָנָיו	וְלֹא־הָיָה	לְבָבוֹ
b^{e}khol-chaṯṯō'wth	'āvîw	'ăsher-'āsāh	l^{e}phānâv	w^{e}lō'-hāyāh	l^{e}vāvô
in all the sins of	his father	that he had done	before him	and it was not	his heart

8400	6196, 3176	435	3626, 3949	1784	1		3706	3937, 4775
adj	prep, pn	n mp, ps 3ms	prep, *n ms*	pn	n ms, ps 3ms	**4.**	cj	prep, prep
שָׁלֵם	עִם־יְהוָה	אֱלֹהָיו	כִּלְבַב	דָּוִד	אָבִיו		כִּי	לְמַעַן
shālēm	'im-y^{e}hwāh	'ĕlōhâv	kilvav	dāwidh	'āvîw		kî	l^{e}ma'an
complete	with Yahweh	his God	like the heart of	David	his ancestor		yet	because of

1784	5598.111	3176	435	3937	5402	904, 3503	3937, 7251.541
pn	v Qal pf 3ms	pn	n mp, ps 3ms	prep, ps 3ms	n ms	prep, pn	prep, v Hiphil inf con
דָּוִד	נָתַן	יְהוָה	אֱלֹהָיו	לוֹ	נִיר	בִּירוּשָׁלִָם	לְהָקִים
dāwidh	nāthan	y^{e}hwāh	'ĕlōhâv	lô	nîr	bîrûshālām	l^{e}hāqîm
David	He gave	Yahweh	his God	to him	a lamp	in Jerusalem	to raise up

881, 1158	313	3937, 6198.541	881, 3503		866	6449.111	1784
do, n ms, ps 3ms	adv, ps 3ms	prep, v Hiphil inf con	do, pn	**5.**	cj	v Qal pf 3ms	pn
אֶת־בְּנוֹ	אַחֲרָיו	וּלְהַעֲמִיד	אֶת־יְרוּשָׁלִָם		אֲשֶׁר	עָשָׂה	דָוִד
'eth-b^{e}nô	'achrâv	ûlăha'ămîdh	'eth-y^{e}rûshālām		'ăsher	'āsāh	dhāwidh
his son	after him	and to establish	Jerusalem		because	he did	David

881, 3596	904, 6084	3176	3940, 5681.111	4623, 3725
do, art, adj	prep, *n fd*	pn	cj, neg part, v Qal pf 3ms	prep, n ms
אֶת־הַיָּשָׁר	בְּעֵינֵי	יְהוָה	וְלֹא־סָר	מִכֹּל
'eth-hayyāshār	b^{e}'ênê	y^{e}hwāh	w^{e}lō'-sār	mikkōl
what is upright	in the eyes of	Yahweh	and he did not turn aside	of everything

866, 6943.311	3725	3219	2522	7828	904, 1745	222
rel part, v Piel pf 3ms, ps 3ms	*n ms*	*n mp*	n mp, ps 3ms	adv	prep, *n ms*	pn
אֲשֶׁר־צִוָּהוּ	כֹּל	יְמֵי	חַיָּיו	רַק	בִּדְבַר	אוּרִיָּה
'ăsher-tsiwwāhû	kōl	y^{e}mê	chayyâv	raq	bidhvar	'ûrîyāh
that He commanded him	the entirety of	the days of	his life	except	in the matter of	Uriah

2958		4560	2030.112	1033, 7628	1033	3493	3725, 3219
art, pn	**6.**	cj, n fs	v Qal pf 3fs	prep, pn	cj, prep	pn	*adj*, *n mp*
הַחִתִּי		וּמִלְחָמָה	הָיְתָה	בֵּין־רְחַבְעָם	וּבֵין	יָרָבְעָם	כָּל־יְמֵי
hachittî		ûmilchāmāh	hāy^{e}thāh	vên-r^{e}chav'ām	ûvên	yārov'ām	kol-y^{e}mê
the Hittite		and war	it was	between Rehoboam	and between	Jeroboam	all the days of

2522		3615	1745	38	3725, 866	6449.111
n mp, ps 3ms	7.	cj, *n ms*	*n mp*	pn	cj, *adj*, rel part	v Qal pf 3ms
חַיָּיו		וְיֶתֶר	דִּבְרֵי	אֲבִיָּם	וְכָל־אֲשֶׁר	עָשָׂה
chayyâv		weyether	divrê	'ăvîyām	wekhol-'ăsher	'āsāh
his life		and the remainder of	the events of	Abijam	and all that	he did

1950B, 3940, 2062	3918.156	6142, 5809	1745	3219	3937, 4567
intrg part, neg part, pers pron	v Qal pass ptc mp	prep, *n ms*	*n mp*	art, n mp	prep, *n mp*
הֲלוֹא־הֵם	כְּתוּבִים	עַל־סֵפֶר	דִּבְרֵי	הַיָּמִים	לְמַלְכֵי
hălô'-hēm	kethûvîm	'al-sēpher	divrê	hayyāmîm	lemalkhê
are they not	things written	on the scroll of	the events of	the days	of the kings of

3171	4560	2030.112	1033	38	1033	3493		8311.121
pn	cj, n fs	v Qal pf 3fs	prep	pn	cj, prep	pn	8.	cj, v Qal impf 3ms
יְהוּדָה	וּמִלְחָמָה	הָיְתָה	בֵּין	אֲבִיָּם	וּבֵין	יָרָבְעָם		וַיִּשְׁכַּב
yehûdhāh	ûmilchāmāh	hāyethāh	bên	'ăvîyām	ûvên	yārov'ām		wayyishkav
Judah	and war	it was	between	Abijam	and between	Jeroboam		then he lay

2. Three years reigned he in Jerusalem. And his mother's name was Maachah, the daughter of Abishalom: ... the granddaughter, *NKJV* ... Maacha the daughter of Abessalom, *Douay* ... a granddaughter of Abishalom, *Beck* ... descendant of Absalom, *JB*.

3. And he walked in all the sins of his father, which he had done before him: ... he followed the sinful example his father had set, *Knox* ... imitated ... had committed, *NAB* ... father before him had committed he also committed, *REB*.

and his heart was not perfect with the LORD his God, as the heart of David his father: ... nor was he faithful to the LORD his God as his ancestor David, *NEB* ... was not completely true, *BB* ... was not at peace with his EVER-LIVING God, *Fenton* ... as his great-grandfather David, *Good News*.

4. Nevertheless for David's sake did the LORD his God give him a lamp in Jerusalem: ... to keep the lamp of the royal dynasty burning, *Knox*.

to set up his son after him, and to establish Jerusalem: ... by raising up a son to succeed him, *NIV* ... to continue Jerusalem, *Tyndale* ... permitting Jerusalem to endure, *NAB* ... by suffering Jerusalem to stand, *Rotherham* ... by giving peace to Jerusalem, *Beck*.

5. Because David did that which was right in the eyes of the LORD, and turned not aside from any thing that he commanded him all the days of his life, save only in the matter of Uriah the Hittite: ... except in the matter, *NRSV* ... had never in all his life disobeyed whatever, *JB* ... except the one time when David sinned against Uriah, *NCV*.

6. And there was war between Rehoboam and Jeroboam all the days of his life: ... during Abijah's lifetime, *NCV* ... There was continuous war, *Berkeley* ... between Roboam and Jeroboam all the time of his life, *Douay* ... continued all the days of his life, *NRSV*.

7. Now the rest of the acts of Abijam, and all that he did, are they not written in the book of the chronicles of the kings of Judah?: ... of the history, *BB* ... in the annals, *REB* ... the scroll of, *Beck* ... of the deeds that were done in the days, *Tyndale*.

And there was war between Abijam and Jeroboam: ... constant war, *NLT* ... fighting between, *NEB*.

---

chronicler adds a great deal more. Jeroboam, he says, went out against him with eight hundred thousand men. Abijam, who had only half the number, stood on Mount Zemaraim in the hill country of Ephraim (2 Chr. 13:3f) and made a speech to Jeroboam and his army. He reproached him with rebellion against his father when he was "young and tender-hearted," and with his golden calves, and his non-Levitical priests. He vaunted the superiority of the temple priests with their holocausts and sweet incense and shewbread and golden candlestick, which priests were now with the army. Jeroboam set an ambush, but at the shout of the men of Judah, he was routed with a loss of five hundred thousand men, after which Abijah recovered "Bethel with the towns thereof" (2 Chr. 13:19), so that the golden calf and its chapel and its priests must have fallen into his power. But it does not seem to have made the least difference. It is certain that "the calf" remained undisturbed till the days of the Assyrian invasion. "The LORD smote him and he died." After this, Abijah waxed mighty, having fourteen wives, twenty-two sons, and sixteen daughters.

38	6196, 1	7196.126	881	904, 6111	1784	4566.121
pn	prep, n mp, ps 3ms	cj, v Qal impf 3mp	do, ps 3ms	prep, *n fs*	pn	cj, v Qal impf 3ms
אֲבִיָּם	עִם־אֲבֹתָיו	וַיִּקְבְּרוּ	אֹתוֹ	בְּעִיר	דָּוִד	וַיִּמְלֹךְ
'ăvîyām	'im-'ăvōthâv	wayyiqōbbᵉrû	'ōthô	bᵉ'îr	dāwidh	wayyimlōkh
Abijam	with his ancestors	and they buried	him	in the city of	David	and he reigned

623	1158	8809		904, 8523	6465	393, 3493	4567	3547
pn	n ms, ps 3ms	prep, ps 3ms		cj, prep, *n fs*	num	prep, pn	*n ms*	pn
אָסָא	בְּנוֹ	תַּחְתָּיו	**9.**	וּבִשְׁנַת	עֶשְׂרִים	לְיָרָבְעָם	מֶלֶךְ	יִשְׂרָאֵל
'āsā'	vᵉnô	tachtâv		ûvishnath	'esrîm	lᵉyārov'ām	melekh	yisrā'ēl
Asa	his son	instead of him		and the year of	twenty	of Jeroboam	the king of	Israel

4566.111	623	4567	3171		727	259	8523	4566.111
v Qal pf 3ms	pn	*n ms*	pn		cj, num	cj, num	n fs	v Qal pf 3ms
מָלַךְ	אָסָא	מֶלֶךְ	יְהוּדָה	**10.**	וְאַרְבָּעִים	וְאַחַת	שָׁנָה	מָלַךְ
mālakh	'āsā'	melekh	yᵉhûdhāh		wᵉ'arbā'îm	wᵉ'achath	shānāh	mālakh
he reigned	Asa	the king of	Judah		and forty	and one	years	he reigned

904, 3503	8428	525	4757	1351, 54
prep, pn	cj, *n ms*	n fs, ps 3ms	pn	*n fs*, pn
בִּירוּשָׁלָם	וְשֵׁם	אִמּוֹ	מַעֲכָה	בַּת־אֲבִישָׁלוֹם
bîrûshālām	wᵉshēm	'immô	ma'ăkhāh	bath-'ăvîshālôm
in Jerusalem	and the name of	his mother	Maacah	the daughter of Abishalom

	6449.121	623	3596	904, 6084	3176	3626, 1784	1
	cj, v Qal impf 3ms	pn	art, adj	prep, *n fd*	pn	prep, pn	n ms, ps 3ms
11.	וַיַּעַשׂ	אָסָא	הַיָּשָׁר	בְּעֵינֵי	יְהוָה	כְּדָוִד	אָבִיו
	wayya'as	'āsā'	hayyāshār	bᵉ'ênê	yᵉhwāh	kᵉdhāwidh	'āvîw
	and he did	Asa	what is upright	in the eyes of	Yahweh	like David	his father

	5882.521	7228	4263, 800	5681.521
	cj, v Hiphil impf 3ms	art, n mp	prep, art, n fs	cj, v Hiphil impf 3ms
12.	וַיַּעֲבֵר	הַקְּדֵשִׁים	מִן־הָאָרֶץ	וַיָּסַר
	wayya'ăvēr	haqqᵉdhēshîm	min-hā'ārets	wayyāsar
	and he caused to pass on	the male cult prostitutes	from the land	and he removed

881, 3725, 1585	866	6449.116	1		1612	881, 4757	525
do, *adj*, art, n mp	rel part	v Qal pf 3cp	n mp, ps 3ms		cj, cj	do, pn	n fs, ps 3ms
אֶת־כָּל־הַגִּלֻּלִים	אֲשֶׁר	עָשׂוּ	אֲבֹתָיו	**13.**	וְגַם	אֶת־מַעֲכָה	אִמּוֹ
'eth-kol-haggillulîm	'ăsher	'āsû	'ăvōthâv		wᵉgham	'eth-ma'ăkhāh	'immô
all the idols	that	they had made	his ancestors		and also	Maacah	his mother

5681.521	4623, 1409	866, 6449.112	4818
cj, v Hiphil impf 3ms, ps 3fs	prep, n fs	rel pron, v Qal pf 3fs	n fs
וַיְסִרֶהָ	מִגְּבִירָה	אֲשֶׁר־עָשְׂתָה	מִפְלֶצֶת
waysireāh	miggᵉvîrāh	'ăsher-'āsᵉthāh	miphletseth
and he removed her	from queen mother	who she had made	a detestable cult image

3937, 867	3901.121	623	881, 4818	8041.121	904, 5337
prep, art, pn	cj, v Qal impf 3ms	pn	do, n fs, ps 3fs	cj, v Qal impf 3ms	prep, *n ms*
לָאֲשֵׁרָה	וַיִּכְרֹת	אָסָא	אֶת־מִפְלַצְתָּהּ	וַיִּשְׂרֹף	בְּנַחַל
lā'ăshērāh	wayyikhrōth	'āsā'	'eth-miphlatstāhh	wayyisrōph	bᵉnachal
for Asherah	and he cut down	Asa	her detestable cult image	then he burned	in the Valley of

7224		1154	3940, 5681.116	7828	3949, 623	2030.111
pn		cj, art, n fp	neg part, v Qal pf 3cp	adv	*n ms*, pn	v Qal pf 3ms
קִדְרוֹן	**14.**	וְהַבָּמוֹת	לֹא־סָרוּ	רַק	לְבַב־אָסָא	הָיָה
qidhrôn		wᵉhabbāmôth	lō'-sārû	raq	lᵉvav-'āsā'	hāyāh
Kidron		but the high places	they were not removed	except	the heart of Asa	it was

8400	6196, 3176	3725, 3219		971.521	881, 7231	1
adj	prep, pn	*adj*, n mp, ps 3ms	15.	cj, v Hiphil impf 3ms	do, *n mp*	n ms, ps 3ms
שָׁלֵם	עִם־יְהוָה	כָּל־יָמָיו		וַיָּבֵא	אֶת־קָדְשֵׁי	אָבִיו
shālēm	'im-y^{e}hwāh	kol-yāmâv		wayyāvē'	'eth-qādh^{e}shê	'āvîw
complete	with Yahweh	all his days		and he brought	the dedicated things of	his father

7231	1041	3176	3826B	2174	3747		4560
cj, n ms, ps 3ms	*n ms*	pn	n ms	cj, n ms	cj, n mp	16.	cj, n fs
וְקָדְשׁוֹ	בֵּית	יְהוָה	כֶּסֶף	וְזָהָב	וְכֵלִים		וּמִלְחָמָה
w^{e}qādh^{e}shô	bêth	y^{e}hwāh	keseph	w^{e}zāhāv	w^{e}khēlîm		ûmilchāmāh
and his dedicated things	the Temple of	Yahweh	silver	and gold	and utensils		and war

8. And Abijam slept with his fathers; and they buried him in the city of David: and Asa his son reigned in his stead: ... Asa succeeded him as king, *Good News* ... put him into the earth in the town of David: and Asa his son became king, *BB* ... fell asleep with his ancestors, *JB* ... the throne passed, *Knox*.

9. And in the twentieth year of Jeroboam king of Israel reigned Asa over Judah: ... Asa began to rule ... in the twentieth year, *NLT* ... Asa became king, *NKJV* ... of Judah, *NIV*.

10. And forty and one years reigned he in Jerusalem. And his mother's name was Maachah, the daughter of Abishalom: ... grandmother's name was Maacah, *NCV* ... granddaughter of Absalom, *Moffatt* ... grandmother was Maacah granddaughter of Abishalom, *REB* ... Maacah descendant of Absalom, *JB*.

11. And Asa did that which was right in the eyes of the LORD, as did David his father: ... the Lord's will, *Knox* ... did what Yahweh regards as right, *JB* ... as his ancestor David had done, *REB* ... what pleased the LORD, *Good News*.

12. And he took away the sodomites out of the land: ... expelled the male shrine prostitutes, *NIV* ... banished the perverted persons from the land, *NKJV* ... put away the male temple prostitutes, *NRSV* ... drove the male sacred prostitutes, *Beck*.

and removed all the idols that his fathers had made: ... did away with all the idols which his predecessors, *NEB* ... his ancestors had made, *NLT* ... the filth of the idols, *Douay*.

13. And also Maachah his mother: ... deposed his grandmother Maacah, *NAB*.

even her he removed from being queen, because she had made an idol in a grove: ... for her worship of Priapus and for dedicating a forest shrine to him, *Knox* ... for the Asherah, *Darby* ... made a monstrous thing to the Sacred Stem, *Rotherham* ... an obscene object made, *REB*.

and Asa destroyed her idol, and burnt it by the brook Kidron: ... burned it in the Kidron Valley, *NIV* ... in the gorge of the Kidron, *NEB*.

14. But the high places were not removed: ... Although the pagan shrines were not completely removed, *NLT* ... hill shrines were not torn down, *Beck* ... did not, however, overturn the Columns, *Fenton* ... places of worship to gods, *NCV*.

nevertheless Asa's heart was perfect with the LORD all his days: ... heart was loyal to the LORD, *NKJV* ... Asa was wholly devoted, *NASB*.

15. And he brought in the things which his father had dedicated, and the things which himself had dedicated, into the house of the LORD,

15:9–15. After this brief and perplexing but apparently eventful reign, Abijah was succeeded by his son Asa, whose long reign of forty-one years was contemporary with the reigns of no less than seven kings of Israel—Nadab, Baasha, Elah, Zimri, Omri, Tibni and Ahab. Asa "did that which was right in the sight of the LORD." Of this he gave an early, decisive and courageous proof.

When he succeeded to the throne at an early age, his grandmother Maachah still held the high position of queen-mother. This great lady inherited the fame and popularity of Absalom and was a princess both of the line of David and of Tolmai, king of Geshur. She was, and always had been, an open idolatress. Asa began his reign with a reformation. He took away the contemptible idols which his fathers had made and suppressed the odious Kedeshim; or he at least made a serious, if an unsuccessful, effort to do so. (That it was not perfectly successful we see from 1 Ki. 22:46.) As to the high places, we have an apparent discrepancy. Here we are told that "they were not removed," whereas the chronicler says that "he took them away out of all the cities of Judah," but afterwards that "the high places were not taken away out of Israel." Asa's heart, however, was perfect with the

2030.112	1033	623	1033	1225	4567, 3547	3725, 3219
v Qal pf 3fs	prep	pn	cj, prep	pn	*n ms*, pn	*adj*, n mp, ps 3mp
הָֽיְתָה	בֵּין	אָסָא	וּבֵין	בַּעְשָׁא	מֶֽלֶךְ־יִשְׂרָאֵל	כָּל־יְמֵיהֶם
hāyethāh	bên	'āsā'	ûvên	ba'āshā'	melekh-yisrā'ēl	kol-yemêhem
it was	between	Asa	and between	Baasha	the king of Israel	all their days

17.

6148.121	1225	4567, 3547	6142, 3171	1161.121	881, 7703
cj, v Qal impf 3ms	pn	*n ms*, pn	prep, pn	cj, v Qal impf 3ms	do, art, pn
וַיַּעַל	בַּעְשָׁא	מֶֽלֶךְ־יִשְׂרָאֵל	עַל־יְהוּדָה	וַיִּבֶן	אֶת־הָרָמָה
wayya'al	ba'āshā'	melekh-yisrā'ēl	'al-yehûdhāh	wayyiven	'eth-hārāmāh
and he went up	Baasha	the king of Israel	against Judah	and he built	the Ramah

3937, 1153	5598.141	3428.151	971.151	3937, 623	4567	3171
prep, neg part	v Qal inf con	v Qal act ptc ms	cj, v Qal act ptc ms	prep, pn	*n ms*	pn
לְבִלְתִּי	תֵּת	יֹצֵא	וָבָא	לְאָסָא	מֶלֶךְ	יְהוּדָה
leviltî	tēth	yōtsē'	wāvā'	le'āsā'	melekh	yehûdhāh
that not	allowing	going out	or coming in	to Asa	the king of	Judah

18.

4089.121	623	881, 3725, 3826B	2174	3613.256
cj, v Qal impf 3ms	pn	do, *adj*, art, n ms	cj, art, n ms	art, v Niphal ptc mp
וַיִּקַּח	אָסָא	אֶת־כָּל־הַכֶּסֶף	וְהַזָּהָב	הַנּוֹתָרִים
wayyiqqach	'āsā'	'eth-kol-hakkeseph	wehazzāhāv	hannôthārîm
and he took	Asa	all the silver	and the gold	the things remaining

904, 212	1041, 3176	881, 212	1041	4567
prep, *n mp*	*n ms*, pn	cj, do, *n mp*	*n ms*	n ms
בְּאוֹצְרוֹת	בֵּית־יְהוָה	וְאֶת־אוֹצְרוֹת	בֵּית	מֶלֶךְ
be'ôtsrôth	bêth-yehwāh	we'eth-'ôtsrôth	bêth	melekh
in the treasuries of	the temple of Yahweh	and the treasuries of	the house of	the king

5598.121	904, 3135, 5860	8365.121	4567	623
cj, v Qal impf 3ms, ps 3mp	prep, *n fs*, n mp, ps 3ms	cj, v Qal impf 3ms, ps 3mp	art, n ms	pn
וַיִּתְּנֵם	בְּיַד־עֲבָדָיו	וַיִּשְׁלָחֵם	הַמֶּלֶךְ	אָסָא
wayyittenēm	beyadh-'ävādhâv	wayyishlāchēm	hammelekh	'āsā'
and he gave them	into the hands of his servants	and he sent them out	the king	Asa

420, 1163	1158, 2996	1158, 2475	4567	782	3553.151
prep, pn	*n ms*, pn	*n ms*, pn	*n ms*	pn	art, v Qal act ptc ms
אֶל־בֶּן־הֲדַד	בֶּן־טַבְרִמֹּן	בֶּן־חֶזְיוֹן	מֶלֶךְ	אֲרָם	הַיֹּשֵׁב
'el-ben-hedhadh	ben-taverimmōn	ben-chezyôn	melekh	'ărām	hayyōshēv
to Ben-Hadad	the son of Tabrimmon	the son of Hezion	the king of	Aram	those dwelling

904, 1802	3937, 569.141	**19.**	1311	1033	1033	1033	1
prep, pn	prep, v Qal inf con		n fs	prep, ps 1cs	cj, prep, ps 2ms	prep	n ms, ps 1cs
בְּדַמֶּשֶׂק	לֵאמֹר		בְּרִית	בֵּינִי	וּבֵינֶךָ	בֵּין	אָבִי
bedhammeseq	lē'mōr		berîth	bênî	ûvênekhā	bên	'āvî
in Damascus	saying		a covenant	between me	and between you	between	my father

1033	1	2079	8365.115	3937	8245	3826B	2174
cj, prep	n ms, ps 2ms	intrj	v Qal pf 1cs	prep, ps 2ms	n ms	n ms	cj, n ms
וּבֵין	אָבִיךָ	הִנֵּה	שָׁלַחְתִּי	לְךָ	שֹׁחַד	כֶּסֶף	וְזָהָב
ûvên	'āvîkhā	hinnēh	shālachtî	lekhā	shōchadh	keseph	wezāhāv
and between	your father	behold	I have sent out	to you	a gift	silver	and gold

2050.131	6815.531	881, 1311	882, 1225	4567, 3547	6148.121
v Qal impv 2ms	v Hiphil impv 2ms	do, n fs, ps 2ms	prep, pn	*n ms*, pn	cj, v Qal juss 3ms
לֵךְ	הָפֵרָה	אֶת־בְּרִיתְךָ	אֶת־בַּעְשָׁא	מֶֽלֶךְ־יִשְׂרָאֵל	וְיַעֲלֶה
lēkh	hāphērāh	'eth-berîthekhā	'eth-ba'āshā'	melekh-yisrā'ēl	weya'ăleh
go	annul	your covenant	with Baasha	the king of Israel	that he may go up

silver, and gold, and vessels: ... his own votive offerings of silver, gold, and various utensils, *NAB* ... silver, gold and sacred vessels in the Temple of Yahweh, *JB* ... his father had made holy, *BB* ... had hallowed, *MAST*.

16. And there was war between Asa and Baasha king of Israel all their days: ... all the time they were kings, *NCV* ... War raged, *Moffatt* ... lifelong war, *Berkeley* ... were constantly at war with each other, *Good News*.

17. And Baasha king of Israel went up against Judah, and built Ramah: ... advanced into Judah, *Fenton* ... invaded Judah and fortified Ramah, *REB* ... marched on Judah, *JB*.

that he might not suffer any to go out or come in to Asa king of Judah: ... to prevent anyone from going out or coming in, *Goodspeed* ... that he might permit no one, *RSV* ... to blockade Asa, *JB* ... might not allow, *KJVII* ... to prevent communication with Asa, *NAB*.

18. Then Asa took all the silver and the gold that were left in the treasures of the house of the LORD, and the treasures of the king's house, and delivered them into the hand of his servants: ... that was left in the storerooms of the LORD's temple, *Beck* ... sent it with some of his officials, *NLT* ... temple of the LORD and of the royal palace. Entrusting them to his ministers, *NAB* ... treasure-chambers of temple and palace, *Knox*.

and king Asa sent them to Ben-hadad, the son of Tabrimon, the son of Hezion, king of Syria, that dwelt at Damascus, saying: ... grandson of Hezion, the king of Aram, who was ruling in Damascus, *NLT* ... whose capital was Damascus, with instructions to say, *NEB*.

19. There is a league between me and thee, and between my father and thy father: ... Let there be a treaty between you and me, *NCV* ... an agreement between me and you, *BB* ... A covenant is between, *Young* ... there is a bond, *Tyndale*.

behold, I have sent unto thee a present of silver and gold; come and break thy league with Baasha king of Israel, that he may depart from me: ... break your alliance, *Moffatt* ... withdraw from me, *NRSV*.

20. So Ben-hadad hearkened unto king Asa: ... responded favorably, *Berkeley* ... therefore listened to King Asa, *Goodspeed* ... agreed to King Asa's request, *NLT*.

and sent the captains of the hosts which he had against the cities of Israel: ... the generals of his forces, *Fenton* ... the captains of his armies, *MAST* ... leaders of his troops, *NAB*.

and smote Ijon, and Dan, and Abel-beth-maachah, and all

LORD all his days. The explanation would seem to be that he made a partial attempt to anticipate the subsequent reformation of Hezekiah, but was defeated by the inveteracy of popular custom. He did, however, take the great step of branding with infamy the impure idolatry of the queen-mother, and he degraded her from her rank. She had made an idol, probably a phallic symbol which Asa indignantly cut down, and burnt it, where all pollutions were destroyed, in the dry Wadi of the Kidron (2 Ki. 23:4, 6, 12; 2 Chr. 29:16). In the fifteenth year of his reign, he dedicated in the Temple "silver and gold and vessels," consecrated by his father and himself for this purpose. He also restored the great altar in the porch of the Temple, which in the course of more than sixty years had fallen into neglect and disrepair.

15:16–22. The land had no rest under this pious king; war was always smoldering between him and Baasha. More alarming to Asa was the action of Baasha in fortifying Ramah (Josh. 18: 25). Ramah, in the heart of Benjamin, was only five miles north of Jerusalem. Baasha had pushed toward Jerusalem, five miles south of Bethel. Had Ramah been left undisturbed, it would have been a thorn in the side of Judah. Asa saw that the demolition of this fortress was a positive necessity. Since he was too weak to effect this, he stripped both his own palace and the Temple of the treasures with which he had himself enriched them, and sent them as a vast bribe to Ben-Hadad I, king of Damascus, begging him to renew the treaty which had existed between their fathers, and to invade the kingdom of Baasha. This step shows to what a depth of weakness Judah had fallen.

The policy was successful. It is easy for us now to condemn it as unpatriotic and short-sighted, but to Asa it seemed a matter of life or death. Ben-Hadad invaded Israel and mastered its territory in the tribe of Naphtali, from Ijon and Abel-Beth-Maachah on the waters of Merom. Baasha, in alarm, abandoned his attempt to blockade Jerusalem and retired to Tirzah for the protection of his own kingdom. Thereupon, Asa proclaimed a levy of all Judah to seize and dismantle Ramah, and with the ample materials which Baasha had amassed, he fortified Geba to the north of Ramah (Josh. 21:17; 2 Ki. 23:8) and Mizpah (probably Neby Samwyl, to the north of the Mount of Olives), where he also sank a deep well for the use of the garrison (Jer. 41:5–9). Into this

4623, 6142	20.	8471.121	1163	420, 4567	623	8365.121
prep, prep, ps 1cs		cj, v Qal impf 3ms	pn	prep, art, n ms	pn	cj, v Qal impf 3ms
מֵעָלָי		וַיִּשְׁמַע	בֶּן־הֲדַד	אֶל־הַמֶּלֶךְ	אָסָא	וַיִּשְׁלַח
mē'ālāy		wayyishma'	ben-hedhadh	'el-hammelekh	'ās̱ā'	wayyishlach
from beside me		and he listened	Ben-Hadad	to the king	Asa	and he sent out

881, 8015	2524	866, 3937	6142, 6111	3547
do, *n mp*	art, n mp	rel part, prep, ps 3ms	prep, *n fp*	pn
אֶת־שָׂרֵי	הַחֲיָלִים	אֲשֶׁר־לוֹ	עַל־עָרֵי	יִשְׂרָאֵל
'eth-sārê	hachyālîm	'ăsher-lô	'al-'ārê	yisrā'ēl
the commanders of	the armies	which to him	against the cities of	Israel

5409.521	881, 6074	881, 1896	881	1078	1078	881	3725, 3797
cj, v Hiphil impf 3ms	do, pn	cj, do, pn	cj, do	pn	pn	cj, do	*adj*, pn
וַיַּךְ	אֶת־עִיּוֹן	וְאֶת־דָּן	וְאֵת	אָבֵל	בֵּית־מַעֲכָה	וְאֵת	כָּל־כִּנְרוֹת
wayyakh	'eth-'îyôn	we'eth-dān	we'ēth	'āvēl	bêth-ma'ăkhāh	we'ēth	kol-kinrôth
and he struck down	Ijon	and Dan	and	Abel	Beth-Maacah	and	all Chinnereth

6142	3725, 800	5503	21.	2030.121	3626, 8471.141	1225	2403.121
prep	*adj, n fs*	pn		cj, v Qal impf 3ms	prep, v Qal inf con	pn	cj, v Qal impf 3ms
עַל	כָּל־אֶרֶץ	נַפְתָּלִי		וַיְהִי	כִּשְׁמֹעַ	בַּעְשָׁא	וַיֶּחְדַּל
'al	kol-'erets	naphtālî		wayhî	kishmōa'	ba'āshā'	wayyechăddal
on	all the land of	Naphtali		and it was	when hearing	Baasha	that he ceased

4623, 1161.141	881, 7703	3553.121	904, 8995	22.	4567	623	8471.511
prep, v Qal inf con	do, art, pn	cj, v Qal impf 3ms	prep, pn		cj, art, n ms	pn	v Hiphil pf 3ms
מִבְּנוֹת	אֶת־הָרָמָה	וַיֵּשֶׁב	בְּתִרְצָה		וְהַמֶּלֶךְ	אָסָא	הִשְׁמִיעַ
mibbenôth	'eth-hārāmāh	wayyēshev	bethirtsāh		wehammelekh	'ās̱ā'	hishmîa'
from building	the Ramah	and he dwelled	in Tirzah		and the king	Asa	he proclaimed

881, 3725, 3171	375	5538	5558.126	881, 63	7703	881, 6320
do, *adj*, pn	*sub*	adj	cj, v Qal impf 3mp	do, *n mp*	art, pn	cj, do, n mp, ps 3fs
אֶת־כָּל־יְהוּדָה	אֵין	נָקִי	וַיִּשְׂאוּ	אֶת־אַבְנֵי	הָרָמָה	וְאֶת־עֵצֶיהָ
'eth-kol-yehûdhāh	'ên	nāqî	wayyis'û	'eth-'avnê	hārāmāh	we'eth-'ētsêāh
all Judah	it was not	exempt	and they carried	the stones of	the Ramah	and its wood

866	1161.111	1225	1161.121	904	4567	623	881, 1419	1175
rel part	v Qal pf 3ms	pn	cj, v Qal impf 3ms	prep, ps 3mp	art, n ms	pn	do, pn	pn
אֲשֶׁר	בָּנָה	בַּעְשָׁא	וַיִּבֶן	בָּם	הַמֶּלֶךְ	אָסָא	אֶת־גֶּבַע	בִּנְיָמִן
'ăsher	bānāh	ba'āshā'	wayyiven	bām	hammelekh	'ās̱ā'	'eth-geva'	binyāmin
which	he built	Baasha	and he built	with them	the king	Asa	Geba	Benjamin

881, 4870	23.	3615	3725, 1745, 623	3725, 1400	3725, 866
cj, do, art, pn		cj, *n ms*	*adj, n ms*, pn	cj, *adj*, n fs, ps 3ms	cj, *adj*, rel part
וְאֶת־הַמִּצְפָּה		וְיֶתֶר	כָּל־דִּבְרֵי־אָסָא	וְכָל־גְּבוּרָתוֹ	וְכָל־אֲשֶׁר
we'eth-hammitspāh		weyether	kol-divrê-'ās̱ā'	wekhol-gevûrāthô	wekhol-'ăsher
and the Mizpah		and the remainder of	all the events of Asa	and all his might	and all that

6449.111	6111	866	1161.111	1950B, 3940, 2065	3918.156
v Qal pf 3ms	cj, art, n fp	rel part	v Qal pf 3ms	intrg part, neg part, pers pron	v Qal pass ptc mp
עָשָׂה	וְהֶעָרִים	אֲשֶׁר	בָּנָה	הֲלֹא־הֵמָּה	כְּתוּבִים
'āsāh	wehe'ārîm	'ăsher	bānāh	hălō'-hēmmāh	khethûvîm
he did	and the cities	which	he built	are they not	things written

6142, 5809	1745	3219	3937, 4567	3171	7828	3937, 6496	2294
prep, *n ms*	*n mp*	art, n mp	prep, *n mp*	pn	adv	prep, *n fs*	n fs, ps 3ms
עַל־סֵפֶר	דִּבְרֵי	הַיָּמִים	לְמַלְכֵי	יְהוּדָה	רַק	לְעֵת	זִקְנָתוֹ
'al-s̱ēpher	divrê	hayyāmîm	lemalkhê	yehûdhāh	raq	le'ēth	ziqnāthô
on the scroll of	the events of	the days	of the kings of	Judah	except	at the time of	his old age

2571.111	881, 7559		8311.121	623	6196, 1	7196.221
v Qal pf 3ms	do, n fd, ps 3ms	**24.**	cj, v Qal impf 3ms	pn	prep, n mp, ps 3ms	cj, v Niphil impf 3ms
חָלָה	אֶת־רַגְלָיו		וַיִּשְׁכַּב	אָסָא	עִם־אֲבֹתָיו	וַיִּקָּבֵר
chālāh	'eth-raghlâv		wayyishkav	'āsā'	'im-'ăvōthâv	wayyiqqāvēr
he became sick	his feet		then he lay	Asa	with his ancestors	and he was buried

6196, 1	904, 6111	1784	1	4566.121	3194	1158
prep, n mp, ps 3ms	prep, *n fs*	pn	n ms, ps 3ms	cj, v Qal impf 3ms	pn	n ms, ps 3ms
עִם־אֲבֹתָיו	בְּעִיר	דָּוִד	אָבִיו	וַיִּמְלֹךְ	יְהוֹשָׁפָט	בְּנוֹ
'im-'ăvōthâv	be'îr	dāwidh	'āvîw	wayyimlōkh	yehôshāphāṯ	benô
with his ancestors	in the city of	David	his father	and he reigned	Jehoshaphat	his son

8809		5247	1158, 3493	4566.111	6142, 3547	904, 8523	8692
prep, ps 3ms	**25.**	cj, pn	*n ms*, pn	v Qal pf 3ms	prep, pn	prep, *n fs*	num
תַּחְתָּיו		וְנָדָב	בֶּן־יָרָבְעָם	מָלַךְ	עַל־יִשְׂרָאֵל	בִּשְׁנַת	שְׁתַּיִם
tachtâv		wenādhāv	ben-yārov'ām	mālakh	'al-yisrā'ēl	bishnath	shettayim
instead of him		and Nadab	the son of Jeroboam	he reigned	over Israel	in the year	two

Cinneroth, with all the land of Naphtali: ... conquered Ijon, *RSV* ... that part of Kinnereth which marches with, *REB* ... ravaged Ijon, Dan, Abel-Beth-Maacah, all Chinneroth, and the whole territory, *JB* ... defeated Ijon, *Beck*.

21. And it came to pass, when Baasha heard thereof, that he left off building of Ramah, and dwelt in Tirzah: ... when the news reached him, went back to Thersa, leaving the defences of Rama half finished, *Knox* ... stopped fortifying Ramah and fell back on Tirzah, *NEB* ... building Ramah, and remained, *NKJV* ... abandoned his project of fortifying Ramah and withdrew, *NLT*.

22. Then king Asa made a proclamation throughout all Judah; none was exempted: ... should be excused, *Tyndale* ... summoned all Judah without exception, *NAB* ... called out all Judah, excusing nobody, *Beck* ... got all Judah together, making every man come, *BB*.

and they took away the stones of Ramah, and the timber thereof, wherewith Baasha had builded; and king Asa built with them Geba of Benjamin, and Mizpah: ... timber with which Baasha had been fortifying Ramah, *JB* ... he used them to fortify Geba of Benjamin and Mizpah, *REB*.

23. The rest of all the acts of Asa, and all his might, and all that he did, and the cities which he built, are they not written in the book of the chronicles of the kings of Judah?: ... the other events of Asa's reign, all his achievements, *NIV* ... the power he wielded, all his history, and the record of the cities, *Knox* ... his courage, and all that he accomplished, *Fenton*.

Nevertheless in the time of his old age he was diseased in his feet: ... Asa had an infirmity, *NAB* ... an ailment, *Beck*.

24. And Asa slept with his fathers, and was buried with his fathers in the city of David his father: and Jehoshaphat his son reigned in his stead: ... rested with his forefathers and was buried with them in the city of his ancestor, *NEB* ... became the next king, *NLT* ... with his ancestors, *NRSV* ... in the royal tombs in David's City, *Good News*.

25. And Nadab the son of Jeroboam began to reign over Israel in the second year of Asa king of Judah, and reigned over Israel two years: ... he was king of

well, Ishmael flung the corpses of the murdered adherents of Gedaliah. He thus effectually protected the frontier of Benjamin.

15:23–24. After a powerful and useful reign, Asa was attacked with gout in his feet two years before his death. The chronicler reproaches him for seeking "not to Yahweh but to the physicians" (2 Chr. 16:12) in his "exceeding great disease." If this was a sin, it is one of which we are unable to estimate the sinfulness from this meager notice. Everything which bears the aspect of a worldly policy is considered foolish.

15:25–34. Jeroboam slept with his fathers and went to his own place, leaving behind him his dreadful epitaph upon the sacred page. His son Nadab succeeded him. In his reign of twenty-two years, the first king of Israel had outlived Rehoboam and his son Abijah. Asa, the great grandson of Solomon, was already on the throne of Judah. Of Nadab we are told next to nothing. The appreciation of the kings of Israel tends to drift into the meager formula that they did that which was evil in the sight of the LORD and walked in the way of Jeroboam, the son of Nebat, and in his sin where-

3937, 623	4567	3171	4566.121	6142, 3547	8523		6449.121
prep, pn	n ms	pn	cj, v Qal impf 3ms	prep, pn	n fd	26.	cj, v Qal impf 3ms
לְאָסָא	מֶלֶךְ	יְהוּדָה	וַיִּמְלֹךְ	עַל־יִשְׂרָאֵל	שְׁנָתָיִם		וַיַּעַשׂ
le'āsā'	melekh	yehûdhāh	wayyimlōkh	'al-yisrā'ēl	shenāthāyim		wayya'as
of Asa	the king of	Judah	and he reigned	over Israel	two years		and he did

7737	904, 6084	3176	2050.121	904, 1932	1	904, 2496
art, adj	prep, n fd	pn	cj, v Qal impf 3ms	prep, n ms	n ms, ps 3ms	cj, prep, n fs, ps 3ms
הָרַע	בְּעֵינֵי	יְהוָה	וַיֵּלֶךְ	בְּדֶרֶךְ	אָבִיו	וּבְחַטָּאתוֹ
hāra'	be'ênê	yehwāh	wayyēlekh	bedherekh	'āvîw	ûvechattā'thô
what is evil	in the eyes of	Yahweh	and he walked	in the way of	his father	and in his sin

866	2490.511	881, 3547		7489.121	6142	1225
rel part	v Hiphil pf 3ms	do, pn	27.	cj, v Qal impf 3ms	prep, ps 3ms	pn
אֲשֶׁר	הֶחֱטִיא	אֶת־יִשְׂרָאֵל		וַיִּקְשֹׁר	עָלָיו	בַּעְשָׁא
'ăsher	hechěṭî'	'eth-yisrā'ēl		wayyiqŏshōr	'ālâv	ba'āshā'
which	he caused to sin	Israel		and he conspired	against him	Baasha

1158, 282	3937, 1041	3551	5409.521	1225	904, 1436
n ms, pn	prep, n ms	pn	cj, v Hiphil impf 3ms, ps 3ms	pn	prep, pn
בֶּן־אֲחִיָּה	לְבֵית	יִשָּׂכָר	וַיַּכֵּהוּ	בַּעְשָׁא	בְּגִבְּתוֹן
ven-'ăchîyāh	levêth	yissākhār	wayyakkēhû	va'āshā'	beghibbethôn
the son of Ahijah	of the household of	Issachar	and he struck him down	Baasha	in Gibbethon

866	3937, 6674	5247	3725, 3547	6961.152	6142, 1436
rel part	prep, pn	cj, pn	cj, adj, pn	v Qal act ptc mp	prep, pn
אֲשֶׁר	לַפְּלִשְׁתִּים	וְנָדָב	וְכָל־יִשְׂרָאֵל	צָרִים	עַל־גִּבְּתוֹן
'ăsher	lappelishtîm	wenādhāv	wekhol-yisrā'ēl	tsārîm	'al-gibbethôn
which	to the Philistines	and Nadab	and all Israel	laying siege	against Gibbethon

	4322.521	1225	904, 8523	8421	3937, 623	4567	3171
28.	cj, v Hiphil impf 3ms, ps 3ms	pn	prep, n fs	num	prep, pn	n ms	pn
	וַיְמִתֵהוּ	בַּעְשָׁא	בִּשְׁנַת	שָׁלֹשׁ	לְאָסָא	מֶלֶךְ	יְהוּדָה
	waymithēhû	va'āshā'	bishnath	shālōsh	le'āsā'	melekh	yehûdhāh
	and he executed him	Baasha	in the year	three	of Asa	the king of	Judah

4566.121	8809		2030.121	3626, 4566.141	5409.511
cj, v Qal impf 3ms	prep, ps 3ms	29.	cj, v Qal impf 3ms	prep, v Qal inf con, ps 3ms	v Hiphil pf 3ms
וַיִּמְלֹךְ	תַּחְתָּיו		וַיְהִי	כְמָלְכוֹ	הִכָּה
wayyimlōkh	tachtâv		wayhî	khemālekhô	hikkāh
and he reigned	instead of him		and it was	when his reigning	he struck down

881, 3725, 1041	3493	3940, 8080.511	3725, 5580	3937, 3493
do, adj, n ms	pn	neg part, v Hiphil pf 3ms	adj, n fs	prep, pn
אֶת־כָּל־בֵּית	יָרָבְעָם	לֹא־הִשְׁאִיר	כָּל־נְשָׁמָה	לְיָרָבְעָם
'eth-kol-bêth	yārov'ām	lō'-hish'îr	kol-neshāmāh	leyārov'ām
all the household of	Jeroboam	he did not leave	any breathing being	to Jeroboam

5912, 8436.511	3626, 1745	3176	866	1744.311
adv, v Hiphil pf 3ms, ps 3ms	prep, n ms	pn	rel part	v Piel pf 3ms
עַד־הִשְׁמִדוֹ	כִּדְבַר	יְהוָה	אֲשֶׁר	דִּבֶּר
'adh-hishmidhô	kidhvar	yehwāh	'ăsher	dibber
until he had exterminated it	according to the word of	Yahweh	which	He had spoken

904, 3135, 5860	282	8296		6142, 2496	3493	866
prep, n fs, n ms, ps 3ms	pn	art, pn	30.	prep, n fp	pn	rel part
בְּיַד־עַבְדּוֹ	אֲחִיָּה	הַשִּׁילֹנִי		עַל־חַטֹּאות	יָרָבְעָם	אֲשֶׁר
beyadh-'avdô	'ăchîyāh	hashshîlōnî		'al-chattō'wth	yārov'ām	'ăsher
by the hand of his servant	Ahijah	the Shilonite		concerning the sins of	Jeroboam	which

2490.111	866	2490.511	881, 3547	904, 3833	866
v Qal pf 3ms	cj, rel pron	v Hiphil pf 3ms	do, pn	prep, n ms, ps 3ms	rel part
חָטָא	וַאֲשֶׁר	הֶחֱטִיא	אֶת־יִשְׂרָאֵל	בְּכַעְסוֹ	אֲשֶׁר
chāṭā'	wa'ăsher	hechĕṭî'	'eth-yisrā'ēl	bekha'ăsô	'ăsher
he sinned	and which	he caused to sin	Israel	in his anger	which

3832.511	881, 3176	435	3547		3615	1745
v Hiphil pf 3ms	do, pn	*n mp*	pn	**31.**	cj, *n ms*	*n mp*
הִכְעִיס	אֶת־יְהוָה	אֱלֹהֵי	יִשְׂרָאֵל		וְיֶתֶר	דִּבְרֵי
hikh'îs	'eth-yehwāh	'ĕlōhê	yisrā'ēl		weyether	divrê
he provoked to anger	Yahweh	the God of	Israel		and the remainder of	the events of

Israel for two years, *BB* ... was king for two years, *Berkeley*.

26. And he did evil in the sight of the Lord, and walked in the way of his father, and in his sin wherewith he made Israel to sin: ... he sinned against the Lord and led Israel into sin, *Good News* ... copying the evil ways, *BB* ... followed in his father's footsteps, *REB* ... what is displeasing to Yahweh; he copied his father's example, *JB*.

27. And Baasha the son of Ahijah, of the house of Issachar, conspired against him: ... made plans to kill Nadab, *NCV* ... plotted against him, *Beck*.

and Baasha smote him at Gibbethon, which belonged to the Philistines; for Nadab and all Israel laid siege to Gibbethon: ... murdered him at Gibethon, belonging to Philistia, *Fenton* ... assassinated him while he and the Israelite army were laying siege, *NLT* ... which Nadab was besieging with all his forces, *NEB*.

28. Even in the third year of Asa king of Judah did Baasha slay him, and reigned in his stead: ... Ba'asha killed him, *RSV* ... put him to death, and became king in his place, *BB* ... Baasa succeeded Nadab, *Knox*.

29. And it came to pass, when he reigned, that he smote all the house of Jeroboam; he left not to Jeroboam any that breathed, until he had destroyed him: ... destroying every living soul and leaving not one survivor, *REB* ... No sooner was he king than he killed all the household of Jeroboam, leaving not a single soul, *Moffatt* ... did not leave a single person alive, *Goodspeed* ... left not so much as one soul of his seed, *Douay*.

according unto the saying of the Lord, which he spake by his servant Ahijah the Shilonite: ... just as Yahweh had foretold through his servant, *JB* ... the Lord had promised, *NLT* ... the warning which the Lord had pronounced, *NAB*.

30. Because of the sins of Jeroboam which he sinned, and which he made Israel sin, by his provocation wherewith he provoked the Lord God of Israel to anger: ... had sinned very much and had led the people of Israel to sin, *NCV* ... led Israel into sin and made the Lord, the God of Israel, angry, *Beck* ... was he punished for defying the Lord God, *Knox*.

31. Now the rest of the acts of Nadab, and all that he did, are they not written in the book of the chronicles of the kings of Israel?: ... the annals, *NIV* ... of the History, *NLT* ... of the words of the days, *Douay* ... recorded in the history of events in the times, *Fenton*.

32. And there was war between Asa and Baasha king of Israel all

with he caused Israel to sin. In the second year of his reign, Nadab was engaged in a wearisome military expedition against Gibbethon in the Shephelah, which belonged to the Philistines. It was a Levitical city in the tribe of Dan, which had been assigned to the Kohathites, and its siege continued for twenty-seven years with no apparent result (Josh. 19:44; 21:23; 1 Ki. 15:27; 16:15). That the Philistines, who had been so utterly crushed by David and who were an insignificant power, should have thus been able to assert themselves once more is a proof of the weakness to which Israel had been reduced. While Nadab was thus occupied, an obscure conspirator, Baasha, son of Ahijah, of the tribe of Issachar, actuated perhaps by tribal jealousy, or stirred up as Jeroboam had been before him and as Jehu was after him by some prophetic message, conspired against him, and slew him. As soon as this military revolt had placed Baasha on the throne, he fulfilled the frightful curse which Ahijah had uttered against the house of Jeroboam. He absolutely exterminated the family of Nebat and left him neither kinsman nor friend to avenge his death. He seems to have been a powerful soldier, and he inflicted severe humiliation on the Southern Kingdom until Asa bribed Benhadad to invade his territory. He reigned at Tirzah for twenty-four years, of which nothing is recorded but the ordinary formula. Toward the

5247	3725, 866	6449.111	1950B, 3940, 2062	3918.156	6142, 5809
pn	cj, *adj*, rel part	v Qal pf 3ms	intrg part, neg part, pers pron	v Qal pass ptc mp	prep, *n ms*
נָדָב	וְכָל־אֲשֶׁר	עָשָׂה	הֲלֹא־הֵם	כְּתוּבִים	עַל־סֵפֶר
nādhāv	wᵉkhol-'ăsher	'āsāh	hălō'-hēm	kᵉthûvîm	'al-sēpher
Nadab	and all that	he did	are they not	things written	on the scroll of

1745	3219	3937, 4567	3547		4560	2030.112	1033	623
n mp	art, n mp	prep, *n mp*	pn		cj, n fs	v Qal pf 3fs	prep	pn
דִּבְרֵי	הַיָּמִים	לְמַלְכֵי	יִשְׂרָאֵל	**32.**	וּמִלְחָמָה	הָיְתָה	בֵּין	אָסָא
divrê	hayyāmîm	lᵉmalkhê	yisrā'ēl		ûmilchāmāh	hāyᵉthāh	bên	'āsā'
the events of	the days	of the kings of	Israel		and war	it was	between	Asa

1033	1225	4567, 3547	3725, 3219		904, 8523	8421	3937, 623
cj, prep	pn	*n ms*, pn	*adj*, n mp, ps 3mp		prep, *n fs*	num	prep, pn
וּבֵין	בַּעְשָׁא	מֶלֶךְ־יִשְׂרָאֵל	כָּל־יְמֵיהֶם	**33.**	בִּשְׁנַת	שָׁלֹשׁ	לְאָסָא
ûvên	ba'ăshā'	melekh-yisrā'ēl	kol-yᵉmêhem		bishnath	shālōsh	lᵉ'āsā'
and between	Baasha	the king of Israel	all their days		in the year	three	of Asa

4567	3171	4566.111	1225	1158, 282	6142, 3725, 3547	904, 8995
n ms	pn	v Qal pf 3ms	pn	*n ms*, pn	prep, *n ms*, pn	prep, pn
מֶלֶךְ	יְהוּדָה	מָלַךְ	בַּעְשָׁא	בֶּן־אֲחִיָּה	עַל־כָּל־יִשְׂרָאֵל	בְּתִרְצָה
melekh	yᵉhûdhāh	mālakh	ba'ăshā'	ven-'ăchîyāh	'al-kol-yisrā'ēl	bᵉthirtsāh
the king of	Judah	he reigned	Baasha	the son of Ahijah	over all Israel	in Tirzah

6465	727	8523		6449.121	7737	904, 6084	3176
num	cj, num	n fs		cj, v Qal impf 3ms	art, adj	prep, *n fd*	pn
עֶשְׂרִים	וְאַרְבַּע	שָׁנָה	**34.**	וַיַּעַשׂ	הָרַע	בְּעֵינֵי	יְהוָה
'esrîm	wᵉ'arba'	shānāh		wayya'as	hāra'	bᵉ'ênê	yᵉhwāh
twenty	and four	years		and he did	what is evil	in the eyes of	Yahweh

2050.121	904, 1932	3493	904, 2496	866	2490.511	881, 3547
cj, v Qal impf 3ms	prep, *n ms*	pn	cj, prep, n fs, ps 3ms	rel part	v Hiphil pf 3ms	do, pn
וַיֵּלֶךְ	בְּדֶרֶךְ	יָרָבְעָם	וּבְחַטָּאתוֹ	אֲשֶׁר	הֶחֱטִיא	אֶת־יִשְׂרָאֵל
wayyēlekh	bᵉdherekh	yārov'ām	ûvᵉchattā'thô	'ăsher	hechĕtî'	'eth-yisrā'ēl
and he walked	in the way of	Jeroboam	and in his sin	which	he caused to sin	Israel

	2030.121	1745, 3176	420, 3167	1158, 2710	6142, 1225
16:1	cj, v Qal impf 3ms	*n ms*, pn	prep, pn	*n ms*, pn	prep, pn
	וַיְהִי	דְבַר־יְהוָה	אֶל־יֵהוּא	בֶן־חֲנָנִי	עַל־בַּעְשָׁא
	wayhî	dhᵉvar-yᵉhwāh	'el-yēhû'	ven-chănānî	'al-ba'ăshā'
	and it was	the word of Yahweh	unto Jehu	the son of Hanani	concerning Baasha

3937, 569.141		3391	866	7597.515	4623, 6312	5598.125
prep, v Qal inf con		cj	rel part	v Hiphil pf 1cs, ps 2ms	prep, art, n ms	cj, v Qal impf 1cs, ps 2ms
לֵאמֹר	**2.**	יַעַן	אֲשֶׁר	הֲרִימֹתִיךָ	מִן־הֶעָפָר	וָאֶתֶּנְךָ
lē'mōr		ya'an	'ăsher	hᵉrîmōthîkhā	min-he'āphār	wā'ettenkhā
saying		because	which	I exalted you	from the dust	and I placed you

5233	6142	6194	3547	2050.123	904, 1932	3493
n ms	prep	n ms, ps 1cs	pn	cj, v Qal impf 2ms	prep, *n ms*	pn
נָגִיד	עַל	עַמִּי	יִשְׂרָאֵל	וַתֵּלֶךְ	בְּדֶרֶךְ	יָרָבְעָם
nāghîdh	'al	'ammî	yisrā'ēl	wattēlekh	bᵉdherekh	yārov'ām
a leader	over	my people	Israel	but you walked	in the way of	Jeroboam

2490.523	881, 6194	3547	3937, 3832.541	904, 2496
cj, v Hiphil impf 2ms	do, n ms, ps 1cs	pn	prep, v Hiphil inf con, ps 1cs	prep, n fp, ps 3mp
וַתַּחֲטִא	אֶת־עַמִּי	יִשְׂרָאֵל	לְהַכְעִיסֵנִי	בְּחַטֹּאתָם
wattachtî'	'eth-'ammî	yisrā'ēl	lᵉhakh'îsēnî	bᵉchattō'thām
and you caused to sin	my people	Israel	to provoke Me to anger	with their sins

3.	2079	1220.551	313	1225	313	1041	5598.115
	intrj, ps 1cs	v Hiphil ptc ms	prep	pn	cj, prep	n ms, ps 3ms	cj, v Qal pf 1cs
	הִנְנִי	מַבְעִיר	אַחֲרֵי	בַעְשָׁא	וְאַחֲרֵי	בֵּיתוֹ	וְנָתַתִּי
	hinenî	mav'îr	'achrê	va'āshā'	we'achrê	vêthô	wenāthattî
	behold I	burning	after	Baasha	and after	his household	and I will put

881, 1041	3626, 1041	3493	1158, 5203	4.	4322.151	3937, 1225
do, n ms, ps 2ms	prep, *n ms*	pn	*n ms*, pn		art, v Qal act ptc ms	prep, pn
אֶת־בֵּיתְךָ	כְּבֵית	יָרָבְעָם	בֶּן־נְבָט		הַמֵּת	לְבַעְשָׁא
'eth-bêthekhā	kevêth	yārov'ām	ben-nevāṭ		hammēth	leva'āshā'
your household	like the household of	Jeroboam	the son of Nebat		the dead one	of Baasha

their days: ... was at war with Asa continually, *Knox* ... all through their reigns, *NEB* ... as long as they lived, *NAB*.

33. In the third year of Asa king of Judah began Baasha the son of Ahijah to reign over all Israel in Tirzah, twenty and four years: ... started to rule over Israel, *Beck* ... became king, *BB* ... Basha-ben-Akhiah began to reign over all Israel in Thirtzah for fourteen years, *Fenton* ... began his twenty-four years' reign, *Berkeley*.

34. And he did evil in the sight of the LORD: ... he did that which displeased, *Tyndale* ... that which was wicked, *Rotherham* ... what was wrong in the eyes, *REB*.

and walked in the way of Jeroboam, and in his sin wherewith he made Israel to sin: ... which he had caused Israel to commit, *NIV* ... imitating the conduct, *NAB* ... copied the example, *JB*.

16:1. Then the word of the LORD came to Jehu the son of Hanani against Baasha, saying: ... spoke ... against King Baasha, *NCV* ... protesting against, *BB* ... message from the LORD was delivered, *NLT*.

2. Forasmuch as I exalted thee out of the dust, and made thee prince over my people Israel: ... I lifted you from the dust and made you supreme, *Moffatt* ... made you leader, *JB*.

and thou hast walked in the way of Jeroboam, and hast made my people Israel to sin, to provoke me to anger with their sins: ... to jealousy, *Goodspeed* ... followed in the footsteps, *REB* ... you have lived in Jeroboam's ways and led My people into sin, *Beck*.

3. Behold, I will take away the posterity of Baasha, and the posterity of his house; and will make thy house like the house of Jeroboam the son of Nebat: ... completely destroy Baasha and his house, *Berkeley* ... utterly sweep away Ba'asha, *RSV* ... see that Baasha and all his family are completely brushed away, *BB* ... consume, *NRSV*.

4. Him that dieth of Baasha in the city shall the dogs eat: ... Those of Baasha's family who die in a town,

close of his reign, he received from the prophet Jehu, the son of Hanani, the message of his doom. Jehu must have been at this time a young prophet. According to the Chronicles, his father Hanani rebuked Asa for the alliance which (as we shall see) he made with the Syrian against Baasha (2 Chr. 16:7–10); and he himself rebuked Jehoshaphat for his alliance with Ahab and lived to be his annalist (2 Chr. 20:34). Like Amos, he lived in Judah, but prophesied also against a king of Israel. He told Baasha that God, who had exalted him out of the dust to be king of Israel, should inflict on his family the same terrible extirpation which He had inflicted on the house of Jeroboam, whose sins he had, nevertheless, followed.

16:1–7. From such meager records of horror there is not much to learn beyond the general truth of the nemesis which dogs the heels of crime; but there is one significant clause which throws great light on the judgment which we are asked to form of these events. The prophet Jehu rebuked Baasha for showing himself false to the destiny to which God had summoned him. He implies, therefore, that Baasha had some divine sanction for the revolution which he headed; and certainly in his slaughter of the house of Jeroboam he was the instrument of a divine decree. Yet we are expressly told that "he provoked the LORD to anger with the work of his hands, in being like the house of Jeroboam, and because he killed him," or, as it is rendered in the Revised Version margin, "because he smote it." This is not the only place where we find that a man may be in one sense commissioned to do a deed of blood, yet in another sense may be held guilty for fulfillment of the commission (cf. 2 Ki. 9:7 with Hos. 1:4). The prophecy of extirpation had been passed, but the cruel agent of its accomplishment was not thereby condoned. God's decrees are car-

904, 6111	404.126	3732	4322.151	3937	904, 7898	404.126
prep, art, n fs	v Qal impf 3mp	art, n mp	cj, art, v Qal act ptc ms	prep, ps 3ms	prep, art, n ms	v Qal impf 3mp
בָּעִיר	יֹאכְלוּ	הַכְּלָבִים	וְהַמֵּת	לוֹ	בַּשָּׂדֶה	יֹאכְלוּ
bā'îr	yō'khelû	hakkelāvîm	wehammēth	lô	bassādheh	yō'khelû
in the city	they will eat	the dogs	and the dead one	of him	in the field	they will eat

5991	8452		3615	1745	1225	866	6449.111
n ms	art, n md	**5.**	cj, *n ms*	*n mp*	pn	cj, rel pron	v Qal pf 3ms
עוֹף	הַשָּׁמָיִם		וְיֶתֶר	דִּבְרֵי	בַּעְשָׁא	וַאֲשֶׁר	עָשָׂה
'ôph	hashshāmāyim		weyether	divrê	va'ăshā'	wa'ăsher	'āsāh
the birds of	the heavens		and the remainder of	the events of	Baasha	and what	he did

1400	1950B, 3940, 2062	3918.156	6142, 5809	1745	3219
cj, n fs, ps 3ms	intrg part, neg part, pers pron	v Qal pass ptc mp	prep, *n ms*	*n mp*	art, n mp
וּגְבוּרָתוֹ	הֲלֹא־הֵם	כְּתוּבִים	עַל־סֵפֶר	דִּבְרֵי	הַיָּמִים
ûghevûrāthô	hălō'-hēm	kethûvîm	'al-sēpher	divrê	hayyāmîm
and his strength	are they not	things written	on the scroll of	the events of	the days

3937, 4567	3547		8311.121	1225	6196, 1	7196.221
prep, *n mp*	pn	**6.**	cj, v Qal impf 3ms	pn	prep, n mp, ps 3ms	cj, v Niphil impf 3ms
לְמַלְכֵי	יִשְׂרָאֵל		וַיִּשְׁכַּב	בַּעְשָׁא	עִם־אֲבֹתָיו	וַיִּקָּבֵר
lemalkhê	yisrā'ēl		wayyishkav	ba'ăshā'	'im-'ăvōthâv	wayyiqqāvēr
of the kings of	Israel		then he lay	Baasha	with his ancestors	and he was buried

904, 8995	4566.121	429	1158	8809		1612	904, 3135, 3167
prep, pn	cj, v Qal impf 3ms	pn	n ms, ps 3ms	prep, ps 3ms	**7.**	cj, cj	prep, *n fs*, pn
בְּתִרְצָה	וַיִּמְלֹךְ	אֵלָה	בְּנוֹ	תַּחְתָּיו		וְגַם	בְּיַד־יֵהוּא
bethirtsāh	wayyimlōkh	'ēlāh	venô	tachtâv		wegham	beyadh-yēhû'
in Tirzah	and he reigned	Elah	his son	instead of him		and also	by the hand of Jehu

1158, 2710	5204	1745, 3176	2030.111	420, 1225	420, 1041
n ms, pn	art, n ms	*n ms*, pn	v Qal pf 3ms	prep, pn	cj, prep, n ms, ps 3ms
בֶּן־חֲנָנִי	הַנָּבִיא	דְּבַר־יְהוָה	הָיָה	אֶל־בַּעְשָׁא	וְאֶל־בֵּיתוֹ
ven-chănānî	hannāvî'	devar-yehwāh	hāyāh	'el-ba'ăshā'	we'el-bêthô
the son of Hanani	the prophet	the word of Yahweh	it was	to Baasha	and to his household

6142	3725, 7750	866, 6449.111	904, 6084	3176	3937, 3832.541
cj, prep	*adj*, art, n fs	rel part, v Qal pf 3ms	prep, *n fd*	pn	prep, v Hiphil inf con, ps 3ms
וְעַל	כָּל־הָרָעָה	אֲשֶׁר־עָשָׂה	בְּעֵינֵי	יְהוָה	לְהַכְעִיסוֹ
we'al	kol-hārā'āh	'ăsher-'āsāh	be'ênê	yehwāh	lehakh'îsô
and concerning	all the evil	that he had done	in the eyes of	Yahweh	to provoke Him to anger

904, 4801	3135	3937, 2030.141	3626, 1041	3493	6142
prep, *n ms*	n fd, ps 3ms	prep, v Qal inf con	prep, *n ms*	pn	cj, prep
בְּמַעֲשֵׂה	יָדָיו	לִהְיוֹת	כְּבֵית	יָרָבְעָם	וְעַל
bema'ăsēh	yādhâv	lihyôth	kevêth	yārov'ām	we'al
with the work of	his hands	to be	like the household of	Jeroboam	and concerning

866, 5409.511	881		904, 8523	6465	8666	8523	3937, 623	4567
rel part, v Hiphil pf 3ms	do, ps 3ms	**8.**	prep, *n fs*	num	cj, num	n fs	prep, pn	*n ms*
אֲשֶׁר־הִכָּה	אֹתוֹ		בִּשְׁנַת	עֶשְׂרִים	וָשֵׁשׁ	שָׁנָה	לְאָסָא	מֶלֶךְ
'ăsher-hikkāh	'ōthô		bishnath	'esrîm	wāshēsh	shānāh	le'āsā'	melekh
that he struck down	him		in the year	twenty	and six	years	of Asa	the king of

3171	4566.111	429	1158, 1225	6142, 3547	904, 8995	8523
pn	v Qal pf 3ms	pn	*n ms*, pn	prep, pn	prep, pn	n fd
יְהוּדָה	מָלַךְ	אֵלָה	בֶּן־בַּעְשָׁא	עַל־יִשְׂרָאֵל	בְּתִרְצָה	שְׁנָתָיִם
yehûdhāh	mālakh	'ēlāh	ven-ba'ăshā'	'al-yisrā'ēl	bethirtsāh	shenāthāyim
Judah	he reigned	Elah	the son of Baasha	over Israel	in Tirzah	two years

9.

7489.121	6142	5860	2259	8015	4414	7681
cj, v Qal impf 3ms	prep, ps 3ms	n ms, ps 3ms	pn	*n ms*	*n fs*	art, n ms
וַיִּקְשֹׁר	עָלָיו	עַבְדּוֹ	זִמְרִי	שַׂר	מַחֲצִית	הָרָכֶב
wayyiqōshōr	'ālâv	'avdô	zimrî	sar	machtsîth	hārākhev
and he conspired	against him	his servant	Zimri	the commander of	half of	the chariots

2000	904, 8995	8685.151	8318	1041	801	866	6142, 1041
cj, pers pron	prep, pn	v Qal act ptc ms	adj	*n ms*	pn	rel pron	prep, art, n ms
וְהוּא	בְּתִרְצָה	שֹׁתֶה	שִׁכּוֹר	בֵּית	אַרְצָא	אֲשֶׁר	עַל־הַבַּיִת
wehû'	vethirtsāh	shōtheh	shikkôr	bêth	'artsā'	'ăsher	'al-habbayith
and he	in Tirzah	drinking	drunk	the household of	Arza	who	over the household

904, 8995	**10.** 971.121	2259	5409.521	4322.521	904, 8523
prep, pn	cj, v Qal impf 3ms	pn	cj, v Hiphil impf 3ms, ps 3ms	cj, v Hiphil impf 3ms, ps 3ms	prep, *n fs*
בְּתִרְצָה	וַיָּבֹא	זִמְרִי	וַיַּכֵּהוּ	וַיְמִיתֵהוּ	בִּשְׁנַת
bethirtsāh	wayyāvō'	zimrî	wayyakkēhû	waymîthēhû	bishnath
in Tirzah	and he entered	Zimri	and he struck him down	and he killed him	in the year

REB ... dogs shall devour him, *NAB* ... shall be food for the dogs, *NEB*.

and him that dieth of his in the fields shall the fowls of the air eat: ... anyone from your family who dies ... will be eaten by birds, *NCV* ... by the vultures, *NLT*.

5. Now the rest of the acts of Baasha, and what he did, and his might, are they not written in the book of the chronicles of the kings of Israel?: ... the Annals, *Moffatt* ... The History, *Good News* ... those are written in the history of events of the times, *Fenton* ... his career, his valour, is this not recorded, *JB*.

6. So Baasha slept with his fathers, and was buried in Tirzah: ... with Thersa for his burying-place, *Knox* ... rested with his ancestors, *NAB*.

and Elah his son reigned in his stead: ... he was succeeded by his son Elah, *NEB* ... succeeded him as king, *NIV* ... became the next king, *NLT*.

7. And also by the hand of the prophet Jehu the son of Hanani came the word of the LORD against Baasha, and against his house: ... the Lord pronounced sentence upon Baasa and his line, *Knox* ... and his family, *Beck*.

even for all the evil that he did in the sight of the LORD, in provoking him to anger with the work of his hands, in being like the house of Jeroboam; and because he killed him: ... because of all the wickedness that he did in the light of the Lord, *Tyndale* ... killed Nadab, *NAB* ... also because he destroyed it, *NRSV* ... because he struck it, *NASB* ... secondly because he had destroyed that House, *JB*.

8. In the twenty and sixth year of Asa king of Judah began Elah the son of Baasha to reign over Israel in Tirzah, two years: ... became king of Israel, *Good News* ... began his two-year reign over Israel, *Berkeley*.

9. And his servant Zimri, captain of half his chariots, conspired against him: ... in his service commanding half the chariotry, plotted against, *NEB* ... made plans to kill him, *NLT* ... half of his war-carriages, made secret designs, *BB*.

ried out as part of the vast scheme of Providence, and He may use guilty hands to fulfill his purposes. King Jehu is his minister of vengeance, but the tiger-like ferocity with which he carried out his work awoke God's anger and received God's punishment. The king of Babylon fulfilled the purpose for which he had been appointed, but his ruthlessness received its just recompense. The wrath of man may accomplish the decrees of God, but it worketh not his righteousness. Herod and Pontius Pilate, Jews and Gentiles, priests and Pharisees, rulers and the mob may rage against Christ, but all they can accomplish is what God allows and his ultimate purpose.

16:8–10. Baasha "slept with his fathers," and his son Elah succeeded him. Elah seems to have been an incapable drunkard and reigned in Tirzah for less than two years. While he was drinking himself drunk, not even secretly in his own palace, but in the house of his chamberlain Arza—a shamelessness which was regarded as an aggravation of his offense (Hos. 7:3–7)—he was murdered by Zimri, the captain of half of his chariots, and the revolting tragedy of massacre was enacted once again. The fact that Baasha was a man of no distinction, but "exalted ... out of the dust" (1 Ki. 16:2), probably added to the weakness of his dynasty.

6465	8124	3937, 623	4567	3171	4566.121	8809
num	cj, num	prep, pn	*n ms*	pn	cj, v Qal impf 3ms	prep, ps 3ms
עֶשְׂרִים	וָשֶׁבַע	לְאָסָא	מֶלֶךְ	יְהוּדָה	וַיִּמְלֹךְ	תַּחְתָּיו
'esrîm	wāsheva'	le'āsā'	melekh	yehûdhāh	wayyimlōkh	tachtâv
twenty	and seven	of Asa	the king of	Judah	and he reigned	instead of him

11.	2030.121	904, 4566.141	3626, 3553.141	6142, 3802	5409.511
	cj, v Qal impf 3ms	prep, v Qal inf con, ps 3ms	prep, v Qal inf con, ps 3ms	prep, n ms, ps 3ms	v Hiphil pf 3ms
	וַיְהִי	בְמָלְכוֹ	כְּשִׁבְתּוֹ	עַל־כִּסְאוֹ	הִכָּה
	wayhî	vemālekhô	keshivtô	'al-kis'ô	hikkāh
	and it was	during his reigning	when his sitting	on his throne	he struck down

881, 3725, 1041	1225	3940, 8080.511	3937	8697.551	904, 7306
do, *adj, n ms*	pn	neg part, v Hiphil pf 3ms	prep, ps 3ms	v Hiphil ptc ms	prep, n ms
אֶת־כָּל־בֵּית	בַּעְשָׁא	לֹא־הִשְׁאִיר	לוֹ	מַשְׁתִּין	בְּקִיר
'eth-kol-bêth	ba'āshā'	lō'-hish'îr	lô	mashtîn	beqîr
all the household of	Baasha	he did not leave	to him	those urinating	on a wall

1381.152	7739	12.	8436.521	2259	881	3725, 1041
cj, v Qal act ptc mp, ps 3ms	cj, n ms, ps 3ms		cj, v Hiphil impf 3ms	pn	do	*adj, n ms*
וְגֹאֲלָיו	וְרֵעֵהוּ		וַיַּשְׁמֵד	זִמְרִי	אֵת	כָּל־בֵּית
weghō'ălâv	werē'ēhû		wayyashmēdh	zimrî	'ēth	kol-bêth
nor his avengers	nor his friends		and he exterminated	Zimri		all the household of

1225	3626, 1745	3176	866	1744.311	420, 1225	904, 3135
pn	prep, *n ms*	pn	rel part	v Piel pf 3ms	prep, pn	prep, *n fs*
בַּעְשָׁא	כִּדְבַר	יְהוָה	אֲשֶׁר	דִּבֶּר	אֶל־בַּעְשָׁא	בְּיַד
ba'āshā'	kidhvar	yehwāh	'ăsher	dibber	'el-ba'āshā'	beyadh
Baasha	according to the word of	Yahweh	which	He had spoken	to Baasha	by the hand of

3167	5204	13.	420	3725, 2496	1225	2496	429	1158	866
pn	art, n ms		prep	*adj, n fp*	pn	cj, *n fp*	pn	n ms, ps 3ms	rel part
יֵהוּא	הַנָּבִיא		אֶל	כָּל־חַטֹּאות	בַּעְשָׁא	וְחַטֹּאות	אֵלָה	בְנוֹ	אֲשֶׁר
yēhû'	hannāvî'		'el	kol-chattō'wth	ba'āshā'	wechattō'wth	'ēlāh	venô	'ăsher
Jehu	the prophet		toward	all the sins of	Baasha	and the sins of	Elah	his son	which

2490.116	866	2490.516	881, 3547	3937, 3832.541	881, 3176
v Qal pf 3cp	cj, rel pron	v Hiphil pf 3cp	do, pn	prep, v Hiphil inf con	do, pn
חָטְאוּ	וַאֲשֶׁר	הֶחֱטִיאוּ	אֶת־יִשְׂרָאֵל	לְהַכְעִיס	אֶת־יְהוָה
chāte'û	wa'ăsher	hechĕtî'û	'eth-yisrā'ēl	lehakh'îs	'eth-yehwāh
they sinned	and which	they caused to sin	Israel	to provoke to anger	Yahweh

435	3547	904, 1961	14.	3615	1745	429	3725, 866
n mp	pn	prep, n mp, ps 3mp		cj, *n ms*	*n mp*	pn	cj, *adj*, rel part
אֱלֹהֵי	יִשְׂרָאֵל	בְּהַבְלֵיהֶם		וְיֶתֶר	דִּבְרֵי	אֵלָה	וְכָל־אֲשֶׁר
'ĕlōhê	yisrā'ēl	behavlêhem		weyether	divrê	'ēlāh	wekhol-'ăsher
the God of	Israel	with their idols		and the remainder of	the events of	Elah	and all that

6449.111	1950B, 3940, 2062	3918.156	6142, 5809	1745	3219
v Qal pf 3ms	intrg part, neg part, pers pron	v Qal pass ptc mp	prep, *n ms*	*n mp*	art, n mp
עָשָׂה	הֲלוֹא־הֵם	כְּתוּבִים	עַל־סֵפֶר	דִּבְרֵי	הַיָּמִים
'āsāh	hălō'-hēm	kethûvîm	'al-sēpher	divrê	hayyāmîm
he did	are they not	things written	on the scroll of	the events of	the days

3937, 4567	3547	15.	904, 8523	6465	8124	8523	3937, 623	4567
prep, *n mp*	pn		prep, *n fs*	num	cj, num	n fs	prep, pn	*n ms*
לְמַלְכֵי	יִשְׂרָאֵל		בִּשְׁנַת	עֶשְׂרִים	וָשֶׁבַע	שָׁנָה	לְאָסָא	מֶלֶךְ
lemalkhê	yisrā'ēl		bishnath	'esrîm	wāsheva'	shānāh	le'āsā'	melekh
of the kings of	Israel		in the year	twenty	and seven	year	of Asa	the king of

as he was in Tirzah, drinking himself drunk in the house of Arza steward of his house in Tirzah: ... getting drunk in the home of Arza, the man in charge of the palace, *NIV* ... drinking himself senseless, *JB* ... into insensibility, *REB* ... who was superintendent of his palace in Thirtzah, *Fenton*.

10. And Zimri went in and smote him, and killed him, in the twenty and seventh year of Asa king of Judah, and reigned in his stead: ... struck him, *NKJV* ... attacked and assassinated him, *REB* ... struck him down dead, *Moffatt*.

11. And it came to pass, when he began to reign, as soon as he sat on his throne, that he slew all the house of Baasha: ... had settled himself ... he killed the whole family, *Fenton* ... Zimri immediately killed the entire royal family, *NLT* ... murdered all the household, *Moffatt*.

he left him not one that pisseth against a wall, neither of his kinsfolks, nor of his friends: ... he did not leave a single male, neither of his relatives, *NASB* ... a single manchild, *MAST* ... a single male of his kinsmen, *RSV* ... not one male child of his relations or his friends kept his life, *BB*.

12. Thus did Zimri destroy all the house of Baasha, according to the word of the LORD, which he spake against Baasha by Jehu the prophet: ... as the Eternal threatened Baasha by the prophet Jehu, *Moffatt* ... By destroying the whole household of Baasha he fulfilled the word, *REB* ... as the LORD had prophesied to Baasha, *NAB*.

13. For all the sins of Baasha, and the sins of Elah his son, by which they sinned, and by which they made Israel to sin, in provoking the LORD God of Israel to anger with their vanities: ... arousing the anger of the LORD ... with their idols, *NLT* ... moving the Lord, the God of Israel, to wrath by their foolish acts, *BB* ... angry because of their worthless idols, *NCV* ... with their nothingnesses, *Berkeley*.

14. Now the rest of the acts of Elah, and all that he did, are they not written in the book of the chronicles of the kings of Israel?: ... of the Annals, *NRSV* ... The History, *Good News* ... his entire career, is this not recorded, *JB* ... of the words of the days, *Douay*.

15. In the twenty and seventh year of Asa king of Judah did Zimri reign seven days in Tirzah. And the people were encamped against Gibbethon, which belonged to the Philistines: ... At the time the army was investing the Philistine city, *REB* ... The army was besieging, *NAB* ... encamped near Gibbethon, a Philistine town, *NIV* ... the people besieging Gebethon a city of, *Tyndale*.

16. And the people that were encamped heard say, Zimri hath conspired, and hath also slain the king: ... Zambri's conspiracy and the king's death, *Knox* ... troops in the field heard of Zimri's conspiracy and the murder, *NEB* ... plotted against the king and murdered him, *NIV* ... not only plotted against but actually killed, *JB*.

16:11–14. As far as can be understood from the meager information available on the subject, we infer that Elah, the son of the powerful Baasha, was a self-indulgent weakling. The army of Israel was encamped against Gibbethon—originally a Levitical town of the Kohathites in the territory of Dan—which they hoped to wrest from the Philistines. It was during the interminable and intermittent siege of this town that Nadab, the son of Jeroboam, had been murdered. Whatever may have been his sins, he was in his proper place leading the armies of Israel. Elah was not there, but in his beautiful palace at Tirzah. It was probably contempt for his incapacity and the bad example of Baasha's successful revolt, that tempted Zimri to murder him as he was drinking himself drunk in the house of his chamberlain, Arza. Zimri was a commander of half the chariots. Probably thinking that he could secure the throne, he slew not only Elah, but every male member of his family. To extinguish any possibility of vengeance, he even massacred all who were known to be friends of the royal house.

16:15–20. It was a consummate crime, and it was followed by swift and fitting judgment. Through that sea of blood Zimri only succeeded in wading to one week's royalty, followed by a shameful and agonizing death. We are told that he did evil in the sight of the LORD by following the sin of Jeroboam's calf-worship. The phrase must be here something of a formula, for in seven days he could hardly have achieved a religious revolution, and every other king of Israel, some of whom have long and prosperous reigns, maintained the unauthorized worship. But Zimri's atrocious revolt had been so ill-considered that it furnished a proverb of the terrible fate of rebels (2 Ki. 9:31). He had not even attempted to secure the assent of the army at Gibbethon. No sooner did the news reach the camp than the soldiers tumultuously refused to accept Zimri as king and elected Omri their captain. Omri instantly broke up the camp and led them to besiege the new king in Tirzah. Zimri saw that his cause was hopeless and took refuge in the fortress attached to the palace (R.V., "the castle of the king's house"). When he saw that even there he

3171	4566.111	2259	8124	3219	904, 8995	6194	2684.152
pn	v Qal pf 3ms	pn	num	n mp	prep, pn	cj, art, n ms	v Qal act ptc mp
יְהוּדָה	מָלַךְ	זִמְרִי	שִׁבְעַת	יָמִים	בְּתִרְצָה	וְהָעָם	חֹנִים
yehûdhāh	mālakh	zimrî	shiv'ath	yāmîm	bethirtsāh	wehā'ām	chōnîm
Judah	he reigned	Zimri	seven	days	in Tirzah	and the people	being encamped

6142, 1436	866	3937, 6674		8471.121	6194	2684.152
prep, pn	rel part	prep, pn	**16.**	cj, v Qal impf 3ms	art, n ms	art, v Qal act ptc mp
עַל־גִּבְּתוֹן	אֲשֶׁר	לַפְּלִשְׁתִּים		וַיִּשְׁמַע	הָעָם	הַחֹנִים
'al-gibbethôn	'ăsher	lappelishtîm		wayyishma'	hā'ām	hachōnîm
against Gibbethon	which	to the Philistines		and they heard	the people	those encamping

3937, 569.141	7489.111	2259	1612	5409.511	881, 4567
prep, v Qal inf con	v Qal pf 3ms	pn	cj, cj	v Hiphil pf 3ms	do, art, n ms
לֵאמֹר	קָשַׁר	זִמְרִי	וְגַם	הִכָּה	אֶת־הַמֶּלֶךְ
lē'mōr	qāshar	zimrî	wegham	hikkāh	'eth-hammelekh
saying	he conspired	Zimri	and also	he struck down	the king

4566.526	3725, 3547	881, 6245	8015, 6893	6142, 3547
cj, v Hiphil impf 3mp	*adj*, pn	do, pn	*n ms*, n ms	prep, pn
וַיַּמְלִכוּ	כָל־יִשְׂרָאֵל	אֶת־עָמְרִי	שַׂר־צָבָא	עַל־יִשְׂרָאֵל
wayyamlikhû	khol-yisrā'ēl	'eth-'omrî	sar-tsāvā'	'al-yisrā'ēl
and they cause him to reign	all Israel	Omri	the commander of the army	over Israel

904, 3219	2000	904, 4402		6148.121	6245	3725, 3547	6196
prep, art, n ms	art, dem pron	prep, art, n ms	**17.**	cj, v Qal impf 3ms	pn	cj, *adj*, pn	prep, ps 3ms
בַּיּוֹם	הַהוּא	בַּמַּחֲנֶה		וַיַּעֲלֶה	עָמְרִי	וְכָל־יִשְׂרָאֵל	עִמּוֹ
bayyôm	hahû'	bammachneh		wayya'ăleh	'omrî	wekhol-yisrā'ēl	'immô
on the day	the that	in the camp		and he went up	Omri	and all Israel	with him

4623, 1436	6961.126	6142, 8995		2030.121	3626, 7495.141	2259
prep, pn	cj, v Qal impf 3mp	prep, pn	**18.**	cj, v Qal impf 3ms	prep, v Qal inf con	pn
מִגִּבְּתוֹן	וַיָּצֻרוּ	עַל־תִּרְצָה		וַיְהִי	כִּרְאוֹת	זִמְרִי
migibbethôn	wayyātsurû	'al-tirtsāh		wayhî	kir'ôth	zimrî
from Gibbethon	and they laid siege	against Tirzah		and it was	when seeing	Zimri

3706, 4058.212	6111	971.121	420, 783	1041, 4567
cj, v Niphal pf 3fs	art, n fs	cj, v Qal impf 3ms	prep, *n ms*	*n ms*, art, n ms
כִּי־נִלְכְּדָה	הָעִיר	וַיָּבֹא	אֶל־אַרְמוֹן	בֵּית־הַמֶּלֶךְ
kî-nilkedhāh	hā'îr	wayyāvō'	'el-'armôn	bêth-hammelekh
that it had been captured	the city	then he entered	to the citadel of	the house of the king

8041.121	6142	881, 1041, 4567	904, 813	4322.121
cj, v Qal impf 3ms	prep, ps 3ms	do, *n ms*, n ms	prep, art, n fs	cj, v Qal impf 3ms
וַיִּשְׂרֹף	עָלָיו	אֶת־בֵּית־מֶלֶךְ	בָּאֵשׁ	וַיָּמֹת
wayyisrōph	'ālâv	'eth-bêth-melekh	bā'ēsh	wayyāmōth
then he burned	on him	the house of the king	with the fire	and he died

	6142, 2496	866	2490.111	3937, 6449.141	7737	904, 6084	3176
19.	prep, n fs, ps 3ms	rel part	v Qal pf 3ms	prep, v Qal inf con	art, adj	prep, *n fd*	pn
	עַל־חַטָּאתוֹ	אֲשֶׁר	חָטָא	לַעֲשׂוֹת	הָרַע	בְּעֵינֵי	יְהוָה
	'al-chaṯṯā'thô	'ăsher	chāṯā'	la'ăsôth	hāra'	be'ênê	yehwāh
	concerning his sin	which	he sinned	to do	what is evil	in the eyes of	Yahweh

3937, 2050.141	904, 1932	3493	904, 2496	866	6449.111	3937, 2490.541
prep, v Qal inf con	prep, *n ms*	pn	cj, prep, n fs, ps 3ms	rel part	v Qal pf 3ms	prep, v Hiphil inf con
לָלֶכֶת	בְּדֶרֶךְ	יָרָבְעָם	וּבְחַטָּאתוֹ	אֲשֶׁר	עָשָׂה	לְהַחֲטִיא
lālekheth	bedherekh	yārov'ām	ûvechaṯṯā'thô	'ăsher	'āsāh	lehachṯî'
to walk	in the way of	Jeroboam	and in his sin	which	he did	to cause to sin

881, 3547 do, pn אֶת־יִשְׂרָאֵל 'eth-yisrā'ēl Israel	**20.**	3615 cj, *n ms* וְיֶתֶר weyether and the remainder of	1745 *n mp* דִּבְרֵי divrê the events of	2259 pn זִמְרִי zimrî Zimri	7490 cj, n ms, ps 3ms וְקִשְׁרוֹ weqishrô and his conspiracy	866 rel part אֲשֶׁר 'ăsher which

7489.111 v Qal pf 3ms קָשָׁר qāshār he conspired	1950B, 3940, 2062 intrg part, neg part, pers pron הֲלֹא־הֵם hălō'-hēm are they not	3918.156 v Qal pass ptc mp כְּתוּבִים kethûvîm things written	6142, 5809 prep, *n ms* עַל־סֵפֶר 'al-sēpher on the scroll of	1745 *n mp* דִּבְרֵי divrê the events of	3219 art, n mp הַיָּמִים hayyāmîm the days

3937, 4567 prep, *n mp* לְמַלְכֵי lemalkhê of the kings of	3547 pn יִשְׂרָאֵל yisrā'ēl Israel	**21.**	226 adv אָז 'āz then	2606.221 v Niphal impf 3ms יֵחָלֵק yēchālēq they were divided	6194 art, n ms הָעָם hā'ām the people	3547 pn יִשְׂרָאֵל yisrā'ēl Israel	3937, 2783 prep, art, n ms לַחֵצִי lachētsî into the half

2783 *n ms* חֲצִי chătsî one half of	6194 art, n ms הָעָם hā'ām the people	2030.111 v Qal pf 3ms הָיָה hāyāh they were	313 prep אַחֲרֵי 'achrê after	8731 pn תִּבְנִי thivnî Tibni	1158, 1564 *n ms*, pn בֶן־גִּינַת ven-gînath the son of Ginath	3937, 4566.541 prep, v Hiphil inf con, ps 3ms לְהַמְלִיכוֹ lehamlîkhô to cause him to reign

wherefore all Israel made Omri, the captain of the host, king over Israel that day in the camp: ... the commander of the army, *NKJV* ... general, *NAB* ... made Amri their king, *Douay*.

17. And Omri went up from Gibbethon, and all Israel with him, and they besieged Tirzah: ... Omri marched up, *NAB* ... his whole force then withdrew, *REB* ... together with all Israel returned, *Berkeley*.

18. And it came to pass, when Zimri saw that the city was taken, that he went into the palace of the king's house, and burnt the king's house over him with fire, and died: ... the royal palace, set the whole of it on fire, *NEB* ... burned the palace over his own head, and died, *JB* ... set the king's house afire upon himself, *Tyndale* ... burned down the king's palace over himself, *Beck*.

19. For his sins which he sinned in doing evil in the sight of the LORD, in walking in the way of Jeroboam, and in his sin which he did, to make Israel to sin: ... following in the footsteps, *REB* ... This happened because of his sins against the LORD, *Good News* ... Zimri died because he had sinned by doing what the LORD said was wrong, *NCV*.

20. Now the rest of the acts of Zimri, and his treason that he wrought, are they not written in the book of the chronicles of the kings of Israel?: ... the story of his plot and of his tyranny, are to be found in the Annals, *Knox* ... other events of Zimri's reign, and the rebellion he carried out, *NIV* ... his conspiracy and tyranny, are they not written in the book of the words, *Douay* ... the secret design he made, *BB*.

21. Then were the people of Israel divided into two parts: half of the people followed Tibni the son of Ginath, to make him king; and half followed Omri: ... forces of Israel divided, *Fenton* ... while the other half supported Omri, *NLT* ... sons of Israel parted into halves, *Young* ... split into two parties, *Moffatt*.

---

could not maintain himself, he preferred speedy death to slow starvation or falling into the hands of his rival. He set fire to the palace and, like Sardanapalus, perished in the flames. (Justin, *Hist.*, 1:3; cf. Herod, 1:176, 7:107; *Liv.*, 21:14. Ewald elaborates out of his own consciousness an extraordinary romance about Zimri and the queen-mother.)

16:21–22. The swift suppression of his treason did not save the unhappy kingdom from anarchy and civil war. However popular Omri might be with the army, he was unacceptable to a large part of the people. They chose as their king a certain Tibni, son of Ginath, who was supported by a powerful brother named Joram. For four years the contest was continued. At the end of that time Tibni and Joram were conquered and killed (Josephus, *Antiquities*, VIII:vii:5, says that Tibni was assassinated, as does the Rabbinic *Seder Olam Rabba*, ch. 17), and Omri began his sole reign, which lasted eight years longer.

2783	313	6245		2480.121	6194	866	313	6245
cj, art, *n ms*	prep	pn	**22.**	cj, v Qal impf 3ms	art, n ms	rel pron	prep	pn
וְהַחֲצִי	אַחֲרֵי	עָמְרִי		וַיֶּחֱזַק	הָעָם	אֲשֶׁר	אַחֲרֵי	עָמְרִי
wehachtsî	'achrê	'omrî		wayyechĕzaq	hā'ām	'ăsher	'achrê	'omrî
and the half of	after	Omri		and they were stronger	the people	who	after	Omri

881, 6194	866	313	8731	1158, 1564	4322.121	8731	4566.121
do, art, n ms	rel pron	prep	pn	*n ms*, pn	cj, v Qal impf 3ms	pn	cj, v Qal impf 3ms
אֶת־הָעָם	אֲשֶׁר	אַחֲרֵי	תִּבְנִי	בֶּן־גִּינַת	וַיָּמָת	תִּבְנִי	וַיִּמְלֹךְ
'eth-hā'ām	'ăsher	'achrê	tivnî	ven-gînath	wayyāmāth	tivnî	wayyimlōkh
the people	who	after	Tibni	the son of Ginath	so he died	Tibni	and he reigned

6245		904, 8523	8421	259	8523	3937, 623	4567	3171	4566.111
pn	**23.**	prep, *n fs*	num	cj, num	n fs	prep, pn	*n ms*	pn	v Qal pf 3ms
עָמְרִי		בִּשְׁנַת	שְׁלֹשִׁים	וְאַחַת	שָׁנָה	לְאָסָא	מֶלֶךְ	יְהוּדָה	מָלַךְ
'omrî		bishnath	shelōshîm	we'achath	shānāh	le'āsā'	melekh	yehûdhāh	mālakh
Omri		in the year	thirty	and one	years	of Asa	the king of	Judah	he reigned

6245	6142, 3547	8692	6462	8523	904, 8995	4566.111	8666, 8523
pn	prep, pn	num	num	n fs	prep, pn	v Qal pf 3ms	num, n fp
עָמְרִי	עַל־יִשְׂרָאֵל	שְׁתֵּים	עֶשְׂרֵה	שָׁנָה	בְּתִרְצָה	מָלָךְ	שֵׁשׁ־שָׁנִים
'omrî	'al-yisrā'ēl	shettêm	'esrēh	shānāh	bethirtsāh	mālakh	shēsh-shānîm
Omri	over Israel	two	ten	years	in Tirzah	he reigned	six years

	7353.121	881, 2098	8497	4623, 882	8492	904, 3724	3826B
24.	cj, v Qal impf 3ms	do, art, n ms	pn	prep, prep	pn	prep, n fd	n ms
	וַיִּקֶן	אֶת־הָהָר	שֹׁמְרוֹן	מֵאֵת	שֶׁמֶר	בְּכִכְּרַיִם	כָּסֶף
	wayyiqen	'eth-hāhār	shōmerôn	mē'eth	shemer	bekhikkerayim	kāseph
	and he bought	the hill	Samaria	from	Shemer	with two talents	silver

1161.121	881, 2098	7410.121	881, 8428	6111	866	1161.111	6142
cj, v Qal impf 3ms	do, art, n ms	cj, v Qal impf 3ms	do, *n ms*	art, n fs	rel part	v Qal pf 3ms	prep
וַיִּבֶן	אֶת־הָהָר	וַיִּקְרָא	אֶת־שֵׁם	הָעִיר	אֲשֶׁר	בָּנָה	עַל
wayyiven	'eth-hāhār	wayyiqŏrā'	'eth-shēm	hā'îr	'ăsher	bānāh	'al
and he built	the hill	and he called	the name of	the city	which	he built	because of

8428, 8492	112	2098	8497		6449.121	6245	7737
n ms, pn	*n mp*	art, n ms	pn	**25.**	cj, v Qal impf 3ms	pn	art, adj
שֵׁם־שֶׁמֶר	אֲדֹנֵי	הָהָר	שֹׁמְרוֹן		וַיַּעֲשֶׂה	עָמְרִי	הָרַע
shem-shemer	'ădhōnê	hāhār	shōmerôn		wayya'ăseh	'omrî	hāra'
the name of Shemer	the owner of	the hill	Samaria		and he did	Omri	what is evil

904, 6084	3176	7778.121	4623, 3725	866	3937, 6686
prep, *n fd*	pn	cj, v Qal impf 3ms	prep, n ms	rel pron	prep, n mp, ps 3ms
בְּעֵינֵי	יְהוָה	וַיָּרַע	מִכֹּל	אֲשֶׁר	לְפָנָיו
be'ênê	yehwāh	wayyāra'	mikkōl	'ăsher	lephānâv
in the eyes of	Yahweh	and he acted more wickedly	than everyone	who	before him

	2050.121	904, 3725, 1932	3493	1158, 5203	904, 2496	866
26.	cj, v Qal impf 3ms	prep, *adj*, *n ms*	pn	*n ms*, pn	cj, prep, n fp, ps 3ms	rel part
	וַיֵּלֶךְ	בְּכָל־דֶּרֶךְ	יָרָבְעָם	בֶּן־נְבָט	וּבְחַטֹּאתָיו	אֲשֶׁר
	wayyēlekh	bekhol-derekh	yārov'ām	ben-nevāṭ	ûvechattō'thâv	'ăsher
	and he walked	in all the ways of	Jeroboam	the son of Nebat	and in his sins	which

2490.511	881, 3547	3937, 3832.541	3176	435	3547
v Hiphil pf 3ms	do, pn	prep, v Hiphil inf con	pn	*n mp*	pn
הֶחֱטִיא	אֶת־יִשְׂרָאֵל	לְהַכְעִיס	אֶת־יְהוָה	אֱלֹהֵי	יִשְׂרָאֵל
hechĕṭî'	'eth-yisrā'ēl	lehakh'îs	'eth-yehwāh	'ĕlōhê	yisrā'ēl
he caused to sin	Israel	to provoke to anger	Yahweh	the God of	Israel

904, 1961		3615	1745	6245	866	6449.111
prep, n mp, ps 3mp	**27.**	cj, *n ms*	*n mp*	pn	rel part	v Qal pf 3ms
בְּהַבְלֵיהֶם		וְיֶתֶר	דִּבְרֵי	עָמְרִי	אֲשֶׁר	עָשָׂה
b^{e}havlêhem		w^{e}yether	divrê	ʻomrî	ʼăsher	ʻāsāh
with their idols		and the remainder of	the events of	Omri	which	he did

1400	866	6449.111	1950B, 3940, 2062	3918.156	6142, 5809
cj, n fs, ps 3ms	rel part	v Qal pf 3ms	intrg part, neg part, pers pron	v Qal pass ptc mp	prep, *n ms*
וּגְבוּרָתוֹ	אֲשֶׁר	עָשָׂה	הֲלֹא־הֵם	כְּתוּבִים	עַל־סֵפֶר
ûgh^{e}vûrāthô	ʼăsher	ʻāsāh	hălōʼ-hēm	k^{e}thûvîm	ʻal-sēpher
and his strength	which	he did	are they not	things written	on the scroll of

22. But the people that followed Omri prevailed against the people that followed Tibni the son of Ginath: ... overcame the people who followed, *RSV* ... force that followed Gomri was stronger, *Fenton* ... those in favor of Omri won out, *Good News*.

so Tibni died, and Omri reigned: ... and Omri became king, *NASB* ... As a result, *Goodspeed* ... lost his life, *REB*.

23. In the thirty and first year of Asa king of Judah began Omri to reign over Israel, twelve years: six years reigned he in Tirzah: ... six years he was ruling, *BB* ... Omri ruled Israel for twelve years, *NCV* ... became king of Israel and reigned, *JB* ... In Thersa he reigned, *Douay*.

24. And he bought the hill Samaria of Shemer for two talents of silver, and built on the hill: ... fortified the hill, *RSV* ... purchased the hill of Samaria from Shemer for 4,250 dollars in silver, *Berkeley*.

and called the name of the city which he built, after the name of Shemer, owner of the hill, Samaria: ... Shemer Lord of the mountaine, *Geneva* ... Samaria in honor of Shemer, *NLT* ... after the name of its former owner, *Beck* ... Semar the Lord of the hill, *Tyndale*.

25. But Omri wrought evil in the eyes of the Lord, and did worse than all that were before him: ... did the thing that was wicked in the eyes of Yahweh, *Rotherham* ... more evil than all who were before, *NRSV* ... worse than anyone, *Moffatt* ... dealt wickedly above all, *MRB*.

26. For he walked in all the way of Jeroboam the son of Nebat, and in his sin wherewith he made Israel to sin, to provoke the Lord God of Israel to anger with their vanities: ... to anger the Lord, *Tyndale* ... by sinning and leading Israel into sin, *Beck* ... every way he copied the example, *JB* ... repeating the sins which he had led Israel to commit, *REB*.

27. Now the rest of the acts of Omri which he did, and his might that he showed, are they not written in the book of the chronicles of the kings of Israel?: ... the record of all the

16:23–28. Omri founded the most conspicuous dynasty of Israel, and so completely identified his name with the Northern Kingdom that it was known to the Assyrians as Beit Khumri, or "the House of Omri." (Athaliah is called "the daughter of Omri.") Jehu, the destroyer of Omri's dynasty, was known as "the son of Omri."

Incidental allusions in the annals of his son show that Omri was engaged in incessant wars against Syria. He was unsuccessful, and Ben-Hadad robbed him of Ramoth Gilead and other cities, enforcing the right of Syrians to have streets of their own even in his new capital of Samaria. (The Arameans have come to be incorrectly called Syrians because the Greeks confused them with the Assyrians.) On the other hand, he was greatly successful on the southeast against the Moabites and their warrior king Chemosh-Gad, the father of Mesha.

Few details of either war are available to us (1 Ki. 20:34). We learn, however, from the famous Moabite stone that Omri began his assault on Moab by capturing Mediba, several miles south of Heshbon. He overran the country, made the king a vassal, and imposed on Moab the enormous annual tribute of 100,000 sheep and 100,000 rams (2 Ki. 3:4). Mesha, in his inscription, recorded that Omri "oppressed Moab many days," and attributed this to the fact that Chemosh was angry with his chosen people.

He stamped his impress deep upon his subjects. It must have meant to him that the alliance with the Tyrians was due, which in his son's reign produced momentous consequences. He "did worse" we are told, "than all [the kings] that were before him" (1 Ki. 16:25). Although he is only charged with walking in the way of Jeroboam, the indignant manner in which the prophet Micah speaks of "the statutes of Omri" as still being kept (Mic. 6:16), seems to prove that his influence on religion was condemned by the prophetic order on special grounds. It is clear that he was a sovereign of far

1745	3219	3937, 4567	3547		8311.121	6245	6196, 1
n mp	art, n mp	prep, *n mp*	pn	**28.**	cj, v Qal impf 3ms	pn	prep, n mp, ps 3ms
דִּבְרֵי	הַיָּמִים	לְמַלְכֵי	יִשְׂרָאֵל		וַיִּשְׁכַּב	עָמְרִי	עִם־אֲבֹתָיו
divrê	hayyāmîm	lemalkhê	yisrā'ēl		wayyishkav	‘omrî	‘im-'ăvōthâv
the events of	the days	of the kings of	Israel		then he lay	Omri	with his ancestors

7196.221	904, 8497	4566.121	255	1158	8809		255
cj, v Niphil impf 3ms	prep, pn	cj, v Qal impf 3ms	pn	n ms, ps 3ms	prep, ps 3ms	**29.**	cj, pn
וַיִּקָּבֵר	בְּשֹׁמְרוֹן	וַיִּמְלֹךְ	אַחְאָב	בְּנוֹ	תַּחְתָּיו		וְאַחְאָב
wayyiqqāvēr	beshōmerôn	wayyimlōkh	'ach'āv	benô	tachtâv		we'ach'āv
and he was buried	in Samaria	and he reigned	Ahab	his son	instead of him		and Ahab

1158, 6245	4566.111	6142, 3547	904, 8523	8421	8470	8523	3937, 623
n ms, pn	v Qal pf 3ms	prep, pn	prep, *n fs*	num	cj, num	n fs	prep, pn
בֶּן־עָמְרִי	מָלַךְ	עַל־יִשְׂרָאֵל	בִּשְׁנַת	שְׁלֹשִׁים	וּשְׁמֹנֶה	שָׁנָה	לְאָסָא
ben-‘omrî	mālakh	‘al-yisrā'ēl	bishnath	shelōshîm	ûshemōneh	shānāh	le'āsā'
the son of Omri	he reigned	over Israel	in the year	thirty	and eight	year	of Asa

4567	3171	4566.121	255	1158, 6245	6142, 3547	904, 8497	6465
n ms	pn	cj, v Qal impf 3ms	pn	*n ms*, pn	prep, pn	prep, pn	num
מֶלֶךְ	יְהוּדָה	וַיִּמְלֹךְ	אַחְאָב	בֶּן־עָמְרִי	עַל־יִשְׂרָאֵל	בְּשֹׁמְרוֹן	עֶשְׂרִים
melekh	yehûdhāh	wayyimlōkh	'ach'āv	ben-‘omrî	‘al-yisrā'ēl	beshōmerôn	‘esrîm
the king of	Judah	and he reigned	Ahab	the son of Omri	over Israel	in Samaria	twenty

8692	8523		6449.121	255	1158, 6245	7737	904, 6084
cj, num	n fs	**30.**	cj, v Qal impf 3ms	pn	*n ms*, pn	art, adj	prep, *n fd*
וּשְׁתַּיִם	שָׁנָה		וַיַּעַשׂ	אַחְאָב	בֶּן־עָמְרִי	הָרַע	בְּעֵינֵי
ûshettayim	shānāh		wayya‘as	'ach'āv	ben-‘omrî	hāra‘	be‘ênê
and two	years		and he did more	Ahab	the son of Omri	what is evil	in the eyes of

3176	4623, 3725	866	3937, 6686		2030.121	1950B, 7327.211
pn	prep, n ms	rel part	prep, n mp, ps 3ms	**31.**	cj, v Qal impf 3ms	intrg part, v Niphal pf 3ms
יְהוָה	מִכֹּל	אֲשֶׁר	לְפָנָיו		וַיְהִי	הֲנָקֵל
yehwāh	mikkōl	'ăsher	lephānâv		wayhî	hănāqēl
Yahweh	than everyone	which	before him		so it was	has it become insignificant

2050.141	904, 2496	3493	1158, 5203	4089.121	828	881, 350
v Qal inf con, ps 3ms	prep, *n fp*	pn	*n ms*, pn	cj, v Qal impf 3ms	n fs	do, pn
לֶכְתּוֹ	בְּחַטֹּאות	יָרָבְעָם	בֶּן־נְבָט	וַיִּקַּח	אִשָּׁה	אֶת־אִיזֶבֶל
lekhtô	bechattō'wth	yārov‘ām	ben-nevāt	wayyiqqach	'ishshāh	'eth-'îzevel
his walking	in the sins of	Jeroboam	the son of Nebat	and he took	a wife	Jezebel

1351, 884	4567	6995	2050.121	5856.121	881, 1197
n fs, pn	*n ms*	pn	cj, v Qal impf 3ms	cj, v Qal impf 3ms	do, art, pn
בַּת־אֶתְבַּעַל	מֶלֶךְ	צִידֹנִים	וַיֵּלֶךְ	וַיַּעֲבֹד	אֶת־הַבַּעַל
bath-'ethba‘al	melekh	tsîdhōnîm	wayyēlekh	wayya‘ăvōdh	'eth-habba‘al
the daughter of Ethbaal	the king of	the Sidonians	and he went	and they served	the Baal

8246.721	3937		7251.521	4326	3937, 1197	1041
cj, v Hithpael impf 3mp	prep, ps 3ms	**32.**	cj, v Hiphil impf 3ms	n ms	prep, art, pn	*n ms*
וַיִּשְׁתַּחוּ	לוֹ		וַיָּקֶם	מִזְבֵּחַ	לַבָּעַל	בֵּית
wayyishtachû	lô		wayyāqem	mizbēach	labbā‘al	bêth
and they worshiped	him		and he erected	an altar	for the Baal	the household of

1197	866	1161.111	904, 8497		6449.121	255	881, 867
art, pn	rel part	v Qal pf 3ms	prep, pn	**33.**	cj, v Qal impf 3ms	pn	do, art, pn
הַבַּעַל	אֲשֶׁר	בָּנָה	בְּשֹׁמְרוֹן		וַיַּעַשׂ	אַחְאָב	אֶת־הָאֲשֵׁרָה
habba‘al	'ăsher	bānāh	beshōmerôn		wayya‘as	'ach'āv	'eth-hā'ăshērāh
the Baal	which	he built	in Samaria		and he made	Ahab	the Asherah

battles he fought, is to be found in the Annals, *Knox* ... of the words of the days, *Douay* ... and all his accomplishments are recorded in The History, *Good News*.

28. So Omri slept with his fathers, and was buried in Samaria: ... rested with his ancestors, *NAB* ... died, *NCV* ... lieth with his fathers, *Young*.

and Ahab his son reigned in his stead: ... succeeded him as king, *NIV* ... reigned in his place, *NKJV*.

29. And in the thirty and eighth year of Asa king of Judah began Ahab the son of Omri to reign over Israel: ... became king, *Berkeley* ... began to rule, *NLT*.

and Ahab the son of Omri reigned over Israel in Samaria twenty and two years: ... was king in Samaria for twenty-two years, *BB*.

30. And Ahab the son of Omri did evil in the sight of the LORD above all that were before him: ... He did more that was wrong in the eyes of the LORD than all his predecessors, *NEB* ... He sinned against, *Good News* ... did the thing that was wicked in the eyes of Yahweh, *Rotherham*.

31. And it came to pass, as if it had been a light thing for him to walk in the sins of Jeroboam the son of Nebat: ... As if it were not enough for him to follow the sinful ways, *REB* ... copying the evil ways ... was a small thing for him, *BB* ... The least that he did was to follow the sinful example, *JB* ... he did even worse things, *NCV*.

that he took to wife Jezebel the daughter of Ethbaal king of the Zidonians, and went and served Baal, and worshipped him: ... began to worship Baal, *NLT* ... goeth and serveth Baal, and boweth himself to it, *Young* ... he actually married Jezebel, a daughter of Ethbaal the king of the Phoenicians, *Moffatt* ... adored him, *Douay*.

32. And he reared up an altar for Baal in the house of Baal, which he had built in Samaria: ... also raised an Altar to Bal, in the Temple of Bal, *Fenton* ... erected and altar to Baal in the temple for Baal, *Berkeley*.

33. And Ahab made a grove: ... the Sacred Stem, *Rotherham* ... also made a sacred pole, *NRSV* ... the Asherah, *NASB* ... a wooden image, *NKJV*.

and Ahab did more to provoke the LORD God of Israel to anger than all the kings of Israel that were before him: ... the jealousy of the LORD, *Goodspeed* ... to arouse the anger of the LORD, *Good News* ... to earn the Lord's displeasure than any king of Israel in earlier times, *Knox*.

---

greater eminence and importance than we might suppose from the meagerness of his annals as here preserved; indeed, for thirty-four years after his accession the history of the Southern Kingdom becomes a mere appendix to that of the Northern.

One conspicuous service he rendered to his subjects was providing them with the city that became their permanent and famous capital. He did this in the sixth year of his reign. The burning of the fortress palace of Tirzah, and the rapidity with which the town had succumbed to its besiegers, may have led him to look out for a site, which was central, strong and beautiful.

Far more important in the eyes of Omri than the beauty of the hill of Samaria was the natural strength of its position. It did not possess the impregnable majesty of Jerusalem, but its height and isolation, permitting of strong fortifications, enabled it to baffle the besieging hosts of the Aramaeans in 901 B.C. and in 892 B.C. For three long years it held out against the mighty Assyrians under Sargon and Shalmanezer. Its capture in 721 B.C. involved the ruin of the whole kingdom in its fall (1 Ki. 20:1; 2 Ki. 6:24). Nebuchadnezzar took it in 554 B.C., after a siege of thirteen years. In later centuries, it partially recovered. Alexander the Great took it, and massacred many of its inhabitants, in 332 B.C.. John Hyrcanus, who took it after a year's siege, tried to demolish it in 129 B.C. After various fortunes, it was splendidly rebuilt by Herod the Great, who called it Sebaste, in honor of Augustus. It still exists under the name of Sebastiyeh (Josephus, *Antiquities*, XV:vii:7).

The new capital marked a new epoch. As completely as Jerusalem had done, it superseded the old local shrines endeared by the immemorial sanctity of their traditions. But as its origin was purely political, it acted unfavorably on the religion of the people. It became a city of idolatry and of luxurious wealth; a city in which Baal worship, with its ritual pomp, diminished the importance of the worship of Yahweh; a city in which corrupted nobles, indulging at wine feasts in their palaces inlaid with ivory, sold the righteous for silver and the needy for a pair of shoes. We are told no more about Omri. After a reign of twelve years, he slept with his fathers, and he was buried in the city which was to be a memorial of his fame for so many centuries for so many centuries.

16:29–33. Omri was succeeded by his son Ahab, whose eventful reign of upwards of twenty years occupies a large space. His name means "brother-father," and has probably some sacred refer-

3362.521	255	3937, 6449.141	3937, 3832.541	881, 3176	435	3547
cj, v Hiphil impf 3ms	pn	prep, v Qal inf con	prep, v Hiphil inf con	do, pn	*n mp*	pn
וַיּוֹסֶף	אַחְאָב	לַעֲשׂוֹת	לְהַכְעִיס	אֶת־יְהוָה	אֱלֹהֵי	יִשְׂרָאֵל
wayyôseph	'ach'āv	la'ăsôth	lehakh'îs	'eth-yehōwāh	'ĕlōhê	yisrā'ēl
and he did again	Ahab	to do	to provoke to anger	Yahweh	the God of	Israel

4623, 3725	4567	3547	866	2030.116	3937, 6686		904, 3219
prep, n ms	*n mp*	pn	rel pron	v Qal pf 3cp	prep, n mp, ps 3ms	**34.**	prep, n mp, ps 3ms
מִכֹּל	מַלְכֵי	יִשְׂרָאֵל	אֲשֶׁר	הָיוּ	לְפָנָיו		בְּיָמָיו
mikkōl	malkhê	yisrā'ēl	'ăsher	hāyû	lephānâv		beyāmâv
than everyone	the kings of	Israel	who	they were	before him		in his days

1161.111	2511	1054	881, 3520	904, 49	1111	3354.311
v Qal pf 3ms	pn	pn	do, pn	prep, pn	n ms, ps 3ms	v Piel pf 3ms, ps 3fs
בָּנָה	חִיאֵל	בֵּית־הָאֱלִי	אֶת־יְרִיחֹה	בַּאֲבִירָם	בְּכֹרוֹ	יִסְּדָהּ
bānāh	chî'ēl	bêth-hā'ĕlî	'eth-yerîchōh	ba'ăvîrām	bekhōrô	yissedhāhh
he built	Hiel	the Bethelite	Jericho	in Abiram	his firstborn	he laid its foundation

904, 7893	7087	5507.511	1878	3626, 1745	3176	866
cj, prep, pn	adj, ps 3ms	v Hiphil pf 3ms	n fp, ps 3fs	prep, *n ms*	pn	rel part
וּבִשְׂגִיב	צְעִירוֹ	הִצִּיב	דְּלָתֶיהָ	כִּדְבַר	יְהוָה	אֲשֶׁר
ûvisghîv	tse'îrô	hitstsîv	delāthêāh	kidhvar	yehwāh	'ăsher
and with Segub	his young one	he stationed	its gates	according to the word of	Yahweh	which

1744.311	904, 3135	3193	1158, 5307		569.121	455
v Piel pf 3ms	prep, *n fs*	pn	*n ms*, pn	**17:1**	cj, v Qal impf 3ms	pn
דִּבֶּר	בְּיַד	יְהוֹשֻׁעַ	בִּן־נוּן		וַיֹּאמֶר	אֵלִיָּהוּ
dibber	beyadh	yehôshua'	bin-nûn		wayyō'mer	'ēlîyāhû
He had spoken	by the hand of	Joshua	the son of Nun		and he said	Elijah

9005	4623, 8785	1609	420, 255	2508, 3176	435	3547
art, pn	prep, *n mp*	pn	prep, pn	adj, pn	*n mp*	pn
הַתִּשְׁבִּי	מִתֹּשָׁבֵי	גִלְעָד	אֶל־אַחְאָב	חַי־יְהוָה	אֱלֹהֵי	יִשְׂרָאֵל
hattishbî	mittōshāvê	ghil'ādh	'el-'ach'āv	chay-yehwāh	'ĕlōhê	yisrā'ēl
the Tishbite	among the dwellers in	Gilead	unto Ahab	Yahweh living	the God of	Israel

866	6198.115	3937, 6686	524, 2030.121	8523	431	3030	4443	3706
rel pron	v Qal pf 1cs	prep, n mp, ps 3ms	cj, v Qal impf 3ms	art, n fp	art, dem pron	n ms	cj, n ms	cj
אֲשֶׁר	עָמַדְתִּי	לְפָנָיו	אִם־יִהְיֶה	הַשָּׁנִים	הָאֵלֶּה	טַל	וּמָטָר	כִּי
'ăsher	'āmadhtî	lephānâv	'im-yihyeh	hashshānîm	hā'ēlleh	tal	ûmātār	kî
Whom	I stand	before Him	if there is	the years	the these	dew	or rain	except

524, 3937, 6552	1745		2030.121	1745, 3176	420
cj, prep, *n ms*	n ms, ps 1cs	**2.**	cj, v Qal impf 3ms	*n ms*, pn	prep, ps 3ms
אִם־לְפִי	דְבָרִי		וַיְהִי	דְבַר־יְהוָה	אֵלָיו
'im-lephî	dhevārî		wayhî	dhevar-yehwāh	'ēlâv
rather of the mouth of	my word		and it was	the word of Yahweh	to him

3937, 569.141		2050.131	4623, 2172	6680.113	3937	7209
prep, v Qal inf con	**3.**	v Qal impv 2ms	prep, adv	cj, v Qal pf 2ms	prep, ps 2ms	adv
לֵאמֹר		לֵךְ	מִזֶּה	וּפָנִיתָ	לְךָ	קֵדְמָה
lē'mōr		lēkh	mizzeh	ûphānîthā	lekhā	qēdhemāh
saying		go	from here	and you will turn	for yourself	eastward

5846.213	904, 5337	3877	866	6142, 6686	3497		2030.111
cj, v Niphal pf 2ms	prep, *n ms*	pn	rel part	prep, *n mp*	art, pn	**4.**	cj, v Qal pf 3ms
וְנִסְתַּרְתָּ	בְּנַחַל	כְּרִית	אֲשֶׁר	עַל־פְּנֵי	הַיַּרְדֵּן		וְהָיָה
wenistartā	benachal	kerîth	'ăsher	'al-penê	hayyardēn		wehāyāh
and you will hide	by the brook of	Cherith	which	opposite	the Jordan		and it will be

34. In his days did Hiel the Beth-elite build Jericho: he laid the foundation thereof in Abiram his firstborn: ... at the cost of Abi'ram, *RSV* ... With the loss of his firstborn, *Beck* ... In Ahab's time, Hiel of Bethel rebuilt Jericho, *NIV*.

and set up the gates thereof in his youngest son Segub: ... setting up of its gates cost him Segub, *REB* ... put its doors in place at the price of, *BB*.

according to the word of the LORD, which he spake by Joshua the son of Nun: ... the message from the LORD concerning Jericho, *NLT* ... exactly as the Eternal had given warning, *Moffatt* ... just as Yahweh had foretold, *JB* ... just as the LORD, speaking ... said it would happen, *NCV*.

17:1. And Elijah the Tishbite, who was of the inhabitants of Gilead, said unto Ahab: ... of Tishbe in Gilead, *NEB* ... word came to Achab from Elias, the man of Thesbe, *Knox* ... was a prophet from the settlers, *NCV*.

As the LORD God of Israel liveth, before whom I stand: ... lives, whom I serve, *NIV* ... in whose sight I stand, *Douay* ... By the life of Yahweh, *JB*.

there shall not be dew nor rain these years, but according to my word: ... save as I appoint it, *Tyndale* ... except by my word, *Berkeley* ... these coming years unless I say so, *Beck* ... as I give orders, *Moffatt*.

2. And the word of the LORD came unto him, saying: ... then said to Elijah, *NAB* ... said to Elijah, *NLT* ... came the word of Yahweh, *Rotherham* ... the Message of the EVER-LIVING, *Fenton*.

3. Get thee hence, and turn thee eastward, and hide thyself by the brook Cherith, that is before Jordan: ... go into hiding in the ravine of Kerith east of the Jordan, *NEB* ... the torrent, *Darby* ... keep yourself in a secret place by the stream, *BB* ... which flows into the Jordan, *NKJV*.

---

ence. He is stigmatized by the historians as a king more wicked than his father. Omri did "worse than all who were before him." He was a brave warrior, and he showed some great qualities during a long and mostly prosperous career. He built cities, and he added to Israel yet another royal residence. He advanced the wealth and prosperity of his subjects. He was highly successful in some of his wars against Syria, and he died in battle against the dangerous enemies of his country. He maintained unbroken, and strengthened by yet closer affinity, the recent alliance with the Southern Kingdom. All this means nothing with the prophetic annalists. They have no word of eulogy for the king who added Baal worship to the sin of Jeroboam. The prominence of Ahab in their record is only due to the fact that he came into dreadful collision with the prophetic order, and with Elijah, the greatest prophet who had yet arisen. The glory and the sins of the warrior king interested the young prophets of the schools solely because they were interwoven with the grand and somber traditions of their mightiest reformer.

The historian traces his ruin to a disastrous alliance. The kings of Judah had followed the bad example of David and had been polygamists. Up to this time, the kings of Israel seem to have been contented with a single wife. The wealth and power of Ahab led him to adopt the costly luxury of a harem, and he had seventy sons (1 Ki. 20:5; 2 Ki. 10:7). This, however, would have been regarded in those days as an excusable offense, or as no offense at all; but just as the growing power of Solomon had been enhanced by marriage with a princess of Egypt, so Ahab was now of sufficient importance to wed a daughter of the King of Tyre. "As if it had been a light thing for him to walk in the sins of Jeroboam the son of Nebat, that he took to wife Jezebel the daughter of Ethbaal king of the Zidonians" (1 Ki. 16:31).

It was an act of policy in which religious considerations went for nothing. There is little doubt that it flattered his pride and the pride of his people, and that Jezebel brought riches with her and pomp and the prestige of luxurious royalty. The permission of Baal worship had been one of the articles of the treaty between Tyre and Israel, which, as we know from Amos, had been made at this time.

The new queen inherited the fanaticism of Baal worship as she inherited the ferocity of her father. From the beginning, she acquired a paramount sway over the weak and luxorious mind of her husband. Under her influence, Ahab built in Samaria a splendid temple and altar to Baal, in which no less than 400 orgiastic priests served the Phoenician idol in splendid vestments, and with the same pompous ritual as in the shrines at Tyre. In front of this temple, to the disgust and horror of all faithful worshipers of Yahweh, stood an Asherah in honor of the goddess, and pillars or obelisks which represented either sunbeams or the reproductive powers of nature. In these ways Ahab "did more to provoke the LORD God to anger than all the kings of Israel that were before him" (1 Ki. 16:30; 2 Ki. 3:2; 10:27).

17:1–2. Suddenly, with abrupt impetuosity, the mighty figure of Elijah the prophet bursts on

4623, 5337	8685.123	881, 6397	6943.315	3937, 3677.341	8427
prep, art, n ms	v Qal impf 2ms	cj, do, art, n mp	v Piel pf 1cs	prep, v Pilpel inf con, ps 2ms	adv
מֵהַנַּחַל	תִּשְׁתֶּה	וְאֶת־הָעֹרְבִים	צִוִּיתִי	לְכַלְכֶּלְךָ	שָׁם
mēhannachal	tishteh	we'eth-hā'ōrevîm	tsiwwîthî	lekhalkelkhā	shām
from the brook	you will drink	and the ravens	I have commanded	to provide for you	there

5.	2050.121	6449.121	3626, 1745	3176	2050.121
	cj, v Qal impf 3ms	cj, v Qal impf 3ms	prep, *n ms*	pn	cj, v Qal impf 3ms
	וַיֵּלֶךְ	וַיַּעַשׂ	כִּדְבַר	יְהוָה	וַיֵּלֶךְ
	wayyēlekh	wayya'as	kidhvar	yehwāh	wayyēlekh
	so he went	and he did	according to the word of	Yahweh	and he went

3553.121	904, 5337	3877	866	6142, 6686	3497	6.	6397
cj, v Qal impf 3ms	prep, *n ms*	pn	rel part	prep, *n mp*	art, pn		cj, art, n mp
וַיֵּשֶׁב	בְּנַחַל	כְּרִית	אֲשֶׁר	עַל־פְּנֵי	הַיַּרְדֵּן		וְהָעֹרְבִים
wayyēshev	benachal	kerîth	'ăsher	'al-penê	hayyardēn		wehā'ōrevîm
and he dwelled	by the brook of	Cherith	which	opposite	the Jordan		and the ravens

971.552	3937	4035	1340	904, 1269	4035	1340	904, 6394
v Hiphil ptc mp	prep, ps 3ms	n ms	cj, n ms	prep, art, n ms	cj, n ms	cj, n ms	prep, art, n ms
מְבִיאִים	לוֹ	לֶחֶם	וּבָשָׂר	בַּבֹּקֶר	וְלֶחֶם	וּבָשָׂר	בָּעָרֶב
mevî'îm	lô	lechem	ûvāsār	babbōqer	welechem	ûvāsār	bā'ārev
bringing	to him	bread	and meat	in the morning	and bread	and meat	in the evening

4623, 5337	8685.121	7.	2030.121	4623, 7377	3219	3111.121
cj, prep, art, n ms	v Qal impf 3ms		cj, v Qal impf 3ms	prep, *n ms*	n mp	cj, v Qal impf 3ms
וּמִן־הַנַּחַל	יִשְׁתֶּה		וַיְהִי	מִקֵּץ	יָמִים	וַיִּיבַשׁ
ûmin-hannachal	yishteh		wayhî	miqqēts	yāmîm	wayyîvash
and from the brook	he drank		and it was	from the end of	days	that it dried up

5337	3706	3940, 2030.111	1700	904, 800	8.	2030.121	1745, 3176
art, n ms	cj	neg part, v Qal pf 3ms	n ms	prep, art, n fs		cj, v Qal impf 3ms	*n ms*, pn
הַנָּחַל	כִּי	לֹא־הָיָה	גֶּשֶׁם	בָּאָרֶץ		וַיְהִי	דְּבַר־יְהוָה
hannāchal	kî	lō'-hāyāh	gheshem	bā'ārets		wayhî	dhevar-yehwāh
the brook	because	there was not	rain	on the land		and it was	the word of Yahweh

4. And it shall be, that thou shalt drink of the brook: … river shall provide drink for thee, *Knox* … of the torrent, *Douay* … from the wadi, *NRSV*.

and I have commanded the ravens to feed thee there: … will instruct the Arabs to supply you with food, *Fenton* … ordered the ravens to feed you, *NIV* … ordered the crows, *Beck* … to provide for you, *NASB*.

5. So he went and did according unto the word of the LORD: … left and did as the LORD had commanded, *NAB* … in obedience to the order of the Eternal, *Moffatt* … Elijah did as the LORD had told him, *REB*.

for he went and dwelt by the brook Cherith, that is before Jordan: … east of the Jordan, *Berkeley* … went to Kerith Ravine, *NCV* … that is on the front of the Jordan, *Young* … camped beside Kerith Brook, *NLT*.

6. And the ravens brought him bread and flesh in the morning, and bread and flesh in the evening: … meat morning and evening, *REB* … The birds brought Elijah bread and meat, *NCV* … Arabs brought him, *Fenton*.

and he drank of the brook: … quenched his thirst at the stream, *JB* … drank of the torrent, *Douay* … from the wadi, *NRSV*.

7. And it came to pass after a while, that the brook dried up: … After a while the stream, *NCV* … After sometime, however, the brook ran dry, *NAB* … that the torrent, *Darby*.

because there had been no rain in the land: … as no rain fell on the country, *Moffatt* … because of the lack of rain, *Good News* … the land was parched, *Knox*.

8. And the word of the LORD came unto him, saying: … Then the LORD said to Elijah, *NLT* … spoke to him, *Beck*.

9. Arise, get thee to Zarephath, which belongeth to Zidon, and dwell there: … up and get thee to Sarephtha a city of Sidon, *Tyndale* … stay there, *NEB*.

behold, I have commanded a widow woman there to sustain thee: … a widow there to feed you, *RSV* … instructed a widow-woman there to provide for you, *Fenton* …

the scene like lightning on the midnight. Like Melchizedek, Elijah was without father, mother or descent. He appears before us unannounced as "Elijah the Tishbite of the inhabitants of Gilead."

The name "Elijah," or, in its fuller Hebrew form, "Elijahu," means "Yahweh is my God." Who he was, other than the man of God, is entirely unknown. So completely lost in mystery is all previous trace of him that Talmudic legends confused him with Phinehas, the son of Aaron, the avenging and fiercely zealous priest; and even identified him with the angel or messenger of Yahweh who appeared to Gideon and ascended in the altar flame.

The name "Tishbite" tells us nothing. No town of Tishbi occurs in Scripture. A Thisbe in the tribe of Naphtali is mentioned as the birthplace of Tobit (Tobit 1:2), giving a lean possibility. The Scripture clearly means to communicate that Elijah's identity, apart from his role as a prophet, is unimportant. In such hallowed loneliness he had learned to fear man little, because he feared God much, and to dwell familiarly on the sterner aspects of religion and morality. The one conscious fact of his mission, the sufficient authentication of his most imperious mandates, was that "he stood before Yahweh." So unexpected were his appearances and disappearances, that in the popular view he only seemed to flash to and fro, or to be swept hither and thither, by the Spirit of the LORD. We may say of him as was said of John the Baptist, that in his manifestation and agency he was like a burning torch; his public life was quite an earthquake; the whole man was a sermon, the voice of one crying in the wilderness. And, like the Baptist, he had been in the deserts, until the day of his showing unto Israel.

Such was the man who delivered to Ahab in one sentence his tremendous message, "As Yahweh, God of Israel, liveth, before whom I stand." Such was the introductory formula, which became proverbial, and which authenticated the prophecy. "There shall not be dew nor rain these years but according to my word." The phrase "to stand before Yahweh" was used of priests: it was applicable to a prophet in a far deeper and less external sense (Ps. 134:1; Heb. 10:11). Drought was one of the recognized divine punishments for idolatrous apostasy. If Israel should fall into disobedience, we read in Deuteronomy, "The LORD shall make the lain of thy land powder and dust; from heaven shall it come down upon thee—until thou be destroyed"; and in Leviticus we read, "If ye will not ... hearken ..., I will make your heaven as iron and your earth as brass" (26:18f). The threat was too significant to need any explanation. The conscience of Ahab could interpret only too readily that prophetic menace.

17:3–7. "Get thee hence, and turn thee eastward, and hide thyself by the brook Cherith, that is before Jordan." The enraged and deluded Ahab and Jezebel longed for the life of the loyal prophet. Elijah needed shelter from the king and queen. He also needed shelter and provision because of the drought which would prove to last over three years. His water supply would be the brook Cherith and his food was provided, ironically, by perhaps the most selfish of all birds. His provision was sure, however, because it was founded on his obedience to God. "So he went and did according unto the word of the LORD" (1 Ki. 17:5). Elijah stayed there until he received further instructions. After a while, the brook ran dry from lack of rain. But God had Elijah's provision already planned for in Zarephath. The blessing he had just experienced, he would now teach to a widow of the Sidonians. Again, obedience would be the key to God's provision.

17:8–9. The fierce drought continued, and "at the end of days" (perhaps years, 1 Ki. 17:7; Lev. 25:29; 1 Sam. 27:7), even the thin trickling of the stream in the clefts of Cherith was dried up. In the language of Job, it felt the glare and vanished (Job 6:17). No miracle was wrought to supply the prophet with water, but once more the providence of God intervened to save his life for the mighty work which still awaited him. He was sent to the region where, nearly a millennium later, the feet of his LORD followed him on a mission of mercy to those other sheep of his flock who were not of the Judean fold.

The word of the LORD prompted him to go to the Sidonian city of Zarephath. Zarephath, the Sarepta of St. Luke, the modern Surafend, lay between Tyre and Sidon, and there the waters would not be wholly dried up, for the fountains of Lebanon were not yet exhausted. Elijah was told that a widow woman would sustain him there. The Baal worshiping queen who had hunted for his life would be least of all likely to search for him in a city of Baal worshipers in the midst of her own people.

420 prep, ps 3ms אֵלָיו 'ēlâv to him	3937, 569.141 prep, v Qal inf con לֵאמֹר lē'mōr saying	**9.**	7251.131 v Qal impv 2ms קוּם qûm rise	2050.131 v Qal impv 2ms לֵךְ lēkh go	7172 pn צָרְפַתָה tsār^{e}phathāh to Zarephath	866 rel part אֲשֶׁר 'ăsher which	3937, 6991 prep, pn לְצִידוֹן l^{e}tsîdhôn to Sidon

3553.113 cj, v Qal pf 2ms וְיָשַׁבְתָּ w^{e}yāshavtā and you must dwell	8427 adv שָׁם shām there	2079 intrj הִנֵּה hinnēh behold	6943.315 v Piel pf 1cs צִוִּיתִי tsiwwîthî I have commanded	8427 adv שָׁם shām there	828 n fs אִשָּׁה 'ishshāh a woman	496 n fs אַלְמָנָה 'almānāh a widow

3937, 3677.341 prep, v Pilpel inf con, ps 2ms לְכַלְכְּלֶךָ l^{e}khalk^{e}lekhā to feed you	**10.**	7251.121 cj, v Qal impf 3ms וַיָּקָם wayyāqām and he rose up	2050.121 cj, v Qal impf 3ms וַיֵּלֶךְ wayyēlekh and he went	7172 pn צָרְפַתָה tsār^{e}phathāh to Zarephath	971.121 cj, v Qal impf 3ms וַיָּבֹא wayyāvō' and he came

420, 6860 prep, *n ms* אֶל־פֶּתַח 'el-pethach to the entrance to	6111 art, n fs הָעִיר hā'îr the city	2079, 8427 cj, intrj, adv וְהִנֵּה־שָׁם w^{e}hinnēh-shām and behold there	828 n fs אִשָּׁה 'ishshāh a woman	496 n fs אַלְמָנָה 'almānāh a widow	7492.353 v Poel ptc fs מְקֹשֶׁשֶׁת m^{e}qōshesheth gathering	6320 n mp עֵצִים 'ētsîm wood

7410.121 cj, v Qal impf 3ms וַיִּקְרָא wayyiqŏrā' and he called	420 prep, ps 3fs אֵלֶיהָ 'ēlêāh to her	569.121 cj, v Qal impf 3ms וַיֹּאמַר wayyō'mar and he said	4089.132, 5167 v Qal impv 2fs, part קְחִי־נָא qŏchî-nā' get please	3937 prep, ps 1cs לִי lî for me	4746, 4448 *sub*, n md מְעַט־מַיִם m^{e}'aṭ-mayim a little water	904, 3747 prep, art, n ms בַּכְּלִי bakk^{e}lî in the vessel

8685.125 cj, v Qal juss 1cs וְאֶשְׁתֶּה w^{e}'eshteh that I may drink	**11.**	2050.122 cj, v Qal impf 3fs וַתֵּלֶךְ wattēlekh and she went	4089.141 prep, v Qal inf con לָקַחַת lāqachath to get	7410.121 cj, v Qal impf 3ms וַיִּקְרָא wayyiqŏrā' and he called	420 prep, ps 3fs אֵלֶיהָ 'ēlêāh to her	569.121 cj, v Qal impf 3ms וַיֹּאמַר wayyō'mar and he said

4089.132, 5167 v Qal impv 2fs, part לִקְחִי־נָא liqŏchî-nā' get please	3937 prep, ps 1cs לִי lî for me	6846, 4035 *n fs*, n ms פַּת־לֶחֶם path-lechem a morsel of bread	904, 3135 prep, n fs, ps 2fs בְּיָדֵךְ b^{e}yādhēkh in your hand	**12.**	569.122 cj, v Qal impf 3fs וַתֹּאמֶר wattō'mer but she said	2508, 3176 *adj*, pn חַי־יְהוָה chay-y^{e}hwāh Yahweh living

435 n mp, ps 2ms אֱלֹהֶיךָ 'ĕlōhêkhā your God	524, 3552, 3937 cj, *sub*, prep, ps 1cs אִם־יֶשׁ־לִי 'im-yesh-lî if there is to me	4734 n ms מָעוֹג mā'ōgh baked bread	3706 cj כִּי kî except	524, 4530 prep, *n ms* אִם־מְלֹא 'im-m^{e}lō' if fulness of	3834, 7343 *n fs*, n ms כַּף־קֶמַח khaph-qemach a handful of flour	904, 3656 prep, art, n fs בַּכַּד bakkadh in the jar

4746, 8467 cj, *sub*, n ms וּמְעַט־שֶׁמֶן ûm^{e}'aṭ-shemen and a little olive oil	904, 7111 prep, art, n fs בַּצַּפָּחַת batstsappāchath in the pitcher	2079 cj, intrj, ps 1cs וְהִנְנִי w^{e}hin^{e}nî now behold I	7492.353 v Poel ptc fs מְקֹשֶׁשֶׁת m^{e}qōshesheth gathering	8530 num שְׁנַיִם sh^{e}nayim two	6320 n mp עֵצִים 'ētsîm sticks	971.115 cj, v Qal pf 1cs וּבָאתִי ûvā'thî then I will go in

6449.115 cj, v Qal pf 1cs, ps 3ms וַעֲשִׂיתִיהוּ wa'ăsîthîhû and I will make it	3937 prep, ps 1cs לִי lî for me	3937, 1158 cj, prep, n ms, ps 1cs וְלִבְנִי w^{e}livnî and for my son	404.119 cj, v Qal pf 1cp, ps 3ms וַאֲכַלְנֻהוּ wa'ăkhalnuhû and we will eat it	4322.119 cj, v Qal pf 1cp וָמָתְנוּ wāmāth^{e}nû then we will die

13.

569.121	420	455	414, 3486.124	971.132	6449.132
cj, v Qal impf 3ms	prep, ps 3fs	pn	adv, v Qal juss 2fs	v Qal impv 2fs	v Qal impv 2fs
וַיֹּאמֶר	אֵלֶיהָ	אֵלִיָּהוּ	אַל־תִּירְאִי	בֹּאִי	עֲשִׂי
wayyō'mer	'ēlêāh	'ēlîyāhû	'al-tîr^{e}'î	bō'î	'ăsî
and he said	to her	Elijah	do not fear	go in	make

3626, 1745	395	6449.132, 3937	4623, 8427	5899	7278	904, 7518
prep, n ms, ps 2fs	adv	v Qal impv 2fs, prep, ps 1cs	prep, adv	n fs	adj	prep, art, adj
כִּדְבָרֵךְ	אַךְ	עֲשִׂי־לִי	מִשָּׁם	עֻגָה	קְטַנָּה	בָרִאשֹׁנָה
khidhvārēkh	'akh	'ăsî-lî	mishshām	'ughāh	qŏṭannāh	vāri'shōnāh
according to your words	only	make for me	from there	a bread cake	small	at the first

3428.514	3937	3937	3937, 1158	6449.124	904, 315
cj, v Hiphil pf 2fs	prep, ps 1cs	cj, prep, ps 2fs	cj, prep, n ms, ps 2fs	v Qal impf 2fs	prep, adv
וְהוֹצֵאתְ	לִי	וְלָךְ	וְלִבְנֵךְ	תַּעֲשִׂי	בָּאַחֲרֹנָה
w^{e}hôtsē'th^{e}	lî	w^{e}lākh	w^{e}livnēkh	ta'ăsî	bā'achrōnāh
and you will bring out	to me	and for you	and for your son	you will make	afterward

given orders to a widow woman there to see that you have food, *BB* ... to maintain thee, *Darby*.

10. So he arose and went to Zarephath. And when he came to the gate of the city: ... As he arrived at the entrance, *NAB* ... to the town gate, *NIV* ... cometh in unto the opening of the city, *Young* ... at the gates of the village, *NLT*.

behold, the widow woman was there gathering of sticks: ... a widow was gathering wood, *Beck* ... he saw a widow gathering firewood, *Good News*.

and he called to her, and said, Fetch me, I pray thee, a little water in a vessel, that I may drink: ... Please bring me a little water in a pitcher to drink, *REB* ... Get me a little water in the jar, *Berkeley* ... in a cup, *NKJV*.

11. And as she was going to fetch it, he called to her, and said: ... to get it, *Beck* ... to bring it, *NRSV* ... to get his water, *NCV*.

Bring me, I pray thee, a morsel of bread in thine hand: ... And get me with it a small bit, *BB* ... Please bring me a piece, *NASB* ... a scrap of bread, *JB* ... too, a mouthful, *Knox*.

12. And she said, As the LORD thy God liveth, I have not a cake: ... By the life of your EVER-LIVING GOD, there is nothing in the house with me, *Fenton* ... I have nothing baked, *RSV* ... no bread, *Douay* ... a single piece of bread, *NLT*.

but an handful of meal in a barrel, and a little oil in a cruse: ... except a handful of flour in the jar and a little oil in the jug, *Berkeley* ... fulness of the hand of meal in a pitcher, and a little oil in a dish, *Young*.

and, behold, I am gathering two sticks: ... I came here to gather some firewood, *Good News*.

that I may go in and dress it for me and my son, that we may eat it, and die: ... to go in and prepare something for myself, *NAB* ... go home and cook this for myself and my boy, *Moffatt*.

13. And Elijah said unto her, Fear not; go and do as thou hast said: ... Do not be afraid; go and do as you have said, *NRSV*.

but make me thereof a little cake first, and bring it unto me, and after make for thee and for thy son: ... but first make a little scone of it for me, *JB* ... a small loaf of bread from the flour you have, *NCV* ... a small cake from what you have, *REB*.

17:10–16. He arrived there faint with hunger and thirst. Seeing a woman gathering sticks near the city gate, he asked her for some water, and as she was going to fetch it he called to her and asked her to also bring him a morsel of bread. The answer revealed the condition of extreme want to which she was reduced. Recognizing that Elijah was an Israelite, and therefore a worshiper of Yahweh, she said, "As Yahweh thy God liveth, I have not a cake, but [only] a handful of meal in the barrel, and a little oil in the cruse." She was gathering a couple of sticks to make one last meal for herself and her son before lying down to die. For drought did not only mean universal anguish, but much actual starvation. It meant, as Joel says, speaking of the desolation caused by locusts, that the cattle groan and perish, and the corn withers, and the seeds rot under their clods.

Strong in faith, Elijah told her not to fear, but first to supply his own more urgent needs, and then to make a meal for herself and her son. Until Yahweh sent rain, the barrel of meal should not

14.

3706	3662	569.111	3176	435	3547	3656	7343	3940
cj	adv	v Qal pf 3ms	pn	*n mp*	pn	*n fs*	art, n ms	neg part
כִּי	כֹּה	אָמַר	יְהוָה	אֱלֹהֵי	יִשְׂרָאֵל	כַּד	הַקֶּמַח	לֹא
kî	khōh	'āmar	yehwāh	'ĕlōhê	yisrā'ēl	kadh	haqqemach	lō'
because	thus	He has said	Yahweh	the God of	Israel	the jar of	the flour	not

3735.122	7111	8467	3940	2741.122	5912	3219
v Qal impf 3fs	cj, *n fs*	art, n ms	neg part	v Qal impf 3fs	adv	*n ms*
תִכְלָה	וְצַפַּחַת	הַשֶּׁמֶן	לֹא	תֶחְסָר	עַד	יוֹם
thikhlāh	wetsappachath	hashshemen	lō'	thechāsār	'adh	yôm
it will come to an end	and the pitcher of	the olive oil	not	it will dwindle	until	the day of

5598.141, 3176	1700	6142, 6686	124	**15.** 2050.122	6449.122
v Qal inf con, pn	n ms	prep, *n mp*	art, n fs	cj, v Qal impf 3fs	cj, v Qal impf 3fs
תֵּתֶן־יְהוָה	גֶּשֶׁם	עַל־פְּנֵי	הָאֲדָמָה	וַתֵּלֶךְ	וַתַּעֲשֶׂה
titten-yehwāh	geshem	'al-penê	hā'ădhāmāh	wattēlekh	watta'ăseh
Yahweh giving	rain	onto the surface of	the land	so she went	and she made

3626, 1745	455	404.122	2026	1041	3219
prep, *n ms*	pn	cj, v Qal impf 3fs	pers pron	cj, n ms, ps 3fs	n mp
כִּדְבַר	אֵלִיָּהוּ	וַתֹּאכַל	הִוא	וּבֵיתָהּ	יָמִים
kidhvar	'ēlîyāhû	wattō'khal	hî'	ûvêthāhh	yāmîm
according to the word of	Elijah	and she ate	she	and her household	days

16.

3656	7343	3940	3735.112	7111	8467	3940
n fs	art, n ms	neg part	v Qal pf 3fs	cj, *n fs*	art, n ms	neg part
כַּד	הַקֶּמַח	לֹא	כָלָתָה	וְצַפַּחַת	הַשֶּׁמֶן	לֹא
kadh	haqqemach	lō'	khālāthāh	wetsappachath	hashshemen	lō'
the jar of	the flour	not	it came to an end	and the pitcher of	the olive oil	not

2741.111	3626, 1745	3176	866	1744.311	904, 3135	455
v Qal pf 3ms	prep, *n ms*	pn	rel part	v Piel pf 3ms	prep, *n fs*	pn
חָסֵר	כִּדְבַר	יְהוָה	אֲשֶׁר	דִּבֶּר	בְּיַד	אֵלִיָּהוּ
chāsēr	kidhvar	yehwāh	'ăsher	dibber	beyadh	'ēlîyāhû
it lacked	according to the word of	Yahweh	which	He had spoken	by the hand of	Elijah

17.

2030.121	313	1745	431	2571.111	1158, 828
cj, v Qal impf 3ms	prep	art, n mp	art, dem pron	v Qal pf 3ms	*n ms*, art, n fs
וַיְהִי	אַחַר	הַדְּבָרִים	הָאֵלֶּה	חָלָה	בֶּן־הָאִשָּׁה
wayhî	'achar	haddevārîm	hā'ēlleh	chālāh	ben-hā'ishshāh
and it was	after	the things	the these	he became sick	the son of the woman

1200	1041	2030.121	2582	2481	4108	5912	866
n fs	art, n ms	cj, v Qal impf 3ms	n ms, ps 3ms	adj	adv	adv	rel part
בַּעֲלַת	הַבָּיִת	וַיְהִי	חָלְיוֹ	חָזָק	מְאֹד	עַד	אֲשֶׁר
ba'ălath	habbāyith	wayhî	chāleyô	chāzāq	me'ōdh	'adh	'ăsher
the matron of	the household	and it was	his illness	severe	very	until	that

3940, 3613.212, 904	5580	**18.** 569.122	420, 455	4242, 3937
neg part, v Niphal pf 3fs, prep, ps 3ms	n fs	cj, v Qal impf 3fs	prep, pn	intrg, prep, ps 1cs
לֹא־נוֹתְרָה־בּוֹ	נְשָׁמָה	וַתֹּאמֶר	אֶל־אֵלִיָּהוּ	מַה־לִּי
lō'-nôthrāh-bô	neshāmāh	wattō'mer	'el-'ēlîyāhû	mah-lî
it was not left in him	a breath	and she said	to Elijah	what to me

3937	382	435	971.113	420	3937, 2226.541
cj, prep, ps 2ms	*n ms*	art, n mp	v Qal pf 2ms	prep, ps 1cs	prep, v Hiphil inf con
וָלָךְ	אִישׁ	הָאֱלֹהִים	בָּאתָ	אֵלַי	לְהַזְכִּיר
wālākh	'îsh	hā'ĕlōhîm	bā'thā	'ēlay	lehazkîr
and to you	O man of	God	you have come	to me	to bring to remembrance

881, 5988 do, n ms, ps 1cs אֶת־עֲוֹנִי 'eth-'ăwōnî my transgression	3937, 4322.541 cj, prep, v Hiphil inf con וּלְהָמִית ûlăhāmîth and to cause to die	881, 1158 do, n ms, ps 1cs אֶת־בְּנִי 'eth-bᵉnî my son	19. 569.121 cj, v Qal impf 3ms וַיֹּאמֶר wayyō'mer and he said	420 prep, ps 3fs אֵלֶיהָ 'ēlêāh to her

5598.132, 3937 v Qal impv 2fs, prep, ps 1cs תְּנִי־לִי tᵉnî-lî give to me	881, 1158 do, n ms, ps 2fs אֶת־בְּנֵךְ 'eth-bᵉnēkh your son	4089.121 cj, v Qal impf 3ms, ps 3ms וַיִּקָּחֵהוּ wayyiqqāchēhû and he took him	4623, 2536 prep, n ms, ps 3fs מֵחֵיקָהּ mēchêqāhh from her bosom

14. For thus saith the LORD God of Israel, The barrel of meal shall not waste: ... jar of flour will never get empty, *Beck* ... bowl of flour shall not be exhausted, *NASB* ... meal shall not be used up, *Moffatt* ... pot of meal shall not waste, *Douay.*

neither shall the cruse of oil fail: ... jug will never lack oil, *Beck* ... jar of oil be empty, *NASB* ... flask of oil give out, *Moffatt* ... be diminished, *Douay.*

until the day that the LORD sendeth rain upon the earth: ... sends rain upon the ground, *Goodspeed* ... gives rain on the land, *NIV.*

15. And she went and did according to the saying of Elijah: and she, and he, and her house, did eat many days: ... she and he and her family had food for a long time, *BB* ... ate again, and again, from that period, *Fenton* ... She was able to eat for a year, and he and her son as well, *NAB* ... continued to eat from her supply of flour and oil, *NLT.*

16. And the barrel of meal wasted not: ... jar of flour was not used up, *NIV* ... meal was not exhausted, *Goodspeed.*

neither did the cruse of oil fail, according to the word of the LORD, which he spake by Elijah: ... there was always enough left in the containers, *NLT* ... jar of oil run dry, *NKJV* ... flask of oil fail, as the word of the LORD foretold, *REB* ... oil never gave out, *Moffatt.*

17. And it came to pass after these things, that the son of the woman, the mistress of the house, fell sick: ... the housewife's son fell sick, *Knox.*

and his sickness was so sore, that there was no breath left in him: ... the sickness was very grievous, *Douay* ... He grew worse and worse and finally stopped breathing, *NCV* ... illness was so severe that in the end he expired, *JB* ... until at last his breathing ceased, *NEB.*

18. And she said unto Elijah, What have I to do with thee, O thou man of God?: ... what have you done to me?, *NLT* ... What made you interfere, *REB* ... why did you do this to me?, *Good News.*

art thou come unto me to call my sin to remembrance, and to slay my son?: ... Did you come to remind me of my sin and kill my son?, *NIV* ... Have you come to me to call attention to my guilt, *NAB.*

19. And he said unto her, Give me thy son. And he took him out of her bosom: ... taking him from her lap, *JB* ... lifting him from her arms, *Moffatt* ... out of her arms, *BB.*

and carried him up into a loft, where he abode, and laid him upon

---

waste, nor the cruse of oil fail. She believed the promise, and for many days, perhaps for two whole years, the prophet continued to be her guest.

17:17–24. But after a time, her boy fell grievously sick, and at last died. His recovery was due to Elijah's prayer. So dreadful a calamity—the smiting of the stay of her home, and the son of her widowhood—filled the woman with terror. She longed to get rid of the presence of this terrible "man of God." The phrase "man of God" is characteristic of the Book of Kings, in which it occurs fifty-three times. It became a normal description of Elijah and Elisha. He must have come, she thought, to bring her sin to remembrance before God, and so to cause Him to slay her son. The prophet was touched by the pathos of her appeal and could not bear that she should look upon him as the cause of her bereavement. "Give me thy son," he said. Taking the dead boy from her arms, he carried him to the chamber which she had set apart for him and laid him on his own bed. Then, after an earnest cry to God, he stretched himself three times over the body of the youth, as though to breathe into his lungs and restore his vital warmth, at the same time praying intensely that "his soul might come into him again." (Compare the similar revivals of life wrought by Elisha [2 Ki. 4:34] and by Paul [Acts 20:10].) His prayer was heard; the boy revived. Carrying him down from the chamber, Elijah had the happiness of restoring him to his widowed mother with the words, "See, thy son liveth."

6148.521	420, 6163	866, 2000	3553.151	8427
cj, v Hiphil impf 3ms, ps 3ms	prep, art, n fs	rel part, pers pron	v Qal act ptc ms	adv
וַיַּעֲלֵהוּ	אֶל־הָעֲלִיָּה	אֲשֶׁר־הוּא	יֹשֵׁב	שָׁם
wayya'ălēhû	'el-hā'ălîyāh	'ăsher-hû'	yōshēv	shām
and he brought him up	to the upper chamber	where he	dwelling	there

8311.521	6142, 4433		7410.121	420, 3176	569.121	3176
cj, v Hiphil impf 3ms, ps 3ms	prep, n fs, ps 3ms	**20.**	cj, v Qal impf 3ms	prep, pn	cj, v Qal impf 3ms	pn
וַיַּשְׁכִּבֵהוּ	עַל־מִטָּתוֹ		וַיִּקְרָא	אֶל־יְהוָה	וַיֹּאמַר	יְהוָה
wayyashkivēhû	'al-mittāthô		wayyiqōrā'	'el-yehwāh	wayyō'mar	yehwāh
and he laid him	on his bed		and he called out	to Yahweh	and he said	Yahweh

435	1950B, 1612	6142, 496	866, 603	1513.751	6196
n mp, ps 1cs	intrg part, cj	prep, art, n fs	rel pron, pers pron	v Hithpael ptc ms	prep, ps 3fs
אֱלֹהָי	הֲגַם	עַל־הָאַלְמָנָה	אֲשֶׁר־אֲנִי	מִתְגּוֹרֵר	עִמָּהּ
'ělōhāy	hăgham	'al-hā'almānāh	'ăsher-'ănî	mithgôrēr	'immāhh
my God	will also	on the widow	whom I	sojourning	with her

7778.513	3937, 4322.541	881, 1158		4200.721	6142, 3315
intrg part, v Hiphil pf 2ms	prep, v Hiphil inf con	do, n ms, ps 3fs	**21.**	cj, v Hithpoel impf 3ms	prep, art, n ms
הֲרֵעוֹתָ	לְהָמִית	אֶת־בְּנָהּ		וַיִּתְמֹדֵד	עַל־הַיֶּלֶד
hărē'ôthā	lehāmîth	'eth-benāhh		wayyithmōdhēdh	'al-hayyeledh
will You bring evil	to kill	her son		and he stretched out	over the child

8421	6718	7410.121	420, 3176	569.121	3176	435	8178.122
num	n fp	cj, v Qal impf 3ms	prep, pn	cj, v Qal impf 3ms	pn	n mp, ps 1cs	v Qal juss 3fs
שָׁלֹשׁ	פְּעָמִים	וַיִּקְרָא	אֶל־יְהוָה	וַיֹּאמַר	יְהוָה	אֱלֹהָי	תָּשָׁב
shālōsh	pe'āmîm	wayyiqōrā'	'el-yehwāh	wayyō'mar	yehwāh	'ělōhāy	tāshāv
three	times	and he called	to Yahweh	and he said	Yahweh	my God	may it return

5167	5497, 3315	2172	6142, 7419		8471.121	3176
part	*n fs*, art, n ms	art, dem pron	prep, n ms, ps 3ms	**22.**	cj, v Qal impf 3ms	pn
נָא	נֶפֶשׁ־הַיֶּלֶד	הַזֶּה	עַל־קִרְבּוֹ		וַיִּשְׁמַע	יְהוָה
nā'	nephesh-hayyeledh	hazzeh	'al-qirbô		wayyishma'	yehwāh
please	the breath of the child	the this	onto his middle		and He heard	Yahweh

904, 7249	455	8178.122	5497, 3315	6142, 7419	2513.121
prep, *n ms*	pn	cj, v Qal impf 3fs	*n fs*, art, n ms	prep, n ms, ps 3ms	cj, v Qal impf 3ms
בְּקוֹל	אֵלִיָּהוּ	וַתָּשָׁב	נֶפֶשׁ־הַיֶּלֶד	עַל־קִרְבּוֹ	וַיֶּחִי
beqôl	'ēlîyāhû	wattāshāv	nephesh-hayyeledh	'al-qirbô	wayyechî
by the voice of	Elijah	and it returned	the breath of the child	onto his middle	and he lived

	4089.121	455	881, 3315	3495.521	4623, 6163
23.	cj, v Qal impf 3ms	pn	do, art, n ms	cj, v Hiphil impf 3ms, ps 3ms	prep, art, n fs
	וַיִּקַּח	אֵלִיָּהוּ	אֶת־הַיֶּלֶד	וַיֹּרִדֵהוּ	מִן־הָעֲלִיָּה
	wayyiqqach	'ēlîyāhû	'eth-hayyeledh	wayyōridhēhû	min-hā'ălîyāh
	and he took	Elijah	the child	and he brought him down	from the upper room

1041	5598.121	3937, 525	569.121	455	7495.132	2508
art, n ms	cj, v Qal impf 3ms, ps 3ms	prep, n fs, ps 3ms	cj, v Qal impf 3ms	pn	v Qal impv 2fs	adj
הַבַּיְתָה	וַיִּתְּנֵהוּ	לְאִמּוֹ	וַיֹּאמֶר	אֵלִיָּהוּ	רְאִי	חַי
habbaythāh	wayyittenēhû	le'immô	wayyō'mer	'ēlîyāhû	re'î	chay
to the house	and he gave him over	to his mother	and he said	Elijah	see	living

1158		569.122	828	420, 455	6498	2172	3156.115	3706
n ms, ps 2fs	**24.**	cj, v Qal impf 3fs	art, n fs	prep, pn	adv	dem pron	v Qal pf 1cs	cj
בְּנֵךְ		וַתֹּאמֶר	הָאִשָּׁה	אֶל־אֵלִיָּהוּ	עַתָּה	זֶה	יָדַעְתִּי	כִּי
benēkh		wattō'mer	hā'ishshāh	'el-'ēlîyāhû	'attāh	zeh	yādha'ttî	kî
your son		and she said	the woman	to Elijah	now	this	I know	that

382	435	887	1745, 3176	904, 6552	583
n ms	n mp	pers pron	cj, *n ms*, pn	prep, n ms, ps 2ms	n fs
אִישׁ	אֱלֹהִים	אַתָּה	וּדְבַר־יְהוָה	בְּפִיךָ	אֱמֶת
'îsh	'ĕlōhîm	'attāh	ûdhevar-yehwāh	bephîkhā	'ĕmeth
a man of	God	you	and the word of Yahweh	in your mouth	truth

	2030.121	3219	7521	1745, 3176	2030.111	420, 455
18:1	cj, v Qal impf 3ms	n mp	adj	cj, *n ms*, pn	v Qal pf 3ms	prep, pn
	וַיְהִי	יָמִים	רַבִּים	וּדְבַר־יְהוָה	הָיָה	אֶל־אֵלִיָּהוּ
	wayhî	yāmîm	rabbîm	ûdhevar-yehwāh	hāyāh	'el-'ēlîyāhû
	and it was	days	many	and the word of Yahweh	it was	to Elijah

his own bed: ... the upper chamber, *Darby* ... to the roof-chamber where his lodging was, *NEB*.

20. And he cried unto the LORD, and said, O LORD my God, hast thou also brought evil upon the widow with whom I sojourn, by slaying her son?: ... have You also brought tragedy on the widow with whom I lodge, *NKJV* ... done this terrible thing to her, *NCV* ... bring trouble even upon this widow, who is all my support, *Knox* ... hast Thou also brought calamity, *NASB*.

21. And he stretched himself upon the child three times, and cried unto the LORD: ... made his prayer to the Lord, *BB* ... measured his whole length upon the child's body, *Knox* ... breathed deeply, *NEB* ... crouched over the child, *Moffatt*.

and said, O LORD my God, I pray thee, let this child's soul come into him again: ... please make this boy live, *Beck* ... let now the life of this child return to him, *Berkeley* ... life breath return to the body, *NAB* ... restore this child to life!, *Good News*.

22. And the LORD heard the voice of Elijah; and the soul of the child came into him again, and he revived: ... he came back to life, *BB* ... the life of the boy came again within him, *Rotherham*.

23. And Elijah took the child, and brought him down out of the chamber into the house: ... from the upper chamber, *NRSV* ... down from the roof, *NEB* ... carried the boy downstairs, *NCV*.

and delivered him unto his mother: and Elijah said, See, thy son liveth: ... See, your son is alive, *NASB* ... See, your son lives!, *NKJV*.

24. And the woman said to Elijah, Now by this I know that thou art a man of God, and that the word of the LORD in thy mouth is truth: ... the EVER-LIVING speaks by your mouth, *Fenton* ... comes truly from your mouth, *NAB* ... the LORD's Word you speak, *Beck* ... his promise on thy lips is true, *Knox*.

18:1. And it came to pass after many days, that the word of the LORD came to Elijah in the third year, saying: ... A long time went by, *JB* ... After a long time, *NIV* ... During the third year without rain, *NCV* ... at last, when two years had gone, *Knox*.

Go, show thyself unto Ahab; and I will send rain upon the earth: ... Tell him that I will soon send rain!, *NLT* ... I may give rain upon the face of the earth, *Douay* ... I will send rain on the country, *JB*.

So remarkable an event not only convinced the woman that Elijah was indeed what she had called him, "a man of God," but also that Yahweh was the true God.

18:1–2. "*Return, ye backsliding children, and I will heal your backslidings. Behold, we come unto thee; for thou art the LORD our God. Truly in vain is salvation hoped for from the hills, and from the multitude of mountains: truly in the LORD our God is the salvation of Israel. For shame hath devoured the labour of our fathers from our youth; their flocks and their herds, their sons and their daughters*" (Jer. 3:22ff).

Elijah stayed long with the Sidonian widow, safe in that obscure concealment and with his simple wants supplied. But at last the word of the LORD came to him with the conviction that the drought had accomplished its appointed end in impressing the souls of king and people and that the time was come for some immense and decisive demonstration against the prevalent apostasy. All his sudden movements, all his stern incisive utterances were swayed by his allegiance to Yahweh before whom he stood, and he now received the command, "Go, show thyself unto Ahab; and I will send rain upon the earth."

To obey such a mandate showed the strength of his faith. It is clear that even before the menace of the drought he had been known, and unfavorably known, to Ahab. The king saw in him a prophet who fearlessly opposed all the idolatrous tendencies

904, 8523	8389	3937, 569.141	2050.131	7495.231	420, 255
prep, art, n fs	art, num	prep, v Qal inf con	v Qal impv 2ms	v Niphal impv 2ms	prep, pn
בַּשָּׁנָה	הַשְּׁלִישִׁית	לֵאמֹר	לֵךְ	הֵרָאֵה	אֶל־אַחְאָב
bashshānāh	hashshᵉlîshîth	lē'mōr	lēkh	hērā'ēh	'el-'ach'āv
in the year	the third	saying	go	appear	to Ahab

5598.125	4443	6142, 6686	124	**2.** 2050.121	455
cj, v Qal juss 1cs	n ms	prep, *n mp*	art, n fs	cj, v Qal impf 3ms	pn
וְאֶתְּנָה	מָטָר	עַל־פְּנֵי	הָאֲדָמָה	וַיֵּלֶךְ	אֵלִיָּהוּ
wᵉ'ettᵉnāh	māṭār	'al-pᵉnê	hā'ădhāmāh	wayyēlekh	'ēlîyāhû
that I may give	rain	on the surface of	the land	so he went	Elijah

3937, 7495.241	420, 255	7743	2481	904, 8497	**3.** 7410.121	255
prep, v Niphal inf con	prep, pn	cj, art, n ms	adj	prep, pn	cj, v Qal impf 3ms	pn
לְהֵרָאוֹת	אֶל־אַחְאָב	וְהָרָעָב	חָזָק	בְּשֹׁמְרוֹן	וַיִּקְרָא	אַחְאָב
lᵉhērā'ōth	'el-'ach'āv	wᵉhārā'āv	chāzāq	bᵉshōmᵉrôn	wayyiqrā'	'ach'āv
to appear	to Ahab	and the famine	severe	in Samaria	and he called	Ahab

420, 5870	866	6142, 1041	5870	2030.111	3495.151	881, 3176
prep, pn	rel pron	prep, art, n ms	cj, pn	v Qal pf 3ms	v Qal act ptc ms	do, pn
אֶל־עֹבַדְיָהוּ	אֲשֶׁר	עַל־הַבָּיִת	וְעֹבַדְיָהוּ	הָיָה	יָרֵא	אֶת־יְהוָה
'el-'ōvadhyāhû	'ăsher	'al-habbāyith	wᵉ'ōvadhyāhû	hāyāh	yārē'	'eth-yᵉhwāh
to Obadiah	who	over the household	and Obadiah	he was	one fearing	Yahweh

4108	**4.** 2030.121	904, 3901.541	350	881	5204	3176
adv	cj, v Qal impf 3ms	prep, v Hiphil inf con	pn	do	*n mp*	pn
מְאֹד	וַיְהִי	בְּהַכְרִית	אִיזֶבֶל	אֵת	נְבִיאֵי	יְהוָה
mᵉ'ōdh	wayhî	bᵉhakhrîth	'îzevel	'ēth	nᵉvî'ê	yᵉhwāh
very	and it was	when cutting off	Jezebel		the prophets of	Yahweh

4089.121	5870	4109	5204	2331.521	2675	382
cj, v Qal impf 3ms	pn	num	n mp	cj, v Hiphil impf 3ms, ps 3mp	num	n ms
וַיִּקַּח	עֹבַדְיָהוּ	מֵאָה	נְבִאִים	וַיַּחְבִּיאֵם	חֲמִשִּׁים	אִישׁ
wayyiqqach	'ōvadhyāhû	mē'āh	nᵉvi'îm	wayyachbî'ēm	chămishshîm	'îsh
that he took	Obadiah	one hundred	prophets	and he hid them	fifty	men

904, 4792	3677.311	4035	4448	**5.** 569.121	255	420, 5870
prep, art, n fs	cj, v Pilpel pf 3ms, ps 3mp	n ms	cj, n mp	cj, v Qal impf 3ms	pn	prep, pn
בַּמְּעָרָה	וְכִלְכְּלָם	לֶחֶם	וָמָיִם	וַיֹּאמֶר	אַחְאָב	אֶל־עֹבַדְיָהוּ
bammᵉ'ārāh	wᵉkhilkᵉlām	lechem	wāmāyim	wayyō'mer	'ach'āv	'el-'ōvadhyāhû
in the cave	and he fed them	food	and water	and he said	Ahab	to Obadiah

2050.131	904, 800	420, 3725, 4754	4448	420	3725, 5337	193
v Qal impv 2ms	prep, art, n fs	prep, *adj*, *n mp*	art, n md	cj, prep	*adj*, art, n mp	adv
לֵךְ	בָּאָרֶץ	אֶל־כָּל־מַעְיְנֵי	הַמַּיִם	וְאֶל	כָּל־הַנְּחָלִים	אוּלַי
lēkh	bā'ārets	'el-kol-ma'ăynê	hammayim	wᵉ'el	kol-hannᵉchālîm	'ûlay
go	throughout the land	to all the springs of	the waters	and to	all the streams	perhaps

4834.120	2785	2513.320	5670	6755	3940	3901.520
v Qal impf 1cp	n ms	cj, v Piel impf 1cp	n ms	cj, n ms	cj, neg part	v Hiphil impf 1cp
נִמְצָא	חָצִיר	וּנְחַיֶּה	סוּס	וָפֶרֶד	וְלוֹא	נַכְרִית
nimtsā'	chātsîr	ûnᵉchayyeh	sûs	wāphered	wᵉlô'	nakhrîth
we will find	grass	and we will keep alive	the horses	and the mules	and not	we will cut off

4623, 966	**6.** 2606.326	3937	881, 800	3937, 5882.141, 904
prep, art, n fs	cj, v Piel impf 3mp	prep, ps 3mp	do, art, n fs	prep, v Qal inf con, prep, ps 3fs
מֵהַבְּהֵמָה	וַיְחַלְּקוּ	לָהֶם	אֶת־הָאָרֶץ	לַעֲבָר־בָּהּ
mēhabbᵉhēmāh	waychallᵉqû	lāhem	'eth-hā'ārets	la'ăvār-bāhh
from the herds	and they divided	for themselves	the land	to pass through on it

2. And Elijah went to show himself unto Ahab. And there was a sore famine in Samaria: ... the famine was severe, *KJVII* ... the famine in Samaria was at its height, *REB* ... By this time there was no food, *NCV* ... Now the famine was raging, *Moffatt* ... famine in Samaria was bitter, *NAB*.

3. And Ahab called Obadiah, which was the governor of his house. (Now Obadiah feared the LORD greatly: ... who was the steward, *Darby* ... who was in charge, *NKJV* ... comptroller of his household, a devout worshipper of the LORD, *NEB*.

4. For it was so, when Jezebel cut off the prophets of the LORD: ... destroyed the Prophets, *Geneva* ... Jezebel ordered the prophets of the LORD exterminated, *Goodspeed* ... Jezebel was massacring the prophets of the Eternal, *Moffatt*.

that Obadiah took an hundred prophets, and hid them by fifty in a cave, and fed them with bread and water.): ... sustained them with food and drink, *REB* ... hiding them in two caves, *Knox*.

5. And Ahab said unto Obadiah, Go into the land, unto all fountains of water, and unto all brooks: ... through the land to all the springs and valleys, *NIV* ... to every spring and gully, *NEB* ... springs of water and to all the wadis, *NRSV* ... every stream bed, *Good News*.

peradventure we may find grass to save the horses and mules alive, that we lose not all the beasts: ... so that we will not have to kill any livestock, *NKJV* ... not lose all the animals, *KJVII* ... not be deprived of the cattle, *Berkeley*.

6. So they divided the land between them to pass throughout it: ... country between them for exploration, *Fenton* ... they went through all the country, covering it, *BB* ... to explore, *NAB* ... to survey it, *NASB*.

Ahab went one way by himself, and Obadiah went another way by himself: ... Abdiah went another, *Tyndale* ... set off in different directions, *Good News*.

7. And as Obadiah was in the way, behold, Elijah met him: ... he was suddenly met by Elijah, *Moffatt* ... suddenly confronted, *REB*.

and he knew him, and fell on his face, and said, Art thou that my lord Elijah?: ... and bowed down with his face on the ground, *Beck* ... Is that you, my master, *Berkeley* ... Recognizing him, Obadiah fell prostrate, *NAB*.

---

into which he had led his easy and faithless people. How terribly intensified Ahab's hatred must have been! Things had, indeed, come to their worst. The "sore famine" in Samaria had reached a point which, if it had not been alleviated, would have led to the utter ruin of the miserable kingdom.

18:3–6. In this crisis, Ahab did all that a king could do. Most of the cattle had perished, but it was essential to save, if possible, some of the horses and mules. No grass was left on the scorched plains, and bare brown hills except where there were fountains and brooks which had not entirely vanished under that copper sky. To these places it was necessary to drive such a remnant of the cattle as it might be still possible to preserve alive. But who could be trusted to rise entirely superior to individual selfishness in such a search? Ahab thought it best to trust no one but himself and his vizier Obadiah. The very name of this high official, Obadjahu, like the common Mohammedan names Abdallah, Abderrahnan, and others, implied that he was "a servant of Yahweh." His conduct answered to his name, for on Jezebel's persecuting attempt to exterminate Yahweh's prophets in their schools or communities, he, "the Sebastian of the Jewish Diocletian," had, at the peril of his own life, taken a hundred of them, concealed them in two of the great limestone caves of Palestine—perhaps in the recesses of Mount Carmel and fed them with bread and water. (Amos 9:3: "And though they hide themselves in the top of Carmel I will search and take them out thence." The phrase shows the security and seclusion of these caves and thickets, the haunt once of lions and bears, and still of leopards and hyaenas.) It is to Ahab's credit that he retained such a man in office, though the touch of timidity which we trace in Obadiah may have concealed the full faithfulness of his personal allegiance to the old worship. Yet that such a man should still hold the post of chamberlain furnishes a fresh proof that Ahab was not himself a worshiper of Baal.

18:7–8. The king and his governor went in opposite directions, each of them unaccompanied, and Obadiah was on his way when he was startled by the sudden appearance of Elijah. He had not previously seen him, but recognizing him by his shaggy locks, his robe of skin, and the awful sternness of his swarthy countenance, he was almost abjectly terrified. Apart from the awe-inspiring aspect and manner of the prophet, this seemed no mere man who stood before him, but the representative of the Eternal, and the wielder of his power. To his contemporaries he appeared like the incarnate vengeance of Yahweh against guilty times, a flash of

255	2050.111	904, 1932	259	3937, 940	5870	2050.111
pn	v Qal pf 3ms	prep, *n ms*	num	prep, n ms, ps 3ms	cj, pn	v Qal pf 3ms
אַחְאָב	הָלַךְ	בְּדֶרֶךְ	אֶחָד	לְבַדּוֹ	וְעֹבַדְיָהוּ	הָלַךְ
'ach'āv	hālakh	bedherekh	'echādh	levaddô	we'ōvadhyāhû	hālakh
Ahab	he walked	on the path of	one	by himself	and Obadiah	he walked

904, 1932, 259	3937, 940	**7.** 2030.121	5870	904, 1932	2079
prep, *n ms*, num	prep, n ms, ps 3ms	cj, v Qal impf 3ms	pn	prep, art, n ms	cj, intrj
בְּדֶרֶךְ־אֶחָד	לְבַדּוֹ	וַיְהִי	עֹבַדְיָהוּ	בַּדֶּרֶךְ	וְהִנֵּה
bedherekh-'echādh	levaddô	wayhî	'ōvadhyāhû	badderekh	wehinnēh
on the path of the other	by himself	and it was	Obadiah	on the path	and behold

455	3937, 7410.141	5422.521	5489.121	6142, 6686
pn	prep, v Qal inf con, ps 3ms	cj, v Hiphil impf 3ms, ps 3ms	cj, v Qal impf 3ms	prep, n mp, ps 3ms
אֵלִיָּהוּ	לִקְרָאתוֹ	וַיַּכִּרֵהוּ	וַיִּפֹּל	עַל־פָּנָיו
'ēlîyāhû	liqŏrā'thô	wayyakkirēhû	wayyippōl	'al-pānâv
Elijah	to meet him	and he recognized him	and he fell	on his face

569.121	1950B, 887	2172	112	455	**8.** 569.121	3937
cj, v Qal impf 3ms	intrg part, pers pron	dem pron	n ms, ps 1cs	pn	cj, v Qal impf 3ms	prep, ps 3ms
וַיֹּאמֶר	הַאַתָּה	זֶה	אֲדֹנִי	אֵלִיָּהוּ	וַיֹּאמֶר	לוֹ
wayyō'mer	ha'attāh	zeh	'ădhōnî	'ēlîyāhû	wayyō'mer	lô
and he said	are you	this one	my master	Elijah	and he said	to him

603	2050.131	569.131	3937, 112	2079	455	**9.** 569.121	4242
pers pron	v Qal impv 2ms	v Qal impv 2ms	prep, n mp, ps 2ms	intrj	pn	cj, v Qal impf 3ms	intrg
אָנִי	לֵךְ	אֱמֹר	לַאדֹנֶיךָ	הִנֵּה	אֵלִיָּהוּ	וַיֹּאמֶר	מֶה
'ānî	lēkh	'ĕmōr	la'dhōnêkhā	hinnēh	'ēlîyāhû	wayyō'mer	meh
I	go	say	to your master	behold	Elijah	and he said	what

2490.115	3706, 887	5598.151	881, 5860	904, 3135, 255
v Qal pf 1cs	cj, pers pron	v Qal act ptc ms	do, n ms, ps 2ms	prep, *n fs*, pn
חָטָאתִי	כִּי־אַתָּה	נֹתֵן	אֶת־עַבְדְּךָ	בְּיַד־אַחְאָב
chāṭā'thî	kî-'attāh	nōthēn	'eth-'avdekhā	beyadh-'ach'āv
have I sinned	that you	giving	your servant	into the hand of Ahab

3937, 4322.541	**10.** 2508	3176	435	524, 3552, 1504	4608	866
prep, v Hiphil inf con, ps 1cs	adj	pn	n mp, ps 2ms	cj, *sub*, n ms	cj, n fs	rel part
לַהֲמִיתֵנִי	חַי	יְהוָה	אֱלֹהֶיךָ	אִם־יֶשׁ־גּוֹי	וּמַמְלָכָה	אֲשֶׁר
lahmîthēnî	chay	yehwāh	'ĕlōhêkhā	'im-yesh-gôy	ûmamlākhāh	'ăsher
to kill me	living	Yahweh	your God	if there is a nation	or a kingdom	which

3940, 8365.111	112	8427	3937, 1272.341	569.116	375
neg part, v Qal pf 3ms	n ms, ps 1cs	adv	prep, v Piel inf con, ps 2ms	cj, v Qal pf 3cp	sub
לֹא־שָׁלַח	אֲדֹנִי	שָׁם	לְבַקֶּשְׁךָ	וְאָמְרוּ	אָיִן
lō'-shālach	'ădhōnî	shām	levaqqeshkhā	we'āmerû	'āyin
he has not sent out	my master	there	to search for you	and they said	he is not

8123.511	881, 4608	881, 1504	3706	3940	4834.121
cj, v Hiphil pf 3ms	do, art, n fs	cj, do, art, n ms	cj	neg part	v Qal impf 3ms, ps 2ms
וְהִשְׁבִּיעַ	אֶת־הַמַּמְלָכָה	וְאֶת־הַגּוֹי	כִּי	לֹא	יִמְצָאֶכָּה
wehishbîa'	'eth-hammamlākhāh	we'eth-haggôy	kî	lō'	yimtsā'ekkāh
and he swore an oath	the kingdom	or the nation	that	not	they found you

11. 6498	887	569.151	2050.131	569.131	3937, 112	2079
cj, adv	pers pron	v Qal act ptc ms	v Qal impv 2ms	v Qal impv 2ms	prep, n mp, ps 2ms	intrj
וְעַתָּה	אַתָּה	אֹמֵר	לֵךְ	אֱמֹר	לַאדֹנֶיךָ	הִנֵּה
we'attāh	'attāh	'ōmēr	lēkh	'ĕmōr	la'dhōnêkhā	hinnēh
and now	you	saying	go	say	to your master	behold

455		2030.111	603	2050.125	4623, 882	7593	3176
pn	**12.**	cj, v Qal pf 3ms	pers pron	v Qal impf 1cs	prep, prep, ps 2ms	cj, *n fs*	pn
אֵלִיָּהוּ		וְהָיָה	אֲנִי	אֵלֵךְ	מֵאִתָּךְ	וְרוּחַ	יְהוָה
'ēlîyāhû		wehāyāh	'ănî	'ēlēkh	mē'ittākh	werûach	yehwāh
Elijah		and it will be	I	I will go	from with you	then the Spirit of	Yahweh

5558.121	6142	866	3940, 3156.125	971.115	3937, 5222.541	3937, 255
v Qal impf 3ms, ps 2ms	prep	rel part	neg part, v Qal impf 1cs	cj, v Qal pf 1cs	prep, v Hiphil inf con	prep, pn
יִשָּׂאֲךָ	עַל	אֲשֶׁר	לֹא־אֵדָע	וּבָאתִי	לְהַגִּיד	לְאַחְאָב
yissā'ăkhā	'al	'ăsher	lō'-'ēdhā'	ûvā'thî	lehaggîdh	le'ach'āv
He will carry you	on	what	I do not know	then I will come	to report	to Ahab

8. And he answered him, I am: go, tell thy lord, Behold, Elijah is here: ... say to your master, *NASB* ... Elias is here, *Douay* ... your master I am here, *NLT* ... your Prince, *Fenton*.

9. And he said, What have I sinned, that thou wouldest deliver thy servant into the hand of Ahab, to slay me?: ... be the cause of my death?, *BB* ... He will put me to death, *NEB* ... put your servant into Ahab's power, *JB*.

10. As the LORD thy God liveth, there is no nation or kingdom, whither my lord hath not sent to seek thee: ... not a tribe or district where my Prince, *Fenton* ... race or realm to which my master, *Knox* ... in search of you, *Moffatt* ... no region, *REB*.

and when they said, He is not there; he took an oath of the kingdom and nation, that they found thee not: ... swear that it found no trace of you, *Berkeley* ... forced the ruler to swear you could not be found in his country, *NCV*.

11. And now thou sayest, Go, tell thy lord, Behold, Elijah is here: ... you tell me to go to my master and say, *NIV* ... you want me to go tell him that you are here?, *Good News*.

12. And it shall come to pass, as soon as I am gone from thee, that the Spirit of the LORD shall carry thee whither I know not: ... I leave you, ... away to who knows where, *NLT* ... may carry you to some other place after I leave, *NCV*.

and so when I come and tell Ahab, and he cannot find thee, he shall slay me: ... he not finding you, will kill me, *Fenton* ... cannot find you, he will put me to death, *Moffatt*.

but I thy servant fear the LORD from my youth: ... although I your servant have revered, *RSV* ... feareth the Lord from his infancy, *Douay* ... have been a worshipper of the LORD from boyhood, *NEB*.

13. Was it not told my lord what I did when Jezebel slew the prophets of the LORD: ... put the LORD's prophets to death, *REB* ... butchered the prophets of Yahweh, *JB* ... was massacring the prophets of the Eternal, *Moffatt*.

how I hid an hundred men of the LORD's prophets by fifty in a cave: ... rescued a hundred of them, by hiding them in two caves, *Knox* ... of the prophets of Yahweh, *Rotherham*.

and fed them with bread and water?: ... sustained them, *Young* ... kept them alive with food and drink?, *NEB* ... provided them, *NASB* ... supplied them, *NAB*.

God's consuming fire. Springing from his chariot, Obadiah fell flat on his face and cried, "Is it thou, my lord Elijah?" "It is I," answered the prophet, not wasting words over his terror and astonishment. "Go, tell thy lord, Behold, Elijah is here."

18:9–16. The message enhanced the alarm. Why had not Elijah shown himself at once to Ahab? Did some terrible vindictive purpose lurk behind his message? Did Elijah confuse the aims and deeds of the minister with those of the king? Why did he dispatch him on an errand which might move Ahab to kill him? Was not Elijah aware, he asks, that Ahab had sent "to every nation and kingdom" to ask if Elijah was there, and when told that he was not there he made them confirm the statement by an oath? (The Septuagint adds that he inflicted vengeance because Elijah was not found: 1 Ki. 18:10.) What would come of such a message if Obadiah conveyed it? No sooner would it be delivered than the wind of the LORD would sweep Elijah away into some new and unknown solitude. (In Bel and the Dragon 33–36, the prophet Habakkuk is said to have been taken invisibly to supply food to Daniel in the den of lions. Then the angel of the LORD took him by the crown and bare him by the hair of his head, and through the vehemency of his spirit.)

Ahab would, in his angry disappointment, put Obadiah to death. Had he deserved such a fate? Had not Elijah heard of his reverence for Yahweh from his youth, and of his saving the hundred

3940	4834.121	2103.111	5860	3495.111	881, 3176
cj, neg part	v Qal impf 3ms, ps 2ms	cj, v Qal pf 3ms, ps 1cs	cj, n ms, ps 2ms	v Qal pf 3ms	do, pn
וְלֹא	יִמְצָאֲךָ	וַהֲרָגָנִי	וְעַבְדְּךָ	יָרֵא	אֶת־יְהוָה
welō'	yimtsā'ăkhā	wahrāghānî	we'avdekhā	yārē'	'eth-yehwāh
and not	he will find you	then he will kill me	yet your servant	he has feared	Yahweh

4623, 5470		1950B, 3940, 5222.611	3937, 112	881	866, 6449.115
prep, n mp, ps 1cs	**13.**	intrg part, neg part, v Hophal pf 3ms	prep, n ms, ps 1cs	do	rel part, v Qal pf 1cs
מִנְּעֻרָי		הֲלֹא־הֻגַּד	לַאדֹנִי	אֵת	אֲשֶׁר־עָשִׂיתִי
minne'urāy		hălō'-huggadh	la'dhōnî	'ēth	'ăsher-'āsîthî
from my youth		has it not been reported	to my master		what I did

904, 2103.141	350	881	5204	3176	2331.525	4623, 5204
prep, v Qal inf con	pn	do	*n mp*	pn	cj, v Hiphil impf 1cs	prep, *n mp*
בַּהֲרֹג	אִיזֶבֶל	אֵת	נְבִיאֵי	יְהוָה	וָאַחְבִּא	מִנְּבִיאֵי
bahrōgh	'îzevel	'ēth	nevî'ê	yehwāh	wā'achbi'	minnevî'ê
when killing	Jezebel		the prophets of	Yahweh	that I hid	from the prophets of

3176	4109	382	2675	2675	382	904, 4792	3677.325
pn	num	n ms	num	num	n ms	prep, art, n fs	cj, v Pilpel impf 1cs, ps 3mp
יְהוָה	מֵאָה	אִישׁ	חֲמִשִּׁים	חֲמִשִּׁים	אִישׁ	בַּמְּעָרָה	וָאֲכַלְכְּלֵם
yehwāh	mē'āh	'îsh	chămishshîm	chămishshîm	'îsh	bamme'ārāh	wā'ăkhalkelēm
Yahweh	one hundred	men	fifty	fifty	men	in the cave	and I fed them

4035	4448		6498	887	569.151	2050.131	569.131
n ms	cj, n mp	**14.**	cj, adv	pers pron	v Qal act ptc ms	v Qal impv 2ms	v Qal impv 2ms
לֶחֶם	וָמָיִם		וְעַתָּה	אַתָּה	אֹמֵר	לֵךְ	אֱמֹר
lechem	wāmāyim		we'attāh	'attāh	'ōmēr	lēkh	'ĕmōr
food	and water		and now	you	saying	go	say

3937, 112	2079	455	2103.111		569.121	455	2508
prep, n mp, ps 2ms	intrj	pn	cj, v Qal pf 3ms, ps 1cs	**15.**	cj, v Qal impf 3ms	pn	adj
לַאדֹנֶיךָ	הִנֵּה	אֵלִיָּהוּ	וַהֲרָגָנִי		וַיֹּאמֶר	אֵלִיָּהוּ	חַי
la'dhōnêkhā	hinnēh	'ēlîyāhû	wahrāghānî		wayyō'mer	'ēlîyāhû	chay
to your master	behold	Elijah	and he will kill me		and he said	Elijah	living

3176	6893	866	6198.115	3937, 6686	3706	3219	7495.225
pn	n mp	rel pron	v Qal pf 1cs	prep, n mp, ps 3ms	cj	art, n ms	v Niphal impf 1cs
יְהוָה	צְבָאוֹת	אֲשֶׁר	עָמַדְתִּי	לְפָנָיו	כִּי	הַיּוֹם	אֵרָאֶה
yehwāh	tsevā'ôth	'ăsher	'āmadhtî	lephānâv	kî	hayyôm	'ērā'eh
Yahweh of	hosts	Whom	I stand	before Him	because	today	I will appear

420		2050.121	5870	3937, 7410.141	255	5222.521, 3937
prep, ps 3ms	**16.**	cj, v Qal impf 3ms	pn	prep, v Qal inf con	pn	cj, v Hiphil impf 3ms, prep, ps 3ms
אֵלָיו		וַיֵּלֶךְ	עֹבַדְיָהוּ	לִקְרַאת	אַחְאָב	וַיַּגֶּד־לוֹ
'ēlâv		wayyēlekh	'ōvadhyāhû	liqōra'th	'ach'āv	wayyaggedh-lô
to him		so he went	Obadiah	to meet	Ahab	and he reported to him

2050.121	255	3937, 7410.141	455		2030.121	3626, 7495.141	255
cj, v Qal impf 3ms	pn	prep, v Qal inf con	pn	**17.**	cj, v Qal impf 3ms	prep, v Qal inf con	pn
וַיֵּלֶךְ	אַחְאָב	לִקְרַאת	אֵלִיָּהוּ		וַיְהִי	כִּרְאוֹת	אַחְאָב
wayyēlekh	'ach'āv	liqōra'th	'ēlîyāhû		wayhî	kir'ôth	'ach'āv
and he went	Ahab	to meet	Elijah		and it was	when seeing	Ahab

881, 455	569.121	255	420	1950B, 887	2172	6138.151
do, pn	cj, v Qal impf 3ms	pn	prep, ps 3ms	intrg part, pers pron	dem pron	v Qal act ptc ms
אֶת־אֵלִיָּהוּ	וַיֹּאמֶר	אַחְאָב	אֵלָיו	הַאַתָּה	זֶה	עֹכֵר
'eth-'ēlîyāhû	wayyō'mer	'ach'āv	'ēlâv	ha'attāh	zeh	'ōkhēr
Elijah	then he said	Ahab	to him	are you	this one	one bringing ruin

3547		569.121	3940	6138.115	881, 3547	3706	524, 887
pn	18.	cj, v Qal impf 3ms	neg part	v Qal pf 1cs	do, pn	cj	cj, pers pron
יִשְׂרָאֵל		וַיֹּאמֶר	לֹא	עָכַרְתִּי	אֶת־יִשְׂרָאֵל	כִּי	אִם־אַתָּה
yisrā'ēl		wayyō'mer	lō'	'ākhartî	'eth-yisrā'ēl	kî	'im-'attāh
Israel		and he said	not	I have ruined	Israel	but	rather you

1041	1	904, 6013.141	881, 4851	3176
cj, *n ms*	n ms, ps 2ms	prep, v Qal inf con, ps 2mp	do, *n fp*	pn
וּבֵית	אָבִיךָ	בַּעֲזָבְכֶם	אֶת־מִצְוֺת	יְהוָה
ûvêth	'āvîkhā	ba'ăzāvekhem	'eth-mitswōth	yehwāh
and the household of	your father	when your abandoning	the commandments of	Yahweh

2050.123	313	1197		6498	8365.131	7192.131	420
cj, v Qal impf 2ms	prep	art, pn	19.	cj, adv	v Qal impv 2ms	v Qal impv 2ms	prep, ps 1cs
וַתֵּלֶךְ	אַחֲרֵי	הַבְּעָלִים		וְעַתָּה	שְׁלַח	קְבֹץ	אֵלַי
wattēlekh	'achrê	habbe'ālîm		we'attāh	shelach	qōvōts	'ēlay
and you walked	after	the Baals		and now	send	gather	to me

14. And now thou sayest, Go, tell thy lord, Behold, Elijah is here: ... tell your master, *NKJV*.

and he shall slay me: ... will kill me, *Darby* ... will put me to death, *BB*.

15. And Elijah said, As the LORD of hosts liveth, before whom I stand: ... Almighty lives, whom I serve, *NIV* ... of armies lives, *Beck*.

I will surely show myself unto him today: ... I will see him now!, *Fenton* ... present myself to Ahab, *NLT* ... swear that I shall show myself to him this day, *REB* ... surely today I appear unto him, *Young*.

16. So Obadiah went to meet Ahab, and told him: and Ahab went to meet Elijah: ... gave him the news, *BB* ... to inform Ahab, *Berkeley* ... gave him the message, *Knox* ... told him where Elijah was, *NCV*.

17. And it came to pass, when Ahab saw Elijah, that Ahab said unto him, Art thou he that troubleth Israel?: ... Is it you, you disturber of Israel?, *NAB* ... You ruin, *Moffatt* ... you scourge, *JB* ... Israel's trouble-maker?, *NLT*.

18. And he answered, I have not troubled Israel; but thou, and thy father's house: ... you and your father's family, *Beck*.

in that ye have forsaken the commandments of the LORD, and thou hast followed Baalim: ... and worshiping the idols of Baal, *Good News* ... because you have deserted Yahweh, *JB* ... of the EVER-LIVING, *Fenton* ... have followed the Baals, *NIV*.

19. Now therefore send, and gather to me all Israel unto mount Carmel: ... summon all Israel to meet me, *NEB*.

and the prophets of Baal four hundred and fifty, and the prophets of the groves four hundred, which eat at Jezebel's table: ... 400 prophets of Asherah who eat, *Beck* ... prophets of the Sacred Stem, *Rotherham* ... forest-shrines, that feed on Jezabel's bounty, *Knox* ... of the goddess Asherah, who are attached to Jezebel's household, *REB*.

prophets at the peril of his life? Why then send him on so dangerous a mission? To these agitated appeals Elijah answered by his customary oath, "As Yahweh of hosts liveth, before whom I stand, I will show myself unto him today." Then Obadiah went and told Ahab, and Ahab with impetuous haste hastened to meet Elijah, knowing that on him depended the fate of his kingdom.

18:17–19. Yet when they met he could not check the burst of anger which sprang to his lips.

"Is it thou, thou troubler of Israel?" he fiercely exclaimed. The phrase had already been applied to Achan (Josh. 7:25). Elijah was not the man to quail before the tyrannical reaction. "I have not troubled Israel," was the undaunted answer, "but thou and thy father's house." The cause of the drought was not the menace of Elijah, but the apostasy of Ahab. It was time that the fatal controversy should be decided. There must be an appeal to the people. Elijah was in a position to dictate, and dictate he did. "Let all Israel," he said, "be summoned to Mount Carmel"; and there he would singly meet in their presence the 450 prophets of Baal, and the 400 prophets of the Asherah, all of whom ate at Jezebel's table (meaning they were maintained at Jezebel's expense). Then and there a great challenge should take place, and the question should be settled forever, whether Baal or Yahweh was to be the national god of Israel. What challenge could be fairer, seeing that Baal was the sun god, the god of fire?

881, 3725, 3547	420, 2098	3890	881, 5204	1197	727	4109
do, *adj*, pn	prep, *n ms*	art, pn	cj, do, *n mp*	art, pn	num	num
אֶת־כָּל־יִשְׂרָאֵל	אֶל־הַר	הַכַּרְמֶל	וְאֶת־נְבִיאֵי	הַבַּעַל	אַרְבַּע	מֵאוֹת
'eth-kol-yisrā'ēl	'el-har	hakkarmel	we'eth-nevî'ê	habba'al	'arba'	mē'ōth
all of Israel	to Mount	the Carmel	and the prophets of	the Baal	four	hundreds

2675	5204	867	727	4109	404.152	8374
cj, num	cj, *n mp*	art, pn	num	num	*v Qal act ptc mp*	*n ms*
וַחֲמִשִּׁים	וּנְבִיאֵי	הָאֲשֵׁרָה	אַרְבַּע	מֵאוֹת	אֹכְלֵי	שֻׁלְחַן
wachmishshîm	ûnevî'ê	hā'ăshērāh	'arba'	mē'ōth	'ōkhelê	shulchan
and fifty	and the prophets of	Asherah	four	hundreds	those eating	the table of

350		8365.121	255	904, 3725, 1158	3547	7192.121
pn	**20.**	cj, v Qal impf 3ms	pn	prep, *adj*, *n mp*	pn	cj, v Qal impf 3ms
אִיזָבֶל		וַיִּשְׁלַח	אַחְאָב	בְּכָל־בְּנֵי	יִשְׂרָאֵל	וַיִּקְבֹּץ
'îzāvel		wayyishlach	'ach'āv	bekhol-benê	yisrā'ēl	wayyiqōbbōts
Jezebel		so he sent out	Ahab	among all the sons of	Israel	and he gathered

881, 5204	420, 2098	3890		5242.121	455	420, 3725, 6194
do, art, n mp	prep, *n ms*	art, pn	**21.**	cj, v Qal impf 3ms	pn	prep, *adj*, art, n ms
אֶת־הַנְּבִיאִים	אֶל־הַר	הַכַּרְמֶל		וַיִּגַּשׁ	אֵלִיָּהוּ	אֶל־כָּל־הָעָם
'eth-hannevî'îm	'el-har	hakkarmel		wayyiggash	'ēlîyāhû	'el-kol-hā'ām
the prophets	to Mount	the Carmel		and he came near	Elijah	to all the people

569.121	5912, 5146	894	6698.152	6142, 8692	5785	524, 3176	435
cj, v Qal impf 3ms	adv, intrg	pers pron	v Qal act ptc mp	prep, num	art, n fp	adv, pn	art, n mp
וַיֹּאמֶר	עַד־מָתַי	אַתֶּם	פֹּסְחִים	עַל־שְׁתֵּי	הַסְּעִפִּים	אִם־יְהוָה	הָאֱלֹהִים
wayyō'mer	'adh-māthay	'attem	pōsechîm	'al-shettê	hasse'ippîm	'im-yehwāh	hā'ĕlōhîm
and he said	until when	you	limping	beside two	the crutches	if Yahweh	God

2050.133	313	524, 1197	2050.133	313	3940, 6257.116
v Qal impv 2mp	prep, ps 3ms	cj, adv, art, pn	v Qal impv 2mp	prep, ps 3ms	cj, neg part, v Qal pf 3cp
לְכוּ	אַחֲרָיו	וְאִם־הַבַּעַל	לְכוּ	אַחֲרָיו	וְלֹא־עָנוּ
lekhû	'achrâv	we'im-habba'al	lekhû	'achrâv	welō'-'ānû
walk	after Him	or if the Baal	walk	after him	but they did not answer

6194	881	1745		569.121	455	420, 6194	603
art, n ms	do, ps 3ms	n ms	**22.**	cj, v Qal impf 3ms	pn	prep, art, n ms	pers pron
הָעָם	אֹתוֹ	דָּבָר		וַיֹּאמֶר	אֵלִיָּהוּ	אֶל־הָעָם	אֲנִי
hā'ām	'ōthô	dāvār		wayyō'mer	'ēlîyāhû	'el-hā'ām	'ănî
the people	him	a word		and he said	Elijah	to the people	I

3613.215	5204	3937, 3176	3937, 940	5204	1197	727, 4109
v Niphal pf 1cs	n ms	prep, pn	prep, n ms, ps 1cs	cj, *n mp*	art, pn	num, num
נוֹתַרְתִּי	נָבִיא	לַיהוָה	לְבַדִּי	וּנְבִיאֵי	הַבַּעַל	אַרְבַּע־מֵאוֹת
nôthartî	nāvî'	layhwāh	levaddî	ûnevî'ê	habba'al	'arba'-mē'ōth
I am remaining	a prophet	to Yahweh	by myself	and the prophets of	the Baal	four hundreds

2675	382		5598.126, 3937	8530	6749	1013.126
cj, num	n ms	**23.**	cj, v Qal juss 3mp, prep, ps 1cp	num	n mp	cj, v Qal juss 3mp
וַחֲמִשִּׁים	אִישׁ		וְיִתְּנוּ־לָנוּ	שְׁנַיִם	פָּרִים	וְיִבְחֲרוּ
wachmishshîm	'îsh		weyittenû-lānû	shenayim	pārîm	weyivchărû
and fifty	men		now let them give to us	two	young bulls	and let them choose

3937	6749	259	5591.326	7947.126
prep, ps 3mp	art, n ms	art, num	cj, v Piel juss 3mp, ps 3ms	cj, v Qal juss 3mp
לָהֶם	הַפָּר	הָאֶחָד	וִינַתְּחֻהוּ	וְיָשִׂימוּ
lāhem	happār	hā'echādh	wînattechuhû	weyāsîmû
for themselves	the young bull	the one	and let them cut it into pieces	and let them place

6142, 6320	813	3940	7947.126	603	6449.125	881, 6749
prep, art, n mp	cj, n ms	neg part	v Qal impf 3mp	cj, pers pron	v Qal impf 1cs	do, art, n ms
עַל־הָעֵצִים	וְאֵשׁ	לֹא	יָשִׂימוּ	וַאֲנִי	אֶעֱשֶׂה	אֶת־הַפָּר
'al-hā'ētsîm	we'ēsh	lō'	yāsîmû	wa'ănî	'e'ĕseh	'eth-happār
on the wood	but a fire	not	they will place	and I	I will prepare	the young bull

259	5598.115	6142, 6320	813	3940	7947.125		7410.117
art, num	cj, v Qal pf 1cs	prep, art, n mp	cj, n ms	neg part	v Qal impf 1cs	**24.**	cj, v Qal pf 2mp
הָאֶחָד	וְנָתַתִּי	עַל־הָעֵצִים	וְאֵשׁ	לֹא	אָשִׂים		וּקְרָאתֶם
hā'echādh	wenāthattî	'al-hā'ētsîm	we'ēsh	lō'	'āsîm		ûqŏrā'them
the other	and I will put	on the wood	but a fire	not	I will place		then you will call

20. So Ahab sent unto all the children of Israel, and gathered the prophets together unto mount Carmel: ... message among all the sons, *NASB* ... called all the Israelites, *NCV* ... throughout the length and breadth, *REB* ... summoned all the people, *NLT*.

21. And Elijah came unto all the people, and said, How long halt ye between two opinions?: ... go limping with two different, *RSV* ... do you mean to hobble first on one leg then on the other?, *JB* ... hesitate, *KJVII* ... waver, *NLT*.

if the Lord be God, follow him: but if Baal, then follow him: ... is the true God, *NCV* ... the Lord is God, worship him, *Good News*.

And the people answered him not a word: ... said nothing, *NIV* ... Not a word did they answer, *REB* ... did not answer, *NAB*.

22. Then said Elijah unto the people, I, even I only, remain a prophet of the Lord; but Baal's prophets are four hundred and fifty men: ... I am the only ... who is left, *NLT* ... am left as a prophet of Yahweh, *JB* ... of the Lord's prophets, *Tyndale*.

23. Let them therefore give us two bullocks: ... Let two bulls be given to us, *RSV* ... give us two oxen, *NASB*.

and let them choose one bullock for themselves, and cut it in pieces, and lay it on wood, and put no fire under: ... without setting fire to it, *REB* ... let them put the meat, *NCV* ... chop it up, laying the pieces, *Moffatt*.

and I will dress the other bullock, and lay it on wood, and put no fire under: ... in my turn shall prepare the other bull, *JB* ... set it on firewood still unkindled, *Knox* ... shall start no fire, *NAB*.

24. And call ye on the name of your gods, and I will call on the name of the Lord: ... You shall invoke your god by name, *NEB*.

18:20–21. Perhaps it never occurred to Ahab to refuse the challenge, or to arrest the hated messenger. The vast assembly was gathered by royal proclamation. There could have been no scene in the land of Israel more strikingly suitable for the purpose than Mount Carmel. It is a ridge of upper oolite, or Jura limestone, which at the eastern extremity rises more than 1600 feet above the sea, sinking down to 600 feet at the western extremity. The prophet speaks of the "excellency of Carmel" (Isa. 33:9; 35:2; Mic. 7:14). Its beauty and fruitfulness are also alluded to (Jer. 46:18; 50:19; Amos 1:2; 9:3; Nah. 1:4; S.S. 7:5).

Here, at early dawn, the prophet of Yahweh, in his solitary grandeur, met the 450 idolatrous priests and their rabble of attendant fanatics in the presence of the half-curious king and the half apostate people. He presented the oft-repeated type of God's servant alone against the world. Megiddo lies in the plain below, and this scene of conflict between good and the powers of evil was an anticipated Armageddon. Most rarely is it otherwise. They who speak smooth things and prophesy deceits may always live at ease in amicable compromise with the world, the flesh and the devil. But the prophet has ever to set his face as a flint against tyrants, mobs, and false prophets intriguing priests, and all who daub tottering walls with untempered mortar, and all who, in days smooth and perilous, softly murmur, "Peace, peace," when there is no peace.

Elijah's first challenge was to the people. "How long," he asked, "do ye totter between two opinions? (1 Ki. 18:21). If Yahweh be God, follow Him; but if Baal, follow him."

Awestruck and ashamed, the multitude kept unbroken silence. Doubtless, it was, in part, the silence of guilt. They knew that they had followed Jezebel into the cruelties of Baal worship and the forbidden lusts by which the land was polluted with the temples of the Asherah.

18:22–26. Receiving no answer to his stern question, Elijah laid down the conditions of the contest. "The prophets of Baal," he said, "are four hun-

904, 8428	435	603	7410.125	904, 8428, 3176	2030.111	435
prep, *n ms*	n mp, ps 2mp	cj, pers pron	v Qal impf 1cs	prep, *n ms*, pn	cj, v Qal pf 3ms	art, n mp
בְּשֵׁם	אֱלֹהֵיכֶם	וַאֲנִי	אֶקְרָא	בְשֵׁם־יְהוָה	וְהָיָה	הָאֱלֹהִים
beshēm	'ĕlōhêkhem	wa'ănî	'eqōrā'	veshēm-yehwāh	wehāyāh	hā'ĕlōhîm
on the name of	your gods	then I	I will call	on the name of Yahweh	and it will be	the God

866, 6257.121	904, 813	2000	435	6257.121	3725, 6194
rel part, v Qal impf 3ms	prep, art, n fs	pers pron	art, n mp	cj, v Qal impf 3ms	*adj*, art, n ms
אֲשֶׁר־יַעֲנֶה	בָאֵשׁ	הוּא	הָאֱלֹהִים	וַיַּעַן	כָּל־הָעָם
'ăsher-ya'ăneh	vā'ēsh	hû'	hā'ĕlōhîm	wayya'an	kol-hā'ām
Who he answers	with the fire	He	the God	and they answered	all the people

569.126	3005	1745	25. 569.121	455	3937, 5204	1197
cj, v Qal impf 3mp	adj	art, n ms	cj, v Qal impf 3ms	pn	prep, *n mp*	art, pn
וַיֹּאמְרוּ	טוֹב	הַדָּבָר	וַיֹּאמֶר	אֵלִיָּהוּ	לִנְבִיאֵי	הַבַּעַל
wayyō'merû	ṭôv	haddāvār	wayyō'mer	'ēlîyāhû	linvî'ê	habba'al
and they said	good	the thing	and he said	Elijah	to the prophets of	the Baal

1013.133	3937	6749	259	6449.133	7518	3706
v Qal impv 2mp	prep, ps 2mp	art, n ms	art, num	cj, v Qal impv 2mp	adv	cj
בַּחֲרוּ	לָכֶם	הַפָּר	הָאֶחָד	וַעֲשׂוּ	רִאשֹׁנָה	כִּי
bachrû	lākhem	happār	hā'echādh	wa'ăsû	ri'shōnāh	kî
choose	for yourselves	the young bull	the one	and prepare	first	because

894	7521	7410.133	904, 8428	435	813	3940	7947.128
pers pron	art, adj	cj, v Qal impv 2mp	prep, n ms	n mp, ps 2mp	cj, n ms	neg part	v Qal impf 2mp
אַתֶּם	הָרַבִּים	וְקִרְאוּ	בְּשֵׁם	אֱלֹהֵיכֶם	וְאֵשׁ	לֹא	תָשִׂימוּ
'attem	hārabbîm	weqir'û	beshēm	'ĕlōhêkhem	we'ēsh	lō'	thāsîmû
you	the many	and call	by name	your gods	but a fire	not	you will place

26. 4089.126	881, 6749	866, 5598.111	3937	6449.126
cj, v Qal impf 3mp	do, art, n ms	rel part, v Qal pf 3ms	prep, ps 3mp	cj, v Qal impf 3mp
וַיִּקְחוּ	אֶת־הַפָּר	אֲשֶׁר־נָתַן	לָהֶם	וַיַּעֲשׂוּ
wayyiqŏchû	'eth-happār	'ăsher-nāthan	lāhem	wayya'ăsû
and they took	the young bull	which he had given	to them	and they prepared

7410.126	904, 8428, 1197	4623, 1269	5912, 6937	3937, 569.141
cj, v Qal impf 3mp	prep, *n ms*, art, pn	prep, art, n ms	cj, adv, art, n md	prep, v Qal inf con
וַיִּקְרְאוּ	בְשֵׁם־הַבַּעַל	מֵהַבֹּקֶר	וְעַד־הַצָּהֳרַיִם	לֵאמֹר
wayyiqŏr'û	veshēm-habba'al	mēhabbōqer	we'adh-hatstsāherayim	lē'mōr
and they called	upon the name of the Baal	from the morning	and until the noontime	saying

1197	6257.131	375	7249	375	6257.151
art, pn	v Qal impv 2ms, ps 1cp	cj, *sub*	n ms	cj, *sub*	v Qal act ptc ms
הַבַּעַל	עֲנֵנוּ	וְאֵין	קוֹל	וְאֵין	עֹנֶה
habba'al	'ănēnû	we'ên	qôl	we'ên	'ōneh
the Baal	answer us	but there was not	a voice	and there was not	answering

6698.326	6142, 4326	866	6449.111	27. 2030.121	904, 6937
cj, v Piel impf 3mp	prep, art, n ms	rel part	v Qal pf 3ms	cj, v Qal impf 3ms	prep, art, n md
וַיְפַסְּחוּ	עַל־הַמִּזְבֵּחַ	אֲשֶׁר	עָשָׂה	וַיְהִי	בַצָּהֳרַיִם
wayphassechû	'al-hammizbēach	'ăsher	'āsāh	wayhî	vatstsāherayim
and they limped	beside the altar	which	they had made	and it was	when the noontime

2130.321	904	455	569.121	7410.131	904, 7249, 1448	3706, 435
cj, v Piel impf 3ms	prep, ps 3mp	pn	cj, v Qal impf 3ms	v Qal impv 2ms	prep, n ms, adj	cj, n mp
וַיְהַתֵּל	בָּהֶם	אֵלִיָּהוּ	וַיֹּאמֶר	קִרְאוּ	בְקוֹל־גָּדוֹל	כִּי־אֱלֹהִים
wayhattēl	bāhem	'ēlîyāhû	wayyō'mer	qir'û	veqôl-gādhôl	kî-'ĕlōhîm
that he mocked	with them	Elijah	and he said	call	with a great voice	because God

and the God that answereth by fire, let him be God: ... who answers by setting fire to the wood is the true God!, *NLT*.

And all the people answered and said, It is well spoken: ... What you say is good, *NIV* ... a good idea, *Fenton* ... The word is good, *Darby* ... a fair test!, *Goodspeed* ... The plan is excellent, *Berkeley*.

25. And Elijah said unto the prophets of Baal, Choose you one bullock for yourselves, and dress it first: ... offer it first, *REB* ... one ox for yourselves and prepare, *NASB*.

for ye are many; and call on the name of your gods, but put no fire under: ... pray to your god, but don't start the fire, *NCV* ... set fire to the wood, *Good News* ... because you are many, *Beck*.

26. And they took the bullock which was given them, and they dressed it: ... ox ... and they prepared it, *NASB* ... and made ready, *Rotherham* ... bull provided for them and offered it, *REB* ... one of the bulls and placed it on the altar, *NLT*.

and called on the name of Baal from morning even until noon, saying, O Baal, hear us: ... they invoked Baal by name from morning, *NEB* ... called to Baal from morn to midday, crying, Baal, answer, *Moffatt* ... and prayed to Baal until noon, *Good News*.

But there was no voice, nor any that answered. And they leaped upon the altar which was made: ... dance as they would on the altar they had built there, *Knox* ... in halting wise about the altar, *MAST* ... performed their hobbling dance, *JB* ... jumping up and down before the altar, *BB*.

27. And it came to pass at noon, that Elijah mocked them, and said: ... playeth on them, and saith, *Young* ... About noon Elijah began to taunt, *Berkeley* ... to make fun of them, *NCV* ... Elias jested at them, saying, *Douay*.

Cry aloud: for he is a god: ... Call with a loud voice, *Young* ... Pray louder, *NCV* ... Cry with a louder voice, *Douay*.

either he is talking, or he is pursuing, or he is in a journey, or peradventure he sleepeth, and must be awaked: ... meditating, or he has wandered away, *NRSV* ... musing, or he is gone aside, *ASV* ... Perhaps he's thinking! Or is busy; or he has gone away!, *Beck*.

28. And they cried aloud, and cut themselves after their manner with knives and lancets, till the blood gushed out upon them: ... as was their custom, gashed themselves with swords and spears until the blood ran, *NEB* ... prophets prayed louder and cut themselves with

---

dred and fifty: I stand alone as a prophet of Yahweh. Let two bullocks be provided for us; they shall slay and dress one, and lay it on wood, but (for there shall be no priestly trickeries today) they shall put no fire under. I, though I be no priest, will slay and dress the other, and lay it on wood, and put no fire under. Then let all of you, Baal priests and people if you will, cry to your idols; I will call on the name of Yahweh. The god that answereth by fire let him be God."

No challenge could be fairer, for what god could be more likely to answer by fire from that blazing sky? The deep murmur of the people expressed their assent. They chose, and slew, and dressed their victim. From morning till noon, many of them with wildly waving arms, others with their foreheads in the dust; they upraised the wild chant of their monotonous invocation, "Baal, hear us! Baal, hear us!" In vain the cry rose and fell, now uttered in soft appealing murmurs, now rising into passionate entreaties. All was silent. There lay the dead bullock. No consuming lightning fell, even when the sun flamed in the zenith of that cloudless sky. There was no voice nor any that answered.

Then they tried still more potent incantations. They began to circle round the altar they had made in one of their solemn dances to the shrill strains of pipe and flute. The rhythmic movements ended in giddy whirls and orgiastic leapings which were a common feature of sensuous heathen worship; dances in which, like modern dervishes, they bounded and yelled and spun round and round till they fell foaming and senseless to the ground. Herodian (*Hist*., v. 3) describes the dance of Heliogabalus round the altar of the Emesene Sun-god, and Apuleius describes at length the fanatic leapings and gashings of the execrable Galli—the eunuch beggar priests of the Syrian goddess. They flew wildly, turning round in circles, so that the loose flowing hair drug through the mire. They first bit themselves on the arm, and they cut themselves with two-edged swords. Then begins a new scene. One of them who surpassed all the rest in frenzy, began to prophesy with sighs and groans. Openly accusing himself of past sins, he wished to punish by the mortifying of the flesh. The people looked on expectantly, but it was all in vain.

18:27–29. Until now, the prophet had remained silent, but when noon came, and still no fire descended, he mocked them. Now was their time!

2000	3706	7945	3706, 7940	3937	3706, 1932
pers pron	cj	n ms	cj, cj, n ms	prep, ps 3ms	cj, cj, n ms
הוּא	כִּי	שִׂיחַ	וְכִי־שִׂיג	לוֹ	וְכִי־דֶרֶךְ
hû'	kî	sîach	wekhî-sîgh	lô	wekhî-dherekh
He	because	a conversation	or because defecation	to him	or because a journey

3937	193	3585	2000	3477		7410.126	904, 7249
prep, ps 3ms	adv	adj	pers pron	cj, v Qal impf 3ms	**28.**	cj, v Qal impf 3mp	prep, n ms
לוֹ	אוּלַי	יָשֵׁן	הוּא	וְיִקָץ		וַיִּקְרְאוּ	בְּקוֹל
lô	'ûlay	yāshēn	hû'	weyiqāts		wayyiqŏr'û	beqôl
to him	perhaps	sleeping	he	but he will wake up		and they called	with a voice

1448	1443.726	3626, 5122	904, 2820	904, 7709
adj	cj, v Hithpoel impf 3mp	prep, n ms, ps 3mp	prep, n fp	cj, prep, art, n mp
גָּדוֹל	וַיִּתְגֹּדְדוּ	כְּמִשְׁפָּטָם	בַּחֲרָבוֹת	וּבָרְמָחִים
gādhôl	wayyithgōdhedhû	kemishpāṭām	bachrāvôth	ûvāremāchîm
great	and they cut themselves	according to their ordinances	with the knives	and with the lances

5912, 8581.141, 1879	6142		2030.121	3626, 5882.141	6937
adv, v Qal inf con, n ms	prep, ps 3mp	**29.**	cj, v Qal impf 3ms	prep, v Qal inf con	art, n md
עַד־שְׁפָךְ־דָּם	עֲלֵיהֶם		וַיְהִי	כַּעֲבֹר	הַצָּהֳרַיִם
'adh-shephākh-dām	'ălêhem		wayhî	ka'ăvōr	hatstsāherayim
until blood gushing out	on them		and it was	when passing	the noontime

5187.726	5912	3937, 6148.141	4647	375, 7249
cj, v Hithpael impf 3mp	adv	prep, v Qal inf con	art, n fs	cj, *sub*, n ms
וַיִּתְנַבְּאוּ	עַד	לַעֲלוֹת	הַמִּנְחָה	וְאֵין־קוֹל
wayyithnabbe'û	'adh	la'ălôth	hamminchāh	we'ên-qôl
then they uttered sayings	until	the going up of	the offering	but there was not a voice

375, 6257.151	375	7478		569.121	455
cj, *sub*, v Qal act ptc ms	cj, *sub*	n ms	**30.**	cj, v Qal impf 3ms	pn
וְאֵין־עֹנֶה	וְאֵין	קָשֶׁב		וַיֹּאמֶר	אֵלִיָּהוּ
we'ên-'ōneh	we'ên	qāshev		wayyō'mer	'ēlîyāhû
neither was there answering	and there was not	attention		and he said	Elijah

3937, 3725, 6194	5242.133	420	5242.126	3725, 6194	420
prep, *adj*, art, n ms	v Qal impv 2mp	prep, ps 1cs	cj, v Qal impf 3mp	*adj*, art, n ms	prep, ps 3ms
לְכָל־הָעָם	גְּשׁוּ	אֵלַי	וַיִּגְּשׁוּ	כָל־הָעָם	אֵלָיו
lekhol-hā'ām	geshû	'ēlay	wayyiggeshû	khol-hā'ām	'ēlâv
to all the people	come near	to me	and they drew near	all the people	to him

7784.321	881, 4326	3176	2117.155		4089.121	455
cj, v Piel impf 3ms	do, *n ms*	pn	art, v Qal pass ptc ms	**31.**	cj, v Qal impf 3ms	pn
וַיְרַפֵּא	אֶת־מִזְבַּח	יְהוָה	הֶהָרוּס		וַיִּקַּח	אֵלִיָּהוּ
wayrappē'	'eth-mizbach	yehwāh	hehārûs		wayyiqqach	'ēlîyāhû
and he repaired	the altar of	Yahweh	the one broken down		and he took	Elijah

8692	6462	63	3626, 4709	8101	1158, 3399	866
num	num	n fp	prep, *n ms*	*n mp*	*n mp*, pn	rel pron
שְׁתֵּים	עֶשְׂרֵה	אֲבָנִים	כְּמִסְפַּר	שִׁבְטֵי	בְנֵי־יַעֲקֹב	אֲשֶׁר
shettêm	'esrēh	'ăvānîm	kemispar	shivṭê	venê-ya'ăqōv	'ăsher
two	ten	stones	according to the number of	the tribes of	the sons of Jacob	who

2030.111	1745, 3176	420	3937, 569.141	3547	2030.121	8428
v Qal pf 3ms	*n ms*, pn	prep, ps 3ms	prep, v Qal inf con	pn	v Qal impf 3ms	n ms, ps 2ms
הָיָה	דְבַר־יְהוָה	אֵלָיו	לֵאמֹר	יִשְׂרָאֵל	יִהְיֶה	שְׁמֶךָ
hāyāh	dhevar-yehwāh	'ēlâv	lē'mōr	yisrā'ēl	yihyeh	shemekhā
it was	the word of Yahweh	to him	saying	Israel	it will be	your name

32.	1161.121 cj, v Qal impf 3ms וַיִּבְנֶה wayyivneh and he built	882, 63 do, art, n fp אֶת־הָאֲבָנִים 'eth-hā'ăvānîm with the stones	4326 n ms מִזְבֵּחַ mizbēach an altar	904, 8428 prep, *n ms* בְּשֵׁם beshēm in the name of	3176 pn יְהוָה yehwāh Yahweh	6449.121 cj, v Qal impf 3ms וַיַּעַשׂ wayya'as and he made	8916 n fs תְּעָלָה te'ālāh a trench

3626, 1041 prep, *n ms* כְּבֵית kevêth like housing for	5613 n fd סָאתַיִם sā'thayim two seahs	2320 n ms זֶרַע zera' seed	5623 adv סָבִיב sāvîv all around	3937, 4326 prep, art, n ms לַמִּזְבֵּחַ lammizbēach to the altar	**33.**	6424.121 cj, v Qal impf 3ms וַיַּעֲרֹךְ wayya'ărōkh and he arranged	881, 6320 do, art, n mp אֶת־הָעֵצִים 'eth-hā'ētsîm the wood

knives and daggers, according to their ritual, *Good News*.

29. And it came to pass, when midday was past, and they prophesied until the time of the offering of the evening sacrifice: ... they raved until the time, *NASB* ... ranted on until the time when the offering is presented, *JB* ... they worked themselves into a prophetic frenzy until the offering of the oblation, *Goodspeed* ... pretended to be prophets, *KJVII*.

that there was neither voice, nor any to answer, nor any that regarded: ... not a sound came, there was no one to answer them, no one to heed them, *Moffatt* ... paid attention, *NKJV* ... still there was no reply, *NLT* ... no one was listening, *NAB*.

30. And Elijah said unto all the people, Come near unto me. And all the people came near unto him: ... Come nigh ... came nigh unto him, *Young* ... drew near, *Rotherham* ... they gathered around him, *NCV*.

And he repaired the altar of the Lord that was broken down: ... had been thrown down, *NRSV* ... rebuilt the LORD's altar that was torn, *Beck* ... mended, *Tyndale* ... which was in ruins, *NIV*.

31. And Elijah took twelve stones, according to the number of the tribes of the sons of Jacob, unto whom the word of the Lord came: ... one to represent each of the tribes of Israel, *NLT* ... corresponding to the number, *Berkeley* ... of the clans, *Moffatt*.

saying, Israel shall be thy name: ... Your name shall be Israel, *Fenton* ... who was named Israel by the word of the Lord, *REB* ... The Lord changed Jacob's name to Israel, *NCV*.

32. And with the stones he built an altar in the name of the Lord: ... of Yahweh, *Rotherham* ... He erected, *Berkeley* ... in honor of the Lord, *NAB*.

and he made a trench about the altar, as great as would contain two measures of seed: ... large enough to hold about three gallons, *NLT* ... of the breadth of two furrows, *Douay* ... the capacity of two homers, *Goodspeed* ... about four gallons of water, *Good News* ... about the space of eighteen hundred square yards, *Moffatt*.

33. And he put the wood in order, and cut the bullock in pieces, and laid him on the wood: ... cutting up the ox, put it, *BB* ... arranged the wood, dismembered the bull, *JB*.

They had been crying for six long hours in their vain repetitions and incantations. Surely they had not shouted loud enough! Baal was a god; some strange accident must have prevented him from hearing the prayer of his miserable priests. Perhaps he was in deep meditation, so that he did not notice those frantic appeals; perhaps he was too busy talking to someone else (v. 27; Others render it "meditating" [De Wette Thenius] or "peevish" [Bahr]. Comp. Hom., Il., 1:423; Od., 1:22, etc.) or was on a journey somewhere; or was asleep and needed to be awakened ; or, he continued with yet more biting sarcasm, and in a scoffing that would have sounded coarse to modern ears, perhaps he had gone aside for a private purpose to relieve himself. He must be called; he must be aroused; he must be made to hear. This instance of grim sarcastic humor is not unique in Scripture.

Such taunts, addressed to this multitude of priests in the hearing of the people, whom they desired to dupe or to convince, drove them to fiercer frenzy. Already the setting sun began to warn them that their hour was past, and failure imminent. They would not succumb without trying the darker sorceries of blood and self-mutilation, which were only resorted to at the most dread extremities. With renewed and redoubled yells, they offered the blood of human sacrifice on their altar, stabbing and gashing themselves with swords and lances, till they became a horrid spectacle. Their clothing and their naked bodies were smeared with gore.

18:30–35. Then Elijah told the sullen and baffled fanatics to stand aside, and he summoned the people to gather around him. There was nothing tumultuous or orgiastic in his proceedings. In strik-

5591.321	881, 6749	7947.121	6142, 6320	569.121	4527.133
cj, v Piel impf 3ms	do, art, n ms	cj, v Qal impf 3ms	prep, art, n mp	cj, v Qal impf 3ms	v Qal impv 2mp
וַיְנַתַּח	אֶת־הַפָּר	וַיָּשֶׂם	עַל־הָעֵצִים	וַיֹּאמֶר	מִלְאוּ
waynattach	'eth-happār	wayyāsem	'al-hā'ētsîm	wayyō'mer	mil'û
and he cut into pieces	the young bull	and he put	on the wood	and he said	fill

727	3656	4448	3441.133	6142, 6150	6142, 6320
num	n mp	n md	cj, v Qal impv 2mp	prep, art, n fs	cj, prep, art, n mp
אַרְבָּעָה	כַדִּים	מַיִם	וְיִצְקוּ	עַל־הָעֹלָה	וְעַל־הָעֵצִים
'arbā'āh	khaddîm	mayim	weyitsqû	'al-hā'ōlāh	we'al-hā'ētsîm
four	jars	water	and pour out	on the burnt offering	and on the wood

	569.121	8521.133	8521.126	569.121	8420.133
34.	cj, v Qal impf 3ms	v Qal impv 2mp	cj, v Qal impf 3mp	cj, v Qal impf 3ms	v Qal impv 2mp
	וַיֹּאמֶר	שְׁנוּ	וַיִּשְׁנוּ	וַיֹּאמֶר	שַׁלֵּשׁוּ
	wayyō'mer	shenû	wayyishnû	wayyō'mer	shallēshû
	and he said	do a second time	and they did a second time	and he said	do a third time

8420.126		2050.126	4448	5623	3937, 4326	1612
cj, v Qal impf 3mp	**35.**	cj, v Qal impf 3mp	art, n md	adv	prep, art, n ms	cj, cj
וַיְשַׁלֵּשׁוּ		וַיֵּלְכוּ	הַמַּיִם	סָבִיב	לַמִּזְבֵּחַ	וְגַם
wayshallēshû		wayyēlekhû	hammayim	sāvîv	lammizbēach	wegham
and they did a third time		and it went	the waters	all around	the altar	and also

881, 8916	4527.311, 4448		2030.121	904, 6148.141	4647
do, art, n fs	v Piel pf 3ms, n mp	**36.**	cj, v Qal impf 3ms	prep, v Qal inf con	art, n fs
אֶת־הַתְּעָלָה	מִלֵּא־מָיִם		וַיְהִי	בַּעֲלוֹת	הַמִּנְחָה
'eth-hatte'ālāh	millē'-māyim		wayhî	ba'ălôth	hamminchāh
the trench	it was full of water		and it was	when the going up of	the offering

5242.121	455	5204	569.121	3176	435	80	3437
cj, v Qal impf 3ms	pn	art, n ms	cj, v Qal impf 3ms	pn	*n mp*	pn	pn
וַיִּגַּשׁ	אֵלִיָּהוּ	הַנָּבִיא	וַיֹּאמַר	יְהוָה	אֱלֹהֵי	אַבְרָהָם	יִצְחָק
wayyiggash	'ēlîyāhû	hannāvî'	wayyō'mar	yehwāh	'ĕlōhê	'avrāhām	yitschāq
that he came near	Elijah	the prophet	and he said	Yahweh	the God of	Abraham	Isaac

3547	3219	3156.221	3706, 887	435	904, 3547	603	5860
cj, pn	art, n ms	v Niphal juss 3ms	cj, pers pron	n mp	prep, pn	cj, pers pron	n ms, ps 2ms
וְיִשְׂרָאֵל	הַיּוֹם	יִוָּדַע	כִּי־אַתָּה	אֱלֹהִים	בְּיִשְׂרָאֵל	וַאֲנִי	עַבְדֶּךָ
weyisrā'ēl	hayyôm	yiwwādha'	kî-'attāh	'ĕlōhîm	beyisrā'ēl	wa'ănî	'avdekhā
and Israel	today	may it be known	that You	God	in Israel	and I	your servant

904, 1745	6449.115	881	3725, 1745	431		6257.131
cj, prep, n mp, ps 2ms	v Qal pf 1cs	do	*adj*, art, n mp	art, dem pron	**37.**	v Qal impv 2ms, ps 1cs
וּבִדְבָרֶיךָ	עָשִׂיתִי	אֵת	כָּל־הַדְּבָרִים	הָאֵלֶּה		עֲנֵנִי
ûvedhivrêkhā	'āsîthî	'ēth	kol-haddevārîm	hā'ēlleh		'ănēnî
and by your words	I did		all the things	the these		answer me

3176	6257.131	3156.126	6194	2172	3706, 887	3176
pn	v Qal impv 2ms, ps 1cs	cj, v Qal juss 3mp	art, n ms	art, dem pron	cj, pers pron	pn
יְהוָה	עֲנֵנִי	וְיֵדְעוּ	הָעָם	הַזֶּה	כִּי־אַתָּה	יְהוָה
yehwāh	'ănēnî	weyēdhe'û	hā'ām	hazzeh	kî-'attāh	yehwāh
O Yahweh	answer me	that they may know	the people	the this	that You	Yahweh

435	887	5621.513	881, 3949	315
art, n mp	cj, pers pron	v Hiphil pf 2ms	do, n ms, ps 3mp	adv
הָאֱלֹהִים	וְאַתָּה	הֲסִבֹּתָ	אֶת־לִבָּם	אֲחֹרַנִּית
hā'ĕlōhîm	we'attāh	hesibbōthā	'eth-libbām	'ăchōranîth
God	and You	you have caused to change direction	their hearts	backward

38.	5489.122 cj, v Qal impf 3fs וַתִּפֹּל wattippōl and it fell	813, 3176 n fs, pn אֵשׁ־יְהוָה 'ēsh-yehwāh the fire of Yahweh	404.122 cj, v Qal impf 3fs וַתֹּאכַל wattō'khal and it devoured	881, 6150 do, art, n fs אֶת־הָעֹלָה 'eth-hā'ōlāh the burnt offering	881, 6320 cj, do, art, n mp וְאֶת־הָעֵצִים we'eth-hā'ētsîm and the wood
	881, 63 cj, do, art, n fp וְאֶת־הָאֲבָנִים we'eth-hā'ăvānîm and the stones	881, 6312 cj, do, art, n ms וְאֶת־הֶעָפָר we'eth-he'āphār and the dust	881, 4448 cj, do, art, n md וְאֶת־הַמַּיִם we'eth-hammayim and the water	866, 8916 rel part, prep, n fs אֲשֶׁר־בַּתְּעָלָה 'ăsher-batte'ālāh which in the trench	4031.312 v Piel pf 3fs לִחֵכָה lichēkhāh it licked up

and said, Fill four barrels with water, and pour it on the burnt sacrifice, and on the wood: ... four pitchers, *Darby* ... four buckets, *Douay* ... four jars ... the whole-offering, *REB* ... over the holocaust, *NAB* ... four waterpots, *NKJV*.

34. And he said, Do it the second time. And they did it the second time. And he said, Do it the third time. And they did it the third time: ... he ordered, and they did it, *NIV* ... Do it once more, *Good News* ... When they had poured it out, *Knox*.

35. And the water ran round about the altar; and he filled the trench also with water: ... trench overflowed to the Altar, *Fenton* ... water ran off the altar and filled the ditch, *NCV* ... the gutter was full of water also, *Tyndale*.

36. And it came to pass at the time of the offering of the evening sacrifice, that Elijah the prophet came near, and said, LORD God of Abraham, Isaac, and of Israel: ... At the hour of the regular sacrifice, *NEB* ... offering of the evening oblation, *ASV*.

let it be known this day that thou art God in Israel, and that I am thy servant: ... give proof this day, *Knox*.

and that I have done all these things at thy word: ... at your bidding, *NRSV* ... by your command, *NAB*.

37. Hear me, O LORD, hear me, that this people may know that thou art the LORD God, and that thou hast turned their heart back again: ... You turn their hearts back to You, *Beck* ... are winning back their hearts, *JB* ... will change their minds, *NCV* ... brought them back to yourself, *NLT*.

38. Then the fire of the LORD fell, and consumed the burnt sacrifice, and the wood, and the stones, and the dust: ... the Eternal's lightning fell, burning up the sacrifice, *Moffatt* ... came down, burning up the offering, *BB*.

and licked up the water that was in the trench: ... swallowing up the very water, *Knox* ... in the gutter, *Tyndale* ... dried up the water in the ditch, *NCV*.

ing contrast with the 450 frantic worshipers, he proceeded in the calmest and most deliberate way. First, in the name of Yahweh, he repaired the old altar, which Jezebel probably had broken down. He did this with twelve stones, one for each of the tribes of Israel. Then he dug a broad trench. Then, when he had prepared his bullock, in order to show the people the impossibility of any deception, such as were common among priests, he told them to drench it three times over with four barrels of water. The drought had been so intense that the water might have been sea water. But Josephus says it was drawn from the still existent spring (*Antiquities*, VIII:xiii:5). Either way, the water was difficult to obtain and hardly an easy commodity to spare. Lastly, at the time of the evening oblation, Elijah briefly offered up one prayer that Yahweh would make it known this day to his backsliding people that He, not Baal, was the God of Israel. He did not use much speaking; he did not adopt the devilish yells and dances and gashings which were abhorrent to God, though they appealed so powerfully to the sensuous imaginations of the multitude. He only raised his eyes to heaven and cried aloud in the hush of expectant stillness.

"Yahweh, God of Abraham, of Isaac, and of Israel,
Let it be known this day that Thou art God in Israel,
And that I am thy servant,
And that I have done all these things at Thy word.
Hear me, Yahweh, hear me.
That this people may know that Thou,
Yahweh, art God,
And that Thou hast turned their heart back again."

18:36–40. The prayer, with its triple invocation of Yahweh's name, and its seven rhythmic lines, was no sooner ended than down streamed the lightning and consumed the bullock and the wood

	7495.121	3725, 6194	5489.126	6142, 6686	569.126	3176
	cj, v Qal impf 3ms	*adj*, art, n ms	cj, v Qal impf 3mp	prep, n mp, ps 3mp	cj, v Qal impf 3mp	pn
39.	וַיַּרְא	כָּל־הָעָם	וַיִּפְּלוּ	עַל־פְּנֵיהֶם	וַיֹּאמְרוּ	יְהוָה
	wayyare'	kol-hā'ām	wayyippelû	'al-penêhem	wayyō'merû	yehwāh
	and they saw	all the people	and they fell	on their faces	and they said	Yahweh

2000	435	3176	2000	435		569.121	455	3937
pers pron	art, n mp	pn	pers pron	art, n mp		cj, v Qal impf 3ms	pn	prep, ps 3mp
הוּא	הָאֱלֹהִים	יְהוָה	הוּא	הָאֱלֹהִים	**40.**	וַיֹּאמֶר	אֵלִיָּהוּ	לָהֶם
hû'	hā'ĕlōhîm	yehwāh	hû'	hā'ĕlōhîm		wayyō'mer	'ēlîyāhû	lāhem
He	God	Yahweh	He	God		and he said	Elijah	to them

8945.133	881, 5204	1197	382	414, 4561.221	4623
v Qal impv 2mp	do, *n mp*	art, pn	n ms	adv, v Niphal juss 3ms	prep, ps 3mp
תִּפְשׂוּ	אֶת־נְבִיאֵי	הַבַּעַל	אִישׁ	אַל־יִמָּלֵט	מֵהֶם
tiphsû	'eth-nevî'ê	habba'al	'îsh	'al-yimmālēṯ	mēhem
seize	the prophets of	the Baal	each one	do not allow them to escape	among them

8945.126	3495.521	455	420, 5337	7312
cj, v Qal impf 3mp, ps 3mp	cj, v Hiphil impf 3ms, ps 3mp	pn	prep, *n ms*	pn
וַיִּתְפְּשׂוּם	וַיּוֹרִדֵם	אֵלִיָּהוּ	אֶל־נַחַל	קִישׁוֹן
wayyithpesûm	wayyôridhēm	'ēlîyāhû	'el-nachal	qîshôn
so they seized them	and he brought them down	Elijah	to the Brook	Kishon

8250.121	8427		569.121	455	3937, 255	6148.131
cj, v Qal impf 3ms, ps 3mp	adv		cj, v Qal impf 3ms	pn	prep, pn	v Qal impv 2ms
וַיִּשְׁחָטֵם	שָׁם	**41.**	וַיֹּאמֶר	אֵלִיָּהוּ	לְאַחְאָב	עֲלֵה
wayyishchāṭēm	shām		wayyō'mer	'ēlîyāhû	le'ach'āv	'ălēh
and he slaughtered them	there		and he said	Elijah	to Ahab	go up

404.131	8685.131	3706, 7249	2066	1700		6148.121
v Qal impv 2ms	cj, v Qal impv 2ms	cj, *n ms*	*n ms*	art, n ms		cj, v Qal impf 3ms
אֱכֹל	וּשְׁתֵה	כִּי־קוֹל	הֲמוֹן	הַגָּשֶׁם	**42.**	וַיַּעֲלֶה
'ĕkhōl	ûshethēh	kî-qôl	hămôn	haggāshem		wayya'ăleh
eat	and drink	because the sound of	the tumult of	the rain		and he went up

255	3937, 404.141	3937, 8685.141	455	6148.111	420, 7513	3890
pn	prep, v Qal inf con	cj, prep, v Qal inf con	cj, pn	v Qal pf 3ms	prep, *n ms*	art, pn
אַחְאָב	לֶאֱכֹל	וְלִשְׁתּוֹת	וְאֵלִיָּהוּ	עָלָה	אֶל־רֹאשׁ	הַכַּרְמֶל
'ach'āv	le'ĕkhōl	welishtôth	we'ēlîyāhû	'ālāh	'el-rō'sh	hakkarmel
Ahab	to eat	and to drink	and Elijah	he went up	to the top of	the Carmel

1487.121	800	7947.121	6686	1033	1314
cj, v Qal impf 3ms	n fs	cj, v Qal impf 3ms	n mp, ps 3ms	prep	n fs, ps 3ms
וַיִּגְהַר	אַרְצָה	וַיָּשֶׂם	פָּנָיו	בֵּין	בִּרְכָו
wayyighhar	'artsāh	wayyāsem	pānāv	bên	berākhô
and he bent down	to the earth	and he put	his face	between	his knees

	569.121	420, 5470	6148.131, 5167	5202.531	1932, 3328
	cj, v Qal impf 3ms	prep, n ms, ps 3ms	v Qal impv 2ms, part	v Hiphil impv 2ms	*n ms*, n ms
43.	וַיֹּאמֶר	אֶל־נַעֲרוֹ	עֲלֵה־נָא	הַבֵּט	דֶּרֶךְ־יָם
	wayyō'mer	'el-na'ărô	'ălēh-nā'	habbēṭ	derekh-yām
	and he said	to his servant	go up please	look at	the way of the sea

6148.121	5202.521	569.121	375	4114	569.121
cj, v Qal impf 3ms	cj, v Hiphil impf 3ms	cj, v Qal impf 3ms	*sub*	indef pron	cj, v Qal impf 3ms
וַיַּעַל	וַיַּבֵּט	וַיֹּאמֶר	אֵין	מְאוּמָה	וַיֹּאמֶר
wayya'al	wayyabbēṭ	wayyō'mer	'ên	me'ûmāh	wayyō'mer
so he went up	and he looked	and he said	there is not	something	and he said

8178.131 v Qal impv 2ms שֻׁב shuv go back	8124 num שֶׁבַע sheva' seven	6718 n fp פְּעָמִים pe'āmîm times	**44.** 2030.121 cj, v Qal impf 3ms וַיְהִי wayhî and it was	904, 8113 prep, art, num בַּשְּׁבִעִית bashshevi'îth when the seventh	569.121 cj, v Qal impf 3ms וַיֹּאמֶר wayyō'mer and he said

2079, 5854 intrj, n fs הִנֵּה־עָב hinnēh-'āv behold a cloud	7278 adj קְטַנָּה qŏṭannāh insignificant	3626, 3834, 382 prep, *n fs*, n ms כְּכַף־אִישׁ kekhaph-'îsh like the palm of a man's hand	6148.153 v Qal act ptc fs עֹלָה 'ōlāh coming up	4623, 3328 prep, n ms מִיָּם mîyām from the sea

39. And when all the people saw it, they fell on their faces: and they said, The LORD, he is the God; the LORD, he is the God: ... the Eternal is God!, *Moffatt* ... fell prostrate, *NAB* ... threw themselves on the ground, *Good News* ... Yahweh he is GOD, *Rotherham*.

40. And Elijah said unto them, Take the prophets of Baal; let not one of them escape: ... Seize the prophets, *NRSV* ... Catch ye the prophets, *Young* ... Arrest the prophets, *Beck*.

And they took them: and Elijah brought them down to the brook Kishon, and slew them there: ... and slaughtered them there in the valley, *NEB* ... seized them ... to the Wadi Kishon, and killed them there, *NRSV* ... and executed them there, *NKJV* ... slit their throats, *NAB*.

41. And Elijah said unto Ahab, Get thee up, eat and drink; for there is a sound of abundance of rain: ... enjoy a good meal! For I hear a mighty rainstorm, *NLT* ... plenty of rain, *KJVII* ... is a murmering sound, *Fenton* ... the noise of the shower, *Young* ... like a storm of rain, *Knox*.

42. So Ahab went up to eat and to drink. And Elijah went up to the top of Carmel: ... Elijah himself climbed to the crest of Carmel, *NEB*.

and he cast himself down upon the earth, and put his face between his knees: ... bowed down on, *Darby* ... crouched down, *Goodspeed* ... bent down to the ground, *NIV* ... bent over toward, *Berkeley*.

43. And said to his servant, Go up now, look toward the sea. And he went up, and looked: ... servant went and returned, *Good News* ... look in the direction of, *BB* ... Climb up and look out to, *NAB*.

and said, There is nothing. And he said, Go again seven times: ... I didn't see anything, *NLT* ... nothing at all, *Berkeley*.

44. And it came to pass at the seventh time, that he said, Behold, there ariseth a little cloud out of

and shattered the stones and burned up the dust and licked up the water in the trenches. With one terror-stricken impulse, the people all prostrated themselves on their faces with the cry, "The LORD, He is God; the LORD, He is God!" This cry was almost identical with the name of the victorious prophet Elijahu, "Yah, He is my God." It is after Elijah's time, and perhaps from his influence, that from this time proper names compounded with Yahweh become almost the rule—as in Ahaziah, Jehoram, Jehu, Jehoahaz, Joash, Pekahiah, etc.

The magnificent narrative in which the interest has been wound up to so high a pitch, and expressed in so lofty a strain of imaginative and dramatic force, ends in a deed of blood. Elijah said to the people, "Take the prophets of Baal; let not one of them escape. And they took them: and Elijah brought them down to the brook Kishon, and slew them there with the sword" (v. 40). It is not necessarily meant that he slew them with his own hand, though indeed he may have done so, as Samuel hewed Agag in pieces before the LORD. His moral responsibility was precisely the same in either case. We are not told that he had any commission from Yahweh to do this, or was called by any voice of the LORD, but neither do we suspect Elijah of doing otherwise. The penalty for being a false prophet was death. Elijah still held to the Covenant, even though most had forsaken it (thus the building of the altar with twelve stones for the twelve tribes). The prophets of Baal indirectly, if not directly, had been the cause of Jezebel's persecution of the prophets of the LORD. The thought of pity would not occur to Elijah any more than it did to Moses in Deuteronomy (Deut. 13:6–9; 17:2ff).

18:41–46. But the terrible excitement of the day was not yet over, nor was the victory completely won. The fire had flashed from heaven, but the long desired rain on which the salvation of land and people depended still showed no signs of falling. And Elijah was pledged to this result. Not until the drought ended could he reach the culmination of his victory over the god of Jezebel's worship.

569.121	6148.131	569.131	420, 255	646.131	3495.131	3940
cj, v Qal impf 3ms	v Qal impv 2ms	v Qal impv 2ms	prep, pn	v Qal impv 2ms	cj, v Qal impv 2ms	cj, neg part
וַיֹּאמֶר	עֲלֵה	אֱמֹר	אֶל־אַחְאָב	אֱסֹר	וָרֵד	וְלֹא
wayyō'mer	'ălēh	'ĕmōr	'el-'ach'āv	'ĕsōr	wārēdh	welō'
and he said	go up	say	to Ahab	tie	and go down	that not

6352.121	1700		2030.121	5912, 3662	5912, 3662	8452
v Qal impf 3ms, ps 2ms	art, n ms	**45.**	cj, v Qal impf 3ms	adv, adv	cj, adv, adv	cj, art, n md
יַעַצָרְכָה	הַגָּשֶׁם		וַיְהִי	עַד־כֹּה	וְעַד־כֹּה	וְהַשָּׁמַיִם
ya'atsārekhāh	haggāshem		wayhî	'adh-kōh	we'adh-kōh	wehashshāmayim
it will hinder you	the rain		and it was	until so	and until so	and the heavens

7222.716	5854	7593	2030.121	1700	1448	7680.121	255
v Hithpael pf 3cp	n mp	cj, n fs	cj, v Qal impf 3ms	n ms	adj	cj, v Qal impf 3ms	pn
הִתְקַדְּרוּ	עָבִים	וְרוּחַ	וַיְהִי	גֶּשֶׁם	גָּדוֹל	וַיִּרְכַּב	אַחְאָב
hithqadderû	'āvîm	werûach	wayhî	geshem	gādhôl	wayyirkav	'ach'āv
they became dark	clouds	and wind	and there was	rain	great	and he rode	Ahab

2050.121	3262		3135, 3176	2030.112	420, 455
cj, v Qal impf 3ms	pn	**46.**	cj, *n fs*, pn	v Qal pf 3fs	prep, pn
וַיֵּלֶךְ	יִזְרְעֶאלָה		וְיַד־יְהוָה	הָיְתָה	אֶל־אֵלִיָּהוּ
wayyēlekh	yizre'e'lāh		weyadh-yehwāh	hāyethāh	'el-'ēlîyāhû
and he went	to Jezreel		and the power of Yahweh	it was	to Elijah

8533.321	5158	7608.121	3937, 6686	255	5912, 971.141
cj, v Piel impf 3ms	n md, ps 3ms	cj, v Qal impf 3ms	prep, *n mp*	pn	adv, v Qal inf con, ps 2ms
וַיְשַׁנֵּס	מָתְנָיו	וַיָּרָץ	לִפְנֵי	אַחְאָב	עַד־בֹּאֲכָה
wayshannēs	māthenâv	wayyārāts	liphnê	'ach'āv	'adh-bō'ăkhāh
and he bound up	his loins	and he ran	before	Ahab	until your coming

3262		5222.521	255	3937, 350	881	3725, 866	6449.111	455
pn	**19:1**	cj, v Hiphil impf 3ms	pn	prep, pn	do	*adj*, rel part	v Qal pf 3ms	pn
יִזְרְעֶאלָה		וַיַּגֵּד	אַחְאָב	לְאִיזֶבֶל	אֵת	כָּל־אֲשֶׁר	עָשָׂה	אֵלִיָּהוּ
yizre'e'lāh		wayyaggēdh	'ach'āv	le'îzevel	'ēth	kol-'ăsher	'āsāh	'ēlîyāhû
to Jezreel		and he told	Ahab	to Jezebel		all that	he had done	Elijah

881	3725, 866	2103.111	881, 3725, 5204	904, 2820		8365.122	350
cj, do	*adj*, rel part	v Qal pf 3ms	do, *adj*, art, n mp	prep, art, n fs	**2.**	cj, v Qal impf 3fs	pn
וְאֵת	כָּל־אֲשֶׁר	הָרַג	אֶת־כָּל־הַנְּבִיאִים	בֶּחָרֶב		וַתִּשְׁלַח	אִיזֶבֶל
we'ēth	kol-'ăsher	hāragh	'eth-kol-hannevî'îm	bechārev		wattishlach	'îzevel
and	all that	he had killed	all the prophets	with the sword		then she sent out	Jezebel

4534	420, 455	3937, 569.141	3662, 6449.126	435	3662	3362.526
n ms	prep, pn	prep, v Qal inf con	adv, v Qal juss 3mp	n mp	cj, adv	v Hiphil juss 3mp
מַלְאָךְ	אֶל־אֵלִיָּהוּ	לֵאמֹר	כֹּה־יַעֲשׂוּן	אֱלֹהִים	וְכֹה	יוֹסִפוּן
mal'ākh	'el-'ēlîyāhû	lē'mōr	kōh-ya'ăsûn	'ĕlōhîm	wekhōh	yôsiphûn
a messenger	to Elijah	saying	thus may they do	gods	and thus	may they add

3706, 3626, 6496	4417	7947.125	881, 5497	3626, 5497	259	4623
cj, prep, art, n fs	adv	v Qal impf 1cs	do, n fs, ps 2ms	prep, *n fs*	num	prep, ps 3mp
כִּי־כָעֵת	מָחָר	אָשִׂים	אֶת־נַפְשְׁךָ	כְּנֶפֶשׁ	אַחַד	מֵהֶם
kî-khā'ēth	māchār	'āsîm	'eth-naphshekhā	kenephesh	'achadh	mēhem
if according to the time	tomorrow	I will make	your life	like the life of	one	of them

	7495.121	7251.121	2050.121	420, 5497	971.121	916	916
3.	cj, v Qal impf 3ms	cj, v Qal impf 3ms	cj, v Qal impf 3ms	prep, n fs, ps 3ms	cj, v Qal impf 3ms	pn	pn
	וַיַּרְא	וַיָּקָם	וַיֵּלֶךְ	אֶל־נַפְשׁוֹ	וַיָּבֹא	בְּאֵר	שֶׁבַע
	wayyare'	wayyāqām	wayyēlekh	'el-naphshô	wayyāvō'	be'ēr	sheva'
	and he saw	and he rose up	and he went	for his life	and he came to	Beer	Sheba

the sea, like a man's hand: ... no bigger than a man's foot-print, *Knox* ... a person's hand, *NRSV* ... like a man's foot, *Douay* ... the size of a human fist, *NCV*.

And he said, Go up, say unto Ahab, Prepare thy chariot, and get thee down, that the rain stop thee not: ... Turn and descend,—or the rain will prevent you, *Fenton*.

45. And it came to pass in the mean while, that the heaven was black with clouds and wind, and there was a great rain. And Ahab rode, and went to Jezreel: ... A heavy wind brought a terrific rainstorm, *NLT* ... there was a great downpour, *Goodspeed* ... rain fell in torrents, *JB*.

46. And the hand of the LORD was on Elijah: ... the power of the LORD had come upon Elijah, *NEB*.

and he girded up his loins, and ran before Ahab to the entrance of Jezreel: ... outran Ahab, *NASB* ... tucking his cloak into his belt, *NIV* ... tightened his clothes around him and ran ahead of King Ahab, *NCV* ... with belt tight round his waist, *Moffatt*.

19:1. And Ahab told Jezebel all that Elijah had done, and withal how he had slain all the prophets with the sword: ... about his slaughter, *Moffatt* ... how he had executed, *NKJV* ... especially how he killed, *Beck* ... put all the prophets to death, *BB*.

2. Then Jezebel sent a messenger unto Elijah, saying, So let the gods do to me, and more also: ... May the gods punish me again and again, *Beck* ... bring unnameable ills on me, *JB*.

if I make not thy life as the life of one of them by tomorrow about this time: ... I don't kill you just as you killed those prophets, *NCV* ...unless by this time tomorrow I have taken your life as you took theirs, *REB*.

3. And when he saw that, he arose, and went for his life: ... in terror rose and ran, *Moffatt* ... Elijah was afraid and fled, *NAB*.

and came to Beer-sheba, which belongeth to Judah, and left his

---

But his faith did not fail him. "Get thee up," he said to Ahab, "eat and drink, for there is a sound of the feet of the rain-storm." Elijah did not join him. He heard, with prophetic ear, the rush of the coming rain, but he had still to wrestle in prayer for the fulfillment of his promise. So he ascended toward the summit where the purple peak of Carmel overlooks the sea, and there he crouched low on the ground in intense prayer, putting his face between his knees. After his first intensity of supplication had spent itself, he said to his attendant, "Go up now, look towards the sea."

The youth went up, and gazed out long and intently, for he knew well that if rain came it would sweep inland from the waters of the Mediterranean, and to an experienced eye the signals of coming storm are patent long before they are noticed by others. But all was as it had been for so many weary and dreadful months. The sea, a sheet of unruffled gold, glared under the setting sun, which still sank through an unclouded sky. Can we not imagine the accent of misgiving and disappointment with which he brought back the one word—"Nothing."

Once more the prophet bowed his face between his knees in prayer, and sent the youth; and again, and yet again, seven times. And each time had come to him the chilling answer: "Nothing." But the seventh time he called out from the mountain summit, "Behold, there ariseth a cloud out of the sea, as small as the palm of a man's hand" (an insignificant measure).

And now, indeed, Elijah knew that his triumph was completed. He bade his servant fly with winged speed to Ahab, and tell him to make ready his chariot at once, lest the burst of the coming rain should flood the river and the road, and prevent him from getting over the rough ground which lay between him and his palace at Jezreel.

Then the blessed storm burst on the parched soil with a sense of infinite refreshfulness which only an Eastern in a thirsty land can fully comprehend. And Ahab mounted his chariot. He had not driven far before the heaven, which had for so long been like brass over an iron globe, was one black mass of clouds driven by the wind, and the drenching rain poured down in sheets. And through the storm the chariot swept, and Elijah girded up his loins, and, filled with a divine impulse of exultation, ran before it, keeping pace with the king's steeds for all those fifteen miles, even after the overwhelming strain of all he had gone through that day. And as through the rifts of rain the king saw his wild dark figure outrunning his swift steeds.

19:1–3. The chariot had reached Jezreel, and at the city gate Elijah stopped. Like his antitype, the great forerunner, John the Baptist, Elijah was a voice in the wilderness; like his Lord that was to be, he loved not cities. Nor was he sure of safety. He knew, in spite of his victory, that a dark hour awaited Ahab when he would have to tell Jezebel that the people had repudiated her idol and that Elijah had slain her 850 priests.

866	3937, 3171	5299.521	881, 5470	8427	**4.** 2000, 2050.111
rel part	prep, pn	cj, v Hiphil impf 3ms	do, n ms, ps 3ms	adv	cj, pers pron, v Qal pf 3ms
אֲשֶׁר	לִיהוּדָה	וַיַּנַּח	אֶת־נַעֲרוֹ	שָׁם	וְהוּא־הָלַךְ
'ăsher	lîhûdhāh	wayyannach	'eth-na'ărô	shām	wehû'-hālakh
which	to Judah	and he left	his servant	there	but he he went

904, 4198	1932	3219	971.121	3553.121	8809	7868
prep, art, n ms	*n ms*	n ms	cj, v Qal impf 3ms	cj, v Qal impf 3ms	prep	n fs
בַּמִּדְבָּר	דֶּרֶךְ	יוֹם	וַיָּבֹא	וַיֵּשֶׁב	תַּחַת	רֹתֶם
bammidhbār	derekh	yôm	wayyāvō'	wayyēshev	tachath	rōthem
in the wilderness	a journey of	a day	and he came	and he sat down	beneath	a broom tree

259	8068.121	881, 5497	3937, 4322.141	569.121	7521	6498
num	cj, v Qal impf 3ms	do, n fs, ps 3ms	prep, v Qal inf con	cj, v Qal impf 3ms	adj	adv
אֶחָת	וַיִּשְׁאַל	אֶת־נַפְשׁוֹ	לָמוּת	וַיֹּאמֶר	רַב	עַתָּה
'echāth	wayyish'al	'eth-naphshô	lāmûth	wayyō'mer	rav	'attāh
one	and he asked	his life	to die	and he said	abundant	now

3176	4089.131	5497	3706, 3940, 3005	609	4623, 1
pn	v Qal impv 2ms	n fs, ps 1cs	cj, neg part, adj	pers pron	prep, n mp, ps 1cs
יְהוָה	קַח	נַפְשִׁי	כִּי־לֹא־טוֹב	אָנֹכִי	מֵאֲבֹתָי
yehwāh	qach	naphshî	kî-lō'-ṭôv	'ānōkhî	mē'ăvōthāy
O Yahweh	take	my life	because not better	I	than my ancestors

5. 8311.121	3583.121	8809	7868	259	2079, 2172
cj, v Qal impf 3ms	cj, v Qal impf 3ms	prep	n fs	num	cj, intrg, dem pron
וַיִּשְׁכַּב	וַיִּישַׁן	תַּחַת	רֹתֶם	אֶחָד	וְהִנֵּה־זֶה
wayyishkav	wayyîshan	tachath	rōthem	'echādh	wehinnēh-zeh
then he lay down	and he slept	beneath	a broom tree	one	but behold this One

4534	5236.151	904	569.121	3937	7251.131	404.131
n ms	v Qal act ptc ms	prep, ps 3ms	cj, v Qal impf 3ms	prep, ps 3ms	v Qal impv 2ms	v Qal impv 2ms
מַלְאָךְ	נֹגֵעַ	בּוֹ	וַיֹּאמֶר	לוֹ	קוּם	אֱכוֹל
mal'ākh	nōghēa'	bô	wayyō'mer	lô	qûm	'ĕkhôl
the Angel	touching	on him	and He said	to him	rise	eat

6. 5202.521	2079	4924	5899	7822	7111	4448
cj, v Hiphil impf 3ms	cj, intrj	n fp, ps 3ms	*n fs*	n fp	cj, *n fs*	n mp
וַיַּבֵּט	וְהִנֵּה	מְרַאֲשֹׁתָיו	עֻגַת	רְצָפִים	וְצַפַּחַת	מָיִם
wayyabbēṭ	wehinnēh	mera'ăshōthâv	'ughath	retsāphîm	wetsappachath	māyim
and he looked	and behold	at his head	a bread cake of	hot stones	and a pitcher of	water

404.121	8685.121	8178.121	8311.121	**7.** 8178.121
cj, v Qal impf 3ms	cj, v Qal impf 3ms	cj, v Qal impf 3ms	cj, v Qal impf 3ms	cj, v Qal impf 3ms
וַיֹּאכַל	וַיֵּשְׁתְּ	וַיָּשָׁב	וַיִּשְׁכָּב	וַיָּשָׁב
wayyō'khal	wayyēsht	wayyāshāv	wayyishkāv	wayyāshāv
and he ate	and he drank	and he returned	and he lay down	and He returned

4534	3176	8529	5236.121, 904	569.121	7251.131
n ms	pn	num	cj, v Qal impf 3ms, prep, ps 3ms	cj, v Qal impf 3ms	v Qal impv 2ms
מַלְאַךְ	יְהוָה	שֵׁנִית	וַיִּגַּע־בּוֹ	וַיֹּאמֶר	קוּם
mal'akh	yehwāh	shēnîth	wayyigga'-bô	wayyō'mer	qûm
the Angel of	Yahweh	a second time	and He touched on him	and He said	rise

404.131	3706	7521	4623	1932	**8.** 7251.121	404.121
v Qal impv 2ms	cj	adj	prep, ps 2ms	art, n ms	cj, v Qal impf 3ms	cj, v Qal impf 3ms
אֱכֹל	כִּי	רַב	מִמְּךָ	הַדָּרֶךְ	וַיָּקָם	וַיֹּאכַל
'ĕkhōl	kî	rav	mimmekhā	haddārekh	wayyāqām	wayyō'khal
eat	because	greater	than you	the journey	and he rose up	and he ate

servant there: ... parting there from his servant, *BB* ... left his attendant, *Fenton.*

4. But he himself went a day's journey into the wilderness, and came and sat down under a juniper tree: ... went forward one day's journey into the desert, *Douay* ... under a solitary, *NRSV* ... a broom tree, *RSV* ... a certain retem-tree, *Young.*

and he requested for himself that he might die: ... wished he were dead, *JB* ... prayed for death, *NEB.*

and said, It is enough; now, O LORD, take away my life; for I am not better than my fathers: ... no better than my ancestors, *NCV.*

5. And as he lay and slept under a juniper tree, behold, then an angel touched him, and said unto him, Arise and eat: ... ordered him to get up and eat, *NAB* ... Get up and have some food, *BB* ... a messenger touching him, who said, *Rotherham* ... bidding him awake and eat, *Knox.*

6. And he looked, and, behold, there was a cake baked on the coals: ... he saw at his head baked cakes, *Fenton* ... bread baked on hot stones, *NLT.*

and a cruse of water at his head. And he did eat and drink, and laid him down again: ... a jug, *KJVII* ... a dish, *Young* ... a pitcher, *NEB* ... a jar, *NRSV.*

7. And the angel of the LORD came again the second time: ... the messenger of Yahweh, *Rotherham.*

and touched him, and said, Arise and eat; because the journey is too great for thee: ... there is a long journey ahead of you, *NLT* ... otherwise the journey will be too much, *NRSV* ... or the journey will be too long, *JB* ... yet a great way to go, *Douay.*

8. And he arose, and did eat and drink, and went in the strength of that meat forty days and forty nights unto Horeb the mount of God: ... to Mount Sinai, the mountain, *NLT* ... till he reached God's own mountain, Horeb, *Knox* ... the food made him strong enough to walk for forty days and nights, *NCV.*

The burst of rage which led her to send the message defeated her own object. The awfulness which invested Elijah, and the supernatural powers on which he relied, when he was engaged in the battles of the LORD, belonged to him only in his public and prophetic capacity. As a man he was but a poor, feeble, lonely subject, whose blood might be shed at any moment. He did not believe God for his own life, but felt that a counter triumph to the Baal worshipers, whom he had so signally humiliated, would be obtained. He fled, and went for his life.

Swift flight was easy to that hardy frame and that trained endurance, even after the fearful day on Carmel and the wild race of fifteen miles from Carmel to Jezreel. It was still night, and cool, and the haunts and byways of the land were known to the solitary and hunted wanderer. "He feared, and he rose, and he went for his life," ninety-five miles to Beersheba, once a town of Simeon, now the southern limit of the kingdom of Judah, thirty-one miles south of Hebron.

19:4. Of what use was life any longer? He had fought for Yahweh, and won, and after all been humiliatingly defeated. He had prophesied the drought, and it had withered and scorched up the erring, afflicted land. He had prayed for the rain, and it had come in a rush of blessing on the reviving fields. In the Wadi Cherith, in the house of the Phoenician widow, he had been divinely supported and sheltered from hot pursuit. He had snatched her boy from death. He had stood before kings, and not been ashamed. He had stretched forth his hands to a disobedient and gainsaying people, and not in vain. He had confounded the rich-vested and royally maintained band of Baal's priests, and in spite of their orgiastic leapings and self-mutilations had put to shame their sun-god under his own burning sun. He had kept pace with Ahab's chariot-steeds as he conducted him, as it were in triumph, through the streaming downpour of that sweeping storm, to his summer capital. Of what use was it all? Was it anything but a splendid and deplorable failure? And he said: "It is enough; now, O LORD, take away my life; for I am not better than my fathers."

19:5–8. *Why art thou cast down, O my soul? and why art thou disquieted within me? hope thou in God: for I shall yet praise him, who is the health of my countenance, and my God* (Ps. 42:11).

"It is enough; now, O LORD, take away my life; for I am not better than my fathers."

The despondency was deeper than personal. It was despair of the world; despair of the fate of the true worship; despair about the future of faith and righteousness; despair of everything. Elijah, in his condition of pitiable weariness, felt himself reduced to entire uncertainty about all God's dealings with him and with mankind. "I am not better than my fathers": they failed one by one, and died, and entered the darkness; and I have failed likewise. To what end did Moses lead this people through the wilderness? Why did the Judges fight and deliver them? Of what use was the wise guid-

8685.121	2050.121	904, 3699	402	2026	727	3219
cj, v Qal impf 3ms	cj, v Qal impf 3ms	prep, *n ms*	art, n fs	art, dem pron	num	n ms
וַיֵּשְׁתְּ	וַיֵּלֶךְ	בְּכֹחַ	הָאֲכִילָה	הַהִיא	אַרְבָּעִים	יוֹם
wayyishteh	wayyēlekh	bekhōach	hā'ăkhîlāh	hahî'	'arbā'îm	yôm
and he drank	and he went	with the strength of	the food	the that	forty	days

727	4050	5912	2098	435	2822		971.121, 8427	420, 4792
cj, num	n ms	prep	*n ms*	art, n mp	pn	9.	cj, v Qal impf 3ms, adv	prep, art, n fs
וְאַרְבָּעִים	לַיְלָה	עַד	הַר	הָאֱלֹהִים	חֹרֵב		וַיָּבֹא־שָׁם	אֶל־הַמְּעָרָה
we'arbā'îm	laylāh	'adh	har	hā'ĕlōhîm	chōrēv		wayyāvō'-shām	'el-hamme'ārāh
and forty	nights	unto	the mount of	God	Horeb		and he came there	into the cave

4053.121	8427	2079	1745, 3176	420	569.121
cj, v Qal impf 3ms	adv	cj, intrj	*n ms*, pn	prep, ps 3ms	cj, v Qal impf 3ms
וַיָּלֶן	שָׁם	וְהִנֵּה	דְּבַר־יְהוָה	אֵלָיו	וַיֹּאמֶר
wayyālen	shām	wehinnēh	dhevar-yehwāh	'ēlâv	wayyō'mer
and he spent the night	there	and behold	the word of Yahweh	to him	and He said

3937	4242, 3937	6553	455		569.121	7349.342
prep, ps 3ms	intrg, prep, ps 2ms	adv	pn	10.	cj, v Qal impf 3ms	v Piel inf abs
לוֹ	מַה־לְּךָ	פֹה	אֵלִיָּהוּ		וַיֹּאמֶר	קַנֹּא
lô	mah-lekhā	phōh	'ēlîyāhû		wayyō'mer	qannō'
to him	what to you	here	Elijah		and he said	being zealous

7349.315	3937, 3176	435	6893	3706, 6013.116
v Piel pf 1cs	prep, pn	*n mp*	n mp	cj, v Qal pf 3cp
קִנֵּאתִי	לַיהוָה	אֱלֹהֵי	צְבָאוֹת	כִּי־עָזְבוּ
qinnē'thî	layhwāh	'ĕlōhê	tsevā'ôth	kî-'āzevû
I have been very zealous	for Yahweh	the God of	hosts	because they abandoned

1311	1158	3547	881, 4326	2117.116
n fs, ps 2ms	*n mp*	pn	do, n mp, ps 2ms	v Qal pf 3cp
בְרִיתְךָ	בְּנֵי	יִשְׂרָאֵל	אֶת־מִזְבְּחֹתֶיךָ	הָרָסוּ
verîthekhā	benê	yisrā'ēl	'eth-mizbechōthêkhā	hārāṣû
your Covenant	the children of	Israel	your altars	they have torn down

881, 5204	2103.116	904, 2820	3613.225	603	3937, 940
cj, do, n mp, ps 2ms	v Qal pf 3cp	prep, art, n fs	cj, v Niphal impf 1cs	pers pron	prep, n ms, ps 1cs
וְאֶת־נְבִיאֶיךָ	הָרְגוּ	בֶחָרֶב	וָאִוָּתֵר	אֲנִי	לְבַדִּי
we'eth-nevî'êkhā	hāreghû	vechārev	wā'iwwāthēr	'ănî	levaddî
and your prophets	they have killed	with the sword	and I am remaining	I	by myself

1272.326	881, 5497	3937, 4089.141		569.121	3428.131
cj, v Piel impf 3mp	do, n fs, ps 1cs	prep, v Qal inf con, ps 3fs	11.	cj, v Qal impf 3ms	v Qal impv 2ms
וַיְבַקְשׁוּ	אֶת־נַפְשִׁי	לְקַחְתָּהּ		וַיֹּאמֶר	צֵא
wayvaqōshû	'eth-naphshî	leqachtāhh		wayyō'mer	tsē'
and they are searching for	my life	to take it		and He said	go out

6198.113	904, 2098	3937, 6686	3176	2079	3176	5882.151
cj, v Qal pf 2ms	prep, art, n ms	prep, *n mp*	pn	cj, intrj	pn	v Qal act ptc ms
וְעָמַדְתָּ	בָהָר	לִפְנֵי	יְהוָה	וְהִנֵּה	יְהוָה	עֹבֵר
we'āmadhtā	vāhār	liphnê	yehwāh	wehinnēh	yehwāh	'ōvēr
and you will stand	on the mountain	before	Yahweh	and behold	Yahweh	passing by

7593	1448	2481	6811.351	2098	8132.351	5748	3937, 6686
cj, n fs	adj	cj, adj	v Piel ptc ms	n mp	cj, v Piel ptc ms	n mp	prep, *n mp*
וְרוּחַ	גְּדוֹלָה	וְחָזָק	מְפָרֵק	הָרִים	וּמְשַׁבֵּר	סְלָעִים	לִפְנֵי
werûach	gedhôlāh	wechāzāq	mephārēq	hārîm	ûmeshabbēr	selā'îm	liphnê
and a wind	great	and strong	tearing apart	the hills	and breaking in pieces	rocks	before

9. And he came thither unto a cave, and lodged there: ... he went into a cave and spent the night, *NIV* ... hole in the rock for the night, *BB* ... where he took shelter, *NAB*.

and, behold, the word of the LORD came to him, and he said unto him, What doest thou here, Elijah?: ... Presently the word, *Berkeley* ... what are you doing here?, *Good News*.

10. And he said, I have been very jealous for the LORD God of hosts: ... very zealous for the EVER-LIVING God of MIGHT, *Fenton* ... I am full of jealous zeal for Yahweh Sabaoth, *JB*.

for the children of Israel have forsaken thy covenant, thrown down thine altars, and slain thy prophets with the sword; and I, even I only, am left; and they seek my life, to take it away: ... put thy prophets to death, *NEB* ... they have sought, *Rotherham* ... are trying to kill me too, *NIV*.

11. And he said, Go forth, and stand upon the mount before the LORD: ... Go outside, *Moffatt*.

And, behold, the LORD passed by, and a great and strong wind rent the mountains, and brake in pieces the rocks before the LORD; but the LORD was not in the wind: ... wind tore into the mountains and broke, *NKJV* ... crushing rocks, *NAB* ... mighty wind was tearing mountains and shattering rocks ahead of, *Beck*.

and after the wind an earthquake; but the LORD was not in the earthquake: ... after the wind came, *Tyndale* ... there was an earth-shock, *BB* ... after the hurricane, an earthquake, *JB*.

12. And after the earthquake a fire; but the LORD was not in the fire: ... Following the earthquake there was fire, *Berkeley*.

---

ance of Samuel? What has come of David's harp, and Solomon's temple and magnificence? It ends, and my work ends, in the despotism of Jezebel, and a nation of apostates!

God pitied his poor suffering servant, and gently led him back to hope and happiness, and restored him to his true self, and to the natural elasticity of his free spirit.

First, he gave his beloved sleep. Elijah lay down and slept. Perhaps this was what he needed most of all.

Next, God provided him with food. When he awoke he saw that at his head, under the broom tree, God had spread him a table in the wilderness. It was a provision, simple indeed, but for his moderate wants more than sufficient—a cake baked on the coals and a cruse of water. The Angel of the LORD touched him, and said, "Arise and eat." He ate and drank, and thus refreshed lay down again to make up, perhaps, for long arrears of unrest. Again, He bade him rise and eat once more, or his strength would fail in the journey which lay before him. For he meant to plunge yet farther into the wilderness. "He arose, and did eat and drink, and went in the strength of that food forty days and forty nights."

Next, God sent him on a hallowed pilgrimage to bathe his weary spirit in the memories of a brighter past.

It does not necessarily require forty days and forty nights, nor anything like so long a period, to get from one day's journey in the wilderness to Horeb, the Mount of God, which was Elijah's destination. The distance does not exceed 180 miles even from Beersheba.

19:9–10. After his wanderings Elijah reached Mount Sinai, and came to "the cave," and took shelter there. The use of the article shows that a particular cave is meant.

And as God had pointed out to him the way to restore his bodily strength by sleep and food, so now He opened before the prophet the remedy of renewed activity. The question of the LORD came to him—it was re-echoed by the voice of his own conscience—"What doest thou here, Elijah?"

"What doest thou?" He was doing nothing! He had, indeed, fled for his life; but was all the rest of his life to be so different from its beginning? Was there, indeed, no more work to be done in Israel or in Judah, and was he tamely to allow Jezebel to be the final mistress of the situation? Was one alien and idolatrous woman to overawe God's people Israel and to snatch from God's prophet all the fruits of his righteous labors? "What doest thou here, Elijah?" Is not the very significance of thy name "Yahweh, He is my God"? Is He to be the God but of one fugitive? "What doest thou here?"

19:11. It was natural that Yahweh should reveal himself to Elijah under the aspect of those awful elemental forces with which his solitary life had made him familiar. No spot in the world is more suitable for those powers in all their fire and magnificence than the knot of mountains which crowd the Sinaitic peninsula with their entangled cliffs. Travelers have borne witness to the overwhelming violence and majesty of the storms which rush and reverberate through the granite gorges of those everlasting hills. It was in such surroundings that Yahweh spoke to the heart of his servant.

3176	3940	904, 7593	3176	313	7593	7783	3940
pn	neg part	prep, art, n fs	pn	cj, adv	art, n fs	n ms	neg part
יְהוָה	לֹא	בָרוּחַ	יְהוָה	וְאַחַר	הָרוּחַ	רַעַשׁ	לֹא
yᵉhwāh	lō'	vārûach	yᵉhwāh	wᵉ'achar	hārûach	ra'ash	lō'
Yahweh	not	in the wind	Yahweh	and after	the wind	an earthquake	not

940, 7783	3176		313	7783	813	3940	904, 813	3176
prep, art, n ms	pn	12.	cj, adv	art, n ms	n fs	neg part	prep, art, n fs	pn
בָרַעַשׁ	יְהוָה		וְאַחַר	הָרַעַשׁ	אֵשׁ	לֹא	בָאֵשׁ	יְהוָה
vāra'ash	yᵉhwāh		wᵉ'achar	hāra'ash	'ēsh	lō'	vā'ēsh	yᵉhwāh
in the earthquake	Yahweh		and after	the earthquake	fire	not	in the fire	Yahweh

313	813	7249	1888	1911		2030.121	3626, 8471.141	455
cj, adv	art, n fs	*n ms*	n fs	adj	13.	cj, v Qal impf 3ms	prep, v Qal inf con	pn
וְאַחַר	הָאֵשׁ	קוֹל	דְּמָמָה	דַקָּה		וַיְהִי	כִּשְׁמֹעַ	אֵלִיָּהוּ
wᵉ'achar	hā'ēsh	qôl	dᵉmāmāh	dhaqqāh		wayhî	kishmōa'	'ēlîyāhû
and after	the fire	a voice of	stillness	small		and it was	when hearing	Elijah

4011.521	6686	904, 152	3428.121	6198.121	6860
cj, v Hiphil impf 3ms	n mp, ps 3ms	prep, n fs, ps 3ms	cj, v Qal impf 3ms	cj, v Qal impf 3ms	*n ms*
וַיָּלֶט	פָּנָיו	בְּאַדַּרְתּוֹ	וַיֵּצֵא	וַיַּעֲמֹד	פֶּתַח
wayyāleṭ	pānâv	bᵉ'addartô	wayyētsē'	wayya'ămōdh	pethach
and he wrapped	his face	with his mantle	then he went out	and he stood	the entrance of

4792	2079	420	7249	569.121	4242, 3937	6553	455
art, n fs	cj, intrj	prep, ps 3ms	n ms	cj, v Qal impf 3ms	intrg, prep, ps 2ms	adv	pn
הַמְּעָרָה	וְהִנֵּה	אֵלָיו	קוֹל	וַיֹּאמֶר	מַה־לְּךָ	פֹה	אֵלִיָּהוּ
hammᵉ'ārāh	wᵉhinnēh	'ēlâv	qôl	wayyō'mer	mah-lᵉkhā	phōh	'ēlîyāhû
the cave	and behold	to him	a voice	and He said	what to you	here	Elijah

	569.121	7349.342	7349.315	3937, 3176	435	6893
14.	cj, v Qal impf 3ms	v Piel inf abs	v Piel pf 1cs	prep, pn	*n mp*	n mp
	וַיֹּאמֶר	קַנֹּא	קִנֵּאתִי	לַיהוָה	אֱלֹהֵי	צְבָאוֹת
	wayyō'mer	qannō'	qinnē'thî	layhwāh	'ĕlōhê	tsᵉvā'ôth
	and he said	being zealous	I have been very zealous	for Yahweh	the God of	hosts

3706, 6013.116	1311	1158	3547	881, 4326
cj, v Qal pf 3cp	n fs, ps 2ms	*n mp*	pn	do, n mp, ps 2ms
כִּי־עָזְבוּ	בְרִיתְךָ	בְּנֵי	יִשְׂרָאֵל	אֶת־מִזְבְּחֹתֶיךָ
kî-'āzᵉvû	vᵉrîthᵉkhā	bᵉnê	yisrā'ēl	'eth-mizbᵉchōthêkhā
because they abandoned	your Covenant	the children of	Israel	your altars

2117.116	881, 5204	2103.116	904, 2820	3613.225
v Qal pf 3cp	cj, do, n mp, ps 2ms	v Qal pf 3cp	prep, art, n fs	cj, v Niphal impf 1cs
הָרָסוּ	וְאֶת־נְבִיאֶיךָ	הָרְגוּ	בֶחָרֶב	וָאִוָּתֵר
hārāsû	wᵉ'eth-nᵉvî'êkhā	hārᵉghû	vechārev	wā'iwwāthēr
they have torn down	and your prophets	they have killed	with the sword	and I am remaining

603	3937, 940	1272.326	881, 5497	3937, 4089.141
pers pron	prep, n ms, ps 1cs	cj, v Piel impf 3mp	do, n fs, ps 1cs	prep, v Qal inf con, ps 3fs
אֲנִי	לְבַדִּי	וַיְבַקְשׁוּ	אֶת־נַפְשִׁי	לְקַחְתָּהּ
'ănî	lᵉvaddî	wayvaqōshû	'eth-naphshî	lᵉqachtāhh
I	by myself	and they are searching for	my life	to take it

	569.121	3176	420	2050.131	8178.131	3937, 1932
15.	cj, v Qal impf 3ms	pn	prep, ps 3ms	v Qal impv 2ms	v Qal impv 2ms	prep, n ms, ps 2ms
	וַיֹּאמֶר	יְהוָה	אֵלָיו	לֵךְ	שׁוּב	לְדַרְכְּךָ
	wayyō'mer	yᵉhwāh	'ēlâv	lēkh	shûv	lᵉdharkᵉkhā
	and He said	Yahweh	to him	go	return	to your journey

4198	1894	971.113	5066.113	881, 2462	3937, 4567
n ms	pn	cj, v Qal pf 2ms	cj, v Qal pf 2ms	do, pn	prep, n ms
מִדְבַּרָה	דַּמָּשֶׂק	וּבָאתָ	וּמָשַׁחְתָּ	אֶת־חֲזָאֵל	לְמֶלֶךְ
midhbārāh	dhammāseq	ûvā'thā	ûmāshachtā	'eth-chăzā'ēl	lemelekh
to the wilderness of	Damascus	and you will come	and you will anoint	Hazael	as king

6142, 782		881	3167	1158, 5437	5066.123	3937, 4567	6142, 3547
prep, pn	16.	cj, do	pn	*n ms*, pn	v Qal impf 2ms	prep, n ms	prep, pn
עַל־אֲרָם		וְאֵת	יֵהוּא	בֶּן־נִמְשִׁי	תִּמְשַׁח	לְמֶלֶךְ	עַל־יִשְׂרָאֵל
'al-'ărām		we'ēth	yēhû'	ven-nimshî	timshach	lemelekh	'al-yisrā'ēl
over Aram		and	Jehu	the son of Nimshi	you will anoint	as king	over Israel

and after the fire a still small voice: ... gentle, quiet, *Beck* ... breath of a light whisper, *Moffatt* ... tiny whispering sound, *NAB* ... quiet, gentle, *NCV* ... sound of a soft breath, *BB* ... light murmuring, *JB*.

13. And it was so, when Elijah heard it, that he wrapped his face in his mantle, and went out, and stood in the entering in of the cave: ... stood in the entrance, *MAST* ... covered his face with his coat, *NCV* ... took his place in the opening of the hole, *BB*.

And, behold, there came a voice unto him, and said, What doest thou here, Elijah?: ... a Voice spoke to him saying, *Beck* ... what are you doing here?, *Good News*.

14. And he said, I have been very jealous for the LORD God of hosts: because the children of Israel have forsaken thy covenant, thrown down thine altars, and slain thy prophets with the sword; and I, even I only, am left; and they seek my life, to take it away: ... have abandoned your covenant, *JB* ... I'm the only one left, and they're trying to kill me, *Beck* ... my soul to have it, *Tyndale*.

15. And the LORD said unto him, Go, return on thy way to the wilderness of Damascus: and when thou comest, anoint Hazael to be king over Syria: ... take the desert road, *Moffatt* ... over Aram, *MAST* ... pour olive oil on Hazael, *NCV* ... through the waste land, *BB*.

16. And Jehu the son of Nimshi shalt thou anoint to be king over Israel: and Elisha the son of Shaphat of Abel-meholah shalt thou anoint to be prophet in thy room: ... in your stead, *KJVII* ... to replace you as my prophet, *NLT* ... consecrate as preacher after you, *Fenton* ... from Abel-Meula, to take thy place, *Knox*.

First "a great and strong wind rent the mountains, and brake in pieces the rocks, before the LORD." And Elijah felt the terror of the scene, as the storm dislodged huge masses of the mountain granite, and sent them rolling and crashing down the hills. But it did not speak to his inmost heart, for "The LORD was not in the wind."

And after the wind an earthquake shook the solid bases of the Sinaitic range. The mountain saw God and trembled. The LORD, in the language of the psalmist, shook the wilderness of Kadesh, the mountains skipped like rams and the little hills like young sheep (Ps. 18:7; 77:18; 97:4; Judg. 5:4; 2 Sam. 22:8). And man never feels so abjectly helpless, he is never reduced to such absolute insignificance, as when the solid earth beneath him, the very emblem of stability, trembles as with a palsy, and cleaves beneath his feet. Once more the soul of Elijah shuddered at the terrific impression of this sign of Yahweh's power. But it had no message for his inmost heart, for "The LORD was not in the earthquake."

19:12–13. And after the earthquake a fire. Yahweh overwhelmed the prophet's senses with the dread magnificence of one of those lucid thunderstorms of which the terrors are never so tremendous as in such mountain scenes, where travelers tell us that the burning air seems transfused into sheets of flame. In that awful muttering and roar of the lurid clouds, that millionfold reverberation of what the psalmist calls "the voice of the LORD," when the lightnings "light the world, and run along the ground," and, in the language of Habakkuk, "God sends abroad his arrows, and the light of his glittering spear, and burning coals go forth under his feet, the lips of man quiver at the voice, and his heart sinks, and he trembles where he stands." And this, too, Elijah must have felt as "the hiding-place of God's power" (Hab. 3:3–16): and yet it did not speak to his inmost heart, for "The LORD was not in the fire."

"And after the fire a still small voice." At once the silence became articulate to his conscience, and repeated to him the reproachful question, "What doest thou here, Elijah?"

19:14–18. Amazed and overwhelmed as he is, he has not yet grasped the meaning of the vision. Something of it perhaps he saw and felt. It breathed

881, 482	1158, 8573	4623, 62C	62C	5066.123	3937, 5204
cj, do, pn	*n ms*, pn	prep, pn	pn	v Qal impf 2ms	prep, n ms
וְאֶת־אֱלִישָׁע	בֶּן־שָׁפָט	מֵאָבֵל	מְחוֹלָה	תִּמְשַׁח	לְנָבִיא
we'eth-'ělîshā‘	ben-shāphāṭ	mē'āvēl	mechôlāh	timshach	lenāvî'
and Elisha	the son of Shaphat	from Abel	Meholah	you will anoint	for a prophet

8809	17.	2030.111	4561.255	4623, 2820	2462	4322.521
prep, ps 2ms		cj, v Qal pf 3ms	art, v Niphal ptc ms	prep, *n fs*	pn	v Hiphil impf 3ms
תַּחְתֶּיךָ		וְהָיָה	הַנִּמְלָט	מֵחֶרֶב	חֲזָאֵל	יָמִית
tachtêkhā		wehāyāh	hanimlāṭ	mēcherev	chăzā'ēl	yāmîth
instead of you		and it will be	the one escaping	from the sword of	Hazael	he will kill

3167	4561.255	4623, 2820	3167	4322.521	482
pn	cj, art, v Niphal ptc ms	prep, *n fs*	pn	v Hiphil impf 3ms	pn
יֵהוּא	וְהַנִּמְלָט	מֵחֶרֶב	יֵהוּא	יָמִית	אֱלִישָׁע
yēhû'	wehanimlāṭ	mēcherev	yēhû'	yāmîth	'ělîshā‘
Jehu	and the one escaping	from the sword of	Jehu	he will kill	Elisha

18.	8080.515	904, 3547	8124	512	3725, 1314	866	3940, 3895.116
	cj, v Hiphil pf 1cs	prep, pn	num	num	*adj*, art, n fd	rel part	neg part, v Qal pf 3cp
	וְהִשְׁאַרְתִּי	בְיִשְׂרָאֵל	שִׁבְעַת	אֲלָפִים	כָּל־הַבִּרְכַּיִם	אֲשֶׁר	לֹא־כָרְעוּ
	wehish'artî	veyisrā'ēl	shiv‘ath	'ălāphîm	kol-habbirkayim	'ăsher	lō'-khāre‘û
	and I have left	in Israel	seven	thousands	all the knees	which	they have not bowed

3937, 1197	3725, 6552	866	3940, 5583.111	3937	19.	2050.121
prep, art, n ms	cj, *adj*, art, n ms	rel part	neg part, v Qal pf 3ms	prep, ps 3ms		cj, v Qal impf 3ms
לַבַּעַל	וְכָל־הַפֶּה	אֲשֶׁר	לֹא־נָשַׁק	לוֹ		וַיֵּלֶךְ
labba‘al	wekhol-happeh	'ăsher	lō'-nāshaq	lô		wayyēlekh
to the Baal	and all the mouths	which	they have not kissed	to him		so he went

4623, 8427	4834.121	881, 482	1158, 8573	2000	2896.151
prep, adv	cj, v Qal impf 3ms	do, pn	*n ms*, pn	cj, pers pron	v Qal act ptc ms
מִשָּׁם	וַיִּמְצָא	אֶת־אֱלִישָׁע	בֶּן־שָׁפָט	וְהוּא	חֹרֵשׁ
mishshām	wayyimtsā'	'eth-'ělîshā‘	ben-shāphāṭ	wehû'	chōrēsh
from there	and he found	Elisha	the son of Shaphat	and he	plowing

8530, 6461	7045	3937, 6686	2000	904, 8530	6461	5882.121
num, num	n mp	prep, n mp, ps 3ms	cj, pers pron	prep, num	art, num	cj, v Qal impf 3ms
שְׁנֵים־עָשָׂר	צְמָדִים	לְפָנָיו	וְהוּא	בִּשְׁנֵים	הֶעָשָׂר	וַיַּעֲבֹר
shenêm-‘āsār	tsemādhîm	lephānâv	wehû'	bishnêm	he‘āsār	wayya‘ăvōr
twelve	pair of oxen	before him	and he	with the two	the ten	and he passed

455	420	8390.521	152	420	20.	6013.121	881, 1267
pn	prep, ps 3ms	cj, v Hiphil impf 3ms	n fs, ps 3ms	prep, ps 3ms		cj, v Qal impf 3ms	do, art, n ms
אֵלִיָּהוּ	אֵלָיו	וַיַּשְׁלֵךְ	אַדַּרְתּוֹ	אֵלָיו		וַיַּעֲזֹב	אֶת־הַבָּקָר
'ēlîyāhû	'ēlâv	wayyashlēkh	'addartô	'ēlâv		wayya‘ăzōv	'eth-habbāqār
Elijah	toward him	and he threw	his mantle	to him		and he left	the oxen

7608.121	313	455	569.121	5583.125	3937, 1
cj, v Qal impf 3ms	prep	pn	cj, v Qal impf 3ms	v Qal juss 1cs, part	prep, n ms, ps 1cs
וַיָּרָץ	אַחֲרֵי	אֵלִיָּהוּ	וַיֹּאמֶר	אֶשְּׁקָה־נָּא	לְאָבִי
wayyārāts	'achrê	'ēlîyāhû	wayyō'mer	'eshsheqāh-nā'	le'āvî
and he ran	after	Elijah	and he said	let me kiss please	my father

3937, 525	2050.125	313	569.121	3937	2050.131
cj, prep, n fs, ps 1cs	cj, v Qal juss 1cs	prep, ps 2ms	cj, v Qal impf 3ms	prep, ps 3ms	v Qal impv 2ms
וּלְאִמִּי	וְאֵלְכָה	אַחֲרֶיךָ	וַיֹּאמֶר	לוֹ	לֵךְ
ûlă'immî	we'ēlekhāh	'achrêkhā	wayyō'mer	lô	lēkh
and my mother	that I may go	after you	and he said	to him	go

17. And it shall come to pass, that him that escapeth the sword of Hazael shall Jehu slay: ... Jehu shall put to death, *NASB* ... any who escape the sword of Jehu, *NIV*.

and him that escapeth from the sword of Jehu shall Elisha slay: ... put to death doth Elisha, *Young* ... shall kill, *NRSV*.

18. Yet I have left me seven thousand in Israel, all the knees which have not bowed unto Baal: ... I reserve, *NIV* ... I will spare, *Berkeley*.

and every mouth which hath not kissed him: ... lips that have never kissed hand to do him worship, *Knox* ... or kissed his idol, *Good News* ... not worshipped him kissing the hands, *Douay*.

19. So he departed thence, and found Elisha the son of Shaphat, who was plowing with twelve yoke of oxen before him, and he with the twelfth: ... plowing a field with a team, *NLT* ... with twelve sets of oxen in his presence, *Fenton* ... he himself was with the last of them, *NEB*.

and Elijah passed by him, and cast his mantle upon him: ... casteth his robe, *Young* ... put his robe on him, *BB* ... threw his cloak over him, *REB*.

20. And he left the oxen, and ran after Elijah, and said, Let me, I pray thee, kiss my father and my mother, and then I will follow thee: ... I beg you, let me kiss, *KJVII* ... Give me leave, he said, to embrace father and mother in parting, *Knox*.

And he said unto him, Go back again: for what have I done to thee?: ... to prevent you?, *NEB* ... consider what I have done to you, *NLT* ... I'm not stopping you!, *Good News* ... for have I done anything, *JB*.

---

something of peace into the despair and tumult of his heart, but he still can only answer as before: "I have been very jealous for the LORD God of hosts: because the children of Israel have forsaken thy covenant, thrown down thine altars, and slain thy prophets with the sword; and I, I only, am left; and they seek my life, to take it away."

Whatever that theophany had taught him, it had not yet fully removed his perplexity. But now God, in tender forbearance, unfolds at any rate the practical issue of the vision. Elijah is to be inactive no longer. He is to find in faithfulness and work the removal of all doubts, and is to learn that man may not abandon his duties, even when they are irksome, even when they seem hopeless, even when they have become intolerable and full of peril. "Go," the LORD said unto him, "return on thy way by the wilderness to Damascus." Did the return involve unknown dangers? Still he must commit his way unto the LORD, and simply be doing good, regardless of all consequences. The saints of old no less had to go forth bearing their cross. Three missions still awaited him.

First, he is to supersede the old dynasty of Ben-Hadad, king of Syria, founded by Solomon's enemy, and to anoint Hazael to be king over Syria.

Next, he is to abolish the dynasty of Omri, and to anoint Jehu, the son of Nimshi, to be king over Israel. Jehu was the grandson of Nimshi, and was the son of Jehoshaphat (2 Ki. 9:2).

Thirdly, and there was deep significance in this behest, and one which must have humiliated to the dust the risings of pride and the half-reproach, so to speak, for inadequate support which had underlain his appeal to Yahweh—he was to anoint Elisha, the son of Shaphat, of Abel-Meholah, to be prophet in his room.

And something of the meaning of these tasks is explained to him. The people of Israel are not yet converted. They still needed the hand of chastisement. The three years' drought had been ineffectual to wean them from their backslidings, and turn their hearts again to the LORD. On the royal house and on the worshipers of Baal should fall the remorseless sword of Jehu. On the whole nation the ruthless invasions of Hazael should press with terrible penalty. And him that escaped from their avenging missions should Elisha slay. The last clause is enigmatic. Elisha can hardly be said directly to have slain any. He lived, on the whole, in friendship with the kings both of Israel and of Aram, and in peace and honor in the cities. But the general idea seems to be that he would carry on the mission of Elijah alike for the guidance and the heaven-directed punishments of kings and nations, and that the famines, raids and humiliations which rendered his nation miserable under the sons of Ahab should be elements of his sacred mission (Isa. 11:4; 49:2; cf. Jer. 1:10; 18:7).

19:19–21. Whether Elijah saw or saw not all that God had meant by the revelation at Horeb, much at any rate was abundantly clear to him, and the path of new duties lay straight before him.

The first of those duties was to anoint Elisha as prophet, and so prepare for the continuation of the task which he had been chosen to inaugurate. He had been bidden to return across the wilderness in the direction of Damascus. Whether he traversed the eastern side of Jordan among his own familiar

				21.	
8178.131	3706	4242, 6449.115	3937	8178.121	4623, 313
v Qal impv 2ms	cj	intrg, v Qal pf 1cs	prep, ps 2ms	cj, v Qal impf 3ms	prep, prep, ps 3ms
שׁוּב	כִּי	מֶה־עָשִׂיתִי	לָךְ	וַיָּשָׁב	מֵאַחֲרָיו
shûv	kî	meh-'āsîthî	lākh	wayyāshāv	mē'achrâv
return	because	what have I done	to you	and he returned	from after him

4089.121	881, 7045	1267	2159.121	904, 3747	1267
cj, v Qal impf 3ms	do, *n ms*	art, n ms	cj, v Qal impf 3ms, ps 3ms	cj, prep, *n ms*	art, n ms
וַיִּקַּח	אֶת־צֶמֶד	הַבָּקָר	וַיִּזְבָּחֵהוּ	וּבִכְלִי	הַבָּקָר
wayyiqqach	'eth-tsemedh	habbāqār	wayyizbāchēhû	ûvikhlî	habbāqār
and he took	the pairs of	the oxen	and he sacrificed them	and with the vessels for	the oxen

1344.311	1340	5598.121	3937, 6194	404.126	7251.121
v Piel pf 3ms, ps 3mp	art, n ms	cj, v Qal impf 3ms	prep, art, n ms	cj, v Qal impf 3mp	cj, v Qal impf 3ms
בִּשְּׁלָם	הַבָּשָׂר	וַיִּתֵּן	לָעָם	וַיֹּאכֵלוּ	וַיָּקָם
bishshelām	habbāsār	wayyittēn	lā'ām	wayyō'khēlû	wayyāqām
he boiled them	the meat	and he gave	to the people	and they ate	and he rose up

				20:1
2050.121	313	455	8664.321	1163
cj, v Qal impf 3ms	prep	pn	cj, v Piel impf 3ms, ps 3ms	cj, pn
וַיֵּלֶךְ	אַחֲרֵי	אֵלִיָּהוּ	וַיְשָׁרְתֵהוּ	וּבֶן־הֲדַד
wayyēlekh	'achrê	'ēlîyāhû	wayshārethēhû	ûven-hedhadh
and he went	after	Elijah	and he ministered to him	now Ben-Hadad

4567, 782	7192.111	881, 3725, 2524	8421	8530	4567	882
n ms, pn	v Qal pf 3ms	do, *adj*, n ms, ps 3ms	cj, num	cj, num	n ms	prep, ps 3ms
מֶלֶךְ־אֲרָם	קָבַץ	אֶת־כָּל־חֵילוֹ	וּשְׁלֹשִׁים	וּשְׁנַיִם	מֶלֶךְ	אִתּוֹ
melekh-'ărām	qāvats	'eth-kol-chêlô	ûshelōshîm	ûshenayim	melekh	'ittô
the king of Aram	he gathered	all his army	and thirty	and two	kings	with him

5670	7681	6148.121	6961.121	6142, 8497	4032.221
cj, n ms	cj, n ms	cj, v Qal impf 3ms	cj, v Qal impf 3ms	prep, pn	cj, v Niphal impf 3ms
וְסוּס	וָרָכֶב	וַיַּעַל	וַיָּצַר	עַל־שֹׁמְרוֹן	וַיִּלָּחֶם
wesûs	wārākhev	wayya'al	wayyātsar	'al-shōmerôn	wayyillāchem
and horses	and chariots	and he went up	and he laid siege	against Samaria	and he fought

	2.				
904	8365.121	4534	420, 255	4567, 3547	6111
prep, ps 3fs	cj, v Qal impf 3ms	n mp	prep, pn	*n ms*, pn	art, n fs
בָּהּ	וַיִּשְׁלַח	מַלְאָכִים	אֶל־אַחְאָב	מֶלֶךְ־יִשְׂרָאֵל	הָעִירָה
bāhh	wayyishlach	mal'ākhîm	'el-'ach'āv	melekh-yisrā'ēl	hā'îrāh
against it	and he sent out	messengers	to Ahab	the king of Israel	to the city

21. And he returned back from him, and took a yoke of oxen, and slew them, and boiled their flesh with the instruments of the oxen, and gave unto the people, and they did eat: ... with the plough of the oxen, *Douay* ... with the yokes … he gave the people a feast, *BB*.

Then he arose, and went after Elijah, and ministered unto him: ... followed Elijah and became his disciple, *REB* ... his helper, *NCV* ... started to follow Elijah and serve him, *Beck* ... as his attendant, *NAB*.

20:1. And Ben-hadad the king of Syria gathered all his host together: and there were thirty and two kings with him, and horses, and chariots: ... mobilized his army, supported by the chariots and horses of thirty-two allied kings, *NLT* ... collected all his forces, and thirty-two Chiefs, *Fenton* ... mustered his whole army, with thirty-two princes at its head, *Knox*.

and he went up and besieged Samaria, and warred against it: ... goeth up and layeth siege against Samaria, and fighteth with it, *Young* ... marched against Samaria to take it by siege or assault, *NEB* ... then he moved, *Berkeley* ... proceeded to invest and attack, *NAB*.

2. And he sent messengers to Ahab king of Israel into the city, and said unto him, Thus saith Ben-hadad: ... inside the city, *Moffatt* ... envoys, *REB* ... representatives into the town, *BB*.

3. Thy silver and thy gold is mine; thy wives also and thy children, even the goodliest, are mine: ... the best are mine, *KJVII* ... your most

hills of Gilead, and then crossed over at Bethshean, where there was a ford, or whether, braving all danger from Jezebel and her emissaries, he passed through the territories of the western tribes, it is certain that we find him next at Abel-Meholah, which was not far from Beth-Shean (1 Ki. 4:12) in the north part of the Jordan valley. This, as he knew, was the home of Elisha, his future successor.

Elijah found him in the heritage of his fathers, plowing the rich level land with twelve yoke of oxen. Eleven were with his servants, and he himself guided the twelfth (1 Ki. 19:19). Elijah must have felt that the youth would have to make a great earthly sacrifice, if he left all this—father and mother and home and lands—to become the disciple and attendant of a wild, wandering and persecuted prophet. He would say nothing to him. He merely left the high road, and "passed over unto him," as he plowed his fields. Reaching him he took off his shaggy garment of skin, and flung it over Elisha's shoulders. The act had a twofold symbolism. It meant the adoption of Elisha by Elijah to be his spiritual son; and it meant a distinct call to the prophetic office.

Elisha did not hesitate long. The mysterious prophet of Carmel—he whose voice was believed to have shut up the heavens, he who had confounded king and priest and people at Carmel—had spoken no word. He had only flung over Elisha the garment of hair, and then stridden back to the road, and gone on his way without once looking back. Soon he would have vanished beyond recall. Elisha decided that he would obey the call of God; that he would not make; "the great refusal." He ran after Elijah, and overtook him, and, accepting the position to which he had been elevated, made but the one human natural request that he might be suffered first to kiss—that is, to bid final farewell to—his father and mother, and then he would follow Elijah.

"Go back again," answered Elijah; "for what have I done to thee?" The words are often explained as a veiled yet severe rebuke, but the words involve no such disapprobation, nor does the context agree with that view of them. His reply simply means, "Go back; it is right, it is natural that thou shouldst thus bid a last farewell before leaving thy home. Thy coming to me must be purely voluntary; I have but cast my mantle over thee, nothing more. Thine own conscience alone can interpret the full meaning of the act, and God will make thy way clear before thy face." And it was thus that Elisha understood the prophet. He went back, and kissed his father and mother. To mark his complete severance from the happy past, he unyoked his pair of oxen, slew them, used the plow and goad and wooden yokes as fuel, boiled the flesh of the oxen, and invited the people to his farewell feast. Then he arose, and went after Elijah, and ministered unto him. He was thence forth recognized as a son of the prophetic schools, and as their future head. His subsequent career belongs entirely to Second Kings.

20:1. The twentieth chapter of the Book of Kings tells us that Ben-Hadad, the Aramean king, accompanied by thirty-two princes of Hittites, Hamathites, and others, gathered together all his host with his horses and chariots, and proclaimed war against Israel. Unable to meet this vast army in the field, Ahab shut himself up in Samaria, and Ben-Hadad went up and besieged it. We do not know which Ben-Hadad this was. It could not have been the grandson of Rezon, whom, fourteen years earlier, King Asa had bribed to attack Baasha in order to divert him from building Ramah. For it is indirectly mentioned that "his father" had taken cities from Omri. It may have been his son or grandson bearing the same religious dynastic name. In any case, the policy of attacking Israel was suicidal. If the kings had possessed the prescient glance of the prophets, they could not have failed to see on the northern horizon the cloud of Assyrian power, which menaced them all with cruel extinction at the hands of that atrocious people. Their true policy would have been to form an offensive and defensive league, instead of coveting one another's dominions. Although Assyria had not yet risen to the zenith of her empire, she was already formidable enough to convince the king of Damascus that he would never be able single-handed to prevent Syria from being crushed before her. Instead of inflicting ruinous losses and humiliations on the tribes of Israel, the dynasty of Rezon, if it had been wise in its day, would have insured their friendly aid against the horrible common enemy of the nations.

20:2–4. When Ben-Hadad had succeeded in reducing Ahab to hopeless straits, he sent him a herald to demand the admission of ambassadors. Their ultimatum was couched in language of the deadliest insult. Ben-Hadad laid insolent claim to everything which Ahab possessed—his silver, his gold, his wives, and the fairest of his children. To save his people from ruin, Ahab sent an answer of the humblest submission. Tyre gave him no help, nor did

569.121	**3937**	**3662**	**569.111**	**1163**		**3826B**	**2174**
cj, v Qal impf 3ms	prep, ps 3ms	adv	v Qal pf 3ms	pn	**3.**	n ms, ps 2ms	cj, n ms, ps 2ms
וַיֹּאמֶר	לוֹ	כֹּה	אָמַר	בֶּן־הֲדַד		כַּסְפְּךָ	וּזְהָבְךָ
wayyō'mer	lô	kōh	'āmar	ben-hᵉdhadh		kaspᵉkhā	ûzăhāvᵉkhā
and he said	to him	thus	he has said	Ben-Hadad		your silver	and your gold

3937, 2000	**5571**	**1158**	**3005**	**3937, 2062**
prep, ps 1cs, pers pron	cj, n fp, ps 2ms	cj, n mp, ps 2ms	art, adj	prep, ps 1cs, pers pron
לִי־הוּא	וְנָשֶׁיךָ	וּבָנֶיךָ	הַטּוֹבִים	לִי־הֵם
lî-hû'	wᵉnāshêkhā	ûvānêkhā	haṯṯôvîm	lî-hēm
to me it	and your women	and your children	the beautiful	to me they

	6257.121	**4567, 3547**	**569.121**	**3626, 1745**	**112**
4.	cj, v Qal impf 3ms	*n ms*, pn	cj, v Qal impf 3ms	prep, n ms, ps 2ms	n ms, ps 1cs
	וַיַּעַן	מֶלֶךְ־יִשְׂרָאֵל	וַיֹּאמֶר	כִּדְבָרְךָ	אֲדֹנִי
	wayya'an	melekh-yisrā'ēl	wayyō'mer	kidhvārᵉkhā	'ădhōnî
	and he answered	the king of Israel	and he said	according to your word	my lord

4567	**3937**	**603**	**3725, 866, 3937**		**8178.126**	**4534**
art, n ms	prep, ps 2ms	pers pron	cj, *adj*, rel part, prep, ps 1cs	**5.**	cj, v Qal impf 3mp	art, n mp
הַמֶּלֶךְ	לְךָ	אֲנִי	וְכָל־אֲשֶׁר־לִי		וַיָּשֻׁבוּ	הַמַּלְאָכִים
hammelekh	lᵉkhā	'ănî	wᵉkhol-'ăsher-lî		wayyāshuvû	hammal'ākhîm
the king	to you	I	and all which to me		and they returned	the messengers

569.126	**3662, 569.111**	**1163**	**3937, 569.141**	**3706, 8365.115**	**420**
cj, v Qal impf 3mp	adv, v Qal pf 3ms	pn	prep, v Qal inf con	cj, v Qal pf 1cs	prep, ps 2ms
וַיֹּאמְרוּ	כֹּה־אָמַר	בֶּן־הֲדַד	לֵאמֹר	כִּי־שָׁלַחְתִּי	אֵלֶיךָ
wayyō'mᵉrû	kōh-'āmar	ben-hᵉdhadh	lē'mōr	kî-shālachtî	'ēlêkhā
and they said	thus He has said	Ben-Hadad	saying	because I sent	to you

3937, 569.141	**3826B**	**2174**	**5571**	**1158**	**3937**
prep, v Qal inf con	n ms, ps 2ms	cj, n ms, ps 2ms	cj, n fp, ps 2ms	cj, n mp, ps 2ms	prep, ps 1cs
לֵאמֹר	כַּסְפְּךָ	וּזְהָבְךָ	וְנָשֶׁיךָ	וּבָנֶיךָ	לִי
lē'mōr	kaspᵉkhā	ûzăhāvᵉkhā	wᵉnāshêkhā	ûvānêkhā	lî
saying	your silver	and your gold	and your women	and your children	to me

5598.123		**3706**	**524, 3626, 6496**	**4417**	**8365.125**	**881, 5860**
v Qal impf 2ms	**6.**	cj	cj, prep, n fs	adv	v Qal impf 1cs	do, n mp, ps 1cs
תִּתֵּן		כִּי	אִם־כָּעֵת	מָחָר	אֶשְׁלַח	אֶת־עֲבָדַי
thittēn		kî	'im-kā'ēth	māchār	'eshlach	'eth-'ăvādhay
you will give		yet	rather according to the time	tomorrow	I will send out	my servants

420	**2769.116**	**881, 1041**	**881**	**1041**	**5860**	**2030.111**
prep, ps 2ms	cj, v Qal pf 3cp	do, n ms, ps 2ms	cj, do	*n mp*	n mp, ps 2ms	cj, v Qal pf 3ms
אֵלֶיךָ	וְחִפְּשׂוּ	אֶת־בֵּיתְךָ	וְאֵת	בָּתֵּי	עֲבָדֶיךָ	וְהָיָה
'ēlêkhā	wᵉchippᵉsû	'eth-bêthᵉkhā	wᵉ'ēth	bāttê	'ăvādhêkhā	wᵉhāyāh
to you	and they will examine	your house	and	the houses of	your servants	and it will be

3725, 4398	**6084**	**7947.126**	**904, 3135**	**4089.116**
adj, n ms	n fd, ps 2ms	v Qal impf 3mp	prep, n fs, ps 3mp	cj, v Qal pf 3cp
כָּל־מַחְמַד	עֵינֶיךָ	יָשִׂימוּ	בְיָדָם	וְלָקָחוּ
kol-machmadh	'ênêkhā	yāsîmû	vᵉyādhām	wᵉlāqāchû
all the desirable objects of	your eyes	they will put	into their hand	and they will take

	7410.121	**4567, 3547**	**3937, 3725, 2292**	**800**	**569.121**
7.	cj, v Qal impf 3ms	*n ms*, pn	prep, *adj*, *n mp*	art, n fs	cj, v Qal impf 3ms
	וַיִּקְרָא	מֶלֶךְ־יִשְׂרָאֵל	לְכָל־זִקְנֵי	הָאָרֶץ	וַיֹּאמֶר
	wayyiqŏrā'	melekh-yisrā'ēl	lᵉkhol-ziqnê	hā'ārets	wayyō'mer
	so he called	the king of Israel	to all the elders of	the land	and he said

beautiful wives and children are also, *NASB* ... remain yours, *JB* ... finest of your sons, *Beck*.

4. And the king of Israel answered and said, My lord, O king, according to thy saying, I am thine, and all that I have: ... As your Majesty says, ... are yours, *Fenton* ... I accept thy terms; all that I have is at thy disposal, *Knox* ... According to your statement ... together with all that I possess, *Goodspeed* ... he can have me and everything I own, *Good News*.

5. And the messengers came again, and said, Thus speaketh Ben-hadad, saying, Although I have sent unto thee, saying: ... The envoys, *NEB* ... the couriers, *NAB* ... the messengers came to Ahab again, *NCV*.

Thou shalt deliver me thy silver, and thy gold, and thy wives, and thy children: ... I have already demanded that you give me, *NLT* ... thy sons, to me thou dost give, *Young* ... sent you an order to hand over, *JB* ... I did not send to ask you, *Moffatt*.

6. Yet I will send my servants unto thee tomorrow about this time: ... nevertheless I will send my servants to you, *NRSV* ... envoys of mine shall visit thee, *Knox* ... And if not by tomorrow at this time, *Fenton* ... Or else I will send, *Tyndale*.

and they shall search thine house, and the houses of thy servants: ... search everywhere in your palace and in the homes of your officers, *NCV* ... send my servants to ransack your house and your servants', *JB* ... plunder your home, *Berkeley* ... my officials to search your palace, *NLT*.

and it shall be, that whatsoever is pleasant in thine eyes, they shall put it in their hand, and take it away: ... whatever they see that pleases them they shall seize and carry off, *Moffatt* ... take away whatever they consider valuable, *NAB* ... lay hands on whatever, *RSV* ... anything that is precious to you, *Beck*.

7. Then the king of Israel called all the elders of the land: ... ancients, *Douay* ... King Ahab called in all the leaders of the country, *Good News* ... sent for all the responsible men, *BB* ... summoned, *NEB*.

and said, Mark, I pray you, and see how this man seeketh mischief: ... and take note how this man is looking for trouble, *Goodspeed* ... You can see the man is bent on picking a quarrel, *REB* ... evil this one is seeking, *Young*.

for he sent unto me for my wives, and for my children, and for my silver, and for my gold; and I denied him not: ... did not refuse, *NIV* ... did not keep them back from, *KJVII*.

8. And all the elders and all the people said unto him, Hearken not unto him, nor consent: ... Don't listen to him or agree to this, *NCV* ... agree to do what he tells you, *Beck* ... give in to any more demands, *NLT*.

Judah. He seems at this time to have been entirely isolated and to have sunk to the nadir of his degradation. "It is true," he said, "my lord, and king; I, and all that I possess, is thine." The depth of humiliation involved in such a concession is the measure of the utter straits to which Ahab was reduced.

20:5–6. Encouraged by this abject demeanor into yet more outrageous insolence, Ben-Hadad sent back his ambassadors with the further menace that he would himself send his messengers next day into Samaria, who should search and rifle not only the palace of Ahab, but the houses of all his servants, from which they should take away everything that was pleasant in their eyes.

20:7. The merciless demand kindled in the breast of the wretched king one last spark of the courage of despair. Nothing could be worse than such a pillage. Death itself seemed preferable. He summoned together all the elders of the land to a great council, to which the people also were invited, and he set the state of things before them. The fact gives us an interesting glimpse into the constitution of the kingdom of Israel. Under ordinary circumstances of prosperity the king was within certain limits despotic; but he might easily be reduced to the necessity of consulting the elders, composed of his greatest subjects (Exo. 3:16), and at these deliberations the people were present as assessors. The king's will, however, determined the ultimate course of action.

Ahab put before his council the desperate condition to which he had been reduced by the Syrian leaguer. He recounted the cruel terms to which he had submitted in order to save his people from destruction. From the second embassage of Ben-Hadad, it was clear that the first demand had only been made in the hope that its refusal would give the Syrians an excuse for pressing on the siege, and delivering the city to ravage and slaughter. Was it their will that the insolent foreign tyrant should have his way, and be permitted without let or hindrance to rifle their houses, and carry away their goodliest sons as eunuchs and their fairest wives as concubines?

20:8–12. The elders saw that even massacre and pillage could hardly be worse than a tame submission to such demands. They plucked up courage and said to Ahab, "Hearken not to him, nor con-

3156.133, 5167	7495.133	3706	7750	2172	1272.351	3706, 8365.111	420
v Qal impv 2mp, part	cj, v Qal impv 2mp	cj	adj	dem pron	v Piel ptc ms	cj, v Qal pf 3ms	prep, ps 1cs
דְּעוּ־נָא	וּרְאוּ	כִּי	רָעָה	זֶה	מְבַקֵּשׁ	כִּי־שָׁלַח	אֵלַי
dᵉ‘û-nā’	ûrᵉ’û	kî	rā‘āh	zeh	mᵉvaqqēsh	kî-shālach	’ēlay
know please	and see	that	evil	this one	seeking	because he sent	to me

3937, 5571	3937, 1158	3937, 3826B	3937, 2174	3940	4661.115
prep, n fp, ps 1cs	cj, prep, n mp, ps 1cs	cj, prep, n ms, ps 1cs	cj, prep, n ms, ps 1cs	cj, neg part	v Qal pf 1cs
לְנָשַׁי	וּלְבָנַי	וּלְכַסְפִּי	וְלִזְהָבִי	וְלֹא	מָנַעְתִּי
lᵉnāshay	ûlăvānay	ûlăkhaspî	wᵉlizhāvî	wᵉlō’	māna‘ăttî
for my women	and for my children	and for my silver	and for my gold	and not	I refused

4623	**8.**	569.126	420	3706, 2292	3725, 6194	414, 8471.123
prep, ps 3ms		cj, v Qal impf 3mp	prep, ps 3ms	*adj*, art, n mp	cj, *adj*, art, n ms	adv, v Qal juss 2ms
מִמֶּנּוּ		וַיֹּאמְרוּ	אֵלָיו	כָּל־הַזְּקֵנִים	וְכָל־הָעָם	אַל־תִּשְׁמַע
mimmennû		wayyō’mᵉrû	’ēlāv	kol-hazzᵉqēnîm	wᵉkhol-hā‘ām	’al-tishma‘
from him		and they said	to him	all the elders	and all the people	do not listen

3940	13.123	**9.**	569.121	3937, 4534	1163	569.133
cj, neg part	v Qal impf 2ms		cj, v Qal impf 3ms	prep, *n mp*	pn	v Qal impv 2mp
וְלוֹא	תֹאבֶה		וַיֹּאמֶר	לְמַלְאֲכֵי	בֶן־הֲדַד	אִמְרוּ
wᵉlô’	thō’veh		wayyō’mer	lᵉmal’ăkhê	ven-hᵉdhadh	’imrû
and not	you will consent		and he said	to the messengers of	Ben-Hadad	say

3937, 112	4567	3725	866, 8365.113	420, 5860	904, 7518	6449.125
prep, n ms, ps 1cs	art, n ms	n ms	rel part, v Qal pf 2ms	prep, n ms, ps 2ms	prep, art, adj	v Qal impf 1cs
לַאדֹנִי	הַמֶּלֶךְ	כֹּל	אֲשֶׁר־שָׁלַחְתָּ	אֶל־עַבְדְּךָ	בָרִאשֹׁנָה	אֶעֱשֶׂה
la’dhōnî	hammelekh	kōl	’ăsher-shālachtā	’el-‘avdᵉkhā	vāri’shōnāh	’e‘ĕseh
to my lord	the king	everything	that you sent	to your servant	at the first	I will do

1745	2172	3940	3310.125	3937, 6449.141	2050.126	4534
cj, art, n ms	art, dem pron	neg part	v Qal impf 1cs	prep, v Qal inf con	cj, v Qal impf 3mp	art, n mp
וְהַדָּבָר	הַזֶּה	לֹא	אוּכַל	לַעֲשׂוֹת	וַיֵּלְכוּ	הַמַּלְאָכִים
wᵉhaddāvār	hazzeh	lō’	’ûkhal	la‘ăsôth	wayyēlᵉkhû	hammal’ākhîm
but the thing	the this	not	I am able	to do	and they went	the messengers

8178.526	1745	**10.**	8365.121	420	1163	569.121
cj, v Hiphil impf 3mp, ps 3ms	n ms		cj, v Qal impf 3ms	prep, ps 3ms	pn	cj, v Qal impf 3ms
וַיְשִׁבֻהוּ	דָּבָר		וַיִּשְׁלַח	אֵלָיו	בֶּן־הֲדַד	וַיֹּאמֶר
wayshivuhû	dāvār		wayyishlach	’ēlāv	ben-hᵉdhadh	wayyō’mer
and they brought to him	words		and he sent out	to him	Ben-Hadad	and he said

3662, 6449.126	3937	435	3662	3362.526	524, 8009.121	6312
adv, v Qal juss 3mp	prep, ps 1cs	n mp	cj, adv	v Hiphil juss 3mp	cj, v Qal impf 3ms	*n ms*
כֹּה־יַעֲשׂוּן	לִי	אֱלֹהִים	וְכֹה	יוֹסִפוּ	אִם־יִשְׂפֹּק	עֲפַר
kōh-ya‘ăsûn	lî	’ĕlōhîm	wᵉkhōh	yôsiphû	’im-yispōq	‘ăphar
thus may they do	to me	gods	and thus	may they add	if it will clap	the dust of

8497	3937, 8545	3937, 3725, 6194	866	904, 7559	**11.**	6257.121
pn	prep, n mp	prep, *adj*, art, n ms	rel pron	prep, n fd, ps 1cs		cj, v Qal impf 3ms
שֹׁמְרוֹן	לִשְׁעָלִים	לְכָל־הָעָם	אֲשֶׁר	בְּרַגְלָי		וַיַּעַן
shōmᵉrôn	lish‘ālîm	lᵉkhol-hā‘ām	’ăsher	bᵉraghlāy		wayya‘an
Samaria	for the handfuls	of all the people	who	beside my feet		and he answered

4567, 3547	569.121	1744.333	414, 2054.721	2391.151
n ms, pn	cj, v Qal impf 3ms	v Piel impv 2mp	adv, v Hithpael juss 3ms	v Qal act ptc ms
מֶלֶךְ־יִשְׂרָאֵל	וַיֹּאמֶר	דַּבְּרוּ	אַל־יִתְהַלֵּל	חֹגֵר
melekh-yisrā’ēl	wayyō’mer	dabbᵉrû	’al-yithhallēl	chōghēr
the king of Israel	and he said	speak	may he not boast	the one girding on

2000 cj, pers pron וְהוּא wᵉhû' that he	2172 art, dem pron הַזֶּה hazzeh the this	881, 1745 do, art, n ms אֶת־הַדָּבָר 'eth-haddāvār the word	3626, 8471.141 prep, v Qal inf con כִּשְׁמֹעַ kishmōa' when hearing	2030.121 cj, v Qal impf 3ms וַיְהִי wayhî and it was	**12.**	3626, 6858.351 prep, v Piel ptc ms כִּמְפַתֵּחַ kimphattēach like the one taking off

7947.133 v Qal impv 2mp שִׂימוּ sîmû place	420, 5860 prep, n mp, ps 3ms אֶל־עֲבָדָיו 'el-'ăvādhâv to his servants	569.121 cj, v Qal impf 3ms וַיֹּאמֶר wayyō'mer and he said	904, 5712 prep, art, n fp בַּסֻּכּוֹת bassukkôth in the booths	4534 cj, art, n mp וְהַמְּלָכִים wᵉhammᵉlākhîm and the kings	2000 pers pron הוּא hû' he	8685.151 v Qal act ptc ms שֹׁתֶה shōtheh drinking

9. Wherefore he said unto the messengers of Ben-hadad, Tell my lord the king, All that thou didst send for to thy servant at the first I will do: ... All you first required of your servant, *JB* ... I agreed to his first demand, *Good News* ... I will agree fully to the first request, *Berkeley* ... I accepted your majesty's demands on the first occasion, *NEB* ... I promised to your officers before, I will do, *Fenton*.

but this thing I may not do. And the messengers departed, and brought him word again: ... I cannot do, *NAB* ... demand I cannot meet, *NIV* ... thing I am not able to do, *Young* ... request I may not do, *Tyndale*.

10. And Ben-hadad sent unto him, and said, The gods do so unto me, and more also: ... Such and such things may the gods do to me, *Douay* ... The gods kill me, *Moffatt* ... punishment be on me, *BB* ... requite me and worse, *Goodspeed*.

if the dust of Samaria shall suffice for handfuls for all the people that follow me: ... for all the people who are at my feet, *Rotherham* ... be enough to all the people … for every man, *Geneva* ... I do not beat Samaria to the dust! I have more than enough warriors here at my back to carry it away, *Knox* ... enough dust is left in Samaria, *REB*.

11. And the king of Israel answered and said, Tell him, Let not him that girdeth on his harness boast himself as he that putteth it off: ... A warrior still dressing for battle should not boast like a warrior who has already won, *NLT* ... puts on his armor boast like the one who takes it off, *NKJV* ... The lame must not think himself a match for the nimble, *NEB* ... The time for boasting is after the battle, *REB*.

12. And it came to pass, when Ben-hadad heard this message, as he was drinking, he and the kings in the pavilions: ... he was drinking with his Generals in the tents, *Fenton* ... feasting in their quarters, *REB* ... temporary shelters, *NASB*.

that he said unto his servants, Set yourselves in array. And they set themselves in array against the city: ... they got ready to attack, *NKJV* ... Besiege me, *Knox* ... took their positions against, *NRSV*.

13. And, behold, there came a prophet unto Ahab king of Israel, saying, Thus saith the Lord, Hast thou seen all this great multitude? behold, I will deliver it into thine hand this day; and thou shalt know that I am the Lord: ... You see this

sent"; and the people shouted their applause to the heroic refusal (cf. Josh. 9:18; Judg. 11:11). The king seems in this instance to have been more despondent than his subjects, perhaps because he was better able than they to gauge the immense military superiority of his invader. Ahab said, "Tell my lord the king, I will submit to his first demands; I may not consent to his final ones."

The ambassadors went to Ben-Hadad, and returned with the fierce menace that their king would shatter Samaria into dust, of which the handfuls would not suffice for each of his soldiers. This pronouncement was delivered in the name of his god (1 Ki. 20:10; 'ĕlōhîm [HED #435] here, doubtless, means the false gods of Ben-Hadad). Ahab replied firmly in a challenging proverb, "Let not him that girdeth on his armor boast himself as he that putteth it off."

The warning proverb was reported to the Aramean king, whilst in the insolent confidence of victory he was drinking himself drunk in his war-booths. The word (sukkûth; HED #5712) implies that they were temporary booths rather than tents. It nettled him to fury. "Attack," he exclaimed. The siege equipment of the day was at once set into motion.

Ahab's heart must have sunk within him, for he knew his impotence, and he knew also the horrors which befell a city taken after desperate resistance. But he was not left unencouraged. The characteristic of the prophets was dauntless confidence in Yahweh.

7947.126	6142, 6111		2079	5204	259	5242.211	420, 255
cj, v Qal impf 3mp	prep, art, n fs	**13.**	cj, intrj	n ms	num	v Niphal pf 3ms	prep, pn
וַיָּשִׂימוּ	עַל־הָעִיר		וְהִנֵּה	נָבִיא	אֶחָד	נִגַּשׁ	אֶל־אַחְאָב
wayyāsîmû	‘al-hā‘îr		wehinnēh	nāvî’	’echādh	niggash	’el-’ach’āv
and they placed	against the city		and behold	a prophet	one	he came near	to Ahab

4567, 3547	569.121	3662	569.111	3176	1950B, 7495.113	881
n ms, pn	cj, v Qal impf 3ms	adv	v Qal pf 3ms	pn	intrg part, v Qal pf 2ms	do
מֶלֶךְ־יִשְׂרָאֵל	וַיֹּאמֶר	כֹּה	אָמַר	יְהוָה	הֲרָאִיתָ	אֵת
melekh-yisrā’ēl	wayyō’mer	kōh	’āmar	yehwāh	hărā’îthā	’ēth
the king of Israel	and he said	thus	He has said	Yahweh	have you seen	

3725, 2066	1448	2172	2079	5598.151	904, 3135	3219
adj, art, n ms	art, adj	art, dem pron	intrj, ps 1cs	v Qal act ptc ms, ps 3ms	prep, n fs, ps 2ms	art, n ms
כָּל־הֶהָמוֹן	הַגָּדוֹל	הַזֶּה	הִנְנִי	נֹתְנוֹ	בְיָדְךָ	הַיּוֹם
kol-hehāmôn	haggādhôl	hazzeh	hinenî	nōthenô	veyādhekhā	hayyôm
all the multitude	the great	the this	behold I	giving it	into your hand	today

3156.113	3706, 603	3176		569.121	255	904, 4449	569.121
cj, v Qal pf 2ms	cj, pers pron	pn	**14.**	cj, v Qal impf 3ms	pn	prep, intrg	cj, v Qal impf 3ms
וְיָדַעְתָּ	כִּי־אֲנִי	יְהוָה		וַיֹּאמֶר	אַחְאָב	בְּמִי	וַיֹּאמֶר
weyādha‘ättā	kî-’ănî	yehwāh		wayyō’mer	’ach’āv	bemî	wayyō’mer
and you will know	that I	Yahweh		and he said	Ahab	by whom	and he said

3662, 569.111	3176	904, 5470	8015	4224	569.121
adv, v Qal pf 3ms	pn	prep, *n mp*	*n mp*	art, n fp	cj, v Qal impf 3ms
כֹּה־אָמַר	יְהוָה	בְּנַעֲרֵי	שָׂרֵי	הַמְּדִינוֹת	וַיֹּאמֶר
kōh-’āmar	yehwāh	bena‘ărê	sārê	hammedhînôth	wayyō’mer
thus He has said	Yahweh	by the servants of	the commanders of	the districts	and he said

4449, 636.121	4560	569.121	887		6734.121	881, 5470
intrg, v Qal impf 3ms	art, n fs	cj, v Qal impf 3ms	pers pron	**15.**	cj, v Qal impf 3ms	do, *n mp*
מִי־יֶאֱסֹר	הַמִּלְחָמָה	וַיֹּאמֶר	אַתָּה		וַיִּפְקֹד	אֶת־נַעֲרֵי
mî-ye’ĕsōr	hammilchāmāh	wayyō’mer	’attāh		wayyiphqōdh	’eth-na‘ărê
who will bind	the war	and he said	you		and he mustered	the servants of

8015	4224	2030.126	4109	8530	8421	313
n mp	art, n fp	cj, v Qal impf 3mp	num	num	cj, num	cj, prep, ps 3mp
שָׂרֵי	הַמְּדִינוֹת	וַיִּהְיוּ	מָאתַיִם	שְׁנַיִם	וּשְׁלֹשִׁים	וְאַחֲרֵיהֶם
sārê	hammedhînôth	wayyihyû	mā’thayim	shenayim	ûshelōshîm	we’achrêhem
the commanders of	the districts	and they were	two hundred	two	and thirty	and after them

6734.111	881, 3725, 6194	3725, 1158	3547	8124	512		3428.126
v Qal pf 3ms	do, *adj*, art, n ms	*adj*, *n mp*	pn	num	num	**16.**	cj, v Qal impf 3mp
פָּקַד	אֶת־כָּל־הָעָם	כָּל־בְּנֵי	יִשְׂרָאֵל	שִׁבְעַת	אֲלָפִים		וַיֵּצְאוּ
pāqadh	’eth-kol-hā‘ām	kol-benê	yisrā’ēl	shiv‘ath	’ălāphîm		wayyētse’û
he mustered	all the people	all the sons of	Israel	seven	thousands		and they went out

904, 6937	1163	8685.151	8318	904, 5712	2000	4534
prep, art, n mp	cj, pn	v Qal act ptc ms	adj	prep, art, n fp	pers pron	cj, art, n mp
בַּצָּהֳרָיִם	וּבֶן־הֲדַד	שֹׁתֶה	שִׁכּוֹר	בַּסֻּכּוֹת	הוּא	וְהַמְּלָכִים
batstsāherāyim	ûven-hedhadh	shōtheh	shikkôr	bassukkôth	hû’	wehammelākhîm
when the noontime	and Ben-Hadad	drinking	drunk	in the booths	he	and the kings

8421, 8530	4567	6038.151	881		3428.126	5470
num, cj, num	n ms	v Qal act ptc ms	do, ps 3ms	**17.**	cj, v Qal impf 3mp	*n mp*
שְׁלֹשִׁים־וּשְׁנַיִם	מֶלֶךְ	עֹזֵר	אֹתוֹ		וַיֵּצְאוּ	נַעֲרֵי
shelōshîm-ûshenayim	melekh	‘ōzēr	’ōthô		wayyētse’û	na‘ărê
thirty and two	kings	helping	him		and they went out	the servants of

8015	4224	904, 7518	8365.121	1163	5222.526
n mp	art, n fp	prep, art, adj	cj, v Qal impf 3ms	pn	cj, v Hiphil impf 3mp
שָׂרֵי	הַמְּדִינוֹת	בָּרִאשֹׁנָה	וַיִּשְׁלַח	בֶּן־הֲדַד	וַיַּגִּידוּ
sārê	hamm^edhînôth	bāri'shōnāh	wayyishlach	ben-h^edhadh	wayyaggîdhû
the commanders of	the districts	at the first	and he sent out	Ben-Hadad	and they reported

3937	3937, 569.141	596	3428.116	4623, 8497	18. 569.121
prep, ps 3ms	prep, v Qal inf con	n mp	v Qal pf 3cp	prep, pn	cj, v Qal impf 3ms
לוֹ	לֵאמֹר	אֲנָשִׁים	יָצְאוּ	מִשֹּׁמְרוֹן	וַיֹּאמֶר
lô	lē'mōr	'ănāshîm	yāts^e'û	mishshōm^erôn	wayyō'mer
to him	saying	men	they have come out	from Samaria	and he said

great rabble? Today I will give it into your hands, *NEB* ... what a great multitude of warriors is here, *Knox* ... great army?, *BB* ... whole mass of people?, *Beck*.

14. And Ahab said, By whom? And he said, Thus saith the LORD, Even by the young men of the princes of the provinces: ... By the Guards of the Provincial Governors, *Fenton* ... young officers of the provincial commanders will do it, *NIV* ... soldiers of your feudal governors, *Moffatt*.

Then he said, Who shall order the battle? And he answered, Thou: ... Who will launch the attack?, *REB* ... co-ordinate the attack?, *JB*.

15. Then he numbered the young men of the princes of the provinces, and they were two hundred and thirty two: ... Ahab mustered the troops of the 232 provincial commanders, *NLT* ... servants of all the chiefs who were over the divisions of the land, *BB* ... young soldiers who were under the district commanders, *Good News*.

and after them he numbered all the people, even all the children of Israel, being seven thousand: ... he mustered all the Israelite soldiery, *NAB* ... After these he reviewed the army, *JB*.

16. And they went out at noon. But Ben-hadad was drinking himself drunk in the pavilions, he and the kings, the thirty and two kings that helped him: ... thirty-two rulers helping him were getting drunk in their tents, *NCV* ... senseless under the awnings, *JB* ... Benhadad and his thirty-two allies, *Good News* ... They made a raid at noon when Benhadad was in his quarters, *Beck*.

17. And the young men of the princes of the provinces went out first; and Ben-hadad sent out, and they told him, saying, There are men come out of Samaria: ... The soldiers of the feudal governors marched in front, *Moffatt* ... Benhadad received word that some men had marched out, *NAB* ... sent out scouts, and they reported to him, *RSV*

20:13–15. In this extreme of peril, a nameless prophet came to Ahab. As though to emphasize the supernatural character of his communication, he pointed to the chariots and archers and the Syrian host—which, if the subsequent numbers are accurate, must have reached the astounding total of 130,000 men—and said, in the name of Yahweh:

> "Hast thou seen all this great multitude?
> Lo! I will deliver it into thine hand today:
> And thou shalt know that I am the LORD."

"By whom?" was the astonished and half-despairing question of the king; and the strange answer was:—

"By the young servants of the provincial governors" (1 Ki. 20:14). It was to be made clear that this was a victory due to the intervention of God, and not won by the power nor the might of man, lest the warriors of Israel should be able to boast of the arm of flesh.

"Who shall lead the assault?" asked the king.

"Thou!" answered the prophet.

Nothing could be wiser than this counsel, now that the nation was brought to the extreme edge of hazard. The veterans, perhaps, were intimidated. They would see more clearly the hopelessness of attempting to cope with that colossal host under its five-and-thirty kings. But now the nation, whose veterans had been driven back, evoked the battle-brunt of its youths. The pages of the district governors were ready to obey orders, ready, like an army of Decii to devote their lives to the cause of their country. They were put in the forefront of the battle, and so pitiable was the depression of the capital that Ahab could only number a paltry army of 7000 soldiers to stand behind their desperate undertaking. Jarchi—more Rabbinico—says that these were the 7000 who had not bowed the knee to Baal.

20:16–21. Their plan was well laid. They went out at noon. At that burning hour, under the intolerable glare and heat of the Syrian sun—and campaigns were only undertaken in spring and sum-

524, 3937, 8361	3428.116	8945.133	2552	524	3937, 4560
cj, prep, n ms	v Qal pf 3cp	v Qal impv 2mp, ps 3mp	adj	cj, cj	prep, n fs
אִם־לְשָׁלוֹם	יָצָאוּ	תִּפְשׂוּם	חַיִּים	וְאִם	לְמִלְחָמָה
'im-l^{e}shālôm	yātsā'û	tiphsûm	chayyîm	w^{e}'im	l^{e}milchāmāh
if for peace	they have come out	seize them	alive	or if	for war

3428.116	2552	8945.133		431	3428.116	4623, 6111
v Qal pf 3cp	adj	v Qal impv 2mp, ps 3mp	**19.**	cj, dem pron	v Qal pf 3cp	prep, art, n fs
יָצָאוּ	חַיִּים	תִּפְשׂוּם		וְאֵלֶּה	יָצְאוּ	מִן־הָעִיר
yātsā'û	chayyîm	tiphsûm		w^{e}'ēlleh	yāts^{e}'û	min-hā'îr
they have come out	alive	seize them		so these	they went out	from the city

5470	8015	4224	2524	866	313
n mp	*n mp*	art, n fp	cj, art, n ms	rel pron	prep, ps 3mp
נַעֲרֵי	שָׂרֵי	הַמְּדִינוֹת	וְהַחַיִל	אֲשֶׁר	אַחֲרֵיהֶם
na'ărê	sārê	hamm^{e}dhînôth	w^{e}hachayil	'ăsher	'achrêhem
the servants of	the commanders of	the districts	and the army	who	after them

	5409.526	382	382	5308.126	782	7579.121
20.	cj, v Hiphil impf 3mp	n ms	n ms, ps 3ms	cj, v Qal impf 3mp	pn	cj, v Qal impf 3ms, ps 3mp
	וַיַּכּוּ	אִישׁ	אִישׁוֹ	וַיָּנֻסוּ	אֲרָם	וַיִּרְדְּפֵם
	wayyakkû	'îsh	'îshô	wayyānusû	'ărām	wayyird^{e}phēm
	and they struck down	each	his man	and they fled	Aram	but they pursued them

3547	4561.221	1163	4567	782	6142, 5670	6821
pn	cj, v Niphal impf 3ms	pn	*n ms*	pn	prep, n ms	cj, n mp
יִשְׂרָאֵל	וַיִּמָּלֵט	בֶּן־הֲדַד	מֶלֶךְ	אֲרָם	עַל־סוּס	וּפָרָשִׁים
yisrā'ēl	wayyimmālēṭ	ben-h^{e}dhadh	melekh	'ărām	'al-sûs	ûphārāshîm
Israel	but he escaped	Ben-Hadad	the king of	Aram	on a horse	and horsemen

	3428.121	4567	3547	5409.521	881, 5670	881, 7681
21.	cj, v Qal impf 3ms	*n ms*	pn	cj, v Hiphil impf 3ms	do, art, n ms	cj, do, art, n ms
	וַיֵּצֵא	מֶלֶךְ	יִשְׂרָאֵל	וַיַּךְ	אֶת־הַסּוּס	וְאֶת־הָרֶכֶב
	wayyētsē'	melekh	yisrā'ēl	wayyakh	'eth-hassûs	w^{e}'eth-hārākhev
	so he went out	the king of	Israel	and he struck down	the horses	and the chariots

5409.521	904, 782	4485	1448		5242.121	5204
cj, Hiphil impf 3ms	prep, pn	n fs	adj	**22.**	cj, v Qal impf 3ms	art, n ms
וְהִכָּה	בַּאֲרָם	מַכָּה	גְדוֹלָה		וַיִּגַּשׁ	הַנָּבִיא
w^{e}hikkāh	va'ărām	makkāh	gh^{e}dhôlāh		wayyiggash	hannāvî'
and he struck down	on Aram	a striking	great		then he came near	the prophet

420, 4567	3547	569.121	3937	2050.131	2480.731
prep, *n ms*	pn	cj, v Qal impf 3ms	prep, ps 3ms	v Qal impv 2ms	v Hithpael impv 2ms
אֶל־מֶלֶךְ	יִשְׂרָאֵל	וַיֹּאמֶר	לוֹ	לֵךְ	הִתְחַזָּק
'el-melekh	yisrā'ēl	wayyō'mer	lô	lēkh	hithchazzaq
to the king of	Israel	and he said	to him	come	strengthen yourself

3156.131	7495.131	881	866, 6449.123	3706	3937, 9007	8523
cj, v Qal impv 2ms	cj, v Qal impv 2ms	do	rel part, v Qal impf 2ms	cj	prep, *n fs*	art, n fs
וְדַע	וּרְאֵה	אֵת	אֲשֶׁר־תַּעֲשֶׂה	כִּי	לִתְשׁוּבַת	הַשָּׁנָה
w^{e}dha'	ûr^{e}'ēh	'ēth	'ăsher-ta'ăseh	kî	lithshûvath	hashshānāh
and know	and see		what you will do	because	at the returning of	the year

4567	782	6148.151	6142		5860	4567, 782
n ms	pn	v Qal act ptc ms	prep, ps 2ms	**23.**	cj, *n mp*	*n ms*, pn
מֶלֶךְ	אֲרָם	עֹלֶה	עָלֶיךָ		וְעַבְדֵי	מֶלֶךְ־אֲרָם
melekh	'ărām	'ōleh	'ālêkhā		w^{e}'avdhê	melekh-'ărām
the king of	Aram	going up	against you		and the servants of	the king of Aram

... the servants of the chiefs who were over the divisions of the land, *BB*.

18. And he said, Whether they be come out for peace, take them alive; or whether they be come out for war, take them alive: ... In either case capture, *NCV* ... gave orders that the men should be taken alive, *Knox* ... if for battle, *NEB* ... if they come for a fight, seize them at once!, *Fenton*.

19. So these young men of the princes of the provinces came out of the city, and the army which followed them: ... they made a sortie from, *JB* ... the young men went out, *REB* ... young leaders, *NKJV* ... had led the army out to fight, *NLT*.

20. And they slew every one his man: and the Syrians fled; and Israel pursued them: ... each one struck down his opponent, *NIV* ... Israelite soldier killed his Aramean opponent, *NLT*.

and Ben-hadad the king of Syria escaped on an horse with the horsemen: ... managed to escape on horseback, *Moffatt* ... a chariot steed, *NAB* ... his horse; so did the cavalry, *Berkeley* ... got away safely, *BB*.

21. And the king of Israel went out, and smote the horses and chariots, and slew the Syrians with a great slaughter: ... defeated Aram with a crushing defeat, *Fenton* ... advanced and captured the horses and chariots, inflicting a heavy, *NEB* ... won a great victory over the men of Syria, *Knox* ... made great destruction among the Aramaeans, *BB*.

22. And the prophet came to the king of Israel, and said unto him, Go, strengthen thyself, and mark, and see what thou doest: ... Build up your forces, *REB* ... reinforce yourself, *Beck* ... Strengthen your position, *NIV*.

for at the return of the year the king of Syria will come up against thee: ... another attack by the king of Aram next spring, *NLT*.

---

mer—it is almost impossible to bear the weight of armor, or to sit on horseback, or to endure the fierce heat of iron chariots. The first little army which issued from the gates of Samaria might rely on the effects of a surprise. Thousands of the Syrian soldiers expecting nothing less than a battle would be unarmed, and taking their siesta. Their chariots and war steeds would be unharnessed and unprepared.

Ben-Hadad was still continuing his heavy drinking bout with his vassal princes, and not one of them was in a condition to give coherent commands. A messenger announced to the band of royal drunkards that "men" were come out of Samaria. They were too few to call them "an army," and the notion of an attack from that poor handful seemed ridiculous. Ben-Hadad thought they were coming to sue for peace, but whether peace or war were their object he gave the contemptuous order to "take them alive."

It was easier said than done. Led by the king at the head of his valorous youths the little host clashed into the midst of the unwieldly, unprepared, ill-handled Syrian host, and by their first slaughter created one of those fearful panics which have often been the destruction of Eastern hosts. The Syrians, whose army was made up of heterogeneous forces, and which could not be managed by thirty-four half-intoxicated feudatories of differing interests and insecure allegiance, was doubtless afraid that internal treachery must have been at work. Like the Midianites, like Zerah's Ethiopian host, like the Edomites in the Valley of Salt, like the Ammonites and Moabites in the wilderness of Tekoa, like the army of Sennacherib, they were instantly flung into irremediable confusion which tended every moment to be more fatal to itself. The little band of the youths and horses of Israel had nothing to do but to slay, and slay, and slay (1 Ki. 20:20). No effective resistance was even attempted. Long before evening, the 130,000 Syrians, with the entangled mass of their chariots and horsemen, were in headlong flight, while Ahab and the people of Israel slaughtered their flying rear. The defeat became an absolute rout. Ben-Hadad himself had a most narrow escape. He could not even wait for his war chariot. He had to fly with a few of his horsemen, and apparently, so the words may imply, on an inferior horse.

What effect was produced on the national mind and on the social religion by this immense deliverance we are not told. Never, certainly, had any nation deeper cause for gratitude to its religious teachers, who alone had not despaired of the commonwealth when everything seemed lost. We would fain know where was Elijah at this crisis, and whether he took any part in it. We cannot tell, but we know that as a rule the sons of the prophets acted together under their chiefs, and that individual impulses were rarely encouraged. The very meaning of the "Schools of the Prophets" was that they were all trained to adopt the same principles and to move together as one body.

20:22. The service rendered by this prophet, whose very name has been buried in undeserved oblivion, did not end here. Perhaps he saw signs of carelessness and undue exultation. He went again to

569.116	420	435	2098	435	6142, 3772	2480.116
v Qal pf 3cp	prep, ps 3ms	*n mp*	n mp	n mp, ps 3mp	prep, adv	v Qal pf 3cp
אָמְרוּ	אֵלָיו	אֱלֹהֵי	הָרִים	אֱלֹהֵיהֶם	עַל־כֵּן	חָזְקוּ
'āmerû	'ēlâv	'ĕlōhê	hārîm	'ĕlōhêhem	'al-kēn	chāzeqû
they said	to him	the gods of	the mountains	their gods	therefore	they were stronger

4623	195	4032.220	882	904, 4473	524, 3940	2480.120
prep, ps 1cp	cj, cj	v Niphal impf 1cp	prep, ps 3mp	prep, art, n ms	cj, neg part	v Qal impf 1cp
מִמֶּנּוּ	וְאוּלָם	נִלָּחֵם	אִתָּם	בַּמִּישׁוֹר	אִם־לֹא	נֶחֱזַק
mimmennû	we'ûlām	nillāchēm	'ittām	bammîshôr	'im-lō'	nechĕzaq
than we	yet but	we will fight	with them	on the plain	if not	we are stronger

4623		881, 1745	2172	6449.131	5681.531	4567	382
prep, ps 3mp		cj, do, art, n ms	art, dem pron	v Qal impv 2ms	v Hiphil impv 2ms	art, n mp	n ms
מֵהֶם	**24.**	וְאֶת־הַדָּבָר	הַזֶּה	עֲשֵׂה	הָסֵר	הַמְּלָכִים	אִישׁ
mēhem		we'eth-haddāvār	hazzeh	'ăsēh	hāsēr	hammelākhîm	'îsh
than they		and the word	the this	do	remove	the kings	each

4623, 4887	7947.131	6589	8809		887
prep, n ms, ps 3ms	cj, v Qal impv 2ms	n mp	prep, ps 3mp		cj, pers pron
מִמְּקֹמוֹ	וְשִׂים	פַּחוֹת	תַּחְתֵּיהֶם	**25.**	וְאַתָּה
mimmeqōmô	wesîm	pachôth	tachtêhem		we'attāh
from his place	and place	governors	instead of them		and you

4630.123, 3937	2524	3626, 2524	5489.151	4623, 881
v Qal impf 2ms, prep, ps 2ms	n ms	prep, art, n ms	art, v Qal act ptc ms	prep, do, ps 2ms
תִּמְנֶה־לְךָ	חַיִל	כַּחַיִל	הַנֹּפֵל	מֵאוֹתָךְ
thimneh-lekhā	chayil	kachayil	hannōphēl	mē'ôthākh
count out for yourself	the army	according to the army	the ones falling	among you

5670	3626, 5670	7681	3626, 7681	4032.220
cj, n ms	prep, art, n ms	cj, n ms	prep, art, n ms	cj, v Niphal juss 1cp
וְסוּס	כַּסּוּס	וְרֶכֶב	כָּרֶכֶב	וְנִלָּחֲמָה
wesûs	kassûs	werekhev	kārekhev	wenillāchămāh
and horses	according to the horses	and chariots	according to the chariots	that we may fight

881	904, 4473	524, 3940	2480.120	4623	8471.121	3937, 7249
do, ps 3mp	prep, art, n ms	cj, neg part	v Qal impf 1cp	prep, ps 3mp	cj, v Qal impf 3ms	prep, n ms, ps 3mp
אוֹתָם	בַּמִּישׁוֹר	אִם־לֹא	נֶחֱזַק	מֵהֶם	וַיִּשְׁמַע	לְקֹלָם
'ôthām	bammîshôr	'im-lō'	nechĕzaq	mēhem	wayyishma'	leqōlām
them	in the plain	if not	we are stronger	than they	and he listened	to their voice

6449.121	3772		2030.121	3937, 9007	8523	6734.121
cj, v Qal impf 3ms	adv		cj, v Qal impf 3ms	prep, *n fs*	art, n fs	cj, v Qal impf 3ms
וַיַּעַשׂ	כֵּן	**26.**	וַיְהִי	לִתְשׁוּבַת	הַשָּׁנָה	וַיִּפְקֹד
wayya'as	kēn		wayhî	lithshûvath	hashshānāh	wayyiphqōdh
and he did	so		and it was	at the returning of	the year	that he mustered

1163	881, 782	6148.121	682	3937, 4560	6196, 3547
pn	do, pn	cj, v Qal impf 3ms	pn	prep, art, n fs	prep, pn
בֶּן־הֲדַד	אֶת־אֲרָם	וַיַּעַל	אֲפֵקָה	לַמִּלְחָמָה	עִם־יִשְׂרָאֵל
ben-hedhadh	'eth-'ărām	wayya'al	'ăphēqāh	lammilchāmāh	'im-yisrā'ēl
Ben-Hadad	Aram	and he went up	to Aphek	into the battle	against Israel

	1158	3547	6734.616	3677.416	2050.126
	cj, *n mp*	pn	v Hothpaal pf 3cp	cj, v Polpal pf 3cp	cj, v Qal impf 3mp
27.	וּבְנֵי	יִשְׂרָאֵל	הָתְפָּקְדוּ	וְכָלְכְּלוּ	וַיֵּלְכוּ
	ûvenê	yisrā'ēl	hātheppāqŏdhû	wekholkelû	wayyēlekhû
	and the sons of	Israel	they were mustered	and they were given provisions	and they went

23. And the servants of the king of Syria said unto him, Their gods are gods of the hills; therefore they were stronger than we: ... of the mountains, *Darby* ... that is why they defeated us, *NEB*.

but let us fight against them in the plain, and surely we shall be stronger than they: ... we can beat them easily on the plains, *NLT* ... have the better of them, *Tyndale* ... best to offer them battle on the low-lying ground, *Knox* ... attack on them in the lowlands, *BB*.

24. And do this thing, Take the kings away, every man out of his place, and put captains in their rooms: ... in their places, *KJVII* ... appoint Generals in their place, *Fenton* ... officers, *REB* ... commanders in place of them, *NRSV*.

25. And number thee an army, like the army that thou hast lost, horse for horse, and chariot for chariot: ... get an army as large as the one you lost, *Beck*.

and we will fight against them in the plain, and surely we shall be stronger than they. And he hearkened unto their voice, and did so: ... this time we will defeat them, *Good News* ... He listened to their advice and acted on it, *NEB* ... He agreed with them and acted accordingly, *NIV* ... plan and followed it, *Berkeley*.

26. And it came to pass at the return of the year, that Ben-hadad numbered the Syrians, and went up to Aphek, to fight against Israel: ... In the spring Ben-hadad mustered the Arameans, *NRSV* ... marched on Aphek, *JB* ... advanced to Aphek to launch their attack, *REB* ... a year had passed, he marshalled the Syrian forces, *Knox*.

27. And the children of Israel were numbered, and were all present, and went against them: ... called to arms and supplied with provisions, *NAB* ... Israelites also had prepared for war, *NCV* ... called up and equipped, *Good News*.

and the children of Israel pitched before them like two little flocks of kids; but the Syrians filled the country: ... looked like two herds of goats, whereas the Aramaeans filled the countryside, *JB* ... camping like goats on the bare heights, *Moffatt* ... but all the country was full of the Aramaeans, *BB*.

28. And there came a man of God, and spake unto the king of Israel, and said, Thus saith the LORD, Because the Syrians have said, The LORD is God of the hills, but he is not God of the valleys: ... not a god of plains, *NAB* ... is a god of the mountains, *Darby*.

---

the king, and warned him that his victory, immense as it had been, was not final. It was no time for him to settle on his lees. The Syrians would assuredly return (Cf. 2 Sam. 11:1). The custom of all countries in the ancient world was to devote only the summer months to military campaigns. There were few or no standing armies. The Assyrians, Babylonians and Persians introduced a gradual revolution in these respects. With increased resources, and the burning determination to avenge their defeat, the Syrians would attack again, believing their god to ultimately be stronger. Let Ahab look well to his army and his fortresses, and prepare himself for the coming shock!

20:23–27. The courtiers of Ben-Hadad found it easy to flatter his pride by furnishing reasons to account for such an alarming overthrow. They had attacked the Israelites on their hills, and the gods of Israel were hill gods. Next time they would take Israel at a disadvantage by fighting only on the plain. Further, the vassal kings were only an element of dissension and weakness. They prevented the handling of the army as one strong machine worked by a single supreme will. Let Ben-Hadad depose from command these incapable weaklings, and put in their place dependent civil officers (pachûth; HED #6589) who would have no thought but to obey orders (1 Ki. 20:24). And so, with trusting heart, let the king collect a fresh army with horses and chariots as powerful as the last. The issue would be certain conquest and dear revenge.

Ben-Hadad followed this advice. The next year he went with his new host and encamped near Aphek. There is an Aphek which lay on the road between Damascus on the east of Jordan on a little plain southeast of the Sea of Galilee. This may have been the town of Issachar, in the valley of Jezreel, where Saul was defeated by the Philistines (1 Sam. 29:1). Israel went out to meet them duly provisioned. The Syrian host spread over the whole country; the Israelite army looked only like two little flocks of kids. Why two? No explanation is given, but the designation may refer to the shepherds' necessity for two flocks—one of sheep and one of goats. It has been conjectured that Judah had sent a separate contingent to help them in their distress.

20:28–30. To strengthen the misgivings of the anxious king of Israel, another nameless prophet came to promise him the victory. Yahweh would convince the Syrians that He was something more than a mere local god of the hills as they had blasphemously said, and Israel would once more be shown that He was indeed the LORD.

3937, 7410.141	2684.126	1158, 3547	5224	3626, 8530
prep, v Qal inf con, ps 3mp	cj, v Qal impf 3mp	*n mp*, pn	prep, ps 3mp	prep, num
לִקְרָאתָם	וַיַּחֲנוּ	בְנֵי־יִשְׂרָאֵל	נֶגְדָּם	כִּשְׁנֵי
liqōrā'thām	wayyachnû	v^{e}nê-yisrā'ēl	neghdām	kishnê
to meet them	and they encamped	the sons of Israel	before them	like two of

2912	6008	782	4527.316	881, 800		5242.121	382
n mp	n fp	cj, pn	v Piel pf 3cp	do, art, n fs	**28.**	cj, v Qal impf 3ms	*n ms*
חֲשִׂפֵי	עִזִּים	וַאֲרָם	מִלְאוּ	אֶת־הָאָרֶץ		וַיִּגַּשׁ	אִישׁ
chăsiphê	'izzîm	wa'ărām	mil'û	'eth-hā'ārets		wayyiggash	'îsh
small flocks of	goats	and Aram	they filled	the land		and he came near	the man of

435	569.121	420, 4567	3547	569.121	3662, 569.111	3176
art, n mp	cj, v Qal impf 3ms	prep, *n ms*	pn	cj, v Qal impf 3ms	adv, v Qal pf 3ms	pn
הָאֱלֹהִים	וַיֹּאמֶר	אֶל־מֶלֶךְ	יִשְׂרָאֵל	וַיֹּאמֶר	כֹּה־אָמַר	יְהוָה
hā'ělōhîm	wayyō'mer	'el-melekh	yisrā'ēl	wayyō'mer	kōh-'āmar	y^{e}hwāh
God	and he said	to the king of	Israel	and he said	thus He has said	Yahweh

3391	866	569.116	782	435	2098	3176	3940, 435	6231
cj	rel part	v Qal pf 3cp	pn	*n mp*	n mp	pn	cj, neg, *n mp*	n mp
יַעַן	אֲשֶׁר	אָמְרוּ	אֲרָם	אֱלֹהֵי	הָרִים	יְהוָה	וְלֹא־אֱלֹהֵי	עֲמָקִים
ya'an	'ăsher	'ām^{e}rû	'ărām	'ělōhê	hārîm	y^{e}hwāh	w^{e}lō'-'ělōhê	'ămāqîm
because	that	they said	Aram	a god of	the mountains	Yahweh	but not a god of	valleys

2000	5598.115	881, 3725, 2066	1448	2172	904, 3135
pers pron	cj, v Qal pf 1cs	do, *adj*, art, n ms	art, adj	art, dem pron	prep, n fs, ps 2ms
הוּא	וְנָתַתִּי	אֶת־כָּל־הֶהָמוֹן	הַגָּדוֹל	הַזֶּה	בְּיָדֶךָ
hû'	w^{e}nāthattî	'eth-kol-hehāmôn	haggādhôl	hazzeh	b^{e}yādhekhā
he	then I will give	all the multitude	the great	the this	into your hand

3156.117	3706, 603	3176		2684.126	431	5415	431
cj, v Qal pf 2mp	cj, pers pron	pn	**29.**	cj, v Qal impf 3mp	dem pron	prep	dem pron
וִידַעְתֶּם	כִּי־אֲנִי	יְהוָה		וַיַּחֲנוּ	אֵלֶּה	נֹכַח	אֵלֶּה
wîdha'ttem	kî-'ănî	y^{e}hwāh		wayyachnû	'ělleh	nōkhach	'ělleh
and you will know	that I	Yahweh		and they encamped	these	in front of	those

8124	3219	2030.121	904, 3219	8113	7414.121	4560
num	n mp	cj, v Qal impf 3ms	prep, art, n ms	art, num	cj, v Qal impf 3ms	art, n fs
שִׁבְעַת	יָמִים	וַיְהִי	בַּיּוֹם	הַשְּׁבִיעִי	וַתִּקְרַב	הַמִּלְחָמָה
shiv'ath	yāmîm	wayhî	bayyôm	hashsh^{e}vî'î	wattiqōrav	hammilchāmāh
seven	days	and it was	on the day	the seventh	that it became near	the war

5409.526	1158, 3547	881, 782	4109, 512	7561	904, 3219
cj, v Hiphil impf 3mp	*n mp*, pn	do, pn	num, num	adj	prep, n ms
וַיַּכּוּ	בְנֵי־יִשְׂרָאֵל	אֶת־אֲרָם	מֵאָה־אֶלֶף	רַגְלִי	בְּיוֹם
wayyakkû	v^{e}nê-yisrā'ēl	'eth-'ărām	mē'āh-'eleph	raghlî	b^{e}yôm
and they struck down	the sons of Israel	Aram	one hundred thousand	infantry	in a day

259		5308.126	3613.256	682	420, 6111	5489.122	2440
num	**30.**	cj, v Qal impf 3mp	art, v Niphal ptc mp	pn	prep, art, n fs	cj, v Qal impf 3fs	art, n fs
אֶחָד		וַיָּנֻסוּ	הַנּוֹתָרִים	אֲפֵקָה	אֶל־הָעִיר	וַתִּפֹּל	הַחוֹמָה
'echādh		wayyānus̱û	hannôthārîm	'ăphēqāh	'el-hā'îr	wattippōl	hachômāh
one		and they fled	those remaining	to Aphek	into the city	but it fell	the wall

6142, 6465	8124	512	382	3613.256	1163	5308.111
prep, num	cj, num	num	n ms	art, v Niphal ptc mp	cj, pn	v Qal pf 3ms
עַל־עֶשְׂרִים	וְשִׁבְעָה	אֶלֶף	אִישׁ	הַנּוֹתָרִים	וּבֶן־הֲדַד	נָס
'al-'esrîm	w^{e}shiv'āh	'eleph	'îsh	hannôthārîm	ûven-h^{e}dhadh	nās̱
on twenty	and seven	thousands	men	those remaining	and Ben-Hadad	he fled

971.121	420, 6111	2410	904, 2410		569.126	420
cj, v Qal impf 3ms	prep, art, n fs	n ms	prep, n ms	**31.**	cj, v Qal impf 3mp	prep, ps 3ms
וַיָּבֹא	אֶל־הָעִיר	חֶדֶר	בְּחָדֶר		וַיֹּאמְרוּ	אֵלָיו
wayyāvō'	'el-hā'îr	chedher	bechādher		wayyō'merû	'ēlâv
and he entered	into the city	an inner room	within an inner room		and they said	to him

5860	2079, 5167	8471.119	3706	4567	1041	3547
n mp, ps 3ms	intrj, part	v Qal pf 1cp	cj	*n mp*	*n ms*	pn
עֲבָדָיו	הִנֵּה־נָא	שָׁמַעְנוּ	כִּי	מַלְכֵי	בֵּית	יִשְׂרָאֵל
'ăvādhâv	hinnēh-nā'	shāma'ănû	kî	malkhê	bêth	yisrā'ēl
his servants	behold please	we have heard	that	the kings of	the household of	Israel

3706, 4567	2721	2062	7947.120	5167	8012	904, 5158	2346
cj, *n mp*	n ms	pers pron	v Qal juss 1cp	part	n mp	prep, n md, ps 1cp	cj, n mp
כִּי־מַלְכֵי	חֶסֶד	הֵם	נָשִׂימָה	נָא	שַׂקִּים	בְּמָתְנֵינוּ	וַחֲבָלִים
kî-malkhê	chesedh	hēm	nāsîmāh	nā'	saqqîm	bemāthenênû	wachvālîm
that kings of	kindness	they	let us put	please	sackcloth	on our loins	and ropes

therefore will I deliver all this great multitude into thine hand, and ye shall know that I am the LORD: ... I shall give all this great host into your hands, *REB* ... great rabble, *NEB* ... I will help you defeat this vast army, *NLT*.

29. And they pitched one over against the other seven days. And so it was, that in the seventh day the battle was joined: ... the battle started, *Beck* ... kept their positions facing one another, *BB*.

and the children of Israel slew of the Syrians an hundred thousand footmen in one day: ... killed 100,000 Syrian foot soldiers in a single day, *Berkeley* ... routed a hundred thousand Syrians that fought on foot, *Knox*.

30. But the rest fled to Aphek, into the city; and there a wall fell upon twenty and seven thousand of the men that were left. And Ben-hadad fled, and came into the city, into an inner chamber: ... took refuge within the city, in an inside room, *NAB* ... in an inner room inside the citadel, *JB* ... ran away to the city and hid in a room, *NCV* ... into a chamber that was within a chamber, *Douay*.

31. And his servants said unto him, Behold now, we have heard that the kings of the house of Israel are merciful kings: ... that they are kind kings, *Young* ... kings of Israel are men to be trusted, *NEB*.

let us, I pray thee, put sackcloth on our loins, and ropes upon our heads, and go out to the king of Israel: peradventure he will save thy life: ... Then perhaps King Ahab will let you live, *NLT* ... spare you life, *NKJV* ... wind rough cord round our heads, *REB*.

32. So they girded sackcloth on their loins, and put ropes on their heads, and came to the king of Israel: ... put on haircloth, and cords,

For seven days, the vast army and the little band of patriots gazed at each other, as the Israelites and Philistines had done in the days of Saul and Goliath. On the seventh day, they joined battle. In what special way the aid of Yahweh seconded the desperate valor of his people who were fighting for their all we do not know, but the result was, once more, their stupendous victory. The army of the Syrians was not only defeated, but practically annihilated. In round numbers, the normal method of counting, 100,000 Syrians fell in the slaughter of that day, and when the remnant took refuge in Aphek, which they had captured, they perished in a sudden crash (perhaps of earthquake) which buried them in the ruins of its fortifications. Rescued, we know not how, from this disaster, Ben-Hadad fled from chamber to chamber.

20:31–32. But it was impossible that he should not be discovered, and therefore his servants persuaded him to throw himself on the mercy of his conqueror. "The kings of Israel," they said; "are, as we have heard, compassionate kings; let us go before the king with sackcloth on our loins, and ropes round our necks, and ask if he will save thy life."

Then Ahab heard from the ambassadors of the king who had once dictated terms to him with such infinite contempt the message: "Thy slave Ben-Hadad saith, I pray thee, let me live." With intense eagerness, the ambassadors, in their sackcloth and their halters, awaited the reply. It came far more favorably than they had dared to hope. Surprised, and perhaps half-touched with pity for so immense a reverse of misfortune, "Is he yet alive?" exclaimed the careless king: "He is my brother!"

904, 7513	3428.120	420, 4567	3547	193	2030.321	881, 5497
prep, n ms, ps 1cp	cj, v Qal juss 1cp	prep, *n ms*	pn	adv	v Piel impf 3ms	do, n fs, ps 2ms
בְּרֹאשֵׁנוּ	וְנֵצֵא	אֶל־מֶלֶךְ	יִשְׂרָאֵל	אוּלַי	יְחַיֶּה	אֶת־נַפְשֶׁךָ
berō'shēnû	wenētsē'	'el-melekh	yisrā'ēl	'ûlay	yechayyeh	'eth-naphshekhā
on our head	and let us go out	to the king of	Israel	perhaps	he will preserve	your life

	2391.126	8012	904, 5158	2346	904, 7513	971.126
32.	cj, v Qal impf 3mp	n mp	prep, n md, ps 3mp	cj, n mp	prep, n mp, ps 3mp	cj, v Qal impf 3mp
	וַיַּחְגְּרוּ	שַׂקִּים	בְּמָתְנֵיהֶם	וַחֲבָלִים	בְּרָאשֵׁיהֶם	וַיָּבֹאוּ
	wayyachgerû	saqqîm	bemāthenêhem	wachvālîm	berā'shêhem	wayyāvō'û
	so they girded	sackcloth	on their loins	and ropes	on their heads	and they came

420, 4567	3547	569.126	5860	1163	569.111	2030.123, 5167
prep, *n ms*	pn	cj, v Qal impf 3mp	n ms, ps 2ms	pn	v Qal pf 3ms	v Qal juss 2ms, part
אֶל־מֶלֶךְ	יִשְׂרָאֵל	וַיֹּאמְרוּ	עַבְדְּךָ	בֶּן־הֲדַד	אָמַר	תְּחִי־נָא
'el-melekh	yisrā'ēl	wayyō'merû	'avdekhā	ven-hedhadh	'āmar	techî-nā'
to the king of	Israel	and they said	your servant	Ben-Hadad	he has said	allow to live please

5497	569.121	1950B, 5968	2508	250	2000		596
n fs, ps 1cs	cj, v Qal impf 3ms	intrg part, adv, ps 3ms	adj	n ms, ps 1cs	pers pron	**33.**	cj, art, n mp
נַפְשִׁי	וַיֹּאמֶר	הַעוֹדֶנּוּ	חַי	אָחִי	הוּא		וְהָאֲנָשִׁים
naphshî	wayyō'mer	ha'ôdhennû	chay	'āchî	hû'		wehā'ănāshîm
my life	and he said	is he still	alive	my brother	he		and the men

5355.326	4257.326	2581.526	1950B, 4623
v Piel impf 3mp	cj, v Piel impf 3mp	cj, v Hiphil impf 3mp	intrg part, prep, ps 3ms
יְנַחֲשׁוּ	וַיְמַהֲרוּ	וַיַּחְלְטוּ	הֲמִמֶּנּוּ
yenachshû	waymahrû	wayyachleṭû	hămimmennû
they were making into an omen	and they hurried	and they received	is from him

569.126	250	1163	569.121	971.133	4089.133
cj, v Qal impf 3mp	n ms, ps 2ms	pn	cj, v Qal impf 3ms	v Qal impv 2mp	v Qal impv 2mp, ps 3ms
וַיֹּאמְרוּ	אָחִיךָ	בֶן־הֲדַד	וַיֹּאמֶר	בֹּאוּ	קָחֻהוּ
wayyō'merû	'āchîkhā	ven-hedhadh	wayyō'mer	bō'û	qāchuhû
and they said	your brother	Ben-Hadad	and he said	go	get him

3428.121	420	1163	6148.521	6142, 4980
cj, v Qal impf 3ms	prep, ps 3ms	pn	cj, v Hiphil impf 3ms, ps 3ms	prep, art, n fs
וַיֵּצֵא	אֵלָיו	בֶּן־הֲדַד	וַיַּעֲלֵהוּ	עַל־הַמֶּרְכָּבָה
wayyētsē'	'ēlāv	ben-hedhadh	wayya'ălēhû	'al-hammerkāvāh
and he came out	to him	Ben-Hadad	and he caused him to come up	onto the chariot

	569.121	420	6111	866, 4089.111, 1	4623, 881	1
34.	cj, v Qal impf 3ms	prep, ps 3ms	art, n fp	rel part, v Qal pf 3ms, n ms, ps 1cs	prep, do	n ms, ps 2ms
	וַיֹּאמֶר	אֵלָיו	הֶעָרִים	אֲשֶׁר־לָקַח־אָבִי	מֵאֵת	אָבִיךָ
	wayyō'mer	'ēlâv	he'ārîm	'ăsher-lāqach-'āvî	mē'ēth	'āvîkhā
	and he said	to him	the cities	which my father took	from	your father

8178.525	2445	7947.123	3937	904, 1894	3626, 866, 7947.111
v Hiphil impf 1cs	cj, n mp	v Qal impf 2ms	prep, ps 2ms	prep, pn	prep, rel part, v Qal pf 3ms
אָשִׁיב	וְחוּצוֹת	תָּשִׂים	לְךָ	בְדַמֶּשֶׂק	כַּאֲשֶׁר־שָׂם
'āshîv	wechûtsôth	tāsîm	lekhā	vedhammeseq	ka'ăsher-sām
I will restore	and streets	you will put	for yourself	in Damascus	like that he put

1	904, 8497	603	904, 1311	8365.325
n ms, ps 1cs	prep, pn	cj, pers pron	prep, art, n fs	v Piel impf 1cs, ps 2ms
אָבִי	בְּשֹׁמְרוֹן	וַאֲנִי	בַּבְּרִית	אֲשַׁלְּחֶךָּ
'āvî	beshōmerôn	wa'ănî	babberîth	'ăshallechekkā
my father	in Samaria	and I	with the covenant	I will send you away

3901.121, 3937	1311	8365.321		382	259
cj, v Qal impf 3ms, prep, ps 3ms	n fs	cj, v Piel impf 3ms, ps 3ms	**35.**	cj, n ms	num
וַיִּכְרָת־לוֹ	בְּרִית	וַיְשַׁלְּחֵהוּ		וְאִישׁ	אֶחָד
wayyikhrāth-lô	v^{e}rîth	wayshall^{e}chēhû		w^{e}'îsh	'echādh
so he cut with him	a covenant	and he sent him away		and a man	one

4623, 1158	5204	569.111	420, 7739	904, 1745	3176
prep, *n mp*	art, n mp	v Qal pf 3ms	prep, n ms, ps 3ms	prep, *n ms*	pn
מִבְּנֵי	הַנְּבִיאִים	אָמַר	אֶל־רֵעֵהוּ	בִּדְבַר	יְהוָה
mibb^{e}nê	hann^{e}vî'îm	'āmar	'el-rē'ēhû	bidhvar	y^{e}hwāh
from the sons of	the prophets	he said	to his fellow	by the word of	Yahweh

BB ... sackcloth on their waists, ropes around their necks, *Beck* ... dressed in rough cloth, *NCV*.

and said, Thy servant Ben-hadad saith, I pray thee, let me live. And he said, Is he yet alive? he is my brother: ... My royal cousin ... is he still alive, *NEB*.

33. Now the men did diligently observe whether any thing would come from him, and did hastily catch it: ... carefully observed and quickly caught it, *KJVII* ... were quick to grasp at this straw of hope, *NLT* ... took it as a good omen, *Darby* ... took the word for good luck, *Tyndale*.

and they said, Thy brother Ben-hadad. Then he said, Go ye, bring him. Then Ben-hadad came forth to him; and he caused him to come up into the chariot: ... Ahab invited him into his chariot, *REB*.

34. And Ben-hadad said unto him, The cities, which my father took from thy father, I will restore; and thou shalt make streets for thee in Damascus, as my father made in Samaria: ... may set up marketplaces for yourself, *NKJV* ... return to Shomeron the suburbs, *Fenton* ... establish bazaars for yourself, *NRSV*.

Then said Ahab, I will send thee away with this covenant. So he made a covenant with him, and sent him away: ... made an appointment, *Tyndale* ... peace with him, and let him go his way, *Knox*.

35. And a certain man of the sons of the prophets said unto his neighbour in the word of the LORD, Smite me, I pray thee. And the man refused to smite him: ... to strike the prophet, *NLT* ... Strike me, please,

20:33–34. The Syrians snatched at the expression as a decisive omen (1 Ki. 20:33). It constituted an absolute end of the feud. It became an implicit promise of that sacred "protection" to which the slightest and most accidental expression constitutes a recognized claim. "Thy brother Ben-Hadad," they earnestly and emphatically repeated. In accordance with Eastern custom and augury their whole end was gained. As far as Ben-Hadad was concerned, he was now safe; as far as Ahab was concerned, the mischief, if mischief it were, was irreparably done.

Ahab could hardly have drawn back even if he wished to do so, but perhaps he was swayed by a fellow feeling for a king. This strange uxorious monarch, with his easily swayed impulses, his fits of schoolboy sullenness and swift repentance, his want of insight into existing conditions, his—if the expression may be excused—happy-go-lucky way of letting questions settle themselves, was, no doubt, a brave warrior, but he was a most incapable statesman. His conduct was perfectly infatuated. Pity is one thing, but the security of a nation should also have been considered. To set free a man endowed with passionate hatred, with immense ambitions, with boundless capacities for trouble, or only to bind him with the packthread of insecure promises, was the conduct of a fool. The pact is vainly dignified with the name of a covenant.

20:35–36. He might ignore guidance, but he could not escape reproof. Again, an unknown monitor from the sons of the prophets was commissioned to bring home to him his error. He did so by an acted parable, which gave concrete force and vividness to the lesson which he desired to convey. Speaking by the word of the LORD, he went to one of his fellows in the school of which the members are here first called "the sons of the prophets," and bade him to wound him. His comrade, not unnaturally, shrank from obeying so strange a command. It must be borne in mind that the mere appeal to an inspiration from Yahweh did not always authenticate itself. Over and over again in the prophetic Books, and in these histories which the Jews call "the earlier prophets," we find that men could profess to act in Yahweh's name, and even perhaps to be sincere in so doing, who were

5409.531	5167	4126.321	382	5409.541
v Hiphil impv 2ms, ps 1cs	part	cj, v Piel impf 3ms	art, n ms	prep, v Hiphil inf con, ps 3ms
הַכֵּינִי	נָא	וַיְמָאֵן	הָאִישׁ	לְהַכֹּתוֹ
hakkênî	nā'	waymā'ēn	hā'îsh	lehakkōthô
strike me	please	but he refused	the man	to strike him

	569.121	3937	3391	866	3940, 8471.113	904, 7249	3176
36.	cj, v Qal impf 3ms	prep, ps 3ms	cj	rel part	neg part, v Qal pf 2ms	prep, *n ms*	pn
	וַיֹּאמֶר	לוֹ	יַעַן	אֲשֶׁר	לֹא־שָׁמַעְתָּ	בְּקוֹל	יְהוָה
	wayyō'mer	lô	ya'an	'ăsher	lō'-shāma'ăttā	beqôl	yehwāh
	and he said	to him	because	that	you did not listen	by the voice of	Yahweh

2079	2050.151	4623, 882	5409.511	765	2050.121
intrj, ps 2ms	v Qal act ptc ms	prep, prep, ps 1cs	cj, v Hiphil pf 3ms, ps 2ms	art, n ms	cj, v Qal impf 3ms
הִנְּךָ	הוֹלֵךְ	מֵאִתִּי	וְהִכְּךָ	הָאַרְיֵה	וַיֵּלֶךְ
hinnekhā	hôlēkh	mē'ittî	wehikkekhā	hā'aryēh	wayyēlekh
behold you	going	from with me	and it will strike you down	the lion	and he went

4623, 703	4834.121	765	5409.521		4834.121
prep, prep, ps 3ms	cj, v Qal impf 3ms, ps 3ms	art, n ms	cj, v Hiphil impf 3ms, ps 3ms	**37.**	cj, v Qal impf 3ms
מֵאֶצְלוֹ	וַיִּמְצָאֵהוּ	הָאַרְיֵה	וַיַּכֵּהוּ		וַיִּמְצָא
mē'etslô	wayyimtsā'ēhû	hā'aryēh	wayyakkēhû		wayyimtsā'
from beside him	and it found him	the lion	and it struck him down		then he found

382	311	569.121	5409.531	5167	5409.521	382
n ms	adj	cj, v Qal impf 3ms	v Hiphil impv 2ms, ps 1cs	part	cj, v Hiphil impf 3ms, ps 3ms	art, n ms
אִישׁ	אַחֵר	וַיֹּאמֶר	הַכֵּינִי	נָא	וַיַּכֵּהוּ	הָאִישׁ
'îsh	'achēr	wayyō'mer	hakkênî	nā'	wayyakkēhû	hā'îsh
a man	another	and he said	strike me	please	and he struck him	the man

5409.542	6728.142		2050.121	5204	6198.121	3937, 4567
v Hiphil inf abs	cj, v Qal inf abs	**38.**	cj, v Qal impf 3ms	art, n ms	cj, v Qal impf 3ms	prep, art, n ms
הַכֵּה	וּפָצֹעַ		וַיֵּלֶךְ	הַנָּבִיא	וַיַּעֲמֹד	לַמֶּלֶךְ
hakkēh	ûphātsōa'		wayyēlekh	hannāvî'	wayya'ămōdh	lammelekh
striking	and wounding		then he went	the prophet	and he stood	for the king

6142, 1932	2769.721	904, 685	6142, 6084		2030.121
prep, art, n ms	cj, v Hithpael impf 3ms	prep, art, n ms	prep, n fd, ps 3ms	**39.**	cj, v Qal impf 3ms
עַל־הַדָּרֶךְ	וַיִּתְחַפֵּשׂ	בָּאֲפֵר	עַל־עֵינָיו		וַיְהִי
'al-haddārekh	wayyithchappēs	bā'ăphēr	'al-'ênâv		wayhî
beside the road	and he disguised himself	with the bandage	over his eyes		and it was

4567	5882.151	2000	7094.111	420, 4567	569.121	5860
art, n ms	v Qal act ptc ms	cj, pers pron	v Qal pf 3ms	prep, art, n ms	cj, v Qal impf 3ms	n ms, ps 2ms
הַמֶּלֶךְ	עֹבֵר	וְהוּא	צָעַק	אֶל־הַמֶּלֶךְ	וַיֹּאמֶר	עַבְדְּךָ
hammelekh	'ōvēr	wehû'	tsā'aq	'el-hammelekh	wayyō'mer	'avdekhā
the king	passing by	and he	he cried out	to the king	and he said	your servant

3428.111	904, 7419, 4560	2079, 382	5681.111	971.521
v Qal pf 3ms	prep, *n ms*, art, n fs	cj, intrj, n ms	v Qal pf 3ms	cj, v Hiphil impf 3ms
יָצָא	בְּקֶרֶב־הַמִּלְחָמָה	וְהִנֵּה־אִישׁ	סָר	וַיָּבֵא
yātsā'	veqerev-hammilchāmāh	wehinnēh-'îsh	sār	wayyāvē'
he went out	into the middle of the battle	and behold a man	he turned aside	and he brought

420	382	569.121	8490.131	881, 382	2172	524, 6734.242
prep, ps 1cs	n ms	cj, v Qal impf 3ms	v Qal impv 2ms	do, art, n ms	art, dem pron	cj, v Niphal inf abs
אֵלַי	אִישׁ	וַיֹּאמֶר	שְׁמֹר	אֶת־הָאִישׁ	הַזֶּה	אִם־הִפָּקֵד
'ēlay	'îsh	wayyō'mer	shemōr	'eth-hā'îsh	hazzeh	'im-hippāqēdh
to me	a man	and he said	keep	the man	the this	if missing

6734.221	2030.112	5497	8809	5497	173	3724, 3826B
v Niphal impf 3ms	cj, v Qal pf 3fs	n fs, ps 2ms	prep	n fs, ps 3ms	cj	*n fs*, n ms
יִפָּקֵד	וְהָיְתָה	נַפְשְׁךָ	תַּחַת	נַפְשׁוֹ	אוֹ	כִּכַּר־כֶּסֶף
yippāqēdh	wehāyethāh	naphshekhā	tachath	naphshô	'ô	khikkar-keseph
he is ever missing	then it will be	your life	instead of	his life	or	a talent of silver

8620.123		2030.121	5860	6449.151	2077	2077	2000
v Qal impf 2ms	40.	cj, v Qal impf 3ms	n ms, ps 2ms	*v Qal act ptc ms*	adv	cj, adv	cj, pers pron
תִּשְׁקוֹל		וַיְהִי	עַבְדְּךָ	עֹשֶׂה	הֵנָּה	וָהֵנָּה	וְהוּא
tishqôl		wayhî	'avdekhā	'ōsēh	hēnnāh	wāhēnnāh	wehû'
you will pay		and it was	your servant	doing	here	and there	then he

NKJV ... I wish you would assault me!, *Fenton* ... Give me a wound, *BB*.

36. Then said he unto him, Because thou hast not obeyed the voice of the Lord: ... you did not listen to the command, *Berkeley*.

behold, as soon as thou art departed from me, a lion shall slay thee. And as soon as he was departed from him, a lion found him, and slew him: ... a lion met him and killed him, *RSV* ... will kill you when you leave me, *NAB* ... the very moment, *JB*.

37. Then he found another man, and said, Smite me, I pray thee. And the man smote him, so that in smiting he wounded him: ... hit him and hurt, *NCV* ... struck him and wounded, *NIV* ... gave him a blow, *BB* ... Strike me a blow, *Knox*.

38. So the prophet departed, and waited for the king by the way, and disguised himself with ashes upon his face: ... a bandage over his eyes, *RSV* ... his headband, *MRB* ... sprinkling dust on his face, *Douay* ... bandaged his face with a cloth, *Good News*.

39. And as the king passed by, he cried unto the king: and he said, Thy servant went out into the midst of the battle; and, behold, a man turned aside, and brought a man unto me, and said, Keep this man: ... One of our men brought an enemy soldier, *NCV* ... a soldier came over to me with a prisoner, *REB* ... brought a fugitive, *Knox*.

if by any means he be missing, then shall thy life be for his life, or else thou shalt pay a talent of silver: ... you will be fined 2,000 dollars in silver, *Berkeley* ... seventy-five pounds, *NLT*.

40. And as thy servant was busy here and there, he was gone. And the king of Israel said unto him, So shall thy judgment be; thyself hast decided it: ... looking here and

mere dupes of their own wills and fancies. It was, in fact, possible for them to become false prophets, without always meaning to be so; and these chances of hallucination—of being misled by a lying spirit—led to fierce contentions in the prophetic communities. "Since you have not obeyed Yahweh's voice," said the man, "the lion shall immediately slay you." "And as soon as he was departed from him the lion found him and slew him." There is nothing impossible in the incident, for in those days lions were common in Palestine, and they multiplied when the country had been depopulated by war.

20:37–42. The prophet then bade another comrade to smite him, and he did so effectually, inflicting a serious wound. The object and necessity of this for his purpose is by no means apparent. Perhaps it was to figure the wound which Ahab had by his conduct wilfully inflicted on himself or on Israel. This was a part of the intended scene in which the prophet meant for a moment to play the role of a soldier who had been wounded in the Syrian war. So he bound up his head with a bandage, (v. 38; This, and not "with ashes upon his face," is the meaning of the Hebrew ['ăphēr, HED #685], not 'ēpher, HED #684) and waited for the king to pass by. An Eastern king is liable at any time to be appealed to by the humblest of his subjects, and the prophet stopped Ahab and stated his imaginary case. "A captain," he, said, "brought me one of his war captives (1 Ki. 20:39), and ordered me to keep him safe. If I failed to do so; I was to pay the forfeit of my life, or to pay as a fine a silver talent. Evidently, therefore, the captive is supposed to be a very important person. But as I was looking here and there the captive escaped." "Be it so," answered Ahab; "you are bound by your own bargain." Thus Ahab, like David, was led to condemn himself out of his own mouth. Then the prophet tore the bandage from his face, and said to Ahab: "Thou art the man! Thus saith Yahweh, I entrusted to thee the man under my ban [chērem, HED #2869], and thou hast let him escape. Thou shalt pay the forfeit. Thy life shall go for his life, thy people for his people."

375 sub, ps 3ms אֵינֶנּוּ 'ênennû he was not	569.121 cj, v Qal impf 3ms וַיֹּאמֶר wayyō'mer and he said	420 prep, ps 3ms אֵלָיו 'ēlâv to him	4567, 3547 *n ms*, pn מֶלֶךְ־יִשְׂרָאֵל melekh-yisrā'ēl the king of Israel	3772 adv כֵּן kēn so	5122 n ms, ps 2ms מִשְׁפָּטֶךָ mishpāṭekhā your judgment	887 pers pron אַתָּה 'attāh you

2888.113 v Qal pf 2ms חָרָצְתָּ chārātsᵉttā you have determined	**41.**	4257.321 cj, v Piel impf 3ms וַיְמַהֵר waymahēr and he hurried	5681.521 cj, v Hiphil impf 3ms וַיָּסַר wayyāsar and he removed	881, 685 do, art, n ms אֶת־הָאֲפֵר 'eth-hā'ăphēr the bandage	4623, 6142 prep, prep מֵעַל mē'al from on	6084 n fd, ps 3ms עֵינָיו 'ênâv his eyes

5422.521 cj, v Hiphil impf 3ms וַיַּכֵּר wayyakkēr and he recognized	881 do, ps 3ms אֹתוֹ 'ōthô him	4567 *n ms* מֶלֶךְ melekh the king of	3547 pn יִשְׂרָאֵל yisrā'ēl Israel	3706 cj כִּי kî that	4623, 5204 prep, art, n mp מֵהַנְּבִאִים mēhannᵉvî'îm from the prophets	2000 pers pron הוּא hû' he

42.	569.121 cj, v Qal impf 3ms וַיֹּאמֶר wayyō'mer and he said	420 prep, ps 3ms אֵלָיו 'ēlâv to him	3662 adv כֹּה kōh thus	569.111 v Qal pf 3ms אָמַר 'āmar He has said	3176 pn יְהוָה yᵉhwāh Yahweh	3391 cj יַעַן ya'an because	8365.313 v Piel pf 2ms שִׁלַּחְתָּ shillachtā you sent away

881, 382, 2869 do, *n ms*, n ms, ps 1cs אֶת־אִישׁ־חֶרְמִי 'eth-'îsh-chermî the man of my devoting to the ban	4623, 3135 prep, n fs מִיָּד mîyādh from the hand	2030.112 cj, v Qal pf 3fs וְהָיְתָה wᵉhāyᵉthāh now it will be	5497 n fs, ps 2ms נַפְשְׁךָ naphshᵉkhā your life	8809 prep תַּחַת tachath instead of	5497 n fs, ps 3ms נַפְשׁוֹ naphshô his life

6194 cj, n ms, ps 2ms וְעַמְּךָ wᵉ'ammᵉkhā and your people	8809 prep תַּחַת tachath instead of	6194 n ms, ps 3ms עַמּוֹ 'ammô his people	**43.**	2050.121 cj, v Qal impf 3ms וַיֵּלֶךְ wayyēlekh and he went	4567, 3547 *n ms*, pn מֶלֶךְ־יִשְׂרָאֵל melekh-yisrā'ēl the king of Israel	6142, 1041 prep, n ms, ps 3ms עַל־בֵּיתוֹ 'al-bêthô unto his house

5821 adj סַר s̱ar incensed	2282 cj, adj וְזָעֵף wᵉzā'ēph and furious	971.121 cj, v Qal impf 3ms וַיָּבֹא wayyāvō' and he came	8497 pn שֹׁמְרוֹנָה shōmᵉrônāh to Samaria	**21:1**	2030.121 cj, v Qal impf 3ms וַיְהִי wayhî and it was	313 prep אַחַר 'achar after	1745 art, n mp הַדְּבָרִים haddᵉvārîm the things

431 art, dem pron הָאֵלֶּה hā'ēlleh the these	3884 n ms כֶּרֶם kerem a vineyard	2030.111 v Qal pf 3ms הָיָה hāyāh it was	3937, 5197 prep, pn לְנָבוֹת lᵉnāvôth to Naboth	3263 art, pn הַיִּזְרְעֵאלִי hayyizrᵉ'ē'lî the Jezreelite	866 rel pron אֲשֶׁר 'ăsher who	904, 3262 prep, pn בְּיִזְרְעֶאל bᵉyizrᵉ'e'l in Jezreel	703 prep אֵצֶל 'ētsel beside

2033 *n ms* הֵיכַל hêkhal the palace of	255 pn אַחְאָב 'ach'āv Ahab	4567 *n ms* מֶלֶךְ melekh the king of	8497 pn שֹׁמְרוֹן shōmᵉrôn Samaria	**2.**	1744.321 cj, v Piel impf 3ms וַיְדַבֵּר waydhabbēr and he spoke	255 pn אַחְאָב 'ach'āv Ahab	420, 5197 prep, pn אֶל־נָבוֹת 'el-nāvôth unto Naboth

3937, 569.141 prep, v Qal inf con לֵאמֹר lē'mōr saying	5598.131, 3937 v Qal impv 2ms, prep, ps 1cs תְּנָה־לִּי tᵉnāh-lî give to me	881, 3884 do, n ms, ps 2ms אֶת־כַּרְמְךָ 'eth-karmᵉkhā your vineyard	2030.121, 3937 cj, v Qal juss 3ms, prep, ps 1cs וִיהִי־לִי wîhî-lî that it may be to me

3937, 1629, 3536	3706	2000	7427	703	1041	5598.125	3937
prep, *n ms*, n ms	cj	pers pron	adj	prep	n ms, ps 1cs	cj, v Qal juss 1cs	prep, ps 2ms
לְגַן־יָרָק	כִּי	הוּא	קָרוֹב	אֵצֶל	בֵּיתִי	וְאֶתְּנָה	לְךָ
leghan-yārāq	kî	hû'	qārôv	'ētsel	bêthî	we'ettenāh	lekhā
for a garden of vegetables	because	it	near	beside	my house	and let me give	to you

8809	3884	3005	4623	524	3005	904, 6084	5598.125, 3937
prep, ps 3ms	n ms	adj	prep, ps 3ms	cj	adj	prep, n fd, ps 2ms	v Qal impf 1cs, prep, ps 2ms
תַּחְתָּיו	כֶּרֶם	טוֹב	מִמֶּנּוּ	אִם	טוֹב	בְּעֵינֶיךָ	אֶתְּנָה־לְּךָ
tachtâv	kerem	ṭôv	mimmennû	'im	ṭôv	be'ênêkhā	'ettenāh-lekhā
instead of it	a vineyard	better	than it	if	good	in your eyes	I will give to you

there, the man disappeared, *NAB* ... That is your sentence then. You have pronounced it yourself, *JB* ... your own verdict, *Beck* ... You are responsible; you have given the decision against, *BB*.

41. And he hasted, and took the ashes away from his face; and the king of Israel discerned him that he was of the prophets: ... took the headband away from his eyes, *MRB* ... wiped off the dust, *Douay* ... recognized him as one, *Goodspeed* ... tore the bandage, *NEB*.

42. And he said unto him, Thus saith the Lord, Because thou hast let go out of thy hand a man whom I appointed to utter destruction, therefore thy life shall go for his life, and thy people for his people: ... your army will be destroyed for letting his army escape, *Good News* ... You freed the man I said should die, so your life will be taken instead of his, *NCV* ... as a substitute for his life, *Beck* ... let a man worthy of death slip through thy hands?, *Knox*.

43. And the king of Israel went to his house heavy and displeased, and came to Samaria: ... went home, gloomy and out of temper, *JB* ... Disturbed and angry, the king of Israel went off homeward, *NAB* ... embittered and angry, *Berkeley* ... Sullen and angry, the king of Israel went to his palace, *NIV*.

21:1. And it came to pass after these things, that Naboth the Jezreelite had a vineyard, which was in Jezreel: ... Some time later there occurred an incident involving Naboth of Jezreel, *REB* ... there was a vineyard owned by a man named Naboth, *Good News*.

hard by the palace of Ahab king of Samaria: ... Close by, *KJVII* ... beside the palace, *NASB* ... near the palace, *Beck* ... adjoining the palace, *Berkeley*.

2. And Ahab spake unto Naboth, saying, Give me thy vineyard, that I may have it for a garden of herbs: ... Sell me your vineyard, and let it be mine for a flower garden, *Fenton* ... so that I may have it for a vegetable garden, *NRSV*.

because it is near unto my house: ... Since your vineyard is so convenient to the palace, *NLT* ... so near adjoining, *Knox*.

and I will give thee for it a better vineyard than it: ... let me give you a better vine-garden in exchange, *BB* ... in its place, *NCV*.

or, if it seem good to thee, I will give thee the worth of it in money: ... of it in silver, *Tyndale* ... the price of it, *NASB* ... silver to the value of this, *Rotherham* ... pay you whatever it is worth, *NIV*.

3. And Naboth said to Ahab, The Lord forbid it me, that I should

20:43. Anger and indignation filled the heart of the king; he went to his house; "heavy and displeased." The phrase, twice applied to him and never used of another, shows that he was liable to characteristic moods of overwhelming rage. It is evident that he did not dare to chastise the audacious offender. Josephus, *Antiquities*, XIII:xv:5, says that Ahab imprisoned and punished the prophet. As a rule the prophets were protected by their sacrosanct position.

"The triumphing of the wicked is short, and the joy of the hypocrite is but for a moment?" (Job 20:5).

21:1–2. Ahab was a builder. He had built cities and palaces, and was specially attached to his palace at Jezreel, which he wished to make the most delightful of summer residences. It was unique in its splendor as the first palace inlaid with ivory. The nation had heard of Solomon's ivory throne, but never till this time of an "ivory palace." But a palace is nothing without pleasant gardens. The neighborhood of Jezreel, as is still shown by the ancient winepresses cut out of the rock in the neighborhood of its ruins, was enriched by vineyards, and one of these vineyards adjoining the palace belonged to a citizen named Naboth. It happened that no other ground would so well have served the purpose of Ahab to make a garden near his palace, and he made Naboth a fair offer for it. "I will give you," he said, "a better vineyard for it, or I will pay you its full value in ingots of silver."

3826B	4378B	2172		569.121	5197	420, 255	2587	3937
n ms	n ms	dem pron	3.	cj, v Qal impf 3ms	pn	prep, pn	sub	prep, ps 1cs
כֶּסֶף	מְחִיר	זֶה		וַיֹּאמֶר	נָבוֹת	אֶל־אַחְאָב	חָלִילָה	לִּי
kheseph	mechîr	zeh		wayyō'mer	nāvôth	'el-'ach'āv	chālîlāh	lî
silver	the price	this		but he said	Naboth	to Ahab	may it be far	to me

4623, 3176	4623, 5598.141	881, 5338	1	3937		971.121
prep, pn	prep, v Qal inf con, ps 1cs	do, *n fs*	n mp, ps 1cs	prep, ps 2ms	4.	cj, v Qal impf 3ms
מֵיְהוָה	מִתִּתִּי	אֶת־נַחֲלַת	אֲבֹתַי	לָךְ		וַיָּבֹא
mêhwāh	mittittî	'eth-nachlath	'ăvōthay	lākh		wayyāvō'
from Yahweh	from my giving	the inheritance of	my ancestors	to you		and he entered

255	420, 1041	5821	2282	6142, 1745	866, 1744.311
pn	prep, n ms, ps 3ms	adj	cj, adj	prep, art, n ms	rel part, v Piel pf 3ms
אַחְאָב	אֶל־בֵּיתוֹ	סַר	וְזָעֵף	עַל־הַדָּבָר	אֲשֶׁר־דִּבֶּר
'ach'āv	'el-bêthô	sar	wezā'ēph	'al-haddāvār	'ăsher-dibber
Ahab	to his house	incensed	and furious	concerning the matter	which he had spoken

420	5197	3263	569.121	3940, 5598.121	3937
prep, ps 3ms	pn	art, pn	cj, v Qal impf 3ms	neg part, v Qal impf 3ms	prep, ps 2ms
אֵלָיו	נָבוֹת	הַיִּזְרְעֵאלִי	וַיֹּאמֶר	לֹא־אֶתֵּן	לְךָ
'ēlâv	nāvôth	hayyizre'ē'lî	wayyō'mer	lō'-'ettēn	lekhā
to him	Naboth	the Jezreelite	for he said	I will not give	to you

881, 5338	1	8311.121	6142, 4433	5621.521
do, *n fs*	n mp, ps 1cs	cj, v Qal impf 3ms	prep, n fs, ps 3ms	cj, v Hiphil impf 3ms
אֶת־נַחֲלַת	אֲבוֹתָי	וַיִּשְׁכַּב	עַל־מִטָּתוֹ	וַיַּסֵּב
'eth-nachlath	'ăvôthāy	wayyishkav	'al-mittāthô	wayyassēv
the inheritance of	my ancestors	then he lay down	on his bed	and he turned aside

881, 6686	3940, 404.111	4035		971.122	420	350	828
do, n mp, ps 3ms	cj, neg part, v Qal pf 3ms	n ms	5.	cj, v Qal impf 3fs	prep, ps 3ms	pn	n fs, ps 3ms
אֶת־פָּנָיו	וְלֹא־אָכַל	לָחֶם		וַתָּבֹא	אֵלָיו	אִיזֶבֶל	אִשְׁתּוֹ
'eth-pānâv	welō'-'ākhal	lāchem		wattāvō'	'ēlâv	'îzevel	'ishtô
his face	and he did not eat	food		so she came	to him	Jezebel	his wife

1744.322	420	4242, 2172	7593	5821	375
cj, v Piel impf 3fs	prep, ps 3ms	intrg, dem pron	n fs, ps 2ms	adj	cj, sub, ps 2ms
וַתְּדַבֵּר	אֵלָיו	מַה־זֶּה	רוּחֲךָ	סָרָה	וְאֵינְךָ
wattedhabbēr	'ēlâv	mah-zeh	rûchăkhā	sārāh	we'ênekhā
and she spoke	to him	what this	your spirit	incensed	and there is not to you

404.151	4035		1744.321	420	3706, 1744.325	420, 5197	3263
v Qal act ptc ms	n ms	6.	cj, v Piel impf 3ms	prep, ps 3fs	cj, v Piel impf 1cs	prep, pn	art, pn
אֹכֵל	לָחֶם		וַיְדַבֵּר	אֵלֶיהָ	כִּי־אֲדַבֵּר	אֶל־נָבוֹת	הַיִּזְרְעֵאלִי
'ōkhēl	lāchem		waydhabbēr	'ēlêāh	kî-'ădhabbēr	'el-nāvôth	hayyizre'ē'lî
eating	food		and he spoke	to her	because I spoke	to Naboth	the Jezreelite

569.125	3937	5598.131, 3937	881, 3884	904, 3826B	173	524, 2760
cj, v Qal impf 1cs	prep, ps 3ms	v Qal impv 2ms, prep, ps 1cs	do, n ms, ps 2ms	prep, n ms	cj	cj, adj
וָאֹמַר	לוֹ	תְּנָה־לִּי	אֶת־כַּרְמְךָ	בְּכֶסֶף	אוֹ	אִם־חָפֵץ
wā'ōmar	lô	tenāh-lî	'eth-karmekhā	bekheseph	'ô	'im-chāphēts
and I said	to him	give to me	your vineyard	with silver	or	if pleased

887	5598.125, 3937	3884	8809	569.121	3940, 5598.125
pers pron	v Qal juss 1cs, prep, ps 2ms	n ms	prep, ps 3ms	cj, v Qal impf 3ms	neg part, v Qal impf 1cs
אַתָּה	אֶתְּנָה־לְּךָ	כֶּרֶם	תַּחְתָּיו	וַיֹּאמֶר	לֹא־אֶתֵּן
'attāh	'ettenāh-lekhā	kherem	tachtâv	wayyō'mer	lō'-'ettēn
you	let me give to you	a vineyard	instead of it	but he said	I will not give

3937	881, 3884	7.	569.122	420	350	828	887	6498
prep, ps 2ms	do, n ms, ps 1cs		cj, v Qal impf 3fs	prep, ps 3ms	pn	n fs, ps 3ms	pers pron	adv
לְךָ	אֶת־כַּרְמִי		וַתֹּאמֶר	אֵלָיו	אִיזֶבֶל	אִשְׁתּוֹ	אַתָּה	עַתָּה
lᵉkhā	'eth-karmî		wattō'mer	'ēlâv	'îzevel	'ishtô	'attāh	'attāh
to you	my vineyard		then she said	to him	Jezebel	his wife	you	now

6449.123	4548	6142, 3547	7251.131	404.131, 4035	3296.121
v Qal impf 2ms	n fs	prep, pn	v Qal impv 2ms	v Qal impv 2ms, n ms	cj, v Qal juss 3ms
תַּעֲשֶׂה	מְלוּכָה	עַל־יִשְׂרָאֵל	קוּם	אֱכָל־לֶחֶם	וְיִטַב
ta'ăseh	mᵉlûkhāh	'al-yisrā'ēl	qûm	'ĕkhāl-lechem	wᵉyiṯav
you execute	the kingship	over Israel	rise	eat food	that it may be pleased

give the inheritance of my fathers unto thee: ... should I give thee the land that was my I fathers' patrimony?, *Knox* ... I inherited this vineyard from my ancestors, *Good News* ... you my ancestral heritage, *NAB*.

4. And Ahab came into his house heavy and displeased because of the word which Naboth the Jezreelite had spoken to him: ... to his house sulky and angry, *KJVII* ... sullen and vexed, *Darby* ... went home gloomy and out of temper, *JB*.

for he had said, I will not give thee the inheritance of my fathers: ... you by ancestral inheritance, *NRSV* ... the heritage, *BB* ... my patrimonial inheritance, *Berkeley*.

And he laid him down upon his bed, and turned away his face, and would eat no bread: ... covered his face, and refused to eat, *REB* ... lay down on the couch, *Beck* ... on his bed sulking, *NIV* ... casting himself, *Douay*.

5. But Jezebel his wife came to him, and said unto him, Why is thy spirit so sad, that thou eatest no bread?: ... What has made you so upset that you are not eating?, *NLT* ... why art thou so froward, that thou eatest no meat?, *Tyndale* ... so sullen that you eat no food?, *NKJV* ... What is the matter, that your spirit is depressed?, *Fenton*.

6. And he said unto her, Because I spake unto Naboth the Jezreelite, and said unto him, Give me thy vineyard for money; or else, if it please thee, I will give thee another vineyard for it: ... Sell me your vineyard, or, if you prefer, I will give you a vineyard in exchange, *NAB* ... for silver, *Rotherham* ... pay for it, or if you like, I will give you, *Beck*.

and he answered, I will not give thee my vineyard: ... But Naboth refused, *NCV* ... he told me that I couldn't have it!, *Good News*.

7. And Jezebel his wife said unto him, Dost thou now govern the kingdom of Israel? arise, and eat bread, and let thine heart be merry: I will give thee the vineyard of Naboth the Jezreelite: ... Some king of Israel you make!, *JB* ... are you not in command, *Moffatt* ... Do you not exercise the kingship over, *Berkeley* ... now reign over, *NASB*.

8. So she wrote letters in Ahab's name, and sealed them with his

21:3. Naboth, however, was perfectly within his rights (Lev. 25:23) in rejecting the offer. It was the inheritance of his fathers, and considerations nothing short of sacred—considerations which then or afterwards found a place in the written statutes of the nation—made it wrong in his judgment to sell it. He sturdily refused the offer of the king. His case was different from that of the Jebusite prince Araunah, who had sold his threshing floor to David, and that of Shemer, who sold the Hill of Samaria to Omri (2 Sam. 24:24; 1 Ki. 16:24).

21:4. A sensible man would have accepted the inevitable, and done the best he could to find a garden elsewhere. But Ahab, who could not bear to be thwarted, came into his house "heavy and displeased." Like an overgrown, sullen boy, he flung himself on his divan, turned his face to the wall, and would not eat.

21:5. News came to Jezebel in her seraglio of her lord's ill-humor, and she came to ask him what dejection in his spirit made him decline to take food.

21:6–7. He told her the sturdy refusal of Naboth, and she broke into a scornful laugh. "Are you king of Israel?" she asked. "Why this is playing at kinghood!" (1 Ki. 21:7). "It is not the way we do things in Tyre. Arise, eat bread, be merry. I will give thee the vineyard of Naboth the Jezreelite."

21:8–10. Did he admire the mannish spirit of the Syrian princess, or did he secretly shrink from it? At any rate, he let Jezebel take her own course. With intrepid insolence she at once wrote a letter in Ahab's name from Samaria, and sent it sealed with his signet to the elders of Jezreel. (The signet was carved with the king's name. Rawlinson aptly compares Lady Macbeth's "Infirm of purpose give me the daggers!") She ordered them to proclaim a fast

3949	603	5598.125	3937	881, 3884	5197	3263
n ms, ps 2ms	pers pron	v Qal impf 1cs	prep, ps 2ms	do, *n ms*	pn	art, pn
לִבְּךָ	אֲנִי	אֶתֵּן	לְךָ	אֶת־כֶּרֶם	נָבוֹת	הַיִּזְרְעֵאלִי
libbekhā	'ănî	'ettēn	lekhā	'eth-kerem	nāvôth	hayyizre'ē'lî
your heart	I	I will give	to you	the vineyard of	Naboth	the Jezreelite

8. 3918.122	5809	904, 8428	255	2964.122	904, 2460
cj, v Qal impf 3fs	n mp	prep, *n ms*	pn	cj, v Qal impf 3fs	prep, n ms, ps 3ms
וַתִּכְתֹּב	סְפָרִים	בְּשֵׁם	אַחְאָב	וַתַּחְתֹּם	בְּחֹתָמוֹ
wattikhtōv	sephārîm	beshēm	'ach'āv	wattachtōm	bechōthāmô
and she wrote	documents	with the name of	Ahab	and she sealed	with his seal

8365.122	5809	420, 2292	420, 2814	866	904, 6111
cj, v Qal impf 3fs	art, n mp	prep, art, n mp	cj, prep, art, n mp	rel pron	prep, n fs, ps 3ms
וַתִּשְׁלַח	הַסְּפָרִים	אֶל־הַזְּקֵנִים	וְאֶל־הַחֹרִים	אֲשֶׁר	בְּעִירוֹ
wattishlach	hasphārîm	'el-hazqēnîm	we'el-hachōrîm	'ăsher	be'îrô
then she sent out	the documents	to the elders	and to the officials	who	in his city

3553.152	882, 5197	9. 3918.122	904, 5809	3937, 569.141
art, v Qal act ptc mp	prep, pn	cj, v Qal impf 3fs	prep, art, n mp	prep, v Qal inf con
הַיֹּשְׁבִים	אֶת־נָבוֹת	וַתִּכְתֹּב	בַּסְּפָרִים	לֵאמֹר
hayyōshevîm	'eth-nāvôth	wattikhtōv	bassephārîm	lē'mōr
those dwelling	Naboth	and she wrote	on the documents	saying

7410.133, 6948	3553.533	881, 5197	904, 7513	6194	10. 3553.533
v Qal impv 2mp, n ms	cj, v Hiphil impv 2mp	do, pn	prep, *n ms*	art, n ms	cj, v Hiphil impv 2mp
קִרְאוּ־צוֹם	וְהוֹשִׁיבוּ	אֶת־נָבוֹת	בְּרֹאשׁ	הָעָם	וְהוֹשִׁיבוּ
qir'û-tsôm	wehôshîvû	'eth-nāvôth	berō'sh	hā'ām	wehôshîvû
proclaim a fast	and cause to sit	Naboth	at the head of	the people	and cause to sit

8530	596	1158, 1139	5224	5967.526
num	n mp	*n mp*, n ms	prep, ps 3ms	cj, v Hiphil juss 3mp, ps 3ms
שְׁנַיִם	אֲנָשִׁים	בְנֵי־בְלִיַּעַל	נֶגְדּוֹ	וִיעִדֻהוּ
shenayim	'ănāshîm	benê-veliya'al	neghdô	wî'idhuhû
two	men	sons of corruption	opposite him	that they may testify about him

3937, 569.141	1313.313	435	4567	3428.533
prep, v Qal inf con	v Piel pf 2ms	n mp	cj, n ms	cj, v Hiphil impv 2mp, ps 3ms
לֵאמֹר	בֵּרַכְתָּ	אֱלֹהִים	וָמֶלֶךְ	וְהוֹצִיאֻהוּ
lē'mōr	bērakhtā	'ĕlōhîm	wāmelekh	wehôtsî'uhû
saying	you have blessed	God	and the king	then take him out

5820.133	4322.121	11. 6449.126	596	6111	2292
cj, v Qal impv 2mp, ps 3ms	cj, v Qal juss 3ms	cj, v Qal impf 3mp	*n mp*	n fs, ps 3ms	art, n mp
וְסִקְלֻהוּ	וְיָמֹת	וַיַּעֲשׂוּ	אַנְשֵׁי	עִירוֹ	הַזְּקֵנִים
wesiqōluhû	weyāmōth	wayya'ăsû	'anshê	'îrô	hazzeqēnîm
and stone him	that he may die	and they did	the men of	his city	the elders

2814	866	3553.152	904, 6111	3626, 866	8365.112	420
cj, art, n mp	rel pron	art, v Qal act ptc mp	prep, n fs, ps 3ms	prep, rel part	v Qal pf 3fs	prep, ps 3mp
וְהַחֹרִים	אֲשֶׁר	הַיֹּשְׁבִים	בְּעִירוֹ	כַּאֲשֶׁר	שָׁלְחָה	אֲלֵיהֶם
wehachōrîm	'ăsher	hayyōshevîm	be'îrô	ka'ăsher	shālechāh	'ălêhem
and the officials	who	those dwelling	in his city	just as	she had sent	to them

350	3626, 866	3918.151	904, 5809	866	8365.112	420
pn	prep, rel part	v Qal pass ptc ms	prep, art, n mp	rel part	v Qal pf 3fs	prep, ps 3mp
אִיזֶבֶל	כַּאֲשֶׁר	כָּתוּב	בַּסְּפָרִים	אֲשֶׁר	שָׁלְחָה	אֲלֵיהֶם
'îzāvel	ka'ăsher	kāthûv	bassephārîm	'ăsher	shālechāh	'ălêhem
Jezebel	just as	what was written	on the documents	which	she sent	to them

12.	7410.116 v Qal pf 3cp קָרְאוּ qāre'û they proclaimed	6948 n ms צוֹם tsôm a fast	3553.516 cj, v Hiphil pf 3cp וְהֹשִׁיבוּ wehōshîvû and they caused to sit	881, 5197 do, pn אֶת־נָבוֹת 'eth-nāvôth Naboth	904, 7513 prep, *n ms* בְּרֹאשׁ berō'sh at the head of	6194 art, n ms הָעָם hā'ām the people
13.	971.126 cj, v Qal impf 3mp וַיָּבֹאוּ wayyāvō'û then they entered	8530 num שְׁנֵי shenê the two of	596 art, n mp הָאֲנָשִׁים hā'ănāshîm the men	1158, 1139 *n mp*, n ms בְּנֵי־בְלִיַּעַל benê-velîya'al sons of corruption	3553.126 cj, v Qal impf 3mp וַיֵּשְׁבוּ wayyēshevû and they sat	5224 prep, ps 3ms נֶגְדּוֹ neghdô opposite him

seal, and sent the letters unto the elders and to the nobles that were in his city, dwelling with Naboth: ... sending it to the sheikhs and the freemen who managed the town, *Moffatt* ... older leaders and important men, *NCV* ... sealed them with his ring; and sent them to the ancients, and the chief men, *Douay* ... responsible men and the chiefs who were in authority, *BB*.

9. And she wrote in the letters, saying, Proclaim a fast, and set Naboth on high among the people: ... set Naboth at the head of, *NAB* ... in a prominent place, *JB* ... a conspicuous place, *Goodspeed* ... of the assembly, *NRSV*.

10. And set two men, sons of Belial, before him, to bear witness against him: ... Seat two troublemakers across from him, *NCV* ... let them bear false witness, *Douay* ... Get a couple of scoundrels to accuse him, *Good News* ... two men, unprincipled men, *Berkeley* ... two wicked men, *Geneva*.

saying, Thou didst blaspheme God and the king. And then carry him out, and stone him, that he may die: ... You have cursed God and the king, *RSV* ... hast reviled, *Rotherham*.

11. And the men of his city, even the elders and the nobles who were the inhabitants in his city, did as Jezebel had sent unto them, and as it was written in the letters which she had sent unto them: ... notables of Naboth's city carried out the instructions, *REB* ... other leaders followed, *NLT* ... who presided, *Goodspeed* ... directed in the letters, *NIV*.

12. They proclaimed a fast, and set Naboth on high among the people: ... at the head of, *NASB* ... sit among the greatest of the townspeople, *Knox* ... gave orders for a day of public sorrow, *BB* ... sit as the first among, *Beck*.

13. And there came in two men, children of Belial, and sat before him: ... and brought the two villains, *Fenton* ... sons of the devil, *Douay* ... Two troublemakers sat across from Naboth, *NCV*.

and the men of Belial witnessed against him, even against Naboth, in the presence of the people, saying, Naboth did blaspheme God and the king: ... two worthless men came in and sat before him, *NASB* ... charged him publicly with cursing, *NEB* ... Naboth hath reviled, *Rotherham*.

Then they carried him forth out of the city, and stoned him with stones, that he died: ... taken outside the town and stoned to death, *Moffatt*.

---

as though to avert some public calamity, and—with a touch of dreadful malice as though to aggravate the horror of his ruin—to exalt Naboth to a conspicuous position in the assembly. They were to get hold of two "sons of worthlessness," professional perjurers, and to accuse Naboth of blasphemy against God and the king. The charge was that "he cursed God and the king." The Hebrew word has both meanings (cf. Exo. 22:28, where some would render 'ělōhîm (HED #435) not "God," but "the judges."). Stoning was the punishment of blasphemy (Lev. 24:16) and took place outside the city (Acts 7:58). His mode of refusing the vineyard might give some colorable pretext to the charge. On the testimony of those two false witnesses, Naboth must be condemned, and then they must drag him outside the city to the pool or tank with his sons and stone them all.

21:11–15. Everything was done by the subservient elders of Jezreel exactly as she had directed. Their fawning readiness to carry out her vile commands is the deadliest incidental proof of the corruption which she and her crew of alien idolaters had wrought in Israel. On that very evening Jezebel received the message, "Naboth is stoned and is dead." By the savage law of those days his innocent sons were involved in his overthrow (2 Ki. 9:26), and his property, left without heirs, reverted by confiscation to the crown (2 Sam. 16:4). "Arise," said the triumphant sorceress, "and take

5967.526	596	1139	881, 5197	5224	6194
cj, Hiphil impf 3mp, ps 3ms	*n mp*	art, n ms	do, pn	prep	art, n ms
וַיְעִדֻהוּ	אַנְשֵׁי	הַבְּלִיַּעַל	אֶת־נָבוֹת	נֶגֶד	הָעָם
way'idhuhû	'anshê	habbelîya'al	'eth-nāvôth	neghedh	hā'ām
and they testified about him	the men of	the corruption	Naboth	before	the people

3937, 569.141	1313.311	5197	435	4567	3428.526
prep, v Qal inf con	v Piel pf 3ms	pn	n mp	cj, n ms	cj, v Hiphil impf 3mp, ps 3ms
לֵאמֹר	בֵּרַךְ	נָבוֹת	אֱלֹהִים	וָמֶלֶךְ	וַיֹּצִאֻהוּ
lē'mōr	bērakh	nāvôth	'ĕlōhîm	wāmelekh	wayyōtsi'uhû
saying	he has blessed	Naboth	God	and the king	and they brought him out

4623, 2445	3937, 6111	5820.126	904, 63	4322.121
prep, n ms	prep, art, n fs	cj, v Qal impf 3mp, ps 3ms	prep, art, n fp	cj, v Qal impf 3ms
מִחוּץ	לָעִיר	וַיִּסְקְלֻהוּ	בָאֲבָנִים	וַיָּמֹת
michûts	lā'îr	wayyisqōluhû	vā'ăvānîm	wayyāmōth
from outside	of the city	and they stoned him	with the stones	and he died

	8365.126	420, 350	3937, 569.141	5820.411	5197	4322.121
14.	cj, v Qal impf 3mp	prep, pn	prep, v Qal inf con	v Pual pf 3ms	pn	cj, v Qal impf 3ms
	וַיִּשְׁלְחוּ	אֶל־אִיזֶבֶל	לֵאמֹר	סֻקַּל	נָבוֹת	וַיָּמֹת
	wayyishlechû	'el-'îzevel	lē'mōr	suqqal	nāvôth	wayyāmōth
	and they sent out	unto Jezebel	saying	he has been stoned	Naboth	and he is dead

	2030.121	3626, 8471.141	350	3706, 5820.411	5197	4322.121
15.	cj, v Qal impf 3ms	prep, v Qal inf con	pn	cj, v Pual pf 3ms	pn	cj, v Qal impf 3ms
	וַיְהִי	כִּשְׁמֹעַ	אִיזֶבֶל	כִּי־סֻקַּל	נָבוֹת	וַיָּמֹת
	wayhî	kishmōa'	'îzevel	kî-suqqal	nāvôth	wayyāmōth
	and it was	when hearing	Jezebel	that he had been stoned	Naboth	and he was dead

569.122	350	420, 255	7251.131	3542.131	881, 3884	5197
cj, v Qal impf 3fs	pn	prep, pn	v Qal impv 2ms	v Qal impv 2ms	do, *n ms*	pn
וַתֹּאמֶר	אִיזֶבֶל	אֶל־אַחְאָב	קוּם	רֵשׁ	אֶת־כֶּרֶם	נָבוֹת
wattō'mer	'îzevel	'el-'ach'āv	qûm	rēsh	'eth-kerem	nāvôth
then she said	Jezebel	to Ahab	rise	take possession of	the vineyard of	Naboth

3263	866	4126.311	3937, 5598.141, 3937	904, 3826B	3706	375	5197
art, pn	rel pron	v Piel pf 3ms	prep, v Qal inf con, ps 2ms	prep, n ms	cj	*sub*	pn
הַיִּזְרְעֵאלִי	אֲשֶׁר	מֵאֵן	לָתֶת־לְךָ	בְכֶסֶף	כִּי	אֵין	נָבוֹת
hayyizre'ē'lî	'ăsher	mē'ēn	lātheth-lekhā	vekheseph	kî	'ên	nāvôth
the Jezreelite	who	he refused	to give to you	with silver	because	he is not	Naboth

2508	3706, 4322.111		2030.121	3626, 8471.141	255	3706	4322.111
adj	cj, v Qal pf 3ms	16.	cj, v Qal impf 3ms	prep, v Qal inf con	pn	cj	v Qal pf 3ms
חַי	כִּי־מֵת		וַיְהִי	כִּשְׁמֹעַ	אַחְאָב	כִּי	מֵת
chay	kî-mēth		wayhî	kishmōa'	'ach'āv	kî	mēth
living	because he is dead		and it was	when hearing	Ahab	that	he was dead

5197	7251.121	255	3937, 3495.141	420, 3884	5197	3263
pn	cj, v Qal impf 3ms	pn	prep, v Qal inf con	prep, *n ms*	pn	art, pn
נָבוֹת	וַיָּקָם	אַחְאָב	לָרֶדֶת	אֶל־כֶּרֶם	נָבוֹת	הַיִּזְרְעֵאלִי
nāvôth	wayyāqām	'ach'āv	lāredheth	'el-kerem	nāvôth	hayyizre'ē'lî
Naboth	that he rose up	Ahab	to go down	to the vineyard of	Naboth	the Jezreelite

3937, 3542.141		2030.121	1745, 3176	420, 455	9005
prep, v Qal inf con, ps 3ms	17.	cj, v Qal impf 3ms	*n ms*, pn	prep, pn	art, pn
לְרִשְׁתּוֹ		וַיְהִי	דְּבַר־יְהוָה	אֶל־אֵלִיָּהוּ	הַתִּשְׁבִּי
lerishtô		wayhî	devar-yehwāh	'el-'ēlîyāhû	hattishbî
to take possession of it		and it was	the word of Yahweh	to Elijah	the Tishbite

3937, 569.141 prep, v Qal inf con לֵאמֹר lē'mōr saying	**18.**	7251.131 v Qal impv 2ms קוּם qûm rise	3495.131 v Qal impv 2ms רֵד rēdh go down	3937, 7410.141 prep, v Qal inf con לִקְרַאת liqōra'th to meet	255 pn אַחְאָב 'ach'āv Ahab	4567, 3547 *n ms*, pn מֶלֶךְ־יִשְׂרָאֵל melekh-yisrā'ēl the king of Israel

866 rel pron אֲשֶׁר 'ăsher who	904, 8497 prep, pn בְּשֹׁמְרוֹן beshōmerôn in Samaria	2079 intrj הִנֵּה hinnēh behold	904, 3884 prep, *n ms* בְּכֶרֶם bekherem in the vineyard of	5197 pn נָבוֹת nāvôth Naboth	866, 3495.111 rel part, v Qal pf 3ms אֲשֶׁר־יָרַד 'ăsher-yāradh where he has gone down	8427 adv שָׁם shām there

3937, 3542.141 prep, v Qal inf con, ps 3ms לְרִשְׁתּוֹ lerishtô to take possession of it	**19.**	1744.313 cj, v Piel pf 2ms וְדִבַּרְתָּ wedhibbartā and you will speak	420 prep, ps 3ms אֵלָיו 'ēlâv to him	3937, 569.141 prep, v Qal inf con לֵאמֹר lē'mōr saying	3662 adv כֹּה kōh thus	569.111 v Qal pf 3ms אָמַר 'āmar He has said

14. Then they sent to Jezebel, saying, Naboth is stoned, and is dead: ... has been stoned to death, *Berkeley* ... put to death, *Good News* ... sent the information, *NAB*.

15. And it came to pass, when Jezebel heard that Naboth was stoned, and was dead, that Jezebel said to Ahab, Arise, take possession of the vineyard of Naboth the Jezreelite, which he refused to give thee for money: for Naboth is not alive, but dead: ... which he denied to give thee for silver, *Tyndale* ... take as your heritage the vine-garden, *BB* ... take over, *Berkeley* ... for yourself the vineyard he would not sell to you, *NCV*.

16. And it came to pass, when Ahab heard that Naboth was dead, that Ahab rose up to go down to the vineyard of Naboth the Jezreelite, to take possession of it: ... went to the vineyard to take it for his own, *NCV* ... as his heritage, *BB* ... to claim it, *NLT*.

17. And the word of the LORD came to Elijah the Tishbite, saying: ... But the LORD said, *NAB* ... Elias the Thesbite, *Douay* ... Elijah, the prophet from Tishbe, *Good News* ... spoke to Elijah from Tishbe, *Beck*.

18. Arise, go down to meet Ahab king of Israel, which is in Samaria: behold, he is in the vineyard of Naboth, whither he is gone down to possess it: ... he has gone to claim it, *Berkeley* ... which he has gone to seize, *Fenton*.

19. And thou shalt speak unto him, saying, Thus saith the LORD, Hast thou killed, and also taken possession?: ... You have committed murder and now you usurp as well, *JB* ... Have you not murdered a man and seized his property?, *NIV* ... Isn't killing Naboth bad enough? Must you rob him, too?, *NLT*.

And thou shalt speak unto him, saying, Thus saith the LORD, In the place where dogs licked the blood of Naboth shall dogs lick thy blood, even thine: ... they will also lick up, *NCV* ... the dogs have lapped up,

possession of the vineyard you wished for. I have given it to you as I promised. Its owner and his sons have died the deaths of blasphemers, and lie crushed under the stones outside Jezreel."

21:16. Caring only for the gratification of his wish, heedless of the means employed, hastily and joyously at early dawn the king arose to seize the coveted vineyard. The dark deed had been done at night, the king was alert with the morning light. In 1 Ki. 21:16, the Septuagint curiously says that "when Ahab heard that Naboth was dead he rent his garments, and clothed himself in sackcloth; and after this he also arose," etc. This mourning for the means but acceptance of the fact would not be in disaccord with Ahab's moral weakness. He rode in his chariot from Samaria to Jezreel, which is but seven miles distant, and he rode in something of military state, for in separate chariots, or else riding in the same chariot, behind him were two war-like youths, Jehu and Bidkar, who were destined to remember the events of that day, and to refer to them four years afterwards, when one had become king and the other his chief commander (2 Ki. 9:25, 36).

21:17–20a. But the king's joy was shortlived!

News of the black crime had come to Elijah, probably in his lonely retreat in some cave at Carmel. He was a man who, though he flamed out on great occasions like a meteor portending ruin to the guilty, lived in general a hidden life. Six years had elapsed since the calling of Elisha, and we have

3176	1950B, 7815.113	1612, 3542.113	1744.313	420
pn	intrg part, v Qal pf 2ms	cj, cj, v Qal pf 2ms	cj, v Piel pf 2ms	prep, ps 3ms
יְהוָה	הֲרָצַחְתָּ	וְגַם־יָרָשְׁתָּ	וְדִבַּרְתָּ	אֵלָיו
yehwāh	herātsachtā	wegham-yārāshettā	wedhibbartā	'ēlâv
Yahweh	have you killed	and also have you taken possession of	and you will speak	to him

3937, 569.141	3662	569.111	3176	904, 4887	866	4094.116	3732
prep, v Qal inf con	adv	v Qal pf 3ms	pn	prep, *n ms*	rel part	v Qal pf 3cp	art, n mp
לֵאמֹר	כֹּה	אָמַר	יְהוָה	בִּמְקוֹם	אֲשֶׁר	לָקְקוּ	הַכְּלָבִים
lē'mōr	kōh	'āmar	yehwāh	bimqôm	'ăsher	lāqōqû	hakkelāvîm
saying	thus	He has said	Yahweh	in the place of	where	they have licked	the dogs

881, 1879	5197	4094.126	3732	881, 1879	1612, 887		569.121
do, *n ms*	pn	v Qal impf 3mp	art, n mp	do, n ms, ps 2ms	cj, pers pron	**20.**	cj, v Qal impf 3ms
אֶת־דַּם	נָבוֹת	יָלֹקּוּ	הַכְּלָבִים	אֶת־דָּמְךָ	גַּם־אָתָּה		וַיֹּאמֶר
'eth-dam	nāvôth	yālōqqû	hakkelāvîm	'eth-dāmekhā	gam-'āttāh		wayyō'mer
the blood of	Naboth	they will lick	the dogs	your blood	also you		and he said

255	420, 455	1950B, 4834.113	342.151	569.121	4834.115
pn	prep, pn	intrg part, v Qal pf 2ms, ps 1cs	v Qal act ptc ms, ps 1cs	cj, v Qal impf 3ms	v Qal pf 1cs
אַחְאָב	אֶל־אֵלִיָּהוּ	הַמְצָאתַנִי	אֹיְבִי	וַיֹּאמֶר	מָצָאתִי
'ach'āv	'el-'ēlîyāhû	hamtso'thanî	'ōyevî	wayyō'mer	mātsā'thî
Ahab	to Elijah	have you found me	my enemy	and he said	I have found

3391	4513.741	3937, 6449.141	7737	904, 6084	3176
cj	v Hithpael inf con, ps 2ms	prep, v Qal inf con	art, adj	prep, *n fs*	pn
יַעַן	הִתְמַכֶּרְךָ	לַעֲשׂוֹת	הָרַע	בְּעֵינֵי	יְהוָה
ya'an	hithmakkerkhā	la'ăsôth	hāra'	be'ênê	yehwāh
because of	your selling yourself	to do	what is evil	in the eyes of	Yahweh

	2079	971.551	420	7750	1220.315	313	3901.515
21.	intrj, ps 1cs	v Hiphil ptc ms	prep, ps 2ms	adj	cj, v Piel pf 1cs	prep, ps 2ms	cj, v Hiphil pf 1cs
	הִנְנִי	מֵבִי	אֵלֶיךָ	רָעָה	וּבִעַרְתִּי	אַחֲרֶיךָ	וְהִכְרַתִּי
	hinenî	mēvî	'ēlêkhā	rā'āh	ûvi'artî	'achrêkhā	wehikhrattî
	behold I	bringing	to you	evil	and I will consume	after you	and I will cut off

3937, 255	8697.551	904, 7306	6352.155	6013.155	904, 3547
prep, pn	v Hiphil ptc ms	prep, n ms	cj, v Qal pass ptc ms	cj, v Qal pass ptc ms	prep, pn
לְאַחְאָב	מַשְׁתִּין	בְּקִיר	וְעָצוּר	וְעָזוּב	בְּיִשְׂרָאֵל
le'ach'āv	mashtîn	beqîr	we'ātsûr	we'āzûv	beyisrā'ēl
from Ahab	those urinating	on a wall	and those bound	and those let loose	in Israel

	5598.115	881, 1041	3626, 1041	3493	1158, 5203
22.	cj, v Qal pf 1cs	do, n ms, ps 2ms	prep, *n ms*	pn	*n ms*, pn
	וְנָתַתִּי	אֶת־בֵּיתְךָ	כְּבֵית	יָרָבְעָם	בֶּן־נְבָט
	wenāthattî	'eth-bêthekhā	kevêth	yārov'ām	ben-nevāṯ
	and I will hand over	your household	like the household of	Jeroboam	the son of Nebat

3626, 1041	1225	1158, 282	420, 3833	866
cj, prep, *n ms*	pn	*n ms*, pn	prep, art, n ms	rel part
וּכְבֵית	בַּעְשָׁא	בֶּן־אֲחִיָּה	אֶל־הַכַּעַס	אֲשֶׁר
ûkhevêth	ba'shā'	ven-'ăchîyāh	'el-hakka'as̱	'ăsher
and like the household of	Baasha	the son of Ahijah	on account of the anger	which

3832.513	2490.523	881, 3547		1612, 3937, 350
v Hiphil pf 2ms	cj, v Hiphil impf 2ms	do, pn	**23.**	cj, cj, prep, pn
הִכְעַסְתָּ	וַתַּחֲטִא	אֶת־יִשְׂרָאֵל		וְגַם־לְאִיזֶבֶל
hikh'as̱tā	wattachṯi'	'eth-yisrā'ēl		wegham-le'îzevel
you have provoked to anger	and you caused to sin	Israel		and also of Jezebel

1744.311	3176	3937, 569.141	3732	404.126	881, 350	904, 2526
v Piel pf 3ms	pn	prep, v Qal inf con	art, n mp	v Qal impf 3mp	do, pn	prep, *n ms*
דִּבֶּר	יְהוָה	לֵאמֹר	הַכְּלָבִים	יֹאכְלוּ	אֶת־אִיזֶבֶל	בְּחֵל
dibber	yehwāh	lē'mōr	hakkelāvîm	yō'khelû	'eth-'îzevel	bechēl
He has spoken	Yahweh	saying	the dogs	they will eat	Jezebel	by the rampart of

3262		4322.151	3937, 255	904, 6111	404.126	3732	4322.151
pn	**24.**	art, v Qal act ptc ms	prep, pn	prep, art, n fs	v Qal impf 3mp	art, n mp	cj, art, v Qal act ptc ms
יִזְרְעֶאל		הַמֵּת	לְאַחְאָב	בָּעִיר	יֹאכְלוּ	הַכְּלָבִים	וְהַמֵּת
yizre'e'l		hammēth	le'ach'āv	bā'îr	yō'khelû	hakkelāvîm	wehammēth
Jezreel		the dead one	of Ahab	in the city	they will eat	the dogs	and the dead one

Rotherham ... there will your blood become the drink of dogs, *BB*.

20. And Ahab said to Elijah, Hast thou found me, O mine enemy? And he answered, I have found thee: ... So you have found me out, *Moffatt* ... Did you find me, my enemy?, *Beck*.

because thou hast sold thyself to work evil in the sight of the Lord: ... sold yourself to do what is evil, *RSV* ... you have given yourself up to doing evil, *NAB* ... committed yourself to do evil, *Berkeley* ... given to work wickedness, *Tyndale*.

21. Behold, I will bring evil upon thee: ... I shall bring disaster on you, *REB* ... And hateful is the ruin I mean to bring, *Knox*.

and will take away thy posterity: ... utterly sweep you away, *NASB* ... send a fire after you, *Fenton* ... will make clean riddance of thee, *Tyndale* ... your children forever, *KJVII* ... I will consume you, *NRSV*.

and will cut off from Ahab him that pisseth against the wall, and him that is shut up and left in Israel: ... and cut off to Ahab those sitting on, *Young* ... every male in Israel, both bond and free, *NKJV* ... He will not let a single one of your male descendants, slave and free alike, survive, *NLT*.

22. And will make thine house like the house of Jeroboam the son of Nebat, and like the house of Baasha the son of Ahijah: ... your family like the family, *BB* ... I shall treat your House as I treated, *JB*.

for the provocation wherewith thou hast provoked me to anger: ... because of the indignation which you have aroused, *Goodspeed* .... you irritated Me, *Berkeley* ... have stirred up my anger, *Good News*.

and made Israel to sin: ... and caused, *Rotherham* ... have led the people, *NCV*.

23. And of Jezebel also spake the Lord, saying, The dogs shall eat Jezebel by the wall of Jezreel: ... The dogs shall eat Jezebel by the rampart, *ASV* ... will devour Jezebel within the boundary, *Beck* ... in the moat, *MAST*.

24. Him that dieth of Ahab in the city the dogs shall eat: ... Of the house of Ahab, those who die in the city will be food for the dogs, *REB* ... The members of your family, *NLT* ... Any of your relatives, *Good News* ... when one of Ahab's line dies, *NAB*.

not once been reminded of his existence. But now he was instantly inspired to protest against the atrocious act of robbery and oppression, and to denounce upon it an awful retribution which not even Baal worship had called forth.

Ahab was at the summit of his hopes. He was about to complete his summer palace and to grasp the fruits of the crime which he had allowed his wife to commit. But at the gate of Naboth's vineyard stood the ominous figure of the prophet in his hairy garb. We can imagine the revulsion of feeling which drove the blood to the king's heart as he instantly felt that he had sinned in vain. The advantage of his crime was snatched from him at the instant of fruition. Half in anger, half in anguish, he cried, "Hast thou found me, O mine enemy?"

21:20b–24. "I have found thee," said the prophet, speaking in Yahweh's name. "Thou hast sold thyself to work evil before me, and I will requite it and extinguish thee before me. Surely the Lord saw yesternight the blood of Naboth and the blood of his sons. Thy dynasty shall be cut off to the last man, like that of Jeroboam, like that of Baasha. Where the dogs licked the blood of Naboth, the dogs shall lick thine. The harlots shall wash themselves in the water which thy blood has stained. Him that dieth of thee in the city the dogs shall eat, and him that dieth in the field shall the vultures rend, and the dogs shall eat Jezebel also in the moat of Jezreel." The desert space outside the walls was where the mongrel dogs prowled on the mounds.

904, 7898	404.126	5991	8452		7828	3940, 2030.111	3626, 255
prep, art, n ms	v Qal impf 3mp	*n ms*	art, n md	**25.**	adv	neg part, v Qal pf 3ms	prep, pn
בַּשָּׂדֶה	יֹאכְלוּ	עוֹף	הַשָּׁמָיִם		רַק	לֹא־הָיָה	כְאַחְאָב
bassādheh	yō'khelû	'ôph	hashshāmāyim		raq	lō'-hāyāh	khe'ach'āv
in the field	they will eat	the birds of	the heavens		surely	he had not been	like Ahab

866	4513.711	3937, 6449.141	7737	904, 6084	3176	866, 5684.512
rel pron	v Hithpael pf 3ms	prep, v Qal inf con	art, adj	prep, *n fd*	pn	rel pron, v Hiphil pf 3fs
אֲשֶׁר	הִתְמַכֵּר	לַעֲשׂוֹת	הָרַע	בְּעֵינֵי	יְהוָה	אֲשֶׁר־הֵסַתָּה
'ăsher	hithmakkēr	la'ăsôth	hāra'	be'ênê	yehwāh	'ăsher-hēsattāh
who	he sold himself	to do	what is evil	in the eyes of	Yahweh	whom she enticed

881	350	828		8911.521	4108	3937, 2050.141	313	1585
do, ps 3ms	pn	n fs, ps 3ms	**26.**	cj, v Hiphil impf 3ms	adv	prep, v Qal inf con	prep	art, n mp
אֹתוֹ	אִיזֶבֶל	אִשְׁתּוֹ		וַיַּתְעֵב	מְאֹד	לָלֶכֶת	אַחֲרֵי	הַגִּלֻּלִים
'ōthô	'îzevel	'ishtô		wayyath'ēv	me'ōdh	lālekheth	'achrê	haggillulîm
him	Jezebel	his wife		and he acted detestably	very	to walk	after	the idols

3626, 3725	866	6449.116	578	866	3542.511	3176
prep, adj	rel part	v Qal pf 3cp	art, pn	rel pron	v Hiphil pf 3ms	pn
כְּכֹל	אֲשֶׁר	עָשׂוּ	הָאֱמֹרִי	אֲשֶׁר	הוֹרִישׁ	יְהוָה
kekhōl	'ăsher	'āsû	hā'ĕmōrî	'ăsher	hôrîsh	yehwāh
according to all	that	they had done	the Amorites	whom	He dispossessed	Yahweh

4623, 6686	1158	3547		2030.121	3626, 8471.141	255	881, 1745
prep, *n mp*	*n mp*	pn	**27.**	cj, v Qal impf 3ms	prep, v Qal inf con	pn	do, art, n mp
מִפְּנֵי	בְּנֵי	יִשְׂרָאֵל		וַיְהִי	כִשְׁמֹעַ	אַחְאָב	אֶת־הַדְּבָרִים
mippenê	benê	yisrā'ēl		wayhî	khishmōa'	'ach'āv	'eth-haddevārîm
from before	the sons of	Israel		and it was	when hearing	Ahab	the words

431	7458	933	7947.121, 8012	6142, 1340	6947.121
art, dem pron	cj, v Qal impf 3ms	n mp, ps 3ms	cj, v Qal impf 3ms, n ms	prep, n ms, ps 3ms	cj, v Qal impf 3ms
הָאֵלֶּה	וַיִּקְרַע	בְּגָדָיו	וַיָּשֶׂם־שַׂק	עַל־בְּשָׂרוֹ	וַיָּצוֹם
hā'ēlleh	wayyiqra'	beghādhâv	wayyāsem-saq	'al-besārô	wayyātsôm
the these	that he tore	his clothes	and he put sackcloth	on his flesh	and he fasted

8311.121	904, 8012	2050.321	330		2030.121
cj, v Qal impf 3ms	prep, art, n ms	cj, v Piel impf 3ms	adv	**28.**	cj, v Qal impf 3ms
וַיִּשְׁכַּב	בַּשָּׂק	וַיְהַלֵּךְ	אַט		וַיְהִי
wayyishkav	bassāq	wayhallēkh	'aṭ		wayhî
and he lay	in the sackcloth	and he walked about	dejectedly		and it was

1745, 3176	420, 455	9005	3937, 569.141		1950B, 7495.113
n ms, pn	prep, pn	art, pn	prep, v Qal inf con	**29.**	intrg part, v Qal pf 2ms
דְּבַר־יְהוָה	אֶל־אֵלִיָּהוּ	הַתִּשְׁבִּי	לֵאמֹר		הֲרָאִיתָ
devar-yehwāh	'el-'ēlîyāhû	hattishbî	lē'mōr		hărā'îthā
the word of Yahweh	to Elijah	the Tishbite	saying		have you seen

3706, 3789.211	255	4623, 3937, 6686	3391	3706, 3789.211
cj, v Niphal pf 3ms	pn	prep, prep, n mp, ps 1cs	cj	cj, v Niphal pf 3ms
כִּי־נִכְנַע	אַחְאָב	מִלְּפָנָי	יַעַן	כִּי־נִכְנַע
kî-nikhna'	'ach'āv	millephānāy	ya'an	kî-nikhna'
that he has humbled himself	Ahab	from before Me	because	that he has humbled himself

4623, 6686	3940, 971.525	7737	904, 3219	904, 3219	1158
prep, n mp, ps 1cs	neg part, v Hiphil impf 1cs	art, adj	prep, n mp, ps 3ms	prep, *n mp*	n ms, ps 3ms
מִפָּנַי	לֹא־אָבִי	הָרָעָה	בְּיָמָיו	בִּימֵי	בְנוֹ
mippānay	lō'-'āvî	hārā'āh	beyāmâv	bîmê	venô
from before Me	I will not bring	the evil	in his days	in the days of	his son

and him that dieth in the field shall the fowls of the air eat: ... the one who dies in the field the birds of heaven shall eat, *NASB* ... the fowls of the skies shall devour, *Fenton* ... anyone of his who dies in the open country, *NRSV*.

25. But there was none like unto Ahab, which did sell himself to work wickedness in the sight of the LORD: ... that gave himself up to doings hateful in the Lord's sight, *Knox* ... There was absolutely no one who sold himself to do evil, *Goodspeed* ... who had chosen so often to do what the LORD said was wrong, *NCV* ... for double dealing and for doing what is displeasing to Yahweh, *JB*.

whom Jezebel his wife stirred up: ... hath moved, *Young* ... pricked him forward, *Tyndale* ... urging him on, *Darby* ... spurred on by, *Beck*.

26. And he did very abominably in following idols, according to all things as did the Amorites: ... He acted most wickedly when he went after, *Berkeley* ... Ahab sinned terribly by worshiping, *NCV* ... He did a very disgusting thing in going after false gods, *BB* ... has foully defiled himself, *Fenton*.

whom the LORD cast out before the children of Israel: ... whom Yahweh dispossessed from before the sons, *Rotherham* ... had driven out of the land as the people of Israel advanced, *Good News* ... from the presence of, *Young*.

27. And it came to pass, when Ahab heard those words, that he rent his clothes, and put sackcloth upon his flesh: ... put haircloth, *Douay* ... he tore his garments and put sackcloth next to his skin, *JB*.

and fasted, and lay in sackcloth, and went softly: ... went about dejectedly, *RSV* ... He even slept in sackcloth and went about in deep mourning, *NLT* ... in sack and went comfortless, *Tyndale* ... went about subdued, *NAB*.

28. And the word of the LORD came to Elijah the Tishbite, saying: ... Then the LORD spoke to Elijah from Tishbe, *Beck*.

29. Seest thou how Ahab humbleth himself before me?: ... I see that Ahab is now sorry for what he has done, *NCV* ... Do you see how Ahab has made himself low, *BB*.

because he humbleth himself before me: ... because he so submitteth, *Tyndale* ... Humbled for my sake, he shall have this reward, *Knox*.

I will not bring the evil in his days: ... this disaster in his day, *NIV* ... in the calamity, *Rotherham* ... upon his house in his own lifetime, *NEB*.

but in his son's days will I bring the evil upon his house: ... in the lifetime of his son, I will bring the calamity, *Berkeley* ... that I will bring disaster on Ahab's family, *Good News*.

21:25–29. It is the duty of prophets to stand before kings and not be ashamed. So had Abraham stood before Nimrod, and Moses before Pharaoh, and Samuel before Saul, and Nathan before David, and Iddo before Jeroboam. So was Isaiah to stand hereafter before Ahaz, and Jeremiah before Jehoiachin, and John the Baptist before Herod, and Paul before Nero. Nor has it been at all otherwise in modern days. So did St. Ignatius confront Trajan, and St. Ambrose brave the Empress Justina, and St. Martin the usurper Maximus, and St. Chrysostom the fierce Eudoxia, and St. Basil the heretic Valens. So, too, in later days, Savonarola could speak the bare bold truth to Lorenzo the Magnificent, and Knox to Mary Queen of Scots, and Bishop Ken to Charles II. But never was any king confronted by so awful a denunciation of doom. Probably the moment that Elijah had uttered it he disappeared; but could not a swift arrow have reached him from Jehu's or Bidkar's bow? We know how they remembered two reigns later the thunder of those awful words, but they would hardly have disobeyed the mandate of their king had he bidden them to seize or slay the prophet. Nothing was further from their thoughts. Elijah had become to Ahab the incarnation of his own awakened conscience, and it spoke to him in the thunders of Sinai. He quailed before the tremendous imprecation. We may well doubt whether he even so much as entered again the vineyard of Naboth; never certainly could he have enjoyed it. He had indeed sold himself to do evil, and, as always happens to such colossal criminals, he had sold himself for naught—as Achan did for a buried robe and a useless ingot, and Judas for the thirty pieces of silver which he could only dash down on the temple floor. Ahab turned away from the vineyard, which might well seem to him haunted by the ghosts of his murdered victims and its clusters full of blood. He rent his clothes, and clad himself in sackcloth, and slept in sackcloth, and went about barefooted with slow steps and bent brow, a stricken man. From then on, as long as he lived, he kept in penitence and humiliation the fateful deed.

"I have not sent these prophets, yet they ran: I have not spoken to them, yet they prophesied. I have heard what the prophets said, that prophesy lies in my name" (Jer. 23:21, 25).

971.525	7737	6142, 1041		3553.126	8421	8523	375
v Hiphil impf 1cs	art, adj	prep, n ms, ps 3ms	**22:1**	cj, v Qal impf 3mp	num	n fp	*sub*
אָבִיא	הָרָעָה	עַל־בֵּיתוֹ		וַיֵּשְׁבוּ	שָׁלֹשׁ	שָׁנִים	אֵין
'āvî'	hārā'āh	'al-bêthô		wayyēshevû	shālōsh	shānîm	'ên
I will bring	the evil	on his household		and they dwelled	three	years	there was not

4560	1033	782	1033	3547		2030.121	904, 8523	8389
n fs	prep	pn	cj, prep	pn	**2.**	cj, v Qal impf 3ms	prep, art, n fs	art, num
מִלְחָמָה	בֵּין	אֲרָם	וּבֵין	יִשְׂרָאֵל		וַיְהִי	בַּשָּׁנָה	הַשְּׁלִישִׁית
milchāmāh	bên	'ărām	ûvên	yisrā'ēl		wayhî	bashshānāh	hashshelîshîth
war	between	Aram	and between	Israel		then it was	in the year	the third

3495.121	3194	4567, 3171	420, 4567	3547		569.121
cj, v Qal impf 3ms	pn	*n ms*, pn	prep, *n ms*	pn	**3.**	cj, v Qal impf 3ms
וַיֵּרֶד	יְהוֹשָׁפָט	מֶלֶךְ־יְהוּדָה	אֶל־מֶלֶךְ	יִשְׂרָאֵל		וַיֹּאמֶר
wayyēredh	yehôshāphāṭ	melekh-yehûdhāh	'el-melekh	yisrā'ēl		wayyō'mer
that he went down	Jehoshaphat	the king of Judah	to the king of	Israel		and he said

4567, 3547	420, 5860	1950B, 3156.117	3706, 3937	7721	7721	601
n ms, pn	prep, n mp, ps 3ms	intrg part, v Qal pf 2mp	cj, prep, ps 1cp	pn	pn	cj, pers pron
מֶלֶךְ־יִשְׂרָאֵל	אֶל־עֲבָדָיו	הַיְדַעְתֶּם	כִּי־לָנוּ	רָמֹת	גִּלְעָד	וַאֲנַחְנוּ
melekh-yisrā'ēl	'el-'ăvādhâv	haydha'ttem	kî-lānû	rāmōth	gil'ādh	wa'ănachnû
the king of Israel	to his servants	do you know	that to us	Ramoth	Gilead	but we

2924	4623, 4089.141	881	4623, 3135	4567	782		569.121
v Hiphil ptc mp	prep, v Qal inf con	do, ps 3fs	prep, *n fs*	*n ms*	pn	**4.**	cj, v Qal impf 3ms
מַחְשִׁים	מִקַּחַת	אֹתָהּ	מִיַּד	מֶלֶךְ	אֲרָם		וַיֹּאמֶר
machshîm	miqqachath	'ōthāhh	mîyadh	melekh	'ărām		wayyō'mer
doing nothing	about taking	it	from the hand of	the king of	Aram		and he said

420, 3194	1950B, 2050.123	882	3937, 4560	7721	7721	569.121
prep, pn	intrg part, v Qal impf 2ms	prep, ps 1cs	prep, art, n fs	pn	pn	cj, v Qal impf 3ms
אֶל־יְהוֹשָׁפָט	הֲתֵלֵךְ	אִתִּי	לַמִּלְחָמָה	רָמֹת	גִּלְעָד	וַיֹּאמֶר
'el-yehôshāphāṭ	hăthēlēkh	'ittî	lammilchāmāh	rāmōth	gil'ādh	wayyō'mer
to Jehoshaphat	will you go	with me	into the battle	Ramoth	Gilead	and he said

3194	420, 4567	3547	3765	3765	3626, 6194	3626, 6194
pn	prep, *n ms*	pn	prep, ps 1cs	prep, ps 2ms	prep, n ms, ps 1cs	prep, n ms, ps 2ms
יְהוֹשָׁפָט	אֶל־מֶלֶךְ	יִשְׂרָאֵל	כָּמוֹנִי	כָמוֹךָ	כְּעַמִּי	כְעַמֶּךָ
yehôshāphāṭ	'el-melekh	yisrā'ēl	kāmônî	khāmôkhā	ke'ammî	khe'ammekhā
Jehoshaphat	to the king of	Israel	like me	like you	like my people	like your people

3626, 5670	3626, 5670		569.121	3194	420, 4567	3547
prep, n mp, ps 1cs	prep, n mp, ps 2ms	**5.**	cj, v Qal impf 3ms	pn	prep, *n ms*	pn
כְּסוּסַי	כְּסוּסֶיךָ		וַיֹּאמֶר	יְהוֹשָׁפָט	אֶל־מֶלֶךְ	יִשְׂרָאֵל
kesûsay	kesûsêkhā		wayyō'mer	yehôshāphāṭ	'el-melekh	yisrā'ēl
like my horses	like your horses		and he said	Jehoshaphat	to the king of	Israel

1938.131, 5167	3626, 3219	881, 1745	3176		7192.121	4567, 3547
v Qal impv 2ms, part	prep, art, n ms	do, *n ms*	pn	**6.**	cj, v Qal impf 3ms	*n ms*, pn
דְּרָשׁ־נָא	כַיּוֹם	אֶת־דְּבַר	יְהוָה		וַיִּקְבֹּץ	מֶלֶךְ־יִשְׂרָאֵל
derāsh-nā'	khayyôm	'eth-devar	yehwāh		wayyiqbbōts	melekh-yisrā'ēl
inquire please	as today	the word of	Yahweh		so he gathered	the king of Israel

881, 5204	3626, 727	4109	382	569.121	420	1950B, 2050.125
do, art, n mp	prep, num	num	n ms	cj, v Qal impf 3ms	prep, ps 3mp	intrg part, v Qal impf 1cs
אֶת־הַנְּבִיאִים	כְּאַרְבַּע	מֵאוֹת	אִישׁ	וַיֹּאמֶר	אֲלֵהֶם	הַאֵלֵךְ
'eth-hannevî'îm	ke'arba'	mē'ôth	'îsh	wayyō'mer	'ălēhem	ha'ēlēkh
the prophets	about four	hundreds	men	and he said	to them	should I go

22:1. And they continued three years without war between Syria and Israel: ... There was peace between Israel and Syria for the next two years, *Good News* ... Now for three years there was no war between Aram and Israel, *BB* ... There was a lull of three years, with no fighting, *JB* ... passed without war, *NASB*.

2. And it came to pass in the third year, that Jehoshaphat the king of Judah came down to the king of Israel: ... went down to visit, *NKJV* ... during a visit from king Josaphat, *Knox*.

3. And the king of Israel said unto his servants, Know ye that Ramoth in Gilead is ours: ... Do you realize that the Arameans are still occupying our city, *NLT* ... know that Ramoth-gilead belongs to us, *Goodspeed*.

and we be still, and take it not out of the hand of the king of Syria?: ... and we keep quiet and do not take it, *RSV* ... Why have we done nothing to get it back?, *NCV* ... Yet we are putting forth no effort to take it from the grasp of the Syrian king, *Berkeley* ... delay in taking it, *Fenton*.

4. And he said unto Jehoshaphat, Wilt thou go with me to battle to Ramoth-gilead?: ... to make war upon, *Rotherham* ... Will you come with me to attack, *JB* ... go with me to fight against, *NIV* ... Shall I have thy aid in attacking Ramoth-Galaad?, *Knox*.

And Jehoshaphat said to the king of Israel, I am as thou art, my people as thy people, my horses as thy horses: ... My troops will be your troops, *Beck* ... You and I are as one, and your people and my people, *NAB* ... What is mine is yours: myself, my people, and my horses, *NEB* ... my men are one with your men, *Moffatt*.

5. And Jehoshaphat said unto the king of Israel, Inquire, I pray thee, at the word of the LORD today: ... But first let's consult the LORD, *Good News* ... Inquire first for the word, *NRSV* ... Let us now get directions from, *BB* ... ask counsel, *Tyndale*.

6. Then the king of Israel gathered the prophets together, about four hundred men, and said unto them: ... invited four hundred men of the Preachers, *Fenton* ... assembled the prophets, *Douay*.

Shall I go against Ramoth-gilead to battle, or shall I forbear?: ...

22:1–2. We now come to the last scene of Ahab's troubled and eventful life. His two immense victories over the Syrians had secured for his harassed kingdom three years of peace, but at the end of that time he began to be convinced that the insecure conditions upon which he had weakly set Ben-Hadad free would never be ratified. The town of Ramoth in Gilead, which was one of great importance as a frontier town of Israel, had, in express defiance of the covenant, been retained by the Syrians, who still refused to give it up. A favorable opportunity, he thought, had now occurred to demand its cession.

This was the friendly visit of Jehoshaphat, king of Judah. It was the first time that a king of Judah had visited the capital of the kings who had revolted from the dynasty of David. It was the first acknowledged close of the old blood-feuds, and the beginning of a friendship and affinity which policy seemed to dictate. After all Ephraim and Judah were brothers, though Ephraim had vexed Judah, and Judah hated Ephraim. Jehoshaphat was rich, prosperous, successful in war. No king since Solomon had attained to anything like his greatness—the reward, it was believed, of his piety and faithfulness. Ahab, too, had proved himself a successful warrior, and the valor of Israel's hosts had, with Yahweh's blessing, extricated their afflicted land from the terrible aggressions of Syria. But how could the little kingdom of Israel hope to hold out against Syria, and to keep Moab in subjection? How could the still smaller and weaker kingdom of Judah keep itself from vassalage to Egypt and from the encroachments of Philistines on the west and Moabites on the east? Could anything but ruin be imminent, if these two nations of Israel and Judah—one in land, one in blood, one in language, in tradition, and in interests—were perpetually to destroy each other with internecine strife? The kings determined to make a league with one another, and to bind it by mutual affinity. It was proposed that Athaliah, daughter of Ahab and Jezebel, should marry Jehoram, the son of Jehoshaphat.

22:3–4. The king of Israel received him with splendid entertainments to all the people (2 Chr. 18:2). Ahab had already broached to his captains the subject of recovering Ramoth-Gilead, and he now took occasion of the king of Judah's visit to invite his cooperation. What advantages and compensations he offered are not stated. It may have been enough to point out that, if Syria once succeeded in crushing Israel, the fate of Judah would not be long postponed. Jehoshaphat, who seems to have been too ready to yield to pressure, answered in a sort of set phrase: "I am as thou art, my people as thy people, ... my horses as thy horses" (cf. 2 Ki. 3:7).

22:5–12. But it is probable that his heart misgave him. He was a truly pious king. He had

6142, 7721	7721	3937, 4560	525, 2403.125	569.126	6148.131
prep, pn	pn	prep, art, n fs	cj, v Qal impf 1cs	cj, v Qal impf 3mp	v Qal impv 2ms
עַל־רָמֹת	גִּלְעָד	לַמִּלְחָמָה	אִם־אֶחְדָּל	וַיֹּאמְרוּ	עֲלֵה
'al-rāmōth	gil'ādh	lammilchāmāh	'im-'echăddāl	wayyō'merû	'ălēh
against Ramoth	Gilead	into the battle	or should I refrain	and they said	go up

5598.121	112	904, 3135	4567		569.121	3194
cj, v Qal juss 3ms	n mp, ps 1cs	prep, *n fs*	art, n ms	**7.**	cj, v Qal impf 3ms	pn
וְיִתֵּן	אֲדֹנָי	בְּיַד	הַמֶּלֶךְ		וַיֹּאמֶר	יְהוֹשָׁפָט
weyittēn	'ădhōnāy	beyadh	hammelekh		wayyō'mer	yehôshāphāṭ
that He may give	my Lord	into the hand of	the king		but he said	Jehoshaphat

1950B, 375	6553	5204	3937, 3176	5968	1938.120	4623, 882
intrg part, sub	adv	n ms	prep, pn	adv	cj, v Qal juss 1cp	prep, prep, ps 3ms
הַאֵין	פֹּה	נָבִיא	לַיהוָה	עוֹד	וְנִדְרְשָׁה	מֵאוֹתוֹ
ha'ên	pōh	nāvî'	layhwāh	'ôdh	wenidhreshāh	mē'ôthô
is there not	here	a prophet	of Yahweh	anymore	that we may inquire	from with him

	569.121	4567, 3547	420, 3194	5968	382, 259	3937, 1938.141
8.	cj, v Qal impf 3ms	*n ms*, pn	prep, pn	adv	n ms, num	prep, v Qal inf con
	וַיֹּאמֶר	מֶלֶךְ־יִשְׂרָאֵל	אֶל־יְהוֹשָׁפָט	עוֹד	אִישׁ־אֶחָד	לִדְרֹשׁ
	wayyō'mer	melekh-yisrā'ēl	'el-yehôshāphāṭ	'ôdh	'îsh-'echādh	lidhrōsh
	and he said	the king of Israel	to Jehoshaphat	still	one man	to inquire

881, 3176	4623, 881	603	7983.115	3706	3940, 5187.711
do, pn	prep, do, ps 3ms	cj, pers pron	v Qal pf 1cs, ps 3ms	cj	neg part, v Hithpael pf 3ms
אֶת־יְהוָה	מֵאֹתוֹ	וַאֲנִי	שְׂנֵאתִיו	כִּי	לֹא־יִתְנַבֵּא
'eth-yehwāh	mē'ōthô	wa'ănî	senē'thîw	kî	lō'-yithnabbē'
Yahweh	from him	but I	I hate him	because	he does not prophesy

6142	3005	3706	524, 7737	4461	1158, 3337	569.121	3194
prep, ps 1cs	adj	cj	cj, n ms	pn	*n ms*, pn	cj, v Qal impf 3ms	pn
עָלַי	טוֹב	כִּי	אִם־רָע	מִיכָיְהוּ	בֶּן־יִמְלָה	וַיֹּאמֶר	יְהוֹשָׁפָט
'ālay	ṭôv	kî	'im-rā'	mîkhāyehû	ben-yimlāh	wayyō'mer	yehôshāphāṭ
concerning me	good	but	only evil	Micaiah	the son of Imlah	and he said	Jehoshaphat

414, 569.121	4567	3772		7410.121	4567	3547	420, 5835	259
adv, v Qal juss 3ms	art, n ms	adv	**9.**	cj, v Qal impf 3ms	*n ms*	pn	prep, n ms	num
אַל־יֹאמַר	הַמֶּלֶךְ	כֵּן		וַיִּקְרָא	מֶלֶךְ	יִשְׂרָאֵל	אֶל־סָרִיס	אֶחָד
'al-yō'mar	hammelekh	kēn		wayyiqōrā'	melekh	yisrā'ēl	'el-sārîs	'echādh
do not say	the king	thus		and he called	the king of	Israel	to a eunuch	one

569.121	4257.331	4461	1158, 3337		4567	3547
cj, v Qal impf 3ms	v Piel impv 2ms	pn	*n ms*, pn	**10.**	cj, *n ms*	pn
וַיֹּאמֶר	מַהֲרָה	מִיכָיְהוּ	בֶן־יִמְלָה		וּמֶלֶךְ	יִשְׂרָאֵל
wayyō'mer	mahrāh	mîkhāyehû	ven-yimlāh		ûmelekh	yisrā'ēl
and he said	act quickly	Micaiah	the son of Imlah		and the king of	Israel

3194	4567, 3171	3553.152	382	6142, 3802	3980.456	933
cj, pn	*n ms*, pn	v Qal act ptc mp	n ms	prep, n ms, ps 3ms	v Pual ptc mp	n mp
וִיהוֹשָׁפָט	מֶלֶךְ־יְהוּדָה	יֹשְׁבִים	אִישׁ	עַל־כִּסְאוֹ	מְלֻבָּשִׁים	בְּגָדִים
wîhôshāphāṭ	melekh-yehûdhāh	yōshevîm	'îsh	'al-kis'ô	melubbāshîm	beghādhîm
and Jehoshaphat	the king of Judah	sitting	each	on his throne	being clothed	clothes

904, 1681	6860	8554	8497	3725, 5204	5187.752
prep, n ms	*n ms*	*n ms*	pn	cj, *adj*, art, n mp	v Hithpael ptc mp
בְּגֹרֶן	פֶּתַח	שַׁעַר	שֹׁמְרוֹן	וְכָל־הַנְּבִיאִים	מִתְנַבְּאִים
beghōren	pethach	sha'ar	shōmerôn	wekhol-hannevî'îm	mithnabbe'îm
on the threshing floor	the entrance of	the gate of	Samaria	and all the prophets	prophesying

Should I go and attack Ramoth in Gilead ... or should I hold back?, *JB* ... fight against Ramoth in Gilead, or not?, *Beck* ... march to attack Ramoth-gilead or shall I give it up?, *Moffatt*.

And they said, Go up; for the Lord shall deliver it into the hand of the king: ... will deliver it over to, *NAB* ... means to make the king's grace master of it, *Knox* ... Go, because the Lord will hand them over to you, *NCV* ... will give you a glorious victory!, *NLT*.

7. And Jehoshaphat said, Is there not here a prophet of the LORD besides, that we might inquire of him?: ... Is there not some other prophet of the LORD around here, *Berkeley* ... here never a Prophet of the Lord more, *Geneva* ... from whom we may get directions?, *BB* ... through whom we may seek guidance?, *NEB*.

8. And the king of Israel said unto Jehoshaphat, There is yet one man, Micaiah the son of Imlah, by whom we may inquire of the LORD: ... ask counsel, *Tyndale* ... There is still, *KJVII* ... through whom we may seek guidance, *REB*.

but I hate him; for he doth not prophesy good concerning me, but evil. And Jehoshaphat said, Let not the king say so: ... for he never preaches good about me, but bad, *Fenton* ... he never prophesies anything favorable about me, but only disaster, *NRSV*.

9. Then the king of Israel called an officer, and said, Hasten hither Micaiah the son of Imlah: ... Bring Micaiah the son of Imlah quickly!, *NKJV* ... and bade him fetch Michaeas the son of Jemla with all speed, *Knox* ... Make haste, and bring hither Micheas, *Douay*.

10. And the king of Israel and Jehoshaphat the king of Judah sat each on his throne, having put on their robes: ... arrayed in, *ASV* ... in full armour, *Moffatt* ... clothed in their robes of state, *NAB* ... Dressed in their royal robes, *NIV*.

in a void place in the entrance of the gate of Samaria: ... in the threshing-floor, at the opening, *Young* ... in an open place at the entrance, *MRB*.

and all the prophets prophesied before them: ... with all the prophets in a state of ecstasy, *JB* ... were acting as prophets, *BB* ... were being moved to prophesy, *Rotherham* ... were standing before them, speaking their messages, *NCV*.

11. And Zedekiah the son of Chenaanah made him horns of iron: and he said: ... had provided

---

swept the Asherahs out of Judah, and endeavored to train his people in the principles of righteousness and the worship of Yahweh. In joining Ahab there must have been in his conscience some unformulated murmur of the reproof which on his return to Jerusalem was addressed to him by Jehu, the son of Hanani, "Shouldst thou help the ungodly, and love them that hate the LORD? Therefore is wrath upon thee from the LORD." But at the beginning of a momentous undertaking he would not be likely to imitate the godless indifference which had led Ahab to take the most fatal steps without seeking the guidance of God. He therefore said to Ahab, "Inquire, I pray thee, of the word of the LORD today."

Ahab could not refuse, and apparently the professional prophets of the schools had been pretty well cajoled or drilled into accordance with his wishes. A great and solemn assembly was summoned. The kings had clothed themselves in their royal robes striped with laticlaves of Tyrian purple (1 Ki. 22:10), and sat on thrones in an open space before the gate of Samaria. About 400 prophets of Yahweh were summoned to prophesy before them. Ahab propounded for their decision the formal and important question, "Shall I go up to Ramoth-Gilead to battle, or shall I forbear?"

With one voice the prophets answered the king according to his idols. Had the gold of Ahab or of Jezebel been at work among them? Had they been in king's houses and succumbed to courtly influences? Or were they carried away by the interested enthusiasm of one or two of their leaders who saw their own account in the matter? Certain it is that on this occasion they showed themselves as false prophets. They used their formula "Thus saith Yahweh" without authority (or shame), and promised Yahweh's aid in vain. The Septuagint has, "The LORD shall deliver into thy hands even the king of Syria." Perhaps, at first, they all said, "Adonai shall deliver it" but afterward, perhaps stung by the doubts of Jehoshaphat, or encouraged by the audacity of Zedekiah, they said, "Yahweh shall deliver it." Conspicuous in his evil ardor was one of them named Zedekiah, son of Chenaanah. To illustrate and emphasize his jubilant prophecies he had made and affixed to his head a pair of iron horns; and as though to symbolize the bull of the House of Ephraim, he said to Ahab, "Thus saith Yahweh. With these shalt thou push the Assyrians until thou have consumed them." (Deuteronomy 33:17, "His glory is like the firstling of his bullock, and his horns are like the horns of unicorns: with them he shall push the people together to the ends of the earth.") And all the prophets prophesied so.

3937, 6686	11.	6449.121	3937	6931	1158, 3792	7451
prep, n mp, ps 3mp		cj, v Qal impf 3ms	prep, ps 3ms	pn	*n ms*, pn	*n fp*
לִפְנֵיהֶם		וַיַּעַשׂ	לוֹ	צִדְקִיָּה	בֶן־כְּנַעֲנָה	קַרְנֵי
liphnêhem		wayya'as	lô	tsidhqîyāh	ven-kᵉna'ănāh	qarnê
before them		and he made	for himself	Zedekiah	the son of Chenaanah	horns of

1298	569.121	3662, 569.111	3176	904, 431	5231.323	881, 782
n ms	cj, v Qal impf 3ms	adv, v Qal pf 3ms	pn	prep, dem pron	v Piel impf 2ms	do, pn
בַּרְזֶל	וַיֹּאמֶר	כֹּה־אָמַר	יְהוָה	בְּאֵלֶּה	תְּנַגַּח	אֶת־אֲרָם
varzel	wayyō'mer	kōh-'āmar	yᵉhwāh	bᵉ'ēlleh	tᵉnaggach	'eth-'ărām
iron	and he said	thus He has said	Yahweh	with these	you will gore	Aram

5912, 3735.341	12.	3725, 5204	5187.252	3772	3937, 569.141
adv, v Piel inf con, ps 3mp		cj, *adj*, art, n mp	v Niphal ptc mp	adv	prep, v Qal inf con
עַד־כַּלֹּתָם		וְכָל־הַנְּבִאִים	נִבְּאִים	כֵּן	לֵאמֹר
'adh-kallōthām		wᵉkhol-hannᵉvi'îm	nibbᵉ'îm	kēn	lē'mōr
until their coming to an end		and all the prophets	prophesying	so	saying

6148.131	7721	7721	7014.531	5598.111	3176	904, 3135
v Qal impv 2ms	pn	pn	cj, v Hiphil impv 2ms	cj, v Qal pf 3ms	pn	prep, *n fs*
עֲלֵה	רָמֹת	גִּלְעָד	וְהַצְלַח	וְנָתַן	יְהוָה	בְּיַד
'ălēh	rāmōth	gil'ādh	wᵉhatslach	wᵉnāthan	yᵉhwāh	bᵉyadh
go up	Ramoth	Gilead	and succeed	for He will give	Yahweh	into the hand of

4567	13.	4534	866, 2050.111	3937, 7410.141	4461	1744.311
art, n ms		cj, art, n ms	rel pron, v Qal pf 3ms	prep, v Qal inf con	pn	v Piel pf 3ms
הַמֶּלֶךְ		וְהַמַּלְאָךְ	אֲשֶׁר־הָלַךְ	לִקְרֹא	מִיכָיְהוּ	דִּבֶּר
hammelekh		wᵉhammal'ākh	'ăsher-hālakh	liqrō'	mîkhāyᵉhû	dibber
the king		and the messenger	who he went	to call	Micaiah	he spoke

420	3937, 569.141	2079, 5167	1745	5204	6552, 259	3005
prep, ps 3ms	prep, v Qal inf con	intrj, part	*n mp*	art, n mp	n ms, num	adj
אֵלָיו	לֵאמֹר	הִנֵּה־נָא	דִּבְרֵי	הַנְּבִיאִים	פֶּה־אֶחָד	טוֹב
'ēlāv	lē'mōr	hinnēh-nā'	divrê	hannᵉvî'îm	peh-'echādh	ṭôv
to him	saying	behold please	the words of	the prophets	one mouth	good

420, 4567	2030.121, 5167	1745	3626, 1745	259	4623
prep, art, n ms	v Qal juss 3ms, part	n mp, ps 2ms	prep, *n ms*	num	prep, ps 3mp
אֶל־הַמֶּלֶךְ	יְהִי־נָא	דְבָרְיךָ	כִּדְבַר	אַחַד	מֵהֶם
'el-hammelekh	yᵉhî-nā'	dhivrêkhā	kidhvar	'achadh	mēhem
to the king	let it be please	your words	according to the word of	one	from them

1744.313	3005	14.	569.121	4461	2508, 3176	3706	881, 866
cj, v Piel pf 2ms	adj		cj, v Qal impf 3ms	pn	*adj*, pn	cj	do, rel part
וְדִבַּרְתָּ	טוֹב		וַיֹּאמֶר	מִיכָיְהוּ	חַי־יְהוָה	כִּי	אֶת־אֲשֶׁר
wᵉdhibbartā	ṭôv		wayyō'mer	mîkhāyᵉhû	chay-yᵉhwāh	kî	'eth-'ăsher
and you will speak	well		but he said	Micaiah	Yahweh living	rather	what

569.121	3176	420	881	1744.325	15.	971.121	420, 4567
v Qal impf 3ms	pn	prep, ps 1cs	do, ps 3ms	v Piel impf 1cs		cj, v Qal impf 3ms	prep, art, n ms
יֹאמַר	יְהוָה	אֵלַי	אֹתוֹ	אֲדַבֵּר		וַיָּבוֹא	אֶל־הַמֶּלֶךְ
yō'mar	yᵉhwāh	'ēlay	'ōthô	'ădhabbēr		wayyāvô'	'el-hammelekh
He is saying	Yahweh	to me	it	I will speak		and he came	to the king

569.121	4567	420	4461	1950B, 2050.120	420, 7721	7721
cj, v Qal impf 3ms	art, n ms	prep, ps 3ms	pn	intrg part, v Qal impf 1cp	prep, pn	pn
וַיֹּאמֶר	הַמֶּלֶךְ	אֵלָיו	מִיכָיְהוּ	הֲנֵלֵךְ	אֶל־רָמֹת	גִּלְעָד
wayyō'mer	hammelekh	'ēlāv	mîkhāyᵉhû	hănēlēkh	'el-rāmōth	gil'ādh
and he said	the king	to him	Micaiah	should we go	to Ramoth	Gilead

himself with a pair of horns fashioned in iron, *Knox*.

Thus saith the LORD, With these shalt thou push the Syrians, until thou have consumed them: ... you shall gore the Syrians until they are destroyed, *Goodspeed* ... horns thou shalt winnow the Sirians until thou have made an end, *Tyndale* ... until they are annihilated, *Berkeley*.

12. And all the prophets prophesied so, saying, Go up to Ramoth-gilead, and prosper: ... and triumph, *NRSV* ... prophesied in like manner, *Douay* ... Attack Ramoth-gilead and win the day, *REB* ... be victorious, *NLT*.

for the LORD shall deliver it into the king's hand: ... will hand the Aramens over to you, *NCV* ... will give it to the power of the king!, *Fenton* ... will give you victory, *Good News* ... Success is sure, for Yahweh has already given it to the king!, *JB*.

13. And the messenger that was gone to call Micaiah spake unto him, saying, Behold now, the words of the prophets declare good unto the king with one mouth: ... with one accord are favorable to the king, *RSV* ... as one man the other prophets are predicting success, *NIV* ... all the prophets with one voice are saying good things, *BB* ... with one mouth, are good towards the king, *Young*.

let thy word, I pray thee, be like the word of one of them, and speak that which is good: ... And mind you agree with them, *NEB* ... let your word be like the word of one of them, and speak favorably, *NASB* ... message be like any one of theirs; say a good word, *Moffatt* ... Please talk like one of them and tell something good, *Beck*.

14. And Micaiah said, As the LORD liveth, what the LORD saith unto me, that will I speak: ... I shall say whatever the LORD tells me, *NAB*.

15. So he came to the king. And the king said unto him, Micaiah, shall we go against Ramoth-gilead to battle, or shall we forbear?: ... should we attack Ramoth in Gilead or not?, *NCV* ... we let it alone?, *Berkeley*.

And he answered him, Go, and prosper: for the LORD shall deliver it into the hand of the king: ... Go up and triumph, *RSV* ... Go to the attack, and a blessing on thy journey!, *Knox* ... will give the king a glorious victory!, *NLT*.

Ahab was deceived and even carried away by the unwonted approval of so many messengers of Yahweh; but Jehoshaphat was not. These 400 prophets who seemed superfluously sufficient to Ahab by no means satisfied the king of Judah. "Is there not," he asked, with uneasy misgiving, "one prophet of the LORD besides, that we might inquire of him?"

And the king of Israel said, "There is yet one man." Had Jehoshaphat been secretly thinking of Elijah? Where was Elijah? He was living, certainly, for he survived even into the reign of Jehoram. But where was Elijah? If Jehoshaphat had thought of him, Ahab at any rate did not care to mention him. Perhaps he was inaccessible, in some lonely unknown retreat of Carmel or of Gilead. Since his fearful message to Ahab, he had not been heard of; but why did he not appear at a national crisis so tremendous as this?

"There is yet one man," said Ahab. "Micaiah, the son of Imlah, by whom we may inquire of the LORD; but I hate him; for he doth not prophesy good concerning me, but evil." Such was the king's most singular comment.

Ahab, as was universally the case in ancient days, thought that the prophet could practically prophesy as he liked, and not merely prophesy, but bring about his own vaticinations. Hence, if a prophet said anything which he disliked, he regarded him as a personal enemy, and, if he dared, he punished him—just as Agamemnon punished Calchas.

Jehoshaphat, however, was still dissatisfied; he wanted further confirmation. "Let not the king say so," he said. If he is a genuine prophet, the king should not hate him, or fancy that he prophesies evil out of malice prepense. Would it not be more satisfactory to hear what he might have to say?

22:13–14. However reluctantly, Ahab saw that he should have to send for Micaiah, and he dispatched a eunuch to hurry him to the scene with all speed. This eunuch, however, seems to have had a kindly disposition. He was good-naturedly anxious that Micaiah should not get into trouble. He advised him, with prudential regard for his own interest, to swim with the stream. "See now," he said, "all the prophets with one mouth are prophesying good to the king. Pray agree with them. Do not spoil everything."

How often has the same base advice been given! How often has it been followed! How certain is its rejection to lead to bitter animosity! One of the most difficult lessons of life is to learn to stand alone when all the prophets are prophesying falsely to please the rulers of the world. Micaiah rose superior to the eunuch's temptation. "As Yahweh lives," he said, "I will speak only what He bids me speak."

22:15–17. He stood before the kings, the eager multitude, the unanimous and passionate prophets;

3937, 4560	524, 2403.120	569.121	420	6148.131	7014.531
prep, art, n fs	cj, v Qal impf 1cp	cj, v Qal impf 3ms	prep, ps 3ms	v Qal impv 2ms	cj, v Qal impv 2ms
לַמִּלְחָמָה	אִם־נֶחְדָּל	וַיֹּאמֶר	אֵלָיו	עֲלֵה	וְהַצְלַח
lammilchāmāh	'im-nechdāl	wayyō'mer	'ēlâv	'ălēh	wehatslach
into the battle	or should we refrain	and he said	to him	go up	and succeed

5598.111	3176	904, 3135	4567	16.	569.121	420	4567
cj, v Qal pf 3ms	pn	prep, *n fs*	art, n ms		cj, v Qal impf 3ms	prep, ps 3ms	art, n ms
וְנָתַן	יְהוָה	בְּיַד	הַמֶּלֶךְ		וַיֹּאמֶר	אֵלָיו	הַמֶּלֶךְ
wenāthan	yehwāh	beyadh	hammelekh		wayyō'mer	'ēlâv	hammelekh
for He will give	Yahweh	into the hand of	the king		and he said	to him	the king

5912, 3626, 4242	6718	603	8123.551	866	3940, 1744.323
adv, prep, intrg	n fp	pers pron	v Hiphil ptc ms, ps 2ms	rel part	neg part, v Piel impf 2ms
עַד־כַּמֶּה	פְּעָמִים	אֲנִי	מַשְׁבִּעֶךָ	אֲשֶׁר	לֹא־תְדַבֵּר
'adh-kammeh	phe'āmîm	'ănî	mashbi'ekhā	'ăsher	lō'-thedhabbēr
until like how many	times	I	causing you to swear	what	you do not speak

420	7828, 583	904, 8428	3176	17.	569.121	7495.115	881, 3725, 3547
prep, ps 1cs	adv, n fs	prep, *n ms*	pn		cj, v Qal impf 3ms	v Qal pf 1cs	do, *adj*, pn
אֵלַי	רַק־אֱמֶת	בְּשֵׁם	יְהוָה		וַיֹּאמֶר	רָאִיתִי	אֶת־כָּל־יִשְׂרָאֵל
'ēlay	raq-'ĕmeth	beshēm	yehwāh		wayyō'mer	rā'îthî	'eth-kol-yisrā'ēl
to me	only truth	in the name of	Yahweh		then he said	I saw	all Israel

6571.252	420, 2098	3626, 6887	866	375, 3937	7749.151
v Niphal ptc mp	prep, art, n mp	prep, art, n ms	rel part	sub, prep, ps 3mp	v Qal act ptc ms
נְפֹצִים	אֶל־הֶהָרִים	כַּצֹּאן	אֲשֶׁר	אֵין־לָהֶם	רֹעֶה
nephōtsîm	'el-hehārîm	katstsō'n	'ăsher	'ên-lāhem	rō'eh
being scattered	toward the mountains	like the sheep	which	there is not to them	a shepherd

569.121	3176	3940, 112	3937, 431	3553.126	382, 3937, 1041
cj, v Qal impf 3ms	pn	neg part, n mp	prep, dem pron	v Qal juss 3mp	n ms, prep, n ms, ps 3ms
וַיֹּאמֶר	יְהוָה	לֹא־אֲדֹנִים	לָאֵלֶּה	יָשׁוּבוּ	אִישׁ־לְבֵיתוֹ
wayyō'mer	yehwāh	lō'-'ădhōnîm	lā'ēlleh	yāshûvû	'îsh-levêthô
and He said	Yahweh	no masters	to these	let them return	each to his household

904, 8361	18.	569.121	4567, 3547	420, 3194	1950B, 3940	569.115
prep, n ms		cj, v Qal impf 3ms	*n ms*, pn	prep, pn	intrg part, neg part	v Qal pf 1cs
בְּשָׁלוֹם		וַיֹּאמֶר	מֶלֶךְ־יִשְׂרָאֵל	אֶל־יְהוֹשָׁפָט	הֲלוֹא	אָמַרְתִּי
beshālôm		wayyō'mer	melekh-yisrā'ēl	'el-yehôshāphāṭ	hălō'	'āmartî
in peace		and he said	the king of Israel	to Jehoshaphat	have not	I said

420	3940, 5187.721	6142	3005	3706	524, 7737	19.	569.121
prep, ps 2ms	neg part, v Hithpael impf 3ms	prep, ps 1cs	adj	cj	cj, n ms		cj, v Qal impf 3ms
אֵלֶיךָ	לוֹא־יִתְנַבֵּא	עָלַי	טוֹב	כִּי	אִם־רָע		וַיֹּאמֶר
'ēlêkhā	lô'-yithnabbē'	'ālay	ṭôv	kî	'im-rā'		wayyō'mer
to you	he will not prophesy	concerning me	good	but	only evil		and he said

3937, 3772	8471.131	1745, 3176	7495.115	881, 3176	3553.151
prep, adv	v Qal impv 2ms	*n ms*, pn	v Qal pf 1cs	do, pn	v Qal act ptc ms
לָכֵן	שְׁמַע	דְּבַר־יְהוָה	רָאִיתִי	אֶת־יְהוָה	יֹשֵׁב
lākhēn	shema'	devar-yehwāh	rā'îthî	'eth-yehwāh	yōshēv
therefore	hear	the word of Yahweh	I have seen	Yahweh	One Who sits

6142, 3802	3725, 6893	8452	6198.151	6142	4623, 3332
prep, n ms, ps 3ms	cj, *adj*, *n ms*	art, n md	v Qal act ptc ms	prep, ps 3ms	prep, n fs, ps 3ms
עַל־כִּסְאוֹ	וְכָל־צְבָא	הַשָּׁמַיִם	עֹמֵד	עָלָיו	מִימִינוֹ
'al-kis'ô	wekhol-tsevā'	hashshāmayim	'ōmēdh	'ālâv	mîmînô
on his throne	and all the host of	the heavens	standing	beside Him	from his right hand

4623, 7972		569.121	3176	4449	6853.321	881, 255
cj, prep, n ms, ps 3ms	20.	cj, v Qal impf 3ms	pn	intrg	v Piel impf 3ms	do, pn
וּמִשְּׂמֹאלוֹ		וַיֹּאמֶר	יְהוָה	מִי	יְפַתֶּה	אֶת־אַחְאָב
ûmissemō'lô		wayyō'mer	yehwāh	mî	yephatteh	'eth-'ach'āv
and from his left hand		and He said	Yahweh	who	he will deceive	Ahab

6148.121	5489.121	904, 7721	7721	569.121	2172	904, 3662
cj, v Qal juss 3ms	cj, v Qal juss 3ms	prep, pn	pn	cj, v Qal impf 3ms	dem pron	prep, adv
וְיַעַל	וְיִפֹּל	בְּרָמֹת	גִּלְעָד	וַיֹּאמֶר	זֶה	בְּכֹה
weya'al	weyippōl	berāmōth	gil'ādh	wayyō'mer	zeh	bekhōh
that he may go up	that he may fall	in Ramoth	Gilead	and he said	this one	with thus

2172	569.151	904, 3662		3428.121	7593	6198.121	3937, 6686
cj, dem pron	v Qal act ptc ms	prep, adv	21.	cj, v Qal impf 3ms	art, n ms	cj, v Qal impf 3ms	prep, *n mp*
וְזֶה	אֹמֵר	בְּכֹה		וַיֵּצֵא	הָרוּחַ	וַיַּעֲמֹד	לִפְנֵי
wezeh	'ōmēr	bekhōh		wayyētsē'	hārûach	wayya'ămōdh	liphnê
and that one	saying	with thus		then it came out	the spirit	and it stood	before

16. And the king said unto him, How many times shall I adjure thee that thou tell me nothing but that which is true in the name of the LORD?: ... How often must I put you on oath to tell me nothing but the truth, *JB* ... Ahab said to Micaiah, How many times do I have to tell you to speak only the truth, *NCV* ... make you swear to tell me, *NRSV*.

17. And he said, I saw all Israel scattered upon the hills, as sheep that have not a shepherd: ... on the mountains, *NLT* ... that strayed because they had no shepherd, *Knox* ... wandering on the mountains like sheep without a keeper, *BB*.

and the LORD said, These have no master: let them return every man to his house in peace: ... let them all go safely home!, *JB* ... These men have no leader, *Good News* ... let each one return, *Berkeley* ... Have these no leader who can lead them back to their homes in safety?, *Fenton*.

18. And the king of Israel said unto Jehoshaphat, Did I not tell thee that he would prophesy no good concerning me, but evil?: ... He never prophecies anything but bad news for me, *NLT* ... still he prophecies ill fortune, never good, *Knox* ... for me, but trouble?, *Berkeley*.

19. And he said, Hear thou therefore the word of the LORD: I saw the LORD sitting on his throne: ... seated on his seat of power, *BB*.

and all the host of heaven standing by him on his right hand and on his left: ... the army of heaven was standing near, *Beck* ... his company of heaven standing about, *Tyndale*.

20. And the LORD said, Who shall persuade Ahab, that he may go up and fall at Ramoth-gilead?: ... entice Ahab, *Darby* ... delude Ahab into marching to his death, *Moffatt*.

And one said on this manner, and another said on that manner: ... one thing, and another said another, *Beck* ... there were many suggestions, *NLT* ... some answered one way, and some another, *JB*.

21. And there came forth a spirit, and stood before the LORD, and said, I will persuade him: ... entice him, *MAST* ... deceive him, *Goodspeed* ... trick him, *NCV*.

---

and there was deep silence when Ahab put to him the question to which the 400 had already shouted an affirmative.

His answer was precisely the same as theirs: "Go up to Ramoth-Gilead and prosper, for the LORD shall deliver it into the hand of the king!" Everyone must have been astonished. But Ahab detected the tone of scorn which rang through the ascenting words and angrily adjured Micaiah to give a true answer in Yahweh's name. "How many times," he cried, "shall I adjure thee that thou tell me nothing but that which is true in Yahweh's name." The "how many times" shows how faithfully Micaiah must have fulfilled his duty of speaking messages of God to his erring king.

So adjured, Micaiah could not be silent, however much the answer might cost him, or however useless it might be. "I saw all Israel," he said, "scattered on the mountain like sheep without a shepherd." And Yahweh said, "These have no master, let every man return to his house in peace."

22:18–23. The vision seemed to hint at the death of the king, and Ahab turned triumphantly to his ally, "Did I not tell you that he would prophesy evil?"

Micaiah justified himself by daring words which startle us, but would not at all have startled those who regarded everything as coming from the immediate action of God, and who could ask, "Shall there be evil in a city, and the LORD hath not done

3176	569.121	603	6853.325		569.121	3176	420
pn	cj, v Qal impf 3ms	pers pron	v Piel impf 1cs, ps 3ms		cj, v Qal impf 3ms	pn	prep, ps 3ms
יְהוָה	וַיֹּאמֶר	אֲנִי	אֲפַתֶּנּוּ	22.	וַיֹּאמֶר	יְהוָה	אֵלָיו
yehwāh	wayyō'mer	'ănî	'ăphattennû		wayyō'mer	yehwāh	'ēlâv
Yahweh	and it said	I	I will deceive him		and He said	Yahweh	to it

904, 4242	569.121	3428.125	2030.115	7593	8632	904, 6552
prep, art, intrg	cj, v Qal impf 3ms	v Qal impf 1cs	cj, v Qal pf 1cs	n ms	n ms	prep, n ms
בַּמָּה	וַיֹּאמֶר	אֵצֵא	וְהָיִיתִי	רוּחַ	שֶׁקֶר	בְּפִי
bammāh	wayyō'mer	'ētsē'	wehāyîthî	rûach	sheqer	bephî
with what	and it said	I will go out	and I will be	a spirit of	a lie	in the mouth of

3725, 5204	569.121	6853.223	1612, 3310.123	3428.131
adj, n mp, ps 3ms	cj, v Qal impf 3ms	v Piel impf 2ms	cj, cj, v Qal impf 2ms	v Qal impv 2ms
כָּל־נְבִיאָיו	וַיֹּאמֶר	תְּפַתֶּה	וְגַם־תּוּכָל	צֵא
kol-nevî'âv	wayyō'mer	tephatteh	wegham-tûkhāl	tsē'
all his prophets	and He said	you will deceive	and also you will be able	go out

6449, 3772		6498	2079	5598.111	3176	7593	8632	904, 6552
cj, v Qal impv 2ms, adv		cj, adv	intrj	v Qal pf 3ms	pn	n ms	n ms	prep, n ms
וַעֲשֵׂה־כֵן	23.	וְעַתָּה	הִנֵּה	נָתַן	יְהוָה	רוּחַ	שֶׁקֶר	בְּפִי
wa'ăsēh-khēn		we'attāh	hinnēh	nāthan	yehwāh	rûach	sheqer	bephî
and do so		and now	behold	He put	Yahweh	a spirit of	a lie	in the mouth of

3725, 5204	431	3176	1744.311	6142	7750
adj, n mp, ps 2ms	dem pron	cj, pn	v Piel pf 3ms	prep, ps 2ms	adj
כָּל־נְבִיאֶיךָ	אֵלֶּה	וַיהוָה	דִּבֶּר	עָלֶיךָ	רָעָה
kol-nevî'êkhā	'ēlleh	wayhwāh	dibber	'ālêkhā	rā'āh
all your prophets	these	and Yahweh	He has spoken	concerning you	evil

	5242.121	6931	1158, 3792	5409.521	881, 4461
	cj, v Qal impf 3ms	pn	n ms, pn	cj, v Hiphil impf 3ms	do, pn
24.	וַיִּגַּשׁ	צִדְקִיָּהוּ	בֶן־כְּנַעֲנָה	וַיַּכֶּה	אֶת־מִיכָיְהוּ
	wayyiggash	tsidhqîyāhû	ven-kena'ănāh	wayyakkeh	'eth-mîkhāyehû
	then he came near	Zedekiah	the son of Chenaanah	and he struck	Micaiah

6142, 4029	569.121	338, 2172	5882.111	7593, 3176	4623, 882
prep, art, n ms	cj, v Qal impf 3ms	intrg, dem pron	v Qal pf 3ms	n fs, pn	prep, prep, ps 1cs
עַל־הַלֶּחִי	וַיֹּאמֶר	אֵי־זֶה	עָבַר	רוּחַ־יְהוָה	מֵאִתִּי
'al-hallechî	wayyō'mer	'ê-zeh	'āvar	rûach-yehwāh	mē'ittî
on the cheek	and he said	where this	He passed	the Spirit of Yahweh	from with me

3937, 1744.341	882		569.121	4461	2079	7495.151	904, 3219
prep, v Piel inf con	prep, ps 2ms		cj, v Qal impf 3ms	pn	intrj, ps 2ms	v Qal act ptc ms	prep, art, n ms
לְדַבֵּר	אוֹתָךְ	25.	וַיֹּאמֶר	מִיכָיְהוּ	הִנְּךָ	רֹאֶה	בַּיּוֹם
ledhabbēr	'ôthākh		wayyō'mer	mîkhāyehû	hinnekhā	rō'eh	bayyôm
to speak	with you		and he said	Micaiah	behold you	seeing	on the day

2000	866	971.123	2410	904, 2410	3937, 2334.241
art, dem pron	rel part	v Qal impf 2ms	n ms	prep, n ms	prep, v Niphal inf con
הַהוּא	אֲשֶׁר	תָּבֹא	חֶדֶר	בְּחֶדֶר	לְהֵחָבֵה
hahû'	'ăsher	tāvō'	chedher	bechedher	lehēchāvēh
the that	which	you will enter	an inner room	within an inner room	to hide yourself

	569.121	4567	3547	4089.131	881, 4460	8178.531
	cj, v Qal impf 3ms	n ms	pn	v Qal impv 2ms	do, pn	cj, v Hiphil impv 2ms, ps 3ms
26.	וַיֹּאמֶר	מֶלֶךְ	יִשְׂרָאֵל	קַח	אֶת־מִיכָיְהוּ	וַהֲשִׁיבֵהוּ
	wayyō'mer	melekh	yisrā'ēl	qach	'eth-mîkhāyehû	wahshîvēhû
	and he said	the king of	Israel	take	Micaiah	and take him back

420, 534	8015, 6111	420, 3204	1158, 4567		569.113	3662
prep, pn	*n ms*, art, n fs	cj, prep, pn	*n ms*, art, n ms		cj, v Qal pf 2ms	adv
אֶל־אָמֹן	שַׂר־הָעִיר	וְאֶל־יוֹאָשׁ	בֶּן־הַמֶּלֶךְ	**27.**	וְאָמַרְתָּ	כֹּה
'el-'āmōn	sar-hā'îr	wᵉ'el-yô'āsh	ben-hammelekh		wᵉ'āmartā	kōh
unto Amon	the official of the city	and unto Joash	the son of the king		and you will say	thus

569.111	4567	7947.133	881, 2172	1041	3728	404.533
v Qal pf 3ms	art, n ms	v Qal impv 2mp	do, dem pron	*n ms*	art, n ms	cj, v Hiphil impv 2mp, ps 3ms
אָמַר	הַמֶּלֶךְ	שִׂימוּ	אֶת־זֶה	בֵּית	הַכֶּלֶא	וְהַאֲכִילֻהוּ
'āmar	hammelekh	sîmû	'eth-zeh	bêth	hakkele'	wᵉha'ăkhîluhû
he has said	the king	put	this one	the house of	the prison	and feed him

22. And the LORD said unto him, Wherewith? And he said, I will go forth, and I will be a lying spirit in the mouth of all his prophets: ... to Ahab's prophets and make them tell lies, *NCV* ... become a spirit of falsehood, *Rotherham* ... Spirit of Deception, *Fenton*.

And he said, Thou shalt persuade him, and prevail also: go forth, and do so: ... shall deceive him and also succeed!, *Goodspeed* ... are to entice him, and you shall succeed, *NRSV* ... You will successfully trick him, *Berkeley*.

23. Now therefore, behold, the LORD hath put a lying spirit in the mouth of all these thy prophets: ... has made these prophets of yours lie to you, *Good News* ... a spirit of deceit, *BB*.

and the LORD hath spoken evil concerning thee: ... has decreed disaster for you, *NRSV* ... has proclaimed, *NASB* ... has determined on thy ruin, *Knox* ... Yahweh has pronounced, *JB*.

24. But Zedekiah the son of Chenaanah went near, and smote Micaiah on the cheek: ... and slapped him in the face, *NCV*.

and said, Which way went the spirit of the LORD from me to speak unto thee?: ... how did the spirit of the LORD pass from me to speak to you?, *REB* ... leave me to talk, *Beck*.

25. And Micaiah said, Behold, thou shalt see in that day, when thou shalt go into an inner chamber to hide thyself: ... go into a chamber within a chamber, *Douay* ... from chamber to chamber, *Tyndale* ... run into an inner room, *NEB* ... the day you seek refuge in, *Berkeley*.

26. And the king of Israel said, Take Micaiah, and carry him back unto Amon the governor of the city, and to Joash the king's son: ... Arrest Micaiah and take him back to Amon, *NLT* ... return him, *NASB* ... Seize Mikaiha, and conduct him to the castle of the Governor, *Fenton* ... send him, *NCV*.

27. And say, Thus saith the king, Put this fellow in the prison: ... with orders from the king that the fellow is to be clapped into prison, *Moffatt* ... they are to imprison him, *Knox* ... Tell them to throw him, *Good News*.

and feed him with bread of affliction and with water of affliction, until I come in peace: ... on nothing but bread and water until I am safely home, *JB* ... cause him to eat bread of oppression, and water of oppression, *Young* ... scanty rations of bread and water until I return in safety, *NAB* ... given prison food till I come again, *BB*.

it?" (Amos 3:6). The prophets were self-deceived, but this would be expressed by saying that Yahweh deceived them. Pharaoh hardened his heart, and God is said to have done it.

He had seen Yahweh on his throne, he said, surrounded by the host of heaven, and asking who would entice Ahab to his fall at Ramoth-Gilead. After various answers, one spirit said, "I will go and be a lying spirit in the mouths of all his prophets, and will entice him." Then Yahweh sent him, so that they all spoke good to the king though Yahweh had spoken evil. God had sent to them all—king, people, prophets—strong delusion that they should believe a lie.

22:24. This stern reproof to all the prophets was more than their leader could endure. Having recourse to the syllogism of violence, Zedekiah strode up to Micaiah and smote the defenseless, isolated, hated man on the cheek (the worst of insults; Job 16:10; Lam. 3:30) with the contemptuous question, "Which way went the spirit of the LORD from me, to speak unto thee?"

22:25. "Behold thou shalt know," was the answer, "on the day when thou shalt flee from chamber to chamber to hide thyself." If the hands of the prophet were bound as he came from the prison, there would have been an infinite dignity in that calm rebuke.

22:26–27. But as though the case was self-evident, and Micaiah's opposition to the 400 prophets proved his guilt, Ahab sent him back to

4035	4041	4448	4041	5912	971.141	904, 8361		569.121
n ms	n ms	cj, *n md*	n ms	adv	v Qal inf con, ps 1cs	prep, n ms	**28.**	cj, v Qal impf 3ms
לֶחֶם	לַחַץ	וּמַיִם	לַחַץ	עַד	בֹּאִי	בְשָׁלוֹם		וַיֹּאמֶר
lechem	lachats	ûmayim	lachats	‘adh	bō’î	vᵉshālôm		wayyō’mer
bread of	oppression	and water of	oppression	until	my coming	in safety		and he said

4461	524, 8178.142	8178.123	904, 8361	3940, 1744.311	3176	904
pn	cj, v Qal inf abs	v Qal impf 2ms	prep, n ms	neg part, v Piel pf 3ms	pn	prep, ps 1cs
מִיכָיְהוּ	אִם־שׁוֹב	תָּשׁוּב	בְּשָׁלוֹם	לֹא־דִבֶּר	יְהוָה	בִּי
mîkhāyᵉhû	’im-shôv	tāshûv	bᵉshālôm	lō’-dhibber	yᵉhwāh	bî
Micaiah	if returning	you at all return	in safety	He has not spoken	Yahweh	by me

569.121	8471.133	6194	3725		6148.121	4567, 3547
cj, v Qal impf 3ms	v Qal impv 2mp	n mp	adj, ps 3mp	**29.**	cj, v Qal impf 3ms	*n ms*, pn
וַיֹּאמֶר	שִׁמְעוּ	עַמִּים	כֻּלָּם		וַיַּעַל	מֶלֶךְ־יִשְׂרָאֵל
wayyō’mer	shim‘û	‘ammîm	kullām		wayya‘al	melekh-yisrā’ēl
and he said	hear	O peoples	all of them		and he went up to	the king of Israel

3194	4567, 3171	7721	7721		569.121	4567	420, 3194
cj, pn	*n ms*, pn	pn	pn	**30.**	cj, v Qal impf 3ms	*n ms*	pn
וִיהוֹשָׁפָט	מֶלֶךְ־יְהוּדָה	רָמֹת	גִּלְעָד		וַיֹּאמֶר	מֶלֶךְ	יִשְׂרָאֵל
wᵉyhôshāphāṭ	melekh-yᵉhûdhāh	rāmōth	gil‘ādh		wayyō’mer	melekh	yisrā’ēl
and Jehoshaphat	the king of Judah	Ramoth	Gilead		and he said	the king of	Israel

3547	2769.742	971.142	904, 4560	887	3980.131
prep, pn	v Hithpael inf abs	cj, v Qal inf abs	prep, art, n fs	cj, pers pron	v Qal impv 2ms
אֶל־יְהוֹשָׁפָט	הִתְחַפֵּשׂ	וָבֹא	בַמִּלְחָמָה	וְאַתָּה	לְבַשׁ
’el-yᵉhôshāphāṭ	hithchappēs	wāvō’	vammilchāmāh	wᵉ’attāh	lᵉvash
to Jehoshaphat	disguise yourself	and enter	into the battle	but you	put on

933	2769.721	4567	3547	971.121	904, 4560
n mp, ps 2ms	cj, v Hithpael impf 3ms	*n ms*	pn	cj, v Qal impf 3ms	prep, art, n fs
בְּגָדֶיךָ	וַיִּתְחַפֵּשׂ	מֶלֶךְ	יִשְׂרָאֵל	וַיָּבוֹא	בַּמִּלְחָמָה
bᵉghādhêkhā	wayyithchappēs	melekh	yisrā’ēl	wayyāvô’	bammilchāmāh
your clothes	and he disguised himself	the king of	Israel	and he entered	into the battle

	4567	782	6943.311	881, 8015	7681
31.	cj, *n ms*	pn	v Piel pf 3ms	do, *n mp*	art, n ms
	וּמֶלֶךְ	אֲרָם	צִוָּה	אֶת־שָׂרֵי	הָרֶכֶב
	ûmelekh	’ărām	tsiwwāh	’eth-sārê	hārekhev
	meanwhile the king of	Aram	he had commanded	the commanders of	the chariots

866, 3937	8421	8530	3937, 569.141	3940	4032.228	882, 7277
rel pron, prep, ps 3ms	num	cj, num	prep, v Qal inf con	neg part	v Niphal impf 2mp	prep, adj
אֲשֶׁר־לוֹ	שְׁלֹשִׁים	וּשְׁנַיִם	לֵאמֹר	לֹא	תִּלָּחֲמוּ	אֶת־קָטֹן
’ăsher-lô	shᵉlōshîm	ûshᵉnayim	lē’mōr	lō’	tillāchămû	’eth-qāṭōn
who to him	thirty	and two	saying	not	you will fight	with insignificant

882, 1448	3706	524, 882, 4567	3547	3937, 940		2030.121
cj, prep, adj	cj	cj, prep, *n ms*	pn	prep, n ms, ps 3ms	**32.**	cj, v Qal impf 3ms
וְאֶת־גָּדוֹל	כִּי	אִם־אֶת־מֶלֶךְ	יִשְׂרָאֵל	לְבַדּוֹ		וַיְהִי
wᵉ’eth-gādhôl	kî	’im-’eth-melekh	yisrā’ēl	lᵉvaddô		wayhî
nor with great	but	only with the king of	Israel	by himself		and it was

3626, 7495.141	8015	7681	881, 3194	2065	569.116	395
prep, v Qal inf con	*n mp*	art, n ms	do, pn	cj, pers pron	v Qal pf 3cp	adv
כִּרְאוֹת	שָׂרֵי	הָרֶכֶב	אֶת־יְהוֹשָׁפָט	וְהֵמָּה	אָמְרוּ	אַךְ
kir’ôth	sārê	hārekhev	’eth-yᵉhôshāphāṭ	wᵉhēmmāh	’āmᵉrû	’akh
when seeing	the commanders of	the chariots	Jehoshaphat	then they	they said	surely

4567, 3547	2000	5681.126	6142	3937, 4032.241	2283.121
n ms, pn	pers pron	cj, v Qal impf 3mp	prep, ps 3ms	prep, v Niphal inf con	cj, v Qal impf 3ms
מֶלֶךְ־יִשְׂרָאֵל	הוּא	וַיָּסֻרוּ	עָלָיו	לְהִלָּחֵם	וַיִּזְעַק
melekh-yisrā'ēl	hû'	wayyāsurû	'ālâv	lehillāchēm	wayyiz'aq
the king of Israel	he	and they turned aside	against him	to fight	and he cried out

3194		2030.121	3626, 7495.141	8015	7681
pn	**33.**	cj, v Qal impf 3ms	prep, v Qal inf con	*n mp*	art, n ms
יְהוֹשָׁפָט		וַיְהִי	כִּרְאוֹת	שָׂרֵי	הָרֶכֶב
yehôshāphāṭ		wayhî	kir'ôth	sārê	hārekhev
Jehoshaphat		and it was	when seeing	the commanders of	the chariots

3706, 3940, 4567	3547	2000	8178.126	4623, 313		382
cj, neg part, *n ms*	pn	pers pron	cj, v Qal impf 3mp	prep, prep, ps 3ms	**34.**	cj, n ms
כִּי־לֹא־מֶלֶךְ	יִשְׂרָאֵל	הוּא	וַיָּשׁוּבוּ	מֵאַחֲרָיו		וְאִישׁ
kî-lō'-melekh	yisrā'ēl	hû'	wayyāshûvû	mē'achrâv		we'îsh
that not the king of	Israel	he	then they turned back	from after him		but a man

28. And Micaiah said, If thou return at all in peace, the LORD hath not spoken by me. And he said, Hearken, O people, every one of you: ... come back safely, *Beck* ... ever return safely, the LORD has not spoken through me, *NIV* ... do indeed return victorious, *Goodspeed.*

29. So the king of Israel and Jehoshaphat the king of Judah went up to Ramoth-gilead: ... attacked Ramoth-gilead, *Berkeley* ... marched on, *NEB.*

30. And the king of Israel said unto Jehoshaphat, I will disguise myself, and enter into the battle: ... make a change in my clothing, so that I do not seem to be the king, *BB* ... change thee and get thee to war, *Tyndale* ... wear other clothes so no one will recognize me, *NCV* ... Take armor, and go, *Douay.*

but put thou on thy robes: ... you wear your royal robes, *NLT* ... put on your own clothes, *NAB* ... put thou on thine apparell, *Geneva.*

And the king of Israel disguised himself, and went into the battle: ... and entered into the battle, *Rotherham.*

31. But the king of Syria commanded his thirty and two captains that had rule over his chariots: ... ordered his thirty-two Officers, *Fenton.*

saying, Fight neither with small nor great, save only with the king of Israel: ... Don't fight with anyone—important or unimportant, *NCV* ... Do not bother to attack anyone, old or young, *Berkeley* ... Press for no other mark, high or low, *Knox* ... with anyone at all except, *NAB.*

32. And it came to pass, when the captains of the chariots saw Jehoshaphat, that they said, Surely it is the king of Israel. And they turned aside to fight against him: and Jehoshaphat cried out: ... So they surrounded him to fight, *Goodspeed* ... making a violent assault they fought, *Douay* ... they went after him, *NLT.*

33. And it came to pass, when the captains of the chariots perceived that it was not the king of Israel, that they turned back from pursuing him: ... they stopped chasing him, *NCV* ... they turned away from him, *Fenton* ... broke off the attack, *NEB* ... their pursuit, *JB.*

34. And a certain man drew a bow at a venture, and smote the king of Israel between the joints of the harness: ... jointed pieces and the breast-plate, *Goodspeed* ... lower

prison. "Issue orders," he said, "to Amon, governor of the city, and Joash, the king's son, to feed him scantily on bread and water till the king's return in peace."

22:28. "If thou return at all in peace," said Micaiah, "Yahweh hath not spoken by me." The words, "And he said, Hearken, O people, every one of you," are omitted in the Septuagint.

22:29–36. Of course, the prophecy of Micaiah came true, and the unanimous 400 had prophesied lies. The expedition was altogether disastrous. Ahab, perhaps knowing by spies how bitterly the Syrians were incensed against him, told Jehoshaphat that he would disguise himself and go into the battle, but begged his ally to wear his robes as was usual with kings. We have no reason to accuse Ahab of any bad or selfish motives here. No doubt Micaiah's prophecy of his approaching death had made him anxious.

Ben-Hadad, with the implacable hatred of one who had received a benefit, was so eager to be avenged on Ahab that he had told his thirty-two

5082.111	904, 7493	3937, 8866	5409.521	881, 4567	3547	1033
v Qal pf 3ms	prep, art, n fs	prep, n ms, ps 3ms	cj, v Hiphil impf 3ms	do, *n ms*	pn	prep
מָשַׁךְ	בַּקֶּשֶׁת	לְתֻמּוֹ	וַיַּכֶּה	אֶת־מֶלֶךְ	יִשְׂרָאֵל	בֵּין
māshakh	baqqesheth	lethummô	wayyakkeh	'eth-melekh	yisrā'ēl	bên
pulled back	with the bow	of his innocence	and he struck down	the king of	Israel	between

1743	1033	8647	569.121	3937, 7682	2089.131
art, n mp	cj, prep	art, n ms	cj, v Qal impf 3ms	prep, n ms, ps 3ms	v Qal impv 2ms
הַדְּבָקִים	וּבֵין	הַשִּׁרְיָן	וַיֹּאמֶר	לְרַכָּבוֹ	הֲפֹךְ
haddevāqîm	ûvên	hashshiryān	wayyō'mer	lerakkāvô	hephōkh
the junctures	even between	the armor	and he said	to his charioteer	turn

3135	3428.531	4623, 4402	3706	2571.615
n fs, ps 2ms	cj, v Hiphil impv 2ms, ps 1cs	prep, art, n ms	cj	v Hophal pf 1cs
יָדְךָ	וְהוֹצִיאֵנִי	מִן־הַמַּחֲנֶה	כִּי	הָחֳלֵיתִי
yādhekhā	wehôtsî'ēnî	min-hammachneh	kî	hāchălēthî
your hand	and take me out	from the encampment	because	I have been weakened

35.	6148.122	4560	904, 3219	2000	4567	2030.111
	cj, v Qal impf 3fs	art, n fs	prep, art, n ms	art, dem pron	cj, art, n ms	v Qal pf 3ms
	וַתַּעֲלֶה	הַמִּלְחָמָה	בַּיּוֹם	הַהוּא	וְהַמֶּלֶךְ	הָיָה
	watta'ăleh	hammilchāmāh	bayyôm	hahû'	wehammelekh	hāyāh
	and it became higher	the battle	on the day	the that	and the king	he was

6198.655	904, 4981	5415	782	4322.121
v Hophal ptc ms	prep, art, n fs	prep	pn	cj, v Qal impf 3ms
מָעֳמָד	בַּמֶּרְכָּבָה	נֹכַח	אֲרָם	וַיָּמָת
mā'ămādh	bammerkāvāh	nōkhach	'ărām	wayyāmāth
being caused to stand	in the chariot	in front of	Aram	but he died

904, 6394	3441.121	1879, 4485	420, 2536	7681
prep, art, n ms	v Qal impf 3ms	*n ms*, art, n fs	prep, *n ms*	art, n ms
בָּעֶרֶב	וַיִּצֶק	דַּם־הַמַּכָּה	אֶל־חֵיק	הָרָכֶב
bā'erev	wayyitseq	dam-hammakkāh	'el-chêq	hārākhev
in the evening	and it flowed	the blood of the wound	to the bottom of	the chariot

36.	5882.121	7726	904, 4402	3626, 971.141
	cj, v Qal impf 3ms	art, n fs	prep, art, n ms	prep, v Qal inf con
	וַיַּעֲבֹר	הָרִנָּה	בַּמַּחֲנֶה	כְּבֹא
	wayya'ăvōr	hārinnāh	bammachneh	kevō'
	and it proceeded to pass through	the lamentation	throughout the camp	when the going of

8507	3937, 569.141	382	420, 6111	382	420, 800	37.	4322.121
art, n ms	prep, v Qal inf con	n ms	prep, n fs, ps 3ms	cj, n ms	prep, n fs, ps 3ms		cj, v Qal impf 3ms
הַשֶּׁמֶשׁ	לֵאמֹר	אִישׁ	אֶל־עִירוֹ	וְאִישׁ	אֶל־אַרְצוֹ		וַיָּמָת
hashshemesh	lē'mōr	'îsh	'el-'îrô	we'îsh	'el-'artsô		wayyāmāth
the sun	saying	each	to his city	and each	to his land		then he died

4567	971.121	8497	7196.126	881, 4567	904, 8497
art, n ms	cj, v Qal impf 3ms	pn	cj, v Qal impf 3mp	do, art, n ms	prep, pn
הַמֶּלֶךְ	וַיָּבוֹא	שֹׁמְרוֹן	וַיִּקְבְּרוּ	אֶת־הַמֶּלֶךְ	בְּשֹׁמְרוֹן
hammelekh	wayyāvô'	shōmerôn	wayyiqbberû	'eth-hammelekh	beshōmerôn
the king	and he entered	Samaria	and they buried	the king	in Samaria

38.	8278.121	881, 7681	6142	1320	8497	4094.126	3732
	cj, v Qal impf 3ms	do, art, n ms	prep	*n fs*	pn	cj, v Qal impf 3mp	art, n mp
	וַיִּשְׁטֹף	אֶת־הָרֶכֶב	עַל	בְּרֵכַת	שֹׁמְרוֹן	וַיָּלֹקּוּ	הַכְּלָבִים
	wayyishṭōph	'eth-hārekhev	'al	berēkhath	shōmerôn	wayyālōqqû	hakkelāvîm
	and they washed off	the chariot	beside	the pool of	Samaria	and they licked	the dogs

881, 1879	2193	7647.116	3626, 1745	3176	866
do, n ms, ps 3ms	cj, art, n fp	v Qal pf 3cp	prep, *n ms*	pn	rel part
אֶת־דָּמוֹ	וְהַזֹּנוֹת	רָחָצוּ	כִּדְבַר	יְהוָה	אֲשֶׁר
'eth-dāmô	w^{e}hazzōnôth	rāchātsû	kidhvar	y^{e}hwāh	'ăsher
his blood	and the prostitutes	they bathed	according to the word of	Yahweh	which

1744.311		3615	1745	255	3725, 866	6449.111
v Piel pf 3ms	**39.**	cj, *n ms*	*n mp*	pn	cj, *adj*, rel part	v Qal pf 3ms
דִּבֵּר		וְיֶתֶר	דִּבְרֵי	אַחְאָב	וְכָל־אֲשֶׁר	עָשָׂה
dibbēr		w^{e}yether	divrê	'ach'āv	w^{e}khol-'ăsher	'āsāh
He had spoken		and the remainder of	the events of	Ahab	and all that	he did

armour and the breastplate, *MAST* ... lungs and the stomach, *Douay* ... drew his bow at random, *REB*.

wherefore he said unto the driver of his chariot, Turn thine hand, and carry me out of the host; for I am wounded: ... Turn around, and carry me out of the battle, *NRSV* ... I am critically wounded, *Berkeley*.

35. And the battle increased that day: ... grew hot, *RSV* ... raged, *NASB* ... fight became more violent, *BB*.

and the king was stayed up in his chariot against the Syrians, and died at even: ... propped up in his chariot facing the Arameans, *NIV* ... That evening he died, *NCV* ... in the afternoon, *Fenton*.

and the blood ran out of the wound into the midst of the chariot: ... from his wound flowed down to the floor, *REB* ... ever into the body of his chariot, *Knox*.

36. And there went a proclamation throughout the host about the going down of the sun: ... a shout went throughout the army, *NKJV* ... a cry went through the army, *Beck* ... a cry spread, *NIV*.

saying, Every man to his city, and every man to his own country: ... back to his town, *JB* ... It's all over—return home!, *NLT* ... to his land, *NAB*.

37. So the king died, and was brought to Samaria; and they buried the king in Samaria: ... was carried back, *Knox* ... put the king's body to rest, *BB* ... they brought the dead king to Shomeron, *Fenton* ... His body was carried to Samaria and buried there, *NCV*.

38. And one washed the chariot in the pool of Samaria; and the dogs licked up his blood: ... dogs came and licked the king's blood, *NLT*.

and they washed his armour: ... the prostitutes washed in it, *JB* ... while the harlots bathed, *NKJV* ... now the harlots washed themselves there, *ASV* ... which was the bathing-place of the loose women, *BB*.

according unto the word of the Lord which he spake: ... as the word of the Lord had declared, *NIV*.

39. Now the rest of the acts of Ahab, and all that he did, and the ivory house which he made, and all the cities that he built, are they not written in the book of the chronicles of the kings of Israel?: ... the annals of Israel's kings, *Beck* ... of the history, *BB* ... of the events of the times, *Fenton* ... of the words of the days, *Douay*.

captains to make his capture their special aim. Seeing a king in his robes, they made a fierce onset on Jehoshaphat and surrounded his chariot. His cries for rescue showed them that he was not Ahab, and they turned away. Second Chronicles 18:31 states, "And the Lord helped him, and God moved them from him." Ahab's disguise did not save him. A Syrian (Josephus calls him Aman) drew a bow with no particular aim, and the arrow smote Ahab in the place between the upper and lower armor. Feeling himself weakening, he ordered his charioteer to turn his hands and drive him out of the increasing roar of the melee. But he would not wholly leave the fight, and with heroic fortitude remained standing in his chariot in spite of agony. All day the blood kept flowing down into the hollow of the chariot. At evening the Syrians had to retire in defeat, but Ahab died. The news of the king's death was proclaimed at sunset by the herald, and the cry was raised which bade the host disband and return home (Josephus, *Antiquities*, VIII:xv:6).

22:37–40. They carried the king's body back to Samaria, and they buried it. They washed the blood-stained chariot in the pool outside the city, and there the dogs licked the king's blood, and the harlot-votaries of Asherah bathed in the blood-dyed waters, as Elijah had prophesied.

So ended the reign of a king who built cities and ivory palaces and fought like a hero against the foes of his country, but who had never known how

1041	8514	866	1161.111	3725, 6111	866	1161.111
cj, *n ms*	art, n fs	rel part	v Qal pf 3ms	cj, *adj*, art, n fp	rel part	v Qal pf 3ms
וּבֵית	הַשֵּׁן	אֲשֶׁר	בָּנָה	וְכָל־הֶעָרִים	אֲשֶׁר	בָּנָה
ûvêth	hashshēn	'ăsher	bānāh	wekhol-he'ārîm	'ăsher	bānāh
and the house of	the ivory	which	he built	and all the cities	that	he built

1950B, 3940, 2062	3918.156	6142, 5809	1745	3219	3937, 4567
intrg part, neg part, pers pron	v Qal pass ptc mp	prep, *n ms*	*n mp*	art, n mp	prep, *n mp*
הֲלוֹא־הֵם	כְּתוּבִים	עַל־סֵפֶר	דִּבְרֵי	הַיָּמִים	לְמַלְכֵי
hălō'-hēm	kethûvîm	'al-s̱ēpher	divrê	hayyāmîm	lemalkhê
are they not	things written	on the scroll of	the events of	the days	of the kings of

3547		8311.121	255	6196, 1	4566.121	275	1158
pn	**40.**	cj, v Qal impf 3ms	pn	prep, n mp, ps 3ms	cj, v Qal impf 3ms	pn	n ms, ps 3ms
יִשְׂרָאֵל		וַיִּשְׁכַּב	אַחְאָב	עִם־אֲבֹתָיו	וַיִּמְלֹךְ	אֲחַזְיָהוּ	בְּנוֹ
yisrā'ēl		wayyishkav	'ach'āv	'im-'ăvōthâv	wayyimlōkh	'ăchazyāhû	venô
Israel		then he lay	Ahab	with his ancestors	and he reigned	Ahaziah	his son

8809		3194	1158, 623	4566.111	6142, 3171	904, 8523	727
prep, ps 3ms	**41.**	cj, pn	*n ms*, pn	v Qal pf 3ms	prep, pn	prep, *n fs*	num
תַּחְתָּיו		וִיהוֹשָׁפָט	בֶּן־אָסָא	מָלַךְ	עַל־יְהוּדָה	בִּשְׁנַת	אַרְבַּע
tachtâv		wîhôshāphāṯ	ben-'ās̱ā'	mālakh	'al-yehûdhāh	bishnath	'arba'
instead of him		and Jehoshaphat	the son of Asa	he reigned	over Judah	in the year	four

3937, 255	4567	3547		3194	1158, 8421	2675	8523
prep, pn	*n ms*	pn	**42.**	pn	*n ms*, num	cj, num	n fs
לְאַחְאָב	מֶלֶךְ	יִשְׂרָאֵל		יְהוֹשָׁפָט	בֶּן־שְׁלֹשִׁים	וְחָמֵשׁ	שָׁנָה
le'ach'āv	melekh	yisrā'ēl		yehôshāphāṯ	ben-shelōshîm	wechāmēsh	shānāh
of Ahab	the king of	Israel		Jehoshaphat	a son of thirty	and five	years

904, 4566.141	6465	2675	8523	4566.111	904, 3503	8428
prep, v Qal inf con, ps 3ms	cj, num	cj, num	n fs	v Qal pf 3ms	prep, pn	cj, *n ms*
בְּמָלְכוֹ	וְעֶשְׂרִים	וְחָמֵשׁ	שָׁנָה	מָלַךְ	בִּירוּשָׁלָם	וְשֵׁם
bemālekhô	we'esrîm	wechāmēsh	shānāh	mālakh	bîrûshālām	weshēm
when his reigning	and twenty	and five	years	he reigned	in Jerusalem	and the name of

525	6019	1351, 8372		2050.121	904, 3725, 1932	623
n fs, ps 3ms	pn	*n fs*, pn	**43.**	cj, v Qal impf 3ms	prep, *adj*, *n ms*	pn
אִמּוֹ	עֲזוּבָה	בַּת־שִׁלְחִי		וַיֵּלֶךְ	בְּכָל־דֶּרֶךְ	אָסָא
'immô	'ăzûvāh	bath-shilchî		wayyēlekh	bekhol-derekh	'ās̱ā'
his mother	Azubah	the daughter of Shilhi		and he walked	in all the ways of	Asa

1	3940, 5681.111	4623	3937, 6449.141	3596	904, 6084
n ms, ps 3ms	neg part, v Qal pf 3ms	prep, ps 3ms	prep, v Qal inf con	art, adj	prep, *n fd*
אָבִיו	לֹא־סָר	מִמֶּנּוּ	לַעֲשׂוֹת	הַיָּשָׁר	בְּעֵינֵי
'āvîw	lō'-s̱ār	mimmennû	la'ăsôth	hayyāshār	be'ênê
his father	he did not turn aside	from them	to do	what is upright	in the eyes of

3176	395	1154	3940, 5681.116	5968	6194	2159.352
pn	adv	art, n fp	neg part, v Qal pf 3cp	adv	art, n ms	v Piel ptc mp
יְהוָה	אַךְ	הַבָּמוֹת	לֹא־סָרוּ	עוֹד	הָעָם	מְזַבְּחִים
yehwāh	'akh	habbāmôth	lō'-s̱ārû	'ôdh	hā'ām	mezabbechîm
Yahweh	only	the high places	they were not removed	still	the people	sacrificing

7281.352	904, 1154		8396.521	3194	6196, 4567
cj, v Piel ptc mp	prep, art, n fp	**44.**	cj, v Hiphil impf 3ms	pn	prep, *n ms*
וּמְקַטְּרִים	בַּבָּמוֹת		וַיַּשְׁלֵם	יְהוֹשָׁפָט	עִם־מֶלֶךְ
ûmeqaṯṯerîm	babbāmôth		wayyashlēm	yehôshāphāṯ	'im-melekh
and burning incense	on the high places		and he made peace	Jehoshaphat	with the king of

3547		3615	1745	3194	1400	866, 6449.111
pn	**45.**	cj, *n ms*	*n mp*	pn	cj, n fs, ps 3ms	rel part, v Qal pf 3ms
יִשְׂרָאֵל		וְיֶתֶר	דִּבְרֵי	יְהוֹשָׁפָט	וּגְבוּרָתוֹ	אֲשֶׁר־עָשָׂה
yisrā'ēl		w^{e}yether	divrê	y^{e}hôshāphāṭ	ûgh^{e}vûrāthô	'ăsher-'āsāh
Israel		and the remainder of	the events of	Jehoshaphat	and his strength	that he had done

866	4032.211	1950B, 3940, 2062	3918.156	6142, 5809	1745
cj, rel pron	v Niphal pf 3ms	intrg part, neg part, pers pron	v Qal pass ptc mp	prep, *n ms*	*n mp*
וַאֲשֶׁר	נִלְחָם	הֲלֹא־הֵם	כְּתוּבִים	עַל־סֵפֶר	דִּבְרֵי
wa'ăsher	nilchām	hălō'-hēm	k^{e}thûvîm	'al-sēpher	divrê
and who	he fought	are they not	things written	on the scroll of	the events of

40. So Ahab slept with his fathers; and Ahaziah his son reigned in his stead: ... buried among his ancestors. Then his son Ahaziah became the next king, *NLT* ... succeeded him as king, *Beck* ... the throne passed to his son Ochozias, *Knox* ... his son became king in his place, *NASB*.

41. And Jehoshaphat the son of Asa began to reign over Judah in the fourth year of Ahab king of Israel: ... during Ahab's fourth year, *NCV* ... rule over Judah in the fourth year of King Ahab's reign in Israel, *NLT*.

42. Jehoshaphat was thirty and five years old when he began to reign; and he reigned twenty and five years in Jerusalem: ... Jehoshafat was thirty-five years old at his coronation, *Fenton* ... came to the throne, *JB*.

And his mother's name was Azubah the daughter of Shilhi: ... the name of his mother, *Rotherham* ... daughter of Salai, *Knox*.

43. And he walked in all the ways of Asa his father; he turned not aside from it, doing that which was right in the eyes of the LORD: ... followed in the footsteps … and did not deviate from them, *REB* ... swerve from them, *NEB* ... stray from them, *NIV* ... the exact path of his father, *Moffatt*.

nevertheless the high places were not taken away; for the people offered and burnt incense yet in the high places: ... the people still sacrificed and offered incense, *NRSV* ... did not destroy the places where gods were worshiped, *NCV* ... Only he did not put the hill altars out of the way, *Tyndale* ... but the pagan places of worship were not destroyed, *Good News*.

44. And Jehoshaphat made peace with the king of Israel: ... he lived on terms of peace, *Knox* ... was at peace, *Darby* ... kept peace, *Beck*.

45. Now the rest of the acts of Jehoshaphat, and his might that he showed, and how he warred, are they not written in the book of the chronicles of the kings of Judah?: ... the words of the days, *Douay* ... his exploits and his wars, *REB* ... they are recorded in the history of events in the days, *Fenton* ... and his worthy deedes that he did, and his battels which hee fought, *Geneva*.

to rule his own house. He had winked at the atrocities committed in his name by his Tyrian queen, had connived at her idolatrous innovations and put no obstacle in the way of her persecutions. The people who might have forgotten or condoned all else never forgot the stoning and spoliation of Naboth and his sons, and his death was regarded as a retribution on this crime.

22:41–53. Before we leave the house of David we must speak of Jehoshaphat, the last king of Judah whose reign is narrated in the First Book of Kings. He was abler, more powerful and more faithful to Yahweh than any of his predecessors, and was alone counted worthy in later ages to rank with Hezekiah and Josiah among the most pious rulers of the Davidic line. The annals of his reign are found chiefly in 2 Chronicles, where his story occupies four long chapters. First Kings compresses all record of him into nine verses, except so far as his fortunes are commingled with the history of Ahab. But both accounts show us a reign which contributed as greatly to the prosperity of Judah as that of Jeroboam II contributed to the prosperity of Israel.

He ascended the throne at the age of thirty-five. He was apparently the only son of Asa, by Azubah, the daughter of Shilhi; for Asa, greatly to his credit, seems to have been the first king of Judah who set his face against the monstrous polygamy of his predecessors, and, so far as we know, contented himself with a single wife. He received the high eulogy that "he turned not aside from doing that which was right in the eyes of the LORD," with the customary qualification that, nevertheless, the people still burnt incense and offerings at the high places, which were not taken away. The chronicler says that he did take them away. This stock contradiction between the two authorities must be accounted for either by a contrast between the effort and its

3219 art, n mp הַיָּמִים hayyāmîm the days	3937, 4567 prep, n mp לְמַלְכֵי lemalkhê of the kings of	3171 pn יְהוּדָה yehûdhāh Judah	**46.**	3615 cj, n ms וְיֶתֶר weyether and the rest of	7228 art, n ms הַקָּדֵשׁ haqqādhēsh the male cult prostitutes	866 rel pron אֲשֶׁר 'ăsher who	8080.211 v Niphal pf 3ms נִשְׁאַר nish'ar they were left

904, 3219 prep, n mp בִּימֵי bîmê in the days of	623 pn אָסָא 'āsā' Asa	1 n ms, ps 3ms אָבִיו 'āvîw his father	1220.311 v Piel pf 3ms בִּעֵר bi'ēr he burned	4263, 800 prep, art, n fs מִן־הָאָרֶץ min-hā'ārets from the land	**47.**	4567 cj, n ms וּמֶלֶךְ ûmelekh and a king	375 sub אֵין 'ên there was not

904, 110 prep, pn בֶּאֱדוֹם be'ĕdhôm in Edom	5507.255 v Niphal ptc ms נִצָּב nitstsāv a deputy	4567 n ms מֶלֶךְ melekh the king	**48.**	3194 pn יְהוֹשָׁפָט yehôshāphāṭ Jehoshaphat	6458.111 v Qal pf 3ms עָשַׂר 'āsār levied a tenth	605 n fp אֳנִיּוֹת 'ănîyôth ships of	8998 pn תַּרְשִׁישׁ tarshîsh Tarshish

3937, 2050.141 prep, v Qal inf con לָלֶכֶת lālekheth to go	209 pn אוֹפִירָה 'ôphîrāh to Ophir	3937, 2174 prep, art, n ms לַזָּהָב lazzāhāv for the gold	3940 cj, neg part וְלֹא welō' but not	2050.111 v Qal pf 3ms הָלָךְ hālākh they went	3706, 8132.212 cj, v Niphal pf 3fs כִּי־נִשְׁבְּרָה kî-nishberāh because they were broken up

605 n fp אֳנִיּוֹת 'ănîyôth the ships	904, 6337 prep, pn בְּעֶצְיוֹן be'etsyôn in Ezion	6337 pn גָּבֶר gāver Geber	**49.**	226 adv אָז 'āz then	569.111 v Qal pf 3ms אָמַר 'āmar he said	275 pn אֲחַזְיָהוּ 'ăchazyāhû Ahaziah	1158, 255 n ms, pn בֶּן־אַחְאָב ven-'ach'āv the son of Ahab	420, 3194 prep, pn אֶל־יְהוֹשָׁפָט 'el-yehôshāphāṭ to Jehoshaphat

2050.126 v Qal juss 3mp יֵלְכוּ yēlekhû let them go	5860 n mp, ps 1cs עֲבָדַי 'ăvādhay my slaves	6196, 5860 prep, n mp, ps 2ms עִם־עֲבָדֶיךָ 'im-'ăvādhêkhā with your slaves	904, 604 prep, art, n fp בָּאֳנִיּוֹת bā'ănîyôth in the ships	3940 cj, neg part וְלֹא welō' but not	13.111 v Qal pf 3ms אָבָה 'āvāh he was willing	3194 pn יְהוֹשָׁפָט yehôshāphāṭ Jehoshaphat

50.	8311.121 cj, v Qal impf 3ms וַיִּשְׁכַּב wayyishkav then he lay	3194 pn יְהוֹשָׁפָט yehôshāphāṭ Jehoshaphat	6196, 1 prep, n mp, ps 3ms עִם־אֲבֹתָיו 'im-'ăvōthâv with his ancestors	7196.221 cj, v Niphal impf 3ms וַיִּקָּבֵר wayyiqqāvēr and he was buried	6196, 1 prep, n mp, ps 3ms עִם־אֲבֹתָיו 'im-'ăvōthâv with his ancestors

904, 6111 prep, n fs בְּעִיר be'îr in the city of	1784 pn דָּוִד dāwidh David	1 n ms, ps 3ms אָבִיו 'āvîw his father	4566.121 cj, v Qal impf 3ms וַיִּמְלֹךְ wayyimlōkh and he reigned	3190 pn יְהוֹרָם yehôrām Jehoram	1158 n ms, ps 3ms בְּנוֹ benô his son	8809 prep, ps 3ms תַּחְתָּיו tachtâv instead of him	**51.**	275 pn אֲחַזְיָהוּ 'ăchazyāhû Ahaziah

1158, 255 n ms, pn בֶּן־אַחְאָב ven-'ach'āv the son of Ahab	4566.111 v Qal pf 3ms מָלַךְ mālakh he reigned	6142, 3547 prep, pn עַל־יִשְׂרָאֵל 'al-yisrā'ēl over Israel	904, 8497 prep, pn בְּשֹׁמְרוֹן beshōmerôn in Samaria	904, 8523 prep, n fs בִּשְׁנַת bishnath in the year	8124 num שְׁבַע sheva' seven	6462 num עֶשְׂרֵה 'esrēh ten	3937, 3194 prep, pn לִיהוֹשָׁפָט lîhôshāphāṭ of Jehoshaphat

4567 n ms מֶלֶךְ melekh the king of	3171 pn יְהוּדָה yehûdhāh Judah	4566.121 cj, v Qal impf 3ms וַיִּמְלֹךְ wayyimlōkh and he reigned	6142, 3547 prep, pn עַל־יִשְׂרָאֵל 'al-yisrā'ēl over Israel	8523 n fd שְׁנָתָיִם shenāthāyim two years	**52.**	6449.121 cj, v Qal impf 3ms וַיַּעַשׂ wayya'as and he did

46. And the remnant of the sodomites, which remained in the days of his father Asa, he took out of the land: ... expelled from the country the rest of the temple-prostitutes, *Moffatt* ... put an end to the rest of those who were used for sex purposes in worship of the gods, *BB* ... rid the land of the rest of the male shrine prostitutes, *NIV* ... forced them to leave, *NCV*.

47. There was then no king in Edom: a deputy was king: ... but an appointed regent, *NAB* ... Since there was no king in Edom at this time to bar his way, *Knox* ... he set up a king, *Young* ... only a viceroy of Jehoshaphat, *NEB* ... he appointed a king, *Fenton*.

48. Jehoshaphat made ships of Tharshish to go to Ophir for gold: but they went not; for the ships were broken at Ezion-geber: ... were wrecked at Eziongeber and never sailed, *Good News* ... never made the voyage since the ships, *JB* ... never set sail, *NCV* ... also built a fleet of trading ships, *NLT*.

49. Then said Ahaziah the son of Ahab unto Jehoshaphat, Let my servants go with thy servants in the ships. But Jehoshaphat would not: ... was not willing, *NASB* ... would not consent, *Berkeley* ... refused, *Beck* ... would not agree, *REB*.

50. And Jehoshaphat slept with his fathers, and was buried with his fathers in the city of David his father: and Jehoram his son reigned in his stead: ... rested with his ancestors, *NAB* ... reigned in his room, *Tyndale* ... became king, *Goodspeed*.

51. Ahaziah the son of Ahab began to reign over Israel in Samaria the seventeenth year of Jehoshaphat king of Judah, and reigned two years over Israel: ... became king over Israel, *BB* ... ruled Israel for two years, *NCV*.

---

failure, or by a distinction between idolatrous high places and those dedicated to the worship of Yahweh to which the people clung with the deep affection which local sanctuaries inspire.

The central fact of Jehoshaphat's history is that "he made peace with the king of Israel." As a piece of ordinary statesmanship, no step could have been more praiseworthy. The sixty-eight years or more which had elapsed since the divinely suggested choice of Jeroboam by the Northern Kingdom had tended to soften old exasperations. The kingdom of Israel was now an established fact, and nothing had become more obvious than that the past could not be undone. Meanwhile, the threatening specter of Syria, under the dynasty of Ben-Hadad, was beginning to throw a dark shadow over both kingdoms. It had become certain that, if they continued to destroy each other by internecine warfare, both would succumb to the foreign invader. Wisely, therefore, and kindly, Jehoshaphat determined to make peace with Ahab, in about the eighth year after his accession; and this policy he consistently maintained to the close of his twenty-five-year reign.

No one surely could blame him for putting an end to an exhaustive civil war between brethren. Indeed, in so doing he was but carrying out the policy which and been dictated to Rehoboam by the prophet Shemaah, when he forbade him to attempt the immense expedition which he had prepared to annihilate Jeroboam. Peace was necessary to the development and happiness of both kingdoms, but even more so to the smaller and weaker, threatened as it was not only by the more distant menace of Syria, but by the might of Egypt on the south and the dangerous predatory warfare of Edom and Moab on the east.

But Jehoshaphat went further than this. He cemented the new peace by an alliance between his young son Jehoram and Athaliah, daughter of Ahab and Jezebel, who was then perhaps under fifteen years of age. At the time of the proposed alliance there is no mention of protest. Micaiah alone among the prophets uttered his stern warning when the expedition to Ramoth-Gilead was actually on foot, and Jehu, son of Hanani, went out to rebuke Jehoshaphat at the close of that disastrous enterprise. It is to the history attributed to this seer and embodied in the annals of Israel that the chronicler refers. "Shouldst thou help the wicked," asked the bold prophet, "and love them that hate the LORD? For this thing wrath is upon thee from the LORD. Nevertheless, there are good things found in thee, in that thou hast put away the Asheroth out of the land, and hast set thy heart to seek God."

Jehoshaphat, in his successful wars, had established the supremacy over Edom which had been all but lost in the days of Solomon. The Edomite Hadad and his successors had not been able to hold their own, and the present kings of Edom were deputies or vassals under the suzerainty of Judea. This once more opened the path to Elath and Ezion-Geber on the gulf of Akaba. Jehoshaphat, in his prosperity, felt a desire to revive the old costly commerce of Solomon with Ophir for gold, almug wood and curious animals (1 Ki. 10:11). For this purpose, he built "ships of Tarshish," i.e., merchant ships, like those

7737	904, 6084	3176	2050.121	904, 1932	1	904, 1932
art, adj	prep, *n fd*	pn	cj, v Qal impf 3ms	prep, *n ms*	n ms, ps 3ms	cj, prep, *n ms*
הָרַע	בְּעֵינֵי	יְהוָה	וַיֵּלֶךְ	בְּדֶרֶךְ	אָבִיו	וּבְדֶרֶךְ
hāra'	be'ênê	yehwāh	wayyēlekh	bedherekh	'āvîw	ûvedherekh
what is evil	in the eyes of	Yahweh	and he walked	in the ways of	his father	and in the ways of

525	904, 1932	3493	1158, 5203	866	2490.511
n fs, ps 3ms	cj, prep, *n ms*	pn	*n ms*, pn	rel pron	v Hiphil pf 3ms
אִמּוֹ	וּבְדֶרֶךְ	יָרָבְעָם	בֶּן־נְבָט	אֲשֶׁר	הֶחֱטִיא
'immô	ûvedherekh	yārov'ām	ben-nevāṯ	'ăsher	hechĕṭî'
his mother	and in the ways of	Jeroboam	the son of Nebat	who	he caused to sin

881, 3547		5856.121	881, 1197	8246.721	3937
do, pn	**53.**	cj, v Qal impf 3ms	do, art, pn	cj, v Hithpael impf 3ms	prep, ps 3ms
אֶת־יִשְׂרָאֵל		וַיַּעֲבֹד	אֶת־הַבַּעַל	וַיִּשְׁתַּחֲוֶה	לוֹ
'eth-yisrā'ēl		wayya'ăvōdh	'eth-habba'al	wayyishtachweh	lô
Israel		and they served	the Baal	and they worshiped	him

3832.521	881, 3176	435	3547	3626, 3725	866, 6449.111
cj, v Hiphil impf 3ms	do, pn	*n mp*	pn	prep, adj	rel part, v Qal pf 3ms
וַיַּכְעֵס	אֶת־יְהוָה	אֱלֹהֵי	יִשְׂרָאֵל	כְּכֹל	אֲשֶׁר־עָשָׂה
wayyakh'ēs̱	'eth-yehwāh	'ĕlōhê	yisrā'ēl	kekhōl	'ăsher-'āsāh
and they provoked to anger	Yahweh	the God of	Israel	according to all	that he had done

52. And he did evil in the sight of the LORD, and walked in the way of his father, and in the way of his mother, and in the way of Jeroboam the son of Nebat, who made Israel to sin: ... defied the Lord's will, following the example of his own father and mother, *Knox* ... what is displeasing to Yahweh, *JB* ... what was wrong in the eyes, *NEB* ... had led Israel into the sin of idolatry, *NLT*.

53. For he served Baal, and worshipped him, and provoked to anger the LORD God of Israel, according to all that his father had done: ... and bowed down to him, *Rotherham* ... vexing the Eternal the God of Israel, exactly as his father, *Moffatt* ... he aroused the anger of, *Good News* ... in all that his ancestors did, *Fenton*.

used for the Phoenician trade between Tyre and Tartessus, to go this long voyage. The ships, however, were wrecked on the reefs of Ezion-Geber. Hearing of this disaster, according to the Book of Kings, Ahaziah made an offer to Jehoshaphat to make the enterprise a joint one—thinking, apparently, that the Israelites, who, perhaps, held Joppa and some of the ports on the coast, would bring more skill and knowledge to bear on the result. But Jehoshaphat had had enough of an attempt which was so dangerous and which offered no solid advantages. He declined Ahaziah's offer.

Jehoshaphat died full of years and honors, leaving seven sons, of whom the eldest was Jehoram. His reign marks a decisive triumph of the prophetic party. The prophets not only felt a fiercely just abhorrence of the abominations of Canaanite idolatry, but wished to establish a theocracy to the exclusion of all local and symbolic worship and reliance on worldly policy.

THE BOOK OF

2 KINGS

Expanded Interlinear
Various Versions
Verse-by-Verse Commentary

THE BOOK OF

2 KINGS מְלָכִים ב

1:1

6839.121	4262	904, 3547	313	4323	255
cj, v Qal impf 3ms	pn	prep, pn	adv	*n ms*	pn
וַיִּפְשַׁע	מוֹאָב	בְּיִשְׂרָאֵל	אַחֲרֵי	מוֹת	אַחְאָב
wayyiphsha‘	mô'āv	beyisrā'ēl	'achrê	môth	'ach'āv
and they revolted	Moab	against Israel	after	the death of	Ahab

2.

5489.121	275	1185	7877	904, 6168	866	904, 8497
cj, v Qal impf 3ms	pn	prep	art, n fs	prep, n fs, ps 3ms	rel part	prep, pn
וַיִּפֹּל	אֲחַזְיָה	בְּעַד	הַשְּׂבָכָה	בַּעֲלִיָּתוֹ	אֲשֶׁר	בְּשֹׁמְרוֹן
wayyippōl	'ăchazyāh	be'adh	hassevākhāh	ba'ălîyāthô	'ăsher	beshōmerôn
and he fell	Ahaziah	through	the lattice	in his upper room	which	in Samaria

2571.121	8365.121	4534	569.121	420	2050.133
cj, v Qal impf 3ms	cj, v Qal impf 3ms	n mp	cj, v Qal impf 3ms	prep, ps 3mp	v Qal impv 2mp
וַיָּחַל	וַיִּשְׁלַח	מַלְאָכִים	וַיֹּאמֶר	אֲלֵהֶם	לְכוּ
wayyāchal	wayyishlach	mal'ākhîm	wayyō'mer	'ălēhem	lekhû
and he was sick	then he sent out	messengers	and he said	to them	go

1938.133	904, 1203B	1203B	435	6376	524, 2513.125	4623, 2582	2172
v Qal impv 2mp	prep, pn	pn	*n mp*	pn	v Qal impf 1cs	prep, n ms	dem pron
דִּרְשׁוּ	בְּבַעַל	זְבוּב	אֱלֹהֵי	עֶקְרוֹן	אִם־אֶחְיֶה	מֵחֳלִי	זֶה
dhirshû	beva'al	zevûv	'ĕlōhê	'eqrôn	'im-'echyeh	mēchălî	zeh
inquire	with Baal	Zebub	the god of	Ekron	if I will live	from sickness	this

3.

4534	3176	1744.311	420, 455	9005	7251.131	6148.131
cj, *n ms*	pn	v Piel pf 3ms	prep, pn	art, pn	v Qal impv 2ms	v Qal impv 2ms
וּמַלְאַךְ	יְהוָה	דִּבֶּר	אֶל־אֵלִיָּה	הַתִּשְׁבִּי	קוּם	עֲלֵה
ûmal'akh	yehwāh	dibber	'el-'ēlîyāh	hattishbî	qûm	'ălēh
and the Angel of	Yahweh	He spoke	to Elijah	the Tishbite	rise	go up

3937, 7410.141	4534	4567, 8497	1744.331	420
prep, v Qal inf con	*n mp*	*n ms*, pn	cj, v Piel impv 2ms	prep, ps 3mp
לִקְרַאת	מַלְאֲכֵי	מֶלֶךְ־שֹׁמְרוֹן	וְדַבֵּר	אֲלֵהֶם
liqōra'th	mal'ăkhê	melekh-shōmerôn	wedhabbēr	'ălēhem
to meet	the messengers of	the king of Samaria	and speak	to them

1:1. Then Moab rebelled against Israel after the death of Ahab: ... Moab broke away from Israel's rule, *NCV* ... Moab revolted against Israel, *Rotherham* ... the nation of Moab declared its independence from Israel, *NLT* ... Moab made itself free from the authority of Israel, *BB*.

2. And Ahaziah fell down through a lattice in his upper chamber that was in Samaria, and was sick: ... through a latticed window in his roof-chamber in Samaria and injured himself, *REB* ... had fallen from the balcony of his upper room, *JB* ... and lay injured, *NRSV* ... through the lattice of his roof terrace, *NAB*.

and he sent messengers, and said unto them, Go, inquire of Baal-zebub the god of Ekron whether I shall recover of this disease: ... if I will get rid of this suffering, *Beck* ... recover from this illness, *Goodspeed* ... recover from this injury, *NIV*.

3. But the angel of the LORD said to Elijah the Tishbite, Arise, go up to meet the messengers of the king of Samaria: ... Go and intercept the king of Samaria's messengers, *JB* ... meet the Ambassadors of the King of Shomeron, *Fenton*.

and say unto them, Is it not because there is not a God in Israel, that ye go to inquire of Baal-zebub the god of Ekron?: ... Is there no God in Israel?, *NLT* ... Is it for lack of a god in Israel that you are going to inquire, *Anchor* ... Has Israel no God of its own, *Knox*.

4. Now therefore thus saith the LORD, Thou shalt not come down from that bed on which thou art

Second Kings begins in the middle of the account of the reign of King Ahaziah. Elijah returns to the scene after several other prophets (most of whom are unnamed) have been prophesying with national import. Second Kings merely marks the continuation of 1 Kings.

1:1–18. *Divine Judgment on King Ahaziah and His Army. Ahaziah, the king of Israel, is introduced in the final three verses of 1 Kings. There is nothing significant concerning the break between 1 Ki. 22:53 and 2 Ki. 1:1. The present section merely represents a continuation of the previous narrative, giving further indication of how King Ahaziah displeased Yahweh, the God of Israel.*

The chapter is a narrative unit with references to the apostasy of King Ahaziah (cf. vv. 3f, 6f, 16) bracketing the narrative proper. The brief comment in v. 1 introduces the striking threefold encounter with fifty-man contingents of soldiers (vv. 9–15), and a statement (vv. 17f) brings the chapter to a close.

1:1. In the first verse of the Book, there is a characteristic chronological synchronism, chronological links between the various kings and kingdoms of the day, between the history of Israel and that of the surrounding nations (Moab in this case). Much of the Books of the Kings is especially concerned with such synchronisms. The death of Ahab took place about 850 B.C. This was a time of Egyptian weakness, and the main enemy of Israel was Aram (whose territory corresponded roughly to the southern part of the modern nation of Syria). The greater empire of Assyria was on the rise, however, and would soon play a major role in the region.

This verse accomplishes two purposes. It introduces two narratives (chs. 1 and 2) concerning the prophets Elijah and Elisha, which in turn serve to prepare the reader for the transfer of authority from the former prophet to the latter. It also serves the wider purpose of signaling the conclusion of one era of Israelite history (the era of the infamous Ahab, son of Omri) and the inauguration of another, leading up, ultimately, to the bloody demise of the dynasty of Omri by King Jehu (see chs. 9–11). Elijah's own prophetic "recommissioning" (as found in 1 Ki. 19:15–18) included both the anointing of Elisha as his own successor and Jehu as the successor to the dynasty of Omri.

1:2. In succinct fashion, the biblical writer presents the background situation. King Ahaziah had ignominiously fallen down, injuring himself, and was in dire need of healing. This would require divine intervention, so he sent for his messengers to consult a false god. Surprisingly, the deity he sought was Baal-Zebub, described here as the god of Ekron. The Hebrew phrase ba'al zevûv (HED #1203B) literally means "lord of the flies," and it corresponds with several NT references (Matt. 10:25; 12:24; Mark 3:22; Luke 11:15) to "Beelzebub" (GED #947) as an epithet for Satan. But Satan is clearly not in view in 2 Ki. 1. Rather, the compound name probably refers to a local manifestation of the prominent Canaanite deity Baal. References to Baal, of course, are found throughout much of the OT, with perhaps the most well-known reference being Elijah's famous contest with the 450 priests of Baal on Mt. Carmel (1 Ki. 18:20–40). The Semitic name "Baal" means "lord," and is probably a short form of the name "Baal-Hadad," "lord of the [thunder]storm" or the like. (Note the irony in 1 Ki. 17–18 on Baal as being entirely powerless to bring much-needed rain to the land of Israel and break the three-year drought announced by Elijah on behalf of Israel's God Yahweh). Scholars differ on what exactly is meant by the reference to "lord of the flies" in the present passage (varying discussions may be found in Cogan and Tadmor, *II Kings*, ABC, 25; Hobbs, WBC, 8; and Gwilym H. Jones, *1 and 2 Kings*, New Century Bible Commentary 2:377). The interpretation usually preferred is that the term is a sarcastic distortion of the more esteemed name, "Baal-Zebul," which means "exalted lord" or the like. Sarcastic corruptions of names are found elsewhere in the OT, the most famous examples being the substitution of the common Hebrew term bōsheth ("shame," HED #1350) for the name Baal in some proper names (contrast "Jerub-Besheth" in 2 Sam. 11:21 with "Jerub-Baal" in Judg. 6:32; and "Ish-Bosheth" in 2 Sam. 2:8 with "Esh-Baal" in 1 Chr. 8:33; 9:39).

Ekron was a Philistine town at this time; in fact, it was one of the five prominent Philistine cities mentioned in 1 Sam. 5–6 as part of the Ark narrative. Why King Ahaziah would consult the deity in that location is not made clear in the present narrative, but it does not significantly affect the interpretation of this passage. The fact that the king of Israel should seek healing from a foreign god was hardly out of character for a descendant of Ahab. God is rightly and understandably jealous of any false, would-be pretenders. The theme of divine jealousy is already brought to the forefront in the very next verse.

1:3–4. Nothing is ever said about any intervention by Baal-Zebub. Rather, it is Yahweh Who acts,

1950B, 4623, 1136	375, 435	904, 3547	894	2050.152	3937, 1938.141
intrg part, prep, neg part	*sub*, n mp	prep, pn	pers pron	v Qal act ptc mp	prep, v Qal inf con
הֲמִבְּלִי	אֵין־אֱלֹהִים	בְּיִשְׂרָאֵל	אַתֶּם	הֹלְכִים	לִדְרֹשׁ
hamibbᵉlî	'ên-'ĕlōhîm	bᵉyisrā'ēl	'attem	hōlᵉkhîm	lidhrōsh
is from none	there is not a God	in Israel	you	going	to inquire

904, 1203B	1203B	435	6376		3937, 3772	3662, 569.111	3176	4433
prep, pn	pn	*n mp*	pn	**4.**	cj, prep, adv	adv, v Qal pf 3ms	pn	art, n fs
בְּבַעַל	זְבוּב	אֱלֹהֵי	עֶקְרוֹן		וְלָכֵן	כֹּה־אָמַר	יְהוָה	הַמִּטָּה
bᵉva'al	zᵉvûv	'ĕlōhê	'eqrôn		wᵉlākhēn	kōh-'āmar	yᵉhwāh	hammiṯṯāh
with Baal	Zebub	the god of	Ekron		now therefore	thus He has said	Yahweh	the bed

866, 6148.113	8427	3940, 3495.123	4623	3706	4322.142
rel part, v Qal pf 2ms	adv	neg part, v Qal impf 2ms	prep, ps 3fs	cj	v Qal inf abs
אֲשֶׁר־עָלִיתָ	שָׁם	לֹא־תֵרֵד	מִמֶּנָּה	כִּי	מוֹת
'ăsher-'ālîthā	shām	lō'-thērēdh	mimmennāh	kî	môth
which you have gone up to	there	you will not come down	from it	rather	dying

4322.123	2050.121	455		8178.126	4534	420
v Qal impf 2ms	cj, v Qal impf 3ms	pn	**5.**	cj, v Qal impf 3mp	art, n mp	prep, ps 3ms
תָּמוּת	וַיֵּלֶךְ	אֵלִיָּה		וַיָּשׁוּבוּ	הַמַּלְאָכִים	אֵלָיו
tāmûth	wayyēlekh	'ēlîyāh		wayyāshûvû	hammal'ākhîm	'ēlāv
you will certainly die	so he went	Elijah		and they returned	the messengers	to him

569.121	420	4242, 2172	8178.117		569.126	420	382
cj, v Qal impf 3ms	prep, ps 3mp	intrg, dem pron	v Qal pf 2mp	**6.**	cj, v Qal impf 3mp	prep, ps 3ms	n ms
וַיֹּאמֶר	אֲלֵיהֶם	מַה־זֶּה	שַׁבְתֶּם		וַיֹּאמְרוּ	אֵלָיו	אִישׁ
wayyō'mer	'ălêhem	mah-zeh	shavtem		wayyō'mᵉrû	'ēlâv	'îsh
and he said	to them	what this	you have returned		and they said	to him	a man

6148.111	3937, 7410.141	569.121	420	2050.133	8178.133
v Qal pf 3ms	prep, v Qal inf con, ps 1cp	cj, v Qal impf 3ms	prep, ps 1cp	v Qal impv 2mp	v Qal impv 2mp
עָלָה	לִקְרָאתֵנוּ	וַיֹּאמֶר	אֵלֵינוּ	לְכוּ	שׁוּבוּ
'ālāh	liqōrā'thēnû	wayyō'mer	'ēlênû	lᵉkhû	shûvû
he came up	to meet us	and he said	to us	go	return

420, 4567	866, 8365.111	881	1744.318	420	3662	569.111
prep, art, n ms	rel pron, v Qal pf 3ms	do, ps 2mp	cj, v Piel pf 2mp	prep, ps 3ms	adv	v Qal pf 3ms
אֶל־הַמֶּלֶךְ	אֲשֶׁר־שָׁלַח	אֶתְכֶם	וְדִבַּרְתֶּם	אֵלָיו	כֹּה	אָמַר
'el-hammelekh	'ăsher-shālach	'ethkhem	wᵉdhibbartem	'ēlâv	kōh	'āmar
to the king	whom he sent	you	and you will speak	to him	thus	He has said

3176	1950B, 4623, 1136	375, 435	904, 3547	887	8365.151	3937, 1938.141
pn	intrg part, prep, neg part	*sub*, n mp	prep, pn	pers pron	v Qal act ptc ms	prep, v Qal inf con
יְהוָה	הֲמִבְּלִי	אֵין־אֱלֹהִים	בְּיִשְׂרָאֵל	אַתָּה	שֹׁלֵחַ	לִדְרֹשׁ
yᵉhwāh	hamibbᵉlî	'ên-'ĕlōhîm	bᵉyisrā'ēl	'attāh	shōlēach	lidhrōsh
Yahweh	is from none	there is not a God	in Israel	you	sending out	to inquire

904, 1203B	1203B	435	6376	3937, 3772	4433	866, 6148.113	8427
prep, pn	pn	*n mp*	pn	prep, adv	art, n fs	rel part, v Qal pf 2ms	adv
בְּבַעַל	זְבוּב	אֱלֹהֵי	עֶקְרוֹן	לָכֵן	הַמִּטָּה	אֲשֶׁר־עָלִיתָ	שָׁם
bᵉva'al	zᵉvûv	'ĕlōhê	'eqrôn	lākhēn	hammiṯṯāh	'ăsher-'ālîthā	shām
with Baal	Zebub	the god of	Ekron	therefore	the bed	which you have gone up to	there

3940, 3495.123	4623	3706, 4322.142	4322.123		1744.321
neg part, v Qal impf 2ms	prep, ps 3fs	cj, v Qal inf abs	v Qal impf 2ms	**7.**	cj, v Piel impf 3ms
לֹא־תֵרֵד	מִמֶּנָּה	כִּי־מוֹת	תָּמוּת		וַיְדַבֵּר
lō'-thērēdh	mimmennāh	kî-môth	tāmûth		waydhabbēr
you will not come down	from it	rather dying	you will certainly die		and he spoke

gone up, but shalt surely die: ... You will never get up from the bed you are lying on, *NCV* ... you must die, *Moffatt* ... but death will certainly come to you, *BB*.

And Elijah departed: ... Then Elijah went, *Berkeley* ... Then Elijah passed on, *Goodspeed* ... Elijah did as the LORD commanded, *Good News*.

5. And when the messengers turned back unto him, he said unto them, Why are ye now turned back?: ... Why did you come back?, *Beck* ... Why have you returned?, *NASB* ... Why have you returned so soon?, *NLT* ... Why are you come back?, *Douay*.

6. And they said unto him, There came a man up to meet us, and said unto us, Go, turn again unto the king that sent you: ... On our way we had a meeting with a man who said, Go back to the king, *BB* ... Go, and return to the king, that sent you, *Douay*.

and say unto him, Thus saith the LORD, Is it not because there is not a God in Israel, that thou sendest to inquire of Baal-zebub the god of Ekron?: ... rebuked him for sending to consult Beelzebub, god of Accaron, as if Israel had no God, *Knox* ... Is it for lack of a god in Israel that you send to inquire of Baal-zebub, *Anchor*.

therefore thou shalt not come down from that bed on which thou art gone up, but shalt surely die: ... death will certainly come to you, *BB* ... You will not recover from your injuries; you will die!, *Good News* ... you will never leave the bed on which you are lying, *NLT*.

7. And he said unto them, What manner of man was he which came up to meet you, and told you these words?: ... What was the man like who came up to you and said these things to you?, *NAB* ... What sort of man was he who came to meet you and told you these things?, *NRSV* ... This man who came up to meet you and spoke to you, what was he like?, *Moffatt*.

---

summoning his messenger, the prophet Elijah. Yahweh gave Elijah an answer to the messengers sent by the king—but an answer phrased in the form of a question: "Is it because there is no God in Israel ...?" This question is repeated twice in this short chapter (vv. 3, 6, 16). The biblical writer focuses on the most important theological issue the Israelites face—where is the God of Israel? To those critics of the OT who decry the violence and bloodshed alleged to have been repeatedly perpetrated by Yahweh, the God of Israel, against his and their enemies, it should be pointed out that the OT believer would have a far greater difficulty if God appeared silent, unresponsive, while the wicked flourished and the righteous suffered. "Where are you, O Yahweh?" seems to be the common refrain of the lament Psalms found in the Psalter. It is not only King Ahaziah of the OT who was tempted to ask the question, "Where is my God?" The chapter focuses at the outset upon this question, and it is indeed Yahweh's honor, and his reputation, that are at stake. Sometimes our lack of prayer to the true God, and our preoccupation with what is not of God, can actually impugn God's honor.

Ahaziah's situation is already bad, but it will soon get worse. First Kings relates that Ahaziah's reign only lasts two years (1 Ki. 22:51), but Yahweh's stern edict in v. 4 still seems abrupt: "You will not leave the sickbed you are on—you will certainly die!" This is an example of one of the activities of the prophet in OT times, i.e., the foretelling of the near-term future. The classic text in Deut. 18:14–22 elucidates an important criterion for authenticating the credentials of a would-be prophet of Yahweh: "If what a prophet proclaims in the name of Yahweh does not take place or come true, that is a message Yahweh has not spoken. That prophet has spoken presumptuously. Do not be afraid of him" (v. 22).

1:5–8. The king's messengers meet Yahweh's messenger. As is so often the case in biblical narrative, the text abounds with irony. The king's messengers are sent to meet with representatives of Baal-Zebub, but there is only one living God in Israel, and his name is Yahweh, not Baal (cf. 1 Ki. 18:22–39; especially vv. 36f). The most aggressive actor in the present text is Yahweh, and by implication, his servant Elijah. The king is surprised (v. 5) at the early return of his servants, yet, when he hears their ominous message (v. 6), he seems to have a pretty good idea whom they have probably encountered (vv. 7f). The description in v. 8 of Elijah as a man "with a garment of hair and with a leather belt around his waist" (NIV; cf. NLT footnote) or "an hairy man, girt with a girdle of leather about his loins" (KJV; cf. NLT text) represents the classic biblical reference to Elijah's "otherworldly" appearance. Cogan and Tadmor argue strongly in their 2 Kings commentary (AB, 26), that the Hebrew ba'al sē'ār (HED #1196, 7998) should be translated "a hairy man," not "a garment of hair." If we follow this interpretation, then the implied contrast is with the presumably bald appearance of Elisha (cf. 2:23ff, below).

420	4242	5122	382	866	6148.111	3937, 7410.141
prep, ps 3mp	intrg	*n ms*	art, n ms	rel pron	v Qal pf 3ms	prep, v Qal inf con, ps 2mp
אֲלֵהֶם	מֶה	מִשְׁפַּט	הָאִישׁ	אֲשֶׁר	עָלָה	לִקְרַאתְכֶם
'ălēhem	meh	mishpaṭ	hā'îsh	'ăsher	'ālāh	liqŏra'th^{e}khem
to them	why	the judgment of	the man	who	he came up	to meet you

1744.321	420	881, 1745	431		569.126	420	382
cj, v Piel impf 3ms	prep, ps 2mp	do, art, n mp	art, dem pron	**8.**	cj, v Qal impf 3mp	prep, ps 3ms	*n ms*
וַיְדַבֵּר	אֲלֵיכֶם	אֶת־הַדְּבָרִים	הָאֵלֶּה		וַיֹּאמְרוּ	אֵלָיו	אִישׁ
waydhabbēr	'ălêkhem	'eth-hadd^{e}vārîm	hā'ēlleh		wayyō'm^{e}rû	'ēlâv	'îsh
and he spoke	to you	the words	the these		and they said	to him	a man of

1196	7998	231	5997	246.155	904, 5158	569.121
n ms	n ms	cj, *n ms*	n ms	v Qal pass ptc ms	prep, n md, ps 3ms	v Qal impf 3ms
בַּעַל	שֵׂעָר	וְאֵזוֹר	עוֹר	אָזוּר	בְּמָתְנָיו	וַיֹּאמַר
ba'al	sē'ār	w^e'ēzôr	'ôr	'āzûr	b^{e}māth^{e}nâv	wayyō'mar
a possessor of	hair	and a loincloth of	leather	girded	on his loins	and he said

455	9005	2000		8365.121	420	8015, 2675	2675
pn	art, pn	pers pron	**9.**	cj, v Qal impf 3ms	prep, ps 3ms	*n ms*, num	cj, num, ps 3ms
אֵלִיָּה	הַתִּשְׁבִּי	הוּא		וַיִּשְׁלַח	אֵלָיו	שַׂר־חֲמִשִּׁים	וַחֲמִשָּׁיו
'ēlîyāh	hattishbî	hû'		wayyishlach	'ēlâv	sar-chămishshîm	wachmishshâv
Elijah	the Tishbite	he		then he sent out	to him	a commander of fifty	and his fifty

6148.121	420	2079	3553.151	6142, 7513	2098	1744.321
cj, v Qal impf 3ms	prep, ps 3ms	cj, intrj	v Qal act ptc ms	prep, *n ms*	art, n ms	cj, v Piel impf 3ms
וַיַּעַל	אֵלָיו	וְהִנֵּה	יֹשֵׁב	עַל־רֹאשׁ	הָהָר	וַיְדַבֵּר
wayya'al	'ēlâv	w^{e}hinnēh	yōshēv	'al-rō'sh	hāhār	waydhabbēr
and he went up	to him	and behold	sitting	on the top of	the hill	and he spoke

420	382	435	4567	1744.311	3495.131		6257.121
prep, ps 3ms	*n ms*	art, n mp	art, n ms	v Piel pf 3ms	v Qal impv 2ms	**10.**	cj, v Qal impf 3ms
אֵלָיו	אִישׁ	הָאֱלֹהִים	הַמֶּלֶךְ	דִּבֶּר	רֵדָה		וַיַּעֲנֶה
'ēlâv	'îsh	hā'ĕlōhîm	hammelekh	dibber	rēdhāh		wayya'ăneh
to him	O man of	God	the king	he has spoken	come down		but he answered

455	1744.321	420, 8015	2675	524, 382	435	603
pn	cj, v Piel impf 3ms	prep, *n ms*	art, num	cj, cj, *n ms*	n mp	pers pron
אֵלִיָּהוּ	וַיְדַבֵּר	אֶל־שַׂר	הַחֲמִשִּׁים	וְאִם־אִישׁ	אֱלֹהִים	אָנִי
'ēlîyāhû	waydhabbēr	'el-sar	hachmishshîm	w^e'im-'îsh	'ĕlōhîm	'ānî
Elijah	and he spoke	to the commander of	the fifty	so if a man of	God	I

3495.122	813	4623, 8452	404.122	881	881, 2675
v Qal juss 3fs	n fs	prep, art, n md	cj, v Qal juss 3fs	do, ps 2ms	cj, do, num, ps 2ms
תֵּרֶד	אֵשׁ	מִן־הַשָּׁמַיִם	וְתֹאכַל	אֹתְךָ	וְאֶת־חֲמִשֶּׁיךָ
tēredh	'ēsh	min-hashshāmayim	w^{e}thō'khal	'ōth^{e}khā	w^e'eth-chămishshêkhā
may it come down	fire	from the heavens	and may it devour	you	and your fifty

3495.122	813	4623, 8452	404.122	881	881, 2675
cj, v Qal impf 3fs	n fs	prep, art, n md	cj, v Qal impf 3fs	do, ps 3ms	cj, do, num, ps 3ms
וַתֵּרֶד	אֵשׁ	מִן־הַשָּׁמַיִם	וַתֹּאכַל	אֹתוֹ	וְאֶת־חֲמִשָּׁיו
wattēredh	'ēsh	min-hashshāmayim	wattō'khal	'ōthô	w^e'eth-chămishshâv
and it came down	fire	from the heavens	and it consumed	him	and his fifty

	8178.121	8365.121	420	8015, 2675	311	2675
11.	cj, v Qal impf 3ms	cj, v Qal impf 3ms	prep, ps 3ms	*n ms*, num	adj	cj, num, ps 3ms
	וַיָּשָׁב	וַיִּשְׁלַח	אֵלָיו	שַׂר־חֲמִשִּׁים	אַחֵר	וַחֲמִשָּׁיו
	wayyāshāv	wayyishlach	'ēlâv	sar-chămishshîm	'achēr	wachmishshâv
	then he returned	and he sent out	to him	a commander of fifty	another	and his fifty

6257.121	1744.321	420	382	435	3662, 569.111	4567
cj, v Qal impf 3ms	cj, v Piel impf 3ms	prep, ps 3ms	*n ms*	art, n mp	adv, v Qal pf 3ms	art, n ms
וַיַּעַן	וַיְדַבֵּר	אֵלָיו	אִישׁ	הָאֱלֹהִים	כֹּה־אָמַר	הַמֶּלֶךְ
wayya'an	waydhabbēr	'ēlâv	'îsh	hā'ělōhîm	kōh-'āmar	hammelekh
and he answered	and he spoke	to him	O man of	God	thus he has said	the king

4259	3495.131		6257.121	455	1744.321	420	524, 382
adv	v Qal impv 2ms	**12.**	cj, v Qal impf 3ms	pn	cj, v Piel impf 3ms	prep, ps 3mp	cj, *n ms*
מְהֵרָה	רֵדָה		וַיַּעַן	אֵלִיָּה	וַיְדַבֵּר	אֲלֵיהֶם	אִם־אִישׁ
mehērāh	rēdhāh		wayya'an	'ēlîyāh	waydhabbēr	'ălêhem	'im-'îsh
quickly	come down		and he answered	Elijah	and he spoke	to them	if a man of

8. And they answered him, He was an hairy man, and girt with a girdle of leather about his loins. And he said, It is Elijah the Tishbite: ... with a leather apron round his waist, *NEB* ... He was a man with a garment of hair and with a leather belt around his waist, *NIV* ... A man covered with hair, *Fenton* ... a man wearing a hair cloak, they answered, and a leather loincloth, *JB*.

9. Then the king sent unto him a captain of fifty with his fifty. And he went up to him: ... king sent a captain at the head of fifty men to find him, *Knox* ... a head of fifty, *Young* ... Thereupon he sent to him a commander of fifty, *Goodspeed* ... Then he sent an army captain with fifty soldiers to arrest him, *NLT*.

and, behold, he sat on the top of an hill: ... The prophet was seated on a hilltop when he found him, *NAB* ... he sat on top of the mount, *Darby*.

And he spake unto him, Thou man of God, the king hath said, Come down: ... Man of God, the king orders you to come down, *NEB* ... the king hath commanded that thou come down, *Douay* ... the king biddeth thee come down, *Tyndale*.

10. And Elijah answered and said to the captain of fifty, If I be a man of God, then let fire come down from heaven, and consume thee and thy fifty. And there came down fire from heaven, and consumed him and his fifty: ... fire came down from heaven and put an end to him and his fifty men, *BB* ... fire descended from heaven and consumed him, *Anchor* ... At once fire came down and killed the officer and his men, *Good News* ... fire came down from heaven and devoured him and his fifty, *Geneva*.

11. Again also he sent unto him another captain of fifty with his fifty. And he answered and said unto him, O man of God, thus hath the king said, Come down quickly: ... He too shouted, Man of God, thus has the king commanded, *Berkeley* ... Man of God, he told him, the king says, Hurry down, *Beck* ... he sent to him another Captain of the Guards, *Fenton* ... Once more the king despatched another captain, *Moffatt*.

12. And Elijah answered and said unto them, If I be a man of God, let fire come down from heaven, and consume thee and thy fifty. And the fire of God came down from heaven, and consumed him and his fifty: ... God's fire came down from heaven and devoured him and his 50, *Beck* ... from God fell from heaven and consumed the man and his company, *REB* ... And lightning fell from heaven and destroyed him, *JB* ... fire of God fell from heaven and killed them all, *NLT*.

1:9–15. These verses record the threefold encounter between the solitary Elijah and the various Israelite military commanders with their accompanying fifty-man companies (such uneven odds remind us of Elijah's solo confrontation with the 450 prophets of Baal in 1 Ki. 18:18ff). This is similar to Queen Esther's threefold opportunity to ask for a favor from King Xerxes (Est. 5:3, 6; 7:2). (A similar threefold pattern of Elijah's repeated remonstrance to Elisha may also be found in the very next chapter of the present Book; see 2 Ki. 2:2, 4, 6.) Quoted in connection with the Esther example, David N. Freedman makes the following apt comment: "The third time is the charm in literary accounts. It is like the acrobat or magician who deliberately fails twice in trying to perform his most difficult feat, before succeeding on the third try. This enhances the suspense and the expectation of the audience, as well as winning for the performance the applause he deserves but is not likely to get if the audience thinks that there is no danger or limited need of skill to succeed" (cited in Carey A. Moore, *Esther*, AB, 58).

The references to the "fire from heaven" in vv. 10, 12 are characteristic of the ministry of Elijah (cf. the "fire from Yahweh" that came down upon Elijah's altar in 1 Ki. 18:38; also cf. the upcoming reference to the "chariot of fires and horses of fire" in 2 Ki. 2:11). A good-sized military company of fifty soldiers and their commander was no match for Elijah alone with his God. The comment in v. 9 about Elijah "sitting on the top of a hill" is also characteristic of the accounts

435	603	3495.122	813	4623, 8452	404.122	881
art, n mp	pers pron	v Qal juss 3fs	n fs	prep, art, n md	cj, v Qal juss 3fs	do, ps 2ms
הָאֱלֹהִים	אֲנִי	תֵּרֶד	אֵשׁ	מִן־הַשָּׁמַיִם	וְתֹאכַל	אֹתְךָ
hā'ĕlōhîm	'ănî	tēredh	'ēsh	min-hashshāmayim	wethō'khal	'ōthekhā
God	I	may it come down	fire	from the heavens	and may it devour	you

881, 2675	3495.122	813, 435	4623, 8452	404.122	881
cj, do, num, ps 2ms	cj, v Qal impf 3fs	*n fs*, n ms	prep, art, n md	cj, v Qal impf 3fs	do, ps 3ms
וְאֶת־חֲמִשֶּׁיךָ	וַתֵּרֶד	אֵשׁ־אֱלֹהִים	מִן־הַשָּׁמַיִם	וַתֹּאכַל	אֹתוֹ
we'eth-chămishshêkhā	wattēredh	'ēsh-'ĕlōhîm	min-hashshāmayim	wattō'khal	'ōthô
and your fifty	and it came down	the fire of God	from the heavens	and it consumed	him

881, 2675		8178.121	8365.121	8015, 2675	8389
cj, do, num, ps 3ms	**13.**	cj, v Qal impf 3ms	cj, v Qal impf 3ms	*n ms*, num	num
וְאֶת־חֲמִשָּׁיו		וַיָּשָׁב	וַיִּשְׁלַח	שַׂר־חֲמִשִּׁים	שְׁלִשִׁים
we'eth-chămishshâv		wayyāshāv	wayyishlach	sar-chămishshîm	shelishîm
and his fifty		then he returned	then he sent out	a commander of fifty	a third

2675	6148.121	971.121	8015, 2675	8389
cj, num, ps 3ms	cj, v Qal impf 3ms	cj, v Qal impf 3ms	*n ms*, art, num	art, num
וַחֲמִשָּׁיו	וַיַּעַל	וַיָּבֹא	שַׂר־הַחֲמִשִּׁים	הַשְּׁלִישִׁי
wachmishshâv	wayya'al	wayyāvō'	sar-hachmishshîm	hashshelîshî
and his fifty	and he went up	and he came	the commander of the fifty	the third

3895.121	6142, 1314	3937, 5224	455	2706.721	420
cj, v Qal impf 3ms	prep, n md, ps 3ms	prep, prep	pn	cj, v Hithpael impf 3ms	prep, ps 3ms
וַיִּכְרַע	עַל־בִּרְכָּיו	לְנֶגֶד	אֵלִיָּהוּ	וַיִּתְחַנֵּן	אֵלָיו
wayyikhra'	'al-birkâv	leneghedh	'ēlîyāhû	wayyithchannēn	'ēlâv
and he kneeled	on his knees	before	Elijah	and he entreated	to him

1744.321	420	382	435	3478.122, 5167	5497	5497
cj, v Piel impf 3ms	prep, ps 3ms	*n ms*	art, n mp	v Qal juss 3fs, part	n fs, ps 1cs	cj, *n fs*
וַיְדַבֵּר	אֵלָיו	אִישׁ	הָאֱלֹהִים	תִּיקַר־נָא	נַפְשִׁי	וְנֶפֶשׁ
waydhabbēr	'ēlâv	'îsh	hā'ĕlōhîm	tîqar-nā'	naphshî	wenephesh
and he spoke	to him	O man of	God	may it be precious	my life	and the life of

5860	431	2675	904, 6084		2079	3495.112	813
n mp, ps 2ms	dem pron	num	prep, n fd, ps 2ms	**14.**	intrj	v Qal pf 3fs	n fs
עֲבָדֶיךָ	אֵלֶּה	חֲמִשִּׁים	בְּעֵינֶיךָ		הִנֵּה	יָרְדָה	אֵשׁ
'ăvādhêkhā	'ēlleh	chămishshîm	be'ênêkhā		hinnēh	yāredhāh	'ēsh
your servants	these	fifty	in your eyes		behold	it has come down	fire

4623, 8452	404.122	881, 8530	8015	2675	7518
prep, art, n md	cj, v Qal impf 3fs	do, num	*n mp*	art, num	art, adj
מִן־הַשָּׁמַיִם	וַתֹּאכַל	אֶת־שְׁנֵי	שָׂרֵי	הַחֲמִשִּׁים	הָרִאשֹׁנִים
min-hashshāmayim	wattō'khal	'eth-shenê	sārê	hachmishshîm	hāri'shōnîm
from the heavens	and it consumed	the two of	the commanders of	the fifty	the first ones

904, 1203B	1203B	435	6376	1950B, 4623, 1136	375, 435	904, 3547
prep, pn	pn	*n mp*	pn	intrg part, prep, neg part	sub, n mp	prep, pn
בְּבַעַל	זְבוּב	אֱלֹהֵי	עֶקְרוֹן	הֲמִבְּלִי	אֵין־אֱלֹהִים	בְּיִשְׂרָאֵל
beva'al	zevûv	'ĕlōhê	'eqrôn	hamibbelî	'ên-'ĕlōhîm	beyisrā'ēl
with Baal	Zebub	the god of	Ekron	is from none	there is no God	in Israel

3937, 1938.141	904, 1745	3937, 3772	4433	866, 6148.113	8427
prep, v Qal inf con	prep, n ms, ps 3ms	prep, adv	art, n fs	rel part, v Qal pf 2ms	adv
לִדְרֹשׁ	בִּדְבָרוֹ	לָכֵן	הַמִּטָּה	אֲשֶׁר־עָלִיתָ	שָׁם
lidhrōsh	bidhvārô	lākhēn	hammiṭṭāh	'ăsher-'ālîthā	shām
to inquire	with his words	therefore	the bed	which you have gone up to	there

881, 2675 cj, do, num, ps 3mp וְאֶת־חֲמִשֵּׁיהֶם we'eth-chămishshêhem and their fifties	6498 cj, adv וְעַתָּה we'attāh but now	3478.122 v Qal juss 3fs תִּיקַר tîqar may it be precious	5497 n fs, ps 1cs נַפְשִׁי naphshî my life	904, 6084 prep, n fd, ps 2ms בְּעֵינֶיךָ be'ênêkhā in your eyes	**15.**	1744.321 cj, v Piel impf 3ms וַיְדַבֵּר waydhabbēr then He spoke

4534 *n ms* מַלְאַךְ mal'akh the Angel of	3176 pn יְהוָה yehwāh Yahweh	420, 455 prep, pn אֶל־אֵלִיָּהוּ 'el-'ēlîyāhû to Elijah	3495.131 v Qal impv 2ms רֵד rēdh go down	882 prep, ps 3ms אוֹתוֹ 'ôthô with him	414, 3486.123 adv, Qal juss 2ms אַל־תִּירָא 'al-tîrā' do not be afraid	4623, 6686 prep, n mp, ps 3ms מִפָּנָיו mippānâv from before him

7251.121 cj, v Qal impf 3ms וַיָּקָם wayyāqām then he rose up	3495.121 cj, v Qal impf 3ms וַיֵּרֶד wayyēredh and he went down	882 prep, ps 3ms אוֹתוֹ 'ôthô with him	420, 4567 prep, art, n ms אֶל־הַמֶּלֶךְ 'el-hammelekh to the king	**16.**	1744.321 cj, v Piel impf 3ms וַיְדַבֵּר waydhabbēr and he spoke	420 prep, ps 3ms אֵלָיו 'ēlâv to him

13. And he sent again a captain of the third fifty with his fifty: ... he sent a third captain with a company of fifty, *Berkeley*.

And the third captain of fifty went up, and came and fell on his knees before Elijah, and besought him: ... captain came and fell down on his knees before Elijah and begged, *NCV* ... and entreated him, *NRSV*.

and said unto him, O man of God, I pray thee, let my life, and the life of these fifty thy servants, be precious in thy sight: ... and have some regard for our lives, *REB* ... please have respect for my life, *NIV* ... be merciful to me and my men. Spare our lives!, *Good News*.

14. Behold, there came fire down from heaven, and burnt up the two captains of the former fifties with their fifties: ... Already fire has come down from heaven, consuming two captains with their companies, *NAB*.

therefore let my life now be precious in thy sight: ... But now, respect my life, *NCV* ... let my life mean something to you!, *NAB* ... so now value my life, *Anchor* ... but now let my life be of value in your eyes, *BB*.

15. And the angel of the LORD said unto Elijah, Go down with him: be not afraid of him. And he arose, and went down with him unto the king: ... fear not for his presence, *Fenton* ... have no fear of him, *BB* ... thou hast nothing to fear. So he set out to accompany the man, *Knox*.

16. And he said unto him, Thus saith the LORD, Forasmuch as thou hast sent messengers to inquire of Baal-zebub the god of Ekron, is it not because there is no God in Israel to inquire of his word?: ... as if there were no god in Israel to consult his word, *Anchor* ... Why did you send messengers to Baal-zebub, the god of Ekron, to ask whether you will get well?, *NLT* ... Is it because there is no God in Israel to ask for His decision?, *Fenton* ... You sent messengers to get help from Baalzebub, *Beck*.

therefore thou shalt not come down off that bed on which thou art gone up, but shalt surely die: ... shalt never leave the bed thou liest on; thou art doomed to die, *Knox* ... will not get well; you will die!, *Good News* ... shalt not come off the bed on which thou art ascended, *Tyndale* ... will never leave the bed you have got into, you are certainly going to die, *JB*.

of Elijah. The prophet often lived in the hills or mountains rather than the cities (cf. 1 Ki. 18; 19:8–18). Elijah's successor, Elisha, was connected not so much with solitude, fire or mountains, as with disciples, water and rivers or springs.

The third commander begged for mercy. Using the same phraseology used by the first two commanders ('îsh hā'ĕlohîm HED #382, 435, "a man of God," i.e., "a true prophet of God") the commander plead, "man of God, please have respect for my life and the lives of these fifty men, your servants" (v. 13). Although the widow of Zarephath used the same phrase ("man of God") for Elijah in 1 Ki. 17:18, 24, the designation is used more frequently of Elijah's successor, Elisha. In the present narrative, Elijah has already risen to the challenge twice, but this third time he refrains. Instead he follows the bidding of the "angel of Yahweh" for the second time in the chapter (cf. v. 3), and he implicitly gives the commander what he has asked for, i.e., the sparing of his life. Surely, Yahweh could also have spared the life of King Ahaziah as well, if only the king had shown half as much faith and boldness as this military commander. The contrast of life spared and death confirmed characterizes these and the next several verses of the present chapter.

3662, 569.111	3176	3391	866, 8365.113	4534	3937, 1938.141
adv, v Qal pf 3ms	pn	cj	rel part, v Qal pf 2ms	n mp	prep, v Qal inf con
כֹּה־אָמַר	יְהוָה	יַעַן	אֲשֶׁר־שָׁלַחְתָּ	מַלְאָכִים	לִדְרֹשׁ
kōh-'āmar	yehwāh	ya'an	'ăsher-shālachtā	mal'ākhîm	lidhrōsh
thus He has said	Yahweh	on account of	that you have sent out	messengers	to inquire

904, 1203B	1203B	435	6376	1950B, 4623, 1136	375, 435	904, 3547
prep, pn	pn	*n mp*	pn	intrg part, prep, neg part	sub, n mp	prep, pn
בְּבַעַל	זְבוּב	אֱלֹהֵי	עֶקְרוֹן	הֲמִבְּלִי	אֵין־אֱלֹהִים	בְּיִשְׂרָאֵל
beva'al	zevûv	'ĕlōhê	'eqrôn	hamibbelî	'ên-'ĕlōhîm	beyisrā'ēl
with Baal	Zebub	the god of	Ekron	is from none	there is no God	in Israel

3937, 1938.141	904, 1745	3937, 3772	4433	866, 6148.113	8427
prep, v Qal inf con	prep, n ms, ps 3ms	prep, adv	art, n fs	rel part, v Qal pf 2ms	adv
לִדְרֹשׁ	בִּדְבָרוֹ	לָכֵן	הַמִּטָּה	אֲשֶׁר־עָלִיתָ	שָׁם
lidherōsh	bidhevārô	lākhēn	hammiṭṭāh	'ăsher-'ālîthā	shām
to inquire	with his word	therefore	the bed	which you have gone up to	there

3940, 3495.123	4623	3706, 4322.142	4322.123		4322.121
neg part, v Qal impf 2ms	prep, ps 3fs	cj, v Qal inf abs	v Qal impf 2ms	**17.**	cj, v Qal impf 3ms
לֹא־תֵרֵד	מִמֶּנָּה	כִּי־מוֹת	תָּמוּת		וַיָּמָת
lō'-thērēdh	mimmennāh	kî-môth	tāmûth		wayyāmāth
you will not come down	from it	rather dying	you will certainly die		then he died

3626, 1745	3176	866, 1744.311	455	4566.121	3190
prep, *n ms*	pn	rel part, v Piel pf 3ms	pn	cj, v Qal impf 3ms	pn
כִּדְבַר	יְהוָה	אֲשֶׁר־דִּבֶּר	אֵלִיָּהוּ	וַיִּמְלֹךְ	יְהוֹרָם
kidhvar	yehwāh	'ăsher-dibber	'ēlîyāhû	wayyimlōkh	yehôrām
according to the word of	Yahweh	that he had spoken	Elijah	and he reigned	Jehoram

8809	904, 8523	8692	3937, 3190	1158, 3194	4567	3171
prep, ps 3ms	prep, *n fs*	num	prep, pn	*n ms*, pn	*n ms*	pn
תַּחְתָּיו	בִּשְׁנַת	שְׁתַּיִם	לִיהוֹרָם	בֶּן־יְהוֹשָׁפָט	מֶלֶךְ	יְהוּדָה
tachtâv	bishnath	shettayim	lîhôrām	ben-yehôshāphāṭ	melekh	yehûdhāh
instead of him	in the year of	two	of Jehoram	the son of Jehoshaphat	the king of	Judah

3706	3940, 2030.111	3937	1158		3615	1745	275
cj	neg part, v Qal pf 3ms	prep, ps 3ms	n ms	**18.**	cj, *n ms*	*n mp*	pn
כִּי	לֹא־הָיָה	לוֹ	בֵּן		וְיֶתֶר	דִּבְרֵי	אֲחַזְיָהוּ
kî	lō'-hāyāh	lô	bēn		weyether	divrê	'ăchazyāhû
because	he was not	to him	a son		and the remainder of	the deeds of	Ahaziah

866	6449.111	1950B, 3940, 2065	3918.156	6142, 5809	1745	3219
rel part	v Qal pf 3ms	intrg part, neg part, pers pron	v Qal pass ptc mp	prep, *n ms*	*n mp*	art, n mp
אֲשֶׁר	עָשָׂה	הֲלוֹא־הֵמָּה	כְּתוּבִים	עַל־סֵפֶר	דִּבְרֵי	הַיָּמִים
'ăsher	'āsāh	hălô'-hēmmāh	khethûvîm	'al-sēpher	divrê	hayyāmîm
which	he did	are they not	things written	on the scroll of	the events of	the days

3937, 4567	3547		2030.121	904, 6148.541	3176	881, 455
prep, *n mp*	pn	**2:1**	cj, v Qal impf 3ms	prep, v Hiphil inf con	pn	do, pn
לְמַלְכֵי	יִשְׂרָאֵל		וַיְהִי	בְּהַעֲלוֹת	יְהוָה	אֶת־אֵלִיָּהוּ
lemalkhê	yisrā'ēl		wayhî	beha'ălôth	yehwāh	'eth-'ēlîyāhû
of the kings of	Israel		and it was	when causing to go up	Yahweh	Elijah

904, 5788	8452	2050.121	455	482	4623, 1577
prep, art, n fs	art, n md	v Qal impf 3ms	pn	cj, pn	prep, art, pn
בַּסְעָרָה	הַשָּׁמָיִם	וַיֵּלֶךְ	אֵלִיָּהוּ	וֶאֱלִישָׁע	מִן־הַגִּלְגָּל
bas'ārāh	hashshāmāyim	wayyēlekh	'ēlîyāhû	we'ĕlîshā'	min-haggilgāl
in the whirlwind	the heavens	and he walked	Elijah	and Elisha	from Gilgal

2.

569.121	455	420, 482	3553.131, 5167	6553	3706	3176
cj, v Qal impf 3ms	pn	prep, pn	v Qal impv 2ms, part	adv	cj	pn
וַיֹּאמֶר	אֵלִיָּהוּ	אֶל־אֱלִישָׁע	שֵׁב־נָא	פֹה	כִּי	יְהוָה
wayyō'mer	'ēlîyāhû	'el-'ĕlîshā'	shēv-nā'	phōh	kî	yehwāh
and he said	Elijah	to Elisha	stay please	here	because	Yahweh

8365.111	5912, 1044	569.121	482	2508, 3176	2508, 5497
v Qal pf 3ms, ps 1cs	prep, pn	cj, v Qal impf 3ms	pn	adj, pn	cj, adj, n fs, ps 2ms
שְׁלָחַנִי	עַד־בֵּית־אֵל	וַיֹּאמֶר	אֱלִישָׁע	חַי־יְהוָה	וְחֵי־נַפְשְׁךָ
shelāchanî	'adh-bêth-'ēl	wayyō'mer	'ĕlîshā'	chay-yehwāh	wechê-naphshekhā
He has sent me	unto Bethel	but he said	Elisha	Yahweh living	and your life living

17. So he died according to the word of the Lord which Elijah had spoken: ... The word of the LORD which Elijah had spoken was fulfilled, and Ahaziah died, *NEB* ... And die he did, exactly as the Eternal had predicted by means of Elijah, *Moffatt*.

And Jehoram reigned in his stead in the second year of Jehoram the son of Jehoshaphat king of Judah; because he had no son: ... And Jehoram became king in his place, *BB* ... so his brother Joram succeeded him as king, *Good News* ... Joram ruled because Ahaziah had no son to take his place, *NCV*.

18. Now the rest of the acts of Ahaziah which he did: ... As for all the other events of Ahaziah's reign, *NIV* ... The rest of the deeds of Ohoziah which he did, *Tyndale* ... Now the rest of the story of Ahaziah the things that he did, *Rotherham* ... Isn't everything else about Ahaziah, what he did, *Beck*.

are they not written in the book of the chronicles of the kings of Israel?: ... are indeed recorded in the annals of the kings of Israel, *Anchor* ... are they not written in the book of the words of the days of the kings of Israel?, *Douay* ... are recorded in The Book of the History of the Kings of Israel, *NLT* ... are written in the history of events of the period of the king of Israel, *Fenton*.

2:1. And it came to pass, when the LORD would take up Elijah into heaven by a whirlwind: ... when Yahweh was about to take up Elijah in a storm into the heavens, *Rotherham* ... Now when the Lord was about to take Elijah up to heaven in a great wind, *BB*.

that Elijah went with Elisha from Gilgal: ... Elijah and Elisha were traveling from Gilgal, *NLT* ... Elijah and Elisha were on their way from Gilgal, *NIV*.

1:16–17a. The king was reminded once again, this time by a personal visit of the prophet, that impending death would still be his fate. How powerless the Israelite and Judahite kings remained in the presence of the prophets of Yahweh! Whether it be King David before Nathan the prophet (2 Sam. 12) or before Gad the seer (ch. 24); or, even more vividly, King Jeroboam I before the unnamed "man of God" of 1 Ki. 13; or King Ahab's unpleasant encounters with Elijah (1 Ki. 18; 20) or with Micaiah (ch. 22), the king stands helpless before the spokesman. What the prophets announce inevitably occurs, and what miracles they perform cannot be stopped or reversed, except at their bidding.

Especially in the area of the institution of holy war, where everything captured must be put "under the ban" (chērem [HED #2869]; see Josh. 6:11–20); the king was specifically required to wait upon the divine oracle for permission to proceed. This, for example, was probably the nature of Saul's sin in 1 Sam. 13:7–14. The voluntary militia was scattering, and Samuel the prophet was delayed in arriving; so Saul proceeded to offer up the burnt offering necessary to initiate combat against the Philistines, without the divine oracle only the prophet could give. It is therefore no surprise to read repeatedly of Israelite and Judahite monarchs powerless before their prophetic counterparts.

1:17b–18. These verses represent characteristic summaries which serve to bring the present discussion of the reign of King Ahaziah to a close. The succession notice of v. 17 includes a characteristic chronological synchronism with the reign of the current king of the other kingdom of God's people. The chronological issues surrounding a number of the kings of the divided monarchy of Israel are difficult, but not unresolvable, as recent scholars have demonstrated (see *Encyclopedia of Bible Difficulties* by Gleason Archer, in particular). A number of scholars enjoy discussing and reevaluating these issues from time to time.

In v. 18, we find a "further reference" notice—such notices are often to be found at the conclusion of the discussions of both the Israelite and the Judahite kings.

524, 6013.125	3495.126	1044		3428.126	1158, 5204
cj, v Qal impf 1cs, ps 2ms	cj, v Qal impf 3mp	pn	3.	cj, v Qal impf 3mp	n mp, art, n mp
אִם־אֶעֶזְבֶךָּ	וַיֵּרְדוּ	בֵּית־אֵל		וַיֵּצְאוּ	בְנֵי־הַנְּבִיאִים
'im-'e'ezvekkā	wayyēredhû	bêth-'ēl		wayyētse'û	venê-hannevî'îm
if I abandon you	so they went down to	Bethel		and they came out	the sons of the prophets

866, 1044	420, 482	569.126	420	1950B, 3156.113	3706	3219
rel pron, pn	prep, pn	cj, v Qal impf 3mp	prep, ps 3ms	intrg part, v Qal pf 2ms	cj	art, n ms
אֲשֶׁר־בֵּית־אֵל	אֶל־אֱלִישָׁע	וַיֹּאמְרוּ	אֵלָיו	הֲיָדַעְתָּ	כִּי	הַיּוֹם
'ăsher-bêth-'ēl	'el-'ĕlîshā'	wayyō'merû	'ēlâv	hăyādha'ăttā	kî	hayyôm
who Bethel	to Elisha	and they said	to him	do you know	that	today

3176	4089.151	881, 112	4623, 6142	7513	569.121	1612, 603
pn	v Qal act ptc ms	do, n mp, ps 2ms	prep, prep	n ms, ps 2ms	cj, v Qal impf 3ms	cj, pers pron
יְהוָה	לֹקֵחַ	אֶת־אֲדֹנֶיךָ	מֵעַל	רֹאשֶׁךָ	וַיֹּאמֶר	גַּם־אֲנִי
yehwāh	lōqēach	'eth-'ădhōnêkhā	mē'al	rō'shekhā	wayyō'mer	gam-'ănî
Yahweh	taking	your master	from over	your head	and he said	also I

3156.115	2924.533		569.121	3937	455	482	3553.131, 5167
v Qal pf 1cs	v Hiphil impv 2mp	4.	cj, v Qal impf 3ms	prep, ps 3ms	pn	pn	v Qal impv 2ms, part
יָדַעְתִּי	הֶחֱשׁוּ		וַיֹּאמֶר	לוֹ	אֵלִיָּהוּ	אֱלִישָׁע	שֵׁב־נָא
yādha'ăttî	hechěshû		wayyō'mer	lô	'ēlîyāhû	'ĕlîshā'	shēv-nā'
I know	be silent		and he said	to him	Elijah	Elisha	stay please

6553	3706	3176	8365.111	3509	569.121	2508, 3176
adv	cj	pn	v Qal pf 3ms, ps 1cs	pn	cj, v Qal impf 3ms	adj, pn
פֹּה	כִּי	יְהוָה	שְׁלָחַנִי	יְרִיחוֹ	וַיֹּאמֶר	חַי־יְהוָה
phōh	kî	yehwāh	shelāchanî	yerîchô	wayyō'mer	chay-yehwāh
here	because	Yahweh	He has sent me to	Jericho	but he said	Yahweh living

2508, 5497	524, 6013.125	971.126	3509		5242.126
cj, adj, n fs, ps 2ms	cj, v Qal impf 1cs, ps 2ms	cj, v Qal impf 3mp	pn	5.	cj, v Qal impf 3mp
וְחֵי־נַפְשְׁךָ	אִם־אֶעֶזְבֶךָּ	וַיָּבֹאוּ	יְרִיחוֹ		וַיִּגְּשׁוּ
wechê-naphshkhā	'im-'e'ezvekkā	wayyāvō'û	yerîchô		wayyiggeshû
and your life living	if I abandon you	so they came to	Jericho		and they drew near

2. And Elijah said unto Elisha, Tarry here, I pray thee; for the Lord hath sent me to Beth-el: ... the Lord has an errand for me at Bethel, *Knox* ... The Lord has told me to go to Bethel, *NCV* ... You stay here, for Yahweh is only sending me to Bethel, *JB* ... for the Lord has sent me as far as Bethel, *NASB*.

And Elisha said unto him, As the Lord liveth, and as thy soul liveth, I will not leave thee: ... and as you yourself are alive, I will not leave you, *Goodspeed* ... I swear by my loyalty to the living Lord and to you that I will not leave you, *Good News* ... As the Lord lives, your life upon it, *NEB*.

So they went down to Beth-el: ... went down country to Bethel, *REB* ... descended to Bethel, *Fenton*.

3. And the sons of the prophets that were at Beth-el came forth to Elisha, and said unto him: ... And the children of the Prophets that were at Bethel, *Geneva* ... where the guild prophets went out to Elisha, *NAB*.

Knowest thou that the Lord will take away thy master from thy head today?: ... Do you know that today the Lord will take away your master from over you?, *RSV* ... Dost thou know that this day the Lord will take away thy master from thee?, *Douay* ... Has it been made clear to you that the Lord is going to take away your master, *BB* ... is taking thy lord from thy head?, *Young*.

And he said, Yea, I know it; hold ye your peace: ... I know it, he said, be still, *Berkeley* ... Yes, I know, he answered, Be silent, *Beck* ... Yes, he answered, only hold your tongues, *Moffatt* ... but do not speak of it, *NIV*.

4. And Elijah said unto him, Elisha, tarry here, I pray thee; for the Lord hath sent me to Jericho: ... Stay here, for the Lord has told me to go to Jericho, *NLT* ... the Lord has ordered me to go to Jericho, *Good News*.

And he said, As the Lord liveth, and as thy soul liveth, I will not leave thee: ... As surely as the Lord lives and as you live, I will not leave you, *NIV* ... I will not be parted from you, *BB* ... As the Lord lives, your life upon it, *NEB*.

So they came to Jericho: ... went on to Jeriko, *Fenton* ... And when they were come to Jericho, *Douay*.

As we know from the Torah, our God is a jealous (or zealous) God. He will tolerate no rivals. As Exo. 34:14 puts it: "Do not worship any other god, for Yahweh, whose name is Jealous, is a jealous God" (cf. Exo. 20:5; Deut. 4:24; 5:9; 6:15). As a jealous husband will not allow his wife to consort with other men, Yahweh will not allow his "wife," Israel, to consort with other gods (of course, in reality there are no other gods, but many in Israel for so long seemed to think otherwise). God's jealousy cannot tolerate shared allegiance. In the present passage, Yahweh cannot tolerate King Ahaziah of Israel consulting any other god, or alleged god, for healing: "Is it because there is no God in Israel for you to consult that you have sent messengers …?" (1 Ki. 1:16; cf. vv. 3, 6). The gods of Israel's neighbors would completely corrupt Yahweh's people until they did not worship Him at all. So it was shortly after the time of Joshua; so it was in the day of Ahaziah; so it is today. Yahweh is the dynamic God, who will act on his own initiative, whether or not we ask, or even wish him to. Sometimes in our weakness we may wish for a God who loves us less, but we have no choice in the matter. God will not ignore wrongdoing or casual flirtations with false providers of security and direction. Our God is a jealous God.

2:1–18. *Elijah taken up into heaven; Elisha takes his place. The focus of interpreters of these verses has traditionally, and quite understandably, been on Elijah's ascension into heaven on a chariot of fire. But the passage also serves to introduce Elisha as indeed receiving the "double portion" of Elijah's spirit, and being entirely worthy to be Elijah's prophetic successor. This most memorable passage is as much about Elisha as it is about Elijah. The present passage consists of an account about Elisha's threefold refusal to abandon his master Elijah (vv. 1–6), which leads directly into an account about the twice-repeated miracle of the dividing of the Jordan (vv. 7–14; these verses in turn bracket Elijah's unique translation into heaven via the chariots of fire), as well as the concluding account of the fifty-man company of prophets who wished to look for Elijah's body (vv. 15–18). The passage clearly focuses more on the apprentice Elisha than it does on the great master Elijah. Note also the repeated references in the present passage to "fifty men of the company of the prophets" in vv. 7, 17. Elijah is once again connected with fire from heaven (v. 11), as he had been in 1 Ki. 18:38 and in 2 Ki. 1:10, 12. Finally, the Elijah accounts tend to emphasize his aloneness as a prophet of the true God Yahweh (not only in his solo confrontation against the Baal prophets in 1 Ki. 18:18ff, but also in his solitary complaint to Yahweh in 19:10, 14). Once again, Elijah seemingly wishes to be left alone in vv. 2, 4, and 6 of the present passage. But the apprentice Elisha this time gets the upper hand. His stubborn persistence carries the day, and Elijah's translation to heaven has therefore both a reliable witness and a proper mourner (v. 12).*

2:1–6. Elijah insists on accompanying Elijah to the Jordan. As commentators often point out, the sequence Gilgal-Bethel-Jericho-Jordan represents a zig-zag route up and down some rugged hills, if one assumes the traditional geographical locations for each site. There is no reason to question the location of Jericho or, of course, the Jordan River (although the precise location of the crossing of this river remains uncertain). But some have questioned the traditional identifications of the "Bethel," and especially, the "Gilgal" of the present text. The place named "Bethel," which in Hebrew means "the house of El [God, HED #418]," is potentially the name for several different sanctuaries in the land of Israel, even though most scholars would link the present "Bethel" reference with the well-known town on the central spine of Israel, north of Jerusalem and south of the hill country of Ephraim. After Jerusalem, Bethel is the second most common place name found in the OT, and its location (Tell Beitin) is strategically significant, since the major north-south road from Hebron, through Jerusalem, and up to Shechem passes through it, and a significant east-west road leading up from Mediterranean coast to the west, and then down to Jericho and the Jordan valley to the east passes just south of it (cf. Harold Brodsky, *Anchor Bible Dictionary*, 1:710–11). The precise location of "Gilgal" of the present passage is less certain, however. Whether it be the famous site of Joshua's first encampment in the valley west of the Jordan River (Josh. 4:19f; cf. 5:9f; 9:6; etc.) or possibly another site (present day Juljulieh) in the hills near Bethel and Shechem (cf. Wade R. Kotter, *Anchor Bible Dictionary*, 2:1023; also, Cogan and Tadmor, AB, 31), scholars remain divided (one compelling argument for the site in the hills is the verb "to go down" [yāradh, HED #3495] used in reference to Bethel in v. 2 of the present passage).

In any case, what matters more than geography is the overall theology of these verses—and that theology surely includes the major theme of godly persistence. The mark of a true disciple is persistence.

1158, 5204	866, 904, 3509	420, 482	569.126	420
n mp, art, n mp	rel pron, prep, pn	prep, pn	cj, v Qal impf 3mp	prep, ps 3ms
בְּנֵי־הַנְּבִיאִים	אֲשֶׁר־בִּירִיחוֹ	אֶל־אֱלִישָׁע	וַיֹּאמְרוּ	אֵלָיו
venê-hannevî'îm	'ăsher-bîrîchô	'el-'ĕlîshā'	wayyō'merû	'ēlâv
the sons of the prophets	who in Jericho	to Elisha	and they said	to him

1950B, 3156.113	3706	3219	3176	4089.151	881, 112	4623, 6142	7513
intrg part, v Qal pf 2ms	cj	art, n ms	pn	v Qal act ptc ms	do, n mp, ps 2ms	prep, prep	n ms, ps 2ms
הֲיָדַעְתָּ	כִּי	הַיּוֹם	יְהוָה	לֹקֵחַ	אֶת־אֲדֹנֶיךָ	מֵעַל	רֹאשֶׁךָ
hăyādha'ättā	kî	hayyôm	yehwāh	lōqēach	'eth-'ădhōnêkhā	mē'al	rō'shekhā
do you know	that	today	Yahweh	taking	your master	from over	your head

569.121	1612, 603	3156.115	2924.533	6.	569.121	3937	455
cj, v Qal impf 3ms	cj, pers pron	v Qal pf 1cs	v Hiphil impv 2mp		cj, v Qal impf 3ms	prep, ps 3ms	pn
וַיֹּאמֶר	גַּם־אֲנִי	יָדַעְתִּי	הֶחֱשׁוּ		וַיֹּאמֶר	לוֹ	אֵלִיָּהוּ
wayyō'mer	gam-'ănî	yādha'ättî	hechěshû		wayyō'mer	lô	'ēlîyāhû
and he said	also I	I know	be silent		and he said	to him	Elijah

3553.131, 5167	6553	3706	3176	8365.111	3497	569.121
v Qal impv 2ms, part	adv	cj	pn	v Qal pf 3ms, ps 1cs	art, pn	cj, v Qal impf 3ms
שֵׁב־נָא	פֹה	כִּי	יְהוָה	שְׁלָחַנִי	הַיַּרְדֵּנָה	וַיֹּאמֶר
shēv-nā'	phōh	kî	yehwāh	shelāchanî	hayyardēnāh	wayyō'mer
stay please	here	because	Yahweh	He has sent me	to the Jordan	but he said

2508, 3176	2508, 5497	524, 6013.125	2050.126	8530
adj, pn	cj, adj, n fs, ps 2ms	cj, v Qal impf 1cs, ps 2ms	cj, v Qal impf 3mp	num, ps 3mp
חַי־יְהוָה	וְחֵי־נַפְשְׁךָ	אִם־אֶעֶזְבֶךָּ	וַיֵּלְכוּ	שְׁנֵיהֶם
chay-yehwāh	wechê-naphshekhā	'im-'e'ezvekkā	wayyēlekhû	shenêhem
Yahweh living	and your life living	if I abandon you	so they walked	the two of them

7.	2675	382	4623, 1158	5204	2050.116	6198.126	4623, 5224
	cj, num	n ms	prep, *n mp*	art, n mp	v Qal pf 3cp	cj, v Qal impf 3mp	prep, prep
	וַחֲמִשִּׁים	אִישׁ	מִבְּנֵי	הַנְּבִיאִים	הָלְכוּ	וַיַּעַמְדוּ	מִנֶּגֶד
	wachmishshîm	'îsh	mibbenê	hannevî'îm	hālekhû	wayya'amdhû	minneghedh
	and fifty	men	from the sons of	the prophets	they went	and they stood	from before

4623, 7632	8530	6198.116	6142, 3497	8.	4089.121	455
prep, adv	cj, num, ps 3mp	v Qal pf 3cp	prep, art, pn		cj, v Qal impf 3ms	pn
מֵרָחוֹק	וּשְׁנֵיהֶם	עָמְדוּ	עַל־הַיַּרְדֵּן		וַיִּקַּח	אֵלִיָּהוּ
mērāchôq	ûshenêhem	'āmedhû	'al-hayyardēn		wayyiqqach	'ēlîyāhû
from far away	and the two of them	they stood	beside the Jordan		and he took	Elijah

881, 152	1604.121	5409.521	881, 4448	2779.226	2077
do, n fs, ps 3ms	cj, v Qal impf 3ms	cj, v Hiphil impf 3ms	do, art, n md	cj, v Niphal impf 3mp	adv
אֶת־אַדַּרְתּוֹ	וַיִּגְלֹם	וַיַּכֶּה	אֶת־הַמַּיִם	וַיֵּחָצוּ	הֵנָּה
'eth-'addartô	wayyighlōm	wayyakkeh	'eth-hammayim	wayyēchātsû	hēnnāh
his mantle	and he rolled up	and he struck	the water	and they divided	here

2077	5882.126	8530	904, 2824	9.	2030.121
cj, adv	cj, v Qal impf 3mp	num, ps 3mp	prep, art, n fs		cj, v Qal impf 3ms
וָהֵנָּה	וַיַּעַבְרוּ	שְׁנֵיהֶם	בֶּחָרָבָה		וַיְהִי
wāhēnnāh	wayya'avrû	shenêhem	bechārāvāh		wayhî
and there	and they passed over	the two of them	on the dry land		and it was

3626, 5882.141	455	569.111	420, 482	8068.131	4242
prep, v Qal inf con, ps 3mp	cj, pn	v Qal pf 3ms	prep, pn	v Qal impv 2ms	intrg
כְעָבְרָם	וְאֵלִיָּהוּ	אָמַר	אֶל־אֱלִישָׁע	שְׁאַל	מָה
khe'āverām	we'ēlîyāhû	'āmar	'el-'ĕlîshā'	she'al	māh
when their passing over	then Elijah	he said	to Elisha	ask	what

5. And the sons of the prophets that were at Jericho came to Elisha, and said unto him: ... The brotherhood of prophets living at Jericho went up to Elisha, *JB* ... the children of the prophets that were at Jericho, *Tyndale* ... the members of the prophetic order who were in Jericho approached Elisha, *Goodspeed*.

Knowest thou that the LORD will take away thy master from thy head today?: ... the LORD is going to take your lord and master from you today?, *REB* ... the LORD will take away your master from over you today?, *NASB* ... Has it been made clear to you that the Lord is going to take away your master, *BB*.

And he answered, Yea, I know it; hold ye your peace: ... I, too, know it, he answered; say no more, *Knox* ... Yes, I know, but don't talk about it, *NCV* ... Quiet!, he answered again. Of course I know it, *NLT* ... Yes, I know; be silent, *NRSV*.

6. And Elijah said unto him, Tarry, I pray thee, here; for the LORD hath sent me to Jordan: ... Come no farther, *BB* ... Remain here, I pray you, *Goodspeed* ... for the Eternal sends me to the Jordan, *Moffatt*.

And he said, As the LORD liveth, and as thy soul liveth, I will not leave thee. And they two went on: ... As the LORD lives, your life upon it, *NEB* ... I swear by my loyalty to the living LORD and to you, *Good News*.

7. And fifty men of the sons of the prophets went, and stood to view afar off: and they two stood by Jordan: ... stood facing them at a distance, *NKJV* ... to look from a distance, *KJVII* ... Fifty of the guild prophets followed, *NAB* ... of the company of prophets, *NRSV* ... from the group of prophets also went, *NLT*.

8. And Elijah took his mantle, and wrapped it together, and smote the waters: ... took off his robe, and, rolling it up, gave the water a blow with it, *BB*.

and they were divided hither and thither, so that they two went over on dry ground: ... water divided to right and left, *NEB* ... the water was parted to the one side and to the other, *RSV* ... The river divided, *NLT*.

9. And it came to pass, when they were gone over, that Elijah said unto Elisha, Ask what I shall do for thee, before I be taken away from thee: ... what can I do for you before I am taken from you?, *NIV*.

And Elisha said, I pray thee, let a double portion of thy spirit be upon me: ... let a special measure of your spirit be on me, *BB* ... let me inherit a double share of your spirit, *NRSV* ... Let there be now a twofold share of your spirit, *Goodspeed* ... let me become your rightful successor, *NLT* ... Let me fall heir to your spirit, *Moffatt*.

Twice (vv. 3, 5) the passage indicates that a company of prophets could discern the future. Twice they gave the "short-term predictions" ("do you know that Yahweh is going to take your master from you today?") which were so essential for authentication of their prophetic call (cf. the comments on 1:3–4). But Elisha alone could discern prophetically the deeper will of his master Elijah (or, even more importantly, the will of his master's God). Three times (vv. 2, 4, and 6), Elisha alone refused to obey the command of his mentor, and all three times there is a strong oath formula attached to Elisha's refusal to obey. The Hebrew phrase underlying "as surely as Yahweh lives, and as you live" forcefully connects the lives of Yahweh, Elisha and Elijah, life being one of the most valuable commodities one could possess. The noted Assyriologist, Donald J. Wiseman, in his Kings commentary (*1 & 2 Kings*, *Tyndale Old Testament Commentary*, 195), notes the likelihood of what we find in the present passage, i.e., "a test of Elisha's faithfulness." Wiseman also notes the NT echoes in Mark 14:29 (Peter's eagerness to remain Christ's disciple, even if all others leave Him—note the reference in the very next verse that Peter will disown his Master three times) and in Matt. 26:38–45 (a threefold admonition to Jesus' disciples to remain alert and faithful). Add to this list the memorable passage in John 21:15–23, with its threefold question that the risen Christ addressed to Peter, "Do you truly love me? ... then feed my sheep. ..." The human master often has reason to question the fundamental loyalty and the faithfulness of his or her disciple—how much more our Savior and our Lord.

2:7–8. Elijah's Moses-like miracle. As is commonly noted, Elijah is often depicted as a Moses figure, and Elisha a Joshua figure (cf. vv. 9f). This is clearly the case here. Elijah divided the waters of the Jordan River, as Moses did the Red (or Reed) Sea (Exo. 14–15), in the sight of the fifty-man company of the prophets "standing at a distance." But, more importantly, this took place in the immediate presence of his stubborn apprentice, Elisha, as well: "The two of them crossed over on dry ground" (v. 8). In the NT, Moses and Elijah are linked together as OT prophets par excellence in the Transfiguration of Christ (cf. Matt. 17:3; Mark 9:4; Luke 9:30f; cf. also Mal. 4:4f for a future prediction of the coming of the Lord, including references to Moses and Elijah in successive verses). Seemingly only Elijah was expected to cross the Jordan on dry ground, but due to the appren-

6449.125, 3937	904, 3071	4089.225	4623, 6196	569.121	482
v Qal impf 1cs, prep, ps 2ms	prep, adv	v Niphal impf 1cs	prep, prep, ps 2ms	cj, v Qal impf 3ms	pn
אֶעֱשֶׂה־לָּךְ	בְּטֶרֶם	אֶלָּקַח	מֵעִמָּךְ	וַיֹּאמֶר	אֱלִישָׁע
'e'ĕseh-lākh	beterem	'ellāqach	mē'immākh	wayyō'mer	'ělîshā'
will I do for you	before	I am taken	from with you	and he said	Elisha

2030.121, 5167	6552, 8530	904, 7593	420		569.121
cj, v Qal juss 3ms, part	*n ms*, num	prep, n fs, ps 2ms	prep, ps 1cs	**10.**	cj, v Qal impf 3ms
וִיהִי־נָא	פִּי־שְׁנַיִם	בְּרוּחֲךָ	אֵלָי		וַיֹּאמֶר
wîhî-nā'	pî-shenayim	berûchăkhā	'ēlāy		wayyō'mer
may it be please	a measure of two	with your spirit	to me		and he said

7481.513	3937, 8068.141	524, 7495.123	881	4089.411	4623, 882
v Hiphil pf 2ms	prep, v Qal inf con	cj, v Qal impf 2ms	do, ps 1cs	v Pual pf 3ms	prep, prep, ps 2fs
הִקְשִׁיתָ	לִשְׁאוֹל	אִם־תִּרְאֶה	אֹתִי	לֻקָּח	מֵאִתָּךְ
hiqŏshîthā	lish'ôl	'im-tir'eh	'ōthî	luqqāch	mē'ittākh
you have made difficult	to ask	if you see	me	it has been taken	from with you

2030.121, 3937	3772	524, 375	3940	2030.121		2030.121	2065
v Qal juss 3ms, prep, ps 2ms	adv	cj, cj, sub	neg part	v Qal impf 3ms	**11.**	cj, v Qal impf 3ms	pers pron
יְהִי־לְךָ	כֵן	וְאִם־אַיִן	לֹא	יִהְיֶה		וַיְהִי	הֵמָּה
yehî-lekhā	khēn	we'im-'ayin	lō'	yihyeh		wayhî	hēmmāh
may it be to you	so	but if it is not	not	it must be		and it was	they

2050.152	2050.142	1744.342	2079	7681, 813	5670	813
v Qal act ptc mp	v Qal inf abs	cj, v Piel inf abs	cj, intrj	*n ms*, n fs	cj, *n mp*	n fs
הֹלְכִים	הָלוֹךְ	וְדַבֵּר	וְהִנֵּה	רֶכֶב־אֵשׁ	וְסוּסֵי	אֵשׁ
hōlekhîm	hālōkh	wedhabbēr	wehinnēh	rekhev-'ēsh	wesûsê	'ēsh
walking	continuing	and speaking	and behold	a chariot of fire	and horses of	fire

6754.526	1033	8530	6148.121	455	904, 5788
cj, v Hiphil impf 3mp	prep	num, ps 3mp	cj, v Qal impf 3ms	pn	prep, art, n fs
וַיַּפְרִדוּ	בֵּין	שְׁנֵיהֶם	וַיַּעַל	אֵלִיָּהוּ	בַּסְעָרָה
wayyaphridhû	bên	shenêhem	wayya'al	'ēlîyāhû	bas'ārāh
and they separated	between	the two of them	and he went up	Elijah	in the whirlwind

8452		482	7495.151	2000	7094.351	1	1
art, n md	**12.**	cj, pn	v Qal act ptc ms	cj, pers pron	v Piel ptc ms	n ms, ps 1cs	n ms, ps 1cs
הַשָּׁמָיִם		וֶאֱלִישָׁע	רֹאֶה	וְהוּא	מְצַעֵק	אָבִי	אָבִי
hashshāmāyim		we'ělîshā'	rō'eh	wehû'	metsa'ēq	'āvî	'āvî
the heavens		and Elisha	seeing	and he	crying out	O my father	O my father

7681	3547	6821	3940	7495.111	5968	2480.521
n ms	pn	cj, n mp, ps 3ms	cj, neg part	v Qal pf 3ms, ps 3ms	adv	cj, v Hiphil impf 3ms
רֶכֶב	יִשְׂרָאֵל	וּפָרָשָׁיו	וְלֹא	רָאָהוּ	עוֹד	וַיַּחֲזֵק
rekhev	yisrā'ēl	ûphārāshâv	welō'	rā'āhû	'ôdh	wayyachzēq
the chariots of	Israel	and their horsemen	then not	he saw him	anymore	and he took hold

904, 933	7458.121	3937, 8530	7459		7597.521	881, 152
prep, n mp, ps 3ms	cj, v Qal impf 3ms, ps 3mp	prep, num	n mp	**13.**	cj, v Hiphil impf 3ms	do, *n fs*
בִּבְגָדָיו	וַיִּקְרָעֵם	לִשְׁנַיִם	קְרָעִים		וַיָּרֶם	אֶת־אַדֶּרֶת
bivghādhâv	wayyiqŏrā'ēm	lishnayim	qŏrā'îm		wayyārem	'eth-'addereth
on his garments	and he tore them	into two	pieces		and he lifted up	the mantle of

455	866	5489.112	4623, 6142	8178.121	6198.121	6142, 8004
pn	rel part	v Qal pf 3fs	prep, prep, ps 3ms	cj, v Qal impf 3ms	cj, v Qal impf 3ms	prep, *n fs*
אֵלִיָּהוּ	אֲשֶׁר	נָפְלָה	מֵעָלָיו	וַיָּשָׁב	וַיַּעֲמֹד	עַל־שְׂפַת
'ēlîyāhû	'ăsher	nāphelāh	mē'ālâv	wayyāshāv	wayya'ămōdh	'al-sephath
Elijah	which	it had fallen	from on him	then he returned	and he stood	on the shore of

10. And he said, Thou hast asked a hard thing: ... That is a difficult request to grant, *Good News* ... It is no light request thou hast made, *Knox*.

nevertheless, if thou see me when I am taken from thee, it shall be so unto thee; but if not, it shall not be so: ... may your wish be granted, *NEB* ... If you see me taken from you, then it will come to you, *Fenton* ... while I am being snatched away from you, *JB*.

11. And it came to pass, as they still went on, and talked, that, behold, there appeared a chariot of fire, and horses of fire, and parted them both asunder: ... a flaming chariot appeared, drawn by flaming horses, *Knox* ... a chariot of fire with horses of fire drove between them, *Moffatt* ... suddenly a chariot of fire appeared, drawn by horses of fire, *NLT* ... behold a fiery chariot and fiery horses parted them both asunder, *Douay*.

and Elijah went up by a whirlwind into heaven: ... Elijah was carried up to heaven in a whirlwind, *REB* ... and Elijah went up in a storm into the heavens, *Rotherham* ... and Eliah ascended in a tempest to the Heavens, *Fenton* ... and Elijah went up to heaven in a great wind, *BB*.

12. And Elisha saw it, and he cried, My father, my father, the chariot of Israel, and the horsemen thereof: ... Chariot of Israel and its chargers!, *JB* ... The chariots and charioteers of Israel!, *NLT* ... Israel's chariots and drivers, *NAB* ... Mighty defender of Israel! You are gone!, *Good News*.

And he saw him no more: and he took hold of his own clothes, and rent them in two pieces: ... Then Elisha grabbed his own clothes and tore them to show how sad he was, *NCV* ... Then he took hold of his own garments and rent them in two pieces, *Darby* ... Then he took hold of his mantle and rent it in two, *NEB*.

13. He took up also the mantle of Elijah that fell from him, and went back, and stood by the bank of Jordan: ... Then he took up Elijah's coat that had fallen from him, *Beck* ... He picked up the cloak which had fallen from Elijah, *REB* ... And he taketh up the robe of Elijah, that fell from off him, *Young*.

---

tice's tenacity and stubbornness, "the two of them crossed over on dry ground." Elisha, a veritable Joshua to Elijah's Moses, was not to be denied.

2:9–10. Elisha's Joshua-like desire. The next event in the account after the crossing of the dry riverbed is Elijah asking his disciple what he could do for him. This was not the actual agenda, but, if Moses can, as it were, change the mind of Yahweh (cf. Num. 14:10–25, especially vv. 17–20), Elisha could change the mind of Elijah. There was, perhaps, more than a little gleam of admiration in Elijah's eye as he looked at his stubborn student and asked, "Tell me, what can I do for you ..." (v. 9). Elisha, of course, was not slow to respond: "Let me inherit a double portion of your spirit" (v. 9). Much misinformation often attends the memorable phrase "double portion" among contemporary preachers. The reference in Deut. 21:17 to what the firstborn son was to receive sheds light on the meaning—a "double share" (pî shenayim [HED #6552, 8530] is identical to the present text) of all the father has. Elisha was thus asking for the status of the "firstborn." The term "son" (bēn, HED #1158), often refers to a member of a guild, order or class, as is frequently the case, for example, in the Book of Proverbs (cf. Prov. 1:8, 10; 2:1; 3:1; etc.; where the term "son" virtually means "dear student," or the like). Elisha was hardly asking for double the amount of the "spirit" or "anointing" that Elijah had. Some emphasize the motif of duality found throughout a number of the Elisha accounts, plus the fact that Elisha seems to have performed twice the miracles Elijah did. But these are literary motifs and features, not strict exegeses of the meaning of the reference here to a "double portion." In support of the "firstborn" interpretation of the "double portion" reference, see the commentaries of Cogan and Tadmor (AB, 32), Hobbs (WBC, 21), Jones (NCBC, 385) and Wiseman (TOTC, 195).

Although Elisha was in no way asking for more power than his master, Elijah, he was properly reminded by his teacher that he had asked for "a difficult thing" (v. 10). It was by no means guaranteed that such a request could or would be granted. Probably, the implicit idea here is that only Yahweh could grant such a request. In any case, the indication that such an audacious request could even be granted would be revealed by the circumstances. In early Israel, what was categorized as a "prophet" was also termed "a seer" (1 Sam. 9:9; rō'eh, HED #7496), i.e., one who could behold spiritual sights in the heavenly realms (perhaps the clearest examples of this would be Micaiah's vision of the heavenly council in 1 Ki. 22:19–23 and Isaiah's vision of the heavenly throne in Isa. 6:1–8; in both cases, the same Hebrew root [rā'āh, "to see," HED #7495] is used of the prophets as they give their oracles). This, therefore, constituted the test Elisha would face: could he too behold visions and sights reserved only for Yahweh's special servants, the prophets? (cf. Amos 3:7f).

2:11–12. Elijah's Moses-like (and Enoch-like) departure. Much mystery attends any theophany

3497	14. 4089.121	881, 152	455	866, 5489.112	4623, 6142
art, pn	cj, v Qal impf 3ms	do, *n fs*	pn	rel part, v Qal pf 3fs	prep, prep, ps 3ms
הַיַּרְדֵּן	וַיִּקַּח	אֶת־אַדֶּרֶת	אֵלִיָּהוּ	אֲשֶׁר־נָפְלָה	מֵעָלָיו
hayyardēn	wayyiqqach	'eth-'addereth	'ēlîyāhû	'ăsher-nāphelāh	mē'ālâv
the Jordan	and he took	the mantle of	Elijah	which it had fallen	from on him

5409.521	881, 4448	569.121	347	3176	435	455	652, 2000
cj, v Hiphil impf 3ms	do, art, n md	v Qal impf 3ms	intrg	pn	*n mp*	pn	cj, pers pron
וַיַּכֶּה	אֶת־הַמַּיִם	וַיֹּאמַר	אַיֵּה	יְהוָה	אֱלֹהֵי	אֵלִיָּהוּ	אַף־הוּא
wayyakkeh	'eth-hammayim	wayyō'mar	'ayyēh	yehwāh	'ĕlōhê	'ēlîyāhû	'aph-hû'
and he struck	the water	and he said	where	Yahweh	the God of	Elijah	also he

5409.521	881, 4448	2779.226	2077	2077	5882.121	482
cj, v Hiphil impf 3ms	do, art, n md	cj, v Niphal impf 3mp	adv	cj, adv	cj, v Qal impf 3ms	pn
וַיַּכֶּה	אֶת־הַמַּיִם	וַיֵּחָצוּ	הֵנָּה	וָהֵנָּה	וַיַּעֲבֹר	אֱלִישָׁע
wayyakkeh	'eth-hammayim	wayyēchātsû	hēnnāh	wāhēnnāh	wayya'ăvōr	'ĕlîshā'
then he struck	the water	and they divided	here	and there	and he passed over	Elisha

15. 7495.126	1158, 5204	866, 904, 3509	4623, 5224	569.126
cj, v Qal impf 3mp, ps 3ms	*n mp*, art, n mp	rel pron, prep, pn	prep, prep	cj, v Qal impf 3mp
וַיִּרְאֻהוּ	בְנֵי־הַנְּבִיאִים	אֲשֶׁר־בִּירִיחוֹ	מִנֶּגֶד	וַיֹּאמְרוּ
wayyir'uhû	venê-hannevî'îm	'ăsher-bîrîchô	minneghedh	wayyō'merû
and they saw him	the sons of the prophets	who in Jericho	from before	and they said

5299.112	7593	455	6142, 482	971.126
v Qal pf 3fs	*n fs*	pn	prep, pn	cj, v Qal impf 3mp
נָחָה	רוּחַ	אֵלִיָּהוּ	עַל־אֱלִישָׁע	וַיָּבֹאוּ
nāchāh	rûach	'ēlîyāhû	'al-'ĕlîshā'	wayyāvō'û
He has come to rest	the Spirit from	Elijah	upon Elisha	and they came

3937, 7410.141	8246.726, 3937	800	16. 569.126
prep, v Qal inf con, ps 3ms	cj, v Hithpael impf 3mp, prep, ps 3ms	n fs	cj, v Qal impf 3mp
לִקְרָאתוֹ	וַיִּשְׁתַּחֲווּ־לוֹ	אַרְצָה	וַיֹּאמְרוּ
liqŏrā'thô	wayyishtachwû-lô	'āretsāh	wayyō'merû
to meet him	and they bowed down to him	to the ground	and they said

14. And he took the mantle of Elijah that fell from him, and smote the waters, and said, Where is the LORD God of Elijah?: ... with this mantle that had fallen from Elias he struck the waters; but they did not part, *Knox* ... After, he took up also the cloak of Elijah, that fell from him, *Geneva* ... And he struck the waters with the mantle of Elias, that had fallen from him, and they were not divided, *Douay* ... Wielding the mantle which had fallen from Elijah, he struck the water in his turn, *NAB*.

and when he also had smitten the waters, they parted hither and thither: and Elisha went over: ... As he struck the water again, it parted and Elisha crossed over, *Berkeley* ... As he struck the water, it divided in two parts, and Elisha crossed over, *Beck* ... it divided to right and left, *JB* ... and at his blow the waters were parted this way and that, *BB*.

15. And when the sons of the prophets which were to view at Jericho saw him: ... And the pupils of the Preachers who were in Jeriko, to the south, saw it, *Fenton* ... When the guild of prophets opposite saw him, *Moffatt* ... When the company of prophets who were at Jericho saw him at a distance, *NRSV*.

they said, The spirit of Elijah doth rest on Elisha: ... Elisha now has the spirit Elijah had, *NCV* ... The spirit of Elijah has settled on Elisha, *REB* ... The power of Elijah is on Elisha, *Good News*.

And they came to meet him, and bowed themselves to the ground before him: ... meeting him, they fell down face to earth, *Knox* ... and went against him and bowed to the earth unto him, *Tyndale* ... they worshipped him, falling to the ground, *Douay* ... and fell on their faces before him, *NEB*.

16. And they said unto him, Behold now, there be with thy servants fifty strong men: ... we your servants have fifty able men, *NIV* ... there are with thy servants fifty valiant men, *Darby* ... there be among thy servants fifty lusty men, *Tyndale* ... there are with thy servants fifty men sons of valour, *Rotherham*.

(visual appearance) of Yahweh, and the present verses are no exception. Elisha described Elijah taken up by "the chariots and horsemen of Israel." Once again, as being the prophet Elijah is connected in Scripture with the phenomenon of fire from heaven (cf. the comments on 1:9–15, above). Fire is also characteristic of divine manifestations in the Pentateuch (cf. Moses' burning bush in Exo. 3:2; also the pillar of fire in Exo. 13:21; 40:38; etc.; and the fire and smoke upon Mt. Sinai in Exo. 19:18). Indeed, Deut. 4:24 reminds us, "Yahweh your God is a consuming fire, a jealous God." But all this is of little help for the present text; although the references to chariots and horses, both of fire (or both of fiery appearance; cf. Ezekiel's vision of the heavenly throne of "fire," as found in Ezek. 1, especially, vv. 4, 27), do seem to invoke military imagery and are perhaps to be connected with the ancient institution of holy war (so Hobbs, WBC, 21). These heavenly apparitions represent the true source of protection for the land of Israel (cf., also, 6:16f). Parallels with the death of Moses (Deut. 34, especially v. 6, "But to this day no one knows where his grave is") and the translation of the ancient patriarch Enoch (Gen. 5:2f), should also be noted.

Wiseman (TOTC, 195f) is surely correct to point out that it was the "whirlwind" that actually took Elijah up into heaven (v. 11; cf. v. 1), not the chariots and horses. The present narrative is not primarily concerned with details of Elijah's translation to heaven, but with the fact that Elisha saw the symbol of God's presence and thus met the condition required by Elijah in v. 10. That is the primary import of Elisha's expression in v. 12. The twofold reference to "my father" communicates Elisha's sense of loss. Almost certainly a respectful reference to Elijah, his teacher, the double form is no doubt a lament. Both it, as well as the subsequent reference to the chariots and horsemen of Israel, are repeated in connection with Elisha's own impending death in 2 Ki. 13:14, in what is clearly a tone of abject mourning.

2:13–14. Elisha's Elijah-like miracle. Just as Joshua eventually proved to be a worthy successor to Moses, Elisha would prove to be a worthy successor to Elijah. Already, we are told that Elisha could indeed "see" visions meant only for a select few, but the present verses give further evidence that Elisha must be reckoned as being in the same league as his great teacher, Elijah. For as Elisha approached the Jordan, to cross back over it to the west, the company of the prophets (v. 15) who were apparently watching as closely as they dared, beheld a second dividing of the waters (similar to that which took place in the day of Joshua; cf. Josh. 3–4). Just as Joshua's miracle was meant to remind his generation of Moses' prior miracle ("Yahweh your God did to the Jordan just what he had done to the Red Sea" [Josh. 4:22]), Elisha's miracle evoked the prior miracle of his mentor, Elijah (the watching company of the prophets properly proclaimed, "The spirit of Elijah is resting on Elisha" [v. 15]). Elisha himself evidently already had the same thing in mind when he struck the water with Elijah's fallen cloak exclaiming, "Where now is Yahweh, the God of Elijah?" (v. 14). The divided waters provided the mute, but positive confirmation to his request—He is still there, in spirit and in power.

Elijah's cloak ('addereth, HED #152) is first mentioned in 1 Ki. 19:13 in connection with his solitary sojourn on Mt. Horeb, as well as in v. 19 of the same chapter, when he throws it around Elisha, whom he has just met for the first time (but whom Yahweh has already designated to be his successor). Although possessing no more magical power than Moses' staff, this cloak evidently served as a sign of Elijah's prophetic authority and commissioning. The cloak evidently served as a visible sign of prophetic succession, both in 1 Ki. 19:19, as well as here in 2 Ki. 2:13f.

2:15–18. Sons of the prophets ask to search for Elijah. Emphasis should be placed here on Elisha's prescience (both in the sense of his prophetic foreknowledge and also in the sense of his acumen as teacher), as well as his patience with the enthusiastic company of prophets. As overeager students often do, they clamored for attention, for a chance to shine before their teacher—after all, did not Elisha himself seem to do much the same thing in vv. 1–6? But these fifty students (again, the number evokes parallels with the preceding chapter) were not in Elisha's category, when it comes to prophetic ability and acuity (although Wiseman, TOTC, 196f, may well be correct to note their proper concern for the possibility of an unburied, hence dishonored, corpse). In any case, Elisha, the new mentor, proved to be at least as forbearing as Elijah, the old mentor, seems to have been in the beginning of the chapter. Both allowed the student(s) to prove themselves, but with varying results. Sometimes students must learn the hard way, as it were. They will not be deterred by good advice, no matter how respected the source. Just after the students cor-

420	2079, 5167	3552, 881, 5860	2675	596	1158, 2524
prep, ps 3ms	intrj, part	*sub*, do, n mp, ps 2ms	num	n mp	*n mp*, n ms
אֵלָיו	הִנֵּה־נָא	יֶשׁ־אֶת־עֲבָדֶיךָ	חֲמִשִּׁים	אֲנָשִׁים	בְּנֵי־חַיִל
'ēlâv	hinnēh-nā'	yēsh-'eth-'ăvādhêkhā	chămishshîm	'ănāshîm	b^{e}nê-chayil
to him	behold please	there are your servants	fifty	men	sons of the army

2050.126	5167	1272.326	881, 112	6678, 5558.111
v Qal juss 3mp	part	cj, v Piel juss 3mp	do, n mp, ps 2ms	cj, v Qal pf 3ms, ps 3ms
יֵלְכוּ	נָא	וִיבַקְשׁוּ	אֶת־אֲדֹנֶיךָ	פֶּן־נְשָׂאוֹ
yēl^{e}khû	nā'	wîvaqōshû	'eth-'ădhōnêkhā	pen-n^{e}sā'ô
may they go	please	and may they search for	your master	so that not He has lifted him up

7593	3176	8390.521	904, 259	2098	173	904, 259
n fs	pn	cj, v Hiphil impf 3ms, ps 3ms	prep, num	art, n mp	cj	prep, num
רוּחַ	יְהוָה	וַיַּשְׁלִכֵהוּ	בְּאַחַד	הֶהָרִים	אוֹ	בְּאַחַת
rûach	y^{e}hwāh	wayyashlikhēhû	b^{e}'achadh	hehārîm	'ô	b^{e}'achath
the Spirit of	Yahweh	but He threw him down	on one of	the mountains	or	into one of

1548	569.121	3940	8365.128	**17.**	6732.126, 904
art, n mp	cj, v Qal impf 3ms	neg part	v Qal impf 2mp		v Qal impf 3mp, prep, ps 3ms
הַגֵּיָאוֹת	וַיֹּאמֶר	לֹא	תִשְׁלָחוּ		וַיִּפְצְרוּ־בוֹ
hagg^{e}yā'ôth	wayyō'mer	lō'	thishlāchû		wayyiphts^{e}rû-vô
the valleys	but he said	not	you will send out		but they urged with him

5912, 991.141	569.121	8365.133	8365.126	2675	382
adv, v Qal inf con	cj, v Qal impf 3ms	v Qal impv 2mp	cj, v Qal impf 3mp	num	n ms
עַד־בֹּשׁ	וַיֹּאמֶר	שְׁלָחוּ	וַיִּשְׁלְחוּ	חֲמִשִּׁים	אִישׁ
'adh-bōsh	wayyō'mer	sh^{e}lāchû	wayyishl^{e}chû	chămishshîm	'îsh
until being ashamed	so he said	send out	and they sent out	fifty	men

1272.326	8421, 3219	3940	4834.116	**18.**	8178.126	420
cj, v Piel impf 3mp	num, n mp	cj, neg part	v Qal pf 3cp, ps 3ms		cj, v Qal impf 3mp	prep, ps 3ms
וַיְבַקְשׁוּ	שְׁלֹשָׁה־יָמִים	וְלֹא	מְצָאֻהוּ		וַיָּשֻׁבוּ	אֵלָיו
wayvaqōshû	sh^{e}lōshāh-yāmîm	w^{e}lō'	m^{e}tsā'uhû		wayyāshuvû	'ēlâv
and they searched	three days	but not	they found him		so they returned	to him

2000	3553.151	904, 3509	569.121	420	1950B, 3940, 569.115	420
cj, pers pron	v Qal act ptc ms	prep, pn	cj, v Qal impf 3ms	prep, ps 3mp	intrg part, neg part, v Qal pf 1cs	prep, ps 2mp
וְהוּא	יֹשֵׁב	בִּירִיחוֹ	וַיֹּאמֶר	אֲלֵהֶם	הֲלוֹא־אָמַרְתִּי	אֲלֵיכֶם
w^{e}hû'	yōshēv	bîrîchô	wayyō'mer	'ălēhem	hălō'-'āmartî	'ălêkhem
and he	staying	in Jericho	and he said	to them	did not I say	to you

414, 2050.128	**19.**	569.126	596	6111	420, 482	2079, 5167
adv, v Qal juss 2mp		cj, v Qal impf 3mp	*n mp*	art, n fs	prep, pn	intrj, part
אַל־תֵּלֵכוּ		וַיֹּאמְרוּ	אַנְשֵׁי	הָעִיר	אֶל־אֱלִישָׁע	הִנֵּה־נָא
'al-tēlēkhû		wayyō'm^{e}rû	'anshê	hā'îr	'el-'ĕlîshā'	hinnēh-nā'
do not go		and they said	the men of	the city	to Elisha	behold please

4319	6111	3005	3626, 866	112	7495.151	4448	7737
n ms	art, n fs	adj	prep, rel part	n ms, ps 1cs	v Qal act ptc ms	cj, art, n md	adj
מוֹשַׁב	הָעִיר	טוֹב	כַּאֲשֶׁר	אֲדֹנִי	רֹאֶה	וְהַמַּיִם	רָעִים
môshav	hā'îr	ṯôv	ka'ăsher	'ădhōnî	rō'eh	w^{e}hammayim	rā'îm
the setting of	the city	good	just as	my master	seeing	but the water	bad

800	8323.353	**20.**	569.121	4089.133, 3937	7016	2413
cj, art, n fs	v Piel ptc fs		cj, v Qal impf 3ms	v Qal impv 2mp, prep, ps 1cs	n fs	adj
וְהָאָרֶץ	מְשַׁכָּלֶת		וַיֹּאמֶר	קְחוּ־לִי	צְלֹחִית	חֲדָשָׁה
w^{e}hā'ārets	m^{e}shakkāleth		wayyō'mer	qōchû-lî	ts^{e}lōchîth	chădhāshāh
and the land	being unproductive		and he said	bring to me	a bowl	new

let them go, we pray thee, and seek thy master: ... will search the wilderness for your master, *NLT* ... be pleased to let them go in search of Elijah, *BB* ... let them go and look for your master, *NCV* ... go out and look for this master of thine, *Knox*.

lest peradventure the spirit of the LORD hath taken him up, and cast him upon some mountain, or into some valley: ... lest the wind of the LORD has taken him up, *Goodspeed* ... it may be that the Spirit of the LORD has caught him up, *RSV* ... the spirit of the LORD has lifted him up, *NEB* ... for fear the spirit of the EVER-LIVING should carry him away, *Fenton*.

And he said, Ye shall not send: ... No, you must not go, Elisha answered, *Good News* ... No, do not send them, *NRSV* ... You shall not send anyone, *NKJV* ... Elisha refused, *Moffatt*.

17. And when they urged him till he was ashamed, he said, Send: ... But they pressed him, till he consented, *Douay* ... they kept urging him, until he was embarrassed, *NAB* ... until he had not the heart to refuse, *NEB* ... begged Elisha until he couldn't refuse them anymore, *NCV*.

They sent therefore fifty men; and they sought three days, but found him not: ... they looked for three days, but did not find him, *KJVII* ... who searched for three days without finding him, *JB* ... for three days they searched in vain, *Knox*.

18. And when they came again to him, (for he tarried at Jericho,) he said unto them: ... they came back to Elisha at Jericho where he was staying, *NCV*.

Did I not say unto you, Go not?: ... did I not say unto you that ye should not go?, *Tyndale* ... Did I not tell you not to go?, *REB* ... Did I not warn you not to send, *Knox*.

19. And the men of the city said unto Elisha, Behold, I pray thee, the situation of this city is pleasant, as my lord seeth: ... This town is located in beautiful natural surroundings, as you can see, *NLT* ... The city's location is a good one, *Anchor* ... The site of the city is fine indeed, *NAB* ... The situation of this town is delightful, *Moffatt*.

but the water is naught, and the ground barren: ... causing the young of the cattle to come to birth dead, *BB* ... the water is bad, and the land is unfruitful, *Goodspeed* ... but the water is polluted and the country is troubled with miscarriages, *NEB* ... and the earth sterile, *Young*.

20. And he said, Bring me a new cruse, and put salt therein. And they brought it to him: ... bring me a new bowl, he said, and put salt into it, *NIV* ... Bring me a new vessel, *Douay* ... Bring me a new jar, *KJVII* ... Bring me a new flask, *Moffatt*.

---

rectly acknowledged the impressive spiritual credentials of their master, Elisha (v. 15), they proceeded to discount altogether his advice (vv. 16f). Human nature has not changed much. Good intentions and misguided zeal can frustrate the leaders of God's people even today. Yet, misguided zeal is surely preferable to spiritual lethargy. More than one church leader has noted that it is easier to redirect an eager volunteer than it is to recruit an unmotivated one. At any rate, after three days, they returned home, unsuccessful in their search. The passage ends with Elisha getting in the last word: in essence, he said, "I told you so." (v. 18). Proper pedagogical technique sometimes includes direct rejoinders to the students—even today. We leave Elisha and the students in Jericho, realizing that (1) Elijah is truly no more—he is in the same category as the patriarch Enoch, who "walked with God; then he was no more, because God took him away" (Gen. 5:24); and (2) Elisha is truly Elijah's successor, endued with a full measure of Yahweh's Spirit and worthy of all proper respect.

2:19–22. Healing of the waters of Jericho. This brief passage introduces a series of miracles brought about by the prophet Elisha, who was, as already noted, particularly concerned with water, whether it be in the form of rivers or springs. The city of Jericho is located just north of the Dead Sea, not far from the Jordan River, but otherwise in a rather desolate region of Israel. A dependable source of sweet water was essential for prosperity for this oasis town. Only a prophet in whom is the very Spirit of Yahweh could effect such a remarkable "healing" (cf. vv. 21f).

In connection with this short passage, it should be noted that the curse against pagan Jericho found in Josh. 6:26 was still in effect, even though it had already been clearly fulfilled in the days of King Ahab, when Hiel of Bethel rebuilt the city at the cost of both his eldest and youngest sons (1 Ki. 16:34). Wiseman notes two possible naturalistic explanations for the sudden "healing" of the spring in Elisha's day—a sudden geological shift clearing up previous radioactivity in the water, or the removal of a parasitic infection. He, however, does not insist on accepting either, or any such explanation. Believing the miracle does not depend on knowing the exact nature of this healing; the "new bowl filled with salt" may have been only symbolic (salt, of

7947.133	8427	4556	4089.126	420		3428.121	420, 4296
cj, v Qal impv 2mp	adv	n ms	cj, v Qal impf 3mp	prep, ps 3ms	21.	cj, v Qal impf 3ms	prep, *n ms*
וְשִׂימוּ	שָׁם	מֶלַח	וַיִּקְחוּ	אֵלָיו		וַיֵּצֵא	אֶל־מוֹצָא
wesîmû	shām	melach	wayyiqŏchû	'ēlâv		wayyētsē'	'el-môtsā'
and put	there	salt	so they got	for him		and he went out	to the outlet of

4448	8390.521, 8427	4556	569.121	3662, 569.111	3176
art, n md	cj, v Hiphil impf 3ms, adv	n ms	cj, v Qal impf 3ms	adv, v Qal pf 3ms	pn
הַמַּיִם	וַיַּשְׁלֶךְ־שָׁם	מֶלַח	וַיֹּאמֶר	כֹּה־אָמַר	יְהוָה
hammayim	wayyashlekh-shām	melach	wayyō'mer	kōh-'āmar	yehwāh
the water	and he threw down there	salt	and he said	thus He has said	Yahweh

7784.315	3937, 4448	431	3940, 2030.121	4623, 8427	5968	4323
v Piel pf 1cs	prep, art, n md	art, dem pron	neg part, v Qal impf 3ms	prep, adv	adv	n ms
רִפֵּאתִי	לַמַּיִם	הָאֵלֶּה	לֹא־יִהְיֶה	מִשָּׁם	עוֹד	מָוֶת
rippi'thî	lammayim	hā'ēlleh	lō'-yihyeh	mishshām	'ôdh	māweth
I have healed	the water	the these	it will not be	from there	anymore	death

8323.353		7784.226	4448	5912	3219	2172
cj, v Piel ptc fs	22.	cj, v Niphal impf 3mp	art, n md	adv	art, n ms	art, dem pron
וּמְשַׁכָּלֶת		וַיֵּרָפוּ	הַמַּיִם	עַד	הַיּוֹם	הַזֶּה
ûmeshakkāleth		wayyērāphû	hammayim	'adh	hayyôm	hazzeh
nor being unproductive		and they were healed	the water	until	the day	the this

3626, 1745	482	866	1744.311		6148.121	4623, 8427
prep, *n ms*	pn	rel part	v Piel pf 3ms	23.	cj, v Qal impf 3ms	prep, adv
כִּדְבַר	אֱלִישָׁע	אֲשֶׁר	דִּבֵּר		וַיַּעַל	מִשָּׁם
kidhvar	'ĕlîshā'	'ăsher	dibbēr		wayya'al	mishshām
according to the word of	Elisha	which	he spoke		and he went up to	from there

1044	2000	6148.151	904, 1932	5470	7277	3428.116	4623, 6111
pn	cj, pers pron	v Qal act ptc ms	prep, art, n ms	cj, n mp	adj	v Qal pf 3cp	prep, art, n fs
בֵּית־אֵל	וְהוּא	עֹלֶה	בַדֶּרֶךְ	וּנְעָרִים	קְטַנִּים	יָצְאוּ	מִן־הָעִיר
bêth-'ēl	wehû'	'ōleh	vadderekh	ûne'ārîm	qŏtanîm	yātse'û	min-hā'îr
Bethel	and he	going up	on the way	and boys	small	they came out	from the city

7330.726, 904	569.126	3937	6148.131	7429	6148.131
cj, v Hithpael impf 3mp, prep, ps 3ms	cj, v Qal impf 3mp	prep, ps 3ms	v Qal impv 2ms	adj	v Qal impv 2ms
וַיִּתְקַלְּסוּ־בוֹ	וַיֹּאמְרוּ	לוֹ	עֲלֵה	קֵרֵחַ	עֲלֵה
wayyithqallesû-vô	wayyō'merû	lô	'ălēh	qērēach	'ălēh
and they ridiculed against him	and they said	to him	go up	O bald one	go up

7429		6680.121	313	7495.121	7327.321
adj	24.	cj, v Qal impf 3ms	prep, ps 3ms	v Qal impf 3ms, ps 3mp	cj, v Piel impf 3ms, ps 3mp
קֵרֵחַ		וַיִּפֶן	אַחֲרָיו	וַיִּרְאֵם	וַיְקַלְלֵם
qērēach		wayyiphen	'achrâv	wayyir'ēm	wayqalelēm
O bald one		and he turned	behind him	and he saw them	and he cursed them

904, 8428	3176	3428.127	8692	1726	4623, 3402	1260.327
prep, *n ms*	pn	cj, v Qal impf 3fp	num	n fp	prep, art, n ms	cj, v Piel impf 3fp
בְּשֵׁם	יְהוָה	וַתֵּצֶאנָה	שְׁתַּיִם	דֻּבִּים	מִן־הַיַּעַר	וַתְּבַקַּעְנָה
beshēm	yehwāh	wattētse'nāh	shettayim	dubbîm	min-hayya'ar	wattevaqqa'ănāh
in the name of	Yahweh	and they came out	two	female bears	from the forest	and they tore

4623	727	8530	3315		2050.121	4623, 8427	420, 2098	3890
prep, ps 3mp	num	cj, num	n mp	25.	cj, v Qal impf 3ms	prep, adv	prep, *n ms*	art, pn
מֵהֶם	אַרְבָּעִים	וּשְׁנֵי	יְלָדִים		וַיֵּלֶךְ	מִשָּׁם	אֶל־הַר	הַכַּרְמֶל
mēhem	'arbā'îm	ûshenê	yeladhîm		wayyēlekh	mishshām	'el-har	hakkarmel
of them	forty	and two	children		and he went	from there	to Mount	the Carmel

21. And he went forth unto the spring of the waters, and cast the salt in there: ... went to the source of the water, threw salt into it, *JB*.

and said, Thus saith the LORD, I have healed these waters; there shall not be from thence any more death or barren land: ... I have purified this water so that death and miscarriage shall no longer come from it, *Berkeley* ... it won't cause death, and it won't keep the land from growing crops, *NCV* ... It shall no longer cause death or sterility, *REB* ... either death or barrenness, *Tyndale*.

22. So the waters were healed unto this day, according to the saying of Elisha which he spake: ... the water is still wholesome today as Elisha declared, *Beck* ... waters have been healthy to this day, *Fenton* ... water was made sweet again to this day, *BB* ... water has remained pure, *NEB*.

23. And he went up from thence unto Beth-el: and as he was going up by the way, there came forth little children out of the city: ... as he climbed up along the road, he was mocked by some young boys, *Knox* ... some small boys came out of the town, *JB*.

and mocked him, and said unto him, Go up, thou bald head; go up, thou bald head: ... Go up, old no-hair, *BB* ... Be off, baldy!, *Anchor* ... Go away, you baldhead! they chanted, *NLT*.

24. And he turned back, and looked on them, and cursed them in the name of the LORD: ... put a curse on them in the name, *NCV*.

And there came forth two she bears out of the wood, and tare forty and two children of them: ... two female bears came out of the forest and tore up forty-two of the boys, *Berkeley* ... tore up 42 of these youths, *Beck* ... and mauled forty-two of them, *REB* ... tore forty-two of the children to pieces, *NAB*.

25. And he went from thence to mount Carmel, and from thence he returned to Samaria: ... Mount Karmel, and afterwards he settled in Shomeron, *Fenton* ... and later returned to Samaria, *Good News*.

---

course, was readily available from the nearby Dead Sea; cf. the enigmatic references to the "covenant of salt" in Num. 18:19; 2 Chr. 13:5). The new bowl may then have represented purity, and the salt, preservation leading to cleansing. But whatever precisely took place at this time, the overall result was evident enough: the region finally enjoyed full health and prosperity. In regard to the overall placement of this story and the next, i.e., one of healing and one of death, see the comments in the next section.

2:23–25. Cursing of the youths of Bethel. In contrast to the preceding passage, this account contains, not a word of blessing or of healing, but a word of cursing and of death. Concerning the overall placement of this passage, as well as the preceding two passages in the present chapter (vv. 1–18, and 19–22), the three accounts represent stages in the progression of the early career of Elisha, and they in turn pivot on the crucial v. 11, where Elijah's departure is briefly described. Thus, everything which takes place before v. 11, including material in the previous chapter, may be seen as symmetrical to everything after v. 11, up to and including the present passage. Thus, in a sense, the present verses correspond with the word of judgment and death given to King Ahaziah in 1:1–8 (also, vv. 16f). The immediately previous passage (2:19–22), which concerns healing and life, corresponds to the passage in 1:9–15, which is ultimately about the sparing of life. But there is a further, more complex parallelism as well: 1:1–8, 16f deal with a king who seeks a word of healing, but the divine response is that of death (hence, a reversal). Likewise, both of these passages end with a "fulfillment formula" (1:17, "according to the word of Yahweh that Elijah had spoken"; and 2:22, "according to the word Elisha had spoken"). But, in the two other parallel passages (1:9–15, and the present passage, 2:23ff), strong, disrespectful challenges are given to the prophet, whether Elijah ordered by the king to "come down," or Elisha taunted by the boys to "go up." The purpose of this literary retracing of the steps of Elijah by Elisha is to identify the latter as the rightful successor of the former. The narrative contains several clear statements to this fact (2:15).

All of God's emissaries know what it is like to be jeered. Obviously, Elisha the prophet was no exception. Whereas Elijah, his predecessor, was mocked by kings and queens (Ahab, Jezebel, and finally, Ahaziah), Elisha suffered the particular ignominy of being mocked by youths. (The "little children" of KJV may not be the most apt rendering of the Hebrew term n[e]'ārîm qŏṯanîm (HED #5470, 7277), "young men," "boys," or the like, although the adjective qŏṯanîm, which literally means "small" or "young," does particularly stress their chronological immaturity. N[e]'ārîm, "youths," otherwise could be as old as late teens or early twenties. In any case, the incredible insolence (especially in a more regimented culture like that of the Israelites) is surely to be stressed—as

4623, 8427	8178.111	8497		3190	1158, 255	4566.111	6142, 3547
cj, prep, adv	v Qal pf 3ms	pn		cj, pn	*n ms*, pn	v Qal pf 3ms	prep, pn
וּמִשָּׁם	שָׁב	שֹׁמְרוֹן	**3:1**	וִיהוֹרָם	בֶּן־אַחְאָב	מָלַךְ	עַל־יִשְׂרָאֵל
ûmishshām	shāv	shômerôn		wîhôrām	ben-'ach'āv	mālakh	'al-yisrā'ēl
and from there	he returned to	Samaria		now Jehoram	the son of Ahab	he reigned	over Israel

904, 8497	904, 8523	8470	6462	3937, 3194	4567	3171	4566.121
prep, pn	prep, *n fs*	num	num	prep, pn	*n ms*	pn	cj, v Qal impf 3ms
בְּשֹׁמְרוֹן	בִּשְׁנַת	שְׁמֹנֶה	עֶשְׂרֵה	לִיהוֹשָׁפָט	מֶלֶךְ	יְהוּדָה	וַיִּמְלֹךְ
beshômerôn	bishnath	shemōneh	'esrēh	lîhôshāphāṭ	melekh	yehûdhāh	wayyimlōkh
in Samaria	in the year of	eight	ten	of Jehoshaphat	the king of	Judah	and he reigned

8692, 6462	8523		6449.121	7737	904, 6084	3176	7828	3940
num, num	n fs		cj, v Qal impf 3ms	art, adj	prep, *n fd*	pn	adv	neg part
שְׁתֵּים־עֶשְׂרֵה	שָׁנָה	**2.**	וַיַּעֲשֶׂה	הָרַע	בְּעֵינֵי	יְהוָה	רַק	לֹא
shettêm-'esrēh	shānāh		wayya'ăseh	hāra'	be'ênê	yehwāh	raq	lō'
twelve	years		and he did	what is evil	in the eyes of	Yahweh	only	not

3626, 1	3626, 525	5681.521	881, 4838	1197	866	6449.111
prep, n ms, ps 3ms	cj, prep, n fs, ps 3ms	cj, v Hiphil impf 3ms	do, *n fs*	art, pn	rel part	v Qal pf 3ms
כְּאָבִיו	וּכְאִמּוֹ	וַיָּסַר	אֶת־מַצְּבַת	הַבַּעַל	אֲשֶׁר	עָשָׂה
khe'āvîw	ûkhe'immô	wayyāsar	'eth-matstsevath	habba'al	'ăsher	'āsāh
like his father	nor like his mother	and he removed	the pillar of	Baal	which	he had made

1		7828	904, 2496	3493	1158, 5203	866, 2490.511	881, 3547
n ms, ps 3ms		adv	prep, *n fp*	pn	*n ms*, pn	rel pron, v Hiphil pf 3ms	do, pn
אָבִיו	**3.**	רַק	בְּחַטֹּאות	יָרָבְעָם	בֶּן־נְבָט	אֲשֶׁר־הֶחֱטִיא	אֶת־יִשְׂרָאֵל
'āvîw		raq	bechattō'wth	yārov'ām	ben-nevāṭ	'ăsher-hechĕṭî'	'eth-yisrā'ēl
his father		only	in the sins of	Jeroboam	the son of Nebat	who he caused to sin	Israel

1740.111	3940, 5681.111	4623		4470	4567, 4262	2030.111
v Qal pf 3ms	neg part, v Qal pf 3ms	prep, ps 3fs		cj, pn	*n ms*, pn	v Qal pf 3ms
דָּבֵק	לֹא־סָר	מִמֶּנָּה	**4.**	וּמֵישַׁע	מֶלֶךְ־מוֹאָב	הָיָה
dāvēq	lō'-sār	mimmennāh		ûmêsha'	melekh-mô'āv	hāyāh
he clung	he did not turn	from it		and Mesha	the king of Moab	he was

5533	3553.511	3937, 4567, 3547	4109, 512	3862
n ms	cj, v Hiphil pf 3ms	prep, *n ms*, pn	num, num	n mp
נֹקֵד	וְהֵשִׁיב	לְמֶלֶךְ־יִשְׂרָאֵל	מֵאָה־אֶלֶף	כָּרִים
nōqēdh	wehēshîv	lemelekh-yisrā'ēl	mē'āh-'eleph	kārîm
a sheep breeder	and he sent back	to the king of Israel	one hundred thousand	male sheep

3:1. Now Jehoram the son of Ahab began to reign over Israel in Samaria the eighteenth year of Jehoshaphat king of Judah: ... became king over Israel, *NASB* ... the eighteenth year of the rule of Jehoshaphat, *BB*.

and reigned twelve years: ... he was king for twelve years, *Berkeley*.

2. And he wrought evil in the sight of the LORD; but not like his father, and like his mother: ... He too defied the Lord's will, *Knox* ... did what the LORD said was wrong, *NCV* ... did the thing that was wicked in the eyes of Yahweh, *Rotherham*.

for he put away the image of Baal that his father had made: ... put away the pillar of Baal, *Beck* ... he did remove the sacred pillar, *REB* ... he overturned the Columns of Bal, *Fenton*.

3. Nevertheless he cleaved unto the sins of Jeroboam the son of Nebat, which made Israel to sin; he departed not therefrom: ... he continued to practise the sins, *JB* ... he did not depart from them, *NASB* ... he never broke away from that, *Moffatt* ... and did not give them up, *NEB*.

4. And Mesha king of Moab was a sheepmaster: ... was a sheep raiser, *Berkeley* ... was a sheep-breeder, *JB*.

and rendered unto the king of Israel an hundred thousand lambs, and an hundred thousand rams, with the wool: ... he had to supply the king of Israel regularly, *REB* ... who used to deliver to the king, *NRSV*.

they repeatedly mocked the prophet, "Go on up, you baldhead." A number of commentators rightly note the contrast of the hairiness of Elijah (2 Ki. 1:8) with the apparently bald appearance of Elisha. Such baldness was most likely a natural condition inasmuch as artificial baldness was legislated against in Israel (Deut. 14:1). Presumably, the repeated taunt, "go on up," referred to the recent ascension of Elijah (note that in these verses, Elisha is retracing the journey both he and his master Elijah had taken earlier in the chapter). In any case, the mocking comments prompted a fearsome reaction both on the part of the prophet as well as his God (2 Ki. 2:24). We are told that the prophet called down a curse on the boys "in the name of Yahweh," in clear contrast with the word of blessing, also in the name of Yahweh in v. 21; and then we are told that two bears came out of the woods and mauled some forty-two of the boys. Wiseman (TOTC, 198) suggests that the number forty-two signifies the size of the "organized mob" which tormented the prophet, not the number of the ill-fated. But such an exact number surely conveys the testimony of an eyewitness.

Two short stories conclude the present chapter of 2 Kings, and their counterparts in the first chapter of the Book. First, causing the death of forty-two boys is hardly to be seen as a characteristic prophetic activity. Suffice it to say that, like the incident of Elijah and the soldiers of Ahaziah (ch. 1), this incident is characterized by excess. Like the touching of the Ark of the Covenant (2 Sam. 6:6f), the ridicule of sacred persons is rewarded by the harshest of punishments.

3:1–27. *The revolt of Moab and its aftermath. This chapter is a generally unified account of King Joram's invasion of the kingdom of Moab and its gruesome results, prefaced by a typical Israelite accession formula in vv. 1ff. The chapter presents one of the most vivid pictures of the powerful role the prophets played during times of warfare in ancient Israel, as well as amply demonstrating the animosity which so often typified relationships between prophet and king (whether in peacetime or during times of war). It also illustrates most effectively the plusses and minuses of coalition politics between neighboring kingdoms which so often took place before the rise of the neo-Assyrian empire. Finally, the chapter conveys most effectively both the extreme horror, as well as the desperate effectiveness, of the barbaric religious rite of child sacrifice. It is to a brief examination of this most memorable chapter that we now turn.*

3:1–3. Jehoram's evil reign over Israel. The first verse of the present chapter represents a formal accession formula for Joram, son of Ahab, king of Israel.

Suggested dates for the accession of Joram generally accord to within a few years. Such dates are largely derived from the extra-biblical evidence attending Joram's successor, the usurper Jehu. Most scholars date Jehu's first year of reign to ca. 841 B.C., which was the year when he paid tribute to the Assyrian king Shalmaneser III, an occasion important enough to be pictured prominently on the Assyrian "Black Obelisk." By means of other extant Assyrian inscriptions, we can calculate that this inglorious event can be closely dated to the year 841. Working backward, then, from that date (assuming once again that it was the first year or so of Jehu's reign), since Joram his predecessor is said to have reigned for a total of twelve years, Joram's accession year must then have taken place in ca. 852 or 851, depending on whether one antedates (i.e., reckons the portion of the civil year in which the king was enthroned as part of his regnal total) or postdates (reckons that period of time as the king's "accession year" and not his first regnal year). Albright shortens Joram's total reign to eight years, citing external historical constraints and the likelihood of scribal confusion, and thus dates Joram's accession at 849.

Verses 2f of the present chapter represent our first example in 2 Kings of a phenomenon we will soon become quite familiar with, i.e., a judgment formula. Characteristically, especially the northern Israelite kings are described by some form of the stock phrase "he did evil in the eyes of Yahweh," often appended with some form of the following statement to elaborate on this "evil": "walking in," "following," "not turning from" or, as here, "clinging to," "the sins of Jeroboam son of Nebat" (i.e., Jeroboam I). As we shall see below, the villain in the fall of Jerusalem to the Babylonians in 586 B.C. is the infamous Judahite king Manasseh. The Israelite king Jeroboam I seems equally to have been considered the chief villain for the eventual fall of the north to Assyria in 722. At least, that is the standard evaluative phrase connected with the discussion of nearly every Israelite king throughout the Books of 1–2 Kings (a quick examination shows that only Elah, Shallum and Hoshea [i.e., three kings out of the total of eighteen kings of Israel who came after Jeroboam I] lack this evaluation).

4109	512	356	7055	5.	2030.121	3626, 4322.141	255
cj, num	num	n mp	n ms		cj, v Qal impf 3ms	prep, v Qal inf con	pn
וּמֵאָה	אֶלֶף	אֵילִים	צָמֶר		וַיְהִי	כְּמוֹת	אַחְאָב
ûmē'āh	'eleph	'êlîm	tsāmer		wayhî	kemôth	'ach'āv
and one hundred	one thousand	male goats	wool		and it was	when the dying of	Ahab

6839.121	4567, 4262	904, 4567	3547	6.	3428.121	4567
cj, v Qal impf 3ms	*n ms*, pn	prep, *n ms*	pn		cj, v Qal impf 3ms	art, n ms
וַיִּפְשַׁע	מֶלֶךְ־מוֹאָב	בְּמֶלֶךְ	יִשְׂרָאֵל		וַיֵּצֵא	הַמֶּלֶךְ
wayyiphsha'	melekh-mô'āv	bemelekh	yisrā'ēl		wayyētsē'	hammelekh
then he revolted	the king of Moab	against the king of	Israel		so he went out	the king

3190	904, 3219	2000	4623, 8497	6734.121	881, 3725, 3547
pn	prep, art, n ms	art, dem pron	prep, pn	cj, v Qal impf 3ms	do, *adj*, pn
יְהוֹרָם	בַּיּוֹם	הַהוּא	מִשֹּׁמְרוֹן	וַיִּפְקֹד	אֶת־כָּל־יִשְׂרָאֵל
yehôrām	bayyôm	hahû'	mishshōmerôn	wayyiphqōdh	'eth-kol-yisrā'ēl
Jehoram	on the day	the that	from Samaria	and he mustered	all Israel

7.	2050.121	8365.121	420, 3194	4567, 3171	3937, 569.141	4567
	cj, v Qal impf 3ms	cj, v Qal impf 3ms	prep, pn	*n ms*, pn	prep, v Qal inf con	*n ms*
	וַיֵּלֶךְ	וַיִּשְׁלַח	אֶל־יְהוֹשָׁפָט	מֶלֶךְ־יְהוּדָה	לֵאמֹר	מֶלֶךְ
	wayyēlekh	wayyishlach	'el-yehôshāphāṯ	melekh-yehûdhāh	lē'mōr	melekh
	and he went	and he sent out	to Jehoshaphat	the king of Judah	saying	the king of

4262	6839.111	904	1950B, 2050.123	882	420, 4262	3937, 4560
pn	v Qal pf 3ms	prep, ps 1cs	intrg part, v Qal impf 2ms	prep, ps 1cs	prep, pn	prep, art, n fs
מוֹאָב	פָּשַׁע	בִּי	הֲתֵלֵךְ	אִתִּי	אֶל־מוֹאָב	לַמִּלְחָמָה
mô'āv	pāsha'	bî	hăthēlēkh	'ittî	'el-mô'āv	lammilchāmāh
Moab	he has revolted	against me	will you go	with me	unto Moab	for the war

569.121	6148.125	3765	3765	3626, 6194	3626, 6194
cj, v Qal impf 3ms	v Qal impf 1cs	prep, ps 1cs	prep, ps 2ms	prep, n ms, ps 1cs	prep, n ms, ps 2ms
וַיֹּאמֶר	אֶעֱלֶה	כָּמוֹנִי	כָמוֹךָ	כְּעַמִּי	כְעַמֶּךָ
wayyō'mer	'e'ĕleh	kāmônî	khāmôkhā	ke'ammî	khe'ammekhā
and he said	I will go	like me	like you	like my people	like your people

3626, 5670	3626, 5670	8.	569.121	338, 2172	1932	6148.120
prep, n mp, ps 1cs	prep, n mp, ps 2ms		cj, v Qal impf 3ms	intrg, dem pron	art, n ms	v Qal impf 1cp
כְּסוּסַי	כְּסוּסֶיךָ		וַיֹּאמֶר	אֵי־זֶה	הַדֶּרֶךְ	נַעֲלֶה
kes̱ûs̱ay	kes̱ûs̱êkhā		wayyō'mer	'ê-zeh	hadderekh	na'ăleh
like my horses	like your horses		and he said	where this	the way	we will go up

569.121	1932	4198	110	9.	2050.121	4567	3547
cj, v Qal impf 3ms	*n ms*	*n ms*	pn		cj, v Qal impf 3ms	*n ms*	pn
וַיֹּאמֶר	דֶּרֶךְ	מִדְבַּר	אֱדוֹם		וַיֵּלֶךְ	מֶלֶךְ	יִשְׂרָאֵל
wayyō'mer	derekh	midhbar	'ĕdhôm		wayyēlekh	melekh	yisrā'ēl
and he said	the way of	the wilderness of	Edom		and he went	the king of	Israel

4567, 3171	4567	110	5621.126	1932	8124	3219
cj, *n ms*, pn	cj, *n ms*	pn	cj, v Qal impf 3mp	*n ms*	num	n mp
וּמֶלֶךְ־יְהוּדָה	וּמֶלֶךְ	אֱדוֹם	וַיָּסֹבּוּ	דֶּרֶךְ	שִׁבְעַת	יָמִים
ûmelekh-yehûdhāh	ûmelekh	'ĕdhôm	wayyās̱ōbbû	derekh	shiv'ath	yāmîm
and the king of Judah	and the king of	Edom	and they went around	a way of	seven	days

3940, 2030.111	4448	3937, 4402	3937, 966	866	904, 7559
cj, neg part, v Qal pf 3ms	n md	prep, art, n ms	cj, prep, art, n fs	rel part	prep, n fd, ps 3mp
וְלֹא־הָיָה	מַיִם	לַמַּחֲנֶה	וְלַבְּהֵמָה	אֲשֶׁר	בְּרַגְלֵיהֶם
welō'-hāyāh	mayim	lammachneh	welabbehēmāh	'ăsher	beraghlêhem
and there was not	water	for the camp	nor for the animals	which	on their feet

5. But it came to pass, when Ahab was dead, that the king of Moab rebelled against the king of Israel: ... when Achab died, he renounced his agreement, *Knox* ... revolted against the king, *Rotherham* ... got free from the authority of the king, *BB* ... he broke the league which he had made, *Douay*.

6. And king Jehoram went out of Samaria the same time, and numbered all Israel: ... and mustered all Israel, *Douay* ... and mobilized all Israel, *NIV* ... and gathered all his troops, *Good News* ... inspected all Israel, *Darby*.

7. And he went and sent to Jehoshaphat the king of Judah, saying, The king of Moab hath rebelled against me: wilt thou go with me against Moab to battle?: ... will you go with me to fight, *Goodspeed* ... Will you help me fight him?, *NLT* ... Will you join me in battle against Moab?, *Anchor* ... Will you join me in attacking Moab?, *NEB*.

And he said, I will go up: I am as thou art, my people as thy people, and my horses as thy horses: ... my troops are yours to command. Even my horses are at your service, *NLT*.

8. And he said, Which way shall we go up?: ... By what route shall we attack?, *NIV* ... which way shall we march?, *RSV*.

And he answered, The way through the wilderness of Edom: ... By the desert of Edom, *Douay* ... By the waste land of Edom, *BB*.

9. So the king of Israel went, and the king of Judah, and the king of Edom: and they fetched a compass of seven days' journey: ... made a circuit of seven day's journey, *MAST* ... they circled about for seven days, *Anchor* ... After their roundabout journey of seven days, *NAB*.

and there was no water for the host, and for the cattle that followed them: ... none left for the men or the pack animals, *Good News* ... nor for the beasts that followed, *ASV* ... no water for the army, *KJVII*.

Ironically, in the present case, there is a lessening of blame assigned to King Joram (a similar phenomenon will be found in connection with Jehu, and with the final king of Israel, Hoshea). Joram, like every other king of Israel, "did evil" in the sight of Yahweh, but, he was not as bad as his parents. In fact, he did some good as well; e.g., he destroyed an idolatrous shrine that his father had made (as we shall see in ch. 23, such idol destruction was particularly the hallmark of the later good king Josiah). Joram's parents were, of course, the notorious King Ahab and his foreign wife Jezebel, about whom very little good has been said. (A few positive comments about Ahab, however, may be found in 1 Ki. 20:1–34, a rather positive account of his heroism against the tyrannical Ben-Hadad, king of Aram; also, in 21:27f, where Ahab's sincere repentance leads to some mitigation of Yahweh's judgment against him; nothing positive can be found in the Books of Kings, or anywhere else, for that matter, about Jezebel). A central concern of the Kings narrative is the destruction of idols and the abolition of the worship of gods other than Yahweh, so that any positive examples are quickly cited to further this agenda, no matter how otherwise unimpressive any given king may have been.

3:4–8. Revolt of Moab; mobilization of Israel and Judah. Cogan and Tadmor (AB, 48) quite properly divide the present chapter into two unequal sections: vv. 1ff, introduction, and vv. 4–27, prophetic narrative. The present verses (vv. 4–8) could themselves be further subdivided as follows: "King Mesha's rebellion" (vv. 4f) and "King Joram's response" (vv. 6ff).

Often after the death of a major king, the vassal states would test the mettle of his successor by means of coordinated rebellion. One particularly well-known occasion in post-exilic times was the terrifying revolt which broke out throughout most of the vast Persian Empire after the death in 522 B.C. of Cambyses (by his own hand) and the accession of Darius I to the throne. References to this may be found in Hag. 2:6f, 21f, dated to Darius' second year, before the Persian king had succeeded in mastering his foes, where Yahweh declares through his prophet, "I will once more shake the heavens and the earth, the sea and the dry land. I will shake all nations ... I will overturn royal thrones and shatter the power of the foreign kingdoms ..." (vv. 6f, 22). In the present text, the rebellion of Moab was probably timed in a similar way in order to test immediately the military prowess of Ahab's son and successor, Joram (or else, the intervening king Ahaziah, whose reign, as we have just seen, barely lasted two years before his own death). Clearly, whatever King Joram's other faults, lack of initiative was not one of them, for he soon organized a formidable coalition and proceeded to attack Moab, not from the north as one might expect, but from the south ("the desert of Edom," v. 8). Here, as elsewhere, rebellions of vassal states would have been dealt with ruthlessly, not only to punish the guilty, but also to serve warning to any and all who otherwise might be so inclined to try

10.	569.121	4567	3547	159	3706, 7410.111	3176	3937, 8421
	cj, v Qal impf 3ms	*n ms*	pn	intrj	cj, v Qal pf 3ms	pn	prep, num
	וַיֹּאמֶר	מֶלֶךְ	יִשְׂרָאֵל	אֲהָהּ	כִּי־קָרָא	יְהוָה	לִשְׁלֹשֶׁת
	wayyō'mer	melekh	yisrā'ēl	'ăhāhh	kî-qārā'	yehwāh	lishlōsheth
	and he said	the king of	Israel	alas	because He has called	Yahweh	to the three of

4567	431	3937, 5598.141	881	904, 3135, 4262	11.	569.121
art, n mp	art, dem pron	prep, v Qal inf con	do, ps 3mp	prep, *n fs*, pn		cj, v Qal impf 3ms
הַמְּלָכִים	הָאֵלֶּה	לָתֵת	אוֹתָם	בְּיַד־מוֹאָב		וַיֹּאמֶר
hammelākhîm	hā'ēlleh	lāthēth	'ôthām	beyadh-mô'āv		wayyō'mer
the kings	the these	to give	them	into the hand of Moab		and he said

3194	1950B, 375	6553	5204	3937, 3176	1938.120	881, 3176
pn	intrg part, sub	adv	n ms	prep, pn	cj, v Qal juss 1cp	do, pn
יְהוֹשָׁפָט	הַאֵין	פֹּה	נָבִיא	לַיהוָה	וְנִדְרְשָׁה	אֶת־יְהוָה
yehôshāphāṭ	ha'ên	pōh	nāvî'	layhwāh	wenidhreshāh	'eth-yehwāh
Jehoshaphat	is there not	here	a prophet	of Yahweh	that we may inquire about	Yahweh

4623, 881	6257.121	259	4623, 5860	4567, 3547	569.121
prep, do, ps 3ms	cj, v Qal impf 3ms	num	prep, *n mp*	*n ms*, pn	cj, v Qal impf 3ms
מֵאוֹתוֹ	וַיַּעַן	אֶחָד	מֵעַבְדֵי	מֶלֶךְ־יִשְׂרָאֵל	וַיֹּאמֶר
mē'ôthô	wayya'an	'echādh	mē'avdhê	melekh-yisrā'ēl	wayyō'mer
from him	and he answered	one	from the servants of	the king of Israel	and he said

6553	482	1158, 8573	866, 3441.111	4448	6142, 3135	455
adv	pn	*n ms*, pn	rel pron, v Qal pf 3ms	n md	prep, *n fp*	pn
פֹּה	אֱלִישָׁע	בֶּן־שָׁפָט	אֲשֶׁר־יָצַק	מַיִם	עַל־יְדֵי	אֵלִיָּהוּ
pōh	'ĕlîshā'	ben-shāphāṭ	'ăsher-yātsaq	mayim	'al-yedhê	'ēlîyāhû
here	Elisha	the son of Shaphat	who he poured out	water	on the hands of	Elijah

12.	569.121	3194	3552	882	1745, 3176	3495.126
	cj, v Qal impf 3ms	pn	sub	prep, ps 3ms	*n ms*, pn	cj, v Qal impf 3mp
	וַיֹּאמֶר	יְהוֹשָׁפָט	יֵשׁ	אוֹתוֹ	דְּבַר־יְהוָה	וַיֵּרְדוּ
	wayyō'mer	yehôshāphāṭ	yēsh	'ôthô	devar-yehwāh	wayyēredhû
	and he said	Jehoshaphat	there is	with him	the word of Yahweh	so they went down

420	4567	3547	3194	4567	110	13.	569.121
prep, ps 3ms	*n ms*	pn	cj, pn	cj, *n ms*	pn		cj, v Qal impf 3ms
אֵלָיו	מֶלֶךְ	יִשְׂרָאֵל	וִיהוֹשָׁפָט	וּמֶלֶךְ	אֱדוֹם		וַיֹּאמֶר
'ēlâv	melekh	yisrā'ēl	wîhôshāphāṭ	ûmelekh	'ĕdhôm		wayyō'mer
to him	the king of	Israel	and Jehoshaphat	and the king of	Edom		and he said

10. And the king of Israel said, Alas! that the LORD hath called these three kings together, to deliver them into the hand of Moab!: … has summoned these three kings to give them into the hand, *Goodspeed* … The LORD has brought the three of us here to let the king of Moab defeat us, *NLT* … only to be handed over to Moab, *NRSV* … only to put us into the power of Moab, *JB*.

11. But Jehoshaphat said, Is there not here a prophet of the LORD, that we may inquire of the LORD by him?: … through whom we may seek the LORD's guidance?, *REB* … no prophet of Yahweh here for us to consult, *JB* … from whom we can get the LORD's help?, *Beck* … We can ask the LORD through him, *NCV*.

And one of the king of Israel's servants answered and said, Here is Elisha the son of Shaphat, which poured water on the hands of Elijah: … one of the officers addressed the king of Israel, *Fenton* … who was servant to Elijah, *BB*.

12. And Jehoshaphat said, The word of the LORD is with him. So the king of Israel and Jehoshaphat and the king of Edom went down to him: … He certainly has YHWH's word!, *Anchor* … went to consult with Elisha, *NLT* … He is a true prophet, *Good News*.

13. And Elisha said unto the king of Israel, What have I to do with thee? get thee to the prophets of thy father, and to the prophets of thy mother: … Why do you come to me?, *Berkeley* … whom thy father and thy mother knew, *Knox*.

the same in the future. This is why Babylonia seemed to have dealt so ruthlessly with Judah after the fall of Jerusalem in 586, putting out the eyes of the captured King Zedekiah, for example (2 Ki. 25:7). They wanted to be sure that word of this harsh punishment would quickly reach the surrounding subject nations. As will be noted in more detail below, Babylonia's subsequent treatment of the defeated Judahites was actually quite lenient.

"Mesha king of Moab" (v. 4) is the same individual who is so prominently featured in the well-known "Moabite Stone," an inscribed black basalt slab with rounded top that contains some thirty-nine lines of text (still the longest ancient inscription ever found in Palestine). It was first discovered in the modern era in 1868 in what is now the kingdom of Jordan. Despite this fortuitous corroboration of the biblical record by archaeology, some problems remain in the coordination of the two sources (for a helpful overview concerning these issues, see Cogan and Tadmor [AB, 50f]; much of the following discussion is indebted to their work). King Mesha noted on the Moabite Stone that, after a long period of oppression by Israel under Omri and "half the days of his son" (presumably Ahab), Mesha succeeded in gaining freedom from the Israelites ("I have triumphed over him [Omri] and his house, and Israel has perished forever"; presumably the coup of Jehu over the house of Omri in ca. 842 is in view here, thus dating the inscription to after this date). Therefore, the Moabite Stone depicts the events of the era of the present text from a somewhat later viewpoint, and it seemingly omits altogether any reference to the Moabite disaster described in the present chapter of 2 Kings (as Cogan and Tadmor point out, "the reason for this omission lies in the very nature of the Moabite document. It is a royal victory stele recording the triumphs of its author [Mesha], initiated by the [Moabite] god Chemosh and sanctified by him" [AB, 50; cf. Horn, *Biblical Archaeology Review*, 57]).

Another important figure in this passage is, of course, King Jehoshaphat of Judah, and it is to a brief discussion of this godly king (cf. his accession and judgment formulas in 1 Ki. 22:41–44) that we now turn. Scholars have long noted the rather close parallels between this chapter of 2 Kings, and 1 Ki. 22, where once again King Jehoshaphat of Judah is allied with an Omride king of Israel (in this case, Ahab) against a common enemy (in this case, Aram), and once again Jehoshaphat takes the initiative in seeking out a prophet of Yahweh (here, Micaiah) to obtain a victory oracle. Once again, the Israelite prophet seemingly has higher regard for the Judahite monarch than his Israelite counterpart, and several of the passages in the two chapters evidence identical phraseology (cf. 1 Ki. 22:4 with 2 Ki. 3:7; and 1 Ki. 22:7 with 2 Ki. 3:11). Not surprisingly, some scholars have suggested that these two accounts are later variants of one and the same event, but the historical differences clearly outweigh the similarities.

In any case, Jehoshaphat's seeming ignorance in 1 Ki. 22:29–33, where he is urged to wear his royal robes into battle, while the Israelite king Ahab disguised himself (presumably as a common soldier), finds no counterpart in the present passage. Even though Jehoshaphat appeared as willing as ever to aid his Israelite counterpart (v. 7). The Judahite king seems more equal in status with Joram than he did with Ahab in the Ramoth-Gilead affair. Certainly, the prophet Elisha seems to think so, for when apprised that (at least in Joram's opinion) "it was Yahweh who called us three kings together to hand us over to Moab," the prophet retorts, "As surely as Yahweh of Hosts lives, whom I serve, if I did not have respect for the presence of Jehoshaphat king of Judah, I would not look at you or even notice you" (v. 14). It is the presence of the Judahite king, which, apparently, eventually saved the day for the kings of Israel and of Edom (the latter unnamed in the present text, but nevertheless undoubtedly representing a welcome third partner in the coalition; cf. v. 9).

3:9–12. Impending disaster for the Israelite coalition. As already pointed out, the coalition of the three kings and their armies followed a southern, circuitous route to engage the enemy (cf. the helpful map in Cogan and Tadmor, AB, 41; they suggest interpreting the reference in v. 8 to the coalition traveling "through the Desert of Edom" as signifying travel via "the Desert of Edom Road," a road south and east of the Dead Sea leading to the eastern desert [see p. 44 of their commentary]). Perhaps Hobbs (WBC, 40) is correct to suggest that such a southern route, through the Negev (Judean) desert and past the southern tip of the Dead Sea, was necessary since the more typical northern approaches, across the Jordan River near Jericho, were firmly in enemy hands. In any case, the lengthy and difficult march soon took its toll. After a "roundabout march" of seven days, there was no

482	420, 4567	3547	4242, 3937	3937	2050.131	420, 5204
pn	prep, *n ms*	pn	intrg, prep, ps 1cs	cj, prep, ps 2ms	v Qal impv 2ms	prep, *n mp*
אֱלִישָׁע	אֶל־מֶלֶךְ	יִשְׂרָאֵל	מַה־לִּי	וָלָךְ	לֵךְ	אֶל־נְבִיאֵי
'ĕlîshā'	'el-melekh	yisrā'ēl	mah-lî	wālākh	lēkh	'el-nevî'ê
Elisha	to the king of	Israel	what to me	and to you	go	to the prophets of

1	420, 5204	525	569.121	3937	4567	3547
n ms, ps 2ms	cj, prep, *n mp*	n fs, ps 2ms	cj, v Qal impf 3ms	prep, ps 3ms	*n ms*	pn
אָבִיךָ	וְאֶל־נְבִיאֵי	אִמֶּךָ	וַיֹּאמֶר	לוֹ	מֶלֶךְ	יִשְׂרָאֵל
'āvîkhā	we'el-nevî'ê	'immekhā	wayyō'mer	lô	melekh	yisrā'ēl
your father	and to the prophets of	your mother	and he said	to him	the king of	Israel

414	3706, 7410.111	3176	3937, 8421	4567	431	3937, 5598.141
adv	cj, v Qal pf 3ms	pn	prep, num	art, n mp	art, dem pron	prep, v Qal inf con
אַל	כִּי־קָרָא	יְהוָה	לִשְׁלֹשֶׁת	הַמְּלָכִים	הָאֵלֶּה	לָתֵת
'al	kî-qārā'	yehwāh	lishlōsheth	hammelākhîm	hā'ēlleh	lāthēth
no	because He has called	Yahweh	to the three of	the kings	the these	to give

881	904, 3135, 4262	**14.**	569.121	482	2508, 3176	6893	866
do, ps 3mp	prep, *n fs*, pn		cj, v Qal impf 3ms	pn	adj, pn	n fp	rel pron
אוֹתָם	בְּיַד־מוֹאָב		וַיֹּאמֶר	אֱלִישָׁע	חַי־יְהוָה	צְבָאוֹת	אֲשֶׁר
'ôthām	beyadh-mô'āv		wayyō'mer	'ĕlîshā'	chay-yehwāh	tsevā'ôth	'ăsher
them	into the hand of Moab		and he said	Elisha	Yahweh living	hosts	whom

6198.115	3937, 6686	3706	4020	6686	3194	4567, 3171	603
v Qal pf 1cs	prep, n mp, ps 3ms	cj	cj	*n mp*	pn	*n ms*, pn	pers pron
עָמַדְתִּי	לְפָנָיו	כִּי	לוּלֵי	פְּנֵי	יְהוֹשָׁפָט	מֶלֶךְ־יְהוּדָה	אֲנִי
'āmadhtî	lephānāv	kî	lûlê	penê	yehôshāphāṭ	melekh-yehûdhāh	'ănî
I stand	before Him	if	if not	the face of	Jehoshaphat	the king of Judah	I

5558.151	524, 5202.525	420	524, 7495.125	**15.**	6498
v Qal act ptc ms	cj, v Hiphil impf 1cs	prep, ps 2ms	cj, cj, v Qal impf 1cs, ps 2ms		cj, adv
נֹשֵׂא	אִם־אַבִּיט	אֵלֶיךָ	וְאִם־אֶרְאֶךָּ		וְעַתָּה
nōsē'	'im-'abbîṭ	'ēlêkhā	we'im-'er'ekkā		we'attāh
lifting up	if I will look	at you	or if I will see you		but now

4089.133, 3937	5235.351	2030.111	3626, 5235.341
v Qal impv 2mp, prep, ps 1cs	v Piel ptc ms	cj, v Qal pf 3ms	prep, v Piel inf con
קְחוּ־לִי	מְנַגֵּן	וְהָיָה	כְּנַגֵּן
qōchû-lî	menaggēn	wehāyāh	kenaggēn
bring to me	a musician	and it was	when playing the stringed instrument

5235.351	2030.122	6142	3135, 3176	**16.**	569.121	3662
art, v Piel ptc ms	cj, v Qal impf 3fs	prep, ps 3ms	*n fs*, pn		cj, v Qal impf 3ms	adv
הַמְנַגֵּן	וַתְּהִי	עָלָיו	יַד־יְהוָה		וַיֹּאמֶר	כֹּה
hamnaggēn	wattehî	'ālâv	yadh-yehwāh		wayyō'mer	kōh
the musician	then it was	upon him	the hand of Yahweh		and he said	thus

569.111	3176	6449.142	5337	2172	1386	1386	**17.**	3706, 3662
v Qal pf 3ms	pn	v Qal inf abs	art, n ms	art, dem pron	n mp	n mp		cj, adv
אָמַר	יְהוָה	עָשֹׂה	הַנַּחַל	הַזֶּה	גֵּבִים	גֵּבִים		כִּי־כֹה
'āmar	yehwāh	'āsōh	hannachal	hazzeh	gēvîm	gēvîm		kî-khōh
He has said	Yahweh	make	the wadi	the this	cisterns	cisterns		because thus

569.111	3176	3940, 7495.128	7593	3940, 7495.128	1700	5337
v Qal pf 3ms	pn	neg part, v Qal impf 2mp	n fs	cj, neg part, v Qal impf 2mp	n ms	cj, art, n ms
אָמַר	יְהוָה	לֹא־תִרְאוּ	רוּחַ	וְלֹא־תִרְאוּ	גֶּשֶׁם	וְהַנַּחַל
'āmar	yehwāh	lō'-thir'û	rûach	welō'-thir'û	gheshem	wehannachal
He has said	Yahweh	you will not see	wind	and you will not see	rain	but the wadi

And the king of Israel said unto him, Nay: for the LORD hath called these three kings together, to deliver them into the hand of Moab: ... summoned us three kings, only to put us into the power of Moab, *JB* ... called us three kings out to put us at the mercy of the Moabites, *REB* ... put them in the grasp of Moab, *NAB*.

14. And Elisha said, As the LORD of hosts liveth, before whom I stand: ... As the LORD of armies lives, *Beck* ... As surely as the LORD All-Powerful lives, whom I serve, *NCV*.

surely, were it not that I regard the presence of Jehoshaphat the king of Judah, I would not look toward thee, nor see thee: ... I would not look your way, I would not notice you, *Moffatt* ... I would not spare a look or a glance for you, *NEB*.

15. But now bring me a minstrel: ... bring me one that can touch the strings, *Rotherham* ... bring me a harp, *Fenton* ... get me a player of music, *BB*.

And it came to pass, when the minstrel played, that the hand of the LORD came upon him: ... when the musician played, *NKJV* ... the power of the LORD, *NRSV*.

16. And he said, Thus saith the LORD, Make this valley full of ditches: ... Dig in this valley ditch after ditch, *JB* ... Make the channel of this torrent full of ditches, *Douay* ... Make this valley full of trenches, *MRB* ... Dig ditches all over this dry stream bed, *Good News*.

17. For thus saith the LORD, Ye shall not see wind, neither shall ye see rain: ... Though you see no wind or rain, *BB* ... No wind shall be perceived, and no rain shall be seen, *Fenton* ... Never a sign shall there be of wind or rain, *Knox*.

yet that valley shall be filled with water: ... yet that dry brook shall be filled with water, *Goodspeed* ... but that stream-bed shall be filled with water, *RSV* ... yet that wadi shall fill up with water, *Anchor* ... this dry ravine shall be so full of water, *Moffatt*.

that ye may drink, both ye, and your cattle, and your beasts: ... and you and your troops and your baggage animals will drink, *JB* ... You will have plenty for yourselves and for your cattle and your other animals, *NLT* ... for you and your army and your pack-animals, *NEB*.

---

more water either for the soldiers or for their animals (v. 9). This is the first instance in the present chapter of the persistent motif of water (or the lack thereof) so characteristic of the narratives about Elisha. Although there are some indications that climatic conditions in biblical Israel were a bit wetter than they are today, the Negev desert has always been a desolate place, with sparse vegetation and few permanent settlements and currently often averaging less than four inches (100 mm) of rain a year, according to the map found in *Moody Atlas of Bible Lands,* 50. Such would also be the case with the Arabah, the rift valley directly south of the Dead Sea and east of the Negev, where Cogan and Tadmor would place the "Desert of Edom Road" (probably the road following wadi Zered to the eastern desert).

At any rate, the allied armies were facing impending disaster, if water was not soon to be found (v. 9). Typically biblical is the terminology Joram employs in v. 10 concerning God: "Has Yahweh called us three kings together only to hand us over to Moab?" Direct, immediate agency is attributed to the deity, whereas we, today, would generally imply only secondary agency to God, recognizing human initiative and the possibility of human error (or, as typically the case in popular Christian terminology, attributing impending disaster almost invariably to the realm of Satan). Nonetheless, Joram's stunning lack of faith is meant to contrast sharply with Jehoshaphat's more rational response, "Is there no prophet of Yahweh with us, that we may inquire of Yahweh through him?" As already noted (see above, on 1:16f), formal inquiry by the prophet of Yahweh was essential for military success in ancient Israel (this is the background, for example, of the prophetic charade found in 1 Ki. 22:6, 13). The response was soon given. One no less than the chief-servant of the great prophet Elijah was present ("Elisha, who used to pour water on the hands of Elijah"; the precise import of this action is uncertain, but it undoubtedly reflects some sort of menial task; cf. 1 Ki. 19:21, where, from the beginning, Elisha was termed Elijah's "attendant" [so NIV; the Hebrew phrase, "and he served him," conveys the idea of his being his "chief assistant" or the like; cf. Brown-Driver-Briggs, 1058]). Note that water is again connected with the Elisha narrative. Also, Elisha is here, as often, introduced in the narrative in response to a crisis.

3:13–19. Elisha's response. After a scornful, preliminary comment concerning Joram (with suitable rejoinder by the king), and then the summons for the harpist to play (vv. 13ff), Elisha gave his oracle (vv. 16–19). Perhaps as clearly as anywhere, we find the contrast between whom the prophet serves (Yahweh of hosts, v. 14) and whom he does not (Joram his earthly king, vv. 13f). The prophet was

2000	4527.221	4448	8685.117	894	4898
art, dem pron	v Niphal impf 3ms	n mp	cj, v Qal pf 2mp	pers pron	cj, n mp, ps 2mp
הַהוּא	יִמָּלֵא	מָיִם	וּשְׁתִיתֶם	אַתֶּם	וּמִקְנֵיכֶם
hahû'	yimmālē'	māyim	ûshethîthem	'attem	ûmiqōnêkhem
the that	it will be filled with	water	and you will drink	you	and your cattle

966		7327.211	2148	904, 6084	3176	5598.111
cj, n fs, ps 2mp	**18.**	cj, v Niphal pf 3ms	dem pron	prep, *n fd*	pn	cj, v Qal pf 3ms
וּבְהֶמְתְּכֶם		וְנָקַל	זֹאת	בְּעֵינֵי	יְהוָה	וְנָתַן
ûvehemtekhem		wenāqal	zō'th	be'ênê	yehwāh	wenāthan
and your animals		and it is trifling	this	in the eyes of	Yahweh	and He will give

881, 4262	904, 3135		5409.517	3725, 6111	4152
do, pn	prep, n fs, ps 2mp	**19.**	cj, v Hiphil pf 2mp	*adj, n fs*	n ms
אֶת־מוֹאָב	בְּיֶדְכֶם		וְהִכִּיתֶם	כָּל־עִיר	מִבְצָר
'eth-mô'āv	beyedhkhem		wehikkîthem	kol-'îr	mivtsār
Moab	into your hand		and you will strike down	all the cities of	fortification

3725, 6111	4143	3725, 6320	3005	5489.528
cj, *adj, n fs*	n ms	cj, *adj*, n ms	adj	v Hiphil impf 2mp
וְכָל־עִיר	מִבְחוֹר	וְכָל־עֵץ	טוֹב	תַּפִּילוּ
wekhol-'îr	mivchôr	wekhol-'ēts	tôv	tappîlû
and all the cities of	choosing	and every tree	good	you will cause to fall

3725, 4754, 4448	5845.128	3725	2610	3009B
cj, *adj, n mp*, n md	v Qal impf 2mp	cj, n ms	art, n fs	art, adj
וְכָל־מַעְיְנֵי־מַיִם	תִּסְתֹּמוּ	וְכֹל	הַחֶלְקָה	הַטּוֹבָה
wekhol-ma'ăynê-mayim	tistōmû	wekhōl	hachelqāh	hattôvāh
and all the springs of water	you will stop up	and everything	the tracts of land	the good

3628.528	904, 63		2030.121	904, 1269	3626, 6148.141
v Hiphil impf 2mp	prep, art, n fp	**20.**	cj, v Qal impf 3ms	prep, art, n ms	prep, v Qal inf con
תַּכְאִבוּ	בָּאֲבָנִים		וַיְהִי	בַבֹּקֶר	כַּעֲלוֹת
takh'ivû	bā'ăvānîm		wayhî	vabbōqer	ka'ălôth
you will inflict	with the stones		and it was	in the morning	when the going up of

4647	2079, 4448	971.152	4623, 1932	110	4527.222	800
art, n fs	cj, intrj, n md	v Qal act ptc mp	prep, *n ms*	pn	cj, v Niphal impf 3fs	art, n fs
הַמִּנְחָה	וְהִנֵּה־מַיִם	בָּאִים	מִדֶּרֶךְ	אֱדוֹם	וַתִּמָּלֵא	הָאָרֶץ
hamminchāh	wehinnēh-mayim	bā'îm	midderekh	'ĕdhôm	wattimmālē'	hā'ārets
the offering	then behold water	coming	from the way of	Edom	and it was filled	the land

882, 4448		3725, 4262	8471.116	3706, 6148.116	4567	3937, 4032.241
prep, art, n mp	**21.**	cj, *adj*, pn	v Qal pf 3cp	cj, v Qal pf 3cp	art, n mp	prep, v Niphal inf con
אֶת־הַמָּיִם		וְכָל־מוֹאָב	שָׁמְעוּ	כִּי־עָלוּ	הַמְּלָכִים	לְהִלָּחֶם
'eth-hammāyim		wekhol-mô'āv	shāme'û	kî-'ālû	hammelākhîm	lehillāchem
with the water		and all Moab	they heard	that they had come up	the kings	to fight

904	7094.226	4623, 3725	2391.151	2383	4767
prep, ps 3mp	cj, v Niphal impf 3mp	prep, n ms	v Qal act ptc ms	n fs	cj, adv
בָּם	וַיִּצָּעֲקוּ	מִכֹּל	חֹגֵר	חֲגֹרָה	וָמָעְלָה
bām	wayyitstsā'ăqû	mikkōl	chōghēr	chăghōrāh	wāma'ălāh
against them	and they were called	from everyone	those girding	a belt	and upward

6198.126	6142, 1397		8326.526	904, 1269	8507	2178.112
cj, v Qal impf 3mp	prep, art, n ms	**22.**	cj, v Hiphil impf 3mp	prep, art, n ms	cj, art, n fs	v Qal pf 3fs
וַיַּעַמְדוּ	עַל־הַגְּבוּל		וַיַּשְׁכִּימוּ	בַבֹּקֶר	וְהַשֶּׁמֶשׁ	זָרְחָה
wayya'amdhû	'al-haggevûl		wayyashkîmû	vabbōqer	wehashshemesh	zārechāh
and they stood	on the border		and they rose early	in the morning	and the sun	it shone

18. And this is but a light thing in the sight of the LORD: ... this is an easy thing for the LORD to do, *Good News* ... But this is a small thing in the sight of the Lord, *Geneva* ... And since the LORD does not consider this enough, *NAB* ... This is only a trifle in the sight of the LORD, *NRSV*.

he will deliver the Moabites also into your hand: ... he shall also give Moab into your hand, *Goodspeed* ... put the Moabites into your power, *Moffatt* ... he means to give you victory over Moab, *Knox* ... put Moab at your mercy, *REB*.

19. And ye shall smite every fenced city, and every choice city: ... and you shall conquer every fortified city, *RSV* ... And you are to put every walled town to destruction, *BB* ... and you shall storm all the fortified cities, and all the best towns, *Fenton* ... And ye shall destroy all strong towns and all goodly cities, *Tyndale*.

and shall fell every good tree, and stop all wells of water: ... and shall cut down every fruitful tree, and shall stop up all the springs of water, *Douay* ... and shall fell every faire tree and shall stop all the fountains of water, *Geneva* ... close up all the springs of water, *Beck*.

and mar every good piece of land with stones: ... and ruin all their good land with stones, *NLT* ... and ruin every fertile plot with stones, *Anchor* ... you will spoil every good piece of land by littering it with stones, *NEB* ... And every goodly heritage shall ye mar with stones, *Rotherham*.

20. And it came to pass in the morning, when the meat offering was offered: ... The next morning,

---

beholden to his God, rather than to any earthly figure. Once again, the contrast between the Omride Joram of Israel and the Davidic Jehoshaphat of Judah is emphasized. If it were not for the southern king, who was loyal to Elisha's God Yahweh, Elisha would not even deign to seek an oracle for his earthly monarch, servants and colleagues ("the utter disrespect for the house of Omri is rarely more clearly expressed" [Hobbs, WBC, 36]).

Not surprisingly, there has been much scholarly interest in the reference in v. 15 to the summoning of the harpist as a preliminary to the act of prophesying. Although some have perhaps overstated the "ecstatic elements" present in such occasions, it is certainly the case that there seem to be clear links between prophesying and music, at least in early Israel. The most commonly cited example is found in 1 Sam 10:1–16, where the youthful Saul is told by Samuel that he will meet a procession of prophets "with lyres, tambourines, flutes and harps being played before them, and they will be prophesying" (v. 5); indeed, Saul himself would prophesy with them, with the Spirit of Yahweh coming upon him "in power," and he would be "changed into a different person" (v. 6). Later on, David would also use the harp to help quiet King Saul during his rages (cf. 1 Sam. 16:16, 23; 18:10f; etc.). While these occurrences do not link up with the act of prophesying, per se, they do correspond with the sending of a "spirit from God" (16:23; cf. vv. 15f). Finally, a note from 1 Chr. 25:1–8 where the "ministry of prophesying" is specifically linked to the accompaniment of harps, lyres and cymbals (v. 1; cf. also v. 3, where the Levitical musician Jeduthun is said to have "prophesied, using the harp in thanking and praising Yahweh"). At least in early monarchical Israel, prophecy and the playing of the harp were apparently rather often closely linked (the fact that so many of the later writing prophets' oracles were in poetic form also may be relevant to this topic).

The resultant oracle of Elisha (2 Ki. 3:16–19) is replete with images of short-term prediction, as one might expect (cf. the comments on 1:3f). Indicating a remarkable reversal of the present situation, Elisha prophesied that the valley would soon be filled with water, not by means of a local rainstorm (although flash-flooding by means of a distant cloudburst is not necessarily altogether precluded), but by a clearly supernatural action or, at least, by remarkably supernatural timing.

A further word concerning the phenomena of "reversals" is appropriate at this point, in light of passages of Scripture such as the "Song of Hannah" (1 Sam. 2:1–10, cf., especially, vv. 6–9). One of the chief activities of Yahweh, the true God of Israel, is to effect "reversals" in the lives of his people—"to comfort the afflicted, and to afflict the comfortable" (cf. Deut. 10:14–22; 32:39). The very name of Yahweh, coming as it does from the verb "to be" (hāyāh, HED #2030), signifies "the Eternal One." And such certainly seems to be the situation envisioned here in 2 Ki. 3:17f. Life-giving water would thus miraculously appear, and rebellious Moab would, as it were, miraculously disappear (the repeated references to destruction in v. 19 represent systematic, comprehensive annihilation of urban and rural regions alike).

3:20–25. Prophetic fulfillment. Whereas there was too little water in v. 9, now there is, perhaps, too much. There is much interest also in this section on the color red, the color of blood. Commentators point out the red color of the sandstone in the region. Many particularly draw atten-

6142, 4448	7495.126	4262	4623, 5224	881, 4448	121	3626, 1879
prep, art, n md	cj, v Qal impf 3mp	pn	prep, prep	do, art, n md	adj	prep, art, n ms
עַל־הַמָּ֫יִם	וַיִּרְאוּ	מוֹאָב	מִנֶּגֶד	אֶת־הַמַּ֫יִם	אֲדֻמִּים	כַּדָּם
'al-hammāyim	wayyir'û	mô'āv	minneghedh	'eth-hammayim	'ădhummîm	kaddām
on the water	and they looked	Moab	from before	the water	red	like the blood

23.	569.126	1879	2172	2817.642	2817.216
	cj, v Qal impf 3mp	n ms	dem pron	v Hophal inf abs	v Niphal pf 3cp
	וַיֹּאמְרוּ	דָּם	זֶה	הָחֳרֵב	נֶחֶרְבוּ
	wayyō'mᵉrû	dām	zeh	hāchărēv	nechervû
	and they said	blood	this	being laid waste	they have been completely laid waste

4567	5409.526	382	881, 7739	6498	8395	4262
art, n mp	cj, v Hiphil impf 3mp	n ms	do, n ms, ps 3ms	cj, adv	prep, art, n ms	pn
הַמְּלָכִים	וַיַּכּוּ	אִישׁ	אֶת־רֵעֵהוּ	וְעַתָּה	לַשָּׁלָל	מוֹאָב
hammᵉlākhîm	wayyakkû	'îsh	'eth-rē'ēhû	wᵉ'attāh	lashshālāl	mô'āv
the kings	and they struck down	each	his fellow	and now	to the booty	O Moab

24.	971.126	420, 4402	3547	7251.126	3547	5409.526
	cj, v Qal impf 3mp	prep, *n ms*	pn	cj, v Qal impf 3mp	pn	cj, v Hiphil impf 3mp
	וַיָּבֹאוּ	אֶל־מַחֲנֵה	יִשְׂרָאֵל	וַיָּקֻמוּ	יִשְׂרָאֵל	וַיַּכּוּ
	wayyāvō'û	'el-machnēh	yisrā'ēl	wayyāqumû	yisrā'ēl	wayyakkû
	and they came	to the camp of	Israel	and they rose up	Israel	and they struck down

881, 4262	5308.126	4623, 6686	971.126, 904	5409.541
do, pn	cj, v Qal impf 3mp	prep, n mp, ps 3mp	cj, v Qal impf 3mp, prep, ps 3fs	cj, v Hiphil inf con
אֶת־מוֹאָב	וַיָּנֻסוּ	מִפְּנֵיהֶם	וַיָּבוֹ־בָהּ	וְהַכּוֹת
'eth-mô'āv	wayyānusû	mippᵉnêhem	wayyāvô-vāhh	wᵉhakkôth
Moab	and they fled	from before them	and they came against them	and striking down

881, 4262	25.	6111	2117.126	3725, 2615	3009B	8390.526
do, pn		cj, art, n fp	cj, v Qal impf 3mp	cj, *adj*, n fs	adj	v Hiphil impf 3mp
אֶת־מוֹאָב		וְהֶעָרִים	יַהֲרֹסוּ	וְכָל־חֶלְקָה	טוֹבָה	יַשְׁלִיכוּ
'eth-mô'āv		wᵉhe'ārîm	yahrōsû	wᵉkhol-chelqāh	tôvāh	yashlîkhû
Moab		and the cities	they tore down	and all the tracts of land	good	they overthrew

382, 63	4527.316	3725, 4754, 4448	5845.126
n ms, n fs, ps 3ms	cj, v Piel pf 3cp, ps 3fs	cj, *adj*, *n ms*, n md	v Qal impf 3mp
אִישׁ־אַבְנוֹ	וּמִלְאוּהָ	וְכָל־מַעְיַן־מַיִם	יִסְתֹּמוּ
'îsh-'avnô	ûmil'ûāh	wᵉkhol-ma'ăyan-mayim	yistōmû
each his stone	and they filled it	and all the springs of water	they stopped up

3725, 6320, 3005	5489.526	5912, 8080.511	63	904, 7309	7309
cj, *adj*, *n ms*, adj	v Hiphil impf 3mp	adv, v Hiphil pf 3ms	n fp, ps 3fs	prep, pn	pn
וְכָל־עֵץ־טוֹב	יַפִּילוּ	עַד־הִשְׁאִיר	אֲבָנֶיהָ	בַּקִּיר	חֲרָשֶׂת
wᵉkhol-'ēts-tôv	yappîlû	'adh-hish'îr	'ăvānêâh	baqqîr	chărāseth
and all the good trees	they caused to fall	until they were left	its stones	in Kir	Hareseth

5621.126	7336	5409.526	26.	7495.121	4567	4262
cj, v Qal impf 3mp	art, n mp	cj, v Hiphil impf 3mp, ps 3fs		cj, v Qal impf 3ms	*n ms*	pn
וַיָּסֹבּוּ	הַקַּלָּעִים	וַיַּכּוּהָ		וַיַּרְא	מֶלֶךְ	מוֹאָב
wayyāsōbû	haqqallā'îm	wayyakkûāh		wayyarᵉ'	melekh	mô'āv
and they surrounded	the slingers	and they struck it down		and he saw	the king of	Moab

3706, 2480.111	4623	4560	4089.121	882	8124, 4109	382
cj, v Qal pf 3ms	prep, ps 3ms	art, n fs	cj, v Qal impf 3ms	prep, ps 3ms	num, num	n ms
כִּי־חָזַק	מִמֶּנּוּ	הַמִּלְחָמָה	וַיִּקַּח	אוֹתוֹ	שְׁבַע־מֵאוֹת	אִישׁ
kî-chāzaq	mimmennû	hammilchāmāh	wayyiqqach	'ôthô	shevaʻ-mē'ôth	'îsh
that it was stronger	than he	the war	and he took	with him	seven hundred	men

about the time for offering the sacrifice, *NIV* ... about the time of offering the oblation, *MRB* ... at the ascending of the morning-present, *Young* ... when the grain offering was offered, *NKJV*.

that, behold, there came water by the way of Edom, and the country was filled with water: ... water came from the direction of Edom, and the whole terrain was flooded, *JB* ... water came flowing from the direction of Edom and covered the ground, *Good News* ... water filled all the plain, *Knox* ... and filled the valley, *NCV*.

21. And when all the Moabites heard that the kings were come up to fight against them: ... hearing that the kings had come to make war against them, *BB* ... all Moab heard that the kings had come to give them battle, *NAB* ... the kings had marched to make war on them, *Anchor* ... the three armies marching against them, *NLT*.

they gathered all that were able to put on armour, and upward: ... and every man old enough to wear a belt and bear arms was called up, *Beck* ... from every one girding on a girdle and upward, *Young* ... all who were old enough to gird themselves, or older, were called to arms, *Berkeley* ... and had convoked an armed force, and had advanced, *Fenton*.

and stood in the border: ... and stationed on the frontier, *NEB* ... and waited in the borders, *Tyndale* ... stood ready to defend their frontier, *Knox*.

22. And they rose up early in the morning, and the sun shone upon the water, and the Moabites saw the water on the other side as red as blood: ... and, seeing the water in front of them red as blood, *Moffatt* ... they saw the water across from them, and it looked red as blood, *NCV* ... making it look as red as blood, *Good News* ... the water looked red-like blood, *NIV*.

23. And they said, This is blood: the kings are surely slain, and they have smitten one another: ... the kings must have fought together, *NRSV* ... The kings are utterly destroyed, *Anchor* ... they have stricken one another, *KJVII* ... The kings must have quarrelled and attacked one another, *REB*.

now therefore, Moab, to the spoil: ... men of Moab, there lies the spoil!, *Knox* ... Let's go and collect the plunder!, *NLT*.

24. And when they came to the camp of Israel: ... when they came to the tents of Israel, *BB* ... when they came to the host of Israel, *Tyndale*.

the Israelites rose up and smote the Moabites, so that they fled before them: ... the Israelites turned out and attacked them and drove the Moabites headlong in flight, *NEB* ... the Israelites sprang up and attacked the Moabites, *Anchor* ... But Israel arose and assailed Moab, *Fenton* ... the Israelites arose and struck the Moabites, *NASB*.

but they went forward smiting the Moabites, even in their country: ... They went into their country and defeated Moab, *Beck* ... and they enter into Moab, so as to smite Moab, *Young* ... as they entered Moab they continued the attack, *NRSV* ... They ranged through the countryside striking down the Moabites, *NAB*.

25. And they beat down the cities: ... they demolished the towns, *Moffatt* ... They tore down the cities, *NCV* ... They razed the towns to the ground, *REB* ... they overthrew the cities, *RSV*.

and on every good piece of land cast every man his stone, and filled it: ... smothered their best plough-

---

tion to the Hebrew wordplay with the name "Edom" in v. 20 from the Hebrew root 'ādhām ('ādhēm, HED #118) that probably underlies both the proper name "Adam" (HED #120) and the common term "man," "humankind" ('ādhām, HED #119) made from the ground.

Whatever the cause of the reddish appearance of the waters, whether of entirely natural or of supernatural causes, the Moabites were completely surprised (Hobbs, WBC, 37, notes that, for the Moabites to see the sun shining on the waters, they must have been looking east—hence the allied armies had apparently completely outflanked them). And they foolishly misread the situation entirely. Knowing that all too often the nations of Israel, Judah and Edom were mutual enemies, not allies, they (certainly providentially, from the Israelite point of view) immediately assumed that victory was theirs (v. 23). This was, to be sure, neither the first nor the last time that such a fatal misconception has completely altered the course of battle. The subsequent verses detail almost word-for-word the fulfillment of Elisha's prophecy.

3:26–27. Mesha's desperate sacrifice; utter defeat averted. Since the phrase "to break through to the king of Edom" (2 Ki. 3:26) seems odd at first glance, some have sought to emend "Edom" to read "Aram." (The names are very close in appearance in Hebrew.) Others have suggested that perhaps Edom had deserted to Moab during the campaign (although the present text does not indicate this). Hobbs (WBC, 37f), however, notes that the Hebrew phrase, as it stands, could well be read "to break through against the king of Edom" (also cf. Cogan and Tadmor, AB, 47, who suggest that the Edomite line may well have been the weakest link in the

8418.151 v Qal act ptc ms שֹׁלֵף shōlēph drawing	2820 n fs חֶרֶב cherev a sword	3937, 1260.541 prep, v Hiphil inf con לְהַבְקִיעַ lehavqîa‘ to divide	420, 4567 prep, *n ms* אֶל־מֶלֶךְ 'el-melekh to the king of	110 pn אֱדוֹם 'ĕdhôm Edom	3940 cj, neg part וְלֹא welō' but not	3310.116 v Qal pf 3mp יָכְלוּ yākhōlû they were able

27.	4089.121 cj, v Qal impf 3ms וַיִּקַּח wayyiqqach and he took	881, 1158 do, n ms, ps 3ms אֶת־בְּנוֹ 'eth-benô his son	1111 art, n ms הַבְּכוֹר habbekhôr the firstborn	866, 4566.121 rel pron, v Qal impf 3ms אֲשֶׁר־יִמְלֹךְ 'ăsher-yimlōkh who he would reign	8809 prep, ps 3ms תַּחְתָּיו tachtâv instead of him

6148.521 cj, v Hiphil impf 3ms, ps 3ms וַיַּעֲלֵהוּ wayya‘ălēhû and he caused him to go up	6150 n fs עֹלָה ‘ōlāh a burnt offering	6142, 2440 prep, art, n fs עַל־הַחֹמָה ‘al-hachōmāh on the wall	2030.121 cj, v Qal impf 3ms וַיְהִי wayhî and it was	7397, 1448 n ms, adj קֶצֶף־גָּדוֹל qetseph-gādhôl great anger

6142, 3547 prep, pn עַל־יִשְׂרָאֵל ‘al-yisrā'ēl against Israel	5450.126 cj, v Qal impf 3mp וַיִּסְעוּ wayyis‘û and they pulled out	4623, 6142 prep, prep, ps 3ms מֵעָלָיו mē‘ālâv from against him	8178.126 cj, v Qal impf 3mp וַיָּשֻׁבוּ wayyāshuvû and they returned	3937, 800 prep, art, n fs לָאָרֶץ lā'ārets to the land

4:1	828 cj, n fs וְאִשָּׁה we'ishshāh and a woman	259 num אַחַת 'achath one	4623, 5571 prep, *n fp* מִנְּשֵׁי minneshê from the women of	1158, 5204 *n mp*, art, n mp בְּנֵי־הַנְּבִיאִים vênê-hannevî'îm the sons of the prophets	7094.112 v Qal pf 3fs צָעֲקָה tsā‘ăqāh she cried out

land, *Knox* ... over all the beautiful gardens they spread stones and destroyed them, *Fenton* ... on every goodly heritage they cast every man his stone, *Rotherham* ... As they passed by a fertile field, every Israelite would throw a stone on it, *Good News*.

and they stopped all the wells of water, and felled all the good trees: ... all the springs of the water they stopped up, every fruit tree they cut down, *Berkeley* ... they stopped all the fountains of water, *MAST* ... cut down all the trees that bore fruit, *Douay* ... they blocked every water-hole and felled every productive tree, *JB*.

only in Kir-haraseth left they the stones thereof; howbeit the slingers went about it, and smote it: ... but even that came under attack, *NLT* ... they left intact the stones of Kir Haraseth, *NKJV* ... they harried Moab until only the men in Kir-hareseth were left, *Goodspeed* ... men armed with slings surrounded it and attacked it as well, *NIV*.

26. And when the king of Moab saw that the battle was too sore for him: ... the war had gone against him, *NEB* ... the battle was too strong for him, *KJVII* ... the war was too much for him, *Anchor* ... the battle was too fierce for him, *NASB*.

he took with him seven hundred men that drew swords: ... seven hundred men armed with swords, *BB* ... seven hundred trained soldiers, *Fenton*.

to break through even unto the king of Edom: but they could not: ... to break through to king of Aram, but he failed, *NAB* ... in the hope of breaking a way out and going to the King of Aram, *JB*.

27. Then he took his eldest son that should have reigned in his stead: ... who would have succeeded him as king, *Beck* ... the heir to the throne, *Moffatt* ... who would have been king after him, *NCV*.

and offered him for a burnt offering upon the wall: ... and causeth him to ascend, *Young* ... offered him up as a sacrifice, *Berkeley* ... as a whole-offering on the city wall, *REB* ... sacrificed him as a burnt offering, *NLT*.

And there was great indignation against Israel: ... The Israelites were filled with such consternation at this sight, *NEB* ... there was great anger against Israel, *KJVII* ... And great wrath came upon Israel, *NRSV* ... for he was furious against Israel, *Fenton*.

and they departed from him, and returned to their own land: ... gave up the siege, *NAB* ... broke camp, *Anchor* ... the Israelites had to leave him alone and return home, *Moffatt* ... let him be, and went back to their own country, *Knox*.

4:1. Now there cried a certain woman of the wives of the sons of

chain of forces encircling the city). In any case, Mesha was by now very desperate, and this provides the context for his horrifying action described in the next verse: the deliberate sacrifice of his eldest son on the city wall, in the sight of the enemy Israelites.

Child sacrifice was an ugly, yet ever-present reality in many of the ancient nations which dwelt in the region of Syria-Palestine. Cogan and Tadmor (AB, 47) note how classical sources reported the frequent sacrifice of children in cities under siege in Phoenicia (present day Lebanon and north-Syria) and her colonies in north Africa (for further discussion of child sacrifice among Israel's neighbors, cf., Stager, "Eroticism and Infanticide at Ashkelon," *Biblical Archaeology Review* [July/August 1991]: 35–53, 72; cf., also, 2 Ki. 16:3, below, for Ahaz's sacrifice of his son). Another well-known example of child sacrifice in the OT, Jephthah's sacrifice of his daughter, his only child (Judg. 11:30–40), belongs rather to the classification of sacrifice offered in fulfillment of a vow.

In his helpful article, also in *Biblical Archaeology Review*, Baruch Margalit ("Why King Mesha of Moab Sacrificed His Oldest Son," [vol. 12, no. 6; November/December 1986], 62–63, 76) quotes a relevant Ugaritic (North Canaanite) prayer to Baal in connection with a besieged city, to the effect that one should offer (among other, lesser sacrifices) "a firstborn [male] child" so that Baal might "drive the [enemy] force from your gates/the aggressor from your walls." Margalit argues from this example that in the present Kings text Mesha was actually following "an integral, if seldom implemented, part of an age-old Canaanite tradition of sacral warfare." Thus, Mesha's conduct should actually be understood as, of all things, "an act of altruism" by religious tradition.

These verses demonstrate the pagans' dependence on religous rites no matter the morality or consequences of their actions. Let us pause here to reflect upon the power of religious tradition. How powerful, for good or for ill, religious tradition can be. As C. S. Lewis reminded us in the context of discussing the inclusion of bitter imprecations (cursings) in the Book of Psalms, "If the divine call does not make us better, it will make us very much worse. Of all bad men, religious bad men are the worst .... It gives a new application to Our Lord's words about 'counting the cost'" (*Reflections on the Psalms*, 32).

Whatever the rationale behind Mesha's shocking action, it seemed to work with terrible effectiveness, for as Margalit points out, "with this horrifying act, Mesha turned defeat into victory. The allied forces retreated and Moab retained its independence for the next two centuries." The relevant text here is 2 Ki. 3:27, which reads in the NIV, "The fury against Israel was great; they withdrew and returned to their own land." But this translation obscures somewhat the possibly intentional ambiguity of the Hebrew. As Cogan and Tadmor (AB, 47) point out, "This clause is one of the most perplexing items in Scripture." The Moabite Stone indicates that the Moabite god, Chemosh, had been angry with his land. The Hebrew text literally reads, "And there was [or came] great wrath [qetseph-gādhôl, HED #7397, 1448] against the Israelites." The question is, where did this wrath come from? Some would say from Chemosh, but that would seem unlikely for an Israelite writer to assert. To do so would have been to admit that a foreign deity was an actual power source rather than nothing (which they are often called) and that Mesha's sacrifice was in this sense efficacious. The Bible, of course, would not say such an absurd statement. False gods have no power whatsoever. Perhaps the reference was indeed left ambiguous, inasmuch as the biblical writer wanted to show that God would not permit an Omride to have an undiluted victory. In spite of the prophet and the decision of God against the Moabites, in the end, Jehoram was not allowed to relish the spoils of the victory, but had to retreat as a result. In any case, what an anticlimactic end to an otherwise stirring narrative of prophetic vindication (as we shall see below, in connection with the tragic case of King Josiah, this is not the only place in 2 Kings where a prophetic note of triumph ends in a very negative way; cf. the comments on 23:26–30). Our God does not always bring us happy endings.

4:1–7. An Israelite widow's debts are paid. The next four and a half chapters of 2 Kings largely center on the notable exploits of Elisha, both in his native land of Israel, and also in the surrounding environs. Despite a number of contrasts between the Elijah and the Elisha narratives concerning various motifs and methods of operation (e.g., Elijah mostly working alone, but Elisha working with disciples and the servant Gehazi), Elisha did imitate his master in one major respect, i.e., by ministering, as God led, to both Israelite and non-Israelite alike. Whereas Jesus our Lord delighted in pointing out to his own contemporaries Elijah's refusal to help out

420, 482	3937, 569.141	5860	382	4322.111	887	3156.113	3706
prep, pn	prep, v Qal inf con	n ms, ps 2ms	n ms, ps 1cs	v Qal pf 3ms	cj, pers pron	v Qal pf 2ms	cj
אֶל־אֱלִישָׁע	לֵאמֹר	עַבְדְּךָ	אִישִׁי	מֵת	וְאַתָּה	יָדַעְתָּ	כִּי
'el-'ělîshā'	lē'mōr	'avdekhā	'îshî	mēth	we'attāh	yādha'ăttā	kî
to Elisha	saying	your servant	my husband	he died	and you	you know	that

5860	2030.111	3486.151	881, 3176	5565.151	971.111
n ms, ps 2ms	v Qal pf 3ms	v Qal act ptc ms	do, pn	cj, art, v Qal act ptc ms	v Qal pf 3ms
עַבְדְּךָ	הָיָה	יְרֵא	אֶת־יְהוָה	וְהַנֹּשֶׁה	בָּא
'avdekhā	hāyāh	yārē'	'eth-yehwāh	wehannōsheh	bā'
your servant	he was	one who fears	Yahweh	and the creditor	he has come

4089.141	881, 8530	3315	3937	3937, 5860		569.121	420
prep, v Qal inf con	do, num	n mp, ps 1cs	prep, ps 3ms	prep, n mp	2.	cj, v Qal impf 3ms	prep, ps 3fs
לָקַחַת	אֶת־שְׁנֵי	יְלָדַי	לוֹ	לַעֲבָדִים		וַיֹּאמֶר	אֵלֶיהָ
lāqachath	'eth-shenê	yelādhay	lô	la'ăvādhîm		wayyō'mer	'ēlêāh
to take	the two of	my children	for himself	for slaves		and he said	to her

482	4242	6449.125, 3937	5222.532	3937	4242, 3552, 3937
pn	intrg	v Qal impf 1cs, prep, ps 2fs	v Hiphil impv 2fs	prep, ps 1cs	intrg, sub, prep, ps 2fs
אֱלִישָׁע	מָה	אֶעֱשֶׂה־לָּךְ	הַגִּידִי	לִי	מַה־יֶּשׁ־לְכִי
'ělîshā'	māh	'e'ěseh-lākh	haggîdhî	lî	mah-yesh-lekhî
Elisha	what	will I do for you	tell	to me	what there is to you

904, 1041	569.122	375	3937, 8569	3725	904, 1041	3706
prep, art, n ms	cj, v Qal impf 3fs	*sub*	prep, n fs, ps 2ms	n ms	prep, art, n ms	cj
בַּבָּיִת	וַתֹּאמֶר	אֵין	לְשִׁפְחָתְךָ	כֹּל	בַּבַּיִת	כִּי
babbāyith	wattō'mer	'ên	leshiphchāthekhā	khōl	babbayith	kî
in the house	and she said	there is not	to your female servant	anything	in the house	except

524, 624	8467		569.121	2050.132	8068.132, 3937	3747
cj, *n ms*	n ms	3.	cj, v Qal impf 3ms	v Qal impv 2fs	v Qal impv 2fs, prep, ps 2fs	n mp
אִם־אָסוּךְ	שָׁמֶן		וַיֹּאמֶר	לְכִי	שַׁאֲלִי־לָךְ	כֵּלִים
'im-'āsûkh	shāmen		wayyō'mer	lekhî	sha'ălî-lākh	kēlîm
only a pot of	olive oil		and he said	go	ask for yourself	vessels

4623, 2445	4623, 881	3725, 8333	3747	7673	414, 4745.524
prep, art, n ms	prep, do	*adj*, n ms, ps 2fs	n mp	adj	adv, v Hiphil juss 2fs
מִן־הַחוּץ	מֵאֵת	כָּל־שְׁכֵנָכִי	כֵּלִים	רֵקִים	אַל־תַּמְעִיטִי
min-hachûts	mē'ēth	kol-shekhēnākhî	kēlîm	rēqîm	'al-tam'îţî
from the outside	from	all your neighbors	vessels	empty	do not make few

	971.114	5646.114	1878	1185	1185, 1158
4.	cj, v Qal pf 2fs	cj, v Qal pf 2fs	art, n fs	prep, ps 2fs	cj, prep, n mp, ps 2fs
	וּבָאת	וְסָגַרְתְּ	הַדֶּלֶת	בַּעֲדֵךְ	וּבְעַד־בָּנַיִךְ
	ûvā'th	wesāghart	haddeleth	ba'ădhēkh	ûve'adh-bānayikh
	and you will go in	and you will shut	the door	behind you	and behind your sons

3441.114	6142	3725, 3747	431	4529	5450.524
cj, v Qal pf 2fs	prep	*adj*, art, n mp	art, dem pron	cj, art, adj	v Hiphil impf 2fs
וְיָצַקְתְּ	עַל	כָּל־הַכֵּלִים	הָאֵלֶּה	וְהַמָּלֵא	תַּסִּיעִי
weyātsaqōtte	'al	kol-hakkēlîm	hā'ēlleh	wehammālē'	tassî'î
and you will pour out	over	all the vessels	the these	and those full	you will pull up

	2050.122	4623, 882	5646.122	1878	1185	1185	1158
5.	cj, v Qal impf 3fs	prep, prep, ps 3ms	cj, v Qal impf 3fs	art, n fs	prep, ps 3fs	cj, prep	n mp, ps 3fs
	וַתֵּלֶךְ	מֵאִתּוֹ	וַתִּסְגֹּר	הַדֶּלֶת	בַּעֲדָהּ	וּבְעַד	בָּנֶיהָ
	wattēlekh	mē'ittô	wattisgōr	haddeleth	ba'ădhāhh	ûve'adh	bānêāh
	and she went	from with him	and she shut	the door	behind her	and behind	her sons

the prophets unto Elisha, saying, Thy servant my husband is dead: ... wife of a member of the prophetic brotherhood appealed to Elisha, *JB* ... a woman, a wife of one of the Preachers, appealed to Alisha, *Fenton*.

and thou knowest that thy servant did fear the LORD: and the creditor is come to take unto him my two sons to be bondmen: ... now his creditor is coming to take my two boys as his slaves, *NIV* ... a man he owed money to has come to take away my two sons as slaves in payment for my husband's debt, *Good News* ... threatening to take my two sons as slaves, *NLT*.

2. And Elisha said unto her, What shall I do for thee? tell me, what hast thou in the house?: ... How can I help you?, *NCV*.

And she said, Thine handmaid hath not any thing in the house, save a pot of oil: ... except a flask of oil, *Goodspeed* ... nothing in the house but a jar of oil, *NKJV* ... nothing left in my house at all but a drop of oil to anoint myself with, *Knox* ... save a pitcher with oil, *Tyndale*.

3. Then he said, Go, borrow thee vessels abroad of all thy neighbours, even empty vessels; borrow not a few: ... borrow vessels of all your neighbors, empty vessels and not too few, *RSV* ... vessels from all the inhabitants of the street,—barrels of a not small capacity, *Fenton* ... borrow vessels from everyone in the neighbourhood, *REB* ... as many empty vessels as you can, *NAB*.

4. And when thou art come in, thou shalt shut the door upon thee and upon thy sons: ... go into your house and shut the door behind you and your sons, *NCV*.

and shalt pour out into all those vessels, and thou shalt set aside that which is full: ... when they are full take them away, *Douay* ... and as each is filled, put it to one side, *NIV* ... whenever one is full, set it aside, *Moffatt*.

5. So she went from him, and shut the door upon her and upon her sons, who brought the vessels to her; and she poured out: ... they passed her the jars and she went on pouring, *JB* ... brought many jars to her, and she filled one after another, *NLT* ... they took the vessels to her and she put oil into them, *BB* ... They kept bringing containers to her, and she poured into them, *Beck*.

---

the Israelites during the three-and-a-half-year drought, rather being led to minister to the Phoenician widow in Zarephath (Luke 4:25f; cf. 1 Ki. 17:1, 7–16). He also noted Elisha's cleansing of the Syrian (or Aramean) leper Naaman, even though there surely were many Israelite lepers whom he did not cleanse (Luke 4:27; cf. 2 Ki. 5). It is, therefore, not only in the NT, but also in the OT, where we find emphasis on the ministry of God's leaders to Jew and Gentile alike (as well as to both male and female, rich and poor, famous and obscure). It is to a story about an obscure, indeed, entirely anonymous widow of a disciple of Elisha, that we now turn.

The present story (2 Ki. 4:1–7) is best taken as a unit, one of the pithy, memorable vignettes. The phrase, "sons of the prophets," as mentioned before, refers to the students of the master prophet (in this case, Elisha). The particular student mentioned in these verses was apparently quite devout (we are told that "he revered Yahweh," not a common thing to do in Israel during the time of Omri). He died penniless, so that his widow had to "cry out to Elisha," as the creditors were about to enslave her two boys to pay off the family debts (v. 1). Let us note in passing that there is no censure whatsoever in the text for the poverty of this family. It was clearly not necessarily due to any lack of faith on their part. Once again, Elisha is called upon to minister in a desperate situation. The prophet often ministered with respect to addressing a crisis situation.

The enslavement of defaulting debtors or their families was practiced throughout the ancient Near East. This was apparently also the case in the land of Israel (Amos 2:6; Neh. 5:1–5; also cf. the metaphor in Isa. 50:1 of Israel herself being sold into slavery to satisfy her creditors). The Torah attempted to put time limits on the length of service of Hebrew slaves (cf. Exo. 21:2f, 7 [seven years for a male slave]; Lev. 25:39–43 [until the Year of Jubilee]); but whether these legal traditions were intended to correct abuse or whether they represented initial directive is hard to determine. The present passage notes that the widow was clearly in great distress, and the prophet himself seemed at first also at a loss to know what to do (v. 2; cf. Cogan and Tadmor [AB, 56]). But it is soon clear that Elisha was being directed by God to have the widow take part in the upcoming miracle. Elisha asked the widow what she had in her house. The widow responded by noting that all she had was a little oil. (Olive oil was considered a staple commodity both for anointing of the body as well as for cooking; cf. the similar comments of the widow of Zarephath to the prophet Elijah in 1 Ki. 17:12.)

Once again, however, the emphasis must be on a little oil: the unusual term 'āsûkh (HED #624)

2062	5242.552	420	2026	3441.553		2030.121	3626, 4527.141
pers pron	v Hiphil ptc mp	prep, ps 3fs	cj, pers pron	v Hiphil ptc fs	**6.**	cj, v Qal impf 3ms	prep, v Qal inf con
הֵם	מַגִּשִׁים	אֵלֶיהָ	וְהִיא	מֵיצָקֶת		וַיְהִי	כִּמְלֹאת
hēm	maggishîm	'ēlêāh	wehî'	mêtsāqeth		wayhî	kimlō'th
they	bringing forward	to her	and she	pouring out		and it was	when filling

3747	569.122	420, 1158	5242.531	420	5968	3747
art, n mp	cj, v Qal impf 3fs	prep, n ms, ps 3fs	art, v Hiphil impv 2ms	prep, ps 1cs	adv	n ms
הַכֵּלִים	וַתֹּאמֶר	אֶל־בְּנָהּ	הַגִּישָׁה	אֵלַי	עוֹד	כֶּלִי
hakkēlîm	wattō'mer	'el-benāhh	haggîshāh	'ēlay	'ôdh	kelî
the vessels	and she said	to her son	bring	to me	still	a vessel

569.121	420	375	5968	3747	6198.121	8467
cj, v Qal impf 3ms	prep, ps 3fs	*sub*	adv	n ms	cj, v Qal impf 3ms	art, n ms
וַיֹּאמֶר	אֵלֶיהָ	אֵין	עוֹד	כֶּלִי	וַיַּעֲמֹד	הַשָּׁמֶן
wayyō'mer	'ēlêāh	'ên	'ôdh	kelî	wayya'ămōdh	hashshāmen
and he said	to her	there is not	anymore	a vessel	then it stayed	the olive oil

	971.122	5222.522	3937, 382	435	569.121	2050.142
7.	cj, v Qal impf 3fs	cj, v Hiphil impf 3fs	prep, *n ms*	art, n mp	cj, v Qal impf 3ms	v Qal impv 2fs
	וַתָּבֹא	וַתַּגֵּד	לְאִישׁ	הָאֱלֹהִים	וַיֹּאמֶר	לְכִי
	wattāvō'	wattaggēdh	le'îsh	hā'ĕlōhîm	wayyō'mer	lekhî
	and she came	and she told	to the man of	God	and he said	go

4513.132	881, 8467	8396.332	881, 5569	879	1158	2513.124
v Qal impv 2fs	do, art, n ms	cj, v Piel impv 2fs	do, n mp, ps 2fs	cj, pers pron	n mp, ps 2fs	v Qal impf 2fs
מִכְרִי	אֶת־הַשֶּׁמֶן	וְשַׁלְּמִי	אֶת־נְשִׁיֵכִי	וְאַתְּ	בְּנֵיכִי	תִּחְיִי
mikhrî	'eth-hashshemen	weshallemî	'eth-nishyēkhî	we'atte	benêkhî	thichăyî
sell	the olive oil	and pay	your debts	and you	your sons	you will live

904, 3613.251		2030.121	3219	5882.121	482	420, 8207	8427
prep, art, v Niphal ptc ms	**8.**	cj, v Qal impf 3ms	art, n ms	cj, v Qal impf 3ms	pn	prep, pn	cj, adv
בַּנּוֹתָר		וַיְהִי	הַיּוֹם	וַיַּעֲבֹר	אֱלִישָׁע	אֶל־שׁוּנֵם	וְשָׁם
bannôthār		wayhî	hayyôm	wayya'ăvōr	'ĕlîshā'	'el-shûnēm	weshām
on what remains		and it was	the day	that he passed on	Elisha	unto Shunem	and there

828	1448	2480.522, 904	3937, 404.141, 4035	2030.121
n fs	adj	cj, v Hiphil impf 3fs, prep, ps 3ms	prep, v Qal inf con, n ms	cj, v Qal impf 3ms
אִשָּׁה	גְדוֹלָה	וַתַּחֲזֶק־בּוֹ	לֶאֱכָל־לָחֶם	וַיְהִי
'ishshāh	ghedhôlāh	wattachzeq-bô	le'ĕkhāl-lāchem	wayhî
a woman	great	and she urged with him	to eat bread	and it was

4623, 1823	5882.141	5681.121	8427	3937, 404.141, 4035
prep, *n ms*	v Qal inf con, ps 3ms	v Qal impf 3ms	adv	prep, v Qal inf con, n ms
מִדֵּי	עָבְרוֹ	יָסֻר	שָׁמָּה	לֶאֱכָל־לָחֶם
middê	'āverô	yāsur	shāmmāh	le'ĕkhāl-lāchem
from enough of	his passing on	he turned aside	to there	to eat bread

	569.122	420, 382	2079, 5167	3156.115	3706	382	435	7202
9.	cj, v Qal impf 3fs	prep, n ms, ps 3fs	intrj, part	v Qal pf 1cs	cj	*n ms*	n mp	adj
	וַתֹּאמֶר	אֶל־אִישָׁהּ	הִנֵּה־נָא	יָדַעְתִּי	כִּי	אִישׁ	אֱלֹהִים	קָדוֹשׁ
	wattō'mer	'el-'îshāhh	hinnēh-nā'	yādha'ăttî	kî	'îsh	'ĕlōhîm	qādhôsh
	and she said	to her husband	behold please	I know	that	the man of	God	holy

2000	5882.151	6142	8878		6449.120, 5167	6168, 7306
pers pron	v Qal act ptc ms	prep, ps 1cp	adv	**10.**	v Qal juss 1cp, part	*n fs*, n ms
הוּא	עֹבֵר	עָלֵינוּ	תָּמִיד		נַעֲשֶׂה־נָּא	עֲלִיַּת־קִיר
hû'	'ōvēr	'ālênû	tāmîdh		na'ăseh-nā'	'ălîyath-qîr
he	passing by	beside us	continually		let us make please	an upper room of walls

6. And it came to pass, when the vessels were full, that she said unto her son, Bring me yet a vessel: ... When the jars were all full, she said to her son, Bring me another jar, *NCV* ... asking one of her sons for a fresh jar, *Knox* ... Soon every container was full to the brim!, *NLT* ... Bring me another cask, *Fenton*.

And he said unto her, There is not a vessel more: ... There is not one more, *Moffatt* ... That was the last one, *Good News* ... There is not a jar left, *NIV*.

And the oil stayed: ... And the flow of oil was stopped, *BB* ... And then the oil ceased, *Tyndale* ... And the oil stood, *Douay*.

7. Then she came and told the man of God. And he said, Go, sell the oil, and pay thy debt, and live thou and thy children of the rest: ... and redeem your boys who are being taken as pledges, *NEB* ... to pay off your creditor; with what remains, you and your children can live, *NAB* ... Go, sell the oil and pay what you owe, *NCV*.

8. And it fell on a day, that Elisha passed to Shunem, where was a great woman: ... there was a woman of high position living there, *BB* ... where a wealthy woman lived, *NRSV* ... came to Sunam, where was a rich woman, *Tyndale* ... where there was a noble woman, *KJVII*.

and she constrained him to eat bread: ... and she layeth hold on him to eat bread, *Young* ... who insisted that he take some food, *Anchor* ... who persuaded him to stay for lunch, *Berkeley* ... that bade him to a meal, and she would take no denial, *Knox*.

And so it was, that as oft as he passed by, he turned in thither to eat bread: ... he used to turn in for a meal whenever he was passing, *Moffatt* ... he stopped there for a meal, *REB* ... he would turn in there to eat food, *RSV* ... he always broke his journey for a meal, *JB*.

9. And she said unto her husband, Behold now, I perceive that this is an holy man of God, which passeth by us continually: ... this man who comes here regularly is a holy man of God, *NEB* ... Since he visits us often, *NAB* ... this man who stops in from time to time is a holy man of God, *NLT*.

---

appears only here (v. 2) in the OT, and it probably refers to a small "flask" for anointing, or the like (Wiseman, TOTC, 202; cf. NIV, "a little oil"). Obviously, without a great miracle, this would be entirely inadequate to live on, let alone sell to pay off the debts. But Elisha was undeterred. He directed the widow to go and ask all the neighbors for empty jars (kēlîm, HED #3747, "[cooking] vessels," size undefined, but certainly not small), making sure that she obtained enough (v. 3). She was then to "go inside" (as Hobbs, WBC, 50, points out, the motif of the "shutting of the door" predominates in these stories; cf. here in vv. 4f, but also in vv. 21 and 33, below, as well as once more in 6:32) and fill all the jars, putting each one to the side when it was full. She did so, and of course all were filled. Only then did the oil stop flowing (vv. 5f; again note the parallels with 1 Ki. 17:15f). This brief, tightly-written story ends with the prophet exhorting the widow to sell the oil and pay her debts. What a remarkable turnaround for that dear woman and her family in some six short verses.

4:8–37. *The Shunammite woman and her son: A miracle of birth and rebirth. We now run into another story about a needy woman, this time wealthy, to be sure, but needy nonetheless. Even in such a patriarchal society, women are prominently featured in the Scriptures when they exhibited faith. And let us not forget that, though God surely has special concern for the poor, He does not forget the God-fearing rich. Joseph so unjustly festered for years in the Egyptian prison (chs. 40–41), but God did not leave him there. The rich, with their many pressures and distractions, so often forget about the problems of the poor, to be sure; but the opposite is all too often the case as well. It is to this poignant story of the wealthy, yet needy, woman, that we now turn.*

The rather lengthy passage finds its sequel in the beginning of ch. 8 (vv. 1–6), below. Once again, just as in the story we just read, the present narrative introduces an unnamed woman (and once again her husband is also unnamed). But at least this time we know the location of the story—the town of Shunem—whence the common designation of the woman as "the Shunammite."

4:8–10. The Shunammite's hospitality. Shunem (present day Sulam) was a village located on the slopes of Mt. Moreh. To the south can be seen the eastern end of the Plain of Jezreel (biblical Armageddon). As Hobbs (WBC, 50) points out, the distance from Mt. Carmel to this place would not normally necessitate a stop for the traveler (being only about 20 miles [32 kilometers] of relatively level road), although the town was conveniently located on the route Elisha probably utilized for his frequent travels throughout this region (this is the force of the phrase "often comes our way" in v. 9, NIV). The "upper room," whose furnishings are so

7277	7947.120	3937	8427	4433	8374	3802	4645
adj	cj, v Qal juss 1cp	prep, ps 3ms	adv	n fs	cj, n ms	cj, n ms	cj, n fs
קְטַנָּה	וְנָשִׂים	לוֹ	שָׁם	מִטָּה	וְשֻׁלְחָן	וְכִסֵּא	וּמְנוֹרָה
qōṯannāh	wenāsîm	lô	shām	mittāh	weshulchān	wekhissē'	ûmenôrāh
small	and let us put	for him	there	a bed	and a table	and a chair	and a lampstand

2030.111	904, 971.141	420	5681.121	8427		2030.121
cj, v Qal pf 3ms	prep, v Qal inf con, ps 3ms	prep, ps 1cp	v Qal impf 3ms	adv	**11.**	cj, v Qal impf 3ms
וְהָיָה	בְּבֹאוֹ	אֵלֵינוּ	יָסוּר	שָׁמָּה		וַיְהִי
wehāyāh	bevō'ô	'ēlênû	yāsûr	shāmmāh		wayhî
and it will be	when his coming	to us	he will turn aside	to there		and it was

3219	971.121	8427	5681.121	420, 6168	8311.121, 8427
art, n ms	cj, v Qal impf 3ms	adv	cj, v Qal impf 3ms	prep, art, n fs	cj, v Qal impf 3ms, adv
הַיּוֹם	וַיָּבֹא	שָׁמָּה	וַיָּסַר	אֶל־הָעֲלִיָּה	וַיִּשְׁכַּב־שָׁמָּה
hayyôm	wayyāvō'	shāmmāh	wayyāsar	'el-hā'ălîyāh	wayyishkav-shāmmāh
the day	and he entered	to there	and he turned aside	to the upper room	and he stayed there

	569.121	420, 1557	5470	7410.131	3937, 8208	2148
12.	cj, v Qal impf 3ms	prep, pn	n ms, ps 3ms	v Qal impv 2ms	prep, art, pn	art, dem pron
	וַיֹּאמֶר	אֶל־גֵּחֲזִי	נַעֲרוֹ	קְרָא	לַשּׁוּנַמִּית	הַזֹּאת
	wayyō'mer	'el-gēchăzî	na'ărô	qŏrā'	lashshûnammîth	hazzō'th
	and he said	to Gehazi	his servant	call	to the Shunammite	the this

7410.121, 3937	6198.122	3937, 6686		569.121	3937
cj, v Qal impf 3ms, prep, ps 3fs	cj, v Qal impf 3fs	prep, n mp, ps 3ms	**13.**	cj, v Qal impf 3ms	prep, ps 3ms
וַיִּקְרָא־לָהּ	וַתַּעֲמֹד	לְפָנָיו		וַיֹּאמֶר	לוֹ
wayyiqŏrā'-lāhh	watta'ămōdh	lephānâv		wayyō'mer	lô
and he called to her	and she stood	before him		and he said	to him

569.131, 5167	420	2079	2829.114	420	881, 3725, 2830	2148
v Qal impv 2ms, part	prep, ps 3fs	intrj	v Qal pf 2fs	prep, ps 1cp	do, *adj*, art, n fs	art, dem pron
אֱמָר־נָא	אֵלֶיהָ	הִנֵּה	חָרַדְתְּ	אֵלֵינוּ	אֶת־כָּל־הַחֲרָדָה	הַזֹּאת
'ĕmār-nā'	'ēlêāh	hinnēh	chāradht	'ēlênû	'eth-kol-hachrādhāh	hazzō'th
say please	to her	behold	you have trembled	for us	all the trembling	the this

4242	3937, 6449.141	3937	1950B, 3552	3937, 1744.341, 3937	420, 4567	173
intrg	prep, v Qal inf con	prep, ps 2ms	intrg part, sub	prep, v Piel inf con, prep, ps 2fs	prep, art, n ms	cj
מֶה	לַעֲשׂוֹת	לָךְ	הֲיֵשׁ	לְדַבֶּר־לָךְ	אֶל־הַמֶּלֶךְ	אוֹ
meh	la'ăsôth	lākh	hăyēsh	ledhabber-lākh	'el-hammelekh	'ô
what	to be done	to you	will it be	speaking for you	to the king	or

420, 8015	6893	569.122	904, 8761	6194	609	3553.153
prep, *n ms*	art, n ms	cj, v Qal impf 3fs	prep, *n ms*	n ms, ps 1cs	pers pron	v Qal act ptc fs
אֶל־שַׂר	הַצָּבָא	וַתֹּאמֶר	בְּתוֹךְ	עַמִּי	אָנֹכִי	יֹשָׁבֶת
'el-sar	hatstsāvā'	wattō'mer	bethôkh	'ammî	'ānōkhî	yōshāveth
to the commander of	the army	and she said	in the midst of	my people	I	dwelling

	569.121	4242	3937, 6449.141	3937	569.121	1557	61	1158
14.	cj, v Qal impf 3ms	cj, intrg	prep, v Qal inf con	prep, ps 3fs	cj, v Qal impf 3ms	pn	adv	n ms
	וַיֹּאמֶר	וּמֶה	לַעֲשׂוֹת	לָהּ	וַיֹּאמֶר	גֵּיחֲזִי	אֲבָל	בֵּן
	wayyō'mer	ûmeh	la'ăsôth	lāhh	wayyō'mer	gêchăzî	'ăvāl	bēn
	and he said	and what	to be done	for her	and he said	Gehazi	truly	a son

375, 3937	382	2290.111		569.121	7410.131, 3937
sub, prep, ps 3fs	cj, n ms, ps 3fs	v Qal pf 3ms	**15.**	cj, v Qal impf 3ms	v Qal impv 2ms, prep, ps 3fs
אֵין־לָהּ	וְאִישָׁהּ	זָקֵן		וַיֹּאמֶר	קְרָא־לָהּ
'ên-lāhh	we'îshāhh	zāqēn		wayyō'mer	qŏrā'-lāhh
there is not to her	and her husband	he is old		and he said	call to her

10. Let us make a little chamber, I pray thee, on the wall; and let us set for him there a bed, and a table, and a stool, and a candlestick: ... Let us make a little room on the roof with walls, *Beck* ... Let us make a small roof chamber with walls, *NRSV* ... Let me furnish the little upper chamber, *Fenton* ... Let's build a small room on the roof, *Good News*.

and it shall be, when he cometh to us, that he shall turn in thither: ... so that when he comes to us, he will be able to go in there, *BB* ... whenever he visits us, he can stay there, *Anchor* ... so that whenever he comes to us, he may rest there, *Berkeley* ... when he cometh to us, he may abide there, *Douay*.

11. And it fell on a day, that he came thither, and he turned into the chamber, and lay there: ... and went to his roof-chamber and lay down to rest, *NEB* ... so he turned aside into the upper chamber, and slept there, *Rotherham* ... and turned to go up to her to rest himself, *Fenton* ... Elisha arrived and stayed in the room overnight, *NAB*.

12. And he said to Gehazi his servant, Call this Shunammite. And when he had called her, she stood before him: ... He called her and she presented herself, *Anchor* ... When he called her and she appeared before the prophet, *REB* ... thus summoned, stood awaiting his audience, *Knox* ... when the servant had called her, she stood in front of him, *NCV*.

13. And he said unto him, Say now unto her, Behold, thou hast been careful for us with all this care: ... Since you have taken all this trouble for us, *NRSV* ... thou hast diligently served us in all things, *Douay* ... You have lavished all this care on us, *NAB* ... she has had in providing for our needs, *Good News*.

what is to be done for thee?: ... what shall we do for thee, *Geneva* ... Now ask her what can we do for her, *NLT* ... what is to be done for you, *BB*.

wouldest thou be spoken for to the king, or to the captain of the host?: ... Shall I speak for you to the king or to the commander-in-chief?, *NEB* ... is it to speak for thee unto the king, or unto the head of host?, *Young* ... Would you be commended to the king or the commander of the army?, *Goodspeed* ... shall some request for you be made to the king or to the captain of the army?, *Berkeley*.

And she answered, I dwell among mine own people: ... I am content where I am, among my own people, *REB* ... I live among my own people, *NASB* ... I reside amongst my own people, *Fenton* ... I dwell among my kinsfolk, *Anchor* ... I have a home among my own people, *NIV*.

14. And he said, What then is to be done for her?: ... What will she then that I do for her?, *Douay* ... Can something be done for her?, *NAB* ... What do you think we can do for her?, *NLT* ... as he wondered what he could do for her, *Knox*.

And Gehazi answered, Verily she hath no child, and her husband is old: ... she has no son, and her husband is an old man, *Good News*.

15. And he said, Call her. And when he had called her, she stood in the door: ... and she standeth at the opening, *Young* ... she stood in the doorway, *NKJV* ... and appeared in the doorway, *REB* ... and in answer to his voice she took her place at the door, *BB*.

16. And he said, About this season, according to the time of life: ... In due time next spring, *Beck* ... by such a time, as soon as the fruit can live, *Tyndale*.

---

carefully described in v. 10, is simply furnished, yet more than adequate for the prophet's needs. As is well-known, both the Old and New Testaments give ample evidence that God's people are to be likewise hospitable to travelers—perhaps the most memorable passage of Scripture in this regard being Heb. 13:2, where we are admonished to show hospitality to strangers, for some may have entertained angels without knowing it. (An allusion to the "three visitors" of Gen. 18 is probably in view here.)

4:11–17. Birth of the Shunammite's son. Elisha's motives in this section are clearly as generous as were the Shunammite's in the previous verses—he simply wished to bless her for blessing him. So he called to his servant Gehazi (this is the first time Gehazi is introduced by name; cf. Hobbs [WBC, 51] for the ambiguous role Gehazi plays in the Elisha narratives—but note here the clearly positive role Gehazi plays in v. 14 in giving his master some discerning advice). After some preliminary inquiries (handled delicately by means of the involvement of the servant), Elisha boldly announced that the Shunammite would have a son "about this time next year" (v. 16). Barrenness was considered a curse in OT times, so such an announcement would surely have been expected to be received joyfully (in addition, a son would maintain family ties to the property—a particularly urgent issue since the husband was up in years [v. 14]). The Shunammite was filled with foreboding, but what Elisha predicted came true. No more than one year later, the Shunammite gave birth to a son, an heir (v. 17). This was once again undoubtedly an occasion for great rejoicing, but not a word of that is even mentioned here in the text. Instead, the earlier ominous worries of the Shunammite still hang in the air.

7410.121, 3937	6198.122	904, 6860	16. 569.121	3937, 4287
cj, v Qal impf 3ms, prep, ps 3fs	cj, v Qal impf 3fs	prep, art, n ms	cj, v Qal impf 3ms	prep, art, n ms
וַיִּקְרָא־לָהּ	וַתַּעֲמֹד	בַּפָּתַח	וַיֹּאמֶר	לַמּוֹעֵד
wayyiqŏrā'-lāhh	watta'ămōdh	bappāthach	wayyō'mer	lammô'ēdh
and he called to her	and she stood	in the entrance	and he said	at the appointed time

2172	3626, 6496	2508	891	2354.153	1158	569.122
art, dem pron	prep, art, *n fs*	adj	pers pron	v Qal act ptc fs	n ms	cj, v Qal impf 3fs
הַזֶּה	כָּעֵת	חַיָּה	אַתִּי	חֹבֶקֶת	בֵּן	וַתֹּאמֶר
hazzeh	kā'ēth	chayyāh	'attᵉ	chōveqeth	bēn	wattō'mer
the this	according to the time of	living	you	embracing	a son	and she said

414, 112	382	435	414, 3694.323	904, 8569
adv, n ms, ps 1cs	*n ms*	art, n mp	adv, v Piel juss 2ms	prep, n fs, ps 2ms
אַל־אֲדֹנִי	אִישׁ	הָאֱלֹהִים	אַל־תְּכַזֵּב	בְּשִׁפְחָתֶךָ
'al-'ădhōnî	'îsh	hā'ĕlōhîm	'al-tᵉkhazzēv	bᵉshiphchāthekhā
no my master	O man of	God	do not lie	against your female servant

17. 2106.121	828	3314.122	1158	3937, 4287	2172
cj, v Qal impf 3fs	art, n fs	cj, v Qal impf 3fs	n ms	prep, art, n ms	art, dem pron
וַתַּהַר	הָאִשָּׁה	וַתֵּלֶד	בֵּן	לַמּוֹעֵד	הַזֶּה
wattahar	hā'ishshāh	watteledh	bēn	lammô'ēdh	hazzeh
and she became pregnant	the woman	and she bore	a son	at the appointed time	the this

3626, 6496	2508	866, 1744.311	420	482	18. 1461.121
prep, art, *n fs*	adj	rel part, v Piel pf 3ms	prep, ps 3fs	pn	cj, v Qal impf 3ms
כָּעֵת	חַיָּה	אֲשֶׁר־דִּבֶּר	אֵלֶיהָ	אֱלִישָׁע	וַיִּגְדַּל
kā'ēth	chayyāh	'ăsher-dibber	'ēlêāh	'ĕlîshā'	wayyighdal
according to the time of	living	which he had spoken	to her	Elisha	and he grew up

3315	2030.121	3219	3428.121	420, 1	420, 7403.152
art, n ms	cj, v Qal impf 3ms	art, n ms	cj, v Qal impf 3ms	prep, n ms, ps 3ms	prep, art, v Qal act ptc mp
הַיָּלֶד	וַיְהִי	הַיּוֹם	וַיֵּצֵא	אֶל־אָבִיו	אֶל־הַקֹּצְרִים
hayyāledh	wayhî	hayyôm	wayyētsē'	'el-'āvîw	'el-haqqōtsᵉrîm
the child	and it was	the day	and he went out	to his father	to the harvesters

19. 569.121	420, 1	7513	7513	569.121	420, 5470
cj, v Qal impf 3ms	prep, n ms, ps 3ms	n ms, ps 1cs	n ms, ps 1cs	cj, v Qal impf 3ms	prep, art, n ms
וַיֹּאמֶר	אֶל־אָבִיו	רֹאשִׁי	רֹאשִׁי	וַיֹּאמֶר	אֶל־הַנַּעַר
wayyō'mer	'el-'āvîw	rō'shî	rō'shî	wayyō'mer	'el-hanna'ar
and he said	to his father	my head	my head	and he said	to the servant

5558.131	420, 525	20. 5558.121	971.521	420, 525
v Qal impv 2ms ps 3ms	prep, n fs, ps 3ms	cj, v Qal impf 3ms, ps 3ms	cj, v Hiphil impf 3ms, ps 3ms	prep, n fs, ps 3ms
שָׂאֵהוּ	אֶל־אִמּוֹ	וַיִּשָּׂאֵהוּ	וַיְבִיאֵהוּ	אֶל־אִמּוֹ
sā'ēhû	'el-'immô	wayyissā'ēhû	wayvî'ēhû	'el-'immô
carry him	to his mother	and he carried him	and he brought him	to his mother

3553.121	6142, 1314	5912, 6937	4322.121	21. 6148.122
cj, v Qal impf 3ms	prep, n fd, ps 3fs	adv, art, n md	cj, v Qal impf 3ms	cj, v Qal impf 3fs
וַיֵּשֶׁב	עַל־בִּרְכֶּיהָ	עַד־הַצָּהֳרָיִם	וַיָּמֹת	וַתַּעַל
wayyēshev	'al-birkêāh	'adh-hatstsāhᵉrayim	wayyāmōth	watta'al
and he sat	on her knees	until noon	and he died	and she went up

8311.522	6142, 4433	382	435	5646.122	1185
cj, v Hiphil impf 3fs, ps 3ms	prep, *n fs*	*n ms*	art, n mp	cj, v Qal impf 3fs	prep, ps 3ms
וַתַּשְׁכִּבֵהוּ	עַל־מִטַּת	אִישׁ	הָאֱלֹהִים	וַתִּסְגֹּר	בַּעֲדוֹ
wattashkivēhû	'al-mittath	'îsh	hā'ĕlōhîm	wattisgōr	ba'ădhô
and she laid him	on the bed of	the man of	God	and she shut	behind him

3428.122	22. 7410.122	420, 382	569.122	8365.131	5167
cj, v Qal impf 3fs	cj, v Qal impf 3fs	prep, n ms, ps 3fs	cj, v Qal impf 3fs	v Qal impv 2ms	part
וַתֵּצֵא	וַתִּקְרָא	אֶל־אִישָׁהּ	וַתֹּאמֶר	שִׁלְחָה	נָא
wattētsē'	wattiqŏrā'	'el-'îshāhh	wattō'mer	shilchāh	nā'
and she went out	and she called	to her husband	and she said	send	please

3937	259	4623, 5470	259	888	7608.125
prep, ps 1cs	num	prep, art, n mp	cj, num	art, n fp	cj, v Qal juss 1cs
לִי	אֶחָד	מִן־הַנְּעָרִים	וְאַחַת	הָאֲתֹנוֹת	וְאָרוּצָה
lî	'echādh	min-hanne'ārîm	we'achath	hā'āthōnôth	we'ārûtsāh
to me	one	from the servants	and one of	the female donkeys	that I may hurry

thou shalt embrace a son: ... you will hold a son in your arms, *JB*.

And she said, Nay, my lord, thou man of God, do not lie unto thine handmaid: ... do not say what is false to your servant, *BB* ... Please don't lie to me like that, *NLT*.

17. And the woman conceived, and bare a son: ... But the woman became pregnant and gave birth to a son, *NCV*.

at that season that Elisha had said unto her, according to the time of life: ... the next season about the time Elisha had told her, *Berkeley* ... as Elisha had foretold, *REB* ... about the same time the next spring, *Goodspeed* ... as Elisha had promised, *NAB*.

18. And when the child was grown, it fell on a day, that he went out to his father to the reapers: ... to where the grain was being cut, *BB* ... who was working with the harvesters, *NLT* ... The child grew up, *Anchor* ... When the child was old enough, he went out one day, *NEB*.

19. And he said unto his father, My head, my head: ... there he complained unto his father, *Tyndale* ... My head aches, my head aches sorely, *Knox* ... My head hurts, *Good News*.

And he said to a lad, Carry him to his mother: ... His father told a servant to carry the child, *REB* ... he ordered his attendant to carry him, *Fenton*.

20. And when he had taken him, and brought him to his mother: ... After the servant had lifted him up and carried him, *NIV*.

he sat on her knees till noon, and then died: ... lay on her lap until midday, *JB* ... he stayed with her until noon, when he died in her lap, *NAB*.

21. And she went up, and laid him on the bed of the man of God: ... The mother took him upstairs, *NAB* ... Then she arose and laid him, *Fenton*.

and shut the door upon him, and went out: ... closed the door on him, and left, *NRSV*.

22. And she called unto her husband, and said, Send me, I pray thee, one of the young men, and one of the asses: ... Let me have a servant and a donkey, *NAB*.

that I may run to the man of God, and come again: ... I must go to the man of God as fast as I can, *NEB* ... I'll be back as soon as I can, *Good News* ... that I may speed to the man of God and return, *Goodspeed* ... that I may quickly go, *RSV*.

4:18–21. Sudden death for the Shunammite's son. Sure enough, disaster struck, and as is so typical of the laconic nature of biblical narrative, it struck quickly (the child, also unnamed, is born in v. 17, and dead by v. 20). Although the exact nature of the son's illness and death is not clearly spelled out, many would point to sunstroke or the like as the cause (the son's head presumably being uncovered when he went out into the field). But the delicate narrative style of the writer does not pause to describe in great detail what happened. Simply put, we are given note that a horrible tragedy occurred. Once again, just as was the case in v. 1 of the present chapter, an innocent person lay dead. But once again, just as also was the case in v. 1 of the present chapter, an enterprising woman did something about it. Surely, if there is any "moral" to the story about the Shunammite here, it is about putting faith to work, refusing to accept the status quo as the final will of God, or of God's servant, the prophet. In accord with the repeated motif found in the previous story, the present woman literally "shut the door" on her dear, dead son in the "upper room," and she went to work.

4:22–30. The Shunammite takes charge. As is remarkably often the case in the Bible, the woman assumes an assertive role. (Whether it be a Sarah or a Deborah or a Tamar [Gen. 38] or a Rizpah [2 Sam. 21:1–14], the OT is replete with strong, enterprising women who literally change the course of history by their words and deeds.) So it is here, in the present instance. The Shunammite told neither her hus-

5912, 382	435	8178.125		569.121	4211	891	2050.153
adv, *n ms*	art, n mp	cj, v Qal juss 1cs	**23.**	cj, v Qal impf 3ms	intrg	pers pron	v Qal act ptc fs
עַד־אִישׁ	הָאֱלֹהִים	וְאָשׁוּבָה		וַיֹּאמֶר	מַדּוּעַ	אַתִּי	הֹלַכְתִּי
'adh-'îsh	hā'ĕlōhîm	we'āshûvāh		wayyō'mer	maddûa'	'atte	hōlakhtî
unto the man of	God	that I may return		and he said	why	you	going

420	3219	3940, 2414	3940	8141	569.122	8361
prep, ps 3ms	art, n ms	neg part, n ms	cj, neg part	n fs	cj, v Qal impf 3fs	n ms
אֵלָיו	הַיּוֹם	לֹא־חֹדֶשׁ	וְלֹא	שַׁבָּת	וַתֹּאמֶר	שָׁלוֹם
'ēlâv	hayyôm	lō'-chōdhesh	welō'	shabbāth	wattō'mer	shālôm
to him	today	not a new moon	and not	Sabbath	and she said	peace

	2372.122	888	569.122	420, 5470	5268.131
24.	cj, v Qal impf 3fs	art, n fs	cj, v Qal impf 3fs	prep, n ms, ps 3fs	v Qal impv 2ms
	וַתַּחֲבֹשׁ	הָאָתוֹן	וַתֹּאמֶר	אֶל־נַעֲרָהּ	נְהַג
	wattachvōsh	hā'āthôn	wattō'mer	'el-na'ărāhh	nehagh
	and she saddled	the female donkey	and she said	to her servant	drive

2050.131	414, 6352.123, 3937	3937, 7680.141	3706	524, 569.115	3937
cj, v Qal impv 2ms	adv, v Qal impf 2ms, prep, ps 1cs	prep, v Qal inf con	cj	cj, v Qal pf 1cs	prep, ps 2ms
וָלֵךְ	אַל־תַּעֲצָר־לִי	לִרְכֹּב	כִּי	אִם־אָמַרְתִּי	לָךְ
wālēkh	'al-ta'ătsār-lî	lirkōv	kî	'im-'āmartî	lākh
and go	do not restrain for me	to ride	except	if I have said	to you

	2050.122	971.122	420, 382	435	420, 2098	3890
25.	cj, v Qal impf 3fs	cj, v Qal impf 3fs	prep, *n ms*	art, n mp	prep, *n ms*	art, pn
	וַתֵּלֶךְ	וַתָּבוֹא	אֶל־אִישׁ	הָאֱלֹהִים	אֶל־הַר	הַכַּרְמֶל
	wattēlekh	wattāvô'	'el-'îsh	hā'ĕlōhîm	'el-har	hakkarmel
	and she went	and she came	to the man of	God	to Mount	the Carmel

2030.121	3626, 7495.141	382, 435	881	4623, 5224	569.121
cj, v Qal impf 3ms	prep, v Qal inf con	*n ms*, art, n mp	do, ps 3fs	prep, prep	cj, v Qal impf 3ms
וַיְהִי	כִּרְאוֹת	אִישׁ־הָאֱלֹהִים	אֹתָהּ	מִנֶּגֶד	וַיֹּאמֶר
wayhî	kir'ôth	'îsh-hā'ĕlōhîm	'ōthāhh	minneghedh	wayyō'mer
and it was	when seeing	the man of God	her	from before	then he said

420, 1557	5470	2079	8208	2044		6498	7608.131, 5167
prep, pn	n ms, ps 3ms	intrj	art, pn	dem pron	**26.**	adv	v Qal impv 2ms, part
אֶל־גֵּיחֲזִי	נַעֲרוֹ	הִנֵּה	הַשּׁוּנַמִּית	הַלָּז		עַתָּה	רוּץ־נָא
'el-gêchăzî	na'ărô	hinnēh	hashshûnammîth	hallāz		'attāh	rûts-nā'
to Gehazi	his servant	behold	the Shunammite	this one		now	run please

3937, 7410.141	569.131, 3937	1950B, 8361	3937	1950B, 8361
prep, v Qal inf con, ps 3fs	cj, v Qal impv 2ms, prep, ps 3fs	intrg part, n ms	prep, ps 2fs	intrg part, n ms
לִקְרָאתָהּ	וֶאֱמָר־לָהּ	הֲשָׁלוֹם	לָךְ	הֲשָׁלוֹם
liqōrā'thāhh	we'ĕmār-lāhh	hăshālôm	lākh	hăshālôm
to meet her	and say to her	is well-being	to you	is well-being

3937, 382	1950B, 8361	3937, 3315	569.122	8361		971.122
prep, n ms, ps 2fs	intrg part, n ms	prep, art, n ms	cj, v Qal impf 3fs	n ms	**27.**	cj, v Qal impf 3fs
לְאִישֵׁךְ	הֲשָׁלוֹם	לַיָּלֶד	וַתֹּאמֶר	שָׁלוֹם		וַתָּבֹא
le'îshēkh	hăshālôm	layyāledh	wattō'mer	shālôm		wattāvō'
to your husband	is well-being	to the child	and she said	well-being		and she came

420, 382	435	420, 2098	2480.522	904, 7559	5242.121
prep, *n ms*	art, n mp	prep, art, n ms	cj, v Hiphil impf 3fs	prep, n fd, ps 3ms	cj, v Qal impf 3ms
אֶל־אִישׁ	הָאֱלֹהִים	אֶל־הָהָר	וַתַּחֲזֵק	בְּרַגְלָיו	וַיִּגַּשׁ
'el-'îsh	hā'ĕlōhîm	'el-hāhār	wattachzēq	beraghlâv	wayyiggash
to the man of	God	to the mountain	and she took hold	on his feet	and he came near

1557	3937, 1990.141	569.121	382	435	7791.531, 3937
pn	prep, v Qal inf con, ps 3fs	cj, v Qal impf 3ms	*n ms*	art, n mp	v Hiphil impv 2ms, prep, ps 3fs
גֵּיחֲזִי	לְהָדְפָהּ	וַיֹּאמֶר	אִישׁ	הָאֱלֹהִים	הַרְפֵּה־לָהּ
gêchăzî	lehādhephāhh	wayyō'mer	'îsh	hā'ĕlōhîm	harpēh-lāhh
Gehazi	to push her	but he said	the man of	God	let her loose

3706, 5497	4947.112, 3937	3176	6180.511	4623	3940
cj, n fs, ps 3fs	v Qal pf 3fs, prep, ps 3fs	cj, pn	v Hiphil pf 3ms	prep, ps 1cs	cj, neg part
כִּי־נַפְשָׁהּ	מָרָה־לָהּ	וַיהוָה	הֶעְלִים	מִמֶּנִּי	וְלֹא
kî-naphshāhh	mārāh-lāhh	wayhwāh	he'ălîm	mimmenî	welō'
because her life	it is bitter to her	and Yahweh	He has hidden	from me	and not

5222.511	3937		569.122	1950B, 8068.115	1158	4623, 881	112
v Hiphil pf 3ms	prep, ps 1cs	**28.**	cj, v Qal impf 3fs	intrg part, v Qal pf 1cs	n ms	prep, do	n ms, ps 1cs
הִגִּיד	לִי		וַתֹּאמֶר	הֲשָׁאַלְתִּי	בֵּן	מֵאֵת	אֲדֹנִי
higgîdh	lî		wattō'mer	hăshā'altî	vēn	mē'ēth	'ădhōnî
He told	to me		and she said	did I request	a son	from	my master

23. And he said, Wherefore wilt thou go to him today?: ... Why go to him today?, *NRSV* ... What is the matter with you that you would go to him?, *Fenton*.

it is neither new moon, nor sabbath. And she said, It shall be well: ... she saith, Peace to thee!, *Young* ... Peace!, *Rotherham* ... It's all right, *NIV*.

24. Then she saddled an ass, and said to her servant, Drive, and go forward: ... Drive fast, *Goodspeed* ... she saddled a donkey, *NKJV*.

slack not thy riding for me, except I bid thee: ... do not hold back for me unless I tell you, *NRSV* ... Don't slow down for me unless I tell you, *NCV*.

25. So she went and came unto the man of God to mount Carmel: ... She kept going till she reached the man of God, *NAB* ... So she departed, *NKJV*.

And it came to pass, when the man of God saw her afar off, that he said to Gehazi his servant, Behold, yonder is that Shunammite: ... That is the Shunammite woman coming, *NEB* ... see, where our servant cometh, *Tyndale* ... There is that woman from Shunem, *Beck*.

26. Run now, I pray thee, to meet her, and say unto her: ... Go quickly to her, *BB* ... run and meet her and ask her, *JB*.

Is it well with thee? is it well with thy husband? is it well with the child? And she answered, It is well: ... Yes, the woman told Gehazi, everything is fine, *NLT* ... Everything is all right, *NCV*.

27. And when she came to the man of God to the hill, she caught him by the feet: but Gehazi came near to thrust her away: ... she clasped him by the knees, *Knox* ... she grabbed hold of his feet. Gehazi stepped forward to push her away, *Anchor*.

And the man of God said, Let her alone; for her soul is vexed within her: ... Something is troubling her deeply, *NLT* ... she is in great distress, *REB*.

and the LORD hath hid it from me, and hath not told me: ... the LORD has hidden the reason from me, *Beck* ... the Lord has kept it secret from me, *BB*.

28. Then she said, Did I desire a son of my lord? did I not say, Do not deceive me?: ... Did I not beg you not to raise my hopes and then dash them?, *REB* ... imploring thee not to cheat me of my hopes?, *Knox* ... Didn't I tell you not to lie to me?, *NCV* ... Why did you tell me he should be sent to me?, *Fenton*.

29. Then he said to Gehazi, Gird up thy loins, and take my staff in thine hand, and go thy way: ... Pull your garment up under your belt, he told Gehazi, and take my rod in your hand, *Beck*.

band (vv. 22f) nor Gehazi (v. 26) what the problem was (once again, the narrator is telling the story, not moralizing about the behavior of the grief-stricken woman). Even Elisha himself had not been forewarned by God concerning her problem (v. 27; a particularly poignant detail to remind us that even the greatest prophets of God were subject to normal human limitations). The theme of extreme haste prominently marked both the Shunammite's visit to the prophet and his servant, as well as their return home to the "upper chamber." But the woman still had the upper hand—her accusation in v. 28 remained unanswered, and her assertion that she would not leave Elisha in v. 30 stood unopposed.

1950B, 3940	569.115	3940	8347.523	881		569.121	3937, 1557
intrg part, neg part	v Qal pf 1cs	neg part	v Hiphil impf 2ms	do, ps 1cs	29.	cj, v Qal impf 3ms	prep, pn
הֲלֹא	אָמַרְתִּי	לֹא	תַשְׁלֶה	אֹתִי		וַיֹּאמֶר	לְגֵיחֲזִי
hălō'	'āmartî	lō'	thashleh	'ōthî		wayyō'mer	leghêchăzî
had not	I said	not	you will mislead	me		and he said	to Gehazi

2391.131	5158	4089.131	5119	904, 3135	2050.131
v Qal impv 2ms	n md, ps 2ms	cj, v Qal impv 2ms	n fs, ps 1cs	prep, n fs, ps 2ms	cj, v Qal impv 2ms
חֲגֹר	מָתְנֶיךָ	וְקַח	מִשְׁעַנְתִּי	בְּיָדְךָ	וָלֵךְ
chăghōr	māthenêkhā	weqach	mish'antî	veyādhekhā	wālēkh
gird	your loins	and take	my staff	in your hand	and go

3706, 4834.123	382	3940	1313.323	3706, 1313.321	382	3940
cj, v Qal impf 2ms	n ms	neg part	v Piel impf 2ms, ps 3ms	cj, cj, v Piel impf 3ms, ps 2ms	n ms	neg part
כִּי־תִמְצָא	אִישׁ	לֹא	תְבָרְכֶנּוּ	וְכִי־יְבָרֶכְךָ	אִישׁ	לֹא
kî-thimtsā'	'îsh	lō'	thevārekhennû	wekhî-yevārekhekhā	'îsh	lō'
when you find	a man	not	you will bless him	and when he blesses you	a man	not

6257.123	7947.113	5119	6142, 6686	5470		569.122
v Qal impf 2ms, ps 3ms	cj, v Qal pf 2ms	n fs, ps 1cs	prep, *n mp*	art, n ms	30.	cj, v Qal impf 3fs
תַעֲנֶנּוּ	וְשַׂמְתָּ	מִשְׁעַנְתִּי	עַל־פְּנֵי	הַנָּעַר		וַתֹּאמֶר
tha'ănennû	wesamtā	mish'antî	'al-penê	hannā'ar		wattō'mer
you will answer him	and you will place	my staff	on the face of	the boy		and she said

525	5470	2508, 3176	2508, 5497	524, 6013.125	7251.121
n fs	art, n ms	adj, pn	cj, adj, n fs, ps 2ms	cj, v Qal impf 1cs, ps 2ms	cj, v Qal impf 3ms
אֵם	הַנַּעַר	חַי־יְהוָה	וְחֵי־נַפְשְׁךָ	אִם־אֶעֶזְבֶךָּ	וַיָּקָם
'ēm	hanna'ar	chay-yehwāh	wechê-naphshekhā	'im-'e'ezvekkā	wayyāqām
the mother of	the boy	Yahweh living	and your life living	if I abandon you	and he rose up

2050.121	313		1557	5882.111	3937, 6686	7947.121
cj, v Qal impf 3ms	prep, ps 3fs	31.	cj, pn	v Qal pf 3ms	prep, n mp, ps 3mp	cj, v Qal impf 3ms
וַיֵּלֶךְ	אַחֲרֶיהָ		וְגֵחֲזִי	עָבַר	לִפְנֵיהֶם	וַיָּשֶׂם
wayyēlekh	'achrêāh		weghēchăzî	'āvar	liphnêhem	wayyāsem
and he went	after her		and Gehazi	he passed on	before them	and he put

881, 5119	6142, 6686	5470	375	7249	375
do, art, n fs	prep, *n mp*	art, n ms	cj, *sub*	n ms	cj, *sub*
אֶת־הַמִּשְׁעֶנֶת	עַל־פְּנֵי	הַנַּעַר	וְאֵין	קוֹל	וְאֵין
'eth-hammish'eneth	'al-penê	hanna'ar	we'ên	qôl	we'ên
the staff	on the face of	the boy	but there was not	a sound	and there was not

7478	8178.121	3937, 7410.141	5222.521, 3937	3937, 569.141
n ms	cj, v Qal impf 3ms	prep, v Qal inf con, ps 3ms	cj, v Hiphil impf 3ms, prep, ps 3ms	prep, v Qal inf con
קָשֶׁב	וַיָּשָׁב	לִקְרָאתוֹ	וַיַּגֶּד־לוֹ	לֵאמֹר
qāshev	wayyāshāv	liqrā'thô	wayyaggedh-lô	lē'mōr
attentiveness	so he returned	to meet him	and he reported to him	saying

3940	7301.511	5470		971.121	482	1041	2079
neg part	v Hiphil pf 3ms	art, n ms	32.	cj, v Qal impf 3ms	pn	art, n ms	cj, intrj
לֹא	הֵקִיץ	הַנָּעַר		וַיָּבֹא	אֱלִישָׁע	הַבַּיְתָה	וְהִנֵּה
lō'	hēqîts	hannā'ar		wayyāvō'	'ělîshā'	habbāyethāh	wehinnēh
not	he has awakened	the boy		and he entered	Elisha	into the house	and behold

5470	4322.111	8311.655	6142, 4433		971.121	5646.121	1878
art, n ms	v Qal pf 3ms	v Hophal ptc ms	prep, n fs, ps 3ms	33.	cj, v Qal impf 3ms	cj, v Qal impf 3ms	art, n fs
הַנַּעַר	מֵת	מֻשְׁכָּב	עַל־מִטָּתוֹ		וַיָּבֹא	וַיִּסְגֹּר	הַדֶּלֶת
hanna'ar	mēth	mushkāv	'al-mittāthô		wayyāvō'	wayyisgōr	haddeleth
the boy	he was dead	being laid	on his bed		and he entered	and he closed	the door

1185 prep בְּעַד be'adh behind	8530 num, ps 3mp שְׁנֵיהֶם shenêhem the two of them	6663.721 cj, v Hithpael impf 3ms וַיִּתְפַּלֵּל wayyithpallēl and he prayed	420, 3176 prep, pn אֶל־יְהוָה 'el-yehwāh to Yahweh	34.	6148.121 cj, v Qal impf 3ms וַיַּעַל wayya'al and he went up	8311.121 cj, v Qal impf 3ms וַיִּשְׁכַּב wayyishkav and he lay
6142, 3315 prep, art, n ms עַל־הַיֶּלֶד 'al-hayyeledh on the child	7947.121 cj, v Qal impf 3ms וַיָּשֶׂם wayyāsem and he put	6552 n ms, ps 3ms פִּיו pîw his mouth	6142, 6552 prep, n ms, ps 3ms עַל־פִּיו 'al-pîw on his mouth		6084 cj, n fd, ps 3ms וְעֵינָיו we'ênâv and his eyes	6142, 6084 prep, n fd, ps 3ms עַל־עֵינָיו 'al-'ênâv on his eyes

if thou meet any man, salute him not; and if any salute thee, answer him not again: ... if anyone greets you, do not answer him, *Anchor.*

and lay my staff upon the face of the child: ... put my stick on the child's face, *BB* ... You are to stretch out my staff over the child, *JB* ... Lay my walking stick on the boy's face, *NCV.*

30. And the mother of the child said, As the Lord liveth, and as thy soul liveth, I will not leave thee: ... I won't go home unless you go with me, *NLT* ... I will not go back without you, *Beck.*

And he arose, and followed her: ... he arose and went after her, *Goodspeed* ... So the two of them started back together, *Good News.*

31. And Gehazi passed on before them, and laid the staff upon the face of the child; but there was neither voice, nor hearing: ... but there was no sound or response, *NIV* ... there was no sound or sign of life, *NAB* ... neither voice, nor sign of attention, *Darby.*

Wherefore he went again to meet him, and told him, saying, The child is not awaked: ... and said, The boy didn't wake up, *Good News* ... The child is not risen, *Douay.*

32. And when Elisha was come into the house, behold, the child was dead, and laid upon his bed: ... he found the boy lying dead, *NAB* ... there was the boy dead, on the bed where he had been laid, *NEB* ... the boy was lying dead on his bed, *NCV.*

33. He went in therefore, and shut the door upon them twain, and prayed unto the Lord: ... went in and closed the door on the two of them, *NRSV* ... and closed the door behind them, *Beck* ... he shut himself in with the boy, *Knox* ... He went in alone and shut the door behind him, *NLT.*

34. And he went up, and lay upon the child, and put his mouth upon his mouth, and his eyes upon his eyes, and his hands upon his hands: ... mouth upon the child's mouth, his eyes upon the child's eyes, and his hands upon the child's hands, *Berkeley.*

and he stretched himself upon the child; and the flesh of the child waxed warm: ... the boy's body grew warm, *NIV* ... bowed over him, and warmed the body of the lad,

4:31–37. The Shunammite's son brought back to life. Again we find echoes with the story in 1 Ki. 17, concerning the widow of Zarephath, whose own son also had tragically died. And once again, the major parallel is the Israelite prophet's ability to reverse the most fundamental curse humankind ever experiences—the awful finality of death. Paul termed it the "last enemy" (1 Cor. 15:26), and he looked forward to the day when Christ would return and put all enemies, including this last enemy, under his feet (indeed, we all still look forward to that day). But, meanwhile, reports of actual resurrections remain few and far between. Yet, we do have one here. Just as Elijah cried out to Yahweh, and Yahweh heard him and brought back to life the widow's boy (1 Ki. 17:21f), so Elisha was also able to do the same here. What Gehazi could not accomplish (v. 31), there again being no censure by the narrator of his "lack of faith" or the like, just the realization that Gehazi was not the prophet of God, Elisha was able to accomplish to the solemn gratitude and delight of the Shunammite (cf. v. 37), i.e., nothing less than the restoration of her son from death to life. As far as the procedure used to effect this resurrection, and the privacy involved, we find the motif of the "shut door" included in the narrative. There are both similarities and differences with the account in 1 Ki. 17. Both occur in upper rooms, both in private, both seemed to necessitate a stretching out or lying on the dead body, and obviously both required prayer to Yahweh. Yet Elisha's account seemed to represent a slow, gradual reviving of the corpse, whereas Elijah's earlier resurrection seemed more immediate. Various methods and lengths of time were used in Jesus'

3834	6142, 3834	1487.121	6142	2657.121	1340
cj, n fd	prep, n fs, ps 3ms	cj, v Qal impf 3ms	prep, ps 3ms	cj, v Qal impf 3ms	*n ms*
וְכַפָּיו	עַל־כַּפּוֹ	וַיִּגְהַר	עָלָיו	וַיָּחָם	בְּשַׂר
wᵉkhappâv	'al-kappô	wayyighhar	'ālâv	wayyāchām	bᵉsar
and his palms	on his palms	and he stretched out	on him	and it became warm	the flesh of

3315		8178.121	2050.121	904, 1041	259	2077	259
art, n ms	**35.**	cj, v Qal impf 3ms	cj, v Qal impf 3ms	prep, art, n ms	num	adv	cj, num
הַיָּלֶד		וַיָּשָׁב	וַיֵּלֶךְ	בַּבַּיִת	אַחַת	הֵנָּה	וְאַחַת
hayyāledh		wayyāshāv	wayyēlekh	babbayith	'achath	hēnnāh	wᵉ'achath
the child		and he returned	and he went	into the house	one time	here	and another time

2077	6148.121	1487.121	6142	2324.321	5470	5912, 8124
adv	cj, v Qal impf 3ms	cj, v Qal impf 3ms	prep, ps 3ms	cj, v Poel impf 3ms	art, n ms	adv, num
הֵנָּה	וַיַּעַל	וַיִּגְהַר	עָלָיו	וַיְזוֹרֵר	הַנַּעַר	עַד־שֶׁבַע
hēnnāh	wayya'al	wayyighhar	'ālâv	wayzôrēr	hanna'ar	'adh-sheva'
there	and he went up	and he stretched out	on him	and he sneezed	the boy	until seven

6718	6860.121	5470	881, 6084		7410.121	420, 1557	569.121
n fp	cj, v Qal impf 3ms	art, n ms	do, n fd, ps 3ms	**36.**	cj, v Qal impf 3ms	prep, pn	cj, v Qal impf 3ms
פְּעָמִים	וַיִּפְקַח	הַנַּעַר	אֶת־עֵינָיו		וַיִּקְרָא	אֶל־גֵּיחֲזִי	וַיֹּאמֶר
pᵉ'āmîm	wayyiphqach	hanna'ar	'eth-'ênâv		wayyiqŏrā'	'el-gêchăzî	wayyō'mer
times	and he opened	the boy	his eyes		and he called	to Gehazi	and he said

7410.131	420, 8208	2148	7410.121	971.122	420
v Qal impv 2ms	prep, art, pn	art, dem pron	cj, v Qal impf 3ms, ps 3fs	cj, v Qal impf 3fs	prep, ps 3ms
קְרָא	אֶל־הַשּׁוּנַמִּית	הַזֹּאת	וַיִּקְרָאֶהָ	וַתָּבוֹא	אֵלָיו
qŏrā'	'el-hashshunammîth	hazzō'th	wayyiqŏrā'eāh	wattāvô'	'ēlâv
call	to the Shunammite	the this	and he called her	and she went	to him

569.121	5558.134	1158		971.122	5489.122	6142, 7559
cj, v Qal impf 3ms	v Qal impv 2fs	n ms, ps 2fs	**37.**	cj, v Qal impf 3fs	cj, v Qal impf 3fs	prep, n fd, ps 3ms
וַיֹּאמֶר	שְׂאִי	בְּנֵךְ		וַתָּבֹא	וַתִּפֹּל	עַל־רַגְלָיו
wayyō'mer	sᵉ'î	vᵉnēkh		wattāvō'	wattippōl	'al-raghlâv
and he said	lift up	your son		and she came	and she fell	on his feet

8246.722	800	5558.122	881, 1158	3428.122
cj, v Hithpael impf 3fs	n fs	cj, v Qal impf 3fs	do, n ms, ps 3fs	cj, v Qal impf 3fs
וַתִּשְׁתַּחוּ	אַרְצָה	וַתִּשָּׂא	אֶת־בְּנָהּ	וַתֵּצֵא
wattishtachû	'ārᵉtsāh	wattissā'	'eth-bᵉnāhh	wattētsē'
and she bowed down	to the ground	and she lifted up	her son	and she went out

	482	8178.111	1577	7743	904, 800	1158	5204
38.	cj, pn	v Qal pf 3ms	art, pn	cj, art, n ms	prep, art, n fs	cj, *n mp*	art, n mp
	וֶאֱלִישָׁע	שָׁב	הַגִּלְגָּלָה	וְהָרָעָב	בָּאָרֶץ	וּבְנֵי	הַנְּבִיאִים
	we'ĕlîshā'	shāv	haggilgālāh	wᵉhārā'āv	bā'ārets	ûvᵉnê	hannᵉvî'îm
	and Elisha	he returned	to the Gilgal	and the famine	in the land	and the sons of	the prophets

3553.152	3937, 6686	569.121	3937, 5470	8570.131	5707	1448
v Qal act ptc mp	prep, n mp, ps 3ms	cj, v Qal impf 3ms	prep, n ms, ps 3ms	v Qal impv 2ms	art, n fs	art, adj
יֹשְׁבִים	לְפָנָיו	וַיֹּאמֶר	לְנַעֲרוֹ	שְׁפֹת	הַסִּיר	הַגְּדוֹלָה
yōshᵉvîm	lᵉphānâv	wayyō'mer	lᵉna'ărô	shᵉphōth	hassîr	haggᵉdhôlāh
sitting	before him	and he said	to his servant	put on	the pot	the great

1344.331	5318	3937, 1158	5204		3428.121	259
cj, v Piel impv 2ms	n ms	prep, *n mp*	art, n mp	**39.**	cj, v Qal impf 3ms	num
וּבַשֵּׁל	נְזִיד	לִבְנֵי	הַנְּבִיאִים		וַיֵּצֵא	אֶחָד
ûvashshēl	nāzîdh	livnê	hannᵉvî'îm		wayyētsē'	'echādh
and boil	something boiled	for the sons of	the prophets		and he went out	one

Fenton ... Soon the boy's skin became warm, *NCV*.

35. Then he returned, and walked in the house to and fro; and went up, and stretched himself upon him: ... paced back and forth in the house, *Goodspeed* ... and lowered himself on to the child seven times in all, *JB*.

and the child sneezed seven times, and the child opened his eyes: ... and breathed into him seven times, *NEB* ... the child gasped seven times, *Douay* ... the boy yawned seven times, *Knox*.

36. And he called Gehazi, and said, Call this Shunammite. So he called her: ... Call this Sunamitess, *Douay* ... Fetch his mother here, *Fenton* ... told him to call the boy's mother, *Good News* ... Call the child's mother!, *NLT*.

And when she was come in unto him, he said, Take up thy son: ... Take your boy, *Beck* ... Pick up your son, *JB* ... bade her take her son into her arms, *Knox* ... Lift up thy son, *Young*.

37. Then she went in, and fell at his feet, and bowed herself to the ground: ... went down on her face to the earth at his feet, *BB* ... She came in and fell at Elisha's feet, bowing facedown to the floor, *NCV* ... and prostrated herself on the ground, *Berkeley* ... She fell at his feet, overwhelmed with gratitude, *NLT*.

and took up her son, and went out: ... Then she picked up her son and went out, *Anchor* ... she took her son and left the room, *NAB*.

38. And Elisha came again to Gilgal: and there was a dearth in the land: ... There was a famine in the country, *Beck* ... there was a famine in that region, *NIV* ... now there was very little food in the land, *BB*.

and the sons of the prophets were sitting before him: ... the children of the prophets dwelt with him, *Tyndale* ... members of the prophetic order were sitting before him, *Goodspeed* ... As the company of prophets was sitting before him, *NRSV* ... a group of prophets was sitting at his feet, *REB*.

and he said unto his servant, Set on the great pot, and seethe pottage for the sons of the prophets: ... Put on a large pot and boil stew for the sons of the prophets, *NASB* ... Set the big pot on the fire and prepare some broth for the company, *NEB* ... Put on the large pot, and boil a mess of food, *Rotherham* ... and make some vegetable stew for the guild prophets, *NAB*.

39. And one went out into the field to gather herbs, and found a wild vine, and gathered thereof wild gourds his lap full: ... gathereth of its gourds of the field—the fulness of his garment, *Young* ... filled the skirt of his garment with bitter-apples, *NEB* ... and picked as many gourds as he could carry, *Good News* ... and gathered from it his lap full of wild colocynths, *Darby*.

and came and shred them into the pot of pottage: ... he cut them up into the pot of vegetable stew, *NAB* ... and sliced them into the pot, *Rotherham* ... he came back and put the fruit, cut up small, into the pot of soup, *BB* ... He cut up the herbs into the kettle, *Berkeley*.

for they knew them not: ... not knowing what they were, *NRSV* ... without realizing they were poisonous, *NLT* ... never enquiring what they were, *Knox* ... they didn't know what kind of fruit it was, *NCV*.

---

own miracles of healing in the NT. While healing still takes place in the church today, we can neither demand God to heal anyone or to bring anyone back to life, nor can we mandate by what means, or at what pace God should effect such miracles. God is sovereign. We must not prevent God's healing power by our apathy or by our unbelief, but neither should we think that God's abilities are limited. That, among other things, is surely the message of the resurrection stories of Elijah and Elisha, as with any miracle of help.

Once again, we will have occasion to return in 8:1–6 to the family of the Shunammite woman. It should be noted here that though she seemingly had no reason to fear the political authorities in v. 13 of the present chapter, the situation will prove to be quite different in the future. Meanwhile, the narrator directs us now to consider two occasions where famine leads the prophet Elisha to effect miracles of food consumption, both of quality (vv. 38–41) and of quantity (vv. 42ff). It is to a brief examination of these two stories that we now turn.

4:38–41. Purifying poisonous food. An occasion of famine necessitated Elisha to purify a pot of stew for the hungry "sons of the prophets" (cf. the comments above, on v. 1 of the present chapter, concerning their probable poverty). This brief story, like all those which surround it, pictures Elisha as a prophet fully equal to whatever challenge he is called upon to face, yet Elisha seemingly made no effort to bring an end to the famine itself. Perhaps, as was also the case in Gen. 12:10 or in Ruth 1:1, this famine is part of the historical context, as it were; thus providing the occasion for acts of faith (the Book of Ruth), or lack of faith (the rest of Gen. 12) by the people of God. That seems to be the sit-

420, 7898	3937, 4092.341	218	4834.121	1655	7898	4092.321	4623
prep, art, n ms	prep, v Piel inf con	n fp	cj, v Qal impf 3ms	*n fs*	n ms	cj, v Piel impf 3ms	prep, ps 3ms
אֶל־הַשָּׂדֶה	לְלַקֵּט	אֹרֹת	וַיִּמְצָא	גֶּפֶן	שָׂדֶה	וַיְלַקֵּט	מִמֶּנּוּ
'el-hassādheh	lelaqqēṯ	'ōrōth	wayyimtsā'	gephen	sādheh	waylaqqēṯ	mimmennû
to the field	to gather	herbs	and he found	a vine of	a field	and he gathered	from it

6748	7898	4530	933	971.121	6642.321	420, 5707
n fp	n ms	*n ms*	n ms, ps 3ms	cj, v Qal impf 3ms	v Piel impf 3ms	prep, *n fs*
פַּקֻּעֹת	שָׂדֶה	מְלֹא	בִּגְדוֹ	וַיָּבֹא	וַיְפַלַּח	אֶל־סִיר
paqqu'ōth	sādheh	melō'	vighdhô	wayyāvō'	wayphallach	'el-sîr
buds of	a field	fullness of	his garment	and he came	and he sliced	into the pot of

5318	3706, 3940	3156.116		3441.126	3937, 596	3937, 404.141
art, n ms	cj, neg part	v Qal pf 3cp		cj, v Qal impf 3mp	prep, n mp	prep, v Qal inf con
הַנָּזִיד	כִּי־לֹא	יָדָעוּ	**40.**	וַיִּצְקוּ	לַאֲנָשִׁים	לֶאֱכוֹל
hannāzîdh	kî-lō'	yādhā'û		wayyitsqû	la'ănāshîm	le'ĕkhôl
the boiled stuff	because not	they knew		and they poured out	for the men	to eat

2030.121	3626, 404.141	4623, 5318	2065	7094.116
cj, v Qal impf 3ms	prep, v Qal inf con, ps 3mp	prep, art, n ms	cj, pers pron	v Qal pf 3cp
וַיְהִי	כְּאָכְלָם	מֵהַנָּזִיד	וְהֵמָּה	צָעָקוּ
wayhî	ke'ākhelām	mēhannāzîdh	wehēmmāh	tsā'āqû
and it was	when their eating	from the boiled stuff	then they	they cried out

569.126	4323	904, 5707	382	435	3940	3310.116
cj, v Qal impf 3mp	n ms	prep, art, n fs	*n ms*	art, n mp	cj, neg part	v Qal pf 3cp
וַיֹּאמְרוּ	מָוֶת	בַּסִּיר	אִישׁ	הָאֱלֹהִים	וְלֹא	יָכְלוּ
wayyō'merû	māweth	bassîr	'îsh	hā'ĕlōhîm	welō'	yākhelû
and they said	death	in the pot	O man of	God	and not	they were able

3937, 404.141		569.121	4089.133, 7343	8390.521	420, 5707
prep, v Qal inf con		cj, v Qal impf 3ms	cj, v Qal impv 2mp, n ms	cj, v Hiphil impf 3ms	prep, art, n fs
לֶאֱכֹל	**41.**	וַיֹּאמֶר	וּקְחוּ־קֶמַח	וַיַּשְׁלֵךְ	אֶל־הַסִּיר
le'ĕkhōl		wayyō'mer	ûqŏchû-qemach	wayyashlēkh	'el-hassîr
to eat		and he said	then take flour	and he threw	into the pot

569.121	3441.131	3937, 6194	404.126	3940	2030.111	1745
cj, v Qal impf 3ms	v Qal impv 2ms	prep, art, n ms	cj, v Qal juss 3mp	cj, neg part	v Qal pf 3ms	n ms
וַיֹּאמֶר	צַק	לָעָם	וְיֹאכֵלוּ	וְלֹא	הָיָה	דָּבָר
wayyō'mer	tsaq	lā'ām	weyō'khēlû	welō'	hāyāh	dāvār
and he said	pour out	for the people	that they may eat	and not	it was	a thing

7737	904, 5707		382	971.111	4623, 1214	1214	971.521	3937, 382
n ms	prep, art, n fs		cj, n ms	v Qal pf 3ms	prep, pn	pn	cj, Hiphil impf 3ms	prep, *n ms*
רָע	בַּסִּיר	**42.**	וְאִישׁ	בָּא	מִבַּעַל	שָׁלִשָׁה	וַיָּבֵא	לְאִישׁ
rā'	bassîr		we'îsh	bā'	mibba'al	shālishāh	wayyāvē'	le'îsh
bad	in the pot		and a man	he came	from Baal	Shalishah	and he brought	to the man of

435	4035	1101	6465, 4035	8002	3889	904, 7139
art, n mp	*n ms*	n mp	num, n ms	n fp	cj, n ms	prep, n ms, ps 3ms
הָאֱלֹהִים	לֶחֶם	בִּכּוּרִים	עֶשְׂרִים־לֶחֶם	שְׂעֹרִים	וְכַרְמֶל	בְּצִקְלֹנוֹ
hā'ĕlōhîm	lechem	bikkûrîm	'esrîm-lechem	se'ōrîm	wekharmel	betsiqōlōnô
God	food of	firstfruits	twenty bread	barley	and fresh grain	in his sack

569.121	5598.131	3937, 6194	404.126		569.121
cj, v Qal impf 3ms	v Qal impv 2ms	prep, art, n ms	cj, v Qal juss 3mp		cj, v Qal impf 3ms
וַיֹּאמֶר	תֵּן	לָעָם	וְיֹאכֵלוּ	**43.**	וַיֹּאמֶר
wayyō'mer	tēn	lā'ām	weyō'khēlû		wayyō'mer
and he said	give	to the people	that they may eat		and he said

40. So they poured out for the men to eat: ... The broth was poured out for the men to eat, *REB* ... Then they served it to the men to eat, *NKJV* ... They then poured the soup out for the men to eat, *JB* ... They poured out the food for the men to eat, *Beck*.

And it came to pass, as they were eating of the pottage: ... And while they were drinking the soup, *BB* ... as they were eating the porridge, *Anchor* ... but when they would have eaten the bunches, *Fenton* ... when they had tasted of the pottage, *Douay*.

that they cried out, and said, O thou man of God, there is death in the pot. And they could not eat thereof: ... they exclaimed to Elisha, It's poisoned!, *Good News*.

41. But he said, Then bring meal. And he cast it into the pot: ... Fetch some meal. He threw it into the pot, *NEB* ... Then bring some flour, *NRSV*.

and he said, Pour out for the people, that they may eat: ... Now it's all right; go ahead and eat, *NLT* ... Pour out, for the company to eat!, *JB*.

And there was no harm in the pot: ... there was no longer anything harmful in the pot, *NAB* ... and there was no evil thing in the pot, *Young* ... all bitterness had left it, *Knox* ... nothing bad came from the pot, *Fenton*.

42. And there came a man from Baal-shalisha, and brought the man of God bread of the firstfruits: ... bringing food of the first fruits to the man of God, *Berkeley* ... made from the first fruits, *NAB* ... bringing the man of God some of the new season's bread, *NEB* ... from the first grain of his harvest, *NLT*.

twenty loaves of barley, and full ears of corn in the husk thereof: ... He also brought fresh grain in his sack, *NCV* ... and new corn in his scrip, *Douay* ... and a sack of garden produce, *Fenton* ... newly ripened grain in his knapsack, *NKJV*.

And he said, Give unto the people, that they may eat: ... Give it to the company to eat, *JB* ... Give these to the people for food, *BB* ... Give this to the people to eat, *REB*.

43. And his servitor said, What, should I set this before an hundred men?: ... and when his servant asked how this would suffice for a hundred mouths, *Knox* ... How can I set this before a hundred men?, *NIV* ... Do you think this is enough for a hundred men?, *Good News* ... Feed one hundred people with only this?, *NLT*.

He said again, Give the people, that they may eat: for thus saith the LORD, They shall eat, and shall leave thereof: ... They will eat and leave some over, *Anchor* ... they shall eat and leave, *Tyndale* ... They shall eat, and shall have to spare, *Darby* ... They are about to eat and to leave remaining, *Rotherham*.

---

uation here, also. The famine was an unchangeable given, and the people of God would either demonstrate faith or lack of faith in response to that given reality. When famine (literal, or metaphorical) strikes in our lives, let us, too, be people of faith, as were Ruth and Elisha in the days of old.

Quite possibly the "Gilgal" that Elisha "returns to" in v. 38 was a location in the hills near Bethel and Shechem, not the location near Jericho (cf. the comments on 2:1–6, above). In any case, it most certainly must have been the same location as that mentioned in 2:1, for in both texts, we find references to the "sons of the prophets." Also, the "servant" of Elisha mentioned in v. 38 may well have been Gehazi (cf. the repeated mention of Gehazi as Elisha's servant in vv. 12ff, 25ff, 29ff, 36). But, once again, we are not certain. The Shunammite narrative breaks off at this point, to be picked up in 8:1–6 (where, not so incidentally, there also is a famine in the land).

Once again, as was the case in Jericho (2:19–22), Elisha was equal to the task. As was the case there, the exact nature of the miracle remains elusive (was the "flour" of v. 41 [NIV], like the "salt" of 2:20, meant to be cleansing?). What counts is that the prophet, led by God's Spirit, was able to remedy the error, and the students enjoyed a delicious meal after all. Once again, there was no "sin" to counteract; only an innocent, yet life-threatening, mistake. Still, the prophet of God was able, no matter what, to overcome adversity, by greatly increasing the oil, by raising the dead, or by purifying the food for the famished students. Indeed, as we shall soon see, he also could multiply loaves of bread to feed a hundred hungry people at one time, with some left over.

4:42–44. Enough food for a hundred people. Evidently the famine continued, whence the great interest in the gift of food from the man of Baal Shalishah. Yet, Elisha continued seemingly to be uninterested in bringing an end to the famine itself. (Contrast Elijah's announcement of the beginning and the end of his three-year drought, in 1 Ki. 17–18.) Some calamities in life are, as it were, inevitable and unavoidable, but we should savor nonetheless the miracles and providential happenings which serve to mitigate such difficult circumstances, even if it be for only a small group of people, or for short periods of time. Our home is in heaven, not on this earth, and we long for the day

8664.351 v Piel ptc ms, ps 3ms מְשָׁרְתוֹ mᵉshārᵉthô his attendant	4242 intrg מָה māh how	5598.125 v Qal impf 1cs אֶתֵּן 'ettēn will I give	2172 dem pron זֶה zeh this	3937, 6686 prep, *n mp* לִפְנֵי liphnê before	4109 num מֵאָה mē'āh one hundred	382 n ms אִישׁ 'îsh men

569.121 cj, v Qal impf 3ms וַיֹּאמֶר wayyō'mer and he said	5598.131 v Qal impv 2ms תֵּן tēn give	3937, 6194 prep, art, n ms לָעָם lā'ām to the people	404.126 cj, v Qal juss 3mp וְיֹאכֵלוּ wᵉyō'khēlû that they may eat	3706 cj כִּי kî because	3662 adv כֹּה khōh thus

569.111 v Qal pf 3ms אָמַר 'āmar He has said	3176 pn יְהוָה yᵉhwāh Yahweh	404.142 v Qal inf abs אָכֹל 'ākhōl eating	3613.542 cj, v Hiphil inf abs וְהוֹתֵר wᵉhôthēr and causing to remain	**44.**	5598.121 cj, v Qal impf 3ms וַיִּתֵּן wayyittēn and he gave	3937, 6686 prep, n mp, ps 3mp לִפְנֵיהֶם liphnêhem before them

404.126 cj, v Qal impf 3mp וַיֹּאכְלוּ wayyō'khᵉlû and they ate	3613.526 cj, v Hiphil impf 3mp וַיּוֹתִרוּ wayyôthirû and they had remaining	3626, 1745 prep, *n ms* כִּדְבַר kidhvar according to the word of	3176 pn יְהוָה yᵉhwāh Yahweh	**5:1**	5465 cj, pn וְנַעֲמָן wᵉna'ămān then Naaman

8015, 6893 *n ms, n ms* שַׂר־צְבָא sar-tsᵉvā' the commander of the host of	4567, 782 *n ms*, pn מֶלֶךְ־אֲרָם melekh-'ărām the king of Aram	2030.111 v Qal pf 3ms הָיָה hāyāh he was	382 n ms אִישׁ 'îsh a man	1448 adj גָּדוֹל gādhôl great	3937, 6686 prep, *n mp* לִפְנֵי liphnê before	112 n mp, ps 3ms אֲדֹנָיו 'ădhōnāv his master

5558.155 cj, *v Qal pass ptc ms* וּנְשֻׂא ûnᵉsu' and being lifted	6686 n mp פָּנִים phānîm the face	3706, 904 cj, prep, ps 3ms כִּי־בוֹ kî-vô because by him	5598.111, 3176 v Qal pf 3ms, pn נָתַן־יְהוָה nāthan-yᵉhwāh Yahweh had given	9009 n fs תְּשׁוּעָה tᵉshû'āh victory	3937, 782 prep, pn לַאֲרָם la'ărām unto Aram

382 cj, art, n ms וְהָאִישׁ wᵉhā'îsh and the man	2030.111 v Qal pf 3ms הָיָה hāyāh he was	1399 *n ms* גִּבּוֹר gibbôr a warrior of	2524 n ms חַיִל chayil the army	7164.455 v Pual ptc ms מְצֹרָע mᵉtsōrā' a diseased man	**2.**	782 cj, pn וַאֲרָם wa'ărām and Aram	3428.116 v Qal pf 3cp יָצְאוּ yātsᵉ'û they went out

44. So he set it before them, and they did eat, and left thereof, according to the word of the LORD: ... He served them; they ate and had some left over, *JB* ... the people ate and had food left over, *NCV* ... they had a meal and there was more than enough, *BB* ... there was plenty for all and some left over, *NLT*.

5:1. Now Naaman, captain of the host of the king of Syria: ... the commander of his army, *NLT* ... commander of the king of Aram's army, *REB*.

was a great man with his master, and honourable: ... and in high favor with his master, *NRSV* ... was a great man before his lord, and accepted of face, *Young* ... highly esteemed and respected by his master, *NAB*.

because by him the LORD had given deliverance unto Syria: ... because by his means the LORD had given victory to Aram, *NEB*.

he was also a mighty man in valour, but he was a leper: ... He was a great soldier, but he suffered from a dreaded skin disease, *Good News*.

2. And the Syrians had gone out by companies, and had brought away captive out of the land of Israel a little maid: ... the Arameans had gone out in bands, *MAST* ... On one of the raids the Aramaeans made they had brought back from the country of Israel a little captive girl, *Beck* ... The Syrians had gone out as marauding bands and had carried off a little girl, *Goodspeed*.

and she waited on Naaman's wife: ... she is before the wife of Naaman, *Young* ... who became an attendant on the wife of Naaman, *Rotherham*.

when God will wipe away the tears from every eye (Rev. 21:4). Meanwhile, let us enjoy the story of how Elisha was able to multiply the loaves to feed a hundred people at one time—with some left over.

The exact location of Baal Shalishah is uncertain. Commentators generally follow the church father Eusebius in identifying the town with Kefr Tilt (Thult) 12 miles (20 kilometers) west of Shechem (cf. Hobbs, WBC, 53), but Cogan and Tadmor believe this identification is probably not accurate (AB, 59). They follow Z. Kallai in preferring a location in the region of Benjamin in the area of Mt. Ephraim, not far from Bethel. This also would correspond more closely to the suggested identification of Elisha's "Gilgal" (in v. 38) with a location near Bethel and Shechem as well. As far as the reference to the "bread baked from the first ripe grain" (v. 42), Hobbs appropriately points out that this would have placed the event chronologically during the time of the barley harvest (Passover time, in March/April), a time when the famine would have been most severely felt.

Once again Elisha's unnamed servant is called upon to bring the food to the people. Their occupations are undefined, but not necessarily "the sons of the prophets" as in the previous passage. Hobbs (WBC, 54) does have a point, however, about the "sons of the prophets" generally being numbered in multiples of fractions of one hundred (cf. 1 Ki. 18:4; 2 Ki. 2:7, 16f). The servant's understandable unbelief that so little food could feed so many people reminds us of the NT disciples who were similarly incredulous (John 6:5–9; cf. Matt. 14:15ff; 15:33f; Mark 6:35–38; 8:4f; Luke 9:12f); whether the servant is to be identified with Gehazi is left unclear. But a miracle once again occurs, as promised prophetically by Yahweh—"they will eat and have some left over." Parallels with Jesus' feedings of the 5000 and the 4000 once again immediately come to mind, with twelve and seven basketfuls of food left over, respectively. When God so directs, God's chosen leaders are both eager and able to supply ample food to their needy followers. In the next several chapters, we will have further occasion to note the parallels between the ministries of Elisha and of Jesus. Suffice it to say at this juncture that as John the Baptist indeed came "in the spirit and in the power of Elijah" (Luke 1:17; cf. Matt. 11:14; Mark 9:11ff), Jesus was often spoken of in terms reminiscent of Elisha (cf. the parallels in the present passage to Jesus' feeding of the multitudes, already cited; also his miraculously meeting the needs of unfortunate women (e.g., Mark 5:24–30; 7:24–30), as well as raising the dead (Mark 5:21–24, 35–43; Luke 7:11–17 [both beloved children]; John 11:38–44). There are also some parallels between the unbelief evidenced by Elisha's servant(s) and Jesus' disciples, as well as the repeated attention both spiritual leaders displayed concerning their theological "students"—whether it be the "sons of the prophets" in Elisha's day, or the twelve apostles in the time of Christ. Great spiritual leaders take great pains to nourish their followers, both physically and spiritually, and our Lord was no exception in this regard.

5:1–27. *Naaman the foreigner healed of leprosy; Gehazi the servant stricken instead. The present chapter is clearly a single narrative unit, with Naaman the Aramean, commander of his nation's army, stricken with leprosy at the beginning of the story and Gehazi the Israelite, the generally reliable servant of Elisha, stricken with the same disease at the story's end. Jesus made reference to the conundrum posed by the present chapter, namely, of Elisha healing a foreigner who was a leper, even though there were surely many lepers in Israel whom Elisha could have, but did not, heal. When one recognizes that the Arameans (or Syrians) were often the bitter enemies of the Israelites during this period of history, one's surprise only deepens. Who was this Aramean who so captured Elisha's attention that he felt led to cleanse him of his disease, and how does all this fit in with Israelite nationalistic theology of the time? It is to these and other questions that we now turn.*

5:1. Introduction: a great man stricken with leprosy. This verse seems to be a remarkable testimony concerning a person an Israelite would normally vilify in the strongest of terms—the commander of the enemy army who, yet, was "a great man in the sight of his master [the king of Aram]," and "highly regarded," since "through him Yahweh had given victory to Aram." Also, he was a "valiant soldier," even though he was smitten with leprosy. First of all, Aram (KJV "Syria"; the OT references to the land of Aram largely coincide with the southern regions of the modern nation of Syria) was usually an enemy of both the northern and southern kingdoms of OT Israel, and that certainly was the case for the Northern Kingdom throughout this era (a quick look at the Elijah and Elisha accounts, along with other references to the Omride and Jehu dynasties in 1 and 2 Kings, resulted in the following references to Aram as enemy: 1 Ki. 20; 22:1–40; 2 Ki. 6:8–23;

1447	8091.126	4623, 800	3547	5472	7277	2030.122
n mp	cj, v Qal impf 3mp	prep, *n fs*	pn	n fs	adj	cj, v Qal impf 3fs
גְדוּדִים	וַיִּשְׁבּוּ	מֵאֶרֶץ	יִשְׂרָאֵל	נַעֲרָה	קְטַנָּה	וַתְּהִי
ghedhûdhîm	wayyishbû	mē'erets	yisrā'ēl	na'ărāh	qŏṭannāh	wattehî
raids	and they carried off	from the land of	Israel	a young woman	small	and she was

3937, 6686	828	5465	3. 569.122	420, 1435	305	112	3937, 6686
prep, *n mp*	*n fs*	pn	cj, v Qal impf 3fs	prep, n fs, ps 3fs	intrj	n ms, ps 1cs	prep, *n mp*
לִפְנֵי	אֵשֶׁת	נַעֲמָן	וַתֹּאמֶר	אֶל־גְּבִרְתָּהּ	אַחֲלֵי	אֲדֹנִי	לִפְנֵי
liphnê	'ēsheth	na'ămān	wattō'mer	'el-gevirtāhh	'achlê	'ădhōnî	liphnê
before	the wife of	Naaman	and she said	to her matron	if only	my master	before

5204	866	904, 8497	226	636.121	881	4623, 7168
art, n ms	rel pron	prep, pn	adv	v Qal impf 3ms	do, ps 3ms	prep, n fs, ps 3ms
הַנָּבִיא	אֲשֶׁר	בְּשֹׁמְרוֹן	אָז	יֶאֱסֹף	אֹתוֹ	מִצָּרַעְתּוֹ
hannāvî'	'ăsher	beshōmerôn	'āz	ye'ĕsōph	'ōthô	mitstsāra'ăttô
the prophet	who	in Samaria	then	he would add to	him	from his skin disease

4. 971.121	5222.521	3937, 112	3937, 569.141	3626, 2148	3626, 2148
cj, v Qal impf 3ms	cj, v Hiphil impf 3ms	prep, n mp, ps 3ms	prep, v Qal inf con	prep, dem pron	cj, prep, dem pron
וַיָּבֹא	וַיַּגֵּד	לַאדֹנָיו	לֵאמֹר	כָּזֹאת	וְכָזֹאת
wayyāvō'	wayyaggēdh	la'dhōnâv	lē'mōr	kāzō'th	wekhāzō'th
and he went	and he reported	to his master	saying	like this	and like that

1744.312	5472	866	4623, 800	3547	5. 569.121
v Piel pf 3fs	art, n fs	rel pron	prep, *n fs*	pn	cj, v Qal impf 3ms
דִּבְּרָה	הַנַּעֲרָה	אֲשֶׁר	מֵאֶרֶץ	יִשְׂרָאֵל	וַיֹּאמֶר
dibberāh	hanna'ărāh	'ăsher	mē'erets	yisrā'ēl	wayyō'mer
she has spoken	the young girl	who	from the land of	Israel	and he said

4567, 782	2050.131, 971.131	8365.125	5809	420, 4567	3547
n ms, pn	v Qal impv 2ms, v Qal impv 2ms	cj, v Qal juss 1cs	n ms	prep, *n ms*	pn
מֶלֶךְ־אֲרָם	לֶךְ־בֹּא	וְאֶשְׁלְחָה	סֵפֶר	אֶל־מֶלֶךְ	יִשְׂרָאֵל
melekh-'ărām	lekh-bō'	we'eshlechāh	sēpher	'el-melekh	yisrā'ēl
the king of Aram	go go	that I may send	a document	to the king of	Israel

2050.121	4089.121	904, 3135	6460	3724, 3826B	8666	512
cj, v Qal impf 3ms	cj, v Qal impf 3ms	prep, n fs, ps 3ms	num	*n fp*, n ms	cj, num	num
וַיֵּלֶךְ	וַיִּקַּח	בְּיָדוֹ	עֶשֶׂר	כִּכְּרֵי־כֶסֶף	וְשֵׁשֶׁת	אֲלָפִים
wayyēlekh	wayyiqqach	beyādhô	'eser	kikkerê-kheseph	weshēsheth	'ălāphîm
and he went	and he took	in his hand	ten	talents of silver	and six of	thousands

3. And she said unto her mistress, Would God my lord were with the prophet that is in Samaria!: … If only my master would present himself to the prophet in Samaria, *NAB*.

for he would recover him of his leprosy: … He would cure him of his leprosy, *NRSV* … he would get rid of the disease for him, *NEB* … he would make him well, *BB*.

4. And one went in, and told his lord, saying, Thus and thus said the maid that is of the land of Israel: … Naaman went and reported to his master what the Israelite girl had said, *REB* … Naaman went to his master, and told him what the Israelite maid had said, *Knox* … She consequently went and reported to her husband, *Fenton* … And she went and told her husband saying, *Tyndale*.

5. And the king of Syria said, Go to, go, and I will send a letter unto the king of Israel: … I will send a letter of introduction for you to carry to the king, *NLT*.

And he departed, and took with him ten talents of silver, and six thousand pieces of gold, and ten changes of raiment: … thirty thousand pieces of silver, six thousand pieces of gold, and ten changes of fine clothes, *Good News* … and ten festal garments, *Goodspeed* … ten robes of honour, *Fenton*.

6. And he brought the letter to the king of Israel, saying, Now when this letter is come unto thee, behold, I have therewith sent Naaman my servant to thee: … when this letter reaches you, know that I am sending Naaman my servant to you, *Anchor*.

6:24–7:20; 8:7–15, 28f; 9:14f; 12:17f; 13:3–7, 17ff, 22–25; 15:37). Clearly, it was not in Israel's self-interest to promote the career of an able military commander of the enemy army. But then why would we find such a narrative in the Hebrew Bible, and, even more fundamentally, why would Israel's God lead his prophet to help out in such a way? The immediate answer is somewhat parochial, to be sure: Israel's king was embarrassed by the request of the foreign king (see v. 7); indeed, he was greatly frightened that there was some sort of plan here to pick a fight with him (even a cursory overview of the above references to strife with Aram would certainly give support for the king's anxieties). The prophetic response in v. 8 is to remind both king and commoner, both Israelite and foreigner, that "there is a prophet in Israel." But the deeper theological import of passages such as the present chapter must also be kept in mind: Israel's God was also the God of Judah and the God over Aram and other nations as well. Once again, the bald statement in the present verse is that "through him [i.e., Naaman the Aramean] Yahweh had given victory to Aram." In the Book of Amos we have clear reminders that Yahweh was the God of not only the Israelites, but also of the Cushites, the Philistines, the Arameans (see Amos 9:7). In Deut. 1–3, Yahweh is said to have given the Moabites and the Ammonites their land, as well as the Edomites (all three of these nations were often enemies of Israel), and in Josh. 4:24, one major reason for Joshua's miraculous crossing of the Jordan River on dry ground (as well as Moses' earlier crossing of the Red [or Reed] Sea) was so that "all the peoples of the earth might know that the hand of Yahweh is powerful." Yahweh cared (and still cares) very much for the spiritual state of the foreigner—and already in the middle of the ninth century B.C., the Israelite narrator recognized as much. Our God has always been a God of love for any and all peoples.

A brief comment on the biblical term "leprosy" is in order, before we move on. As the footnotes to the most recent English translations make clear, biblical references to "leprosy" seem to presuppose some sort of skin disease, or family of skin diseases, at once wider, and also often less debilitating, than the modern usage of the term would signify. Hobbs' comments (WBC, 63) are particularly helpful here, and the following discussion is largely indebted to them. There seem to be many forms of biblical "leprosy," and Naaman's affliction is not easy to categorize. In contrast to what modern medicine categorizes as "leprosy," or "Hansen's disease," whose symptoms include painful, blotchy, widespread infection of the joints of the body, eventually resulting in loss of limbs and gross disfigurement, Naaman seemed to have some sort of skin disease which resulted in a whiteness, and possible dryness of the skin tissues (cf. v. 27). Seemingly, his affliction was such that he did not have to be quarantined; indeed, his career seems not to have suffered much from the affliction (in contrast to subsequent examples of separations of lepers from society below in 7:3 and in 15:5). Cogan and Tadmor (AB, 63) flatly state that "true leprosy" (Hansen's disease), does not appear in the Bible, and that the ancient Near Eastern terms translated as "leprosy" probably refer to various skin diseases such as psoriasis and vitiligo—and the ouster of such "lepers" from society "may have been prompted more by aesthetics than by concerns for contagion." (One should also note that the ritual statutes found in Lev. 13–14 refer both to these various human skin diseases, as well as various kinds of molds and fungi [NIV, "mildew"] on clothing and in buildings.)

5:2–7. An earnest letter to the king of Israel, seeking the prophet of God. All this starts with the innocent comments of a captured Israelite servant girl. God often uses the most unlikely messengers and witnesses for his purposes, and we often have no idea what our innocent testimony may bring about, both in the short and in the long run (e.g., the comments of servants, for both good and ill, figure quite prominently in the present chapter). Due to the testimony of that unnamed servant girl, the Israelite king probably had more than one sleepless night over the next several months (cf. v. 7), and Gehazi and his descendants would eventually be marked by the disfiguring curse of leprosy "forever" (v. 27); but Naaman the Aramean would also be cured of his affliction, as well as gain new found reverence for Yahweh the God of Israel, indeed, the only real God in the entire world (vv. 15–18). Both Israel and Aram, moreover, as well as countless readers ever since, would come to know in a fresher and deeper way that "there is a prophet in Israel" (v. 8). But before all that comes to pass, one should recognize the careful and lavish preparations which Naaman and his leader, the unnamed king of Aram made, including the generous gifts—some 750 pounds (340 kilograms) of silver and about 150 pounds (70 kilograms) of gold, plus the

2174	6460	2588	933	6.	971.521	5809	420, 4567	3547
n ms	cj, num	n fp	n mp		cj, v Hiphil impf 3ms	art, n ms	prep, *n ms*	pn
זָהָב	וְעֶשֶׂר	חֲלִיפוֹת	בְגָדִים		וַיָּבֵא	הַסֵּפֶר	אֶל־מֶלֶךְ	יִשְׂרָאֵל
zāhāv	we‘eser	chălîphôth	beghādhîm		wayyāvē'	hassēpher	'el-melekh	yisrā'ēl
gold	and ten	changes	clothes		and he brought	the document	to the king of	Israel

3937, 569.141	6498	3626, 971.141	5809	2172	420	2079
prep, v Qal inf con	cj, adv	prep, v Qal inf con	art, n ms	art, dem pron	prep, ps 2ms	intrj
לֵאמֹר	וְעַתָּה	כְּבוֹא	הַסֵּפֶר	הַזֶּה	אֵלֶיךָ	הִנֵּה
lē'mōr	we‘attāh	kevô'	hassēpher	hazzeh	'ēlêkhā	hinnēh
saying	and now	when coming	the document	the this	to you	behold

8365.115	420	881, 5465	5860	636.113	4623, 7168
v Qal pf 1cs	prep, ps 2ms	do, pn	n ms, ps 1cs	cj, v Qal pf 2ms, ps 3ms	prep, n fs, ps 3ms
שָׁלַחְתִּי	אֵלֶיךָ	אֶת־נַעֲמָן	עַבְדִּי	וַאֲסַפְתּוֹ	מִצָּרַעְתּוֹ
shālachtî	'ēlêkhā	'eth-na‘ămān	‘avdî	wa'ăsaphtô	mitstsāra‘ttô
I have sent	to you	Naaman	my servant	and you will add to him	from his skin disease

7.	2030.121	3626, 7410.141	4567, 3547	881, 5809	7458	933
	cj, v Qal impf 3ms	prep, v Qal inf con	*n ms*, pn	do, art, n ms	cj, v Qal impf 3ms	n mp, ps 3ms
	וַיְהִי	כִּקְרֹא	מֶלֶךְ־יִשְׂרָאֵל	אֶת־הַסֵּפֶר	וַיִּקְרַע	בְּגָדָיו
	wayhî	kiqŏrō'	melekh-yisrā'ēl	'eth-hassēpher	wayyiqŏra‘	beghādhâv
	and it was	when reading	the king of Israel	the document	that he tore	his clothes

569.121	1950B, 435	603	3937, 4322.541	3937, 2513.541	3706, 2172
cj, v Qal impf 3ms	intrg part, n mp	pers pron	prep, v Hiphil inf con	cj, prep, v Hiphil inf con	cj, dem pron
וַיֹּאמֶר	הַאֱלֹהִים	אָנִי	לְהָמִית	וּלְהַחֲיוֹת	כִּי־זֶה
wayyō'mer	ha'ĕlōhîm	'ānî	lehāmîth	ûlăhachyôth	kî-zeh
and he said	am God	I	to cause to die	or to cause to live	that this one

8365.151	420	3937, 636.141	382	4623, 7168	3706
v Qal act ptc ms	prep, ps 1cs	prep, v Qal inf con	n ms	prep, n fs, ps 3ms	cj
שֹׁלֵחַ	אֵלַי	לֶאֱסֹף	אִישׁ	מִצָּרַעְתּוֹ	כִּי
shōlēach	'ēlay	le'ĕsōph	'îsh	mitstsāra‘ttô	kî
sending	to me	to add to	a man	from his skin disease	except

395, 3156.133, 5167	7495.133	3706, 589.751	2000	3937	8.	2030.121
adv, v Qal impv 2mp, part	cj, v Qal impv 2mp	cj, v Hithpael ptc ms	pers pron	prep, ps 1cs		cj, v Qal impf 3ms
אַךְ־דְּעוּ־נָא	וּרְאוּ	כִּי־מִתְאַנֶּה	הוּא	לִי		וַיְהִי
'akh-de‘û-nā'	ûre'û	kî-mith'anneh	hû'	lî		wayhî
only know please	and see	that happening	he	to me		and it was

3626, 8471.141	482	382, 435	3706, 7458.111	4567, 3547	881, 933
prep, v Qal inf con	pn	*n ms*, art, n mp	cj, v Qal pf 3ms	*n ms*, pn	do, n mp, ps 3ms
כִּשְׁמֹעַ	אֱלִישָׁע	אִישׁ־הָאֱלֹהִים	כִּי־קָרַע	מֶלֶךְ־יִשְׂרָאֵל	אֶת־בְּגָדָיו
kishmōa‘	'ĕlîshā‘	'îsh-hā'ĕlōhîm	kî-qāra‘	melekh-yisrā'ēl	'eth-beghādhâv
when hearing	Elisha	the man of God	that he had torn	the king of Israel	his clothes

8365.121	420, 4567	3937, 569.141	4066	7458.113	933
cj, v Qal impf 3ms	prep, art, n ms	prep, v Qal inf con	intrg	v Qal pf 2ms	n mp, ps 2ms
וַיִּשְׁלַח	אֶל־הַמֶּלֶךְ	לֵאמֹר	לָמָּה	קָרַעְתָּ	בְּגָדֶיךָ
wayyishlach	'el-hammelekh	lē'mōr	lāmmāh	qāra‘ttā	beghādhêkhā
then he sent out	to the king	saying	why	have you torn	your clothes

971.121, 5167	420	3156.121	3706	3552	5204	904, 3547
v Qal juss 3ms, part	prep, ps 1cs	cj, v Qal juss 3ms	cj	sub	n ms	prep, pn
יָבֹא־נָא	אֵלַי	וְיֵדַע	כִּי	יֵשׁ	נָבִיא	בְּיִשְׂרָאֵל
yāvō'-nā'	'ēlay	weyēdha‘	kî	yēsh	nāvî'	beyisrā'ēl
let him come please	to me	that he may know	that	there is	a prophet	in Israel

9.				
971.121	5465	904, 5670	904, 7681	6198.121
cj, v Qal impf 3ms	pn	prep, n ms, ps 3ms	cj, prep, n ms, ps 3ms	cj, v Qal impf 3ms
וַיָּבֹא	נַעֲמָן	בְּסוּסוֹ	וּבְרִכְבּוֹ	וַיַּעֲמֹד
wayyāvō'	na'ămān	besûsô	ûverikhbô	wayya'ămōdh
and he came	Naaman	with his horse	and with his chariot	and he stood

		10.			
6860, 1041	3937, 482	8365.121	420	482	4534
n ms, art, n ms	prep, pn	cj, v Qal impf 3ms	prep, ps 3ms	pn	n ms
פֶּתַח־הַבַּיִת	לֶאֱלִישָׁע	וַיִּשְׁלַח	אֵלָיו	אֱלִישָׁע	מַלְאָךְ
pethach-habbayith	le'ĕlîshā'	wayyishlach	'ēlâv	'ĕlîshā'	mal'ākh
the entrance of the house	of Elisha	then he sent out	to him	Elisha	a messenger

that thou mayest recover him of his leprosy: ... that you may drive out his leprosy, *Berkeley* ... for you to cure him of his skin-disease, *JB* ... so you can heal him of his skin disease, *NCV*.

7. And it came to pass, when the king of Israel had read the letter, that he rent his clothes, and said, Am I God, to kill and to make alive, that this man doth send unto me to recover a man of his leprosy?: ... to deliver a man from his leprosy?, *Tyndale* ... with power to kill men and bring them to life again, that he should send a leper to me to be cured?, *Knox*.

wherefore consider, I pray you, and see how he seeketh a quarrel against me: ... Surely you must see that he is picking a quarrel with me, *Anchor* ... he is looking for a cause of war, *BB* ... he seeks an occasion against me, *Darby*.

8. And it was so, when Elisha the man of God had heard that the king of Israel had rent his clothes, that he sent to the king: ... had torn his robes, *NIV*.

saying, Wherefore hast thou rent thy clothes?: ... Why have you torn your clothes?, *NCV* ... Why are you so upset?, *NLT*.

let him come now to me, and he shall know that there is a prophet in Israel: ... and find out there's a prophet in Israel, *Beck*.

9. So Naaman came with his horses and with his chariot, and stood at the door of the house of Elisha: ... and halted at the door of Elisha's house, *RSV* ... with all his horses and his carriages, *BB* ... and stopped at the entrance to Elisha's house, *Good News* ... and halted at the entrance, *NRSV*.

10. And Elisha sent a messenger unto him, saying, Go and wash in Jordan seven times, and thy flesh shall come again to thee, and thou shalt be clean: ... and your body shall be well and clean again, *Berkeley* ... Go and bathe seven times in the Jordan, *JB* ... your flesh shall be restored to you, and be clean, *Fenton* ... your flesh will be healthy again and clean, *Beck*.

10 sets of clothing. All this would be a major factor in regard to Gehazi's greed (how typical of material excess—so often meant to coerce for good, but all too often ending up tempting for evil).

5:8–10. Elisha's message to the king and Naaman. Despite the understandable worries of the Israelite king, the motives behind the letter and the visit were peaceable enough. Once again, the witness of the anonymous servant girl led to major headaches for the king. The king's rhetorical questions, "Am I God? Can I kill and bring back to life?" (v. 7), remind us of the previous chapter, where Elisha, as Yahweh's public representative, brought about that very thing (concerning the king's clear grasp of the nature of Yahweh to effect "reversals," cf. the comments on 3:13–19; passages such as Deut. 32:39, where Yahweh declares, "I put to death and I bring to life, I have wounded and I will heal, and no one can deliver out of my hand," may have been particularly on the king's mind). More to the present point, kings, even Israelite kings, cannot cure leprosy; only God can. But, the king seems to have forgotten that there was a prophet in Israel, who could, by God's power, do that very thing. And that prophet, entirely unsolicited by the king (at least, as far as we know), sent his own messages, to both king and Aramean commander. First, to the king: why have you torn your robes? (As is well-known, such actions bespeak grief and despair.) Send the foreign officer to the one with real power, the prophet urged. And to the official himself, Elisha communicates through the closed door, as it were (so Naaman's complaint in v. 11; concerning the motif of the closed door in the Elisha materials, cf. above, on 4:1–7): wash seven times in the Jordan River, and you will be healed. Quite a curt message for the visiting dignitary who brought the lavish gifts (apparently never even seen by the prophet). Not surprisingly, Naaman's first reac-

Number	Parsing	Hebrew	Transliteration	Translation
3937, 569.141	prep, v Qal inf con	לֵאמֹר	lē'mōr	saying
2050.142	v Qal inf abs	הָלוֹךְ	hālôkh	go
7647.113	v Qal pf 2ms	וְרָחַצְתָּ	werāchatstā	and you will wash
8124, 6718	num, n fp	שֶׁבַע־פְּעָמִים	sheva'-pe'āmîm	seven times
904, 3497	prep, art, pn	בַּיַּרְדֵּן	bayyardēn	in the Jordan
8178.121	cj, v Qal impf 3ms	וְיָשֹׁב	weyāshōv	and it will return
1340	n ms, ps 2ms	בְּשָׂרְךָ	besārekhā	your flesh
3937	prep, ps 2ms	לְךָ	lekhā	to you
3000.131	cj, v Qal impv 2ms	וּטְהָר	ûṭehār	and be clean
11.				
7395.121	v Qal impf 3ms	וַיִּקְצֹף	wayyiqtsōph	and he was angry
5465	pn	נַעֲמָן	na'ămān	Naaman
2050.121	cj, v Qal impf 3ms	וַיֵּלַךְ	wayyēlakh	and he went
569.121	cj, v Qal impf 3ms	וַיֹּאמֶר	wayyō'mer	and he said
2079	intrj	הִנֵּה	hinnēh	behold
569.115	v Qal pf 1cs	אָמַרְתִּי	'āmartî	I said
420	prep, ps 1cs	אֵלַי	'ēlay	to myself
3428.121	v Qal impf 3ms	יֵצֵא	yētsē'	he will surely come out
3428.142	v Qal inf abs	יָצוֹא	yātsô'	coming out
6198.111	cj, v Qal pf 3ms	וְעָמַד	we'āmadh	and he will stand
7410.111	cj, v Qal pf 3ms	וְקָרָא	weqārā'	and he will call
904, 8428, 3176	prep, *n ms*, pn	בְּשֵׁם־יְהוָה	beshēm-yehwāh	on the name of Yahweh
435	n mp, ps 3ms	אֱלֹהָיו	'ĕlōhâv	his God
5311.511	cj, v Hiphil pf 3ms	וְהֵנִיף	wehēnîph	and he will wave
3135	n fs, ps 3ms	יָדוֹ	yādhô	his hand
420, 4887	prep, art, n ms	אֶל־הַמָּקוֹם	'el-hammāqôm	toward the place
636.111	cj, v Qal pf 3ms	וְאָסַף	we'āsaph	and he will add
7164.455	art, v Pual ptc ms	הַמְּצֹרָע	hammetsōrā'	what is diseased
12.				
1950B, 3940	intrg part, neg part	הֲלֹא	hălō'	are not
3005	adj	טוֹב	ṯôv	better
66	pn	אֲבָנָה	'ăvānāh	Abana
6804	cj, pn	וּפַרְפַּר	ûpharpar	and Pharpar
5282	*n mp*	נַהֲרוֹת	nahrôth	the rivers of
1894	pn	דַּמֶּשֶׂק	dammeseq	Damascus
4623, 3725	prep, *n ms*	מִכֹּל	mikkōl	than all
4448	*n md*	מֵימֵי	mêmê	the waters of
3547	pn	יִשְׂרָאֵל	yisrā'ēl	Israel
1950B, 3940, 7647.125	intrg part, neg part, v Qal impf 1cs	הֲלֹא־אֶרְחַץ	hălō'-'erchats	should I not wash
904	prep, ps 3mp	בָּהֶם	bāhem	in them
3000.115	cj, v Qal pf 1cs	וְטָהָרְתִּי	weṭāhārettî	then I will be clean
6680.121	cj, v Qal impf 3ms	וַיִּפֶן	wayyiphen	and he turned
2050.121	cj, v Qal impf 3ms	וַיֵּלֶךְ	wayyēlekh	and he went
904, 2735	prep, n fs	בְּחֵמָה	bechēmāh	in wrath
13.				
5242.126	cj, v Qal impf 3mp	וַיִּגְּשׁוּ	wayyiggeshû	and they drew near
5860	n mp, ps 3ms	עֲבָדָיו	'ăvādhâv	his servants
1744.326	cj, v Piel impf 3mp	וַיְדַבְּרוּ	waydhabberû	and they spoke
420	prep, ps 3ms	אֵלָיו	'ēlâv	to him
569.126	cj, v Qal impf 3mp	וַיֹּאמְרוּ	wayyō'merû	and they said
1	n ms, ps 1cs	אָבִי	'āvî	O my father
1745	n ms	דָּבָר	dāvār	a thing
1448	adj	גָּדוֹל	gādhôl	great
5204	art, n ms	הַנָּבִיא	hannāvî'	the prophet
1744.311	v Piel pf 3ms	דִּבֶּר	dibber	he has spoken
420	prep, ps 2ms	אֵלֶיךָ	'ēlêkhā	to you
1950B, 3940	intrg part, neg part	הֲלוֹא	hălô'	would not
6449.123	v Qal impf 2ms	תַעֲשֶׂה	tha'ăseh	you would do
652	cj, adv	וְאַף	we'aph	then also
3706, 569.111	cj, v Qal pf 3ms	כִּי־אָמַר	kî-'āmar	when he has said
420	prep, ps 2ms	אֵלֶיךָ	'ēlêkhā	to you
7647.131	v Qal impv 2ms	רְחַץ	rechats	wash
3000.131	cj, v Qal impv 2ms	וּטְהָר	ûṭehār	and be clean
14.				
3495.121	cj, v Qal impf 3ms	וַיֵּרֶד	wayyēredh	then he went down
2991.121	cj, v Qal impf 3ms	וַיִּטְבֹּל	wayyiṭbōl	and he dipped
904, 3497	prep, art, pn	בַּיַּרְדֵּן	bayyardēn	in the Jordan
8124	num	שֶׁבַע	sheva'	seven

11. But Naaman was wroth, and went away, and said: ... Naaman became angry, *NRSV* ... Naaman was furious, *NEB* ... Naaman was enraged and left, *Goodspeed*.

Behold, I thought, He will surely come out to me: ... surely come out to meet me!, *NLT*.

and stand, and call on the name of the LORD his God, and strike his hand over the place, and recover the leper: ... invoke the LORD his God, and would move his hand over the spot, and thus cure the leprosy, *NAB*.

12. Are not Abana and Pharpar, rivers of Damascus, better than all the waters of Israel?: ... such water as is not to be found in Israel?, *Knox* ... better than all the brooks of Israel?, *Fenton*.

may I not wash in them, and be clean?: ... I could have washed in them and been cured!, *Good News*.

So he turned and went away in a rage: ... he turned, and departed in displeasure, *Geneva* ... so turning, he went away in wrath, *BB*.

13. And his servants came near, and spake unto him: ... his officers tried to reason with him, *NLT*.

and said, My father, if the prophet had bid thee do some great thing, wouldest thou not have done it?: ... had commanded you to do something difficult, would you not have done it?, *NRSV*.

how much rather then, when he saith to thee, Wash, and be clean?: ... when he tells you, Wash and be cleansed!, *NIV* ... After all, he only told you, Wash, and you will be clean, *NCV* ... Bathe, and you will become clean, *JB*.

14. Then went he down, and dipped himself seven times in Jordan, according to the saying of the man of God: ... plunged into the Jordan seven times, *NAB*.

and his flesh came again like unto the flesh of a little child, and he was clean: ... turn back as the flesh of a little youth, *Young* ... became clean like that of a young boy, *NIV* ... restored like the flesh of a little child, *NASB*.

15. And he returned to the man of God, he and all his company, and came, and stood before him: ... coming back with all his retinue, he stood there in the presence of God's servant, *Knox*.

and he said, Behold, now I know that there is no God in all the earth, but in Israel: ... no god anywhere in the world except in Israel, *REB*.

now therefore, I pray thee, take a blessing of thy servant: ... Will you accept a token of gratitude, *NEB* ... Now please accept my gifts, *NLT* ... a present from your servant, *Beck*.

---

tion to this was anger at the remarkably cavalier and perfunctory treatment Elisha had given him. What kind of response was this for such a distinguished foreign guest? Hobbs (WBC, 65) comments, "His preparations for the journey—the diplomatic involvement of the king, the gift he has brought—all seem rejected in the most off-hand way by the prophet."

5:11–14. Naaman's servants give him sage advice. Reference has just been given to Naaman's angry response to the prophetic pronouncement. He expected far more personal attention, far more ritual than he received from Elisha. How often we expect the same from God, or from God's anointed servant. How disappointing an answer to prayer may seem, or a conversation with a respected pastor or teacher. But, as we already know, appearances can be very deceiving. All the hocus-pocus, all the "abracadabra," all the magic rituals in the world, may lead to nothing, whereas the simple directive, "go, wash ..." may make all the difference in the world, if God is truly in it.

Once again, we run into servants more astute than their master (v. 13). Even though the narrow, slow-flowing Jordan River is much less impressive than the "rivers of Damascus" which descend, clear and strong, from the snow-covered Amanus Mountains (cf. Cogan and Tadmor, AB, 64–65, on the textual difficulties attending the biblical references to the names "Abana and Pharpar" for the rivers), what counts is obedience to the prophetic word. "If he had commanded some great thing ...," then there would have been compliance. Naaman, like so many after him, forgot that it is in the small things that God tests us ("'not by might, nor by power, but by my Spirit,' says Yahweh of Hosts. ... 'Who despises the day of small things?'" [Zech. 4:6, 10]). To Naaman's credit, he listened to the servants, and did as Elisha commanded, washing seven times in the Jordan (some compare these actions to the rituals in Lev. 14, with their repeated references to cleansing by water, and to seven sprinklings, and waiting seven days, etc., but there the references are to priestly certification of prior healing, not to any healing itself). And indeed he was healed, just as the prophet predicted, "and his flesh was restored and became clean like that of a young boy" (v. 14).

6718	3626, 1745	382	435	8178.121	1340
n fp	prep, *n ms*	*n ms*	art, n mp	cj, v Qal impf 3ms	n ms, ps 3ms
פְּעָמִים	כִּדְבַר	אִישׁ	הָאֱלֹהִים	וַיָּשָׁב	בְּשָׂרוֹ
pe'āmîm	kidhvar	'îsh	hā'ělōhîm	wayyāshāv	besārô
times	according to the word of	the man of	God	and it returned	his flesh

3626, 1340	5470	7277	3000.121		8178.121	420, 382
prep, *n ms*	n ms	adj	cj, v Qal impf 3ms	**15.**	cj, v Qal impf 3ms	prep, *n ms*
כִּבְשַׂר	נַעַר	קָטֹן	וַיִּטְהָר		וַיָּשָׁב	אֶל־אִישׁ
kivsar	na'ar	qāṭōn	wayyiṭhār		wayyāshāv	'el-'îsh
like the flesh of	a child	small	and he was clean		then he returned	to the man of

435	2000	3725, 4402	971.121	6198.121	3937, 6686
art, n mp	pers pron	cj, *adj*, n ms, ps 3ms	cj, v Qal impf 3ms	cj, v Qal impf 3ms	prep, n mp, ps 3ms
הָאֱלֹהִים	הוּא	וְכָל־מַחֲנֵהוּ	וַיָּבֹא	וַיַּעֲמֹד	לְפָנָיו
hā'ělōhîm	hû'	wekhol-machnēhû	wayyāvō'	wayya'ămōdh	lephānâv
God	he	and all his camp	and he came	and he stood	before him

569.121	2079, 5167	3156.115	3706	375	435	904, 3725, 800
cj, v Qal impf 3ms	intrj, part	v Qal pf 1cs	cj	*sub*	n mp	prep, *adj*, art, n fs
וַיֹּאמֶר	הִנֵּה־נָא	יָדַעְתִּי	כִּי	אֵין	אֱלֹהִים	בְּכָל־הָאָרֶץ
wayyō'mer	hinnēh-nā'	yādha'ttî	kî	'ên	'ělōhîm	bekhol-hā'ārets
and he said	behold please	I know	that	there is not	a God	throughout all the earth

3706	524, 904, 3547	6498	4089.131, 5167	1318	4623, 881	5860
cj	cj, prep, pn	cj, adv	v Qal impv 2ms, part	n fs	prep, do	n ms, ps 2ms
כִּי	אִם־בְּיִשְׂרָאֵל	וְעַתָּה	קַח־נָא	בְרָכָה	מֵאֵת	עַבְדֶּךָ
kî	'im-beyisrā'ēl	we'attāh	qach-nā'	verākhāh	mē'ēth	'avdekhā
except	only in Israel	so now	take please	a gift	from	your servant

	569.121	2508, 3176	866, 6198.115	3937, 6686	524, 4089.125
16.	cj, v Qal impf 3ms	adj, pn	rel pron, v Qal pf 1cs	prep, n mp, ps 3ms	cj, v Qal impf 1cs
	וַיֹּאמֶר	חַי־יְהוָה	אֲשֶׁר־עָמַדְתִּי	לְפָנָיו	אִם־אֶקָּח
	wayyō'mer	chay-yehwāh	'ăsher-'āmadhtî	lephānâv	'im-'eqqāch
	and he said	Yahweh living	Whom I stand	before Him	if I will take

6732.121, 904	4089.141	4126.321		569.121	5465
cj, v Qal impf 3ms, prep, ps 3ms	prep, v Qal inf con	cj, v Piel impf 3ms	**17.**	cj, v Qal impf 3ms	pn
וַיִּפְצַר־בּוֹ	לָקַחַת	וַיְמָאֵן		וַיֹּאמֶר	נַעֲמָן
wayyiphtsar-bô	lāqachath	waymā'ēn		wayyō'mer	na'ămān
and he urged on him	to take	but he refused		and he said	Naaman

3940	5598.621, 5167	3937, 5860	5014	7045, 6755	124
cj, neg part	v Hophal juss 3ms, part	prep, n ms, ps 2ms	*n ms*	*n ms*, n mp	n fs
וָלֹא	יֻתַּן־נָא	לְעַבְדְּךָ	מַשָּׂא	צֶמֶד־פְּרָדִים	אֲדָמָה
wālō'	yuttan-nā'	le'avdekhā	massā'	tsemedh-perādhîm	'ădhāmāh
then no	may it be given please	to your servant	a burden of	a team of mules	the ground

3706	3940, 6449.121	5968	5860	6150	2160	3937, 435
cj	neg part, v Qal impf 3ms	adv	n ms, ps 2ms	n fs	cj, n ms	prep, n mp
כִּי	לוֹא־יַעֲשֶׂה	עוֹד	עַבְדְּךָ	עֹלָה	וָזֶבַח	לֵאלֹהִים
kî	lô'-ya'ăseh	'ôdh	'avdekhā	'ōlāh	wāzevach	lē'lōhîm
because	I will not make	anymore	your servant	a burnt offering	or a sacrifice	to gods

311	3706	524, 3937, 3176		3937, 1745	2172	5739.121	3176
adj	cj	cj, prep, pn	**18.**	prep, art, n ms	art, dem pron	v Qal juss 3ms	pn
אֲחֵרִים	כִּי	אִם־לַיהוָה		לַדָּבָר	הַזֶּה	יִסְלַח	יְהוָה
'ăchērîm	kî	'im-layhwāh		laddāvār	hazzeh	yislach	yehwāh
others	except	only to Yahweh		for the matter	the this	may He forgive	Yahweh

3937, 5860 prep, n ms, ps 2ms לְעַבְדְּךָ le'avdekhā your servant	904, 971.141 prep, v Qal inf con בְּבוֹא bevô' when entering	112 n ms, ps 1cs אֲדֹנִי 'ădhōnî my master	1041, 7706 *n ms*, pn בֵּית־רִמּוֹן vêth-rimmôn the temple of Rimmon	3937, 8249.741 prep, v Hithpael inf con לְהִשְׁתַּחֲוֹת lehishtachwōth to worship	8427 adv שָׁמָּה shāmmāh to there
2000 cj, pers pron וְהוּא wehû' and he	8550.255 v Niphal ptc ms נִשְׁעָן nish'ān leaning	6142, 3135 prep, n fs, ps 1cs עַל־יָדִי 'al-yādhî on my hand	8249.715 cj, v Hithpael pf 1cs וְהִשְׁתַּחֲוֵיתִי wehishtachwêthî then I bow down	1041 *n ms* בֵּית bêth the temple of	7706 pn רִמֹּן rimmōn Rimmon

16. But he said, As the LORD liveth, before whom I stand, I will receive none: ... As YHWH lives, whom I serve, I will not accept anything, *Anchor* ... I will take nothing from you, *BB* ... I will not take it, *Beck* ... I swear that I will not accept a gift, *Good News*.

And he urged him to take it; but he refused: ... Even though he pressed him to accept it, *Berkeley* ... the other would have constrained him to receive: but he would not do it, *Tyndale* ... Naaman urged him to take the gift, *NCV* ... I will accept nothing from thee; nor would any pleading bring him to consent, *Knox*.

17. And Naaman said, Shall there not then, I pray thee, be given to thy servant two mules' burden of earth?: ... allow your servant to be given as much earth as two mules may carry, *JB* ... let your servant at least be given two mules' load of earth, *NASB* ... allow me to load two of my mules with earth from this place, *NLT*.

for thy servant will henceforth offer neither burnt offering nor sacrifice unto other gods, but unto the LORD: ... will not offer holocaust, or victim to other gods, *Douay* ... will never after now make offering and sacrifice to another God except the EVER-LIVING, *Fenton* ... for I shall no longer offer whole-offering or sacrifice to any god but the LORD, *REB* ... will henceforth offer neither ascending-offering nor sacrifice to other gods, *Rotherham*.

18. In this thing the LORD pardon thy servant: ... and may Yahweh forgive your servant for this, *JB* ... may your servant have the Lord's forgiveness for this one thing, *BB* ... Herein the Lord be mercifull unto thy servant, *Geneva* ... be propitious, I pray thee, to thy servant, *Young*.

that when my master goeth into the house of Rimmon to worship there, and he leaneth on my hand, and I bow myself in the house of Rimmon: ... as my master does reverence, in Remmon's temple, *Knox* ... When my master enters the temple of Rimmon to bow down, *NIV*.

when I bow down myself in the house of Rimmon, the LORD pardon thy servant in this thing: ... may the LORD forgive your servant in this matter, *Berkeley* ... let the Lord I pray thee be merciful unto thy servant in this case, *Tyndale* ... Surely the LORD will forgive me, *Good News* ... may the LORD pardon me when I bow, too, *NLT*.

5:15–19a. Naaman's praise for Israel's God and for his prophet. Naaman, to his credit, gives credit where credit is due—to Israel's God and to his representative, the Israelite prophet (perhaps Naaman's servants deserve some credit, too, but at least they are able to hear Naaman call himself a "servant" of Elisha, when they accompany him back to the prophet's house). Naaman's bold statement of faith is true monotheism: "I now know that there is no God in all the world except in Israel" (v. 15). Naaman then urged Elisha to accept a gift. (It should be recalled that he had brought with him generous amounts of gold and silver, plus ten sets of clothing; cf. vv. 2–7.) But Elisha repeatedly refused the commander's offering—the miracles of God are not for hire—and Naaman finally turned to another topic: how is Yahweh to be worshiped in a foreign land, under pagan domination? Although the image to the two muleloads of Israelite dirt to be transported to Damascus would surely bring a smile to the reader (Yahweh, the universal God, is best worshiped on local soil?), Naaman truly demonstrated the enthusiasm (and the naiveté) of the new convert. How often do we both enjoy and envy the words and actions of those who have just come to the Lord in repentance and faith! Let us never lose that enthusiasm and innocent faith, even as we become more sophisticated in our Bible knowledge and Christian conduct.

The Aramean god Rimmon is an epithet for Baal Hadad, the Canaanite storm god (Cogan and Tadmor, AB, 65, suggest that "Rimmon" is derived from the Semitic root rmm, "to thunder"). The name "Rimmon" appears also in the personal name

904, 8249.741	1041	7706	5739.121, 5167	3176	3937, 5860
prep, v Hithpael inf con, ps 1cs	*n ms*	pn	v Qal juss 3ms, part	pn	prep, n ms, ps 2ms
בְּהִשְׁתַּחֲוָיָתִי	בֵּית	רִמֹּן	יִסְלַח־נָא	יְהוָה	לְעַבְדְּךָ
behishtachwāyāthî	bêth	rimmōn	yislach-nā'	yehwāh	le'avdekhā
when my bowing down	the temple of	Rimmon	may He forgive please	Yahweh	your servant

904, 1745	2172		569.121	3937	2050.131	3937, 8361	2050.121
prep, art, n ms	art, dem pron	**19.**	cj, v Qal impf 3ms	prep, ps 3ms	v Qal impv 2ms	prep, n ms	cj, v Qal impf 3ms
בַּדָּבָר	הַזֶּה		וַיֹּאמֶר	לוֹ	לֵךְ	לְשָׁלוֹם	וַיֵּלֶךְ
baddāvār	hazzeh		wayyō'mer	lô	lēkh	leshālôm	wayyēlekh
in the matter	the this		and he said	to him	go	peace	and he went

4623, 882	3650, 800		569.121	1557	5470	482
prep, prep, ps 3ms	*n fs*, n fs	**20.**	cj, v Qal impf 3ms	pn	*n ms*	pn
מֵאִתּוֹ	כִּבְרַת־אָרֶץ		וַיֹּאמֶר	גֵּיחֲזִי	נַעַר	אֱלִישָׁע
mē'ittô	kivrath-'ārets		wayyō'mer	gêchăzî	na'ar	'ĕlîshā'
from with him	a distance of land		and he said	Gehazi	the servant of	Elisha

382, 435	2079	2910.111	112	881, 5465	784	2172
n ms, art, n mp	intrj	v Qal pf 3ms	n ms, ps 1cs	do, pn	art, pn	art, dem pron
אִישׁ־הָאֱלֹהִים	הִנֵּה	חָשַׂךְ	אֲדֹנִי	אֶת־נַעֲמָן	הָאֲרַמִּי	הַזֶּה
'îsh-hā'ĕlōhîm	hinnēh	chāsakh	'ădhōnî	'eth-na'ămān	hā'ărammî	hazzeh
the man of God	behold	he has spared	my master	Naaman	the Aramean	the this

4623, 4089.141	4623, 3135	881	866, 971.511	2508, 3176	3708, 7608.115
prep, v Qal inf con	prep, n fs, ps 3ms	do	rel part, v Hiphil pf 3ms	adj, pn	cj, v Qal pf 1cs
מִקַּחַת	מִיָּדוֹ	אֵת	אֲשֶׁר־הֵבִיא	חַי־יְהוָה	כִּי־אִם־רַצְתִּי
miqqachath	mîyādhô	'ēth	'ăsher-hēvî'	chay-yehwāh	kî-'im-ratstî
from taking	from his hand		what he brought	Yahweh living	except I run

313	4089.115	4623, 882	4114		7579.121	1557	313
prep, ps 3ms	cj, prep, v Qal pf 1cs	prep, prep, ps 3ms	indef pron	**21.**	cj, v Qal impf 3ms	pn	adv
אַחֲרָיו	וְלָקַחְתִּי	מֵאִתּוֹ	מְאוּמָה		וַיִּרְדֹּף	גֵּיחֲזִי	אַחֲרֵי
'achrâv	welāqachtî	mē'ittô	me'ûmāh		wayyirdōph	gêchăzî	'achrê
after him	and I take	from with him	something		and he pursued	Gehazi	after

5465	7495.121	5465	7608.151	313	5489.121	4623, 6142
pn	cj, v Qal impf 3ms	pn	v Qal act ptc ms	prep, ps 3ms	cj, v Qal impf 3ms	prep, prep
נַעֲמָן	וַיִּרְאֶה	נַעֲמָן	רָץ	אַחֲרָיו	וַיִּפֹּל	מֵעַל
na'ămān	wayyir'eh	na'ămān	rāts	'achrâv	wayyippōl	mē'al
Naaman	when he saw	Naaman	running	after him	then he fell	from on

4981	3937, 7410.141	569.121	1950B, 8361		569.121	8361
art, n fs	prep, v Qal inf con, ps 3ms	cj, v Qal impf 3ms	intrg part, n ms	**22.**	cj, v Qal impf 3ms	n ms
הַמֶּרְכָּבָה	לִקְרָאתוֹ	וַיֹּאמֶר	הֲשָׁלוֹם		וַיֹּאמֶר	שָׁלוֹם
hammerkāvāh	liqōrā'thô	wayyō'mer	hăshālôm		wayyō'mer	shālôm
the chariot	to meet him	and he said	is peace		and he said	peace

112	8365.111	3937, 569.141	2079	6498	2172	971.116	420
n ms, ps 1cs	v Qal pf 3ms, ps 1cs	prep, v Qal inf con	intrj	adv	dem pron	v Qal pf 3cp	prep, ps 1cs
אֲדֹנִי	שִׁלְחַנִי	לֵאמֹר	הִנֵּה	עַתָּה	זֶה	בָּאוּ	אֵלַי
'ădhōnî	shelāchanî	lē'mōr	hinnēh	'attāh	zeh	bā'û	'ēlay
my master	he has sent me	saying	behold	now	this	they have come	to me

8530, 5470	4623, 2098	688	4623, 1158	5204	5598.131, 5167
num, n mp	prep, *n ms*	pn	prep, *n mp*	art, n mp	v Qal impv 2ms, part
שְׁנֵי־נְעָרִים	מֵהַר	אֶפְרָיִם	מִבְּנֵי	הַנְּבִיאִים	תְּנָה־נָּא
shenê-ne'ārîm	mēhar	'ephrayim	mibbenê	hannevî'îm	tenāh-nā'
two young men	from the hills of	Ephraim	from the sons of	the prophets	give please

19. And he said unto him, Go in peace: ... Go and prosper!, *Rotherham* ... Go on thy way, said Eliseus, and peace go with thee, *Knox* ... Farewell, said Elisha, *Moffatt*.

So he departed from him a little way: ... So he departed with his loads of earth, *Fenton* ... After Naaman had traveled some distance, *NIV* ... and he goeth from him a kibrath of land, *Young* ... So hee departed from him about halfe a dayes journey, *Geneva*.

20. But Gehazi, the servant of Elisha the man of God, said, Behold, my master hath spared Naaman this Syrian: ... My master has let that Aramean Naaman off too lightly, *NRSV* ... Now my master has taken nothing from Naaman, *BB* ... My master should not have let this Aramean get away, *NLT* ... has my master let this Aramaean, Naaman, go scot-free, *NEB*.

in not receiving at his hands that which he brought: ... by not taking from him what he brought, *Beck* ... without accepting what he brought?, *REB* ... declining to accept his present!, *Moffatt* ... without paying a thing!, *Good News*.

but, as the Lord liveth, I will run after him, and take somewhat of him: ... and accept of him something, *Rotherham* ... and take something of him, *Douay* ... and get something out of him, *JB*.

21. So Gehazi followed after Naaman: ... So Gehazi pursued Naaman, *NKJV* ... So after Naaman Giezi went, *Knox* ... Ghikhazi consequently ran after Naman, *Fenton* ... So Gehazi set off after him, *NLT*.

And when Naaman saw him running after him, he lighted down from the chariot to meet him: ... he got down from the chariot, *NIV* ... he jumped down from the chariot, *NRSV* ... he sprang down from the chariot, *Darby* ... he got down from his carriage and went after him, *BB*.

and said, Is all well?: ... Is everything all right?, *Beck* ... Is there peace?, *Young* ... Is anything wrong?, *REB* ... Is everything well, *Anchor*.

22. And he said, All is well. My master hath sent me, saying: ... Nothing, replied Gehazi, *REB* ... Everything is all right, *NCV* ... Yes, but my master has sent me, *NRSV*.

Behold, even now there be come to me from mount Ephraim two young men of the sons of the prophets: ... two young men of the company of prophets from the hill-country of Ephraim have just arrived, *NEB* ... two young members of the prophet's guild from the uplands of Ephraim have just come to him, *Moffatt* ... Here are two young prophets but now come to visit me, *Knox*.

give them, I pray thee, a talent of silver, and two changes of garments: ... He would like 75 pounds of silver and two sets of clothing to give to them, *NLT* ... give me therefore a talent of silver and two Robes of Honour, *Fenton* ... Let me have 2,000 dollars in silver and two suits of clothes for them, *Berkeley*.

"Tabrimmon," father of the Aramean king Ben-Hadad ("son of [the god] Hadad") in 1 Ki. 15:18. For further discussion of the Canaanite god Baal Hadad, see the comments on 1:2.

5:19b–25a. A deceitful appeal from a greedy servant. Alas, we now proceed from the sublime to what is indeed ridiculous. How often when an unbeliever comes to faith, we rejoice, and then we are forced to reckon with a believer who has succumbed to sin—whether it be avarice, as here, or lust, or pride, or whatever. Gehazi is confronted with the same temptation Elisha was (cf. Hobbs, WBC, 67), with the closely related Hebrew verbal root (pārats, HED #6805), "to urge," found in v. 23, as that found in v. 16 for Elisha (pātsar, HED #6732), also probably meaning "to urge," or the like. As Naaman "urged" Elisha repeatedly to accept the gift, so he also (after being solicited by Gehazi) "urged" the servant to take double the money he had asked for. Up to this point, we have had prescient servants and obtuse masters, by and large, but now we have a prescient master and a very obtuse servant. Naaman's servants led him to be healed of leprosy, despite their master's temper and pride. But Elisha's servant, who had repeatedly seen his master's miracles, wanted, it seems, to profit selfishly by them; so he acted on his own volition and in secret (or so he thought). We may have a bit of sympathy for Gehazi, yet we have absolutely no reason to commend his enterprise—and the final judgment of leprosy seems only fitting for this most "unprofitable servant" of God (cf. Matt. 25:30).

Naaman was well on his way home when Gehazi caught up to him (vv. 19ff). He graciously descended from his chariot to meet the pursuing servant. Gehazi spun a tale about two visiting "sons of the prophets" (v. 22)—a cunning touch, since we have read much about these groups of students over the previous three chapters, and we will return to them again in the very next story (6:1–7). By now, we know that Elisha cared deeply for both the spiritual and the physical needs of these students, so two of the students could possibly warrant necessitating a fair amount of money, and two sets of clothing. (For comments about the motif of "twos" in these Elisha stories, and especially in the present chapter, as well, cf. the comments on 13:14–21.)

3937	3724, 3826B	8692	2588	933		569.121	5465
prep, ps 3mp	*n fs*, n ms	cj, num	*n fp*	n mp		cj, v Qal impf 3ms	pn
לָהֶם	כִּכַּר־כֶּסֶף	וּשְׁתֵּי	חֲלִפוֹת	בְּגָדִים	**23.**	וַיֹּאמֶר	נַעֲמָן
lāhem	kikkar-keseph	ûshettê	chăliphôth	beghādhîm		wayyō'mer	na'ămān
to them	a talent of silver	and two	changes of	clothes		and he said	Naaman

3082.531	4089.131	3724	6805.121, 904	6961.121
v Hiphil impv 2ms	v Qal impv 2ms	n fd	cj, v Qal impf 3ms, prep, ps 3ms	cj, v Qal impf 3ms
הוֹאֵל	קַח	כִּכָּרַיִם	וַיִּפְרָץ־בּוֹ	וַיָּצַר
hô'ēl	qach	kikkārāyim	wayyiphrāts-bô	wayyātsar
decide	take	two talents	and he broke through with him	and he tied

3724	3826B	904, 8530	2857	8692	2588	933	5598.121
n fd	n ms	prep, num	n mp	cj, num	*n fp*	n mp	cj, v Qal impf 3ms
כִּכְּרַיִם	כֶּסֶף	בִּשְׁנֵי	חֲרִטִים	וּשְׁתֵּי	חֲלִפוֹת	בְּגָדִים	וַיִּתֵּן
kikkerayim	keseph	bishnê	chărițîm	ûshettê	chăliphôth	beghādhîm	wayyittēn
two talents	silver	in two	money bags	and two	changes of	clothes	and he gave

420, 8530	5470	5558.126	3937, 6686		971.121	420, 6308
prep, num	n mp, ps 3ms	cj, v Qal impf 3mp	prep, n mp, ps 3ms		cj, v Qal impf 3ms	prep, art, n ms
אֶל־שְׁנֵי	נְעָרָיו	וַיִּשְׂאוּ	לְפָנָיו	**24.**	וַיָּבֹא	אֶל־הָעֹפֶל
'el-shenê	ne'ārâv	wayyis'û	lephānâv		wayyāvō'	'el-hā'ōphel
to the two of	his servants	and they carried	before him		and he came	to the hill

4089.121	4623, 3135	6734.121	904, 1041	8365.321	881, 596
cj, v Qal impf 3ms	prep, n fs, ps 3mp	cj, v Qal impf 3ms	prep, art, n ms	cj, v Piel impf 3ms	do, art, n mp
וַיִּקַּח	מִיָּדָם	וַיִּפְקֹד	בַּבָּיִת	וַיְשַׁלַּח	אֶת־הָאֲנָשִׁים
wayyiqqach	mîyādhām	wayyiphqōdh	babbāyith	wayshallach	'eth-hā'ănāshîm
and he took	from their hand	and he gathered	in the house	and he sent	the men

2050.126		2000, 971.111	6198.121	420, 112	569.121
cj, v Qal impf 3mp		cj, pers pron, v Qal pf 3ms	cj, v Qal impf 3ms	prep, n mp, ps 3ms	cj, v Qal impf 3ms
וַיֵּלֵכוּ	**25.**	וְהוּא־בָא	וַיַּעֲמֹד	אֶל־אֲדֹנָיו	וַיֹּאמֶר
wayyēlēkhû		wehû'-vā'	wayya'ămōdh	'el-'ădhōnâv	wayyō'mer
and they went		but he he entered	and he stood	to his master	and he said

420	482	4623, 586	1557	569.121	3940, 2050.111	5860	590
prep, ps 3ms	pn	prep, intrg	pn	cj, v Qal impf 3ms	neg part, v Qal pf 3ms	n ms, ps 2ms	adv
אֵלָיו	אֱלִישָׁע	מֵאַן	גֵּחֲזִי	וַיֹּאמֶר	לֹא־הָלַךְ	עַבְדְּךָ	אָנֶה
'ēlâv	'ĕlîshā'	mē'ān	gēchăzî	wayyō'mer	lō'-hālakh	'avdekhā	'āneh
to him	Elisha	from where	Gehazi	and he said	he has not gone	your servant	where

590		569.121	420	3940, 3949	2050.111	3626, 866
cj, adv		cj, v Qal impf 3ms	prep, ps 3ms	neg part, n ms, ps 1cs	v Qal pf 3ms	prep, rel part
וָאָנָה	**26.**	וַיֹּאמֶר	אֵלָיו	לֹא־לִבִּי	הָלַךְ	כַּאֲשֶׁר
wā'ānāh		wayyō'mer	'ēlâv	lō'-libbî	hālakh	ka'ăsher
or where		and he said	to him	not my heart	it went	when

2089.111, 382	4623, 6142	4981	3937, 7410.141	1950B, 6496	4089.141
v Qal pf 3ms, n ms	prep, prep	n fs, ps 3ms	prep, v Qal inf con, ps 2ms	intrg, part, n fs	prep, v Qal inf con
הָפַךְ־אִישׁ	מֵעַל	מֶרְכַּבְתּוֹ	לִקְרָאתֶךָ	הַעֵת	לָקַחַת
hāphakh-'îsh	mē'al	merkavtô	liqōrā'thekhā	ha'ēth	lāqachath
the man turned	from on	his chariot	to meet you	is a time	for the taking of

881, 3826B	4089.141	933	2215	3884	6887	1267
do, art, n ms	cj, v Qal inf con	n mp	cj, n mp	cj, n mp	cj, n fs	cj, n ms
אֶת־הַכֶּסֶף	וְלָקַחַת	בְּגָדִים	וְזֵיתִים	וּכְרָמִים	וְצֹאן	וּבָקָר
'eth-hakkeseph	welāqachath	beghādhîm	wezêthîm	ûkherāmîm	wetsō'n	ûvāqār
the silver	and the taking of	clothes	and olive trees	and vineyards	and sheep	and oxen

23. And Naaman said, Be content, take two talents: ... By all means; take two talents, *NEB* ... Please take six thousand pieces of silver, *Good News* ... Allow me to give you eight hundred pounds, *Moffatt* ... please take one hundred fifty pounds, *NCV*.

And he urged him, and bound two talents of silver in two bags, with two changes of garments: ... and pressed him, tying up the two talents of silver in two bags with the two festal robes, *JB* ... then tied up the two talents of silver in two bags, with two sets of clothing, *NIV*.

and laid them upon two of his servants; and they bare them before him: ... and handed them to two of his servants; and they carried them on ahead of him, *NKJV* ... and gave them to two of his servants, and they walked ahead carrying them, *REB* ... and delivered them unto two of his servants, to bear it before him, *Tyndale*.

24. And when he came to the tower, he took them from their hand: ... When Gehazi came to the citadel he took them from the two servants, *NEB* ... Gehazi took the gifts from the servants, *NLT* ... When they reached the hill where Elisha lived, Gehazi took the two bags, *Good News*.

and bestowed them in the house: ... and put them away in the house, *BB* ... deposited them in the house, *NASB* ... and stowed them in the house, *Darby* ... stored them inside, *NRSV*.

and he let the men go, and they departed: ... and dismissed the men and they departed, *Fenton* ... letting the servants go their way, *Moffatt* ... and sent them away on their journey, *Knox* ... sendeth away the men, and they go, *Young*.

25. But he went in, and stood before his master. And Elisha said unto him, Whence comest thou, Gehazi?: ... Where did you go, Gehazi?, *NKJV* ... Where have you been, *RSV*.

And he said, Thy servant went no whither: ... I took no journey, *Knox* ... Your servant has not gone anywhere, *Anchor* ... Your servant went nowhere, *NASB*.

26. And he said unto him, Went not mine heart with thee, when the man turned again from his chariot to meet thee?: ... Did I not go with you in spirit, *RSV* ... Was not my heart present there, *JB*.

Is it a time to receive money, and to receive garments, and oliveyards, and vineyards, and sheep, and oxen, and menservants, and maidservants?: ... olive groves and vineyards and sheep and cattle and male and female slaves?, *Anchor* ... Is this a time for you to take money? And take Robes? And Olive-yards, and Vineyards?, *Fenton* ... Is it not true that you have the money?, *NEB*.

Naaman "urged" the servant to take double the money he had originally requested. Two talents of silver (probably about 150 pounds [70 kilograms]) was indeed a lot of money. Omri purchased the "hill of Samaria" to be the site of his capital city for two talents of silver (1 Ki. 16:24). The generosity of Naaman is all-too-typical of a new believer in the faith: "Naaman now assumes the role of a naive dupe" is Hobbs' comment on v. 20 (WBC, 66). Our God surely judges harshly anyone who preys on new believers in the faith ("but if anyone causes one of these little ones who believe in me to sin, it would be better for him to have a large millstone hung around his neck and to be drowned in the depths of the sea"—Jesus' comments on those who would hurt the "little children" who have come to him [Matt. 18:6]). Once again, we have almost a monotonous litany of duality in v. 23 of the present passage: two talents, two bags, two sets of clothing, two servants. Gehazi had the "loot" secreted away when he stood before his master (v. 25). It would have been most unenviable to be in Gehazi's sandals when he confronted the seer.

5:25b–27. Prophetic pronouncement of eternal judgment on dishonest Gehazi. Wiseman (TOTC, 208) delineates well Gehazi's sins as follows: avarice (v. 22), deception (v. 23) and derogation (belittling) of superiors ("this Aramean," v. 20), also, swearing deceitfully by the name of Yahweh ("as surely as Yahweh lives," v. 20; contrast Elisha's identical phrase in v. 16, when he refuses to accept any gift from Naaman). As Wiseman concludes: "Naaman was more faithful to his new LORD than Gehazi was to his." What a sad indictment for a supposedly faithful servant of God.

Elisha responds in v. 26 that his "spirit" (so NIV, cf. NLB; the Hebrew term is generally translated "heart," and it refers to the inward person, including his or her will, intellect and emotions) was there with Gehazi when Naaman alighted from his chariot to give him the gifts; thus, he knew all along that Gehazi was lying. The Israelite prophet had earlier been termed a "seer," i.e., one who could "see" spiritual sights in the heavenly realms (cf. the comments on 2:9f, also note how Elisha was able to reveal the heavenly horses and chariots of fire to his frightened servant in 6:17). Elisha could also, evidently, "see" quite well what were normally faraway earthly events (contrast, however, 4:27), at least in regard to

5860	8569		7168	5465
cj, n mp	cj, n fp	**27.**	cj, *n fs*	pn
וַעֲבָדִים	וּשְׁפָחוֹת		וְצָרַעַת	נַעֲמָן
wa‘ăvādhîm	ûshephāchôth		wetsāra‘ath	na‘ămān
and male servants	and female servants		and the skin disease of	Naaman

1740.122, 904	904, 2320	3937, 5986	3428.121
v Qal impf 3fs, prep, ps 2ms	cj, prep, n ms, ps 2ms	prep, n ms	cj, v Qal impf 3ms
תִּדְבַּק־בְּךָ	וּבְזַרְעֲךָ	לְעוֹלָם	וַיֵּצֵא
tidhbaq-bekhā	ûvezar‘ăkhā	le‘ôlām	wayyētsē’
it will cling on you	and on your descendants	unto eternity	and he went out

4623, 3937, 6686	7164.455	3706, 8345		569.126	1158, 5204
prep, prep, n mp, ps 3ms	v Pual ptc ms	prep, art, n ms	**6:1**	cj, v Qal impf 3mp	*n mp*, art, n mp
מִלְּפָנָיו	מְצֹרָע	כַּשָּׁלֶג		וַיֹּאמְרוּ	בְנֵי־הַנְּבִיאִים
millephānâv	metsōrā‘	kashshālegh		wayyō’merû	venê-hannevî’îm
from before him	a diseased man	like the snow		and they said	the sons of the prophets

420, 482	2079, 5167	4887	866	601	3553.152	8427	3937, 6686
prep, pn	intrj, part	art, n ms	rel part	pers pron	v Qal act ptc mp	adv	prep, n mp, ps 2ms
אֶל־אֱלִישָׁע	הִנֵּה־נָא	הַמָּקוֹם	אֲשֶׁר	אֲנַחְנוּ	יֹשְׁבִים	שָׁם	לְפָנֶיךָ
’el-’ĕlîshā‘	hinnēh-nā’	hammāqôm	’ăsher	’ănachnû	yōshevîm	shām	lephānêkhā
to Elisha	behold please	the place	where	we	dwelling	there	before you

7140	4623		2050.120, 5167	5912, 3497	4089.120	4623, 8427	382	7264
adj	prep, ps 1cp	**2.**	v Qal juss 1cp, part	prep, art, pn	cj, v Qal juss 1cp	prep, adv	n ms	n fs
צַר	מִמֶּנּוּ		נֵלְכָה־נָּא	עַד־הַיַּרְדֵּן	וְנִקְחָה	מִשָּׁם	אִישׁ	קוֹרָה
tsar	mimmennû		nēlekhāh-nā’	‘adh-hayyardēn	weniqŏchāh	mishshām	’îsh	qôrāh
narrower	than us		let us go please	unto the Jordan	and let us take	from there	each	a beam

259	6449.120, 3937	8427	4887	3937, 3553.141	8427	569.121
num	cj, v Qal juss 1cp, prep, ps 1cp	adv	n ms	prep, v Qal inf con	adv	cj, v Qal impf 3ms
אֶחָת	וְנַעֲשֶׂה־לָּנוּ	שָׁם	מָקוֹם	לָשֶׁבֶת	שָׁם	וַיֹּאמֶר
’echāth	wena‘ăseh-lānû	shām	māqôm	lāsheveth	shām	wayyō’mer
one	and let us make for ourselves	there	a place	for dwelling	there	and he said

2050.133		569.121	259	3082.531	5167	2050.131
v Qal impv 2mp	**3.**	cj, v Qal impf 3ms	art, num	v Hiphil impv 2ms	part	cj, v Qal impv 2ms
לְכוּ		וַיֹּאמֶר	הָאֶחָד	הוֹאֶל	נָא	וְלֵךְ
lēkhû		wayyō’mer	hā’echādh	hô’el	nā’	welēkh
go		and he said	the one	decide	please	and go

882, 5860	569.121	603	2050.125		2050.121	882
prep, n mp, ps 2ms	cj, v Qal impf 3ms	pers pron	v Qal impf 1cs	**4.**	cj, v Qal impf 3ms	prep, ps 3mp
אֶת־עֲבָדֶיךָ	וַיֹּאמֶר	אֲנִי	אֵלֵךְ		וַיֵּלֶךְ	אִתָּם
’eth-‘ăvādhêkhā	wayyō’mer	’ănî	’ēlēkh		wayyēlekh	’ittām
with your servants	and he said	I	I will go		and he went	with them

971.126	3497	1535.126	6320		2030.121	259
cj, v Qal impf 3mp	art, pn	cj, v Qal impf 3mp	art, n mp	**5.**	cj, v Qal impf 3ms	art, num
וַיָּבֹאוּ	הַיַּרְדֵּנָה	וַיִּגְזְרוּ	הָעֵצִים		וַיְהִי	הָאֶחָד
wayyāvō’û	hayyardēnāh	wayyighzerû	hā‘ētsîm		wayhî	hā’echādh
and they came	to the Jordan	and they cut	the trees		and it was	the one

5489.551	7264	881, 1298	5489.111	420, 4448	7094.121	569.121
v Hiphil ptc ms	art, n fs	cj, do, art, n ms	v Qal pf 3ms	prep, art, n mp	cj, v Qal impf 3ms	cj, v Qal impf 3ms
מַפִּיל	הַקּוֹרָה	וְאֶת־הַבַּרְזֶל	נָפַל	אֶל־הַמָּיִם	וַיִּצְעַק	וַיֹּאמֶר
mappîl	haqqôrāh	we’eth-habbarzel	nāphal	’el-hammāyim	wayyits‘aq	wayyō’mer
causing to fall	the beam	and the iron	it fell	to the water	and he cried out	and he said

27. The leprosy therefore of Naaman shall cleave unto thee, and unto thy seed for ever: ... shall cling to you and your descendants forever, *NKJV* ... leprosy of Naaman shall also stick to thee, *Douay* ... Naaman's disease will come upon you, and you and your descendants will have it forever!, *Good News* ... the disease of Naaman the leper will take you in its grip, *BB*.

And he went out from his presence a leper as white as snow: ... left his presence white as snow from skin-disease, *JB*.

6:1. And the sons of the prophets said unto Elisha, Behold now, the place where we dwell with thee is too strait for us: ... where we live with you is too small for us, *KJVII* ... place before you where we dwell is too limited for us, *Goodspeed* ... they had no room to live there in his company, *Knox* ... There is not enough room for us to continue to live here with you, *NAB*.

2. Let us go, we pray thee, unto Jordan, and take thence every man a beam: ... and get each of us a log, *Moffatt* ... to the Jordan River, where there are plenty of logs, *NLT*.

and let us make us a place there, where we may dwell: ... and let's build a place there to live, *NCV* ... a place wherein we may sit, *Rotherham* ... and construct for us a residence to settle in, *Fenton*.

And he answered, Go ye: ... All right, Elisha answered, *Good News*.

3. And one said, Be content, I pray thee, and go with thy servants. And he answered, I will go: ... Please consent to go with your servants, *NKJV* ... Please, sir, come with us, *REB* ... I will go along, *Berkeley* ... Will you please come with your servants, *Anchor*.

4. So he went with them. And when they came to Jordan, they cut down wood: ... they came to the Jordan and cut down the trees, *Darby* ... they reached the Jordan, and began felling wood, *Knox* ... On reaching the Jordan they began cutting down timber, *JB* ... they got to work cutting down trees, *BB*.

5. But as one was felling a beam, the axe head fell into the water: ... felling a tree trunk, the iron axhead slipped into the water, *NAB* ... as one man was swinging his axe, *Moffatt* ... felling the timber the axe fell into the stream, *Fenton*.

Gehazi's travels. Possibly, also, the use of the Hebrew term lev is meant to point to Elisha's love and concern for Gehazi, as well as his dismay over his servant's sin. Of all Gehazi's shortcomings, apparently the most grievous to his master was that of greed, for that is what Elisha focuses on in the rest of the verse, "Is this the time ...?" The list of wealth and prosperity listed here finds its counterparts elsewhere in the biblical literature (Deut. 6:11f; 8:8; Josh. 24:13; 1 Sam. 8:14–17). These items are seen as normally gifts from God (Deut. 8:8; Josh. 24:13), but they could well become occasions for apostasy (Deut. 6:11; cf. Neh. 9:25) or signs of self-seeking avarice (1 Sam. 8:14–17). This last alternative, sadly, proved to be the case here. So Naaman's leprosy, whatever the exact medical nature it may have been, was now to cling to Gehazi. He, like Naaman before him, could still appear in society (the next clear reference to Gehazi occurs in 8:4, below, where he is conversing with the king about the exploits of his master), but his name, and that of his family, would be forever linked with that dreaded disease. May we, especially those of us who live in very materialistic societies, learn from the example of Gehazi not to be greedy concerning the gifts and blessings of God. (For a summary of Gehazi's various roles in the Elisha narratives, see comments on 8:1–6.)

6:1–7. A borrowed axhead made to float. We are now back in the category of short Elisha stories about the "sons of the prophets" (cf. 4:1–7, 38–41, and possibly 42ff; also cf. the references in vv. 2–18 to several of these groups). Once again, they appear to be a needy lot, and once again Elisha was called upon to help one of them out.

As in parts of chs. 2 and 5, above, much of the action is centered around the Jordan River. Although it is possible to understand v. 2 as merely the location of obtaining wood to build in a location other than the Jordan valley, the more likely possibility is that the students wished to relocate their place of study to that place. Hobbs, WBC, 76, points out that the Jordan valley has never been known for its supply of wood, the western slopes of the central highlands undoubtedly providing a clearly better source of supply. In any case, the problem which led to the prophetic miracle was, for once, a good one—too many prophetic students, thus rendering the present meeting place entirely too small. Sometimes "good problems," especially those which attend the growth of churches or schools, can still lead to as many heartaches as the more typically negative problems, yet who would not rather deal with the problems of overcrowding, rather than those of not having enough people?

159	112	2000	8068.155		569.121	382, 435	590
intrj	n ms, ps 1cs	cj, pers pron	v Qal pass ptc ms	6.	cj, v Qal impf 3ms	*n ms*, art, n mp	intrg
אֲהָהּ	אֲדֹנִי	וְהוּא	שָׁאוּל		וַיֹּאמֶר	אִישׁ־הָאֱלֹהִים	אָנָה
'ăhāhh	'ădhōnî	wehû'	shā'ûl		wayyō'mer	'îsh-hā'ĕlōhîm	'ānāh
alas	my master	and it	something asked for		and he said	the man of God	where

5489.111	7495.521	881, 4887	7378.121, 6320	8390.521, 8427
v Qal pf 3ms	cj, v Hiphil impf 3ms, ps 3ms	do, art, n ms	cj, v Qal impf 3ms, n ms	cj, v Hiphil impf 3ms, adv
נָפַל	וַיַּרְאֵהוּ	אֶת־הַמָּקוֹם	וַיִּקְצָב־עֵץ	וַיַּשְׁלֶךְ־שָׁמָּה
nāphāl	wayyar'ēhû	'eth-hammāqôm	wayyiqŏtsāv-'ēts	wayyashlekh-shāmmāh
it fell	and he showed him	the place	and he cut a stick	and he threw to there

6950.521	1298		569.121	7597.531	3937	8365.121
cj, v Hiphil impf 3ms	art, n ms	7.	cj, v Qal impf 3ms	v Hiphil impv 2ms	prep, ps 2ms	cj, v Qal impf 3ms
וַיָּצֶף	הַבַּרְזֶל		וַיֹּאמֶר	הָרֶם	לָךְ	וַיִּשְׁלַח
wayyātseph	habbarzel		wayyō'mer	hārem	lākh	wayyishlach
and it caused to float	the iron		and he said	lift up	for yourself	so he stretched out

3135	4089.121		4567	782	2030.111	4032.255
n fs, ps 3ms	cj, v Qal impf 3ms, ps 3ms	8.	cj, *n ms*	pn	v Qal pf 3ms	v Niphal ptc ms
יָדוֹ	וַיִּקָּחֵהוּ		וּמֶלֶךְ	אֲרָם	הָיָה	נִלְחָם
yādhô	wayyiqqāchēhû		ûmelekh	'ărām	hāyāh	nilchām
his hand	and he took it		and the king of	Aram	he was	fighting

904, 3547	3398.221	420, 5860	3937, 569.141	420, 4887	6667
prep, pn	cj, v Niphal impf 3ms	prep, n mp, ps 3ms	prep, v Qal inf con	prep, n ms	indef pron
בְּיִשְׂרָאֵל	וַיִּוָּעַץ	אֶל־עֲבָדָיו	לֵאמֹר	אֶל־מְקוֹם	פְּלֹנִי
beyisrā'ēl	wayyiwwā'ats	'el-'ăvādhâv	lē'mōr	'el-meqôm	pelōnî
against Israel	and he counseled	to his servants	saying	to a place	a certain place

498	8802		8365.121	382	435
adj	n fs, ps 1cs	9.	cj, v Qal impf 3ms	*n ms*	art, n mp
אַלְמֹנִי	תַּחֲנֹתִי		וַיִּשְׁלַח	אִישׁ	הָאֱלֹהִים
'almōnî	tachnōthî		wayyishlach	'îsh	hā'ĕlōhîm
a particular one	my supplication for victory		then he sent out	the man of	God

420, 4567	3547	3937, 569.141	8490.231	5882.141	4887
prep, *n ms*	pn	prep, v Qal inf con	art, v Niphal impv 2ms	prep, v Qal inf con	art, n ms
אֶל־מֶלֶךְ	יִשְׂרָאֵל	לֵאמֹר	הִשָּׁמֶר	מֵעֲבֹר	הַמָּקוֹם
'el-melekh	yisrā'ēl	lē'mōr	hishshāmer	mē'ăvōr	hammāqôm
to the king of	Israel	saying	take heed	from passing by	the place

2172	3706, 8427	782	5368		8365.121	4567	3547
art, dem pron	cj, adv	pn	adj	10.	cj, v Qal impf 3ms	*n ms*	pn
הַזֶּה	כִּי־שָׁם	אֲרָם	נְחִתִּים		וַיִּשְׁלַח	מֶלֶךְ	יִשְׂרָאֵל
hazzeh	kî-shām	'ărām	nechittîm		wayyishlach	melekh	yisrā'ēl
the this	because there	Aram	deployed		then he sent out	the king of	Israel

420, 4887	866	569.111, 3937	382, 435	2178.511	8490.211
prep, art, n ms	rel part	v Qal pf 3ms, prep, ps 3ms	*n ms*, art, n mp	cj, v Hiphil pf 3ms, ps 3ms	cj, v Niphal pf 3ms
אֶל־הַמָּקוֹם	אֲשֶׁר	אָמַר־לוֹ	אִישׁ־הָאֱלֹהִים	וְהִזְהִירֹה	וְנִשְׁמַר
'el-hammāqôm	'ăsher	'āmar-lô	'îsh-hā'ĕlōhîm	wehizhîroh	wenishmar
to the place	which	he had said to him	the man of God	and he warned him	so he was careful

8427	3940	259	3940	8692		5786.221	3949	4567, 782
adv	neg part	num	cj, neg part	num	11.	cj, v Niphal impf 3ms	*n ms*	*n ms*, pn
שָׁם	לֹא	אַחַת	וְלֹא	שְׁתָּיִם		וַיִּסָּעֵר	לֵב	מֶלֶךְ־אֲרָם
shām	lō'	'achath	welō'	shettāyim		wayyissā'ēr	lēv	melekh-'ărām
there	not	once	and not	twice		and it was raging	the heart of	the king of Aram

rowed that ax!, *NCV* ... for it was lent me, *Tyndale*.

6. And the man of God said, Where fell it? And he showed him the place: ... Where did it go in, *BB* ... Where did it fall?, *NEB*.

And he cut down a stick, and cast it in thither; and the iron did swim: ... threw it in there, and made the iron float, *NASB* ... threw it in at that point and made the iron axehead float, *JB* ... Then the ax head rose to the surface and floated, *NLT*.

7. Therefore said he, Take it up to thee. And he put out his hand, and took it: ... Pick it up! So he reached out and took it, *Anchor* ... Lift it out, *NIV* ... It floats for you, *Fenton* ... the man put out his hand and lifted it, *Moffatt*.

8. Then the king of Syria warred against Israel, and took counsel with his servants: ... He conferred with his officers, *JB* ... king of Aram was making war on Israel, he held a conference with his staff, *NEB* ... was fighting against Israel he advised his officers, *Beck*.

saying, In such and such a place shall be my camp: ... I will be waiting in secret in some named place, *BB*

The present brief passage, curiously, leaves a number of questions unanswered: perhaps, most basically, did the students finally finish their new meeting place? Also, why did they want to move into that area anyway? Also, why was Elisha asked to accompany them? Such loose ends were evidently not the concern of the narrator, who basically wished to present Elisha once again as "one who responds immediately and decisively to need." Thus, the description of the background setting leading up to the problem of the lost axhead is relatively lengthy (vv. 1–5), but the solution is told briefly and abruptly (vv. 6f). The prophet of God is always and ever able to effect a solution in the face of need. Yet, Elisha was not without limitations: for example, he had to ascertain the spot where the axhead was lost by means of a question. And the follower was told to retrieve the axhead himself. But it was Elisha who cut the stick and threw it into the designated area, thus causing the axhead to float. (This is the third time in the accounts that something is "thrown" to effect a miracle; in 2:21, salt was "thrown" from the new bowl into the water to purify Jericho's spring; and in 4:41, flour was "thrown" into the pot full of poisonous stew—the same Hebrew term is used in all three places.)

Notice, once again, the lack of censure on the part of the narrator concerning the situation—it was not his place to assign guilt. Was the student negligent in regard to a loose ax-handle, or just particularly unlucky? What does it matter, here? The story celebrates God's grace, in the person and work of God's prophetic representative. In our everyday lives and work, God will manifest his grace, even when we are sometimes lax in our duties (and sometimes God may surprise us by a totally unexpected manifestation of his grace and love for us). That is probably the real message of this heartwarming story. As far as the actual operation of the miracle, Cogan and Tadmor (AB, 70) appropriately cite at length the words of the medieval rabbi David Kimhi: "Why didn't he throw the wooden handle of the ax there to begin with? Why did he have to cut a piece of wood to size? It is apparent that miracles are performed by (the use) of new devices; cf. the new flask (2:20). He cut the stick so that it would be like the handle of the ax that had fallen, and so the stick would enter the eye of the ax. When the handle entered it, the ax head floated together with its handle. ..."

In summary, it would indeed be nice, would it not, to have a "man of God" such as Elisha present when we undertake our building programs. (Maybe that explains why the students invited him to their construction site in v. 3.) But we do have God's Spirit. When pesky problems come our way, and come they will, let us remember that God's Spirit, whether by means of miracle or simple divine intuition, will guide and protect us—all we have to do is to call out in faith in our time of need.

6:8–23. *Elisha opening and closing the eyes of friend and foe alike. The motif of blindness, literal and metaphorical, repeatedly characterizes this memorable story. Who among us would not appreciate visual reassurance as to the reality of the divine world of angels, thus reminding us that "those who are with us are more than those who are with them [our opponents]" (v. 16). And who would not wish for the power to blind our enemies to be able to lead them into a trap, then cause them to see again? (cf. vv. 18ff). Finally, who would not desire to have the compassion to block the murder of these thus-incapacitated enemy soldiers, indeed, to serve them a great banquet? (cf. vv. 21ff). Following is this story of blindness and of sight, both literal and spiritual.*

6:8–10. Elisha "sees" the enemy plans. As mentioned earlier, the Israelite prophet was formerly designated a "seer" (e.g., cf. the most recent

6142, 1745	2172	7410.121	420, 5860	569.121	420
prep, art, n ms	art, dem pron	cj, v Qal impf 3ms	prep, n mp, ps 3ms	cj, v Qal impf 3ms	prep, ps 3mp
עַל־הַדָּבָר	הַזֶּה	וַיִּקְרָא	אֶל־עֲבָדָיו	וַיֹּאמֶר	אֲלֵיהֶם
'al-haddāvār	hazzeh	wayyiqŏrā'	'el-'ăvādhâv	wayyō'mer	'ălêhem
concerning the matter	the this	and he called	to his servants	and he said	to them

1950B, 3940	5222.527	3937	4449	4623, 8340	420, 4567	3547
intrg part, neg part	v Hiphil impf 2mp	prep, ps 1cs	intrg	prep, rel part, ps 1cp	prep, *n ms*	pn
הֲלוֹא	תַּגִּידוּ	לִי	מִי	מִשֶּׁלָּנוּ	אֶל־מֶלֶךְ	יִשְׂרָאֵל
hălô'	taggîdhû	lî	mî	mishshellānû	'el-melekh	yisrā'ēl
will not	you report	to me	who	who of us	to the king of	Israel

	569.121	259	4623, 5860	3940	112	4567	3706, 482
12.	cj, v Qal impf 3ms	num	prep, n mp, ps 3ms	neg part	n ms, ps 1cs	art, n ms	cj, pn
	וַיֹּאמֶר	אַחַד	מֵעֲבָדָיו	לוֹא	אֲדֹנִי	הַמֶּלֶךְ	כִּי־אֱלִישָׁע
	wayyō'mer	'achadh	mē'ăvādhâv	lô'	'ădhōnî	hammelekh	kî-'ĕlîshā'
	and he said	one	from his servants	no	my master	the king	rather Elisha

5204	866	904, 3547	5222.521	3937, 4567	3547	1745	866
art, n ms	rel pron	prep, pn	v Hiphil impf 3ms	prep, *n ms*	pn	art, n mp	rel part
הַנָּבִיא	אֲשֶׁר	בְּיִשְׂרָאֵל	יַגִּיד	לְמֶלֶךְ	יִשְׂרָאֵל	אֶת־הַדְּבָרִים	אֲשֶׁר
hannāvî'	'ăsher	b^{e}yisrā'ēl	yaggîdh	l^{e}melekh	yisrā'ēl	'eth-hadd^{e}vārîm	'ăsher
the prophet	who	in Israel	he reports	to the king of	Israel	the words	which

1744.323	904, 2410	5085		569.121	2050.133
v Piel impf 2ms	prep, *n ms*	n ms, ps 2ms	**13.**	cj, v Qal impf 3ms	v Qal impv 2mp
תְּדַבֵּר	בַּחֲדַר	מִשְׁכָּבֶךָ		וַיֹּאמֶר	לְכוּ
t^{e}dhabbēr	bachdhar	mishkāvekhā		wayyō'mer	l^{e}khû
you are speaking	in the inner room of	your chamber		and he said	go

7495.133	354	2000	8365.125	4089.125
cj, v Qal impv 2mp	adv	pers pron	cj, v Qal juss 1cs	cj, v Qal juss 1cs, ps 3ms
וּרְאוּ	אֵיכֹה	הוּא	וְאֶשְׁלַח	וְאֶקָּחֵהוּ
ûr^{e}'û	'êkhōh	hû'	w^{e}'eshlach	w^{e}'eqqāchēhû
and see	where	he	that I may send out	that I may get him

5222.621, 3937	3937, 569.141	2079	904, 1949		8365.121, 8427
cj, v Hophal impf 3ms, prep, ps 3ms	prep, v Qal inf con	intrj	prep, pn	**14.**	cj, v Qal impf 3ms, adv
וַיֻּגַּד־לוֹ	לֵאמֹר	הִנֵּה	בְדֹתָן		וַיִּשְׁלַח־שָׁמָּה
wayyuggadh-lô	lē'mōr	hinnēh	v^{e}dhōthān		wayyishlach-shāmmāh
and it was reported to him	saying	behold	in Dothan		and he sent out to there

5670	7681	2524	3633	971.126	4050	5545.526
n mp	cj, n ms	cj, n ms	adj	cj, v Qal impf 3mp	n ms	cj, v Hiphil impf 3mp
סוּסִים	וְרֶכֶב	וְחַיִל	כָּבֵד	וַיָּבֹאוּ	לַיְלָה	וַיַּקִּפוּ
sûsîm	w^{e}rekhev	w^{e}chayil	kāvēdh	wayyāvō'û	laylāh	wayyaqqiphû
horses	and chariots	and an army	heavy	and they came	at night	and they surrounded

6142, 6111		8326.521	8664.351	382	435	3937, 7251.141
prep, art, n fs	**15.**	cj, v Hiphil impf 3ms	*v Piel ptc ms*	*n ms*	art, n mp	prep, v Qal inf con
עַל־הָעִיר		וַיַּשְׁכֵּם	מְשָׁרֵת	אִישׁ	הָאֱלֹהִים	לָקוּם
'al-hā'îr		wayyashkēm	m^{e}shārēth	'îsh	hā'ĕlōhîm	lāqûm
against the city		and he rose early	the assistant of	the man of	God	to rise

3428.121	2079, 2524	5621.151	881, 6111	5670	7681
cj, v Qal impf 3ms	cj, intrj, n ms	v Qal act ptc ms	do, art, n fs	cj, n ms	cj, n ms
וַיֵּצֵא	וְהִנֵּה־חַיִל	סוֹבֵב	אֶת־הָעִיר	וְסוּס	וָרָכֶב
wayyētsē'	w^{e}hinnēh-chayil	sôvēv	'eth-hā'îr	w^{e}sûs	wārākhev
and he went out	and behold an army	being all around	the city	and horses	and chariots

... In such and such a place let us lay ambushes, *Douay* ... I mean to attack in such and such a direction, *REB*.

9. And the man of God sent unto the king of Israel, saying, Beware that thou pass not such a place; for thither the Syrians are come down: ... Be careful not to pass by that place, for the Aramaeans attack there, *Anchor* ... The man of God, however, informed the king of Israel, *Berkeley* ... are planning to mobilize their troops there, *NLT* ... Syrians were waiting in ambush there, *Good News*.

10. And the king of Israel sent to the place which the man of God told him and warned him of, and saved himself there, not once nor twice: ... the king took special precautions every time he found himself near that place, *REB* ... he used to warn him, so that he saved himself there more than once or twice, *RSV* ... Time and again Elisha warned the king, so that he was on his guard in such places, *NIV* ... More than once or twice he warned such a place so that it was on the alert, *NRSV*.

11. Therefore the heart of the king of Syria was sore troubled for this thing: ... Greatly disturbed over this, the king of Aram, *NAB* ... the heart of the king of Aram is tossed about concerning this thing, *Young* ... the mind of the king of Syria was agitated because of this fact, *Goodspeed* ... disquieted concerning this thing, *Rotherham*.

and he called his servants, and said unto them, Will ye not show me which of us is for the king of Israel?: ... at last he summoned his council and asked, was there no learning the name of this traitor, *Knox*.

12. And one of his servants said, None, my lord, O king: ... No one, my lord king, answered one of the officers, *NAB* ... None of us, my lord king! said an officer, *Moffatt*.

but Elisha, the prophet that is in Israel, telleth the king of Israel the words that thou speakest in thy bedchamber: ... tells the king of Israel the words that you speak in your bedroom, *NKJV* ... what you say even in the privacy of your own room, *Good News*.

13. And he said, Go and spy where he is, that I may send and fetch him: ... go and find out where he is, so that I can send and take him prisoner, *Knox* ... that I may send and take him, *Goodspeed* ... I will send and capture him, *Fenton* ... we will send troops to seize him, *NLT*.

And it was told him, saying, Behold, he is in Dothan: ... The servants came back and reported, He is in Dothan, *NCV*.

14. Therefore sent he thither horses, and chariots, and a great host: and they came by night, and compassed the city about: ... and a great army there, and they came by night and surrounded the city, *NKJV* ... he sent a strong force there, *REB* ... Then he sent there, horses, chariots, and a powerful army. They arrived by night, *Berkeley* ... and these, arriving during the night, surrounded the town, *JB*.

15. And when the servant of the man of God was risen early, and gone forth, behold, an host compassed the city both with horses

---

comments on 5:25). Once again, Elisha saw as no one else could—and this time it was the enemy Arameans who suffered. Time after time, the enemy plans were revealed to the Israelite king (vv. 9f), with the result that the Aramean king became convinced there was a spy among his officers (v. 11; we cannot but smile at the frustration such prophetic revelations must have brought to the enemy camp). As is often the case in the Elisha narratives, neither king is named.

6:11–14. The enemy seeks out Elisha. The image of all those Arameans in hot pursuit of Elisha in Dothan is rather humorous: "Then he sent horses and chariots and a strong force there" (v. 14). All this to capture one person. (But, it should be recalled that a total of 150 soldiers, albeit in three separate contingents, were sent to capture the prophet Elijah in ch. 1.) Dothan (modern Tell Dothan) is located about 10 miles (16 kilometers) north of Samaria, on the western branch of the mountain road which goes from Shechem through Samaria from the south, and through Ibleam to the Plain of Jezreel to the north.

The fact that the Arameans were able to find the Israelite prophet so quickly indicates that it was not only Israel who had a good intelligence system—although the king of Aram probably did not quite know "the very words" the Israelite king spoke "in his bedroom," as one of the Aramean officials reported Elisha could ascertain concerning the Aramean king (v. 12; the image of the bedroom is, of course, a very intimate one—cf. Ecc. 10:20 for similar concerns about secrecy).

6:15–17. Elisha causes his servant to see heavenly sights. Not surprisingly, Elisha's servant was terrified when he discovered that an enemy army with horses and chariots had surrounded the city. Once again, such a large force seems unnecessary to capture one person. But the prophet was, as usual, not worried. He could see things the servant normally could not, and so he responded, "Don't be afraid ... those who are with us are more than those who are with them" (v. 16). The NT counterpart may be found in 1 John 4:4, "You [the believers] have overcome them [the enemy],

569.121	5470	420	159	112	353	6449.120
cj, v Qal impf 3ms	n ms, ps 3ms	prep, ps 3ms	intrj	n ms, ps 1cs	intrg	v Qal impf 1cp
וַיֹּאמֶר	נַעֲרוֹ	אֵלָיו	אֲהָהּ	אֲדֹנִי	אֵיכָה	נַעֲשֶׂה
wayyō'mer	na'ărô	'ēlâv	'ăhāhh	'ădhōnî	'êkhāh	na'ăseh
and he said	his servant	to him	alas	my master	what	will we do

16.	569.121	414, 3486.123	3706	7521	866	882	4623, 866	882
	cj, v Qal impf 3ms	adv, v Qal juss 2ms	cj	adj	rel pron	prep, ps 1cp	prep, rel pron	prep, ps 3mp
	וַיֹּאמֶר	אַל־תִּירָא	כִּי	רַבִּים	אֲשֶׁר	אִתָּנוּ	מֵאֲשֶׁר	אוֹתָם
	wayyō'mer	'al-tîrā'	kî	rabbîm	'ăsher	'ittānû	mē'ăsher	'ôthām
	and he said	do not be afraid	because	more	who	with us	than who	with them

17.	6663.721	482	569.121	3176	6741.131, 5167	881, 6084
	cj, v Hithpael impf 3ms	pn	v Qal impf 3ms	pn	v Qal impv 2ms, part	do, n fd, ps 3ms
	וַיִּתְפַּלֵּל	אֱלִישָׁע	וַיֹּאמַר	יְהוָה	פְּקַח־נָא	אֶת־עֵינָיו
	wayyithpallēl	'ĕlîshā'	wayyō'mar	y^{e}hwāh	p^{e}qach-nā'	'eth-'ênâv
	and he prayed	Elisha	and he said	O Yahweh	open please	his eyes

7495.121	6860.121	3176	881, 6084	5470	7495.121	2079
cj, v Qal juss 3ms	cj, v Qal impf 3ms	pn	do, *n fd*	art, n ms	cj, v Qal impf 3ms	cj, intrj
וְיִרְאֶה	וַיִּפְקַח	יְהוָה	אֶת־עֵינֵי	הַנַּעַר	וַיַּרְא	וְהִנֵּה
w^{e}yir'eh	wayyiphqach	y^{e}hwāh	'eth-'ênêy	hanna'ar	wayyar^e'	w^{e}hinnēh
that he may see	and He opened	Yahweh	the eyes of	the servant	and he saw	and behold

2098	4527.151	5670	7681	813	5623	482
art, n ms	v Qal act ptc ms	n mp	cj, *n ms*	n fs	adv	pn
הָהָר	מָלֵא	סוּסִים	וְרֶכֶב	אֵשׁ	סְבִיבֹת	אֱלִישָׁע
hāhār	mālē'	sûsîm	w^{e}rekhev	'ēsh	s^{e}vîvōth	'ĕlîshā'
the hills	being full of	horses	and chariots of	fire	all around	Elisha

18.	3495.126	420	6663.721	482	420, 3176	569.121
	cj, v Qal impf 3mp	prep, ps 3ms	cj, v Hithpael impf 3ms	pn	prep, pn	v Qal impf 3ms
	וַיֵּרְדוּ	אֵלָיו	וַיִּתְפַּלֵּל	אֱלִישָׁע	אֶל־יְהוָה	וַיֹּאמַר
	wayyēr^{e}dhû	'ēlâv	wayyithpallēl	'ĕlîshā'	'el-y^{e}hwāh	wayyō'mar
	and they came down	against him	but he prayed	Elisha	to Yahweh	and he said

5409.531, 5167	881, 1504, 2172	904, 5770	5409.521
v Hiphil impv 2ms, part	do, art, n ms, art, dem pron	prep, art, n mp	cj, v Hiphil impf 3ms, ps 3mp
הַךְ־נָא	אֶת־הַגּוֹי־הַזֶּה	בַּסַּנְוֵרִים	וַיַּכֵּם
hakh-nā'	'eth-haggôy-hazzeh	bassanwērîm	wayyakkēm
strike down please	this nation	with the blindness	and He struck them down

904, 5770	3626, 1745	482	19.	569.121	420	482
prep, art, n mp	prep, *n ms*	pn		cj, v Qal impf 3ms	prep, ps 3mp	pn
בַּסַּנְוֵרִים	כִּדְבַר	אֱלִישָׁע		וַיֹּאמֶר	אֲלֵהֶם	אֱלִישָׁע
bassanwērîm	kidhvar	'ĕlîshā'		wayyō'mer	'ălēhem	'ĕlîshā'
with the blindness	according to the word of	Elisha		and he said	to them	Elisha

3940	2172	1932	3940	2173	6111	2050.133	313
neg part	dem pron	art, n ms	cj, neg part	dem pron	art, n fs	v Qal impv 2mp	prep, ps 1cs
לֹא	זֶה	הַדֶּרֶךְ	וְלֹא	זֹה	הָעִיר	לְכוּ	אַחֲרַי
lō'	zeh	hadderekh	w^{e}lō'	zōh	hā'îr	l^{e}khû	'achray
not	this	the way	and not	this	the city	come	after me

2050.525	881	420, 382	866	1272.328	2050.521
cj, v Hiphil juss 1cs	do, ps 2mp	prep, art, n ms	rel pron	v Piel impf 2mp	cj, v Hiphil impf 3ms
וְאוֹלִיכָה	אֶתְכֶם	אֶל־הָאִישׁ	אֲשֶׁר	תְּבַקֵּשׁוּן	וַיֹּלֶךְ
w^e'ôlîkhāh	'ethkhem	'el-hā'îsh	'ăsher	t^{e}vaqqēshûn	wayyōlekh
that I may cause to go	you	to the man	whom	you are seeking for	and he caused to go

and chariots: ... the attendant of the man of God rose early and went forth, behold, an army surrounded the city, *Darby* ... When the disciple of the man of God rose early in the morning and went out, he saw a force with horses, *NEB*.

And his servant said unto him, Alas, my master! how shall we do?: ... Oh, my master, what can we do?, *NCV* ... Ah, my lord, what will we do now?, *NLT* ... How can we do anything, *Beck*.

16. And he answered, Fear not: for they that be with us are more than they that be with them: ... for there are more on our side than on theirs, *JB* ... The army that fights for us is larger than the one against us, *NCV* ... there are more with us than with them, *Tyndale* ... we have more on our side than they on theirs, *Knox* ... Our side outnumbers theirs, *NAB*.

17. And Elisha prayed, and said, LORD, I pray thee, open his eyes, that he may see: ... open his eyes and let him see, *NEB*.

And the LORD opened the eyes of the young man; and he saw: ... YHWH opened the eyes of the attendant, *Anchor* ... opened the eyes of the servant, *NRSV*.

and, behold, the mountain was full of horses and chariots of fire round about Elisha: ... The mountain was full of fiery horses and chariots around Elisha, *Beck* ... he saw the hills covered with horses and chariots, *REB*.

18. And when they came down to him, Elisha prayed unto the LORD: ... and the enemies came down to him, *Douay* ... when the Aramaeans came down to Elisha, he made a prayer, *BB* ... when the Syrians came down against him, *RSV*.

and said, Smite this people, I pray thee, with blindness. And he smote them with blindness according to the word of Elisha: ... Strike this people with blindness, I pray, *NASB* ... I beg you to strike these people sun-blind, *JB*.

19. And Elisha said unto them, This is not the way, neither is this the city: ... You are on the wrong road; this is not the city, *NEB* ... You have come the wrong way! This isn't the right city!, *NLT*.

follow me, and I will bring you to the man whom ye seek: ... I may take you to the man you are searching for, *BB* ... March after me and I will lead you to the man, *Fenton*.

But he led them to Samaria: ... So he brought them to Samaria, *Berkeley*.

---

because the one who is in you is greater than the one who is in the world." We can rest assured that those on our side are stronger than the enemy. Divine support and protection is available to God's people at times of testing (also cf. Ps. 91:11; Acts 7:56; Rom. 8:31).

The metaphors of eyesight/blindness are rarely more sublimely juxtaposed than they are here. The servant saw only the enemy and was blind to spiritual realities, whereas the prophet could see that the enemy has always been outpowered by heavenly forces, and he simply asked Yahweh both to open the servant's eyes (v. 17) and to close the Arameans' physical eyes (v. 18). As we are reminded once again by the present narrative, things are rarely as they seem (to our own all-too-limited eyesight). This observation sheds its own light, for example, on the plight of the patriarch Job, as recorded in the Book of that name—Job himself had no idea what had transpired in the heavenly realms between Yahweh and "the Satan," as described in the first two chapters of the Book. (Such an observation is, however, not entirely encouraging for either Job or his so-called "comforters"—for God's ways are often "past finding out" [Rom. 11:33].) In regard to the heavenly "horses and chariots of fire," cf. above, on 2:11f, in regard to their appearance at Elijah's translation into heaven, suffice it to say here, that fire is frequently connected with divine images and appearances throughout both Testaments of the Bible.

6:18–20. The enemy blinded, captured, and then their sight restored. As just noted, Elisha now prayed for physical blindness for the enemy. The unusual term for "blindness" used twice in v. 18 (s̱anwērîm, HED #5770, which Cogan and Tadmor [AB, 74], note is a loanword from Akkadian, and which they translate as "a blinding light") is used in only one other place in the OT (Gen. 19:11, again of divine agency). In both places, the effect is immediate, entirely debilitating, but of short duration (cf. the blinding of Saul on the road to Damascus by the bright light from heaven, as a likely NT parallel [Acts 9:3–9]).

Whatever exactly might have taken place, the enemy was obviously completely disoriented as a result (v. 19). They were willing to be led directly into the enemy capital. Elisha, of course, told them a lie (once again, the narrator tells the story, and rarely moralizes about it), but surely the perspective here is that of the humorous bewilderment of the enemy, not that of careful moral distinctions being made for the sake of edification.

881	8497		2030.121	3626, 971.141	8497	569.121	482
do, ps 3mp	pn	**20.**	cj, v Qal impf 3ms	prep, v Qal inf con	pn	cj, v Qal impf 3ms	pn
אוֹתָם	שֹׁמְרוֹנָה		וַיְהִי	כְּבֹאָם	שֹׁמְרוֹן	וַיֹּאמֶר	אֱלִישָׁע
'ôthām	shōmerônāh		wayhî	kevō'ām	shōmerôn	wayyō'mer	'ĕlîshā'
them	to Samaria		and it was	when entering	Samaria	then he said	Elisha

3176	6741.131	881, 6084, 431	7495.126	6741.121	3176
pn	v Qal impv 2ms	do, *n fd*, dem pron	cj, v Qal juss 3mp	cj, v Qal impf 3ms	pn
יְהוָה	פְּקַח	אֶת־עֵינֵי־אֵלֶּה	וְיִרְאוּ	וַיִּפְקַח	יְהוָה
yehwāh	peqach	'eth-'ênê-'ēlleh	weyir'û	wayyiphqach	yehwāh
Yahweh	open	the eyes of these	that they may see	and He opened	Yahweh

881, 6084	7495.126	2079	904, 8761	8497		569.121
do, n fd, ps 3mp	cj, v Qal impf 3mp	cj, intrj	prep, *n ms*	pn	**21.**	cj, v Qal impf 3ms
אֶת־עֵינֵיהֶם	וַיִּרְאוּ	וְהִנֵּה	בְּתוֹךְ	שֹׁמְרוֹן		וַיֹּאמֶר
'eth-'ênêhem	wayyir'û	wehinnēh	bethôkh	shōmerôn		wayyō'mer
their eyes	and they looked	and behold	in the midst of	Samaria		and he said

4567, 3547	420, 482	3626, 7495.141	881	1950B, 5409.525
n ms, pn	prep, pn	prep, v Qal inf con, ps 3ms	do, ps 3mp	intrg part, v Hiphil juss 1cs
מֶלֶךְ־יִשְׂרָאֵל	אֶל־אֱלִישָׁע	כִּרְאֹתוֹ	אוֹתָם	הַאַכֶּה
melekh-yisrā'ēl	'el-'ĕlîshā'	kir'ōthô	'ôthām	ha'akkeh
the king of Israel	to Elisha	when his seeing	them	should I strike down

5409.525	1		569.121	3940	5409.523	1950B, 866
v Hiphil impf 1cs	n ms, ps 1cs	**22.**	cj, v Qal impf 3ms	neg part	v Hiphil impf 2ms	intrg part, rel pron
אַכֶּה	אָבִי		וַיֹּאמֶר	לֹא	תַכֶּה	הַאֲשֶׁר
'akkeh	'āvî		wayyō'mer	lō'	thakkeh	ha'ăsher
I will strike down	O my father		and he said	not	you will strike down	will whom

8091.113	904, 2820	904, 7493	887	5409.551	7947.131
v Qal pf 2ms	prep, n fs, ps 2ms	cj, prep, n fs, ps 2ms	pers pron	v Hiphil ptc ms	v Qal impv 2ms
שָׁבִיתָ	בְּחַרְבְּךָ	וּבְקַשְׁתְּךָ	אַתָּה	מַכֶּה	שִׂים
shāvîthā	becharbekhā	ûveqashtekhā	'attāh	makkeh	sîm
you have taken captive	with your sword	or with your bow	you	striking down	put

4035	4448	3937, 6686	404.126	8685.126	2050.126
n ms	cj, n md	prep, n mp, ps 3mp	cj, v Qal juss 3mp	cj, v Qal juss 3mp	cj, v Qal juss 3mp
לֶחֶם	וָמַיִם	לִפְנֵיהֶם	וְיֹאכְלוּ	וְיִשְׁתּוּ	וְיֵלְכוּ
lechem	wāmayim	liphnêhem	weyō'khelû	weyishtû	weyēlekhû
bread	and water	before them	that they may eat	and they may drink	that they may go

420, 112		3868.121	3937	3871	1448	404.126
prep, n mp, ps 3mp	**23.**	cj, v Qal impf 3ms	prep, ps 3mp	n fs	adj	cj, v Qal impf 3mp
אֶל־אֲדֹנֵיהֶם		וַיִּכְרֶה	לָהֶם	כֵּרָה	גְדוֹלָה	וַיֹּאכְלוּ
'el-'ădhōnêhem		wayyikhreh	lāhem	kērāh	ghedhôlāh	wayyō'khelû
to their master		and he obtained	for them	a feast	great	and they ate

8685.126	8365.321	2050.126	420, 112	3940, 3362.116
~cj, v Qal impf 3mp	cj, v Piel impf 3ms, ps 3mp	cj, v Qal impf 3mp	prep, n mp, ps 3mp	cj, neg part, v Qal pf 3cp
וַיִּשְׁתּוּ	וַיְשַׁלְּחֵם	וַיֵּלְכוּ	אֶל־אֲדֹנֵיהֶם	וְלֹא־יָסְפוּ
wayyishtû	wayshallechēm	wayyēlekhû	'el-'ădhōnêhem	welō'-yāsephû
and they drank	and he sent them	and they went	to their master	and they did not do again

5968	1447	782	3937, 971.141	904, 800	3547		2030.121
adv	*n mp*	pn	prep, v Qal inf con	prep, *n fs*	pn	**24.**	cj, v Qal impf 3ms
עוֹד	גְּדוּדֵי	אֲרָם	לָבוֹא	בְּאֶרֶץ	יִשְׂרָאֵל		וַיְהִי
'ôdh	gedhûdhê	'ărām	lāvô'	be'erets	yisrā'ēl		wayhî
anymore	the raiders of	Aram	to enter	in the land of	Israel		and it was

20. And it came to pass, when they were come into Samaria, that Elisha said, LORD, open the eyes of these men, that they may see: ... As soon as they had entered the city, *Good News*.

And the LORD opened their eyes, and they saw; and, behold, they were in the midst of Samaria: ... they saw that they were inside Samaria, *Anchor* ... they looked, and there they were, inside Samaria, *NIV* ... they saw they were in the market-place of Shomeron, *Fenton*.

21. And the king of Israel said unto Elisha, when he saw them, My father, shall I smite them? shall I smite them?: ... Shall I kill them, my father?, *NAB* ... shall I strike them down?, *Knox* ... Shall I cut them down?, *Moffatt* ... Shall I cut them off? Shall I assail them, father?, *Fenton*.

22. And he answered, Thou shalt not smite them: wouldest thou smite those whom thou hast taken captive with thy sword and with thy bow?: ... would you slay those whom you have not taken prisoner with your sword, *Goodspeed* ... Would you cut down prisoners you never captured, *Moffatt* ... Not even soldiers you had captured in combat would you put to death, *Good News* ... Would you destroy those whom you have not taken prisoner with your own sword, *REB*.

set bread and water before them, that they may eat and drink, and go to their master: ... Give them food and drink and send them home again, *NLT*.

23. And he prepared great provision for them: and when they had eaten and drunk, he sent them away, and they went to their master: ... he prepared a great feast for them, *NKJV* ... spread a great feast of food, and they ate and drank. Then he dismissed them, and they went to their Prince, *Fenton*.

So the bands of Syria came no more into the land of Israel: ... No more Aramean raiders came into the land of Israel, *NAB* ... The soldiers of Aram did not come anymore into the land, *NCV* ... From that time Aramaean raids on Israel ceased, *REB*.

24. And it came to pass after this, that Ben-hadad king of Syria gathered all his host, and went up, and besieged Samaria: ... Ben-hadad king of Syria assembled all his army, *Goodspeed* ... Benhadad of Aram mobilized his entire army, *NLT* ... mustered his entire army; he marched against Samaria, *NRSV*.

6:21–23. Elisha "sees to it"—a day of celebration, not slaughter, leading to the cessation of enemy oppression. By v. 20, the blind can again see, and they can indeed see that they are now in the enemy capital, surrounded by Israelite forces. Whether the (again unnamed) king of Israel remained spiritually blind or not, his question to Elisha was somewhat understandable, if predictably bloodthirsty: "Shall I kill them, my father? Shall I kill them?" (v. 21). The reference to the prophet as spiritual father (or teacher) to the king (the terms "father" and "son" often refer to the teacher and the pupil, respectively, in Hebrew thought; this is especially true in the Wisdom literature [e.g., the Books of Job, Proverbs and Ecclesiastes]), is particularly to be noted; it is, of course, a term of high respect and regard (cf. its use in 5:13). After all, the king had just been handed an incredible victory without a fight (in the very next story, however, the Israelite king will come to think very differently of the prophet; cf. v. 31). The king's thirst for blood-revenge is understandable, if disappointing (already in the OT, mercy for one's enemies is enjoined; cf., e.g., Exo. 23:4f; Prov. 16:7; 24:17f; and especially, Prov. 25:21f; cf Rom. 12:20).

Elisha did not start this war—his role merely was that of a "seer" helping out his king. So it is entirely fitting that he help him out once again, this time by advising mercy, not revenge (v. 22). In the ancient Near East, prisoners of war were not wantonly murdered; rather they were spared as spoils of war, and often used as slaves (cf. 5:2). Whether Elisha's motive was that of genuine humanitarianism, or rather that of "embarrassing his foes with kindness" (cf. Hobbs), the end result was the same: the fame of Yahweh and of his prophet beyond the borders of Israel was further reinforced. As Cogan and Tadmor (AB, 75) argue, "The Arameans are [Elisha's] prisoners, not the king's; they are spared so that they, like Naaman, may spread the word of his greatness. It is small wonder that a subsequent narrative told of Elisha being so handsomely received in Damascus (8:7ff)." The story concludes with the reminder that the Arameans no longer sent raiding parties into the territory of Israel, and, whether this newfound restraint resulted from an act of reciprocity to the graciousness of Elisha's prior actions or from respect for the awesome powers he displayed (or from both), the Arameans finally realized that Israel would never be overcome, as long as she had such a prophet on her side. Let us likewise be faithful to our civil authorities, as God so leads (cf. Rom. 13:1–7), by displaying both faithfulness and generosity to friend and foe alike.

311, 3772	7192.121	1163	4567, 782	881, 3725, 4402	6148.121
adv, adv	cj, v Qal impf 3ms	pn	*n ms*, pn	do, *adj*, n ms, ps 3ms	cj, v Qal impf 3ms
אַחֲרֵי־כֵן	וַיִּקְבֹּץ	בֶּן־הֲדַד	מֶלֶךְ־אֲרָם	אֶת־כָּל־מַחֲנֵהוּ	וַיַּעַל
'achrê-khēn	wayyiqŏbbōts	ben-h^{e}dhadh	melekh-'ărām	'eth-kol-machnēhû	wayya'al
afterward	that he gathered	Ben-Hadad	the king of Aram	all his camp	and he went up

6961.121	6142, 8497		2030.121	7743	1448	904, 8497	2079
cj, v Qal impf 3ms	prep, pn	**25.**	cj, v Qal impf 3ms	n ms	adj	prep, pn	cj, intrj
וַיָּצַר	עַל־שֹׁמְרוֹן		וַיְהִי	רָעָב	גָּדוֹל	בְּשֹׁמְרוֹן	וְהִנֵּה
wayyātsar	'al-shōm^{e}rôn		wayhî	rā'āv	gādhôl	b^{e}shōm^{e}rôn	w^{e}hinnēh
and he besieged	against Samaria		and it was	a famine	great	in Samaria	and behold

6961.152	6142	5912	2030.141	7513, 2645	904, 8470	3826B
v Qal act ptc mp	prep, ps 3fs	adv	v Qal inf con	*n ms*, n ms	prep, num	n ms
צָרִים	עָלֶיהָ	עַד	הֱיוֹת	רֹאשׁ־חֲמוֹר	בִּשְׁמֹנִים	כֶּסֶף
tsārîm	'ālêāh	'adh	hĕyôth	rō'sh-chămôr	bishmōnîm	kese̲ph
besieging	against it	until	being	the head of a donkey	with eighty	silver

7544	7180	2858	904, 2675, 3826B		2030.121	4567
cj, *n ms*	art, n ms	n mp	prep, num, n ms	**26.**	cj, v Qal impf 3ms	*n ms*
וְרֹבַע	הַקַּב	חֲרֵיוֹנִים	בַּחֲמִשָּׁה־כָסֶף		וַיְהִי	מֶלֶךְ
w^{e}rōva'	haqqav	chărêyônîm	bachmishshāh-khāse̲ph		wayhî	melekh
and the fourth part of	the kab	dung	with five silver		and it was	the king of

3547	5882.151	6142, 2440	828	7094.112	420	3937, 569.141
pn	v Qal act ptc ms	prep, art, n fs	cj, n fs	v Qal pf 3fs	prep, ps 3ms	prep, v Qal inf con
יִשְׂרָאֵל	עֹבֵר	עַל־הַחֹמָה	וְאִשָּׁה	צָעֲקָה	אֵלָיו	לֵאמֹר
yisrā'ēl	'ōvēr	'al-hachōmāh	w^{e}'ishshāh	tsā'ăqāh	'ēlāv	lē'mōr
Israel	passing by	beside the wall	and a woman	she cried out	to him	saying

3588.531	112	4567		569.121	414, 3588.521	3176
v Hiphil impv 2ms	n ms, ps 1cs	art, n ms	**27.**	cj, v Qal impf 3ms	adv, v Hiphil juss 3ms	pn
הוֹשִׁיעָה	אֲדֹנִי	הַמֶּלֶךְ		וַיֹּאמֶר	אַל־יוֹשִׁעֵךְ	יְהוָה
hôshî'āh	'ădhōnî	hammelekh		wayyō'mer	'al-yôshi'ēkh	y^{e}hwāh
save	my master	the king		and he said	may He not save you	Yahweh

4623, 376	3588.525	1950B, 4623, 1681	173	4623, 3449
prep, intrg	v Hiphil impf 1cs, ps 2fs	intrg part, prep, art, n ms	cj	prep, art, n ms
מֵאַיִן	אוֹשִׁיעֵךְ	הֲמִן־הַגֹּרֶן	אוֹ	מִן־הַיָּקֶב
mē'ayin	'ôshî'ēkh	hămin-haggōren	'ô	min-hayyāqev
from where	will I save you	will from the threshing floor	or	from the winepress

25. And there was a great famine in Samaria: ... There was a shortage of food in Samaria, *NCV* ... The city was near starvation, *NEB*.

and, behold, they besieged it, until an ass's head was sold for fourscore pieces of silver: ... that a donkey's head brought fifty dollars in silver, *Berkeley*.

and the fourth part of a cab of dove's dung for five pieces of silver: ... or five for a pint of dove's droppings, *Knox* ... a quarter of a kab of dove manure for 5 shekels of silver, *Beck* ... a quarter of a kab of locust-beans for five shekels, *NEB*.

26. And as the king of Israel was passing by upon the wall, there cried a woman unto him, saying, Help, my lord, O king: ... Save me, my lord O king, *Douay* ... Please help me, my lord the king!, *NLT* ... a woman appealed to him, saying, Help! your Majesty!, *Fenton* ... a woman yelled out to him, Help me, my master and king!, *NCV*.

27. And he said, If the LORD do not help thee, whence shall I help thee?: ... No! Let YHWH help you! From where can I get help for you, *Anchor* ... Out of what can I help you?, *Goodspeed*.

out of the barnfloor, or out of the winepress?: ... from the grain-floor or the grape-crusher, *BB* ... With something from the threshing floor, *Beck* ... Do I have any wheat or wine?, *Good News*.

28. And the king said unto her, What aileth thee?: ... What is your trouble?, *RSV* ... What is the matter?, *JB* ... What is your complaint?, *NRSV*.

6:24–7:20. *Siege in Samaria and its aftermath. A lengthy story now commands our attention, one which, in its entirety, spans some thirty verses in two different chapters of the Book. Therefore, many commentators on the Books of Kings include ch. 7 with the last ten verses of ch. 6 as part of the same story.*

The story is lengthy and somewhat complex, with two related parts. The first (6:24–33) gives the extent of the siege-induced-famine in the Israelite capital city of Samaria; whereas the second, a carefully written account of the miraculous lifting of the famine within one day (7:1–20), represents the outworking of the word of the prophet Elisha. Following is a brief analysis of both of these sections.

6:24–33. *Part I. Israelite's king powerless to break the famine. This section may be divided into the following three subsections: vv. 24f, 26–30, and 31ff; it is of more than passing interest that the story puts off any reference to the prophet until v. 31, where the incredibly frustrated king is calling for his immediate demise, in no uncertain terms. Thus the delay heightens interest in the reader as to what, again behind closed doors (concerning this motif in the Elisha stories, see above, on 4:1–7), Elisha will do or say about the king, and the account ends with the king about ready to take action, "Why should I wait for Yahweh any longer?" (v. 33). It is at that point, and not until, that we hear Elisha's incredible statement about food prices returning to near normal, by this time the next day (in sharp contrast to the beginning of the present account, where the famine has led to outrageous prices for the most unsavory of foods). Thus, concern for food prices serves as a unifying motif between the two parts of the story.*

6:24–25. Introduction: Famine as a result of the Aramean siege. The present events take place "some time later" than the events of the previous story, which concludes with the Arameans at peace with Israel. Historical reconstructions of the events and personages alluded to in these Elisha stories are notoriously hard to sustain, but there may well have been a period of some several decades between these two stories. In any case, we have quite a different military situation envisioned in the present passage—massive warfare, and desperate siege. Indeed, as just noted, the most unpalatable of food products—donkey's heads, and bird dung—are cited, along with their simply incredible prices on the market, to illustrate starkly the severity of the famine. Once again, it is the Arameans, this time under Ben-Hadad the king (often identified as "Ben-Hadad III" by contemporary scholars, although the historical reconstruction underlying this numerical designation is far from certain; cf. Wayne T. Pitard, *Anchor Bible Dictionary,* 1:339ff, and the sources cited there), who are at war. They had seemingly overrun the northern kingdom of Israel, even to the point of subjecting the capital city of Samaria to a brutal and protracted siege. Concerning the consumption of normally discarded items during famine, Cogan and Tadmor (AB, 79) cite the Babylonians "gnawing leather straps," as well as resorting to cannibalism, during Ashurbanipal's siege of the city in ca. 650 B.C. (also cf. the graphic depictions of the result of siege in the covenant curses in Lev. 26:25–29; and in Deut. 28:53–57). The proper translation of the term "dove's dung" in the present passage (v. 25) is disputed, with the strong possibility that it was a popular name for normally inedible husks, perhaps of the (false) carob plant. Beyond speculation, however, the more specific term may refer to the most common type of bird dung. Hobbs, however, prefers the more literal meaning for both terms, with the "dove's dung" (or "pigeon dung") probably used for fuel. In any case, the passing reference to cannibalism in the next section amply illustrates the extremely desperate state of the people during this time.

6:26–31. The king unable to help a desperate, traumatized woman. Focus for the balance of this part of the story will be on the (again unnamed) Israelite king, and, just as was the case in 5:7 (cf. the comments on 5:8ff), the king was entirely powerless (so his own words in v. 27) to do much of anything to lift the siege and break the famine (except, to tear his clothes in despair, wear sackcloth and call for the head of the prophet Elisha). Once again, a concrete detail reinforces most vividly the desperate plight of the inhabitants of the city. This time a woman calls out to the king to seek legal redress for a wrong she has just suffered at the hands of her neighbor (whence the appeal to the king). More specifically, it concerns a recent deception her neighbor has perpetrated on her, concerning their children. It seems that they both had agreed to eat her son yesterday, and then the neighbor's son today. But the neighbor reneged on the agreement, and had hidden her own son away. The plaintiff's apparent lack of feeling concerning the death of her own son only under-

28. 569.121, 3937	4567	4242, 3937	569.122	828	2148
cj, v Qal impf 3ms, prep, ps 3fs	art, n ms	intrg, prep, ps 2fs	cj, v Qal impf 3fs	art, n fs	art, dem pron
וַיֹּאמֶר־לָהּ	הַמֶּלֶךְ	מַה־לָּךְ	וַתֹּאמֶר	הָאִשָּׁה	הַזֹּאת
wayyō'mer-lāhh	hammelekh	mah-lākh	wattō'mer	hā'ishshāh	hazzō'th
and he said to her	the king	what to you	and she said	the woman	the this

569.112	420	5598.132	881, 1158	404.120	3219	881, 1158
v Qal pf 3fs	prep, ps 1cs	v Qal impv 2fs	do, n ms, ps 2fs	cj, v Qal juss 1cp, ps 3ms	art, n ms	cj, do, n ms, ps 1cs
אָמְרָה	אֵלַי	תְּנִי	אֶת־בְּנֵךְ	וְנֹאכְלֶנּוּ	הַיּוֹם	וְאֶת־בְּנִי
'āmerāh	'ēlay	tenî	'eth-benēkh	wenō'khelennû	hayyôm	we'eth-benî
she said	to me	give	your son	and let us eat him	today	and my son

404.120	4417	**29.** 1344.320	881, 1158	404.120	569.125
v Qal juss 1cp	adv	cj, v Piel impf 1cp	do, n ms, ps 1cs	cj, v Qal impf 1cp, ps 3ms	cj, v Qal impf 1cs
נֹאכַל	מָחָר	וַנְּבַשֵּׁל	אֶת־בְּנִי	וַנֹּאכְלֵהוּ	וָאֹמַר
nō'khal	māchār	wannevashshēl	'eth-benî	wannō'khelēhû	wā'ōmar
let us eat	tomorrow	and we boiled	my son	and we ate him	and I said

420	904, 3219	311	5598.132	881, 1158	404.120
prep, ps 3fs	prep, art, n ms	art, adj	v Qal impv 2fs	do, n ms, ps 2fs	cj, v Qal impf 1cp, ps 3ms
אֵלֶיהָ	בַּיּוֹם	הָאַחֵר	תְּנִי	אֶת־בְּנֵךְ	וְנֹאכְלֶנּוּ
'ēlêāh	bayyôm	hā'achēr	tenî	'eth-benēkh	wenō'khelennû
to her	on the day	the following	give	your son	and let us eat him

2334.522	881, 1158	**30.** 2030.121	3626, 8471.141	4567	881, 1745
cj, v Hiphil impf 3fs	do, n ms, ps 3fs	cj, v Qal impf 3ms	prep, v Qal inf con	art, n ms	do, *n mp*
וַתַּחְבִּא	אֶת־בְּנָהּ	וַיְהִי	כִּשְׁמֹעַ	הַמֶּלֶךְ	אֶת־דִּבְרֵי
wattachbi'	'eth-benāhh	wayhî	khishmōa'	hammelekh	'eth-divrê
but she hid	her son	and it was	when hearing	the king	the words of

828	7458	881, 933	2000	5882.151	6142, 2440
art, n fs	cj, v Qal impf 3ms	do, n mp, ps 3ms	cj, pers pron	v Qal act ptc ms	prep, art, n fs
הָאִשָּׁה	וַיִּקְרַע	אֶת־בְּגָדָיו	וְהוּא	עֹבֵר	עַל־הַחֹמָה
hā'ishshāh	wayyiqra'	'eth-beghādhâv	wehû'	'ōvēr	'al-hachōmāh
the woman	that he tore	his clothes	and he	passing by	beside the wall

7495.121	6194	2079	8012	6142, 1340	4623, 1041
cj, v Qal impf 3ms	art, n ms	cj, intrj	art, n ms	prep, n ms, ps 3ms	prep, n ms
וַיַּרְא	הָעָם	וְהִנֵּה	הַשַּׂק	עַל־בְּשָׂרוֹ	מִבָּיִת
wayyare'	hā'ām	wehinnēh	hassaq	'al-besārô	mibbāyith
and they saw	the people	and behold	the sackcloth	on his flesh	from a house

31. 569.121	3662, 6449.121, 3937	435	3662	3362.521	524, 6198.121
cj, v Qal impf 3ms	adv, v Qal juss 3ms, prep, ps 1cs	n mp	cj, adv	v Hiphil juss 3ms	cj, v Qal impf 3ms
וַיֹּאמֶר	כֹּה־יַעֲשֶׂה־לִּי	אֱלֹהִים	וְכֹה	יוֹסִף	אִם־יַעֲמֹד
wayyō'mer	kōh-ya'ăseh-lî	'ĕlōhîm	wekhōh	yôsiph	'im-ya'ămōdh
and he said	thus may He do to me	God	and thus	may He add	if it stands

7513	482	1158, 8573	6142	3219	**32.** 482	3553.151
n ms	pn	*n ms*, pn	prep, ps 3ms	art, n ms	cj, pn	v Qal act ptc ms
רֹאשׁ	אֱלִישָׁע	בֶּן־שָׁפָט	עָלָיו	הַיּוֹם	וֶאֱלִישָׁע	יֹשֵׁב
rō'sh	'ĕlîshā'	ben-shāphāṭ	'ālâv	hayyôm	we'ĕlîshā'	yōshēv
the head of	Elisha	the son of Shaphat	on him	today	and Elisha	sitting

904, 1041	2292	3553.152	882	8365.121	382
prep, n ms, ps 3ms	cj, art, n mp	v Qal act ptc mp	prep, ps 3ms	cj, v Qal impf 3ms	n ms
בְּבֵיתוֹ	וְהַזְּקֵנִים	יֹשְׁבִים	אִתּוֹ	וַיִּשְׁלַח	אִישׁ
bevêthô	wehazzeqēnîm	yōshevîm	'ittô	wayyishlach	'îsh
in his house	and the elders	sitting	with him	and he sent out	a man

And she answered, This woman said unto me, Give thy son, that we may eat him today, and we will eat my son tomorrow: ... This woman proposed that we eat my son one day and her son the next, *NLT* ... This woman who is with me bade me kill my son, to be food for us that day, *Knox*.

29. So we boiled my son, and did eat him: ... we cooked my son and we ate him, *Anchor* ... so we dressed my son and did eat him, *Tyndale*.

and I said unto her on the next day, Give thy son, that we may eat him: ... Now give up your child for us to eat, *REB*.

and she hath hid her son: ... but she has put her son in a secret place, *BB* ... but she has hidden her son, *NKJV*.

30. And it came to pass, when the king heard the words of the woman, that he rent his clothes: ... he tore his garments, *Goodspeed* ... he tore his clothes in grief, *NCV*.

and he passed by upon the wall, and the people looked, and, behold, he had sackcloth within upon his flesh: ... he made his way along the battlements the people, one and all, could see how his shirt underneath was of sackcloth, *Knox* ... people noticed that he was wearing sackcloth next his skin, *Moffatt*.

31. Then he said, God do so and more also to me, if the head of Elisha the son of Shaphat shall stand on him this day: ... remains on him today, *NKJV* ... isn't cut off from his body today!, *NCV* ... if Elisha is not beheaded before the day is over!, *Good News* ... if I don't execute Elisha son of Shaphat this very day, *NLT*.

32. But Elisha sat in his house, and the elders sat with him; and the king sent a man from before him: ... was sitting in his house in conference with the elders, *NAB* ... The king had dispatched one of those at court, *REB*.

but ere the messenger came to him, he said to the elders, See ye how this son of a murderer hath sent to take away mine head?: ... see how this son of a murderer has sent someone to tear off my head?, *Beck*.

look, when the messenger cometh, shut the door, and hold him fast at the door: is not the sound of his master's feet behind him?: ... shut the door and keep him back with the door, *Berkeley*.

---

scores all the more the incredible pathos of her situation (Hobbs, WBC, 80). Imagine being called upon to deal with such a horrifying "legal" case. Such a juridical conundrum could only further traumatize the king (vv. 30f), who, apparently without a word of reply, could only tear his garments in grief and dismay (thus revealing the sackcloth underneath) and with an oath call for the immediate execution of Elisha the prophet.

The wearing of sackcloth, probably a garment of goat's hair or camel's hair, and generally dark in color (cf. W. L. Reed, *Interpreter's Dictionary of the Bible*, 4:147), is a custom found throughout the Bible, and it usually conveyed the idea of abject grief and mourning. A particularly memorable, almost comic depiction of the wearing of sackcloth may be found in the Book of Jonah (3:5–9), where all the Ninevites, whether king or commoner—and even including the animals—put on sackcloth in response to Jonah's preaching (thus infuriating the reluctant prophet all the more, as they repent and thus avert the very destruction he had prophesied and personally looked forward to).

6:32–33. Elisha the prophet predicts the king's arrival. As already noted in the introduction to the present passage, the motif of the "closed door" (v. 32) occurs elsewhere a number of times in the Elisha narratives. Here it serves to emphasize the prophet's calmness and serenity, in sharp contrast with all who surrounded him in the besieged city (presumably the "elders" who called upon Elisha [cf. v. 32] were hardly as calm as he was). With a quick, offhand "short-term" prediction (concerning this common feature in the prophetic narratives, see above, on 1:3f), the prophet foretold the arrival of both the king's messenger, as well as that of the king himself. Uncharacteristically, Elisha used the designation "this murderer" (literally, "son of a murderer," but, the term "son of" often means "partaking of the characteristics of" or the like) for the king. His epithet is certainly prescient in light of the king's prior comments (v. 31), but harsh nonetheless. Possibly he meant the phrase literally, the king (presumably, Joram) being one of the sons of the murderer Ahab, but in light of the rest of his statement, probably the king's own murderous impulses were in view. The entire narrative communicates an atmosphere of harsh opposition otherwise not found in the Elisha material.

A translational note on v. 33a—inasmuch as the Hebrew words for "messenger" (mal'ākh, HED #4534) and "king" (melekh, HED #4567) are easily confused, the reference in the Masoretic text to the "messenger" arriving, but evidently the "king" speaking, has led some (e.g., NRSV, also Cogan and Tadmor, AB) to emend the text to read, "the king came down to him and said ..." (NIV, with its cus-

4623, 3937, 6686	904, 3071	971.121	4534	420	2000	569.111
prep, prep, n mp, ps 3ms	prep, adv	v Qal impf 3ms	art, n ms	prep, ps 3ms	cj, pers pron	v Qal pf 3ms
מִלְּפָנָיו	בְּטֶרֶם	יָבֹא	הַמַּלְאָךְ	אֵלָיו	וְהוּא	אָמַר
millephānâv	beṭerem	yāvō'	hammal'ākh	'ēlâv	wehû'	'āmar
from before him	before	he entered	the messenger	to him	and he	he said

420, 2292	1950B, 7495.117	3706, 8365.111	1158, 7815.351	2172
prep, art, n mp	intrg part, v Qal pf 2mp	cj, v Qal pf 3ms	*n ms*, art, v Piel ptc ms	art, dem pron
אֶל־הַזְּקֵנִים	הַרְאִיתֶם	כִּי־שָׁלַח	בֶּן־הַמְרַצֵּחַ	הַזֶּה
'el-hazzeqēnîm	harre'îthem	kî-shālach	ben-hamratstsēach	hazzeh
to the elders	do you see	that he has sent out	the son of the murderer	the this

3937, 5681.541	881, 7513	7495.133	3626, 971.141	4534	5646.133
prep, v Hiphil inf con	do, n ms, ps 1cs	v Qal impv 2mp	prep, v Qal inf con	art, n ms	v Qal impv 2mp
לְהָסִיר	אֶת־רֹאשִׁי	רְאוּ	כְּבֹא	הַמַּלְאָךְ	סִגְרוּ
lehāsîr	'eth-rō'shî	re'û	kevō'	hammal'ākh	sighrû
to remove	my head	see	when coming	the messenger	shut

1878	4040.117	881	904, 1878	1950B, 3940	7249	7559
art, n fs	cj, v Qal pf 2mp	do, ps 3ms	prep, art, n fs	intrg part, neg part	*n ms*	*n fd*
הַדֶּלֶת	וּלְחַצְתֶּם	אֹתוֹ	בַּדֶּלֶת	הֲלוֹא	קוֹל	רַגְלֵי
haddeleth	ûlăchatstem	'ōthô	baddeleth	hălô'	qôl	raghlēy
the door	and you will push	him	with the door	is not	the sound of	the feet of

112	313		5968	1744.351	6196	2079	4534
n mp, ps 3ms	prep, ps 3ms	**33.**	adv, ps 3ms	v Piel ptc ms	prep, ps 3mp	cj, intrj	art, n ms
אֲדֹנָיו	אַחֲרָיו		עוֹדֶנּוּ	מְדַבֵּר	עִמָּם	וְהִנֵּה	הַמַּלְאָךְ
'ădhōnâv	'achrâv		'ôdhennû	medhabbēr	'immām	wehinnēh	hammal'ākh
his master	after him		still he	speaking	with them	and behold	the messenger

3495.151	420	569.121	2079, 2148	7750	4623, 881	3176
v Qal act ptc ms	prep, ps 3ms	cj, v Qal impf 3ms	intrj, dem pron	art, n fs	prep, do	pn
יֹרֵד	אֵלָיו	וַיֹּאמֶר	הִנֵּה־זֹאת	הָרָעָה	מֵאֵת	יְהוָה
yōrēdh	'ēlâv	wayyō'mer	hinnēh-zō'th	hārā'āh	mē'ēth	yehwāh
coming down	to him	and he said	behold this	the evil	from	Yahweh

4242, 3282.525	3937, 3176	5968		569.121	482	8471.133
intrg, v Hiphil impf 1cs	prep, pn	adv	**7:1**	cj, v Qal impf 3ms	pn	v Qal impv 2mp
מָה־אוֹחִיל	לַיהוָה	עוֹד		וַיֹּאמֶר	אֱלִישָׁע	שִׁמְעוּ
māh-'ôchîl	layhwāh	'ôdh		wayyō'mer	'ĕlîshā'	shim'û
how will I wait	for Yahweh	anymore		and he said	Elisha	listen to

1745, 3176	3662	569.111	3176	3626, 6496	4417	5613, 5755
n ms, pn	adv	v Qal pf 3ms	pn	prep, art, *n fs*	adv	n fs, n fs
דְּבַר־יְהוָה	כֹּה	אָמַר	יְהוָה	כָּעֵת	מָחָר	סְאָה־סֹלֶת
devar-yehwāh	kōh	'āmar	yehwāh	kā'ēth	māchār	se'āh-sōleth
the word of Yahweh	thus	He has said	Yahweh	according to the time of	tomorrow	a seah of flour

904, 8621	5613	8002	904, 8621	904, 8554	8497
prep, n ms	cj, n fd	n fp	prep, n ms	prep, *n ms*	pn
בְּשֶׁקֶל	וְסָאתַיִם	שְׂעֹרִים	בְּשֶׁקֶל	בְּשַׁעַר	שֹׁמְרוֹן
besheqel	wesā'thayim	se'ōrîm	besheqel	besha'ar	shōmerôn
with a shekel	and two seahs	barley	with a shekel	by the gate of	Samaria

	6257.121	8388	866, 3937, 4567	8550.255	6142, 3135	881, 382
2.	cj, v Qal impf 3ms	art, n ms	rel pron, prep, n ms	v Niphal ptc ms	prep, n fs, ps 3ms	do, *n ms*
	וַיַּעַן	הַשָּׁלִישׁ	אֲשֶׁר־לַמֶּלֶךְ	נִשְׁעָן	עַל־יָדוֹ	אֶת־אִישׁ
	wayya'an	hashshālîsh	'ăsher-lammelekh	nish'ān	'al-yādhô	'eth-'îsh
	and he answered	the adjutant	who to the king	leaning	on his hand	the man of

33. And while he yet talked with them, behold, the messenger came down unto him: ... While he was still speaking with them, the king came down, *NRSV* ... He was still actually speaking, when the king arrived, *JB*.

and he said, Behold, this evil is of the LORD; what should I wait for the LORD any longer?: ... wait any longer for him to do something?, *Good News* ... Why should I longer trust on the EVER-LIVING, *Fenton* ... Why should I wait any longer for him to help us?, *REB*.

7:1. Then Elisha said, Hear ye the word of the LORD; Thus saith the LORD: ... Give ear to, *BB* ... Listen to, *NASB*.

Tomorrow about this time shall a measure of fine flour be sold for a shekel, and two measures of barley for a shekel, in the gate of Samaria: ... a peck of fine meal may be purchased at the gate of Samaria for a dollar and two pecks of barley for a dollar, *Berkeley* ... in the markets of Samaria, five quarts of fine flour will cost only half an ounce of silver, *NLT* ... a silver piece will buy a peck of wheat, *Knox*.

2. Then a lord on whose hand the king leaned answered the man of God, and said, Behold, if the LORD would make windows in heaven, might this thing be?: ... Even if YHWH were to make floodgates in the sky, could this come to pass, *Anchor* ... made windows in the sky, could this word come true, *JB* ... such a thing could not happen, *NEB*.

... **And he said, Behold, thou shalt see it with thine eyes, but shalt not eat thereof:** ... You shall see it with your own eyes, but you shall not eat of it, *RSV* ... but you will not have a taste of the food, *BB*.

---

tomary half-brackets indicating an interpretational addition, adds the phrase "the king" instead; cf. also NLT). Much could be said for either option, but following the more difficult reading, we see both the messenger and the king arriving at about the same time. In any case, the present chapter (and the first part of the present story) comes to a close with the king still breathing threats against the prophet. But such a king could not be allowed to have the last word in the story. Note how the repeated statement of Elisha to the king's "officer" both begins and ends the rest of the story in ch. 7 (see vv. 2 and 19). We can surely feel sorry for both king and commoner in that pathetic, famine-stricken town, but it was the prophet—not the king—who represented the true God of that town, and we hasten on to the next part of the story to hear how Elisha the prophet answered the irate king.

7:1–20. Part II. The Israelite prophet predicts an immediate end to the famine. A prophetic statement by Elijah both begins and ends this part of the story (vv. 2 and 19). In both instances, the prophet tells the king's officer that he will see with his own eyes the end of the famine, but he will not eat any of the food. But, in fact, another similar bracketing repetition (or inclusio; see below for a definition of the term) is also to be found here in the present passage: in both vv. 1 and 18 (cf., also, v. 16), Elisha's comments about food prices returning to near normal are to be found. The motif of food prices binds together the overall story as well (6:24–7:20). Note the reference to the exorbitant prices for some very unappetizing commodities in 6:25, contrasted with the repeated emphasis on more normal prices (the very next day.) in 7:16, 18.

The literary term "inclusio" (Latin for "confinement," or "inclusion") refers to a rhetorical feature signaling by means of repetition of a key word or phrase (whether it be in exact or in closely parallel vocabulary), the beginning and end of a narrative unit or poem. Sometimes inclusios are termed "inclusions" or "bookending devices." One of the most dramatic inclusios in the Bible may be found at the beginning and end of Ps. 8, where we read in both the first and the last verses of the Psalm the repeated refrain, "O Yahweh, our Lord, how majestic is your name in all the earth." The alert reader of the English text will notice inclusios throughout the Bible (as well as in other ancient and modern literary works, especially in stories and essays, not to mention oral/visual media such as movies and videos). Somehow, especially in the spoken media, helping the audience to sense that one is returning (in some sense) back to the beginning of the story or presentation is a very effective method to bring the performance to a close. Thus, in the present narrative, clear inclusios may be found in vv. 1 and 18 of the chapter, as well as in vv. 2 and 19. Inclusios generally bespeak a carefully written literary work, as the present chapter gives other evidence of being.

7:1–2. Introduction: The amazing prophetic oracle is announced by Elisha. As if Elisha had actually overheard the king's exclamation of 6:31, where he swore by an oath to Yahweh that the prophet had less than a day to live, Elisha announced that "by this time tomorrow," the prices of flour and barley will be drastically reduced—indeed, pretty close to normal, it would seem (but see below). Such a dramatic development is, of course, seemingly out of the ques-

435	569.121	2079	3176	6449.151	724	904, 8452
art, n mp	v Qal impf 3ms	intrj	pn	v Qal act ptc ms	n fp	prep, art, n md
הָאֱלֹהִים	וַיֹּאמַר	הִנֵּה	יְהוָה	עֹשֶׂה	אֲרֻבּוֹת	בַּשָּׁמַיִם
hā'ĕlōhîm	wayyō'mar	hinnēh	y^{e}hwāh	'ōseh	'ărubbôth	bashshāmayim
God	and he said	behold	Yahweh	One Who makes	windows	in the heavens

1950B, 2030.121	1745	2172	569.121	2079	7495.151
intrg part, v Qal impf 3ms	art, n ms	art, dem pron	cj, v Qal impf 3ms	intrj, ps 2ms	v Qal act ptc ms
הֲיִהְיֶה	הַדָּבָר	הַזֶּה	וַיֹּאמֶר	הִנְּכָה	רֹאֶה
hăyihyeh	haddāvār	hazzeh	wayyō'mer	hinn^{e}khāh	rō'eh
will it be	the thing	the this	and he said	behold you	seeing

904, 6084	4623, 8427	3940	404.123		727	596	2030.116
prep, n fd, ps 2ms	cj, prep, adv	neg part	v Qal impf 2ms		cj, num	n mp	v Qal pf 3cp
בְּעֵינֶיךָ	וּמִשָּׁם	לֹא	תֹאכֵל	3.	וְאַרְבָּעָה	אֲנָשִׁים	הָיוּ
b^{e}'ênêkhā	ûmishshām	lō'	thō'khēl		w^{e}'arbā'āh	'ănāshîm	hāyû
with your eyes	but from there	not	you will eat		and four	men	they were

7164.456	6860	8554	569.126	382	420, 7739	4242	601
v Pual ptc mp	*n ms*	art, n ms	cj, v Qal impf 3mp	n ms	prep, n ms, ps 3ms	intrg	pers pron
מְצֹרָעִים	פֶּתַח	הַשָּׁעַר	וַיֹּאמְרוּ	אִישׁ	אֶל־רֵעֵהוּ	מָה	אֲנַחְנוּ
m^{e}tsōrā'îm	pethach	hashshā'ar	wayyō'm^{e}rû	'îsh	'el-rē'ēhû	māh	'ănachnû
diseased men	the entrance of	the gate	and they said	each	to his fellow	why	we

3553.152	6553	5912, 4322.119		524, 569.119	971.120	6111	7743
v Qal act ptc mp	adv	prep, v Qal pf 1cp		cj, v Qal pf 1cp	v Qal impf 1cp	art, n fs	cj, art, n ms
יֹשְׁבִים	פֹּה	עַד־מָתְנוּ	4.	אִם־אָמַרְנוּ	נָבוֹא	הָעִיר	וְהָרָעָב
yōsh^{e}vîm	pōh	'adh-māth^{e}nû		'im-'āmarnû	nāvô'	hā'îr	w^{e}hārā'āv
sitting	here	until we will die		if we say	we will enter	the city	and the famine

904, 6111	4322.110	8427	524, 3553.110	6553	4322.110	6498	2050.133
prep, art, n fs	cj, v Qal pf 1cp	adv	cj, cj, v Qal pf 1cp	adv	cj, v Qal pf 1cp	cj, adv	v Qal impv 2mp
בָּעִיר	וָמַתְנוּ	שָׁם	וְאִם־יָשַׁבְנוּ	פֹה	וָמָתְנוּ	וְעַתָּה	לְכוּ
bā'îr	wāmathnû	shām	w^{e}'im-yāshavnû	phōh	wāmāth^{e}nû	w^{e}'attāh	l^{e}khû
in the city	and we will die	there	or if we sit	here	then we will die	so now	come

5489.120	420, 4402	782	524, 2513.326	2513.120
cj, v Qal juss 1cp	prep, *n ms*	pn	cj, v Piel impf 3mp, ps 1cp	v Qal impf 1cp
וְנִפְּלָה	אֶל־מַחֲנֵה	אֲרָם	אִם־יְחַיֻּנוּ	נִחְיֶה
w^{e}nipp^{e}lāh	'el-machnēh	'ărām	'im-y^{e}chayyunû	nichăyeh
and let us fall	to the camp of	Aram	if they preserve us	we will live

524, 4322.526	4322.119		7251.126	904, 5582	3937, 971.141
cj, cj, v Hiphil impf 3mp, ps 1cp	cj, v Qal pf 1cp		cj, v Qal impf 3mp	prep, art, n ms	prep, v Qal inf con
וְאִם־יְמִיתֻנוּ	וָמָתְנוּ	5.	וַיָּקוּמוּ	בַנֶּשֶׁף	לָבוֹא
w^{e}'im-y^{e}mîthunû	wāmāth^{e}nû		wayyāqûmû	vannesheph	lāvô'
but if they kill us	then we die		and they rose up	during the twilight	to go

420, 4402	782	971.126	5912, 7381	4402	782	2079
prep, *n ms*	pn	cj, v Qal impf 3mp	prep, *n ms*	*n ms*	pn	cj, intrj
אֶל־מַחֲנֵה	אֲרָם	וַיָּבֹאוּ	עַד־קְצֵה	מַחֲנֵה	אֲרָם	וְהִנֵּה
'el-machnēh	'ărām	wayyāvō'û	'adh-qōtsēh	machnēh	'ărām	w^{e}hinnēh
to the camp of	Aram	and they came	unto the edge of	the camp of	Aram	and behold

375, 8427	382		112	8471.511	881, 4402	782
sub, adv	n ms		cj, n mp, ps 1cs	v Hiphil pf 3ms	do, *n ms*	pn
אֵין־שָׁם	אִישׁ	6.	וַאדֹנָי	הִשְׁמִיעַ	אֶת־מַחֲנֵה	אֲרָם
'ên-shām	'îsh		wa'dhōnāy	hishmîa'	'eth-machnēh	'ărām
there was not there	a man		for my Lord	He had caused to hear	the camp of	Aram

3. And there were four leprous men at the entering in of the gate: ... for they were afflicted with virulent skin-disease, *JB* ... who were suffering from a dreaded skin disease, *Good News*.

and they said one to another, Why sit we here until we die?: ... Why stay here, *NIV* ... Why should we stay here and wait for death, *REB* ... Wherever we turn we shall go to death, *Fenton*.

4. If we say, We will enter into the city, then the famine is in the city, and we shall die there: and if we sit still here, we die also: ... There is no food in the city, *NCV*.

Now therefore come, and let us fall unto the host of the Syrians: ... Come, let us desert to the Aramaean camp, *Anchor* ... let us surrender to the army of the Syrians, *NKJV*.

if they save us alive, we shall live; and if they kill us, we shall but die: ... If they spare us, we shall live, *Douay* ... If they let us live, so much the better. But if they kill us, we would have died anyway, *NLT*.

5. And they rose up in the twilight, to go unto the camp of the Syrians: ... they got up to advance to the Syrian camp, *Berkeley* ... that evening they went out to the camp, *NLT* ... So, when night fell, they ventured out, *Knox*.

and when they were come to the uttermost part of the camp of Syria, behold, there was no man there: ... there was not a person there, *Anchor* ... there was no one there, *RSV*.

6. For the Lord had made the host of the Syrians to hear a noise of chariots, and a noise of horses, even the noise of a great host: ... the noise of a great army, *NKJV* ... hear what sounded like the advance of a large army with horses and chariots, *Good News*.

and they said one to another, Lo, the king of Israel hath hired against us the kings of the Hittites, and the kings of the Egyptians, to come upon us: ... and the kings of the borderlands to fight us, *NAB* ... and the kings of Muzri to attack us, *Moffatt*.

---

tion in the midst of a protracted siege. "Even if Yahweh opened the floodgates of heaven, could this happen?" is the quite reasonable response of the king's official in v. 2. As we have already noted, this statement of understandable unbelief prompts another remarkable short-term prophecy: "You will see it with your own eyes, but you will not eat any of it" (v. 2). As if to savor once again the conundrum Elisha put the official in, the narrator repeats both his unbelieving response about the "floodgates of heaven," as well as Elisha's prophetic response about his "seeing but not eating," nearly word for word at the end of the account (v. 19).

The consensus of the commentators seems to be that Elisha's prices for flour (or "meal," or "choice flour," s̱ōleth, HED #5755) and for barley (sᵉʻōrîm, HED #8002) were still noticeably higher than during peacetime, although still astoundingly much lower than would be the case during a severe famine. The reference to the "floodgates of the heavens" recalls the image of God damming up the rain in the heavenly realms (cf. Gen. 7:11; 8:2), both in reference to the flood of Noah; also Mal. 3:10, in reference of Yahweh pouring out agricultural blessing on those who bring in the full "storehouse tithe"—the tithe paid every third year for the sake of the needy, whether Israelite (lay or Levite) or foreign-born (cf. *The Complete Biblical Library—OT*, "Joshua Judges Ruth," 221)—when we neglect to pay this tithe, we in essence rob God. Thus, in the present passage, the king's officer flatly denies that Elisha's prophecy could come to pass, even if Yahweh should perform the most amazing of heavenly miracles. But, he would soon learn otherwise.

7:3–11. Two lepers make an astounding discovery. The actions of these lepers can be compared to the other occasions in the Elisha stories where persons of relatively low social standing point the way to a resolution of a serious problem (e.g., the young servant girl who informed Naaman's wife about the prophet in Samaria who could heal her master's leprosy [5:2f] or Naaman's own servants who later persuaded him to obey the prophet's instructions to wash in the Jordan [5:13f] or the official of the Israelite king who informed King Jehoshaphat of Judah that Elisha was present on the Moabite expedition [3:11]). We encounter yet another example of this phenomenon in v. 13 of the present chapter, when the king's officer suggests sending out a patrol for reconnaissance to verify the lepers' story about the departure of the Arameans. So often, the seemingly insignificant figures in literature and in life may make all the difference in the world (a good biblical example is that of the unnamed individual in Gen. 37:15ff who just happened to know which city the brothers of the youthful Joseph had moved on to with their flocks, thereby dooming Joseph himself in the short-term to slavery and imprisonment in Egypt, but, in the long-term, enabling him to save at least two civi-

7249	7681	7249	5670	7249	2524	1448	569.126	382
n ms	n ms	n ms	n ms	n ms	n ms	adj	cj, v Qal impf 3mp	n ms
קוֹל	רֶכֶב	קוֹל	סוּס	קוֹל	חָיִל	גָּדוֹל	וַיֹּאמְרוּ	אִישׁ
qôl	rekhev	qôl	sûs	qôl	chayil	gādhôl	wayyō'merû	'îsh
the sound of	chariots	the sound of	horses	the sound of	an army	great	and they said	each

420, 250	2079	7963.111, 6142	4567	3547	881, 4567	2958
prep, n ms, ps 3ms	intrj	v Qal pf 3ms, prep, ps 1cp	n ms	pn	do, n mp	art, pn
אֶל־אָחִיו	הִנֵּה	שָׂכַר־עָלֵינוּ	מֶלֶךְ	יִשְׂרָאֵל	אֶת־מַלְכֵי	הַחִתִּים
'el-'āchîw	hinnēh	sākhar-'ālênû	melekh	yisrā'ēl	'eth-malkhê	hachittîm
to his brother	behold	he has hired against us	the king of	Israel	the kings of	the Hittites

881, 4567	4875	3937, 971.141	6142	7. 7251.126	5308.126
cj, do, n mp	pn	prep, v Qal inf con	prep, ps 1cp	cj, v Qal impf 3mp	cj, v Qal impf 3mp
וְאֶת־מַלְכֵי	מִצְרַיִם	לָבוֹא	עָלֵינוּ	וַיָּקוּמוּ	וַיָּנוּסוּ
we'eth-malkhê	mitsrayim	lāvô'	'ālênû	wayyāqûmû	wayyānûsû
and the kings of	Egypt	to come	against us	and they rose up	and they fled

904, 5582	6013.126	881, 164	881, 5670	881, 2645
prep, art, n ms	cj, v Qal impf 3mp	do, n mp, ps 3mp	cj, do, n mp, ps 3mp	cj, do, n mp, ps 3mp
בַנֶּשֶׁף	וַיַּעַזְבוּ	אֶת־אָהֳלֵיהֶם	וְאֶת־סוּסֵיהֶם	וְאֶת־חֲמֹרֵיהֶם
vannesheph	wayya'azvû	'eth-'āhelêhem	we'eth-sûsêhem	we'eth-chămōrêhem
during the twilight	so they left behind	their tents	and their horses	and their donkeys

4402	3626, 866, 2026	5308.126	420, 5497	8. 971.126
art, n ms	prep, rel part, pers pron	cj, v Qal impf 3mp	prep, n fs, ps 3mp	cj, v Qal impf 3mp
הַמַּחֲנֶה	כַּאֲשֶׁר־הִיא	וַיָּנֻסוּ	אֶל־נַפְשָׁם	וַיָּבֹאוּ
hammachneh	ka'ăsher-hî'	wayyānusû	'el-naphshām	wayyāvō'û
the camp	just as it	and they fled	toward their life	and they came

7164.456	431	5912, 7381	4402	971.126	420, 164	259
art, v Pual ptc mp	art, dem pron	prep, n ms	art, n ms	cj, v Qal impf 3mp	prep, n ms	num
הַמְצֹרָעִים	הָאֵלֶּה	עַד־קְצֵה	הַמַּחֲנֶה	וַיָּבֹאוּ	אֶל־אֹהֶל	אֶחָד
hamtsōrā'îm	hā'ēlleh	'adh-qŏtsēh	hammachneh	wayyāvō'û	'el-'ōhel	'echādh
the diseased men	the these	unto the edge of	the camp	and they came	to a tent	one

404.126	8685.126	5558.126	4623, 8427	3826B	2174	933
cj, v Qal impf 3mp	cj, v Qal impf 3mp	cj, v Qal impf 3mp	prep, adv	n ms	cj, n ms	cj, n mp
וַיֹּאכְלוּ	וַיִּשְׁתּוּ	וַיִּשְׂאוּ	מִשָּׁם	כֶּסֶף	וְזָהָב	וּבְגָדִים
wayyō'khelû	wayyishtû	wayyis'û	mishshām	keseph	wezāhāv	ûveghādhîm
and they ate	and they drank	and they carried	from there	silver	and gold	and garments

2050.126	3045.526	8178.126	971.126	420, 164	311
cj, v Qal impf 3mp	cj, v Hiphil impf 3mp	cj, v Qal impf 3mp	cj, v Qal impf 3mp	prep, n ms	adj
וַיֵּלְכוּ	וַיַּטְמִנוּ	וַיָּשֻׁבוּ	וַיָּבֹאוּ	אֶל־אֹהֶל	אַחֵר
wayyēlekhû	wayyatminû	wayyāshuvû	wayyāvō'û	'el-'ōhel	'achēr
and they went	and they hid	and they returned	and they came	to a tent	another

5558.126	4623, 8427	2050.126	3045.526	9. 569.126	382
cj, v Qal impf 3mp	prep, adv	cj, v Qal impf 3mp	cj, v Hiphil impf 3mp	cj, v Qal impf 3mp	n ms
וַיִּשְׂאוּ	מִשָּׁם	וַיֵּלְכוּ	וַיַּטְמִנוּ	וַיֹּאמְרוּ	אִישׁ
wayyis'û	mishshām	wayyēlekhû	wayyatminû	wayyō'merû	'îsh
and they carried	from there	and they went	and they hid	then they said	each

420, 7739	3940, 3772	601	6449.152	3219	2172	3219, 1342
prep, n ms, ps 3ms	neg part, adv	pers pron	v Qal act ptc mp	art, n ms	art, dem pron	n ms, n fs
אֶל־רֵעֵהוּ	לֹא־כֵן	אֲנַחְנוּ	עֹשִׂים	הַיּוֹם	הַזֶּה	יוֹם־בְּשֹׂרָה
'el-rē'ēhû	lō'-khēn	'ănachnû	'ōsîm	hayyôm	hazzeh	yôm-besōrāh
to his fellow	not so	we	doing	the day	the this	a day of good news

7. Wherefore they arose and fled in the twilight, and left their tents: ... they rose up and fled in the dusk, *Darby* ... So they panicked and fled into the night, abandoning their tents, *NLT.*

and their horses, and their asses, even the camp as it was, and fled for their life: ... leaving their tents, horses, and donkeys. They left the camp standing and ran for their lives, *NCV* ... Leaving the camp as it stood, *REB.*

8. And when these lepers came to the uttermost part of the camp, they went into one tent, and did eat and drink: ... came to the outskirts of the camp, they went into one tent and ate and drank, *NKJV* ... came to the edge of the camp, *Beck.*

and carried thence silver, and gold, and raiment, and went and hid it: ... and carried away silver and gold and clothing and went and hid them, *Goodspeed.*

and came again, and entered into another tent, and carried thence also, and went and hid it: ... came back to another tent, plundered that too, and hid away their plunder, *Knox* ... another tent which they also stripped, hiding its contents, *Moffatt.*

9. Then they said one to another, We do not well: this day is a day of good tidings, and we hold our peace: ... We are not doing right. This is a day of good news, and we are keeping silent, *NAB* ... and we are not telling, *KJVII.*

if we tarry till the morning light, some mischief will come upon us: ... punishment will overtake us, *Goodspeed* ... If we wait until the sun comes up, we'll be discovered, *NCV.*

now therefore come, that we may go and tell the king's household: ... and report us to the palace of the king, *Fenton* ... let's go back and tell the people at the palace, *NLT.*

---

lizations from perishing in the famine). Sometimes God indeed works in the most mysterious of ways and by means of the most unlikely of heroes. Such is the case here—God uses four lepers to announce his salvation of his city, Samaria.

Although, as we have seen in ch. 5 (cf. comments on 5:1), biblical "leprosy" did not necessarily exclude the person from society (again, cf. the example of Naaman; also Gehazi's leprous condition at the end of ch. 5, which seemingly did not prevent him from meeting with the king in 8:4f). Still, the present chapter seems unequivocally to present four lepers who have been permanently banished from Samarian society, as well as the ironic developments for the city that take place as a direct result of their status as outcasts of society. If the lepers had not been so desperate for food, yet so reluctant to re-enter the city, they would not have even considered the possibility of defecting to the Aramean camp (vv. 3f). This is not the last time in the present story where desperation leads a subordinate to advocate a wise course of action (cf., once again, the king's official in v. 13). Sometimes, as in the case of the story of Ruth (especially in Ruth 2), desperation causes one to undertake bold and risky actions one would never consider otherwise (cf., also, the Book of Esther).

The story continues by means of a series of probable and improbable events—humans acting in a typical fashion when faced with very atypical circumstances and the prior divine action which led to those improbable circumstances mentioned almost as an aside. The lepers made their way to the enemy camp—but they found it deserted (only then does the narrator inform us of how the Israelite God had caused the Arameans to hear the sounds of chariots and horses and a great army so that they panicked and fled the scene in great haste, even leaving behind the horses and donkeys they would normally have taken with them [cf. vv. 6f]). The lepers did as we also might have done (if we thought no authority figure were around); they feasted and celebrated, and carried off booty, and hid it, and then they looked for more (v. 8).

A brief note on the reference to the "Hittites and the Egyptians" in v. 6—commentators often suggest that the term here for "Egyptians" (mitsrayim, HED #4874) may instead have been a reference to the "Musrites," a people allegedly living in north Syria or in Anatolia (modern Turkey) at the time (cf. NIV footnote to 1 Ki. 10:28, in reference to Solomon's horses imported from "Egypt"). Cogan and Tadmor (AB, 82f), however, quite convincingly argue for the traditional rendering "Hittites and Egyptians," pointing out that the kingdom of Musri had already been conquered by the Assyrian king Ashur-Dan II in the late tenth century B.C. and annexed to his kingdom. As for the "Hittites," the reference could not have been to the great Hittite empire of the second millennium B.C. in Anatolia, for that had been largely dissipated by this time. Biblical references to the "Hittites" would have to be to the remnants which survived in numerous small principalities in northern Syria (Hobbs, WBC, 90).

But even despised lepers have consciences, and our four unlikely heroes eventually recognized

2000	601	2924.552	2542.319	5912, 214	1269
pers pron	cj, pers pron	v Hiphil ptc mp	cj, v Piel pf 1cp	adv, *n ms*	art, n ms
הוּא	וַאֲנַחְנוּ	מַחְשִׁים	וְחִכִּינוּ	עַד־אוֹר	הַבֹּקֶר
hû'	wa'ănachnû	machshîm	wechikkînû	'adh-'ôr	habbōqer
it	and we	being silent	and we will wait	until the light of	the morning

4834.111	5988	6498	2050.133	971.120	5222.520
cj, v Qal pf 3ms, ps 1cp	n ms	cj, adv	v Qal impv 2mp	cj, v Qal juss 1cp	cj, v Hiphil juss 1cp
וּמְצָאָנוּ	עָוֹן	וְעַתָּה	לְכוּ	וְנָבֹאָה	וְנַגִּידָה
ûmetsā'ānû	'āwôn	we'attāh	lekhû	wenāvō'āh	wenaggîdhāh
then it will find us	guilt	so now	come	and let us go	and let us report to

1041	4567		971.126	7410.126	420, 8219	6111
n ms	art, n ms	**10.**	cj, v Qal impf 3mp	cj, v Qal impf 3mp	prep, *n ms*	art, n fs
בֵּית	הַמֶּלֶךְ		וַיָּבֹאוּ	וַיִּקְרְאוּ	אֶל־שֹׁעֵר	הָעִיר
bêth	hammelekh		wayyāvō'û	wayyiqŏr'û	'el-shō'ēr	hā'îr
the household of	the king		and they came	and they called	to the gatekeeper of	the city

5222.526	3937	3937, 569.141	971.119	420, 4402	782	2079
cj, v Hiphil impf 3mp	prep, ps 3mp	prep, v Qal inf con	v Qal pf 1cp	prep, *n ms*	pn	cj, intrj
וַיַּגִּידוּ	לָהֶם	לֵאמֹר	בָּאנוּ	אֶל־מַחֲנֵה	אֲרָם	וְהִנֵּה
wayyaggîdhû	lāhem	lē'mōr	bā'nû	'el-machnēh	'ărām	wehinnēh
and they reported	to them	saying	we entered	to the camp of	Aram	and behold

375, 8427	382	7249	119	3706	524, 5670	646.155
sub, adv	n ms	cj, *n ms*	n ms	cj	cj, art, n ms	v Qal pass ptc ms
אֵין־שָׁם	אִישׁ	וְקוֹל	אָדָם	כִּי	אִם־הַסּוּס	אָסוּר
'ên-shām	'îsh	weqôl	'ādhām	kî	'im-hassûs	'āsûr
there was not there	a man	nor the sound of	a man	except	only the horses	tied

2645	646.155	164	3626, 866, 2062		7410.121
cj, art, n ms	v Qal pass ptc ms	cj, n mp	prep, rel part, pers pron	**11.**	cj, v Qal impf 3ms
וְהַחֲמוֹר	אָסוּר	וְאֹהָלִים	כַּאֲשֶׁר־הֵמָּה		וַיִּקְרָא
wehachmôr	'āsûr	we'ōhālîm	ka'ăsher-hēmmāh		wayyiqŏrā'
and the donkeys	tied	and tents	just as they		and he called

8219	5222.526	1041	4567	6687		7251.121
art, n mp	cj, v Hiphil impf 3mp	*n ms*	art, n ms	adv	**12.**	cj, v Qal impf 3ms
הַשֹּׁעֲרִים	וַיַּגִּידוּ	בֵּית	הַמֶּלֶךְ	פְּנִימָה		וַיָּקָם
hashshō'ărîm	wayyaggîdhû	bêth	hammelekh	penîmāh		wayyāqām
the gatekeepers	and they reported to	the household of	the king	inside		and he rose up

4567	4050	569.121	420, 5860	5222.525, 5167	3937	881
art, n ms	n ms	cj, v Qal impf 3ms	prep, n mp, ps 3ms	v Hiphil juss 1cs, part	prep, ps 2mp	do
הַמֶּלֶךְ	לַיְלָה	וַיֹּאמֶר	אֶל־עֲבָדָיו	אַגִּידָה־נָּא	לָכֶם	אֵת
hammelekh	laylāh	wayyō'mer	'el-'ăvādhâv	'aggîdhāh-nā'	lākhem	'ēth
the king	at night	and he said	to his servants	let me report please	to you	

866, 6449.116	3937	782	3156.116	3706, 7743	601	3428.126
rel part, v Qal pf 3cp	prep, ps 1cp	pn	v Qal pf 3cp	cj, adj	pers pron	cj, v Qal impf 3mp
אֲשֶׁר־עָשׂוּ	לָנוּ	אֲרָם	יָדְעוּ	כִּי־רְעֵבִים	אֲנָחְנוּ	וַיֵּצְאוּ
'ăsher-'āsû	lānû	'ărām	yādhe'û	kî-re'ēvîm	'ănachnû	wayyētse'û
what they have done	to us	Aram	they know	that hungry	we	and they went out

4623, 4402	3937, 2334.241	904, 7898	3937, 569.141	3706, 3428.126	4623, 6111
prep, art, n ms	prep, v Niphal inf con	prep, art, n fs	prep, v Qal inf con	cj, v Qal impf 3mp	prep, art, n fs
מִן־הַמַּחֲנֶה	לְהֵחָבֵה	בְהַשָּׂדֶה	לֵאמֹר	כִּי־יֵצְאוּ	מִן־הָעִיר
min-hammachneh	lehēchāvēh	vehassādheh	lē'mōr	kî-yētse'û	min-hā'îr
from the camp	to hide themselves	in the field	saying	when they come out	from the city

8945.120	2508	420, 6111	971.120		6257.121	259
cj, v Qal impf 1cp, ps 3mp	adj	cj, prep, art, n fs	v Qal impf 1cp	**13.**	cj, v Qal impf 3ms	num
וְנִתְפְּשֵׂם	חַיִּים	וְאֶל־הָעִיר	נָבֹא		וַיַּעַן	אֶחָד
w^{e}nithp^{e}sēm	chayyîm	w^{e}'el-hā'îr	nāvō'		wayya'an	'echādh
then we will capture them	alive	and to the city	we will enter		and he answered	one

4623, 5860	569.121	4089.126, 5167	2675	4623, 5670	8080.256
prep, n mp, ps 3ms	cj, v Qal impf 3ms	cj, v Qal juss 3mp, part	num	prep, art, n mp	art, v Niphal ptc mp
מֵעֲבָדָיו	וַיֹּאמֶר	וְיִקְחוּ־נָא	חֲמִשָּׁה	מִן־הַסּוּסִים	הַנִּשְׁאָרִים
mē'ăvādhâv	wayyō'mer	w^{e}yiqŏchû-nā'	chămishshāh	min-hassûsîm	hanish^{e}'ārîm
from his servants	and he said	let us take please	five	from the horses	those remaining

10. So they came and called unto the porter of the city: ... and call unto the gatekeeper of the city, *Young*.

and they told them, saying, We came to the camp of the Syrians: ... went to the Aramean camp, *NCV*.

and, behold, there was no man there, neither voice of man, but horses tied, and asses tied, and the tents as they were: ... there was not there a man nor sound of human being, *Rotherham* ... and didn't see or hear anybody, *Good News* ... found not one man in it and had heard no human voice: nothing but horses and donkeys tethered, *REB*.

11. And he called the porters; and they told it to the king's house within: ... the gatekeepers shouted and told it to the king's household, *Berkeley* ... shouted the news, and it was reported within the palace, *NIV* ... the watch called out and gave the news, *NEB* ... Then the guards of the gate went, *Douay*.

12. And the king arose in the night, and said unto his servants, I will now show you what the Syrians have done to us: ... what the Arameans have prepared against us, *NRSV* ... Let me tell you what the Aramaeans have prepared for us, he told his officers, *Beck*.

They know that we be hungry; therefore are they gone out of the camp to hide themselves in the field: ... They have knowledge that we are without food; and so they have gone out of their tents, and are waiting secretly in the open country, *BB* ... They know we are starving, so they have left the camp to hide, *JB*.

saying, When they come out of the city, we shall catch them alive, and get into the city: ... we will take them alive and then enter the city, *Anchor*.

13. And one of his servants answered and said, Let some take, I pray thee, five of the horses that remain, which are left in the city: ... Send out a party of men with some of the horses that are left, *REB* ... of his officers replied, We had better send out scouts to check into this, *NLT* ... one of his counsellors said, There are still half a dozen horses left in the city, *Knox*.

that they simply must share their good fortune with the rest of their fellow citizens (v. 9); they also recognized that they might face dire reprisals if they did not speak out. They shouted the news to the city gatekeepers (presumably their leprosy preventing closer contact), who eventually informed the king (vv. 10ff), who, predictably, and somewhat understandably (cf. comments in connection with vv. 12–16), misinterpreted the good tidings as only an enemy trick. Thus, the burlesque scenes, which up to now have dominated the narrative, threaten to come to an abrupt end, due to the gloomy "realism" of the king. But, providentially, another obscure underling spoke up and, once again with the common sense which seemingly only severe circumstances can engender, suggested that the king's officers investigate the story. What is there to lose? We (like the four lepers, in vv. 3f) are only doomed to die anyway.

7:12–16. The king's officers corroborate the incredible story. The king heeded the wise words of his officer, and commissioned a small reconnaissance party to investigate the situation (v. 14). They reported back that the Arameans had indeed disappeared, and that the road all the way to the Jordan River was strewn with abandoned clothing and equipment (v. 15). The Israelites, naturally, plundered the Aramean camp (that is, whatever was left over and not hidden or carried off by the four lepers).

Thus, despite a number of intriguing, agonizing vicissitudes, Elisha's word came true (v.16). Flour and barley sold at fairly reasonable prices, only one day after the desperate woman had complained to the king about her neighbor's son not being available as promised for food consumption. But there was a further word of Elisha yet to be fulfilled—the king's officer beholding such a situation with his own eyes, but not being able to partake of any of the

866	8080.216, 904	2079	3626, 3725, 2066	3547	866
rel part	v Niphal pf 3cp, prep, ps 3fs	intrj, ps 3mp	prep, *adj*, art, *n ms*	pn	rel pron
אֲשֶׁר	נִשְׁאֲרוּ־בָהּ	הִנָּם	כְּכָל־הֶהָמוֹן	יִשְׂרָאֵל	אֲשֶׁר
'ăsher	nish'ărû-vāhh	hinnām	kᵉkhol-hehāmôn	yisrā'ēl	'ăsher
which	they have been left in it	behold they	like all the multitude of	Israel	who

8080.216, 904	2079	3626, 3725, 2066	3547	866, 8882.116
v Niphal pf 3cp, prep, ps 3fs	intrj, ps 3mp	prep, *adj*, *n ms*	pn	rel pron, v Qal pf 3cp
נִשְׁאֲרוּ־בָהּ	הִנָּם	כְּכָל־הֲמוֹן	יִשְׂרָאֵל	אֲשֶׁר־תָּמּוּ
nish'ărû-vāhh	hinnām	kᵉkhol-hᵉmôn	yisrā'ēl	'ăsher-tāmmû
they have been left in it	behold they	like all the multitude of	Israel	who they are finished

8365.120	7495.120		4089.126	8530	7681	5670	8365.121
cj, v Qal juss 1cp	cj, v Qal juss 1cp	**14.**	cj, v Qal impf 3mp	num	*n ms*	n mp	cj, v Qal impf 3ms
וְנִשְׁלְחָה	וְנִרְאֶה		וַיִּקְחוּ	שְׁנֵי	רֶכֶב	סוּסִים	וַיִּשְׁלַח
wᵉnishlᵉchāh	wᵉnir'eh		wayyiqŏchû	shᵉnê	rekhev	sûsîm	wayyishlach
and let us send out	and let us see		and they took	two	chariots of	horses	and he sent out

4567	313	4402, 782	3937, 569.141	2050.133	7495.133
art, n ms	adv	*n ms*, pn	prep, v Qal inf con	v Qal impv 2mp	cj, v Qal impv 2mp
הַמֶּלֶךְ	אַחֲרֵי	מַחֲנֵה־אֲרָם	לֵאמֹר	לְכוּ	וּרְאוּ
hammelekh	'achrê	machnēh-'ărām	lē'mōr	lᵉkhû	ûrᵉ'û
the king	after	the army of Aram	saying	go	and see

	2050.126	313	5912, 3497	2079	3725, 1932	4529	933
15.	cj, v Qal impf 3mp	prep, ps 3mp	prep, art, pn	cj, intrj	*adj*, art, n ms	adj	n mp
	וַיֵּלְכוּ	אַחֲרֵיהֶם	עַד־הַיַּרְדֵּן	וְהִנֵּה	כָל־הַדֶּרֶךְ	מְלֵאָה	בְגָדִים
	wayyēlᵉkhû	'achrêhem	'adh-hayyardēn	wᵉhinnēh	khol-hadderekh	mᵉlē'āh	vᵉghādhîm
	and they went	after them	unto the Jordan	and behold	all the way	full	clothes

3747	866, 8390.516	782	904, 2753.141	8178.126
cj, n mp	rel part, v Hiphil pf 3cp	pn	prep, v Qal inf con, ps 3mp	cj, v Qal impf 3mp
וְכֵלִים	אֲשֶׁר־הִשְׁלִיכוּ	אֲרָם	בְּהֵחָפְזָם	וַיָּשֻׁבוּ
wᵉkhēlîm	'ăsher-hishlîkhû	'ărām	bᵉhēchāphᵉzām	wayyāshuvû
and weapons	which they had thrown down	Aram	during their hurrying away	and they returned

4534	5222.526	3937, 4567		3428.121	6194
art, n mp	cj, v Hiphil impf 3mp	prep, art, n ms	**16.**	cj, v Qal impf 3ms	art, n ms
הַמַּלְאָכִים	וַיַּגִּדוּ	לַמֶּלֶךְ		וַיֵּצֵא	הָעָם
hammal'ākhîm	wayyaggidhû	lammelekh		wayyētsē'	hā'ām
the messengers	and they reported	to the king		and they went out	the people

997.126	881	4402	782	2030.121	5613, 5755	904, 8621
cj, v Qal impf 3mp	do	*n ms*	pn	cj, v Qal impf 3ms	*n fs*, n fs	prep, n ms
וַיָּבֹזּוּ	אֵת	מַחֲנֵה	אֲרָם	וַיְהִי	סְאָה־סֹלֶת	בְּשֶׁקֶל
wayyāvōzzû	'ēth	machnēh	'ărām	wayhî	sᵉ'āh-sōleth	bᵉsheqel
and they plundered		the camp of	Aram	and it was	a seah of flour	with a shekel

5613	8002	904, 8621	3626, 1745	3176		4567
cj, n fd	n fp	prep, n ms	prep, *n ms*	pn	**17.**	cj, art, n ms
וְסָאתַיִם	שְׂעֹרִים	בְּשֶׁקֶל	כִּדְבַר	יְהוָה		וְהַמֶּלֶךְ
wᵉsā'thayim	sᵉ'ōrîm	bᵉsheqel	kidhvar	yᵉhwāh		wᵉhammelekh
and two seahs	barley	with a shekel	according to the word of	Yahweh		and the king

6734.511	881, 8388	866, 8550.251	6142, 3135	6142, 8554
v Hiphil pf 3ms	do, art, n ms	rel part, v Niphal ptc ms	prep, n fs, ps 3ms	prep, art, n ms
הִפְקִיד	אֶת־הַשָּׁלִישׁ	אֲשֶׁר־נִשְׁעָן	עַל־יָדוֹ	עַל־הַשַּׁעַר
hiphqîdh	'eth-hashshālîsh	'ăsher-nish'ān	'al-yādhô	'al-hashsha'ar
he had summoned	the adjutant	whom being leaned on	on his hand	beside the gate

7717.126	6194	904, 8554	4322.121	3626, 866	1744.311
cj, v Qal impf 3mp, ps 3ms	art, n ms	prep, art, n ms	cj, v Qal impf 3ms	prep, rel part	v Piel pf 3ms
וַיִּרְמְסֻהוּ	הָעָם	בַּשַּׁעַר	וַיָּמֹת	כַּאֲשֶׁר	דִּבֶּר
wayyirmᵉsuhû	hā'ām	bashsha'ar	wayyāmōth	ka'ăsher	dibber
and they trampled him	the people	in the gate	and he died	just as	he had spoken

382	435	866	1744.311	904, 3495.141	4567	420
n ms	art, n mp	rel pron	v Piel pf 3ms	prep, v Qal inf con	art, n ms	prep, ps 3ms
אִישׁ	הָאֱלֹהִים	אֲשֶׁר	דִּבֶּר	בְּרֶדֶת	הַמֶּלֶךְ	אֵלָיו
'îsh	hā'ĕlōhîm	'ăsher	dibber	bᵉredheth	hammelekh	'ēlâv
the man of	God	who	he had spoken	when coming down	the king	to him

18.

2030.121	3626, 1744.341	382	435	420, 4567	3937, 569.141
cj, v Qal impf 3ms	prep, v Piel inf con	*n ms*	art, n mp	prep, art, n ms	prep, v Qal inf con
וַיְהִי	כְּדַבֵּר	אִישׁ	הָאֱלֹהִים	אֶל־הַמֶּלֶךְ	לֵאמֹר
wayhî	kᵉdhabbēr	'îsh	hā'ĕlōhîm	'el-hammelekh	lē'mōr
and it was	when speaking	the man of	God	to the king	saying

(behold, they are as all the multitude of Israel that are left in it: behold, I say, they are even as all the multitude of the Israelites that are consumed:) and let us send and see: ... but if they fall into a trap, they will be like the whole multitude of Israel which has perished, *Berkeley* ... since those left here will suffer the fate of the whole multitude of Israel that have perished already, *NRSV* ... Let's send them to see what has happened, *NCV*.

14. They took therefore two chariot horses; and the king sent after the host of the Syrians, saying, Go and see: ... He commanded the drivers, Go and find out what has happened, *NIV* ... Let them go and see, *NEB* ... king sent after the army of the Arameans, *NASB* ... took two mounted men, and the king sent them after the army of the Syrians, *RSV*.

15. And they went after them unto Jordan: and, lo, all the way was full of garments and vessels, which the Syrians had cast away in their haste: ... finding the whole way strewn with clothes and gear which the Aramaeans had thrown away in their panic, *JB* ... the entire way was filled with clothing and equipment which the Aramaeans had thrown off, *Anchor* ... had thrown away in their mad rush to escape, *NLT*.

And the messengers returned, and told the king: ... those who were sent went back and gave the news to the king, *BB* ... The scouts returned and informed the king, *JB*.

16. And the people went out, and spoiled the tents of the Syrians: ... and plundered the camp of the Arameans, *NAB* ... and robbed the tents of the Sirians, *Tyndale* ... took valuables from the Aramean camp, *NCV* ... rushed out and looted the Syrian camp, *Good News*.

So a measure of fine flour was sold for a shekel, and two measures of barley for a shekel, according to the word of the LORD: ... So a seah of fine flour was sold for a shekel, and two seahs of barley for a shekel, *NKJV* ... a silver piece for a peck of wheat, a silver piece for two pecks of barley, *Knox* ... a peck of fine flour was sold for only half-a-crown, two pecks of barley were sold for only half-a-crown, *Moffatt* ... a bushel of fine flour was sold for a stater, and two bushels of barley for a stater, *Douay*.

17. And the king appointed the lord on whose hand he leaned to have the charge of the gate: ... put the city gate under the command of the officer who was his personal attendant, Good News ... appointed the general upon whose arm he rested over the gate, *Fenton* ... appointed his officer to control the traffic at the gate, *NLT* ... appointed his aid, on whose arm he leaned, *Beck*.

and the people trode upon him in the gate, and he died, as the man of God had said, who spake when the king came down to him: ... but the people trampled the officer to death,

---

food. And it is to that final prophetic fulfillment that the narrator now turns.

7:17–20. Conclusion: Elisha's oracle confirmed to the last detail. Some commentators have seen all or part of this section as being added at a later date. But it makes a fitting conclusion to the overall account, which, once again, started in 6:24. The skeptical official in v. 2 somewhat understandably questioned Elisha's bold prophecy about the fall in food prices, and he had, received in return a second prophecy of personal catastrophe (he would see it, but not be able to eat it [v. 2]). So it turns out, here in v. 17. The king places at the city gate that very official (apparently a very trusted one, according to the idiom found both here and also in v. 2, which speaks of him as the one "on whose arm the king was leaning" [cf. also Naaman as the Aramean king's "right-hand man" in 5:18—using the same phraseology as here]). But the

5613	8002	904, 8621	5613, 5755	904, 8621	2030.121
n fd	n fp	prep, n ms	cj, n fs, n fs	prep, n ms	v Qal impf 3ms
סָאתַיִם	שְׂעֹרִים	בְּשֶׁקֶל	וּסְאָה־סֹלֶת	בְּשֶׁקֶל	יִהְיֶה
sā'thayim	se'ōrîm	besheqel	ûse'āh-sōleth	besheqel	yihyeh
two seahs	barley	with a shekel	and a seah of flour	with a shekel	it will be

3626, 6496	4417	904, 8554	8497		6257.121	8388
prep, art, n fs	adv	prep, n ms	pn	**19.**	cj, v Qal impf 3ms	art, n ms
כָּעֵת	מָחָר	בְּשַׁעַר	שֹׁמְרוֹן		וַיַּעַן	הַשָּׁלִישׁ
kā'ēth	māchār	besha'ar	shōmerôn		wayya'an	hashshālîsh
according to the time of	tomorrow	by the gate of	Samaria		and he answered	the adjutant

881, 382	435	569.121	2079	3176	6449.151	724
do, n ms	art, n mp	v Qal impf 3ms	cj, intrj	pn	v Qal act ptc ms	n fp
אֶת־אִישׁ	הָאֱלֹהִים	וַיֹּאמַר	וְהִנֵּה	יְהוָה	עֹשֶׂה	אֲרֻבּוֹת
'eth-'îsh	hā'ĕlōhîm	wayyō'mar	wehinnēh	yehwāh	'ōseh	'ărubbôth
the man of	God	and he said	and behold	Yahweh	One Who makes	windows

904, 8452	1950B, 2030.121	3626, 1745	2172	569.121
prep, art, n md	intrg part, v Qal impf 3ms	prep, art, n ms	art, dem pron	cj, v Qal impf 3ms
בַּשָּׁמַיִם	הֲיִהְיֶה	כַּדָּבָר	הַזֶּה	וַיֹּאמֶר
bashshāmayim	hăyihyeh	kaddāvār	hazzeh	wayyō'mer
in the heavens	will it be	according to the word	the this	and he said

2079	7495.151	904, 6084	4623, 8427	3940	404.123
intrj, ps 2ms	v Qal act ptc ms	prep, n fd, ps 2ms	cj, prep, adv	neg part	v Qal impf 2ms
הִנְּךָ	רֹאֶה	בְּעֵינֶיךָ	וּמִשָּׁם	לֹא	תֹאכֵל
hinnekhā	rō'eh	be'ênêkhā	ûmishshām	lō'	thō'khēl
behold you	seeing	with your eyes	but from there	not	you will eat

	2030.121, 3937	3772	7717.126	881	6194	904, 8554
20.	cj, v Qal impf 3ms, prep, ps 3ms	adv	cj, v Qal impf 3mp	do, ps 3ms	art, n ms	prep, art, n ms
	וַיְהִי־לוֹ	כֵּן	וַיִּרְמְסוּ	אֹתוֹ	הָעָם	בַּשַּׁעַר
	wayhî-lô	kēn	wayyirmesû	'ōthô	hā'ām	bashsha'ar
	and it happened to him	thus	and they trampled	him	the people	in the gate

4322.121		482	1744.311	420, 828	866, 2513.511
cj, v Qal impf 3ms	**8:1**	cj, pn	v Piel pf 3ms	prep, art, n fs	rel pron, v Hiphil pf 3ms
וַיָּמֹת		וֶאֱלִישָׁע	דִּבֶּר	אֶל־הָאִשָּׁה	אֲשֶׁר־הֶחֱיָה
wayyāmōth		we'ĕlîshā'	dibber	'el-hā'ishshāh	'ăsher-hechĕyāh
and he died		and Elisha	he had spoken	to the woman	whom he had caused to live

881, 1158	3937, 569.141	7251.132	2050.132	891	1041
do, n ms, ps 3fs	prep, v Qal inf con	v Qal impv 2fs	cj, v Qal impv 2fs	pers pron	cj, n ms, ps 2fs
אֶת־בְּנָהּ	לֵאמֹר	קוּמִי	וּלְכִי	אַתִּי	וּבֵיתֵךְ
'eth-benāhh	lē'mōr	qûmî	ûlākhî	'attî	ûvêthēkh
her son	saying	rise	and go	you	and your household

1513.132	904, 866	1513.124	3706, 7410.111	3176	3937, 7743
cj, v Qal impv 2fs	prep, rel part	v Qal impf 2fs	cj, v Qal pf 3ms	pn	prep, art, n ms
וְגוּרִי	בַּאֲשֶׁר	תָּגוּרִי	כִּי־קָרָא	יְהוָה	לָרָעָב
weghûrî	ba'ăsher	tāghûrî	kî-qārā'	yehwāh	lārā'āv
and sojourn	where	you will sojourn	because He has called	Yahweh	for the famine

1612, 971.111	420, 800	8124	8523		7251.122	828	6449.122
cj, cj, v Qal pf 3ms	prep, art, n fs	num	n fp	**2.**	cj, v Qal impf 3fs	art, n fs	cj, v Qal impf 3fs
וְגַם־בָּא	אֶל־הָאָרֶץ	שֶׁבַע	שָׁנִים		וַתָּקָם	הָאִשָּׁה	וַתַּעַשׂ
wegham-bā'	'el-hā'ārets	sheva'	shānîm		wattāqām	hā'ishshāh	watta'as
and also it will enter	into the land	seven	years		and she rose up	the woman	and she did

NCV ... he was crushed to death there under the feet of the people, *BB*.

18. And it came to pass as the man of God had spoken to the king, saying, Two measures of barley for a shekel, and a measure of fine flour for a shekel, shall be tomorrow about this time in the gate of Samaria: ... Two seahs of barley will sell for a shekel, and one seah of fine flour for a shekel, *NAB* ... two bushels of barley for a sickle and a bushel of flour for another, *Tyndale* ... five quarts of fine flour will cost half an ounce of silver, and ten quarts of barley grain cost half an ounce of silver, *NLT*.

19. And that lord answered the man of God, and said, Now, behold, if the LORD should make windows in heaven, might such a thing be?: ... Perhaps the Lord means to open the flood-gates of heaven, *Knox* ... if Yahweh were making windows in heaven, could it be according to this word, *Rotherham* ... Even if the LORD were to open windows in the sky, *REB* ... Even if Yahweh were to make flood gates in the sky, could this come to pass, *Anchor*.

And he said, Behold, thou shalt see it with thine eyes, but shalt not eat thereof: ... You shall see that sight, but you shall not eat the food, *Moffatt* ... but you will eat none of it, *Beck* ... Your eyes will see it, but you will not have a taste of the food, *BB*.

20. And so it fell out unto him: for the people trode upon him in the gate, and he died: ... the people trampled him in the gate, *NKJV* ... the people tread him down in the gate, *Young*.

8:1. Then spake Elisha unto the woman, whose son he had restored to life: ... he had raised to life, *JB* ... he had revived, *Anchor* ... he had brought back to life, *Good News*.

saying, Arise, and go thou and thine household, and sojourn wheresoever thou canst sojourn: ... Go away, you and your family, and stay wherever you can stay, *Beck* ... Go away at once with your household and find lodging where you can, *NEB* ... Take your family and move to some other place, *NLT* ... and stay abroad wherever you can, *Moffatt*.

for the LORD hath called for a famine; and it shall also come upon the land seven years: ... there will be a great need of food in the land; and this will go on for seven years, *BB* ... that will last for seven years, *NIV* ... a time without food, *NCV* ... the Lord has drought in store for us, which will fall upon this land, *Knox*.

2. And the woman arose, and did after the saying of the man of God: ... The woman hurried to do what the man of God had told her, *JB* ... The woman acted at once on the word, *REB* ... The woman got ready and did as the man of God said, *NAB*.

and she went with her household, and sojourned in the land of the Philistines seven years: ... she and her household went and lived, *Anchor* ... she and her household stayed, *Berkeley* ... gone with her family to live in Philistia, *Good News* ... and dwelt, *NKJV*.

---

official was trampled by the excited citizens of the city, as they rushed out to plunder the enemy camp, just as Elisha had intimated. In repetitive phrases, the narrator twice belabors the point (cf. vv. 17, 20), "The people trampled him in the gateway, and he died." What a sad epithet for anyone to have to bear.

8:1–6. Conclusion of the story of the Shunammite woman and her family: Famine and its aftermath. These brief verses represent a sequel to the fairly lengthy and very inspirational story concerning the birth of the Shunammite's son, and the resurrection of that son from the dead by the prophet Elisha (4:8–37). This time, we are told that famine compelled the woman and her family to leave the land of Israel and to stay in the land of the Philistines for some seven years. (This may well be the same famine spoken of in 4:38, although others link it to the siege of Samaria and its environs in 6:25ff.) Once the Shunammite returned, she had to go to the king to "beg" to get her house and land back, and it took Gehazi's providentially timed invocation of the name and reputation of Elisha the prophet to compel the king into granting her full justice. Note that Elisha himself made no appearance and played no active role in the narrative other than to give the initial advice to the woman and her family to flee the land. But his name and reputation was enough. By the end of this brief story the king promised to restore everything to the woman and her family, including any lost income.

T. R. Hobbs (WBC, 96ff) has suggested a most interesting interpretation for this carefully written story. Noting that Elisha's initial advice (in v. 1) actually led to the problem the woman faced upon her return (of course, she and her family meanwhile did avoid the ravages of famine), Hobbs points out that "the prophet inadvertently caused the problem, and his role in the solution to the problem is a passive one." Indeed, "in this narrative it is the king, not the prophet, who provides a very practical solution to her problem of dispossession," and "if anyone is legitimized in this narrative, it is the king, not Elisha." He also showed that this story follows quite closely the features of the

3626, 1745	382	435	2050.122	2026	1041
prep, *n ms*	*n ms*	art, n mp	cj, v Qal impf 3fs	pers pron	cj, n ms, ps 3fs
כִּדְבַר	אִישׁ	הָאֱלֹהִים	וַתֵּלֶךְ	הִיא	וּבֵיתָהּ
kidhvar	'îsh	hā'ĕlōhîm	wattēlekh	hî'	ûvêthāhh
according to the word of	the man of	God	and she went	she	and her household

1513.122	904, 800, 6674	8124	8523		2030.121	4623, 7381
v Qal impf 3fs	prep, *n fs*, pn	num	n fp	**3.**	cj, v Qal impf 3ms	prep, *n ms*
וַתָּגָר	בְּאֶרֶץ־פְּלִשְׁתִּים	שֶׁבַע	שָׁנִים		וַיְהִי	מִקְצֵה
wattāghār	be'erets-pelishtîm	sheva'	shānîm		wayhî	miqŏtsēh
and she sojourned	in the land of the Philistines	seven	years		and it was	from the end of

8124	8523	8178.122	828	4623, 800	6674	3428.122
num	n fp	cj, v Qal impf 3fs	art, n fs	prep, *n fs*	pn	cj, v Qal impf 3fs
שֶׁבַע	שָׁנִים	וַתָּשָׁב	הָאִשָּׁה	מֵאֶרֶץ	פְּלִשְׁתִּים	וַתֵּצֵא
sheva'	shānîm	wattāshāv	hā'ishshāh	mē'erets	pelishtîm	wattētsē'
seven	years	then she returned	the woman	from the land of	the Philistines	and she went out

3937, 7094.141	420, 4567	420, 1041	420, 7898		4567	1744.351
prep, v Qal inf con	prep, art, n ms	prep, n ms, ps 3fs	cj, prep, n ms, ps 3fs	**4.**	cj, art, n ms	v Piel ptc ms
לִצְעֹק	אֶל־הַמֶּלֶךְ	אֶל־בֵּיתָהּ	וְאֶל־שָׂדָהּ		וְהַמֶּלֶךְ	מְדַבֵּר
lits'ōq	'el-hammelekh	'el-bêthāhh	we'el-sādhāhh		wehammelekh	medhabbēr
to cry out	to the king	for her household	and for her field		and the king	speaking

420, 1557	5470	382, 435	3937, 569.141	5807.331, 5167	3937	881
prep, pn	*n ms*	*n ms*, art, n mp	prep, v Qal inf con	v Piel impv 2ms, part	prep, ps 1cs	do
אֶל־גֵּחֲזִי	נַעַר	אִישׁ־הָאֱלֹהִים	לֵאמֹר	סַפְּרָה־נָּא	לִי	אֵת
'el-gēchăzî	na'ar	'îsh-hā'ĕlōhîm	lē'mōr	sapperāh-nā'	lî	'ēth
to Gehazi	the servant of	the man of God	saying	recount please	to me	

3725, 1448	866, 6449.111	482		2030.121	2000	5807.351	3937, 4567
adj, art, adj	rel part, v Qal pf 3ms	pn	**5.**	cj, v Qal impf 3ms	pers pron	v Piel ptc ms	prep, art, n ms
כָּל־הַגְּדֹלוֹת	אֲשֶׁר־עָשָׂה	אֱלִישָׁע		וַיְהִי	הוּא	מְסַפֵּר	לַמֶּלֶךְ
kol-haggedhōlôth	'ăsher-'āsāh	'ĕlîshā'		wayhî	hû'	mesappēr	lammelekh
all the great	that he has done	Elisha		and it was	he	recounting	to the king

881	866, 2513.511	881, 4322.151	2079	828
do	rel pron, v Hiphil pf 3ms	do, art, v Qal act ptc ms	cj, intrj	art, n fs
אֵת	אֲשֶׁר־הֶחֱיָה	אֶת־הַמֵּת	וְהִנֵּה	הָאִשָּׁה
'ēth	'ăsher-hechĕyāh	'eth-hammēth	wehinnēh	hā'ishshāh
	whom he had caused to live	the dead one	and behold	the woman

866, 2513.511	881, 1158	7094.153	420, 4567	6142, 1041
rel pron, v Hiphil pf 3ms	do, n ms, ps 3fs	v Qal act ptc fs	prep, art, n ms	prep, n ms, ps 3fs
אֲשֶׁר־הֶחֱיָה	אֶת־בְּנָהּ	צֹעֶקֶת	אֶל־הַמֶּלֶךְ	עַל־בֵּיתָהּ
'ăsher-hechĕyāh	'eth-benāhh	tsō'eqeth	'el-hammelekh	'al-bêthāhh
whom he had caused to live	her son	crying out	to the king	concerning her household

6142, 7898	569.121	1557	112	4567	2148	828
cj, prep, n ms, ps 3fs	cj, v Qal impf 3ms	pn	n ms, ps 1cs	art, n ms	dem pron	art, n fs
וְעַל־שָׂדָהּ	וַיֹּאמֶר	גֵּחֲזִי	אֲדֹנִי	הַמֶּלֶךְ	זֹאת	הָאִשָּׁה
we'al-sādhāhh	wayyō'mer	gēchăzî	'ădhōnî	hammelekh	zō'th	hā'ishshāh
and concerning her field	and he said	Gehazi	my master	the king	this	the woman

2172, 1158	866, 2513.511	482		8068.121	4567
cj, dem pron, n ms, ps 3fs	rel pron, v Hiphil pf 3ms	pn	**6.**	cj, v Qal impf 3ms	art, n ms
וְזֶה־בְּנָהּ	אֲשֶׁר־הֶחֱיָה	אֱלִישָׁע		וַיִּשְׁאַל	הַמֶּלֶךְ
wezeh-benāhh	'ăsher-hechĕyāh	'ĕlîshā'		wayyish'al	hammelekh
and this her son	whom he caused to live	Elisha		and he asked	the king

3. And it came to pass at the seven years' end, that the woman returned out of the land of the Philistines: ... After the end of the famine she returned to the land of Israel, *NLT* ... At the end of the seven years, when the woman returned from the land, *NRSV*.

and she went forth to cry unto the king for her house and for her land: ... she sought and audience of the king to appeal for the return of, *NEB* ... and went to beg the king, *NCV* ... to make outcry unto the king, concerning her house and concerning her field, *Rotherham* ... she went out to speak to the king, *Tyndale*.

4. And the king talked with Gehazi the servant of the man of God, saying, Tell me, I pray thee, all the great things that Elisha hath done: ... all the great acts, *Geneva* ... asking him to tell him all the great deeds of Elisha, *Moffatt* ... Relate to me, *Goodspeed* ... tell the story of all Eliseus' marvellous deeds, *Knox*.

5. And it came to pass, as he was telling the king how he had restored a dead body to life: ... the story of how Elisha had given life to the dead, *BB* ... about the time Elisha had brought a boy back to life, *NLT* ... how he had raised one dead to life, *Douay* ... Elisha had brought a dead person back to life, *Good News*.

that, behold, the woman, whose son he had restored to life, cried to the king for her house and for her land: ... the woman whose son Elisha had raised lodged her claim with the king, *JB* ... appealed to the king for her house and field, *NASB* ... came to beg, *NIV* ... began making an outcry, *Rotherham*.

And Gehazi said, My lord, O king, this is the woman, and this is her son, whom Elisha restored to life: ... whom Elisha brought back to life, *NEB* ... whom Elisha revived, *Young* ... which Eliseus brought to life again, *Tyndale*.

6. And when the king asked the woman, she told him. So the king appointed unto her a certain officer, saying: ... With that the king placed an official at her disposal, *NAB* ... charged one of his own chamberlains, *Knox* ... when the king committed her to an Officer, *Fenton* ... the king appointed her an eunuch, *Douay*.

Restore all that was hers, and all the fruits of the field since the day that she left the land, even until now: ... and all the revenue of the land since the day that she left the country, *Darby* ... Give the woman everything that is hers, the king said. Give her all the money made from her land, *NCV* ... Give back all that she hath, and all the increase of the field, *Young* ... she got back all her property and all the produce that her farm had yielded, *Moffatt*.

---

initial story found in ch. 4 (the story of the multiplication of the oil to pay the unnamed widow's debts), in which the prophet is depicted as the "problem-solver par excellence" (all quotes from Hobbs, 97); the present story, however, "provides a clear reversal of the prophet's power and reduces the prophet to a very human level" (p. 98).

At first glance, there is a lot to be said for Hobbs' novel reading of the text. Elisha is indeed mostly conspicuous by his absence, and the king does appear in a relatively positive light (which is not usually the case in the Elisha stories). However, a closer look at vv. 4f, where Gehazi just happens to be rehearsing the great deeds of the prophet (admittedly, at the king's prompting) and where the woman herself and her son make a providentially timed appearance (she has been gone for some seven years, after all), demonstrates that something more subtle than Hobbs' king/prophet dichotomy is taking place here. As will be the case in the very next story (vv. 7–15; also cf. 9:1–13; 13:14–19), Elisha is now, both directly and indirectly, greatly influencing the future behavior of kings, both Israelite and foreign. What he has done, and what he continues to do, have an immediate, as well as a long term effect on the future history of Israel and her neighbors. Such is the case here, in the present passage, as well. Elisha's past actions, with their remarkable long-term effects, greatly affect the present and the future. Who would not deny that the woman would have had much greater difficulty in securing a sympathetic audience with the king, not to mention receiving her property back in its entirety, if Elisha's remarkable name and reputation had not happened to be the topic of discussion? The present narrative presents positively the role of the prophet, even in a situation where he is physically absent, as the major guarantor of the woman's legal and moral property rights (note once again that such matters are clearly on Elisha's mind even in 4:13), and it is the king who is forced to acquiesce in her recovery of that property in full. The story once again vindicates the prophet vis-à-vis the king. No prophet, no recovery of house or land. Still, the king plays a relatively positive role in the story as well—but even this reflects well on the prior actions of the prophet in support of the monarchy (cf., grudgingly, in 3:13f, but more willingly in 5:7f and very willingly in 6:9f, 21ff). And as far as Elisha initially "causing the problem" inadvertently, well, life is messy, and famines do come, and Elisha's role was proactive and preventative—both for the woman and for her

3937, 828	5807.322, 3937	5598.121, 3937	4567	5835	259
prep, art, n fs	cj, v Piel impf 3fs, prep, ps 3ms	cj, v Qal impf 3ms, prep, ps 3fs	art, n ms	n ms	num
לָאִשָּׁה	וַתְּסַפֶּר־לוֹ	וַיִּתֶּן־לָהּ	הַמֶּלֶךְ	סָרִיס	אֶחָד
lā'ishshāh	wattesapper-lô	wayyitten-lāhh	hammelekh	sārîs	'echādh
to the woman	and she recounted to him	and he gave to her	the king	a eunuch	one

3937, 569.141	8178.531	881, 3725, 866, 3937	881	3725, 8721	7898
prep, v Qal inf con	v Hiphil impv 2ms	do, *adj*, rel part, prep, ps 3fs	cj, do	*adj*, *n fp*	art, n ms
לֵאמֹר	הָשֵׁיב	אֶת־כָּל־אֲשֶׁר־לָהּ	וְאֵת	כָּל־תְּבוּאֹת	הַשָּׂדֶה
lē'mōr	hāshēv	'eth-kol-'ăsher-lāhh	we'ēth	kol-tevû'ōth	hassādheh
saying	return	all which to her	and	all the produce of	the field

4623, 3219	6013.112	881, 800	5912, 6498		971.121	482	1894
prep, n ms	v Qal pf 3fs	do, art, n fs	cj, adv, adv	**7.**	cj, v Qal impf 3ms	pn	pn
מִיּוֹם	עָזְבָה	אֶת־הָאָרֶץ	וְעַד־עָתָּה		וַיָּבֹא	אֱלִישָׁע	דַּמֶּשֶׂק
mîyôm	'āzevāh	'eth-hā'ārets	we'adh-'āttāh		wayyāvō'	'ĕlîshā'	dammeseq
from a day	she left	the land	even until now		and he entered	Elisha	Damascus

1163	4567, 782	2571.151	5222.621, 3937	3937, 569.141
cj, pn	*n ms*, pn	v Qal act ptc ms	cj, v Hophal impf 3ms, prep, ps 3ms	prep, v Qal inf con
וּבֶן־הֲדַד	מֶלֶךְ־אֲרָם	חֹלֶה	וַיֻּגַּד־לוֹ	לֵאמֹר
ûven-hedhadh	melekh-'ărām	chōleh	wayyuggadh-lô	lē'mōr
and Ben-Hadad	the king of Aram	sick	and it was reported to him	saying

971.111	382	435	5912, 2077		569.121	4567	420, 2462
v Qal pf 3ms	*n ms*	art, n mp	prep, adv	**8.**	cj, v Qal impf 3ms	art, n ms	prep, pn
בָּא	אִישׁ	הָאֱלֹהִים	עַד־הֵנָּה		וַיֹּאמֶר	הַמֶּלֶךְ	אֶל־חֲזָהאֵל
bā'	'îsh	hā'ĕlōhîm	'adh-hēnnāh		wayyō'mer	hammelekh	'el-chăzāh'ēl
he has come	the man of	God	unto here		and he said	the king	to Hazael

4089.131	904, 3135	4647	2050.131	3937, 7410.141	382	435
v Qal impv 2ms	prep, n fs, ps 2ms	n fs	cj, v Qal impv 2ms	prep, v Qal inf con	*n ms*	art, n mp
קַח	בְּיָדְךָ	מִנְחָה	וְלֵךְ	לִקְרַאת	אִישׁ	הָאֱלֹהִים
qach	beyādhekhā	minchāh	welēkh	liqŏra'th	'îsh	hā'ĕlōhîm
take	in your hand	a tribute	and go	to meet	the man of	God

1938.113	881, 3176	4623, 881	3937, 569.141	1950B, 2513.125	4623, 2582
cj, v Qal pf 2ms	do, pn	prep, do, ps 3ms	prep, v Qal inf con	intrg part, v Qal impf 1cs	prep, n ms
וְדָרַשְׁתָּ	אֶת־יְהוָה	מֵאוֹתוֹ	לֵאמֹר	הַאֶחְיֶה	מֵחֳלִי
wedhārashtā	'eth-yehwāh	mē'ôthô	lē'mōr	ha'echăyeh	mēchălî
and you will inquire	Yahweh	from him	saying	will I live	from sickness

7. And Elisha came to Damascus; and Ben-Hadad the king of Syria was sick: ... While King Ben-hadad of Aram was ill, *NRSV* ... where King Ben-hadad lay sick, *NLT* ... Benhadad the king of Siria being sick, *Tyndale*.

and it was told him, saying, The man of God is come hither: ... he was told the man of God had arrived, *Moffatt* ... when he heard that the servant of God was there, *Knox* ... The man of God hath come as far as this place, *Rotherham* ... when he was informed, The man of God has come here, *Berkeley*.

8. And the king said unto Hazael, Take a present in thine hand, and go, meet the man of God: ... Take a gift to the prophet, *Good News* ... Take a present with you, *Fenton* ... Take an offering with you, *BB*.

and inquire of the LORD by him, saying, Shall I recover of this disease?: ... Have him consult the LORD as to whether I shall recover from this sickness, *NAB* ... Do I revive from this sickness, *Young* ... Can I recover from this my illness, *Douay* ... tell him to ask the LORD if I will get well again, *NLT*.

9. So Hazael went to meet him, and took a present with him, even of every good thing of Damascus, forty camels' burden, and came and stood before him, and said: ... taking with him a gift of forty camels loaded, *NCV* ... and gifts went too, all the best Damascus had to offer, *Knox* ... all sorts of valuable things, *Berkeley* ... taking with him as a gift forty camel-loads of all kinds of Damascus wares, *REB*.

Thy son Ben-Hadad king of Syria hath sent me to thee, saying, Shall I recover of this disease?: ... from

family. We cannot hold him accountable for illegal actions made by others. (Expropriation of property was routinely condemned by the prophets; cf. Elijah's harsh words to Ahab and Jezebel concerning the seizing of Naboth's vineyard in 1 Ki. 21:18–24; also cf. Isa. 5:8; Mic. 2:1f; and the Torah legislation in Lev. 25:8–17; Num. 27:5–11; Deut. 27:17.)

This is the final time Elisha's servant Gehazi is mentioned in 2 Kings, and a summarizing word about his role would therefore be in order. Gehazi has appeared by name in a total of three Elisha stories—or in a sense, in only two stories, if 4:8–37 and 8:1–6 are considered as two parts of the same story, as suggested. His only other explicit appearance was in the Naaman narrative in ch. 5. (Unnamed servants of Elisha also make inconsequential appearances in 4:38, 43 [NIV]; and 6:15.) In both parts of the story about the Shunammite woman, Gehazi's role is actually quite positive. There is no criticism of his words or actions anywhere, and, on two different occasions, his contributions to the story are particularly positive. First of all, in 4:14, when Elisha is casting about for some way to reward the Shunammite for her kind hospitality, Gehazi directs his master's attention to the advanced age of the Shunammite's husband, as well as to the fact that she was still childless. This, of course, redirects the narrative toward concern for a son for the woman. When the son later tragically dies, Gehazi does seem to act in an insensitive manner in 4:27, trying to push away the Shunammite from the prophet's presence, but Gehazi had just been assured by the woman that everything was all right, so his insensitivity is hardly purposeful. (This is also the case when he is unable to effect the resurrection of the son in 4:32—he is only a servant, after all, not the prophet himself—and he is just following Elisha's orders when he places the staff on the boy's face.) As for Gehazi's second major contribution, that of course is to be found in the present passage. Here, Gehazi's responses to the king's questions concerning Elisha's past miracles play a major and very positive role in effecting the woman's eventual recovery of her family's property. Thus, at least in the Shunammite stories, Gehazi is an obedient and devoted servant, who occasionally plays a more active role in Elisha's prophetic ministry as well.

But this, of course, is emphatically not the case in the Naaman account in ch. 5. Here Gehazi is roundly condemned by prophet and narrator alike for his greed and deception (cf. comments on 5:19–25, and 5:25ff). Gehazi's sins were avarice, deception, derogation of superiors and swearing deceitfully by the name of Yahweh; and of all these shortcomings, the most serious was, at least in Elisha's opinion, that of avarice or greed. Such a sin can, and in this case did, lead to the others, and such a sin surely has ruined more careers and ministries than that of Gehazi. Reflect carefully upon the dangers of such a perspective in our own all too materialistic culture of today. It would seem that, as a result of this brief summary, it may well take only one serious occasion for sin to torpedo quite effectively one's entire future vocation—in the present instance, one greedy grab at wealth leading to the lifetime (indeed the perpetual) ignominy of leprosy in Gehazi and in his descendants. That is too high a price to pay for any momentary monetary attraction.

8:7–15. *Elisha's international ministry and its ramifications. Reference has just been given to Elisha's ministry with and to kings, both foreign and domestic. In perhaps the oddest single narrative about Elisha, the prophet here helps hasten the day when Hazael takes over as king of Aram. Elisha foresaw as much, but even he was powerless either to stop Hazael's apparent murder of his master, or put an end to Aram's future plundering of Israel. The story of Ben-Hadad's illness and death brings to mind King Ahaziah's similar plight in 2 Ki. 1, both kings ironically seeking healing from foreign gods, and both failing in the attempt. Following is a brief discussion of the background and lessons of this peculiar account.*

8:7–8. King Ben-Hadad's illness; his inquiry of Yahweh, God of Israel. Damascus was the capital of Israel's most powerful enemy, the nation of Aram (concerning the frequently hostile relationship between Israel and Aram, see comments on 5:1). Although Elisha had earlier healed Naaman, the respected Aramean military commander, of his leprosy, he did not seek to do so of his own volition, but rather as the result of (among other things) the Israelite king's prior embarrassment (cf. 5:7f). The emphasis there was on the sovereignty of the Israelite God Yahweh and on his prophet, Elisha, over against any and all disease. But here, the very same prophet seeks to visit the foreign capital of Damascus seemingly of his own accord (conceivably the commission Yahweh gave to Elijah in 1 Ki. 19:15 to "go to the Desert of [or wilderness to] Damascus … and anoint Hazael king over Aram," weighed heavily in this decision as well—especially inasmuch as it was never fulfilled by the elder prophet). In any case, there is

2172		2050.121	2462	3937, 7410.141	4089.121	4647
dem pron	**9.**	cj, v Qal impf 3ms	pn	prep, v Qal inf con, ps 3ms	cj, v Qal impf 3ms	n fs
זֶה		וַיֵּלֶךְ	חֲזָאֵל	לִקְרָאתוֹ	וַיִּקַּח	מִנְחָה
zeh		wayyēlekh	chăzā'ēl	liqŏrā'thô	wayyiqqach	minchāh
this		and he walked	Hazael	to meet him	and he took	a tribute

904, 3135	3725, 3008	1894	5014	727	1622
prep, n fs, ps 3ms	cj, *adj*, *n ms*	pn	*n ms*	num	n ms
בְּיָדוֹ	וְכָל־טוּב	דַּמֶּשֶׂק	מַשָּׂא	אַרְבָּעִים	גָּמָל
v[e]yādhô	w[e]khol-ṭûv	dammeseq	massā'	'arbā'îm	gāmāl
in his hand	and all the good things of	Damascus	a burden of	forty	camels

971.121	6198.121	3937, 6686	569.121	1158	1163
cj, v Qal impf 3ms	cj, v Qal impf 3ms	prep, n mp, ps 3ms	cj, v Qal impf 3ms	n ms, ps 2ms	pn
וַיָּבֹא	וַיַּעֲמֹד	לְפָנָיו	וַיֹּאמֶר	בִּנְךָ	בֶּן־הֲדַד
wayyāvō'	wayya'ămōdh	l[e]phānâv	wayyō'mer	binkhā	ven-h[e]dhadh
and he came	and he stood	before him	and he said	your son	Ben-Hadad

4567, 782	8365.111	420	3937, 569.141	1950B, 2513.125	4623, 2582
n ms, pn	v Qal pf 3ms, ps 1cs	prep, ps 2ms	prep, v Qal inf con	intrg part, v Qal impf 1cs	prep, n ms
מֶלֶךְ־אֲרָם	שְׁלָחַנִי	אֵלֶיךָ	לֵאמֹר	הַאֶחְיֶה	מֵחֳלִי
melekh-'ărām	sh[e]lāchanî	'ēlêkhā	lē'mōr	ha'echăyeh	mēchălî
the king of Aram	he has sent me	to you	saying	will I live	from sickness

2172		569.121	420	482	2050.131	569.131, 3940	2513.142
dem pron	**10.**	cj, v Qal impf 3ms	prep, ps 3ms	pn	v Qal impv 2ms	v Qal impv 2ms, neg part	v Qal inf abs
זֶה		וַיֹּאמֶר	אֵלָיו	אֱלִישָׁע	לֵךְ	אֱמָר־לֹא	חָיֹה
zeh		wayyō'mer	'ēlâv	'ĕlîshā'	lēkh	'ĕmār-lō'	chāyōh
this		and he said	to him	Elisha	go	say no	living

2513.123	7495.511	3176	3706, 4322.142	4322.121
v Qal impf 2ms	cj, v Hiphil pf 3ms, ps 1cs	pn	cj, v Qal inf abs	v Qal impf 3ms
תִּחְיֶה	וְהִרְאַנִי	יְהוָה	כִּי־מוֹת	יָמוּת
thichăyeh	w[e]hir'anî	y[e]hwāh	kî-môth	yāmûth
you will certainly live	but He has shown me	Yahweh	rather dying	he will certainly die

	6198.521	881, 6686	7947.121	5912, 991.141
11.	cj, v Hiphil impf 3ms	do, n mp, ps 3ms	cj, v Qal impf 3ms	adv, v Qal inf con
	וַיַּעֲמֵד	אֶת־פָּנָיו	וַיָּשֶׂם	עַד־בֹּשׁ
	wayya'ămēdh	'eth-pānâv	wayyāsem	'adh-bōsh
	and he caused to be motionless	his face	and he set	until being ashamed

1098.121	382	435		569.121	2462	4211	112
cj, v Qal impf 3ms	*n ms*	art, n mp	**12.**	cj, v Qal impf 3ms	pn	intrg	n ms, ps 1cs
וַיֵּבְךְּ	אִישׁ	הָאֱלֹהִים		וַיֹּאמֶר	חֲזָאֵל	מַדּוּעַ	אֲדֹנִי
wayyēvk	'îsh	hā'ĕlōhîm		wayyō'mer	chăzā'ēl	maddûa'	'ădhōnî
and he wept	the man of	God		and he said	Hazael	why	my master

1098.151	569.121	3706, 3156.115	881	866, 6449.123	3937, 1158
v Qal act ptc ms	cj, v Qal impf 3ms	cj, v Qal pf 1cs	do	rel part, v Qal impf 2ms	prep, *n mp*
בֹּכֶה	וַיֹּאמֶר	כִּי־יָדַעְתִּי	אֵת	אֲשֶׁר־תַּעֲשֶׂה	לִבְנֵי
vōkheh	wayyō'mer	kî-yādha'ättî	'ēth	'ăsher-ta'ăseh	livnê
weeping	and he said	because I know		what you will do	to the children of

3547	7737	4152	8365.323	904, 813	1005	904, 2820
pn	adj	n mp, ps 3mp	v Piel impf 2ms	prep, art, n fs	cj, n mp, ps 3mp	prep, art, n fs
יִשְׂרָאֵל	רָעָה	מִבְצְרֵיהֶם	תְּשַׁלַּח	בָּאֵשׁ	וּבַחֻרֵיהֶם	בַּחֶרֶב
yisrā'ēl	rā'āh	mivts[e]rêhem	t[e]shallach	bā'ēsh	ûvachurêhem	bacherev
Israel	evil	their fortresses	you will send	with the fire	and their young men	with the sword

this illness, *NRSV* ... from this sickness, *Rotherham* ... Will I be cured of this illness, *Beck*.

10. And Elisha said unto him, Go, say unto him, Thou mayest certainly recover: howbeit the LORD hath shown me that he shall surely die: ... However, the LORD has showed me that he will in fact die, *NAB* ... he will certainly recover though the Eternal has revealed to me that he will certainly die, *Moffatt* ... The LORD has revealed to me that he will die; but go to him and tell him that he will recover, *Good News* ... You will not live, for the EVER-LIVING has shown me, *Fenton*.

11. And he settled his countenance stedfastly, until he was ashamed: and the man of God wept: ... he fixed his gaze and stared at him, *Goodspeed* ... his face became fixed till he looked confused, *Beck* ... The man of God stood there with set face like a man stunned, until he could bear it no longer, *NEB* ... He stared at him with a fixed gaze until Hazael felt ashamed, *NIV*.

12. And Hazael said, Why weepeth my lord? And he answered, Because I know the evil that thou wilt do unto the children of Israel: ... do you weep, sir? said Hazael. He answered,

---

not the slightest suggestion that Elisha went to the enemy city out of the will of God. And, in sharp contrast with the "seeing and blinding" incidents in 6:8–23, the Arameans now knew full well who Elisha was. So it is no surprise, that in language virtually identical to that of Ahaziah in 1:2, Ben-Hadad commissioned his emissary Hazael to ask whether or not he would recover from his illness (v. 8). Concerning the probable identity of this Ben-Hadad, see Cogan and Tadmor, AB, 92; they follow the commonly accepted convention of labeling him "Ben-Hadad II," but there are some serious questions concerning this enumeration. In any case, this particular king, known as "Adad-idri of Damascus" in the contemporary Assyrian inscriptions "Ben-Hadad" was probably his throne name, gave Shalmaneser III much opposition in the latter's attempts to take over southern Syria during the years 853–845. But in Shalmaneser's eighteenth year, 841, one "Hazael of Damascus, son of a nobody" [cf. Wiseman, TOTC, 214] was in control of the Aramean city. Clearly, Hazael's coup had already taken place by this time.

8:9–10. Hazael's inquiry; Elisha's surprising response. As bidden, Hazael "took a gift" ("forty camel-loads," a very generous offering; indeed, "worthy of royalty" [Cogan and Tadmor, AB, 90]; they go on to suggest that it "can only be the product of the storyteller's fancy"; but, as Wiseman, TOTC, 213, points out, this "audience gift" may well have been a bribe to obtain an oracle from Yahweh). Hazael also asked the question he was told to ask: would the king die? The reference to "your son" is in line with courtly etiquette. But Hazael was hardly ready for Elisha's response (or was he? perhaps assassination was already on his mind?). Elisha's answer in v. 10 is perplexing: he tells Hazael to say one thing, but to be aware of another. He is to say the current king will live, but he is to be apprised of the fact that he will die, instead. How are we to understand this apparent subterfuge? Despite attempts at softening the Hebrew (cf. NIV footnote), it certainly seems the case that Elisha told Hazael to lie, to say that Ben-Hadad would recover, when they both knew he would not (good, albeit somewhat technical discussions of the Masoretic text, the versions, and the medieval and modern commentators may be found in Cogan and Tadmor [AB, 90], and in Hobbs [WBC, 95, n. 10.b]). As Cogan and Tadmor point out, "The storyteller had no difficulty with a man of God involved in international political affairs, sometimes dealing underhandedly" (cf. a similar situation in 1 Sam. 16:1ff, where Yahweh tells Samuel the prophet what to say if and when Saul objects to his visit to Bethlehem to anoint one of the sons of Jesse as king). Some commentators (e.g., Jones, NCBC, 3444) point out that Elisha is not technically advocating lying—after all Ben-Hadad did not die of the illness he had contracted, but rather by another cause—assassination. But there is, in my opinion, another way to handle the present text as well. The main point is that Elisha knew full well what Hazael was about to do, both against his own master the king, as well as against Israel in the future (cf. vv. 11ff). Thus the present statement is probably in line with Jesus' advice to Judas Iscariot in John 13:27, "What you are about to do, do quickly." Jesus was hardly telling Judas to hurry up and make the decision to betray him. Rather He was demonstrating that he knew all along what was in Judas' mind, and that Judas was determined to accomplish his dastardly deed. He might as well get on with it. This is probably the gist of Elisha's curious response to Hazael in v. 10 of the present text. Elisha could see the future, and there was no stopping Hazael, so he might as well get on with it. Go ahead, lie to the king, and then kill him—you are going to do it anyway.

8:11–13. Elisha's further revelation to and about Hazael. As was the case with the upset

2103.123	5985	7660.323	2107	1260.323
v Qal impf 2ms	cj, n mp, ps 3mp	v Piel impf 2ms	cj, adj, ps 3mp	v Piel impf 2ms
תַּהֲרֹג	וְעֹלְלֵיהֶם	תְּרַטֵּשׁ	וְהָרֹתֵיהֶם	תְּבַקֵּעַ
tahrōgh	we'ōlelêhem	terattēsh	wehārōthêhem	tevaqqēa'
you will kill	and their children	you will dash in pieces	and their pregnant	you will split open

13.	569.121	2462	3706	4242	5860	3732	3706	6449.121	1745
	cj, v Qal impf 3ms	pn	cj	intrg	n ms, ps 2ms	art, n ms	cj	v Qal impf 3ms	art, n ms
	וַיֹּאמֶר	חֲזָהאֵל	כִּי	מָה	עַבְדְּךָ	הַכֶּלֶב	כִּי	יַעֲשֶׂה	הַדָּבָר
	wayyō'mer	chăzāh'ēl	kî	māh	'avdekhā	hakkelev	kî	ya'ăseh	haddāvār
	and he said	Hazael	because	what	your servant	the dog	that	he will do	the thing

1448	2172	569.121	482	7495.511	3176	881	4567
art, adj	art, dem pron	cj, v Qal impf 3ms	pn	v Hiphil pf 3ms, ps 1cs	pn	do, ps 2ms	n ms
הַגָּדוֹל	הַזֶּה	וַיֹּאמֶר	אֱלִישָׁע	הִרְאַנִי	יְהוָה	אֹתְךָ	מֶלֶךְ
haggādhôl	hazzeh	wayyō'mer	'ĕlîshā'	hir'anî	yehwāh	'ōthekhā	melekh
the great	the this	and he said	Elisha	He has shown me	Yahweh	you	a king

6142, 482	14.	2050.121	4623, 881	482	971.121	420, 112
prep, pn		cj, v Qal impf 3ms	prep, do	pn	cj, v Qal impf 3ms	prep, n mp, ps 3ms
עַל־אֲרָם		וַיֵּלֶךְ	מֵאֵת	אֱלִישָׁע	וַיָּבֹא	אֶל־אֲדֹנָיו
'al-'ărām		wayyēlekh	mē'ēth	'ĕlîshā'	wayyāvō'	'el-'ădhōnāv
over Aram		and he went	from	Elisha	and he came	to his master

569.121	3937	4242, 569.111	3937	482	569.121	569.111
cj, v Qal impf 3ms	prep, ps 3ms	intrg, v Qal pf 3ms	prep, ps 2ms	pn	cj, v Qal impf 3ms	v Qal pf 3ms
וַיֹּאמֶר	לוֹ	מָה־אָמַר	לְךָ	אֱלִישָׁע	וַיֹּאמֶר	אָמַר
wayyō'mer	lô	māh-'āmar	lekhā	'ĕlîshā'	wayyō'mer	'āmar
and he said	to him	what has he said	to you	Elisha	and he said	he said

3937	2513.142	2513.123	15.	2030.121	4623, 4420	4089.121
prep, ps 1cs	v Qal inf abs	v Qal impf 2ms		cj, v Qal impf 3ms	prep, n fs	cj, v Qal impf 3ms
לִי	חָיֹה	תִּחְיֶה		וַיְהִי	מִמָּחֳרָת	וַיִּקַּח
lî	chāyōh	thichāyeh		wayhî	mimmāchărāth	wayyiqqach
to me	living	you will certainly live		and it was	on the next day	and he took

4483	2991.121	904, 4448	6816.121	6142, 6686	4322.121
art, n ms	cj, v Qal impf 3ms	prep, art, n md	cj, v Qal impf 3ms	prep, n mp, ps 3ms	cj, v Qal impf 3ms
הַמַּכְבֵּר	וַיִּטְבֹּל	בַּמַּיִם	וַיִּפְרֹשׂ	עַל־פָּנָיו	וַיָּמֹת
hammakhbēr	wayyitbōl	bammayim	wayyiphrōs	'al-pānâv	wayyāmōth
the cloth	and he dipped	with the water	and he spread	on his face	and he died

4566.121	2462	8809	16.	904, 8523	2675	3937, 3245
cj, v Qal impf 3ms	pn	prep, ps 3ms		cj, prep, *n fs*	num	prep, pn
וַיִּמְלֹךְ	חֲזָהאֵל	תַּחְתָּיו		וּבִשְׁנַת	חָמֵשׁ	לְיוֹרָם
wayyimlōkh	chăzāh'ēl	tachtâv		ûvishnath	chāmēsh	leyôrām
and he reigned	Hazael	instead of him		and in the year of	five	of Joram

Because I know the harm you will do to the Israelites, *REB* ... I know what cruelty you will do, *Fenton*.

their strong holds wilt thou set on fire, and their young men wilt thou slay with the sword, and wilt dash their children, and rip up their women with child: ... little children you will dash in pieces, and their pregnant women you will rip open, *Berkeley* ... burn their fortified cities, kill their young men, dash their children to the ground, *NLT* ... set fire to their towns; and murder their youths with the sword; and tear their infants to pieces, *Fenton*.

13. And Hazael said, But what, is thy servant a dog, that he should do this great thing?: ... But I am a dog, a mere nobody; how can I do this great thing, *NEB* ... that he should do this gross thing, *NKJV*.

And Elisha answered, The LORD hath shown me that thou shalt be king over Syria: ... The Lord has made it clear to me that you will be king, *BB*.

14. So he departed from Elisha, and came to his master; who said to him, What said Elisha to thee?: ... Hazael went back to Benhadad, who asked him, What did Elisha say, *Good News*.

And he answered, He told me that thou shouldest surely recover: ... said to me that you would certainly live, *Goodspeed*.

15. And it came to pass on the morrow, that he took a thick cloth, and dipped it in water, and spread it on his face, so that he died: ... he took a blanket and, after dipping it in water, laid it over the king's face, *REB* ... soaked it in water, and smothered the king, *Good News* ... Hazael took the bed-cover, and making it wet with water, put it over Ben-hadad's face, causing his death, *BB*.

and Hazael reigned in his stead: ... Hazael succeeded him as king, *Beck* ... reigned in his place, *NKJV* ... became the next king of Aram, *NLT*.

16. And in the fifth year of Joram the son of Ahab king of Israel, Jehoshaphat being then king of Judah, Jehoram the son of Jehoshaphat king of Judah began to reign: ... While Jehoshaphat was king in Judah, Jehoram son of

---

Amos (cf. Amos 7:1–9; 8:1ff) and the weeping Jeremiah (Jer. 8:21–9:2), merely knowing the future does not automatically mean one has the power to alter it. So Elisha stared at Hazael, and then started weeping (v. 11). He could foresee that this "son of a nobody," this "dog," would soon become king, and would greatly oppress the land of Israel. Even if somehow this was the judgmental will of Yahweh, even if Israel somehow deserved it, still the prophet wept at the prospect. And, of course, the melancholy prophecy of v. 12 did come true—setting fire to the fortified cities, killing the children, ripping open pregnant women (alas, the standard, stark depiction of warfare at this time—cf. Hos. 10:14; 13:16; Amos 1:13; and concerning Hazael's future deprivations of Israel, cf. 2 Ki. 10:32f; 13:3, 7, 19, 22; also cf. 12:17f [against Judah]). Hobbs (WBC, 102; cf. the references in Cogan and Tadmor, AB, 91) points out that Hazael's self-designation as a "mere dog" was probably not a gesture of humility, but merely that of an inferior addressing a superior (the ancients had utter contempt for those creatures; cf. the Jews' later designation of the Gentiles as "dogs," and how that is turned on its head [to Jesus' own amazement and amusement] in Matt. 15:21–28).

8:14–15. Hazael kills his master, and succeeds him as king. The traditional interpretation is that Hazael indeed assassinated his master Ben-Hadad, but some disagree with this view (as Wiseman [TOTC, 215] acknowledged, "the manner of Ben-Hadad's death is disputed"). Cogan and Tadmor (AB, 91) point out that medieval commentators understood Hazael as "merely applying cool compresses to his fevered lord" when the latter died. But "this interpretation sounds like an attempt to place the man of God above any suspicion of complicity in the death of the Aramean king." Although the Hebrew term (makhber, HED #4483) for "thick cloth" (NIV) is only used here in the OT, and could mean "[mosquito] netting" or the like, it seems unlikely that the usurper Hazael of the Bible (besides the references already given, also cf. Amos 1:3ff) and of the ancient Near Eastern inscriptions, would be that solicitous of his master. And thus, in a miserable way, were the instructions to Elijah recorded in 1 Ki. 19:15ff beginning to be fulfilled ("anoint Hazael ... anoint Jehu ... Jehu will put to death any who escape the sword of Hazael"). Alas, we will soon see bloodshed in the land of Israel at the hand of Jehu (chs. 9–10) which will make Hazael's deeds fade into relative insignificance. But before we get to that, we have to look at the two accession notices which conclude the present chapter.

8:16–24. *Accession, judgment, and burial notices for Jehoram, king of Judah. Great pains are taken to erect a scaffold of chronological notices concerning the kings of the divided monarchy. Even at the risk of occasional literary confusion, each of the kings of either kingdom is introduced in chronological order, and such is the case here. Jehoram of Judah (not to be confused with Joram of Israel, who was first introduced in 3:1ff) followed Jehoshaphat his father (cf. 1 Ki. 22:41–50) in the Judahite dynasty of David. Atypical of the Judahite accession notices, we find no reference to the queen mother (contrast Ahaziah's notice in v. 26; also Jehoshaphat's notice in 1 Ki. 22:42, etc.), but otherwise, we have the typical formulas: accession notice, with synchronism (vv. 16f; concerning such synchronisms, cf. comments on 1:1), Judahite judgment formula (vv. 18f) bolstered by a brief summary of important events in his reign (vv. 20ff) and concluding burial notice (with a "further reference" notice; cf. discussion on 1:17f).*

8:16–17. Accession formula. There are differences in the accession formulas of Judahite kings and Israelite kings. First, the Judahite formulas usually include the age at accession, whereas

1158, 255	4567	3547	3194	4567	3171	4566.111	3190
n ms, pn	*n ms*	pn	cj, pn	*n ms*	pn	v Qal pf 3ms	pn
בֶּן־אַחְאָב	מֶלֶךְ	יִשְׂרָאֵל	וִיהוֹשָׁפָט	מֶלֶךְ	יְהוּדָה	מָלַךְ	יְהוֹרָם
ben-'ach'āv	melekh	yisrā'ēl	wîhôshāphāṭ	melekh	yehûdhāh	mālakh	yehôrām
the son of Ahab	the king of	Israel	and Jehoshaphat	the king of	Judah	he reigned	Jehoram

1158, 3194	4567	3171		1158, 8421	8692	8523	2030.111
n ms, pn	*n ms*	pn		*n ms*, num	cj, num	n fs	v Qal pf 3ms
בֶּן־יְהוֹשָׁפָט	מֶלֶךְ	יְהוּדָה	**17.**	בֶּן־שְׁלֹשִׁים	וּשְׁתַּיִם	שָׁנָה	הָיָה
ben-yehôshāphāṭ	melekh	yehûdhāh		ben-sheloshîm	ûshettayim	shānāh	hāyāh
the son of Jehoshaphat	the king of	Judah		a son of thirty	and two	years	he was

904, 4566.141	8470	8523	4566.111	904, 3503		2050.121
prep, v Qal inf con, ps 3ms	cj, num	n fs	v Qal pf 3ms	prep, pn		cj, v Qal impf 3ms
בְמָלְכוֹ	וּשְׁמֹנֶה	שָׁנָה	מָלַךְ	בִּירוּשָׁלָם	**18.**	וַיֵּלֶךְ
vemālekhô	ûshemōneh	shānāh	mālakh	bîrûshālām		wayyēlekh
when his reigning	and eight	years	he reigned	in Jerusalem		and he walked

904, 1932	4567	3547	3626, 866	6449.116	1041	255	3706
prep, *n ms*	*n mp*	pn	prep, rel part	v Qal pf 3cp	*n ms*	pn	cj
בְּדֶרֶךְ	מַלְכֵי	יִשְׂרָאֵל	כַּאֲשֶׁר	עָשׂוּ	בֵּית	אַחְאָב	כִּי
bedherekh	malkhê	yisrā'ēl	ka'ăsher	'āsû	bêth	'ach'āv	kî
in the way of	the kings of	Israel	just as	they had done	the household of	Ahab	because

1351, 255	2030.112, 3937	3937, 828	6449.121	7737	904, 6084
n fs, pn	v Qal pf 3fs, prep, ps 3ms	prep, n fs	cj, v Qal impf 3ms	art, adj	prep, *n fd*
בַּת־אַחְאָב	הָיְתָה־לּוֹ	לְאִשָּׁה	וַיַּעַשׂ	הָרַע	בְּעֵינֵי
bath-'ach'āv	hāyethāh-lô	le'ishshāh	wayya'as	hāra'	be'ênê
the daughter of Ahab	she was to him	for a wife	and he did	what is evil	in the eyes of

3176		3940, 13.111	3176	8271.541	881, 3171	3937, 4775
pn		cj, neg part, v Qal pf 3ms	pn	prep, v Hiphil inf con	do, pn	prep, prep
יְהוָה	**19.**	וְלֹא־אָבָה	יְהוָה	לְהַשְׁחִית	אֶת־יְהוּדָה	לְמַעַן
yehwāh		welō'-'āvāh	yehwāh	lehashchîth	'eth-yehûdhāh	lema'an
Yahweh		but He was not willing	Yahweh	to destroy	Judah	on account of

1784	5860	3626, 866	569.111, 3937	3937, 5598.141	3937	5402
pn	n ms, ps 3ms	prep, rel part	v Qal pf 3ms, prep, ps 3ms	prep, v Qal inf con	prep, ps 3ms	n ms
דָּוִד	עַבְדּוֹ	כַּאֲשֶׁר	אָמַר־לוֹ	לָתֵת	לוֹ	נִיר
dāwidh	'avdô	ka'ăsher	'āmar-lô	lāthēth	lô	nîr
David	his servant	just as	He said to him	to give	to him	a lamp

3937, 1158	3725, 3219		904, 3219	6839.111	110	4623, 8809
prep, n mp, ps 3ms	*adj*, art, n mp		prep, n mp, ps 3ms	v Qal pf 3ms	pn	prep, prep
לְבָנָיו	כָּל־הַיָּמִים	**20.**	בְּיָמָיו	פָּשַׁע	אֱדוֹם	מִתַּחַת
levānâv	kol-hayyāmîm		beyāmâv	pāsha'	'ĕdhôm	mittachath
for his sons	all the days		in his days	they revolted	Edom	from under

3135, 3171	4566.526	6142	4567		5882.121	3245
n fs, pn	cj, v Hiphil impf 3mp	prep, ps 3mp	n ms		cj, v Qal impf 3ms	pn
יַד־יְהוּדָה	וַיַּמְלִכוּ	עֲלֵיהֶם	מֶלֶךְ	**21.**	וַיַּעֲבֹר	יוֹרָם
yadh-yehûdhāh	wayyamlikhû	'ălêhem	melekh		wayya'ăvōr	yôrām
the hand of Judah	and they caused to reign	over them	a king		and he passed over	Joram

7088	3725, 7681	6196	2030.121, 2000	7251.111	4050
pn	cj, *adj*, art, n ms	prep, ps 3ms	cj, v Qal impf 3ms, pers pron	v Qal pf 3ms	n ms
צָעִירָה	וְכָל־הָרֶכֶב	עִמּוֹ	וַיְהִי־הוּא	קָם	לַיְלָה
tsā'îrāh	wekhol-hārekhev	'immô	wayhî-hû'	qām	laylāh
to Zair	and all the chariots	with him	and it was he	he rose up	at night

Jehoshaphat became king of Judah, *NCV* ... Joram, Achab's son, king of Israel (and Josaphat, king of Juda), that Josaphat's son Joram became king, *Knox* ... began to reign over Judah in conjunction with Jehoshafat, as kings of Judah, *Fenton* ... Joram was the son of Ahab, *NLT*.

17. Thirty and two years old was he when he began to reign; and he reigned eight years in Jerusalem: ... He was thirty-two years old when he became king, *RSV* ... when he came to the throne, *JB* ... he was ruling in Jerusalem for eight years, *BB* ... when he started to rule, *Beck*.

18. And he walked in the way of the kings of Israel, as did the house of Ahab: ... He lived on the lines of the kings of Israel, following the dynasty of Ahab, *Moffatt*.

for the daughter of Ahab was his wife: and he did evil in the sight of the LORD: ... since the sister of Ahab was his wife, *NAB* ... he had married a daughter of Achab's. So he defied the Lord's will, *Knox* ... did the thing that was wicked in the eyes of Yahweh, *Rotherham* ... he did that displeased the Lord, *Tyndale*.

19. Yet the LORD would not destroy Judah for David his servant's sake: ... it was not the Lord's purpose to send destruction on Judah, *BB*.

as he promised him to give him always a light, and to his children: ... to give him always a lamp for his sons, *Darby* ... would leave him a lamp in the LORD's presence for all time, *NAB* ... promised that one of David's descendants would always rule, *NCV*.

20. In his days Edom revolted from under the hand of Judah, and made a king over themselves: ... revolted against the rule of Judah, and set up a king of their own, *NRSV*

---

the Israelite formulas never do; and second, the Israelite formulas consistently place the length of the king's reign at the end of each notice, while the Judahite formulas never do (this last detail is somewhat obscured in the more idiomatic English translations such as the NIV and the NLT, which rework the Hebrew word order for the sake of smoothness and clarity). Thus we find both in the Hebrew original of the present passage (vv. 16f), as well as of the next (vv. 25f), the words "in Jerusalem" following the regnal total of "eight years," and "one year," respectively.

8:18–19. Judgment notice. In contrast to the Israelite notices with the oft-repeated reference to the sins of Jeroboam son of Nebat, a number of the Judahite formulas condemn, as here, those Judahite kings who "walked in the way of the kings of Israel" (cf. Ahaz in 16:3; also, with some variation in the wording, Ahaziah in v. 27). Others, especially the later formulas, condemn kings who were "following the detestable ways of the nations Yahweh had driven out before the Israelites" (again Ahaz, in 16:3; also Manasseh, in 21:2) or who acted wickedly "just as their father[s] had done" (cf. Abijam in 1 Ki. 15:3; also Amon in 2 Ki. 21:20; as well as all the kings who followed Josiah—Jehoahaz [23:32]; Jehoiakim [23:37]; Jehoiachin [24:9]; and finally Zedekiah [24:19]). But, again in clear contrast to the nearly universal condemnation of the Israelite kings, a significant number of the Judahite kings (but, alas, neither Jehoram nor Ahaziah in the present chapter) received praise (cf. Asa in 1 Ki. 15:11; also, Jehoshaphat [with some reservations, 22:43]; Jehoash [2 Ki. 12:2]; Amaziah [14:3, but with serious reservations]; Azariah [or Uzziah; 15:3]; Jotham [15:34]; Hezekiah [18:3; cf. v. 5]; and finally, Josiah [22:2; cf. 23:25]). In the present text, the "daughter of Ahab" whom Jehoram of Judah married (v. 18) was none other than the infamous Athaliah (cf. v. 26; Athaliah, of course, is the villainous queen-[grand]mother of ch. 11).

The reference to the "lamp" (nîr, (HED #5402) "for David and his sons" in v. 19 is again a theme of 1 and 2 Kings (cf. 1 Ki. 11:36; 15:4). Although translations such as "yoke" or "dominion" or the like have been suggested for the Hebrew term, probably the traditional translation "lamp" should be retained (cf. Cogan and Tadmor, AB, 95). In any case, the overall meaning is clear enough—despite the failings of the current Davidic king, Yahweh would remain faithful to his original covenant with David (cf. 2 Sam. 7). Cogan and Tadmor would see the "promise of a remnant" in these Davidic prophecies of hope, and Wiseman (TOTC, 138, in reference to 1 Ki. 11:36) would see the "lamp" as symbolic of continuing life, continuous succession, and (especially in reference to 1 Ki. 15:4), divine guidance (note also that in the two references in 1 Kings, the city of Jerusalem is also prominently featured). Such repeated references to the Davidic hope must have been a source of considerable encouragement for the audience after the debacle of 586 (the Babylonian destruction of Jerusalem and the Solomonic temple). Exilic and post-exilic references to Davidides such as Sheshbazzar and Zerubbabel (cf. Ezra 1:8, 11; 3:8; Hag. 2:2–5, 23; Zech. 4:6–10; etc.) as chosen by Yahweh and prominent in the Judahite community would also confirm this impression.

8:20–22. Summary statements concerning revolt in Edom and Libnah. As suggested earlier,

5409.521	881, 110	5621.151	420	881	8015
cj, v Hiphil impf 3ms	do, pn	art, v Qal act ptc ms	prep, ps 3ms	cj, do	*n mp*
וַיַּכֶּה	אֶת־אֱדוֹם	הַסֹּבֵיב	אֵלָיו	וְאֵת	שָׂרֵי
wayyakkeh	'eth-'ĕdhôm	hassōvêv	'ēlâv	we'ēth	sārê
and he struck down	Edom	those surrounding	to it	and	the commanders of

7681	5308.121	6194	3937, 164	22.	6839.121	110
art, n ms	cj, v Qal impf 3ms	art, n ms	prep, n mp, ps 3ms		cj, v Qal impf 3ms	pn
הָרֶכֶב	וַיָּנָס	הָעָם	לְאֹהָלָיו		וַיִּפְשַׁע	אֱדוֹם
hārekhev	wayyānās	hā'ām	le'ōhālâv		wayyiphsha'	'ĕdhôm
the chariots	and they fled	the people	to their tents		and they revolted	Edom

4623, 8809	3135, 3171	5912	3219	2172	226	6839.122	3975	904, 6496
prep, prep	*n fs*, pn	adv	art, n ms	art, dem pron	adv	v Qal impf 3fs	pn	prep, art, n fs
מִתַּחַת	יַד־יְהוּדָה	עַד	הַיּוֹם	הַזֶּה	אָז	תִּפְשַׁע	לִבְנָה	בָּעֵת
mittachath	yadh-yehûdhāh	'adh	hayyôm	hazzeh	'āz	tiphsha'	livnāh	bā'ēth
from under	the hand of Judah	until	the day	the this	then	they revolted	Libnah	at the time

2026	23.	3615	1745	3245	3725, 866	6449.111
art, dem pron		cj, *n ms*	*n mp*	pn	cj, *adj*, rel part	v Qal pf 3ms
הַהִיא		וְיֶתֶר	דִּבְרֵי	יוֹרָם	וְכָל־אֲשֶׁר	עָשָׂה
hahî'		weyether	divrê	yôrām	wekhol-'ăsher	'āsāh
the that		and the remainder of	the events of	Joram	and all which	he did

1950B, 3940, 2062	3918.156	6142, 5809	1745	3219	3937, 4567
intrg part, neg part, pers pron	v Qal pass ptc mp	prep, *n ms*	*n mp*	art, n mp	prep, *n mp*
הֲלוֹא־הֵם	כְּתוּבִים	עַל־סֵפֶר	דִּבְרֵי	הַיָּמִים	לְמַלְכֵי
hălô'-hēm	kethûvîm	'al-sēpher	divrê	hayyāmîm	lemalkhê
are they not	things written	on the scroll of	the events of	the days	of the kings of

3171	24.	8311.121	3245	6196, 1	7196.221	6196, 1
pn		cj, v Qal impf 3ms	pn	prep, n mp, ps 3ms	cj, v Niphil impf 3ms	prep, n mp, ps 3ms
יְהוּדָה		וַיִּשְׁכַּב	יוֹרָם	עִם־אֲבֹתָיו	וַיִּקָּבֵר	עִם־אֲבֹתָיו
yehûdhāh		wayyishkav	yôrām	'im-'ăvōthâv	wayyiqqāvēr	'im-'ăvōthâv
Judah		and he lay	Joram	with his ancestors	and he was buried	with his ancestors

904, 6111	1784	4566.121	275	1158	8809	25.	904, 8523
prep, *n fs*	pn	cj, v Qal impf 3ms	pn	n ms, ps 3ms	prep, ps 3ms		prep, *n fs*
בְּעִיר	דָּוִד	וַיִּמְלֹךְ	אֲחַזְיָהוּ	בְּנוֹ	תַּחְתָּיו		בִּשְׁנַת
be'îr	dāwidh	wayyimlōkh	'ăchazyāhû	venô	tachtâv		bishnath
in the city of	David	and he reigned	Ahaziah	his son	instead of him		in the year of

8692, 6462	8523	3937, 3245	1158, 255	4567	3547	4566.111	275
num, num	n fs	prep, pn	*n ms*, pn	*n ms*	pn	v Qal pf 3ms	pn
שְׁתֵּים־עֶשְׂרֵה	שָׁנָה	לְיוֹרָם	בֶּן־אַחְאָב	מֶלֶךְ	יִשְׂרָאֵל	מָלַךְ	אֲחַזְיָהוּ
shettêm-'esrēh	shānāh	leyōrām	ben-'ach'āv	melekh	yisrā'ēl	mālakh	'ăchazyāhû
twelve	years	of Joram	the son of Ahab	the king of	Israel	he reigned	Ahaziah

1158, 3190	4567	3171	26.	1158, 6465	8692	8523	275
n ms, pn	*n ms*	pn		*n ms*, num	cj, num	n fs	pn
בֶּן־יְהוֹרָם	מֶלֶךְ	יְהוּדָה		בֶּן־עֶשְׂרִים	וּשְׁתַּיִם	שָׁנָה	אֲחַזְיָהוּ
ven-yehôrām	melekh	yehûdhāh		ben-'esrîm	ûshettayim	shānāh	'ăchazyāhû
the son of Jehoram	the king of	Judah		a son of twenty	and two	years	Ahaziah

904, 4566.141	8523	259	4566.111	904, 3503	8428	525
prep, v Qal inf con, ps 3ms	cj, n fs	num	v Qal pf 3ms	prep, pn	cj, *n ms*	n fs, ps 3ms
בְּמָלְכוֹ	וְשָׁנָה	אַחַת	מָלַךְ	בִּירוּשָׁלִָם	וְשֵׁם	אִמּוֹ
vemālekhô	weshānāh	'achath	mālakh	bîrûshālām	weshēm	'immô
when his reigning	and a year	one	he reigned	in Jerusalem	and the name of	his mother

... the Edomites renounced their allegiance to Juda and set up a king of their own choice, *Knox* ... Edom rebelled against the authority of Judah, *Anchor* ... threw off the domination of Judah, *JB*.

21. So Joram went over to Zair, and all the chariots with him: ... Joram with all his chariots pushed on to Zair, *REB*.

and he rose by night, and smote the Edomites which compassed him about, and the captains of the chariots: ... the Edomites with the captains of their chariots surrounded him, *Beck* ... broke through the Edomites who had surrounded him, *Goodspeed* ... destroyed the Edomites around him together with their chariot officers, *Berkeley*.

and the people fled into their tents: ... his army, however, fled back home, *NIV*.

22. Yet Edom revolted from under the hand of Judah unto this day. Then Libnah revolted at the same time: ... So Edom has remained independent of Judah, *NEB* ... Thus Edom has been in revolt against Judah's authority, *NKJV* ... Edom made themselves free from the rule of Judah, *BB* ... Edom threw off the domination of Judah, remaining free to the present day, *JB*.

23. And the rest of the acts of Joram, and all that he did, are they not written in the book of the chronicles of the kings of Judah?: ... the annals of the kings, *NIV* ... the History of the Kings of Judah, *NLT* ... the words of the days of the kings of Juda, *Douay* ... the history of events in the days of the kings, *Fenton*.

24. And Joram slept with his fathers, and was buried with his fathers in the city of David: ... Jehoram died and was buried in the royal tombs, *Good News* ... he was laid to rest with his father, and shared their burying-place in the Keep of David, *Knox*.

and Ahaziah his son reigned in his stead: ... Ahaziah became king in his place, *Berkeley* ... Ahaziah his son succeeded him, *Anchor*.

25. In the twelfth year of Joram the son of Ahab king of Israel did Ahaziah the son of Jehoram king of Judah begin to reign: ... son of Joram, king of Judah, started to rule, *Beck* ... Ochozias son of Joram king of Juda, *Douay* ... Ahaziah son of Jehoram became king of Judah during the twelfth year Joram son of Ahab was king of Israel, *NCV*.

26. Two and twenty years old was Ahaziah when he began to reign; and he reigned one year in Jerusalem: ... when he came to the throne, *Knox* ... when he became king, and he was ruling in Jerusalem, *BB*.

And his mother's name was Athaliah, the daughter of Omri king of Israel: ... a granddaughter of Omri king of Israel, *NCV* ... the daughter of King Ahab and granddaughter of King Omri of Israel, *Good News*.

---

this additional material was intended to bolster his perspective of the "evil" of King Jehoram in the eyes of Yahweh—note how ignominious was his military campaign against the nation of Edom (who, previously, had no king [1 Ki. 22:47]; Cogan and Tadmor, AB, 97, point out that Edom may well have been emboldened in her revolt by the example of Moab [2 Ki. 3]). Also, the insurrection at Libnah (v. 22), located as it is on the Philistine border, may hint at monarchical instability. As Hobbs (WBC, 106) points out, the writer takes pains here to show how the sins of the house of Omri now influence the southern as well as the northern kingdom: "Israelite and Judean power continues to be whittled away."

8:23–24. Concluding burial notice. As is typically the case for most of the kings of either kingdom, a "further reference" notice concludes the discussion of the king's reign, just before the stereotypical burial notice (once again, cf. discussion on 17f, above, concerning these "further reference" notices). For the Judahite kings, burial in the city of Jerusalem (occasionally, for the later kings, with further details of the tomb's location) is mentioned for sixteen out of the twenty-one kings from David to the exile (curiously, Hezekiah's burial location is not specified in 2 Kings; cf. 2 Ki. 20:21; 2 Chr. 32:33 which has him buried in Jerusalem; Jehoahaz died in Egypt; Jehoiakim's burial location is not specified in the Masoretic text; and Jehoiachin and Zedekiah, of course, eventually died in Babylonian captivity).

8:25–29. Accession and judgment notices for Ahaziah king of Judah. Akin to the previous section, we find brief notices concerning the next king of Judah, once again with judgment predominating. Ahaziah's accession formula comprises vv. 25f; and a judgment notice is found in v. 27, with a brief summary of the occasion which led up to the end of his very short reign in vv. 28f (which in turn are largely repeated in 9:14ff). For the continuing story of Ahaziah's death and burial, one must continue down to 9:27f.

This time, the Judahite accession formula includes a reference to the queen mother, the infamous Athaliah (contrast, vv. 16f). Only four of the total of twenty-one Judahite kings from David to

6510	1351, 6245	4567	3547		2050.121	904, 1932
pn	n fs, pn	n ms	pn		cj, v Qal impf 3ms	prep, n ms
עֲתַלְיָהוּ	בַּת־עָמְרִי	מֶלֶךְ	יִשְׂרָאֵל	**27.**	וַיֵּלֶךְ	בְּדֶרֶךְ
‘ăthalyāhû	bath-‘omrî	melekh	yisrā’ēl		wayyēlekh	bedherekh
Athaliah	the daughter of Omri	the king of	Israel		and he walked	in the way of

1041	255	6449.121	7737	904, 6084	3176
n ms	pn	cj, v Qal impf 3ms	art, adj	prep, n fd	pn
בֵּית	אַחְאָב	וַיַּעַשׂ	הָרַע	בְּעֵינֵי	יְהוָה
bêth	'ach'āv	wayya‘as	hāra‘	be‘ênê	yehwāh
the household of	Ahab	and he did	what is evil	in the eyes of	Yahweh

3626, 1041	255	3706	2968	1041, 255	2000
prep, n ms	pn	cj	n ms	n ms, pn	pers pron
כְּבֵית	אַחְאָב	כִּי	חֲתַן	בֵּית־אַחְאָב	הוּא
kevêth	'ach'āv	kî	chăthan	bêth-'ach'āv	hû'
like the household of	Ahab	because	the son-in-law of	the household of Ahab	he

	2050.121	882, 3245	1158, 255	3937, 4560	6196, 2462	4567, 782
	cj, v Qal impf 3ms	prep, pn	n ms, pn	prep, art, n fs	prep, pn	n ms, pn
28.	וַיֵּלֶךְ	אֶת־יוֹרָם	בֶּן־אַחְאָב	לַמִּלְחָמָה	עִם־חֲזָהאֵל	מֶלֶךְ־אֲרָם
	wayyēlekh	'eth-yôrām	ben-'ach'āv	lammilchāmāh	‘im-chăzāh'ēl	melekh-'ărām
	and he went	with Joram	the son of Ahab	for the war	with Hazael	the king of Aram

904, 7721	7721	5409.526	782	881, 3245		8178.121	3245
prep, pn	pn	cj, v Hiphil impf 3mp	pn	do, pn		cj, v Qal impf 3ms	pn
בְּרָמֹת	גִּלְעָד	וַיַּכּוּ	אֲרַמִּים	אֶת־יוֹרָם	**29.**	וַיָּשָׁב	יוֹרָם
berāmōth	gil‘ādh	wayyakkû	'ărammîm	'eth-yôrām		wayyāshāv	yôrām
in Ramoth	Gilead	and they struck	the Arameans	Joram		then he returned	Joram

4567	3937, 7784.741	904, 3262	4623, 4485	866	5409.526
art, n ms	prep, v Hithpael inf con	prep, pn	prep, art, n mp	rel part	v Hiphil impf 3mp, ps 3ms
הַמֶּלֶךְ	לְהִתְרַפֵּא	בְּיִזְרְעֶאל	מִן־הַמַּכִּים	אֲשֶׁר	יַכֻּהוּ
hammelekh	lehithrappē'	veyizre'e'l	min-hammakkîm	'ăsher	yakkuhû
the king	to be healed	in Jezreel	from the wounds	which	they had struck him

782	904, 7703	904, 4032.241	882, 2462	4567	782	275
pn	prep, art, pn	prep, v Niphal inf con, ps 3ms	prep, pn	n ms	pn	cj, pn
אֲרַמִּים	בָּרָמָה	בְּהִלָּחֲמוֹ	אֶת־חֲזָהאֵל	מֶלֶךְ	אֲרָם	וַאֲחַזְיָהוּ
'ărammîm	bārāmāh	behillāchămô	'eth-chăzāh'ēl	melekh	'ărām	wa'ăchazyāhû
the Arameans	in Ramah	when his fighting	with Hazael	the king of	Aram	and Ahaziah

1158, 3190	4567	3171	3495.111	3937, 7495.141	881, 3245
n ms, pn	n ms	pn	v Qal pf 3ms	prep, v Qal inf con	do, pn
בֶּן־יְהוֹרָם	מֶלֶךְ	יְהוּדָה	יָרַד	לִרְאוֹת	אֶת־יוֹרָם
ven-yehôrām	melekh	yehûdhāh	yāradh	lir'ôth	'eth-yôrām
the son of Jehoram	the king of	Judah	he went down	to see	Joram

1158, 255	904, 3262	3706, 2571.151	2000		482	5204	7410.111
n ms, pn	prep, pn	cj, v Qal act ptc ms	pers pron		cj, pn	art, n ms	v Qal pf 3ms
בֶּן־אַחְאָב	בְּיִזְרְעֶאל	כִּי־חֹלֶה	הוּא	**9:1**	וֶאֱלִישָׁע	הַנָּבִיא	קָרָא
ben-'ach'āv	beyizre'e'l	kî-chōleh	hû'		we'ĕlîshā‘	hannāvî'	qārā'
the son of Ahab	in Jezreel	because sick	he		and Elisha	the prophet	he called

3937, 259	4623, 1158	5204	569.121	3937	2391.131	5158
cj, num	prep, n mp	art, n mp	cj, v Qal impf 3ms	prep, ps 3ms	v Qal impv 2ms	n md, ps 2ms
לְאַחַד	מִבְּנֵי	הַנְּבִיאִים	וַיֹּאמֶר	לוֹ	חֲגֹר	מָתְנֶיךָ
le'achadh	mibbenê	hannevî'îm	wayyō'mer	lô	chăghōr	māthenêkhā
to one	from the sons of	the prophets	and he said	to him	gird	your loins

27. And he walked in the way of the house of Ahab, and did evil in the sight of the LORD, as did the house of Ahab: ... He lived on the lines of the dynasty of Ahab, *Moffatt* ... and did the thing that was wicked in the eyes of Yahweh, *Rotherham* ... did what was displeasing, *Anchor*.

for he was the son-in-law of the house of Ahab: ... he was related to them by marriage, *NAB* ... he had married a wife of that family, *Moffatt*.

28. And he went with Joram the son of Ahab to the war against Hazael king of Syria in Ramoth-gilead: ... he went to fight against Hazael, *Knox* ... King Joram returned to be cured, *Fenton*.

and the Syrians wounded Joram: ... The Arameans, *NCV* ... but the Aramaeans wounded Jehoram, *JB* ... When King Joram was wounded in the battle, *NLT*.

29. And king Joram went back to be healed in Jezreel of the wounds which the Syrians had given him at Ramah, when he fought against Hazael king of Syria: ... the Syrians had given him in Ra-mah, *KJVII* ... that the Arameans had inflicted on him, *NRSV* ... from the wounds which the bowmen had given him, *BB*.

And Ahaziah the son of Jehoram king of Judah went down to see Joram the son of Ahab in Jezreel, because he was sick: ... down to Jezreel to visit him there in his illness, *NAB*.

9:1. And Elisha the prophet called one of the children of the prophets, and said unto him, Gird up thy loins, and take this box of oil in thine hand, and go to Ramoth-gilead: ... Get yourself ready, and take this flask of oil with you, *Anchor* ... take this vial of oil in thy hand, *ASV* ... Fasten your belt around your waist, and take this flask of olive oil with you, *Beck* ... Tuck your cloak into your belt, take this flask of oil with you and go, *NIV*.

2. And when thou comest thither, look out there Jehu the son of

---

the exile lack references to the queen mother in their accession formulas (David, Solomon, Jehoram and Ahaz). Another synchronism between King Ahaziah of Judah and King Joram of Israel may be found in 9:29, but there the Hebrew text reads "the eleventh year," instead of the "twelfth" year as here.

The judgment notice (v. 27) is similar (but not identical) to that of Jehoram, yet again the "house of Ahab" is largely to blame for Ahaziah's brief and disastrous reign (the name "Ahab" appears some three times in this single verse in the Masoretic text).

The present passage concludes with a brief summary of Ahaziah's alliance with King Joram of Israel against King Hazael of Aram. Joram was wounded at Ramoth Gilead (cf. the similar fate of King Ahab in 1 Ki. 22:29–38), and Ahaziah, whose wife was Ahab's daughter, went to see the wounded king in his winter palace in Jezreel. (The city of Jezreel, located in the valley of that name, would have been a logical site for Ahab's winter palace [cf. 1 Ki. 21:1] because of the warmer winter weather in the valley; the hill of Samaria, with its cooling breezes, would, however, have been considerably more comfortable in the summertime.) Thus ends ch. 8, with King Ahaziah of Judah visiting Israel. The writer, however, with his "literary bridge" between the end of this chapter and the middle of the lengthy Jehu narrative in the next two chapters (i.e., the close literary parallels between 8:28f and 9:14ff), clearly expects the reader to continue to learn about the circumstances leading to Ahaziah's quick demise at the hands of none other than the usurper Jehu, the scourge of the Omride dynasty, and the instrument of the sovereign will of Yahweh.

9:1–10:36. *Jehu anointed and acclaimed as king over Israel: Judgment on the house of Omri and on the worshipers of Baal. In sharp contrast to the four short sections of ch. 8, the present lengthy narrative encompasses the entirety of the next two chapters, and its importance to the history of Israel (and Judah) is commensurate to its length. For here, finally we have Yahweh's judgment on the house of Omri, and it proves to be a fierce and bloody judgment. The words of Elijah the prophet, particularly concerning Jezebel, cry out for fulfillment, and the reader can only agonize as that wicked woman still escapes judgment. But by the end of ch. 9, the woman is dead, and just as Elijah had prophesied, "Dogs devoured Jezebel's flesh." A further prophecy of Elijah was explicitly fulfilled when the rest of Ahab's family met their death as well (cf. 10:10, 17). Indeed, after all this bloodshed, Yahweh's words to Jehu are startling, "You have done well in accomplishing what is right in my eyes and have done to the house of Ahab all I had in mind to do. ..." (v. 30). Who is this Jehu, who executes so fiercely the will of God? This, and other related issues, will now be addressed.*

9:1–13. Jehu anointed to be king over Israel. This passage represents the completion of Yahweh's commission to Elijah given in 1 Ki. 19:15–18. Once again, emphasis on the fearsome fulfillment of Elijah's prophecies of judgment is a mark of the Jehu narrative. Both explicit (9:36f; 10:10, 17) and

4089.131	6620	8467	2172	904, 3135	2050.131	7721
cj, v Qal impv 2ms	*n ms*	art, n ms	art, dem pron	prep, n fs, ps 2ms	cj, v Qal impv 2ms	pn
וְקַח	פַּךְ	הַשֶּׁמֶן	הַזֶּה	בְּיָדֶךָ	וְלֵךְ	רָמֹת
weqach	pakh	hashshemen	hazzeh	beyādhekhā	welēkh	rāmōth
and take	a jug of	the olive oil	the this	in your hands	and go to	Ramoth

7721	2.	971.113	8427	7495.131, 8427	3167	1158, 3194
pn		cj, v Qal pf 2ms	adv	cj, v Qal impv 2ms, adv	pn	*n ms*, pn
גִּלְעָד		וּבָאתָ	שָׁמָּה	וּרְאֵה־שָׁם	יֵהוּא	בֶּן־יְהוֹשָׁפָט
gil'ādh		ûvā'thā	shāmmāh	ûre'ēh-shām	yēhû'	ven-yehôshāphāṭ
Gilead		and you will go	to there	and you will see there	Jehu	the son of Jehoshaphat

1158, 5437	971.113	7251.513	4623, 8761	250
n ms, pn	cj, v Qal pf 2ms	cj, v Hiphil pf 2ms, ps 3ms	prep, *n ms*	n mp, ps 3ms
בֶּן־נִמְשִׁי	וּבָאתָ	וַהֲקֵמֹתוֹ	מִתּוֹךְ	אֶחָיו
ben-nimshî	ûvā'thā	wahqēmōthô	mittôkh	'echâv
the son of Nimshi	and you will go	and you will cause him to rise	from the midst of	his brothers

971.513	881	2410	904, 2410	3.	4089.113
cj, v Hiphil pf 2ms	do, ps 3ms	n ms	prep, n ms		cj, v Qal pf 2ms
וְהֵבֵיאתָ	אֹתוֹ	חֶדֶר	בְּחָדֶר		וְלָקַחְתָּ
wehēvê'thā	'ōthô	chedher	bechādher		welāqachtā
and you will cause to enter	him	an inner room	within an inner room		and you must take

6620, 8467	3441.113	6142, 7513	569.113	3662, 569.111
n ms, art, n ms	cj, v Qal pf 2ms	prep, n ms, ps 3ms	cj, v Qal pf 2ms	adv, v Qal pf 3ms
פַּךְ־הַשֶּׁמֶן	וְיָצַקְתָּ	עַל־רֹאשׁוֹ	וְאָמַרְתָּ	כֹּה־אָמַר
phakh-hashshemen	weyātsaqōttā	'al-rō'shô	we'āmartā	kōh-'āmar
a jug of the olive oil	and you will pour out	on his head	and you will say	thus He has said

3176	5066.115	3937, 4567	420, 3547	6858.113	1878
pn	v Qal pf 1cs, ps 2ms	prep, n ms	prep, pn	cj, v Qal pf 2ms	art, n fs
יְהוָה	מְשַׁחְתִּיךָ	לְמֶלֶךְ	אֶל־יִשְׂרָאֵל	וּפָתַחְתָּ	הַדֶּלֶת
yehwāh	meshachtîkhā	lemelekh	'el-yisrā'ēl	ûphāthachtā	haddeleth
Yahweh	I have anointed you	a king	to Israel	then you will open	the door

5308.113	3940	2542.323	4.	2050.121	5470	5470
cj, v Qal pf 2ms	cj, neg part	v Piel impf 2ms		cj, v Qal impf 3ms	art, n ms	art, *n ms*
וְנַסְתָּה	וְלֹא	תְחַכֶּה		וַיֵּלֶךְ	הַנַּעַר	הַנַּעַר
wenastāh	welō'	thechakkeh		wayyēlekh	hanna'ar	hanna'ar
and you will flee	and not	you will wait		and he went to	the servant	the servant of

5204	7721	7721	5.	971.121	2079	8015	2524
art, n ms	pn	pn		cj, v Qal impf 3ms	cj, intrj	*n mp*	art, n ms
הַנָּבִיא	רָמֹת	גִּלְעָד		וַיָּבֹא	וְהִנֵּה	שָׂרֵי	הַחַיִל
hannāvî'	rāmōth	gil'ādh		wayyāvō'	wehinnēh	sārê	hachayil
the prophet	Ramoth	Gilead		and he entered	and behold	the commanders of	the army

3553.152	569.121	1745	3937	420	8015	569.121
v Qal act ptc mp	cj, v Qal impf 3ms	n ms	prep, ps 1cs	prep, ps 2ms	art, n ms	cj, v Qal impf 3ms
יֹשְׁבִים	וַיֹּאמֶר	דָּבָר	לִי	אֵלֶיךָ	הַשָּׂר	וַיֹּאמֶר
yōshevîm	wayyō'mer	dāvār	lî	'ēlêkhā	hassār	wayyō'mer
sitting	and he said	a word	to me	to you	the commander	and he said

3167	420, 4449	4623, 3725	569.121	420	8015	6.	7251.121
pn	prep, intrg	prep, adj, ps 1cp	cj, v Qal impf 3ms	prep, ps 2ms	art, n ms		cj, v Qal impf 3ms
יֵהוּא	אֶל־מִי	מִכֻּלָּנוּ	וַיֹּאמֶר	אֵלֶיךָ	הַשָּׂר		וַיָּקָם
yēhû'	'el-mî	mikkullānû	wayyō'mer	'ēlêkhā	hassār		wayyāqām
Jehu	to whom	among all of us	and he said	to you	the commander		and he rose up

Jehoshaphat the son of Nimshi, and go in, and make him arise up from among his brethren, and carry him to an inner chamber: ... when you arrive at that place, *NKJV* ... and get him to leave his companions, and take him into, *NRSV* ... lead him through to an inner room, *REB* ... take him with you to a private room, *Fenton*.

3. Then take the box of oil, and pour it on his head, and say, Thus saith the LORD, I have anointed thee king over Israel. Then open the door, and flee, and tarry not: ... take the flask and pour the oil on his head and say, This is the word of the LORD: I anoint you king over Israel, *NEB* ... taking the little bottle of oil, thou shalt pour it on his head, *Douay* ... open the door and run; don't delay, *NIV* ... do not linger, *Moffatt*.

4. So the young man, even the young man the prophet, went to Ramoth-gilead: ... the prophet went to, *RSV* ... the attendant, the prophet's attendant, went to, *Anchor* ... the youth, the young Preacher went to, *Fenton*.

5. And when he came, behold, the captains of the host were sitting; and he said, I have an errand to thee, O captain. And Jehu said, Unto which of all us? And he said, To thee, O captain: ... he found the army officers in a conference. He said, Sir, I have a message for you, *Good News* ... the commanders of the army were in session. I have a word for you, O commander, *Goodspeed* ... I have something to say to you, *BB* ... Jehu asked, For which one of us?, *NCV*.

6. And he arose, and went into the house; and he poured the oil on his head, and said unto him, Thus saith the LORD God of Israel, I have anointed thee king over the people of the LORD, even over Israel: ... the two of them went indoors, and the young prophet poured the olive oil on Jehu's head, *Good News* ... Jehu rose up, and went into the inner room; where the prophet forthwith poured the oil over his head, *Knox* ... The Eternal, the God of Israel, hereby declares, I anoint you king over the Eternal's people, over Israel, *Moffatt* ... he arose, and went into the chamber, *Douay*.

---

implicit (9:3, 6–10, 21, 25f) references to his prophecies abound in these two chapters. Even though an unnamed disciple of Elisha, who himself was a disciple of Elijah, actually did the anointing of Jehu, Elijah's own implicit commissioning is felt to be present. (First Kings 9:6–10 is directed mainly at the calamitous events attending the era of Elijah.) Finally, the deaths and persecutions of Yahweh's prophets, and all his servants in the days of Ahab and Jezebel will be avenged (9:7).

"Jehu, son of Omri," is prominently featured on the Black Obelisk of Shalmaneser III as paying tribute to the Assyrian king (also cf. comments on 3:1ff and the references cited there). To be sure, we immediately recognize that the usurper Jehu was hardly a literal descendant of the dynasty of Omri—quite the contrary. But as Cogan and Tadmor note, "It is not possible that the Assyrian scribes were unaware that Jehu had seized the throne in Samaria. Rather they chose to designate Israel by the term ["Omri"] or ["house of Omri"], after Israel's first successful dynast." And Cogan and Tadmor are probably correct to follow M. Weippert's rejection of Kyle McCarter's conjecture that the Assyrians were referring to Joram, not Jehu in these references. Once again, the inglorious event of Jehu paying tribute to the Assyrian king may be closely dated (by the Assyrian records) to the year 841 B.C., which was probably the first year of Jehu's reign.

The double reference in vv. 2, 14 to Jehu's ancestors, "Jehu son of Jehoshaphat, the son of Nimshi" is unusual. Usually only the father's name appears in a patronymic. Perhaps the grandfather was better known in the community. Jehu is elsewhere simply called "son of Nimshi" (1 Ki. 19:16; 2 Ki. 9:20; 2 Chr. 22:7). Alternatively, "Nimshi" may have been a clan name. Hobbs (WBC, 114) suggested that both the names "Jehu" (possibly meaning, "Yahweh is the one") and "Jehoshaphat" (his father's name) reflect the conservative religious circles from which the army commander came. ("Jehoshaphat" is usually understood to mean "Yahweh judges" or "Yahweh has judged," probably in the sense of bringing about justice, punishment, vindication, and the like.)

For the final time, we run into the "sons of the prophets" in the Elisha material. References to the "sons of the prophets" may be found in 2 Ki. 2:3, 5, 7, 15; 4:1, 38; 5:22; 6:1; and here in 9:1. One more reference may be found in 1 Ki. 20:35, but apparently not connected with the prophet. Also cf. Amos 7:14, where Amos says to the Bethelite priest Amaziah that he is "neither a prophet nor the son of a prophet" (but cf. Douglas Stuart's translation [*Hosea-Jonah*, WBC, 376f, "No, I am a prophet though I am not a professional prophet"). In Hobbs' helpful excursus on "the sons of the prophets" (WBC, 25ff), he concludes that, at least in the Elisha accounts, they were the "lay supporters" of the prophet, scattered throughout the country, and some "even assuming the rare function of prophecy" (cf. also comments on 2:1–6). In any case, an anony-

971.121	1041	3441.121	8467	420, 7513	569.121
cj, v Qal impf 3ms	art, n ms	cj, v Qal impf 3ms	art, n ms	prep, n ms, ps 3ms	cj, v Qal impf 3ms
וַיָּבֹא	הַבַּיְתָה	וַיִּצֹק	הַשֶּׁמֶן	אֶל־רֹאשׁוֹ	וַיֹּאמֶר
wayyāvō'	habbaythāh	wayyitsōq	hashshemen	'el-rō'shô	wayyō'mer
and he entered	to the house	and he poured out	the olive oil	to his head	and he said

3937	3662, 569.111	3176	435	3547	5066.115	3937, 4567
prep, ps 3ms	adv, v Qal pf 3ms	pn	*n mp*	pn	v Qal pf 1cs, ps 2ms	prep, n ms
לוֹ	כֹּה־אָמַר	יְהוָה	אֱלֹהֵי	יִשְׂרָאֵל	מְשַׁחְתִּיךָ	לְמֶלֶךְ
lô	kōh-'āmar	y^{e}hwāh	'ĕlōhê	yisrā'ēl	m^{e}shachtîkhā	l^{e}melekh
to him	thus He has said	Yahweh	the God of	Israel	I have anointed you	a king

420, 6194	3176	420, 3547		5409.513	881, 1041	255
prep, *n ms*	pn	prep, pn		cj, v Hiphil pf 2ms	do, *n ms*	pn
אֶל־עַם	יְהוָה	אֶל־יִשְׂרָאֵל	**7.**	וְהִכִּיתָה	אֶת־בֵּית	אַחְאָב
'el-'am	y^{e}hwāh	'el-yisrā'ēl		w^{e}hikkîthāh	'eth-bêth	'ach'āv
to the people of	Yahweh	to Israel		and you will strike down	the household of	Ahab

112	5541.315	1879	5860	5204	1879
n mp, ps 2ms	cj, v Piel pf 1cs	*n mp*	n mp, ps 1cs	art, n mp	cj, *n mp*
אֲדֹנֶיךָ	וְנִקַּמְתִּי	דְּמֵי	עֲבָדַי	הַנְּבִיאִים	וּדְמֵי
'ădhōnêkhā	w^{e}niqqamtî	d^{e}mê	'ăvādhay	hann^{e}vî'îm	ûdh^{e}mê
your master	and I will avenge	the blood of	my servants	the prophets	and the blood of

3725, 5860	3176	4623, 3135	350		6.111	3725, 1041
adj, n mp	pn	prep, *n fs*	pn		cj, v Qal pf 3ms	*adj, n ms*
כָּל־עַבְדֵי	יְהוָה	מִיַּד	אִיזָבֶל	**8.**	וְאָבַד	כָּל־בֵּית
kol-'avdhê	y^{e}hwāh	mîyadh	'îzāvel		w^{e}'āvadh	kol-bêth
all the servants of	Yahweh	from the hand of	Jezebel		and it will perish	all the household of

255	3918.515	3937, 255	8697.551	904, 7306	6352.155	6013.155
pn	cj, v Hiphil pf 1cs	prep, pn	v Hiphil ptc ms	prep, n ms	cj, v Qal pass ptc ms	cj, v Qal pass ptc ms
אַחְאָב	וְהִכְרַתִּי	לְאַחְאָב	מַשְׁתִּין	בְּקִיר	וְעָצוּר	וְעָזוּב
'ach'āv	w^{e}hikhrattî	l^{e}'ach'āv	mashtîn	b^{e}qîr	w^{e}'ātsûr	w^{e}'āzûv
Ahab	and I will cut off	of Ahab	urinating	on a wall	and those bound	and those freed

904, 3547		5598.115	1041	255	3626, 1041	3493
prep, pn		cj, v Qal pf 1cs	*n ms*	pn	prep, *n ms*	pn
בְּיִשְׂרָאֵל	**9.**	וְנָתַתִּי	אֶת־בֵּית	אַחְאָב	כְּבֵית	יָרָבְעָם
b^{e}yisrā'ēl		w^{e}nāthattî	'eth-bêth	'ach'āv	k^{e}vêth	yārov'ām
in Israel		then I will give	the household of	Ahab	like the household of	Jeroboam

1158, 5203	3626, 1041	1225	1158, 282		881, 350
n ms, pn	cj, prep, *n ms*	pn	*n ms*, pn		cj, do, pn
בֶּן־נְבָט	וּכְבֵית	בַּעְשָׁא	בֶּן־אֲחִיָּה	**10.**	וְאֶת־אִיזֶבֶל
ben-n^{e}vāṯ	ûkh^{e}vêth	ba'ăshā'	ven-'ăchîyāh		w^{e}'eth-'îzevel
the son of Nebat	and like the household of	Baasha	the son of Ahijah		and Jezebel

404.126	3732	904, 2610	3262	375	7196.151
v Qal impf 3mp	art, n mp	prep, *n ms*	pn	cj, *sub*	v Qal act ptc ms
יֹאכְלוּ	הַכְּלָבִים	בְּחֵלֶק	יִזְרְעֶאל	וְאֵין	קֹבֵר
yō'kh^{e}lû	hakk^{e}lāvîm	b^{e}chēleq	yizr^{e}'e'l	w^{e}'ên	qōvēr
they will eat	the dogs	on the portion of	Jezreel	and there is not	one who buries

6858.121	1878	5308.121		3167	3428.111	420, 5860	112
cj, v Qal impf 3ms	art, n fs	cj, v Qal impf 3ms		cj, pn	v Qal pf 3ms	prep, *n mp*	n mp, ps 3ms
וַיִּפְתַּח	הַדֶּלֶת	וַיָּנֹס	**11.**	וְיֵהוּא	יָצָא	אֶל־עַבְדֵי	אֲדֹנָיו
wayyiphtach	haddeleth	wayyānōs		w^{e}yēhû'	yātsā'	'el-'avdhê	'ădhōnâv
and he opened	the door	and it fled		and Jehu	he came out	to the servants of	his master

7. And thou shalt smite the house of Ahab thy master, that I may avenge the blood of my servants the prophets, and the blood of all the servants of the LORD, at the hand of Jezebel: ... You must destroy the family of Ahab your master. I will punish Jezebel for the deaths of my servants the prophets and for all the LORD's servants who were murdered, *NCV* ... strike down the house of Ahab your master, and I will take vengeance on Jezebel, *NEB* ... In this way, I will avenge the murder of my prophets and all the LORD's servants who were killed by Jezebel, *NLT* ... see that the family of Ahab your master is cut off, so that I may take from Jezebel payment, *BB*.

8. For the whole house of Ahab shall perish: and I will cut off from Ahab him that pisseth against the wall, and him that is shut up and left in Israel: ... All of Ahab's family will perish, and I will cut down every male coming from Ahab, bound or free, in Israel, *Beck* ... shall be destroyed; I will cut off from Ahab every male, bond and free, *Berkeley* ... All Ahab's race I mean to destroy, sparing no male issue of his, free man or bondman in the realm of Israel, *Knox* ... I will cut off every male in Ahab's line, whether slave or freeman in Israel, *NAB*.

9. And I will make the house of Ahab like the house of Jeroboam the son of Nebat, and like the house of Baasha the son of Ahijah: ... I will make Ahab's family like the family of Jeroboam, *NCV* ... I will destroy the family of Ahab as I destroyed the families of Jeroboam, *NLT*.

10. And the dogs shall eat Jezebel in the portion of Jezreel, and there shall be none to bury her. And he opened the door, and fled: ... in the vicinity of Jezreel, and nobody will bury her. Then he opened the door and ran away, *Beck* ... dogs shall devour Jezebel in the district of Jezreel, *Berkeley* ... Jezebel will never be buried; her body will be eaten by dogs in the territory of Jezreel, *Good News* ... in the field of Jezreel; no one will bury her. With this, he opened the door and made his escape, *JB*.

11. Then Jehu came forth to the servants of his lord: and one said unto him, Is all well? wherefore came this mad fellow to thee? And he said unto them, Ye know the man, and his communication: ... Jehu went outside to the servants of his master, *Anchor* ... why did this man, who is off his head, come to you? And he said to them, You have knowledge of the man and of his talk, *BB* ... Why did this crazy fellow come to you, *Beck* ... Oh you know how a fellow like that talks, *Moffatt*.

---

mous member of this group was commissioned by Elisha to "take this flask of oil with you … look for Jehu … take him into an inner room … pour the oil on his head" (vv. 1ff). As the chapter unfolds, we realize that nothing less than a royal anointing is to take place (once again, so predicted in 1 Ki. 19:16). Jehu is to succeed Joram as king over Israel.

But the "son of the prophet" was to accomplish his task quickly (v. 3), and secretly (v. 2; the "inner room" is literally in Hebrew, "a room within a room"). Perhaps this is yet another example of the "closed door motif" found throughout the Elisha narratives (also cf. v. 10). (For the "closed door motif," cf. above, on 4:1–7.) Wiseman (TOTC, 219) points out that such secrecy would allow Jehu to choose his own time when to go public with the announcement. Also, Babylonian coronation ceremonies took place partly in an inner room, and partly in public in the temple court. In v. 6, the anointing is accomplished. The unnamed prophet then declared that Jehu was anointed "over Yahweh's people Israel" for the purpose of destroying the whole house of Ahab, including "every last male," plus Jezebel (vv. 6–10). Then the prophet fled, apparently as quickly and as quietly as he had come. Obviously, even proper prophetic anointing of a usurper to the throne was most assuredly a dangerous task.

Jehu's fellow officers asked him, "Is everything all right?" (literally, "Is there peace?"). The appearance of a prophet was significant, yet they then labeled him a "madman" (meshuggā', "a crazy one," HED #8154). Especially in the early period, the prophets were known for their wild and peculiar behavior (cf. 1 Sam. 10:6, 10f). The present comments by the soldiers were probably along the lines of tough talk or "locker room" banter among the battle-scarred commanders. "Hey, Jehu, what's up. Why did that crazy prophet come to visit you?"

Jehu responded with a vague demurral: "Oh, it was nothing—you know how those types are." But then, when the officers pressed him further, he blurted out the truth. His comrades responded spontaneously when Jehu told them of the anointing. They took off their cloaks and blew the trumpet and shouted, "Jehu is king!" Such an overwhelming response probably demonstrated that there was unrest even before the appearance of the prophet. Presumably, the spreading of the garments (there are no parallels to this anywhere else in the OT, but cf. the NT references in Matt. 21:8; Mark 11:8; and Luke 19:36 to the crowd's adulation of Christ on Palm Sunday) indicated their recognition of Jehu as king and their loyalty to him. The blowing of the trumpet and the shout of acclamation were regular

569.121	3937	1950B, 8361	4211	971.111, 8154.455	2172
cj, v Qal impf 3ms	prep, ps 3ms	intrg part, n ms	intrg	v Qal pf 3ms, art, v Pual ptc ms	art, dem pron
וַיֹּאמֶר	לוֹ	הֲשָׁלוֹם	מַדּוּעַ	בָּא־הַמְשֻׁגָּע	הַזֶּה
wayyō'mer	lô	hăshālôm	maddûa'	bā'-hamshuggā'	hazzeh
and he said	to him	is peace	why	did the insane man come	the this

420	569.121	420	894	3156.117	881, 382	881, 7945
prep, ps 2ms	cj, v Qal impf 3ms	prep, ps 3mp	pers pron	v Qal pf 2mp	do, art, n ms	cj, do, n ms, ps 3ms
אֵלֶיךָ	וַיֹּאמֶר	אֲלֵיהֶם	אַתֶּם	יְדַעְתֶּם	אֶת־הָאִישׁ	וְאֶת־שִׂיחוֹ
'ēlêkhā	wayyō'mer	'ălêhem	'attem	yedha'ättem	'eth-hā'îsh	we'eth-sîchô
to you	and he said	to them	you	you know	the man	and his talk

12. 569.126	8632	5222.531, 5167	3937	569.121	3626, 2148
cj, v Qal impf 3mp	n ms	v Hiphil impv 2ms, part	prep, ps 1cp	cj, v Qal impf 3ms	prep, dem pron
וַיֹּאמְרוּ	שֶׁקֶר	הַגֶּד־נָא	לָנוּ	וַיֹּאמֶר	כָּזֹאת
wayyō'merû	sheqer	haggedh-nā'	lānû	wayyō'mer	kāzō'th
and they said	a lie	tell please	to us	and he said	like this

3626, 2148	569.111	420	3937, 569.141	3662	569.111	3176
cj, prep, dem pron	v Qal pf 3ms	prep, ps 1cs	prep, v Qal inf con	adv	v Qal pf 3ms	pn
וְכָזֹאת	אָמַר	אֵלַי	לֵאמֹר	כֹּה	אָמַר	יְהוָה
wekhāzō'th	'āmar	'ēlay	lē'mōr	kōh	'āmar	yehwāh
and like that	he said	to me	saying	thus	He has said	Yahweh

5066.115	3937, 4567	420, 3547	13. 4257.326	4089.126	382
v Qal pf 1cs, ps 2ms	n ms	prep, pn	cj, v Piel impf 3mp	cj, v Qal impf 3mp	n ms
מְשַׁחְתִּיךָ	לְמֶלֶךְ	אֶל־יִשְׂרָאֵל	וַיְמַהֲרוּ	וַיִּקְחוּ	אִישׁ
meshachtîkhā	lemelekh	'el-yisrā'ēl	waymahrû	wayyiqŏchû	'îsh
I have anointed you	as king	to Israel	and they hurried	and they took	each

933	7947.126	8809	420, 1678	4765	8965.126
n ms, ps 3ms	cj, v Qal impf 3mp	prep, ps 3ms	prep, *n ms*	art, n fp	cj, v Qal impf 3mp
בִּגְדוֹ	וַיָּשִׂימוּ	תַּחְתָּיו	אֶל־גֶּרֶם	הַמַּעֲלוֹת	וַיִּתְקְעוּ
bighdhô	wayyāsîmû	thachtâv	'el-gerem	hamma'ălôth	wayyithqŏ'û
his garment	and they put	beneath him	to the bone of	the stairs	and they blew

904, 8223	569.126	4566.111	3167	14. 7489.721	3167
prep, art, n ms	cj, v Qal impf 3mp	v Qal pf 3ms	pn	cj, v Hithpael impf 3ms	pn
בַּשּׁוֹפָר	וַיֹּאמְרוּ	מָלַךְ	יֵהוּא	וַיִּתְקַשֵּׁר	יֵהוּא
bashshôphār	wayyō'merû	mālakh	yēhû'	wayyithqashshēr	yēhû'
into the ram's horn	and they said	he is king	Jehu	and he conspired	Jehu

1158, 3194	1158, 5437	420, 3245	3245	2030.111	8490.151
n ms, pn	*n ms*, pn	prep, pn	cj, pn	v Qal pf 3ms	v Qal act ptc ms
בֶּן־יְהוֹשָׁפָט	בֶּן־נִמְשִׁי	אֶל־יוֹרָם	וְיוֹרָם	הָיָה	שֹׁמֵר
ben-yehôshāphāṭ	ben-nimshî	'el-yôrām	weyôrām	hāyāh	shōmēr
the son of Jehoshaphat	the son of Nimshi	against Joram	and Joram	he was	guarding

904, 7721	7721	2000	3725, 3547	4623, 6686	2462	4567, 782
prep, pn	pn	pers pron	cj, *adj*, pn	prep, *n mp*	pn	*n ms*, pn
בְּרָמֹת	גִּלְעָד	הוּא	וְכָל־יִשְׂרָאֵל	מִפְּנֵי	חֲזָאֵל	מֶלֶךְ־אֲרָם
berāmōth	gil'ādh	hû'	wekhol-yisrā'ēl	mippenê	chăzā'ēl	melekh-'ărām
in Ramoth	Gilead	he	and all Israel	from before	Hazael	the king of Aram

15. 8178.121	3190	4567	3937, 7784.741	904, 3262	4623, 4485	866
cj, v Qal impf 3ms	pn	art, n ms	prep, v Hithpael inf con	prep, pn	prep, art, n mp	rel part
וַיָּשָׁב	יְהוֹרָם	הַמֶּלֶךְ	לְהִתְרַפֵּא	בְּיִזְרְעֶאל	מִן־הַמַּכִּים	אֲשֶׁר
wayyāshāv	yehôrām	hammelekh	lehithrappē'	viyezre'e'l	min-hammakkîm	'āsher
but he returned	Jehoram	the king	to be healed	in Jezreel	from the wounds	which

5409.526	782	904, 4032.241	881, 2462	4567	782
v Hiphil impf 3mp, ps 3ms	pn	prep, v Niphal inf con, ps 3ms	do, pn	*n ms*	pn
יַכֻּהוּ	אֲרַמִּים	בְּהִלָּחֲמוֹ	אֶת־חֲזָאֵל	מֶלֶךְ	אֲרָם
yakkuhû	'ărammîm	behillāchămô	'eth-chăzā'ēl	melekh	'ărām
they had struck him	the Arameans	when his fighting	Hazael	the king of	Aram

569.121	3167	524, 3552	5497	414, 3428.121	6654	4623, 6111
cj, v Qal impf 3ms	pn	cj, *sub*	n fs, ps 2mp	adv, v Qal juss 3ms	n ms	prep, art, n fs
וַיֹּאמֶר	יֵהוּא	אִם־יֵשׁ	נַפְשְׁכֶם	אַל־יֵצֵא	פָּלִיט	מִן־הָעִיר
wayyō'mer	yēhû'	'im-yēsh	naphshekhem	'al-yētsē'	phālîṭ	min-hā'îr
and he said	Jehu	if there is	your life	let him not go out	an escapee	from the city

12. And they said, It is false; tell us now. And he said, Thus and thus spake he to me, saying, Thus saith the LORD, I have anointed thee king over Israel: ... They answered, That's not true. Tell us, *NCV* ... You are lying, they said; come, tell us what it was, *Moffat* ... So he told them what the young man had said to him, *NAB* ... Jehu said, Here is what he told me, *NIV.*

13. Then they hasted, and took every man his garment, and put it under him on the top of the stairs, and blew with trumpets, saying, Jehu is king: ... Then hurriedly they all took their cloaks and spread them for him on the bare steps; and they blew the trumpet, and proclaimed, *NRSV* ... they sounded the trumpet and shouted, Jehu, *REB* ... they blew the horn and said, *Anchor* ... everyone took his robe and put it under him on the top of the steps, *BB.*

14. So Jehu the son of Jehoshaphat the son of Nimshi conspired against Joram. (Now Joram had kept Ramoth-gilead, he and all Israel, because of Hazael king of Syria: ... plotted against Joram, *Beck* ... while Joram, together with all Israel, was holding Ramoth-gilead against Hazael, *Goodspeed* ... son of Namsi, entered into a conspiracy against Joram. (Joram himself had been in command of the Israelite army that held Ramoth-Galaad, *Knox* ... Now Joram had besieged Ramoth Galaad, he and all Israel fighting, *Douay* ... made plans against Joram. Now Joram and all Israel had been defending Ramoth in Gilead from Hazael king of Aram, *NCV.*

15. But king Joram was returned to be healed in Jezreel of the wounds which the Syrians had given him, when he fought with Hazael king of Syria.) And Jehu said, If it be your minds, then let none go forth nor escape out of the city to go to tell it in Jezreel: ... to heal from the injuries the Arameans had given him when he fought against Hazael king of Aram. Jehu said, If you agree with this, don't let anyone leave the city. They might tell the news in Jezreel, *NCV* ... King Jehoram had returned to Jezreel to recover, *NEB* ... If this is the way you feel, don't let anyone slip out, *NIV* ...

features of the public accession ritual. After the sounding of the shophar, or ram's horn, the people would indicate their formal recognition of, and submission to, the new king by ritual acclamation, "Long live the king!" (cf., e.g., 1 Ki. 1:34, 39).

9:14–29. Jehu kills Kings Joram of Israel and Ahaziah of Judah. This section includes substantial parallels with the end of ch. 8 (see above, on 8:25–29; once again, the narrator includes the "literary bridge" between 8:28f and 9:14ff to link the present account of the death of Ahaziah with his accession and judgment notices at the end of the previous chapter). The pace of the narrative is as quick as that of Jehu's chariot driving (cf. v. 20), with quick confrontations leading to bloody results. Yet the narrator ensures that numerous allusions to Elijah's condemnation of the house of Ahab will not go unnoticed. Both the place (the plot of ground that had belonged to Naboth the Jezreelite; cf. 1 Ki. 21) and the time ("yesterday ..." [v. 26]) are eerily appropriate. Just as Ahab's own fate at Ramoth Gilead was prophetically ordained (1 Ki. 22:19–38), his son and his son-in-law are both fated to die on the same day, and fleeing from the same person. God's ways will not be thwarted.

A key term throughout this entire section is the familiar Hebrew word, shālôm, which can be variously translated as "peace," "welfare," "fullness," "prosperity," "health," "safety," or the like (the verbal root reflects the concepts of fullness, and completeness; also recompense, retribution, or the like). This rich and comprehensive term figures prominently in the following phrase repeated throughout chs. 9–10: literally, "Is there peace?" (hăshālôm, HED #1950B, 8361). This phrase (one word in Hebrew—the noun shālôm plus what is termed the he-interrogative prefix, which indicates a question) is repeated five times in ch. 9, plus once without the prefix. The same term with a preposition or definite article occurs another four

3937, 2050.141	3937, 5222.541	904, 3262		7680.121	3167	2050.121
prep, v Qal inf con	prep, v Hiphil inf con	prep, pn	**16.**	cj, v Qal impf 3ms	pn	cj, v Qal impf 3ms
לָלֶכֶת	לַגִּיד	בְּיִזְרְעֶאל		וַיִּרְכַּב	יֵהוּא	וַיֵּלֶךְ
lālekheth	laggîdh	beyizre'e'l		wayyirkav	yēhû'	wayyēlekh
to go	to report	in Jezreel		and he rode	Jehu	and he went

3262	3706	3245	8311.151	8427	275	4567	3171
pn	cj	pn	v Qal act ptc ms	adv	cj, pn	*n ms*	pn
יִזְרְעֶאלָה	כִּי	יוֹרָם	שֹׁכֵב	שָׁמָּה	וַאֲחַזְיָה	מֶלֶךְ	יְהוּדָה
yizre'e'lāh	kî	yôrām	shōkhēv	shāmmāh	wa'ăchazyāh	melekh	yehûdhāh
to Jezreel	because	Joram	lying	to there	and Ahaziah	the king of	Judah

3495.111	3937, 7495.141	881, 3245		7099.151	6198.151	6142, 4166
v Qal pf 3ms	prep, v Qal inf con	do, pn	**17.**	cj, art, v Qal act ptc ms	v Qal act ptc ms	prep, art, n ms
יָרַד	לִרְאוֹת	אֶת־יוֹרָם		וְהַצֹּפֶה	עֹמֵד	עַל־הַמִּגְדָּל
yāradh	lir'ôth	'eth-yôrām		wehatstsōpheh	'ōmēdh	'al-hammighdāl
he went down	to see	Joram		and the watchman	standing	on the tower

904, 3262	7495.121	881, 8599	3167	904, 971.141	569.121
prep, pn	cj, v Qal impf 3ms	do, *n fs*	pn	prep, v Qal inf con, ps 3ms	cj, v Qal impf 3ms
בְּיִזְרְעֶאל	וַיַּרְא	אֶת־שִׁפְעַת	יֵהוּא	בְּבֹאוֹ	וַיֹּאמֶר
beyizre'e'l	wayyare'	'eth-shiph'ath	yēhû'	bevō'ô	wayyō'mer
in Jezreel	and he saw	the company of	Jehu	when his coming	and he said

8599	603	7495.151	569.121	3190	4089.131	7682
n fs	pers pron	v Qal act ptc ms	cj, v Qal impf 3ms	pn	v Qal impv 2ms	n ms
שִׁפְעַת	אֲנִי	רֹאֶה	וַיֹּאמֶר	יְהוֹרָם	קַח	רַכָּב
shiph'ath	'ănî	rō'eh	wayyō'mer	yehôrām	qach	rakkāv
a company	I	seeing	and he said	Jehoram	take	a charioteer

8365.131	3937, 7410.141	569.121	1950B, 8361		2050.121
cj, v Qal impv 2ms	prep, v Qal inf con, ps 3mp	cj, v Qal impf 3ms	intrg part, n ms	**18.**	cj, v Qal impf 3ms
וּשְׁלַח	לִקְרָאתָם	וְיֹאמַר	הֲשָׁלוֹם		וַיֵּלֶךְ
ûshelach	liqŏrā'thām	weyō'mar	hăshālôm		wayyēlekh
and send out	to meet them	and they will say	is peace		and he went

7680.151	5670	3937, 7410.141	569.121	3662, 569.111	4567
v Qal act ptc ms	art, n ms	prep, v Qal inf con, ps 3ms	cj, v Qal impf 3ms	adv, v Qal pf 3ms	art, n ms
רֹכֵב	הַסּוּס	לִקְרָאתוֹ	וַיֹּאמֶר	כֹּה־אָמַר	הַמֶּלֶךְ
rōkhēv	hassûs	liqŏrā'thô	wayyō'mer	kōh-'āmar	hammelekh
a rider	the horse	to meet him	and he said	thus he has said	the king

1950B, 8361	569.121	3167	4242, 3937	3937, 8361	5621.131	420, 313
intrg part, n ms	cj, v Qal impf 3ms	pn	intrg, prep, ps 2ms	cj, prep, n ms	v Qal impv 2ms	prep, prep, ps 1cs
הֲשָׁלוֹם	וַיֹּאמֶר	יֵהוּא	מַה־לְּךָ	וּלְשָׁלוֹם	סֹב	אֶל־אַחֲרָי
hăshālôm	wayyō'mer	yēhû'	mah-lekhā	ûlăshālôm	sōv	'el-'achrāy
is peace	and he said	Jehu	what to you	and to peace	turn around	to behind me

5222.521	7099.151	3937, 569.141	971.111, 4534	5912, 2062
cj, v Hiphil impf 3ms	art, v Qal act ptc ms	prep, v Qal inf con	v Qal pf 3ms, art, n ms	prep, pers pron
וַיַּגֵּד	הַצֹּפֶה	לֵאמֹר	בָּא־הַמַּלְאָךְ	עַד־הֵם
wayyaggēdh	hatstsōpheh	lē'mōr	bā'-hammal'ākh	'adh-hēm
and he reported	the watchman	saying	the messenger came	unto them

3940, 8178.111		8365.121	7680.151	5670	8529	971.121
cj, neg part, v Qal pf 3ms	**19.**	cj, v Qal impf 3ms	v Qal act ptc ms	n ms	num	cj, v Qal impf 3ms
וְלֹא־שָׁב		וַיִּשְׁלַח	רֹכֵב	סוּס	שֵׁנִי	וַיָּבֹא
welō'-shāv		wayyishlach	rōkhēv	sûs	shēnî	wayyāvō'
but he has not returned		then he sent out	a rider	a horse	a second	and he came

420	569.121	3662, 569.111	4567	8361	569.121	3167
prep, ps 3mp	cj, v Qal impf 3ms	adv, v Qal pf 3ms	art, n ms	n ms	cj, v Qal impf 3ms	pn
אֲלֵהֶם	וַיֹּאמֶר	כֹּה־אָמַר	הַמֶּלֶךְ	שָׁלוֹם	וַיֹּאמֶר	יֵהוּא
'ălēhem	wayyō'mer	kōh-'āmar	hammelekh	shālôm	wayyō'mer	yēhû'
to them	and he said	thus he has said	the king	peace	and he said	Jehu

4242, 3937	3937, 8361	5621.131	420, 313		5222.521	7099.151
intrg, prep, ps 2ms	cj, prep, n ms	v Qal impv 2ms	prep, prep, ps 1cs	20.	cj, v Hiphil impf 3ms	art, v Qal act ptc ms
מַה־לְּךָ	וּלְשָׁלוֹם	סֹב	אֶל־אַחֲרָי		וַיַּגֵּד	הַצֹּפֶה
mah-lᵉkhā	ûlăshālôm	sōv	'el-'achrāy		wayaggēdh	hatstsōpheh
what to you	and to peace	turn around	to behind me		and he reported	the watchman

If you are so minded, let no one leave, *NKJV*.

16. So Jehu rode in a chariot, and went to Jezreel; for Joram lay there. And Ahaziah king of Judah was come down to see Joram: ... who was lying there wounded. King Ahaziah of Judah was there too, for he had gone to visit him, *NLT* ... Joram was lying ill, *NRSV* ... Joram was laid up, *Anchor* ... Jehu got into his carriage, *BB*.

17. And there stood a watchman on the tower in Jezreel, and he spied the company of Jehu as he came, and said, I see a company ... saw Jehu and his band coming, and said, I see a band of people, *BB* ... saw Jehu and his men approaching. I see some men riding up!, *Good News* ... saw the troop of Jehu coming and reported, I see chariots, *NAB*.

And Joram said, Take an horseman, and send to meet them, and let him say, Is it peace? ... Take a driver, Joram said, and send him to meet them and ask, Is everything well, *Beck* ... to find out if they are friends or enemies, *Good News* ... Get a driver, Joram said, and send him to meet them and to ask whether all is well, *NAB*.

18. So there went one on horseback to meet him, and said, Thus saith the king, Is it peace? And Jehu said, What hast thou to do with peace? turn thee behind me. And the watchman told, saying, The messenger came to them, but he cometh not again: ... Is all in order? Jehu said, Why bother yourself with order? Come along behind me. The lookout reported, *NCV* ... Peace? What is peace to you? Fall in behind me. Thereupon the watchman reported, *NEB* ... Turn around and follow me, *NKJV* ... What concern is it of yours whether all is well? *Anchor*.

19. Then he sent out a second on horseback, which came to them, and said, Thus saith the king, Is it peace? And Jehu answered, What hast thou to do with peace? turn thee behind me: ... come after me, *BB* ... he sent out a second driver. When he came to them, he said, The king asks, Is everything well? What is it to you? Jehu asked. Turn around and follow me, *Beck* ... What have you to do with well-being? replied Jehu. Swing around, *Berkeley* ... Talk not of peace; pass on behind me and follow, *Knox*.

20. And the watchman told, saying, He came even unto them, and cometh not again: and the driving is like the driving of Jehu the son of Nimshi; for he driveth furiously: ... He reached them, but he is not returning, *Moffatt* ... driving is like that of Jehu, son of Nimshi, in its fury, *NAB* ... He drives as if he were crazy, *NCV* ... like a madman, *NIV*.

times—for a total of ten occurrences of the noun (plus an additional verbal occurrence) in a thirty-two-verse span (9:11–10:13), namely, 9:11, 17f, 19, 22, 26 (the verbal form); 31; 10:13. Once again, the term shālôm (HED #8361) can be variously translated, and in 9:11 it is a simple greeting (NIV, "Is everything all right?"). So, in the present narrative, the litany, "Is everything all right?" or "Do you come in peace?" (9:11, 17ff, 22, 31; cf. 10:13), often alternates with the rejoinder "What do you have to do with peace?" or "How can there be peace …?" (9:18f, 22). Finally, the verbal form wᵉshillamtî (HED #8396) "and I will seek retribution" (NIV, "and I will make [you] pay"), is also found once again in 9:26.

Alert attention to these repeating phrases (in good Hebrew style, the forms and word order vary slightly in the repetitions) indicates the flow of the narrative: in 9:11, "Is everything all right?" leads to the impromptu coronation ritual (literally, "Is there peace?"—no, there is not—well, then, "Jehu is [the next] king"). Then in 9:18, the first emissary asks Jehu at Joram's command, "Do you come in peace?" which leads to the response, "What do you have to do with peace?" And this same interchange is essentially repeated with the second emissary in v. 19, and finally the king himself in v. 22. Thus three queries and three responses (concerning the motif of three's; see comments on 1:9–15), all of which culminate in

3937, 569.141	971.111	5912, 420	3940, 8178.111	4635
prep, v Qal inf con	v Qal pf 3ms	adv, prep, ps 3mp	cj, neg part, v Qal pf 3ms	cj, art, n ms
לֵאמֹר	בָּא	עַד־אֲלֵיהֶם	וְלֹא־שָׁב	וְהַמִּנְהָג
lē'mōr	bā'	'adh-'ălêhem	welō'-shāv	wehamminhāgh
saying	he came	until to them	but he has not returned	and the driving

3626, 4635	3167	1158, 5437	3706	904, 8155	5268.121
prep, *n ms*	pn	*n ms*, pn	cj	prep, n ms	v Qal impf 3ms
כְּמִנְהַג	יֵהוּא	בֶן־נִמְשִׁי	כִּי	בְשִׁגָּעוֹן	יִנְהָג
keminhagh	yēhû'	ven-nimshî	kî	veshiggā'ôn	yinhāgh
like the driving of	Jehu	the son of Nimshi	because	with insanity	he is driving

21. 569.121	3190	646.131	646.121	7681	3428.121	3190
cj, v Qal impf 3ms	pn	v Qal impv 2ms	cj, v Qal impf 3ms	n ms, ps 3ms	cj, v Qal impf 3ms	pn
וַיֹּאמֶר	יְהוֹרָם	אֱסֹר	וַיֶּאְסֹר	רִכְבּוֹ	וַיֵּצֵא	יְהוֹרָם
wayyō'mer	yehôrām	'ĕsōr	wayye'ăsōr	rikhbô	wayyētsē'	yehôrām
and he said	Jehoram	tie	and they tied	his chariot	and he went out	Jehoram

4567, 3547	275	4567, 3171	382	904, 7681	3428.126
n ms, pn	cj, pn	*n ms*, pn	n ms	prep, n ms, ps 3ms	cj, v Qal impf 3mp
מֶלֶךְ־יִשְׂרָאֵל	וַאֲחַזְיָהוּ	מֶלֶךְ־יְהוּדָה	אִישׁ	בְּרִכְבּוֹ	וַיֵּצְאוּ
melekh-yisrā'ēl	wa'ăchazyāhû	melekh-yehûdhāh	'îsh	berikhbô	wayyētse'û
the king of Israel	and Ahaziah	the king of Judah	each	in his chariot	and they went out

3937, 7410.141	3167	4834.126	904, 2610	5197	3263
prep, v Qal inf con	pn	cj, v Qal impf 3mp, ps 3ms	prep, *n fs*	pn	art, pn
לִקְרַאת	יֵהוּא	וַיִּמְצָאֻהוּ	בְּחֶלְקַת	נָבוֹת	הַיִּזְרְעֵאלִי
liqŏra'th	yēhû'	wayyimtsā'uhû	bechelqath	nāvôth	hayyizre'ē'lî
to meet	Jehu	and they found him	on the portion of	Naboth	the Jezreelite

22. 2030.121	3626, 7495.141	3190	881, 3167	569.121	1950B, 8361	3167
cj, v Qal impf 3ms	prep, v Qal inf con	pn	do, pn	cj, v Qal impf 3ms	intrg part, n ms	pn
וַיְהִי	כִּרְאוֹת	יְהוֹרָם	אֶת־יֵהוּא	וַיֹּאמֶר	הֲשָׁלוֹם	יֵהוּא
wayhî	kir'ôth	yehôrām	'eth-yēhû'	wayyō'mer	hăshālôm	yēhû'
and it was	when seeing	Jehoram	Jehu	then he said	is peace	Jehu

569.121	4242	8361	5912, 2267	350	525
cj, v Qal impf 3ms	intrg	art, n ms	adv, *n mp*	pn	n fs, ps 2ms
וַיֹּאמֶר	מָה	הַשָּׁלוֹם	עַד־זְנוּנֵי	אִיזֶבֶל	אִמְּךָ
wayyō'mer	māh	hashshālôm	'adh-zenûnê	'îzevel	'immekhā
and he said	what	the peace	as long as the prostitutions of	Jezebel	your mother

3914	7521	**23.** 2089.121	3190	3135	5308.121
cj, n mp, ps 3fs	art, adj	cj, v Qal impf 3ms	pn	n fd, ps 3ms	cj, v Qal impf 3ms
וּכְשָׁפֶיהָ	הָרַבִּים	וַיַּהֲפֹךְ	יְהוֹרָם	יָדָיו	וַיָּנֹס
ûkheshāphêāh	hārabbîm	wayyahphōkh	yehôrām	yādhâv	wayyānōs
and her sorceries	the many	and he turned	Jehoram	his hands	and he fled

569.121	420, 275	4983	275	**24.** 3167	4527.311	3135
cj, v Qal impf 3ms	prep, pn	n fs	pn	cj, pn	v Piel pf 3ms	n fs, ps 3ms
וַיֹּאמֶר	אֶל־אֲחַזְיָהוּ	מִרְמָה	אֲחַזְיָה	וְיֵהוּא	מִלֵּא	יָדוֹ
wayyō'mer	'el-'ăchazyāhû	mirmāh	'ăchazyāh	weyēhû'	millē'	yādhô
and he said	to Ahaziah	deceit	Ahaziah	and Jehu	he filled	his hand

904, 7493	5409.521	881, 3190	1033	2307	3428.121	2784
prep, art, n fs	cj, v Hiphil impf 3ms	do, pn	prep	n fp, ps 3ms	cj, v Qal impf 3ms	art, n ms
בַּקֶּשֶׁת	וַיַּךְ	אֶת־יְהוֹרָם	בֵּין	זְרֹעָיו	וַיֵּצֵא	הַחֵצִי
vaqqesheth	wayyakh	'eth-yehôrām	bên	zerō'āv	wayyētsē'	hachētsî
with the bow	and he struck down	Joram	between	his arms	and it went out	the arrow

4623, 3949 prep, n ms, ps 3ms מִלִּבּוֹ millibbô from his heart	3895.121 cj, v Qal impf 3ms וַיִּכְרַע wayyikhra' and he kneeled	904, 7681 prep, n ms, ps 3ms בְּרִכְבּוֹ berikhbô in his chariot	25.	569.121 cj, v Qal impf 3ms וַיֹּאמֶר wayyō'mer and he said	420, 956 prep, pn אֶל־בִּדְקַר 'el-bidhqar to Bidkar	8388 n ms, ps 3ms שָׁלִשֹׁה shelōshāh his adjutant

5558.131 v Qal impv 2ms שָׂא sā' lift	8390.531 v Hiphil impv 2ms, ps 3ms הַשְׁלִכֵהוּ hashlikhēhû throw him down	904, 2610 prep, n fs בְּחֶלְקַת bechelqath on the portion of	7898 n ms שְׂדֵה sedhēh the field of	5197 pn נָבוֹת nāvôth Naboth	3263 art, pn הַיִּזְרְעֵאלִי hayyizre'ē'lî the Jezreelite

21. And Joram said, Make ready. And his chariot was made ready: ... Hitch up! They hitched up his chariot, *Anchor* ... they made his carriage ready, *BB* ... Joram exclaimed, Harness! And they harnessed his chariot, *Fenton* ... Prepare my chariot, *NAB*.

And Joram king of Israel and Ahaziah king of Judah went out, each in his chariot, and they went out against Jehu, and met him in the portion of Naboth the Jezreelite: ... they came face to face with him at the field of Naboth, *BB* ... they went out to meet Jehu, *NASB* ... at the property of Naboth the Jezreelite, *NCV* ... met him by the plot of Naboth of Jezreel, *NEB*.

22. And it came to pass, when Joram saw Jehu, that he said, Is it peace, Jehu? And he answered, What peace, so long as the whoredoms of thy mother Jezebel and her witchcrafts are so many?: ... Is all well, *Anchor* ... How can there be peace, Jehu replied, as long as all the idolatry and witchcraft of your mother Jezebel abound, *NIV* ... What peace, as long as the harlotries of your mother Jezebel, *NKJV* ... and sorceries of your mother Jezebel continue, *NRSV*.

23. And Joram turned his hands, and fled, and said to Ahaziah, There is treachery, O Ahaziah: ... Joram, turning his horses in flight, said to Ahaziah, Broken faith, *BB* ... Joram turned his chariot around and tried to flee, saying to Ahaziah, Treason, *Beck* ... It is a rebellion, Ahaziah, *Fenton* ... Joram turned the horses to run away and yelled to Ahaziah, It's a trick, *NCV*.

24. And Jehu drew a bow with his full strength, and smote Jehoram between his arms, and the arrow went out at his heart, and he sunk down in his chariot: ... shot Jehoram between the shoulders; the arrow pierced his heart and he slumped down, *REB* ... he collapsed, *Anchor* ... the arrow came out at his breast. And he fell down three fold, *Tyndale* ... and with all his strength sent an arrow, wounding Joram, *BB*.

25. Then said Jehu to Bidkar his captain, Take up, and cast him in the portion of the field of Naboth the Jezreelite: for remember how that, when I and thou rode together after Ahab his father, the LORD laid this burden upon him: ... Bidkar his lieutenant, Take him up, and cast him on the property of, *Berkeley* ... Get his body and throw it in the field that belonged to Naboth, *Good News* ... the Lord put this fate on him, *BB* ... Remember how I and you used to drive our teams behind his father Ahab and the LORD gave this judgment against him, *Beck*.

26. Surely I have seen yesterday the blood of Naboth, and the blood of his sons, saith the LORD; and I

Jehu's scathing indictment of Joram in v. 22, "How can there be peace as long as all the idolatry and witchcraft of your mother Jezebel abound?" Joram's response to his cohort Ahaziah in the next verse is but a single word: "treachery" (mirmāh, HED #4983). Is there peace? No, there is treachery (NLT, "Treason"). Of course, the word has two meanings here. There cannot be peace as long as the treachery of Jezebel is unavenged. Surface peace currently hides treachery against Yahweh, against his prophets and against his people. So, the surface peace must be broken, so that true peace can result. The treachery of Jehu leads to the peace of Yahweh. This, if anything, is the major theme of the Jehu narrative.

Jehu himself is certainly pictured as a "man on a mission." Even his chariot driving style (cf. v. 20) is like that of a "madman." (The Hebrew expression veshiggā'ôn is from the same verbal root as the reference to the unnamed prophet in v. 11, HED #8154.)

Jehu's killing of King Joram in v. 24 was deliberate assassination, and he commanded his assistant Bidkar to throw the body on Naboth's plot of ground. The otherwise unknown prophetic word of Yahweh recorded in v. 26 was thus fulfilled, along with, of course, Elijah's well-known condemnation in 1 Ki. 21:17–24. As Hobbs notes, inclusion of the present prophetic utterance would probably indicate that there was widespread resistance to Ahab's godless rule.

3706, 2226.131	603	887	881	7680.152	7045	313	255
cj, v Qal impv 2ms	pers pron	cj, pers pron	do	v Qal act ptc mp	n mp	adv	pn
כִּי־זְכֹר	אֲנִי	וָאַתָּה	אֵת	רֹכְבִים	צְמָדִים	אַחֲרֵי	אַחְאָב
kî-z^{e}khōr	'ănî	wā'attāh	'ēth	rōkh^{e}vîm	ts^{e}mādhîm	'achrê	'ach'āv
because remember	I	and you		riding	pairs	after	Ahab

1	3176	5558.111	6142	881, 5014	2172		524, 3940
n ms, ps 3ms	cj, pn	v Qal pf 3ms	prep, ps 3ms	do, art, n ms	art, dem pron	26.	cj, neg part
אָבִיו	וַיהוָה	נָשָׂא	עָלָיו	אֶת־הַמַּשָּׂא	הַזֶּה		אִם־לֹא
'āvîw	wayhwāh	nāsā'	'ālâv	'eth-hammassā'	hazzeh		'im-lō'
his father	and Yahweh	He had lifted up	against him	the oracle	the this		if not

881, 1879	5197	881, 1879	1158	7495.115	582
do, *n ms*	pn	cj, do, *n mp*	n mp, ps 3ms	v Qal pf 1cs	adv
אֶת־דְּמֵי	נָבוֹת	וְאֶת־דְּמֵי	בָּנָיו	רָאִיתִי	אֶמֶשׁ
'eth-d^{e}mê	nāvôth	w^{e}'eth-d^{e}mê	vānâv	rā'îthî	'emesh
the blood of	Naboth	and the blood of	his sons	I have seen	yesterday

5177, 3176	8396.315	3937	904, 2610	2148
n ms, pn	cj, v Piel pf 1cs	prep, ps 2ms	prep, art, n fs	art, dem pron
נְאֻם־יְהוָה	וְשִׁלַּמְתִּי	לְךָ	בַּחֶלְקָה	הַזֹּאת
n^{e}'um-y^{e}hwāh	w^{e}shillamtî	l^{e}khā	bachelqāh	hazzō'th
the declaration of Yahweh	and I will recompense	to you	on the portion	the this

5177, 3176	6498	5558.131	8390.531	904, 2610
n ms, pn	cj, adv	v Qal impv 2ms	v Hiphil impv 2ms, ps 3ms	prep, art, n fs
נְאֻם־יְהוָה	וְעַתָּה	שָׂא	הַשְׁלִכֵהוּ	בַּחֶלְקָה
n^{e}'um-y^{e}hwāh	w^{e}'attāh	sā'	hashlikhēhû	bachelqāh
the declaration of Yahweh	but now	lift	throw him down	on the portion

3626, 1745	3176		275	4567, 3171	7495.111	5308.121
prep, *n ms*	pn	27.	cj, pn	*n ms*, pn	v Qal pf 3ms	cj, v Qal impf 3ms
כִּדְבַר	יְהוָה		וַאֲחַזְיָה	מֶלֶךְ־יְהוּדָה	רָאָה	וַיָּנָס
kidhvar	y^{e}hwāh		wa'ăchazyāh	melekh-y^{e}hûdhāh	rā'āh	wayyānās
according to the word of	Yahweh		and Ahaziah	the king of Judah	he saw	and he fled

1932	1057	1057	7579.121	313	3167	569.121	1612, 881
n ms	pn	pn	cj, v Qal impf 3ms	prep, ps 3ms	pn	cj, v Qal impf 3ms	cj, do, ps 3ms
דֶּרֶךְ	בֵּית	הַגָּן	וַיִּרְדֹּף	אַחֲרָיו	יֵהוּא	וַיֹּאמֶר	גַּם־אֹתוֹ
derekh	bêth	haggān	wayyirdōph	'achrâv	yēhû'	wayyō'mer	gam-'ōthô
the way of	Beth	Hagan	and he pursued	after him	Jehu	and he said	also him

5409.533	420, 4981	904, 4765, 1516	866	882, 3099	5308.121
v Hiphil impv 2mp, ps 3ms	prep, art, n fs	prep, *n ms*, pn	rel part	prep, pn	cj, v Qal impf 3ms
הַכֻּהוּ	אֶל־הַמֶּרְכָּבָה	בְּמַעֲלֵה־גוּר	אֲשֶׁר	אֶת־יִבְלְעָם	וַיָּנָס
hakkuhû	'el-hammerkāvāh	b^{e}ma'ălēh-ghûr	'ăsher	'eth-yivl^{e}'ām	wayyānās
strike him down	to the chariot	at the ascent of Gur	which	near Ibleam	and he fled to

4163	4322.121	8427		7680.526	881	5860	3503
pn	cj, v Qal impf 3ms	adv	28.	cj, v Hiphil impf 3mp	do, ps 3ms	n mp, ps 3ms	pn
מְגִדּוֹ	וַיָּמָת	שָׁם		וַיַּרְכִּבוּ	אֹתוֹ	עֲבָדָיו	יְרוּשָׁלָמָה
m^{e}ghiddô	wayyāmāth	shām		wayyarkivû	'ōthô	'ăvādhâv	y^{e}rûshālāmāh
Meggido	and he died	there		and they caused to ride	him	his servants	to Jerusalem

7196.126	881	904, 7185	6196, 1	904, 6111	1784
cj, v Qal impf 3mp	do, ps 3ms	prep, n fs, ps 3ms	prep, n mp, ps 3ms	prep, *n fs*	pn
וַיִּקְבְּרוּ	אֹתוֹ	בִּקְבֻרָתוֹ	עִם־אֲבֹתָיו	בְּעִיר	דָּוִד
wayyiqbb^{e}rû	'ōthô	viqōvurāthô	'im-'ăvōthâv	b^{e}'îr	dāwidh
and they buried	him	in his tomb	with his ancestors	in the city of	David

29.	904, 8523 cj, prep, *n fs* וּבִשְׁנַת ûvishnath and in the year of	259 num אַחַת 'achath one	6462 num עֶשְׂרֵה 'esrēh ten	8523 n fs שָׁנָה shānāh years	3937, 3245 prep, pn לְיוֹרָם leyôrām of Joram	1158, 255 *n ms*, pn בֶּן־אַחְאָב ben-'ach'āv the son of Ahab	4566.111 v Qal pf 3ms מָלַךְ mālakh he reigned	275 pn אֲחַזְיָה 'ăchazyāh Ahaziah

6142, 3171 prep, pn עַל־יְהוּדָה 'al-yehûdhāh over Judah	30.	971.121 cj, v Qal impf 3ms וַיָּבוֹא wayyāvô' and he came	3167 pn יֵהוּא yēhû' Jehu	3262 pn יִזְרְעֶאלָה yizre'e'lāh to Jezreel	350 cj, pn וְאִיזֶבֶל we'îzevel and Jezebel	8471.112 v Qal pf 3fs שָׁמְעָה shāme'āh she heard	7947.122 cj, v Qal impf 3fs וַתָּשֶׂם wattāsem and she put

will requite thee in this plat, saith the LORD: ... in this very field, *Goodspeed* ... punish you in this plot of ground, *Moffatt* ... repay you for it, *NAB* ... surely make you pay, *NIV*.

Now therefore take and cast him into the plat of ground, according to the word of the LORD: ... pick him up, and throw him into the field, *JB* ... fling him on this plot, *Moffatt* ... pick him up and throw him into it and thus fulfil, *NEB* ... throw him out on Naboth's field, just as the LORD said, *NLT*.

27. But when Ahaziah the king of Judah saw this, he fled by the way of the garden house: ... in the direction of Beth-haggan, *NRSV* ... King Ahaziah saw what happened, so he fled in his chariot toward the town of Beth Haggan, *Good News* ... As for Ahaziah, king of Juda, he fled at the sight, past the lodge of the royal garden, *Knox*.

And Jehu followed after him, and said, Smite him also in the chariot. And they did so at the going up to Gur, which is by Ibleam. And he fled to Megiddo, and died there: ... Jehu pursued him and said, Get him too. They shot him down in his chariot on the road up the valley near Ibleam, but he escaped, *REB* ... Put him to death in the same way; and they gave him a death-wound in his carriage, on the slope, *BB* ... Shoot him, too. So they shot him in his chariot at the upward slope of Gur, *Berkeley* ... Kill him too! Jehu ordered his men, and they wounded him as he drove his chariot, *Good News*.

28. And his servants carried him in a chariot to Jerusalem, and buried him in his sepulchre with his fathers in the city of David: ... His officials took him, *NLT* ... in his tomb beside his fathers, *Moffatt* ... in the tomb of his ancestors, *NAB* ... with his forefathers, *NEB*.

29. And in the eleventh year of Joram the son of Ahab began Ahaziah to reign over Judah: ... of the rule of Joram, the son of Ahab, Ahaziah became king, *BB*.

30. And when Jehu was come to Jezreel, Jezebel heard of it; and she painted her face, and tired her head, and looked out at a window: ... painted her eyelashes and adorned her head and peered out, *Goodspeed* ... she shadowed her eyes, adorned her hair, and looked down, *NAB* ... She put on her eye makeup and fixed her hair, *NCV* ... painted her eyes and dressed her hair, *NEB*.

The present passage ends with a brief note concerning the death of King Ahaziah as well (vv. 27f). He was wounded as he fled south, presumably toward Jerusalem ("Ibleam" is located in the territory of Manasseh, and is probably to be located just south of the modern town of Jenin, some seven miles or so [ten kilometers] directly south of Jezreel). He died in Megiddo, the important town located on the strategic mountain pass southwest of the Jezreel valley. Megiddo was the site of an important Solomonic city (1 Ki. 4:12, cf. 9:15). Later, in a tragic occasion, King Josiah of Judah, the hero of the Kings narrative, died there, also (see 2 Ki. 23:29f; cf. the longer account in 2 Chr. 35:20–25). Ahaziah was not the only Judahite king to lose his life at Megiddo.

9:30–37. Jezebel the queen mother killed. This is, perhaps, one of the most well-known parts of the Book of 2 Kings, for who has not heard of "wicked Queen Jezebel" and her long-awaited demise? Elijah, of course, in 1 Ki. 21:23, predicted that "dogs would devour Jezebel by the wall of Jezreel" (just as they would also lick up the blood of her dead husband Ahab [1 Ki. 21:19; fulfilled in 22:38—some see Joram's body thrown on Naboth's plot of ground in v. 26 of the present chapter as a delayed fulfillment of Elijah's words; cf. Yahweh's change of heart concerning Ahab, as recorded in 1 Ki. 21:29]). But we have had to wait some nine chapters to read of Jezebel's promised execution. As will be recalled, Jezebel was not originally an Israelite; she was the daughter of the Phoenician king Itto-Baal (1 Ki. 16:31, "Ethbaal, king of the Sidonians"). Since she was a Baal worshiper all her life, her antipathy to the Yahwistic prophets during the time of Elijah (e.g., 1 Ki. 18–19) is more under-

904, 6563	6084	3296.522	881, 7513	8625.522	1185
prep, art, n ms	n fd, ps 3fs	cj, v Hiphil impf 3fs	do, n ms, ps 3fs	cj, v Hiphil impf 3fs	prep
בַּפּוּךְ	עֵינֶיהָ	וַתֵּיטֶב	אֶת־רֹאשָׁהּ	וַתַּשְׁקֵף	בְּעַד
bappûkh	'ênêāh	wattêṯev	'eth-rō'shāhh	wattashqēph	be'adh
with the eye-paint	her eyes	and she made lovely	her head	and she looked down	behind

2574		3167	971.111	904, 8554	569.122	1950B, 8361	2259
art, n ms	**31.**	cj, pn	v Qal pf 3ms	prep, art, n ms	cj, v Qal impf 3fs	intrg part, n ms	pn
הַחַלּוֹן		וְיֵהוּא	בָּא	בַּשַּׁעַר	וַתֹּאמֶר	הֲשָׁלוֹם	זִמְרִי
hachallôn		weyēhû'	bā'	vashshā'ar	wattō'mer	hăshālôm	zimrî
the window		and Jehu	he entered	in the gate	and she said	is peace	Zimri

2103.151	112		5558.121	6686	420, 2574	569.121	4449
v Qal act ptc ms	n mp, ps 3ms	**32.**	cj, v Qal impf 3ms	n mp, ps 3ms	prep, art, n ms	cj, v Qal impf 3ms	intrg
הֹרֵג	אֲדֹנָיו		וַיִּשָּׂא	פָּנָיו	אֶל־הַחַלּוֹן	וַיֹּאמֶר	מִי
hōrēgh	'ădhōnâv		wayyissā'	phānâv	'el-hachallôn	wayyō'mer	mî
a killer	his master		and he lifted up	his face	to the window	and he said	who

882	4449	8625.526	420	8530	8421	5835
prep, ps 1cs	intrg	cj, v Hiphil impf 3mp	prep, ps 3ms	num	num	n mp
אִתִּי	מִי	וַיַּשְׁקִיפוּ	אֵלָיו	שְׁנַיִם	שְׁלֹשָׁה	סָרִיסִים
'ittî	mî	wayyashqîphû	'ēlâv	shenayim	shelōshāh	sārîsîm
with me	who	and they looked down	to him	two	three	eunuchs

	569.121	8447.133	8447.126	5317.121	4623, 1879
33.	cj, v Qal impf 3ms	v Qal impv 2mp, ps 3fs	cj, v Qal impf 3mp, ps 3fs	cj, v Qal impf 3ms	prep, n ms, ps 3fs
	וַיֹּאמֶר	שִׁמְטֻהָ	וַיִּשְׁמְטוּהָ	וַיִּז	מִדָּמָהּ
	wayyō'mer	shimṯuhâv	wayyishmeṯûāh	wayyiz	middāmāhh
	and he said	drop her	and they dropped her	and it spattered	from her blood

420, 7306	420, 5670	7717.121		971.121	404.121
prep, art, n ms	cj, prep, art, n mp	cj, v Qal impf 3ms, ps 3fs	**34.**	cj, v Qal impf 3ms	cj, v Qal impf 3ms
אֶל־הַקִּיר	וְאֶל־הַסּוּסִים	וַיִּרְמְסֶנָּה		וַיָּבֹא	וַיֹּאכַל
'el-haqqîr	we'el-hassûsîm	wayyirmesennāh		wayyāvō'	wayyō'khal
to the wall	and to the horses	and they trampled her		and he entered	and he ate

8685.121	569.121	6734.133, 5167	881, 803.157	2148
cj, v Qal impf 3ms	cj, v Qal impf 3ms	v Qal impv 2mp, part	do, art, v Qal pass ptc fs	art, dem pron
וַיֵּשְׁתְּ	וַיֹּאמֶר	פִּקְדוּ־נָא	אֶת־הָאֲרוּרָה	הַזֹּאת
wayyēsht	wayyō'mer	piqŏdhû-nā'	'eth-hā'ărûrāh	hazzō'th
and he drank	and he said	gather up please	the cursed woman	the this

7196.133	3706	1351, 4567	2026		2050.126
cj, v Qal impv 2mp, ps 3fs	cj	*n fs*, n ms	pers pron	**35.**	cj, v Qal impf 3mp
וְקִבְרוּהָ	כִּי	בַּת־מֶלֶךְ	הִיא		וַיֵּלְכוּ
weqivrûāh	kî	vath-melekh	hî'		wayyēlekhû
and bury her	because	the daughter of the king	she		and they went

3937, 7196.141	3940, 4834.116	904	3706	524, 1578	7559
prep, v Qal inf con, ps 3fs	cj, neg part, v Qal pf 3cp	prep, ps 3fs	cj	cj, art, n fs	cj, art, n fd
לְקָבְרָהּ	וְלֹא־מָצְאוּ	בָהּ	כִּי	אִם־הַגֻּלְגֹּלֶת	וְהָרַגְלַיִם
leqāverāhh	welō'-mātse'û	vāhh	kî	'im-haggulgōleth	wehāraghlayim
to bury her	but they did not find	of her	except	only her skull	and the feet

3834	3135		8178.126	5222.526	3937	569.121
cj, *n fp*	art, n fd	**36.**	cj, v Qal impf 3mp	cj, v Hiphil impf 3mp	prep, ps 3ms	cj, v Qal impf 3ms
וְכַפּוֹת	הַיָּדָיִם		וַיָּשֻׁבוּ	וַיַּגִּידוּ	לוֹ	וַיֹּאמֶר
wekhappôth	hayyādhāyim		wayyāshuvû	wayyaggîdhû	lô	wayyō'mer
and the palms of	the hands		and they returned	and they reported	to him	and he said

1745, 3176 *n ms*, pn דְּבַר־יְהוָה dᵉvar-yᵉhwāh the word of Yahweh	2000 pers pron הוּא hû' it	866 rel part אֲשֶׁר 'ăsher which	1744.311 v Piel pf 3ms דִּבֶּר dibber He spoke	904, 3135, 5860 prep, *n fs*, n ms, ps 3ms בְּיַד־עַבְדּוֹ bᵉyadh-'avdô by the hand of his servant	455 pn אֵלִיָּהוּ 'ēlîyāhû Elijah	9005 art, pn הַתִּשְׁבִּי hattishbî the Tishbite

3937, 569.141 prep, v Qal inf con לֵאמֹר lē'mōr saying	904, 2610 prep, *n ms* בְּחֵלֶק bᵉchēleq on the portion of	3262 pn יִזְרְעֶאל yizrᵉ'e'l Jezreel	404.126 v Qal impf 3mp יֹאכְלוּ yō'khᵉlû they will eat	3732 art, n mp הַכְּלָבִים hakkᵉlāvîm the dogs	881, 1340 do, *n ms* אֶת־בְּשַׂר 'eth-bᵉsar the flesh of	350 pn אִיזָבֶל 'îzāvel Jezebel

31. And as Jehu entered in at the gate, she said, Had Zimri peace, who slew his master? ... when Jehu was coming into the town, she said, Is all well, O Zimri, taker of your master's life, *BB* ... his master's killer, *Anchor* ... murderer of your master, *Moffatt* ... Can there be peace for Zambri, that hath killed, *Douay*.

32. And he lifted up his face to the window, and said, Who is on my side? who? And there looked out to him two or three eunuchs: ... Two or three servants looked out the window at Jehu, *NCV* ... two or three officials, *JB* ... Jehu looked up and saw her at the window and shouted, *NLT* ... Who is with me, *Berkeley* ... he raised his eyes, *Goodspeed*.

33. And he said, Throw her down. So they threw her down: and some of her blood was sprinkled on the wall, and on the horses: and he trode her under foot: ... Throw her down headlong, *Douay* ... they sent her down with force, and her blood went in a shower on the wall and on the horses; and she was crushed under their feet, *BB* ... Jehu rode over her, *JB* ... the horses trampled her, *Knox*.

34. And when he was come in, he did eat and drink, and said, Go, see now this cursed woman, and bury her: for she is a king's daughter: ... he, going into the palace to eat and drink there, gave the word, Go find the accursed woman's body, and give it burial, *Knox* ... Take care of this cursed woman, *Beck* ... Attend now to this accursed woman, *Berkeley* ... because she is, *NCV*.

35. And they went to bury her: but they found no more of her than the skull, and the feet, and the palms of her hands: ... they found nothing except her, *NIV* ... they went to put her body into the earth, but nothing of her was to be seen, only the bones of her head, and, *BB* ... the extremities of her hands, *Douay*.

36. Wherefore they came again, and told him. And he said, This is the word of the LORD, which he spake by his servant Elijah the Tishbite, saying, In the portion of Jezreel shall dogs eat the flesh of Jezebel: ... they came back and gave him word of it, *BB* ... they returned, *Berkeley* ...

standable (concerning Baal-Hadad, the storm god, cf. comments on 1:2). Also, since she was of foreign birth, her incredible insensitivity to the ancestral land rights of Naboth (cf. 1 Ki. 21; note the active role she played in Ahab's seizure of the property in vv. 5–16) is somewhat more understandable as well, if still hard to forgive. Although some scholars have suggested quite seriously that the wedding song we now call Ps. 45 may well have been originally written in her honor (cf., e.g., vv. 10ff, where the unnamed bride is clearly of foreign, and possibly of Phoenician, birth), her name has long since become synonymous with feminine cruelty and despotism (cf., e.g., Rev. 2:20).

The scene of the queen at the upstairs window of the palace is a familiar one in ancient Near Eastern art (which usually pictured such females as prostitutes; cf. the verbal image of Prov. 7:6ff). Jezebel, of course, was dressed and made-up for the occasion (v. 30). She addressed the usurper Jehu with an appropriate epithet (v. 31), "Have you come in peace, Zimri, you murderer of your master?" This is the final reference to shālôm in this chapter (cf. comments on vv. 14–29). "Zimri" was undoubtedly a reference to the usurper in 1 Ki. 16:19f, again a military commander who had killed his king, Elah son of Baasha, as well as the rest of Baasha's family, but who, himself, was killed only seven days later, according to the Masoretic text, by Jezebel's father-in-law, Omri (but cf. Wiseman for a different identification for Jezebel's use of the name "Zimri"). In any case, we must acknowledge a certain grudging admiration for the self-assurance and courage of Queen Jezebel up to the end. "The idea is that (as) a queen, (she) meets her destiny in full regalia and made up for the occasion" (David Noel Freedman, as quoted by Cogan and Tadmor [AB, 112]).

Jehu's courage and determination was equal to Jezebel's, however. He called the "eunuchs" (cf. Cogan and Tadmor for a defense of this traditional

37.	2030.112	5215	350	3626, 1889	6142, 6686	7898	904, 2610
	cj, v Qal pf 3fs	*n fs*	pn	prep, n ms	prep, *n mp*	art, n ms	prep, *n ms*
	וְהָיְתָ	נִבְלַת	אִיזֶבֶל	כְּדֹמֶן	עַל־פְּנֵי	הַשָּׂדֶה	בְּחֵלֶק
	wehāyāth	nivlath	'îzevel	kedhōmen	'al-penê	hassādheh	bechēleq
	and it will be	the corpse of	Jezebel	like dung	on the surface of	the field	on the portion of

3262	866	3940, 569.126	2148	350	10:1	3937, 255	8124	1158
pn	rel part	neg part, v Qal impf 3mp	dem pron	pn		cj, prep, pn	num	n mp
יִזְרְעֶאל	אֲשֶׁר	לֹא־יֹאמְרוּ	זֹאת	אִיזָבֶל		וּלְאַחְאָב	שִׁבְעִים	בָנִים
yizre'e'l	'ăsher	lō'-yō'merû	zō'th	'îzāvel		ûlă'ach'āv	shiv'îm	bānîm
Jezreel	that	they will not say	this	Jezebel		now to Ahab	seventy	sons

904, 8497	3918.121	3167	5809	8365.121	8497	420, 8015
prep, pn	cj, v Qal impf 3ms	pn	n mp	cj, v Qal impf 3ms	pn	prep, *n mp*
בְּשֹׁמְרוֹן	וַיִּכְתֹּב	יֵהוּא	סְפָרִים	וַיִּשְׁלַח	שֹׁמְרוֹן	אֶל־שָׂרֵי
beshōmerôn	wayyikhtōv	yēhû'	sephārîm	wayyishlach	shōmerôn	'el-sārê
in Samaria	and he wrote	Jehu	documents	and he sent out to	Samaria	to the officials of

3262	2292	420, 548.152	255	3937, 569.141	2.	6498
pn	art, n mp	cj, prep, art, v Qal act ptc mp	pn	prep, v Qal inf con		cj, adv
יִזְרְעֶאל	הַזְּקֵנִים	וְאֶל־הָאֹמְנִים	אַחְאָב	לֵאמֹר		וְעַתָּה
yizre'e'l	hazzeqēnîm	we'el-hā'ōmenîm	'ach'āv	lē'mōr		we'attāh
Jezreel	the elders	and to the faithful ones	Ahab	saying		and now

904, 971.141	5809	2172	420	882	1158	112
prep, v Qal inf con	art, n ms	art, dem pron	prep, ps 2mp	cj, prep, ps 2mp	*n mp*	n mp, ps 2mp
בְּבֹא	הַסֵּפֶר	הַזֶּה	אֲלֵיכֶם	וְאִתְּכֶם	בְּנֵי	אֲדֹנֵיכֶם
bevō'	hassēpher	hazzeh	'ălêkhem	we'ittekhem	benê	'ădhōnêkhem
when coming	the document	the this	to you	and with you	the sons of	your master

882	7681	5670	6111	4152	5584
cj, prep, ps 2mp	art, n ms	cj, art, n mp	cj, *n fs*	n ms	cj, art, n ms
וְאִתְּכֶם	הָרֶכֶב	וְהַסּוּסִים	וְעִיר	מִבְצָר	וְהַנָּשֶׁק
we'ittekhem	hārekhev	wehassûsîm	we'îr	mivtsār	wehannāsheq
and with you	the chariots	and the horses	and cities of	fortification	and the weapons

3.	7495.117	3005	3596	4623, 1158	112
	cj, v Qal pf 2mp	art, adj	cj, art, adj	prep, *n mp*	n mp, ps 2mp
	וּרְאִיתֶם	הַטּוֹב	וְהַיָּשָׁר	מִבְּנֵי	אֲדֹנֵיכֶם
	ûre'îthem	hattôv	wehayyāshār	mibbenê	'ădhōnêkhem
	and you will see	what is good	and the most upright	from the sons of	your master

7947.117	6142, 3802	1	4032.233	6142, 1041
cj, v Qal pf 2mp	prep, *n ms*	n ms, ps 3ms	cj, v Niphal impv 2mp	prep, *n ms*
וְשַׂמְתֶּם	עַל־כִּסֵּא	אָבִיו	וְהִלָּחֲמוּ	עַל־בֵּית
wesamtem	'al-kissē'	'āvîw	wehillāchămû	'al-bêth
and you will appoint	on the throne of	his father	and fight	concerning the household of

112	4.	7495.126	4108	4108	569.126	2079	8530	4567
n mp, ps 2mp		cj, v Qal impf 3mp	adv	adv	cj, v Qal impf 3mp	intrj	num	art, n mp
אֲדֹנֵיכֶם		וַיִּרְאוּ	מְאֹד	מְאֹד	וַיֹּאמְרוּ	הִנֵּה	שְׁנֵי	הַמְּלָכִים
'ădhōnêkhem		wayyir'û	me'ōdh	me'ōdh	wayyō'merû	hinnēh	shenê	hammelākhîm
your master		and they looked	very	very	and they said	behold	the two of	the kings

3940	6198.116	3937, 6686	351	6198.120	601	5.	8365.121
neg part	v Qal pf 3cp	prep, n mp, ps 3ms	cj, intrg	v Qal impf 1cp	pers pron		cj, v Qal impf 3ms
לֹא	עָמְדוּ	לְפָנָיו	וְאֵיךְ	נַעֲמֹד	אֲנַחְנוּ		וַיִּשְׁלַח
lō'	'āmedhû	lephānâv	we'êkh	na'ămōdh	'ănachănû		wayyishlach
not	they stood	before him	so how	will we stand	we		then he sent out

Dogs shall devour the flesh of Jezebel in the plot of Jezreel, *Anchor* ... Dogs will eat Jezebel's body in the territory of Jezreel, *Good News*.

37. And the carcase of Jezebel shall be as dung upon the face of the field in the portion of Jezreel; so that they shall not say, This is Jezebel: ... Jezebel's body will be like refuse on the ground, *NIV* ... so that no one will be able to say, *JB* ... her corpse shall lie like dung on the ground, for the passers-by to wonder whether this is indeed Jezebel, *Knox* ... Her body will be like manure on the field, *NCV*.

10:1. And Ahab had seventy sons in Samaria. And Jehu wrote letters, and sent to Samaria, unto the rulers of Jezreel, to the elders, and to them that brought up Ahab's children, saying: ... and to those who reared Ahab's sons, *NKJV* ... and to the guardians of the sons of Ahab, *NRSV* ... to the rulers of the town, and to the responsible men, and to those who had the care of the sons of Ahab, *BB*.

2. Now as soon as this letter cometh to you, seeing your master's sons are with you, and there are with you chariots and horses, a fenced city also, and armour: ... fortified cities, and weapons, *Beck* ... when you receive this letter, since you have charge of your master's sons, ... and equipment, *Berkeley*.

3. Look even out the best and meetest of your master's sons, and set him on his father's throne, and fight for your master's house: ... choose the best, and him that shall please you most of, *Douay* ... and most worthy person among your master's sons, and make him king. Then fight for your master's family, *NCV* ... most upright of your master's sons, *BB* ... choose the one of the princes who is best and most just, *Beck*.

4. But they were exceedingly afraid, and said, Behold, two kings stood not before him: how then shall we stand? ... trembling in great fear, they said, *Berkeley* ... The rulers of Samaria were terrified. How can we oppose Jehu, they said, when neither King Joram nor King Ahaziah could, *Good News* ... They were overcome with fright and said, If two kings could not withstand him, how can we?, *NAB* ... they were panic-stricken, *Goodspeed*.

5. And he that was over the house, and he that was over the city, the elders also, and the bringers up of the children, sent to Jehu, saying, We are thy servants, and will do all that thou shalt bid us; we will not make any king: do thou that which is good in thine eyes: ... the comptroller of the household and the governor of the city, with the elders and the tutors, *NEB* ... all that you say to us we will do, *NASB* ... do whatever you think is best, *NCV* ... Do whatever pleases you, *Anchor*.

---

translation of s̲ārîs̲, HED #5835) to "throw her down" (v. 33). And so they did. The narrator takes special interest in relaying the details concerning the fate of her corpse, as it is both trampled by horses and devoured by dogs (vv. 33–37; once again these verses are linked closely to Elijah's prophecy in 1 Ki. 21:17–24). "The report of the end of Jezebel is characterized by its complete frankness in its depiction of the absolute disdain in which Jehu held the woman" (Hobbs, WBC, 118). But after some reflection (and after his meal was over), Jehu did command her proper burial—she was of royal birth after all. Notice, also, the haunting parallel of Saul's concubine Rizpah in this regard, namely, her devotion in protecting the exposed bodies of Saul's seven sons (two of which were her own children) from the deprivations of the birds and the wild animals, until King David commanded that they be given a proper burial, and, "after that, God answered prayer in behalf of the land" (1 Sam. 21:1–14). Jezebel, in sharp contrast, had no such protector, human or divine. "Do not be deceived: God cannot be mocked. A person reaps what he sows" (Gal. 6:7).

10:1–17. Children of the house of Ahab killed, as well as the relatives of King Ahaziah. The death of Jezebel was not the end of bloodshed. Wholesale killing continued throughout much of the present chapter, as well. Perhaps Jezebel was correct: we have here a veritable Zimri, who worked so hard to kill off his master's entire family (1 Ki. 16:11; cf. 2 Ki. 9:8f). Yet, echoing throughout all these barbarities is the comment that King Jehu did what was right in accomplishing the will of Yahweh, especially in regard to the house of Ahab (v. 30).

The story of the deaths of Ahab's sons is told vividly and powerfully, with the details of Jehu's letters (especially the second one) truly taken to heart by the terrified recipients (e.g., all-too-literally bringing in the "heads" of their master's sons). It is to a brief overview of these potent, yet gloomy verses that we now turn.

There is some confusion in the versions concerning where the letters were sent, and to whom (cf. footnotes in NIV and NLT). Commentators suspect this confusion stems partly from the uncertain location of "the officials of Jezreel." Were they in Samaria seeking advice from the royal officials in the capital? (so Kimhi, as cited by Cogan and Tadmor [AB, 113]; they, however, follow the Greek Lucianic readings [as does NLT] in reading "[to the officials] of the city" instead of "[to the officials] of Jezreel" as in the Masoretic text). But, inasmuch as

866, 6142, 1041	866	6142, 6111	2292	548.152	420, 3167
rel pron, prep, art, n ms	cj, rel pron	prep, art, n fs	cj, art, n mp	cj, art, v Qal act ptc mp	prep, pn
אֲשֶׁר־עַל־הַבַּיִת	וַאֲשֶׁר	עַל־הָעִיר	וְהַזְּקֵנִים	וְהָאֹמְנִים	אֶל־יֵהוּא
'ăsher-'al-habbayith	wa'ăsher	'al-hā'îr	wehazzeqēnîm	wehā'ōmenîm	'el-yēhû'
who over the household	and who	over the city	and the elders	and the faithful ones	to Jehu

3937, 569.141	5860	601	3725	866, 569.123	420
prep, v Qal inf con	n mp, ps 2ms	pers pron	cj, n ms	rel part, v Qal impf 2ms	prep, ps 1cp
לֵאמֹר	עֲבָדֶיךָ	אֲנַחְנוּ	וְכֹל	אֲשֶׁר־תֹּאמַר	אֵלֵינוּ
lē'mōr	'ăvādhêkhā	'ănachnû	wekhōl	'ăsher-tō'mar	'ēlênû
saying	your servants	we	and everything	that you say	to us

6449.120	3940, 4566.520	382	3005	904, 6084	6449.131
v Qal impf 1cp	neg part, v Hiphil impf 1cp	n ms	art, adj	prep, n fd, ps 2ms	v Qal impv 2ms
נַעֲשֶׂה	לֹא־נַמְלִיךְ	אִישׁ	הַטּוֹב	בְּעֵינֶיךָ	עֲשֵׂה
na'ăseh	lō'-namlîkh	'îsh	hattôv	be'ênêkhā	'ăsēh
we will do	we will not cause to reign	a man	what is good	in your eyes	do

6. 3918.121	420	5809	8529	3937, 569.141	524, 3937	894
cj, v Qal impf 3ms	prep, ps 3mp	n ms	num	prep, v Qal inf con	cj, prep, ps 1cs	pers pron
וַיִּכְתֹּב	אֲלֵיהֶם	סֵפֶר	שֵׁנִית	לֵאמֹר	אִם־לִי	אַתֶּם
wayyikhtōv	'ălêhem	sēpher	shēnîth	lē'mōr	'im-lî	'attem
and he wrote	to them	a document	a second	saying	if to me	you

3937, 7249	894	8471.152	4089.133	881, 7513	596
cj, prep, n ms, ps 1cs	pers pron	v Qal act ptc mp	v Qal impv 2mp	do, *n mp*	*n mp*
וּלְקֹלִי	אַתֶּם	שֹׁמְעִים	קְחוּ	אֶת־רָאשֵׁי	אַנְשֵׁי
ûlăqōlî	'attem	shōme'îm	qŏchû	'eth-rā'shê	'anshê
and to my voice	you	listening	take	the heads of	the men of

1158, 112	971.133	420	3626, 6496	4417
n mp, n mp, ps 2mp	cj, v Qal impv 2mp	prep, ps 1cs	prep, art, *n fs*	adv
בְּנֵי־אֲדֹנֵיכֶם	וּבֹאוּ	אֵלַי	כָּעֵת	מָחָר
venê-'ădhōnêkhem	ûvō'û	'ēlay	kā'ēth	māchār
the sons of your master	and come	to me	according to the time of	tomorrow

3262	1158	4567	8124	382	881, 1448	6111
pn	cj, *n mp*	art, n ms	num	n ms	do, *adj*	art, n fs
יִזְרְעֶאלָה	וּבְנֵי	הַמֶּלֶךְ	שִׁבְעִים	אִישׁ	אֶת־גְּדֹלֵי	הָעִיר
yizre'e'lāh	ûvenê	hammelekh	shiv'îm	'îsh	'eth-gedhōlê	hā'îr
to Jezreel	and the sons of	the king	seventy	men	the great of	the city

1461.352	881	7. 2030.121	3626, 971.141	5809	420
v Piel ptc mp	do, ps 3mp	cj, v Qal impf 3ms	prep, v Qal inf con	art, n ms	prep, ps 3mp
מְגַדְּלִים	אוֹתָם	וַיְהִי	כְּבֹא	הַסֵּפֶר	אֲלֵיהֶם
meghaddelîm	'ôthām	wayhî	kevō'	hassēpher	'ălêhem
those causing to grow up	them	and it was	when coming	the document	to them

4089.126	881, 1158	4567	8250.126	8124	382	7947.126
cj, v Qal impf 3mp	do, *n mp*	art, n ms	cj, v Qal impf 3mp	num	n ms	cj, v Qal impf 3mp
וַיִּקְחוּ	אֶת־בְּנֵי	הַמֶּלֶךְ	וַיִּשְׁחֲטוּ	שִׁבְעִים	אִישׁ	וַיָּשִׂימוּ
wayyiqŏchû	'eth-benê	hammelekh	wayyishchătû	shiv'îm	'îsh	wayyāsîmû
then they took	the sons of	the king	and they slaughtered	seventy	men	and they put

881, 7513	904, 1783	8365.126	420	3262	8. 971.121
do, n mp, ps 3mp	prep, art, n mp	cj, v Qal impf 3mp	prep, ps 3ms	pn	cj, v Qal impf 3ms
אֶת־רָאשֵׁיהֶם	בַּדּוּדִים	וַיִּשְׁלְחוּ	אֵלָיו	יִזְרְעֶאלָה	וַיָּבֹא
'eth-rā'shêhem	baddûdhîm	wayyishlechû	'ēlāv	yizre'e'lāh	wayyāvō'
their heads	in the baskets	and they sent out	to him	to Jezreel	and he came

4534	5222.521, 3937	3937, 569.141	971.516	7513
art, n ms	cj, v Hiphil impf 3ms, prep, ps 3ms	prep, v Qal inf con	v Hiphil pf 3cp	*n mp*
הַמַּלְאָךְ	וַיַּגֶּד־לוֹ	לֵאמֹר	הֵבִיאוּ	רָאשֵׁי
hammal'ākh	wayyaggedh-lô	lē'mōr	hēvî'û	rā'shê
the messenger	and he reported to him	saying	they have brought	the heads of

1158, 4567	569.121	7947.133	881	8530	6915	6860
n mp, art, n ms	cj, v Qal impf 3ms	v Qal impv 2mp	do, ps 3mp	num	n mp	*n ms*
בְנֵי־הַמֶּלֶךְ	וַיֹּאמֶר	שִׂימוּ	אֹתָם	שְׁנֵי	צִבֻּרִים	פֶּתַח
vᵉnê-hammelekh	wayyō'mer	sîmû	'ōthām	shᵉnê	tsibburîm	pethach
the sons of the king	and he said	place	them	two	heaps	the entrance of

6. Then he wrote a letter the second time to them, saying, If ye be mine, and if ye will hearken unto my voice, take ye the heads of the men your master's sons, and come to me to Jezreel by tomorrow this time: ... If you are on my side, and if you will do my orders, come to me at Jezreel by this time tomorrow, *BB* ... if you are for me and are ready to listen to me, *Beck* ... and if you are prepared to accept orders from me, *JB* ... If you are loyal lieges of mine, cut off the heads of the princes, and bring them to me, *Knox*.

Now the king's sons, being seventy persons, were with the great men of the city, which brought them up: ... who had the care of them, *BB* ... the magnates of the city who were responsible for their upbringing, *Berkeley* ... These leading men of the city had the seventy princes in their keeping, *Knox* ... in the care of prominent men of the city, who were rearing them, *NAB*.

7. And it came to pass, when the letter came to them, that they took the king's sons, and slew seventy persons, and put their heads in baskets, and sent him them to Jezreel: ... When the letter reached them, they took the princes and slaughtered all seventy men, *Anchor* ... they took the king's sons and put them to death, *BB* ... they killed all seventy, *Knox* ... and butchered all seventy, *JB*.

8. And there came a messenger, and told him, saying, They have brought the heads of the king's sons. And he said, Lay ye them in two heaps at the entering in of the gate until the morning: ... at the entrance of the gate, *Moffatt* ... Pile them in two heaps at the entrance of the city, *NAB* ... the city gate, *NEB* ... Put them down in two masses at the doorway of the town, *BB*.

9. And it came to pass in the morning, that he went out, and stood,

the Masoretic text is, once again, the more difficult text, it probably should be preferred. In any case, as the commentators point out, Jehu's letters follow the scribal conventions of the time (cf. Wiseman, TOTC, 225; Cogan and Tadmor, AB, 113; also cf. Hobbs' helpful excursus on the "Form of the Letter in 2 Kings 5" [WBC, 62]; Hobbs' observations also apply to the present chapter of the Book).

The number "seventy" for the "sons" (or male relatives) of Ahab seems high, although such a large family would not be without precedent. In an eighth century B.C. Aramean text, one Bar-Rakib, king of Sam'al, attests that his father Panammu seized the throne by killing his father and "his seventy brothers" (cf. Cogan and Tadmor, AB, 113; also cf. Abimelech's murder of Jerub-Baal's [Gideon's] "seventy sons" [Abimelech's half-brothers] in Judg. 9:5).

Jehu's first letter (vv. 2f) represents a master stroke of indirection. By ostensibly urging the officials to prepare energetically to fight for "their master's house," it effectively undermined that very possibility. The high officials respond in v. 4, "If two kings could not resist him, how can we?" The response of the officers could be wise, since they felt that Jehu had the upper hand. Perhaps it resulted from their cowardice. Probably, however, it shows that the rebellion was more widespread than is apparent from the text. As Cogan and Tadmor (AB, 120) point out, "the clarion call" of the rebellion against the house of Ahab which echoes throughout the present two chapters is vengeance for the blood of Naboth. The confiscation of Naboth's prosperity is just one example of the poor way Ahab ruled. Such chronic problems as miscarriage of justice, excesses of lifestyle, and expensive building projects eventually took their toll on the loyalty of the public.

Jehu's second letter (v. 6a), sent in response to the officials' conciliatory reply to his first letter, was once again, masterfully composed. Perhaps unconsciously echoing the fierce determination of the late Jezebel herself in 1 Ki. 19:2 ("by this time tomorrow ..."; the wording in the Hebrew is identical), Jehu insists that the officials bring the "heads" of "your master's sons" to him in Jezreel within twenty-four

8554	5912, 1269		2030.121	904, 1269	3428.121	6198.121
art, n ms	adv, art, n ms	**9.**	cj, v Qal impf 3ms	prep, art, n ms	cj, v Qal impf 3ms	cj, v Qal impf 3ms
הַשַּׁעַר	עַד־הַבֹּקֶר		וַיְהִי	בַבֹּקֶר	וַיֵּצֵא	וַיַּעֲמֹד
hashsha‘ar	‘adh-habbōqer		wayhî	vabbōqer	wayyētsē’	wayya‘ămōdh
the gate	until the morning		and it was	in the morning	that he went out	and he stood

569.121	420, 3725, 6194	6926	894	2079	603	7489.115
cj, v Qal impf 3ms	prep, *adj*, art, n ms	adj	pers pron	intrj	pers pron	v Qal pf 1cs
וַיֹּאמֶר	אֶל־כָּל־הָעָם	צַדִּקִים	אַתֶּם	הִנֵּה	אֲנִי	קָשַׁרְתִּי
wayyō’mer	’el-kol-hā‘ām	tsaddiqîm	’attem	hinnēh	’ănî	qāshartî
and he said	to all the people	innocent	you	behold	I	I conspired

6142, 112	2103.125	4449	5409.511	881, 3725, 431
prep, n ms, ps 1cs	cj, v Qal impf 1cs, ps 3ms	cj, intrg	v Hiphil pf 3ms	do, *adj*, dem pron
עַל־אֲדֹנִי	וָאֶהַרְגֵהוּ	וּמִי	הִכָּה	אֶת־כָּל־אֵלֶּה
‘al-’ădhōnî	wā’ehreghēhû	ûmî	hikkāh	’eth-kol-’ēlleh
against my master	and I killed him	but who	he struck down	all these

	3156.133	660	3706	3940	5489.121	4623, 1745	3176	800
10.	v Qal impv 2mp	adv	cj	neg part	v Qal impf 3ms	prep, *n ms*	pn	n fs
	דְּעוּ	אֵפוֹא	כִּי	לֹא	יִפֹּל	מִדְּבַר	יְהוָה	אַרְצָה
	de‘û	’ēphô’	kî	lō’	yippōl	middevar	yehwāh	’artsāh
	know	now	that	not	it will fall	from the word of	Yahweh	to the earth

866, 1744.311	3176	6142, 1041	255	3176	6449.111
rel part, v Piel pf 3ms	pn	prep, *n ms*	pn	cj, pn	v Qal pf 3ms
אֲשֶׁר־דִּבֶּר	יְהוָה	עַל־בֵּית	אַחְאָב	וַיהוָה	עָשָׂה
’ăsher-dibber	yehwāh	‘al-bêth	’ach’āv	wayhwāh	‘āsāh
which He has spoken	Yahweh	concerning the household of	Ahab	and Yahweh	He has done

881	866	1744.311	904, 3135	5860	455		5409.521	3167
do	rel part	v Piel pf 3ms	prep, *n fs*	n ms, ps 3ms	pn	**11.**	cj, v Hiphil impf 3ms	pn
אֵת	אֲשֶׁר	דִּבֶּר	בְּיַד	עַבְדּוֹ	אֵלִיָּהוּ		וַיַּךְ	יֵהוּא
’ēth	’ăsher	dibber	beyadh	‘avdô	’ēlîyāhû		wayyakh	yēhû’
	what	He spoke	by the hand of	his servant	Elijah		and he struck down	Jehu

881	3725, 8080.256	3937, 1041, 255	904, 3262	3725, 1448
do	*adj*, art, v Niphal ptc mp	prep, *n ms*, pn	prep, pn	cj, *adj*, adj, ps 3ms
אֵת	כָּל־הַנִּשְׁאָרִים	לְבֵית־אַחְאָב	בְּיִזְרְעֶאל	וְכָל־גְּדֹלָיו
’ēth	kol-hanish’ārîm	levêth-’ach’āv	beyizre‘e’l	wekhol-gedhōlâv
	all those remaining	of the house of Ahab	in Jezreel	and all his great ones

3156.456	3669	5912, 1153	8080.511, 3937	8032
cj, v Pual ptc mp, ps 3ms	cj, n mp, ps 3ms	adv, neg part	v Hiphil pf 3ms, prep, ps 3ms	n ms
וּמְיֻדָּעָיו	וְכֹהֲנָיו	עַד־בִּלְתִּי	הִשְׁאִיר־לוֹ	שָׂרִיד
ûmeyuddā‘âv	wekhōhenâv	‘adh-biltî	hish’îr-lô	sārîdh
and those known by him	and his priests	until not	he left of them	a survivor

	7251.121	971.121	2050.121	8497	2000	1086
12.	cj, v Qal impf 3ms	cj, v Qal impf 3ms	cj, v Qal impf 3ms	pn	pers pron	pn
	וַיָּקָם	וַיָּבֹא	וַיֵּלֶךְ	שֹׁמְרוֹן	הוּא	בֵּית־עֵקֶד
	wayyāqām	wayyāvō’	wayyēlekh	shōmerôn	hû’	bêth-‘ēqedh
	and he rose up	and he came	and he went to	Samaria	he	Beth-Eked

7749.152	904, 1932		3167	4834.111	881, 250	275
art, v Qal act ptc mp	prep, art, n ms	**13.**	cj, pn	v Qal pf 3ms	do, *n mp*	pn
הָרֹעִים	בַּדָּרֶךְ		וְיֵהוּא	מָצָא	אֶת־אֲחֵי	אֲחַזְיָהוּ
hārō‘îm	baddārekh		weyēhû’	mātsā’	’eth-’āchê	’ăchazyāhû
the shepherds	on the way		and Jehu	he found	the brothers of	Ahaziah

and said to all the people, Ye be righteous: ... upright men, *BB* ... innocent, *Beck* ... blameless, *Berkeley* ... all honourable men, *Fenton*.

behold, I conspired against my master, and slew him: but who slew all these? ... I made designs against my master, and put him to death; but who is responsible for the death of all these, *BB* ... I have plotted against my master and killed him, but who killed all these, *Beck* ... I made plans, *NCV*.

10. Know now that there shall fall unto the earth nothing of the word of the LORD, which the LORD spake concerning the house of Ahab: for the LORD hath done that which he spake by his servant Elijah: ... Be sure then that every word which the LORD has spoken against the house of Ahab shall be fulfilled, *NEB* ... against the house of Ahab will fail, *NIV* ... about the family of Ahab will be without effect, *BB* ... everything that the Lord said about the descendants of Ahab will come true. The LORD has done what he promised through his prophet Elijah, *Good News*.

11. So Jehu slew all that remained of the house of Ahab in Jezreel, and all his great men, and his kinsfolks, and his priests, until he left him none remaining: ... Jehu then killed every member of the House of Ahab surviving in Jezreel, all his leading men, his close friends, his priests; he did not leave a single one alive, *JB* ... of Ahab's family in Jezreel who was still alive, *NCV* ... So Ahab was left without a single survivor, *NLT* ... all the rest of the seed of Ahab in Jezreel, and all his relations and, *BB*.

12. And he arose and departed, and came to Samaria. And as he was at the shearing house in the way: ... Jehu left and went to Samaria, *NCV* ... and on the way there, when he had reached a shepherds' shelter, *NEB* ... And when he was on the way, *Beck* ... the shepherds' lodging by the road, *Knox*.

13. Jehu met with the brethren of Ahaziah king of Judah, and said, Who are ye? And they answered, We are the brethren of Ahaziah; and we go down to salute the children of the king and the children of the queen: ... We are the relatives of Ahaziah, and we have come down to meet the families, *NIV* ... We are the kin of Ahaziah; we have come down to visit the royal princes and the sons of the queen mother, *NRSV* ... we have come down to pay our respects, *REB* ... to inquire after the welfare of, *Anchor*.

---

hours. As Hobbs (WBC, 127) points out, Jehu's second letter is apparently intentionally ambiguous. The word for "heads" in Hebrew comes from the common term rō'sh (HED #7513), and it can mean "leaders" or, literally, their "heads." (We have the same semantic range in English.) The officials delivered the actual "heads" of the unfortunate juveniles in baskets to Jehu in Jezreel. Jehu then had them piled up in two piles at the entrance of the city gate (probably one pile on each side of the city gate itself—the city gate opened into a courtyard where much of the commerce and legal business of the city would be transacted [cf. Gen. 23:10–20; Ruth 4:1–12; etc.]). What a graphic visual reminder to the people of Jehu's fierce determination to be their king, as well as the extreme methods he would use to attain that goal! (To be fair to him, it should be noted that such bloodthirsty methods were probably essential in that cultural setting; such a procedure was not without parallel elsewhere in the ancient Near East.)

Jehu's speech to the citizens of Jezreel (vv. 9f) yet again reveals both his cleverness and the moral ambiguities attending his usurpation of the throne. Yes, he personally was guilty of conspiring against the king himself, but the local leadership was just as guilty in regard to the murdering of all royal personages represented by the piled-up heads. Thus, they implicated themselves, and, in essence, were as guilty as he. Verse 10 of the present chapter is yet again a reference to the fulfillment of Elijah's original prophecy against the house of Ahab. And, just as was the case with King Hazael of Aram in 8:7f, 14f (cf. comments on those verses), Yahweh's original instructions to Elijah in 1 Ki. 19:15–18, finally are fulfilled.

But relatives of the late King Ahaziah of Judah were still alive (cf. vv. 12ff; the use of shālôm in v. 13 is the last occurrence of this significant word in the present chapters; cf. analysis in 9:14–29). The relatives were innocently seeking the shālôm of the king and queen mother (i.e., Joram and Jezebel). But, they were in for a shock. Not only did those distinguished personages suddenly "rest in peace" (events have transpired so quickly that the present group of visiting relatives probably had no idea that they were dead [but see Hobbs, WBC, 128, for a very different interpretation]), and presently, so would their would-be visitors. Indeed, we soon read of "forty-two men" being slaughtered at the well of Beth Eked (v. 14; any comparison with the forty-two boys mauled by the bears in 2:23ff is probably farfetched). The location of "Beth Eked" (in fact, even the proper translation of the name) site is uncertain, but it is generally placed near the modern town of Jenin, south of Jezreel. Monotonously, we read once again, "He left no survivor."

4567, 3171	**569.121**	**4449**	**894**	**569.126**	**250**	**275**
n ms, pn	cj, v Qal impf 3ms	intrg	pers pron	cj, v Qal impf 3mp	*n mp*	pn
מֶלֶךְ־יְהוּדָה	וַיֹּאמֶר	מִי	אַתֶּם	וַיֹּאמְרוּ	אֲחֵי	אֲחַזְיָהוּ
melekh-yehûdhāh	wayyō'mer	mî	'attem	wayyō'merû	'ăchê	'ăchazyāhû
the king of Judah	and he said	who	you	and they said	the brothers of	Ahaziah

601	**3495.120**	**3937, 8361**	**1158, 4567**	**1158**
pers pron	cj, v Qal impf 1cp	prep, *n ms*	*n mp*, art, n ms	cj, *n mp*
אֲנַחְנוּ	וַנֵּרֶד	לִשְׁלוֹם	בְּנֵי־הַמֶּלֶךְ	וּבְנֵי
'ănachnû	wannēredh	lishlôm	benê-hammelekh	ûvenê
we	and we came down	about the well-being of	the sons of the king	and the sons of

1409		**569.121**	**8945.131**	**2508**	**8945.126**
art, n fs	**14.**	cj, v Qal impf 3ms	v Qal impv 2ms, ps 3mp	adj	cj, v Qal impf 3mp, ps 3mp
הַגְּבִירָה		וַיֹּאמֶר	תִּפְשׂוּם	חַיִּים	וַיִּתְפְּשׂוּם
haggevîrāh		wayyō'mer	tiphsûm	chayyîm	wayyithpesûm
the queen mother		and he said	capture them	alive	and they captured them

2508	**8250.126**	**420, 988**	**1086**	**727**	**8530**	**382**
adj	cj, v Qal impf 3mp, ps 3mp	prep, *n ms*	pn	num	cj, num	n ms
חַיִּים	וַיִּשְׁחָטוּם	אֶל־בּוֹר	בֵּית־עֵקֶד	אַרְבָּעִים	וּשְׁנַיִם	אִישׁ
chayyîm	wayyishchāṭûm	'el-bôr	bêth-'ēqedh	'arbā'îm	ûshenayim	'îsh
alive	and they slaughtered them	at the pit of	Beth-Eked	forty	and two	men

3940, 8080.511	**382**	**4623**		**2050.121**	**4623, 8427**	**4834.121**
cj, neg part, v Hiphil pf 3ms	n ms	prep, ps 3mp	**15.**	cj, v Qal impf 3ms	prep, adv	cj, v Qal impf 3ms
וְלֹא־הִשְׁאִיר	אִישׁ	מֵהֶם		וַיֵּלֶךְ	מִשָּׁם	וַיִּמְצָא
welō'-hish'îr	'îsh	mēhem		wayyēlekh	mishshām	wayyimtsā'
and he did not leave	a man	from them		and he went	from there	and he found

881, 3184	**1158, 7683**	**3937, 7410.141**	**1313.321**	**569.121**
do, pn	*n ms*, pn	prep, v Qal inf con, ps 3ms	cj, v Piel impf 3ms, ps 3ms	cj, v Qal impf 3ms
אֶת־יְהוֹנָדָב	בֶּן־רֵכָב	לִקְרָאתוֹ	וַיְבָרְכֵהוּ	וַיֹּאמֶר
'eth-yehônādhāv	ben-rēkhāv	liqŏrā'thô	wayvārekhēhû	wayyō'mer
Jonadab	the son of Rechab	to meet him	and he blessed him	and he said

420	**1950B, 3552**	**881, 3949**	**3596**	**3626, 866**	**3949**	**6196, 3949**
prep, ps 3ms	intrg part, sub	do, n ms, ps 2ms	adj	prep, rel part	n ms, ps 1cs	prep, n ms, ps 2ms
אֵלָיו	הֲיֵשׁ	אֶת־לְבָבְךָ	יָשָׁר	כַּאֲשֶׁר	לְבָבִי	עִם־לְבָבֶךָ
'ēlâv	hăyēsh	'eth-levāvekhā	yāshār	ka'ăsher	levāvî	'im-levāvekhā
to him	will it be	your heart	upright	just as	my heart	with your heart

569.121	**3184**	**3552**	**3552**	**5598.131**	**881, 3135**	**5598.121**	**3135**
cj, v Qal impf 3ms	pn	sub	cj, sub	v Qal impv 2ms	do, n fs, ps 2ms	cj, v Qal impf 3ms	n fs, ps 3ms
וַיֹּאמֶר	יְהוֹנָדָב	יֵשׁ	וָיֵשׁ	תְּנָה	אֶת־יָדֶךָ	וַיִּתֵּן	יָדוֹ
wayyō'mer	yehônādhāv	yēsh	wāyēsh	tenāh	'eth-yādhekhā	wayyittēn	yādhô
and he said	Jonadab	it is	and it is	give	your hand	and he gave	his hand

6148.521	**420**	**420, 4981**		**569.121**	**2050.131**
cj, v Hiphil impf 3ms, ps 3ms	prep, ps 3ms	prep, art, n fs	**16.**	cj, v Qal impf 3ms	v Qal impv 2ms
וַיַּעֲלֵהוּ	אֵלָיו	אֶל־הַמֶּרְכָּבָה		וַיֹּאמֶר	לְכָה
wayya'ălēhû	'ēlâv	'el-hammerkāvāh		wayyō'mer	lekhāh
and he caused him to go up	to him	to the chariot		and he said	come

882	**7495.131**	**904, 7352**	**3937, 3176**	**7680.526**	**881**
prep, ps 1cs	cj, v Qal impv 2ms	prep, n fs, ps 1cs	prep, pn	cj, v Hiphil impf 3mp	do, ps 3ms
אִתִּי	וּרְאֵה	בְּקִנְאָתִי	לַיהוָה	וַיַּרְכִּבוּ	אֹתוֹ
'ittî	ûre'ēh	beqin'āthî	layhwāh	wayyarkivû	'ōthô
with me	and see	with my zeal	for Yahweh	and they caused to ride	him

904, 7681		971.121	8497	5409.521	881, 3725, 8080.256
prep, n ms, ps 3ms	17.	cj, v Qal impf 3ms	pn	cj, v Hiphil impf 3ms	do, *adj*, art, v Niphal ptc mp
בְּרִכְבּוֹ		וַיָּבֹא	שֹׁמְרוֹן	וַיַּךְ	אֶת־כָּל־הַנִּשְׁאָרִים
berikhbô		wayyāvō'	shōmerôn	wayyakh	'eth-kol-hanish'ārîm
in his chariot		and he came to	Samaria	and he struck down	all those remaining

3937, 255	904, 8497	5912, 8436.511	3626, 1745	3176	866
prep, pn	prep, pn	adv, v Hiphil pf 3ms, ps 3ms	prep, *n ms*	pn	rel part
לְאַחְאָב	בְּשֹׁמְרוֹן	עַד־הִשְׁמִידוֹ	כִּדְבַר	יְהוָה	אֲשֶׁר
le'ach'āv	beshōmerôn	'adh-hishmîdhô	kidhvar	yehwāh	'ăsher
to Ahab	in Samaria	until he had annihilated him	according to the word of	Yahweh	which

14. And he said, Take them alive. And they took them alive, and slew them at the pit of the shearing house, even two and forty men: neither left he any of them: ... killed 42 of them at a cistern near the shearing-place and didn't leave a one, *Beck* ... he slaughtered them at the storage-well of Beth-Eked, *JB* ... and put them to death in the water-hole, *BB* ... he spared not one of them, *Berkeley*.

15. And when he was departed thence, He lighted on Jehonadab the son of Rechab coming to meet him: and he saluted him, and said to him, Is thine heart right, as my heart is with thy heart? ... Leaving there, he came on Jehonadab son of Rechab who was on his way to meet him. He greeted him and said, Is you heart true to mine, as my heart is to yours, *JB* ... honestly with me, as I am honestly with you, *Moffatt* ... sincerely disposed toward me, as I am toward you, *NAB* ... as good a friend to me as I am to you, *NCV*.

And Jehonadab answered, It is. If it be, give me thine hand. And he gave him his hand; and he took him up to him into the chariot.: ... Give me thy hand, and lifted him up, by his outstretched hand, *Knox* ... drew him up, *NAB* ... helped him up, *NIV* ... pulled him into, *NCV*.

16. And he said, Come with me, and see my zeal for the Lord. So they made him ride in his chariot: ... You can see how strong my feelings are, *NCV* ... see how devoted I am, *NLT* ... see how I am on fire for the Lord's cause, *BB*.

17. And when he came to Samaria, he slew all that remained unto Ahab in Samaria, till he had destroyed him, according to the saying of the Lord, which he spake to Elijah: ... he killed all the survivors of Ahab in Samaria; he exterminated it completely, *Berkeley* ... When they arrived there, Jehu killed all of Ahab's relatives, not sparing even one, *Good News* ... he murdered all the survivors of Ahab in Samaria, till Ahab's house was wiped out, as the Eternal had given orders by Elijah, *Moffatt* ... of Ahab's line, doing away with them completely and thus fulfilling the prophecy which the Lord had spoken to, *NAB*.

18. And Jehu gathered all the people together, and said unto them, Ahab served Baal a little; but Jehu shall serve him much: ...

It is with some relief that we can now turn to a brief passage (vv. 15ff) focusing on friendship, not bloodshed. Jehu's meeting with "Jehonadab son of Recab," who "was on his way to meet him" (note the irony of this would-be visitor's fate as being diametrically the opposite of the would-be visitors in the previous several verses), bespeaks of an ally seeking out the new king, to be of service to him. Hobbs (WBC, 128f, following a suggestion made by F. S. Frick) argues rather convincingly that the phrase usually translated "son of Recab" actually may well have originally signified a member of the chariot corps (the Hebrew root is usually associated with chariotry, HED #7680), or else of the chariot-making guild. Note Jehu's mention of his own longstanding service as a chariot rider under Ahab in 9:25. Further mention of the "Recabites" may be found in Jer. 35, where their longstanding faithfulness to their ancestor's commands is contrasted to the faithlessness of Judah to the commands of Yahweh. Commentators generally note that both Jehu and Jehonadab seem to represent a more primitive or "puritanical" strain within Israel, thus making them natural allies (v. 15; the "giving of the hand," i.e., the shaking of hands, is shown on Assyrian reliefs as a sign of agreement by equal parties pledging their mutual trust [so Wiseman, TOTC, 227, who cites Ezra 10:19 and Ezek. 17:18 as biblical parallels]). Mention has already been made of Jehu's "zeal for Yahweh" in v. 16 of the present passage (see above, on 9:14–29). We will soon see what bloodthirsty direction this "zeal" was to take (cf. vv. 23ff). The final verse of this passage once again links Jehu's actions to Elijah's prior prophecies (cf. introductory remarks to chs. 9–10; also cf. 9:1–13).

2 Kings 10:18–22

1744.311	420, 455		7192.121	3167	881, 3725, 6194	569.121
v Piel pf 3ms	prep, pn	18.	cj, v Qal impf 3ms	pn	do, *adj*, art, n ms	cj, v Qal impf 3ms
דִּבֶּר	אֶל־אֵלִיָּהוּ		וַיִּקְבֹּץ	יֵהוּא	אֶת־כָּל־הָעָם	וַיֹּאמֶר
dibber	'el-'ēlîyāhû		wayyiqŏbbōts	yēhû'	'eth-kol-hā'ām	wayyō'mer
He had spoken	to Elijah		and he gathered	Jehu	all the people	and he said

420	255	5856.111	881, 1197	4746	3167	5856.121	7528.542
prep, ps 3mp	pn	v Qal pf 3ms	do, art, pn	sub	pn	v Qal impf 3ms, ps 3ms	v Hiphil inf abs
אֲלֵהֶם	אַחְאָב	עָבַד	אֶת־הַבַּעַל	מְעָט	יֵהוּא	יַעַבְדֶנּוּ	הַרְבֵּה
'ălēhem	'ach'āv	'āvadh	'eth-habba'al	m^{e}'āt	yēhû'	ya'avdhennû	harbēh
to them	Ahab	he served	the Baal	little	Jehu	he will serve him	making abundant

	6498	3725, 5204	1197	3725, 5856.152	3725, 3669
19.	cj, adv	*adj, n mp*	art, pn	*adj*, v Qal act ptc mp, ps 3ms	cj, *adj*, n mp, ps 3ms
	וְעַתָּה	כָּל־נְבִיאֵי	הַבַּעַל	כָּל־עֹבְדָיו	וְכָל־כֹּהֲנָיו
	w^{e}'attāh	khol-n^{e}vî'ê	habba'al	kol-'ōv^{e}dhāv	w^{e}khol-kōh^{e}nâv
	and now	all the prophets of	the Baal	all those serving him	and all his priests

7410.133	420	382	414, 6734.221	3706	2160	1448	3937
v Qal impv 2mp	prep, ps 1cs	n ms	adv, v Niphal juss 3ms	cj	n ms	adj	prep, ps 1cs
קִרְאוּ	אֵלַי	אִישׁ	אַל־יִפָּקֵד	כִּי	זֶבַח	גָּדוֹל	לִי
qir'û	'ēlay	'îsh	'al-yippāqēdh	kî	zevach	gādhôl	lî
call	to me	a man	may he not be mustered	because	a sacrifice	great	to me

3937, 1197	3725	866, 6734.221	3940	2513.121	3167	6449.111
prep, art, n ms	n ms	rel pron, v Niphal impf 3ms	neg part	v Qal impf 3ms	cj, pn	v Qal pf 3ms
לַבַּעַל	כֹּל	אֲשֶׁר־יִפָּקֵד	לֹא	יִחְיֶה	וְיֵהוּא	עָשָׂה
labba'al	kōl	'ăsher-yippāqēdh	lō'	yichăyeh	w^{e}yēhû'	'āsāh
for the Baal	everyone	who he is mustered	not	he will live	and Jehu	he acted

904, 6360	3937, 4775	6.541	881, 5856.152	1197		569.121
prep, n fs	prep, prep	v Hiphil inf con	do, *v Qal act ptc mp*	art, pn	20.	cj, v Qal impf 3ms
בְּעָקְבָּה	לְמַעַן	הַאֲבִיד	אֶת־עֹבְדֵי	הַבַּעַל		וַיֹּאמֶר
v^{e}'āqŏbbāh	l^{e}ma'an	ha'ăvîdh	'eth-'ōv^{e}dhê	habbā'al		wayyō'mer
with cunning	so that	to cause to perish	the servants of	the Baal		and he said

3167	7227.333	6355	3937, 1197	7410.126		8365.121
pn	v Piel impv 2mp	n fs	prep, art, n ms	cj, v Qal impf 3mp	21.	cj, v Qal impf 3ms
יֵהוּא	קַדְּשׁוּ	עֲצָרָה	לַבַּעַל	וַיִּקְרָאוּ		וַיִּשְׁלַח
yēhû'	qadd^{e}shû	'ătsārāh	labba'al	wayyiqŏrā'û		wayyishlach
Jehu	sanctify	a cultic assembly	for the Baal	and they proclaimed		and he sent out

3167	904, 3725, 3547	971.126	3725, 5856.152	1197	3940, 8080.211
pn	prep, *adj*, pn	cj, v Qal impf 3mp	*adj, v Qal act ptc mp*	art, pn	cj, neg part, v Niphal pf 3ms
יֵהוּא	בְּכָל־יִשְׂרָאֵל	וַיָּבֹאוּ	כָּל־עֹבְדֵי	הַבַּעַל	וְלֹא־נִשְׁאַר
yēhû'	b^{e}khol-yisrā'ēl	wayyāvō'û	kol-'ōv^{e}dhê	habba'al	w^{e}lō'-nish'ar
Jehu	in all Israel	and they came	all the servants of	the Baal	and he did not remain

382	866	3940, 971.111	971.126	1041	1197	4527.221
n ms	rel pron	neg part, v Qal pf 3ms	cj, v Qal impf 3mp	*n ms*	art, pn	cj, v Niphal impf 3ms
אִישׁ	אֲשֶׁר	לֹא־בָא	וַיָּבֹאוּ	בֵּית	הַבַּעַל	וַיִּמָּלֵא
'îsh	'ăsher	lō'-vā'	wayyāvō'û	bêth	habba'al	wayyimmālē'
a man	who	he did not come	and they entered	the temple of	the Baal	and it was filled

1041, 1197	6552	3937, 6552		569.121	3937, 866	6142, 4599
n ms, art, pn	n ms	prep, n ms	22.	cj, v Qal impf 3ms	prep, rel pron	prep, art, n fs
בֵּית־הַבַּעַל	פֶּה	לָפֶה		וַיֹּאמֶר	לַאֲשֶׁר	עַל־הַמֶּלְתָּחָה
vêth-habba'al	peh	lāpheh		wayyō'mer	la'ăsher	'al-hammeltāchāh
the temple of the Baal	a mouth	to a mouth		and he said	to who	over the costumes

Jehu summoned all the people, *Berkeley* ... Jehu called a meeting of all the people of the city and said to them, Ahab hardly worshiped Baal at all compared to the way I will worship him, *NLT* ... Ahab offered Baal small service; but Jehu will offer much more, *NRSV* ... Ahab was Baal's servant in a small way, but Jehu will be his servant on a great scale, *BB*.

19. Now therefore call unto me all the prophets of Baal, all his servants, and all his priests; let none be wanting: ... summon for me all Baal's prophets, all his worshipers, and, *NAB* ... let not one be missing, *Berkeley* ... let none be absent, *Goodspeed* ... let no one keep away, *BB*.

for I have a great sacrifice to do to Baal; whosoever shall be wanting, he shall not live: ... I am preparing a great sacrifice for Baal. Every one who is missing shall forfeit his life, *Berkeley* ... whoever is absent, *Goodspeed* ... Anyone who fails to come will no longer live, *NIV* ... I have a great offering to make to Baal; anyone who is not present, will be put to death, *BB*.

But Jehu did it in subtlety, to the intent that he might destroy the worshippers of Baal: ... deceptively in order to destroy the servants of Baal, *Berkeley* ... with deliberate cunning in order to wipe out, *Goodspeed* ... This was a trick on Jehu's part to destroy the devotees of Baal, *JB* ... Jehu did this craftily, *Douay*.

20. And Jehu said, Proclaim a solemn assembly for Baal. And they proclaimed it: ... Let there be a special holy meeting for the worship of Baal. So a public statement was made, *BB* ... a day of worship in honor of Baal, *Good News* ... Summon a sacred assembly for Baal, *JB* ... Proclaim a festival for Baal, *Douay*.

21. And Jehu sent through all Israel: and all the worshippers of Baal came, so that there was not a man left that came not: ... Jehu sent word, *Anchor* ... not one kept away, *BB* ... there wasn't anyone left behind who didn't come, *Beck* ... sent messengers throughout Israel, and all the devotees of Baal arrived, not a man was left who did not attend, *JB*.

And they came into the house of Baal; and the house of Baal was full from one end to another: ... from end to end, *Anchor* ... and went to the Temple of Bal and filled the Temple of Bal all over, *Fenton* ... They crowded into the temple of Baal until it was full from wall to wall, *JB* ... All the worshipers of Baal without exception came into the temple of Baal, which was filled to capacity, *NAB*.

22. And he said unto him that was over the vestry, Bring forth vestments for all the worshippers of Baal. And he brought them forth vestments: ... to the one who was in charge of the wardrobe. Bring out garments for, *NASB* ... to the man who kept the robes, Bring out robes for, *NCV* ... for all the ministers of Baal, *NIV* ... He then said to the Superintendent of the Wardrobe, Bring out uniforms, *Fenton*.

10:18–27. Clergy and worshipers of Baal killed. Yet again, Jehu's clever but savage actions are both fascinating and repulsive. By now, the whole house of Ahab, and many of the house of Ahaziah, had been exterminated, but, seemingly, there still remained most of the clergy and the laity loyal to the Canaanite god Baal (concerning Jezebel's devotion to her ancestral god Baal-Hadad, see comments on 9:30–37). So Jehu and his new ally Jehonadab got to work. Once again, he summoned the future victims (v. 18ff), this time the prophets, ministers and priests of Baal. They all arrived, though by now it seems that few would wish to disobey any "invitation" from this new king. Besides, Jehu claimed that he wished to serve Baal more fervently than did his predecessors ("Ahab served Baal a little; Jehu will serve him much" [v. 18]; Hobbs [WBC, 129] points out that Ahab, after all, did give Yahwistic names to his sons Ahaziah and Joram). Any usurper, especially one who must have alienated so many by his bloodthirsty actions, would have been expected to show some sort of allegiance to his predecessors' religious sensibilities—hence, the particularly seductive nature of Jehu's prevarication in v. 18 ("whatever you may think of me, I will be even more loyal to the Baal religion than the preceding kings were—you can depend on that"). Commentators (e.g., Hobbs, WBC, 129) often point out the macabre wordplays in the Hebrew text (such as zevach [HED #2160] in v. 19, which normally means "sacrifice" can also mean "slaughter" [especially of apostates]; also the similar sounding Hebrew verbs 'āvadh [HED #5856], "to serve," and 'āvadh [HED #6], "to perish," or, in the causative stem, "to destroy"). Both the clergy and the laity were sucked into his lies, and soon joined their political compatriots "resting in peace." Once again, to be fair to Jehu, religious factions of the day often resorted to mass bloodshed (cf. Elijah's slaughter of the 450 prophets of Baal in 1 Ki. 18:40, and references to Jezebel's slaughtering of the Yahwistic prophets previously in the same chapter; vv. 4, 13; also her infamous threat to Elijah himself in 19:2).

The ruse worked like a charm (v. 21). After ensuring that there were no Yahweh worshipers in the crowd (Wiseman [TOTC, 227] is probably correct in his preference for the translation "wor-

3428.531	3961	3937, 3725	5856.152	1197	3428.521	3937
v Hiphil impv 2ms	n ms	prep, n ms	*v Qal act ptc mp*	art, pn	cj, v Hiphil impf 3ms	prep, ps 3mp
הוֹצֵא	לְבוּשׁ	לְכֹל	עֹבְדֵי	הַבָּעַל	וַיֹּצֵא	לָהֶם
hôtsē'	levûsh	lekhōl	'ōvedhê	habbā'al	wayyōtsē'	lāhem
bring out	clothes	for everyone	the servants of	the Baal	and he brought out	to them

4540		971.121	3167	3184	1158, 7683	1041	1197
art, n ms	23.	cj, v Qal impf 3ms	pn	cj, pn	*n ms*, pn	*n ms*	art, pn
הַמַּלְבּוּשׁ		וַיָּבֹא	יֵהוּא	וִיהוֹנָדָב	בֶּן־רֵכָב	בֵּית	הַבָּעַל
hammalbûsh		wayyāvō'	yēhû'	wîhônādhāv	ben-rēkhāv	bêth	habbā'al
the clothing		and he entered	Jehu	and Jonadab	the son of Rechab	the temple of	the Baal

569.121	3937, 5856.152	1197	2769.333	7495.133
cj, v Qal impf 3ms	prep, *v Qal act ptc mp*	art, pn	v Piel impv 2mp	cj, v Qal impv 2mp
וַיֹּאמֶר	לְעֹבְדֵי	הַבַּעַל	חַפְּשׂוּ	וּרְאוּ
wayyō'mer	le'ōvedhê	habba'al	chappesû	ûre'û
and he said	to the servants of	the Baal	search	and see

6678, 3552, 6553	6196	4623, 5860	3176	3706	524, 5856.152
adv, sub, adv	prep, ps 2mp	prep, *n mp*	pn	cj	cj, *v Qal act ptc mp*
פֶּן־יֶשׁ־פֹּה	עִמָּכֶם	מֵעַבְדֵי	יְהוָה	כִּי	אִם־עֹבְדֵי
pen-yesh-pōh	'immākhem	mē'avdhê	yehwāh	kî	'im-'ōvedhê
so that there is not here	with you	from the servants of	Yahweh	except	only the servants of

1197	3937, 940		971.126	3937, 6449.141	2160	6150
art, pn	prep, n ms, ps 3mp	24.	cj, v Qal impf 3mp	prep, v Qal inf con	n mp	cj, n fp
הַבַּעַל	לְבַדָּם		וַיָּבֹאוּ	לַעֲשׂוֹת	זְבָחִים	וְעֹלוֹת
habba'al	levaddām		wayyāvō'û	la'ăsôth	zevāchîm	we'ōlôth
the Baal	by themselves		and they entered	to make	sacrifices	and burnt offerings

3167	7947.111, 3937	904, 2445	8470	382	569.121	382
cj, pn	v Qal pf 3ms, prep, ps 3ms	prep, art, n ms	num	n ms	cj, v Qal impf 3ms	art, n ms
וְיֵהוּא	שָׂם־לוֹ	בַחוּץ	שְׁמֹנִים	אִישׁ	וַיֹּאמֶר	הָאִישׁ
weyēhû'	sām-lô	vachûts	shemōnîm	'îsh	wayyō'mer	hā'îsh
and Jehu	he had stationed for himself	in the street	eighty	men	and he said	the man

866, 4561.221	4623, 596	866	603	971.551	6142, 3135
rel pron, v Niphal impf 3ms	prep, art, n mp	rel pron	pers pron	v Hiphil ptc ms	prep, n fd, ps 2mp
אֲשֶׁר־יִמָּלֵט	מִן־הָאֲנָשִׁים	אֲשֶׁר	אֲנִי	מֵבִיא	עַל־יְדֵיכֶם
'ăsher-yimmālēṭ	min-hā'ănāshîm	'ăsher	'ănî	mēvî'	'al-yedhêkhem
who he allows to escape	among the men	whom	I	causing to go	opposite your hands

5497	8809	5497		2030.121	3626, 3735.141	3937, 6449.141
n fs, ps 3ms	prep	n fs, ps 3ms	25.	cj, v Qal impf 3ms	prep, v Qal inf con, ps 3ms	prep, v Qal inf con
נַפְשׁוֹ	תַּחַת	נַפְשׁוֹ		וַיְהִי	כְּכַלֹּתוֹ	לַעֲשׂוֹת
naphshô	tachath	naphshô		wayhî	kekhallōthô	la'ăsôth
his life	instead of	his life		and it was	when his finishing	to make

6150	569.121	3167	3937, 7608.152	3937, 8388	971.133
art, n fs	cj, v Qal impf 3ms	pn	prep, art, v Qal act ptc mp	cj, prep, n mp	v Qal impv 2mp
הָעֹלָה	וַיֹּאמֶר	יֵהוּא	לָרָצִים	וְלַשָּׁלִשִׁים	בֹּאוּ
hā'ōlāh	wayyō'mer	yēhû'	lārātsîm	welashshālishîm	bō'û
the burnt offering	and he said	Jehu	to the runners	and to the adjutants	enter

5409.533	382	414, 3428.121	5409.526
v Hiphil impv 2mp, ps 3mp	n ms	adv, v Qal juss 3ms	cj, v Hiphil impf 3mp, ps 3mp
הַכּוּם	אִישׁ	אַל־יֵצֵא	וַיַּכּוּם
hakkûm	'îsh	'al-yētsē'	wayyakkûm
strike them down	a man	do not let him go out	and they struck them down

3937, 6686, 2820 prep, *n ms*, n fs לְפִי־חָרֶב lephî-chārev with the edge of the sword	8390.526 cj, v Hiphil impf 3mp וַיַּשְׁלִכוּ wayyashlikhû and they threw	7608.152 art, v Qal act ptc mp הָרָצִים hārātsîm the runners	8388 cj, art, n mp וְהַשָּׁלִשִׁים wehashshālishîm and the adjutants	2050.126 cj, v Qal impf 3mp וַיֵּלְכוּ wayyēlekhû and they went

5912, 6111 adv, *n fs* עַד־עִיר 'adh-'îr unto the city of	1158, 1197 *n ms*, art, pn בֵּית־הַבָּעַל bêth-habbā'al the temple of the Baal	**26.**	3428.526 cj, v Hiphil impf 3mp וַיֹּצִאוּ wayyōtsi'û and they caused to go out	881, 4838 do, *n fp* אֶת־מַצְּבוֹת 'eth-matstsevôth the pillars of

23. And Jehu went, and Jehonadab the son of Rechab, into the house of Baal, and said unto the worshippers of Baal, Search, and look that there be here with you none of the servants of the LORD, but the worshippers of Baal only: ... Make quite sure that there are no devotees of Yahweh in here with you, but only devotees of Baal, *JB* ... Make sure that only worshipers of Baal are present and that no worshiper of the LORD has come in, *Good News* ... Look carefully and make sure that there are no servants of the LORD here with you, but only the ministers of Baal, *NEB* ... Make a search with care, *BB*.

24. And when they went in to offer sacrifices and burnt offerings, Jehu appointed fourscore men without, and said, If any of the men whom I have brought into your hands escape, he that letteth him go, his life shall be for the life of him: ... Jehu had put eighty men outside, and said to them, If any man whom I give into your hands gets away, the life of him who lets him go will be the price of his life, *BB* ... you will pay for his life with yours, *Beck* ... Whoever lets one of the people go whom I am now putting within your clutches, will pay for it with his life, *JB* ... If you let any of my quarry slip through your hands, *Knox*.

25. And it came to pass, as soon as he had made an end of offering the burnt offering, that Jehu said to the guard and to the captains, Go in, and slay them; let none come forth: ... let no one out, *Moffatt* ... Let no one escape, *NAB* ... Go in and kill the worshipers of Baal, *NCV* ... Jehu ordered the guards and the lieutenants to go and cut them all down, *NEB*.

And they smote them with the edge of the sword; and the guard and the captains cast them out, and went to the city of the house of Baal: ... killed the worshipers of Baal with the sword and threw their bodies out, *NCV* ... and went into the inner room of the temple of Baal, *NKJV* ... and officers dragged their bodies outside, *NLT* ... they went into the holy place of, *BB*.

26. And they brought forth the images out of the house of Baal, and burned them: ... the sacred pillar of the temple of Baal, *Beck* ... brought out the sacred pole, *Goodspeed* ... brought forth columns, *Darby* ... took out Baal's statue from the temple, to burn it, *Knox*.

shipers" instead of NIV's "ministers" here; also cf. NRSV; NLT), Jehu offered the burnt offering (v. 25). It should be noted that kings not rarely presided over such offerings; cf. the extreme case of Solomon offering up tens of thousands of "peace" offerings in 1 Ki. 8:63, as well as the burnt offerings and grain offerings of v. 64. But Jehu had more than the deaths of animals on his mind in the present passage. Into the temple of Baal crammed with clergy and lay worshipers (cf. v. 21), Jehu sent his guards and officers to massacre the people and desecrate permanently the sacred objects (vv. 26f; probably the "sacred stone" of NIV is better understood as a "sacred pillar" or the like [so Wiseman, TOTC, 228; cf. NLT]). If it was made of stone, it could have been "burned," then "demolished" by pouring cold water on the already heated object (so Jones, NCBC, 471; citing John Gray). The famous Moabite Stone suffered such a fate in the hands of the local Arabs in 1868. Finally, the temple area was turned into a "latrine" (v. 27; NIV; NRSV), or "public toilet" (NLT) which remains "to this day." Although such an odoriferous image certainly catches the reader's eye or ear, the Hebrew probably signifies something more along the lines of a "public dump" (cf. Cogan and Tadmor, AB, 116; also Wiseman, TOTC, 228—the Hebrew term mōchor'ôth [HED #4418, in the Kethiv or "written" text preserved by the Masoretes] is found only here in the Hebrew Bible). In any case, the temple location (which, by the way, is still unknown; the numerous excavations of Samaria that have taken place have yet to uncover the site [cf. Hobbs, WBC, 129], which actually may have been situated on one of the mountains outside of the city [so Yigael Yadin, as cited in Cogan and Tadmor, AB, 116]) was

1158, 1197	8041.126		5606.126	881	4838	1197
n ms, art, pn	cj, v Qal impf 3mp, ps 3fs	**27.**	cj, v Qal impf 3mp	do	*n fs*	art, pn
בֵּית־הַבַּעַל	וַיִּשְׂרְפוּהָ		וַיִּתְּצוּ	אֵת	מַצְּבַת	הַבָּעַל
bêth-habba'al	wayyisrephûāh		wayyittetsû	'ēth	matstsevath	habbā'al
the temple of the Baal	and they burned it		and they tore down		the pillar of	the Baal

5606.126	1041	1197	7947.126	3937, 4418	5912, 3219
cj, v Qal impf 3mp	*n ms*	art, pn	cj, v Qal impf 3mp, ps 3ms	prep, n fp	adv, art, n ms
וַיִּתְּצוּ	אֶת־בֵּית	הַבַּעַל	וַיְשִׂמֻהוּ	לְמַחֲרָאוֹת	עַד־הַיּוֹם
wayyittetsû	'eth-bêth	habba'al	waysimuhû	lemachărā'ôth	'adh-hayyôm
and they tore down	the temple of	the Baal	and they made it into	for a latrine	until today

	8436.521	3167	881, 1197	4623, 3547		7828	2491	3493
28.	cj, v Hiphil impf 3ms	pn	do, art, pn	prep, pn	**29.**	adv	*n mp*	pn
	וַיַּשְׁמֵד	יֵהוּא	אֶת־הַבַּעַל	מִיִּשְׂרָאֵל		רַק	חֲטָאֵי	יָרָבְעָם
	wayyashmēdh	yēhû'	'eth-habba'al	mîyisrā'ēl		raq	chăṭā'ê	yārov'ām
	and he destroyed	Jehu	the Baal	from Israel		only	the sins of	Jeroboam

1158, 5203	866	2490.511	881, 3547	3940, 5681.111	3167	4623, 313
n ms, pn	rel part	v Hiphil pf 3ms	do, pn	neg part, v Qal pf 3ms	pn	prep, prep, ps 3mp
בֶּן־נְבָט	אֲשֶׁר	הֶחֱטִיא	אֶת־יִשְׂרָאֵל	לֹא־סָר	יֵהוּא	מֵאַחֲרֵיהֶם
ben-nevāṭ	'ăsher	hechĕṭî'	'eth-yisrā'ēl	lō'-sār	yēhû'	mē'achrêhem
the son of Nebat	which	he caused to sin	Israel	he did not turn	Jehu	from after them

5903	2174	866	1044	866	904, 1896		569.121	3176
n mp	art, n ms	rel part	pn	cj, rel part	prep, pn	**30.**	cj, v Qal impf 3ms	pn
עֶגְלֵי	הַזָּהָב	אֲשֶׁר	בֵּית־אֵל	וַאֲשֶׁר	בְּדָן		וַיֹּאמֶר	יְהוָה
'eghlê	hazzāhāv	'ăsher	bêth-'ēl	wa'ăsher	bedhān		wayyō'mer	yehwāh
the calves of	the gold	which	Bethel	and which	in Dan		and he said	Yahweh

420, 3167	3391	866, 3004.513	3937, 6449.141	3596	904, 6084
prep, pn	cj	rel part, v Hiphil pf 2ms	prep, v Qal inf con	art, adj	prep, n fd, ps 1cs
אֶל־יֵהוּא	יַעַן	אֲשֶׁר־הֱטִיבֹתָ	לַעֲשׂוֹת	הַיָּשָׁר	בְּעֵינַי
'el-yēhû'	ya'an	'ăsher-hĕṭîvōthā	la'ăsôth	hayyāshār	be'ênay
to Jehu	because	that you have made good	to do	what is right	in my eyes

3626, 3725	866	904, 3949	6449.113	3937, 1041	255
prep, n ms	rel part	prep, n ms, ps 1cs	v Qal pf 2ms	prep, *n ms*	pn
כְּכֹל	אֲשֶׁר	בִּלְבָבִי	עָשִׂיתָ	לְבֵית	אַחְאָב
kekhōl	'ăsher	bilvāvî	'āsîthā	levêth	'ach'āv
according to everything	which	in my heart	you have done	to the household of	Ahab

1158	7536	3553.126	3937	6142, 3802	3547		3167	3940
n mp	n mp	v Qal impf 3mp	prep, ps 2ms	prep, *n ms*	pn	**31.**	cj, pn	neg part
בְּנֵי	רְבִעִים	יֵשְׁבוּ	לְךָ	עַל־כִּסֵּא	יִשְׂרָאֵל		וְיֵהוּא	לֹא
benê	revi'îm	yēshevû	lekhā	'al-kissē'	yisrā'ēl		weyēhû'	lō'
the sons of	fourth	they will sit	of you	on the throne of	Israel		but Jehu	not

8490.111	3937, 2050.141	904, 8784, 3176	435, 3547	904, 3725, 3949
v Qal pf 3ms	prep, v Qal inf con	prep, *n fs*, pn	*n mp*, pn	prep, *adj*, n ms, ps 3ms
שָׁמַר	לָלֶכֶת	בְּתוֹרַת־יְהוָה	אֱלֹהֵי־יִשְׂרָאֵל	בְּכָל־לְבָבוֹ
shāmar	lālekheth	bethôrath-yehwāh	'ĕlōhê-yisrā'ēl	bekhol-levāvô
he was careful	to walk	in the Law of Yahweh	the God of Israel	with all his heart

3940	5681.111	4623, 6142	2496	3493	866	2490.511	881, 3547
neg part	v Qal pf 3ms	prep, prep	*n fp*	pn	rel part	v Hiphil pf 3ms	do, pn
לֹא	סָר	מֵעַל	חַטֹּאות	יָרָבְעָם	אֲשֶׁר	הֶחֱטִיא	אֶת־יִשְׂרָאֵל
lō'	sār	mē'al	chaṭṭō'wth	yārov'ām	'ăsher	hechĕṭî'	'eth-yisrā'ēl
not	he turned aside	from beside	the sins of	Jeroboam	which	he caused to sin	Israel

27. And they brake down the image of Baal, and brake down the house of Baal, and made it a draught house unto this day: ... demolishing the pillar of Baal, and destroying the temple of Baal till it became a latrine, *Moffatt* ... they smashed the stele of Baal, tore down the building, *NAB* ... they made it into a sewage pit, as it is today, *NCV* ... made it a refuse dump, *NKJV.*

28. Thus Jehu destroyed Baal out of Israel: ... wiped out Baal from Israel, *NRSV* ... stamped out the worship of Baal, *REB* ... destroyed every trace of Baal worship, *NLT* ... rooted out Baal, *Anchor.*

29. Howbeit from the sins of Jeroboam the son of Nebat, who made Israel to sin, Jehu departed not from after them, to wit, the golden calves that were in Beth-el, and that were in Dan: ... Jehu did not keep himself from all the sins of Jeroboam, the son of Nebat, and the evil he made Israel do; the gold oxen were still in, *BB* ... he did not remove the sins of Jeroboam, *Berkeley* ... Jehu did not give up the sins into which Jeroboam son of Nebat had led Israel, *JB* ... he would not forgo the sins of Jeroboam son of Nabat, that taught Israel to sin; at Bethel and at Dan the golden calves had their worship still, *Knox*.

30. And the LORD said unto Jehu, Because thou hast done well in executing that which is right in mine eyes, and hast done unto the house of Ahab according to all that was in mine heart, thy children of the fourth generation shall sit on the throne of Israel: ... in carrying out my will, punishing the house of Ahab exactly as I intended, *Moffatt* ... what I deem right, and have treated the house of Ahab as I desire, your sons to, *NAB* ... in obeying what I said was right. You have done to the family of Ahab as I wanted. Because of this, your descendants as far as your great-great-grandchildren will be kings of Israel, *NCV* ... in accomplishing what is right in my eyes and have done to the house of Ahab all I had in mind to do, *NIV.*

31. But Jehu took no heed to walk in the law of the LORD God of Israel with all his heart: for he departed not from the sins of Jeroboam, which made Israel to sin: ... Jehu did not take care to keep the law of the Lord with all his heart: he did not keep himself, *BB* ... Jehu wasn't careful to live, *Beck* ... he did not turn, *Goodspeed* ... Jehu, however, did not faithfully and wholeheartedly follow the law of Yahweh, *JB*.

---

clearly and notoriously rendered unsuitable for future worship. The "bathroom humor" of Elijah in 1 Ki. 18:27, concerning the reasons the god Baal was being unresponsive to his prophets' prayers ("perhaps … he is relieving himself" [NLT]), may find an ironic parallel here.

10:28–36. Conclusion to the Jehu narrative: Yahweh's approval and Yahweh's judgment. These verses certainly seem to betray the ambivalent attitude the writer has toward King Jehu. Clearly he, on the one hand, appreciated most certainly his "zeal for Yahweh," especially over against the previous apostasy of the house of Ahab and Jezebel, with their relentless persecution of Yahwism and their ceaseless encouragement of Baal worship. Yet, on the other hand, Jehu's bloodthirsty ways seemed to have been too much, even by the standards of the day. So it is that we have a "pro" and "con" sequence here. In v. 28, Jehu is positively cited for his destruction of Baal worship in Israel, but in the next verse, he is condemned, as so many of his predecessors were, for succumbing to the "sin of Jeroboam [I] son of Nebat," i.e., the worship of idols. In v. 30, he is highly praised by Yahweh for his faithfulness and dedication. But again, in the very next verse, he is condemned for not fully keeping the Law, again just like Jeroboam I (once again, some fifteen out of the total of eighteen kings who came after Jeroboam I in the north are condemned in these terms; cf. comments on 3:1ff). Then the narrator begins to cite a negative example (in vv. 32f) to support his thesis of how Israel began to decline in Jehu's day (brief notices concerning the various political expansions and declines of both Israel and Judah are plenteous indeed; cf. comments on 8:20ff, above; also cf. 3:25; 14:22, 25, 28; 15:16, 19f, 29, 37; etc.). The chapter then closes with what can be termed a "further reference" statement (v. 34; cf. comments on 1:17f); then a burial notice (v. 35); and, finally, a belated notice concerning Jehu's regnal total. And thus, this lengthy section, comprising some two chapters, and some seventy-three verses, finally draws to a close. Both Israel and Judah are radically changed kingdoms, largely due to the remarkable zeal and the incredible barbarity of Jehu son of Nimshi.

A few notes about specific verses in this section: The prophecy of the "four generations" in v. 30, although perhaps indeed a "parody" (so Hobbs, WBC, 126) of the Davidic promise of an eternal dynasty in the south (cf. David's charge to Solomon in 1 Ki. 2:1–4; also the classic text in 2 Sam. 7), nonetheless represents by far the longest of the roughly nine "dynasties" which ruled the north (some of these "dynasties," of course, comprised only one person). Comparisons of Albright's and

32.	904, 3219	2062	2591.511	3176	3937, 7380.341	904, 3547
	prep, art, n mp	art, dem pron	v Hiphil pf 3ms	pn	prep, v Piel inf con	prep, pn
	בַּיָּמִים	הָהֵם	הֵחֵל	יְהוָה	לְקַצּוֹת	בְּיִשְׂרָאֵל
	bayyāmîm	hāhēm	hēchēl	yehwāh	leqatstsôth	beyisrā'ēl
	in the days	the those	He began	Yahweh	to cut off pieces	in Israel

5409.521	2462	904, 3725, 1397	3547	33.	4623, 3497
cj, v Hiphil impf 3ms, ps 3mp	pn	prep, *adj*, *n ms*	pn		prep, art, pn
וַיַּכֵּם	חֲזָאֵל	בְּכָל־גְּבוּל	יִשְׂרָאֵל		מִן־הַיַּרְדֵּן
wayyakkēm	chăzā'ēl	bekhol-gevûl	yisrā'ēl		min-hayyardēn
and he struck them down	Hazael	within all the borders of	Israel		from the Jordan

4350	8507	881	3725, 800	1609	1455	7499
n ms	art, n ms	do	adj, *n fs*	art, pn	art, pn	cj, art, pn
מִזְרַח	הַשֶּׁמֶשׁ	אֵת	כָּל־אֶרֶץ	הַגִּלְעָד	הַגָּדִי	וְהָראוּבֵנִי
mizrach	hashshemesh	'ēth	kol-'erets	haggil'ādh	haggādhî	wehāru'wvēnî
the rising of	the sun		all the land of	the Gilead	the Gadites	and the Reubenites

4668	4623, 6416	866	6142, 5337	792	1609	1347
cj, art, pn	prep, pn	rel part	prep, *n ms*	pn	cj, art, pn	cj, art, pn
וְהַמְנַשִּׁי	מֵעֲרֹעֵר	אֲשֶׁר	עַל־נַחַל	אַרְנֹן	וְהַגִּלְעָד	וְהַבָּשָׁן
wehamnashshî	mē'ărō'ēr	'ăsher	'al-nachal	'arnōn	wehaggil'ādh	wehabbāshān
and the Manassites	from Aroer	which	beside the Wadi	Arnon	and the Gilead	and the Bashan

34.	3615	1745	3167	3725, 866	6449.111	3725, 1400
	cj, *n ms*	*n mp*	pn	cj, *adj*, rel part	v Qal pf 3ms	cj, *adj*, n fs, ps 3ms
	וְיֶתֶר	דִּבְרֵי	יֵהוּא	וְכָל־אֲשֶׁר	עָשָׂה	וְכָל־גְּבוּרָתוֹ
	weyether	divrê	yēhû'	wekhol-'ăsher	'āsāh	wekhol-gevûrāthô
	and the remainder of	the events of	Jehu	and all which	he did	and all his strength

1950B, 3940, 2062	3918.156	6142, 5809	1745	3219	3937, 4567
intrg part, neg part, pers pron	v Qal pass ptc mp	prep, *n ms*	*n mp*	art, n mp	prep, *n mp*
הֲלוֹא־הֵם	כְּתוּבִים	עַל־סֵפֶר	דִּבְרֵי	הַיָּמִים	לְמַלְכֵי
hălô'-hēm	kethûvîm	'al-sēpher	divrê	hayyāmîm	lemalkhê
are they not	things written	on the scroll of	the events of	the days	of the kings of

3547	35.	8311.121	3167	6196, 1	7196.126	881	904, 8497
pn		cj, v Qal impf 3ms	pn	prep, n mp, ps 3ms	cj, v Qal impf 3mp	do, ps 3ms	prep, pn
יִשְׂרָאֵל		וַיִּשְׁכַּב	יֵהוּא	עִם־אֲבֹתָיו	וַיִּקְבְּרוּ	אֹתוֹ	בְּשֹׁמְרוֹן
yisrā'ēl		wayyishkav	yēhû'	'im-'ăvōthâv	wayyiqōbberû	'ōthô	beshōmerôn
Israel		and he lay	Jehu	with his ancestors	and they buried	him	in Samaria

32. In those days the LORD began to cut Israel short: and Hazael smote them in all the coasts of Israel: ... At that time the Lord began to dismember Israel, *NAB* ... the LORD began to be weary of Israel; and Hazael ravaged them in all, *Douay* ... Hazael struck them in all, *KJVII* ... Hazael defeated them everywhere, all over the territory of Israel, *Moffatt*.

33. From Jordan eastward, all the land of Gilead, the Gadites, and the Reubenites, and the Manassites, from Aroer, which is by the river Arnon, even Gilead and Bashan: ... taking all the land of the Jordan known as the land of Gilead, *NCV* ... all the country of Gilead, *Beck*.

34. Now the rest of the acts of Jehu, and all that he did, and all his might, are they not written in the book of the chronicles of the kings of Israel? ... the affairs of Jehu, and all that he did, and all his achievements, they are recorded in the history of the events of the times, *Fenton* ... his valor and all his accomplishments, *NAB* ... and his strength, *Douay* ... everything he did and all his victories, *NCV*.

35. And Jehu slept with his fathers: and they buried him in Samaria. And Jehoahaz his son reigned in his stead: ... rested with his forefathers, *NEB* ... When Jehu died, he was buried with his ancestors in Samaria, *NLT* ... Jehoahaz his son succeeded him as king, *NIV* ... in his place, *NKJV*.

36. And the time that Jehu reigned over Israel in Samaria was twenty and eight years: ... twenty-eight years, *NRSV* ... Jehu's rule over Israel, *BB* ... was king of Israel, *Beck*.

Thiele's chronologies show that Jehu's dynasty lasted a minimum of eighty-nine years (ninety-nine years according to my own chronological calculations). This is no small length of time, and it should further be recalled that at least one of Jehu's descendants, namely Jeroboam II (cf. 2 Ki. 14:23–29, and especially vv. 25, 28), was one of the most powerful monarchs the land of Israel had ever known. (Subsequent reference to the "four generation" prophecy may be found in 15:12.)

In vv. 32f, Aramean successes in the Transjordanian regions of Gad, Reuben and east Manasseh (comprising the entire region of Gilead, from the Arnon Gorge east of the Dead Sea in the south, to Bashan near the Sea of Galilee in the north) are interpreted as Yahweh's judgment against Jehu, particularly due to his lack of fidelity to the Torah (v. 31; cf. the so-called "Law of the King" in Deut. 17:14–20, especially vv. 18ff which promise a long reign for any king and his descendants who remain faithful to the Law). As is commonly pointed out (cf., e.g., John E. Hartley, *Theological Wordbook of the Old Testament*, 1:403ff), the Hebrew term tôrāh (HED #8784), which is often translated as "Law," is better understood as "Teachings." The Law represents divine guidance—authoritative, to be sure, but guidance, nonetheless. It is hardly a list of inflexible rules guaranteeing a life free of misfortune and heartache. Still, it represents par excellence the will, advice and instructions of Yahweh our God. Neglect of the Law would lead to disaster, but love of and devotion to the Law would lead to continued success and prosperity (Josh. 1:6–9; Ps. 1:2f, 6). And this Jehu did not do. He did not keep the Law "with all his heart" (in clear contrast to David; cf. 1 Ki. 11:4, 6, 38; 14:8; 15:3, 5; etc.). Therefore, we are not surprised to read about continued Aramean oppression in the reign of Jehu's son, Jehoahaz (cf. 13:3, 22)—Moab was now apparently free to the south (cf. the Moabite Stone; also, 2 Ki. 13:20), as is Edom as well (cf. 8:22); and the Arameans controlled the entirety of the northern Trans-jordan. Thus nothing north or east of the Jordan River was in Israelite (or Judahite) hands. It was not until the reign of Jehoash, son of Jehoahaz, that we read of Israelite successes in the region (13:25). And that was only because of the grace and compassion of Yahweh the God of Israel: "To this day he has been unwilling to destroy [Israel] or banish them from his presence" (13:23). Our God is, and always has been, a God of love and mercy.

11:1–21. *Athaliah the Queen Mother versus Jehoiada the High Priest: Contending for the Kingship of Judah, the Life of King Joash, and the Future of the Davidic Dynasty. With the beginning of this chapter, attention is now directed toward the southern kingdom of Judah—more particularly, with the stirring story of the accession of the youthful King Joash to the throne. Actually both (chs. 11–12) deal with King Joash of Judah, but, inasmuch as a formal accession formula opens ch. 12 (12:1 in the English text, but 12:2 in the Hebrew), each chapter will be treated separately. Jehoiada the high priest is an important figure in this narrative, for in sharp contrast with most of the high priests in pre-exilic Israel (who rather appropriately basically remain unmentioned in the narratives), Jehoiada played a very active role in saving the Davidic dynasty from the wrath of the enraged queen mother, Athaliah (who, of course, was bitterly mourning the death of her son Ahaziah, as well as so many of his relatives, at the hands of King Jehu [cf. 9:27ff; 10:12ff]). As was the case in the previous two chapters, strong and vigorous actions by both men and women—for good and for ill—predominate.*

The present chapter is clearly a single narrative unit, with the possible exception of the last verse (11:21 in the English text, but 12:1 in the Hebrew text). The story is once again told vividly, with detailed dialogue interspersed with quickly moving action sequences. Indeed, here we gain perhaps the clearest perspective of the temple and palace bureaucracies in pre-exilic Israel anywhere in Scripture. After a brief introduction (vv. 1ff), the narrative of the youthful Joash's coronation day takes center stage (vv. 4–21). References to Joash's seventh year seem to bracket this latter passage, forming an inclusio (for a brief definition of "inclusio," cf. introductory comments on 7:1–20). All in all, 2 Ki. 11 demonstrates Yahweh's faithfulness to the covenant of David, ensuring survival of David's descendant Joash even in the midst of seemingly total disaster. There are no prophets nor any prophetic messages in the chapter, but the hand of Yahweh is, in retrospect, evident throughout. Such is life sometimes, leadership walking in faith as best they can, and, after the crises are over, looking back on the goodness and the faithfulness of God.

4566.121	3168	1158	8809		3219	866	4566.111
cj, v Qal impf 3ms	pn	n ms, ps 3ms	prep, ps 3ms	**36.**	cj, art, n mp	rel part	v Qal pf 3ms
וַיִּמְלֹךְ	יְהוֹאָחָז	בְּנוֹ	תַּחְתָּיו		וְהַיָּמִים	אֲשֶׁר	מָלַךְ
wayyimlōkh	yehô'āchāz	benô	tachtâv		wehayyāmîm	'ăsher	mālakh
and he reigned	Jehoahaz	his son	instead of him		and the days	which	he reigned

3167	6142, 3547	6465	8470, 8523	904, 8497		6510	525
pn	prep, pn	num	cj, num, n fs	prep, pn	**11:1**	cj, pn	*n fs*
יֵהוּא	עַל־יִשְׂרָאֵל	עֶשְׂרִים	וּשְׁמֹנֶה־שָׁנָה	בְּשֹׁמְרוֹן		וַעֲתַלְיָה	אֵם
yēhû'	'al-yisrā'ēl	'esrîm	ûshemōneh-shānāh	beshōmerôn		wa'ăthalyāh	'ēm
Jehu	over Israel	twenty	and eight years	in Samaria		and Athaliah	the mother of

275	7495.112	3706	4322.111	1158	7251.122	6.322	881
pn	cj, v Qal pf 3fs	cj	v Qal pf 3ms	n ms, ps 3fs	cj, v Qal impf 3fs	cj, v Piel impf 3fs	do
אֲחַזְיָהוּ	וּרָאֲתָה	כִּי	מֵת	בְּנָהּ	וַתָּקָם	וַתְּאַבֵּד	אֵת
'ăchazyāhû	ûrā'ăthāh	kî	mēth	benāhh	wattāqām	watte'abbēdh	'ēth
Ahaziah	when she saw	that	he died	her son	then she rose up	and she annihilated	

3725, 2320	4608		4089.122	3191	1351, 4567, 3245
adj, n ms	art, n fs	**2.**	cj, v Qal impf 3fs	pn	*n fs*, n ms, pn
כָּל־זֶרַע	הַמַּמְלָכָה		וַתִּקַּח	יְהוֹשֶׁבַע	בַּת־הַמֶּלֶךְ־יוֹרָם
kol-zera'	hammamlākhāh		wattiqqach	yehôsheva'	bath-hammelekh-yôrām
all the descendants of	the kingdom		but she took	Jehosheba	the daughter of the king Joram

269	275	881, 3204	1158, 275	1630.122	881
n fs	pn	do, pn	*n ms*, pn	cj, v Qal impf 3fs	do, ps 3ms
אֲחוֹת	אֲחַזְיָהוּ	אֶת־יוֹאָשׁ	בֶּן־אֲחַזְיָה	וַתִּגְנֹב	אֹתוֹ
'ăchôth	'ăchazyāhû	'eth-yô'āsh	ben-'ăchazyāh	wattighnōv	'ōthô
the sister of	Ahaziah	Joash	the son of Ahaziah	and she stole	him

4623, 8761	1158, 4567	4604	881	881, 3352.553
prep, *n ms*	*n mp*, art, n ms	art, n mp	do, ps 3ms	cj, do, v Hiphil ptc fs, ps 3ms
מִתּוֹךְ	בְּנֵי־הַמֶּלֶךְ	הַמְּמוֹתְתִים	אֹתוֹ	וְאֶת־מֵינִקְתּוֹ
mittôkh	benê-hammelekh	hammamôthethîm	'ōthô	we'eth-mêniqōttô
from the midst of	the sons of the king	the deaths	him	and his nurse

904, 2410	4433	5846.526	881	4623, 6686	6510	3940
prep, *n ms*	art, n fp	cj, v Hiphil impf 3mp	do, ps 3ms	prep, *n mp*	pn	cj, neg part
בַּחֲדַר	הַמִּטּוֹת	וַיַּסְתִּרוּ	אֹתוֹ	מִפְּנֵי	עֲתַלְיָהוּ	וְלֹא
bachdhar	hammittôth	wayyastirû	'ōthô	mippenê	'ăthalyāhû	welō'
in the inner room of	the beds	and they hid	him	from before	Athaliah	and not

4322.611		2030.121	882	1041	3176	2331.751	8666	8523
v Hophal pf 3ms	**3.**	cj, v Qal impf 3ms	prep, ps 3fs	*n ms*	pn	v Hithpael ptc ms	num	n fp
הוּמָת		וַיְהִי	אִתָּהּ	בֵּית	יְהוָה	מִתְחַבֵּא	שֵׁשׁ	שָׁנִים
hûmāth		wayhî	'ittāhh	bêth	yehwāh	mithchabbē'	shēsh	shānîm
he was killed		and he was	with her	the temple of	Yahweh	hiding	six	years

6510	4566.153	6142, 800		904, 8523	8113	8365.111	3179
cj, pn	v Qal act ptc fs	prep, art, n fs	**4.**	cj, prep, art, n fs	art, num	v Qal pf 3ms	pn
וַעֲתַלְיָה	מֹלֶכֶת	עַל־הָאָרֶץ		וּבַשָּׁנָה	הַשְּׁבִיעִית	שָׁלַח	יְהוֹיָדָע
wa'ăthalyāh	mōlekheth	'al-hā'ārets		ûvashshānāh	hashshevî'îth	shālach	yehôyādhā'
and Athaliah	reigning	over the land		and in the year	the seventh	he sent out	Jehoiada

4089.121	881, 8015	4119	3937, 3876	3937, 7608.152
cj, v Qal impf 3ms	do, *n mp*	art, num	prep, art, pn	cj, prep, v Qal act ptc mp
וַיִּקַּח	אֶת־שָׂרֵי	הַמֵּאוֹת	לַכָּרִי	וְלָרָצִים
wayyiqqach	'eth-sārê	hammē'yôth	lakkārî	welārātsîm
and he got	the commanders of	the hundreds	of the Carites	and of the runners

11:1. And when Athaliah the mother of Ahaziah saw that her son was dead, she arose and destroyed all the seed royal: ... the seed of the kingdom, *KJVII* ... put all the princes of the royal house to death, *Knox* ... she began to kill off the whole royal family, *NAB* ... the royal offspring, *NASB*.

2. But Jehosheba, the daughter of king Joram, sister of Ahaziah, took Joash the son of Ahaziah, and stole him from among the king's sons which were slain; and they hid him, even him and his nurse, in the bedchamber from Athaliah, so that he was not slain: ... away from among the princes who were being murdered, *NEB* ... in a bedroom to hide him from Athaliah, so he was not killed, *NCV* ... took Ahaziah's infant son, Joash, and stole him away from among the rest of the king's children, who were about to be killed, *NLT* ... where he was hidden from Athaliah and escaped death, *REB*.

3. And he was with her hid in the house of the LORD six years. And Athaliah did reign over the land: ... ruled the country, *Anchor* ... for six years, she kept him safe, *BB* ... Jehosheba took care of the boy and kept him hidden in the Temple, while Athaliah ruled as queen, *Good News* ... governed the country, *JB*.

4. And the seventh year Jehoiada sent and fetched the rulers over hundreds, with the captains and the guard, and brought them to him into the house of the LORD: ... the commanders of the army and the royal bodyguard, took them into the temple, *Knox* ... summoned the captains of the Carians and of the guards. He had them come, *NAB* ... of the bodyguards and the escorts, *NKJV*.

and made a covenant with them, and took an oath of them in the house of the LORD, and showed them the king's son: ... He made a pact with them, put them on oath, *JB* ... he made a compact with them, obliging them to swear by the temple of the Eternal, *Moffatt* ... exacted from them a sworn commitment, *NAB* ... made an agreement with them. He made them promise loyalty, *NCV*.

11:1–3. Introduction: Athaliah takes over as queen in Judah; her daughter Jehosheba hides the baby Prince Joash for six years. As just noted, strong personalities predominate in the Joash narrative, and such is certainly the case in these few introductory verses. The writer seems totally uninterested in the "reign" of Queen Athaliah (daughter of the infamous Ahab and Jezebel [cf. above, 8:18, 26]); no regnal accession formula is ever given for her reign. All the writer stresses is the fact that she tried to exterminate the entire royal family of Judah. However, another strong and capable woman, by the name of Jehosheba (and quite possibly Athaliah's very own daughter [she is described quite specifically in v. 2 as "daughter of King Jehoram and sister of Ahaziah"; cf. Cogan and Tadmor, AB, 126]), succeeds in thwarting her mother's will. Once again, strong women, for good or for ill, are prominently featured in these introductory verses. As in the cases of Sarah and Ruth, Deborah and Esther, Priscilla and the Virgin Mary, the Bible is replete with strong and vigorous female personalities.

We gain further information from the chronicler's version of this story (cf. 2 Chr. 22:10ff). There we are told quite explicitly that Jehosheba (there spelled Jehoshabeath) was wife of the high priest Jehoiada (v. 11). The young Prince Joash was apparently hidden in or near the temple of Yahweh for his first six years (cf. vv. 2f of the present passage in 2 Kings—the "bedroom" of v. 2 probably being in the priests' dormitory or the like [cf. Hobbs, WBC, 138], or else in the actual apartment of the high priest himself [Cogan and Tadmor, AB, 126]). In any case, hiding the infant prince in the temple area gives further support to the identification made in 2 Chronicles that Jehosheba was married to the high priest. As Sarah Japhet, in her fine Chonicles commentary (*Old Testament Library*, 828f), points out, that the writer "passed in silence over this detail is no indication that it is inauthentic."

The attention to detail that characterizes the rest of the chapter contrasts vividly to the brief treatment given the actions of Athaliah. This gives legitimacy to the reign of Joash, in contrast to that of Athaliah. Once again, emphases and omissions are crucial features of any given narrative. We should always take note both what a given text does dwell on, and what it passes over in silence.

11:4–12. The high priest Jehoiada prepares carefully for young Joash's coronation day. As noted above, one could well argue that the entirety of 11:4–21 is a single unit, but for the purposes of ease in discussion, the narrative is divided into the present three subsections. Yet again, vigorous personalities predominate—this time the high priest Jehoiada. Again, there is not a hint of prophetic authorization (or lack of same) for his preparations. Overriding concerns for the preservation of the Davidic dynasty precluded this. In general, it is hard to overestimate the contrast between the

971.521	881	420	1041	3176	3901.121	3937
cj, Hiphil impf 3ms	do, ps 3mp	prep, ps 3ms	*n ms*	pn	cj, v Qal impf 3ms	prep, ps 3mp
וַיָּבֵא	אֹתָם	אֵלָיו	בֵּית	יְהוָה	וַיִּכְרֹת	לָהֶם
wayyāvē'	'ōthām	'ēlâv	bêth	yᵉhwāh	wayyikhrōth	lāhem
and he brought	them	to him	the temple of	Yahweh	and he cut	for them

1311	8123.521	881	904, 1041	3176	7495.521
n fs	cj, v Hiphil impf 3ms	do, ps 3mp	prep, *n ms*	pn	cj, v Hiphil impf 3ms
בְּרִית	וַיַּשְׁבַּע	אֹתָם	בְּבֵית	יְהוָה	וַיַּרְא
bᵉrîth	wayyashba'	'ōthām	bᵉvêth	yᵉhwāh	wayyarᵉ'
a covenant	and he caused to swear	them	in the temple of	Yahweh	and he showed

881	881, 1158, 4567		6943.321	3937, 569.141	2172	1745
do, ps 3mp	do, *n ms*, art, n ms	**5.**	cj, v Piel impf 3ms, ps 3mp	prep, v Qal inf con	dem pron	art, n ms
אֹתָם	אֶת־בֶּן־הַמֶּלֶךְ		וַיְצַוֵּם	לֵאמֹר	זֶה	הַדָּבָר
'ōthām	'eth-ben-hammelekh		waytsawwēm	lē'mōr	zeh	haddāvār
them	the son of the king		and he commanded them	saying	this	the thing

866	6449.128	8389	4623	971.152	8141
rel part	v Qal impf 2mp	art, n fs	prep, ps 2mp	*v Qal act ptc mp*	art, n fs
אֲשֶׁר	תַּעֲשׂוּן	הַשְּׁלִשִׁית	מִכֶּם	בָּאֵי	הַשַּׁבָּת
'ăsher	ta'ăsûn	hashshᵉlishîth	mikkem	bā'ê	hashshabbāth
which	you will do	the third part	of you	those going into	the Sabbath

8490.152	5111	1041	4567		8389
cj, *v Qal act ptc mp*	*n fs*	*n ms*	art, n ms	**6.**	cj, art, n fs
וְשֹׁמְרֵי	מִשְׁמֶרֶת	בֵּית	הַמֶּלֶךְ		וְהַשְּׁלִשִׁית
wᵉshōmᵉrê	mishmereth	bêth	hammelekh		wᵉhashshᵉlishîth
and those who keep watch for	the guarding of	the household of	the king		and the third part

904, 8554	5683	8389	904, 8554	313	7608.152	8490.117
prep, *n ms*	pn	cj, art, n fs	prep, art, n ms	prep	art, v Qal act ptc mp	cj, v Qal pf 2mp
בְּשַׁעַר	סוּר	וְהַשְּׁלִשִׁית	בַּשַּׁעַר	אַחַר	הָרָצִים	וּשְׁמַרְתֶּם
bᵉsha'ar	sûr	wᵉhashshᵉlishîth	bashsha'ar	'achar	hārātsîm	ûshᵉmartem
by the gate of	Sur	and the third part	in the gate	behind	the runners	and you will guard

881, 5111	1041	4685		8692	3135	904	3725
do, *n fs*	art, n ms	adv	**7.**	cj, num	art, n fp	prep, ps 2mp	n ms
אֶת־מִשְׁמֶרֶת	הַבַּיִת	מַסָּח		וּשְׁתֵּי	הַיָּדוֹת	בָּכֶם	כֹּל
'eth-mishmereth	habbayith	massāch		ûshᵉttê	hayyādhôth	bākhem	kōl
the guarding of	the household	alternatively		and two	the parts	among you	everyone

3428.152	8141	8490.116	881, 5111	1041, 3176
v Qal act ptc mp	art, n fs	cj, v Qal pf 3cp	do, *n fs*	*n ms*, pn
יֹצְאֵי	הַשַּׁבָּת	וְשָׁמְרוּ	אֶת־מִשְׁמֶרֶת	בֵּית־יְהוָה
yōtsᵉ'ê	hashshabbāth	wᵉshāmᵉrû	'eth-mishmereth	bêth-yᵉhwāh
those going out on	the Sabbath	and they will guard	the duty of	the temple of Yahweh

420, 4567		5545.517	6142, 4567	5623	382	3747
prep, art, n ms	**8.**	cj, v Hiphil pf 2mp	prep, art, n ms	adv	n ms	cj, n mp, ps 3ms
אֶל־הַמֶּלֶךְ		וְהִקַּפְתֶּם	עַל־הַמֶּלֶךְ	סָבִיב	אִישׁ	וְכֵלָיו
'el-hammelekh		wᵉhiqqaphtem	'al-hammelekh	sāvîv	'îsh	wᵉkhēlâv
to the king		and you will surround	beside the king	all around	each	and his weapons

904, 3135	971.151	420, 7901	4322.621	2030.133
prep, n fs, ps 3ms	cj, v Qal act ptc ms	prep, art, n fp	v Hophal impf 3ms	cj, v Qal impv 2mp
בְּיָדוֹ	וְהַבָּא	אֶל־הַשְּׂדֵרוֹת	יוּמָת	וִהְיוּ
bᵉyādhô	wᵉhabbā'	'el-hassᵉdhērôth	yûmāth	wihyû
in his hand	and the one entering	into the ranks	he will be executed	and be

5. And he commanded them, saying, This is the thing that ye shall do; A third part of you that enter in on the sabbath shall even be keepers of the watch of the king's house: ... he gave them their directions, *Knox* ... who come on duty on the sabbath will keep guard over the palace, *Anchor* ... Come on the Sabbath and fix the Guards to guard the king's palace, *Fenton* ... who come on duty on the Sabbath must mount guard at the royal palace, *JB*.

6. And a third part shall be at the gate of Sur; and a third part at the gate behind the guard: so shall ye keep the watch of the house, that it be not broken down: ... the running guard, *Beck* ... the bodyguard, *Berkeley* ... This way you will guard the Temple, *NCV* ... and the other third at the gate with the outrunners, *NEB*.

7. And two parts of all you that go forth on the sabbath, even they shall keep the watch of the house of the LORD about the king: ... you who are in the other two companies that normally go off Sabbath duty are all to guard the temple for the king, *NIV* ... the two contingents of you who go off duty on the Sabbath, *NKJV* ... all who leave on the Sabbath, must provide a watch over the king at the LORD's temple, *Beck* ... Two detachments of all of you, *Berkeley*.

8. And ye shall compass the king round about, every man with his weapons in his hand: and he that cometh within the ranges, let him be slain: and be ye with the king as he goeth out and as he cometh in: ... whoever comes to the ranks, *Anchor* ... Stay with the king at all times, *Beck* ... any one intruding into the ranks, *Berkeley* ... You are to guard King Joash with drawn swords and stay with him wherever he goes. Anyone who comes near you is to be killed, *Good News*.

---

remarkable dynastic stability in pre-exilic Judah (some 424 years from the accession of David to the throne, possibly in 1010, to the fall of Jerusalem in 586) over against the equally remarkable dynastic instability of the Northern Kingdom, Israel, which altogether lasted a much shorter time (some 210 years from the accession of Jeroboam I in ca. 932 to the fall of Samaria in 722). Surely, this contrast helps explain the relative religious conservatism and stability of the south (at least after Solomon's death) over against the religious pluralism and instability of the north.

In any case, Jehoiada's successful thwarting of Queen Athaliah corresponds rather closely to Jehu's earlier coup in the north. As G. H. Jones (NCBC, 475, following J. A. Montgomery) points out, "Whereas the revolt in the north was led by Jehu, a soldier, who took advantage of the opposition to the Omride dynasty fanned by the prophetic movement, the coup d'état ["stroke against the state"] in the south was a combined effort by the people, the priesthood and the palace guards. The movement in the north although inspired by the prophets, failed but the movement in the south, because it had been organized by the priesthood and involved military personnel and the populace, and was to a large degree a movement supported by the religious establishment, had a more permanent success"

As is commonly noted, the temple precincts adjoined the palace, and so there was inevitable overlap between temple personnel and the royal guard. Thus, Jehoiada the high priest was able to summon the military officials, including the "Carites" (on this term, see below), as well as the rest of the royal escorts (literally, the "outrunners," rātsîm (HED #7608), including the various shifts of the palace guards, each apparently serving one week out of three (so Cogan and Tadmor [AB, 127], who, following A. B. Ehrlich, note the similar setup for the forced labor battalions in the days of Solomon [cf. 1 Ki. 5:13f]). It should be noted, however, that some of the details found in vv. 5ff of the present chapter are hard to delineate (cf. Hobbs WBC, 139f, whose suggestions, however, basically agree with Cogan and Tadmor). In any case, all of the shifts were apparently to report to duty on this occasion (even those who normally have the day off), and their various guard stations are then specified: for those normally on duty, one third should report to the royal palace, one third to the "Sur" gate (but see below), and one third to the gate "behind the guard." For the two-thirds who would normally have been off duty, they should all report to the Temple, to be ready to protect the young king (and, possibly to be less conspicuous than if they had assembled in the more public locations). What is clear in all this is the meticulous forethought involved in the plans and the need to put the leaders "under oath" to be faithful to the king and to the high priest (v. 4).

Brief notes on the "Carites" (v. 4) and the "Sur Gate" (v. 6): both of these terms, while very defensible translations of the Hebrew, are disputed. Most commentators understand the "Carites" (kārî, HED #3876) as foreign mercenaries from Caria in southwest Asia Minor (cf. Wiseman, TOTC, 231), and perhaps analogous to the "Kerethites" in the days of King David (cf. 2 Sam. 20:23, Kethiv [concerning the term "kethiv," which means "written" in Aramaic, cf. on 10:18–27]). David's "Kerethites and

882, 4567	904, 3428.141	904, 971.141		6449.126
prep, art, n ms	prep, v Qal inf con, ps 3ms	cj, v Qal inf con, ps 3ms	**9.**	cj, v Qal impf 3mp
אֶת־הַמֶּלֶךְ	בְּצֵאתוֹ	וּבְבֹאוֹ		וַיַּעֲשׂוּ
'eth-hammelekh	betsē'thô	ûvevō'ô		wayya'ăsû
with the king	when his going out	and when his coming in		and they did

8015	4119	3626, 3725	866, 6943.311	3179
n mp	art, num	prep, n ms	rel part, v Piel pf 3ms	pn
שָׂרֵי	הַמֵּאוֹת	כְּכֹל	אֲשֶׁר־צִוָּה	יְהוֹיָדָע
sārê	hammē'yôth	kekhōl	'ăsher-tsiwwāh	yehôyādhā'
the commanders of	the hundreds	according to everything	that he had commanded	Jehoiada

3669	4089.126	382	881, 596	971.152	8141	6196
art, n ms	cj, v Qal impf 3mp	n ms	do, n mp, ps 3ms	*v Qal act ptc mp*	art, n fs	prep
הַכֹּהֵן	וַיִּקְחוּ	אִישׁ	אֶת־אֲנָשָׁיו	בָּאֵי	הַשַּׁבָּת	עִם
hakkōhēn	wayyiqŏchû	'îsh	'eth-'ănāshâv	bā'ê	hashshabbāth	'im
the priest	and they got	each	his men	those going into	the Sabbath	with

3428.152	8141	971.126	420, 3179	3669		5598.121
v Qal act ptc mp	art, n fs	cj, v Qal impf 3mp	prep, pn	art, n ms	**10.**	cj, v Qal impf 3ms
יֹצְאֵי	הַשַּׁבָּת	וַיָּבֹאוּ	אֶל־יְהוֹיָדָע	הַכֹּהֵן		וַיִּתֵּן
yōtse'ê	hashshabbāth	wayyāvō'û	'el-yehôyādhā'	hakkōhēn		wayyittēn
those going out of	the Sabbath	and they came	to Jehoiada	the priest		and he gave

3669	3937, 8015	4119	881, 2698	881, 8377	866	3937, 4567
art, n ms	prep, *n mp*	art, num	do, art, n fs	cj, do, art, n mp	rel part	prep, art, n ms
הַכֹּהֵן	לְשָׂרֵי	הַמֵּאוֹת	אֶת־הַחֲנִית	וְאֶת־הַשְּׁלָטִים	אֲשֶׁר	לַמֶּלֶךְ
hakkōhēn	lesārê	hammē'yôth	'eth-hachnîth	we'eth-hashshelāṭîm	'ăsher	lammelekh
the priest	to the commanders of	the hundreds	the spears	and the shields	which	to the king

1784	866	904, 1041	3176		6198.126	7608.152	382
pn	rel part	prep, *n ms*	pn	**11.**	cj, v Qal impf 3mp	art, v Qal act ptc mp	n ms
דָּוִד	אֲשֶׁר	בְּבֵית	יְהוָה		וַיַּעַמְדוּ	הָרָצִים	אִישׁ
dāwidh	'ăsher	bevêth	yehwāh		wayya'amdhû	hārātsîm	'îsh
David	which	in the temple of	Yahweh		and they stood	the runners	each

3747	904, 3135	4623, 3931	1041	3342	5912, 3931
cj, n mp, ps 3ms	prep, n fs, ps 3ms	prep, *n fs*	art, n ms	art, n fs	prep, *n fs*
וְכֵלָיו	בְּיָדוֹ	מִכֶּתֶף	הַבַּיִת	הַיְמָנִית	עַד־כֶּתֶף
wekhēlâv	beyādhô	mikketheph	habbayith	haymānîth	'adh-ketheph
and his weapons	in his hand	from the side of	the house	the right side	unto the side of

1041	7974	3937, 4326	3937, 1041	6142, 4567	5623
art, n ms	art, n fs	prep, art, n ms	cj, prep, art, n ms	prep, art, n ms	adv
הַבַּיִת	הַשְּׂמָאלִית	לַמִּזְבֵּחַ	וְלַבָּיִת	עַל־הַמֶּלֶךְ	סָבִיב
habbayith	hassemā'lîth	lammizbēach	welabbāyith	'al-hammelekh	s̱āvîv
the house	the left side	to the altar	and to the house	unto the king	all around

	3428.521	881, 1158, 4567	5598.121	6142	881, 5325
12.	cj, v Hiphil impf 3ms	do, *n ms*, art, n ms	cj, v Qal impf 3ms	prep, ps 3ms	do, art, n ms
	וַיּוֹצִא	אֶת־בֶּן־הַמֶּלֶךְ	וַיִּתֵּן	עָלָיו	אֶת־הַנֵּזֶר
	wayyôtsi'	'eth-ben-hammelekh	wayyittēn	'ālâv	'eth-hannēzer
	and he brought out	the son of the king	and he placed	on him	the diadem

881, 5925	4566.526	881	5066.126
cj, do, art, n fs	cj, v Hiphil impf 3mp	do, ps 3ms	cj, v Qal impf 3mp, ps 3ms
וְאֶת־הָעֵדוּת	וַיַּמְלִכוּ	אֹתוֹ	וַיִּמְשְׁחֻהוּ
we'eth-hā'ēdhûth	wayyamlikhû	'ōthô	wayyimshāchuhû
and the testimony	and they caused to reign	him	and they anointed him

5409.526, 3834	569.126	2513.121	4567		8471.122	6510
cj, v Hiphil impf 3mp, n fs	cj, v Qal impf 3mp	v Qal juss 3ms	art, n ms		cj, v Qal impf 3fs	pn
וַיַּכּוּ־כָף	וַיֹּאמְרוּ	יְחִי	הַמֶּלֶךְ	**13.**	וַתִּשְׁמַע	עֲתַלְיָה
wayyakkû-khāph	wayyō'm^{e}rû	y^{e}chî	hammelekh		wattishma'	'ăthalyāh
and they struck hands	and they said	may he live	the king		and she heard	Athaliah

881, 7249	7608.152	6194	971.122	420, 6194	1041	3176
do, *n ms*	art, v Qal act ptc mp	art, n ms	cj, v Qal impf 3fs	prep, art, n ms	*n ms*	pn
אֶת־קוֹל	הָרָצִין	הָעָם	וַתָּבֹא	אֶל־הָעָם	בֵּית	יְהוָה
'eth-qôl	hārātsîn	hā'ām	wattāvō'	'el-hā'ām	bêth	y^{e}hwāh
the sound of	the runners	the people	and she came	to the people	the temple of	Yahweh

9. And the captains over the hundreds did according to all things that Jehoiada the priest commanded: and they took every man his men that were to come in on the sabbath, with them that should go out on the sabbath, and came to Jehoiada the priest: ... The regimental commanders did everything as Jehoiada the priest had ordered, *JB* ... the centurions did, *Douay* ... The commanders over a hundred men obeyed everything, *NCV* ... each one brought his men, those coming on duty … and those going off duty … and reported to, *JB*.

10. And to the captains over hundreds did the priest give king David's spears and shields, that were in the temple of the LORD: ... The priest handed the captains the spears and shields belonging to king David, which had lain in the temple of the Eternal, *Moffatt* ... the priest delivered, *RSV* ... spears and quivers, *Anchor* ... spears and body-covers, *BB*.

11. And the guard stood, every man with his weapons in his hand, round about the king, from the right corner of the temple to the left corner of the temple, along by the altar and the temple: ... from the south end of the House to the north end of the House, at the altar and the house, all about the king, *Anchor* ... the armed men took up their positions, every man with his instruments of war in his hand, *BB* ... to right and to left of altar and temple stood armed men ready to protect the king, *Knox*.

12. And he brought forth the king's son, and put the crown upon him, and gave him the testimony: ... and the insignia upon him, *NAB* ... diadem upon him, *Douay* ... a copy of the agreement, *NCV* ... he presented him with a copy of the covenant, *NIV*.

and they made him king, and anointed him; and they clapped their hands, and said, God save the king: ... Long live the king, *Moffatt* ... They appointed him king and poured olive oil on him, *NCV* ... and they all,

Pelethites," however, are usually seen as coming from Crete (the "Kerethites," sometimes spelled "Cherethites" [k^{e}rēthî, HED #3903]) and the Aegean regions further west (the "Pelethites" perhaps originally "Philistines" who, themselves, had come from that area). In any case, Cogan and Tadmor (AB, 126) are probably correct to label the Carites as "the traditional 'Swiss guard' of the Davidides," loyal to the family from the earliest times. As for the "Sur Gate," such a gate is otherwise unknown, and in the Chronicles parallel (2 Chr. 23:5), it is termed the "Foundation Gate" (shā'ar s̱ûr [HED #8554, 5683] in Kings, but sha'ar hays̱ôdh [HED #8554, 3356] in Chronicles). But the Chronicles' reading is also not without problems. There is no parallel elsewhere for the "Foundation Gate," either. Some would connect the "Sur Gate" of the present text to the "Horse Gate" (derekh-m^{e}vô' hass̱ûs̱îm [HED #1932, 4264, 5670] literally, "the way of the entrance of the horses") in v. 16 below; but, with our present lack of knowledge concerning pre-exilic gates in Jerusalem, this certainty still eludes us.

The present section ends with the coronation service well in progress (v. 12). The guards were carefully stationed throughout the palace, Temple and city (but Wiseman, TOTC, 231, would see the reference to Athaliah's leaving the palace seemingly unhindered, as perhaps suggesting that it was left minimally guarded), and the people thronged the Temple, cheering the new king, who had been given the crown and "a copy of the Covenant" (once again, cf. the so-called "Law of the King" in Deut. 17:14–20, and especially vv. 18ff, which reminded the king that he was to have "a copy of this Torah" with him and read it all the days of his life, so that his reign, and the reign of his descendants, might be long in the land [cf. comments on 10:28–36]). (For further comments on the coronation service in pre-exilic Israel, as well as elsewhere in the ancient Near East, see Wiseman, TOTC, 232; as already noted, there seems to have been both a private and a public component to the ceremony.)

11:13–16. The surprised Queen Athaliah seized and put to death. Perhaps because the palace was relatively unguarded, the queen mother

	7495.122	2079	4567	6198.151	6142, 6204	3626, 5122
14.	cj, v Qal impf 3fs	cj, intrj	art, n ms	v Qal act ptc ms	prep, art, n ms	prep, art, n ms
	וַתֵּרֶא	וְהִנֵּה	הַמֶּלֶךְ	עֹמֵד	עַל־הָעַמּוּד	כַּמִּשְׁפָּט
	wattēre'	wehinnēh	hammelekh	‘ōmēdh	‘al-hā‘ammûdh	kammishpāṭ
	and she looked	and behold	the king	standing	beside the pillar	like the custom

8015	2792	420, 4567	3725, 6194	800	7976
cj, art, n mp	cj, art, n fp	prep, art, n ms	cj, *adj*, *n ms*	art, n fs	adj
וְהַשָּׂרִים	וְהַחֲצֹצְרוֹת	אֶל־הַמֶּלֶךְ	וְכָל־עַם	הָאָרֶץ	שָׂמֵחַ
wehassārîm	wehachtsōtserôth	'el-hammelekh	wekhol-‘am	hā'ārets	sāmēach
and the commanders	and the trumpets	toward the king	and all the people of	the land	rejoicing

8965.151	904, 2792	7458.122	6510	881, 933	7410.122
cj, v Qal act ptc ms	prep, art, n fp	cj, v Qal impf 3fs	pn	do, n mp, ps 3fs	cj, v Qal impf 3fs
וְתֹקֵעַ	בַּחֲצֹצְרוֹת	וַתִּקְרַע	עֲתַלְיָה	אֶת־בְּגָדֶיהָ	וַתִּקְרָא
wethōqēa‘	bachtsōtserôth	wattiqra‘	‘athalyāh	'eth-beghādhêāh	wattiqrā'
and blowing	with the trumpets	and she tore	Athaliah	her clothes	and she called

7490	7490		6943.321	3179	3669	881, 8015
n ms	n ms	**15.**	cj, v Piel impf 3ms	pn	art, n ms	cj, *n mp*
קֶשֶׁר	קָשֶׁר		וַיְצַו	יְהוֹיָדָע	הַכֹּהֵן	אֶת־שָׂרֵי
qesher	qāsher		waytsaw	yehôyādhā‘	hakkōhēn	'eth-sārê
conspiracy	conspiracy		and he commanded	Jehoiada	the priest	the commanders of

4119	6734.156	2524	569.121	420	3428.533	881
art, n fp	*v Qal pass ptc mp*	art, n ms	cj, v Qal impf 3ms	prep, ps 3mp	v Hiphil impv 2mp	do, ps 3fs
הַמֵּיאוֹת	פְּקֻדֵי	הַחַיִל	וַיֹּאמֶר	אֲלֵיהֶם	הוֹצִיאוּ	אֹתָהּ
hammê'ôth	pequdhê	hachayil	wayyō'mer	'ălêhem	hôtsî'û	'ōthāhh
the hundreds	those mustered of	the army	and he said	to them	bring out	her

420, 4623, 1041	3937, 7901	971.151	313	4322.151	904, 2820
prep, prep, n ms	prep, art, n fp	cj, art, v Qal act ptc ms	prep, ps 3fs	art, v Qal act ptc ms	prep, art, n fs
אֶל־מִבֵּית	לַשְּׂדֵרֹת	וְהַבָּא	אַחֲרֶיהָ	הָמֵת	בֶּחָרֶב
'el-mibbêth	lassedhērōth	wehabbā'	'achrêāh	hāmēth	bechārev
to from the house	to the ranks	and the one coming	after her	the dead man	with the sword

3706	569.111	3669	414, 4322.622	1041	3176
cj	v Qal pf 3ms	art, n ms	adv, v Hophal juss 3fs	*n ms*	pn
כִּי	אָמַר	הַכֹּהֵן	אַל־תּוּמַת	בֵּית	יְהוָה
kî	'āmar	hakkōhēn	'al-tûmath	bêth	yehwāh
because	he said	the priest	may she not be executed	the temple of	Yahweh

	7947.126	3937	3135	971.122	1932, 4136	5670
16.	cj, v Qal impf 3mp	prep, ps 3fs	n fd	cj, v Qal impf 3fs	*n ms*, *n ms*	art, n mp
	וַיָּשִׂמוּ	לָהּ	יָדַיִם	וַתָּבוֹא	דֶּרֶךְ־מְבוֹא	הַסּוּסִים
	wayyāsimû	lāhh	yādhayim	wattāvô'	derekh-mevô'	hassûsîm
	and they put	to her	hands	and she went	the way of the entrance of	the horses

1041	4567	4322.622	8427		3901.121	3179	881, 1311
n ms	art, n ms	cj, v Hophal impf 3fs	adv	**17.**	cj, v Qal impf 3ms	pn	do, art, n fs
בֵּית	הַמֶּלֶךְ	וַתּוּמַת	שָׁם		וַיִּכְרֹת	יְהוֹיָדָע	אֶת־הַבְּרִית
bêth	hammelekh	wattûmath	shām		wayyikhrōth	yehôyādhā‘	'eth-habberîth
the house of	the king	and she was executed	there		and he cut	Jehoiada	the covenant

1033	3176	1033	4567	1033	6194	3937, 2030.141	3937, 6194
prep	pn	cj, prep	art, n ms	cj, prep	art, n ms	prep, v Qal inf con	prep, n ms
בֵּין	יְהוָה	וּבֵין	הַמֶּלֶךְ	וּבֵין	הָעָם	לִהְיוֹת	לְעָם
bên	yehwāh	ûvên	hammelekh	ûvên	hā‘ām	lihyôth	le‘ām
between	Yahweh	and between	the king	and between	the people	to be	a people

making sounds of joy with their hands, said, Long life to the king, *BB*.

13. And when Athaliah heard the noise of the guard and of the people, she came to the people into the temple of the LORD: ... and other troops, *Beck* ... of the couriers and of the people, *Darby* ... heard the shout of the troops and crowd, *Fenton* ... the stir in which the soldiers made in going about their errand reached the ears of Athalia; and she made her way into, *Knox*.

14. And when she looked, behold, the king stood by a pillar, as the manner was, and the princes and the trumpeters by the king, and all the people of the land rejoiced, and blew with trumpets: ... there she saw the king standing on the platform, as was the custom, with the captains, *Moffatt* ... people of the land were very happy, *NCV* ... and the leaders and, *NKJV* ... she saw the newly crowned king standing in his place of authority, *NLT*.

and Athaliah rent her clothes, and cried, Treason, Treason: ... she tore her garments and cried out, *NAB* ... cried: A conspiracy, a conspiracy, *Douay* ... tore her clothes and screamed, Traitors! Traitors, *NCV* ... tore her robes, *NIV*.

15. But Jehoiada the priest commanded the captains of the hundreds, the officers of the host, and said unto them, Have her forth without the ranges: and him that followeth her kill with the sword: ... who were set over the army, Bring her out between the ranks, and kill with the sword anyone who follows her, *NRSV* ... gave orders to the captains in command of the troops: Bring her outside the precincts and put to the sword anyone in attendance on her, *REB* ... who were placed in authority over the army, saying, Take her outside the lines, and let anyone who goes after her, *BB* ... Take her out under guard, *Beck*.

For the priest had said, Let her not be slain in the house of the LORD: ... put to death, *REB* ... She should not be put to death in, *Anchor* ... not be killed in the LORD's temple, *Beck* ... the priest forbade her to be killed inside the temple, *Moffatt*.

16. And they laid hands on her; and she went by the way by the which the horses came into the king's house: and there was she slain: ... She was led out forcibly to the horse gate of the royal palace, where she was put to death, *NAB* ... they seized her, and when she arrived at the horses' entrance of, *NASB* ... was killed, *NKJV* ... they arrested her and brought her on the way through the horses' entrance, *Beck*.

17. And Jehoiada made a covenant between the LORD and the king and the people, that they should be the LORD's people; between the king also and the people: ... would remain Yahweh's people, *JB* ... that bound king and people to the Lord,

---

was able to attend the ceremony (or at least the public portion). She was, of course, horrified at what she saw. Presumably, she had no idea that Joash was even alive, let alone being crowned king over Judah. In any case, she tore her robes (i.e., in grief and despair; cf. the actions of the king of Israel in 5:7; also in 6:30, above), and she shouted "Treason. Treason" (qesher [HED #7490] "conspiracy," "collusion"). One is reminded of King Joram's words about Jehu ("Treachery, Ahaziah!") in 9:23. (In fact, in regard to the placing of trusted guards in and around the Temple, parallels with Jehu's similar action in 10:18–27 concerning the Baal temple in Samaria also come to mind.) Jehoiada, of course, was ready for this. He commanded the royal guard to remove Athaliah from the temple area and to kill any who would show support for her (v. 15). Thus, they brought her out to the previously mentioned "Horse Gate" (cf. NIV's "as she reached the place where the horses enter the palace grounds;" Cogan and Tadmor, AB, 130, locate the Horse Gate east of the Ophel, which itself is just south of the temple mount), and there she was executed. Thus ends, most decisively, official royal influence of the house of Ahab and Jezebel on the land of Judah (cf. the destruction of the temple of Baal in v. 18, below). How ironic that it had taken some seven additional years to rid the southern nation of Judah of Baalism than it had taken the northern nation of Israel.

Commentators often note the parallel references to the "pillar" ('ammûdh, HED #6204) here in v. 14 and also in 23:3, both in contexts of formal covenant renewal (of Joash and of King Josiah). Hobbs (WBC, 142) would see some kind of "column, podium, or platform" as probably in view, but one cannot be certain. A reference to one of the two famous bronze columns of Solomon's temple (1 Ki. 7:15–22) seems unlikely. At any rate, the "custom" was evidently well-known at the time, so once again, our sources are less descriptive than we today might wish. "Brevity is the soul of wit," and also the heart of Hebrew storytelling.

11:17–21. Conclusion: Covenant with Yahweh, and peace in the land. With Athaliah executed and the Davidic king safely enthroned, the remnants of Baal worship could now be eliminated from the land. As already noted, the fact that a Baal temple was found in Judah (with its only mention being here, we cannot be sure where the temple was more specifically

3937, 3176	1033	4567	1033	6194	18.	971.126
prep, pn	cj, prep	art, n ms	cj, prep	art, n ms		cj, v Qal impf 3mp
לַיהוָה	וּבֵין	הַמֶּלֶךְ	וּבֵין	הָעָם		וַיָּבֹאוּ
layhwāh	ûvên	hammelekh	ûvên	hā'ām		wayyāvō'û
to Yahweh	and between	the king	and between	the people		and they went to

3725, 6194	800	1158, 1197	5606.126	881, 4326
adj, n ms	art, n fs	*n ms*, art, pn	cj, v Qal impf 3mp, ps 3ms	do, n mp, ps 3ms
כָּל־עַם	הָאָרֶץ	בֵּית־הַבַּעַל	וַיִּתְּצֻהוּ	אֶת־מִזְבְּחֹתוֹ
khol-'am	hā'ārets	bêth-habba'al	wayyittetsuhû	'eth-mizbechōthô
all the people of	the land	the temple of the Baal	and they tore it down	its altars

881, 7021	8132.316	3296.542	881	5151	3669	1197
cj, do, n mp, ps 3ms	v Piel pf 3cp	v Hiphil inf abs	cj, do	pn	n ms	art, pn
וְאֶת־צְלָמָיו	שִׁבְּרוּ	הֵיטֵב	וְאֵת	מַתָּן	כֹּהֵן	הַבַּעַל
we'eth-tselāmâv	shibberû	hêṯēv	we'ēth	mattān	kōhēn	habba'al
and its images	they broke in pieces	causing to go well	and	Mattan	a priest	the Baal

2103.116	3937, 6686	4326	7947.121	3669	6735	6142, 1041
v Qal pf 3cp	prep, *n mp*	art, n mp	cj, v Qal impf 3ms	art, n ms	n fp	prep, *n ms*
הָרְגוּ	לִפְנֵי	הַמִּזְבְּחוֹת	וַיָּשֶׂם	הַכֹּהֵן	פְּקֻדּוֹת	עַל־בֵּית
hāreghû	liphnê	hammizbechôth	wayyāsem	hakkōhēn	pequddôth	'al-bêth
they killed	before	the altars	and he put	the priest	sentries	beside the temple of

3176	19.	4089.121	881, 8015	4109	881, 3876
pn		cj, v Qal impf 3ms	do, *n mp*	art, num	cj, do, art, pn
יְהוָה		וַיִּקַּח	אֶת־שָׂרֵי	הַמֵּאוֹת	וְאֶת־הַכָּרִי
yehwāh		wayyiqqach	'eth-sārê	hammē'ôth	we'eth-hakkārî
Yahweh		and he took	the commanders of	the hundreds	and the Carites

881, 7608.152	881	3725, 6194	800	3495.526	881, 4567
cj, do, art, v Qal act ptc mp	cj, do	*adj, n ms*	art, n fs	cj, v Hiphil impf 3mp	do, art, n ms
וְאֶת־הָרָצִים	וְאֵת	כָּל־עַם	הָאָרֶץ	וַיֹּרִידוּ	אֶת־הַמֶּלֶךְ
we'eth-hārātsîm	we'ēth	kol-'am	hā'ārets	wayyōrîdhû	'eth-hammelekh
and the runners	and	all the people of	the land	and they brought down	the king

4623, 1041	3176	971.126	1932, 8554	7608.152
prep, *n ms*	pn	cj, v Qal impf 3mp	*n ms, n ms*	art, v Qal act ptc mp
מִבֵּית	יְהוָה	וַיָּבוֹאוּ	דֶּרֶךְ־שַׁעַר	הָרָצִים
mibbêth	yehwāh	wayyāvô'û	derekh-sha'ar	hārātsîm
from the temple of	Yahweh	and they entered	the way of the gate of	the runners

1041	4567	3553.121	6142, 3802	4567	20.	7975.121
n ms	art, n ms	cj, v Qal impf 3ms	prep, *n ms*	art, n mp		cj, v Qal impf 3ms
בֵּית	הַמֶּלֶךְ	וַיֵּשֶׁב	עַל־כִּסֵּא	הַמְּלָכִים		וַיִּשְׂמַח
bêth	hammelekh	wayyēshev	'al-kissē'	hammelākhîm		wayyismach
the house of	the king	and he sat	on the throne of	the kings		and they were glad

3725, 6194, 800	6111	8618.112	881, 6510	4322.516
adj, n ms, art, n fs	cj, art, n fs	v Qal pf 3fs	cj, do, pn	v Hiphil pf 3cp
כָּל־עַם־הָאָרֶץ	וְהָעִיר	שָׁקָטָה	וְאֶת־עֲתַלְיָהוּ	הֵמִיתוּ
kol-'am-hā'ārets	wehā'îr	shāqāṭāh	we'eth-'athalyāhû	hēmîthû
all the people of the land	and the city	it had rest	and Athaliah	they had executed

904, 2820	1041	4567	21.	1158, 8124	8523	3169	904, 4566.141
prep, art, n fs	*n ms*	n ms		*n ms*, num	n fp	pn	prep, v Qal inf con, ps 3ms
בַחֶרֶב	בֵּית	מֶלֶךְ		בֶּן־שֶׁבַע	שָׁנִים	יְהוֹאָשׁ	בְּמָלְכוֹ
vacherev	bêth	melekh		ben-sheva'	shānîm	yehô'āsh	bemālekhô
with the sword	the house of	the king		a son of seven	years	Jehoash	when his reigning

Knox ... a compact, *Moffatt* ... as one party and the king and the people as the other, *NAB*.

18. And all the people of the land went into the house of Baal, and brake it down; his altars and his images brake they in pieces thoroughly, and slew Mattan the priest of Baal before the altars. And the priest appointed officers over the house of the Lord: ... and tore it down, *NASB* ... smashing the altars and idols. They also killed Mattan, the priest of Baal, in front of the altars, *NCV* ... Then Jehoiada set a watch, *NEB* ... posted guards at the temple, *NIV*.

19. And he took the rulers over hundreds, and the captains, and the guard, and all the people of the land; and they brought down the king from the house of the Lord, and came by the way of the gate of the guard to the king's house. And he sat on the throne of the kings: ... and they came down with the king ... through the doorway of the armed men, *BB* ... he sat on the royal throne, *Anchor* ... of the shieldbearers into the palace, *Douay* ... marching through the gate, *NRSV*.

20. And all the people of the land rejoiced, and the city was in quiet: and they slew Athaliah with the sword beside the king's house: ... the country were delighted and the city was quiet. They had killed Athaliah with the sword at the royal palace, *Beck* ... and the city was peaceful after they had killed Athaliah, *Berkeley* ... and the City was content, when they had killed, *Fenton* ... All the people were filled with happiness, and the city was quiet, *Good News*.

21. Seven years old was Jehoash when he began to reign: ... he became king, *NKJV* ... he was crowned, *Fenton* ... he came to the throne, *JB*.

---

located, but seemingly it was in or near the city of Jerusalem; for possible archaeological sites, cf. Cogan and Tadmor, AB, 130), speaks strongly of the influence of Athaliah and of her parents (Josephus, *Antiquities*, IX:154 maintained that Athaliah herself had built the temple, but there is no independent evidence for this). The fact that the name of its presiding priest was Mattan further suggests that Jezebel's cult had made significant inroads into the Israelite religion. In the southern desert, one could worship Baal, the storm-god, all year, as fervently as the priests did on Mt. Carmel in the days of Elijah [cf. 1 Ki. 18:25–29], but hardly see any rainfall. The rainfall in the Negeb today can be less than four inches a year, but whether it was so then cannot be known for sure. But the pagan temple was indeed destroyed, and the priest executed, and further plans were instituted to protect the temple of Yahweh from any future retaliation (vv. 18f). The young king took his place on the throne; the people rejoiced; and there was "quiet" in the city of Jerusalem (the Hebrew verbal root shāqaṯ [HED #8618], "to be or become quiet," often connotes the idea of "tranquility" or "being untroubled," or the like); for Queen Athaliah was now dead, and Joash, her grand-nephew, was now king of the land (vv. 20f). But the real heroes of this chapter are neither the now-deceased queen, nor the new king, but the high priest Jehoiada, and, not least, his wife (and Athaliah's daughter) Jehosheba. God often uses the most unlikely people, and the most surprising relationships, to change the course of history.

12:1–21. *Joash the king commissions repair of the temple of Yahweh. This is the second chapter concerning King Joash of Judah, but the first chapter which presents him as old enough to take charge of his own affairs (it will be recalled that he was crowned king at the tender age of seven). Nonetheless, Jehoiada the high priest was also still very much in the picture, and we are immediately apprised that Joash did what pleased Yahweh "all the years Jehoiada the priest instructed him" (v. 2). According to the chronicler, Joash's later military defeats at the hands of the redoubtable Hazael, king of Aram (vv. 17f), took place after Jehoiada's death (2 Chr. 24:17–25), although such is not explicitly mentioned in the present account in Kings. At any rate, even with the commendable concern King Joash demonstrated for repairing and refurbishing the Temple, as well as for the careful allocation of monetary resources for this purpose (vv. 4–16), the chapter ends on a depressing note. All these temple furnishings and temple treasures, both from him and from his predecessors, had to be given to the foreign king Hazael (concerning Hazael, and his deprivations of Israel and Judah, cf. comments on 8:11ff). What a gloomy conclusion to a basically upbeat narrative—but such are, alas, all too often the realities of life (shades of the pathetic end of the good King Josiah must be mentioned at this point; cf. chs. 22–23). Joash was ultimately assassinated, and his son Amaziah came to the throne, who himself followed the example, not of his famous ancestor David, but of his immediate father Joash (14:3). Such a melancholy epitaph for the promising start that King Joash was privileged to experience. Let us, therefore, learn from his examples—both good and ill—so we will not be ultimately ensnared by any future actions we may undertake.*

12:1	904, 8523, 8124 prep, n fs, num בִּשְׁנַת־שֶׁבַע bishnath-sheva' in the year of seven	3937, 3167 prep, pn לְיֵהוּא leyēhû' of Jehu	4566.111 v Qal pf 3ms מָלַךְ mālakh he reigned	3169 pn יְהוֹאָשׁ yehô'āsh Jehoash	727 cj, num וְאַרְבָּעִים we'arbā'îm and forty	8523 n fs שָׁנָה shānāh years	4566.111 v Qal pf 3ms מָלַךְ mālakh he reigned

904, 3503 prep, pn בִּירוּשָׁלָם bîrûshālām in Jerusalem	8428 cj, n ms וְשֵׁם weshēm and the name of	525 n fs, ps 3ms אִמּוֹ 'immô his mother	6908 pn צִבְיָה tsivyāh Zibiah	4623, 916 prep, pn מִבְּאֵר mibbe'ēr from Beer	916 pn שָׁבַע shāva' Sheba	2.	6449.121 cj, v Qal impf 3ms וַיַּעַשׂ wayya'as and he did	3169 pn יְהוֹאָשׁ yehô'āsh Jehoash

3596 art, adj הַיָּשָׁר hayyāshār what is right	904, 6084 prep, n fd בְּעֵינֵי be'ênê in the eyes of	3176 pn יְהוָה yehwāh Yahweh	3725, 3219 adj, n mp, ps 3ms כָּל־יָמָיו kol-yāmâv all his days	866 rel part אֲשֶׁר 'ăsher what	3498.511 v Hiphil pf 3ms, ps 3ms הוֹרָהוּ hôrāhû he taught him	3179 pn יְהוֹיָדָע yehôyādhā' Jehoiada

3669 art, n ms הַכֹּהֵן hakkōhēn the priest	3.	7828 adv רַק raq only	1154 art, n fp הַבָּמוֹת habbāmôth the high places	3940, 5681.116 neg part, v Qal pf 3cp לֹא־סָרוּ lō'-sārû they did not turn aside	5968 adv עוֹד 'ôdh still	6194 art, n ms הָעָם hā'ām the people	2159.352 v Piel ptc mp מְזַבְּחִים mezabbechîm sacrificing

7281.352 cj, v Piel ptc mp וּמְקַטְּרִים ûmeqatterîm and burning incense	904, 1154 prep, art, n fp בַּבָּמוֹת babbāmôth on the high places	4.	569.121 cj, v Qal impf 3ms וַיֹּאמֶר wayyō'mer and he said	3169 pn יְהוֹאָשׁ yehô'āsh Jehoash	420, 3669 prep, art, n mp אֶל־הַכֹּהֲנִים 'el-hakkōhenîm to the priests	3725 n ms כֹּל kōl everything

3826B n ms כֶּסֶף keseph silver	7231 art, n mp הַקֳּדָשִׁים haqqedhāshîm the consecrated things	866, 971.621 rel part, v Hophal impf 3ms אֲשֶׁר־יוּבָא 'ăsher-yûvā' which it is brought to	1041, 3176 n ms, pn בֵּית־יְהוָה vêth-yehwāh the temple of Yahweh	3826B n ms כֶּסֶף keseph silver	5882.151 v Qal act ptc ms עוֹבֵר 'ôvēr passing

382 n ms אִישׁ 'îsh each	3826B n ms כֶּסֶף keseph the silver of	5497 n fp נַפְשׁוֹת naphshôth the people	6425 n ms, ps 3ms עֶרְכּוֹ 'erkô his value	3725, 3826B adj, n ms כָּל־כֶּסֶף kol-keseph all the silver	866 rel part אֲשֶׁר 'ăsher which	6148.521 v Hiphil impf 3ms יַעֲלֶה ya'ăleh he will bring up	6142 prep עַל 'al because of

3949, 382 n ms, n ms לֶב־אִישׁ lev-'îsh the heart of the man	3937, 971.541 prep, v Hiphil inf con לְהָבִיא lehāvî' to bring to	1041 n ms בֵּית bêth the temple of	3176 pn יְהוָה yehwāh Yahweh	5.	4089.126 v Qal juss 3mp יִקְחוּ yiqōchû let them take	3937 prep, ps 3mp לָהֶם lāhem for themselves

3669 art, n mp הַכֹּהֲנִים hakkōhenîm the priests	382 n ms אִישׁ 'îsh each	4623, 881 prep, do מֵאֵת mē'ēth from	4515 n ms, ps 3ms מַכָּרוֹ makkārô his acquaintance	2062 cj, pers pron וְהֵם wehēm and they	2480.326 v Piel impf 3mp יְחַזְּקוּ yechazzequ they will make strong	881, 955 do, n ms אֶת־בֶּדֶק 'eth-bedheq the breaches of

1041 art, n ms הַבַּיִת habbayith the temple	3937, 3725 prep, n ms לְכֹל lekhōl of everything	866, 4834.221 rel part, v Niphal impf 3ms אֲשֶׁר־יִמָּצֵא 'ăsher-yimmātsē' which it is found	8427 adv שָׁם shām there	955 n ms בָּדֶק bādheq breaches	6.	2030.121 cj, v Qal impf 3ms וַיְהִי wayhî and it was	904, 8523 prep, n fs בִּשְׁנַת bishnath in the year of

12:1. In the seventh year of Jehu Jehoash began to reign; and forty years reigned he in Jerusalem. And his mother's name was Zibiah of Beer-sheba: ... Jehoash became king, *BB* ... the reign of King Jehu of Israel, Joash became king of Judah, and he ruled, *Good News*.

2. And Jehoash did that which was right in the sight of the LORD all his days wherein Jehoiada the priest instructed him: ... was pleasing to the LORD as long as he lived, because the priest Jehoiada guided him, *NAB* ... taught him, *Douay* ... informed him, *Tyndale* ... he was guided by the teaching of, *BB*.

3. But the high places were not taken away: the people still sacrificed and burnt incense in the high places: ... continued to offer sacrifices and incense, *Beck* ... high places were not removed, *Darby* ... the pagan places of worship were not destroyed, *Good News* ... were not abolished, *JB*.

4. And Jehoash said to the priests, All the money of the dedicated things that is brought into the house of the LORD, even the money of every one that passeth the account, the money that every man is set at, and all the money that cometh into any man's heart to bring into the house of the LORD: ... For the priests Joash made this rule: All the funds for sacred purposes that are brought to the temple of the LORD: the census tax, personal redemption money, and whatever funds are freely brought to the temple of the LORD, *NAB* ... of the sanctified things, which is brought into the temple of the Lord by those that pass, which is offerd for the price of a soul and which of their own accord and of their own free heart, *Douay* ... This includes the money each person owes in taxes and the money each person promises or brings freely, *NCV* ... of the holy things, which comes into the house of the Lord, the amount fixed for every man's payment, *BB*.

5. Let the priests take it to them, every man of his acquaintance: and let them repair the breaches of the house, wheresoever any breach shall be found: ... Each of the priests should take it from his friends and repair the temple wherever it may be found to be damaged, *Beck* ... receive for themselves, each from his constituency, *Berkeley* ... each from his own clients. However, they must make whatever repairs on the temple may prove necessary, *NAB* ... will take the money from the people he serves, *NCV*.

6. But it was so, that in the three and twentieth year of king Jehoash the priests had not repaired the breaches of the house: ... by the twenty-third year of King Joash the priests still had not repaired the temple, *NIV* ... the damages of, *NKJV* ... had not made good the damaged parts of, *BB* ... the breaks, *KJVII*.

12:1–3. Introduction: Accession and judgment formulas. As already noted (cf. comments on 8:16f), the accession notices for Judahite monarchs differed systematically from their Israelite counterparts. Such is the case here, with Joash's length of reign (in this case, forty years) placed before the phrase "in Jerusalem" (so the Hebrew word order; contrast NIV, which changes the word order for the sake of a more idiomatic translation). And again, we find reference to the name of the queen mother in most of the Judahite formulas, as is the case here (concerning the inclusion of such names in the Judahite accession formulas, cf. above, on 8:25–29).

A typical judgment notice follows in vv. 2f. Here, as is sometimes the case for the southern kings, the notice is relatively positive. At least as long as Jehoiada the high priest was alive, and as long as King Joash followed Jehoiada's instructions (the Hebrew verbal root used here, hārāh [HED #3498], meaning "to teach" or "to instruct," also underlies the familiar term "Torah"; cf. earlier comments about "Torah" as "Teachings" in connection with 10:28–36). As long as that was the case, Joash did "what was right in the eyes of Yahweh" (even at that, Joash was in relatively exalted company; of the nineteen Judahite kings who followed Solomon, only eight merited this positive statement—Asa; Jehoshaphat [with some reservations]; Joash here [again with reservations]; Amaziah [with definite reservations]; Azariah, or Uzziah [with reservations]; Jotham [with reservations]; Hezekiah; and finally Josiah [these last two kings spoken of in the most glowing of terms; cf. 2 Ki. 18:3, 5f; and 22:2; 23:25; respectively]). Here King Joash (along with six other Judahite kings [besides Rehoboam and Manasseh who actively built or rebuilt the high places]) is condemned for his inactivity, so to speak, for he did not remove the high places. These "high places" presumably were for the worship of Yahweh, not other gods (cf. Hobbs, WBC, 151).

12:4–16. Repair of the temple. This section is the heart of the chapter, and the initial impulse for temple repair was clearly the king's (if Jehoiada was behind Joash's command, there is no hint of it in the text; in fact in v. 7, the high priest is upbraided for his seeming inactivity in the matter, although admittedly, Jehoiada was quite advanced in age by this time; cf. 2 Chr. 24:15). Joash's initial command is found in vv. 4f (Hebrew, vv. 5f) of the present text; although no time indication is given,

6465	8421	8523	3937, 4567	3169	3940, 2480.316	3669
num	cj, num	n fs	prep, art, n ms	pn	neg part, v Piel pf 3cp	art, n mp
עֶשְׂרִים	וְשָׁלֹשׁ	שָׁנָה	לַמֶּלֶךְ	יְהוֹאָשׁ	לֹא־חִזְּקוּ	הַכֹּהֲנִים
'esrîm	weshālōsh	shānāh	lammelekh	yehô'āsh	lō'-chizzeqû	hakkōhenîm
twenty	and three	years	to the king	Jehoash	they had not made strong	the priests

881, 955	1041		7410.121	4567	3169	3937, 3179	3669
do, *n ms*	art, n ms	**7.**	cj, v Qal impf 3ms	art, n ms	pn	prep, pn	art, n ms
אֶת־בֶּדֶק	הַבָּיִת		וַיִּקְרָא	הַמֶּלֶךְ	יְהוֹאָשׁ	לִיהוֹיָדָע	הַכֹּהֵן
'eth-bedheq	habbāyith		wayyiqōrā'	hammelekh	yehô'āsh	lîhôyādhā'	hakkōhēn
the breaches of	the Temple		and he called	the king	Jehoash	for Jehoiada	the priest

3937, 3669	569.121	420	4211	375	2480.352
cj, prep, n mp	cj, v Qal impf 3ms	prep, ps 3mp	intrg	sub, ps 3mp	v Piel ptc mp
וְלַכֹּהֲנִים	וַיֹּאמֶר	אֲלֵהֶם	מַדּוּעַ	אֵינְכֶם	מְחַזְּקִים
welakkōhenîm	wayyō'mer	'ălēhem	maddûa'	'ênekhem	mechazzeqîm
and for the priests	and he said	to them	why	there is not of you	ones making strong

881, 955	1041	6498	414, 4089.128, 3826B	4623, 881	4515
do, *n ms*	art, n ms	cj, adv	adv, v Qal juss 2mp, n ms	prep, do	n mp, ps 2mp
אֶת־בֶּדֶק	הַבָּיִת	וְעַתָּה	אַל־תִּקְחוּ־כֶסֶף	מֵאֵת	מַכָּרֵיכֶם
'eth-bedheq	habbāyith	we'attāh	'al-tiqōchû-kheseph	mē'ēth	makkārêkhem
the breaches of	the Temple	and now	do not take silver	from	your acquaintances

3706, 3937, 955	1041	5598.128		224.226	3669
cj, prep, *n ms*	art, n ms	v Qal impf 2mp, ps 3ms	**8.**	cj, v Niphal impf 3mp	art, n mp
כִּי־לְבֶדֶק	הַבַּיִת	תִּתְּנֻהוּ		וַיֵּאֹתוּ	הַכֹּהֲנִים
kî-levedheq	habbayith	tittenuhû		wayyē'ōthû	hakkōhenîm
except for the breaches of	the Temple	you will hand it over		and they agreed	the priests

3937, 1153	4089.141, 3826B	4623, 881	6194	3937, 1153	2480.341	881, 955
prep, neg part	v Qal inf con, n ms	prep, do	art, n ms	cj, prep, neg part	v Piel inf con	do, *n ms*
לְבִלְתִּי	קְחַת־כֶּסֶף	מֵאֵת	הָעָם	וּלְבִלְתִּי	חַזֵּק	אֶת־בֶּדֶק
leviltî	qōchath-keseph	mē'ēth	hā'ām	ûlāviltî	chazzēq	'eth-bedheq
to not	to take silver	from	the people	and to not	to make strong	the breaches of

1041		4089.121	3179	3669	751	259	5529.121	2815
art, n ms	**9.**	cj, v Qal impf 3ms	pn	art, n ms	n ms	num	cj, v Qal impf 3ms	n ms
הַבָּיִת		וַיִּקַּח	יְהוֹיָדָע	הַכֹּהֵן	אֲרוֹן	אֶחָד	וַיִּקֹּב	חֹר
habbāyith		wayyiqqach	yehôyādhā'	hakkōhēn	'ārôn	'echādh	wayyiqqōv	chōr
the Temple		and he took	Jehoiada	the priest	a chest	one	and he bored	a hole

904, 1878	5598.121	881	703	4326	904, 3332
prep, n fs, ps 3ms	cj, v Qal impf 3ms	do, ps 3ms	prep	art, n ms	prep, art, n fs
בְּדַלְתּוֹ	וַיִּתֵּן	אֹתוֹ	אֵצֶל	הַמִּזְבֵּחַ	בַּיָּמִין
bedhaltô	wayyittēn	'ōthô	'ētsel	hammizbēach	bayyāmîn
in its lid	and he set	it	beside	the altar	on the right side

904, 971.141, 382	1041	3176	5598.116, 8427	3669	8490.152
prep, v Qal inf con, n ms	*n ms*	pn	cj, v Qal pf 3cp, adv	art, n mp	*v Qal act ptc mp*
בְּבוֹא־אִישׁ	בֵּית	יְהוָה	וְנָתְנוּ־שָׁמָּה	הַכֹּהֲנִים	שֹׁמְרֵי
bevô'-'îsh	bêth	yehwāh	wenāthenû-shāmmāh	hakkōhenîm	shōmerê
by a man entering	the temple of	Yahweh	and they gave to there	the priests	those guarding

5790	881, 3725, 3826B	971.655	1041, 3176		2030.121
art, n ms	do, *adj*, art, n ms	art, v Hophal ptc ms	*n ms*, pn	**10.**	cj, v Qal impf 3ms
הַסַּף	אֶת־כָּל־הַכֶּסֶף	הַמּוּבָא	בֵּית־יְהוָה		וַיְהִי
hassaph	'eth-kol-hakkeseph	hammûvā'	vêth-yehwāh		wayhî
the threshold	all the silver	what was brought into	the temple of Yahweh		and it was

7. Then king Jehoash called for Jehoiada the priest, and the other priests, and said unto them, Why repair ye not the breaches of the house? ... What means it that you have not made good the temple's needs, *Knox* ... Why aren't you repairing the damage, *NCV* ... what is damaged in the house?, *BB*.

now therefore receive no more money of your acquaintance, but deliver it for the breaches of the house: ... Instead of accepting money from your customers, hand it over for the repair of the temple, *Moffatt* ... You must no longer take funds from your clients, *NAB* ... from the people you serve, *NCV* ... from your treasurers, *NIV*.

8. And the priests consented to receive no more money of the people, neither to repair the breaches of the house: ... priests made an agreement to take no more money from the people, and not to make good what was damaged in the house, *BB* ... nor to be responsible for the repair, *Beck* ... It was ordered, then, that the priests should no longer receive the gifts, and no longer be answerable for the repairs, *Knox* ... nor to undertake the repairs, *NEB*.

9. But Jehoiada the priest took a chest, and bored a hole in the lid of it, and set it beside the altar, on the right side as one cometh into the house of the LORD: ... making a hole in the cover of it, *BB* ... took a box, *Good News* ... put it beside the doorpost at the right side as one entered, *Goodspeed* ... placed it beside the pillar, to the right of the entry to the Temple, *JB*.

and the priests that kept the door put therein all the money that was brought into the house of the LORD: ... who guarded the threshold put in it the money that was brought to the LORD's temple, *Beck* ... who served as door-keepers, *Berkeley* ... on duty at the entrance put in the box all the money given by the worshippers, *Good News*.

10. And it was so, when they saw that there was much money in the chest, that the king's scribe and the high priest came up, and they put up in bags, and told the money that was found in the house of the LORD: ... the royal secretary and the high priest came, counted the money that had been brought into the temple of the LORD and, *NIV* ... noting the amount of all the money there was, *BB* ... royal secretary and the high

---

presumably it took place quite early in Joash's reign. In any case, even by the twenty-third year of the king (when he was now twenty-nine or thirty years of age), we are told that the Temple was still unrepaired (v. 6). That is a long time to wait, by anyone's reckoning. Sometimes, possibly, the status quo becomes too comfortable, even for the most godly of leaders, especially if they are living quite comfortably (cf. the three sources of income listed for the priests in v. 4; cf. Hobbs [WBC, 152], and Cogan and Tadmor [AB, 137] for lengthy discussions of some of the difficulties found in the Hebrew text for this verse).

As already noted, decades had passed and no repairs had taken place. So the king again took the initiative. He summoned Jehoiada and the other priests and insisted that they accept no more money, but hand it over for temple repair, which would be effected by others (vv. 6ff). Certainly, Joash had gone more than "the second mile" in this endeavor. It is hard, sometimes, for Christian leadership to know when to step in to bring about change, and when to remain patient. At least, no one could accuse Joash of being hasty to reprimand the priestly hierarchy in the matter.

Now a new plan began to take shape (vv. 9–12), this time under the auspices of Jehoiada. In my experience, even the most godly of individuals will often profit from a (gentle, and appropriate) reprimand, from time to time. We are reminded in Prov. 9:8f, "Do not rebuke a mocker or he will hate you; rebuke a wise man and he will love you. Instruct a wise man and he will be wiser still; teach a righteous man and he will add to his learning" (cf. also Prov. 17:10; 19:25; and 25:11f). In any case, Jehoiada could no longer be charged with inactivity (removing the regular sources of income for the priests undoubtedly would catch his, and their, attention). Jehoiada had a "collection box" ('ărôn [HED #751]) built, and placed near the altar, so that the priests could place any money donated to the Temple there (as Hobbs [WBC, 153] points out, this was still the age before coinage, so we should think along the lines of offerings of silver and gold which had to be weighed to determine their value [cf. the Hebrew term sheqel which originally came from the verb shāqal, HED #8620, "to weigh out"]). "Cash boxes" such as this were a regular feature of temples in first millennium Mesopotamia (Cogan and Tadmor, AB, 138, note that secular authorities would also be used to collect the funds).

Further innovations included the use of two different high officials (one "secular," the other "religious") to count the money (again, this would have been done by weighing it), and to put it into bags (v. 10). The "royal secretary" (sōphēr hammelekh, HED #5810, 4567) would have, of course, answered directly to the king ("his presence indicates the way

3626, 7495.141	3706, 7521	3826B	904, 751	6148.121	5810	4567
prep, v Qal inf con, ps 3mp	cj, adj	art, n ms	prep, art, n ms	cj, v Qal impf 3ms	*n ms*	art, n ms
כִּרְאוֹתָם	כִּי־רַב	הַכֶּסֶף	בָּאָרוֹן	וַיַּעַל	סֹפֵר	הַמֶּלֶךְ
kir'ôthām	kî-rav	hakkes̱eph	bā'ārôn	wayya'al	s̱ōphēr	hammelekh
when their seeing	that great	the silver	in the chest	then they went up	the scribe of	the king

3669	1448	6961.126	4630.126	881, 3826B	4834.255
cj, art, n ms	art, adj	cj, v Qal impf 3mp	cj, v Qal impf 3mp	do, art, n ms	art, v Niphal ptc ms
וְהַכֹּהֵן	הַגָּדוֹל	וַיָּצֻרוּ	וַיִּמְנוּ	אֶת־הַכֶּסֶף	הַנִּמְצָא
wehakkōhēn	haggādhôl	wayyātsurû	wayyimnû	'eth-hakkes̱eph	hanimtsā'
and the priest	the great	and they tied	and they counted	the silver	what was found

1041, 3176		5598.116	3826B	8834.455	6142, 3135
n ms, pn	**11.**	cj, v Qal pf 3cp	art, n ms	art, v Pual ptc ms	prep, *n fs*
בֵית־יְהוָה		וְנָתְנוּ	אֶת־הַכֶּסֶף	הַמְתֻכָּן	עַל־יַד
vêth-yehwāh		wenāthenû	'eth-hakkes̱eph	hamthukkān	'al-yadh
the temple of Yahweh		and they gave	the silver	what was denominated	onto the hands of

6449.152	4536	6734.155	1041	3176	3428.526
v Qal act ptc mp	art, n fs	art, v Qal pass ptc ms	*n ms*	pn	cj, v Hiphil impf 3mp, ps 3ms
עֹשֵׂי	הַמְּלָאכָה	הַפְּקֻדִים	בֵּית	יְהוָה	וַיּוֹצִיאֻהוּ
'ōsê	hammelā'khāh	happequdhîm	bêth	yehwāh	wayyôtsî'uhû
the doers of	the duties	those appointed	the temple of	Yahweh	and they brought it out

3937, 2900	6320	3937, 1161.152	6449.152	1041	3176
prep, *n mp*	art, n ms	cj, prep, art, v Qal act ptc mp	art, v Qal act ptc mp	*n ms*	pn
לְחָרָשֵׁי	הָעֵץ	וְלַבֹּנִים	הָעֹשִׂים	בֵּית	יְהוָה
lechārāshê	hā'ēts	welabbōnîm	hā'ōsîm	bêth	yehwāh
to the workers of	the wood	and to the builders	the makers	the temple of	Yahweh

	3937, 1473.152	3937, 2778.152	63	3937, 7353.141	6320
12.	cj, prep, art, v Qal act ptc mp	cj, prep, *v Qal act ptc mp*	art, n fs	cj, prep, v Qal inf con	n mp
	וְלַגֹּדְרִים	וּלְחֹצְבֵי	הָאֶבֶן	וְלִקְנוֹת	עֵצִים
	welaggōdherîm	ûlăchōtsevê	hā'even	weliqnôth	'ētsîm
	and to the masons	and to the hewers of	the stone	and to buy	wood

63	4412	3937, 2480.341	881, 955	1041, 3176
cj, *n fp*	n ms	prep, v Piel inf con	do, *n ms*	*n ms*, pn
וְאַבְנֵי	מַחְצֵב	לְחַזֵּק	אֶת־בֶּדֶק	בֵּית־יְהוָה
we'avnê	machtsēv	lechazzēq	'eth-bedheq	bêth-yehwāh
and stones of	squared stone	to make strong	the breaches of	the temple of Yahweh

3937, 3725	866, 3428.121	6142, 1041	3937, 2486		395	3940
cj, prep, n ms	rel part, v Qal impf 3ms	prep, art, n ms	prep, n fs	**13.**	adv	neg part
וּלְכֹל	אֲשֶׁר־יֵצֵא	עַל־הַבַּיִת	לְחָזְקָה		אַךְ	לֹא
ûlăkhōl	'ăsher-yētsē'	'al-habbayith	lechāzeqāh		'akh	lō'
and everything	which it went out	concerning the Temple	for strengthening		only	not

6449.221	1041	3176	5789	3826B	4345	4353	2792
v Niphal impf 3ms	*n ms*	pn	*n fp*	n ms	n fp	n mp	n fp
יֵעָשֶׂה	בֵּית	יְהוָה	סִפּוֹת	כֶּסֶף	מְזַמְּרוֹת	מִזְרָקוֹת	חֲצֹצְרוֹת
yē'āseh	bêth	yehwāh	s̱ippôth	kes̱eph	mezammerôth	mizrāqôth	chătsōtserôth
it was made	the temple of	Yahweh	bowls of	silver	hooks	basins	trumpets

3725, 3747	2174	3747, 3826B	4623, 3826B	971.655
adj, n ms	n ms	cj, *n ms*, n ms	prep, art, n ms	art, v Hophal ptc ms
כָּל־כְּלִי	זָהָב	וּכְלִי־כָסֶף	מִן־הַכֶּסֶף	הַמּוּבָא
kol-kelî	zāhāv	ûkhelî-khās̱eph	min-hakkes̱eph	hammûvā'
all the vessels of	gold	and vessels of silver	from the silver	what was brought into

priest would come up, make it into ingots and evaluate the money, *Berkeley*.

11. And they gave the money, being told, into the hands of them that did the work, that had the oversight of the house of the LORD: ... the money which was measured out they gave regularly to those who were responsible for overseeing the work, *BB* ... When the amount had been determined, they gave the money to the men appointed to supervise the work on the temple, *NIV* ... when its value had been duly reckoned, they paid over to the master-builders, *Knox* ... they gave the silver to the foremen over the work, *NEB*.

and they laid it out to the carpenters and builders, that wrought upon the house of the LORD: ... they used it to pay the, *Beck* ... working on the Temple, *JB* ... who distributed it to the carpenters and masons that worked in the Lord's house and carried out the repairs, *Knox*.

12. And to masons, and hewers of stone, and to buy timber and hewed stone to repair the breaches of the house of the LORD, and for all that was laid out for the house to repair it: ... They purchased timber and dressed stone for the repair of the temple of the LORD, and met all the other expenses of restoring the temple, *NIV* ... and quarried stone, *NRSV* ... and they paid any other expenses related to the Temple's restoration, *NLT* ... and for all other expenditures needed, *Anchor*.

13. Howbeit there were not made for the house of the LORD bowls of silver, snuffers, basins, trumpets, any vessels of gold, or vessels of silver, of the money that was brought into the house of the LORD: ... But the money was not used for making silver cups or scissors or basins or wind instruments or, *BB* ... None of the funds brought to the temple of the LORD were used there to make, *NAB* ... wick trimmers, bowls, *NCV* ... into the temple was not spent, *NIV*.

---

in which the king governed the affairs of the temple" [Hobbs]). Cogan and Tadmor note that in a letter to King Esarhaddon (680–669), reference is made to the fact that the royal delegate was to be accompanied by a priest when checking the gold available to repair the temple at Uruk. The principle of double signatures on checks in some churches would be a modern adaptation of this practice. As the reader undoubtedly is well aware, church parishioners deserve complete reassurance that their money is handled carefully and correctly. Such reassurance the high priest Jehoiada belatedly guaranteed with the revised procedure described here.

The counted money was then given directly to the construction supervisors, who in turn gave it to the workmen (vv. 11f). As promised earlier, the priests themselves no longer supervised the repairs of the Temple, nor collected the money (v. 8). Whether it be the high priest planning carefully the accession of the youthful King Joash in the previous chapter, or the king urging on the high priest to complete the temple repairs, each had his own calling and profession, yet each acted properly to bring about positive change in the other's sphere of influence. We should be open to the same kind of thing—acting as professionals in our own line of work, to be sure, yet carefully, prayerfully intervening (only when God leads us, of course) in the affairs of others. Thus the Kingdom of God continues to grow and flourish.

The final four verses of this section (vv. 13–16) reinforce the very careful allocation of the donated funds for temple repair. The "complete honesty" on the part of the contractors is emphasized (so that no formal accounting was required; this apparently was not the usual practice); also, non-use of the donated money for any ornamental and ritual objects (again, perhaps the opposite had been the case previously). Sometimes we can glean from various emphases in the text what might have transpired differently in earlier times. That is an acceptable, if admittedly risky, procedure when studying the Bible, so we must be careful when we do this, lest we build moral or doctrinal teachings from what are essentially "arguments from silence." Such arguments are built on negative evidence—from what a text does not say, but perhaps what one would have expected it to say. Such arguments are not necessarily invalid, but they are generally quite weak. Still, we are probably on relatively safe ground here: we know that for years, even decades, inappropriate use was made of the funds designated for temple repair, and we know that major changes in both collection and auditing procedures were instituted. So, the additional features which the present narrator draws attention to are probably noteworthy changes from prior practice. (Certainly the emphasis on no formal accounting procedures in v. 15 would not be the norm in ancient Israel—nor should it be the norm in the church today.) Like the refreshing dilemma mentioned in Exo. 36:3–7 concerning another fund-raising occasion, this time for the Tabernacle, such was presumably the exception, not the norm (Moses had to tell the people not to give anymore, since they already had more than enough). In any case, the final verse in this section (v. 16) reminds us that the

1041, 3176	14.	3706, 3937, 6449.152	4536	5598.126
n ms, pn		cj, prep, *v Qal act ptc mp*	art, n fs	v Qal impf 3mp, ps 3ms
בֵּית־יְהוָה		כִּי־לְעֹשֵׂי	הַמְּלָאכָה	יִתְּנֻהוּ
vêth-yehwāh		kî-le'ōsê	hammelā'khāh	yittenuhû
the temple of Yahweh		for to the doers of	the duties	they gave it

2480.316, 904	881, 1041	3176	15.	3940	2913.316
cj, v Piel pf 3cp, prep, ps 3ms	do, *n ms*	pn		cj, neg part	v Piel pf 3cp
וְחִזְּקוּ־בוֹ	אֶת־בֵּית	יְהוָה		וְלֹא	יְחַשְּׁבוּ
wechizzeqû-vô	'eth-bêth	yehwāh		welō'	yechashshevû
and they made strong with it	the temple of	Yahweh		and not	they thought about

881, 596	866	5598.126	881, 3826B	6142, 3135	3937, 5598.141
do, art, n mp	rel pron	v Qal impf 3mp	do, art, n ms	prep, n fs, ps 3mp	prep, v Qal inf con
אֶת־הָאֲנָשִׁים	אֲשֶׁר	יִתְּנוּ	אֶת־הַכֶּסֶף	עַל־יָדָם	לָתֵת
'eth-hā'ănāshîm	'ăsher	yittenû	'eth-hakkeseph	'al-yādhām	lāthēth
the men	who	they gave	the silver	on their hand	to give

3937, 6449.152	4536	3706	904, 536	2062	6449.152	16.	3826B
prep, *v Qal act ptc mp*	art, n fs	cj	prep, art, n fs	pers pron	v Qal act ptc mp		*n ms*
לְעֹשֵׂי	הַמְּלָאכָה	כִּי	בֶּאֱמֻנָה	הֵם	עֹשִׂים		כֶּסֶף
le'ōsê	hammelā'khāh	kî	ve'ĕmunāh	hēm	'ōsîm		keseph
to the doers of	the duties	because	with truth	they	doing		the silver of

844	3826B	2496	3940	971.621	1041
n ms	cj, *n ms*	n fp	neg part	v Hophal impf 3ms	*n ms*
אָשָׁם	וְכֶסֶף	חַטָּאוֹת	לֹא	יוּבָא	בֵּית
'āshām	wekheseph	chattā'ōth	lō'	yûvā'	bêth
the guilt offerings	and the silver of	the sin offerings	not	they were brought into	the temple of

3176	3937, 3669	2030.126	17.	226	6148.121	2462	4567	782
pn	prep, art, n mp	v Qal impf 3mp		adv	v Qal impf 3ms	pn	*n ms*	pn
יְהוָה	לַכֹּהֲנִים	יִהְיוּ		אָז	יַעֲלֶה	חֲזָאֵל	מֶלֶךְ	אֲרָם
yehwāh	lakkōhenîm	yihyû		'āz	ya'ăleh	chăzā'ēl	melekh	'ărām
Yahweh	to the priests	they were		then	he went up	Hazael	the king of	Aram

4032.221	6142, 1709	4058.121	7947.121	2462	6686
cj, v Niphal impf 3ms	prep, pn	cj, v Qal impf 3ms, ps 3fs	cj, v Qal impf 3ms	pn	n mp, ps 3ms
וַיִּלָּחֶם	עַל־גַּת	וַיִּלְכְּדָהּ	וַיָּשֶׂם	חֲזָאֵל	פָּנָיו
wayyillāchem	'al-gath	wayyilkedhāhh	wayyāsem	chăzā'ēl	pānâv
and he fought	against Gath	and he captured it	and he set	Hazael	his face

3937, 6148.141	6142, 3503	18.	4089.121	3169	4567, 3171	881
prep, v Qal inf con	prep, pn		cj, v Qal impf 3ms	pn	*n ms*, pn	do
לַעֲלוֹת	עַל־יְרוּשָׁלָם		וַיִּקַּח	יְהוֹאָשׁ	מֶלֶךְ־יְהוּדָה	אֵת
la'ălôth	'al-yerûshālām		wayyiqqach	yehô'āsh	melekh-yehûdhāh	'ēth
to go up	against Jerusalem		and he took	Jehoash	the king of Judah	

3725, 7231	866, 7227.516	3194	3190	275
adj, art, n mp	rel part, v Hiphil pf 3cp	pn	pn	cj, pn
כָּל־הַקֳּדָשִׁים	אֲשֶׁר־הִקְדִּישׁוּ	יְהוֹשָׁפָט	וִיהוֹרָם	וַאֲחַזְיָהוּ
kol-haqqedhāshîm	'ăsher-hiqŏddîshû	yehôshāphāt	wîhôrām	wa'ăchazyāhû
all the consecrated things	which they had consecrated	Jehoshaphat	Jehoram	and Ahaziah

1	4567	3171	881, 7231	881	3725, 2174
n mp, ps 3ms	*n mp*	pn	cj, do, n mp, ps 3ms	cj, do	*adj*, art, n ms
אֲבֹתָיו	מַלְכֵי	יְהוּדָה	וְאֶת־קֳדָשָׁיו	וְאֵת	כָּל־הַזָּהָב
'ăvōthâv	malkhê	yehûdhāh	we'eth-qōdhāshâv	we'ēth	kol-hazzāhāv
his ancestors	the kings of	Judah	and his consecrated things	and	all the gold

4834.255	904, 212	1041, 3176	1041	4567
art, v Niphal ptc ms	prep, *n mp*	*n ms*, pn	cj, *n ms*	art, n ms
הַנִּמְצָא	בְּאֹצְרוֹת	בֵּית־יְהוָה	וּבֵית	הַמֶּלֶךְ
hanimtsā'	be'ōtserôth	bêth-yehwāh	ûvêth	hammelekh
what was found	in the treasuries of	the temple of Yahweh	and the house of	the king

8365.121	3937, 2462	4567	782	6148.121	4623, 6142	3503
cj, v Qal impf 3ms	prep, pn	*n ms*	pn	cj, v Qal impf 3ms	prep, prep	pn
וַיִּשְׁלַח	לַחֲזָאֵל	מֶלֶךְ	אֲרָם	וַיַּעַל	מֵעַל	יְרוּשָׁלָם
wayyishlach	lachzā'ēl	melekh	'ărām	wayya'al	mē'al	yerûshālām
and he sent out	to Hazael	the king of	Aram	and he went up	from against	Jerusalem

14. But they gave that to the workmen, and repaired therewith the house of the LORD: ... that was given to the workers, *NRSV* ... they used it for paying the workmen and for the repairs, *REB* ... who were building up the house, *BB* ... It was paid out, *NLT.*

15. Moreover they reckoned not with the men, into whose hand they delivered the money to be bestowed on workmen: for they dealt faithfully: ... They didn't ask the men to whom they entrusted the money to pay the workers to give an account, because they were honest, *Beck* ... They required no accounting from the men, *Berkeley* ... there was no need to require them to account for the funds, *Good News* ... No accounts were kept with the men to whom the money was paid over to be spent on the workmen, *JB.*

16. The trespass money and sin money was not brought into the house of the LORD: it was the priests': ... the fines paid for fault or wrong done were not put into the treasury, since these belonged to the priests as of right, *Knox* ... and guilt-offerings were not brought into the temple of the Eternal, *Moffatt* ... they brought not into the temple of, *Douay* ... from the penalty offerings and, *NCV.*

17. Then Hazael king of Syria went up, and fought against Gath, and took it: and Hazael set his face to go up to Jerusalem: ... came up and attacked Gath, *NEB* ... Then he turned to attack Jerusalem, *NIV* ... went to war against Gath and captured it, *NLT* ... he was also determined to attack Jerusalem, *Beck.*

18. And Jehoash king of Judah took all the hallowed things that Jehoshaphat, and Jehoram, and Ahaziah, his fathers, kings of Judah, had dedicated: ... gifts, *Beck* ... sacred treasures, *Berkeley* ... consecrations, *Fenton* ... offerings, *Good News.*

and his own hallowed things, and all the gold that was found in the treasures of the house of the LORD, and in the king's house: ... dedicated things and all the gold that could be found in the store rooms, *Beck* ... together with his own sacred treasures and all the gold deposited, *Berkeley* ... consecrations, *Fenton* ... offerings, *Good News.*

and sent it to Hazael king of Syria: and he went away from Jerusalem: ... so that he might leave Jerusalem, *Berkeley* ... so he retreated, *Fenton* ... as a gift to King Hazael who then led his army, *Good News.*

priests did not starve; they continued to receive their normal income from the sin and guilt offerings. Yet the irony lingers—construction contractors who are more trustworthy than priests. What an indictment against the religious professionals of that day—an indictment sadly repeated from time to time throughout history!

12:17–18. Later debacle at the hands of Hazael. Alas, how quickly circumstances can deteriorate, at least, that is the impression we get in these two abrupt verses (as noted earlier, the Chronicles account has more information, especially in regard to the death of Jehoiada, and the serious deterioration that took place in Joash's reign after that time; cf. 2 Chr. 24:17–25). Mention has already been made several times of the exceptional career of King Hazael of Syria (cf., especially, comments on 8:11ff); the fact that here he captured Gath (one of the five major Philistine cities, but whose exact location still somewhat disputed) implies movement toward Jerusalem from the west (probably the easiest way to advance against the southern capital). "This incursion of Hazael into the south is quite possibly connected with the chaotic state of affairs in the north after the death of Jehu and the accession of his son Jehoahaz" (Hobbs, WBC, 155; cf. comments on 13:1ff). The next verse indicates the extreme cost paid by King Joash to buy off the invader: "All the sacred objects dedicated by his fathers ... and the gifts he himself had dedicated, and all the gold found in the treasuries of the temple of Yahweh and of the royal palace"—all sent off to Hazael, who then withdrew from Jerusalem. What a fearsome price to pay, and what an incredible anticlimax to an otherwise upbeat nar-

	3615	1745	3204	3725, 866	6449.111	1950B, 3940, 2062
19.	cj, *n ms*	*n mp*	pn	cj, *adj*, rel part	v Qal pf 3ms	intrg part, neg part, pers pron
	וְיֶתֶר	דִּבְרֵי	יוֹאָשׁ	וְכָל־אֲשֶׁר	עָשָׂה	הֲלוֹא־הֵם
	weyether	divrê	yô'āsh	wekhol-'ăsher	'āsāh	hălô'-hēm
	and the remainder of	the events of	Joash	and all which	he did	are they not

3918.156	6142, 5809	1745	3219	3937, 4567	3171
v Qal pass ptc mp	prep, *n ms*	*n mp*	art, n mp	prep, *n mp*	pn
כְּתוּבִים	עַל־סֵפֶר	דִּבְרֵי	הַיָּמִים	לְמַלְכֵי	יְהוּדָה
kethûvîm	'al-sēpher	divrê	hayyāmîm	lemalkhê	yehûdhāh
things written	on the scroll of	the events of	the days	of the kings of	Judah

	7251.126	5860	7489.126, 7490	5409.526
20.	cj, v Qal impf 3mp	n mp, ps 3ms	cj, v Qal impf 3mp, n ms	cj, v Hiphil impf 3mp
	וַיָּקֻמוּ	עֲבָדָיו	וַיִּקְשְׁרוּ־קָשֶׁר	וַיַּכּוּ
	wayyāqumû	'ăvādhâv	wayyiqōshrû-qāsher	wayyakkû
	and they arose	his servants	and they conspired a conspiracy	and they struck down

881, 3204	1041	1076	3495.151	5730		3210
do, pn	*n ms*	pn	art, v Qal act ptc ms	pn	**21.**	cj, pn
אֶת־יוֹאָשׁ	בֵּית	מִלֹּא	הַיֹּרֵד	סִלָּא		וְיוֹזָבָד
'eth-yô'āsh	bêth	millō'	hayyôrēdh	sillā'		weyôzāvādh
Joash	the house of	Millo	the one going down to	Silla		and Jozabad

1158, 8486	3177	1158, 8205	5860	5409.516
n ms, pn	cj, pn	*n ms*, pn	n mp, ps 3ms	v Hiphil pf 3cp, ps 3ms
בֶּן־שִׁמְעָת	וִיהוֹזָבָד	בֶּן־שֹׁמֵר	עֲבָדָיו	הִכֻּהוּ
ben-shim'āth	wîhôzāvādh	ben-shōmēr	'ăvādhâv	hikkuhû
the son of Shimeath	and Jehozabad	the son of Shomer	his servants	they struck him down

4322.121	7196.126	881	6196, 1	904, 6111	1784	4566.121
cj, v Qal impf 3ms	cj, v Qal impf 3mp	do, ps 3ms	prep, n mp, ps 3ms	prep, *n fs*	pn	cj, v Qal impf 3ms
וַיָּמֹת	וַיִּקְבְּרוּ	אֹתוֹ	עִם־אֲבֹתָיו	בְּעִיר	דָּוִד	וַיִּמְלֹךְ
wayyāmōth	wayyiqōbberû	'ōthô	'im-'ăvōthâv	be'îr	dāwidh	wayyimlōkh
and he died	and they buried	him	with his ancestors	in the city of	David	and he reigned

568	1158	8809		904, 8523	6465	8421	8523	3937, 3204
pn	n ms, ps 3ms	prep, ps 3ms	**13:1**	prep, *n fs*	num	cj, num	n fs	prep, pn
אֲמַצְיָה	בְּנוֹ	תַּחְתָּיו		בִּשְׁנַת	עֶשְׂרִים	וְשָׁלֹשׁ	שָׁנָה	לְיוֹאָשׁ
'ămatsyāh	venô	tachtâv		bishnath	'esrîm	weshālōsh	shānāh	leyô'āsh
Amaziah	his son	instead of him		in the year of	twenty	and three	years	of Joash

1158, 275	4567	3171	4566.111	3168	1158, 3167	6142, 3547
n ms, pn	*n ms*	pn	v Qal pf 3ms	pn	*n ms*, pn	prep, pn
בֶּן־אֲחַזְיָהוּ	מֶלֶךְ	יְהוּדָה	מָלַךְ	יְהוֹאָחָז	בֶּן־יֵהוּא	עַל־יִשְׂרָאֵל
ben-'ăchazyāhû	melekh	yehûdhāh	mālakh	yehô'āchāz	ben-yēhû'	'al-yisrā'ēl
the son of Ahaziah	the king of	Judah	he reigned	Jehoahaz	the son of Jehu	over Israel

904, 8497	8124	6462	8523		6449.121	7737	904, 6084	3176
prep, pn	num	num	n fs	**2.**	cj, v Qal impf 3ms	art, adj	prep, *n fd*	pn
בְּשֹׁמְרוֹן	שְׁבַע	עֶשְׂרֵה	שָׁנָה		וַיַּעַשׂ	הָרַע	בְּעֵינֵי	יְהוָה
beshōmerôn	sheva'	'esrēh	shānāh		wayya'as	hāra'	be'ênê	yehwāh
in Samaria	seven	ten	years		and he did	what is evil	in the eyes of	Yahweh

2050.121	313	2496	3493	1158, 5203	866, 2490.511	881, 3547
cj, v Qal impf 3ms	prep	*n fp*	pn	*n ms*, pn	rel pron, v Hiphil pf 3ms	do, pn
וַיֵּלֶךְ	אַחַר	חַטֹּאת	יָרָבְעָם	בֶּן־נְבָט	אֲשֶׁר־הֶחֱטִיא	אֶת־יִשְׂרָאֵל
wayyēlekh	'achar	chattō'th	yārov'ām	ben-nevāt	'ăsher-hechĕtî'	'eth-yisrā'ēl
and he walked	after	the sins of	Jeroboam	the son of Nebat	who he caused to sin	Israel

19. And the rest of the acts of Joash, and all that he did, are they not written in the book of the chronicles of the kings of Judah? ... the records of Joash, *Goodspeed* ... the history of Joash, his entire career, is this not recorded in, *JB* ... are they not described, *Moffatt* ... in the book of the history, *NCV.*

20. And his servants arose, and made a conspiracy, and slew Joash in the house of Millo, which goeth down to Silla: ... revolted against him and struck him down, *NEB* ... His officials conspired against him and assassinated him at Beth Millo on the road down to Silla, *NIV* ... his officers plotted against him, *NLT* ... his servants made a secret design and put Joash to death, *BB.*

21. For Jozachar the son of Shimeath, and Jehozabad the son of Shomer, his servants, smote him, and he died; and they buried him with his fathers in the city of David: and Amaziah his son reigned in his stead: ... came to him and put him to death; and they put him into the earth, *BB* ... his own attendants, gave him his death-blow, *Knox* ... succeeded him as king, *Beck* ... became king in his place, *Berkeley.*

13:1. In the three and twentieth year of Joash the son of Ahaziah king of Judah Jehoahaz the son of Jehu began to reign over Israel in Samaria, and reigned seventeen years: ... In the twenty-third year of Joash, *BB* ... Jehoahaz son of Jehu became king over Israel in Samaria for seventeen years, *Anchor* ... Jehoahaz, Jehu's son, started to rule over Israel, *Beck.*

2. And he did that which was evil in the sight of the LORD, and followed the sins of Jeroboam the son of Nebat, which made Israel to sin; he departed not therefrom: ... He did what is displeasing to Yahweh and copied the sin into which Jeroboam son of Nebat had led Israel; he did not give it up, *JB* ... he did not turn from them, *Goodspeed* ... He defied the Lord's will, following the sinful example of Jeroboam, son of Nabat, that taught Israel to sin, and never departing from it, *Knox* ... he did not abandon these sinful practices, *Moffatt.*

---

rative. All the care and concern to repair and refurbish the Temple, all, virtually, for naught. A sobering reminder, this, of the horrifying vicissitudes of life, especially for one who does not remain in the clear will of God. All for naught.

12:19–21. Conclusion: "Further reference" and burial notices. The end of King Joash's reign turned out so differently than what one would have expected for such a person of great promise. Joash, like his father Ahaziah, was assassinated, but at least Ahaziah died on the battlefield, at the hands of an enemy usurper. Joash, on the other hand, died at the hands of his own officials (in 2 Chr. 24:25, Joash is said to have been wounded by the attacking Arameans, and then assassinated by his own officers because of his commissioning the murder of the prophet Zechariah son of Jehoiada, who had announced to him the judgment of Yahweh for idolatry). But once again, none of this is in Kings, just the bald fact that Joash paid off Hazael at a dear price, and he was put to death apparently somewhere in the greater city of Jerusalem (for the possible locations of the obscure "Beth Millo," and the even more obscure "road down to Silla," cf. Cogan and Tadmor, AB, 139, who suggest that the first name signified a prominent building on the "Millo," or "filling," which was the area filled in and supported by terraces on the eastern slope of the City of David, i.e., Jerusalem south of the temple mount; cf. 1 Ki. 9:15, 24; and especially 11:27). The chronicler records that Joash died ignominiously in his own bed, location otherwise unspecified (2 Chr. 24:25). Apart from the execution of Queen Athaliah, who was regarded as an usurper anyway, this is the first example of a Judahite king killed by conspirators; alas, he would be followed by his own son Amaziah (14:19), and, much later, by Amon son of Manasseh (21:23). In every case, the assassinated king was succeeded by his son—another example of the remarkable stability of the Davidic dynasty over more than four centuries until the Babylonian exile (some 424 years; cf. comments on 11:4–12). (Concerning the familiar "further reference" notice in v. 19, cf. comments on 1:17f. Once again all these sources have long since disappeared. And concerning the burial notice which concludes the chapter, cf. comments on 8:23f.)

13:1–9. Jehoahaz King of Israel: Accession, judgment, deliverance and burial notices. We now move into a chapter filled with short notices pertaining to the northern kingdom of Israel (concerning 2 Kings' "leapfrog" chronological procedure, first dealing with the north, then the south, then the north, etc.; cf. comments on 8:16–24, above). It should be recalled that the framework of the Book is relentlessly chronological, even occasionally at the risk of some confusion on the part of the reader (cf. the present chapter, where King Jehoash of Israel is dead and buried in v. 13, but alive and well in v. 25).

Much of this material is quite formulaic, and can be discussed rather quickly. But there is the danger by such a procedure of neglecting the original

3940, 5681.111	4623		2835.121, 653	3176	904, 3547
neg part, v Qal pf 3ms	prep, ps 3fs	3.	cj, v Qal impf 3ms, *n ms*	pn	prep, pn
לֹא־סָר	מִמֶּנָּה		וַיִּחַר־אַף	יְהוָה	בְּיִשְׂרָאֵל
lō'-s̱ār	mimmennāh		wayyichar-'aph	yehwāh	beyisrā'ēl
he did not turn	from them		and it became hot the nose of	Yahweh	against Israel

5598.121	904, 3135	2462	4567, 782	904, 3135
cj, v Qal impf 3ms, ps 3mp	prep, *n fs*	pn	*n ms*, pn	cj, prep, *n fs*
וַיִּתְּנֵם	בְּיַד	חֲזָאֵל	מֶלֶךְ־אֲרָם	וּבְיַד
wayyittenēm	beyadh	chăzā'ēl	melekh-'ărām	ûveyadh
and He gave them	into the hand of	Hazael	the king of Aram	and into the hand of

1163	1158, 2462	3725, 3219		2571.321	3168	881, 6686	3176
pn	*n ms*, pn	*adj*, art, n mp	4.	cj, v Piel impf 3ms	pn	do, *n mp*	pn
בֶּן־הֲדַד	בֶּן־חֲזָאֵל	כָּל־הַיָּמִים		וַיְחַל	יְהוֹאָחָז	אֶת־פְּנֵי	יְהוָה
ben-hedhadh	ben-chăzā'ēl	kol-hayyāmîm		waychal	yehô'āchāz	'eth-penê	yehwāh
Ben-Hadad	the son of Hazael	all the days		and he entreated	Jehoahaz	the face of	Yahweh

8471.121	420	3176	3706	7495.111	881, 4041	3547
cj, v Qal impf 3ms	prep, ps 3ms	pn	cj	v Qal pf 3ms	do, *n ms*	pn
וַיִּשְׁמַע	אֵלָיו	יְהוָה	כִּי	רָאָה	אֶת־לַחַץ	יִשְׂרָאֵל
wayyishma'	'ēlâv	yehwāh	kî	rā'āh	'eth-lachats	yisrā'ēl
and He listened	to him	Yahweh	because	He saw	the oppression of	Israel

3706, 4040.111	881	4567	782		5598.121	3176	3937, 3547
cj, v Qal pf 3ms	do, ps 3mp	*n ms*	pn	5.	cj, v Qal impf 3ms	pn	prep, pn
כִּי־לָחַץ	אֹתָם	מֶלֶךְ	אֲרָם		וַיִּתֵּן	יְהוָה	לְיִשְׂרָאֵל
kî-lāchats	'ōthām	melekh	'ărām		wayyittēn	yehwāh	leyisrā'ēl
that he oppressed	them	the king of	Aram		and He gave	Yahweh	to Israel

3588.551	3428.126	4623, 8809	3135, 782	3553.126
v Hiphil ptc ms	cj, v Qal impf 3mp	prep, prep	*n fs*, pn	cj, v Qal impf 3mp
מוֹשִׁיעַ	וַיֵּצְאוּ	מִתַּחַת	יַד־אֲרָם	וַיֵּשְׁבוּ
môshîa'	wayyētse'û	mittachath	yadh-'ărām	wayyēshevû
a savior	and they went out	from beneath	the hand of Aram	and they dwelled

1158, 3547	904, 164	3626, 8873	8425		395
n mp, pn	prep, n mp, ps 3mp	prep, adv	adv	6.	adv
בְנֵי־יִשְׂרָאֵל	בְּאָהֳלֵיהֶם	כִּתְמוֹל	שִׁלְשׁוֹם		אַךְ
venê-yisrā'ēl	be'āhelêhem	kithmôl	shilshôm		'akh
the children of Israel	in their tents	like previously	three days ago		only

3940, 5681.116	4623, 2496	1041, 3493	866, 2490.511
neg part, v Qal pf 3cp	prep, *n fp*	*n ms*, pn	rel part, v Hiphil pf 3ms
לֹא־סָרוּ	מֵחַטֹּאות	בֵּית־יָרָבְעָם	אֲשֶׁר־הֶחֱטִי
lō'-s̱ārû	mēchaṯṯō'wth	bêth-yārov'ām	'ăsher-hechĕṭî
they did not turn aside	from the sins of	the household of Jeroboam	which he caused to sin

881, 3547	904	2050.111	1612	867	6198.112	904, 8497		3706
do, pn	prep, ps 3fs	v Qal pf 3ms	cj, cj	art, pn	v Qal pf 3fs	prep, pn	7.	cj
אֶת־יִשְׂרָאֵל	בָּהּ	הָלָךְ	וְגַם	הָאֲשֵׁרָה	עָמְדָה	בְּשֹׁמְרוֹן		כִּי
'eth-yisrā'ēl	bāhh	hālākh	wegham	hā'ăshērāh	'āmedhāh	beshōmerôn		kî
Israel	in them	he walked	and also	the Asherah	it stood	in Samaria		because

3940	8080.511	3937, 3168	6194	3706	524, 2675	6821	6463	7681
neg part	v Hiphil pf 3ms	prep, pn	n ms	cj	cj, num	n mp	cj, num	n ms
לֹא	הִשְׁאִיר	לִיהוֹאָחָז	עָם	כִּי	אִם־חֲמִשִּׁים	פָּרָשִׁים	וַעֲשָׂרָה	רֶכֶב
lō'	hish'îr	lîhô'āchāz	'ām	kî	'im-chămishshîm	pārāshîm	wa'ăsārāh	rekhev
not	it was left	to Jehoahaz	a people	except	only fifty	horsemen	and ten	chariots

3. And the anger of the LORD was kindled against Israel, and he delivered them into the hand of Hazael king of Syria, and into the hand of Ben-hadad the son of Hazael, all their days: ... The LORD was angry with Israel and for a long time left them in the power of Hazael, *NAB* ... the wrath of the Lord was kindled, *Douay* ... the LORD was roused to anger against Israel and he made them subject for some years to Hazael, *NEB* ... the LORD's anger burned against Israel, *NIV.*

4. And Jehoahaz besought the LORD, and the LORD hearkened unto him: for he saw the oppression of Israel, because the king of Syria oppressed them: ... The LORD could see how terribly the king of Aram was oppressing Israel, *NLT* ... he saw how cruelly Israel was crushed by the king of Aram, *BB* ... the EVER-LIVING pitied the distress of Israel. For the kings of Aram distressed them, *Fenton.* ... Jehoahaz pleaded with the LORD, and the LORD listened to him, *NKJV* ... Jehoahaz prayed for the LORD's help, and the LORD heard his prayer, *NLT* ... Jehoahaz entreated the LORD, and the LORD heeded him, *NRSV* ... Jehoahaz prayed for the LORD's favor, and the LORD listened to him, *Berkeley.*

5. (And the LORD gave Israel a saviour, so that they went out from under the hand of the Syrians: and the children of Israel dwelt in their tents, as beforetime: ... gave Israel a deliverer, *Goodspeed* ... gave Israel a saviour who freed them from the grip of Aram, and the Israelites lived in their tents as in the past, *JB* ... Israelites lived in their own homes as they had before, *NIV* ... they were freed from the authority of Aram, *Anchor.*

6. Nevertheless they departed not from the sins of the house of Jeroboam, who made Israel sin, but walked therein: and there remained the grove also in Samaria.): ... they did not give up the sin of Jeroboam, *BB* ... but they lived in it, *Beck* ... but kept on committing them; and the image of the goddess Asherah remained in Samaria, *Good News* ... while the shame-images too remained standing in Samaria, *Berkeley.*

7. Neither did he leave of the people to Jehoahaz but fifty horsemen, and ten chariots, and ten thousand footmen; for the king of Syria had destroyed them, and had made them like the dust by threshing: ... making them like dust trampled under foot, *JB* ... sweeping them away like chaff on the threshing-floor, *Knox* ... in the barnfloor, *Douay* ... crushed them like dust, *Anchor.*

---

historical import of every stereotypical accession or burial notice. These were kings of God's people, after all, and the present chapter includes two who reigned in Israel for significant periods of time. An Israelite accession notice (v. 1) is followed by a typical Israelite judgment formula (v. 2); but then a less formulaic discussion of Israel's oppression again at the hands of the Arameans, coupled with Jehoahaz's "seeking the favor of Yahweh" and Yahweh's gracious response, comprises most of the balance of the present section (vv. 3–7). Predictable "further reference" and burial notices then conclude the passage (vv. 8f). (Concerning Israelite accession formulas, cf. above, on 8:16f; and concerning Israelite judgment notices, cf. above, on 3:1ff. Briefly discussed are the "further reference" notices in comments on 1:17f, and discussed later at some length are the Israelite burial formulas.)

The name Jehoahaz probably means "Yahweh has taken hold of," "Yahweh has overcome," or the like; its shortened form is "Ahaz" (e.g., the name of the infamous southern Davidic king, son of Jotham and father of Hezekiah; cf. ch. 16). The name "Ahaziah" also comes from the same Hebrew root (cf. the Israelite king of that name in 2 Ki. 1, and his Judahite counterpart in 8:25–29); and we will run into another "Jehoahaz," this time a Judahite king who reigns only some three months, in 23:31–35, below. The name "Jehoahaz" is also attested on a late seventh-century stamp seal (cf. Cogan and Tadmor, AB, 142). Suggested dates for the accession of the present king vary only slightly, from 815 (Albright) to 814 (Thiele).

As just noted, Yahweh's judgment against Israel during this time was particularly manifested by the strong military pressure exerted by the Arameans. We have already read about King Hazael's repeated oppression of the Israelites (and even the Judahites; cf. above, on 8:11ff), and we will soon read about his successor, Ben-Hadad (see 13:24, below; this Ben-Hadad is conventionally labeled "Ben-Hadad III," although, as we have already seen [see above, on 6:24f], there are serious objections to this enumeration). In any case, we read here in v. 3, that Yahweh's "anger" was thus manifested "for a long time"; yet in the very next verse, King Jehoahaz "sought Yahweh's favor," and Yahweh "listened to him" (shades of Yahweh's hearkening even to the evil King Ahab in 1 Ki. 21:27ff). As we shall again be reminded in the case of the wicked King Manasseh of Judah (at least according to the chronicler's account; cf. 2 Chr. 33:12f), it is seemingly never too late to seek the grace of the Lord, no matter what our previous actions

6460	512	7561	3706	6.311	4567	782
cj, num	num	n ms	cj	v Piel pf 3ms, ps 3mp	*n ms*	pn
וַעֲשֶׂרֶת	אֲלָפִים	רַגְלִי	כִּי	אִבְּדָם	מֶלֶךְ	אֲרָם
wa'ăsereth	'ălāphîm	raghlî	kî	'ibb^{e}dhām	melekh	'ărām
and ten	thousands	infantry	because	he had caused them to perish	the king of	Aram

7947.121	3626, 6312	3937, 1813.141		3615	1745
cj, v Qal impf 3ms, ps 3mp	prep, art, n ms	prep, v Qal inf con	**8.**	cj, *n ms*	*n mp*
וַיְשִׂמֵם	כֶּעָפָר	לָדֻשׁ		וְיֶתֶר	דִּבְרֵי
waysimēm	ke'āphār	lādhush		w^{e}yether	divrê
and he made them	like the dust	of threshing		and the remainder of	the events of

3168	3725, 866	6449.111	1400	1950B, 3940, 2062	3918.156
pn	cj, *adj*, rel part	v Qal pf 3ms	cj, n fs, ps 3ms	intrg part, neg part, pers pron	v Qal pass ptc mp
יְהוֹאָחָז	וְכָל־אֲשֶׁר	עָשָׂה	וּגְבוּרָתוֹ	הֲלוֹא־הֵם	כְּתוּבִים
y^{e}hô'āchāz	w^{e}khol-'ăsher	'āsāh	ûgh^{e}vûrāthô	hălô'-hēm	k^{e}thûvîm
Jehoahaz	and all which	he did	and his strength	are they not	things written

6142, 5809	1745	3219	3937, 4567	3547		8311.121	3168
prep, *n ms*	*n mp*	art, n mp	prep, *n mp*	pn	**9.**	cj, v Qal impf 3ms	pn
עַל־סֵפֶר	דִּבְרֵי	הַיָּמִים	לְמַלְכֵי	יִשְׂרָאֵל		וַיִּשְׁכַּב	יְהוֹאָחָז
'al-s̲ēpher	divrê	hayyāmîm	l^{e}malkhê	yisrā'ēl		wayyishkav	y^{e}hô'āchāz
on the scroll of	the events of	the days	of the kings of	Israel		and he lay	Jehoahaz

6196, 1	7196.126	904, 8497	4566.121	3204	1158
prep, n mp, ps 3ms	cj, v Qal impf 3mp, ps 3ms	prep, pn	cj, v Qal impf 3ms	pn	n ms, ps 3ms
עִם־אֲבֹתָיו	וַיִּקְבְּרֻהוּ	בְּשֹׁמְרוֹן	וַיִּמְלֹךְ	יוֹאָשׁ	בְּנוֹ
'im-'ăvōthâv	wayyiqōbb^{e}ruhû	b^{e}shōm^{e}rôn	wayyimlōkh	yô'āsh	b^{e}nô
with his ancestors	and they buried him	in Samaria	and he reigned	Joash	his son

8809		904, 8523	8421	8124	8523	3937, 3204	4567	3171
prep, ps 3ms	**10.**	prep, *n fs*	num	cj, num	n fs	prep, pn	*n ms*	pn
תַּחְתָּיו		בִּשְׁנַת	שְׁלֹשִׁים	וָשֶׁבַע	שָׁנָה	לְיוֹאָשׁ	מֶלֶךְ	יְהוּדָה
tachtâv		bishnath	sh^{e}lōshîm	wāsheva'	shānāh	l^{e}yô'āsh	melekh	y^{e}hûdhāh
instead of him		in the year of	thirty	and seven	years	of Joash	the king of	Judah

4566.111	3169	1158, 3168	6142, 3547	904, 8497	8666	6462	8523
v Qal pf 3ms	pn	*n ms*, pn	prep, pn	prep, pn	num	num	n fs
מָלַךְ	יְהוֹאָשׁ	בֶּן־יְהוֹאָחָז	עַל־יִשְׂרָאֵל	בְּשֹׁמְרוֹן	שֵׁשׁ	עֶשְׂרֵה	שָׁנָה
mālakh	y^{e}hô'āsh	ben-y^{e}hô'āchāz	'al-yisrā'ēl	b^{e}shōm^{e}rôn	shēsh	'esrēh	shānāh
he reigned	Jehoash	the son of Jehoahaz	over Israel	in Samaria	six	ten	years

	6449.121	7737	904, 6084	3176	3940	5681.111
11.	cj, v Qal impf 3ms	art, adj	prep, *n fd*	pn	neg part	v Qal pf 3ms
	וַיַּעֲשֶׂה	הָרַע	בְּעֵינֵי	יְהוָה	לֹא	סָר
	wayya'ăseh	hāra'	b^{e}'ênê	y^{e}hwāh	lō'	s̲ār
	and he did	what is evil	in the eyes of	Yahweh	not	he turned aside

4623, 3725, 2496	3493	1158, 5203	866, 2490.511	881, 3547	904
prep, *adj*, *n fp*	pn	*n ms*, pn	rel pron, v Hiphil pf 3ms	do, pn	prep, ps 3fs
מִכָּל־חַטֹּאות	יָרָבְעָם	בֶּן־נְבָט	אֲשֶׁר־הֶחֱטִיא	אֶת־יִשְׂרָאֵל	בָּהּ
mikkol-chat̲t̲ō'wth	yārov'ām	ben-n^{e}vāt̲	'ăsher-hechĕt̲î'	'eth-yisrā'ēl	bāhh
from all the sins of	Jeroboam	the son of Nebat	who he caused to sin	Israel	in them

2050.111		3615	1745	3204	3725, 866	6449.111
v Qal pf 3ms	**12.**	cj, *n ms*	*n mp*	pn	cj, *adj*, rel part	v Qal pf 3ms
הָלָךְ		וְיֶתֶר	דִּבְרֵי	יוֹאָשׁ	וְכָל־אֲשֶׁר	עָשָׂה
hālākh		w^{e}yether	divrê	yô'āsh	w^{e}khol-'ăsher	'āsāh
he walked		and the remainder of	the events of	Joash	and all which	he did

8. Now the rest of the acts of Jehoahaz, and all that he did, and his might, are they not written in the book of the chronicles of the kings of Israel?: ... all he did, and his great power, *BB* ... Isn't everything else about Jehoahaz, including all he did and the strength he showed, written in the annals of Israel's kings?, *Beck* ... The remainder of the affairs of Jhoakhaz, and all he did, and his courage, are recorded, *Fenton* ... all his history, and the record of his great deeds, is to be found, *Knox*.

9. And Jehoahaz slept with his fathers; and they buried him in Samaria: and Joash his son reigned in his stead: ... rested with his ancestors, *NAB* ... Jehoahaz died and was buried in Samaria, and his son Jehoash became king in his place, *NCV* ... he was succeeded by his son Jehoash, *NEB* ... reigned in his place, *NKJV*.

10. In the thirty and seventh year of Joash king of Judah began Jehoash the son of Jehoahaz to reign over Israel in Samaria, and reigned sixteen years: ... thirty-seventh year, *Anchor* ... Joash, the son of Jehoahaz, became king over Israel in Samaria, ruling for sixteen years, *BB* ... and was king for 16 years, *Beck*.

11. And he did that which was evil in the sight of the Lord; he departed not from all the sins of Jeroboam the son of Nebat, who made Israel sin: but he walked therein: ... He did wrong before the LORD and didn't turn away from any of the sins by which Jeroboam made Israel sin, but continued to practice them, *Beck* ... he persisted in it, *JB* ... He defied the Lord's will, and would not abandon the sins of Jeroboam, son of Nabat, that taught Israel to sin; he clung to them yet, *Knox* ... he did what the Lord said was wrong. He did not stop doing the same sins Jeroboam son of Nebat had done. Jeroboam had led Israel to sin, and Jehoash continued to do the same thing, *NCV*.

12. And the rest of the acts of Joash, and all that he did, and his

---

in life or in leadership may have been. Thus, in the present case, King Jehoahaz of Israel turned to the ancestral God of his people, and the marvelous love and compassion of that God were clearly displayed yet one more time (the theme of Yahweh's repeated concern for the northern nation of Israel is mentioned again in v. 23, below, as well as in 14:26f; we today, in our understandable focus on God's continued faithfulness to the southern kingdom of Judah, tend to overlook these repeated references to God's unconditional love for the Northern Kingdom, as well).

We are then told in v. 5 that Yahweh provided a "deliverer" (môshîa', HED #3588, a term not used elsewhere in 1–2 Kings, but used several times in the Books of Judges and 1 Samuel; cf. Judg. 3:9, 15; 12:3; 1 Sam. 10:19)—for the sake of his severely oppressed people Israel. (The identity of the present "deliverer" is unknown, but an attractive suggestion is to link Jehoahaz's act of contrition in v. 4 of the present text with the unnamed king's grief and despair in 6:30, during the horrific siege of Samaria [so Cogan and Tadmor, AB, 85, 144]. If this be the case, at least some further light can be shed on both the appalling pressure Israel faced at this time, as well as the incredible answer to prayer Yahweh provided when that siege was miraculously lifted the very next day [cf. ch. 7].) In any case, we are further reminded that the "amazing grace" of our God seemingly knows no bounds. It is all the more depressing to read then of Israel's return to apostasy and idol worship in v. 6 of the present passage—once again, shades of the sin of Jeroboam I. (Cogan and Tadmor [AB, 144] understand v. 7 as a kind of "footnote" to the text, illustrating how feeble the forces under Jehoahaz had become under Aramean oppression; they suggest that it was added at a later date).

As already noted, v. 8 of the present text represents a "further reference" formula, and v. 9 an Israelite burial notice. As of yet, this last formula has gone unexamined at any length in 2 Kings. (The Israelite kings Ahaziah [cf. 1:17] and Joram [cf. 9:24ff] had no such formal burial notices as such. Also, here Jehu's notice [10:35] was passed over with little comment. [Comment is made, however, on the Judahite burial notices at some length, in connection with 8:23f, above]). Like their southern counterparts, some of the Israelite kings have formal burial notices appended to the discussions of their reigns (but only nine notices out of a total of nineteen kings, from Jeroboam I to the Assyrian exile, in contrast to the fifteen formal notices for the nineteen Judahite kings after Solomon). Five of these notices include the place of burial (once, Tirzah [1 Ki. 16:6]; four times, Samaria [1 Ki. 16:28; 2 Ki. 10:35; 13:9, 13; cf. the parallel in 14:16]), and all nine give the name of the deceased king's successor (invariably his son; usurpers are never featured). None of the assassinated kings have formal burial notices (and of the nine kings with burial notices [Jeroboam I, Baasha, Omri, Ahab, Jehu, Jehoahaz, Jehoash, Jeroboam II and Menahem], only Ahab evidently died a violent death; cf. 1 Ki. 22:34–38).

13:10–13. Jehoash king of Israel: Accession, judgment and burial notices. As was the case in the immediately preceding section, most of the present

1400	866	4032.211	6196	568	4567, 3171
cj, n fs, ps 3ms	rel part	v Niphal pf 3ms	prep	pn	*n ms*, pn
וּגְבוּרָתוֹ	אֲשֶׁר	נִלְחָם	עִם	אֲמַצְיָה	מֶלֶךְ־יְהוּדָה
ûghevûrāthô	'ăsher	nilcham	'im	'ămatsyāh	melekh-yehûdhāh
and his strength	which	he fought	against	Amaziah	the king of Judah

1950B, 3940, 2062	3918.156	6142, 5809	1745	3219	3937, 4567
intrg part, neg part, pers pron	v Qal pass ptc mp	prep, *n ms*	*n mp*	art, n mp	prep, *n mp*
הֲלוֹא־הֵם	כְּתוּבִים	עַל־סֵפֶר	דִּבְרֵי	הַיָּמִים	לְמַלְכֵי
hălô'-hēm	kethûvîm	'al-sēpher	divrê	hayyāmîm	lemalkhê
are they not	things written	on the scroll of	the events of	the days	of the kings of

3547		8311.121	3204	6196, 1	3493	3553.111
pn	13.	cj, v Qal impf 3ms	pn	prep, n mp, ps 3ms	cj, pn	v Qal pf 3ms
יִשְׂרָאֵל		וַיִּשְׁכַּב	יוֹאָשׁ	עִם־אֲבֹתָיו	וְיָרָבְעָם	יָשַׁב
yisrā'ēl		wayyishkav	yô'āsh	'im-'ăvōthâv	weyārov'ām	yāshav
Israel		and he lay	Joash	with his ancestors	and Jeroboam	he sat

6142, 3802	7196.221	3204	904, 8497	6196	4567	3547		482
prep, n ms, ps 3ms	cj, v Niphil impf 3ms	pn	prep, pn	prep	*n mp*	pn	14.	cj, pn
עַל־כִּסְאוֹ	וַיִּקָּבֵר	יוֹאָשׁ	בְּשֹׁמְרוֹן	עִם	מַלְכֵי	יִשְׂרָאֵל		וֶאֱלִישָׁע
'al-kis'ô	wayyiqqāvēr	yô'āsh	beshōmerôn	'im	malkhê	yisrā'ēl		we'ĕlîshā'
on his throne	and he was buried	Joash	in Samaria	with	the kings of	Israel		and Elisha

2571.111	881, 2582	866	4322.121	904	3495.121	420
v Qal pf 3ms	do, n ms, ps 3ms	rel part	v Qal impf 3ms	prep, ps 3ms	cj, v Qal impf 3ms	prep, ps 3ms
חָלָה	אֶת־חָלְיוֹ	אֲשֶׁר	יָמוּת	בּוֹ	וַיֵּרֶד	אֵלָיו
chālāh	'eth-chāleyô	'ăsher	yāmûth	bô	wayyēredh	'ēlâv
he was sick	with his sickness	which	he would die	with it	and he went down	to him

3204	4567, 3547	1098.121	6142, 6686	569.121	1	1
pn	*n ms*, pn	cj, v Qal impf 3ms	prep, n mp, ps 3ms	v Qal impf 3ms	n ms, ps 1cs	n ms, ps 1cs
יוֹאָשׁ	מֶלֶךְ־יִשְׂרָאֵל	וַיֵּבְךְּ	עַל־פָּנָיו	וַיֹּאמַר	אָבִי	אָבִי
yô'āsh	melekh-yisrā'ēl	wayyēvekke	'al-pānâv	wayyō'mar	'āvî	'āvî
Joash	the king of Israel	and he wept	on his face	and he said	O my father	O my father

7681	3547	6821		569.121	3937	482
n ms	pn	cj, n mp, ps 3ms	15.	cj, v Qal impf 3ms	prep, ps 3ms	pn
רֶכֶב	יִשְׂרָאֵל	וּפָרָשָׁיו		וַיֹּאמֶר	לוֹ	אֱלִישָׁע
rekhev	yisrā'ēl	ûphārāshâv		wayyō'mer	lô	'ĕlîshā'
the chariots of	Israel	and their horsemen		and he said	to him	Elisha

4089.131	7493	2777	4089.121	420	7493	2777
v Qal impv 2ms	n fs	cj, n mp	cj, v Qal impf 3ms	prep, ps 3ms	n fs	cj, n mp
קַח	קֶשֶׁת	וְחִצִּים	וַיִּקַּח	אֵלָיו	קֶשֶׁת	וְחִצִּים
qach	qesheth	wechitstsîm	wayyiqqach	'ēlâv	qesheth	wechitstsîm
take	the bow	and arrows	and he took	to him	the bow	and arrows

	569.121	3937, 4567	3547	7680.531	3135	6142, 7493
16.	cj, v Qal impf 3ms	prep, *n ms*	pn	v Hiphil impv 2ms	n fs, ps 2ms	prep, art, n fs
	וַיֹּאמֶר	לְמֶלֶךְ	יִשְׂרָאֵל	הַרְכֵּב	יָדְךָ	עַל־הַקֶּשֶׁת
	wayyō'mer	lemelekh	yisrā'ēl	harkēv	yādhekhā	'al-haqqesheth
	and he said	to the king of	Israel	mount	your hand	on the bow

7680.521	3135	7947.121	482	3135	6142, 3135	4567
cj, v Hiphil impf 3ms	n fs, ps 3ms	cj, v Qal impf 3ms	pn	n fd, ps 3ms	prep, *n fd*	art, n ms
וַיַּרְכֵּב	יָדוֹ	וַיָּשֶׂם	אֱלִישָׁע	יָדָיו	עַל־יְדֵי	הַמֶּלֶךְ
wayyarkēv	yādhô	wayyāsem	'ĕlîshā'	yādhâv	'al-yedhê	hammelekh
and he mounted	his hand	and he put	Elisha	his hands	on the hands of	the king

might wherewith he fought against Amaziah king of Judah, are they not written in the book of the chronicles of the kings of Israel?: ... Isn't everything else about Joash, including all he did and the ability with which he fought against Amaziah king of Judah written in, *Beck* ... all that he did, and his courage, *Fenton* ... The other events of the reign of Jehoash, all his achievements, his exploits and his war with Amaziah king of Judah, are recorded in, *NEB* ... Everything else that Jehoash did, including his bravery in the war against King Amaziah of Judah, is recorded, *Good News*.

13. And Joash slept with his fathers; and Jeroboam sat upon his throne: and Joash was buried in Samaria with the kings of Israel: ... Jeroboam ascended his throne, *JB* ... He was laid to rest with his fathers, *Knox* ... rested with his ancestors, *NAB* ... Jehoash died, and Jeroboam took his place on the throne, *NCV*.

14. Now Elisha was fallen sick of his sickness whereof he died: ... Elisha fell ill and lay on his deathbed, *NEB* ... was suffering from the illness from which he died, *NIV* ... became ill with the disease which was the cause of his death, *BB* ... was confined at the time with the illness of which he was to die, *Berkeley*.

And Joash the king of Israel came down unto him, and wept over his face, and said, O my father, my father, the chariot of Israel, and the horsemen thereof: ... The chariots and horsemen of Israel!, *NIV* ... King Jehoash of Israel visited him and wept over him, *NLT* ... came down to him, and weeping over him said, *BB* ... went down to see him and wept in his presence, sobbing, *Berkeley*.

15. And Elisha said unto him, Take bow and arrows. And he took unto him bow and arrows: ... Get a bow and, *Good News* ... Bring bow, *JB* ... fetch bow, *Knox* ... And the king did as he was told, *NLT*.

16. And he said to the king of Israel, Put thine hand upon the bow. And he put his hand upon it: and Elisha put his hands upon the king's hands: ... Draw the bow; and he drew it, *NRSV* ... Take hold of the bow, *Berkeley* ... get ready to shoot, *Good News* ... As the king held the bow, Elisha placed his hands over the king's hands, *NAB*.

---

material is quite formulaic, and need be discussed only briefly. A typical Israelite accession notice (v. 10) leads into the stereotypical Israelite judgment formula (v. 11; "not turning away from the sins of Jeroboam son of Nebat"). Next is the concluding "further reference" formula (v. 12), with its "teaser" notice concerning the "war against Amaziah king of Judah" (cf. 14:8–14, with v. 15 of that chapter virtually identical to the present v. 12); and finally we read Jehoash's burial notice in v. 13 (virtually the same as 14:16). If it had not been for the additional material in the next chapter, we would know very little about the "achievements" (cf. v. 12) of this Israelite king.

King Jehoash of Israel is featured briefly not only in the present section, but also in the Elisha material in the rest of the chapter (especially cf. vv. 14–19, 25, below), and, as just noted, also in the Amaziah material in the next chapter (14:8–16). Rarely do we have the compartmentalized nature of the biblical writer's organizational process better illustrated, with each Israelite and Judahite king discussed in turn, generally introduced with an accession notice and concluded with a burial notice; then the next king in chronological order, etc. (Chapter 15, below, is another excellent example of this procedure, with a total of seven kings in relentless chronological order, each with synchronisms to the opposite kingdom introducing his reign.) Inasmuch as the discussion has largely centered on the Elijah and Elisha materials up to this point, this chronological backbone has been less obvious in the first half of 2 Kings.

13:14–19. Conclusion of the Elisha narratives cycle: Prediction of limited victory for King Jehoash of Israel, and resurrection of an anonymous Israelite. These final verses about Elisha are curiously located, for no mention of Elisha has been made since the beginning of ch. 9. It is possible the writer felt he had to wait to the present point to insert this Elisha material, since it mentioned King Jehoash of Israel by name, and Jehoash's regnal formulas do not appear until the beginning of the present chapter. At any rate, we once again, and for the final time, encounter the Israelite prophet who had such an effect on the political history of both Israel and Aram. Once again, the subject is Israelite defeat and Aramean resurgence, but, thankfully, that will not always prove to be the case.

It will be recalled that we have already encountered the refrain, "My father. My father. The chariots and horsemen of Israel" (v. 14); Elisha said the very same thing when his mentor, the prophet Elijah was taken from him (cf. above, on 2:11f). Here, however, it is the Israelite king who utters this refrain concerning the dying Elisha. The true source of Israel's protection was not the earthly chariots and horsemen in the army, but the heavenly protection

17.	569.121	6858.131	2574	7209	6858.121	569.121
	cj, v Qal impf 3ms	v Qal impv 2ms	art, n ms	adv	cj, v Qal impf 3ms	cj, v Qal impf 3ms
	וַיֹּאמֶר	פְּתַח	הַחַלּוֹן	קֵדְמָה	וַיִּפְתָּח	וַיֹּאמֶר
	wayyō'mer	pethach	hachallôn	qēdhemāh	wayyiphtāch	wayyō'mer
	and he said	open	the window	eastward	and he opened	and he said

482	3498.131	3498.521	569.121	2777, 9009	3937, 3176
pn	v Qal impv 2ms	cj, v Hiphil impf 3ms	cj, v Qal impf 3ms	*n ms*, n fs	prep, pn
אֱלִישָׁע	יְרֵה	וַיּוֹר	וַיֹּאמֶר	חֵץ־תְּשׁוּעָה	לַיהוָה
'ĕlîshā'	yerēh	wayyôr	wayyō'mer	chēts-teshû'āh	layhwāh
Elisha	shoot	and he shot	and he said	an arrow of deliverance	of Yahweh

2777	9009	904, 782	5409.513	881, 782	904, 682
cj, *n ms*	n fs	prep, pn	cj, v Hiphil pf 2ms	do, pn	prep, pn
וְחֵץ	תְּשׁוּעָה	בַאֲרָם	וְהִכִּיתָ	אֶת־אֲרָם	בַּאֲפֵק
wechēts	teshû'āh	va'ărām	wehikkîthā	'eth-'ărām	ba'ăphēq
and an arrow of	deliverance	over Aram	and you will strike	Aram	in Aphek

5912, 3735.342	18.	569.121	4089.131	2777	4089.121	569.121
adv, v Piel inf abs		cj, v Qal impf 3ms	v Qal impv 2ms	art, n mp	cj, v Qal impf 3ms	cj, v Qal impf 3ms
עַד־כַּלֵּה		וַיֹּאמֶר	קַח	הַחִצִּים	וַיִּקָּח	וַיֹּאמֶר
'adh-kallēh		wayyō'mer	qach	hachitstsîm	wayyiqqāch	wayyō'mer
until making an end		and he said	take	the arrows	and he took	and he said

3937, 4567, 3547	5409.531, 800	5409.521	8421, 6718	6198.121
prep, *n ms*, pn	v Hiphil impv 2ms, n fs	cj, v Hiphil impf 3ms	num, n fp	cj, v Qal impf 3ms
לְמֶלֶךְ־יִשְׂרָאֵל	הַךְ־אַרְצָה	וַיַּךְ	שָׁלֹשׁ־פְּעָמִים	וַיַּעֲמֹד
lemelekh-yisrā'ēl	hakh-'artsāh	wayyakh	shālōsh-pe'āmîm	wayya'ămōdh
to the king of Israel	strike to the ground	and he struck	three times	and he stood

19.	7395.121	6142	382	435	569.121	3937, 5409.541
	v Qal impf 3ms	prep, ps 3ms	*n ms*	art, n mp	cj, v Qal impf 3ms	prep, v Hiphil inf con
	וַיִּקְצֹף	עָלָיו	אִישׁ	הָאֱלֹהִים	וַיֹּאמֶר	לְהַכּוֹת
	wayyiqtsōph	'ālâv	'îsh	hā'ĕlōhîm	wayyō'mer	lehakkôth
	and he was angry	concerning him	the man of	God	and he said	to strike

2675	173, 8666	6718	226	5409.513	881, 782	5912, 3735.342
num	cj, num	n fp	adv	v Hiphil pf 2ms	do, pn	adv, v Piel inf abs
חָמֵשׁ	אוֹ־שֵׁשׁ	פְּעָמִים	אָז	הִכִּיתָ	אֶת־אֲרָם	עַד־כַּלֵּה
chāmēsh	'ô-shēsh	pe'āmîm	'āz	hikkîthā	'eth-'ărām	'adh-kallēh
five	or six	times	then	you would have struck down	Aram	until making an end

17. And he said, Open the window eastward. And he opened it. Then Elisha said, Shoot. And he shot. And he said, The arrow of the LORD's deliverance, and the arrow of deliverance from Syria: for thou shalt smite the Syrians in Aphek, till thou have consumed them: ... The Lord's arrow of salvation, of salvation over Aram; for you will overcome the Aramaeans in Aphek and put an end to them, *BB* ... Defeat the Aramaeans at Aphek till you wipe them out, *Beck* ... You are the LORD's arrow, with which he will win victory over Syria. You will fight the Syrians in Aphek until you defeat them, *Good News* ... This is the LORD's arrow, full of victory over Aram, for you will completely conquer the Arameans at Aphek, *NLT*.

18. And he said, Take the arrows. And he took them. And he said unto the king of Israel, Smite upon the ground. And he smote thrice, and stayed: ... Strike the ground with them; he struck three times, and stopped, *NRSV* ... Send them down into the earth; and he did so three times and no more, *BB* ... Smash them on the ground, *Beck* ... Shoot at the ground! So he shot three times, then stopped, *Fenton*.

19. And the man of God was wroth with him, and said, Thou shouldest have smitten five or six times: ... MAN of GOD was angry, *Fenton* ... was enraged at him, *Goodspeed* ... was furious with him, *NEB* ... You should have struck half a dozen times, *JB*.

then hadst thou smitten Syria till thou hadst consumed it: whereas now thou shalt smite Syria but thrice: ... you would have defeated

always available when needed (cf. also 6:16f, "Those who are with us are more than those who are with them"). By now, King Jehoash was very clear about one thing: a prophet like Elisha, even at his advanced age (Wiseman [TOTC, 241] calculated that by this time Elisha's ministry had spanned more than sixty years), is worth more than the greatest number of youthful warriors, or the largest number of horses and chariots (how much more, then, than the currently decrepit state of the Israelite military, as reflected in v. 7). Hobbs (WBC, 169) quotes Josephus' apt comment (*Antiquities*, IX, 179): "Because of him, he said, they had never had to use arms against the foe, but through his prophecies they had overcome the enemy without battle. But now he was departing this life and leaving him unarmed before the Syrians and the enemies under them." The primacy of the prophet of God even over the king is rarely more clearly illustrated.

In vv. 15–19, Elisha commissions the king to perform two symbolic actions: shooting the bow through the window and striking the ground with the arrows. Both represent future victories over the Arameans: "Such actions are a 'miniature' of the events they depict" (Hobbs, following H. W. Robinson). Even on his deathbed, Elisha seemed more exuberant than the more youthful King Jehoash. He placed his own hands over the king's hands when shooting the arrow (cf. 4:34, above, where the prophet stretched out over the Shunammite's dead boy, "mouth to mouth, eyes to eyes, hands to hands"); and he reprimanded the king sharply when the latter struck the ground only three times with the arrows ("you should have struck the ground five or six times ..."). Ironic indeed is the fact that these are the last recorded words of this dear prophet—and perhaps even more ironic is the fact that Elisha died very much alone. He was not surrounded by his supporters at his death as was Elijah. The prophet Elijah, whose ministry was usually characterized by solitary activity, left this earth with supporters assembled, whereas Elisha, whose trademark was the repeated association with the "sons of the prophets," died very much in solitude (v. 20). One never knows when an established pattern may be altered, either by accident or by design.

A theme of duality pervades the Elisha narratives, and a discussion of that topic now follows. In ch. 2, Elisha asks for a "double portion" of Elijah's spirit (cf. on 2:9f, above). This clearly represented the inheritance of the first-born son. Commentators and preachers, however, have long noted that the motif of duality, seems to be well represented in the subsequent Elisha stories. For example, Elijah raised one person from the dead (the son of the widow of Zarephath [1 Ki. 17:17–24]), but Elisha two (the Shunammite's son [2 Ki. 4:18–37] and the unnamed Israelite in the present text). Elijah is reckoned to have performed five miracles, but Elisha ten (cf. Wiseman, TOTC, 45; also cf. the statement from Sirach, quoted above, at 2:9f). In 2:23ff, there are two she-bears which mauled the Bethelite youths; in the Naaman passage (ch. 5) there are a pair of mules (in v. 17), two young men (in v. 22a), two sets of clothing (in v. 22b), two talents in two bags, and again two sets of clothing, given to two servants (all in v. 23). Less impressive examples may be found in 4:1 (the widow's two sons liable for debt-slavery); in 4:34f (Elisha stretching out on the dead boy two times); in 4:43 (a hundred men fed, possibly representing two companies of fifty "sons of the prophets," but the text does not say anything about this method of reckoning), and finally in 7:14 (two chariots sent out). Certainly, the intriguing story in the present passage (vv. 20f) about the second occasion a resurrection occurred in connection with Elisha is more than coincidental. But these are literary parallels, not strict exegeses of the reference to the "double portion" in 2:9. We cannot allegorize the Scriptures to entertain our audiences; rather we must seek, as best we can, to ascertain the strict grammatical-historical meaning, in order to edify them. And the meaning of the "double-portion" reference is clearly that of the inheritance of the first-born son, Elisha sought to be the "first-born" disciple of Elijah, his true successor, nothing more (anything more would be arrogant and presumptive). It is therefore not surprising that we find Moses and Elijah (not, e.g., Joshua and Elisha) at the Transfiguration of our Lord (Matt. 17:3, etc.). Both Joshua and Elisha were exemplary leaders, to be sure, but they were not the same as Moses, the prophet par excellence (cf. Deut. 34:10ff), and Elijah, the promised forerunner of the Messiah (Mal. 4:5f).

13:20–21. Hobbs (WBC, 170) rightly points out that the revival of the corpse in vv. 20f is "unlike anything else in the Scriptures"; he understood it as, among other things, a foretaste of the revival the nation of Israel would experience, especially as recounted in the next chapter. The

6498	8421	6718	5409.523	881, 782		4322.121	482
cj, adv	num	n fp	v Hiphil impf 2ms	do, pn	20.	cj, v Qal impf 3ms	pn
וְעַתָּה	שָׁלֹשׁ	פְּעָמִים	תַּכֶּה	אֶת־אֲרָם		וַיָּמָת	אֱלִישָׁע
we'attāh	shālōsh	pe'āmîm	takkeh	'eth-'ărām		wayyāmāth	'ĕlîshā'
but now	three	times	you will strike	Aram		and he died	Elisha

7196.126	1447	4262	971.126	904, 800	971.111	8523
cj, v Qal impf 3mp, ps 3ms	cj, *n mp*	pn	v Qal impf 3mp	prep, art, n fs	v Qal pf 3ms	n fs
וַיִּקְבְּרֻהוּ	וּגְדוּדֵי	מוֹאָב	יָבֹאוּ	בָאָרֶץ	בָּא	שָׁנָה
wayyiqōbberuhû	ûghedhûdhê	mô'āv	yāvō'û	vā'ārets	bā'	shānāh
and they buried him	and raiders of	Moab	they entered	in the land	it had come	a year

	2030.121	2062	7196.152	382	2079	7495.116	881, 1447
21.	cj, v Qal impf 3ms	pers pron	v Qal act ptc mp	n ms	cj, intrj	v Qal pf 3cp	do, art, n ms
	וַיְהִי	הֵם	קֹבְרִים	אִישׁ	וְהִנֵּה	רָאוּ	אֶת־הַגְּדוּד
	wayhî	hēm	qōverîm	'îsh	wehinnēh	rā'û	'eth-haggedhûdh
	and it was	they	burying	a man	and behold	they saw	the raiding party

8390.526	881, 382	904, 7197	482	2050.121	5236.121
cj, v Hiphil impf 3mp	do, art, n ms	prep, *n ms*	pn	cj, v Qal impf 3ms	cj, v Qal impf 3ms
וַיַּשְׁלִיכוּ	אֶת־הָאִישׁ	בְּקֶבֶר	אֱלִישָׁע	וַיֵּלֶךְ	וַיִּגַּע
wayyashlîkhû	'eth-hā'îsh	beqever	'ĕlîshā'	wayyēlekh	wayyigga'
and they threw	the man	in the tomb of	Elisha	and he proceeded	and he touched

382	904, 6344	482	2513.121	7251.121	6142, 7559
art, n ms	prep, *n fp*	pn	cj, v Qal impf 3ms	cj, v Qal impf 3ms	prep, n fd, ps 3ms
הָאִישׁ	בְּעַצְמוֹת	אֱלִישָׁע	וַיְחִי	וַיָּקָם	עַל־רַגְלָיו
hā'îsh	be'atsmôth	'ĕlîshā'	waychî	wayyāqām	'al-raghlāv
the man	on the bones of	Elisha	and he lived	and he rose up	on his feet

	2462	4567	782	4040.111	881, 3547	3725	3219
22.	cj, pn	*n ms*	pn	v Qal pf 3ms	do, pn	*n ms*	*n mp*
	וַחֲזָאֵל	מֶלֶךְ	אֲרָם	לָחַץ	אֶת־יִשְׂרָאֵל	כֹּל	יְמֵי
	wachzā'ēl	melekh	'ărām	lāchats	'eth-yisrā'ēl	kōl	yemê
	and Hazael	the king of	Aram	he oppressed	Israel	the entirety of	the days of

3168		2706.121	3176	881	7638.321
pn	23.	cj, v Qal impf 3ms	pn	do, ps 3mp	cj, v Piel impf 3ms, ps 3mp
יְהוֹאָחָז		וַיָּחָן	יְהוָה	אֹתָם	וַיְרַחֲמֵם
yehô'āchāz		wayyāchān	yehwāh	'ōthām	wayrachmēm
Jehoahaz		but He had compassion on	Yahweh	them	and He was merciful to them

6680.121	420	3937, 4775	1311	882, 80	3437	3399
cj, v Qal impf 3ms	prep, ps 3mp	prep, prep	n fs, ps 3ms	prep, pn	pn	cj, pn
וַיִּפֶן	אֲלֵיהֶם	לְמַעַן	בְּרִיתוֹ	אֶת־אַבְרָהָם	יִצְחָק	וְיַעֲקֹב
wayyiphen	'ălêhem	lema'an	berîthô	'eth-'avrāhām	yitschāq	weya'ăqōv
and He turned	to them	on account of	his covenant	with Abraham	Isaac	and Jacob

3940	13.111	8271.541	3940, 8390.511
cj, neg part	v Qal pf 3ms	v Hiphil inf con, ps 3mp	cj, neg part, v Hiphil pf 3ms, ps 3mp
וְלֹא	אָבָה	הַשְׁחִיתָם	וְלֹא־הִשְׁלִיכָם
welō'	'āvāh	hashchîthām	welō'-hishlîkhām
and not	He was willing	to allow them to be ravaged	and He did not throw them

4623, 6142, 6686	5912, 6498		4322.121	2462	4567, 782
prep, prep, n mp, ps 3ms	prep, adv	24.	cj, v Qal impf 3ms	pn	*n ms*, pn
מֵעַל־פָּנָיו	עַד־עַתָּה		וַיָּמָת	חֲזָאֵל	מֶלֶךְ־אֲרָם
mē'al-pānâv	'adh-'attāh		wayyāmāth	chăzā'ēl	melekh-'ărām
from beside his presence	until now		then he died	Hazael	the king of Aram

Aram to destruction; but now you have only defeated Aram three times, *Fenton* ... you would have won complete victory over the Syrians, *Good News* ... you would have struck down Aram and destroyed it, *Moffatt* ... you would have defeated Aram utterly; as it is, you will strike Aram three times and no more, *NEB*.

20. And Elisha died, and they buried him. And the bands of the Moabites invaded the land at the coming in of the year: ... death came to Elisha and they put his body into the earth. Now in the spring of the year, armed bands of Moabites frequently came, overrunning the land, *BB* ... the raiding bands from Moab invaded the land in the spring of the year, *NKJV* ... Bands of Moabites were making incursions into the country every year, *JB*.

21. And it came to pass, as they were burying a man, that, behold, they spied a band of men; and they cast the man into the sepulchre of Elisha: ... Some of these appearing suddenly when a dead man was being carried out to his funeral, the bearers took fright, and threw the corpse into the first grave they could find; it was that of Elisha, *Knox* ... they cast the dead man into the grave of Elisha, and everyone went off, *NAB* ... they saw a marauding band, *NASB* ... they saw a group of Moabites, *NCV*.

and when the man was let down, and touched the bones of Elisha, he revived, and stood up on his feet: ... no sooner had it touched the prophet's bones, than the dead man came to life again, and rose to his feet, *Knox* ... when the man came in contact with the bones of Elisha, he came back to life and rose to his feet, *NAB* ... dead man revived and jumped to his feet!, *NLT*.

22. But Hazael king of Syria oppressed Israel all the days of Jehoahaz: ... afflicted Israel all the days of, *Douay* ... Israel was crushed under the power of Hazael, *BB* ... as long as Jehoahaz ruled, *Beck* ... throughout the lifetime of Jehoahaz, *JB*.

23. And the Lord was gracious unto them, and had compassion on them, and had respect unto them, because of his covenant with Abraham, Isaac, and Jacob: ... had mercy on them, and returned to them because of his covenant, *Douay* ... was kind to the Israelites; he had mercy on them and helped them because of his agreement with, *NCV* ... was gracious and took pity on them; because of his covenant, *NEB* ... was gracious to them and had compassion and showed concern for them because of his covenant, *NIV*.

and would not destroy them, neither cast he them from his presence as yet: ... nor utterly cast them away, unto this present time, *Douay* ... To this day he has never wanted to

---

accounts in the Bible concerning Elisha begin with an account about his deadly curse (2:23ff), and it closes with one about life-giving contact with his dead bones. But, probably a better way to delineate this correspondence is as follows: (A) life-giving water restored at Jericho (2:19–22); (B) deadly curse at Bethel (2:23ff); (B') angry censure for King Jehoash (13:14–19); and, finally, (A') life-giving restoration at his grave. Thus, we find an inversion (AB, then B'A'), which is so typical of Hebrew narrative structure.

Presumably, Elisha has been dead for some time, since the narrator speaks of his "bones." Modern western audiences of Scripture are often unaware of the biblical custom of reburial of the bones of the deceased some time after the original internment of the body in the family tomb. Particularly helpful here are the following comments of E. F. Campbell (*Ruth*, AB, 74f, in connection with Ruth's bold assertion that "even death will not separate you [Naomi] and me"): "Family tombs were the dominant feature, and after decomposition of the flesh was complete, bones were gathered in a common repository in the tomb, either in an ossuary or in a pit cut out of the rock in the floor of the tomb. A body might be placed in the tomb to decompose, or, if the family member died at some distance from home, the body could be interred at the distant spot and then the bones gathered up several months later for transport to the family tomb and deposit in the repository." This, by the way, is likely the practice underlying the common biblical cliché of a person being "gathered to one's fathers" (cf. Deut. 32:50; Judg. 2:10; etc.; also comments on 2 Ki. 22:20). The term "to gather" (ʾāsaph HED #636) was therefore meant to be taken quite literally. The bones were carefully gathered together for proper reburial (cf., once again, the Rizpah narrative in 2 Sam. 21:1–14, where King David eventually commissions a proper burial for the bones of Saul's seven sons; see, also, comments on Jezebel's demise in 2 Ki. 9:30–37). In the present passage, the final conundrum of the Elisha narrative may be simply put: "Out of death comes life" (Hobbs, WBC, 172).

13:22–25. Concluding note on King Hazael and Ben-Hadad of Aram and on King Jehoash of Israel: Further evidence concerning Yahweh's graciousness toward his people Israel. As already prophesied in vv. 17, 19, Israel would finally experience significant victories against their perennial enemy Aram. Whether it be under King Hazael, or his successor Ben-Hadad (concerning this latter

4566.121	1163	1158	8809		8178.121	3169
cj, v Qal impf 3ms	pn	n ms, ps 3ms	prep, ps 3ms	**25.**	cj, v Qal impf 3ms	pn
וַיִּמְלֹךְ	בֶּן־הֲדַד	בְּנוֹ	תַּחְתָּיו		וַיָּשָׁב	יְהוֹאָשׁ
wayyimlōkh	ben-hᵉdhadh	bᵉnô	tachtâv		wayyāshāv	yᵉhô'āsh
and he reigned	Ben-Hadad	his son	instead of him		then he returned	Jehoash

1158, 3168	4089.121	881, 6111	4623, 3135	1163	1158, 2462
n ms, pn	cj, v Qal impf 3ms	do, art, n fp	prep, *n fs*	pn	*n ms*, pn
בֶּן־יְהוֹאָחָז	וַיִּקַּח	אֶת־הֶעָרִים	מִיַּד	בֶּן־הֲדַד	בֶּן־חֲזָאֵל
ben-yᵉhô'āchāz	wayyiqqach	'eth-he'ārîm	mîyadh	ben-hᵉdhadh	ben-chăzā'ēl
the son of Jehoahaz	and he took	the cities	from the hand of	Ben-Hadad	the son of Hazael

866	4089.111	4623, 3135	3168	1	904, 4560	8421	6718
rel part	v Qal pf 3ms	prep, *n fs*	pn	n ms, ps 3ms	prep, art, n fs	num	n fp
אֲשֶׁר	לָקַח	מִיַּד	יְהוֹאָחָז	אָבִיו	בַּמִּלְחָמָה	שָׁלֹשׁ	פְּעָמִים
'āsher	lāqach	mîyadh	yᵉhô'āchāz	'āvîw	bammilchāmāh	shālōsh	pᵉ'āmîm
which	he took	from the hand of	Jehoahaz	his father	in the battle	three	times

5409.511	3204	8178.521	881, 6111	3547		904, 8523
v Hiphil pf 3ms, ps 3ms	pn	cj, v Hiphil impf 3ms	do, *n fp*	pn	**14:1**	prep, *n fs*
הִכָּהוּ	יוֹאָשׁ	וַיָּשֶׁב	אֶת־עָרֵי	יִשְׂרָאֵל		בִּשְׁנַת
hikkāhû	yô'āsh	wayyāshev	'eth-'ārê	yisrā'ēl		bishnath
he struck him	Joash	and he caused to return	the cities of	Israel		in the year of

8692	3937, 3204	1158, 3202	4567	3547	4566.111	568	1158, 3204
num	prep, pn	*n ms*, pn	*n ms*	pn	v Qal pf 3ms	pn	*n ms*, pn
שְׁתַּיִם	לְיוֹאָשׁ	בֶּן־יוֹאָחָז	מֶלֶךְ	יִשְׂרָאֵל	מָלַךְ	אֲמַצְיָהוּ	בֶן־יוֹאָשׁ
shᵉttayim	lᵉyô'āsh	ben-yô'āchāz	melekh	yisrā'ēl	mālakh	'ămatsyāhû	ven-yô'āsh
two	to Joash	the son of Joahaz	the king of	Israel	he reigned	Amaziah	the son of Joash

4567	3171		1158, 6465	2675	8523	2030.111	904, 4566.141
n ms	pn	**2.**	*n ms*, num	cj, num	n fs	v Qal pf 3ms	prep, v Qal inf con, ps 3ms
מֶלֶךְ	יְהוּדָה		בֶּן־עֶשְׂרִים	וְחָמֵשׁ	שָׁנָה	הָיָה	בְמָלְכוֹ
melekh	yᵉhûdhāh		ben-'esrîm	wᵉchāmēsh	shānāh	hāyāh	vᵉmālᵉkhô
the king of	Judah		a son of twenty	and five	years	he was	when his reigning

6465	9013	8523	4566.111	904, 3503	8428	525	3188
cj, num	cj, num	n fs	v Qal pf 3ms	prep, pn	cj, *n ms*	n fs, ps 3ms	pn
וְעֶשְׂרִים	וָתֵשַׁע	שָׁנָה	מָלַךְ	בִּירוּשָׁלָם	וְשֵׁם	אִמּוֹ	יְהוֹעַדִּין
wᵉ'esrîm	wāthēsha'	shānāh	mālakh	bîrûshālām	wᵉshēm	'immô	yᵉhô'addîn
and twenty	and nine	years	he reigned	in Jerusalem	and the name of	his mother	Jehoaddin

4623, 3503		6449.121	3596	904, 6084	3176	7828	3940	3626, 1784
prep, pn	**3.**	cj, v Qal impf 3ms	art, adj	prep, *n fd*	pn	adv	neg part	prep, pn
מִן־יְרוּשָׁלָם		וַיַּעַשׂ	הַיָּשָׁר	בְּעֵינֵי	יְהוָה	רַק	לֹא	כְּדָוִד
min-yᵉrûshālām		wayya'as	hayyāshār	bᵉ'ênê	yᵉhwāh	raq	lō'	kᵉdhāwidh
from Jerusalem		and he did	what is right	in the eyes of	Yahweh	only	not	like David

destroy them or reject them, *NCV* ... he looked on them with favour and was unwilling to destroy them; nor has he even yet banished them from his sight, *NEB* ... and so has not rid himself of them until now, *Anchor*.

24. So Hazael king of Syria died; and Benhadad his son reigned in his stead: ... Hazael, king of Aram, came to his end; and Ben-hadad his son became king in his place, *BB* ... his son Benhadad succeeded him as king, *Beck* ... reigned after him, *Fenton*.

25. And Jehoash the son of Jehoahaz took again out of the hand of Ben-hadad the son of Hazael the cities, which he had taken out of the hand of Jehoahaz his father by war. Three times did Joash beat him, and recovered the cities of Israel: ... Jehoash son of Jehoahaz recaptured the towns which Hazael had seized from his father Jehoahaz by force of arms, *JB* ... took back from Ben-hadad, son of Hazael, the cities which Hazael had taken in battle from his father Jehoahaz, *NAB* ... three times

Joas was victorious, and restored the lost cities to Israel, *Knox* ... He defeated Ben-Hadad three times and took back the cities of Israel, *NCV.*

14:1. In the second year of Joash son of Jehoahaz king of Israel reigned Amaziah the son of Joash king of Judah: ... Amaziah son of Joash king of Judah became king, *Anchor* ... began to rule, *Beck* ... the throne of Joas, king of Juda, passed to his son Amasias, *Knox.*

2. He was twenty and five years old when he began to reign, and reigned twenty and nine years in Jerusalem. And his mother's name was Jehoaddan of Jerusalem: ... twenty-five years old when he became king, *NAB* ... he ruled twenty-nine years in Jerusalem, *NCV* ... she was from Jerusalem, *NIV.*

3. And he did that which was right in the sight of the LORD, yet not like David his father: he did according to all things as Joash his father did: ... did what was right in the eyes of the Lord, *BB* ... but not so well as David his father, *Berkeley* ... In everything he followed the example of his father Joash, *NIV* ... he was not like his ancestor King David; instead, he did what his father Joash had done, *Good News.*

4. Howbeit the high places were not taken away: as yet the people did sacrifice and burnt incense on the

---

name, cf. above, on 6:24f), Yahweh remained "unwilling" to destroy Israel completely (v. 23), and thus the chapter ends on a relatively positive note, with the Israelites recapturing the towns that had been previously lost to the Arameans. Three times Jehoash defeated Ben-Hadad, just as the dying prophet Elisha had promised.

Hazael's death is usually dated to ca. 806 B.C. By this time, the Assyrian empire was again on the march, with its new king Adad-Nirari III campaigning in the west in 805–803, and again in 796. Indeed, it was probably in the year 796 that Adad-Nirari was able to enter the Aramean capital of Damascus itself, and, according to the Calah slab, receive tribute from "Mari' king of Damascus" (i.e., Ben-Hadad). The Tell al-Rimah stele also makes reference to the paying of tribute by King Jehoash of Israel at this time as well: "[Adad-nirari received] ... tribute from Mari' of Damascus, Joash of Samaria, the Tyrians, and the Sidonians." Cogan and Tadmor posit the following historical reconstruction for this period—Ben-Hadad of Aram first withdrawing his siege of Samaria and its king Jehoahaz in response to the Assyrian campaigns in North Syria between 805 and 803; then in 796, Ben-Hadad paying tribute to the victorious Assyrian king, Adad-Nirari, prompting Jehoash, who was then on the throne in Samaria, to do the same. Later, but still suffering from their earlier reversals to Assyria, Aram suffered a threefold defeat by Jehoash at Aphek. But even those defeats did not eliminate Aram as a power in southern Syria—it served as a target for repeated Assyrian campaigns in 773, 772, 765, and 755. By this time, Jeroboam II was on the throne in Israel, and he is the one who is credited as bringing the entire area under the dominion of Samaria (cf. 14:23–29).

Theologically, the present text once again reminds us of God's eternal and incomprehensible love for his people—as well as his wondrous faithfulness to the covenant of "Abraham, Isaac and Jacob" (v. 23; these patriarchs are mentioned in only one other spot in the Books of 1–2 Kings—in the Elijah episode on Mt. Carmel in 1 Ki. 18:36, where the prophet prays for the people to behold Yahweh's power once again). The pattern for complete political and military dependence upon Yahweh is clear—the only way to defeat Aram (or later, Assyria or Babylon) is to rely radically upon the love and faithfulness of Yahweh the God of Israel. "To this day" he has been unwilling to destroy his wayward children, or to banish them completely from his presence.

14:1–22. *Amaziah King of Judah: Success, failure, and eventual assassination. Once again, we move back south, to a discussion of the Judahite king Amaziah (strict chronological constraints again compel this "leapfrog" approach, inasmuch as Amaziah came to the throne before the death of Jehoash of Israel [concerning this approach, cf. on 8:16–24]). The typical Judahite accession and judgment formulas usher in both positive and then negative examples of Amaziah's reign—in many respects "he did according to all things as Joash his father did" (v. 3). Alas, just like his father, his reign started out on a pious note, but then eventually deteriorated into military embarrassment, and he too died at the hands of assassins. Yet Yahweh remained faithful, and Amaziah's son Azariah (also known as Uzziah) was able to ascend the throne as his successor.*

14:1–4. Introduction. The name "Amaziah" means "Yahweh is strong" or the like ('ămatsyah[î], HED #568); its short form appears as "Amoz," the name of Isaiah's father (cf. Isa. 1:1). Suggested dates for King Amaziah's accession vary slightly, with Albright's date of 800 a bit higher than Thiele's date of 796. The formulaic

1	3626, 3725	866, 6449.111	3204	1	6449.111		7828
n ms, ps 3ms	prep, n ms	rel part, v Qal pf 3ms	pn	n ms, ps 3ms	v Qal pf 3ms	4.	adv
אָבִיו	כְּכֹל	אֲשֶׁר־עָשָׂה	יוֹאָשׁ	אָבִיו	עָשָׂה		רַק
'āvîw	k^{e}khōl	'ăsher-'āsāh	yô'āsh	'āvîw	'āsāh		raq
his father	according to everything	which he did	Joash	his father	he did		only

1154	3940, 5681.116	5968	6194	2159.352	7281.352
art, n fp	neg part, v Qal pf 3cp	adv	art, n ms	v Piel ptc mp	cj, v Piel ptc mp
הַבָּמוֹת	לֹא־סָרוּ	עוֹד	הָעָם	מְזַבְּחִים	וּמְקַטְּרִים
habbāmôth	lō'-s̱ārû	'ôdh	hā'ām	m^{e}zabb^{e}chîm	ûm^{e}qat̲t̲^{e}rîm
the high places	they did not turn aside from	still	the people	sacrificing	and burning incense

904, 1154		2030.121	3626, 866	2480.112	4608	904, 3135
prep, art, n fp	5.	cj, v Qal impf 3ms	prep, rel part	v Qal pf 3fs	art, n fs	prep, n fs, ps 3ms
בַּבָּמוֹת		וַיְהִי	כַּאֲשֶׁר	חָזְקָה	הַמַּמְלָכָה	בְּיָדוֹ
babbāmôth		wayhî	ka'ăsher	chāz^{e}qāh	hammamlākhāh	b^{e}yādhô
on the high places		and it was	when	it was firm	the kingdom	in his hand

5409.521	881, 5860	5409.552	881, 4567	1
cj, v Hiphil impf 3ms	do, n mp, ps 3ms	art, v Hiphil ptc mp	do, art, n ms	n ms, ps 3ms
וַיַּךְ	אֶת־עֲבָדָיו	הַמַּכִּים	אֶת־הַמֶּלֶךְ	אָבִיו
wayyakh	'eth-'ăvādhâv	hammakkîm	'eth-hammelekh	'āvîw
then he struck down	his servants	the ones striking down	the king	his father

	881, 1158	5409.552	3940	4322.511	3626, 3918.155
6.	cj, do, *n mp*	art, v Hiphil ptc mp	neg part	v Hiphil pf 3ms	prep, art, v Qal pass ptc ms
	וְאֶת־בְּנֵי	הַמַּכִּים	לֹא	הֵמִית	כַּכָּתוּב
	w^{e}'eth-b^{e}nê	hammakkîm	lō'	hēmîth	kakkāthûv
	but the sons of	the ones striking down	not	he killed	according to what was written

904, 5809	8784, 5057	866, 6943.311	3176	3937, 569.141
prep, *n ms*	*n fs*, pn	rel part, v Piel pf 3ms	pn	prep, v Qal inf con
בְּסֵפֶר	תּוֹרַת־מֹשֶׁה	אֲשֶׁר־צִוָּה	יְהוָה	לֵאמֹר
b^{e}s̱ēpher	tôrath-mōsheh	'ăsher-tsiwwāh	y^{e}hwāh	lē'mōr
on the scroll of	the Law of Moses	which He had commanded	Yahweh	saying

3940, 4322.626	1	6142, 1158	1158	3940, 4322.626
neg part, v Hophal impf 3mp	n mp	prep, n mp	cj, n mp	neg part, v Hophal impf 3mp
לֹא־יוּמְתוּ	אָבוֹת	עַל־בָּנִים	וּבָנִים	לֹא־יוּמְתוּ
lō'-yûmthû	'āvôth	'al-bānîm	ûvānîm	lō'-yûmthû
they must not be executed	fathers	on account of sons	and sons	they must not be executed

6142, 1	3706	524, 382	904, 2491	4322.121		2000, 5409.511
prep, n mp	cj	cj, n ms	prep, n ms, ps 3ms	v Qal impf 3ms	7.	pers pron, v Hiphil pf 3ms
עַל־אָבוֹת	כִּי	אִם־אִישׁ	בְּחֶטְאוֹ	יָמוּת		הוּא־הִכָּה
'al-'āvôth	kî	'im-'îsh	b^{e}chet̲'ô	yāmûth		hû'-hikkāh
on account of fathers	except	only a man	because of his sin	he will die		he he struck down

881, 110	904, 1550	6467	512	8945.111	881, 5749
do, pn	prep, pn	num	num	cj, v Qal pf 3ms	do, art, pn
אֶת־אֱדוֹם	בְּגֵיא־הַמֶּלַח	עֲשֶׂרֶת	אֲלָפִים	וְתָפַשׂ	אֶת־הַסֶּלַע
'eth-'ĕdhôm	b^{e}ghê'-hammelach	'ăsereth	'ălāphîm	w^{e}thāphas	'eth-has̱s̱ela'
Edom	in the Valley of the Salt	ten	thousands	and he captured	the Sela

904, 4560	7410.121	881, 8428	3485	5912	3219	2172		226
prep, art, n fs	cj, v Qal impf 3ms	do, n ms, ps 3fs	pn	adv	art, n ms	art, dem pron	8.	adv
בַּמִּלְחָמָה	וַיִּקְרָא	אֶת־שְׁמָהּ	יָקְתְאֵל	עַד	הַיּוֹם	הַזֶּה		אָז
bammilchāmāh	wayyiqōrā'	'eth-sh^{e}māhh	yāqōth'ēl	'adh	hayyôm	hazzeh		'āz
in the battle	and he called	its name	Joktheel	until	the day	the this		then

high places: ... high places were not removed, *Goodspeed* ... were not abolished, *JB* ... shrines were not removed, *Moffatt* ... places where gods were worshiped were not removed, *NCV.*

5. And it came to pass, as soon as the kingdom was confirmed in his hand, that he slew his servants which had slain the king his father: ... When the royal power was firmly in his grasp, he put to death those of his servants who had murdered the king, *NEB* ... he executed the officials who had murdered his father, *NIV* ... as soon as the kingdom was established in his hand, *NKJV* ... When Amaziah was well established as king, he executed the men who had assassinated his father, *NLT.*

6. But the children of the murderers he slew not: ... he did not put to death the children of the murderers, *NRSV* ... he did not put to death the sons of the attackers, *Anchor* ... he did not kill the children of the servants, *KJVII.*

according unto that which is written in the book of the law of Moses, wherein the LORD commanded, saying, The fathers shall not be put to death for the children, nor the children be put to death for the fathers; but every man shall be put to death for his own sin: ... The parents shall not be put to death for the children, or the children be put to death for the parents, *NRSV* ... but a man is to be put to death for the sin which he himself has done, *BB* ... You shall not kill the parents on account of their children; and you shall not kill the children on account of their parents, *Fenton* ... each must be put to death for his own crime, *JB.*

7. He slew of Edom in the valley of salt ten thousand, and took Selah by war, and called the name of it Joktheel unto this day: ... He defeated ten thousand Edomites, *NEB* ... In battle Amaziah killed ten thousand Edomites, *NCV* ... He also conquered Sela and changed its name to Joktheel, as it is called to this day, *NLT* ... and seized Sela by war, *Fenton.*

---

accession formula in v. 2 typically includes the age at accession and the name of the queen mother (cf. comments on 8:16–24; also on 8:25–29). And, as already noted (cf. comments on 12:1–21), Amaziah's judgment notice (vv. 3f) is relatively positive—he did "that which was right in the eyes of the LORD," but not as completely as the godly King David of old, but more as his immediate father King Joash. Once again, we are also reminded that the high places were not removed (for a listing of the "good" Judahite kings, cf. above, on 12:1ff concerning the preoccupation of the writer with removal of high places, cf. comments on the reign of Josiah [ch. 22]).

14:5–7. Early successes. We have here a direct citation from the "Book of the Law of Moses" justifying Amaziah's enlightened policy of not punishing children for the sins of their parents (Deut. 24:16; cf. Ezek. 18:1–20). Yet, this notice stands in some tension with other perspectives found in the Pentateuch, especially the reference in the Ten Commandments that the Israelites were not to make for themselves any idol (KJV, "graven image") or bow down to them or worship them, for Yahweh is a "jealous God" (cf. comments on the crucial nature of Yahweh's jealousy on 1:17f), and He will punish the children for the sin of the parents to the third and fourth generation of those who "hate" him, while, on the other hand, showing love to "a thousand generations" (KJV, "to thousands") of those who "love [him] and keep [his] commandments" (Exo. 20:4ff; and Deut. 5:8ff—probably the "thousand generations" of NIV should be preferred in light of the explicit parallel in Deut. 7:9). Similar thoughts are expressed in Exo. 34:6f where Yahweh is most memorably described as "merciful and gracious, longsuffering, and abundant in goodness and truth, keeping mercy for thousands, forgiving iniquity and transgression and sin," yet not leaving the guilty unpunished, but "visiting the iniquity of the fathers upon the children, and upon the children's children, unto the third and to the fourth generation" (also cf. Moses' close paraphrase of these very words in Num. 14:18 when he beseeches Yahweh to forgive the Israelites). How are we to understand this clear tension between punishment of children to the third and fourth generation in the latter examples, but not punishing children for the sins of the parents in the former examples?

Such questions go beyond the scope of a brief commentary such as the present one, yet, this issue is crucial in connection with our understanding the import of v. 6 of the present chapter, and it also resonates strongly in the present day, as we contemplate Jesus' startling words about loving our enemies (Matt. 5:44). Some tentative observations and conclusions are necessary. First of all, the issue is not necessarily simply an issue of different sources, or strands in the Pentateuch, or in the Hebrew Bible as a whole. Therefore, these alternative tendencies must be regarded as traditions stemming from the earliest of days (even if some of their formulations, such as Ezek. 18 may be rather late). The following factors relate to these divergent the-

Number	Grammar	Hebrew	Transliteration	Translation
4567	n ms	מֶלֶךְ	melekh	the king of
1158, 3167	n ms, pn	בֶּן־יֵהוּא	ben-yēhû'	the son of Jehu
1158, 3168	n ms, pn	בֶּן־יְהוֹאָחָז	ben-yehô'āchāz	the son of Jehoahaz
420, 3169	prep, pn	אֶל־יְהוֹאָשׁ	'el-yehô'āsh	to Jehoash
4534	n mp	מַלְאָכִים	mal'ākhîm	messengers
568	pn	אֲמַצְיָה	'ămatsyāh	Amaziah
8365.111	v Qal pf 3ms	שָׁלַח	shālach	he sent out
3547	pn	יִשְׂרָאֵל	yisrā'ēl	Israel
3937, 569.141	prep, v Qal inf con	לֵאמֹר	lē'mōr	saying
2050.131	v Qal impv 2ms	לְכָה	lekhāh	come
7495.720	v Hithpael juss 1cp	נִתְרָאֶה	nithrā'eh	let us see each other
6686	n mp	פָּנִים	phānîm	faces
9.				
8365.121	cj, v Qal impf 3ms	וַיִּשְׁלַח	wayyishlach	and he sent out
3169	pn	יְהוֹאָשׁ	yehô'āsh	Jehoash
4567, 3547	n ms, pn	מֶלֶךְ־יִשְׂרָאֵל	melekh-yisrā'ēl	the king of Israel
420, 568	prep, pn	אֶל־אֲמַצְיָהוּ	'el-'ămatsyāhû	to Amaziah
4567, 3171	n ms, pn	מֶלֶךְ־יְהוּדָה	melekh-yehûdhāh	the king of Judah
3937, 569.141	prep, v Qal inf con	לֵאמֹר	lē'mōr	saying
2430	art, n ms	הַחוֹחַ	hachôach	the thornbush
866	rel part	אֲשֶׁר	'ăsher	which
904, 3976	prep, art, pn	בַּלְּבָנוֹן	ballevānôn	in the Lebanon
8365.111	v Qal pf 3ms	שָׁלַח	shālach	he sent out
420, 753	prep, art, n ms	אֶל־הָאֶרֶז	'el-hā'erez	to the cedar
866	rel part	אֲשֶׁר	'ăsher	which
904, 3976	prep, art, pn	בַּלְּבָנוֹן	ballevānôn	in the Lebanon
3937, 569.141	prep, v Qal inf con	לֵאמֹר	lē'mōr	saying
5598.131, 881, 1351	v Qal impv 2ms, do, n fs, ps 2ms	תְּנָה־אֶת־בִּתְּךָ	tenāh-'eth-bittekhā	give your daughter
3937, 1158	prep, n ms, ps 1cs	לִבְנִי	livnî	to my son
3937, 828	prep, n fs	לְאִשָּׁה	le'ishshāh	for a wife
5882.122	cj, v Qal impf 3fs	וַתַּעֲבֹר	watta'ăvōr	and it passed by
2516	n fs	חַיַּת	chayyath	a beast of
7898	art, n ms	הַשָּׂדֶה	hassādheh	the field
866	rel part	אֲשֶׁר	'ăsher	which
904, 3976	prep, art, pn	בַּלְּבָנוֹן	ballevānôn	in the Lebanon
7717.122	cj, v Qal impf 3fs	וַתִּרְמֹס	wattirmōs	and it trampled
881, 2430	do, art, n ms	אֶת־הַחוֹחַ	'eth-hachôach	the thornbush
10.				
5409.542	v Hiphil inf abs	הַכֵּה	hakkēh	striking down
5409.513	v Hiphil pf 2ms	הִכִּיתָ	hikkîthā	you have certainly struck down
881, 110	do, pn	אֶת־אֱדוֹם	'eth-'ĕdhôm	Edom
5558.111	cj, v Qal pf 3ms, ps 2ms	וּנְשָׂאֲךָ	ûnesā'ăkhā	and it has lifted you up
3949	n ms, ps 2ms	לִבֶּךָ	libbekhā	your heart
3632.231	v Niphal impv 2ms	הִכָּבֵד	hikkāvēdh	be honored
3553.131	cj, v Qal impv 2ms	וְשֵׁב	weshēv	and sit
904, 1041	prep, n ms, ps 2ms	בְּבֵיתֶךָ	bevêthekhā	in your house

8. Then Amaziah sent messengers to Jehoash, the son of Jehoahaz son of Jehu, king of Israel, saying, Come, let us look one another in the face: ... sent messengers to King Jehoash of Israel, challenging him to fight, *Good News* ... Come and make a trial of strength!, *JB* ... Come, meet me face to face, *NIV* ... let us face one another in battle, *NKJV.*

9. And Jehoash the king of Israel sent to Amaziah king of Judah, saying, The thistle that was in Lebanon sent to the cedar that was in Lebanon, saying, Give thy daughter to my son to wife: ... sent this reply to Amaziah king of Judah, *Berkeley* ... A thorn bush on Lebanon sent to a cedar on Lebanon, saying, *NRSV* ... Let your daughter marry my son, *Beck* ... Once a thorn bush on the Lebanon Mountains sent a message to a cedar: Give your daughter in marriage to my son, *Good News.*

and there passed by a wild beast that was in Lebanon, and trode down the thistle: ... a wild animal of Lebanon passed by and trampled down the thorn bush, *NRSV* ... a beast from the woodland in Lebanon went by, crushing the thorn under his feet, *BB* ... a wild animal came along and trampled on the thistle, *Beck* ... A wild animal passed by and trampled the bush down, *Good News.*

10. Thou hast indeed smitten Edom, and thine heart hath lifted thee up: ... You have indeed conquered Edom and it has turned your head, *Goodspeed* ... You have conquered Edom and now aspire to even greater glory, *JB* ... now thy heart is puffed up with pride, *Knox* ... your heart has become proud, *NASB.*

ological tendencies. First, Yahweh from the beginning is clearly a God of love and compassion, even though He is clearly also fundamentally a jealous God. Secondly, the "third and fourth generations" references are found in connection with God's jealousy, and primarily in the Ten Commandments—more precisely in what is usually termed the second commandment (or part of the first commandment in Roman Catholic and Lutheran enumeration), the commandment against making images of God. Such a prohibition (usually termed "aniconic" by biblical scholars) undoubtedly stems from the earliest days of the Israelite religion, and it represents the very essence of the new faith (note that any modern attempts to image or to explain the essence or the very nature of the One True God, whether they be pictorial or verbal [such as some theologies] may well fall into this category as well). The "third and the fourth generation" would then refer to anyone alive at any given moment—at most four generations of an extended family would be alive to face the wrath of an angry God for violation of this most basic of tenets (and once again, even in the Scriptures which make reference to such stern judgment, invariably one reads almost immediately a reference to God's love for "thousands" or for "thousands of generations" of those who love him and keep his commandments). On the other hand, the passages of Scripture which make reference to the children not suffering for the sins of the parents (most basically, Deut. 24:16, with both the present text in 2 Kings, as well as the Ezekiel passage (ch. 18, especially vv. 1–20, the clear borrowers from Deuteronomy) likewise point to the essence of the Israelite religion, celebrating a God of love, of compassion and of forgiveness. Even King Amaziah recognized that children were not to be executed because of their parents' actions ("Amaziah's restraint was, therefore, not due to a new departure in jurisprudence ... but to the existence of an ancient law demanding such restraint," so Jones, NCBC, 508). Contemporary Assyrian practice included advocating execution of the entire family for instigators of insurrection (cf. the treaty of Esarhaddon as cited by Jones—"seize and slay the perpetrators of rebellion. You will destroy their name and their seed from the land"); such practices were also practiced in Israel (cf. the melancholy examples of Achan's family in Josh. 7; also the Rizpah tradition in 2 Sam. 21:1–9; and, not least, the Jehu narratives here in 2 Kings [e.g., 9:26; 10:11, 17]). Still, even the OT points beyond such sweeping retaliation, and, despite whatever else may be said about King Amaziah, the Kings narrator rightly lauds his restraint in v. 6 of the present chapter. As Wiseman (TOTC, 244) notes, despite the pressures and practices of former times and of foreign cultures, those who follow the law of God will dare to be distinctive.

Brief mention is then made in v. 7 as to Amaziah's military success against the Edomites. The land of Edom was last mentioned in 8:20ff, where they are said to have rebelled against King Jehoram of Judah, and to have set up their own king. When Jehoram campaigned against them, he lost disastrously, and their rebellion continued "to this day." That notice referred to events which took place probably a good forty years prior to the accession of the current king. Hobbs (WBC, 179) notes the archival flavor of the present verse, as well as the similar reference found in 14:25. All these verses give evidence of renewed Judahite and Israelite military power (but, in the present instance, Edom seems again lost to Judah by the time of King Ahaz; cf. 16:6). The present verse, of course, also sets the stage for Amaziah's apparent hubris over against the land of Israel, and the clear change of fortune for both king and nation which was the result.

14:8–14. Ignominious defeat at the hands of Israel. The present verses demonstrate how Amaziah's military success against the Edomites seemed to lead directly to his arrogant message to Jehoash, king of Israel, "Come, let us look one another in the face" (v. 8; probably meant as a battle challenge [so Cogan and Tadmor, AB, 156; but cf. Hobbs, WBC, 180]). The chronicler presents some additional information in 2 Chr. 25:5–24 concerning both Amaziah's Edomite incursion as well as his confrontation with Jehoash. Inasmuch as this information stands in some tension with the chronicler's overall theology some theorize that it stems from an extra-biblical source. Such sources, however, are not consistent with the point of the passage. The chronicler focuses clearly on Amaziah's worship of Edomite gods as the major reason for his defeat by the Israelites.

In the present text, the major reason for Amaziah's "challenge" to the Israelites in v. 8 may be the Edomite victory itself. As is so often the case, success can lead to pride and arrogance; and again, as is so often the case, this pride and arrogance can lead directly to disaster. As the famous verse of the Book

4066	1667.723	904, 7750	5489.213	887	3171
cj, intrg	v Hithpael impf 2ms	prep, n fs	cj, v Qal pf 2ms	pers pron	cj, pn
וְלָמָּה	תִתְגָּרֶה	בְּרָעָה	וְנָפַלְתָּה	אַתָּה	וִיהוּדָה
welāmmāh	thithgāreh	berā'āh	wenāphaltāh	'attāh	wîhûdhāh
and why	cause contention for yourself	with evil	then you will fall	you	and Judah

6196		3940, 8471.111	568	6148.121	3169	4567, 3547
prep, ps 2ms	11.	cj, neg part, v Qal pf 3ms	pn	cj, v Qal impf 3ms	pn	*n ms*, pn
עִמָּךְ		וְלֹא־שָׁמַע	אֲמַצְיָהוּ	וַיַּעַל	יְהוֹאָשׁ	מֶלֶךְ־יִשְׂרָאֵל
'immākh		welō'-shāma'	'ămatsyāhû	wayya'al	yehô'āsh	melekh-yisrā'ēl
with you		but he did not listen	Amaziah	so he went up	Jehoash	the king of Israel

7495.726	6686	2000	568	4567, 3171	904, 1094	1094
cj, v Hithpael impf 3mp	n mp	pers pron	cj, pn	*n ms*, pn	prep, pn	pn
וַיִּתְרָאוּ	פָּנִים	הוּא	וַאֲמַצְיָהוּ	מֶלֶךְ־יְהוּדָה	בְּבֵית	שֶׁמֶשׁ
wayyithrā'û	phānîm	hû'	wa'ămatsyāhû	melekh-yehûdhāh	bevêth	shemesh
and they saw each other	faces	he	and Amaziah	the king of Judah	in Beth	Shemesh

866	3937, 3171		5238.221	3171	3937, 6686	3547	5308.126	382
rel part	prep, pn	12.	cj, v Niphal impf 3ms	pn	prep, *n mp*	pn	cj, v Qal impf 3mp	n ms
אֲשֶׁר	לִיהוּדָה		וַיִּנָּגֶף	יְהוּדָה	לִפְנֵי	יִשְׂרָאֵל	וַיָּנֻסוּ	אִישׁ
'ăsher	lîhûdhāh		wayyinnāgeph	yehûdhāh	liphnê	yisrā'ēl	wayyānusû	'îsh
which	to Judah		and they were struck	Judah	before	Israel	and they fled	each

3937, 164		881	568	4567, 3171	1158, 3169	1158, 275
prep, n ms, ps 3ms	13.	cj, do	pn	*n ms*, pn	*n ms*, pn	*n ms*, pn
לְאֹהָלוֹ		וְאֵת	אֲמַצְיָהוּ	מֶלֶךְ־יְהוּדָה	בֶּן־יְהוֹאָשׁ	בֶּן־אֲחַזְיָהוּ
le'āhelô		we'ēth	'ămatsyāhû	melekh-yehûdhāh	ben-yehô'āsh	ben-'ăchazyāhû
to his tent		and	Amaziah	the king of Judah	the son of Jehoash	the son of Ahaziah

8945.111	3169	4567, 3547	904, 1094	1094	971.126	3503
v Qal pf 3ms	pn	*n ms*, pn	prep, pn	pn	cj, v Qal impf 3mp	pn
תָּפַשׂ	יְהוֹאָשׁ	מֶלֶךְ־יִשְׂרָאֵל	בְּבֵית	שָׁמֶשׁ	וַיָּבֹאוּ	יְרוּשָׁלַם
tāphas	yehô'āsh	melekh-yisrā'ēl	bevêth	shāmesh	wayyāvō'û	yerûshālam
he captured	Jehoash	the king of Israel	at Beth	Shemesh	and they entered	Jerusalem

6805.121	904, 2440	3503	904, 8554	688	5912, 8554
cj, v Qal impf 3ms	prep, *n fs*	pn	prep, *n ms*	pn	prep, *n ms*
וַיִּפְרֹץ	בְּחוֹמַת	יְרוּשָׁלַם	בְּשַׁעַר	אֶפְרַיִם	עַד־שַׁעַר
wayyiphrōts	bechômath	yerûshālam	besha'ar	'ephrayim	'adh-sha'ar
and he broke through	through the wall of	Jerusalem	by the Gate of	Ephraim	unto the Gate of

6682	727	4109	527		4089.111	881, 3725, 2174, 3826B	881
art, n fs	num	num	n fs	14.	cj, v Qal pf 3ms	do, *adj*, art, n ms, cj, art, n ms	cj, do
הַפִּנָּה	אַרְבַּע	מֵאוֹת	אַמָּה		וְלָקַח	אֶת־כָּל־הַזָּהָב־וְהַכֶּסֶף	וְאֵת
happinnāh	'arba'	mē'ôth	'ammāh		welāqach	'eth-kol-hazzāhāv-wehakkeseph	we'ēth
the Corner	four	hundreds	cubits		and he took	all the gold and the silver	and

3725, 3747	4834.256	1041, 3176	904, 212	1041
adj, art, n mp	art, v Niphal ptc mp	*n ms*, pn	cj, prep, *n mp*	*n ms*
כָּל־הַכֵּלִים	הַנִּמְצְאִים	בֵּית־יְהוָה	וּבְאֹצְרוֹת	בֵּית
kol-hakkēlîm	hanimtse'îm	bêth-yehwāh	ûve'ōtserôth	bêth
all the vessels	those found	the temple of Yahweh	and in the treasuries of	the house of

4567	881	1158	8927	8178.121	8497		3615
art, n ms	cj, do	*n mp*	art, n fp	cj, v Qal impf 3ms	pn	15.	cj, *n ms*
הַמֶּלֶךְ	וְאֵת	בְּנֵי	הַתַּעֲרֻבוֹת	וַיָּשָׁב	שֹׁמְרוֹנָה		וְיֶתֶר
hammelekh	we'ēth	benê	hatta'ăruvôth	wayyāshāv	shōmerônāh		weyether
the king	and	the sons of	the hostages	and he returned	to Samaria		and the remainder of

glory of this, and tarry at home: ... Adorn yourself, but remain at home, *Goodspeed* ... Stay where you belong!, *JB* ... Enjoy your glory and stay at home, *NASB* ... Stay at home and brag, *NCV.*

for why shouldest thou meddle to thy hurt, that thou shouldest fall, even thou, and Judah with thee?: ... why should you court trouble, so that you and Judah with you should fall?, *Goodspeed* ... Why challenge disaster, to your own and Judah's ruin?, *JB* ... why should you provoke trouble so that you, even you, should fall, and Judah with you?, *NASB* ... Don't ask for trouble, or you and Judah will be defeated, *NCV.*

11. But Amaziah would not hear. Therefore Jehoash king of Israel went up; and he and Amaziah king of Judah looked one another in the face at Beth-shemesh, which belongeth to Judah: ... Amaziah would not listen, *NEB* ... did not take heed, *Anchor* ... gave no attention, *BB* ... Jehoash king of Israel attacked, *NIV* ... he and Amaziah king of Judah met in battle at Beth-shemesh, *Beck.*

12. And Judah was put to the worse before Israel; and they fled every man to their tents: ... Judah was defeated by Israel, *Berkeley* ... everyone fled to his house, *Fenton* ... its army scattered and fled for home, *NLT* ... Judah was overcome before Israel, *BB.*

13. And Jehoash king of Israel took Amaziah king of Judah, the son of Jehoash the son of Ahaziah, at Beth-shemesh, and came to Jerusalem, and brake down the wall of Jerusalem from the gate of Ephraim unto the corner gate, four hundred cubits: ... Jehoash, king of Israel, captured Amaziah, *Goodspeed* ... he demolished four hundred cubits of the city wall, *JB* ... Jehoash took Amaziah prisoner, advanced on Jerusalem, and tore down the city wall, *Good News* ... made a gap in the walls four hundred cubits long, *Knox* ... a section about six hundred feet long, *NIV.*

14. And he took all the gold and silver, and all the vessels that were found in the house of the Lord, and in the treasures of the king's house, and hostages, and returned to Samaria: ... seized all the gold

---

of Proverbs reminds us: "Pride goeth before destruction, and an haughty spirit before a fall" (Prov. 16:18; also cf. 13:10; 16:19; 29:23). Although we know that Proverbs must date considerably later than the time of Amaziah (cf. the reference to the "men of Hezekiah" in Prov. 25:1), many of these proverbs were surely known (or should have been known) by the king. In any case, here is another proverb Amaziah should have taken to heart: "where no counsel is, the people fall: but in the multitude of counsellors there is safety" (11:14). Yet King Amaziah disregarded the wise words of his soon-to-be adversary, King Jehoash of Israel (vv. 9f of the present passage)—"Thou hast indeed smitten Edom, and thine heart hath lifted thee up: glory of this, and tarry at home: for why shouldest thou meddle to thy hurt, that thou shouldest fall, even thou, and Judah with thee?" And Jehoash prefaced this direct advice by what may well be termed a "fable" ("a story not founded on fact but allied to parable and allegory" [Wiseman, TOTC, 245]) concerning the immense contrast between the stately cedar tree of Lebanon, and the lowly thistle plant. A wild beast easily trampled the thistle underfoot, and this presumably would also happen to the "thistle king" Amaziah. Perhaps the best-known fable in the Bible is that told by Jotham, lone-surviving son of Jerub-Baal (Gideon), to the citizens of Shechem about ready to crown Abimelech, son of Jerub-Baal by a concubine, as king. That fable describes the various categories of trees and vines who turned down the chance to become king over the plant kingdom (Judg. 9:8–15). Only the thornbush responded positively to the opportunity for such political power, since the other trees (olive, fig, grapevine) clearly had more important contributions to make. Other possible examples of fables in the Bible cited by Wiseman are in Isa. 10:15; Ezek. 17:3–8; 19:1–9.

In any event, Amaziah spurned Jehoash's apt advice, and the kings faced off at Beth Shemesh (the town nearly due west of Jerusalem and directly in the path of one of the best approaches to the city). Cogan and Tadmor (AB, 156) take the additional phrase "to Judah" (v. 11) as evidence for the northern provenance of the tradition. Alas, the results of the battle were, as predicted, absolute disaster for Judah: the king was captured, the wall of Jerusalem breached, the Temple and palace looted, and hostages taken back to Samaria (vv. 13f). (The "Ephraim Gate" of Jerusalem probably was located in the center of the northern wall of Jerusalem, and the "Corner Gate" probably in the northwest corner [Cogan and Tadmor, AB, 157]. Destruction of this part of the wall was especially significant inasmuch as Jerusalem was most vulnerable to attack from the north.) According to available sources, this was the first time that Jerusalem had actually been penetrated by a foreign force since David's original capture of the city. A "thistle king" indeed.

14:15–22. Concluding remarks concerning King Amaziah (as well as concerning Jehoash, king

1745	3169	866	6449.111	1400	866	4032.211	6196
n mp	pn	rel part	v Qal pf 3ms	cj, n fs, ps 3ms	cj, rel part	v Niphal pf 3ms	prep
דִּבְרֵי	יְהוֹאָשׁ	אֲשֶׁר	עָשָׂה	וּגְבוּרָתוֹ	וַאֲשֶׁר	נִלְחַם	עִם
divrê	yehô'āsh	'ăsher	'āsāh	ûghevûrāthô	wa'ăsher	nilcham	'im
the events of	Jehoash	which	he did	and his strength	and where	he fought	with

568	4567, 3171	1950B, 2062	3918.156	6142, 5809
pn	*n ms*, pn	intrg part, neg part, pers pron	v Qal pass ptc mp	prep, *n ms*
אֲמַצְיָהוּ	מֶלֶךְ־יְהוּדָה	הֲלֹא־הֵם	כְּתוּבִים	עַל־סֵפֶר
'ămatsyāhû	melekh-yehûdhāh	hălō'-hēm	kethûvîm	'al-sēpher
Amaziah	the king of Judah	are they not	things written	on the scroll of

1745	3219	3937, 4567	3547		8311.121	3169	6196, 1
n mp	art, n mp	prep, *n mp*	pn	**16.**	cj, v Qal impf 3ms	pn	prep, n mp, ps 3ms
דִּבְרֵי	הַיָּמִים	לְמַלְכֵי	יִשְׂרָאֵל		וַיִּשְׁכַּב	יְהוֹאָשׁ	עִם־אֲבֹתָיו
divrê	hayyāmîm	lemalkhê	yisrā'ēl		wayyishkav	yehô'āsh	'im-'ăvōthâv
the events of	the days	of the kings of	Israel		and he lay	Jehoash	with his ancestors

7196.221	904, 8497	6196	4567	3547	4566.121	3493	1158
cj, v Niphal impf 3ms	prep, pn	prep	*n mp*	pn	cj, v Qal impf 3ms	pn	n ms, ps 3ms
וַיִּקָּבֵר	בְּשֹׁמְרוֹן	עִם	מַלְכֵי	יִשְׂרָאֵל	וַיִּמְלֹךְ	יָרָבְעָם	בְּנוֹ
wayyiqqāvēr	beshōmerôn	'im	malkhê	yisrā'ēl	wayyimlōkh	yārov'ām	benô
and he was buried	in Samaria	with	the kings of	Israel	and he reigned	Jeroboam	his son

8809		2513.121	568	1158, 3204	4567	3171	313
prep, ps 3ms	**17.**	cj, v Qal impf 3ms	pn	*n ms*, pn	*n ms*	pn	adv
תַּחְתָּיו		וַיְחִי	אֲמַצְיָהוּ	בֶּן־יוֹאָשׁ	מֶלֶךְ	יְהוּדָה	אַחֲרֵי
tachtâv		waychî	'ămatsyāhû	ven-yô'āsh	melekh	yehûdhāh	'achrê
instead of him		and he lived	Amaziah	the son of Joash	the king of	Judah	after

4323	3169	1158, 3168	4567	3547	2675	6462	8523
n ms	pn	*n ms*, pn	*n ms*	pn	num	num	n fs
מוֹת	יְהוֹאָשׁ	בֶּן־יְהוֹאָחָז	מֶלֶךְ	יִשְׂרָאֵל	חָמֵשׁ	עֶשְׂרֵה	שָׁנָה
môth	yehô'āsh	ben-yehô'āchāz	melekh	yisrā'ēl	chămēsh	'esrēh	shānāh
the death of	Jehoash	the son of Jehoahaz	the king of	Israel	five	ten	years

	3615	1745	568	1950B, 3940, 2062	3918.156
18.	cj, *n ms*	*n mp*	pn	intrg part, neg part, pers pron	v Qal pass ptc mp
	וְיֶתֶר	דִּבְרֵי	אֲמַצְיָהוּ	הֲלֹא־הֵם	כְּתוּבִים
	weyether	divrê	'ămatsyāhû	hălō'-hēm	kethûvîm
	and the remainder of	the events of	Amaziah	are they not	things written

6142, 5809	1745	3219	3937, 4567	3171		7489.126
prep, *n ms*	*n mp*	art, n mp	prep, *n mp*	pn	**19.**	cj, v Qal impf 3mp
עַל־סֵפֶר	דִּבְרֵי	הַיָּמִים	לְמַלְכֵי	יְהוּדָה		וַיִּקְשְׁרוּ
'al-sēpher	divrê	hayyāmîm	lemalkhê	yehûdhāh		wayyiqŏshrû
on the scroll of	the events of	the days	of the kings of	Judah		and they conspired

6142	7490	904, 3503	5308.121	4061	8365.126	313
prep, ps 3ms	n ms	prep, pn	cj, v Qal impf 3ms	pn	cj, v Qal impf 3mp	prep, ps 3ms
עָלָיו	קֶשֶׁר	בִּירוּשָׁלַםִ	וַיָּנָס	לָכִישָׁה	וַיִּשְׁלְחוּ	אַחֲרָיו
'ālâv	qesher	bîrûshālam	wayyānās	lākhîshāh	wayyishlechû	'achrâv
against them	a conspiracy	in Jerusalem	and he fled	to Lachish	and they sent out	after him

4061	4322.526	8427		5558.126	881	6142, 5670
pn	cj, v Hiphil impf 3mp, ps 3ms	adv	**20.**	cj, v Qal impf 3mp	do, ps 3ms	prep, art, n mp
לָכִישָׁה	וַיְמִתֻהוּ	שָׁם		וַיִּשָׂאוּ	אֹתוֹ	עַל־הַסּוּסִים
lākhîshāh	waymithuhû	shām		wayyis'û	'ōthô	'al-hassûsîm
to Lachish	and they executed him	there		and they lifted up	him	onto the horses

and silver, *NRSV* ... gold and silver, all the articles that were found, *NKJV* ... gold and silver and all the vessels which were in the house of the Lord and in the store-house of the king, together with those whose lives would be the price of broken faith, and went back to, *BB* ... took all the silver and gold he could find, all the temple equipment and all the palace treasures, and carried them back to, *Good News*.

15. Now the rest of the acts of Jehoash which he did, and his might, and how he fought with Amaziah king of Judah, are they not written in the book of the chronicles of the kings of Israel?: ... his valor, and how he fought, *NAB* ... The other acts of Jehoash and his victories, including his war against Amaziah king of Judah, are written, *NCV* ... and all his achievements, his exploits and his wars with Amaziah king of Judah, are recorded, *NEB* ... the other affairs of Jhoash, what he did, and his achievements, and how he fought, *Fenton*.

16. And Jehoash slept with his fathers, and was buried in Samaria with the kings of Israel; and Jeroboam his son reigned in his stead: ... slept with his ancestors, *Anchor* ... went to rest with his fathers, *BB* ... Jeroboam succeeded him as king, *Beck* ... became king in his place, *Berkeley*.

17. And Amaziah the son of Joash king of Judah lived after the death of Jehoash son of Jehoahaz king of Israel fifteen years: ... reigned over Judah after the death of Jhoash-ben-Ahaziah, *Fenton* ... lived for fifteen years after the death of, *Moffatt* ... survived Jehoash, ... by fifteen, *NAB*.

18. And the rest of the acts of Amaziah, are they not written in the book of the chronicles of the kings of Judah?: ... The other things Amaziah did are written in the book of the history of, *NCV* ... other events of Amaziah's reign are recorded in the annals of the kings of, *NEB* ... the rest of the deeds of Amaziah, are they not written, *NRSV* ... are they not told in the book of, *Berkeley*.

19. Now they made a conspiracy against him in Jerusalem: and he fled to Lachish; but they sent after him to Lachish, and slew him there: ... murdered him there, *Fenton* ... There was a plot in Jerusalem to assassinate Amaziah, so he fled to the city of Lachish, but his enemies followed him there and killed him, *Good News* ... people in Jerusalem made plans against him. So he ran away to the town of Lachish, *NCV* ... they made a secret design against him in Jerusalem, *BB*.

20. And they brought him on horses: and he was buried at Jerusalem with his fathers in the city of David: ... They, however, carried him with the horseman to Jerusalem and buried him

---

of Israel, and Azariah, king of Judah). These verses include a mishmash of formulas, burial notices for two separate kings, and further reference formulas, plus brief "footnotes" of related material. As already noted (see 13:10–13), vv. 15f of the present chapter represent the second mention of what seem to be the typical "further reference" and burial formulas for the Israelite king, Jehoash (v. 15 accords quite closely with 13:12, and v. 16 with 13:13).

Much ink has been spilled concerning the curious chronological notice in v. 17 of the present chapter ("Amaziah ... lived after the death of Jehoash ... fifteen years"). Indeed, this verse provides one of the crucial linchpins for E. R. Thiele's theory concerning lengthy coregencies for this period of Israelite history (e.g., he posits only five years of sole reign for King Amaziah, and the rest of his twenty-nine years were actually spent in a coregency with his son Azariah, with nary a hint of this, however, in the biblical text). Thiele's theories have been quite influential in corroborating biblical and secular histories. Such "justifications," however, are important only with regard to constructing biblical chronology; reconstructing due to doubting the Bible's reliability is fallacious reasoning. The odd term "[Amaziah] lived" (chāyāh, HED #2513), not the usual term "Amaziah reigned" (mālakh, HED #4566; cf. 1:17; 3:1; 15:13; etc.), does, perhaps contain a clue to the chronology.

Perhaps the northern provenance of the preceding material is germane to this verse. Obviously, the writer has little respect for Amaziah, the "thistle king," and he probably sees him as lucky to have even survived the battle with Jehoash king of Israel—hence, the archival note that he "lived" (in the sense of "endured"?) for another fifteen years after the death of Jehoash. Reading anything more into the verb here, such as an indication of a coregency, is most likely unwarranted. As Hobbs (WBC, 181) points out, "As it stands, the statement means no more than Amaziah outlived his former foe by fifteen years. There is nothing to indicate that he was in any way bereft of power during this time."

Alas, Amaziah, like his father, eventually was assassinated (vv. 19f). Once again, details are lacking, so the commentators are tempted to speculate. For example, was this conspiracy the result of the military fiasco against Israel? (The chronicler adds, "Now after the time that Amaziah did turn away from following the Lord they made a conspiracy against him" [2 Chr. 25:27], but the

7196.221	904, 3503	6196, 1	904, 6111	1784		4089.126
cj, v Niphil impf 3ms	prep, pn	prep, n mp, ps 3ms	prep, *n fs*	pn	**21.**	cj, v Qal impf 3mp
וַיִּקָּבֵר	בִירוּשָׁלִַם	עִם־אֲבֹתָיו	בְּעִיר	דָּוִד		וַיִּקְחוּ
wayyiqqāvēr	bîrûshālam	'im-'ăvōthâv	be'îr	dāwidh		wayyiqŏchû
and he was buried	in Jerusalem	with his ancestors	in the city of	David		and they took

3725, 6194	3171	881, 6051	2000	1158, 8666	6462	8523
adj, n ms	pn	do, pn	cj, pers pron	*n ms*, num	num	n fs
כָּל־עַם	יְהוּדָה	אֶת־עֲזַרְיָה	וְהוּא	בֶּן־שֵׁשׁ	עֶשְׂרֵה	שָׁנָה
kol-'am	yehûdhāh	'eth-'ăzaryāh	wehû'	ben-shēsh	'esrēh	shānāh
all the people of	Judah	Azariah	and he	a son of six	ten	years

4566.526	881	8809	1	568		2000	1161.111
cj, v Hiphil impf 3mp	do, ps 3ms	prep	n ms, ps 3ms	pn	**22.**	pers pron	v Qal pf 3ms
וַיַּמְלִכוּ	אֹתוֹ	תַּחַת	אָבִיו	אֲמַצְיָהוּ		הוּא	בָּנָה
wayyamlikhû	'ōthô	tachath	'āvîw	'ămatsyāhû		hû'	bānāh
and they caused to reign	him	instead of	his father	Amaziah		he	he built

881, 369	8178.521	3937, 3171	313	8311.141, 4567	6196, 1
do, pn	cj, v Hiphil impf 3ms, ps 3fs	prep, pn	adv	v Qal inf con, art, n ms	prep, n mp, ps 3ms
אֶת־אֵילַת	וַיְשִׁבֶהָ	לִיהוּדָה	אַחֲרֵי	שְׁכַב־הַמֶּלֶךְ	עִם־אֲבֹתָיו
'eth-'êlath	wayshiveāh	lîhûdhāh	'achrê	shekhav-hammelekh	'im-'ăvōthâv
Elath	and he caused it to return	to Judah	after	the lying of the king	with his ancestors

	904, 8523	2675, 6462	8523	3937, 568	1158, 3204	4567	3171
23.	prep, *n fs*	num, num	n fs	prep, pn	*n ms*, pn	*n ms*	pn
	בִּשְׁנַת	חֲמֵשׁ־עֶשְׂרֵה	שָׁנָה	לַאֲמַצְיָהוּ	בֶן־יוֹאָשׁ	מֶלֶךְ	יְהוּדָה
	bishnath	chămēsh-'esrēh	shānāh	la'ămatsyāhû	ven-yô'āsh	melekh	yehûdhāh
	in the year of	fifteen	years	of Amaziah	the son of Joash	the king of	Judah

4566.111	3493	1158, 3204	4567, 3547	904, 8497	727	259	8523
v Qal pf 3ms	pn	*n ms*, pn	*n ms*, pn	prep, pn	num	cj, num	n fs
מָלַךְ	יָרָבְעָם	בֶּן־יוֹאָשׁ	מֶלֶךְ־יִשְׂרָאֵל	בְּשֹׁמְרוֹן	אַרְבָּעִים	וְאַחַת	שָׁנָה
mālakh	yārov'ām	ben-yô'āsh	melekh-yisrā'ēl	beshōmerôn	'arbā'îm	we'achath	shānāh
he reigned	Jeroboam	the son of Joash	the king of Israel	in Samaria	forty	and one	years

	6449.121	7737	904, 6084	3176	3940	5681.111
24.	cj, v Qal impf 3ms	art, adj	prep, *n fd*	pn	neg part	v Qal pf 3ms
	וַיַּעַשׂ	הָרַע	בְּעֵינֵי	יְהוָה	לֹא	סָר
	wayya'as	hāra'	be'ênê	yehwāh	lō'	sār
	and he did	what is evil	in the eyes of	Yahweh	not	he turned aside

4623, 3725, 2496	3493	1158, 5203	866	2490.511	881, 3547
prep, *adj, n fp*	pn	*n ms*, pn	rel part	v Hiphil pf 3ms	do, pn
מִכָּל־חַטֹּאות	יָרָבְעָם	בֶּן־נְבָט	אֲשֶׁר	הֶחֱטִיא	אֶת־יִשְׂרָאֵל
mikkol-chattō'wth	yārov'ām	ben-nevāt	'ăsher	hechětî'	'eth-yisrā'ēl
from all the sins of	Jeroboam	the son of Nebat	which	he caused to sin	Israel

	2000	8178.511	881, 1397	3547	4623, 3937, 971.141	2679
25.	pers pron	v Hiphil pf 3ms	do, *n ms*	pn	prep, prep, v Qal inf con	pn
	הוּא	הֵשִׁיב	אֶת־גְּבוּל	יִשְׂרָאֵל	מִלְּבוֹא	חֲמָת
	hû'	hēshîv	'eth-gevûl	yisrā'ēl	millevô'	chămāth
	he	he caused to return	the border of	Israel	from to entering	Hamath

5912, 3328	6400	3626, 1745	3176	435	3547	866
prep, *n ms*	art, n ms	prep, *n ms*	pn	*n mp*	pn	rel part
עַד־יָם	הָעֲרָבָה	כִּדְבַר	יְהוָה	אֱלֹהֵי	יִשְׂרָאֵל	אֲשֶׁר
'adh-yām	hā'ărāvāh	kidhvar	yehwāh	'ĕlōhê	yisrā'ēl	'ăsher
unto the sea of	the Arabah	according to the word of	Yahweh	the God of	Israel	which

with, *Fenton* ... was buried in the royal tombs in David's City, *Good News* ... He was then transported by horse and buried ... with his ancestors, *JB* ... They brought his body back on horses, *NCV.*

21. And all the people of Judah took Azariah, which was sixteen years old, and made him king instead of his father Amaziah: ... made him king in succession to his father, *NEB* ... king in place of his father, *NIV* ... crowned him in place of his father, *Fenton* ... people of Judah then chose Uzziah, *JB*.

22. He built Elath, and restored it to Judah, after that the king slept with his fathers: ... rebuilt the town of Elath and made it part of Judah again after Amaziah died, *NCV* ... rested with his ancestors, *NAB* ... rested with his forefathers, *NEB* ... He was the builder of Elath, which he got back for Judah after the death of the king, *BB*.

23. In the fifteenth year of Amaziah the son of Joash king of Judah Jeroboam the son of Joash king of Israel began to reign in Samaria, and reigned forty and one years: ... started to rule in Samaria, *Beck* ... became king of Israel in Samaria, *JB*.

24. And he did that which was evil in the sight of the LORD: he departed not from all the sins of Jeroboam the son of Nebat, who made Israel to sin: ... He did what was wrong before the LORD. He didn't turn from any of the sins of Jeroboam, *Beck* ... He sinned against the LORD, following the wicked example of his predecessor King Jeroboam son of Nebat, who led Israel into sin, *Good News* ... He did what is displeasing to Yahweh and did not give up any of the sins into which Jeroboam son of Nebat had led Israel, *JB* ... he did what the LORD said was wrong. Jeroboam son of Nebat had led Israel to sin, and Jeroboam son of Jehoash did not stop doing the same sins, *NCV.*

25. He restored the coast of Israel from the entering of Hamath unto the sea of the plain, according to the word of the LORD God of Israel, which he spake by the hand of his servant Jonah, the son of Amittai, the prophet, which was of Gath-hepher: ... He re-established the frontiers of Israel from Lebo-hamath to the Sea of the Arabah, in fulfilment of the word of, *NEB* ... restored the boundaries of Israel from Lebo Hamath to the Sea of the Arabah, in accordance with the word of, *NIV* ... restored the territory of Israel from the entrance of Hamath to the Sea of the Arabah, *NKJV* ... reconquered all the territory that had belonged to Israel, from Hamath Pass in the north to the Dead Sea in the south. This was what the LORD, the God of Israel, had promised through his servant the prophet Jonah, son of Amittai from Gath Hepher, *Good News*.

26. For the LORD saw the affliction of Israel, that it was very bitter: for

---

added phrase merely represents reiteration of the theme of idolatry which pervades their discussion of the king's downfall.) Amaziah's defeat, however, took place at least fifteen years previously, and while "memories are long in the Middle East," and while such a lengthy period of time for retaliation is not totally out of the question, reasonable certitude still remains beyond our grasp. In any case, the fact that Amaziah was forced to flee to Lachish (an important garrison city some thirty miles [fifty kilometers] southwest of Jerusalem) implies a widespread threat to the king's life. The passage ends with the king's death and respectful internment of his bones in the "City of David," the traditional site for burial of the Judahite kings until the time of Hezekiah. (Concerning the procedure involved in transferring Amaziah's remains back to Jerusalem, cf. comments concerning the practice of reinterring the bones, on 13:14–21.)

Some believe King Amaziah may have seen himself as the next David, or a king as great as David, able to unite the two nations of Israel and Judah (maybe that was why he attacked Jehoash). But Amaziah was obviously no David (we have already been warned about that in v. 3). "That Jesus had Amaziah in mind when he talked of counting the cost before going to war [cf. Luke 14:31f] is a most tempting possibility." And that warning certainly did apply in Amaziah's case: "Not only is he unlike David in his piety, but he is also challenging a king whose dynasty has been promised longevity for at least two more generations" (cf. the promise made in 11:30 to King Jehu; also cf. 13:5, 23). As Hobbs concludes, "The promise of success for Amaziah is evidently nil."

14:23–29. Jeroboam II, king of Israel. Yet again we seem to have the "bare bones" treatment of what secular historians would have deemed one of the most important kings, politically and militarily, of either kingdom. A typically Israelite accession formula (v. 23) leads to the very predictable Israelite judgment notice (v. 24), followed by a brief archival note concerning the extent of his conquests (v. 24; cf. on 10:28–36; also cf. on 13:22–25). Of more than passing interest to the student of biblical prophecy is the observation that this verse also contains the only reference to the prophet Jonah, apart from the book of that name. The next two verses (vv. 26f) return to what is by now a rather familiar theme of Yahweh's love and concern for his nation Israel (see discussion on 13:1–9; also on 13:22–25); then a "further reference" notice (v. 28, including

1744.311	904, 3135, 5860	3226	1158, 585	5204	866	4623, 1710
v Piel pf 3ms	prep, *n fs*, n ms, ps 3ms	pn	*n ms*, pn	art, n ms	rel pron	prep, pn
דִּבֶּר	בְּיַד־עַבְדּוֹ	יוֹנָה	בֶּן־אֲמִתַּי	הַנָּבִיא	אֲשֶׁר	מִגַּת
dibber	beyadh-'avdô	yônāh	ven-'ămittay	hannāvî'	'ăsher	miggath
He spoke	by the hand of his servant	Jonah	the son of Amittai	the prophet	who	from Gath

1710		3706, 7495.111	3176	881, 6271	3547	4947.151	4108
art, pn	26.	cj, v Qal pf 3ms	pn	do, *n ms*	pn	v Qal act ptc ms	adv
הַחֵפֶר		כִּי־רָאָה	יְהוָה	אֶת־עֳנִי	יִשְׂרָאֵל	מֹרֶה	מְאֹד
hachēpher		kî-rā'āh	yehwāh	'eth-'ănî	yisrā'ēl	mōreh	me'ōdh
Hepher		because He saw	Yahweh	the affliction of	Israel	being bitter	very

675	6352.155	675	6013.155	375	6038.151	3937, 3547
cj, n ms	v Qal pass ptc ms	cj, n ms	v Qal pass ptc ms	cj, *sub*	v Qal act ptc ms	prep, pn
וְאֶפֶס	עָצוּר	וְאֶפֶס	עָזוּב	וְאֵין	עֹזֵר	לְיִשְׂרָאֵל
we'ephes	'ātsûr	we'ephes	'āzûv	we'ên	'ōzēr	leyisrā'ēl
and an end	the one bound	and an end	the one freed	and there was not	a helper	for Israel

	3940, 1744.311	3176	3937, 4364.141	881, 8428	3547	4623, 8809
27.	cj, neg part, v Piel pf 3ms	pn	prep, v Qal inf con	do, *n ms*	pn	prep, prep
	וְלֹא־דִבֶּר	יְהוָה	לִמְחוֹת	אֶת־שֵׁם	יִשְׂרָאֵל	מִתַּחַת
	welō'-dhibber	yehwāh	limchôth	'eth-shēm	yisrā'ēl	mittachath
	and He had not spoken	Yahweh	to wipe away	the name of	Israel	from beneath

8452	3588.521	904, 3135	3493	1158, 3204
art, n md	cj, v Hiphil impf 3ms, ps 3mp	prep, *n fs*	pn	*n ms*, pn
הַשָּׁמָיִם	וַיּוֹשִׁיעֵם	בְּיַד	יָרָבְעָם	בֶּן־יוֹאָשׁ
hashshāmāyim	wayyôshî'ēm	beyadh	yārov'ām	ben-yô'āsh
the heavens	and He saved them	by the hand of	Jeroboam	the son of Joash

	3615	1745	3493	3725, 866	6449.111	1400
28.	cj, *n ms*	*n mp*	pn	cj, *adj*, rel part	v Qal pf 3ms	cj, n fs, ps 3ms
	וְיֶתֶר	דִּבְרֵי	יָרָבְעָם	וְכָל־אֲשֶׁר	עָשָׂה	וּגְבוּרָתוֹ
	weyether	divrê	yārov'ām	wekhol-'ăsher	'āsāh	ûghevûrāthô
	and the remainder of	the events of	Jeroboam	and all which	he did	and his strength

866, 4032.211	866	8178.511	881, 1894	881, 2679	3937, 3171
rel part, v Niphal pf 3ms	cj, rel part	v Hiphil pf 3ms	do, pn	cj, do, pn	prep, pn
אֲשֶׁר־נִלְחָם	וַאֲשֶׁר	הֵשִׁיב	אֶת־דַּמֶּשֶׂק	וְאֶת־חֲמָת	לִיהוּדָה
'ăsher-nilchām	wa'ăsher	hēshîv	'eth-dammeseq	we'eth-chămāth	lîhûdhāh
which he fought	and that	he caused to return	Damascus	and Hamath	to Judah

there was not any shut up, nor any left, nor any helper for Israel: ... had seen how very bitter the affliction of Israel was, with no one, either fettered or free, to come to Israel's help, *JB* ... the Lord has not been blind to the affliction, past all endurance, that has fallen on Israel, bondman and free man alike perishing with none to succour them, *Knox* ... saw the very bitter affliction of Israel, where there was neither slave nor freeman, no one at all to help Israel, *NAB* ... LORD had seen how the Israelites, both slave and free, were suffering terribly. No one was left who could help Israel, *NCV*.

27. And the LORD said not that he would blot out the name of Israel from under heaven: but he saved them by the hand of Jeroboam the son of Joash: ... the LORD had promised not to wipe out Israel's name from the world, and so He saved them by Jeroboam, *Beck* ... the Lord had not said that the name of Israel was to be taken away from the earth; but he gave them a saviour in Jeroboam, the son of Joash, *BB* ... indeed He delivered them through the hand of Jeroboam, *Berkeley* ... He rescued it by the hand of Jerabam-ben-Joash, *Fenton*.

28. Now the rest of the acts of Jeroboam, and all that he did, and his might, how he warred, and how he recovered Damascus, and Hamath, which belonged to Judah, for Israel, are they not written in the book of the chronicles of the kings of Israel?: ... The rest of the history of Jeroboam, his entire career, his prowess, what wars he waged, how he brought Damascus and Hamath back to their allegiance to Judah and Israel, is this not recorded in, *JB* ... all his history, and the record of his great deeds, how he fought and how he restored to Israel all of

some more noteworthy conquests), and an Israelite burial formula (v. 29) conclude the passage.

Evidently, the name "Jeroboam" must have been perceived in a positive way at the time, inasmuch as the present king bears it (today's ritualistic denouncement of "Jeroboam son of Nebat" in the judgment formulas may shadow this). The name "Jeroboam" (yārov'ām HED #3493) is usually understood to mean "may the people be great" or the like, but other possibilities include "may the people multiply," or "he who fights the people's battle" (i.e., against the tyranny of Rehoboam king of Judah [cf. 1 Ki. 12]); cf. M. Aberback and L. Smolar, *The Interpreter's Dictionary of the Bible*, Supplementary Volume, 473. A stamp seal "of exquisite design" belonging to one "Shema," a courtier of the king, has been recovered at Megiddo; its inscription reads, "Belonging to Shema, servant of Jeroboam," and its image of a roaring lion dominates the seal impression (cf. Cogan and Tadmor, AB, 160; also Plate 12 [a]).

Dates for the accession of Jeroboam II range more widely than those for his predecessors, depending on whether one posits a coregency with his father Jehoash (e.g., Thiele who dated Jeroboam's coregency to 793, and his sole reign to 782), or not (e.g., Albright's date of 786).

Once again, Jeroboam II proved to be a very important king in the history of the Northern Kingdom, Israel. As Cogan and Tadmor (AB, 162) points out: "Jeroboam II's forty-one year reign, the longest of all kings of Israel, is presented tersely and in no way proportionally to his notable accomplishments in political and military affairs. He pursued the policies of his father Joash; in the north he warred with Aram and pushed beyond Damascus into central Syria, and in Trans-Jordan he extended his control to the Dead Sea.... The statement that Jeroboam 'restored the boundaries of Israel from Lebo-hamath to the Sea of the Arabah' (v. 25), the ideal borders of the Promised Land and the farthest limits of the United Monarchy, reflects an ideology which saw the Israelite king as achieving the glories of David and Solomon." (Let the reader note the irony of such northern success expressed in Davidic terms over against the inept failures of Amaziah, the Davidic descendant, as just described earlier in this same chapter.)

Furthermore, the prophecies of Amos, although curiously unmentioned anywhere in 1–2 Kings, definitely must be dated to this time (cf. Amos 1; 7:10). The situation is one of a prosperous nation. In sharp contrast to the nationalistic prophets such as Jonah son of Amittai (once again, cf. v. 25 of the present text), Amos of Tekoa prophesied boldly of the fall of Jeroboam and his dynasty, and the exile of the nation of Israel (cf. the strong words of Amos 7:10–17).

The so-called Samaria Ostraca are also probably to be dated around this time as well, and they, too, seem to picture taxation of Jeroboam's subjects for the maintenance of extravagant lifestyles, including the lavish use of wine and fine cosmetic oils (cf. Amos 6:6; also Ivan T. Kaufman, *Anchor Bible Dictionary*, 65:921–26). Archaeological excavations at Samaria confirm this picture of extravagant living; as John Bright (*A History of Israel*, 259) points out, "The splendid buildings and costly ivory inlays of Phoenician or Damascene origin unearthed at Samaria show that Amos did not exaggerate the luxury that Israel's upper classes enjoyed." It was already noted in connection with the story of Amaziah earlier in the present chapter, that "pride goeth before destruction." That, of course, is no less true for the northern nation of Israel. Yes, the era of Jeroboam II was one of the most prosperous ever known in that land (at least for the upper class). But within less than thirty years, that nation not only knew abject poverty and military disaster, but it came to know firsthand Assyrian exile, and, as Amos once again put it, "Hear this word, ye kine of Bashan, that are in the mountains of Samaria, which oppress the poor, which crush the needy, which say to their masters, Bring, and let us drink. The Lord God hath sworn by his holiness, that, lo, the days shall come upon you, that he will take you away with hooks, and your posterity with fishhooks. And ye shall go out at the breaches, every cow at that which is before her; and ye shall cast them into the palace, saith the LORD" (Amos 4:1ff; the reference to the women as "cows of Bashan" was not meant to be insulting per se, but rather a graphic reminder of their well-fed appearances.). So it is today—we know what luxury is, and we also know the widening chasm between rich and poor. Let us not think that we are immune from the judgments of an OT Amos or a NT James ("Go to now, ye rich men, weep and howl for your miseries that shall come upon you. ... Ye have heaped treasure together for the last days. Behold, the hire of the labourers who have reaped down your fields, which is of you kept back by fraud, crieth: ... ye have lived in pleasure on the earth, and been wanton; ye have nourished your hearts, as in a day of slaughter" Jam. 5:1–5). Let us heed the Word of the Lord.

904, 3547	1950B, 3940, 2062	3918.156	6142, 5809	1745	3219
prep, pn	intrg part, neg part, pers pron	v Qal pass ptc mp	prep, *n ms*	*n mp*	art, n mp
בְּיִשְׂרָאֵל	הֲלֹא־הֵם	כְּתוּבִים	עַל־סֵפֶר	דִּבְרֵי	הַיָּמִים
beyisrā'ēl	hălō'-hēm	kethûvîm	'al-sēpher	divrê	hayyāmîm
in Israel	are they not	things written	on the scroll of	the events of	the days

3937, 4567	3547		8311.121	3493	6196, 1	6196	4567
prep, *n mp*	pn	**29.**	cj, v Qal impf 3ms	pn	prep, n mp, ps 3ms	prep	*n mp*
לְמַלְכֵי	יִשְׂרָאֵל		וַיִּשְׁכַּב	יָרָבְעָם	עִם־אֲבֹתָיו	עִם	מַלְכֵי
lemalkhê	yisrā'ēl		wayyishkav	yārov'ām	'im-'ăvōthâv	'im	malkhê
of the kings of	Israel		and he lay	Jeroboam	with his ancestors	with	the kings of

3547	4566.121	2232	1158	8809		904, 8523	6465
pn	cj, v Qal impf 3ms	pn	n ms, ps 3ms	prep, ps 3ms	**15:1**	prep, *n fs*	num
יִשְׂרָאֵל	וַיִּמְלֹךְ	זְכַרְיָה	בְּנוֹ	תַּחְתָּיו		בִּשְׁנַת	עֶשְׂרִים
yisrā'ēl	wayyimlōkh	zekharyāh	venô	tachtâv		bishnath	'esrîm
Israel	and he reigned	Zechariah	his son	instead of him		in the year of	twenty

8124	8523	3937, 3493	4567	3547	4566.111	6051	1158, 568
cj, num	n fs	prep, pn	*n ms*	pn	v Qal pf 3ms	pn	*n ms*, pn
וָשֶׁבַע	שָׁנָה	לְיָרָבְעָם	מֶלֶךְ	יִשְׂרָאֵל	מָלַךְ	עֲזַרְיָה	בֶּן־אֲמַצְיָה
wāsheva'	shānāh	leyārov'ām	melekh	yisrā'ēl	mālakh	'ăzaryāh	ven-'ămatsyāh
and seven	years	of Jeroboam	the king of	Israel	he reigned	Azariah	the son of Amaziah

4567	3171		1158, 8666	6462	8523	2030.111	904, 4566.141
n ms	pn	**2.**	*n ms*, num	num	n fs	v Qal pf 3ms	prep, v Qal inf con, ps 3ms
מֶלֶךְ	יְהוּדָה		בֶּן־שֵׁשׁ	עֶשְׂרֵה	שָׁנָה	הָיָה	בְמָלְכוֹ
melekh	yehûdhāh		ben-shēsh	'esrēh	shānāh	hāyāh	vemālekhô
the king of	Judah		a son of six	ten	years	he was	when his reigning

2675	8692	8523	4566.111	904, 3503	8428	525	3312
cj, num	cj, num	n fs	v Qal pf 3ms	prep, pn	cj, *n ms*	n fs, ps 3ms	pn
וַחֲמִשִּׁים	וּשְׁתַּיִם	שָׁנָה	מָלַךְ	בִּירוּשָׁלָם	וְשֵׁם	אִמּוֹ	יְכָלְיָהוּ
wachmishshîm	ûshettayim	shānāh	mālakh	bîrûshālām	weshēm	'immô	yekholyāhû
and fifty	and two	years	he reigned	in Jerusalem	and the name of	his mother	Jecoliah

4623, 3503		6449.121	3596	904, 6084	3176	3626, 3725
prep, pn	**3.**	cj, v Qal impf 3ms	art, adj	prep, *n fd*	pn	prep, n ms
מִירוּשָׁלָם		וַיַּעַשׂ	הַיָּשָׁר	בְּעֵינֵי	יְהוָה	כְּכֹל
mîrûshālām		wayya'as	hayyāshār	be'ênê	yehwāh	kekhōl
of Jerusalem		and he did	what is right	in the eyes of	Yahweh	according to everything

866, 6449.111	568	1		7828	1154	3940, 5681.116
rel part, v Qal pf 3ms	pn	n ms, ps 3ms	**4.**	adv	art, n fp	neg part, v Qal pf 3cp
אֲשֶׁר־עָשָׂה	אֲמַצְיָהוּ	אָבִיו		רַק	הַבָּמוֹת	לֹא־סָרוּ
'ăsher-'āsāh	'ămatsyāhû	'āvîw		raq	habbāmôth	lō'-sārû
which he did	Amaziah	his father		only	the high places	they did not turn aside from

5968	6194	2159.352	7281.352	904, 1154		5236.321	3176
adv	art, n ms	v Piel ptc mp	cj, v Piel ptc mp	prep, art, n fp	**5.**	cj, v Piel impf 3ms	pn
עוֹד	הָעָם	מְזַבְּחִים	וּמְקַטְּרִים	בַּבָּמוֹת		וַיְנַגַּע	יְהוָה
'ōdh	hā'ām	mezabbechîm	ûmeqatterîm	babbāmôth		waynagga'	yehwāh
still	the people	sacrificing	and burning incense	on the high places		and He struck	Yahweh

881, 4567	2030.121	7164.455	5912, 3219	4323	3553.121
do, art, n ms	cj, v Qal impf 3ms	v Pual ptc ms	adv, *n ms*	n ms, ps 3ms	cj, v Qal impf 3ms
אֶת־הַמֶּלֶךְ	וַיְהִי	מְצֹרָע	עַד־יוֹם	מֹתוֹ	וַיֵּשֶׁב
'eth-hammelekh	wayhî	metsōrā'	'adh-yôm	mōthô	wayyēshev
the king	and he was	a diseased man	until the day of	his death	and he dwelled

Damascus and Emath that once belonged to the Jewish kingdom, is to be found in the Annals of the kings of Israel, *Knox* ... his valor and all his accomplishments, how he fought, *NAB* ... Everything else that Jeroboam II did, his brave battles, and how he restored Damascus and Hamath to Israel, are all recorded in The History of the Kings, *Good News*.

29. And Jeroboam slept with his fathers, even with the kings of Israel; and Zachariah his son reigned in his stead: ... died and was buried with his ancestors, the kings of Israel, *NCV* ... rested with his fore-fathers, *NEB* ... Zechariah his son became king in his place, *NASB*.

15:1. In the twenty and seventh year of Jeroboam king of Israel began Azariah son of Amaziah king of Judah to reign: ... Azariah ... became king, *Anchor* ... started to rule as king of Judah, *Beck* ... succeeded his father Amasias on the throne of Juda, *Knox*.

2. Sixteen years old was he when he began to reign, and he reigned two and fifty years in Jerusalem. And his mother's name was Jecholiah of Jerusalem: ... 16 years old when he started to rule, *Beck* ... sixteen years old at his coronation, *Fenton*.

3. And he did that which was right in the sight of the Lord, according to all that his father Amaziah had done: ... did that which was pleasing before the Lord, *Douay* ... did what the Lord said was right, just as his father Amaziah had done, *NCV* ... Following the example of his father, *Good News*.

4. Save that the high places were not removed: the people sacrificed and burnt incense still on the high places: ... except that the high places

---

15:1–38. *Since most of this chapter consists of stereotypical regnal formulas (twenty-six and one-half verses out of a total of thirty-eight verses for the chapter), the following brief references should prove to be of significant value for the reader: Judahite accession notices (cf. vv. 1f, 32f) are discussed in comments on 8:16–24 and 8:25–29. Judahite judgment formulas (cf. 15:3f, 34f) are reviewed briefly at 12:1ff (Hebrew, 12:2ff) while "further reference" notices for either kingdom (cf. 15:6, 11, 15, 21, 26, 31, 36) are discussed at 1:17f. Finally, Judahite burial notices (cf. 15:7, 38) are examined briefly at 8:23f. For the Israelite kings, their accession notices (cf. 15:8, 13, 17, 23, 27) are discussed at 13:1–9; while their judgment formulas (cf. 15:9, 18, 24, 28) are examined at 3:1ff. Israelite burial notices (cf. 15:22) are looked at briefly at 13:1–9; while the archival-style material for the kings of either kingdom (15:5, 16, 19f, 29, 35, 37), also the accounts of assassinations (15:10, 14, 25, 30) find some parallels from ch. 14 (cp. 14:5ff). Thus, not counting the last two categories of archival-style material, still over two-thirds of the present chapter consists of stereotypical notices and formulas; and, once the last two categories are added in, only one verse remains unaccounted for—namely v. 12, which is a brief prophetic notice acknowledging the fulfillment of Yahweh's word to Jehu in 10:30 (cf. comments on 10:28–36).*

15:1–7. Azariah (or Uzziah), king of Judah. Judahite accession formula, vv. 1f; Judahite judgment notice, vv. 3f; "further reference" notice, v. 6; Judahite burial formula, v. 7. The name "Azariah" (usually interpreted as "Yahweh has helped," or the like) is used some eight times in 2 Kings, and "Uzziah" ("Yahweh is my strength," or the like) some four times. The chronicler, however, clearly prefers the name "Uzziah," using it some thirteen times, and using the name "Azariah" only once (namely, in the list of Davidic kings in 1 Chr. 3:12). References to "Uzziah" are also found three times in Isaiah, once in Hosea, once in Amos and once in Zechariah. The Assyrian inscriptions attest the form "Azariah" as the rebel king who confronted Tiglath-Pileser III in north Syria in 739/38 (cf. Cogan and Tadmor [AB, 165], who also cite the work of G. Brin to the effect that the two names "Azariah" and "Uzziah" represent two Hebrew roots ['āzar, HED #6038 and 'āzaz, HED #6022] which are semantically quite closely related to each other [both convey the sense of "victory, valor, strength"], and therefore one need not assume that the king adopted a second name as a throne name or the like—heretofore a common suggestion proposed by biblical scholars).

Suggested dates for Azariah's accession range from 783 (Albright) to 767 (Thiele, sole reign), but the issue of coregencies for Azariah remains uncertain (e.g., whether there is some overlap with his father Amaziah; most scholars do recognize that v. 5 of the present chapter probably signifies some sort of coregency with his son Jotham). The length of reign for Azariah, fifty-two years, is also difficult, even with coregencies with Amaziah and with Jotham (Albright lowers it to a more likely forty-two; whereas Cogan and Tadmor posit coregencies with Amaziah, Jotham and even Ahaz; cf. AB, 166). Such issues are of more than antiquarian interest when one confronts the familiar text of Isa. 6:1, "In the year that king Uzziah died I saw also the Lord"; did it take place in ca. 742

904, 1041	2776	3251	1158, 4567	6142, 1041	8570.151
prep, *n ms*	art, n fs	cj, pn	*n ms*, art, n ms	prep, art, n ms	v Qal act ptc ms
בְּבֵית	הַחָפְשִׁית	וְיוֹתָם	בֶּן־הַמֶּלֶךְ	עַל־הַבַּיִת	שֹׁפֵט
bevêth	hachāpheshîth	weyôthām	ben-hammelekh	ʿal-habbayith	shōphēṯ
in the house of	the separation	and Jotham	the son of the king	over the household	judging

881, 6194	800		3615	1745	6051	3725, 866	6449.111
do, *n ms*	art, n fs	**6.**	cj, *n ms*	*n mp*	pn	cj, *adj*, rel part	v Qal pf 3ms
אֶת־עַם	הָאָרֶץ		וְיֶתֶר	דִּבְרֵי	עֲזַרְיָהוּ	וְכָל־אֲשֶׁר	עָשָׂה
ʾeth-ʿam	hāʾārets		weyether	divrê	ʿăzaryāhû	wekhol-ʾăsher	ʿāsāh
the people of	the land		and the remainder of	the events of	Azariah	and all which	he did

1950B, 3940, 2062	3918.156	6142, 5809	1745	3219	3937, 4567
intrg part, neg part, pers pron	v Qal pass ptc mp	prep, *n ms*	*n mp*	art, n mp	prep, *n mp*
הֲלֹא־הֵם	כְּתוּבִים	עַל־סֵפֶר	דִּבְרֵי	הַיָּמִים	לְמַלְכֵי
hălōʾ-hēm	kethûvîm	ʿal-sēpher	divrê	hayyāmîm	lemalkhê
are they not	things written	on the scroll of	the events of	the days	of the kings of

3171		8311.121	6051	6196, 1	7196.126	881
pn	**7.**	cj, v Qal impf 3ms	pn	prep, n mp, ps 3ms	cj, v Qal impf 3mp	do, ps 3ms
יְהוּדָה		וַיִּשְׁכַּב	עֲזַרְיָה	עִם־אֲבֹתָיו	וַיִּקְבְּרוּ	אֹתוֹ
yehûdhāh		wayyishkav	ʿăzaryāh	ʿim-ʾăvōthâv	wayyiqōbberû	ʾōthô
Judah		and he lay	Azariah	with his ancestors	and they buried	him

6196, 1	904, 6111	1784	4566.121	3251	1158	8809
prep, n mp, ps 3ms	prep, *n fs*	pn	cj, v Qal impf 3ms	pn	n ms, ps 3ms	prep, ps 3ms
עִם־אֲבֹתָיו	בְּעִיר	דָּוִד	וַיִּמְלֹךְ	יוֹתָם	בְּנוֹ	תַּחְתָּיו
ʿim-ʾăvōthâv	beʿîr	dāwidh	wayyimlōkh	yôthām	benô	tachtâv
with his ancestors	in the city of	David	and he reigned	Jotham	his son	instead of him

	904, 8523	8421	8470	8523	3937, 6051	4567	3171	4566.111
8.	prep, *n fs*	num	cj, num	n fs	prep, pn	*n ms*	pn	v Qal pf 3ms
	בִּשְׁנַת	שְׁלֹשִׁים	וּשְׁמֹנֶה	שָׁנָה	לַעֲזַרְיָהוּ	מֶלֶךְ	יְהוּדָה	מָלַךְ
	bishnath	shelōshîm	ûshemōneh	shānāh	laʿăzaryāhû	melekh	yehûdhāh	mālakh
	in the year of	thirty	and eight	years	of Azariah	the king of	Judah	he reigned

2232	1158, 3493	6142, 3547	904, 8497	8666	2414		6449.121
pn	*n ms*, pn	prep, pn	prep, pn	num	n mp	**9.**	cj, v Qal impf 3ms
זְכַרְיָהוּ	בֶּן־יָרָבְעָם	עַל־יִשְׂרָאֵל	בְּשֹׁמְרוֹן	שִׁשָּׁה	חֳדָשִׁים		וַיַּעַשׂ
zekharyāhû	ven-yārovʿām	ʿal-yisrāʾēl	beshōmerôn	shishshāh	chŏdhāshîm		wayyaʿas
Zechariah	the son of Jeroboam	over Israel	in Samaria	six	months		and he did

7737	904, 6084	3176	3626, 866	6449.116	1	3940	5681.111
art, adj	prep, *n fd*	pn	prep, rel part	v Qal pf 3cp	n mp, ps 3ms	neg part	v Qal pf 3ms
הָרַע	בְּעֵינֵי	יְהוָה	כַּאֲשֶׁר	עָשׂוּ	אֲבֹתָיו	לֹא	סָר
hāraʿ	beʿênê	yehwāh	kaʾăsher	ʿāsû	ʾăvōthâv	lōʾ	s̱ār
what is evil	in the eyes of	Yahweh	just as	they had done	his fathers	not	he turned aside

4623, 2496	3493	1158, 5203	866	2490.511	881, 3547
prep, *n fp*	pn	*n ms*, pn	rel part	v Hiphil pf 3ms	do, pn
מֵחַטֹּאות	יָרָבְעָם	בֶּן־נְבָט	אֲשֶׁר	הֶחֱטִיא	אֶת־יִשְׂרָאֵל
mēchaṯṯōʾwth	yārovʿām	ben-nevāṯ	ʾăsher	hechĕṯîʾ	ʾeth-yisrāʾēl
from the sins of	Jeroboam	the son of Nebat	which	he caused to sin	Israel

	7489.121	6142	8362	1158, 3113	5409.521
10.	cj, v Qal impf 3ms	prep, ps 3ms	pn	*n ms*, pn	cj, v Hiphil impf 3ms, ps 3ms
	וַיִּקְשֹׁר	עָלָיו	שַׁלֻּם	בֶּן־יָבֵישׁ	וַיַּכֵּהוּ
	wayyiqōshōr	ʿālâv	shallum	ben-yāvēsh	wayyakkēhû
	and he conspired	against him	Shallum	the son of Jabesh	and he struck him down

were not removed, *KJVII* ... but did not destroy the hill-shrines, *Knox* ... the places where gods were worshiped were not removed, *NCV*.

5. And the LORD smote the king, so that he was a leper unto the day of his death, and dwelt in a several house: ... LORD struck the king, ... lived in a separate house, *NRSV* ... sent disease on the king ... afflicted the king, *Fenton* ... struck Uzziah with a dreaded skin disease that stayed with him the rest of his life. He lived in a separate house, relieved of all duties, *Good News* ... He lived confined to his room, *JB* ... was living separately in his private house, *BB*.

And Jotham the king's son was over the house, judging the people of the land: ... managed the palace and also governed the country, *Beck* ... was Chief-Justice for the public, *Fenton* ... the crown prince, was over the household, *Goodspeed* ... had charge of the palace, *Knox*.

6. And the rest of the acts of Azariah, and all that he did, are they not written in the book of the chronicles of the kings of Judah?: ... and all his accomplishments, are recorded, *NAB* ... the history, *NCV* ... and events of Azariah's reign are recorded in the annals, *NEB*.

7. So Azariah slept with his fathers; and they buried him with his fathers in the city of David: and Jotham his son reigned in his stead: ... became king in his place, *Berkeley* ... his ancestors, *Fenton* ... in the royal burial ground in David's City, *Good News*.

8. In the thirty and eighth year of Azariah king of Judah did Zachariah the son of Jeroboam

---

(as Albright argues), or in 740 (Thiele), or as late as 733 (Cogan and Tadmor). Some date before 735 would be necessary to squeeze in the Syro-Ephraimite War in that year (with Tiglath-Pileser marching down the coast in 734 to response to King Ahaz' requests for help [cf. 16:7ff; also cf. Isa. 7:17–25; it should be noted, however, that Cogan and Tadmor (AB, 191) question whether Ahaz necessarily asked for Assyrian aid that early]. For further discussion on the Syro-Ephraimite War, cf. on vv. 27–31).

A brief comment has already been made on the nature of biblical "leprosy" (cf. on 5:1). As noted, various degrees of social stigma attended this disease, with the four Samarian lepers in 7:3f seemingly excluded from the city, but Gehazi, Elisha's servant (5:27) probably not (cf. 8:4ff, where he meets with the king—but some date that event before his punishment at the end of ch. 5); and, finally, the example of Naaman himself able to move about quite freely and meet with whomever he chose (5:1). Apparently, in the present instance, Azariah's leprosy must have been fairly severe, for he was indeed excluded from palace and Temple (in fact, he was afflicted with leprosy and permanently excluded from the Temple as a direct result of his attempt to burn incense there [2 Chr. 26:16–21]). He was also compelled to live in a "separate house" (cf. Cogan and Tadmor, AB, 167) until the day of his death (which could have been many years later, even some twenty-five years according to the reckoning of Cogan and Tadmor). Hobbs (WBC, 194) notes, however, that standards for leprosy may well have been more stringent for kings than for commoners: "A monarch whose skin (i.e., outer limits) was thus affected would have been a very inadequate symbol of the Davidic ideology."

As is evident, the present account has little else to say about this important, and clearly long-lived, Judahite king. Azariah's long and apparently profitable reign does not take any more space than the writer's description of the reigns of Zechariah or Shallum of Israel who reigned for a fraction of the time. The brief notation of the king, comparable with the earlier treatment of Jeroboam, Azariah's contemporary in the north (see 14:23–29), serves the literary purpose of showing how Judah was moving swiftly along to the final stages of the disintegration of the northern country of Israel. The discussion of evil kings serves to show the inevitable self-destruction to which such behavior always leads.

Much more information about Azariah may be found in 2 Chr. 26, with its twenty-three verses devoted solely to this king. Some note that Azariah emerged as a militant king who transformed the national power extending borders to the west and south, reaching the Mediterranean coast at Ashdod and the Red Sea at Eilat (2 Ki. 14:22). Of particular note is the collaboration of Judah and Israel in the census in Trans-Jordan, in the Gilead and Bashan (1 Chr. 5:17), evidence for the joint resettling of the grazing areas formerly controlled by Aram-Damascus. Also in the mountainous and semiarid areas of Judah, Azariah developed agricultural projects and cattle raising. He was, in the words of the Chronicler's unusual accolade, a 'lover of the soil' (2 Chr. 26:10). Quite a remarkable king, this Azariah, who indeed, by and large, "did that which was right in the sight of the LORD," (cf. v. 3 of the present passage).

15:8–12. Zechariah, king of Israel. Israelite accession formula, v. 8; Israelite judgment notice, v. 9; archival-style assassination notice, v. 10; "further reference" notice, v. 11.

7188, 6194	4322.521	4566.121	8809
n ms, n ms	cj, v Hiphil impf 3ms, ps 3ms	cj, v Qal impf 3ms	prep, ps 3ms
קָבָל־עָם	וַיְמִיתֵהוּ	וַיִּמְלֹךְ	תַּחְתָּיו
qāvāle-ʿām	waymîthēhû	wayyimlōkh	tachtāv
an undertaking for the people	and he executed him	and he reigned	instead of him

11.	3615	1745	2232	2079	3918.156	6142, 5809
	cj, *n ms*	*n mp*	pn	intrj, ps 3mp	v Qal pass ptc mp	prep, *n ms*
	וְיֶתֶר	דִּבְרֵי	זְכַרְיָה	הִנָּם	כְּתוּבִים	עַל־סֵפֶר
	weyether	divrê	zekharyāh	hinnām	kethûvîm	ʿal-sēpher
	and the remainder of	the events of	Zechariah	behold they	things written	on the scroll of

1745	3219	3937, 4567	3547	**12.**	2000	1745, 3176	866
n mp	art, n mp	prep, *n mp*	pn		pers pron	*n ms*, pn	rel part
דִּבְרֵי	הַיָּמִים	לְמַלְכֵי	יִשְׂרָאֵל		הוּא	דְּבַר־יְהוָה	אֲשֶׁר
divrê	hayyāmîm	lemalkhê	yisrāʾēl		hûʾ	dhevar-yehwāh	ʾăsher
the events of	the days	of the kings of	Israel		it	the word of Yahweh	which

1744.311	420, 3167	3937, 569.141	1158	7536	3553.126	3937
v Piel pf 3ms	prep, pn	prep, v Qal inf con	*n mp*	num	v Qal impf 3mp	prep, ps 2ms
דִּבֶּר	אֶל־יֵהוּא	לֵאמֹר	בְּנֵי	רְבִיעִים	יֵשְׁבוּ	לְךָ
dibber	ʾel-yēhûʾ	lēʾmōr	benê	revîʿîm	yēshevû	lekhā
He spoke	to Jehu	saying	the sons of	the fourth	they will sit	to you

6142, 3802	3547	2030.121, 3772	**13.**	8362	1158, 3113	4566.111
prep, *n ms*	pn	cj, v Qal impf 3ms, adv		pn	*n ms*, pn	v Qal pf 3ms
עַל־כִּסֵּא	יִשְׂרָאֵל	וַיְהִי־כֵן		שַׁלּוּם	בֶּן־יָבֵישׁ	מָלַךְ
ʿal-kissēʾ	yisrāʾēl	wayhî-khēn		shallûm	ben-yāvêsh	mālakh
on the throne of	Israel	and it was so		Shallum	the son of Jabesh	he reigned

904, 8523	8421	9013	8523	3937, 6030	4567	3171	4566.121
prep, *n fs*	num	cj, num	n fs	prep, pn	*n ms*	pn	cj, v Qal impf 3ms
בִּשְׁנַת	שְׁלֹשִׁים	וָתֵשַׁע	שָׁנָה	לְעֻזִּיָּה	מֶלֶךְ	יְהוּדָה	וַיִּמְלֹךְ
bishnath	shelōshîm	wāthēshaʿ	shānāh	leʿuzzîyāh	melekh	yehûdhāh	wayyimlōkh
in the year of	thirty	and nine	years	of Uzziah	the king of	Judah	and he reigned

3505, 3219	904, 8497	**14.**	6148.121	4650	1158, 1455	4623, 8995
n ms, n mp	prep, pn		cj, v Qal impf 3ms	pn	*n ms*, pn	prep, pn
יֶרַח־יָמִים	בְּשֹׁמְרוֹן		וַיַּעַל	מְנַחֵם	בֶּן־גָּדִי	מִתִּרְצָה
yerach-yāmîm	beshōmerôn		wayyaʿal	menachēm	ben-gādhî	mittirtsāh
a month of days	in Samaria		and he went up	Menahem	the son of Gadi	from Tirzah

971.121	8497	5409.521	881, 8362	1158, 3113	904, 8497
cj, v Qal impf 3ms	pn	cj, v Hiphil impf 3ms	do, pn	*n ms*, pn	prep, pn
וַיָּבֹא	שֹׁמְרוֹן	וַיַּךְ	אֶת־שַׁלּוּם	בֶּן־יָבֵישׁ	בְּשֹׁמְרוֹן
wayyāvōʾ	shōmerôn	wayyakh	ʾeth-shallûm	ben-yāvêsh	beshōmerôn
and he entered	Samaria	and he struck down	Shallum	the son of Jabesh	in Samaria

4322.521	4566.121	8809	**15.**	3615	1745
cj, v Hiphil impf 3ms, ps 3ms	cj, v Qal impf 3ms	prep, ps 3ms		cj, *n ms*	*n mp*
וַיְמִיתֵהוּ	וַיִּמְלֹךְ	תַּחְתָּיו		וְיֶתֶר	דִּבְרֵי
waymîthēhû	wayyimlōkh	tachtāv		weyether	divrê
and he executed him	and he reigned	instead of him		and the remainder of	the events of

8362	7490	866	7489.111	2079	3918.156	6142, 5809
pn	cj, n ms, ps 3ms	rel part	v Qal pf 3ms	intrj, ps 3mp	v Qal pass ptc mp	prep, *n ms*
שַׁלּוּם	וְקִשְׁרוֹ	אֲשֶׁר	קָשָׁר	הִנָּם	כְּתֻבִים	עַל־סֵפֶר
shallûm	weqishrô	ʾăsher	qāshār	hinnām	kethuvîm	ʿal-sēpher
Shallum	and his conspiracy	which	he conspired	behold they	things written	on the scroll of

reign over Israel in Samaria six months: ... became king over Israel in Samaria and reigned six months, *NEB*.

9. And he did that which was evil in the sight of the LORD, as his fathers had done: he departed not from the sins of Jeroboam the son of Nebat, who made Israel to sin: ... He did wrong before the LORD, *Beck* ... he did not turn away, *Berkeley* ... did what is displeasing to Yahweh, as his fathers had done; he did not give up the sins, *JB* ... He defied the Lord's will, like his fathers before him, *Knox*.

10. And Shallum the son of Jabesh conspired against him, and smote him before the people, and slew him, and reigned in his stead: ... made plans against Zechariah and killed him in front of, *NCV* ... attacked and killed him at Ibleam, and reigned in his place, *NAB* ... assassinated him and succeeded him as king, *NIV* ... in public, and became the next king, *NLT*.

11. And the rest of the acts of Zachariah, behold, they are written in the book of the chronicles of the kings of Israel: ... rest of the history of Zechariah is recorded in the annals, *Anchor* ... see, they are told, *Berkeley* ... rest of the affairs of Zakeriah are recorded in the history of events during the period of, *Fenton* ... in The History of, *Good News*.

12. This was the word of the LORD which he spake unto Jehu, saying, Thy sons shall sit on the throne of Israel unto the fourth generation. And so it came to pass: ... Thus the LORD's promise to Jehu, Your descendants to the fourth generation shall sit upon the throne of Israel, was fulfilled, *NAB* ... Thy heirs shall keep the throne of Israel till the fourth generation; and so it proved, *Knox* ... down to your great-great-grandchildren will be kings of Israel, and the LORD's word came true, *NCV*.

13. Shallum the son of Jabesh began to reign in the nine and thirtieth year of Uzziah king of Judah; and he reigned a full month in Samaria: ... to rule over Israel in the thirty-ninth year of King Uzziah's reign, *NLT* ... he was ruling in Samaria for the space of one month, *BB* ... he was king for a whole month, *Beck*.

14. For Menahem the son of Gadi went up from Tirzah, and came to Samaria, and smote Shallum the son of Jabesh in Samaria, and slew him, and reigned in his stead: ... marched from Tirzah, entered Samaria, murdered Shallum son of Jabesh there and succeeded him, *JB* ... he cut down Shallum son of Jabesh, killed him, and became king in his place, *Berkeley* ... assassinated Shallum, *Good News*.

15. And the rest of the acts of Shallum, and his conspiracy which he made, behold, they are written in the book of the chronicles of the kings of Israel: ... what else Sellum did, all the history of his secret conspiracy, is to be found in the Annals, *Knox* ... his secret plans, *NCV* ... other events of Shallum's reign, *NEB* ... and the secret design which he made, are recorded, *BB*.

There are, depending on how one counts them, some thirty different Zechariahs in the OT. The name means "Yahweh has remembered," or the like; but not much needs to be remembered about this particular king—except, as alluded to here in v. 12, that he was the fifth and the final king from the dynasty of Jehu (actually, then, at least for his brief six months on the throne, part of that "fourth generation" promised Jehu in 10:30).

15:13–16. Shallum, king of Israel. Israelite accession formula, v. 13; archival-style assassination notice, v. 14; "further reference" notice, v. 15.

Again, very little needs to be said here, other than to note the almost pedantic desire for completeness listing of all the kings of both kingdoms. Ironically, more is said here about Menahem (cf. comments on vv. 17–22) than about Shallum in the present section. The name "Shallum" is related to the familiar Hebrew root shālôm, HED #8396; cf. on 9:14–29 for an extensive examination of this important term. As noted there, the basic idea is that of "completeness," or "wholeness," whence the likely meanings of the name "Shallum" as "the requited one," or "he for whom compensation is made" (Robert Althann, *Anchor Bible Dictionary*, 5:1154).

15:17–22. Menahem, king of Israel. Israelite accession formula, v. 17; Israelite judgment notice, v. 18; archival-style assassination notice, v. 10; "further reference" notice, v. 21; Israelite burial formula; v. 22.

As just noted, a few significant facts concerning Menahem may be found in the previous section—especially his bloodthirsty actions mentioned in v. 16. The ugly reference to his "ripping open all the pregnant women" finds a parallel in 8:12, in connection with King Hazael of Aram; however, the precise location where Menahem's barbarous activity took place is uncertain, with NRSV and NIV reading "Tiphsah" (a faraway city on the Euphrates river), but NLT preferring "Tappuah" (a city much closer, on the Ephraim-Manasseh border; cf. Cogan and Tadmor [AB, 171], who strongly argue for this reading). Once again, Menahem's vicious actions against the defeated city are understandably repugnant to modern sensitivities (although, similar actions in our

1745	3219	3937, 4567	3547		226	5409.521, 4650	881, 8942
n mp	art, n mp	prep, *n mp*	pn	**16.**	adv	v Hiphil impf 3ms, pn	do, pn
דִּבְרֵי	הַיָּמִים	לְמַלְכֵי	יִשְׂרָאֵל		אָז	יַכֶּה־מְנַחֵם	אֶת־תִּפְסַח
divrê	hayyāmîm	lemalkhê	yisrā'ēl		'āz	yakkeh-menachēm	'eth-tiphsach
the events of	the days	of the kings of	Israel		then	Menahem struck	Tiphsah

881, 3725, 866, 904	881, 1397	4623, 8995	3706	3940	6858.111
cj, do, *adj*, rel pron, prep, ps 3fs	cj, do, n mp, ps 3fs	prep, pn	cj	neg part	v Qal pf 3ms
וְאֶת־כָּל־אֲשֶׁר־בָּהּ	וְאֶת־גְּבוּלֶיהָ	מִתִּרְצָה	כִּי	לֹא	פָּתַח
we'eth-kol-'ăsher-bāhh	we'eth-gevûlêāh	mittirtsāh	kî	lō'	phāthach
and all who in it	and its territories	from Tirzah	because	not	they opened

5409.521	881	3725, 2107	1260.311		904, 8523	8421
cj, v Hiphil impf 3ms	do	*adj*, art, adj, ps 3fs	v Piel pf 3ms	**17.**	prep, *n fs*	num
וַיַּךְ	אֵת	כָּל־הֶהָרוֹתֶיהָ	בִּקֵּעַ		בִּשְׁנַת	שְׁלֹשִׁים
wayyakh	'ēth	kol-hehārôthêāh	biqqēa'		bishnath	shelōshîm
so he struck down		all its pregnant women	he split open		in the year of	thirty

9013	8523	3937, 6051	4567	3171	4566.111	4650	1158, 1455
cj, num	n fs	prep, pn	*n ms*	pn	v Qal pf 3ms	pn	*n ms*, pn
וָתֵשַׁע	שָׁנָה	לַעֲזַרְיָה	מֶלֶךְ	יְהוּדָה	מָלַךְ	מְנַחֵם	בֶּן־גָּדִי
wāthēsha'	shānāh	la'ăzaryāh	melekh	yehûdhāh	mālakh	menachēm	ben-gādhî
and nine	years	of Azariah	the king of	Judah	he reigned	Menahem	the son of Gadi

6142, 3547	6460	8523	904, 8497		6449.121	7737	904, 6084	3176
prep, pn	num	n fp	prep, pn	**18.**	cj, v Qal impf 3ms	art, adj	prep, *n fd*	pn
עַל־יִשְׂרָאֵל	עֶשֶׂר	שָׁנִים	בְּשֹׁמְרוֹן		וַיַּעַשׂ	הָרַע	בְּעֵינֵי	יְהוָה
'al-yisrā'ēl	'eser	shānîm	beshōmerôn		wayya'as	hāra'	be'ênê	yehwāh
over Israel	ten	years	in Samaria		and he did	what is evil	in the eyes of	Yahweh

3940	5681.111	4623, 6142	2496	3493	1158, 5203	866, 2490.511
neg part	v Qal pf 3ms	prep, prep	*n fp*	pn	*n ms*, pn	rel pron, v Hiphil pf 3ms
לֹא	סָר	מֵעַל	חַטֹּאות	יָרָבְעָם	בֶּן־נְבָט	אֲשֶׁר־הֶחֱטִיא
lō'	sār	mē'al	chattō'wth	yārov'ām	ben-nevāt	'ăsher-hechĕtî'
not	he turned aside	from beside	the sins of	Jeroboam	the son of Nebat	who he caused to sin

881, 3547	3725, 3219		971.111	6565	4567, 831	6142, 800
do, pn	*adj*, n mp, ps 3ms	**19.**	v Qal pf 3ms	pn	*n ms*, pn	prep, art, n fs
אֶת־יִשְׂרָאֵל	כָּל־יָמָיו		בָּא	פוּל	מֶלֶךְ־אַשּׁוּר	עַל־הָאָרֶץ
'eth-yisrā'ēl	kol-yāmâv		bā'	phûl	melekh-'ashshûr	'al-hā'ārets
Israel	all his days		he came	Pul	the king of Assyria	against the land

5598.121	4650	3937, 6565	512	3724, 3826B	3937, 2030.141	3135
cj, v Qal impf 3ms	pn	prep, pn	num	*n fs*, n ms	prep, v Qal inf con	n fd, ps 3ms
וַיִּתֵּן	מְנַחֵם	לְפוּל	אֶלֶף	כִּכַּר־כָּסֶף	לִהְיוֹת	יָדָיו
wayyittēn	menachēm	lephûl	'eleph	kikkar-kāseph	lihyôth	yādhâv
and he gave	Menahem	to Pul	one thousand	talents of silver	to be	his hands

882	3937, 2480.541	4608	904, 3135		3428.521
prep, ps 3ms	prep, v Hiphil inf con	art, n fs	prep, n fs, ps 3ms	**20.**	cj, v Hiphil impf 3ms
אִתּוֹ	לְהַחֲזִיק	הַמַּמְלָכָה	בְּיָדוֹ		וַיֹּצֵא
'ittô	lehachzîq	hammamlākhāh	beyādhô		wayyōtsē'
with him	to make firm	the kingdom	in his hand		and he caused to go out

4650	881, 3826B	6142, 3547	6142	3725, 1399	2524
pn	do, art, n ms	prep, pn	prep	*adj*, *n mp*	art, n ms
מְנַחֵם	אֶת־הַכֶּסֶף	עַל־יִשְׂרָאֵל	עַל	כָּל־גִּבּוֹרֵי	הַחַיִל
menachēm	'eth-hakkeseph	'al-yisrā'ēl	'al	kol-gibbôrê	hachayil
Menahem	the silver	opposite Israel	opposite	all the mighty men of	the wealth

16. Then Menahem smote Tiphsah, and all that were therein, and the coasts thereof from Tirzah: ... sent destruction on Tappuah and all the people in it, and its limits, *BB* ... conquered Tiphsah and all who were there and its territory near Tirzah, *Beck* ... sacked Tappuah—killing all who were in it—and its territory from Tirzah onwards, *JB* ... punished Tappuah, all the inhabitants of the town and of its whole district, *NAB*.

because they opened not to him, therefore he smote it: ... they would not let him come in, *BB* ... he destroyed it, *Beck* ... if a city refused to open, he razed it, *Berkeley* ... because they did not surrender, *Fenton* ... it had not opened its gates to him; he sacked the town, *JB*.

and all the women therein that were with child he ripped up: ... with child cut open, *BB* ... ripping open all the pregnant women, *Beck* ... with child, he disemboweled, *Goodspeed* ... ripped up the wombs, too, *Knox*.

17. In the nine and thirtieth year of Azariah king of Judah began Menahem the son of Gadi to reign over Israel, and reigned ten years in Samaria: ... In the thirty-ninth year, *NRSV* ... became king over Israel, *NASB* ... began to rule, *NLT*.

18. And he did that which was evil in the sight of the Lord: he departed not all his days from the sins of Jeroboam the son of Nebat, who made Israel to sin: ... what was displeasing to Yahweh, *Anchor* ... did not keep himself from the sin, *BB* ... wrong before the LORD and all his life didn't give up the, *Beck* ... sinned against the Lord, following the wicked example of King Jeroboam son of Nebat, who led Israel into sin to the day of his death, *Good News*.

19. And Pul the king of Assyria came against the land: ... invaded the country, *JB* ... through his reign the country suffered invasion by Phul, *Knox*.

and Menahem gave Pul a thousand talents of silver, that his hand might be with him to confirm the kingdom in his hand: ... in return for his support in strengthening his hold on the royal power, *JB* ... to establish the kingdom under his rule, *Goodspeed* ... to win support for his claim to the throne, *Knox* ... to gain his help in confirming his royal power, *Moffatt*.

20. And Menahem exacted the money of Israel, even of all the mighty men of wealth, of each man fifty shekels of silver, to give to the king of Assyria: ... laid a tax upon Israel, on all that were mighty and rich, *Douay* ... taxed Israel to pay about one and one-fourth pounds of silver to each soldier, *NCV* ... extorted the money from the rich of Israel, demanding that each of them pay twenty ounces of silver in the form of a special tax, *NLT* ... levied the silver, *Anchor*.

So the king of Assyria turned back, and stayed not there in the land: ... king left, *NCV* ... withdrew without occupying the country, *NEB* ... stayed in the land no longer, *NIV* ... from attacking Israel and did not stay, *NLT*.

21. And the rest of the acts of Menahem, and all that he did, are they not written in the book of the chronicles of the kings of Israel?: ... history and everything he did, aren't they recorded, *Beck* ... are they

---

own century are not that hard to find), it should be borne in mind that such were commonly a feature of warfare in the ancient Near East. As Hobbs (WBC, 197) notes, "Such deeds were regarded as the right of the victor, and ought not to be judged by modern philosophies of international conflict. ... Siege warfare, perfected by the Assyrian at this time, was a particularly horrible form of conflict. Slaughter of civilians of towns under siege was something the Assyrians had added to their repertoire of warfare."

In vv. 19f, "Pul" (the powerful Assyrian monarch Tiglath-Pileser III [744–727]), makes his first appearance in the Bible. As Cogan and Tadmor (AB, 171f) note, "Pul" was a short form of Tiglath-Pileser's name, also known in late cuneiform sources, and it is a well-attested Assyrian name meaning "limestone (block)." It probably did not represent a throne name of the Assyrian king (as is commonly argued), and it may well have been associated in folk etymology with the term "Pileser" as a nickname. ("Tiglath-Pileser" itself is the Hebrew rendering [cf. comments on v. 29] of the Assyrian phrase Tukulti-apil-esharra, which may be translated "My trust is in the firstborn of the shrine Esharra" [the temple of the god Ashur in the city of that name].) We may be reminded of Jesus' nickname for Cephas (Aramaic, "rock," or "stone"), as "Peter" (Greek petros, GED #3935, again "rock," or "stone"; cf. Matt. 16:18; Mark 3:16).

Menahem's tribute of a thousand talents of silver for Tiglath-Pileser (v. 19), though huge (about 7 tons [34 metric tons]; cf. comments on 5:19–25), is not an implausible sum (Cogan and Tadmor [AB, 172] note that it was similar to Tiglath-Pileser's tribute exacted from Hulli king of Tabal—10 talents of gold, and 1000 talents of silver—or from Metenna king of Tyre—50 or 150 talents of gold and 2000 talents of silver; and, inasmuch as both of these kings were also usurpers, their payments bought Assyrian support, hence legitimization of their rule).

3937, 5598.141	3937, 4567	831	2675	8621	3826B	3937, 382	259
prep, v Qal inf con	prep, *n ms*	pn	num	n mp	n ms	prep, n ms	num
לָתֵת	לְמֶלֶךְ	אַשּׁוּר	חֲמִשִּׁים	שְׁקָלִים	כֶּסֶף	לְאִישׁ	אֶחָד
lāthēth	lemelekh	'ashshûr	chămishshîm	sheqālîm	keseph	le'îsh	'echādh
to give	to the king of	Assyria	fifty	shekels	silver	to a man	one

8178.121	4567	831	3940, 6198.111	8427	904, 800
cj, v Qal impf 3ms	*n ms*	pn	cj, neg part, v Qal pf 3ms	adv	prep, art, n fs
וַיָּשָׁב	מֶלֶךְ	אַשּׁוּר	וְלֹא־עָמַד	שָׁם	בָּאָרֶץ
wayyāshāv	melekh	'ashshûr	welō'-'āmadh	shām	bā'ārets
then he returned	the king of	Assyria	and he did not station	there	in the land

	3615	1745	4650	3725, 866	6449.111
21.	cj, *n ms*	*n mp*	pn	cj, *adj*, rel part	v Qal pf 3ms
	וְיֶתֶר	דִּבְרֵי	מְנַחֵם	וְכָל־אֲשֶׁר	עָשָׂה
	weyether	divrê	menachēm	wekhol-'ăsher	'āsāh
	and the remainder of	the events of	Menahem	and all which	he did

1950B, 3940, 2062	3918.156	6142, 5809	1745	3219	3937, 4567
intrg part, neg part, pers pron	v Qal pass ptc mp	prep, *n ms*	*n mp*	art, n mp	prep, *n mp*
הֲלוֹא־הֵם	כְּתוּבִים	עַל־סֵפֶר	דִּבְרֵי	הַיָּמִים	לְמַלְכֵי
hălô'-hēm	kethûvîm	'al-sēpher	divrê	hayyāmîm	lemalkhê
are they not	things written	on the scroll of	the events of	the days	of the kings of

3547		8311.121	4650	6196, 1	4566.121	6744	1158
pn	**22.**	cj, v Qal impf 3ms	pn	prep, n mp, ps 3ms	cj, v Qal impf 3ms	pn	n ms, ps 3ms
יִשְׂרָאֵל		וַיִּשְׁכַּב	מְנַחֵם	עִם־אֲבֹתָיו	וַיִּמְלֹךְ	פְּקַחְיָה	בְּנוֹ
yisrā'ēl		wayyishkav	menachēm	'im-'ăvōthâv	wayyimlōkh	peqachyāh	venô
Israel		and he lay	Menahem	with his ancestors	and he reigned	Pekahiah	his son

8809		904, 8523	2675	8523	3937, 6051	4567	3171	4566.111
prep, ps 3ms	**23.**	prep, *n fs*	num	n fs	prep, pn	*n ms*	pn	v Qal pf 3ms
תַּחְתָּיו		בִּשְׁנַת	חֲמִשִּׁים	שָׁנָה	לַעֲזַרְיָה	מֶלֶךְ	יְהוּדָה	מָלַךְ
tachtâv		bishnath	chămishshîm	shānāh	la'ăzaryāh	melekh	yehûdhāh	mālakh
instead of him		in the year of	fifty	years	of Azariah	the king of	Judah	he reigned

6744	1158, 4650	6142, 3547	904, 8497	8530		6449.121
pn	*n ms*, pn	prep, pn	prep, pn	n fd	**24.**	cj, v Qal impf 3ms
פְּקַחְיָה	בֶּן־מְנַחֵם	עַל־יִשְׂרָאֵל	בְּשֹׁמְרוֹן	שְׁנָתָיִם		וַיַּעַשׂ
peqachyāh	ven-menachēm	'al-yisrā'ēl	beshōmerôn	shenāthāyim		wayya'as
Pekahiah	the son of Menahem	over Israel	in Samaria	two years		and he did

7737	904, 6084	3176	3940	5681.111	4623, 2496	3493
art, adj	prep, *n fd*	pn	neg part	v Qal pf 3ms	prep, *n fp*	pn
הָרַע	בְּעֵינֵי	יְהוָה	לֹא	סָר	מֵחַטֹּאות	יָרָבְעָם
hāra'	be'ênê	yehwāh	lō'	sār	mēchattō'wth	yārov'ām
what is evil	in the eyes of	Yahweh	not	he turned aside	from the sins of	Jeroboam

1158, 5203	866	2490.511	881, 3547		7489.121	6142	6742
n ms, pn	rel part	v Hiphil pf 3ms	do, pn	**25.**	cj, v Qal impf 3ms	prep, ps 3ms	pn
בֶּן־נְבָט	אֲשֶׁר	הֶחֱטִיא	אֶת־יִשְׂרָאֵל		וַיִּקְשֹׁר	עָלָיו	פֶּקַח
ben-nevāt	'ăsher	hechĕtî'	'eth-yisrā'ēl		wayyiqōshōr	'ālâv	peqach
the son of Nebat	which	he caused to sin	Israel		and he conspired	against him	Pekah

1158, 7714	8388	5409.521	904, 8497	904, 783
n ms, pn	n ms, ps 3ms	cj, v Hiphil impf 3ms, ps 3ms	prep, pn	prep, *n ms*
בֶּן־רְמַלְיָהוּ	שָׁלִישׁוֹ	וַיַּכֵּהוּ	בְשֹׁמְרוֹן	בְּאַרְמוֹן
ben-remalyāhû	shālîshô	wayyakkēhû	veshōmerôn	be'armôn
the son of Remaliah	his adjutant	and he struck him down	in Samaria	in the citadel of

not told, *Berkeley* ... As to the other affairs of Menakham, and all that he did, they are related in the history of events of the days, *Fenton* ... in The History of, *Good News*.

22. And Menahem slept with his fathers; and Pekahiah his son reigned in his stead: ... fell asleep with his ancestors; his son Pekahiah succeeded him, *JB* ... he was laid to rest, *Knox* ... reigned instead of him, *Moffatt* ... Menahem died, and his son Pekahiah became king in his place, *NCV*.

23. In the fiftieth year of Azariah king of Judah Pekahiah the son of Menahem began to reign over Israel in Samaria, and reigned two years: ... became king over Israel in Samaria, *NEB*.

24. And he did that which was evil in the sight of the LORD: he departed not from the sins of Jeroboam the son of Nebat, who made Israel to sin: ... did what was displeasing to Yahweh; he did not stray from the sinful ways, *Anchor* ... wrong before the LORD. He didn't give up, *Beck* ... He sinned against the LORD, following the wicked example of King Jeroboam, *Good News* ... he defied the Lord's will, and would not forgo, *Knox*.

25. But Pekah the son of Remaliah, a captain of his, conspired against him, and smote him in Samaria, in the palace of the king's house, with Argob and Arieh, and with him fifty men of the Gileadites: ... was one of Pekahiah's captains, and he made plans against, *NCV* ... made a secret design against him, attacking him in the king's great house, *BB* ... Taking fifty men of Gilead with him, he assassinated Pekahiah, along with Argob and Arieh, in the citadel of the royal palace, *NIV* ... an officer of his, *NKJV*.

and he killed him, and reigned in his room: ... Pekah killed Pekahiah and succeeded him as king, *NIV* ... reigned in his place, *NKJV* ... he put him to death and became king, *BB*.

26. And the rest of the acts of Pekahiah, and all that he did, behold, they are written in the book of the chronicles of the kings of Israel: ... history and everything he did you will find written in the annals of, *Beck* ... The other affairs of Pekahiah, and all that he did, are recorded in the history of events during the period, *Fenton* ... The rest of the history of Pekahiah, his entire career, *JB* ... are described in, *Moffatt*.

Menahem's surrender here is usually connected to the one recorded in the annals of Tiglath-Pileser in which Menahem and other kings of the west paid tribute to the Assyrian monarch. Cogan and Tadmor date this reference to the year 738, but they note that a recently discovered stele from Iran gives a similar list of tribute bearers, and possibly should be dated to an earlier year. The fifty-shekel assessment (v. 20) would be the equivalent of the cost of a slave at current Assyrian prices (Wiseman, TOTC, 255). If the "wealthy men" had to defray the entire cost, approximately 60,000 such must have paid the price, although some of the payment may well have come from the royal treasury or such. But Hobbs (WBC, 198ff) takes clear exception to the traditional understanding of vv. 19f presupposed above; he argues, quite plausibly, that the talent paid by Menahem was to buy Assyrian military aid against Pekah's rival kingdom to the east (see comments on vv. 27–31), with the fifty shekel price being the cost of a single Assyrian mercenary (the term translated "every wealthy man" in the NIV (kol-gibbôr-hachayil, HED #3725, 1399, 2524, "all the mighty men of valor," or the like) may more naturally have meant "soldiers," than the landed gentry, as the traditional interpretation of this passage would necessitate. In any case, any anxiety by Menahem concerning military pressures from the east proved prescient in the second year of his son, Pekahiah (see the next section).

15:23–26. Pekahiah, king of Israel. Israelite accession formula, v. 23; Israelite judgment notice, v. 24; archival-style assassination notice, v. 25; "further reference" notice, v. 26.

Once again, only the briefest of notes need to be included here. The entire discussion of Pekahiah consists of stereotypical formulas, including the familiar "archival-style assassination notice." Menahem's short-lived dynasty (a total of twelve years or so) fell to one Pekah, along with fifty fellow assassins from the land of Gilead (in Trans-jordan). Yet again, we have a dynastic change, the third in the last fourteen or so years. Most scholars would connect the prophesying of Hosea with this time; indeed, Hosea's comments concerning Yahweh giving and taking away Israelite kings by compulsion seem relevant: "Where is your king, that he may save you? Where are your rulers in all your towns, of whom you said, 'Give me a king and princes?' So in my anger I gave you a king, and in my wrath I took him away" (Hos. 13:10f). Both the names "Pekahiah" and "Pekah" (the shortened form) mean "Yahweh opened [the eyes]," or "Yahweh is open-eyed or alert"; cf. Dennis T. Olson, *Anchor Bible Dictionary*, 5:214ff. (For Hobbs' interpretation of Menahem's attempts to procure Assyrian mercenaries to counteract military pressure from the east, cf. above, on vv. 17–22.)

382	2675	6196	881, 766	881, 732	1041, 4567
n ms	num	cj, prep, ps 3ms	cj, do, art, pn	do, pn	n ms, n ms
אִישׁ	חֲמִשִּׁים	וְעִמּוֹ	וְאֶת־הָאַרְיֵה	אֶת־אַרְגֹּב	בֵּית־מֶלֶךְ
'îsh	chămishshîm	we'immô	we'eth-hā'aryēh	'eth-'argōv	bêth-melekh
men	fifty	and with him	and Arieh	Argob	the house of the king

8809	4566.121	4322.521	1610	4623, 1158
prep, ps 3ms	cj, v Qal impf 3ms	cj, v Hiphil impf 3ms, ps 3ms	pn	prep, n mp
תַּחְתָּיו	וַיִּמְלֹךְ	וַיְמִיתֵהוּ	גִּלְעָדִים	מִבְּנֵי
tachtâv	wayyimlōkh	waymîthēhû	ghil'ādhîm	mibbenê
instead of him	and he reigned	and he executed him	Gileadites	from the sons of

26.

2079	6449.111	3725, 866	6744	1745	3615
intrj, ps 3mp	v Qal pf 3ms	cj, adj, rel part	pn	n mp	cj, n ms
הִנָּם	עָשָׂה	וְכָל־אֲשֶׁר	פְּקַחְיָה	דִּבְרֵי	וְיֶתֶר
hinnām	'āsāh	wekhol-'ăsher	pheqachyāh	divrê	weyether
behold they	he did	and all which	Pekahiah	the events of	and the remainder of

3547	3937, 4567	3219	1745	6142, 5809	3918.156
pn	prep, n mp	art, n mp	n mp	prep, n ms	v Qal pass ptc mp
יִשְׂרָאֵל	לְמַלְכֵי	הַיָּמִים	דִּבְרֵי	עַל־סֵפֶר	כְּתוּבִים
yisrā'ēl	lemalkhê	hayyāmîm	divrê	'al-sēpher	kethûvîm
Israel	of the kings of	the days	the events of	on the scroll of	things written

27.

4566.111	3171	4567	3937, 6051	8523	8692	2675	904, 8523
v Qal pf 3ms	pn	n ms	prep, pn	n fs	cj, num	num	prep, n fs
מָלַךְ	יְהוּדָה	מֶלֶךְ	לַעֲזַרְיָה	שָׁנָה	וּשְׁתַּיִם	חֲמִשִּׁים	בִּשְׁנַת
mālakh	yehûdhāh	melekh	la'ăzaryāh	shānāh	ûshettayim	chămishshîm	bishnath
he reigned	Judah	the king of	of Azariah	years	and two	fifty	in the year of

28. 6449.121	8523	6465	904, 8497	6142, 3547	1158, 7714	6742
cj, v Qal impf 3ms	n fs	num	prep, pn	prep, pn	n ms, pn	pn
וַיַּעַשׂ	שָׁנָה	עֶשְׂרִים	בְּשֹׁמְרוֹן	עַל־יִשְׂרָאֵל	בֶּן־רְמַלְיָהוּ	פֶּקַח
wayya'as	shānāh	'esrîm	beshōmerôn	'al-yisrā'ēl	ben-remalyāhû	peqach
and he did	years	twenty	in Samaria	over Israel	the son of Remaliah	Pekah

3493	4623, 2496	5681.111	3940	3176	904, 6084	7737
pn	prep, n fp	v Qal pf 3ms	neg part	pn	prep, n fd	art, adj
יָרָבְעָם	מִן־חַטֹּאות	סָר	לֹא	יְהוָה	בְּעֵינֵי	הָרַע
yārov'ām	min-chattō'wth	sār	lō'	yehwāh	be'ênê	hāra'
Jeroboam	from the sins of	he turned aside	not	Yahweh	in the eyes of	what is evil

6742	29. 904, 3219	881, 3547	2490.511	866	1158, 5203
pn	prep, n mp	do, pn	v Hiphil pf 3ms	rel part	n ms, pn
פֶּקַח	בִּימֵי	אֶת־יִשְׂרָאֵל	הֶחֱטִיא	אֲשֶׁר	בֶּן־נְבָט
peqach	bîmê	'eth-yisrā'ēl	hechĕtî'	'ăsher	ben-nevāt
Pekah	in the days of	Israel	he caused to sin	which	the son of Nebat

881, 6074	4089.121	831	4567	8736	8736	971.111	4567, 3547
do, pn	cj, v Qal impf 3ms	pn	n ms	pn	pn	v Qal pf 3ms	n ms, pn
אֶת־עִיּוֹן	וַיִּקַּח	אַשּׁוּר	מֶלֶךְ	פִּלְאֶסֶר	תִּגְלַת	בָּא	מֶלֶךְ־יִשְׂרָאֵל
'eth-'îyôn	wayyiqqach	'ashshûr	melekh	pil'eser	tighlath	bā'	melekh-yisrā'ēl
Ijon	and he took	Assyria	the king of	Pileser	Tiglath	he came	the king of Israel

881, 1609	881, 2780	881, 7230	881, 3348	1078	881, 1078
cj, do, art, pn	cj, do, pn	cj, do, pn	cj, do, pn	pn	cj, do, pn
וְאֶת־הַגִּלְעָד	וְאֶת־חָצוֹר	וְאֶת־קֶדֶשׁ	וְאֶת־יָנוֹחַ	בֵּית־מַעֲכָה	וְאֶת־אָבֵל
we'eth-haggil'ādh	we'eth-chātsôr	we'eth-qedhesh	we'eth-yānôach	bêth-ma'ăkhāh	we'eth-'āvēl
and the Gilead	and Hazor	and Kedesh	and Janoah	Beth-Maacah	and Abel

881, 1592 cj, do, art, pn וְאֶת־הַגָּלִילָה we'eth-haggālîlāh and the Galilee	3725 *n ms* כֹּל kōl the entirety of	800 *n fs* אֶרֶץ 'erets the land of	5503 pn נַפְתָּלִי naphtālî Naphtali	1580.521 cj, v Hiphil impf 3ms, ps 3mp וַיַּגְלֵם wayyaghlēm and he deported them	831 pn אַשּׁוּרָה 'ashshûrāh to Assyria

30.

7489.121, 7490 cj, v Qal impf 3ms, n ms וַיִּקְשָׁר־קֶשֶׁר wayyiqŏshār-qesher then he conspired a conspiracy	2021 pn הוֹשֵׁעַ hôshēa' Hoshea	1158, 429 *n ms*, pn בֶּן־אֵלָה ben-'ēlāh the son of Elah	6142, 6742 prep, pn עַל־פֶּקַח 'al-peqach against Pekah	1158, 7714 *n ms*, pn בֶּן־רְמַלְיָהוּ ben-remalyāhû the son of Remaliah

5409.521 cj, v Hiphil impf 3ms, ps 3ms וַיַּכֵּהוּ wayyakkēhû and he struck him down	4322.521 cj, v Hiphil impf 3ms, ps 3ms וַיְמִיתֵהוּ waymîthēhû and he executed him	4566.121 cj, v Qal impf 3ms וַיִּמְלֹךְ wayyimlōkh and he reigned	8809 prep, ps 3ms תַּחְתָּיו tachtâv instead of him	904, 8523 prep, *n fs* בִּשְׁנַת bishnath in the year of

27. In the two and fiftieth year of Azariah king of Judah Pekah the son of Remaliah began to reign over Israel in Samaria, and reigned twenty years: ... In the fifty-second year, *NIV* ... became king, *NASB* ... Pekah ruled twenty years, *NCV*.

28. And he did that which was evil in the sight of the LORD: he departed not from the sins of Jeroboam the son of Nebat, who made Israel to sin: ... was displeasing to Yahweh; he did not stray from the sinful ways, *Anchor* ... He did wrong before the LORD. He didn't give up the sins, *Beck* ... He sinned against the LORD, following the wicked example, *Good News* ... had led Israel to sin, and Pekah did not stop doing the same sins, *NCV*.

29. In the days of Pekah king of Israel came Tiglath-pileser king of Assyria, and took Ijon, and Abel-beth-maachah, and Janoah, and Kedesh, and Hazor, and Gilead, and Galilee, all the land of Naphtali, and carried them captive to Assyria: ... deported the people, *NIV* ... took the people to Assyria as captives, *NLT* ... He exiled their population, *Anchor* ... brought their inhabitants up, *Berkeley*.

30. And Hoshea the son of Elah made a conspiracy against Pekah the son of Remaliah, and smote him, and slew him, and reigned in his stead, in the twentieth year of Jotham the son of Uzziah: ... assailed and murdered him, and reigned in his place, *Fenton* ... plotted against King Pekah, assassinated him, and succeeded him as king, *Good News* ... overcame him and slew him, *Goodspeed* ... he attacked and killed him, and reigned in his place, *NAB*.

31. And the rest of the acts of Pekah, and all that he did, behold, they are written in the book of the chronicles of the kings of Israel: ... is written in the book of the history, *NCV* ... events of Pekah's reign are recorded in the annals, *NEB* ... history and everything he did you will find written, *Beck* ... As to the other affairs of Pekakh, and all that he did, they are related in the history of the events of the times, *Fenton*.

15:27–31. Pekah, king of Israel. Israelite accession formula, v. 27; Israelite judgment notice, v. 28; archival-style assassination notice, v. 30; "further reference" notice, v. 31.

For the meaning of the name "Pekah," see comments on vv. 17–22. As noted there, Pekah came with assassins from Gilead in Trans-jordan to take over the Israelite kingdom. This Pekah was one of the architects of the so-called Syro-Ephraimite War (cf. Isa. 7:1–6, especially v. 2) in which King Rezin of Aram and Pekah of Israel banded together against Judah, apparently during the waning days of the reign of King Jotham (cf. v. 37), as well as most definitely in the early days of his successor, King Ahaz (cf. 16:5f). They tried to pressure Judah into joining their opposition to the expanding Assyrian empire under Tiglath-Pileser (other allies in this rebellion included Kashpuna, Tyre, Ashkelon and perhaps even Egypt [cf. Henri Cazelles, *Anchor Bible Dictionary*, 6:282–85]). Isaiah the prophet counseled King Ahaz to firmly reject those pressures, for Yahweh predicted that the makeshift coalition would soon fall apart; and Isaiah then urged Ahaz to ask Yahweh for a sign, "whether in the deepest depths or in the highest heights," to confirm the veracity of his prophecy (see Isa. 7:7–11; once again, we find the familiar test of "short-term prediction"; cf. comments on 1:3f, above). Ahaz piously refused, but Isaiah gave him a sign anyway: "a virgin shall conceive, and

6465	3937, 3251	1158, 6030		3615	1745, 6742
num עֶשְׂרִים ‘esrîm twenty	prep, pn לְיוֹתָם leyôthām of Jotham	*n ms*, pn בֶּן־עֻזִּיָּה ben-‘uzîyāh the son of Uzziah	**31.**	cj, *n ms* וְיֶתֶר weyether and the remainder of	*n mp*, pn דִּבְרֵי־פֶקַח divrê-pheqach the events of Pekah

3725, 866	6449.111	2079	3918.156	6142, 5809	1745	3219
cj, *adj*, rel part וְכָל־אֲשֶׁר wekhol-'ăsher and all which	v Qal pf 3ms עָשָׂה ‘āsāh he did	intrj, ps 3mp הִנָּם hinnām behold they	v Qal pass ptc mp כְּתוּבִים kethûvîm things written	prep, *n ms* עַל־סֵפֶר ‘al-sēpher on the scroll of	*n mp* דִּבְרֵי divrê the events of	art, n mp הַיָּמִים hayyāmîm the days

3937, 4567	3547		904, 8523	8692	3937, 6742	1158, 7714	4567
prep, *n mp* לְמַלְכֵי lemalkhê of the kings of	pn יִשְׂרָאֵל yisrā'ēl Israel	**32.**	prep, *n fs* בִּשְׁנַת bishnath in the year of	num שְׁתַּיִם shettayim two	prep, pn לְפֶקַח lepheqach of Pekah	*n ms*, pn בֶּן־רְמַלְיָהוּ ben-remalyāhû the son of Remaliah	*n ms* מֶלֶךְ melekh the king of

3547	4566.111	3251	1158, 6030	4567	3171		1158, 6465
pn יִשְׂרָאֵל yisrā'ēl Israel	v Qal pf 3ms מָלַךְ mālakh he reigned	pn יוֹתָם yôthām Jotham	*n ms*, pn בֶּן־עֻזִּיָּהוּ ben-‘uzîyāhû the son of Uzziah	*n ms* מֶלֶךְ melekh the king of	pn יְהוּדָה yehûdhāh Judah	**33.**	*n ms*, num בֶּן־עֶשְׂרִים ben-‘esrîm a son of twenty

2675	8523	2030.111	904, 4566.141	8666, 6462	8523	4566.111
cj, num וְחָמֵשׁ wechāmēsh and five	n fs שָׁנָה shānāh years	v Qal pf 3ms הָיָה hāyāh he was	prep, v Qal inf con, ps 3ms בְּמָלְכוֹ vemālekhô when his reigning	num, num וְשֵׁשׁ־עֶשְׂרֵה weshēsh-‘esrēh and sixteen	n fs שָׁנָה shānāh years	v Qal pf 3ms מָלַךְ mālakh he reigned

904, 3503	8428	525	3502	1351, 6923		6449.121
prep, pn בִּירוּשָׁלָם bîrûshālām in Jerusalem	cj, *n ms* וְשֵׁם weshēm and the name of	n fs, ps 3ms אִמּוֹ 'immô his mother	pn יְרוּשָׁא yerûshā' Jerusha	*n fs*, pn בַּת־צָדוֹק bath-tsādhôq the daughter of Zadok	**34.**	cj, v Qal impf 3ms וַיַּעַשׂ wayya‘as and he did

3596	904, 6084	3176	3626, 3725	866, 6449.111	6030
art, adj הַיָּשָׁר hayyāshār what is right	prep, *n fd* בְּעֵינֵי be‘ênê in the eyes of	pn יְהוָה yehwāh Yahweh	prep, n ms כְּכֹל kekhōl according to everything	rel part, v Qal pf 3ms אֲשֶׁר־עָשָׂה 'ăsher-‘āsāh which he had done	pn עֻזִּיָּהוּ ‘uzîyāhû Uzziah

1	6449.111		7828	1154	3940	5681.116	5968	6194
n ms, ps 3ms אָבִיו 'āvîw his father	v Qal pf 3ms עָשָׂה ‘āsāh he did	**35.**	adv רַק raq only	art, n fp הַבָּמוֹת habbāmôth the high places	neg part לֹא lō' not	v Qal pf 3cp סָרוּ sārû they turned aside	adv עוֹד ‘ôdh still	art, n ms הָעָם hā‘ām the people

2159.352	7281.352	904, 1154	2000	1161.111	881, 8554
v Piel ptc mp מְזַבְּחִים mezabbechîm sacrificing	cj, v Piel ptc mp וּמְקַטְּרִים ûmeqatterîm and burning incense	prep, art, n fp בַּבָּמוֹת babbāmôth on the high places	pers pron הוּא hû' he	v Qal pf 3ms בָּנָה bānāh he built	do, *n ms* אֶת־שַׁעַר 'eth-sha‘ar the gate of

1041, 3176	6169		3615	1745	3251	866
n ms, pn בֵּית־יְהוָה bêth-yehwāh the temple of Yahweh	art, adj הָעֶלְיוֹן hā‘elyôn the upper	**36.**	cj, *n ms* וְיֶתֶר weyether and the remainder of	*n mp* דִּבְרֵי divrê the events of	pn יוֹתָם yôthām Jotham	rel part אֲשֶׁר 'ăsher which

6449.111	1950B, 3940, 2062	3918.156	6142, 5809	1745	3219
v Qal pf 3ms	intrg part, neg part, pers pron	v Qal pass ptc mp	prep, *n ms*	*n mp*	art, n mp
עָשָׂה	הֲלֹא־הֵם	כְּתוּבִים	עַל־סֵפֶר	דִּבְרֵי	הַיָּמִים
'āsāh	hălō'-hēm	kᵉthûvîm	'al-sēpher	divrê	hayyāmîm
he did	are they not	things written	on the scroll of	the events of	the days

3937, 4567	3171		904, 3219	2062	2591.511	3176	3937, 8365.541
prep, *n mp*	pn	**37.**	prep, art, n mp	art, dem pron	v Hiphil pf 3ms	pn	prep, v Hiphil inf con
לְמַלְכֵי	יְהוּדָה		בַּיָּמִים	הָהֵם	הֵחֵל	יְהוָה	לְהַשְׁלִיחַ
lᵉmalkhê	yᵉhûdhāh		bayyāmîm	hāhēm	hēchēl	yᵉhwāh	lᵉhashlîach
of the kings of	Judah		in the days	the those	He began	Yahweh	to send

32. In the second year of Pekah the son of Remaliah king of Israel began Jotham the son of Uzziah king of Judah to reign: ... came to the throne of Juda, *Knox* ... became king, *Good News* ... became king of Judah during the second year Pekah son of, *NCV*.

33. Five and twenty years old was he when he began to reign, and he reigned sixteen years in Jerusalem. And his mother's name was Jerusha, the daughter of Zadok: ... He was twenty-five years old when he came to the throne, *NEB* ... when he became king, *NIV* ... and he was ruling, *BB*.

34. And he did that which was right in the sight of the LORD: he did according to all that his father Uzziah had done: ... He obeyed the Lord's will, following in all things the example, *Knox* ... Following the example of his father Uzziah, Jotham did what was pleasing to the LORD, *Good News* ... he did exactly as, *Moffatt* ... He pleased the LORD, *NAB*.

35. Howbeit the high places were not removed: the people sacrificed and burned incense still in the high places. He built the higher gate of the house of the LORD: ... the places where gods were worshiped, *NCV* ... the hill-shrines were allowed to remain, *NEB* ... Jotham rebuilt the Upper Gate of the temple, *NIV* ... He was the builder of the higher doorway, *BB*.

36. Now the rest of the acts of Jotham, and all that he did, are they not written in the book of the chronicles of the kings of Judah?: ... history and everything he did, aren't they recorded in the annals, *Beck* ... the rest of the affairs, *Fenton* ... his entire career, is this not recorded, *JB* ... are they not all described, *Moffatt*.

37. In those days the LORD began to send against Judah Rezin the king of Syria, and Pekah the son of Remaliah: ... It was at that time that the LORD first loosed Rezin, *NAB* ... the LORD started, *Beck* ... It was while he was king that the LORD first sent, *Good News*.

bear a son, and call his name Immanuel" (Isa. 7:13f); and, as noted earlier, Isaiah ends ch. 7 of his Book with a clear warning about soliciting help from Assyria (which Ahaz nonetheless does anyway, as noted in 2 Ki. 16:7ff).

Jumping ahead to the time of Ahaz, vv. 29f of the present chapter describe Tiglath-Pileser's (for the meaning of his name, and its relation to "Pul," cf. on vv. 17–21) march against Pekah partly in response to Ahaz's pleadings. What is not said here is that he captured Damascus in 732 after a two-year siege, probably before Pekah was assassinated, (but almost certainly after Tiglath-Pileser captured "Gilead and Galilee, including all the land of Naphtali" (v. 29). The people were deported to Assyria—the first time we read of this in the Bible. Deportation of captive peoples is well documented as early as the ninth century, but the scope here is unusual. Tiglath-Pileser deported people from the west and replaced them with people from the east and south. The purpose of this policy was to break the deported populations' dependence on their native lands and create a dependence on Syria in an effort to make the captives Assyrians. We will, of course, have future occasion to return to this melancholy issue, in connection with ch. 17.

15:32–38. Jotham, king of Judah. Judahite accession formula, vv. 32f; Judahite judgment notice, vv. 34f; "further reference" notice, v. 36; Judahite burial formula, v. 38.

We finally return to a Judahite king, albeit most probably a coregent throughout most or all of his life (cf. above, on Azariah, vv. 1–7). Yet again, the present passage consists mostly of standard formulas, with only two additional archival notes (in v. 35, we are informed that Jotham rebuilt the "Upper Gate" to the Temple; and in v. 37, the reference to the beginning of the Syro-Ephraimite War [cf. above, on vv. 27–31] is to be found). Once again, much more can be found about this Judahite king in the chronicler's work (cf. 2 Chr. 27:1–9), including the completion of other building projects in Jerusalem and around

904, 3171	7819	4567	782	881	6742	1158, 7714		8311.121
prep, pn	pn	*n ms*	pn	cj, do	pn	*n ms*, pn	**38.**	cj, v Qal impf 3ms
בִּיהוּדָה	רְצִין	מֶלֶךְ	אֲרָם	וְאֵת	פֶּקַח	בֶּן־רְמַלְיָהוּ		וַיִּשְׁכַּב
bîhûdhāh	retsîn	melekh	'ărām	we'ēth	peqach	ben-remalyāhû		wayyishkav
into Judah	Rezin	the king of	Aram	and	Pekah	the son of Remaliah		and he lay

3251	6196, 1	7196.221	6196, 1	904, 6111	1784	1
pn	prep, n mp, ps 3ms	cj, v Niphil impf 3ms	prep, n mp, ps 3ms	prep, *n fs*	pn	n ms, ps 3ms
יוֹתָם	עִם־אֲבֹתָיו	וַיִּקָּבֵר	עִם־אֲבֹתָיו	בְּעִיר	דָּוִד	אָבִיו
yôthām	'im-'ăvōthâv	wayyiqqāvēr	'im-'ăvōthâv	be'îr	dāwidh	'āvîw
Jotham	with his ancestors	and he was buried	with his ancestors	in the city of	David	his ancestor

4566.121	271	1158	8809		904, 8523	8124, 6462	8523
cj, v Qal impf 3ms	pn	n ms, ps 3ms	prep, ps 3ms	**16:1**	prep, *n fs*	num, num	n fs
וַיִּמְלֹךְ	אָחָז	בְּנוֹ	תַּחְתָּיו		בִּשְׁנַת	שְׁבַע־עֶשְׂרֵה	שָׁנָה
wayyimlōkh	'āchāz	benô	tachtâv		bishnath	sheva'-'esrēh	shānāh
and he reigned	Ahaz	his son	instead of him		in the year of	seventeen	years

3937, 6742	1158, 7714	4566.111	271	1158, 3251	4567	3171
prep, pn	*n ms*, pn	v Qal pf 3ms	pn	*n ms*, pn	*n ms*	pn
לְפֶקַח	בֶּן־רְמַלְיָהוּ	מָלַךְ	אָחָז	בֶּן־יוֹתָם	מֶלֶךְ	יְהוּדָה
lepheqach	ben-remalyāhû	mālakh	'āchāz	ben-yôthām	melekh	yehûdhāh
of Pekah	the son of Remaliah	he reigned	Ahaz	the son of Jotham	the king of	Judah

	1158, 6465	8523	271	904, 4566.141	8666, 6462	8523	4566.111
2.	*n ms*, num	n fs	pn	prep, v Qal inf con, ps 3ms	num, num	n fs	v Qal pf 3ms
	בֶּן־עֶשְׂרִים	שָׁנָה	אָחָז	בְּמָלְכוֹ	וְשֵׁשׁ־עֶשְׂרֵה	שָׁנָה	מָלַךְ
	ben-'esrîm	shānāh	'āchāz	bemālekhô	weshēsh-'esrēh	shānāh	mālakh
	a son of twenty	years	Ahaz	when his reigning	and sixteen	years	he reigned

904, 3503	3940, 6449.111	3596	904, 6084	3176	435	3626, 1784
prep, pn	cj, neg part, v Qal pf 3ms	art, adj	prep, *n fd*	pn	n mp, ps 3ms	prep, pn
בִּירוּשָׁלָם	וְלֹא־עָשָׂה	הַיָּשָׁר	בְּעֵינֵי	יְהוָה	אֱלֹהָיו	כְּדָוִד
bîrûshālām	welō'-'āsāh	hayyāshār	be'ênê	yehwāh	'ĕlōhâv	kedhāwidh
in Jerusalem	and he did not do	what is right	in the eyes of	Yahweh	his God	like David

1		2050.121	904, 1932	4567	3547	1612	881, 1158
n ms, ps 3ms	**3.**	cj, v Qal impf 3ms	prep, *n ms*	*n mp*	pn	cj, cj	do, n ms, ps 3ms
אָבִיו		וַיֵּלֶךְ	בְּדֶרֶךְ	מַלְכֵי	יִשְׂרָאֵל	וְגַם	אֶת־בְּנוֹ
'āvîw		wayyēlekh	bedherekh	malkhê	yisrā'ēl	wegham	'eth-benô
his father		and he walked	in the way of	the kings of	Israel	and also	his son

5882.511	904, 813	3626, 8774	1504	866
v Hiphil pf 3ms	prep, art, n fs	prep, *n fp*	art, n mp	rel part
הֶעֱבִיר	בָּאֵשׁ	כְּתֹעֲבוֹת	הַגּוֹיִם	אֲשֶׁר
he'ĕvîr	bā'ēsh	kethō'ăvôth	haggôyim	'ăsher
he caused to pass through	in the fire	like the detestable things of	the nations	which

3542.511	3176	881	4623, 6686	1158	3547		2159.321
v Hiphil pf 3ms	pn	do, ps 3mp	prep, *n mp*	*n mp*	pn	**4.**	cj, v Piel impf 3ms
הוֹרִישׁ	יְהוָה	אֹתָם	מִפְּנֵי	בְּנֵי	יִשְׂרָאֵל		וַיְזַבֵּחַ
hôrîsh	yehwāh	'ōthām	mippenê	benê	yisrā'ēl		wayzabbēach
He dispossessed	Yahweh	them	from before	the sons of	Israel		and he sacrificed

7281.321	904, 1154	6142, 1421	8809	3725, 6320	7776
cj, v Piel impf 3ms	prep, art, n fp	cj, prep, art, n fp	cj, prep	*adj*, n ms	adj
וַיְקַטֵּר	בַּבָּמוֹת	וְעַל־הַגְּבָעוֹת	וְתַחַת	כָּל־עֵץ	רַעֲנָן
wayqattēr	babbāmôth	we'al-haggevā'ôth	wethachath	kol-'ēts	ra'ănān
and he burned incense	on the high places	and on the hills	and beneath	all the trees	luxuriant

38. And Jotham slept with his fathers, and was buried with his fathers in the city of David his father: and Ahaz his son reigned in his stead: ... fell asleep with his ancestors, *JB* ... with them in his forefather's, *NAB* ... the throne passed to his son Achaz, *Knox* ... reigned instead of him, *Moffatt*.

16:1. In the seventeenth year of Pekah the son of Remaliah Ahaz the son of Jotham king of Judah began to reign: ... became king, *Anchor* ... came to the throne of Juda, *Knox*.

2. Twenty years old was Ahaz when he began to reign, and reigned sixteen years in Jerusalem, and did not that which was right in the sight of the LORD his God, like David his father: ... came to the throne, *NEB* ... Unlike David his father, he did not do, *NIV* ... He did not do what was pleasing, *Anchor* ... He didn't do what was right in the presence, *Beck*.

3. But he walked in the way of the kings of Israel, yea, and made his son to pass through the fire, according to the abominations of the heathen, whom the LORD cast out from before the children of Israel: ... He followed the path of the kings of Israel, and even passed his children, *Fenton* ... dispossessed, *Berkeley* ... and followed the example of the kings of Israel. He even sacrificed his own son as a burnt offering to idols, imitating the disgusting practice of the people whom the LORD had driven out of the land as the Israelites advanced, *Good News* ... he lived on the lines of the kings of Israel, and he actually burned his son alive in sacrifice, following the abominable practice of the nations whom the Eternal had dispossessed to make room for Israel, *Moffatt*.

4. And he sacrificed and burnt incense in the high places, and on the hills, and under every green tree: ... at the places where gods were worshiped, *NCV* ... under every leafy tree, *NAB* ... He slaughtered and burnt sacrifices at the hill-shrines and on the hill-tops and under every spreading tree, *NEB* ... at the pagan shrines, *NLT*.

---

the nation of Judah and his decisive defeat of the Ammonites, with his imposition of substantial tribute upon them for three years. The chronicler, however, makes no mention of the material found in v. 37, keeping all references to the Syro-Ephraimite War to the time of Jotham's son Ahaz (cf. the extensive account found in 2 Chr. 28:5–15 to the disasters Ahaz faced from both Aram and Israel). Instead, the chronicler gives this simple epitaph for King Jotham: "Jotham grew powerful because he walked steadfastly before Yahweh his God" (2 Chr. 27:6). If only that could be our simple epitaph at the end of our lives, too.

16:1–20. *Ahaz, the apostate king of Judah. We now continue the story of the Judahite monarchy, but this time with a completely reprobate king. He was religious, to be sure—relentlessly religious, in fact. But he was far from being faithful to the true God Yahweh. He followed, not David his ancestor, but rather the kings of Israel, even to the point of "sacrificing his own son in the fire" (cf. v. 3, NIV). He also followed the ways of the nations the Israelites dispossessed so long ago, offering sacrifices and worshiping seemingly at every location possible (cf. v. 4). Ahaz was truly a wicked king from the point of view of the writer of 2 Kings, and the relatively great detail included in the description of his reign only provides more grist for the mill. To be religiously fervent and devout—carelessly and uncritically—can actually be an abomination to Yahweh our God.*

16:1–4. Introduction: Judahite accession formula (vv. 1–2a); Judahite judgment notice with corroborating details (vv. 2b–4). For references to prior discussions of these formulas, see the introduction to ch. 15. Ahaz's accession formula lacks any reference to the queen mother, a curious omission (such are also lacking in connection with David, Solomon and Jehoram; cf. on 8:25–29). Suggested dates for Ahaz's accession vary from scholar to scholar, depending on how one reckons the regnal data for Azariah and Jotham (cf. on 15:1–7), as well as how one handles the issue of the accession of Hezekiah (cf. discussion on 18:1–4). Suffice it to note here that Albright preferred 735 for Ahaz's accession; Thiele, 732 (with a co-regency with Jotham in 735); and Cogan and Tadmor, 743. It is hard to date Ahaz's accession much earlier than 736 if one takes seriously the reference in 15:37 to Rezin king of Aram and Pekah (king of Israel) son of Remaliah pressuring Judah already in the days of Jotham. Compare Hobbs' brief excursus on the issue (WBC, 204f), for a good overview.

As already noted, the verdict on Ahaz is unrelentingly negative. The Judahite judgment notice explicitly contrasts him to his ancestor David, one of only four kings to be so contrasted (the three others were Solomon [1 Ki. 11:4], Abijam [15:3], and Amaziah [14:3; but Amaziah nonetheless does receive some praise]). And once again, Ahaz is compared to the "kings of Israel"—only one other Judahite king (Jehoram in 8:18; but also cf. Ahaziah in 8:27) is so negatively characterized. Finally, Ahaz is characterized as "following the detestable ways of the nations Yahweh had driven out before

5.	226	6148.121	7819	4567, 782	6742	1158, 7714	4567, 3547
	adv	v Qal impf 3ms	pn	*n ms*, pn	cj, pn	*n ms*, pn	*n ms*, pn
	אָז	יַעֲלֶה	רְצִין	מֶלֶךְ־אֲרָם	וּפֶקַח	בֶּן־רְמַלְיָהוּ	מֶלֶךְ־יִשְׂרָאֵל
	'āz	ya'ăleh	retsîn	melekh-'ărām	ûpheqach	ben-remalyāhû	melekh-yisrā'ēl
	then	he came up to	Rezin	the king of Aram	and Pekah	the son of Remaliah	the king of Israel

3503	3937, 4560	6961.126	6142, 271	3940	3310.116
pn	prep, art, n fs	cj, v Qal impf 3mp	prep, pn	cj, neg part	v Qal pf 3cp
יְרוּשָׁלַם	לַמִּלְחָמָה	וַיָּצֻרוּ	עַל־אָחָז	וְלֹא	יָכְלוּ
yerûshālam	lammilchāmāh	wayyātsurû	'al-'āchāz	welō'	yākhelû
Jerusalem	to the battle	and they besieged	against Ahaz	and not	they were able

3937, 4032.241	**6.**	904, 6496	2026	8178.511	7819	4567, 782
prep, v Niphal inf con		prep, art, n fs	art, dem pron	v Hiphil pf 3ms	pn	*n ms*, pn
לְהִלָּחֵם		בָּעֵת	הַהִיא	הֵשִׁיב	רְצִין	מֶלֶךְ־אֲרָם
lehillāchēm		bā'ēth	hahî'	hēshîv	retsîn	melekh-'ărām
to fight		at the time	the that	he caused to return	Rezin	the king of Aram

881, 369	3937, 782	5577.321	881, 3173	4623, 363	784	971.116
do, pn	prep, pn	cj, v Piel impf 3ms	do, pn	prep, pn	cj, pn	v Qal pf 3cp
אֶת־אֵילַת	לַאֲרָם	וַיְנַשֵּׁל	אֶת־הַיְהוּדִים	מֵאֵילוֹת	וַאֲרַמִּים	בָּאוּ
'eth-'êlath	la'ărām	waynashshēl	'eth-hayhûdhîm	mē'êlôth	wa'ărammîm	bā'û
Elath	to Aram	and he drove away	the Jews	from Elath	and the Arameans	they came

369	3553.126	8427	5912	3219	2172	**7.**	8365.121	271	4534
pn	cj, v Qal impf 3mp	adv	adv	art, n ms	art, dem pron		cj, v Qal impf 3ms	pn	n mp
אֵילַת	וַיֵּשְׁבוּ	שָׁם	עַד	הַיּוֹם	הַזֶּה		וַיִּשְׁלַח	אָחָז	מַלְאָכִים
'êlath	wayyēshevû	shām	'adh	hayyôm	hazzeh		wayyishlach	'āchāz	mal'ākhîm
Elath	and they dwelled	there	until	the day	the this		and he sent out	Ahaz	messengers

420, 8736	8736	4567, 831	3937, 569.141	5860	1158	603
prep, pn	pn	*n ms*, pn	prep, v Qal inf con	n ms, ps 2ms	cj, n ms, ps 2ms	pers pron
אֶל־תִּגְלַת	פְּלֶסֶר	מֶלֶךְ־אַשּׁוּר	לֵאמֹר	עַבְדְּךָ	וּבִנְךָ	אָנִי
'el-tighlath	peleser	melekh-'ashshûr	lē'mōr	'avdekhā	ûvinekhā	'ānî
to Tiglath	Pileser	the king of Assyria	saying	your servant	and your son	I

6148.131	3588.531	4623, 3834	4567, 782	4623, 3834
v Qal impv 2ms	cj, v Hiphil impv 2ms, ps 1cs	prep, *n fs*	*n ms*, pn	cj, prep, *n fs*
עֲלֵה	וְהוֹשִׁעֵנִי	מִכַּף	מֶלֶךְ־אֲרָם	וּמִכַּף
'ălēh	wehôshi'ēnî	mikkaph	melekh-'ărām	ûmikkaph
come up	and deliver me	from the palm of	the king of Aram	and from the palm of

4567	3547	7251.152	6142	**8.**	4089.121	271	881, 3826B
n ms	pn	art, v Qal act ptc mp	prep, ps 1cs		cj, v Qal impf 3ms	pn	do, art, n ms
מֶלֶךְ	יִשְׂרָאֵל	הַקּוֹמִים	עָלָי		וַיִּקַּח	אָחָז	אֶת־הַכֶּסֶף
melekh	yisrā'ēl	haqqômîm	'ālāy		wayyiqqach	'āchāz	'eth-hakkeseph
the king of	Israel	those rising up	against me		and he took	Ahaz	the silver

881, 2174	4834.255	1041	3176	904, 212	1041
cj, do, art, n ms	art, v Niphal ptc ms	*n ms*	pn	cj, prep, *n mp*	*n ms*
וְאֶת־הַזָּהָב	הַנִּמְצָא	בֵּית	יְהוָה	וּבְאֹצְרוֹת	בֵּית
we'eth-hazzāhāv	hanimtsā'	bêth	yehwāh	ûve'ōtserôth	bêth
and the gold	what was found	the temple of	Yahweh	and in the treasuries of	the household of

4567	8365.121	3937, 4567, 831	8245	**9.**	8471.121	420
art, n ms	cj, v Qal impf 3ms	prep, *n ms*, pn	n ms		cj, v Qal impf 3ms	prep, ps 3ms
הַמֶּלֶךְ	וַיִּשְׁלַח	לְמֶלֶךְ־אַשּׁוּר	שֹׁחַד		וַיִּשְׁמַע	אֵלָיו
hammelekh	wayyishlach	lemelekh-'ashshûr	shōchadh		wayyishma'	'ēlāv
the king	and he sent out	to the king of Assyria	a bribe		and he listened	to him

5. Then Rezin king of Syria and Pekah son of Remaliah king of Israel came up to Jerusalem to war: and they besieged Ahaz, but could not overcome him: conquer him, *NRSV* ... attacked Jerusalem and besieged Ahaz but could not bring him to battle, *REB* ... they were not able to attack, *Anchor* ... they made an attack on Ahaz, shutting him in, *BB*.

6. At that time Rezin king of Syria recovered Elath to Syria, and drave the Jews from Elath: and the Syrians came to Elath, and dwelt there unto this day: ... King Rezin of Aram gave Elath back to Edom, driving the Judeans out, *Beck* ... regained Elath for Edom, clearing the Jews completely out of Elath, *Berkeley* ... and settled them, *Fenton* ... The Edomites settled in Elath and still live there, *Good News*.

7. So Ahaz sent messengers to Tiglath-pileser king of Assyria, saying, I am thy servant and thy son: come up, and save me out of the hand of the king of Syria, and out of the hand of the king of Israel, which rise up against me: ... and your friend, *NCV* ... and vassal, *NIV* ... deliver me ... who are besieging me, *Goodspeed* ... rescue me from the king of Aram and the king of Israel who are making war on me, *JB*.

8. And Ahaz took the silver and gold that was found in the house of the LORD, and in the treasures of the king's house, and sent it for a present to the king of Assyria: ... LORD's temple and in storerooms of the king's palace, *Beck* ... deposited in, *Berkeley* ... and sent a bribe, *Anchor* ... sent them as an offering, *BB*.

9. And the king of Assyria hearkened unto him: for the king of Assyria went up against Damascus, and took it, and carried the people of it captive to Kir, and slew Rezin: ... listened to him, *Goodspeed* ... granted his request and, marching on Damascus, captured it; he deported its population to Kir and put Razon to death, *JB* ... Tiglath Pileser, in answer to Ahaz' plea, marched out with his army against Damascus, captured it, killed King Rezin, and took the people to Kir as prisoners, *Good News* ... and carried the people of it away into exile to Kir, *NASB*.

---

the Israelites" (cf. Manasseh in 21:2, below). Surely, Ahaz is depicted as evil incarnate, as it were. If we need more convincing, the writer immediately adds that Ahaz (literally) "made his son pass through the fire" (v. 6), a phrase traditionally understood as child sacrifice, although the exact meaning of the phrase remains unclear (cf. Hobbs, WBC, 213). (For further discussion of this heinous rite, see above, on 3:26f.)

The name "Ahaz" means "[Yahweh] holds," or "[Yahweh] has overcome," or the like (cf. comments on 13:1–9; as noted there, the name "Ahaziah" also comes from the same Hebrew root). Scholars such as W. F. Albright have emphasized that Ahaz's name is probably a short form of the name "Jehoahaz"; in fact, in his influential "Chronology" article (*Bulletin of the American Schools of Oriental Research*, 100 [1945], 16–22), Albright calls the present king "Jehoahaz I," and the later Jehoahaz (successor to Josiah) "Jehoahaz II."

16:5–9. The Syro-Ephraimite War. Both the background and the result of this war were previously discussed (cf. on 15:27–31; also cf. the brief reference in comments on 15:32–38 concerning the chronicler's treatment of Ahaz in 2 Chr. 28:5–15 [and see below for more on this last point]). Seemingly, the enemy coalition was threatening Judah before Ahaz came to the throne, although the onus for the decision to solicit help from Assyria is evidently his alone (once again, cf. Isa. 7). But to be fair to this relatively young king, he did face a fearsome enemy coalition as soon as he ascended to the throne, and he had thus some hard decisions to make very early in his reign. Still, with a prophetic adviser as worthy as Isaiah by his side, one would have hoped that Ahaz would have taken his advice more seriously (it seems that generally, even from the time of David himself, the Judahite kings would have "court prophets" available to consult for determining the will of Yahweh—once again emblematic of the "uneasy compromise" between king and prophet discussed on 1:16f).

As just noted, only the prophet could deliver the divine oracle, and Isaiah surely does that in 7:7ff of his Book: "It will not take place, it will not happen .... If you do not stand firm in your faith, you will not stand at all" (vv. 7, 9). But in this same passage in Isaiah, there is an important detail concerning the enemy coalition which has not yet been pointed out. It seems that Kings Rezin and Pekah had already picked out a successor to the young Judahite King Ahaz, namely one "son of Tabeel." Notice that the actual name "Pekah" is never mentioned by Isaiah, only the dismissive epithet "son of Remaliah," thus emphasizing his being a usurper to the throne. (Also, cf. Isa. 7:6; the name "Tabeel" refers to the Phoenician king Ittoba'al [also known as Ethbaal II; cf. H. J. Katzenstein, *Anchor Bible Dictionary*, 6:686–92.) This detail sheds further light on Ahaz's evident alarm (cf. vv. 7f of the pre-

4567	831	6148.121	4567	831	420, 1894	8945.121
n ms	pn	cj, v Qal impf 3ms	*n ms*	pn	prep, pn	cj, v Qal impf 3ms, ps 3fs
מֶלֶךְ	אַשּׁוּר	וַיַּעַל	מֶלֶךְ	אַשּׁוּר	אֶל־דַּמֶּשֶׂק	וַיִּתְפְּשֶׂהָ
melekh	'ashshûr	wayya'al	melekh	'ashshûr	'el-dammeseq	wayyithpeseāh
the king of	Assyria	and he went up	the king of	Assyria	unto Damascus	and he captured it

1580.521	7307	881, 7819	4322.511		2050.121	4567	271
cj, v Hiphil impf 3ms, ps 3fs	pn	cj, do, pn	v Hiphil pf 3ms	**10.**	cj, v Qal impf 3ms	art, n ms	pn
וַיַּגְלֶהָ	קִירָה	וְאֶת־רְצִין	הֵמִית		וַיֵּלֶךְ	הַמֶּלֶךְ	אָחָז
wayyaghleāh	qîrāh	we'eth-retsîn	hēmîth		wayyēlekh	hammelekh	'āchāz
and he deported it	to Kir	and Rezin	he executed		and he went to	the king	Ahaz

3937, 7410.141	8736	8736	4567, 831	1802	7495.121	881, 4326
prep, v Qal inf con	pn	pn	*n ms*, pn	pn	cj, v Qal impf 3ms	do, art, n ms
לִקְרַאת	תִּגְלַת	פִּלְאֶסֶר	מֶלֶךְ־אַשּׁוּר	דּוּמֶּשֶׂק	וַיַּרְא	אֶת־הַמִּזְבֵּחַ
liqōra'th	tighlath	pil'eser	melekh-'ashshûr	dûmmeseq	wayyare'	'eth-hammizbēach
to meet	Tiglath	Pileser	the king of Assyria	Damascus	and he saw	the altar

866	904, 1894	8365.121	4567	271	420, 222	3669	881, 1883
rel part	prep, pn	cj, v Qal impf 3ms	art, n ms	pn	prep, pn	art, n ms	do, *n fs*
אֲשֶׁר	בְּדַמָּשֶׂק	וַיִּשְׁלַח	הַמֶּלֶךְ	אָחָז	אֶל־אוּרִיָּה	הַכֹּהֵן	אֶת־דְּמוּת
'ăsher	bedhammāseq	wayyishlach	hammelekh	'āchāz	'el-'ûrîyāh	hakkōhēn	'eth-demûth
which	in Damascus	and he sent out	the king	Ahaz	to Uriah	the priest	a likeness of

4326	881, 8732	3937, 3725, 4801		1161.121	222	3669
art, n ms	cj, do, n fs, ps 3ms	prep, *adj*, n ms, ps 3ms	**11.**	cj, v Qal impf 3ms	pn	art, n ms
הַמִּזְבֵּחַ	וְאֶת־תַּבְנִיתוֹ	לְכָל־מַעֲשֵׂהוּ		וַיִּבֶן	אוּרִיָּה	הַכֹּהֵן
hammizbēach	we'eth-tavnîthô	lekhol-ma'ăsēhû		wayyiven	'ûrîyāh	hakkōhēn
the altar	and its pattern	of all its workmanship		and he built	Uriah	the priest

881, 4326	3626, 3725	866, 8365.111	4567	271	4623, 1894
do, art, n ms	prep, n ms	rel pron, v Qal pf 3ms	art, n ms	pn	prep, pn
אֶת־הַמִּזְבֵּחַ	כְּכֹל	אֲשֶׁר־שָׁלַח	הַמֶּלֶךְ	אָחָז	מִדַּמֶּשֶׂק
'eth-hammizbēach	kekhōl	'ăsher-shālach	hammelekh	'āchāz	middammeseq
the altar	according to everything	that he sent	the king	Ahaz	from Damascus

3772	6449.111	222	3669	5912, 971.141	4567, 271	4623, 1894
adv	v Qal pf 3ms	pn	art, n ms	adv, v Qal inf con	art, n ms, pn	prep, pn
כֵּן	עָשָׂה	אוּרִיָּה	הַכֹּהֵן	עַד־בּוֹא	הַמֶּלֶךְ־אָחָז	מִדַּמָּשֶׂק
kēn	'āsāh	'ûrîyāh	hakkōhēn	'adh-bô'	hammelekh-'āchāz	middammāseq
so	he made	Uriah	the priest	until the coming of	the king Ahaz	from Damascus

	971.121	4567	4623, 1894	7495.121	4567	881, 4326
12.	cj, v Qal impf 3ms	art, n ms	prep, pn	cj, v Qal impf 3ms	art, n ms	do, art, n ms
	וַיָּבֹא	הַמֶּלֶךְ	מִדַּמֶּשֶׂק	וַיַּרְא	הַמֶּלֶךְ	אֶת־הַמִּזְבֵּחַ
	wayyāvō'	hammelekh	middammeseq	wayyare'	hammelekh	'eth-hammizbēach
	and he came	the king	from Damascus	and he saw	the king	the altar

7414.121	4567	6142, 4326	6148.121	6142
cj, v Qal impf 3ms	art, n ms	prep, art, n ms	cj, v Qal impf 3ms	prep, ps 3ms
וַיִּקְרַב	הַמֶּלֶךְ	עַל־הַמִּזְבֵּחַ	וַיַּעַל	עָלָיו
wayyiqōrav	hammelekh	'al-hammizbēach	wayya'al	'ālâv
and he came near	the king	beside the altar	and he went up	on it

	7281.521	881, 6150	881, 4647	5445.521
13.	cj, v Hiphil impf 3ms	do, n fs, ps 3ms	cj, do, n fs, ps 3ms	cj, v Hiphil impf 3ms
	וַיַּקְטֵר	אֶת־עֹלָתוֹ	וְאֶת־מִנְחָתוֹ	וַיַּסֵּךְ
	wayyaqṭēr	'eth-'ōlāthô	we'eth-minchāthô	wayyassēkh
	and he sent up in smoke	his burnt offering	and his offering	and he poured out

10. And king Ahaz went to Damascus to meet Tiglath-pileser king of Assyria, and saw an altar that was at Damascus: and king Ahaz sent to Urijah the priest the fashion of the altar, and the pattern of it, according to all the workmanship thereof: ... he sent plans and a pattern of this altar to, *NCV* ... sent to Uriah the priest a sketch of the altar, with detailed plans for its construction, *NIV* ... sent a model of the altar and a plan with all details, *Anchor* ... giving the design of it and all the details of its structure, *BB*.

11. And Urijah the priest built an altar according to all that king Ahaz had sent from Damascus: so Urijah the priest made it against king Ahaz came from Damascus: ... made it exactly according to all the directions King Ahaz sent from Damascus and waited for King Ahaz to come home from, *Beck* ... Uriah built an altar just like it and finished it before Ahaz returned, *Good News* ... constructed the altar; all the instructions sent by King Ahaz from Damascus were carried out, *JB* ... and had it ready, *Moffatt*.

12. And when the king was come from Damascus, the king saw the altar: and the king approached to the altar, and offered thereon: ... returned from Damascus, he inspected, *Berkeley* ... and ascended it, *Anchor* ... he went up on it and made an offering on it, *BB* ... went to see it and did reverence to it, *Knox*.

13. And he burnt his burnt offering and his meat offering, and poured his drink offering, and sprinkled the blood of his peace offerings, upon the altar: ... grain offerings and ... the blood of his fellowship offerings, *NCV* ... his libation, and he splashed the blood of his recompense-offerings, *Moffatt* ... of his communion sacrifices, *JB* ... and his meal offering; he poured out his libation, and he dashed the blood of his offering of well-being against, *Anchor*.

---

sent text), as he desperately solicited help from Assyria, even stripping the silver and gold from Temple and palace for a gift (shōchadh, HED #8245, "bribe"; cf. Cogan and Tadmor, AB, 188) to the Assyrian king Tiglath-Pileser III.

Meanwhile, vv. 5f of the present passage succinctly present Rezin and Pekah as able to set siege even to the capital city Jerusalem (but evidently not succeeding in overpowering it; but, cf. 2 Chr. 28:5–15, where the chronicler there emphasizes the many prisoners and the great spoil Ahaz lost, especially to Samaria). But, even according to the Kings account, the allied enemies were depicted as clearly being able to strike deep into Judahite territory, wresting the city of Elath, the southern seaport on the Gulf of Aqaba, from the Judahites—with the result that the Edomites gained their freedom "to this day" (v. 6; Cogan and Tadmor, AB, 186, however, wish to follow the Qere [cf., on 10:18–27] reading in the Masoretic text, which speaks of the "Edomites," not the "Arameans" taking over the city [cf. also NRSV; NLT]). (For the previous vicissitudes of the Edomites, cf. above, on 8:20ff; also on 14:5ff.) In any case, as we have already seen, Tiglath-Pileser indeed marched to the west in 734, as well as again in 733, but it was not until 732 that he was able to conquer Damascus, after a two-year siege (cf. v. 9 of the present passage). Thus ends most ignominiously the grandiose scheme of the anti-Assyrian coalition—as Isaiah had prophesied, "It will not take place, it will not happen" (Isa. 7:7). (Concerning the deportation of inhabitants of defeated nations as Assyrian policy, see on 15:27–31.)

16:10–18. King Ahaz's visit to Damascus; resulting modifications in the Jerusalem temple. As Hobbs (WBC, 215) points out, "Everything in the chapter up to this point has been a preface for what follows." Quite probably, Ahaz's visit coincided with Tiglath-Pileser's takeover of the city, which once again took place in the year 732. (Cogan and Tadmor [AB, 192] suggest Ahaz traveled there to greet the victorious king.) In a move mystifying to the modern reader, Ahaz saw an altar there (in the defeated city, it should be recalled), liked it, had sketches made, and had it copied for the Jerusalem temple (cf. vv. 10f; analogous to this is Amaziah's curious devotion to the defeated Edomite deities in the chronicler's description of his reign [see 2 Chr. 25:14ff; and cf. comments on 14:8–14]).

Why would victorious kings seek to imitate the worship of defeated countries? First of all, the adoption of such worship would not necessarily be an indication of subservience to Assyria (cf. Hobbs). Even though Ahaz's earlier statement to Tiglath-Pileser, "I am your servant and vassal" (v. 7, NIV; the term for "vassal" is literally, "son") is quite likely to indicate subservience (but note the caveats both of Hobbs [WBC, 214], as well as of Cogan and Tadmor [AB, 187]), the present imitation of an Aramean altar is most likely not. Cogan and Tadmor (AB, 193) seem to be right on target here. They suggest that Ahaz's copying of the altar was an example of Israel's acculturation to the Assyrian Empire. This practice continued into the reign of King Manasseh in the seventh century. Even the high priest Uriah (vv. 11, 16; apparently a friend of Isaiah,

5447	2323.121	881, 1879, 8399	866, 3937
do, n ms, ps 3ms	cj, v Qal impf 3ms	do, *n ms*, art, n mp	rel part, prep, ps 3ms
אֶת־נִסְכּוֹ	וַיִּזְרֹק	אֶת־דַּם־הַשְּׁלָמִים	אֲשֶׁר־לוֹ
'eth-nis̲kô	wayyizrōq	'eth-dam-hashsh^{e}lāmîm	'ăsher-lô
his drink offering	and he sprinkled	the blood of the peace offering	which to him

6142, 4326		881	4326	5361	866	3937, 6686	3176
prep, art, n ms	**14.**	cj, do	art, n ms	art, n fs	rel part	prep, *n mp*	pn
עַל־הַמִּזְבֵּחַ		וְאֵת	הַמִּזְבַּח	הַנְּחֹשֶׁת	אֲשֶׁר	לִפְנֵי	יְהוָה
'al-hammizbēach		w^{e}'ēth	hammizbach	hann^{e}chōsheth	'ăsher	liphnê	y^{e}hwāh
on the altar		and	the altar	the bronze	which	before	Yahweh

7414.521	4623, 881	6686	1041	4623, 1033	4326
cj, v Hiphil impf 3ms	prep, do	*n mp*	art, n ms	prep, prep	art, n ms
וַיַּקְרֵב	מֵאֵת	פְּנֵי	הַבַּיִת	מִבֵּין	הַמִּזְבֵּחַ
wayyaqōrēv	mē'ēth	p^{e}nê	habbayith	mibbên	hammizbēach
and he brought near	from	the front of	the house	from between	the altar

4623, 1033	1041	3176	5598.121	881	6142, 3525	4326
cj, prep, prep	*n ms*	pn	cj, v Qal impf 3ms	do, ps 3ms	prep, *n fs*	art, n ms
וּמִבֵּין	בֵּית	יְהוָה	וַיִּתֵּן	אֹתוֹ	עַל־יֶרֶךְ	הַמִּזְבֵּחַ
ûmibbên	bêth	y^{e}hwāh	wayyittēn	'ōthô	'al-yerekh	hammizbēach
and from between	the temple of	Yahweh	and he placed	it	on the side of	the altar

7103		6943.121	4567, 271	881, 222	3669	3937, 569.141
n fs	**15.**	cj, v Piel impf 3ms, ps 3ms	art, n ms, pn	do, pn	art, n ms	prep, v Qal inf con
צָפוֹנָה		וַיְצַוֵּהוּ	הַמֶּלֶךְ־אָחָז	אֶת־אוּרִיָּה	הַכֹּהֵן	לֵאמֹר
tsāphônāh		waytsawwēhû	hammelekh-'āchāz	'eth-'ûrîyāh	hakkōhēn	lē'mōr
northward		and he commanded him	the king Ahaz	Uriah	the priest	saying

6142	4326	1448	7281.531	881, 6150, 1269
prep	art, n ms	art, adj	v Hiphil impv 2ms	do, *n fs*, art, n ms
עַל	הַמִּזְבֵּחַ	הַגָּדוֹל	הַקְטֵר	אֶת־עֹלַת־הַבֹּקֶר
'al	hammizbēach	haggādhôl	haqōṭēr	'eth-'ōlath-habbōqer
on	the altar	the great	cause to go up in smoke	the burnt offering of the morning

881, 4647	6394	881, 6150	4567	881, 4647
cj, do, *n fs*	art, n ms	cj, do, *n fs*	art, n ms	cj, do, n fs, ps 3ms
וְאֶת־מִנְחַת	הָעֶרֶב	וְאֶת־עֹלַת	הַמֶּלֶךְ	וְאֶת־מִנְחָתוֹ
w^{e}'eth-minchath	hā'erev	w^{e}'eth-'ōlath	hammelekh	w^{e}'eth-minchāthô
and the grain offering of	the evening	and the burnt offering of	the king	and his grain offering

881	6150	3725, 6194	800	4647
cj, do	*n fs*	*adj*, *n ms*	art, n fs	cj, n fs, ps 3mp
וְאֵת	עֹלַת	כָּל־עַם	הָאָרֶץ	וּמִנְחָתָם
w^{e}'ēth	'ōlath	kol-'am	hā'ārets	ûminchāthām
and	the burnt offering of	all the people of	the land	and their grain offering

5447	3725, 1879	6150	3725, 1879, 2160
cj, n mp, ps 3mp	cj, *adj*, *n ms*	n fs	cj, *adj*, *n ms*, n ms
וְנִסְכֵּיהֶם	וְכָל־דַּם	עֹלָה	וְכָל־דַּם־זֶבַח
w^{e}nis̲kêhem	w^{e}khol-dam	'ōlāh	w^{e}khol-dam-zevach
and their drink offerings	and all the blood of	the burnt offering	and all the blood of the sacrifice

6142	2323.123	4326	5361	2030.121, 3937	3937, 1266.341
prep, ps 3ms	v Qal impf 2ms	cj, *n ms*	art, n fs	v Qal impf 3ms, prep, ps 1cs	prep, v Piel inf con
עָלָיו	תִּזְרֹק	וּמִזְבַּח	הַנְּחֹשֶׁת	יִהְיֶה־לִּי	לְבַקֵּר
'ālâv	tizrōq	ûmizbach	hann^{e}chōsheth	yihyeh-lî	l^{e}vaqqēr
on it	you will sprinkle	but the altar of	the bronze	it will be to me	to seek

14. And he brought also the brasen altar, which was before the LORD, from the forefront of the house, from between the altar and the house of the LORD, and put it on the north side of the altar: ... he moved from its place—in front of the temple, *Beck* ... The bronze altar dedicated to the LORD was between the new altar and the Temple, so Ahaz moved it to the north side of his new altar, *Good News* ... that stood ever in the Lord's presence opposite the tabernacle, away from its place between the new altar and the temple, *Knox*.

15. And king Ahaz commanded Urijah the priest, saying, Upon the great altar burn the morning burnt offering, and the evening meat offering, and the king's burnt sacrifice, and his meat offering, with the burnt offering of all the people of the land, and their meat offering, and their drink offerings; and sprinkle upon it all the blood of the burnt offering, and all the blood of the sacrifice: and the brasen altar shall be for me to inquire by: ... while the bronze altar was to serve for the king's divination, *Moffatt* ... I will use the bronze altar to ask questions of God, *NCV* ... for seeking guidance, *NIV* ... will be only for my personal use, *NLT*.

---

cf. Isa. 8:2) seems willing to comply with Ahaz's wishes. What is it about the spirit of assimilation which so pervades the human personality—why is it that we, whether in the church, or in the world, wish to be so in tune with the latest fads? Let us ever be diligent concerning importing the latest thing into our worship, and into our lives. But let us, on the other hand, not turn into reactionaries, about whom Jesus spoke concerning putting new wine into old wineskins when He said that they will only complain "the old is good" (Luke 5:39). And as for that business of Amaziah worshiping the Edomite gods—probably Raymond B. Dillard (*2 Chronicles*, WBC, 201) is on target here when he points out that in the ancient Near East, the deities of an enemy nation were often described as abandoning their people, and coming to the aid of the attacking force; hence, Amaziah's worship of the gods whom he thought were on his side.

Hobbs (WBC, 216f) notes the detailed nature of the present narrative (vv. 10–18), likening it to the source probably underlying much of chs. 11–12, above. He further argues against outright apostasy being envisioned here ("no hint is given in the account that the altar was to be used for anything other than Yahwistic worship"), noting that the various offerings listed in vv. 13 and 15 line up quite nicely with other OT sacrificial practices. Indeed, the purpose of the new altar appears to solve the problem, already addressed in 1 Ki. 8:64, of the inadequate size of the bronze altar: "From this account [e.g., v. 15] the motivation of Ahaz was clearly not apostasy, since the organization of the sacrifice that follows is consistent with the other legislation on sacrifice in the OT." And as Cogan and Tadmor, AB, 192f, point out, "The rites described here as practiced upon the new altar are typically Israelite ... and do not contradict what is known of the accepted practice of the Jerusalem temple. Mesopotamian ritual, including that of Assyria, did not admit whole burnt offerings and blood sprinkling." But then why were Ahaz's actions so strongly criticized, citing this altar innovation as noteworthy support for condemning the king? Again, Cogan and Tadmor write, "Ahaz's innovations, by no means idolatrous or syncretistic, are criticized, it would seem, because they upset the order of things in the Temple as established by Solomon." Ahaz had violated the standards of temple worship that the biblical writers held. In order to please the king of Assyria, Ahaz compromised the fidelity of his nation's religious practices.

Verse 18 of the present chapter is difficult and merits closer examination. Why did Ahaz "take away the Sabbath canopy," etc., "in deference to the king of Assyria"? The short answer is, we are not sure. Some (e.g., Cogan and Tadmor, AB, 190; cf. Jones, NCBC, 541f; also Wiseman, TOTC, 263f) would see the temple alterations (in vv. 17f) as necessary to pay the heavy tribute in metal to the Assyrian king, while others (e.g., Hobbs, WBC, 218) would maintain the Hebrew here is unlikely to bear that much weight, "An attitude of subservience, or even fear, but [the expression here] cannot bear the weight of 'paying tribute.'" As far as what exactly the "Sabbath canopy" represented, again commentators differ as to what is meant by this difficult phrase. Possibly, some sort of "metal awning" may have been in view (so, Cogan and Tadmor); but, once again, we simply are not sure. In general, however, it does seem that at least some of the temple modifications Ahaz made were for the sake of paying off his new "friend," Tiglath-Pileser. In the colorful words, once again, of Isaiah the prophet, "In that day the LORD will use a razor hired from beyond the River [i.e., the Euphrates River]—the king of Assyria—to shave your head and the hair of your legs, and to take off your beards also"

16.	6449.121	222	3669	3626, 3725	866, 6943.311	4567
	cj, v Qal impf 3ms	pn	art, n ms	prep, n ms	rel part, v Piel pf 3ms	art, n ms
	וַיַּעַשׂ	אוּרִיָּה	הַכֹּהֵן	כְּכֹל	אֲשֶׁר־צִוָּה	הַמֶּלֶךְ
	wayya'as	'ûrîyāh	hakkōhēn	kekhōl	'ăsher-tsiwwāh	hammelekh
	and he did	Uriah	the priest	according to everything	that he had commanded	the king

271	17.	7401.321	4567	271	881, 4675	4488	5681.521
pn		cj, v Piel impf 3ms	art, n ms	pn	do, art, n fp	art, n fp	cj, v Hiphil impf 3ms
אָחָז		וַיְקַצֵּץ	הַמֶּלֶךְ	אָחָז	אֶת־הַמִּסְגְּרוֹת	הַמְּכֹנוֹת	וַיָּסַר
'āchāz		wayqatstsēts	hammelekh	'āchāz	'eth-hammisgerôth	hammekhōnôth	wayyāsar
Ahaz		and he cut off	the king	Ahaz	the frames	the bases	and he removed

4623, 6142	881, 3715	881, 3328	3495.511	4623, 6142	1267	5361	866
prep, prep, ps 3mp	cj, do, n ms	cj, do, art, n ms	v Hiphil pf 3ms	prep, prep	art, n ms	art, n fs	rel part
מֵעֲלֵיהֶם	וְאֶת־הַכִּיֹּר	וְאֶת־הַיָּם	הוֹרִד	מֵעַל	הַבָּקָר	הַנְּחֹשֶׁת	אֲשֶׁר
mē'ălêhem	we'eth-hakkiyyor	we'eth-hayyām	hôridh	mē'al	habbāqār	hannechōsheth	'ăsher
from on them	and the laver	and the sea	he took down	from on	the oxen	the bronze	which

8809	5598.121	881	6142	5000	63	18.	881, 4466
prep, ps 3fs	cj, v Qal impf 3ms	do, ps 3ms	prep	*n fs*	n fp		cj, do, *n ms*
תַּחְתֶּיהָ	וַיִּתֵּן	אֹתוֹ	עַל	מַרְצֶפֶת	אֲבָנִים		וְאֶת־מֵיסַךְ
tachtêāh	wayyittēn	'ōthô	'al	martsepheth	'ăvānîm		we'eth-mîsakh
beneath it	and he placed	it	on	a pavement of	stones		and the pavilion of

8141	866, 1161.116	904, 1041	881, 4136	4567	2535
art, n fs	rel part, v Qal pf 3cp	prep, art, n ms	cj, do, *n ms*	art, n ms	art, adj
הַשַּׁבָּת	אֲשֶׁר־בָּנוּ	בַּבַּיִת	וְאֶת־מְבוֹא	הַמֶּלֶךְ	הַחִיצוֹנָה
hashshabbāth	'ăsher-bānû	vabbayith	we'eth-mevô'	hammelekh	hachîtsônāh
the Sabbath	which they had built	in the house	and the entrance for	the king	the outer

5621.511	1041	3176	4623, 6686	4567	831
v Hiphil pf 3ms	*n ms*	pn	prep, *n mp*	*n ms*	pn
הֵסֵב	בֵּית	יְהוָה	מִפְּנֵי	מֶלֶךְ	אַשּׁוּר
hēsēv	bêth	yehwāh	mippenê	melekh	'ashshûr
he turned back to	the temple of	Yahweh	from before	the king of	Assyria

19.	3615	1745	271	866	6449.111	1950B, 3940, 2062
	cj, *n ms*	*n mp*	pn	rel part	v Qal pf 3ms	intrg part, neg part, pers pron
	וְיֶתֶר	דִּבְרֵי	אָחָז	אֲשֶׁר	עָשָׂה	הֲלֹא־הֵם
	weyether	divrê	'āchāz	'ăsher	'āsāh	hălō'-hēm
	and the remainder of	the events of	Ahaz	which	he did	are they not

3918.156	6142, 5809	1745	3219	3937, 4567	3171
v Qal pass ptc mp	prep, *n ms*	*n mp*	art, n mp	prep, *n mp*	pn
כְּתוּבִים	עַל־סֵפֶר	דִּבְרֵי	הַיָּמִים	לְמַלְכֵי	יְהוּדָה
kethûvîm	'al-sēpher	divrê	hayyāmîm	lemalkhê	yehûdhāh
things written	on the scroll of	the events of	the days	of the kings of	Judah

20.	8311.121	271	6196, 1	7196.221	6196, 1	904, 6111
	cj, v Qal impf 3ms	pn	prep, n mp, ps 3ms	cj, v Niphil impf 3ms	prep, n mp, ps 3ms	prep, *n fs*
	וַיִּשְׁכַּב	אָחָז	עִם־אֲבֹתָיו	וַיִּקָּבֵר	עִם־אֲבֹתָיו	בְּעִיר
	wayyishkav	'āchāz	'im-'ăvōthâv	wayyiqqāvēr	'im-'ăvōthâv	be'îr
	and he lay	Ahaz	with his ancestors	and he was buried	with his ancestors	in the city of

1784	4566.121	2488	1158	8809	17:1	904, 8523	8692
pn	cj, v Qal impf 3ms	pn	n ms, ps 3ms	prep, ps 3ms		prep, *n fs*	num
דָּוִד	וַיִּמְלֹךְ	חִזְקִיָּהוּ	בְּנוֹ	תַּחְתָּיו		בִּשְׁנַת	שְׁתֵּים
dāwidh	wayyimlōkh	chizqîyāhû	venô	tachtâv		bishnath	shettêm
David	and he reigned	Hezekiah	his son	instead of him		in the year of	two

16. Thus did Urijah the priest, according to all that king Ahaz commanded: ... priest Uriah did everything, *NRSV* ... carried out all the king's orders, *REB* ... followed all the instructions, *Moffatt* ... all his bidding, *Knox*.

17. And king Ahaz cut off the borders of the bases, and removed the laver from off them: ... detached the frames from, *NAB* ... took off the side panels from the bases and removed the washing bowls, *NCV* ... the basins from the movable stands, *NIV* ... stripped off the frames of the wheeled stands, *Anchor.*

and took down the sea from off the brasen oxen that were under it, and put it upon a pavement of stones: ... that supported it, and set it on a stone pavement, *NAB* ... He also took the large bowl, which was called the Sea, off the bronze bulls that held it up, and he put it on a stone base, *NCV* ... great water-vessel from off the brass oxen, *BB*.

18. And the covert for the sabbath that they had built in the house, and the king's entry without, turned he from the house of the LORD for the king of Assyria: ... The covered walk used on the Sabbath, which had been built at the temple, as well as the outer entrance for the king, Ahaz removed from the LORD's temple on account, *Beck* ... and the king's entrance from the outside, he turned around in, *Berkeley* ... the intervening screen which was built between the Temple and the royal entrance to the Court that surrounded the House of the EVER-LIVING, *Fenton* ... in order to please the Assyrian emperor, Ahaz also removed from the Temple the platform for the royal throne and closed up the king's private entrance to the Temple, *Good News*.

19. Now the rest of the acts of Ahaz which he did, are they not written in the book of the chronicles of the kings of Judah?: ... history of Ahaz, his entire career, is this not recorded in the Book of the Annals, *JB* ... book of the history, *NCV* ... other acts and events of the reign of Ahaz, *NEB* ... other things that Ahaz did are related in the history of events in the period, *Fenton*.

20. And Ahaz slept with his fathers, and was buried with his fathers in the city of David: and Hezekiah his son reigned in his stead: ... with his ancestors, *Anchor* ... went to rest with his fathers, and was put into the earth with, *BB* ... succeeded him as king, *Beck* ... became king in his place, *Berkeley*.

17:1. In the twelfth year of Ahaz king of Judah began Hoshea the son of Elah to reign in Samaria over Israel nine years: ... became king over Israel, *Anchor* ... started to rule in Samaria, *Beck* ... began his nine years' reign over Israel, *Moffatt* ... began to reign in Samaria upon Israel, and continued nine years, *Tyndale*.

(Isa. 7:20; the reference, of course, is to Tiglath-Pileser and his successors, and to their depredations of the land of Judah).

16:19–20. Conclusion: Judahite "further reference" notice (v. 19); Judahite burial notice (v. 20). Little more needs to be said here (as noted above, the introduction to ch. 15, above, gives references to prior discussions of these formulas). The next chapter contains only some six verses about Hoshea, the last king of Israel—who reigned only nine years, and who saw his capital city ransacked by Assyria, by the very successor of the Assyrian king who helped out King Ahaz of Judah. And, in contrast to Ahaz's peaceful burial in the city of Jerusalem, Hoshea died in exile—the result of sins of syncretism, disloyalty and idolatry, the very kinds of sins which Ahaz succeeded in bringing into the Davidic kingdom, due to his inexperience, perhaps, but also due to his unfaith. To quote the prophet Isaiah once more, "If you do not stand firm in your faith, you will not stand at all" (Isa. 7:9). It would take Ahaz's son Hezekiah to stand firm against another Assyrian king, Sennacherib, some thirty years subsequent to this time (cf. 18:13–19:37), and it would take another word from the prophet Isaiah to encourage him—successfully, this time—to wait upon the miracle-working God. We still must wait upon him in faith, to deliver us from all his, and our, enemies.

17:1–6. Hoshea the last king of Israel. As just noted, these six short verses represent the swan song for the nation of Israel. Founded, as it were, in ca. 932 B.C., the nation in its 210 or so years experienced nineteen kings, and nine changes of dynasty (cf. comments on 10:28–36). Most of these nineteen kings received a negative evaluation from the writer, while none of them received a positive evaluation. So Hoshea's judgment formula (v. 2), while once again negative, is noteworthy in its "qualified disapproval" (only Jehu seems to merit qualified praise ; cf. 10:28–31). More than likely, the pathos attending the end of the reign of King Hoshea largely accounts for the relaxation of blame in this passage. Preceding the judgment formula is our last example of an Israelite accession formula (v. 1). (Once again, cf. the introduction to ch. 15 for references to prior discussions of these formulas.) The rest of this short section consists of a brief account of Shalmaneser's siege of Samaria, its rationale (i.e., disloyalty on the part of Hoshea) and its results

6462	3937, 271	4567	3171	4566.111	2021	1158, 429	904, 8497
num	prep, pn	n ms	pn	v Qal pf 3ms	pn	n ms, pn	prep, pn
עֶשְׂרֵה	לְאָחָז	מֶלֶךְ	יְהוּדָה	מָלַךְ	הוֹשֵׁעַ	בֶּן־אֵלָה	בְּשֹׁמְרוֹן
'esrēh	le'āchāz	melekh	yehûdhāh	mālakh	hôshēa'	ben-'ēlāh	veshōmerôn
ten	of Ahaz	the king of	Judah	he reigned	Hoshea	the son of Elah	in Samaria

6142, 3547	9013	8523	2.	6449.121	7737	904, 6084	3176	7828	3940
prep, pn	num	n fp		cj, v Qal impf 3ms	art, adj	prep, n fd	pn	adv	neg part
עַל־יִשְׂרָאֵל	תֵּשַׁע	שָׁנִים		וַיַּעַשׂ	הָרַע	בְּעֵינֵי	יְהוָה	רַק	לֹא
'al-yisrā'ēl	tēsha'	shānîm		wayya'as	hāra'	be'ênê	yehwāh	raq	lō'
over Israel	nine	years		and he did	what is evil	in the eyes of	Yahweh	only	not

3626, 4567	3547	866	2030.116	3937, 6686	3.	6142	6148.111
prep, n mp	pn	rel pron	v Qal pf 3cp	prep, n mp, ps 3ms		prep, ps 3ms	v Qal pf 3ms
כְּמַלְכֵי	יִשְׂרָאֵל	אֲשֶׁר	הָיוּ	לְפָנָיו		עָלָיו	עָלָה
kemalkhê	yisrā'ēl	'ăsher	hāyû	lephānâv		'ālâv	'ālāh
like the kings of	Israel	who	they were	before him		against him	he came up

8415	4567	831	2030.121, 3937	2021	5860
pn	n ms	pn	cj, v Qal impf 3ms, prep, ps 3ms	pn	n ms
שַׁלְמַנְאֶסֶר	מֶלֶךְ	אַשּׁוּר	וַיְהִי־לוֹ	הוֹשֵׁעַ	עֶבֶד
shalman'eser	melekh	'ashshûr	wayhî-lô	hôshēa'	'evedh
Shalmaneser	the king of	Assyria	and he was to him	Hoshea	a servant

8178.521	3937	4647	4.	4834.121	4567, 831	904, 2021
cj, v Hiphil impf 3ms	prep, ps 3ms	n fs		cj, v Qal impf 3ms	n ms, pn	prep, pn
וַיָּשֶׁב	לוֹ	מִנְחָה		וַיִּמְצָא	מֶלֶךְ־אַשּׁוּר	בְּהוֹשֵׁעַ
wayyāshev	lô	minchāh		wayyimtsā'	melekh-'ashshûr	behôshēa'
and he caused to return	to him	a tribute		and he found	the king of Assyria	in Hoshea

7490	866	8365.111	4534	420, 5655	4567, 4875
n ms	rel part	v Qal pf 3ms	n mp	prep, pn	n ms, pn
קֶשֶׁר	אֲשֶׁר	שָׁלַח	מַלְאָכִים	אֶל־סוֹא	מֶלֶךְ־מִצְרָיִם
qesher	'ăsher	shālach	mal'ākhîm	'el-sô'	melekh-mitsrayim
a conspiracy	because	he sent out	messengers	to So	the king of Egypt

3940, 6148.511	4647	3937, 4567	831	3626, 8523	904, 8523
cj, neg part, v Hiphil pf 3ms	n fs	prep, n ms	pn	prep, n fs	prep, n fs
וְלֹא־הֶעֱלָה	מִנְחָה	לְמֶלֶךְ	אַשּׁוּר	כְּשָׁנָה	בְּשָׁנָה
welō'-he'ĕlāh	minchāh	lemelekh	'ashshûr	keshānāh	veshānāh
and he did not cause to go up	a tribute	to the king of	Assyria	like a year	in a year

6352.121	4567	831	646.126	1041	3728
cj, v Qal impf 3ms, ps 3ms	n ms	pn	cj, v Qal impf 3mp, ps 3ms	n ms	n ms
וַיַּעַצְרֵהוּ	מֶלֶךְ	אַשּׁוּר	וַיַּאַסְרֵהוּ	בֵּית	כֶּלֶא
wayya'atsrēhû	melekh	'ashshûr	wayya'asrēhû	bêth	kele'
so he bound him	the king of	Assyria	and he imprisoned him	the house of	the prison

5.	6148.121	4567, 831	904, 3725, 800	6148.121	8497
	cj, v Qal impf 3ms	n ms, pn	prep, adj, art, n fs	cj, v Qal impf 3ms	pn
	וַיַּעַל	מֶלֶךְ־אַשּׁוּר	בְּכָל־הָאָרֶץ	וַיַּעַל	שֹׁמְרוֹן
	wayya'al	melekh-'ashshûr	bekhol-hā'ārets	wayya'al	shōmerôn
	and he went up	the king of Assyria	throughout all the land	and he went up to	Samaria

6961.121	6142	8421	8523	6.	904, 8523	9012	3937, 2021	4058.111
cj, v Qal impf 3ms	prep, ps 3fs	num	n fp		prep, n fs	art, num	prep, pn	v Qal pf 3ms
וַיָּצַר	עָלֶיהָ	שָׁלֹשׁ	שָׁנִים		בִּשְׁנַת	הַתְּשִׁיעִית	לְהוֹשֵׁעַ	לָכַד
wayyātsar	'ālêāh	shālōsh	shānîm		bishnath	hattshî'îth	lehôshēa'	lākhadh
and he besieged	against it	three	years		in the year of	the ninth	of Hoshea	he captured

2. And he did that which was evil in the sight of the Lord, but not as the kings of Israel that were before him: ... displeasing to Yahweh, *Anchor* ... wrong before the LORD, *Beck* ... defied the Lord's will, *Knox* ... though not like the preceding kings of Israel, *JB* ... He sinned against the Lord, but not as much as the kings who had ruled Israel before him, *Good News*.

3. Against him came up Shalmaneser king of Assyria; and Hoshea became his servant, and gave him presents: ... This king was attacked by Salmanasar, *Knox* ... Hoshea submitted to him and offered tribute, *Moffatt* ... vassal, and paid him tribute, *NRSV* ... paid him tribute money, *NKJV*.

4. And the king of Assyria found conspiracy in Hoshea: ... Hoshea was being disloyal to him, *REB* ... found treachery, *RSV* ... Hoshea was plotting rebellion against him, *Berkeley* ... was playing a double game with him, *JB*.

for he had sent messengers to So king of Egypt, and brought no present to the king of Assyria, as he had done year by year: ... had sent representatives, *BB* ... sending envoys to the king of Egypt at So, and withholding the annual tribute which he had been paying, *REB* ... withheld the yearly tribute, *Anchor*.

therefore the king of Assyria shut him up, and bound him in prison: ... seized and imprisoned him, *REB* ... arrested him and put him in, *Anchor* ... put in chains, *BB* ... kept him in custody as a prisoner, *Moffatt*.

5. Then the king of Assyria came up throughout all the land, and went up to Samaria, and besieged it three years: ... overran the whole country, *Beck* ... invaded the whole country, and ravaged it, *Fenton* ... occupied the whole land and attacked, *NAB* ... laid it under siege, *Berkeley*.

6. In the ninth year of Hoshea the king of Assyria took Samaria, and carried Israel away into Assyria, and placed them in Halah and in Habor by the river of Gozan, and in the cities of the Medes: ... cap-

---

(the fall of the city after a three-year siege and the deportation of the inhabitants of Israel).

Most commentators date Hoshea's reign from the year 732 or 731, and the fall of Samaria exactly a decade later. Presumably Hoshea's nine-year reign implies that he was either removed from his kingship (possibly deported; cf. v. 4) before the city fell, or else that the final year or two of the siege were not reckoned as part of his regnal total.

The name "Hoshea" means "May Yahweh save" or "Yahweh saves," in either case a sad irony; the name is related to the familiar names "Joshua" and "Isaiah," as well as, of course, the name of the prophet Hosea (the names of the prophet and of the present king are identical in Hebrew [hôshēaʻ, HED #2021]). King Hoshea's nemesis, Shalmaneser V, reigned from 727 to 722, and he was the son of the infamous Tiglath-Pileser III (cf. on 15:17–22). He apparently died either during or shortly after the siege of Samaria. Cogan and Tadmor (AB, 197) argue that the siege of Samaria ended in the winter of 722/21, with the city's surrender to Shalmaneser, but because of the king's death, final determination of the city's status was postponed for two years. Sargon II (721–705), his successor, recaptured the city in 720, in his first campaign to the west, and deportations took place sometime after that (for the Assyrian policy of wholesale transfer of subject populations, cf. above, on 15:27–31).

Probably, the most important historical issue alluded to here, besides the fall of Samaria itself, would be the reference to "envoys sent to So king of Egypt" (v. 4, NIV). The reference to "So" is probably not to "[King O]so[rkon]" (so Kitchen; cf. Wiseman, TOTC, 265), but probably to the western delta capital of "Sais" (so NIV footnote; cf. also Cogan and Tadmor, AB, 196; Hobbs, WBC, 229; Jones, NCBC, 546f). It must be borne in mind that there were at least two, possibly three, different Pharaohs on various thrones at this time. Hoshea was very likely playing one Pharaoh against another (no matter how one interprets the phrase "So king of Egypt"), as well as the land of Egypt against the land of Assyria. Be that as it may, the end result was obviously complete disaster. Egypt, once again, proved to be a "broken reed" which "pierces the hand" of any who would lean on it (so 2 Ki. 18:21; cf. Isa. 36:6, quoting the taunts of the Assyrian "field commander" in the days of Hezekiah). Apparent Assyrian weakness attending the death of Tiglath-Pileser III proved sadly illusory. As Cogan and Tadmor (AB, 200) quote the Assyrian accounts of these events (as restored from two separate inscriptions): "With the strength of my gods, I [Sargon] fought with and defeated the Samarians, who had come to an agreement with a hostile king not to be my vassals and not to pay tribute, and who opened hostilities (against me). I took captive 27,290 of its inhabitants. From among them, I organized fifty chariots as a royal unit, and the rest of them I resettled within Assyria. The city of Samaria I rebuilt and repopulated more than before; I brought people there from the lands which I had conquered. I placed my courtier over them as

4567, 831	881, 8497	1580.521	881, 3547	831
n ms, pn	do, pn	cj, v Hiphil impf 3ms	do, pn	pn
מֶלֶךְ־אַשּׁוּר	אֶת־שֹׁמְרוֹן	וַיֶּגֶל	אֶת־יִשְׂרָאֵל	אַשּׁוּרָה
melekh-'ashshûr	'eth-shōmᵉrôn	wayyeghel	'eth-yisrā'ēl	'ashshûrāh
the king of Assyria	Samaria	and he deported	Israel	to Assyria

3553.521	881	904, 2578	904, 2336	5282	1502	6111
cj, v Hiphil impf 3ms	do, ps 3mp	prep, pn	cj, prep, pn	n ms	pn	cj, n fp
וַיֹּשֶׁב	אֹתָם	בַּחְלַח	וּבְחָבוֹר	נְהַר	גּוֹזָן	וְעָרֵי
wayyōshev	'ōthām	bachlach	ûvᵉchāvôr	nᵉhar	gôzān	wᵉ'ārê
and he caused to dwell	them	in Halah	and in Habor	the River	Gozan	and the cities of

4216		2030.121	3706, 2490.116	1158, 3547	3937, 3176
pn	**7.**	cj, v Qal impf 3ms	cj, v Qal pf 3cp	n mp, pn	prep, pn
מָדָי		וַיְהִי	כִּי־חָטְאוּ	בְנֵי־יִשְׂרָאֵל	לַיהוָה
mādhāy		wayhî	kî-chāṭᵉ'û	vᵉnê-yisrā'ēl	layhwāh
Medes		and it was	because they had sinned	the children of Israel	against Yahweh

435	6148.551	881	4623, 800	4875	4623, 8809
n mp, ps 3mp	art, v Hiphil ptc ms	do, ps 3mp	prep, n fs	pn	prep, prep
אֱלֹהֵיהֶם	הַמַּעֲלֶה	אֹתָם	מֵאֶרֶץ	מִצְרַיִם	מִתַּחַת
'ĕlōhêhem	hamma'ăleh	'ōthām	mē'erets	mitsrayim	mittachath
their God	the One Who caused to go up	them	from the land of	Egypt	from beneath

3135	6799	4567, 4875	3486.126	435	311		2050.126
n fs	pn	n ms, pn	cj, v Qal impf 3mp	n mp	adj	**8.**	cj, v Qal impf 3mp
יַד	פַּרְעֹה	מֶלֶךְ־מִצְרָיִם	וַיִּירְאוּ	אֱלֹהִים	אֲחֵרִים		וַיֵּלְכוּ
yadh	par'ōh	melekh-mitsrāyim	wayyîr'û	'ĕlōhîm	'ăchērîm		wayyēlᵉkhû
the hand of	Pharaoh	the king of Egypt	and they feared	gods	others		and they walked

904, 2807	1504	866	3542.511	3176	4623, 6686	1158	3547
prep, n fp	art, n mp	rel pron	v Hiphil pf 3ms	pn	prep, n mp	n mp	pn
בְּחֻקּוֹת	הַגּוֹיִם	אֲשֶׁר	הוֹרִישׁ	יְהוָה	מִפְּנֵי	בְּנֵי	יִשְׂרָאֵל
bᵉchuqqôth	haggôyim	'ăsher	hôrîsh	yᵉhwāh	mippᵉnê	bᵉnê	yisrā'ēl
in the statutes of	the nations	whom	He dispossessed	Yahweh	from before	the sons of	Israel

4567	3547	866	6449.116		2749.326	1158, 3547
cj, n mp	pn	rel part	v Qal pf 3cp	**9.**	cj, v Piel impf 3mp	n mp, pn
וּמַלְכֵי	יִשְׂרָאֵל	אֲשֶׁר	עָשׂוּ		וַיְחַפְּאוּ	בְנֵי־יִשְׂרָאֵל
ûmalkhê	yisrā'ēl	'ăsher	'āsû		waychappe'û	vᵉnê-yisrā'ēl
and the kings of	Israel	which	they made		and they acted secretly	the children of Israel

1745	866	3940, 3772	6142, 3176	435	1161.126	3937	1154
n mp	rel part	neg part, adv	prep, pn	n mp, ps 3mp	cj, v Qal impf 3mp	prep, ps 3mp	n fp
דְּבָרִים	אֲשֶׁר	לֹא־כֵן	עַל־יְהוָה	אֱלֹהֵיהֶם	וַיִּבְנוּ	לָהֶם	בָּמוֹת
dᵉvārîm	'ăsher	lō'-khēn	'al-yᵉhwāh	'ĕlōhêhem	wayyivnû	lāhem	bāmôth
things	which	not so	against Yahweh	their God	and they built	to them	high places

904, 3725, 6111	4623, 4166	5526.152	5912, 6111	4152
prep, adj, n fp, ps 3mp	prep, n ms	v Qal act ptc mp	prep, n fs	n ms
בְּכָל־עָרֵיהֶם	מִמִּגְדַּל	נוֹצְרִים	עַד־עִיר	מִבְצָר
bᵉkhol-'ārêhem	mimmighdal	nôtsrîm	'adh-'îr	mivtsār
in all their cities	from a tower of	guarding	unto the city of	fortification

	5507.526	3937	4838	867	6142	3725, 1421	1393
10.	cj, v Hiphil impf 3mp	prep, ps 3mp	n fp	cj, pn	prep	adj, n fs	n fs
	וַיַּצִּבוּ	לָהֶם	מַצֵּבוֹת	וַאֲשֵׁרִים	עַל	כָּל־גִּבְעָה	גְבֹהָה
	wayyatstsivû	lāhem	matstsēvôth	wa'ăshērîm	'al	kol-giv'āh	ghᵉvōhāh
	and they stationed	to them	pillars	and Asherah poles	on	every hill	high

tured Samaria and deported its people to Assyria and settled them, *NEB* ... Samaria fell, and the people of Israel were exiled to Assyria, *NLT* ... took the people captive, *Beck* ... Israelites carried off to the Assyrian country, *Knox*.

7. For so it was, that the children of Israel had sinned against the LORD their God, which had brought them up out of the land of Egypt, from under the hand of Pharaoh king of Egypt, and had feared other gods: ... The wrath of God was upon Israel, *Moffatt* ... had rescued them from the power of the king of Egypt, but the Israelites had honored other gods, *NCV* ... the domination, *NAB* ... they worshipped strange gods, *Douay*.

8. And walked in the statutes of the heathen, whom the LORD cast out from before the children of Israel, and of the kings of Israel, which they had made: ... Living by the rules of the nations, *BB* ... lived according to the customs, *Beck* ... whom they had appointed, *Berkeley* ... whom the LORD dispossessed before the Israelites, *Goodspeed*.

9. And the children of Israel did secretly those things that were not right against the LORD their God: ... They adopted unlawful practices toward, *NAB* ... offended the Lord their God, *Douay* ... were not pleasing, *NLT* ... the LORD their God disapproved of, *Good News*.

and they built them high places in all their cities, from the tower of the watchmen to the fenced city: ... making themselves mountain shrines in all their townships, *Knox* ... settlements, the watchtowers as well as the walled cities, *NAB* ... from villages to large towns, *Moffatt* ... to fortified town, *JB*.

10. And they set them up images and groves in every high hill, and under every green tree: ... setting up obelisks and sacred poles, *Moffatt* ... sacred pillars and sacred poles, *Goodspeed* ... luxuriant tree, *JB* ... leafy tree, *NAB*.

11. And there they burnt incense in all the high places, as did the heathen whom the LORD carried away before them: ... as the nations whom the LORD had driven out, *NIV* ... made offerings, *NRSV* ... Lord sent away, *BB* ... had removed, *Berkeley*.

---

governor, and imposed tax and tribute upon them, just as if they were Assyrian. I also had them trained in proper conduct."

The above account is quoted at length, because it will illustrate quite nicely the Assyrian point of view concerning the deportation and resettlement of Israelite and foreign populations in and from this area. (For the point of view of the captive, see below.) The later "Samaritans" of the NT era ultimately traced their lineage partly from these events. The stigma of being "halfbreeds" (from the Jewish point of view), however elitist and ethnically prejudiced it may be, contains more than a grain of truth (the radicalness of, e.g., the Parable of the Good Samaritan [Luke 10:25–37] stems largely from those prejudices; also cf. Jesus' radical friendship with the Samaritan woman at Jacob's well [John 4:1–42]). It is simply amazing the later reverberations an abortive attempt at freedom brought about—Hoshea's misjudging the world political scene of his day led to major ethnic repercussions in Jesus' day, not to mention our own. Actions have consequences—often far-reaching consequences.

17:7–41. *An Extended Editorial: Why the North Fell to Assyria. As just noted, the fall of Samaria led to major repercussions both in the north and elsewhere. Not least, the reasons for the fall consume the better part of this section, with vv. 7–23 an extended treatise on why Yahweh permitted, indeed caused, the destruction and the exile of his people Israel. Appended to these verses is another extended editorial examination of the results of this disaster, with foreign peoples brought in to repopulate the land, and the seemingly inevitable syncretism (religious blending and compromise) which resulted. It is to this unique portion of Scripture—extended editorial, not extended narrative—that is examined below.*

17:7–23. Reasons for the fall of the nation of Israel: Idolatry and disobedience. Rather than a verse-by-verse analysis, a listing of the various reasons Israel was doomed to destruction is more beneficial. The present "editorial" is at times repetitive, but even in its repetitions, its melancholy eloquence speaks afresh to any age which might be tempted to compromise or to wander from the revealed truth. For the Israelites could not plead ignorance (even if, as they say, "ignorance of the law is no excuse"). No, they could not plead ignorance—for both the Law and the Prophets bore repeated and eloquent witness against their behavior, time and time again.

The key rubric throughout this passage is of course the sin of Israel (v. 7; cf. v. 21, where both the noun and the verb appear). Israel "knew better": they had no excuse. It should be noted that their sins are largely those of worship, of religious practice. They worshiped too much, they worshiped in too many places and they clearly worshiped too many gods.

8809	3725, 6320	7776		7281.326, 8427	904, 3725, 1154
cj, prep	*adj*, n ms	adj		cj, v Piel impf 3mp, adv	prep, *adj*, n fp
וְתַחַת	כָּל־עֵץ	רַעֲנָן	**11.**	וַיְקַטְּרוּ־שָׁם	בְּכָל־בָּמוֹת
wethachath	kol-'ēts	ra'ănān		wayqatterû-shām	bekhol-bāmôth
and beneath	every tree	luxuriant		and they burned incense there	on all the high places

3626, 1504	866, 1580.511	3176	4623, 6686	6449.126
prep, art, n mp	rel pron, v Hiphil pf 3ms	pn	prep, n mp, ps 3mp	cj, v Qal impf 3mp
כַּגּוֹיִם	אֲשֶׁר־הֶגְלָה	יְהוָה	מִפְּנֵיהֶם	וַיַּעֲשׂוּ
kaggôyim	'ăsher-heghlāh	yehwāh	mippenêhem	wayya'ăsû
like the nations	whom He had caused to depart	Yahweh	from before them	and they did

1745	7737	3937, 3832.541	881, 3176		5856.126	1585	866
n mp	adj	prep, v Hiphil inf con	do, pn		cj, v Qal impf 3mp	art, n mp	rel part
דְּבָרִים	רָעִים	לְהַכְעִיס	אֶת־יְהוָה	**12.**	וַיַּעַבְדוּ	הַגִּלֻּלִים	אֲשֶׁר
devārîm	rā'îm	lehakh'îs	'eth-yehwāh		wayya'avdhû	haggillulîm	'ăsher
things	evil	to provoke to anger	Yahweh		and they served	the idols	which

569.111	3176	3937	3940	6449.128	881, 1745	2172
v Qal pf 3ms	pn	prep, ps 3mp	neg part	v Qal impf 2mp	do, art, n ms	art, dem pron
אָמַר	יְהוָה	לָהֶם	לֹא	תַעֲשׂוּ	אֶת־הַדָּבָר	הַזֶּה
'āmar	yehwāh	lāhem	lō'	tha'ăsû	'eth-haddāvār	hazzeh
He has said	Yahweh	to them	not	you will do	the thing	the this

	5967.521	3176	904, 3547	904, 3171	904, 3135	3725, 5204
13.	cj, v Hiphil impf 3ms	pn	prep, pn	cj, prep, pn	prep, *n fs*	*adj*, n ms, ps 3ms
	וַיָּעַד	יְהוָה	בְּיִשְׂרָאֵל	וּבִיהוּדָה	בְּיַד	כָּל־נְבִיאוֹ
	wayyā'adh	yehwāh	beyisrā'ēl	ûvîhûdhāh	beyadh	kol-nevî'ô
	and He testified	Yahweh	against Israel	and against Judah	by the hand of	all his prophets

3725, 2463.151	3937, 569.141	8178.133	4623, 1932	7737	8490.133
adj, v Qal act ptc ms	prep, v Qal inf con	v Qal impv 2mp	prep, n mp, ps 2mp	art, adj	cj, v Qal impv 2mp
כָל־חֹזֶה	לֵאמֹר	שֻׁבוּ	מִדַּרְכֵיכֶם	הָרָעִים	וְשִׁמְרוּ
khol-chōzeh	lē'mōr	shuvû	middarkhêkhem	hārā'îm	weshimrû
all the seers	saying	turn back	from your ways	the evil	and observe

4851	2807	3626, 3725, 8784	866	6943.315
n fp, ps 1cs	n fp, ps 1cs	prep, *adj*, art, n fs	rel part	v Piel pf 1cs
מִצְוֹתַי	חֻקּוֹתַי	כְּכָל־הַתּוֹרָה	אֲשֶׁר	צִוִּיתִי
mitswōthay	chuqqôthay	kekhol-hattôrāh	'ăsher	tsiwwîthî
my commandments	my statutes	according to all the Law	which	I have commanded

881, 1	866	8365.115	420	904, 3135	5860	5204
do, n mp, ps 2mp	cj, rel part	v Qal pf 1cs	prep, ps 2mp	prep, *n fs*	n mp, ps 1cs	art, n mp
אֶת־אֲבֹתֵיכֶם	וַאֲשֶׁר	שָׁלַחְתִּי	אֲלֵיכֶם	בְּיַד	עֲבָדַי	הַנְּבִיאִים
'eth-'ăvōthêkhem	wa'ăsher	shālachtî	'ălêkhem	beyadh	'ăvādhay	hannevî'îm
your fathers	and which	I have sent	to you	by the hand of	my servants	the prophets

	3940	8471.116	7481.526	881, 6439	3626, 6439	1
14.	cj, neg part	v Qal pf 3cp	cj, v Hiphil impf 3mp	do, n ms, ps 3mp	prep, *n ms*	n mp, ps 3mp
	וְלֹא	שָׁמֵעוּ	וַיַּקְשׁוּ	אֶת־עָרְפָּם	כְּעֹרֶף	אֲבוֹתָם
	welō'	shāmē'û	wayyaqōshû	'eth-'āreppām	ke'ōreph	'ăvôthām
	and not	they listened	and they made stiff	their necks	like the necks of	their ancestors

866	3940	548.516	904, 3176	435		4128.126	881, 2807
rel pron	neg part	v Hiphil pf 3cp	prep, pn	n mp, ps 3mp		cj, v Qal impf 3mp	do, n mp, ps 3ms
אֲשֶׁר	לֹא	הֶאֱמִינוּ	בַּיהוָה	אֱלֹהֵיהֶם	**15.**	וַיִּמְאֲסוּ	אֶת־חֻקָּיו
'ăsher	lō'	he'ĕmînû	bayhwāh	'ĕlōhêhem		wayyim'ăsû	'eth-chuqqāv
who	not	they believed	in Yahweh	their God		but they despised	his statutes

and wrought wicked things to provoke the LORD to anger: ... did wicked, *NIV* ... had done many evil things, arousing, *NLT* ... moving the Lord to wrath, *BB* ... the LORD's jealousy, *Goodspeed*.

12. For they served idols, whereof the LORD had said unto them, Ye shall not do this thing: ... they worshipped abominations, *Douay* ... despite the LORD's specific and repeated warnings, *NLT* ... the Lord had forbidden expressly, *Knox* ... made themselves servants of disgusting things, *BB*.

13. Yet the LORD testified against Israel, and against Judah, by all the prophets, and by all the seers, saying: ... warned Israel and Judah, *Anchor* ... he gave witness to Israel and, *BB* ... solemnly charged Israel and, *NEB*.

Turn ye from your evil ways, and keep my commandments and my statutes, according to all the law which I commanded your fathers, and which I sent to you by my servants the prophets: ... Give up your evil, *NAB* ... do my orders and keep my rules, and be guided by the law, *BB* ... Institutions, according to the perfect laws that I ordained for your ancestors, *Fenton* ... Come back from these graceless ways, follow precept and observance of mine, *Knox*.

14. Notwithstanding they would not hear, but hardened their necks, like to the neck of their fathers, that did not believe in the LORD their God: ... they did not listen. They were as stiff-necked as their ancestors had been, who did not trust Yahweh, *Anchor* ... who had no faith in the Lord, *BB* ... refused to listen, getting as stubborn as their fathers, *Beck* ... who did not remain faithful, *Berkeley*.

15. And they rejected his statutes, and his covenant that he made with their fathers, and his testimonies which he testified against them: ... and his decrees which he decreed for them, *Goodspeed* ... They despised his laws and the covenant which he had made with their ancestors and the warnings, *JB* ... the LORD's laws and the agreement he had made with, *NCV*.

and they followed vanity, and became vain, and went after the heathen that were round about them, concerning whom the LORD had charged them, that they should not do like them: ... Pursuing futility, they themselves became futile through copying the nations round them, although Yahweh had ordered them not to, *JB* ... they followed worthless idols and became worthless themselves; they imitated the nations round about them, *NEB* ... they betook themselves, and learned false ways, *Knox* ... had commanded them not to imitate, *NAB*.

As Jones (NCBC, 548f) points out, already in vv. 7f, Israel's sin is contrasted with Yahweh's graciousness. Yahweh had brought them "up out of Egypt from under the power of Pharaoh king of Egypt," and yet they followed the religious practices "of the nations Yahweh had driven out before them," as well as the practices "that the kings of Israel had introduced." (Note that this same double indictment is lodged against King Ahaz of Judah in 16:3.) Thus Yahweh had given them (1) deliverance from bondage, (2) a wonderful land and (3) kings and dominion. But they spurned these gifts and, in essence, spurned the Giver as well. The following represents ways these Israelites spurned both gift and Giver:

Whatever the translation of v. 9 (NIV, "the Israelites secretly did things against Yahweh their God that were not right" [cf. KJV, NRSV, NLT]; Cogan and Tadmor [AB, 205], however, prefer, "the Israelites ascribed untruths to Yahweh their God." The Hebrew term commonly translated "secret" [waychappe'û, HED #2749] is used only here in the OT), the first, and clearly most heinous sin Israel committed was that of her continued worship at the high places (vv. 9ff, also cf. vv. 29, 32). The improper acts listed here [in vv. 9ff] are not idolatrous worship only, but are, as usual, assimilation of foreign practices introduced into Israelite religion after the fashion of the nations. Already in Deut. 12:2ff, the strongest of injunctions is issued against such worship (and let it be noted that Deut. 12 itself strategically introduces the major "specific stipulations" section of that covenant book [chs. 12–26]). Both here and in Deut. 12 (cf. also the repeated refrain in 1 Ki. 3:2f; 11:7f; 12:31f; 13:32ff; 14:23f; 15:14; 22:43; 2 Ki. 12:3; 14:4; 15:4, 35; 16:4), the chief sin is clearly that of syncretistic worship at the high places. Probably the term "high place," although commonly used to translate the Hebrew term bāmāh [HED #1154], is not the most accurate or appropriate term to use; the more generic terms "sanctuary" or "shrine" are preferable, if less colorful [cf. W. Boyd Barrick, *Anchor Bible Dictionary*, 3:196–200.)

Another continuing charge Yahweh had against his people was in regard to their persistent worship of idols (vv. 12, 15f; also cf. v. 40). Whether these "idols" represented Yahweh or foreign gods (see the next section), they were still abhorrent to the true God. What is generally described as the "Second Commandment" (Exo. 20:4f; cf. Deut. 5:8ff; above, on 14:5ff) clearly forbids any attempts to "image

881, 1311	866	3901.111	882, 1	881	5926	866
cj, do, n fs, ps 3ms	rel part	v Qal pf 3ms	prep, n mp, ps 3mp	cj, do	n fp, ps 3ms	rel part
וְאֶת־בְּרִיתוֹ	אֲשֶׁר	כָּרַת	אֶת־אֲבוֹתָם	וְאֵת	עֵדְוֹתָיו	אֲשֶׁר
we'eth-berîthô	'ăsher	kārath	'eth-'ăvôthām	we'ēth	'ēdhewōthâv	'ăsher
and his Covenant	which	He cut	with their fathers	and	his testimonies	which

5967.511	904	2050.126	313	1961	1960.126	313
v Hiphil pf 3ms	prep, ps 3mp	cj, v Qal impf 3mp	adv	art, n ms	cj, v Qal impf 3mp	cj, prep
הֵעִיד	בָּם	וַיֵּלְכוּ	אַחֲרֵי	הַהֶבֶל	וַיֶּהְבָּלוּ	וְאַחֲרֵי
hē'îdh	bām	wayyēlekhû	'achrê	hahevel	wayyehbālû	we'achrê
He had testified	against them	and they walked	after	the vanity	and they acted vainly	and after

1504	866	5623	866	6943.311	3176	881	3937, 1153
art, n mp	rel pron	prep, ps 3mp	rel pron	v Piel pf 3ms	pn	do, ps 3mp	prep, neg part
הַגּוֹיִם	אֲשֶׁר	סְבִיבֹתָם	אֲשֶׁר	צִוָּה	יְהוָה	אֹתָם	לְבִלְתִּי
haggôyim	'ăsher	sevîvōthām	'ăsher	tsiwwāh	yehwāh	'ōthām	leviltî
the nations	who	all around them	whom	He had commanded	Yahweh	them	that not

6449.141	3626		6013.126	881, 3725, 4851	3176	435
v Qal inf con	prep, ps 3mp	**16.**	cj, v Qal impf 3mp	do, *adj*, *n fp*	pn	n mp, ps 3mp
עֲשׂוֹת	כָּהֶם		וַיַּעַזְבוּ	אֶת־כָּל־מִצְוֹת	יְהוָה	אֱלֹהֵיהֶם
'ăsôth	kāhem		wayya'azvû	'eth-kol-mitswōth	yehwāh	'ĕlōhêhem
to do	like them		and they abandoned	all the commandments of	Yahweh	their God

6449.126	3937	4691	8530	5903	6449.126	867
cj, v Qal impf 3mp	prep, ps 3mp	n fs	num	n mp	cj, v Qal impf 3mp	pn
וַיַּעֲשׂוּ	לָהֶם	מַסֵּכָה	שְׁנֵים	עֲגָלִים	וַיַּעֲשׂוּ	אֲשֵׁירָה
wayya'ăsû	lāhem	massēkhāh	shenêm	'ăghālîm	wayya'ăsû	'ăshērāh
and they made	for themselves	cast images	two	calves	and they made	Asherah

8246.726	3937, 3725, 6893	8452	5856.126	881, 1197
cj, v Hithpael impf 3mp	prep, *adj*, n ms	art, n md	cj, v Qal impf 3mp	do, art, pn
וַיִּשְׁתַּחֲווּ	לְכָל־צְבָא	הַשָּׁמַיִם	וַיַּעַבְדוּ	אֶת־הַבָּעַל
wayyishtachwû	lekhol-tsevā'	hashshāmayim	wayya'avdhû	'eth-habbā'al
and they worshiped	all the host of	the heavens	and they served	the Baal

	5882.526	881, 1158	881, 1351	904, 813
17.	cj, v Hiphil impf 3mp	do, n mp, ps 3mp	cj, do, n fp, ps 3mp	prep, art, n fs
	וַיַּעֲבִירוּ	אֶת־בְּנֵיהֶם	וְאֶת־בְּנוֹתֵיהֶם	בָּאֵשׁ
	wayya'ăvîrû	'eth-benêhem	we'eth-benôthêhem	bā'ēsh
	and they caused to pass through	their sons	and their daughters	in the fire

7364.126	7365	5355.326	4513.726
cj, v Qal impf 3mp	n mp	cj, v Piel impf 3mp	cj, v Hithpael impf 3mp
וַיִּקְסְמוּ	קְסָמִים	וַיְנַחֵשׁוּ	וַיִּתְמַכְּרוּ
wayyiqōsmû	qōsāmîm	waynachēshû	wayyithmakkerû
and they divined	divinations	and they practiced sorceries	and they sold themselves

3937, 6449.141	7737	904, 6084	3176	3937, 3832.541
prep, v Qal inf con	art, adj	prep, *n fd*	pn	prep, v Hiphil inf con, ps 3ms
לַעֲשׂוֹת	הָרַע	בְּעֵינֵי	יְהוָה	לְהַכְעִיסוֹ
la'ăsôth	hāra'	be'ênê	yehwāh	lehakh'îsô
to do	what is evil	in the eyes of	Yahweh	to provoke Him to anger

	613.721	3176	4108	904, 3547	5861.521	4623, 6142
18.	cj, v Hithpael impf 3ms	pn	adv	prep, pn	cj, v Hiphil impf 3ms, ps 3mp	prep, prep
	וַיִּתְאַנַּף	יְהוָה	מְאֹד	בְּיִשְׂרָאֵל	וַיְסִרֵם	מֵעַל
	wayyith'annaph	yehwāh	me'ōdh	beyisrā'ēl	waysirēm	mē'al
	and He became angry	Yahweh	very	with Israel	and He removed them	from beside

6686	3940	8080.211	7828	8101	3171	3937, 940	19. 1612, 3171
n mp, ps 3ms	neg part	v Niphal pf 3ms	adv	*n ms*	pn	prep, n ms, ps 3ms	cj, pn
פָּנָיו	לֹא	נִשְׁאַר	רַק	שֵׁבֶט	יְהוּדָה	לְבַדּוֹ	גַּם־יְהוּדָה
pānâv	lō'	nish'ar	raq	shēveṯ	yehûdhāh	levaddô	gam-yehûdhāh
his presence	not	it remained	only	the tribe of	Judah	by itself	also Judah

3940	8490.111	881, 4851	3176	435	2050.126
neg part	v Qal pf 3ms	do, *n fp*	pn	n mp, ps 3mp	cj, v Qal impf 3mp
לֹא	שָׁמַר	אֶת־מִצְוֺת	יְהוָה	אֱלֹהֵיהֶם	וַיֵּלְכוּ
lō'	shāmar	'eth-mitswōth	yehwāh	'ĕlōhêhem	wayyēlekhû
not	they observed	the commandments of	Yahweh	their God	and they walked

16. And they left all the commandments of the LORD their God, and made them molten images, even two calves, and made a grove, and worshipped all the host of heaven, and served Baal: ... Forsaking every commandment, *NEB* ... defied all the commands, *NLT* ... two idols cast in the shape of calves, and an Asherah pole. They bowed down to all the starry hosts, and, *NIV* ... they made a sacred pole, *NRSV.*

17. And they caused their sons and their daughters to pass through the fire, and used divination and enchantments: ... and augury, *NRSV* ... and sorcery, *Anchor* ... they made use of secret arts and unnatural powers, *BB* ... sacrificed their sons and daughters in fire, practiced fortune-telling, and used charms, *Beck.*

and sold themselves to do evil in the sight of the LORD, to provoke him to anger: ... gave themselves up to doing evil in the eyes of the Lord, till he was moved to wrath, *BB* ... they abandoned themselves to do wrong before, *Beck* ... to jealousy, *Goodspeed* ... his vengeance, *Knox.*

18. Therefore the LORD was very angry with Israel, and removed them out of his sight: there was none left but the tribe of Judah only: ... was furious with Israel, *Moffatt* ... from his presence, *NCV* ... LORD was incensed against Israel and banished them, *NEB* ... his face was turned away from them, *BB.*

19. Also Judah kept not the commandments of the LORD their God, but walked in the statutes of Israel which they made: ... practiced by the Israelites, *Anchor* ... did not keep the orders of the Lord their God, but were guided by the rules, *BB* ... they followed the practices which Israel had adopted, *Berkeley* ... followed the same customs, *Fenton.*

God"—whether pictorially, graphically or even verbally. Such the Israelites did, nonetheless, as did all of their neighbors; and thus they caused great anger on the part of their God (cf. vv. 12, 16ff, of the present passage).

Directly related to the Israelite preoccupation with idols was their preoccupation with the gods of their neighbors, whether Baal (v. 16; for a discussion of the storm god Baal-Hadad, cf. on 1:2) or the Asherah (cf. vv. 10, 16; references here may be to the Canaanite goddess Asherah, consort of the high god El, and/or her sacred object, probably a stylized tree) or the "starry host" (v. 16; cf. 21:3, below; Cogan and Tadmor [AB, 266], contrary to many, would see Canaanite more than Mesopotamian influence here). I suspect the one issue (idols) tended to blend into the other (foreign gods), again a spirit of syncretism, of religious compromise. We today likewise must guard against such religious compromise, and the temptation to blend together different traditions and perspectives uncritically. Once Yahweh was allowed to be imaged (presumably the calf-idols of Jeroboam I [v. 16; cf. 1 Ki. 12:28f] were images of Yahweh, not Baal or some other god; cf. in the days of Moses and Aaron [Exo. 32:2–6], when Aaron described the golden-calf festival as "a festival to Yahweh" [v. 5]), he became just another god, and his uniqueness became irretrievably obscured.

Another sin of the Israelites involved pagan practices. What may be described as "pagan practices" are the following: setting up sacred stones and Asherah poles (v. 10; cf. comments on the goddess Asherah); also "burning incense" (v. 11, NIV; but NRSV's "making offerings" is probably a better translation); sacrificing their children "in the fire" (v. 17, NIV; concerning this expression, cf. comments on 16:1–4); and, finally, practicing divination and sorcery (v. 17; such actions in trying to ascertain—and affect—the future are, of course, roundly condemned in the Law; cf. Deut. 18:9–14).

The present editorial emphasizes the fact that the Israelites knew to avoid these practices, especially by its repeated references to the prophets (cf. vv. 12–15, 23). They had been repeatedly warned,

904, 2807	3547	866	6449.116		4128.121	3176
prep, *n fp*	pn	rel part	v Qal pf 3cp	**20.**	cj, v Qal impf 3ms	pn
בְּחֻקּוֹת	יִשְׂרָאֵל	אֲשֶׁר	עָשׂוּ		וַיִּמְאַס	יְהוָה
bechuqqôth	yisrā'ēl	'ăsher	'āsû		wayyim'as	yehwāh
in the statutes of	Israel	which	they had done		and He rejected	Yahweh

904, 3725, 2320	3547	6257.321	5598.121
prep, *adj*, *n ms*	pn	cj, v Piel impf 3ms, ps 3mp	cj, v Qal impf 3ms, ps 3mp
בְּכָל־זֶרַע	יִשְׂרָאֵל	וַיְעַנֵּם	וַיִּתְּנֵם
bekhol-zera'	yisrā'ēl	way'annēm	wayyittenēm
against all the descendants of	Israel	and He afflicted them	and He gave them

904, 3135, 8536.152	5912	866	8390.511	4623, 6686
prep, *n fs*, v Qal act ptc mp	adv	rel part	v Hiphil pf 3ms, ps 3mp	prep, n mp, ps 3ms
בְּיַד־שֹׁסִים	עַד	אֲשֶׁר	הִשְׁלִיכָם	מִפָּנָיו
beyadh-shōsîm	'adh	'ăsher	hishlîkhām	mippānâv
into the hand of plunderers	until	that	He threw them away	from his presence

	3706, 7458.111	3547	4623, 6142	1041	1784	4566.526
21.	cj, v Qal pf 3ms	pn	prep, prep	*n ms*	pn	cj, v Hiphil impf 3mp
	כִּי־קָרַע	יִשְׂרָאֵל	מֵעַל	בֵּית	דָּוִד	וַיַּמְלִיכוּ
	kî-qāra'	yisrā'ēl	mē'al	bêth	dāwidh	wayyamlîkhû
	when He had torn	Israel	from beside	the household of	David	then they caused to rule

881, 3493	1158, 5203	5245.521	3493	881, 3547	4623, 313	3176
do, pn	*n ms*, pn	cj, v Hiphil impf 3ms	pn	do, pn	prep, prep	pn
אֶת־יָרָבְעָם	בֶּן־נְבָט	וַיַּדֵּא	יָרָבְעָם	אֶת־יִשְׂרָאֵל	מֵאַחֲרֵי	יְהוָה
'eth-yārov'ām	ben-nevāt	wayyaddē'	yārov'ām	'eth-yisrā'ēl	mē'achrê	yehwāh
Jeroboam	the son of Nebat	and he prevented	Jeroboam	Israel	from after	Yahweh

2490.511	2494	1448		2050.126	1158	3547
cj, v Hiphil pf 3ms, ps 3mp	n fs	adj	**22.**	cj, v Qal impf 3mp	*n mp*	pn
וְהֶחֱטִיאָם	חֲטָאָה	גְדוֹלָה		וַיֵּלְכוּ	בְּנֵי	יִשְׂרָאֵל
wehechĕtî'ām	chătā'āh	ghedhôlāh		wayyēlekhû	benê	yisrā'ēl
and he caused them to sin	sin	great		and they walked	the children of	Israel

904, 3725, 2496	3493	866	6449.111	3940, 5681.116	4623		5912
prep, *adj*, *n fp*	pn	rel part	v Qal pf 3ms	neg part, v Qal pf 3cp	prep, ps 3fs	**23.**	adv
בְּכָל־חַטֹּאות	יָרָבְעָם	אֲשֶׁר	עָשָׂה	לֹא־סָרוּ	מִמֶּנָּה		עַד
bekhol-chattō'wth	yārov'ām	'ăsher	'āsāh	lō'-sārû	mimmennāh		'adh
in all the sins of	Jeroboam	which	he did	they did not turn aside from	from them		until

866, 5681.511	3176	881, 3547	4623, 6142	6686	3626, 866	1744.311
rel part, v Hiphil pf 3ms	pn	do, pn	prep, prep	n mp, ps 3ms	prep, rel part	v Piel pf 3ms
אֲשֶׁר־הֵסִיר	יְהוָה	אֶת־יִשְׂרָאֵל	מֵעַל	פָּנָיו	כַּאֲשֶׁר	דִּבֶּר
'ăsher-hēsîr	yehwāh	'eth-yisrā'ēl	mē'al	pānâv	ka'ăsher	dibber
that He removed	Yahweh	Israel	from beside	his presence	just as	He had spoken

904, 3135	3725, 5860	5204	1580.121	3547	4623, 6142	124
prep, *n fs*	*adj*, n mp, ps 3ms	art, n mp	cj, v Qal impf 3ms	pn	prep, prep	n fs, ps 3ms
בְּיַד	כָּל־עֲבָדָיו	הַנְּבִיאִים	וַיִּגֶל	יִשְׂרָאֵל	מֵעַל	אַדְמָתוֹ
beyadh	kol-'ăvādhâv	hannevî'îm	wayyighel	yisrā'ēl	mē'al	'adhmāthô
by the hand of	all his servants	the prophets	and He exiled	Israel	from on	their land

831	5912	3219	2172		971.521	4567, 831	4623, 928
pn	adv	art, n ms	art, dem pron	**24.**	cj, Hiphil impf 3ms	*n ms*, pn	prep, pn
אַשּׁוּרָה	עַד	הַיּוֹם	הַזֶּה		וַיָּבֵא	מֶלֶךְ־אַשּׁוּר	מִבָּבֶל
'ashshûrāh	'adh	hayyôm	hazzeh		wayyāvē'	melekh-'ashshûr	mibbāvel
to Assyria	until	the day	the this		and he brought	the king of Assyria	from Babylon

4623, 3693	4623, 5960	4623, 2679	5816	3553.521
cj, prep, pn	cj, prep, pn	cj, prep, pn	cj, pn	cj, v Hiphil impf 3ms
וּמִכּוּתָה	וּמֵעַוָּא	וּמֵחֲמָת	וּסְפַרְוַיִם	וַיֹּשֶׁב
ûmikkûthāh	ûmē'awwā'	ûmēchămāth	ûsepharwayim	wayyōshev
and from Cuth	and from Avva	and from Hamath	and Sepharvaim	and he caused to dwell

904, 6111	8497	8809	1158	3547	3542.126
prep, *n fp*	pn	prep	*n mp*	pn	cj, v Qal impf 3mp
בְּעָרֵי	שֹׁמְרוֹן	תַּחַת	בְּנֵי	יִשְׂרָאֵל	וַיִּרְשׁוּ
be'ārê	shōmerôn	tachath	benê	yisrā'ēl	wayyirshû
in the cities of	Samaria	instead of	the children of	Israel	and they took possession of

881, 8497	3553.126	904, 6111		2030.121	904, 8795
do, pn	cj, v Qal impf 3mp	prep, n fp, ps 3fs		cj, v Qal impf 3ms	prep, *n fs*
אֶת־שֹׁמְרוֹן	וַיֵּשְׁבוּ	בְּעָרֶיהָ	**25.**	וַיְהִי	בִּתְחִלַּת
'eth-shōmerôn	wayyēshevû	be'ārêāh		wayhî	bithchillath
Samaria	and they dwelled	in its cities		and it was	in the beginning of

20. And the LORD rejected all the seed of Israel, and afflicted them, and delivered them into the hand of spoilers, until he had cast them out of his sight: ... the whole race, *Goodspeed* ... the people of, *NIV* ... All Israel's race, then, the Lord cast off; humbled them, and left them at the spoiler's mercy; was ready, at last, to banish them from his presence altogether, *Knox* ... finally casting them out from before him, *NAB*.

21. For he rent Israel from the house of David; and they made Jeroboam the son of Nebat king: and Jeroboam drave Israel from following the LORD, and made them sin a great sin: ... he tore, *NEB* ... Jeroboam enticed, *NIV* ... commit a great sin, *NKJV* ... caused them to, *Anchor*.

22. For the children of Israel walked in all the sins of Jeroboam which he did; they departed not from them: ... went on with all the sins which Jeroboam did; they did not keep themselves, *BB* ... did not turn away, *Berkeley* ... continued to practice all the sins he had committed, *Good News* ... To his evil example the men of Israel clung, *Knox*.

23. Until the LORD removed Israel out of his sight, as he had said by all his servants the prophets: ... from his face, as he had spoken in the hand, *Douay* ... banished the Israelites from his presence, *NEB* ... as he had threatened by, *Moffatt* ... as he had foretold, *NAB*.

So was Israel carried away out of their own land to Assyria unto this day: ... went into exile from their native soil, *NAB* ... were taken from their homeland into exile, *NIV* ... they have been there to this day, *NCV*.

24. And the king of Assyria brought men from Babylon, and from Cuthah, and from Ava, and from Hamath, and from Sepharvaim, and placed them in the cities of Samaria instead of the children of Israel: ... brought people, *NKJV* ... settled them, *Anchor* ... put them in the towns, *BB* ... had them live in the towns of Samaria, replacing the Israelites, *Beck*.

and they possessed Samaria, and dwelt in the cities thereof: ... they got Samaria for their heritage, living in its towns, *BB* ... They took over, *Beck* ... occupied, *NEB*.

25. And so it was at the beginning of their dwelling there, that they feared not the LORD: ... they did not give worship, *BB* ... When they first came to live there, they did not revere, *Berkeley* ... the new comers who were settled there did not reverence the EVER-LIVING, *Fenton* ... did not pay homage, *NEB* ... did not venerate, *NAB*.

time and again, by the prophets sent from Yahweh (note the double reference to "my servants the prophets" in vv. 13, 23). They knew, or should have known, that Yahweh was angry (vv. 11, 17f). They had been warned many times. They were without excuse. Even Judah (v. 19) was in danger; as the prophets had warned Israel (alas, to no avail), the example of Israel was to warn Judah (alas, once again, ultimately to no avail). Perhaps the theme could well be simply summarized as, "they knew better." They were without excuse.

17:24–41. Results of the fall of the nation of Israel: Syncretism and Disobedience. The balance of the chapter mainly focuses on the peoples brought into the land by the Assyrians and their religious misadventures. Here, "they did not know better." They too were syncretistic, but they had some excuse—they were pagans from birth, after all (cf. vv. 24ff, 29–33). They did not know any better. But they too were without excuse, for Yahweh showed them, even them, the proper way to worship Him. He sent lions (v. 25), with the result that the king of Assyria sought

3553.141	8427	3940	3486.116	881, 3176	8365.321	3176	904
v Qal inf con, ps 3mp	adv	neg part	v Qal pf 3cp	do, pn	cj, v Piel impf 3ms	pn	prep, ps 3mp
שִׁבְתָּם	שָׁם	לֹא	יָרְאוּ	אֶת־יְהוָה	וַיְשַׁלַּח	יְהוָה	בָּהֶם
shivtām	shām	lō'	yārᵉ'û	'eth-yᵉhwāh	wayshallach	yᵉhwāh	bāhem
their dwelling	there	not	they feared	Yahweh	but He sent	Yahweh	among them

881, 761	2030.126	2103.152	904		569.126	3937, 4567
do, art, n fp	cj, v Qal impf 3mp	v Qal act ptc mp	prep, ps 3mp	**26.**	cj, v Qal impf 3mp	prep, *n ms*
אֶת־הָאֲרָיוֹת	וַיִּהְיוּ	הֹרְגִים	בָּהֶם		וַיֹּאמְרוּ	לְמֶלֶךְ
'eth-hā'ărāyôth	wayyihyû	hōrᵉghîm	bāhem		wayyō'mᵉrû	lᵉmelekh
the lions	and they were	killers	among them		and they said	to the king of

831	3937, 569.141	1504	866	1580.513	3553.523
pn	prep, v Qal inf con	art, n mp	rel part	v Hiphil pf 2ms	cj, v Hiphil impf 2ms
אַשּׁוּר	לֵאמֹר	הַגּוֹיִם	אֲשֶׁר	הִגְלִיתָ	וַתּוֹשֶׁב
'ashshûr	lē'mōr	haggôyim	'ăsher	highlîthā	wattôshev
Assyria	saying	the nations	which	you have deported to	and you have made to dwell

904, 6111	8497	3940	3156.116	881, 5122	435	800
prep, *n fp*	pn	neg part	v Qal pf 3cp	do, *n ms*	*n mp*	art, n fs
בְּעָרֵי	שֹׁמְרוֹן	לֹא	יָדְעוּ	אֶת־מִשְׁפַּט	אֱלֹהֵי	הָאָרֶץ
bᵉ'ārê	shōmᵉrôn	lō'	yādhᵉ'û	'eth-mishpaṭ	'ĕlōhê	hā'ārets
in the cities of	Samaria	not	they know	the ordinance of	the God of	the land

8365.321, 904	881, 761	2079	4322.552	881	3626, 866
cj, v Piel impf 3ms, prep, ps 3mp	do, art, n fp	cj, intrj, ps 3mp	v Hiphil ptc mp	do, ps 3mp	prep, rel part
וַיְשַׁלַּח־בָּם	אֶת־הָאֲרָיוֹת	וְהִנָּם	מְמִיתִים	אוֹתָם	כַּאֲשֶׁר
wayshallach-bām	'eth-hā'ărāyôth	wᵉhinnām	mᵉmîthîm	'ôthām	ka'ăsher
and he has sent among them	the lions	and behold they	killing	them	because

375	3156.152	881, 5122	435	800
sub, ps 3mp	v Qal act ptc mp	do, *n ms*	*n mp*	art, n fs
אֵינָם	יֹדְעִים	אֶת־מִשְׁפַּט	אֱלֹהֵי	הָאָרֶץ
'ênām	yōdhᵉ'îm	'eth-mishpaṭ	'ĕlōhê	hā'ārets
there is not of them	ones who know	the ordinance of	the God of	the land

	6943.321	4567, 831	3937, 569.141	2050.533	8427	259
27.	cj, v Piel impf 3ms	*n ms*, pn	prep, v Qal inf con	v Hiphil impv 2mp	adv	num
	וַיְצַו	מֶלֶךְ־אַשּׁוּר	לֵאמֹר	הֹלִיכוּ	שָׁמָּה	אֶחָד
	waytsaw	melekh-'ashshûr	lē'mōr	hōlîkhû	shāmmāh	'echādh
	and he commanded	the king of Assyria	saying	cause to go	to there	one

4623, 3669	866	1580.517	4623, 8427	2050.126	3553.126
prep, art, n mp	rel pron	v Hiphil pf 2mp	prep, adv	cj, v Qal juss 3mp	cj, v Qal juss 3mp
מֵהַכֹּהֲנִים	אֲשֶׁר	הִגְלִיתֶם	מִשָּׁם	וְיֵלְכוּ	וְיֵשְׁבוּ
mēhakkōhᵉnîm	'ăsher	highlîthem	mishshām	wᵉyēlᵉkhû	wᵉyēshᵉvû
from the priests	whom	you have deported	from there	that they may go	and they may dwell

8427	3498.521	881, 5122	435	800		971.121	259
adv	cj, v Hiphil juss 3ms, ps 3mp	do, *n ms*	*n mp*	art, n fs	**28.**	cj, v Qal impf 3ms	num
שָׁם	וְיֹרֵם	אֶת־מִשְׁפַּט	אֱלֹהֵי	הָאָרֶץ		וַיָּבֹא	אֶחָד
shām	wᵉyōrēm	'eth-mishpaṭ	'ĕlōhê	hā'ārets		wayyāvō'	'echādh
there	and he may teach them	the ordinance of	the God of	the land		and he came	one

4623, 3669	866	1580.516	4623, 8497	3553.121	904, 1044
prep, pn	rel pron	v Hiphil pf 3cp	prep, pn	cj, v Qal impf 3ms	prep, pn
מֵהַכֹּהֲנִים	אֲשֶׁר	הִגְלוּ	מִשֹּׁמְרוֹן	וַיֵּשֶׁב	בְּבֵית־אֵל
mēhakkōhᵉnîm	'ăsher	highlû	mishshōmᵉrôn	wayyēshev	bᵉvêth-'ēl
from the priests	whom	they had deported	from Samaria	and he dwelled	in Bethel

2030.121	3498.551	881	351	3486.126	881, 3176		2030.126
cj, v Qal impf 3ms	v Hiphil ptc ms	do, ps 3mp	intrg	v Qal juss 3mp	do, pn	29.	cj, v Qal impf 3mp
וַיְהִי	מוֹרֶה	אֹתָם	אֵיךְ	יִירְאוּ	אֶת־יְהוָה		וַיִּהְיוּ
wayhî	môreh	'ōthām	'êkh	yîr^{e}'û	'eth-y^{e}hwāh		wayyihyû
and he was	teaching	them	how	they should fear	Yahweh		but they were

6449.152	1504	1504	435	5299.526	904, 1041
v Qal act ptc mp	n ms	n ms	n mp, ps 3ms	cj, v Hiphil impf 3mp	prep, *n ms*
עֹשִׂים	גּוֹי	גּוֹי	אֱלֹהָיו	וַיַּנִּיחוּ	בְּבֵית
'ōsîm	gôy	gôy	'ĕlōhâv	wayyanîchû	b^{e}vêth
doing	a nation	a nation	its gods	and they caused to stay	in the temple of

therefore the LORD sent lions among them, which slew some of them: ... causing the death of some of them, *BB* ... that killed some of them, *Beck* ... a plague of lions, that preyed upon them, *Knox* ... some of the people, *NIV.*

26. Wherefore they spake to the king of Assyria, saying, The nations which thou hast removed, and placed in the cities of Samaria, know not the manner of the God of the land: ... do not know the rituals, *NKJV* ... do not know how to worship, *NLT* ... do not know the law of, *NRSV* ... did not know the established usage, *REB*.

therefore he hath sent lions among them, and, behold, they slay them, because they know not the manner of the God of the land: ... indeed, they are killing them because they do not know the rituals, *NKJV* ... do not know the law, *NRSV* ... They are preying upon them, because they do not know the rites of the local god!, *Anchor* ... to destroy them because they have not worshiped him correctly, *NLT.*

27. Then the king of Assyria commanded, saying, Carry thither one of the priests whom ye brought from thence: ... gave orders, *BB* ... Send back one of the priests we brought as prisoners, *Good News* ... whom I carried away from there, *Goodspeed* ... whom I deported, *NAB*.

and let them go and dwell there, and let him teach them the manner of the God of the land: ... and live there and teach them how to worship the god of the country, *Beck* ... the law of, *Berkeley* ... the religion of, *Moffatt* ... and reside there, and teach them the decrees of the GOD, *Fenton*.

28. Then one of the priests whom they had carried away from Samaria came and dwelt in Beth-el, and taught them how they should fear the LORD: ... had been carried away captive, *Douay* ... the people how to honor, *NCV* ... how to worship, *NIV* ... how to revere Yahweh, *Anchor.*

29. Howbeit every nation made gods of their own, and put them in the houses of the high places which the Samaritans had made, every nation in their cities wherein they dwelt: ... continued to make its own idols, and they set them in the shrines, *Beck* ... set them up in the sanctuary of, *Berkeley* ... in their towns where they resided, *Fenton* ... each nation would fashion the image of its own god, *Knox*.

out an exiled Samarian priest to send back to teach the people "what the god of the land requires" (vv. 27f). Imagine that—a pagan Assyrian king showing more respect for the "god of the land" than the Israelites did. Why is it that pagans often show more respect for God than we Christians do? Does "familiarity breed contempt" even in the religious realm?

Yet again, even with their worship of Yahweh, the newcomers remained faithful to their old ways. Again the operative word here is "syncretism." The pagans had no trouble adding worship of the new god to their ancestral religions. What is one more god? Their gods, it should be recalled, were not jealous, like Yahweh was and is. To quote Trent Butler once again (cf. comments on Yahweh's jealousy, above, on 1:17f): "Yahweh's uniqueness lies in his jealousy over against his worshipers. ... He will not share them with any other god."

Insightful comments such as this help explain the parting themes of vv. 34–41 of the present chapter. These dislocated peoples were then in Yahweh's land, yet they persisted in worshiping their ancestral gods, too. They were originally ignorant of Yahweh's ways, but now, they too, are without excuse. They now know the ways of the covenant God, so the writer can now quote the Law, as it were, to them too. (This entire section is replete with covenant language.) Indeed, the fate of the Israelites stood as warning to them too: "Do not forget the covenant. ... Do not worship other gods. ... Worship Yahweh alone. ... Be careful always to keep the decrees, the ordinances, the laws, and the commands he wrote for you. ..." (vv. 35–39; notice that the prohibition against worshiping other gods is repeated no less than three times in this short section). The chapter closes with the

1154	866	6449.116	8505	1504	1504	904, 6111	866
art, n fp	rel part	v Qal pf 3cp	art, pn	n ms	n ms	prep, n fp, ps 3mp	rel part
הַבָּמוֹת	אֲשֶׁר	עָשׂוּ	הַשֹּׁמְרֹנִים	גּוֹי	גּוֹי	בְּעָרֵיהֶם	אֲשֶׁר
habbāmôth	'ăsher	‘āsû	hashshōmᵉrōnîm	gôy	gôy	bᵉ'ārêhem	'ăsher
the high places	which	they had made	the Samaritans	a nation	a nation	in their cities	which

2062	3553.152	8427		596	928	6449.116	881, 5715	5715
pers pron	v Qal act ptc mp	adv	**30.**	cj, *n mp*	pn	v Qal pf 3cp	do, pn	pn
הֵם	יֹשְׁבִים	שָׁם		וְאַנְשֵׁי	בָבֶל	עָשׂוּ	אֶת־סֻכּוֹת	בְּנוֹת
hēm	yōshᵉvîm	shām		wᵉ'anshê	vāvel	‘āsû	'eth-sukkôth	bᵉnôth
they	dwelling	there		and the men of	Babylon	they made	Succoth	Benoth

382, 3693	6449.116	881, 5554	596	2679	6449.116	881, 835
cj, *n mp*, pn	v Qal pf 3cp	do, pn	cj, *n mp*	pn	v Qal pf 3cp	do, pn
וְאַנְשֵׁי־כוּת	עָשׂוּ	אֶת־נֵרְגַל	וְאַנְשֵׁי	חֲמָת	עָשׂוּ	אֶת־אֲשִׁימָא
wᵉ'anshê-khûth	‘āsû	'eth-nērᵉghal	wᵉ'anshê	chămāth	‘āsû	'eth-'ăshîmā'
and the men of Cuth	they made	Nergal	and the men of	Hamath	they made	Ashima

	5977	6449.116	5201	881, 9002	5817	8041.152
31.	cj, art, pn	v Qal pf 3cp	pn	cj, do, pn	cj, art, pn	v Qal act ptc mp
	וְהָעַוִּים	עָשׂוּ	נִבְחַז	וְאֶת־תַּרְתָּק	וְהַסְפַרְוִים	שֹׂרְפִים
	wᵉhā‘awwîm	‘āsû	nivchaz	wᵉ'eth-tartāq	wᵉhaspharwîm	sōrᵉphîm
	and the Avvim	they made	Nibhaz	and Tartak	and the Sepharvaim	burning

881, 1158	904, 813	3937, 149	6279	438	5817
do, n mp, ps 3mp	prep, art, n fs	prep, pn	cj, pn	*n ms*	pn
אֶת־בְּנֵיהֶם	בָּאֵשׁ	לְאַדְרַמֶּלֶךְ	וַעֲנַמֶּלֶךְ	אֱלֹהַּ	סְפַרִים
'eth-bᵉnêhem	bā'ēsh	lᵉ'adhrammelekh	wa‘ănammelekh	'ĕlōahh	sᵉpharîm
their children	in the fire	to Adrammelech	and Anammelech	the god of	Sepharvaim

	2030.126	3486.152	881, 3176	6449.126	3937	4623, 7382
32.	cj, v Qal impf 3mp	v Qal act ptc mp	do, pn	cj, v Qal impf 3mp	prep, ps 3mp	prep, n fp, ps 3mp
	וַיִּהְיוּ	יְרֵאִים	אֶת־יְהוָה	וַיַּעֲשׂוּ	לָהֶם	מִקְצוֹתָם
	wayyihyû	yᵉrē'îm	'eth-yᵉhwāh	wayya‘ăsû	lāhem	miqōtsôthām
	and they became	ones who fear	Yahweh	and they made	for themselves	among their borders

3669	1154	2030.126	6449.152	3937	904, 1041	1154
n mp	n fp	cj, v Qal impf 3mp	v Qal act ptc mp	prep, ps 3mp	prep, *n ms*	art, n fp
כֹּהֲנֵי	בָמוֹת	וַיִּהְיוּ	עֹשִׂים	לָהֶם	בְּבֵית	הַבָּמוֹת
kōhᵉnê	vāmôth	wayyihyû	‘ōsîm	lāhem	bᵉvêth	habbāmôth
priests of	high places	and they were	doing	for them	in the temple of	the high places

	881, 3176	2030.116	3486.152	881, 435	2030.116	5856.152
33.	do, pn	v Qal pf 3cp	v Qal act ptc mp	cj, do, n mp, ps 3mp	v Qal pf 3cp	v Qal act ptc mp
	אֶת־יְהוָה	הָיוּ	יְרֵאִים	וְאֶת־אֱלֹהֵיהֶם	הָיוּ	עֹבְדִים
	'eth-yᵉhwāh	hāyû	yᵉrē'îm	wᵉ'eth-'ĕlōhêhem	hāyû	‘ōvᵉdhîm
	Yahweh	they were	ones who fear	and their gods	they were	ones who serve

3626, 5122	1504	866, 1580.516	881	4623, 8427		5912	3219
prep, *n ms*	art, n mp	rel part, v Hiphil pf 3cp	do, ps 3mp	prep, adv	**34.**	adv	art, n ms
כְּמִשְׁפַּט	הַגּוֹיִם	אֲשֶׁר־הִגְלוּ	אֹתָם	מִשָּׁם		עַד	הַיּוֹם
kᵉmishpaṯ	haggôyim	'ăsher-highlû	'ōthām	mishshām		‘adh	hayyôm
like the customs of	the nations	who they had deported	them	from there		until	the day

2172	2062	6449.152	3626, 5122	7518	375
art, dem pron	pers pron	v Qal act ptc mp	prep, art, n mp	art, adj	sub, ps 3mp
הַזֶּה	הֵם	עֹשִׂים	כַּמִּשְׁפָּטִים	הָרִאשֹׁנִים	אֵינָם
hazzeh	hēm	‘ōsîm	kammishpāṭîm	hāri'shōnîm	'ênām
the this	they	doing	according to the customs	the former	there was not of them

3486.152	881, 3176	375	6449.152	3626, 2807
v Qal act ptc mp	do, pn	cj, neg part, ps 3mp	v Qal act ptc mp	prep, n fp, ps 3mp
יְרֵאִים	אֶת־יְהוָה	וְאֵינָם	עֹשִׂים	כְּחֻקֹּתָם
yᵉrēʾîm	'eth-yᵉhwāh	wᵉʾênām	ʿōsîm	kᵉchuqqōthām
ones who fear	Yahweh	and there was not of them	ones who acted	according to their statutes

3626, 5122	3626, 8784	3626, 4851
cj, prep, n ms, ps 3mp	cj, prep, art, n fs	cj, prep, art, n fs
וּכְמִשְׁפָּטָם	וְכַתּוֹרָה	וְכַמִּצְוָה
ûkhᵉmishpāṭām	wᵉkhattôrāh	wᵉkhammitswāh
or according to their ordinances	or according to the Law	or according to the commandments

866	6943.311	3176	881, 1158	3399	866, 7947.111	8428
rel part	v Piel pf 3ms	pn	do, *n mp*	pn	rel part, v Qal pf 3ms	n ms, ps 3ms
אֲשֶׁר	צִוָּה	יְהוָה	אֶת־בְּנֵי	יַעֲקֹב	אֲשֶׁר־שָׂם	שְׁמוֹ
'āsher	tsiwwāh	yᵉhwāh	'eth-bᵉnê	ya'ăqōv	'ăsher-sām	shᵉmô
which	He had commanded	Yahweh	the children of	Jacob	whom He had designated	his name

3547	35. 3901.121	3176	882	1311	6943.321
pn	cj, v Qal impf 3ms	pn	prep, ps 3mp	n fs	cj, v Piel impf 3ms, ps 3mp
יִשְׂרָאֵל	וַיִּכְרֹת	יְהוָה	אִתָּם	בְּרִית	וַיְצַוֵּם
yisrā'ēl	wayyikhrōth	yᵉhwāh	'ittām	bᵉrîth	waytsawwēm
Israel	for He cut	Yahweh	with them	a covenant	and He commanded them

3937, 569.141	3940	3486.128	435	311	3940, 8246.728	3937
prep, v Qal inf con	neg part	v Qal impf 2mp	n mp	adj	cj, neg part, v Hithpael impf 2mp	prep, ps 3mp
לֵאמֹר	לֹא	תִירְאוּ	אֱלֹהִים	אֲחֵרִים	וְלֹא־תִשְׁתַּחֲווּ	לָהֶם
lē'mōr	lō'	thîr'û	'ĕlōhîm	'ăchērîm	wᵉlō'-thishtachwû	lāhem
saying	not	you must fear	gods	others	and you must not bow down	to them

30. And the men of Babylon made Succoth-benoth, and the men of Cuth made Nergal, and the men of Hamath made Ashima: ... Babylonians made Marduk and his consort, *NAB* ... people from Babylon made Succoth Benoth their god. The people from Cuthah worshiped Nergal. The people of Hamath worshiped Ashima, *NCV*.

31. And the Avites made Nibhaz and Tartak, and the Sepharvites burnt their children in fire to Adrammelech and Anammelech, the gods of Sepharvaim: ... people of Sepharvaim sacrificed their children as burnt offerings, *Good News* ... caused their children to pass through the fire of sacrifice, *JB* ... offered their own children, *Knox* ... immolated their children by fire, *NAB*.

32. So they feared the LORD, and made unto themselves of the lowest of them priests of the high places, which sacrificed for them in the houses of the high places: ... they worshipped, *Douay* ... While still paying homage to the LORD, they appointed people from every class to act as priests of the hill-shrines and they resorted to them there, *NEB* ... who acted for them, *NASB* ... in the temples of, *Goodspeed*.

33. They feared the LORD, and served their own gods, after the manner of the nations whom they carried away from thence: ... worshiped the LORD, *NIV* ... revered Yahweh, *Anchor* ... according to the rituals of the nations from among, *NKJV* ... they continued to follow the religious customs of the nations from which they came, *NLT*.

34. Unto this day they do after the former manners: ... follow the(ir) earlier practices, *Anchor* ... go on in their old ways, *BB* ... still do just as they've done from the beginning, *Beck* ... the old habits still cling, *Knox* ... still carry on their old customs, *Good News*.

they fear not the LORD: ... do not revere Yahweh, *Anchor* ... not worshipping, *BB* ... did not venerate, *NAB* ... do not pay homage to, *NEB*.

neither do they after their statutes, or after their ordinances, or after the law and commandment which the LORD commanded the children of Jacob, whom he named Israel: ... and their practice—the Teaching and the command which Yahweh commanded the sons, *Anchor* ... or keeping his orders or his ways or the law and the rule, *BB* ... or do according to the decrees and rules, the law and the commandments the LORD prescribed for the descendants, *Beck* ... whose name he changed, *Berkeley*.

35. With whom the LORD had made a covenant, and charged them, saying, Ye shall not fear other gods, nor bow yourselves to them, nor serve them, nor sacrifice to them: ... made an agreement with them, *BB* ... You must not venerate,

3940	5856.128	3940	2159.128	3937		3706
cj, neg part	v Qal impf 2mp, ps 3mp	cj, neg part	v Qal impf 2mp	prep, ps 3mp		cj
וְלֹא	תַעַבְדוּם	וְלֹא	תִזְבְּחוּ	לָהֶם	**36.**	כִּי
welō'	tha'avdhûm	welō'	thizbechû	lāhem		kî
and not	you must serve them	and not	you must sacrifice	to them		rather

524, 881, 3176	866	6148.511	881	4623, 800	4875	904, 3699	1448
cj, do, pn	rel pron	v Hiphil pf 3ms	do, ps 2mp	prep, *n fs*	pn	prep, n ms	adj
אִם־אֶת־יְהוָה	אֲשֶׁר	הֶעֱלָה	אֶתְכֶם	מֵאֶרֶץ	מִצְרַיִם	בְּכֹחַ	גָּדוֹל
'im-'eth-yehwāh	'ăsher	he'ĕlāh	'ethkhem	mē'erets	mitsrayim	bekhōach	gādhôl
only Yahweh	Who	He brought out	you	from the land of	Egypt	with strength	great

904, 2307	5371.157	881	3486.128	3937	8246.728
cj, prep, n fs	v Qal pass ptc fs	do, ps 3ms	v Qal impf 2mp	cj, prep, ps 3ms	v Hithpael impf 2mp
וּבִזְרוֹעַ	נְטוּיָה	אֹתוֹ	תִירָאוּ	וְלוֹ	תִשְׁתַּחֲווּ
ûvizerôa'	netûyāh	'ōthô	thîrā'û	welô	thishtachwû
and with an arm	extended	Him	you must fear	and to Him	you must bow down

3937	2159.128		881, 2807	881, 5122	8784
cj, prep, ps 3ms	v Qal impf 2mp		cj, do, art, n mp	cj, do, art, n mp	cj, art, n fs
וְלוֹ	תִזְבָּחוּ	**37.**	וְאֶת־הַחֻקִּים	וְאֶת־הַמִּשְׁפָּטִים	וְהַתּוֹרָה
welô	thizbāchû		we'eth-hachuqqîm	we'eth-hammishpāṯîm	wehattôrāh
and to Him	you must sacrifice		and the statutes	and the ordinances	and the Law

4851	866	3918.111	3937	8490.128	3937, 6449.141
cj, art, n fs	rel part	v Qal pf 3ms	prep, ps 2mp	v Qal impf 2mp	prep, v Qal inf con
וְהַמִּצְוָה	אֲשֶׁר	כָּתַב	לָכֶם	תִּשְׁמְרוּן	לַעֲשׂוֹת
wehammitswāh	'ăsher	kāthav	lākhem	tishmerûn	la'ăsôth
and the commandments	which	He has written	to you	you must be careful	to do

3725, 3219	3940	3486.128	435	311		1311	866, 3918.115
adj, art, n mp	cj, neg part	v Qal impf 2mp	n mp	adj		cj, art, n fs	rel part, v Qal pf 1cs
כָּל־הַיָּמִים	וְלֹא	תִירְאוּ	אֱלֹהִים	אֲחֵרִים	**38.**	וְהַבְּרִית	אֲשֶׁר־כָּרַתִּי
kol-hayyāmîm	welō'	thîre'û	'ĕlōhîm	'ăchērîm		wehabberîth	'ăsher-kārattî
all the days	and not	you must fear	gods	others		and the Covenant	which I have cut

882	3940	8319.128	3940	3486.128	435	311		3706
prep, ps 2mp	neg part	v Qal impf 2mp	cj, neg part	v Qal impf 2mp	n mp	adj		cj
אִתְּכֶם	לֹא	תִשְׁכָּחוּ	וְלֹא	תִירְאוּ	אֱלֹהִים	אֲחֵרִים	**39.**	כִּי
'ittekhem	lō'	thishkāchû	welō'	thîre'û	'ĕlōhîm	'ăchērîm		kî
with you	not	you must forget	and not	you must fear	gods	others		rather

524, 881, 3176	435	3486.128	2000	5522.521	881	4623, 3135
cj, do, pn	n mp, ps 2mp	v Qal impf 2mp	cj, pers pron	v Hiphil impf 3ms	do, ps 2mp	prep, *n fs*
אִם־אֶת־יְהוָה	אֱלֹהֵיכֶם	תִּירָאוּ	וְהוּא	יַצִּיל	אֶתְכֶם	מִיַּד
'im-'eth-yehwāh	'ĕlōhêkhem	tîrā'û	wehû'	yatstsîl	'ethkhem	mîyadh
only Yahweh	your God	you must fear	and He	He will rescue	you	from the hand of

3725, 342.152		3940	8471.116	3706	524, 3626, 5122	7518
adj, v Qal act ptc mp, ps 2mp		cj, neg part	v Qal pf 3cp	cj	cj, prep, n ms, ps 3mp	art, adj
כָּל־אֹיְבֵיכֶם	**40.**	וְלֹא	שָׁמֵעוּ	כִּי	אִם־כְּמִשְׁפָּטָם	הָרִאשׁוֹן
kol-'ōyevêkhem		welō'	shāmē'û	kî	'im-kemishpāṭām	hāri'shôn
all your enemies		but not	they listened	rather	only like their ordinance	the former

2062	6449.152		2030.126	1504	431	3486.152	881, 3176
pers pron	v Qal act ptc mp		cj, v Qal impf 3mp	art, n mp	art, dem pron	v Qal act ptc mp	do, pn
הֵם	עֹשִׂים	**41.**	וַיִּהְיוּ	הַגּוֹיִם	הָאֵלֶּה	יְרֵאִים	אֶת־יְהוָה
hēm	'ōsîm		wayyihyû	haggôyim	hā'ēlleh	yerē'îm	'eth-yehwāh
they	doing		and they were	the nations	the these	ones who fear	Yahweh

881, 6702	2030.116	5856.152	1612, 1158	1158	1158
cj, do, n mp, ps 3mp	v Qal pf 3cp	v Qal act ptc mp	cj, n mp, ps 3mp	cj, *n mp*	n mp, ps 3mp
וְאֶת־פְּסִילֵיהֶם	הָיוּ	עֹבְדִים	גַּם־בְּנֵיהֶם	וּבְנֵי	בְנֵיהֶם
weʼeth-pesîlêhem	hāyû	ʻōvedhîm	gam-benêhem	ûvenê	venêhem
and their idols	they were	ones who serve	also their sons	and the sons of	their sons

3626, 866	6449.116	1	2062	6449.152	5912	3219	2172
prep, rel part	v Qal pf 3cp	n mp, ps 3mp	pers pron	v Qal act ptc mp	adv	art, n ms	art, dem pron
כַּאֲשֶׁר	עָשׂוּ	אֲבֹתָם	הֵם	עֹשִׂים	עַד	הַיּוֹם	הַזֶּה
ka'ăsher	ʻāsû	ʼăvōthām	hēm	ʻōsîm	ʻadh	hayyôm	hazzeh
just as	they had done	their ancestors	they	doing	until	the day	the this

NAB ... Do not worship, *NIV* ... Do not revere, *Anchor*.

36. But the LORD, who brought you up out of the land of Egypt with great power and a stretched out arm, him shall ye fear, and him shall ye worship, and to him shall ye do sacrifice: ... and him shall you adore, *Douay* ... Worship the LORD who brought you up out of the land of Egypt with great power and strength. Bow down to him, *NCV* ... he is your God, to whom you are to give worship and make offerings, *BB* ... you must revere the LORD, *Berkeley*.

37. And the statutes, and the ordinances, and the law, and the commandment, which he wrote for you, ye shall observe to do for evermore; and ye shall not fear other gods: ... You shall not obey, *Good News* ... you shall be careful to, *Goodspeed* ... and ritual, ... and to which you are always to conform; you are not to worship alien gods, *JB* ... you must be mindful always to keep the rules, the rites, *Moffatt*.

38. And the covenant that I have made with you ye shall not forget; neither shall ye fear other gods: ... Do not forget the agreement I made with you, and do not honor, *NCV* ... worship strange gods, *Douay* ... shall not pay homage to, *NEB* ... do not revere, *Anchor*.

39. But the LORD your God ye shall fear; and he shall deliver you out of the hand of all your enemies: ... give worship to the Lord your God; for it is he who will give you salvation from the hands of all who are against you, *BB* ... He will rescue you, *Beck* ... revere the LORD your God, for He it was, *Berkeley* ... from the clutches of, *JB*.

40. Howbeit they did not hearken, but they did after their former manner: ... would not listen and still followed their old rites, *JB* ... paid no heed; old custom was still the rule they lived by, *Knox* ... continued in their earlier, *NAB* ... followed after their former way, *KJVII*.

41. So these nations feared the LORD, and served their graven images, both their children, and their children's children: as did their fathers, so do they unto this day: ... Even while these people were worshiping the LORD, they were serving their idols. To this day their children and grandchildren continue to, *NIV* ... their carved images, *NKJV* ... to do as their ancestors did, *NRSV* ... these nations revered Yahweh, *Anchor*.

melancholy refrain that they, too, would not listen. Rather, they too persisted in their former practices. Yes, they worshiped Yahweh (v. 41), but they worshiped idols, too (idols of Yahweh, or idols of other gods—the text is unclear, perhaps purposely so—ultimately, perhaps it does not matter that much anyway). "To this day" their descendants do the same. Despite some curious claims to the contrary, both the Israelites ("the ten lost tribes") and virtually all of their "Samaritan" replacements, are now lost to history. We still hear of the Jews and of the Israelis, but we do not hear any more of the ancient Israelites nor of the Samaritans. They "would not listen" (vv. 14, 40), and thus they are no more.

18:1–20:21. *Hezekiah King of Judah: A Man of Great Faith and Prayer. We now move into the final section of the Books of 1–2 Kings. More specifically, we turn to the three-chapter discussion of King Hezekiah of Judah. It is not coincidental that, apart from Solomon, Hezekiah receives more space in 1–2 Kings than any other king of either kingdom, even the godly King Josiah of Judah (see 22:1–23:30, below; to be sure, references to King Ahab of Israel stretch out over some seven chapters of 1 Kings, from 16:29 to 22:40, but most of these chapters represent material about Elijah, and they mention Ahab only incidentally). For King Hezekiah accomplished what no other king was able to accomplish up to this point—he was able to stand up to the full might of the king of Assyria, and live to tell the tale. So it is with great delight that we now turn to an overview of these faith-affirming chapters of Scripture.*

	2030.121	904, 8523	8421	3937, 2021	1158, 429	4567	3547
18:1	cj, v Qal impf 3ms	prep, *n fs*	num	prep, pn	*n ms*, pn	*n ms*	pn
	וַיְהִי	בִּשְׁנַת	שָׁלֹשׁ	לְהוֹשֵׁעַ	בֶּן־אֵלָה	מֶלֶךְ	יִשְׂרָאֵל
	wayhî	bishnath	shālōsh	lehôshēaʻ	ben-'ēlāh	melekh	yisrā'ēl
	and it was	in the year of	three	of Hoshea	the son of Elah	the king of	Israel

4566.111	2488	1158, 271	4567	3171		1158, 6465	2675	8523
v Qal pf 3ms	pn	*n ms*, pn	*n ms*	pn	**2.**	*n ms*, num	cj, num	n fs
מָלַךְ	חִזְקִיָּה	בֶּן־אָחָז	מֶלֶךְ	יְהוּדָה		בֶּן־עֶשְׂרִים	וְחָמֵשׁ	שָׁנָה
mālakh	chizqîyāh	ven-'āchāz	melekh	yehûdhāh		ben-ʻesrîm	wechāmēsh	shānāh
he reigned	Hezekiah	the son of Ahaz	the king of	Judah		a son of twenty	and five	years

2030.111	904, 4566.141	6465	9013	8523	4566.111	904, 3503
v Qal pf 3ms	prep, v Qal inf con, ps 3ms	cj, num	cj, num	n fs	v Qal pf 3ms	prep, pn
הָיָה	בְמָלְכוֹ	וְעֶשְׂרִים	וָתֵשַׁע	שָׁנָה	מָלַךְ	בִּירוּשָׁלָם
hāyāh	vemālekhô	weʻesrîm	wāthēshaʻ	shānāh	mālakh	bîrûshālām
he was	when his reigning	and twenty	and nine	years	he reigned	in Jerusalem

8428	525	20	1351, 2232		6449.121	3596
cj, *n ms*	n fs, ps 3ms	pn	*n fs*, pn	**3.**	cj, v Qal impf 3ms	art, adj
וְשֵׁם	אִמּוֹ	אֲבִי	בַּת־זְכַרְיָה		וַיַּעַשׂ	הַיָּשָׁר
weshēm	'immô	'ăvî	bath-zekharyāh		wayya'as	hayyāshār
and the name of	his mother	Abi	the daughter of Zechariah		and he did	what is right

904, 6084	3176	3626, 3725	866, 6449.111	1784	1		2000
prep, *n fd*	pn	prep, n ms	rel part, v Qal pf 3ms	pn	n ms, ps 3ms	**4.**	pers pron
בְּעֵינֵי	יְהוָה	כְּכֹל	אֲשֶׁר־עָשָׂה	דָּוִד	אָבִיו		הוּא
beʻênê	yehwāh	kekhōl	'ăsher-ʻāsāh	dāwidh	'āvîw		hû'
in the eyes of	Yahweh	according to everything	which he did	David	his father		he

5681.511	881, 1154	8132.311	881, 4851	3901.111	881, 867
v Hiphil pf 3ms	do, art, n fp	cj, v Piel pf 3ms	do, art, n fp	cj, v Qal pf 3ms	do, art, pn
הֵסִיר	אֶת־הַבָּמוֹת	וְשִׁבַּר	אֶת־הַמַּצֵּבֹת	וְכָרַת	אֶת־הָאֲשֵׁרָה
hēsîr	'eth-habbāmôth	weshibbar	'eth-hammatstsēvōth	wekhārath	'eth-hā'ăshērāh
he removed	the high places	and he smashed	the pillars	and he cut down	the Asherah

3936.311	5357	5361	866, 6449.111	5057	3706	5912, 3219
cj, v Piel pf 3ms	*n ms*	art, n fs	rel part, v Qal pf 3ms	pn	cj	adv, art, n mp
וְכִתַּת	נְחַשׁ	הַנְּחֹשֶׁת	אֲשֶׁר־עָשָׂה	מֹשֶׁה	כִּי	עַד־הַיָּמִים
wekhittath	nechash	hannechōsheth	'ăsher-ʻāsāh	mōsheh	kî	ʻadh-hayyāmîm
and he hammered	the serpent of	the bronze	which he had made	Moses	because	until the days

2065	2030.116	1158, 3547	7281.352	3937
art, pers pron	v Qal pf 3cp	*n mp*, pn	v Piel ptc mp	prep, ps 3ms
הָהֵמָּה	הָיוּ	בְנֵי־יִשְׂרָאֵל	מְקַטְּרִים	לוֹ
hāhēmmāh	hāyû	venê-yisrā'ēl	meqatterîm	lô
the those	they were	the children of Israel	burning incense	to it

7410.121, 3937	5364		904, 3176	435, 3547	1019.111	313
cj, v Qal impf 3ms, prep, ps 3ms	pn	**5.**	prep, pn	*n mp*, pn	v Qal pf 3ms	cj, prep, ps 3ms
וַיִּקְרָא־לוֹ	נְחֻשְׁתָּן		בַּיהוָה	אֱלֹהֵי־יִשְׂרָאֵל	בָּטָח	וְאַחֲרָיו
wayyiqōrā'-lô	nechushtān		bayhwāh	'ĕlōhê-yisrā'ēl	bātach	we'achrāv
and he called it	Nehushtan		in Yahweh	the God of Israel	he trusted	and after him

3940, 2030.111	3765	904, 3725	4567	3171	866	2030.116
neg part, v Qal pf 3ms	prep, ps 3ms	prep, n ms	*n mp*	pn	cj, rel pron	v Qal pf 3cp
לֹא־הָיָה	כָמֹהוּ	בְּכֹל	מַלְכֵי	יְהוּדָה	וַאֲשֶׁר	הָיוּ
lō'-hāyāh	khāmōhû	bekhōl	malkhê	yehûdhāh	wa'ăsher	hāyû
he was not	like him	among everyone	the kings of	Judah	nor who	they were

18:1. Now it came to pass in the third year of Hoshea son of Elah king of Israel, that Hezekiah the son of Ahaz king of Judah began to reign: ... became king, *NASB* ... In the third year of Osee, son of Ela, king Achaz of Juda was succeeded by his son, *Knox*.

2. Twenty and five years old was he when he began to reign; and he reigned twenty and nine years in Jerusalem. His mother's name also was Abi, the daughter of Zachariah: ... He was 25 years old when he became king, *Beck* ... came to the throne, *JB* ... ruling in Jerusalem for twenty-nine years, *BB*.

3. And he did that which was right in the sight of the LORD, according to all that David his father did: ... He pleased the LORD, just as his forefather, *NAB* ... as his ancestor, *NRSV* ... Following the example of his ancestor King David, he did what was pleasing, *Good News* ... Here was one that obeyed the Lord's will no less than his father, *Knox*.

4. He removed the high places, and brake the images, and cut down the groves, and brake in pieces the brasen serpent that Moses had made: ... taken away, and the stone pillars broken to bits, and the Asherah cut down; and the brass snake which Moses had made was crushed to powder at his order, *BB* ... destroyed the high places, and broke the statues in pieces, *Douay* ... suppressed the hill-shrines, smashed the sacred pillars, cut down every sacred pole and, *NEB* ... broke down the pillars, cut off the shame images, and crushed, *Berkeley*.

for unto those days the children of Israel did burn incense to it: and he called it Nehushtan: ... Israelites in those days sacrificed to it, *Moffatt* ... up to that time the Israelites had been burning, *NIV* ... people of Israel had begun to worship it, *NLT* ... children of Israel had offerings, *BB*.

5. He trusted in the LORD God of Israel: ... adhered to the EVER-LIVING, *Fenton* ... had faith in the Lord, *BB*.

so that after him was none like him among all the kings of Judah, nor any that were before him: ... No king of Judah after him could be compared with him, *JB* ... never was a king of Juda to rival him, *Knox*.

18:1–12. *Introduction to the reign of the godly King Hezekiah. A typical Judahite accession formula (vv.1f) leads into a glowing judgment formula (v. 3; cf. v. 5), with archival-style corroborating details (vv. 4, 6ff). An excerpt from the previous chapter (vv. 9–12 [vv. 9ff accord quite closely with 17:5f; and v. 12 nicely summarizes the rest of the chapter]) round out the introduction.*

18:1–12. Accession and judgment formulas for King Hezekiah. Once again, see the introduction to ch. 15, above, for references to prior discussions of these formulas. The judgment notice for King Hezekiah (chizqîyā(hû), HED #2488, "Yahweh strengthens," or "Yahweh is my strength") is entirely positive, comparing him to his "father" David (only two other kings [Asa, 1 Ki. 15:11; and, of course, Josiah, 2 Ki. 22:2] are in this category). The writer by no means glosses over the failings of the historical King David (cf. 1 Ki. 15:5), but he never gives even a hint that David was ever disloyal to his God Yahweh (cf. the positive statements about David in passages such as 1 Ki. 11:6; 14:8f). David's undivided devotion to his God, as well as his astonishing skills as poet, warrior and leader of people (cf. the incredible loyalty described in 2 Sam. 23:13–17, for example), makes David a natural hero in Kings, not to mention the Chronicles, which idealizes him even more completely. (Concerning the theme of King Hezekiah's "incomparability" as found in v. 5 of the present passage [i.e., "there was no one like him among all the kings of Judah, either before him or after him"], see introductory comments on 19:14–34.)

From Assyrian records it is clear that Sennacherib's invasion was in 701 B.C. Because Hezekiah reigned as co-ruler with his father Ahaz, the sixth year of that co-reign was 722 B.C. However, when Ahaz died in 715 B.C., Hezekiah began his full reign and began counting the years of his reign over again, thus the twenty-nine years of his reign lasted to 686. Second Chronicles 29:3 tells us, "In the first month of the first year of his reign, he opened the doors of the Temple of the LORD and repaired them" (NIV). This was followed by a great revival and the celebration of the Passover. None of this would have been allowed by the wicked King Ahaz, so his death made possible the inauguration of a new era, and 715 B.C. was declared to be Hezekiah's first year—so the fourteenth year was 701 B.C., the fourth year of the reign of Sennacherib.

As long as Sargon was on the throne of Assyria, Hezekiah accepted the treaty made by Ahaz (2 Ki. 16:7) and continued to pay tribute to Assyria. But when Sennacherib came to the throne in 705 B.C. and found it necessary to give his attention to the Chaldean usurpation of Babylon—which was in the opposite direction from Judah—Hezekiah decided to break with Assyria and sent no more tribute (2 Ki. 18:7). Because Egypt under Piankhi seemed to have gained strength, he made an alliance with Egypt for their protection against Assyria. At the same time, he

3937, 6686	6. 1740.121	904, 3176	3940, 5681.111	4623, 313
prep, n mp, ps 3ms	cj, v Qal impf 3ms	prep, pn	neg part, v Qal pf 3ms	prep, prep, ps 3ms
לְפָנָיו	וַיִּדְבַּק	בַּיהוָה	לֹא־סָר	מֵאַחֲרָיו
lephānâv	wayyidhbaq	bayhwāh	lō’-sār	mē’achrâv
before him	and he clung	with Yahweh	he did not turn	from after Him

8490.121	4851	866, 6943.311	3176	881, 5057
cj, v Qal impf 3ms	n fp, ps 3ms	rel part, v Piel pf 3ms	pn	do, pn
וַיִּשְׁמֹר	מִצְוֺתָיו	אֲשֶׁר־צִוָּה	יְהוָה	אֶת־מֹשֶׁה
wayyishmōr	mitswōthâv	’ăsher-tsiwwāh	yehwāh	’eth-mōsheh
and he observed	his commandments	that He had commanded	Yahweh	Moses

7. 2030.111	3176	6196	904, 3725	866, 3428.121	7959.521
cj, v Qal pf 3ms	pn	prep, ps 3ms	prep, n ms	rel part, v Qal impf 3ms	v Hiphil impf 3ms
וְהָיָה	יְהוָה	עִמּוֹ	בְּכֹל	אֲשֶׁר־יֵצֵא	יַשְׂכִּיל
wehāyāh	yehwāh	‘immô	bekhōl	’ăsher-yētsē’	yaskîl
and He was	Yahweh	with him	in everything	where he went out	and He caused to succeed

4937.121	904, 4567, 831	3940	5856.111	8. 2000, 5409.511
cj, v Qal impf 3ms	prep, *n ms*, pn	cj, neg part	v Qal pf 3ms, ps 3ms	pers pron, v Hiphil pf 3ms
וַיִּמְרֹד	בְּמֶלֶךְ־אַשּׁוּר	וְלֹא	עֲבָדוֹ	הוּא־הִכָּה
wayyimrōdh	bemelekh-’ashshûr	welō’	‘ăvādhô	hû’-hikkāh
and he rebelled	against the king of Assyria	and not	he served him	he he struck down

881, 6674	5912, 6017	881, 1397	4623, 4166	5526.152	5912, 6111
do, pn	prep, pn	cj, do, n mp, ps 3fs	prep, *n ms*	v Qal act ptc mp	prep, *n fs*
אֶת־פְּלִשְׁתִּים	עַד־עַזָּה	וְאֶת־גְּבוּלֶיהָ	מִמִּגְדַּל	נוֹצְרִים	עַד־עִיר
’eth-pelishtîm	‘adh-‘azzāh	we’eth-gevûlêāh	mimmighdal	nôtsrîm	‘adh-‘îr
Philistines	unto Gaza	and its borders	from the tower of	guarding	unto the city of

4152	9. 2030.121	904, 8523	7536	3937, 4567	2488	2026
n ms	cj, v Qal impf 3ms	prep, art, n fs	art, num	prep, art, n ms	pn	pers pron
מִבְצָר	וַיְהִי	בַּשָּׁנָה	הָרְבִיעִית	לַמֶּלֶךְ	חִזְקִיָּהוּ	הִיא
mivtsār	wayhî	bashshānāh	hārevî‘îth	lammelekh	chizqîyāhû	hî’
fortification	and it was	in the year	the fourth	to the king	Hezekiah	it

8523	8113	3937, 2021	1158, 429	4567	3547	6148.111	8415
art, n fs	art, num	prep, pn	*n ms*, pn	*n ms*	pn	v Qal pf 3ms	pn
הַשָּׁנָה	הַשְּׁבִיעִית	לְהוֹשֵׁעַ	בֶּן־אֵלָה	מֶלֶךְ	יִשְׂרָאֵל	עָלָה	שַׁלְמַנְאֶסֶר
hashshānāh	hashshevî‘îth	lehôshēa‘	ben-’ēlāh	melekh	yisrā’ēl	‘ālāh	shalman’eser
the year	the seventh	of Hoshea	the son of Elah	the king of	Israel	he went up	Shalmaneser

4567, 831	6142, 8497	6961.121	6142	10. 4058.126
n ms, pn	prep, pn	cj, v Qal impf 3ms	prep, ps 3fs	cj, v Qal impf 3mp, ps 3fs
מֶלֶךְ־אַשּׁוּר	עַל־שֹׁמְרוֹן	וַיָּצַר	עָלֶיהָ	וַיִּלְכְּדֻהָ
melekh-’ashshûr	‘al-shōmerôn	wayyātsar	‘ālêāh	wayyilkedhuāh
the king of Assyria	unto Samaria	and he laid siege	against it	and they captured it

4623, 7381	8421	8523	904, 8523, 8666	3937, 2488	2026	8523, 9013
prep, *n ms*	num	n fp	prep, *n fs*, num	prep, pn	pers pron	*n fs*, num
מִקְצֵה	שָׁלֹשׁ	שָׁנִים	בִּשְׁנַת־שֵׁשׁ	לְחִזְקִיָּה	הִיא	שְׁנַת־תֵּשַׁע
miqōtsēh	shālōsh	shānîm	bishnath-shēsh	lechizqîyāh	hî’	shenath-tēsha‘
from the end of	three	years	in the year of six	of Hezekiah	it	the year of nine

3937, 2021	4567	3547	4058.212	8497	11. 1580.521
prep, pn	*n ms*	pn	v Niphal pf 3fs	pn	cj, v Hiphil impf 3ms
לְהוֹשֵׁעַ	מֶלֶךְ	יִשְׂרָאֵל	נִלְכְּדָה	שֹׁמְרוֹן	וַיֶּגֶל
lehôshēa‘	melekh	yisrā’ēl	nilkedhāh	shōmerôn	wayyeghel
of Hoshea	the king of	Israel	it was captured	Samaria	and he deported

6. For he clave to the LORD, and departed not from following him: ... was loyal to Yahweh; he did not turn away, *Anchor* ... never gave up, *Moffatt* ... his heart was fixed, *BB* ... clung to, *KJVII* ... was devoted to Yahweh, *JB*.

but kept his commandments, which the LORD commanded Moses: ... he did his orders which the Lord gave, *BB* ... observed, *NAB* ... regarded, *Fenton*.

7. And the LORD was with him; and he prospered whithersoever he went forth: ... in all that he set out to do, *NAB* ... he was successful in whatever he undertook, *NIV* ... wherever he went, *NKJV* ... whatsoever he took in hand he did it wisely, *Tyndale*.

and he rebelled against the king of Assyria, and served him not: ... and was no longer subject to him, *REB* ... He revolted against the king of Assyria and refused to pay him tribute, *NLT* ... was his vassal no longer, *Anchor* ... was his servant no longer, *BB*.

8. He smote the Philistines, even unto Gaza, and the borders thereof, from the tower of the watchmen to the fenced city: ... defeated, *Berkeley* ... overcame the, *BB* ... conquered the, *Fenton* ... beat the Philistines back to Gaza, laying their territory waste from watchtower to fortified town, *JB*.

9. And it came to pass in the fourth year of king Hezekiah, which was the seventh year of Hoshea son of Elah king of Israel, that Shalmaneser king of Assyria came up against Samaria, and besieged it: ... attacked Samaria, *NAB* ... Samaria was captured, *NEB* ... marched against, *NIV* ... laid siege to it, *Anchor*.

10. And at the end of three years they took it: even in the sixth year of Hezekiah, that is the ninth year of Hoshea king of Israel, Samaria was taken: ... was captured, *Knox* ... Samaria fell, *JB* ... the ninth year of Hosea king of Israel, was Samaria won, *Tyndale* ... of Hezekiah's rule, *BB*.

11. And the king of Assyria did carry away Israel unto Assyria, and put them in Halah and in Habor by the river of Gozan, and in the cities of the Medes: ... into exile, *NASB* ... deported the Israelites to Assyria and settled them, *REB* ... captive, *NKJV* ... away as prisoners, *Beck*.

---

defeated the Philistines and took control of their territory as far as Gaza (2 Ki. 18:8).

After only six months, however, Sennacherib drove out Merodach-Baladan, regained control of Babylon and headed west. His real objective was the wealth of Egypt, but he was taking control of countries on the way. He gave Judah special attention because, according to his records, Hezekiah tried to stop him. When the Philistine, King Padi of Ekron, attempted to keep the city from joining Hezekiah's revolt against Assyria, Hezekiah put him in chains and imprisoned him in Jerusalem.

But Sennacherib's annals tell how he conquered Ekron, defeated an Egyptian army at Eltekeh (about thirty-two miles west-northwest of Jerusalem), scattered the other mercenary troops Hezekiah had hired, and then turned his attention to the fortified cities of Judah (attacking and capturing them all). Sennacherib's annals state that he captured forty-six of them plus many unwalled villages and took 200,146 people captive. Second Kings 18:14ff adds that while Sennacherib was besieging Lachish about thirty miles southwest of Jerusalem, Hezekiah sent a message to him saying, "I have done wrong. Withdraw from me, and I will pay whatever you demand of me" (NIV). Sennacherib demanded 300 talents (up to ten metric tons) of silver and thirty talents of gold, which Hezekiah paid by taking all the silver from the Temple of the LORD as well as from the treasuries of the royal palace and by stripping the gold from the doors and doorposts of the Temple. Sennacherib also wrote that he forced Hezekiah to give Padi up and Padi was restored to his throne in Ekron.

It must have been at this time that Hezekiah became sick and was told by Isaiah that he was going to die (2 Ki. 20:2; cf. Isa. 38:1). The Bible in both 2 Kings and Isaiah finishes up the history of Sennacherib's campaigns and then goes back to tell of the sickness as a background for the coming of the envoys from Merodach-Baladan who had proclaimed himself king of Babylon for the third time. But Hezekiah's prayer and tears brought God's promise of fifteen added years and assurance that God would deliver him and Jerusalem "out of the hand of the king of Assyria" (Isa. 38:5f). Hezekiah declared this to the people to encourage them to put their faith in the LORD.

The more important themes are reform and rebellion. Hezekiah promptly and decisively moved to obliterate all pagan shrines, as well as the dubious places of Yahweh worship (cf. 2 Chr. 29:3, "in the first month of the first year of his reign"). Naturally, the "high places" are mentioned first here in the discussion (v. 4). It will be recalled that the "high places" were particularly abhorrent (cf. list of some eleven citations in 1–2 Kings to this effect in comments on 17:7–23). Concomitant to this were the "sacred stones" (Hebrew, matstevôth, probably to be

Number	Parsing	Hebrew	Transliteration	English
904, 2336	cj, prep, pn	וּבְחָבוֹר	ûvechāvôr	and in Habor
904, 2578	prep, pn	בַּחְלַח	bachlach	in Halah
5341.521	cj, v Hiphil impf 3ms, ps 3mp	וַיַּנְחֵם	wayyanchēm	and he made them settle
831	pn	אַשּׁוּרָה	'ashshûrāh	to Assyria
881, 3547	do, pn	אֶת־יִשְׂרָאֵל	'eth-yisrā'ēl	Israel
4567, 831	*n ms*, pn	מֶלֶךְ־אַשּׁוּר	melekh-'ashshûr	the king of Assyria

Number	Parsing	Hebrew	Transliteration	English
904, 7249	prep, *n ms*	בְּקוֹל	beqôl	by the voice of
3940, 8471.116	neg part, v Qal pf 3cp	לֹא־שָׁמְעוּ	lō'-shāme'û	they did not listen
866	rel part	אֲשֶׁר	'ăsher	that
6142	prep	עַל	'al	because
12.				
4216	pn	מָדָי	mādhāy	Medes
6111	cj, *n fp*	וְעָרֵי	we'ārê	and the cities of
1502	pn	גּוֹזָן	gôzān	Gozan
5282	*n ms*	נְהַר	nehar	the River

Number	Parsing	Hebrew	Transliteration	English
5057	pn	מֹשֶׁה	mōsheh	Moses
6943.311	v Piel pf 3ms	צִוָּה	tsiwwāh	he had commanded
3725, 866	*adj*, rel part	כָּל־אֲשֶׁר	kol-'ăsher	all that
881	do	אֵת	'ēth	
881, 1311	do, n fs, ps 3ms	אֶת־בְּרִיתוֹ	'eth-berîthô	his Covenant
5882.126	cj, v Qal impf 3mp	וַיַּעַבְרוּ	wayya'avrû	and they violated
435	n mp, ps 3mp	אֱלֹהֵיהֶם	'ĕlōhêhem	their God
3176	pn	יְהוָה	yehwāh	Yahweh

Number	Parsing	Hebrew	Transliteration	English
6462	num	עֶשְׂרֵה	'esrēh	ten
904, 727	cj, prep, num	וּבְאַרְבַּע	ûve'arba'	and in four
13.				
6449.116	v Qal pf 3cp	עָשׂוּ	'āsû	they did
3940	cj, neg part	וְלֹא	welō'	and not
8471.116	v Qal pf 3cp	שָׁמְעוּ	shāme'û	they listened
3940	cj, neg part	וְלֹא	welō'	and not
3176	pn	יְהוָה	yehwāh	Yahweh
5860	*n ms*	עֶבֶד	'evedh	the servant of

Number	Parsing	Hebrew	Transliteration	English
6142	prep	עַל	'al	against
4567, 831	*n ms*, pn	מֶלֶךְ־אַשּׁוּר	melekh-'ashshûr	the king of Assyria
5771	pn	סַנְחֵרִיב	sanchērîv	Sennacherib
6148.111	v Qal pf 3ms	עָלָה	'ālāh	he went up
2488	pn	חִזְקִיָּה	chizqîyāh	Hezekiah
3937, 4567	prep, art, n ms	לַמֶּלֶךְ	lammelekh	of the king
8523	n fs	שָׁנָה	shānāh	years

Number	Parsing	Hebrew	Transliteration	English
2488	pn	חִזְקִיָּה	chizqîyāh	Hezekiah
8365.121	cj, v Qal impf 3ms	וַיִּשְׁלַח	wayyishlach	and he sent out
14.				
8945.121	cj, v Qal impf 3ms, ps 3mp	וַיִּתְפְּשֵׂם	wayyithpesēm	and he captured them
1245.158	art, v Qal pass ptc fp	הַבְּצֻרוֹת	habbetsurôth	the fortified
3171	pn	יְהוּדָה	yehûdhāh	Judah
3725, 6111	*adj*, *n fp*	כָּל־עָרֵי	kol-'ārê	all the cities of

Number	Parsing	Hebrew	Transliteration	English
8178.131	v Qal impv 2ms	שׁוּב	shûv	return
2490.115	v Qal pf 1cs	חָטָאתִי	chātā'thî	I have sinned
3937, 569.141	prep, v Qal inf con	לֵאמֹר	lē'mōr	saying
4061	pn	לָכִישָׁה	lākhîshāh	to Lachish
420, 4567, 831	prep, *n ms*, pn	אֶל־מֶלֶךְ־אַשּׁוּר	'el-melekh-'ashshûr	to the king of Assyria
4567, 3171	*n ms*, pn	מֶלֶךְ־יְהוּדָה	melekh-yehûdhāh	the king of Judah

Number	Parsing	Hebrew	Transliteration	English
7947.121	cj, v Qal impf 3ms	וַיָּשֶׂם	wayyāsem	and he put
5558.125	v Qal impf 1cs	אֶשָּׂא	'essā'	I will bear
6142	prep, ps 1cs	עָלַי	'ālay	upon me
866, 5598.123	rel part, v Qal impf 2ms	אֲשֶׁר־תִּתֵּן	'ăsher-tittēn	what you appoint
881	do	אֵת	'ēth	
4623, 6142	prep, prep, ps 1cs	מֵעָלַי	mē'ālay	from beside me

Number	Parsing	Hebrew	Transliteration	English
3724, 3826B	*n fs*, n ms	כִּכַּר־כֶּסֶף	kikkar-keseph	talents of silver
4109	num	מֵאוֹת	mē'ôth	hundreds
8421	num	שְׁלֹשׁ	shelōsh	three
4567, 3171	*n ms*, pn	מֶלֶךְ־יְהוּדָה	melekh-yehûdhāh	the king of Judah
6142, 2488	prep, pn	עַל־חִזְקִיָּה	'al-chizqîyāh	upon Hezekiah
4567, 831	*n ms*, pn	מֶלֶךְ־אַשּׁוּר	melekh-'ashshûr	the king of Assyria

Number	Parsing	Hebrew	Transliteration	English
4834.255	art, v Niphal ptc ms	הַנִּמְצָא	hanimtsā'	what was found
881, 3725, 3826B	do, *adj*, art, n ms	אֶת־כָּל־הַכֶּסֶף	'eth-kol-hakkeseph	all the silver
2488	pn	חִזְקִיָּה	chizqîyāh	Hezekiah
5598.121	cj, v Qal impf 3ms	וַיִּתֵּן	wayyittēn	and he gave
15.				
2174	n ms	זָהָב	zāhāv	gold
3724	*n fs*	כִּכַּר	kikkar	talents of
8421	cj, num	וּשְׁלֹשִׁים	ûshelōshîm	and thirty

12. Because they obeyed not the voice of the LORD their God: ... refused to listen to, *Berkeley* ... paid no heed to the Lord's bidding, *Knox* ... hearkened not to, *MAST* ... had not heeded the warning of the LORD, *NAB*.

but transgressed his covenant: ... broke, *Good News* ... had broken his compact, *Moffatt* ... violated, *NEB*.

and all that Moses the servant of the LORD commanded, and would not hear them, nor do them: ... They neither listened to it nor practiced it, *Berkeley* ... they would not listen, nor obey, *Fenton* ... would neither listen nor keep it, *Goodspeed* ... not heeding and not fulfilling the commandments, *NAB*.

13. Now in the fourteenth year of king Hezekiah did Sennacherib king of Assyria come up against all the fenced cities of Judah, and took them: ... came to attack the fortified cities of Judah and conquered them, *NLT* ... captured them, *NRSV* ... all the strong cities, *Tyndale* ... seized them, *Anchor*.

14. And Hezekiah king of Judah sent to the king of Assyria to Lachish, saying, I have offended; return from me: ... sent a message to, *Good News* ... I have done wrong; give up attacking me, *BB* ... Go away and leave me alone, *Beck* ... Withdraw, *Berkeley*.

that which thou puttest on me will I bear: ... I will undergo, *BB* ... I'll do anything you demand of me, *Beck* ... whatever you prescribe for me, *Berkeley* ... what you impose upon me, I will pay, *Fenton*.

And the king of Assyria appointed unto Hezekiah king of Judah three hundred talents of silver and thirty talents of gold: ... the payment he was to make was fixed by the king of Assyria, *BB* ... exacted three hundred, *JB* ... demanded from Hezekiah, *Beck* ... made Hezekiah, king of Judah, pay, *Goodspeed*.

15. And Hezekiah gave him all the silver that was found in the house of the LORD, and in the treasures of the king's house: ... paid him all the funds there were in the temple, *NAB* ... and in the treasuries of the royal palace, *NIV* ... stored in, *Anchor* ... all the money deposited, *Berkeley*.

16. At that time did Hezekiah cut off the gold from the doors of the

---

translated "sacred pillars" or the like; cf. Hobbs, WBC, 232), and the "Asherah poles" (again some cult object, this time made out of wood). Finally, Hezekiah also destroyed the so-called "Nehushtan," (v. 4, NIV), the "bronze snake Moses had made" (nᵉchōsheth, HED #5361; Hobbs [WBC, 252] colorfully translates it as "The Brass Thing"). Apparently it was a particularly notorious idol (cf. Num. 21:9; Cogan and Tadmor [AB, 217] cite M. Haran's stress on the association of snakes with fertility rites, and how popular such rites apparently were in ancient Judah). Needless to say, merely linking a popular object or tradition with a venerable name (in this case, Moses) is no guarantee of either its authenticity or its appropriateness.

In contrast to prior scholarship, the theme in these verses of "reform and rebellion" need not signify that such religious reforms indicated removal of Assyrian religious objects from Judah. (Some scholars had earlier argued for the necessity of religious observation of Assyrian gods as part of any vassal treaty with the Assyrian overlords and the repudiation of the former as necessary precursor for repudiation of the latter.) Hobbs (p. 251) is particularly eloquent on this topic. He rightly stressed the "radical reorganization of the native Judean cultus" as what is basically envisioned in these verses. Still, vv.7f do decisively point to rebellion against Assyria as the other major item on Hezekiah's reform agenda. Just after a review of the previous chapter of 2 Kings, the reader well knows how risky such a move can be. Interestingly, we are apprised of Hezekiah's move against Assyria in line with an analogous move against Philistia as well (actually this last reference is probably to Hezekiah's military activity around 705 or later; cf. H. J. Katzenstein, *Anchor Bible Dictionary*, 5:327; also Cogan and Tadmor, AB, 217, 221f).

18:13–19:37. *Siege of Jerusalem by Sennacherib king of Assyria. As Hobbs (WBC, 247) points out, v. 13 is closely parallel to v. 9, above. This parallel structure emphasizes the inherent comparison between Israel and Judah already encountered in ch. 17, above. As Hobbs further notes, "The possibility of Judah now suffering the same fate as Israel at the hands of the Assyrians looms large." This section now begins a lengthy parallel with the Book of Isaiah, as well (2 Ki. 18:13, 17–37; Isa. 36; 2 Ki. 19; Isa. 37; 2 Ki. 20:1–11; Isa. 38 [with a major addition]; 2 Ki. 20:12–19; Isa. 39).*

18:13–16. Introduction to the Sennacherib account: Hezekiah accommodated the Assyrian king. Sennacherib came to the throne in 704. Hezekiah was already on the throne when Samaria fell to the Assyrians in 722. Attempts to emend the number "fourteen" to "twenty-four" or the like, while possible, should be resisted. Some purport that the present data in v. 13 was originally appended to the stories

1041, 3176	904, 212	1041	4567	16. 904, 6496
n ms, pn	cj, prep, *n mp*	*n ms*	art, n ms	prep, art, n fs
בֵּית־יְהוָה	וּבְאֹצְרוֹת	בֵּית	הַמֶּלֶךְ	בָּעֵת
vêth-yehwāh	ûve'ōtserôth	bêth	hammelekh	bā'ēth
the temple of Yahweh	and in the treasuries of	the household of	the king	at the time

2026	7401.311	2488	881, 1878	2033	3176	881, 559	866
art, dem pron	v Piel pf 3ms	pn	do, *n fp*	*n ms*	pn	cj, do, art, *n fp*	rel part
הַהִיא	קִצַּץ	חִזְקִיָּה	אֶת־דַּלְתוֹת	הֵיכַל	יְהוָה	וְאֶת־הָאֹמְנוֹת	אֲשֶׁר
hahî'	qitstsats	chizqîyāh	'eth-dalthôth	hêkhal	yehwāh	we'eth-hā'ōmenôth	'āsher
the that	he cut off	Hezekiah	the doors of	the temple of	Yahweh	and the doorposts	which

7099.311	2488	4567	3171	5598.121	3937, 4567	831
v Piel pf 3ms	pn	*n ms*	pn	cj, v Qal impf 3ms, ps 3mp	prep, *n ms*	pn
צִפָּה	חִזְקִיָּה	מֶלֶךְ	יְהוּדָה	וַיִּתְּנֵם	לְמֶלֶךְ	אַשּׁוּר
tsippāh	chizqîyāh	melekh	yehûdhāh	wayyittenēm	lemelekh	'ashshûr
he had overlaid	Hezekiah	the king of	Judah	and he gave them	to the king of	Assyria

17. 8365.121	4567, 831	881, 9001	881, 7521, 5835	881, 7551
cj, v Qal impf 3ms	*n ms*, pn	do, pn	cj, do, adj, n ms	cj, do, n ms
וַיִּשְׁלַח	מֶלֶךְ־אַשּׁוּר	אֶת־תַּרְתָּן	וְאֶת־רַב־סָרִיס	וְאֶת־רַב־שָׁקֵה
wayyishlach	melekh-'ashshûr	'eth-tartān	we'eth-rav-sārîs	we'eth-rav-shāqēh
and he sent out to	the king of Assyria	Tartan	and the rab-saris	and the rab-shakeh

4623, 4061	420, 4567	2488	904, 2524	3633	3503	6148.126
prep, pn	prep, art, n ms	pn	prep, n ms	adj	pn	cj, v Qal impf 3mp
מִן־לָכִישׁ	אֶל־הַמֶּלֶךְ	חִזְקִיָּהוּ	בְּחֵיל	כָּבֵד	יְרוּשָׁלִָם	וַיַּעֲלוּ
min-lākhîsh	'el-hammelekh	chizqîyāhû	bechêl	kāvēdh	yerûshālām	wayya'ălû
from Lachish	to the king	Hezekiah	with an army	massive	Jerusalem	and they went up

971.126	3503	6148.126	971.126	6198.126	904, 8916
cj, v Qal impf 3mp	pn	cj, v Qal impf 3mp	cj, v Qal impf 3mp	cj, v Qal impf 3mp	prep, *n fs*
וַיָּבֹאוּ	יְרוּשָׁלִָם	וַיַּעֲלוּ	וַיָּבֹאוּ	וַיַּעַמְדוּ	בִּתְעָלַת
wayyāvō'û	yerûshālam	wayya'ălû	wayyāvō'û	wayya'amdhû	bith'ālath
and they came to	Jerusalem	and they went up	and they came	and they stood	by the conduit of

1320	6169	866	904, 4697	7898	3645.151	18. 7410.126
art, n fs	art, adj	rel part	prep, *n fs*	*n ms*	v Qal act ptc ms	cj, v Qal impf 3mp
הַבְּרֵכָה	הָעֶלְיוֹנָה	אֲשֶׁר	בִּמְסִלַּת	שְׂדֵה	כוֹבֵס	וַיִּקְרְאוּ
habberēkhāh	hā'elyônāh	'ăsher	bimsillath	sedhēh	khôvēs	wayyiqōr'û
the pool	the upper	which	on the highway of	the field of	the fuller	and they called

420, 4567	3428.121	420	476	1158, 2619	866	6142, 1041
prep, art, n ms	cj, v Qal impf 3ms	prep, ps 3mp	pn	*n ms*, pn	rel pron	prep, art, n fs
אֶל־הַמֶּלֶךְ	וַיֵּצֵא	אֲלֵהֶם	אֶלְיָקִים	בֶּן־חִלְקִיָּהוּ	אֲשֶׁר	עַל־הַבָּיִת
'el-hammelekh	wayyētsē'	'ălēhem	'elyāqîm	ben-chilqîyāhû	'ăsher	'al-habbāyith
to the king	and he went out	to them	Eliakim	the son of Hilkiah	who	over the household

temple of the LORD, and from the pillars which Hezekiah king of Judah had overlaid, and gave it to the king of Assyria: ... and of the doorposts, … had covered with plating, *Beck* ... stripped it, *Fenton* ... broke up, too, the temple doors, with the golden plates he himself had nailed to them, *Knox* ... stripped the facing from the leaves and jambs, *JB*.

17. And the king of Assyria sent Tartan and Rabsaris and Rabshakeh from Lachish to king Hezekiah with a great host against Jerusalem: ... the general, the lord chamberlain, and the commander, *NAB* ... with a strong force, *NEB* ... with a great army, *NKJV* ... huge army, *NLT*.

And they went up and came to Jerusalem: ... They marched up, *REB* ... went up and arrived at Jerusalem, *Berkeley*.

And when they were come up, they came and stood by the conduit of the upper pool, which is in the highway of the fuller's field: ... at the canal of the upper pool on the road that goes to the laundryman's field, *Beck* ... on the causeway which leads to the Fuller's Field, *NEB* ... at the aqueduct of the Upper Pool, on the road to the Washerman's Field, *NIV* ... stopped beside the aqueduct that feeds water into the upper pool, near the road leading to the field where cloth is bleached, *NLT*.

18. And when they had called to the king, there came out to them Eliakim the son of Hilkiah, which was over the household, and Shebna the scribe, and Joah the son of Asaph the recorder: ... in charge of the palace, *Good News* ... stewart, *Goodspeed* ... controller of the royal, *Knox* ... master, *NAB*.

19. And Rab-shakeh said unto them, Speak ye now to Hezekiah, Thus saith the great king, the king of Assyria, What confidence is this wherein thou trustest?: ... Tell Hezekiah that this is the message of the Great King, *NEB* ... On what do you base this confidence of yours?, *NRSV* ... that makes thee so bold?, *Knox* ... In what are you placing your hope?, *BB*.

---

found in ch. 20. But Sennacherib invaded Judah twice, according to the text of 1 Kings, compared with Isaiah 36–39, and archaeological evidence.

It is imperative that we do not allow such chronological discussions to detract from the more important issues. In essence, at least in these brief, initial verses, Hezekiah gives up a lot (both money and prestige) when the new Assyrian king Sennacherib puts serious pressure on him. Once again, an Israelite or Judahite king gave up when the times got tough. Times were very tough to be sure. In fact, according to Sennacherib's own annals, in his "third campaign" (i.e., in 701) he conquered from "Hezekiah, the Judean, who had not submitted to my yoke" some "forty-six of his fortified walled cities"; and further, "I took out 200,150 people, young and old, male and female, horses, mules, donkeys, camels, cattle, and sheep, without number, and counted them as spoil. Himself, I locked him up within Jerusalem, his royal city; like a bird in a cage I surrounded him with earthworks, and made it unthinkable for him to exit by the city gate. His cities which I had despoiled, I cut off from his land and gave them to Mitinti, king of Ashdod [etc.; here other kings are listed], and thus diminished his land. I imposed upon him in addition to the former tribute, yearly payment of dues and gifts for my lordship [and here Sennacherib lovingly lists entry after entry of tribute, including 30 talents of gold, and 800 talents of silver]. [In conclusion,] he [Hezekiah] dispatched his personal messenger to deliver the tribute and to do obeisance" (translation, courtesy of Cogan and Tadmor, AB, 338f, from the Rassan Prism Inscription).

As is universally acknowledged, these events correspond with vv. 13–16 of the present Kings passage. The monumental wall relief from the palace of Sennacherib in Nineveh commemorated Sennacherib's takeover of the city of Lachish (cf. v. 14) and the deportation of its inhabitants; the campaign apparently took place under the personal direction of the king (cf. Cogan and Tadmor, AB, 229; also Plate 10). Of course, both this artwork as well as the Rassan Prism Inscription quoted above indicate by their strategic choice of emphasis and by their implicit silence the following fact: the rebel Hezekiah's capital city of Jerusalem was never captured. Yes, Hezekiah was shut up "like a bird in a cage," and yes, Hezekiah paid much tribute (30 talents of gold according to both the Bible and the Assyrian annals, and 300 talents of silver according to the present text [v. 14], but 800 talents according to Sennacherib's inscription [some have seen here evidence for a difference in weight between the Assyrian silver talent and the Hebrew talent), but Hezekiah remained uncaptured, and he still sat on the throne in his city of Jerusalem (needless to say, this was neither the normal—nor the desired—fate for defeated covenant-violators). Still, so far, we are in distressingly familiar territory. King Ahaz had also paid a fearsome cost in 16:8, as he emptied the treasuries of both palace and Temple to buy off an Assyrian king (indeed, here in v. 16, Hezekiah has to resort to stripping off the rich metal overlay of the Temple to help pay the tribute; truly an ignominious and embarrassing action, to be sure). But, the present narrative has barely started. We will have much more to read and to ponder.

18:17–37. The rab-shakeh called Sennacherib "the great king." Then he proceeded with Sennacherib's message, trying to break down the confidence and trust Hezekiah had placed in the LORD. Sennacherib was right in that Hezekiah's strategy and military strength had already proved meaningless before his armies. He was really saying that Hezekiah was foolish to depend on anyone to help him in his rebellion against Sennacherib.

Sennacherib was also right in saying that it was foolish to depend on Egypt. The comparison of leaning on a splintered reed meant that Pharaoh would only take advantage of those who depended on him and would turn against them.

8121	5810	3201	1158, 637	4339		569.121
cj, pn	art, n ms	cj, pn	*n ms*, pn	art, n ms		cj, v Qal impf 3ms
וְשֶׁבְנָה	הַסֹּפֵר	וְיוֹאָח	בֶּן־אָסָף	הַמַּזְכִּיר	**19.**	וַיֹּאמֶר
wᵉshevnāh	hassōphēr	wᵉyô'āch	ben-'āsāph	hammazkîr		wayyō'mer
and Shebna	the secretary	and Joah	the son of Asaph	the record keeper		and he said

420	7551	569.133, 5167	420, 2488	3662, 569.111	4567	1448
prep, ps 3mp	n ms	v Qal impv 2mp, part	prep, pn	adv, v Qal pf 3ms	art, n ms	art, adj
אֲלֵהֶם	רַב־שָׁקֵה	אִמְרוּ־נָא	אֶל־חִזְקִיָּהוּ	כֹּה־אָמַר	הַמֶּלֶךְ	הַגָּדוֹל
'ălēhem	rav-shāqēh	'imrû-nā'	'el-chizqîyāhû	kōh-'āmar	hammelekh	haggādhôl
to them	rab-shakeh	say please	to Hezekiah	thus he has said	the king	the great

4567	831	4242	1023	2172	866	1019.113		569.113
n ms	pn	intrg	art, n ms	art, dem pron	rel part	v Qal pf 2ms		v Qal pf 2ms
מֶלֶךְ	אַשּׁוּר	מָה	הַבִּטָּחוֹן	הַזֶּה	אֲשֶׁר	בָּטָחְתָּ	**20.**	אָמַרְתָּ
melekh	'ashshûr	māh	habbittāchôn	hazzeh	'ăsher	bātachăttā		'āmartā
the king of	Assyria	what	the trust	the this	which	you have trusted in		you have said

395, 1745, 8004	6332	1400	3937, 4560	6498	6142, 4449	1019.113	3706
cj, *n ms*, n fd	n fs	cj, n fs	prep, art, n fs	adv	prep, intrg	v Qal pf 2ms	cj
אַךְ־דְּבַר־שְׂפָתַיִם	עֵצָה	וּגְבוּרָה	לַמִּלְחָמָה	עַתָּה	עַל־מִי	בָטַחְתָּ	כִּי
'akh-dᵉvar-sᵉphāthayim	'ētsāh	ûghᵉvûrāh	lammilchāmāh	'attāh	'al-mî	vātachtā	kî
only words of lips	strategy	and strength	for the war	now	on whom	have you depended	that

4937.113	904		6498	2079	1019.113	3937	6142, 5120
v Qal pf 2ms	prep, ps 1cs		adv	intrj	v Qal pf 2ms	prep, ps 2ms	prep, *n fs*
מָרַדְתָּ	בִּי	**21.**	עַתָּה	הִנֵּה	בָטַחְתָּ	לְּךָ	עַל־מִשְׁעֶנֶת
māradhtā	bî		'attāh	hinnēh	vātachtā	lᵉkhā	'al-mish'eneth
you have rebelled	against me		now	behold	you have depended	for yourself	on the staff of

7354	7827.155	2172	6142, 4875	866	5759.221	382	6142
art, n ms	art, v Qal pass ptc ms	art, dem pron	prep, pn	rel pron	Niphal impf 3ms	n ms	prep, ps 3ms
הַקָּנֶה	הָרָצוּץ	הַזֶּה	עַל־מִצְרַיִם	אֲשֶׁר	יִסָּמֵךְ	אִישׁ	עָלָיו
haqqāneh	hārātsûts	hazzeh	'al-mitsrayim	'ăsher	yissāmēkh	'îsh	'ālâv
the reed	the broken	the this	upon Egypt	who	he leans on	a man	on it

971.111	904, 3834	5529.111	3772	6799	4567, 4875
cj, v Qal pf 3ms	prep, n fs, ps 3ms	cj, v Qal pf 3ms, ps 3fs	adv	pn	*n ms*, pn
וּבָא	בְכַפּוֹ	וּנְקָבָהּ	כֵּן	פַּרְעֹה	מֶלֶךְ־מִצְרַיִם
ûvā'	vᵉkhappô	ûnᵉqāvāhh	kēn	par'ōh	melekh-mitsrayim
then it will enter	into his palm	and it will pierce it	so	Pharaoh	the king of Egypt

3937, 3725, 1019.152	6142		3706, 569.128	420	420, 3176	435
prep, *adj*, art, v Qal act ptc mp	prep, ps 3ms		cj, cj, v Qal impf 2mp	prep, ps 1cs	prep, pn	n mp, ps 1cp
לְכָל־הַבֹּטְחִים	עָלָיו	**22.**	וְכִי־תֹאמְרוּן	אֵלַי	אֶל־יְהוָה	אֱלֹהֵינוּ
lᵉkhol-habbōtᵉchîm	'ālâv		wᵉkhî-thō'mᵉrûn	'ēlay	'el-yᵉhwāh	'ĕlōhênû
to all those depending	on him		and if you say	to me	to Yahweh	our God

1019.119	1950B, 3940, 2000	866	5681.511	2488	881, 1154
v Qal pf 1cp	intrg part, neg part, pers pron	rel pron	v Hiphil pf 3ms	pn	do, n fp, ps 3ms
בָּטָחְנוּ	הֲלוֹא־הוּא	אֲשֶׁר	הֵסִיר	חִזְקִיָּהוּ	אֶת־בָּמֹתָיו
bātāchănû	hălô'-hû'	'ăsher	hēsîr	chizqîyāhû	'eth-bāmōthâv
we trust	is it not He	Whom	he has removed	Hezekiah	his high places

881, 4326	569.121	3937, 3171	3937, 3503	3937, 6686	4326
cj, do, n fp, ps 3ms	cj, v Qal impf 3ms	prep, pn	cj, prep, pn	prep, *n mp*	art, n ms
וְאֶת־מִזְבְּחֹתָיו	וַיֹּאמֶר	לִיהוּדָה	וְלִירוּשָׁלַםִ	לִפְנֵי	הַמִּזְבֵּחַ
wᵉ'eth-mizbᵉchōthâv	wayyō'mer	lîhûdhāh	wᵉlîrûshālam	liphnê	hammizbēach
and his altars	and he said	to Judah	and to Jerusalem	before	the altar

20. Thou sayest, (but they are but vain words,) I have counsel and strength for the war: ... Do you think a few words dropped from the lips are as good as strategy and strength in battle?, *Beck* ... You think mere lip service is advice and, *Berkeley* ... Do you think empty words are as good as strategy and military strength?, *JB* ... only empty words, *NASB*.

Now on whom dost thou trust, that thou rebellest against me?: ... enough to rebel, *Beck* ... do you have confidence, *Berkeley* ... rely when you revolted from me, *Fenton* ... for support in your rebellion, *NEB*.

21. Now, behold, thou trustest upon the staff of this bruised reed, even upon Egypt: ... put your trust in this splintered reed staff, *Anchor* ... you are basing your hope on that broken rod, *BB* ... you rely on the staff of this crushed reed, *NASB* ... you are depending on Egypt, *NIV*.

on which if a man lean, it will go into his hand, and pierce it: ... it pierces his palm and punctures it, *Anchor* ... which will go through a man's hand if he makes use of it for a support, *BB* ... which pricks and pierces the hand of whoever leans on it, *JB* ... that will splinter and run into a man's hand, if he presses on it, *Knox*.

so is Pharaoh king of Egypt unto all that trust on him: ... put their faith in him, *BB* ... That is what the king of Egypt is like when anyone relies on him, *Good News* ... depend on him, *NIV*.

22. But if ye say unto me, We trust in the Lord Our God: ... We rely on, *NAB* ... We are depending on, *NIV* ... Our hope is in, *BB*.

is not that he, whose high places and whose altars Hezekiah hath taken away: ... whose high places and altars Hezekiah got rid of, *Beck* ... not been suppressed by Hezekiah, *JB* ... Is he not the God whose hill-shrines and altars Ezechias has cleared away, *Knox* ... Hezekiah has removed, *RSV*.

and hath said to Judah and Jerusalem, Ye shall worship before this altar in Jerusalem?: ... gave orders to, *Berkeley* ... commanding, *NAB* ... bidding Juda and Jerusalem worship at one altar, *Knox* ... telling Judah and Jerusalem that they must prostrate themselves before this, *NEB*.

Sennacherib knew what was going on in Jerusalem. During the great revival, Hezekiah had taken away the shrines and high places, which were formerly dedicated to Baal. The Israelites made them places for worship to the Lord, but they mixed worship (worshiped both the Lord and other gods). Mixed worship was an abomination to the Lord and Hezekiah was right in destroying these shrines. Sennacherib, however, missed the point. The demand to offer sacrifices at the Temple in Jerusalem only was intended to be a witness to the pagan world that there was only one true Temple because there is only one true God. However, those shrines had been popular before the revival, and Sennacherib hoped there was still enough feeling for them among the common people that they could be encouraged not to listen to Hezekiah.

The rab-shakeh then asked Hezekiah to make a wager with Sennacherib, and the rab-shakeh would give 2000 horses to him if he could set riders on them. This was really an invitation to surrender and to join Sennacherib's army as it continued on toward Egypt. It was common for the Assyrians to invite conquered people to join their army and recoup losses at the next place.

The rab-shakeh emphasizes that this would be a much better deal than depending on Egypt for chariots and horsemen.

Part of the psychological warfare of ancient kings was to declare that the gods of the people they were attacking had sent them to do it. Cyrus did this when he was approaching Babylon, claiming that their gods, Bel and Nebo, had sent him to deliver them from the misrule of Nabonidus and Belshazzar. Cyrus was successful in this, and the people of Babylon threw open the gates and welcomed his army, giving Cyrus himself a triumphal entry complete with palm branches. But Sennacherib was not as subtle. He claimed that the Lord had sent him to destroy Judah. No doubt he knew of Isaiah's earlier prophecies, where God said Assyria was a rod in his angry hand (Isa. 10:5); however, he did not pay attention to the rest of the prophecy, which was against Assyria.

Aramaic was the language of trade, commerce, advanced education and political communication between countries from before the time of Abraham down to the time of Alexander the Great. The delegation from Hezekiah asked the rab-shakeh to speak in Aramaic because they did not want to upset the people of Jerusalem who were sitting on the wall and who would spread the rab-shakeh's threats throughout the city.

The rab-shakeh's reply was even more threatening. He saw that Hezekiah and the Jerusalem leaders did not intend to give in. Therefore, he and his army would besiege Jerusalem and cut them off from supplies until there was nothing else to eat or drink.

2172	8246.728	904, 3503		6498	6386.731	5167	882, 112
art, dem pron	v Hithpael impf 2mp	prep, pn		cj, adv	v Hithpael impv 2ms	part	prep, n ms, ps 1cs
הַזֶּה	תִּשְׁתַּחֲוּוּ	בִּירוּשָׁלָם	**23.**	וְעַתָּה	הִתְעָרֶב	נָא	אֶת־אֲדֹנִי
hazzeh	tishtachwû	bîrûshālām		we'attāh	hith'ārev	nā'	'eth-'ădhōnî
the this	you will worship	in Jerusalem		and now	make a wager	please	with my master

881, 4567	831	5598.125	3937	512	5670	524, 3310.123
do, *n ms*	pn	cj, v Qal juss 1cs	prep, ps 2ms	num	n mp	cj, v Qal impf 2ms
אֶת־מֶלֶךְ	אַשּׁוּר	וְאֶתְּנָה	לְךָ	אַלְפַּיִם	סוּסִים	אִם־תּוּכַל
'eth-melekh	'ashshûr	we'ettenāh	lekhā	'alpayim	sûsîm	'im-tûkhal
the king of	Assyria	and let me give	to you	two thousand	horses	if you are able

3937, 5598.141	3937	7680.152	6142		351	8178.523	881
prep, v Qal inf con	prep, ps 2ms	v Qal act ptc mp	prep, ps 3mp		cj, intrg	v Hiphil impf 2ms	do
לָתֵת	לְךָ	רֹכְבִים	עֲלֵיהֶם	**24.**	וְאֵיךְ	תָּשִׁיב	אֵת
lātheth	lekhā	rōkhevîm	'ălêhem		we'êkh	tāshîv	'ēth
to give	for yourself	riders	on them		and how	will you turn back	

6686	6589	259	5860	112	7278	1019.123
n mp	*n ms*	num	*n mp*	n ms, ps 1cs	art, adj	cj, v Qal impf 2ms
פְּנֵי	פַּחַת	אַחַד	עַבְדֵי	אֲדֹנִי	הַקְּטַנִּים	וַתִּבְטַח
penê	phachath	'achadh	'avdhê	'ădhōnî	haqqetanîm	wattivtach
the face of	a governor of	one	the slaves of	my master	the insignificant	since you depend

3937	6142, 4875	3937, 7681	3937, 6821		6498	1950B, 4623, 1146	3176
prep, ps 2ms	prep, pn	prep, n ms	cj, prep, n mp		adv	intrg part, prep, prep	pn
לְךָ	עַל־מִצְרַיִם	לְרֶכֶב	וּלְפָרָשִׁים	**25.**	עַתָּה	הֲמִבַּלְעֲדֵי	יְהוָה
lekhā	'al-mitsrayim	lerekhev	ûlephārāshîm		'attāh	hămibbal'ădhê	yehwāh
for yourself	upon Egypt	for chariots	and for horsemen		now	was it apart from	Yahweh

6148.115	6142, 4887	2172	3937, 8271.541	3176	569.111	420
v Qal pf 1cs	prep, art, n ms	art, dem pron	prep, v Hiphil inf con, ps 3ms	pn	v Qal pf 3ms	prep, ps 1cs
עָלִיתִי	עַל־הַמָּקוֹם	הַזֶּה	לְהַשְׁחִתוֹ	יְהוָה	אָמַר	אֵלַי
'ālîthî	'al-hammāqôm	hazzeh	lehashchithô	yehwāh	'āmar	'ēlay
I came up	against the place	the this	to destroy it	Yahweh	He said	to me

6148.131	6142, 800	2148	8271.531		569.121	476
v Qal impv 2ms	prep, art, n fs	art, dem pron	cj, v Hiphil impv 2ms, ps 3fs		cj, v Qal impf 3ms	pn
עֲלֵה	עַל־הָאָרֶץ	הַזֹּאת	וְהַשְׁחִיתָהּ	**26.**	וַיֹּאמֶר	אֶלְיָקִים
'ălēh	'al-hā'ārets	hazzō'th	wehashchîthāhh		wayyō'mer	'elyāqîm
go up	unto the land	the this	and destroy it		and he said	Eliakim

1158, 2619	8121	3201	420, 7551	1744.331, 5167	420, 5860
n ms, pn	cj, pn	cj, pn	prep, n ms	v Piel impv 2ms, part	prep, n mp, ps 2ms
בֶּן־חִלְקִיָּהוּ	וְשֶׁבְנָה	וְיוֹאָח	אֶל־רַב־שָׁקֵה	דַּבֶּר־נָא	אֶל־עֲבָדֶיךָ
ben-chilqîyāhû	weshevnāh	weyô'āch	'el-rav-shāqēh	dabber-nā'	'el-'ăvādhêkhā
the son of Hilkiah	and Shebna	and Joah	to rab-shakeh	speak please	to your servants

785	3706	8471.152	601	414, 1744.323	6196	3173
pn	cj	v Qal act ptc mp	pers pron	cj, adv, v Piel juss 2ms	prep, ps 1cp	pn
אֲרָמִית	כִּי	שֹׁמְעִים	אֲנָחְנוּ	וְאַל־תְּדַבֵּר	עִמָּנוּ	יְהוּדִית
'ărāmîth	kî	shōme'îm	'ănāchnû	we'al-tedhabbēr	'immānû	yehûdhîth
Aramaic	because	ones who understand	we	but do not speak	with us	Jewish language

904, 238	6194	866	6142, 2440		569.121	420	7551
prep, *n fd*	art, n ms	rel pron	prep, art, n fs		cj, v Qal impf 3ms	prep, ps 3mp	n ms
בְּאָזְנֵי	הָעָם	אֲשֶׁר	עַל־הַחֹמָה	**27.**	וַיֹּאמֶר	אֲלֵיהֶם	רַב־שָׁקֵה
be'āzenê	hā'ām	'ăsher	'al-hachōmāh		wayyō'mer	'ălêhem	rav-shāqēh
in the ears of	the people	who	on the wall		but he said	to them	rab-shakeh

1950B, 6142 intrg part, prep הַעַל ha'al is it about	112 n ms, ps 2ms אֲדֹנֶיךָ 'ădhōnêkhā your master	420 cj, prep, ps 2ms וְאֵלֶיךָ wᵉ'ēlêkhā and to you	8365.111 v Qal pf 3ms, ps 1cs שְׁלָחַנִי shᵉlāchanî he sent me	112 n mp, ps 1cs אֲדֹנִי 'ădhōnî my master	3937, 1744.341 prep, v Piel inf con לְדַבֵּר lᵉdhabbēr to speak
881, 1745 do, art, n mp אֶת־הַדְּבָרִים 'eth-haddᵉvārîm the words	431 art, dem pron הָאֵלֶּה hā'ēlleh the these	1950B, 3940 intrg part, neg part הֲלֹא hălō' is not	6142, 596 prep, art, n mp עַל־הָאֲנָשִׁים 'al-hā'ănāshîm about the men	3553.152 art, v Qal act ptc mp הַיֹּשְׁבִים hayyōshᵉvîm those sitting	6142, 2440 prep, art, n fs עַל־הַחֹמָה 'al-hachōmāh on the wall

23. Now therefore, I pray thee, give pledges to my lord the king of Assyria: ... make a wager with my master, *MAST* ... make a bargain, *NASB* ... take a chance, *BB* ... make a bet, *Beck*.

and I will deliver thee two thousand horses, if thou be able on thy part to set riders upon them: ... if you can find riders, *NEB* ... I will give you two thousand horses—if you can, *NIV* ... to put horsemen on them, *BB* ... find that many men to ride, *Good News*.

24. How then wilt thou turn away the face of one captain of the least of my master's servants, and put thy trust on Egypt for chariots and for horsemen?: ... you repulse the attack of, *Goodspeed* ... repel a single one of the least of my master's soldiers?, *JB* ... reject the authority of even the least of my master's servants and rely on, *REB* ... turn down one of my master's minor servants, *Anchor*.

25. Am I now come up without the Lord against this place to destroy it?: ... without the Lord's consent, *Berkeley* ... dost thou doubt that I have the Lord's warrant to subdue this land?, *Knox* ... Was it without the Lord's will that I have come up, *NAB* ... do you think we have invaded your land without the Lord's direction? *NLT*.

The Lord said to me, Go up against this land, and destroy it: ... It was the Lord himself who sent word to me, Make war on this land, and subdue it, *Knox* ... The Lord himself told me to march against this country, *NIV* ... and make it waste, *BB*.

26. Then said Eliakim the son of Hilkiah, and Shebna, and Joah, unto Rab-shakeh, Speak, I pray thee, to thy servants in the Syrian language; for we understand it: ... speak Aramaic with your servants, *Anchor* ... we know it well, *Knox* ... that tongue, *Douay*.

and talk not with us in the Jews' language in the ears of the people that are on the wall: ... Don't speak to us in Hebrew, *NIV* ... while the people on the wall are listening, *Beck* ... do not speak to us in the Judean tongue within hearing distance of, *Berkeley* ... within earshot of the people on the ramparts, *JB*.

27. But Rab-shakeh said unto them, Hath my master sent me to thy master, and to thee, to speak these words?: ... Do you think you and the king are the only ones the emperor sent me to say all these things to?, *Good News* ... Did my master send me to tell only your master and you these things?, *Beck*.

hath he not sent me to the men which sit on the wall: ... people sitting on the ramparts, *JB* ... men that keep on the walls, *Tyndale*.

that they may eat their own dung: ... who will have to eat their excrement, *Good News* ... doomed with you to, *Goodspeed* ... their own filth, *NIV* ... waste, *NKJV*.

and drink their own piss with you?: ... their own urine, *Darby* ... drink the water of their feet, *KJVII* ...

The words of the rab-shakeh clearly show that Hezekiah's sickness came after his giving of tribute. Before that time, he was trusting in Egypt and not in the Lord. The inclusion of gold and silver from the Temple also showed he was not trusting in the Lord when he made the treaty with Sennacherib. Hezekiah's healing and God's promise made the difference. But Sennacherib tried to break down the confidence of the people in God's promise by saying that Hezekiah could not deliver them and that they must not let Hezekiah persuade them to trust in the Lord.

Again the people were told not to listen to Hezekiah. If they would make peace with Sennacherib, he would let them live in peace until he returned from this campaign, undoubtedly expecting to return triumphantly from Egypt. Then he would carry out the Assyrian policy of moving people around and resettling them. He promised that he would take them to a land as good as their own, where they could grow grapes and wheat as they did in the land of Judah. He probably had Babylonia in mind, for he had just removed 208,000 people from Babylonia, and it was

3937, 404.141	881, 2816	3937, 8685.141	881, 8299	6196		6198.121
prep, v Qal inf con	do, n mp, ps 3mp	cj, prep, v Qal inf con	do, n mp, ps 3mp	prep, ps 2mp	**28.**	cj, v Qal impf 3ms
לֶאֱכֹל	אֶת־חֲרֵיהֶם	וְלִשְׁתּוֹת	אֶת־שֵׁינֵיהֶם	עִמָּכֶם		וַיַּעֲמֹד
le'ĕkhōl	'eth-chărêhem	welishtôth	'eth-shênêhem	'immākhem		wayya'ămōdh
to eat	their dung	and to drink	their urine	with you		and he stood up

7551	7410.121	904, 7249, 1448	3173	1744.321	569.121
n ms	cj, v Qal impf 3ms	prep, n ms, adj	pn	cj, v Piel impf 3ms	cj, v Qal impf 3ms
רַב־שָׁקֵה	וַיִּקְרָא	בְּקוֹל־גָּדוֹל	יְהוּדִית	וַיְדַבֵּר	וַיֹּאמֶר
rav-shāqēh	wayyiqrā'	veqôl-gādhôl	yehûdhîth	waydhabbēr	wayyō'mer
rab-shakeh	and he called	with a loud voice	Jewish language	and he spoke	and he said

8471.133	1745, 4567	1448	4567	831		3662	569.111
v Qal impv 2mp	*n ms*, art, n ms	art, adj	*n ms*	pn	**29.**	adv	v Qal pf 3ms
שִׁמְעוּ	דְּבַר־הַמֶּלֶךְ	הַגָּדוֹל	מֶלֶךְ	אַשּׁוּר		כֹּה	אָמַר
shim'û	devar-hammelekh	haggādhôl	melekh	'ashshûr		kōh	'āmar
hear	the words of the king	the great	the king of	Assyria		thus	he has said

4567	414, 5565.521	3937	2488	3706, 3940	3310.121
art, n ms	adv, v Hiphil juss 3ms	prep, ps 2mp	pn	cj, neg part	v Qal impf 3ms
הַמֶּלֶךְ	אַל־יַשִּׁיא	לָכֶם	חִזְקִיָּהוּ	כִּי־לֹא	יוּכַל
hammelekh	'al-yashshî'	lākhem	chizqîyāhû	kî-lō'	yûkhal
the king	do not let him deceive	you	Hezekiah	because not	he is able

3937, 5522.541	881	4623, 3135		414, 1019.521	881
prep, v Hiphil inf con	do, ps 2mp	prep, n fs	**30.**	cj, adv, v Hiphil juss 3ms	do, ps 2mp
לְהַצִּיל	אֶתְכֶם	מִיָּדוֹ		וְאַל־יַבְטַח	אֶתְכֶם
lehatstsîl	'ethkhem	mîyādhô		we'al-yavtach	'ethkhem
to rescue	you	from his hand		and do not let him cause to trust	you

2488	420, 3176	3937, 569.141	5522.542	5522.521	3176	3940
pn	prep, pn	prep, v Qal inf con	v Hiphil inf abs	v Hiphil impf 3ms, ps 1cp	pn	cj, neg part
חִזְקִיָּהוּ	אֶל־יְהוָה	לֵאמֹר	הַצֵּל	יַצִּילֵנוּ	יְהוָה	וְלֹא
chizqîyāhû	'el-yehwāh	lē'mōr	hatstsēl	yatstsîlēnû	yehwāh	welō'
Hezekiah	to Yahweh	saying	rescuing	He will surely rescue us	Yahweh	and not

5598.222	881, 6111	2148	904, 3135	4567	831
v Niphal impf 3fs	do, art, n fs	art, dem pron	prep, *n fs*	*n ms*	pn
תִנָּתֵן	אֶת־הָעִיר	הַזֹּאת	בְּיַד	מֶלֶךְ	אַשּׁוּר
thinnāthēn	'eth-hā'îr	hazzō'th	beyadh	melekh	'ashshûr
it will be given	the city	the this	into the hand of	the king of	Assyria

	414, 8471.128	420, 2488	3706	3662	569.111	4567	831
31.	adv, v Qal juss 2mp	prep, pn	cj	adv	v Qal pf 3ms	*n ms*	pn
	אַל־תִּשְׁמְעוּ	אֶל־חִזְקִיָּהוּ	כִּי	כֹה	אָמַר	מֶלֶךְ	אַשּׁוּר
	'al-tishme'û	'el-chizqîyāhû	kî	khōh	'āmar	melekh	'ashshûr
	do not listen	to Hezekiah	because	thus	he has said	the king of	Assyria

6449.133, 882	1318	3428.133	420	404.133	382, 1655
v Qal impv 2mp, prep, ps 1cs	n fs	cj, v Qal impv 2mp	prep, ps 1cs	cj, v Qal impv 2mp	*n ms*, n fs, ps 3ms
עֲשׂוּ־אִתִּי	בְרָכָה	וּצְאוּ	אֵלַי	וְאִכְלוּ	אִישׁ־גַּפְנוֹ
'ăsû-'ittî	verākhāh	ûtse'û	'ēlay	we'ikhlû	'îsh-gaphnô
make with me	a blessing	and come out	to me	and eat	each his vine

382	8711	8685.133	382	4448, 988		5912, 971.141
cj, n ms	n fs, ps 3ms	cj, v Qal impv 2mp	n ms	*n mp*, n ms, ps 3ms	**32.**	adv, v Qal inf con, ps 1cs
וְאִישׁ	תְּאֵנָתוֹ	וּשְׁתוּ	אִישׁ	מֵי־בוֹרוֹ		עַד־בֹּאִי
we'îsh	te'ēnāthô	ûshethû	'îsh	mê-vôrô		'adh-bō'î
and each	his fig tree	and drink	each	the water of his cistern		until my coming

4089.115	881	420, 800	3626, 800	800	1765	8822	800
cj, prep, v Qal pf 1cs	do, ps 2mp	prep, n fs	prep, n fs, ps 2mp	*n fs*	n ms	cj, n ms	*n fs*
וְלָקַחְתִּי	אֶתְכֶם	אֶל־אֶרֶץ	כְּאַרְצְכֶם	אֶרֶץ	דָּגָן	וְתִירוֹשׁ	אֶרֶץ
wᵉlāqachtî	'ethkhem	'el-'erets	kᵉ'artsᵉkhem	'erets	dāghān	wᵉthîrôsh	'erets
and I will take	you	to a land	like your land	a land of	grain	and new wine	a land of

4035	3884	800	2215	3432	1756	2513.133	3940
n ms	cj, n mp	*n fs*	*n ms*	n ms	cj, n ms	cj, v Qal impv 2mp	cj, neg part
לֶחֶם	וּכְרָמִים	אֶרֶץ	זֵית	יִצְהָר	וּדְבַשׁ	וִחְיוּ	וְלֹא
lechem	ûkhᵉrāmîm	'erets	zêth	yitshār	ûdhᵉvash	wichăyû	wᵉlō'
bread	and vineyards	a land of	olive trees of	olive oil	and honey	and live	and not

4322.128	414, 8471.128	420, 2488	3706, 5684.521	881	3937, 569.141
v Qal impf 2mp	cj, adv, v Qal juss 2mp	prep, pn	cj, v Hiphil impf 3ms	do, ps 2mp	prep, v Qal inf con
תָּמֻתוּ	וְאַל־תִּשְׁמְעוּ	אֶל־חִזְקִיָּהוּ	כִּי־יַסִּית	אֶתְכֶם	לֵאמֹר
thāmuthû	wᵉ'al-tishmᵉ'û	'el-chizqîyāhû	kî-yassîth	'ethkhem	lē'mōr
you will die	and do not listen	to Hezekiah	because he will deceive	you	saying

3176	5522.521		1950B, 5522.542	5522.516	435
pn	v Hiphil impf 3ms, ps 1cp	33.	intrg part, v Hiphil inf abs	v Hiphil pf 3cp	*n mp*
יְהוָה	יַצִּילֵנוּ		הַהַצֵּל	הִצִּילוּ	אֱלֹהֵי
yᵉhwāh	yatstsîlēnû		hahatstsēl	hitstsîlû	'ĕlōhê
Yahweh	He will rescue us		have delivering	they ever delivered	the gods of

waste, *NKJV* ... ventings of their own bodies, *Knox*.

28. Then Rab-shakeh stood and cried with a loud voice in the Jews' language, and spake, saying, Hear the word of the great king, the king of Assyria: ... drew himself up and shouted loudly in the Judaean language, Listen, *JB* ... stepped forward, shouting aloud, *Moffatt* ... shouted in Hebrew, *NEB* ... called out … in the language of Judah, *NRSV*.

29. Thus saith the king, Let not Hezekiah deceive you: ... mislead you, *Fenton* ... delude you, *JB* ... Do not be taken in by Hezekiah, *REB* ... Do not be tricked by, *BB*.

for he shall not be able to deliver you out of his hand: ... there is no salvation for you in him, *BB* ... cannot save you from me, *Anchor* ... is not able to deliver you, *Fenton* ... will be powerless to save you from my clutches, *JB*.

30. Neither let Hezekiah make you trust in the LORD, saying, The LORD will surely deliver us: ... induce you to trust in, *Moffatt* ... persuade you to rely on the LORD, and tell you that the LORD will save you, *NEB* ... Do not permit Hezekiah to make you have confidence in the LORD with the promise, *Berkeley* ... is certain to bring you aid, *Knox*.

and this city shall not be delivered into the hand of the king of Assyria: ... and prevent this town from falling into the, *Moffatt* ... this city will never be surrendered to the king, *NEB* ... he will stop our Assyrian army from capturing your city, *Good News* ... fall into the king of Assyria's clutches, *JB*.

31. Hearken not to Hezekiah: ... Do not listen to, *NAB* ... Do not give ear to, *BB*.

for thus saith the king of Assyria, Make an agreement with me by a present: ... peace with me and surrender!, *NAB* ... Do with me that which is for your advantage, *Douay* ... Deal kindly with me, *Tyndale* ... Seek my favor, *KJVII*.

and come out to me, and then eat ye every man of his own vine, and every one of his fig tree, and drink ye every one the waters of his cistern: ... water from his own well, *NCV* ... water of his spring, *BB* ... I will allow each of you to continue eating from your own garden and drinking from, *NLT* ... let everyone eat of his own grapes, and everyone his own figs, *Fenton*.

32. Until I come and take you away to a land like your own land, a land of corn and wine, a land of bread and vineyards, a land of oil olive and of honey, that ye may live, and not die: ... I come to transfer you, *Anchor* ... grain and new wine, *NASB* ... a fruitful land, and plentiful in, *Douay* ... life for you all, instead of death, *NEB* ... Choose life and not death!, *NIV*.

and hearken not unto Hezekiah, when he persuadeth you, saying, The LORD will deliver us: ... he will only mislead you by telling you that the LORD will save you, *NEB* ... when he incites you by saying, Yahweh will save us!, *Anchor* ... Give no attention to, *BB* ... when he wants to seduce you with his, The LORD will deliver us, *Berkeley*.

33. Hath any of the gods of the nations delivered at all his land out of the hand of the king of Assyria?: ... any one of their countries, *Fenton*

1504	382	881, 800	4623, 3135	4567	831	**34.**	347
art, n mp	n ms	do, n fs, ps 3ms	prep, *n fs*	*n ms*	pn		intrg
הַגּוֹיִם	אִישׁ	אֶת־אַרְצוֹ	מִיַּד	מֶלֶךְ	אַשּׁוּר		אַיֵּה
haggôyim	'îsh	'eth-'artsô	mîyadh	melekh	'ashshûr		'ayyēh
the nations	a single man	his land	from the hand of	the king of	Assyria		where

435	2679	798	347	435	5816	2083	5973
n mp	pn	cj, pn	intrg	*n mp*	pn	pn	cj, pn
אֱלֹהֵי	חֲמָת	וְאַרְפָּד	אַיֵּה	אֱלֹהֵי	סְפַרְוַיִם	הֵנַע	וְעִוָּה
'ĕlōhê	chămāth	we'arpādh	'ayyēh	'ĕlōhê	sepharwayim	hēna'	we'iwwāh
the gods of	Hamath	and Arpad	where	the gods of	Sepharvaim	Hena	and Ivvah

3706, 5522.516	881, 8497	4623, 3135	**35.**	4449	904, 3725, 435	800
cj, v Hiphil pf 3cp	do, pn	prep, n fs, ps 1cs		intrg	prep, *adj*, *n mp*	art, n fp
כִּי־הִצִּילוּ	אֶת־שֹׁמְרוֹן	מִיָּדִי		מִי	בְּכָל־אֱלֹהֵי	הָאֲרָצוֹת
kî-hitstsîlû	'eth-shōmerôn	mîyādhî		mî	bekhol-'ĕlōhê	hā'ărātsôth
that they have rescued	Samaria	from my hand		who	among all the gods of	the lands

866, 5522.516	881, 800	4623, 3135	3706, 5522.521	3176	881, 3503
rel pron, v Hiphil pf 3cp	do, n fs, ps 3mp	prep, n fs, ps 1cs	cj, v Hiphil impf 3ms	pn	do, pn
אֲשֶׁר־הִצִּילוּ	אֶת־אַרְצָם	מִיָּדִי	כִּי־יַצִּיל	יְהוָה	אֶת־יְרוּשָׁלַם
'ăsher-hitstsîlû	'eth-'artsām	mîyādhî	kî-yatstsîl	yehwāh	'eth-yerûshālam
who they rescued	their land	from my hand	that He will rescue	Yahweh	Jerusalem

4623, 3135	**36.**	2896.516	6194	3940, 6257.116	881	1745
prep, n fs, ps 1cs		cj, v Hiphil pf 3cp	art, n ms	cj, neg part, v Qal pf 3cp	do, ps 3ms	n ms
מִיָּדִי		וְהֶחֱרִישׁוּ	הָעָם	וְלֹא־עָנוּ	אֹתוֹ	דָּבָר
mîyādhî		wehecherîshû	hā'ām	welō'-'ānû	'ōthô	dāvār
from my hand		but they were silent	the people	and they did not answer	him	a word

3706, 4851	4567	2026	3937, 569.141	3940	6257.128
cj, *n fs*	art, n ms	pers pron	prep, v Qal inf con	neg part	v Qal impf 2mp, ps 3ms
כִּי־מִצְוַת	הַמֶּלֶךְ	הִיא	לֵאמֹר	לֹא	תַעֲנֻהוּ
kî-mitswath	hammelekh	hî'	lē'mōr	lō'	tha'ănuhû
because the commandment of	the king	it	saying	not	you will answer him

37.	971.121	476	1158, 2619	866, 6142, 1041	8120
	cj, v Qal impf 3ms	pn	*n ms*, pn	rel pron, prep, art, n ms	cj, pn
	וַיָּבֹא	אֶלְיָקִים	בֶּן־חִלְקִיָּה	אֲשֶׁר־עַל־הַבָּיִת	וְשֶׁבְנָא
	wayyāvō'	'elyāqîm	ben-chilqîyāh	'ăsher-'al-habbayith	weshevnā'
	and he went	Eliakim	the son of Hilkiah	who over the household	and Shebna

5810	3201	1158, 637	4339	420, 2488	7458.156
art, n ms	cj, pn	*n ms*, pn	art, n ms	prep, pn	*v Qal pass ptc mp*
הַסֹּפֵר	וְיוֹאָח	בֶּן־אָסָף	הַמַּזְכִּיר	אֶל־חִזְקִיָּהוּ	קְרוּעֵי
hassōphēr	weyô'āch	ben-'āsāph	hammazkîr	'el-chizqîyāhû	qōrû'ê
the secretary	and Joah	the son of Asaph	the record keeper	to Hezekiah	torn of

933	5222.526	3937	1745	7551	**19:1**	2030.121
n mp	cj, v Hiphil impf 3mp	prep, ps 3ms	*n mp*	n ms		cj, v Qal impf 3ms
בְגָדִים	וַיַּגִּדוּ	לוֹ	דִּבְרֵי	רַב־שָׁקֵה		וַיְהִי
veghādhîm	wayyaggidhû	lô	divrê	rav-shāqēh		wayhî
clothes	and they reported	to him	the words of	rab-shakeh		and it was

3626, 8471.141	4567	2488	7458	881, 933	3803.721
prep, v Qal inf con	art, n ms	pn	cj, v Qal impf 3ms	do, n mp, ps 3ms	cj, v Hithpael impf 3ms
כִּשְׁמֹעַ	הַמֶּלֶךְ	חִזְקִיָּהוּ	וַיִּקְרַע	אֶת־בְּגָדָיו	וַיִּתְכַּס
kishmōa'	hammelekh	chizqîyāhû	wayyiqra'	'eth-beghādhâv	wayyithkas
when hearing	the king	Hezekiah	then he tore	his clothes	and he covered himself

... been able to save his country, *JB* ... ever rescued his land, *NAB* ... saved his people from the power, *NCV.*

34. Where are the gods of Hamath, and of Arpad? where are the gods of Sepharvaim, Hena, and Ivah? have they delivered Samaria out of mine hand?: ... rescued Samaria, *NIV* ... kept Samaria, *BB* ... Did they save Samaria from me?, *REB* ... save Samaria from my clutches?, *JB.*

35. Who are they among all the gods of the countries, that have delivered their country out of mine hand, that the LORD should deliver Jerusalem out of mine hand?: ... Which of the gods for all these lands ever rescued his land, *NAB* ... When did any of the gods of all these countries ever save their country from our emperor? Then what makes you think the LORD can save Jerusalem?, *Good News* ... Of all the local gods, which ones have saved their countries from my clutches, for Yahweh to be, *JB* ... in the world has delivered his country when I threatened it, that you should trust in the Lord's deliverance, when I threaten Jerusalem?, *Knox.*

36. But the people held their peace, and answered him not a word: ... they made no reply, *Moffatt* ... were silent, *NASB* ... and didn't answer him, *Beck* ... said nothing in reply, *NIV.*

for the king's commandment was, saying, Answer him not: ... had ordered them to make no answer, *Moffatt* ... Do not reply to him, *Berkeley* ... had given strict orders that they were not, *Knox.*

37. Then came Eliakim the son of Hilkiah, which was over the household, and Shebna the scribe, and Joah the son of Asaph the recorder, to Hezekiah with their clothes rent, and told him the words of Rab-shakeh: ... who was in charge of the palace, *NRSV* ... comptroller, *REB* ... their clothes torn, *NKJV* ... clothes in despair, *NLT.*

19:1. And it came to pass, when king Hezekiah heard it, that he rent his clothes, and covered himself with sackcloth, and went into the house of the LORD: ... Hezekiah heard their report, *REB* ... took off his robe, and put on haircloth, *BB* ... tore his clothes, *Beck* ... rent his garments, *Anchor.*

2. And he sent Eliakim, which was over the household: ... manager of the house, *Berkeley* ... Superintendent of the Palace, *Fenton* ... palace administrator, *NIV* ... controller of the household, *Knox* ... master of the palace, *NAB.*

and Shebna the scribe, and the elders of the priests, covered with sackcloth, to Isaiah the prophet the son of Amoz: ... wearing sackcloth, *JB* ... robed in, *Moffatt* ... dressed in, *NLT* ... rough cloth, *NCV.*

Assyrian policy to move other people in to take the place of those captives who were displaced.

Again Sennacherib referred to Hezekiah's declaration of the promise of Isa. 38:6. But he still missed the point. He could not imagine that the God worshiped in the little country of Judah could be greater than the gods worshiped in the countries he had already conquered. The gods of those countries had not been able to save their lands from the great king of Assyria. Sennacherib implied that he was greater than any god. Therefore, he suggested that the LORD could not be any different and could not save Jerusalem from him.

The people made no answer to these taunts and threats. Hezekiah had commanded them not to answer him. By obeying the king and thus trusting God along with him, they took a new stand of faith. God would indeed deliver them.

The war party had been discredited. The Egyptians were no help. Now Isaiah had an audience with a new heart and a new spirit. He was soon able to give them the comfort of Isa. 40 and following.

The threats of Sennacherib were serious. The rab-shakeh had an army ready to besiege Jerusalem. The three who had met with the rab-shakeh then tore their clothes—probably the front of their tunics were torn open as a sign of grief and debasement because of Sennacherib's blasphemy. Then they reported to Hezekiah what the rab-shakeh said.

19:1–8. Response of Hezekiah and Isaiah: Earnest prayer and a prophecy of deliverance. As just noted, we still await the reaction of the king to the scandalous (yet oddly logical) accusations of the rab-shakeh. The king took those accusations to heart. He joined his three officials in tearing his garments (cf. 2 Ki. 18:37), and he donned sackcloth (on this custom, again a sign of grief and mourning, cf. comments on 6:26–31). They wisely sought out the one individual who could help them, the prophet Isaiah (19:2; this is the first reference to the "prince of prophets" in 1–2 Kings). As Hobbs (WBC, 274) points out, "The abruptness with which Isaiah is introduced here, and the way in which Elijah is introduced in 1 Ki. 17:1, would imply that they were well-known figures to the original readers." Still, the relationship between Hezekiah the king and Isaiah the prophet remains somewhat problematic. As H. H. Rowley points out, in Hezekiah's time, the prophet Isaiah seemed to display an ambivalent attitude toward the invad-

904, 8012	971.121	1041	3176		8365.121	881, 476
prep, art, n ms	cj, v Qal impf 3ms	*n ms*	pn	**2.**	cj, v Qal impf 3ms	do, pn
בַּשָּׂק	וַיָּבֹא	בֵּית	יְהוָה		וַיִּשְׁלַח	אֶת־אֶלְיָקִים
bassāq	wayyāvō'	bêth	y^{e}hwāh		wayyishlach	'eth-'elyāqîm
with sackcloth	and he entered	the temple of	Yahweh		and he sent	Eliakim

866, 6142, 1041	8120	5810	881	2292	3669
rel part, prep, art, n ms	cj, pn	art, n ms	cj, do	*n mp*	art, n mp
אֲשֶׁר־עַל־הַבָּיִת	וְשֶׁבְנָא	הַסֹּפֵר	וְאֵת	זִקְנֵי	הַכֹּהֲנִים
'ăsher-'al-habbayith	w^{e}shevnā'	hassōphēr	w^{e}'ēth	ziqnê	hakkōh^{e}nîm
who over the household	and Shebna	the secretary	and	the elders of	the priests

3803.752	904, 8012	420, 3591	5204	1158, 537
v Hithpael ptc mp	prep, art, n mp	prep, pn	art, n ms	*n ms*, pn
מִתְכַּסִּים	בַּשַּׂקִּים	אֶל־יְשַׁעְיָהוּ	הַנָּבִיא	בֶּן־אָמוֹץ
mithkassîm	bassaqqîm	'el-y^{e}sha'ăyāhû	hannāvî'	ben-'āmôts
covering themselves	with the sackcloth	to Isaiah	the prophet	the son of Amoz

	569.126	420	3662	569.111	2488	3219, 7150	8762
3.	cj, v Qal impf 3mp	prep, ps 3ms	adv	v Qal pf 3ms	pn	*n ms*, n fs	cj, n fs
	וַיֹּאמְרוּ	אֵלָיו	כֹּה	אָמַר	חִזְקִיָּהוּ	יוֹם־צָרָה	וְתוֹכֵחָה
	wayyō'm^{e}rû	'ēlāv	kōh	'āmar	chizqîyāhû	yôm-tsārāh	w^{e}thôkhēchāh
	and they said	to him	thus	He has said	Hezekiah	a day of distress	and rebuke

5181	3219	2172	3706	971.116	1158
cj, n fs	art, n ms	art, dem pron	cj	v Qal pf 3cp	n mp
וּנְאָצָה	הַיּוֹם	הַזֶּה	כִּי	בָּאוּ	בָנִים
ûn^{e}'ātsāh	hayyôm	hazzeh	kî	vā'û	vānîm
and disgrace	the day	the this	because	they have come	children

5912, 5052	3699	375	3937, 3314.141		193	8471.121
prep, n ms	cj, n ms	sub	prep, v Qal inf con	**4.**	adv	v Qal impf 3ms
עַד־מַשְׁבֵּר	וְכֹחַ	אַיִן	לְלֵדָה		אוּלַי	יִשְׁמַע
'adh-mashbēr	w^{e}khōach	'ayin	l^{e}lēdhāh		'ûlay	yishma'
unto the opening of the womb	but strength	there is not	to give birth		perhaps	He heard

3176	435	881	3725, 1745	7551	866	8365.111	4567, 831
pn	n mp, ps 2ms	do	*adj, n mp*	n ms	rel pron	v Qal pf 3ms, ps 3ms	*n ms*, pn
יְהוָה	אֱלֹהֶיךָ	אֵת	כָּל־דִּבְרֵי	רַב־שָׁקֵה	אֲשֶׁר	שְׁלָחוֹ	מֶלֶךְ־אַשּׁוּר
y^{e}hwāh	'ĕlōhêkhā	'ēth	kol-divrê	rav-shāqēh	'ăsher	sh^{e}lāchô	melekh-'ashshûr
Yahweh	your God		all the words of	rab-shakeh	whom	he sent him	the king of Assyria

112	3937, 2884.341	435	2508	3306.511	904, 1745	866
n mp, ps 3ms	prep, v Piel inf con	n mp	adj	cj, v Hiphil pf 3ms	prep, art, n mp	rel part
אֲדֹנָיו	לְחָרֵף	אֱלֹהִים	חַי	וְהוֹכִיחַ	בַּדְּבָרִים	אֲשֶׁר
'ădhōnâv	l^{e}chārēph	'ĕlōhîm	chay	w^{e}hôkhîach	badd^{e}vārîm	'ăsher
his master	to revile	God	living	and He will reprove	about the words	which

8471.111	3176	435	5558.113	8940	1185	8086	4834.257
v Qal pf 3ms	pn	n mp, ps 2ms	cj, v Qal pf 2ms	n fs	prep	art, n fs	art, v Niphal ptc fs
שָׁמַע	יְהוָה	אֱלֹהֶיךָ	וְנָשָׂאתָ	תְפִלָּה	בְּעַד	הַשְּׁאֵרִית	הַנִּמְצָאָה
shāma'	y^{e}hwāh	'ĕlōhêkhā	w^{e}nāsā'thā	th^{e}phillāh	b^{e}'adh	hashsh^{e}'ērîth	hanimtsā'āh
He heard	Yahweh	your God	and you will lift up	a prayer	for	the remnant	the ones found

	971.126	5860	4567	2488	420, 3591		569.121
5.	cj, v Qal impf 3mp	*n mp*	art, n ms	pn	prep, pn	**6.**	cj, v Qal impf 3ms
	וַיָּבֹאוּ	עַבְדֵי	הַמֶּלֶךְ	חִזְקִיָּהוּ	אֶל־יְשַׁעְיָהוּ		וַיֹּאמֶר
	wayyāvō'û	'avdhê	hammelekh	chizqîyāhû	'el-y^{e}sha'ayāhû		wayyō'mer
	and they came	the servants of	the king	Hezekiah	to Isaiah		and he said

3937	3591	3662	569.128	420, 112	3662	569.111	3176
prep, ps 3mp	pn	adv	v Qal impf 2mp	prep, n mp, ps 2mp	adv	v Qal pf 3ms	pn
לָהֶם	יְשַׁעְיָהוּ	כֹּה	תֹּאמְרוּן	אֶל־אֲדֹנֵיכֶם	כֹּה	אָמַר	יְהוָה
lāhem	yesha'ăyāhû	kōh	thō'merûn	'el-'ădhōnêkhem	kōh	'āmar	yehwāh
to them	Isaiah	thus	you will say	to your master	thus	He has said	Yahweh

414, 3486.123	4623, 6686	1745	866	8471.113	866	1472.316
adv, Qal juss 2ms	prep, *n mp*	art, n mp	rel part	v Qal pf 2ms	rel part	v Piel pf 3cp
אַל־תִּירָא	מִפְּנֵי	הַדְּבָרִים	אֲשֶׁר	שָׁמַעְתָּ	אֲשֶׁר	גִּדְּפוּ
'al-tîrā'	mippenê	haddevārîm	'ăsher	shāma'ăttā	'ăsher	giddephû
do not be afraid	from before	the words	which	you heard	which	they have blasphemed

3. And they said unto him, Thus saith Hezekiah, This day is a day of trouble: ... distress, *NRSV* ... tribulation, *Tyndale* ... suffering, *Good News.*

and of rebuke: ... reproof, *REB* ... punishment, *BB* ... reproach, *Berkeley* ... discipline, *Moffatt.*

and blasphemy: ... disgrace, *NRSV* ... contumely, *ASV* ... contempt, *NEB* ... dishonor, *Berkeley* ... shame, *BB.*

for the children are come to the birth, and there is not strength to bring forth: ... the mothers have no power to be delivered, *Tyndale* ... Children have come to the breach, but there is no strength, *Anchor* ... We are like a woman who is ready to give birth, but is too weak to do it, *Good News* ... no strength to deliver, *NASB.*

4. It may be the LORD thy God will hear all the words of Rab-shakeh: ... hear everything the general said, *Beck* ... listen to all the words of the chief of staff, *Berkeley* ... give ear to the words, *BB* ... heard all the utterances of Rabshakah, *Fenton.*

whom the king of Assyria his master hath sent to reproach the living God: ... defy the living God, *Beck* ... ridicule, *Berkeley* ... insult, *Goodspeed* ... blaspheme, *Knox.*

and will reprove the words which the LORD thy God hath heard: ... may the LORD your God punish him for what He heard him say, *Beck* ... have a reply for the words, *Berkeley* ... will rebuke the words, *Darby* ... Surely the Lord thy God has listened to the reproaches he uttered, *Knox.*

wherefore lift up thy prayer for the remnant that are left: ... Raise thy voice, then, in prayer for the poor remnant that is left, *Knox* ... pray for those who are still left, *Beck* ... offer a prayer, *NASB* ... for those who still survive, *NEB.*

5. So the servants of king Hezekiah came to Isaiah: ... Hezekiah's ministers went to, *JB* ... Hezekiah's officials came, *NIV* ... Hezekiah's men, *Beck* ... related to Isaiah, *Fenton.*

6. And Isaiah said unto them, Thus shall ye say to your master, Thus saith the LORD, Be not afraid of the words which thou hast heard: ... Do not be dismayed, *Knox* ... frightened, *NAB* ... alarmed, *REB* ... troubled, *BB* ... disturbed, *NLT.*

with which the servants of the king of Assyria have blasphemed me: ... spoken against me, *NCV* ... reviled me, *RSV* ... railed on me, *Tyndale* ... mocked Me, *Beck.*

---

ing Assyrians. In some places he counseled surrender (e.g., Isa. 10:5ff; 18:1–6; 22:1–14; 30:1–5), but in other places he counseled defiance (e.g., 10:8f; 31:1ff, 8f). Hezekiah had violated his oath to his Assyrian overlord, but in this case, Sennacherib was wrong for breaking the terms of surrender. In addition to that, he blasphemed Yahweh. Thus Isaiah counseled resistance.

In any case, the Judahite officials, including the king, were understandably quite desperate (vv. 3f of the present passage). They asked Isaiah to pray for "the remnant that still survives." (As we shall soon see, Hezekiah is pictured as a king particularly personified as a person of prayer.) Isaiah had recognized the "blasphemy" of the Assyrian officials (v. 6). He counseled fearlessness. (Cf. his words to King Ahaz, Hezekiah's father, in Isa. 7:9 which state, "If ye will not believe, surely ye shall not be established.") He also prophesied that a miracle would take place—the king of Assyria would hear a negative report and return home, and there Yahweh would have him assassinated with the sword (v. 7). (The "report" is detailed in v. 9, but the return and the assassination is described in vv. 36f, at the very end of the present chapter.) Yet again, a "short-term prediction" attested the authenticity of the prophet of Yahweh as well as the accuracy of his message. Meanwhile, the Assyrian king had apparently taken Lachish (v. 8), for he had moved on to Libnah, a town probably on the route to Jerusalem (this is disputed, however, inasmuch as the precise location of Libnah is still uncertain; cf. Hobbs, WBC, 275f). In any case, Sennacherib would soon have trouble on his hands from an unexpected source: Egypt.

5470	4567, 831	881		2079	5598.151	904	7593
n mp	*n ms*, pn	do, ps 1cs	**7.**	intrj, ps 1cs	v Qal act ptc ms	prep, ps 3ms	n fs
נַעֲרֵי	מֶלֶךְ־אַשּׁוּר	אֹתִי		הִנְנִי	נֹתֵן	בּוֹ	רוּחַ
na'ărê	melekh-'ashshûr	'ōthî		hin^{e}nî	nōthēn	bô	rûach
the boys of	the king of Assyria	Me		behold I	putting	in him	a spirit

8471.111	8444	8178.111	3937, 800	5489.515
cj, v Qal pf 3ms	n fs	cj, v Qal pf 3ms	prep, n fs, ps 3ms	cj, v Hiphil pf 1cs, ps 3ms
וְשָׁמַע	שְׁמוּעָה	וְשָׁב	לְאַרְצוֹ	וְהִפַּלְתִּיו
w^{e}shāma‘	sh^{e}mû‘āh	w^{e}shāv	l^{e}'artsô	w^{e}hippaltîw
and he will hear	news	and he will return	to his land	and I will cause him to fall

904, 2820	904, 800		8178.121	7551	4834.121	881, 4567	831
prep, art, n fs	prep, n fs, ps 3ms	**8.**	cj, v Qal impf 3ms	n ms	cj, v Qal impf 3ms	do, *n ms*	pn
בַּחֶרֶב	בְּאַרְצוֹ		וַיָּשָׁב	רַב־שָׁקֵה	וַיִּמְצָא	אֶת־מֶלֶךְ	אַשּׁוּר
bacherev	b^{e}'artsô		wayyāshāv	rav-shāqēh	wayyimtsā'	'eth-melekh	'ashshûr
by the sword	in his land		and he returned	rab-shakeh	and he found	the king of	Assyria

4032.255	6142, 3975	3706	8471.111	3706	5450.111	4623, 4061
v Niphal ptc ms	prep, pn	cj	v Qal pf 3ms	cj	v Qal pf 3ms	prep, pn
נִלְחָם	עַל־לִבְנָה	כִּי	שָׁמַע	כִּי	נָסַע	מִלָּכִישׁ
nilchām	'al-livnāh	kî	shāma‘	kî	nāsa‘	millākhîsh
fighting	against Libnah	because	he heard	that	he pulled out	from Lachish

	8471.121	420, 8977	4567, 3688	3937, 569.141	2079	3428.111
9.	cj, v Qal impf 3ms	prep, pn	*n ms*, pn	prep, v Qal inf con	intrj	v Qal pf 3ms
	וַיִּשְׁמַע	אֶל־תִּרְהָקָה	מֶלֶךְ־כּוּשׁ	לֵאמֹר	הִנֵּה	יָצָא
	wayyishma‘	'el-tirhāqāh	melekh-kûsh	lē'mōr	hinnēh	yātsā'
	and he heard	about Tirhakah	the king of Cush	saying	behold	he went out

3937, 4032.241	882	8178.121	8365.121	4534	420, 2488
prep, v Niphal inf con	prep, ps 2ms	cj, v Qal impf 3ms	cj, v Qal impf 3ms	n mp	prep, pn
לְהִלָּחֵם	אִתָּךְ	וַיָּשָׁב	וַיִּשְׁלַח	מַלְאָכִים	אֶל־חִזְקִיָּהוּ
l^{e}hillāchēm	'ittākh	wayyāshāv	wayyishlach	mal'ākhîm	'el-chizqîyāhû
to fight	against you	then he returned	and he sent out	messengers	to Hezekiah

3937, 569.141		3662	569.128	420, 2488	4567, 3171	3937, 569.141
prep, v Qal inf con	**10.**	adv	v Qal impf 2mp	prep, pn	*n ms*, pn	prep, v Qal inf con
לֵאמֹר		כֹּה	תֹאמְרוּן	אֶל־חִזְקִיָּהוּ	מֶלֶךְ־יְהוּדָה	לֵאמֹר
lē'mōr		kōh	thō'm^{e}rûn	'el-chizqîyāhû	melekh-y^{e}hûdhāh	lē'mōr
saying		thus	you will say	to Hezekiah	the king of Judah	saying

414, 5565.521	435	866	887	1019.151	904
adv, v Hiphil juss 3ms, ps 2ms	n mp, ps 2ms	rel pron	pers pron	v Qal act ptc ms	prep, ps 3ms
אַל־יַשִּׁאֲךָ	אֱלֹהֶיךָ	אֲשֶׁר	אַתָּה	בֹּטֵחַ	בּוֹ
'al-yashshi'ăkhā	'ĕlōhêkhā	'ăsher	'attāh	bōṭeach	bô
do not allow Him to deceive you	your God	Whom	you	trusting	in Him

3937, 569.141	3940	5598.222	3503	904, 3135	4567	831
prep, v Qal inf con	neg part	v Niphal impf 3fs	pn	prep, *n fs*	*n ms*	pn
לֵאמֹר	לֹא	תִנָּתֵן	יְרוּשָׁלַם	בְּיַד	מֶלֶךְ	אַשּׁוּר
lē'mōr	lō'	thinnāthēn	y^{e}rûshālam	b^{e}yadh	melekh	'ashshûr
saying	not	it will be given	Jerusalem	into the hand of	the king of	Assyria

	2079	887	8471.113	881	866	6449.116	4567	831
11.	intrj	pers pron	v Qal pf 2ms	do	rel part	v Qal pf 3cp	*n mp*	pn
	הִנֵּה	אַתָּה	שָׁמַעְתָּ	אֵת	אֲשֶׁר	עָשׂוּ	מַלְכֵי	אַשּׁוּר
	hinnēh	'attāh	shāma‘ttā	'ēth	'ăsher	'āsû	malkhê	'ashshûr
	behold	you	you have heard		what	they have done	the kings of	Assyria

3937, 3725, 800 prep, *adj*, art, n fp לְכָל־הָאֲרָצוֹת lekhol-hā'ărātsôth to all the lands	3937, 2868.541 prep, v Hiphil inf con, ps 3mp לְהַחֲרִימָם lehachrîmām to destroy them	887 cj, pers pron וְאַתָּה we'attāh yet you	5522.223 v Niphal impf 2ms תִּנָּצֵל tinnātsēl you will be rescued	**12.**	1950B, 5522.116 intrg part, v Hiphil pf 3cp הַהִצִּילוּ hahitstsîlû have they rescued

881 do, ps 3mp אֹתָם 'ōthām them	435 *n mp* אֱלֹהֵי 'ĕlōhê the gods of	1504 art, n mp הַגּוֹיִם haggôyim the nations	866 rel part אֲשֶׁר 'ăsher which	8271.516 v Hiphil pf 3cp שִׁחֲתוּ shichăthû they destroyed	1 n mp, ps 1cs אֲבוֹתַי 'ăvôthay my ancestors	881, 1502 do, pn אֶת־גּוֹזָן 'eth-gôzān Gozan	881, 2115 cj, do, pn וְאֶת־חָרָן we'eth-chārān and Haran

7. Behold, I will send a blast upon him: ... put a spirit in him, *Berkeley* ... send a wind upon him, *Fenton* ... will dispirit him, *Moffatt* ... I myself will move against him, *NLT.*

and he shall hear a rumour, and shall return to his own land: ... shall hear tidings, *Darby* ... hear its report, *Fenton* ... on the strength of a rumour, he will go back to his own country, *JB* ... shall hear a message, *Douay* ... withdraw to his own country, *NEB.*

and I will cause him to fall by the sword in his own land: ... overthrow him with the sword, *Berkeley* ... the sword shall make an end of him, *Knox* ... I will have him cut down with the sword, *NIV* ... will have him killed with a sword, *NLT.*

8. So Rab-shakeh returned, and found the king of Assyria warring against Libnah: ... fighting against Libnah, *NRSV* ... attacking Libnah, *REB* ... engaged in battle at Libnah, *Anchor* ... making war against, *BB* ... besieging Libnah, *NAB.*

for he had heard that he was departed from Lachish: ... had left Lachish, *NRSV* ... had moved camp from Lachish, *REB* ... had gone away from, *BB* ... had withdrawn from, *NAB.*

9. And when he heard say of Tirhakah king of Ethiopia, Behold, he is come out to fight against thee: he sent messengers again unto Hezekiah, saying: ... Look, he has come out to make war with you, *NKJV* ... He has set out to do battle with you, *Anchor* ... was coming to attack him, *NCV* ... make war on him, *NEB.*

10. Thus shall ye speak to Hezekiah king of Judah, saying, Let not thy God in whom thou trustest deceive thee: ... Do not let your God on whom you rely deceive you, *NRSV* ... Let not your God, in whom is your faith, give you a false hope, *BB* ... in whom you have confidence deceive you, *Berkeley* ... How can you be deluded by your god on whom you rely, *NEB.*

saying, Jerusalem shall not be delivered into the hand of the king of Assyria: ... will not be handed over to, *NIV* ... will not fall into the hands of, *REB* ... will not fall into the king of Assyria's clutches, *JB.*

11. Behold, thou hast heard what the kings of Assyria have done to all lands, by destroying them utterly: ... exterminating their people, *NEB* ... devoting them to destruction, *JB* ... they doomed them!, *NAB* ... how they have laid them waste, *Douay.*

and shalt thou be delivered?: ... will you be kept safe?, *BB* ... shall you escape?, *Fenton* ... will you be spared?, *NASB* ... how can you be saved?, *Beck.*

12. Have the gods of the nations delivered them which my fathers have destroyed; as Gozan, and Haran, and Rezeph, and the children of Eden which were in Thelasar?: ... What saving power had the gods of those old peoples my

19:9–13. A second Assyrian propaganda piece: No other city-state ever delivered out of their hands. In 18:19–25, the rab-shakeh had made two scornful challenges: (1) where is Egypt? and (2) where is Yahweh? Isaiah's answer, in vv. 6f of the present chapter, begins to address the rab-shakeh's second query, but we have heard nothing so far in response to his first. In the present section, however, we find a brief and enigmatic note concerning one "Tirhakah, the Cushite king of Egypt" (v. 9, NIV). Tirhakah (Egyptian Taharqa, the third and most powerful Pharaoh of the Twenty-fifth [Ethiopian or Nubian] Dynasty) did not become king until the year 690 or so. The writer takes pains to assert that the Egyptians, for once, were not "a splintered reed of a staff" (as the rab-shakeh asserts in 18:21). Their military pressure was rather a significant factor in Sennacherib's eventual withdrawal from the field.

We once again find a communication from Sennacherib to Hezekiah, this time, a letter (vv. 9–13); Hezekiah's heartfelt and pious response (vv. 14–19); Isaiah's stirring prophetic message of deliverance (vv. 20–34); and Yahweh's sudden devastation of the Assyrian camp (v. 35). A number of commentators have noted the tone of both directness and desperation in Sennacherib's message in these

7823	1158, 5943	866	904, 8844		248	4567, 2679
cj, pn	cj, n mp, pn	rel pron	prep, pn	13.	intrg	n ms, pn
וְרֶצֶף	וּבְנֵי־עֶדֶן	אֲשֶׁר	בִּתְלַאשָּׂר		אַיּוֹ	מֶלֶךְ־חֲמָת
weretseph	ûvenê-ʻedhen	'ăsher	bithla'ssār		'ayyô	melekh-chămāth
and Rezeph	and the children of Eden	who	in Telassar		where	the king of Hamath

4567	798	4567	3937, 6111	5816	2083	5973
cj, n ms	pn	cj, n ms	prep, art, n fs	pn	pn	cj, pn
וּמֶלֶךְ	אַרְפָּד	וּמֶלֶךְ	לָעִיר	סְפַרְוָיִם	הֵנַע	וְעִוָּה
ûmelekh	'arpādh	ûmelekh	lā'îr	sepharwāyim	hēna'	we'iwwāh
and the king of	Arpad	and the king of	of the city of	Sepharvaim	Hena	and Ivvah

	4089.121	2488	881, 5809	4623, 3135	4534
14.	cj, v Qal impf 3ms	pn	do, art, n mp	prep, n fs	art, n mp
	וַיִּקַּח	חִזְקִיָּהוּ	אֶת־הַסְּפָרִים	מִיַּד	הַמַּלְאָכִים
	wayyiqqach	chizqîyāhû	'eth-hassephārîm	mîyadh	hammal'ākhîm
	and he received	Hezekiah	the letters	from the hand of	the messengers

7410.121	6148.121	1041	3176	6816.121	2488
cj, v Qal impf 3ms, ps 3mp	cj, v Qal impf 3ms	n ms	pn	cj, v Qal impf 3ms, ps 3ms	pn
וַיִּקְרָאֵם	וַיַּעַל	בֵּית	יְהוָה	וַיִּפְרְשֵׂהוּ	חִזְקִיָּהוּ
wayyiqōrā'ēm	wayya'al	bêth	yehwāh	wayyiphresēhû	chizqîyāhû
and he read them	and he went up to	the temple of	Yahweh	and he spread it out	Hezekiah

3937, 6686	3176		6663.721	2488	3937, 6686	3176	569.121
prep, n mp	pn	15.	cj, v Hithpael impf 3ms	pn	prep, n mp	pn	v Qal impf 3ms
לִפְנֵי	יְהוָה		וַיִּתְפַּלֵּל	חִזְקִיָּהוּ	לִפְנֵי	יְהוָה	וַיֹּאמַר
liphnê	yehwāh		wayyithpallēl	chizqîyāhû	liphnê	yehwāh	wayyō'mar
before	Yahweh		and he prayed	Hezekiah	before	Yahweh	and he said

3176	435	3547	3553.151	3872	887, 2000	435
pn	n mp	pn	v Qal act ptc ms	art, n mp	pers pron, pers pron	art, n mp
יְהוָה	אֱלֹהֵי	יִשְׂרָאֵל	יֹשֵׁב	הַכְּרֻבִים	אַתָּה־הוּא	הָאֱלֹהִים
yehwāh	'ĕlōhê	yisrā'ēl	yōshēv	hakkeruvîm	'attāh-hû'	hā'ĕlōhîm
O Yahweh	the God of	Israel	sitting on	the cherubim	You He	the God

3937, 940	3937, 3725	4608	800	887	6449.113	881, 8452
prep, n ms, ps 2ms	prep, n ms	n fp	art, n fs	pers pron	v Qal pf 2ms	do, art, n mp
לְבַדְּךָ	לְכֹל	מַמְלְכוֹת	הָאָרֶץ	אַתָּה	עָשִׂיתָ	אֶת־הַשָּׁמַיִם
levaddekhā	lekhōl	mamlekhôth	hā'ārets	'attāh	'āsîthā	'eth-hashshāmayim
only You	of the entirety of	the kingdoms of	the earth	You	You made	the heavens

881, 800		5371.531	3176	238	8471.131	6741.131	3176
cj, do, art, n fs	16.	v Hiphil impv 2ms	pn	n fs, ps 2ms	v Qal impv 2ms	v Qal impv 2ms	pn
וְאֶת־הָאָרֶץ		הַטֵּה	יְהוָה	אָזְנְךָ	וּשְׁמָע	פְּקַח	יְהוָה
we'eth-hā'ārets		hattēh	yehwāh	'oznekhā	ûshemā'	peqach	yehwāh
and the earth		incline	O Yahweh	your ear	and hear	open	O Yahweh

6084	7495.131	8471.131	881	1745	5771	866
n fd, ps 2ms	cj, v Qal impv 2ms	cj, v Qal impv 2ms	do	n mp	pn	rel pron
עֵינֶיךָ	וּרְאֵה	וּשְׁמַע	אֵת	דִּבְרֵי	סַנְחֵרִיב	אֲשֶׁר
'ênêkhā	ûre'ēh	ûshema'	'ēth	divrê	sanchērîv	'ăsher
your eyes	and see	and hear		the words of	Sennacherib	who

8365.111	3937, 2884.341	435	2508		561	3176
v Qal pf 3ms, ps 3ms	prep, v Piel inf con	n mp	adj	17.	adv	pn
שְׁלָחוֹ	לְחָרֵף	אֱלֹהִים	חַי		אָמְנָם	יְהוָה
shelāchô	lechārēph	'ĕlōhîm	chāy		'āmenām	yehwāh
he sent him	to revile	God	the living		truly	O Yahweh

2817.516	4567	831	881, 1504	881, 800		5598.116
v Hiphil pf 3cp	*n mp*	pn	do, art, n mp	cj, do, n fs, ps 3mp	**18.**	cj, v Qal pf 3cp
הֶחֱרִיבוּ	מַלְכֵי	אַשּׁוּר	אֶת־הַגּוֹיִם	וְאֶת־אַרְצָם		וְנָתְנוּ
hechěrîvû	malkhê	'ashshûr	'eth-haggôyim	we'eth-'artsām		wenāthenû
they have laid waste	the kings of	Assyria	the nations	and their land		and they put

881, 435	904, 813	3706	3940	435	2065	3706	524, 4801
do, n mp, ps 3mp	prep, art, n fs	cj	neg part	n mp	pers pron	cj	cj, *n ms*
אֶת־אֱלֹהֵיהֶם	בָּאֵשׁ	כִּי	לֹא	אֱלֹהִים	הֵמָּה	כִּי	אִם־מַעֲשֵׂה
'eth-'ělōhêhem	bā'ēsh	kî	lō'	'ělōhîm	hēmmāh	kî	'im-ma'ăsēh
their gods	in the fire	because	not	gods	they	but	rather a work of

fathers overthrew, *Knox* ... gods of other nations rescued them, *NLT* ... whom my ancestors devastated, *JB* ... my forefathers destroyed, *NEB*.

13. Where is the king of Hamath, and the king of Arpad, and the king of the city of Sepharvaim, of Hena, and Ivah?: ... town of Sepharvaim, *BB* ... the kings who governed the city of Sepharvaim, *Knox*.

14. And Hezekiah received the letter of the hand of the messengers, and read it: ... took the letter from the messengers' hands, *JB* ... took the letter from the hands of those who had come with it, *BB* ... from the hands of the Ambassadors, *Fenton* ... On receiving this letter from the messengers, Hezekiah read it, *Moffatt*.

and Hezekiah went up into the house of the LORD, and spread it before the LORD: ... went to the Temple, placed the letter there in the presence of the LORD, *Good News* ... held them out open in the Lord's presence, *Knox* ... laid it abroad before the Lord, *Tyndale* ... opening the letter there before the Lord, *BB*.

15. And Hezekiah prayed before the LORD: ... said this prayer in the presence of Yahweh, *JB* ... he prayed in his sight, *Douay* ... offered this prayer, *NEB*.

and said, O LORD God of Israel, which dwellest between the cherubims: ... who art seated upon the cherubim, *Goodspeed* ... enthroned on the winged creatures, *JB* ... the One who dwells between the cherubim, *NKJV* ... on Your throne above angels, *Beck*.

thou art the God, even thou alone, of all the kingdoms of the earth; thou hast made heaven and earth: ... you alone are God of all the kingdoms of the world, *JB* ... heaven and earth are of thy fashioning, *Knox* ... thou art the God, thou only, of all realms on earth, *Moffatt* ... thou, the Same, thou alone art the God of all the kingdoms of the earth, *Darby*.

16. LORD, bow down thine ear, and hear: open, LORD, thine eyes, and see: ... Incline Thine ear, O LORD, and listen, *Berkeley* ... look at what is happening to us, *Good News* ... Give ear, and listen, *Knox* ... Bend thine ear, O Eternal, listen!, *Moffatt*.

and hear the words of Sennacherib, which hath sent him to reproach the living God: ... Listen to the message that Sennacherib has sent to taunt the living God, *Anchor* ... take note of all the words of Sennacherib who has sent men to say evil against the living God, *BB* ... who sent someone to defy the living God, *Beck* ... to insult the God of Life!, *Fenton*.

17. Of a truth, LORD, the kings of Assyria have destroyed the nations and their lands: ... have laid waste the nations, *NKJV* ... devastated the nations, *NASB* ... have destroyed many nations, made their lands desolate, *Good News* ... have brought ruin on whole nations, and the lands they lived in, *Knox*.

18. And have cast their gods into the fire: for they were no gods: ... gods that were no gods at all, *Moffatt* ... they have consigned their gods to the fire, *NEB* ... thrown their gods into, *NIV* ... hurled, *NRSV*.

verses. Perhaps he himself was feeling the heat from the Egyptian advance. In any case, we are back on familiar ground: "Let not thy God in whom thou trustest deceive thee, saying, Jerusalem shall not be delivered into the hand of the king of Assyria" (v. 10). Once again, we hear the familiar refrain of the previously defeated countries, whose gods did not rescue them from the Assyrians (vv. 11ff).

19:14–34. A second response of Hezekiah and Isaiah: Earnest prayer, and triumphal prophecy of deliverance. Nonetheless, Hezekiah (rightly, of course) takes this latest missive of Sennacherib seriously, spreading it "before the LORD" (v. 14; Wiseman, TOTC, 281, compares this to the contemporary Mesopotamian practice of placing letters in the temple to be read by the god). Hezekiah then prayed. Hezekiah was a man of prayer. (Remember, the statement in 18:5 that "there was no one like him [Hezekiah] either before him or after him"?).

Hezekiah's prayer (vv. 15–19) is an excellent model for us to emulate. As Hobbs (WBC, 270f) points out, we find here first "invocation" (v. 15),

Number	Grammar	Hebrew	Transliteration	English
3176	pn	יְהוָה	yehwāh	O Yahweh
6498	cj, adv	וְעַתָּה	we‘attāh	and now
19.				
6.326	cj, v Piel impf 3mp, ps 3mp	וַיְאַבְּדוּם	way’abbedhûm	so they completely destroyed them
63	cj, n fs	וָאֶבֶן	wā’even	and stone
6320	n ms	עֵץ	‘ēts	wood
3135, 119	*n fd*, n ms	יְדֵי־אָדָם	yedhê-’ādhām	the hands of a man

Number	Grammar	Hebrew	Transliteration	English
3725, 4608	*adj, n fp*	כָּל־מַמְלְכוֹת	kol-mamlekhôth	all the kingdoms of
3156.126	cj, v Qal impf 3mp	וְיֵדְעוּ	weyēdhe‘û	and they will know
4623, 3135	prep, n fs, ps 3ms	מִיָּדוֹ	mîyādhô	from his hand
5167	part	נָא	nā’	please
3588.531	v Hiphil impv 2ms, ps 1cp	הוֹשִׁיעֵנוּ	hôshî‘ēnû	save us
435	n mp, ps 1cp	אֱלֹהֵינוּ	’ĕlōhênû	our God

Number	Grammar	Hebrew	Transliteration	English
3591	pn	יְשַׁעְיָהוּ	yesha‘ăyāhû	Isaiah
8365.121	cj, v Qal impf 3ms	וַיִּשְׁלַח	wayyishlach	and he sent
20.				
3937, 940	prep, n ms, ps 2ms	לְבַדֶּךָ	levaddekhā	only You
435	n mp	אֱלֹהִים	’ĕlōhîm	God
3176	pn	יְהוָה	yehwāh	Yahweh
887	pers pron	אַתָּה	’attāh	You
3706	cj	כִּי	kî	that
800	art, n fs	הָאָרֶץ	hā’ārets	the earth

Number	Grammar	Hebrew	Transliteration	English
3547	pn	יִשְׂרָאֵל	yisrā’ēl	Israel
435	*n mp*	אֱלֹהֵי	’ĕlōhê	the God of
3176	pn	יְהוָה	yehwāh	Yahweh
3662, 569.111	adv, v Qal pf 3ms	כֹּה־אָמַר	kōh-’āmar	thus He has said
3937, 569.141	prep, v Qal inf con	לֵאמֹר	lē’mōr	saying
420, 2488	prep, pn	אֶל־חִזְקִיָּהוּ	’el-chizqîyāhû	to Hezekiah
1158, 537	*n ms*, pn	בֶּן־אָמוֹץ	ven-’āmôts	the son of Amoz

Number	Grammar	Hebrew	Transliteration	English
2172	dem pron	זֶה	zeh	this
21.				
8471.115	v Qal pf 1cs	שָׁמַעְתִּי	shāmā‘ttî	I heard
4567, 831	*n ms*, pn	מֶלֶךְ־אַשּׁוּר	melekh-’ashshûr	the king of Assyria
420, 5771	prep, pn	אֶל־סַנְחֵרִב	’el-sanchēriv	about Sennacherib
420	prep, ps 1cs	אֵלַי	’ēlay	to Me
6663.713	v Hithpael pf 2ms	הִתְפַּלַּלְתָּ	hithpallaltā	you prayed
866	rel pron	אֲשֶׁר	’ăsher	Whom

Number	Grammar	Hebrew	Transliteration	English
4074.112	v Qal pf 3fs	לָעֲגָה	lā‘ăghāh	she ridicules
3937	prep, ps 2ms	לְךָ	lekhā	you
995.112	v Qal pf 3fs	בָּזָה	bāzāh	she despises
6142	prep, ps 3ms	עָלָיו	‘ālâv	concerning him
3176	pn	יְהוָה	yehwāh	Yahweh
866, 1744.311	rel part, v Piel pf 3ms	אֲשֶׁר־דִּבֶּר	’ăsher-dibber	which He has spoken
1745	art, n ms	הַדָּבָר	haddāvār	the word

Number	Grammar	Hebrew	Transliteration	English
1351	*n fs*	בַּת	bath	the daughter of
5309.512	v Hiphil pf 3fs	הֵנִיעָה	hēnî‘āh	she shakes
7513	n ms	רֹאשׁ	rō’sh	a head
313	prep, ps 2ms	אַחֲרֶיךָ	’achrêkhā	behind you
1351, 6995	*n fs*, pn	בַּת־צִיּוֹן	bath-tsîyôn	the daughter of Zion
1359	*n fs*	בְּתוּלַת	bethûlath	the virgin
3937	prep, ps 2ms	לְךָ	lekhā	you

Number	Grammar	Hebrew	Transliteration	English
6142, 4449	cj, prep, intrg	וְעַל־מִי	we‘al-mî	and against whom
1472.313	cj, v Piel pf 2ms	וְגִדַּפְתָּ	weghiddaphtā	and have you blasphemed
2884.313	v Piel pf 2ms	חֵרַפְתָּ	chēraphtā	have you reviled
881, 4449	do, intrg	אֶת־מִי	’eth-mî	whom
22.				
3503	pn	יְרוּשָׁלָם	yerûshālām	Jerusalem

Number	Grammar	Hebrew	Transliteration	English
6142, 7202	prep, *n ms*	עַל־קְדוֹשׁ	‘al-qōdhôsh	against the Holy One of
6084	n fd, ps 2ms	עֵינֶיךָ	‘ênêkhā	your eyes
4953	adv	מָרוֹם	mārôm	on high
5558.123	cj, v Qal impf 2ms	וַתִּשָּׂא	wattissā’	and have you lifted up
7249	n ms	קוֹל	qôl	a voice
7597.513	v Hiphil pf 2ms	הֲרִימוֹתָ	herîmôthā	have you raised

Number	Grammar	Hebrew	Transliteration	English
569.121	cj, v Qal impf 3ms	וַתֹּאמֶר	wattō’mer	and you said
112	n mp, ps 1cs	אֲדֹנָי	’ădhōnāy	the Lord
2884.313	v Piel pf 2ms	חֵרַפְתָּ	chēraphtā	have you reviled
4534	n mp, ps 2ms	מַלְאָכֶיךָ	mal’ākhêkhā	your messengers
904, 3135	prep, *n fs*	בְּיַד	beyadh	by the hand of
23.				
3547	pn	יִשְׂרָאֵל	yisrā’ēl	Israel

but the work of men's hands, wood and stone: therefore they have destroyed them: ... mere things of wood and stone that men had made, *Moffatt* ... the work of human hands, *NAB* ... man's handicraft, *Anchor* ... only wood and rock statues that people made, *NCV* ... wood and stone, fashioned by men's hands, *NIV.*

19. Now therefore, O LORD our God, I beseech thee: ... I beg you, *JB* ... I pray, *NASB* ... please, *Beck.*

save thou us out of his hand, that all the kingdoms of the earth may know that thou art the LORD God, even thou only: ... deliver us from his hand, *Berkeley* ... rescue us, *Good News* ... it may be clear to all the kingdoms of the earth that you and only you, O Lord, are God, *BB* ... you alone are God, *JB.*

20. Then Isaiah the son of Amoz sent to Hezekiah, saying, Thus saith the LORD God of Israel, That which thou hast prayed to me against Sennacherib king of Assyria I have heard: ... sent word to Ezechias, *Knox* ... sent Hezekiah this message, *Moffatt* ... in answer to your prayer for help against Sennacherib, king of Assyria: I have listened!, *NAB* ... I have heard your prayer concerning, *NIV.*

21. This is the word that the LORD hath spoken concerning him; The virgin the daughter of Zion hath despised thee, and laughed thee to scorn: ... This is what the Lord has to say of him, *Knox* ... virgin daughter of Zion disdains you, *REB* ... In the eyes of the virgin daughter of Zion you are shamed and laughed at, *BB* ... The city of Jerusalem laughs at you, Sennacherib, and makes fun of you, *Good News.*

the daughter of Jerusalem hath shaken her head at thee: ... shaken her head behind your back!, *NKJV* ... she tosses her head—behind your back, *NRSV* ... wags her head behind you, *RSV* ... shakes her head after you, *Anchor.*

22. Whom hast thou reproached and blasphemed?: ... insulted and blasphemed, *Moffatt* ... taunted and blasphemed?, *NEB* ... mocked and reviled?, *NRSV* ... Against whom have you said evil and bitter things?, *BB.*

and against whom hast thou exalted thy voice, and lifted up thine eyes on high? even against the Holy One of Israel: ... at whom have you dared raise your voice, and lift your eyes on high?, *Moffatt* ... And haughtily lifted up your eyes?, *NASB* ... Against whom have you clamoured, casting haughty glances at the Holy One of Israel?, *NEB* ... and lifted your eyes in pride?, *NIV* ... Against whom did you raise an outcry, *REB.*

23. By thy messengers thou hast reproached the Lord: ... taunted Yahweh, *Anchor* ... you defy the LORD, *Beck* ... insulted, *Goodspeed* ... mocked, *KJVII.*

and hast said, With the multitude of my chariots I am come up to the height of the mountains, to the sides of Lebanon, and will cut down the tall cedar trees thereof, and the choice fir trees thereof: ... With my countless chariots I'll ride up to the top of the mountains, the distant parts of Lebanon, *Beck* ... I scaled the highest mountains, the remotest parts, *Berkeley* ... I ascended the mountain heights, the recesses, *Goodspeed* ... I have climbed the mountain-tops, the utmost peaks, *JB.*

---

then "complaint" (vv. 16ff) and finally "supplication" (v. 19). There are similarities of the ending of this prayer with that of Elijah in 1 Ki. 18:36f; both besought Yahweh to act dramatically and decisively so that all would recognize the uniqueness of the One True God. Already, in his opening invocation (v. 15), Hezekiah cites the traditional epithet, "LORD God of Israel, which dwellest between the cherubims" (cf. also, Ezek. 1, where Yahweh on his heavenly throne sits in glory above the cherubim). Then Hezekiah, in a heartfelt lament, implored Yahweh to give heed to his prayer. Once again, this was one of those occasions where one feels compelled to ask, "Where are you, O God?" Most of Judah was in enemy hands and Jerusalem herself severely threatened—where are you, O God? Two things may be pointed out here: first, the living God had truly been "insulted" by Sennacherib's words (v. 16), and second, Hezekiah's concern was for "all kingdoms on earth," not merely his own (v. 19). What Yahweh was to do for Judah and for Jerusalem would stand as testimony to all nations, especially those who had recently tasted defeat at the hands of the dreaded and arrogant Assyrians.

Isaiah's prophecy (vv. 20–34) concludes this lengthy section. The prophet immediately cites Hezekiah's prayer as impetus for Yahweh's response (v. 20). Then he went into magnificent poetic detail as to how "virgin daughter Zion" (a better translation than the traditional "virgin daughter of Zion," for Zion [or Jerusalem] is herself the daughter [cities were considered "daughters" of the state]) would insolently "toss her head" at the fleeing Assyrians. Thus Sennacherib's proud invasion would end in the people of Jerusalem taunting the one who had taunted them.

Assyria's sin was pride; they had let their remarkable military successes go to their head

904, 7681	7681	603	6148.115	4953	2098	3526
prep, n ms	n ms, ps 1cs	pers pron	v Qal pf 3ms	*n ms*	n mp	*n fd*
בְּרֶכֶב	רִכְבִּי	אֲנִי	עָלִיתִי	מְרוֹם	הָרִים	יַרְכְּתֵי
berekhev	rikhbî	'ănî	'ālîthî	merôm	hārîm	yarkethê
with chariots	my chariots	I	I went up to	the heights of	the mountains	the remote parts of

3976	3918.125	7253	753	4143	1293	971.125
pn	cj, v Qal impf 1cs	*n fs*	n mp, ps 3ms	*n ms*	n mp, ps 3ms	cj, v Qal impf 1cs
לְבָנוֹן	וְאֶכְרֹת	קוֹמַת	אֲרָזָיו	מִבְחוֹר	בְּרֹשָׁיו	וְאָבוֹאָה
levānôn	we'ekhrōth	qômath	'ărāzâv	mivchôr	berōshâv	we'āvô'āh
Lebanon	and I cut off	the height of	its cedars	the choice of	its pines	and I came to

4550	7377	3402	3888		603	7262.115
n ms	n ms, ps 3ms	*n ms*	n ms, ps 3ms		pers pron	v Qal pf 1cs
מְלוֹן	קִצֹּה	יַעַר	כַּרְמִלּוֹ	**24.**	אֲנִי	קַרְתִּי
melôn	qitstsōh	ya'ar	karmillô		'ănî	qartî
the lodging place of	its extremities	the forest of	its fertile field		I	I dug for water

8685.115	4448	2197.152	2817.525	904, 3834, 6718	3725
cj, v Qal pf 1cs	n md	v Qal act ptc mp	cj, v Hiphil impf 1cs	prep, *n fs*, n fp, ps 1cs	*n ms*
וְשָׁתִיתִי	מַיִם	זָרִים	וְאַחְרִב	בְּכַף־פְּעָמַי	כֹּל
weshāthîthî	mayim	zārîm	we'achriv	bekhaph-pe'āmay	kōl
and I drank	water	being strange	and I dried up	with the sole of my foot	the entirety of

3083	4858		1950B, 3940, 8471.113	3937, 4623, 7632	881	6449.115
n mp	pn		intrg part, neg part, v Qal pf 2ms	prep, prep, n ms	do, ps 3fs	v Qal pf 1cs
יְאֹרֵי	מָצוֹר	**25.**	הֲלֹא־שָׁמַעְתָּ	לְמֵרָחוֹק	אֹתָהּ	עָשִׂיתִי
ye'ōrê	mātsôr		helō'-shāma'ttā	lemērāchôq	'ōthāhh	'āsîthî
the streams of	lower Egypt		have you not heard	from long ago	it	I did

3937, 4623, 4448	7208	3443.115	6498	971.515	2030.122
prep, prep, *n mp*	n ms	cj, v Qal pf 1cs, ps 3fs	adv	v Hiphil pf 1cs, ps 3fs	cj, v Qal impf 3fs
לְמִימֵי	קֶדֶם	וִיצַרְתִּיהָ	עַתָּה	הֲבֵיאתִיהָ	וּתְהִי
lemîmê	qedhem	wîtsartîāh	'attāh	hevê'thîāh	ûthehî
of from the days of	antiquity	and I thought it	now	I have brought it	and it will be

3937, 8059.541	1569	5510.256	6111	1245.158		3553.152
prep, v Hiphil inf con	n mp	v Niphal ptc mp	n fp	v Qal pass ptc fp		cj, v Qal act ptc mp, ps 3fp
לַהְשׁוֹת	גַּלִּים	נִצִּים	עָרִים	בְּצֻרוֹת	**26.**	וְיֹשְׁבֵיהֶן
lahshôth	gallîm	nitstsîm	'ārîm	betsurôth		weyōshevêhen
causing to lay waste	rubble	devastated	cities	fortified		and their dwellers

7405, 3135	2973.116	991.116	2030.116	6448	7898
adj, n fs	v Qal pf 3cp	cj, v Qal pf 3cp	v Qal pf 3cp	*n ms*	n ms
קִצְרֵי־יָד	חַתּוּ	וַיֵּבֹשׁוּ	הָיוּ	עֵשֶׂב	שָׂדֶה
qitsrê-yādh	chattû	wayyēvōshû	hāyû	'ēsev	sādheh
short of hand	they were dismayed	and they were ashamed	they were	plants of	a field

3537	1940	2785	1437	8166	3937, 6686
cj, *n ms*	n ms	*n ms*	n mp	cj, n fs	prep, *n mp*
וִירַק	דֶּשֶׁא	חֲצִיר	גַּגּוֹת	וּשְׁדֵפָה	לִפְנֵי
wîraq	deshe'	chătsîr	gaggôth	ûshedhēphāh	liphnê
and green growth of	vegetation	grass of	rooftops	and something dried up	before

7339		3553.141	3428.141	971.141	3156.115
n fs		cj, v Qal inf con, ps 2ms	cj, v Qal inf con, ps 2ms	cj, v Qal inf con, ps 2ms	v Qal pf 1cs
קָמָה	**27.**	וְשִׁבְתְּךָ	וְצֵאתְךָ	וּבֹאֲךָ	יָדַעְתִּי
qāmāh		weshivtekhā	wetsē'thekhā	ûvō'ăkhā	yādhā'ttî
the standing grain		and your sitting	and your going out	and your coming in	I know

881	7553.741	420		3391	7553.741	420
cj, do	v Hithpael inf con, ps 2ms	prep, ps 1cs	28.	cj	v Hithpael inf con, ps 2ms	prep, ps 1cs
וְאֵת	הִתְרַגֶּזְךָ	אֵלָי		יַעַן	הִתְרַגֶּזְךָ	אֵלַי
we'ēth	hithraggezkhā	'ēlāy		ya'an	hithraggezkhā	'ēlay
and	your raging	against Me		because	your raging	against Me

8077	6148.111	904, 238	7947.115	2489	904, 653
cj, n ms, ps 2ms	v Qal pf 3ms	prep, n fd, ps 1cs	cj, v Qal pf 1cs	n ms, ps 1cs	prep, n ms, ps 2ms
וְשַׁאֲנַנְךָ	עָלָה	בְאָזְנָי	וְשַׂמְתִּי	חַחִי	בְּאַפֶּךָ
wesha'ănankhā	'ālāh	ve'āzenāy	wesamtî	chachî	be'appekhā
and your arrogance	it went up	in my ears	I will establish	my hook	in your nose

and I will enter into the lodgings of his borders, and into the forest of his Carmel: ... I came to its remotest lodge, its cultivated forest, *Berkeley* ... into the forest and its fruitful field, *KJVII* ... will enter into his farthest lodging place, *MRB* ... I will enter the extremity of its borders, To its fruitful forest, *NKJV*.

24. I have digged and drunk strange waters, and with the sole of my feet have I dried up all the rivers of besieged places: ... sparkling waters, *Fenton* ... foreign waters, *NASB* ... rivers of fenced places, *KJVII* ... have dug wells and drunk the waters of a foreign land, *NEB*.

25. Hast thou not heard long ago how I have done it, and of ancient times that I have formed it?: ... Have you not heard? Long ago I ordained it. In days of old I planned it, *NIV* ... In ancient days, I fashioned it, *Anchor* ... Long ago I prepared for this and planned it in the past, *Beck* ... from days of old I actually planned it, *JB*.

now have I brought it to pass, that thou shouldest be to lay waste fenced cities into ruinous heaps: ... I have given effect to my design, so that by you strong towns might be turned into masses of broken walls, *BB* ... Now I have brought it about, *Anchor* ... now I have made it happen, *Beck* ... that you have turned fortified cities into piles of stone, *NIV*.

26. Therefore their inhabitants were of small power, they were dismayed and confounded: ... they were fearful and put to shame, *KJVII* ... inhabitants were short of strength, *NASB* ... were weak of hand, they trembled and were confounded, *Douay* ... disheartened and ashamed, *NEB*.

they were as the grass of the field, and as the green herb, as the grass on the housetops, and as corn blasted before it be grown up: ... like grain blasted before it was grown up, *KJVII* ... frail as meadow grass, or the stalks that grow on the housetop, withering before they can ripen, *Knox* ... Becoming like the plants of the field, like the green growth, like the scorched grass on the housetops, *NAB* ... they were as the vegetation of the field, *NASB*.

27. But I know thy abode, and thy going out, and thy coming in, and thy rage against me: ... where you stay and when you come and go and how you rage against me, *NIV* ... I know your dwelling place, *NKJV* ... I know your rising up and your sitting down, your going out and your coming in, *REB* ... I know everything about you, what you do and where you go, *Good News*.

28. Because thy rage against me and thy tumult is come up into mine ears: ... your uproar rings in my ears, *Anchor* ... thine arrogance is come up into mine ears, *Darby* ... your words of pride have come up to my ears, *BB* ... I hear your cocky talk, *Beck*.

therefore I will put my hook in thy nose, and my bridle in thy lips, and I will turn thee back by the way by

(vv. 22ff). Assyria had been "the rod of [Yahweh's] anger" (cf. Isa. 10:5), but now they had gone too far (vv. 12–19), and their pride had misled them greatly ("Shall the axe boast itself against him that heweth therewith? or shall the saw magnify itself against him that shaketh it?" [v. 15]). They were doomed; just as Yahweh long ago ordained their successes (vv. 25f), He now ordained their own disaster (vv. 27f; the images of a "hook in your nose" and a "bit in your mouth" are familiar ones of Assyria's own treatment of her defeated enemies). And Isaiah, playing on the "tender plant" metaphor (cf. 2 Ki. 19:26), gives the short-term prediction that a "remnant" (a familiar image in the Isaiah prophecies; cf. Isa. 1:7ff; 6:11ff; 10:20ff; 11:11f; etc.) would once again "take root downward, and bear fruit upward" and, by the third year, enjoy bountiful crops and harvests, as in peacetime (vv. 29f). It was the "zeal of the LORD of hosts" which would accomplish this (v. 31, cf. Isa. 9:7).

Isaiah's concluding comments (vv. 32ff) are as problematic as they are memorable, if we assume that Sennacherib did besiege the city of Jerusalem, as he himself seemed to claim (of course, he never claimed to have taken the city). But Cogan and Tadmor (AB, 238; also cf. their excursus, 246–51) point out that, even from

5141	904, 8004	8178.515	904, 1932	866, 971.113
cj, n ms, ps 1cs	prep, n fd, ps 2ms	cj, v Hiphil pf 1cs, ps 2ms	prep, art, n ms	rel part, v Qal pf 2ms
וּמִתְגִּי	בִּשְׂפָתֶיךָ	וַהֲשִׁבֹתִיךָ	בַּדֶּרֶךְ	אֲשֶׁר־בָּאתָ
ûmithgî	bisphāthêkhā	wahshivōthîkhā	badderekh	'ăsher-bā'thā
and my bridle	in your lips	and I will make you return	on the way	which you came

904		2172, 3937	225	404.142	8523	5798
prep, ps 3fs	29.	cj, dem pron, prep, ps 2ms	art, n ms	v Qal inf abs	art, n fs	n ms
בָּהּ		וְזֶה־לְּךָ	הָאוֹת	אָכוֹל	הַשָּׁנָה	סָפִיחַ
bāhh		wezeh-lekhā	hā'ôth	'ākhôl	hashshānāh	sāphîach
on it		and this to you	the sign	eating	the year	volunteer grain

904, 8523	8529	5690	904, 8523	8389	2319.133	7403.133
cj, prep, art, n fs	art, num	n ms	cj, prep, art, n fs	art, num	v Qal impv 2mp	cj, v Qal impv 2mp
וּבַשָּׁנָה	הַשֵּׁנִית	סָחִישׁ	וּבַשָּׁנָה	הַשְּׁלִישִׁית	זִרְעוּ	וְקִצְרוּ
ûvashshānāh	hashshēnîth	sāchîsh	ûvashshānāh	hashshelîshîth	zir'û	wiqitsrû
and in the year	the second	wild grain	and in the year	the third	sow	and reap

5378.133	3884	404.133	6780		3362.112	6656
cj, v Qal impv 2mp	n mp	cj, v Qal impv 2mp	n ms, ps 3mp	30.	cj, v Qal pf 3fs	*n fs*
וְנִטְעוּ	כְרָמִים	וְאִכְלוּ	פִּרְיָם		וְיָסְפָה	פְּלֵיטַת
wenit'û	kherāmîm	we'ikhlû	phiryām		weyāsephāh	pelêtath
and plant	vineyards	and eat	their fruit		and it will do again	the fugitives of

1041, 3171	8080.257	8659	3937, 4432	6449.111	6780	3937, 4762
n ms, pn	art, v Niphal ptc fs	n ms	prep, adv	cj, v Qal pf 3ms	n ms	prep, adv
בֵּית־יְהוּדָה	הַנִּשְׁאָרָה	שֹׁרֶשׁ	לְמָטָּה	וְעָשָׂה	פְרִי	לְמָעְלָה
bêth-yehûdhāh	hanish'ārāh	shōresh	lemattāh	we'āsāh	pherî	lemā'ālāh
the household of Judah	the remnant	a root	below	and it will produce	fruit	to upward

	3706	4623, 3503	3428.122	8086	6656	4623, 2098	6995
31.	cj	prep, pn	v Qal impf 3fs	n fs	cj, n fs	prep, *n ms*	pn
	כִּי	מִירוּשָׁלַם	תֵּצֵא	שְׁאֵרִית	וּפְלֵיטָה	מֵהַר	צִיּוֹן
	kî	mîrûshālam	tētsē'	she'ērîth	ûphelêtāh	mēhar	tsîyôn
	because	from Jerusalem	it will go out	a remnant	and fugitives	from Mount	Zion

7352	3176	6893	6449.122, 2148		3937, 3772	3662, 569.111	3176
n fs	pn	n fp	v Qal impf 3fs, dem pron	32.	prep, adv	adv, v Qal pf 3ms	pn
קִנְאַת	יְהוָה	צְבָאוֹתה	תַּעֲשֶׂה־זֹּאת		לָכֵן	כֹּה־אָמַר	יְהוָה
qin'ath	yehwāh	tsevā'ôthh	ta'ăseh-zō'th		lākhēn	kōh-'āmar	yehwāh
the zeal of	Yahweh of	hosts	it will accomplish this		therefore	thus He has said	Yahweh

420, 4567	831	3940	971.121	420, 6111	2148	3940, 3498.521
prep, *n ms*	pn	neg part	v Qal impf 3ms	prep, art, n fs	art, dem pron	cj, neg part, v Hiphil impf 3ms
אֶל־מֶלֶךְ	אַשּׁוּר	לֹא	יָבֹא	אֶל־הָעִיר	הַזֹּאת	וְלֹא־יוֹרֶה
'el-melekh	'ashshûr	lō'	yāvō'	'el-hā'îr	hazzō'th	welō'-yôreh
to the king of	Assyria	not	he will enter	to the city	the this	neither will he shoot

8427	2777	3940, 7207.321	4182	3940, 8581.121	6142
adv	n ms	cj, neg part, v Piel impf 3ms, ps 3fs	n ms	cj, neg part, v Qal impf 3ms	prep, ps 3fs
שָׁם	חֵץ	וְלֹא־יְקַדְּמֶנָּה	מָגֵן	וְלֹא־יִשְׁפֹּךְ	עָלֶיהָ
shām	chēts	welō'-yeqaddemennāh	māghēn	welō'-yishpōkh	'ālêāh
there	an arrow	nor will it appear before it	a shield	neither will he pile up	against it

5745		904, 1932	866, 971.111	904	8178.121	420, 6111
n fs	33.	prep, art, n ms	rel part, v Qal pf 3ms	prep, ps 3fs	v Qal impf 3ms	cj, prep, art, n fs
סֹלְלָה		בַּדֶּרֶךְ	אֲשֶׁר־יָבֹא	בָּהּ	יָשׁוּב	וְאֶל־הָעִיר
sōlelāh		badderekh	'ăsher-yāvō'	bāhh	yāshûv	we'el-hā'îr
a siege-mound		on the way	which he came	on it	he will return	and to the city

2148 art, dem pron הַזֹּאת hazzō'th the this	3940 neg part לֹא lō' not	971.121 v Qal impf 3ms יָבֹא yāvō' he will come	5177, 3176 *n ms*, pn נְאֻם־יְהוָה ne'um-yehwāh the declaration of Yahweh	**34.** 1639.115 cj, v Qal pf 1cs וְגַנּוֹתִי weghannôthî and I will defend	
420, 6111 prep, art, n fs אֶל־הָעִיר 'el-hā'îr toward the city	2148 art, dem pron הַזֹּאת hazzō'th the this	3937, 3588.541 prep, v Hiphil inf con, ps 3fs לְהוֹשִׁיעָהּ lehôshî'āhh to save it	3937, 4775 prep, prep, ps 1cs לְמַעֲנִי lema'ănî for my sake	3937, 4775 cj, prep, prep וּלְמַעַן ûlăma'an and for the sake of	1784 pn דָּוִד dāwidh David

which thou camest: ... put a hook through your nostrils and a muzzle on your lips, and make you return by the road by which you came, *JB* ... and my cord in your lips, *BB* ... My bit in your jaws, And by the way that you came, lead you back!, *Fenton* ... and turn you back on the very road by which you came, *Anchor.*

29. And this shall be a sign unto thee, Ye shall eat this year such things as grow of themselves, and in the second year that which springeth of the same: ... You shall have proof of this: for while you feed this year on casual grains, and next year on what springs from casual grains, *Moffatt* ... this year you shall eat the aftergrowth, next year, what grows of itself, *NAB* ... this year you shall eat shed grain and in the second year what is self-sown, *NEB* ... This year you will eat what grows by itself, and the second year what springs from that, *NIV.*

and in the third year sow ye, and reap, and plant vineyards, and eat the fruits thereof: ... you can sow and reap a crop, you can plant vineyards and enjoy their fruit, *Moffatt* ... plant grain and harvest it. Plant vineyards and eat their fruit, *NCV* ... you will put in your seed and get in the grain and make vine-gardens and take of their fruit, *BB* ... plant vineyards, and eat the produce, *Beck.*

30. And the remnant that is escaped of the house of Judah shall yet again take root downward, and bear fruit upward: ... The survivors of the house of Judah who are left shall again take root downwards, *Berkeley* ... will bring forth new roots below and fruits above, *JB* ... shall once more strike down its roots and then rise to be fruitful, *Moffatt* ... shall strike fresh root under ground and yield fruit above ground, *NEB.*

31. For out of Jerusalem shall go forth a remnant, and they that escape out of mount Zion: the zeal of the LORD of hosts shall do this: ... a remnant shall emerge out of Jerusalem, *Anchor* ... zeal of the Lord Almighty will accomplish this, *NIV* ... power of the LORD will do this, *Fenton* ... passion of the LORD Almighty will make this happen, *NLT.*

32. Therefore thus saith the LORD concerning the king of Assyria, He shall not come into this city, nor shoot an arrow there, nor come before it with shield, nor cast a bank against it: ... nor cast a mound against it, *MAST* ... confront it with no shield, throw up no earthwork against it, *JB* ... no shield-protected host shall storm it, no earth-works shall be cast up around it, *Knox* ... nor cast a trench about it, *Douay.*

33. By the way that he came, by the same shall he return, and shall not come into this city, saith the LORD: ... By the way he came he will go back, *REB* ... shall go back again the way he came, *Tyndale* ... shall go back by the same road he came, *Anchor* ... and he will not get into this town, *BB.*

34. For I will defend this city, to save it, for mine own sake, and for

Sennacherib's own account, apparently no actual assault upon the city of Jerusalem employing siege works ever took place. Isaiah's prediction in v. 32 did come true: "He shall not come into ... nor shoot an arrow ... [nor] come before it with shield, nor cast a bank against it." In any case, whatever the precise course of events in the summer of 701, the final brief passage of the present chapter makes it obvious that the Assyrian army was soon compelled to quit the field altogether, as the "angel of Yahweh" went forth and put to death an immense number of their cohorts ("Yahweh's angel/messenger" [Hebrew, mal'ākh, HED #4534] seeks redress from Sennacherib's "messengers" [plural of the same term in Hebrew], who had come to "taunt the living God" [cf. v. 16]).

19:35–37. Conclusion to the Sennacherib account: The Assyrian camp annihilated, and the Assyrian king assassinated. Isaiah's prophecies and Hezekiah's prayers were evidently answered quickly and impressively (concerning the "angel of Yahweh," see the preceding section). As to what exactly took place under that hot summer sun, it was clearly sudden, entirely unexpected and incredibly devastating. The vast number mentioned (185,000) staggers the imagination, for the entire army of

5860 n ms, ps 1cs עַבְדִּי 'avdî my servant	**35.**	2030.121 cj, v Qal impf 3ms וַיְהִי wayhî and it was	904, 4050 prep, art, n ms בַּלַּיְלָה ballaylāh in the night	2000 art, dem pron הַהוּא hahû' the that	3428.121 cj, v Qal impf 3ms וַיֵּצֵא wayyētsē' that He went out	4534 *n ms* מַלְאַךְ mal'akh the Angel of	3176 pn יְהוָה yehwāh Yahweh

5409.521 cj, v Hiphil impf 3ms וַיַּךְ wayyakh and He struck down	904, 4402 prep, *n ms* בְּמַחֲנֵה bemachnēh in the camp of	831 pn אַשּׁוּר 'ashshûr Assyria	4109 num מֵאָה mē'āh one hundred	8470 num שְׁמוֹנִים shemônîm eighty	2675 cj, num וַחֲמִשָּׁה wachmishshāh and five	512 num אָלֶף 'āleph thousands

8326.526 cj, v Hiphil impf 3mp וַיַּשְׁכִּימוּ wayyashkîmû and they rose early	904, 1269 prep, art, n ms בַבֹּקֶר vabbōqer in the morning	2079 cj, intrj וְהִנֵּה wehinnēh and behold	3725 adj, ps 3mp כֻּלָּם khullām all of them	6538 n mp פְּגָרִים peghārîm corpses	4322.152 v Qal act ptc mp מֵתִים mēthîm dead men

36.	5450.121 cj, v Qal impf 3ms וַיִּסַּע wayyissa' so he pulled out	2050.121 cj, v Qal impf 3ms וַיֵּלֶךְ wayyēlekh and he went	8178.121 cj, v Qal impf 3ms וַיָּשָׁב wayyāshāv then he returned	5771 pn סַנְחֵרִיב sanchērîv Sennacherib	4567, 831 *n ms*, pn מֶלֶךְ־אַשּׁוּר melekh-'ashshûr the king of Assyria

3553.121 cj, v Qal impf 3ms וַיֵּשֶׁב wayyēshev and he dwelled	904, 5398 prep, pn בְּנִינְוֵה benînewēh in Nineveh	**37.**	2030.121 cj, v Qal impf 3ms וַיְהִי wayhî and it was	2000 pers pron הוּא hû' he	8246.751 v Hithpael ptc ms מִשְׁתַּחֲוֶה mishtachweh worshiping	1041 *n ms* בֵּית bêth the temple of	5451 pn נִסְרֹךְ nisrōkh Nisroch

435 n mp, ps 3ms אֱלֹהָיו 'ĕlōhâv his god	149 cj, pn וְאַדְרַמֶּלֶךְ we'adhrammelekh and Adrammelech	8016 cj, pn וְשַׂרְאֶצֶר wesar'etser and Sharezer	1158 n mp, ps 3ms בָּנָיו bānâv his sons	5409.516 v Hiphil pf 3cp, ps 3ms הִכֻּהוּ hikkuhû they struck him down	904, 2820 prep, art, n fs בַחֶרֶב vacherev with the sword

2065 cj, pers pron וְהֵמָּה wehēmmāh and they	4561.216 v Niphal pf 3cp נִמְלְטוּ nimletû they escaped to	800 *n fs* אֶרֶץ 'erets the land of	804 pn אֲרָרָט 'ărārāt Ararat	4566.121 cj, v Qal impf 3ms וַיִּמְלֹךְ wayyimlōkh and he reigned	649 pn אֵסַר־חַדֹּן 'ēsar-chaddōn Esarhaddon	1158 n ms, ps 3ms בְּנוֹ benô his son

8809 prep, ps 3ms תַּחְתָּיו tachtâv instead of him	**20:1**	904, 3219 prep, art, n mp בַּיָּמִים bayyāmîm in the days	2062 art, dem pron הָהֵם hāhēm the those	2571.111 v Qal pf 3ms חָלָה chālāh he became sick	2488 pn חִזְקִיָּהוּ chizqîyāhû Hezekiah	3937, 4322.141 prep, v Qal inf con לָמוּת lāmûth unto dying

971.121 cj, v Qal impf 3ms וַיָּבֹא wayyāvō' and he came	420 prep, ps 3ms אֵלָיו 'ēlâv to him	3591 pn יְשַׁעְיָהוּ yesha'yāhû Isaiah	1158, 537 *n ms*, pn בֶּן־אָמוֹץ ven-'āmôts the son of Amoz	5204 art, n ms הַנָּבִיא hannāvî' the prophet	569.121 cj, v Qal impf 3ms וַיֹּאמֶר wayyō'mer and he said	420 prep, ps 3ms אֵלָיו 'ēlâv to him

3662, 569.111 adv, v Qal pf 3ms כֹּה־אָמַר kōh-'āmar thus He has said	3176 pn יְהוָה yehwāh Yahweh	6943.331 v Piel impv 2ms צַו tsaw command	3937, 1041 prep, n ms, ps 2ms לְבֵיתֶךָ levêthekhā your household	3706 cj כִּי kî because	4322.151 v Qal act ptc ms מֵת mēth dying	887 pers pron אַתָּה 'attāh you	3940 cj, neg part וְלֹא welō' and not

my servant David's sake: ... I will shield this city, *Beck* ... to spare it for My sake, *Berkeley* ... defend this city and protect it, *Good News* ... I will keep guard over this city and deliver it, for my own honour, *Knox*.

35. And it came to pass that night, that the angel of the LORD went out, and smote in the camp of the Assyrians an hundred fourscore and five thousand: ... went out and put to death a hundred and eighty-five thousand men, *NIV* ... struck the Assyrian camp, *Anchor* ... slew in the camp of the Assyrians, *Goodspeed* ... killed in the camp of, *NKJV*.

and when they arose early in the morning, behold, they were all dead corpses: ... dead bodies, *ASV* ... when morning dawned, they all lay dead, *NEB* ... At daybreak there were dead bodies all about, *Anchor* ... When the people got up the next morning, *NIV*.

36. So Sennacherib king of Assyria departed, and went and returned, and dwelt at Nineveh: ... left, went home, and lived at Nineveh, *NRSV* ... broke camp and marched away; he went back to Nineveh and remained there, *REB* ... went back to his place at Nineveh, *BB* ... struck camp and left; he returned home and stayed in Nineveh, *JB*.

37. And it came to pass, as he was worshipping in the house of Nisroch his god, that Adrammelech and Sharezer his sons smote him with the sword: ... struck him, *KJVII* ... slew him, *NAB* ... killed him, *NASB* ... murdered him, *NEB* ... drew their swords on him, *Knox*.

and they escaped into the land of Armenia. And Esar-haddon his son reigned in his stead: ... reigned in his place, *NKJV* ... became king in his place, *NASB* ... the throne passed to his son, *Knox* ... He was succeeded by his son, *NEB*.

20:1. In those days was Hezekiah sick unto death: ... became mortally ill, *REB* ... became sick and was at the point of death, *RSV* ... was ill and near death, *BB* ... deathly ill, *NLT*.

And the prophet Isaiah the son of Amoz came to him, and said unto

---

Shalmaneser III. Some have tried to suggest that the force only numbered some 120,000 men, others suggest the possible translation, "a hundred and eighty-five officers." The issue of large biblical numbers continues to be debated. However, despite attempts to reinterpret the Hebrew term for "thousand" ('eleph, HED #512) as referring to a "clan," or to a military unit numbering less than 1000 men, the text should not be doubted simply because a number seems large. (Concerning the relationship of this Assyrian debacle in 701 with the story in Herodotus concerning Sennacherib's retreat from Egypt due to a "multitude of field mice" swarming over the Assyrian camp and devouring their quivers, their bowstrings, and the handles of their shields [also cf. Josephus, *Antiquities*, X:19] Cogan and Tadmor, AB, 250f, largely discount the story's historicity [e.g., Sennacherib never even campaigned as far south as Egypt].)

At any rate, Sennacherib was clearly forced to withdraw precipitously and return to Nineveh (v. 36). Some time later, Sennacherib lay dead at the hands of his son(s) in the temple of "Nisroch" (for details, as best as can be determined from the extant Assyrian evidence, see the full note in Cogan and Tadmor, AB, 239f; apparently one "Arad-Ninlil," bypassed in the line of succession in favor of Esarhaddon, a younger son, did the deed). In any case, the insolent words of the rab-shakeh in ch. 18, at the instigation of his Assyrian master, proved to be entirely false and misleading. Yahweh, the true God, will not abandon his people, who cry out to him day and night (cf. Luke 18:7). Our God is ever faithful.

20:1–11. *Life-threatening illness announced by Isaiah the prophet. It has already been suggested that these three Hezekiah chapters in 2 Ki. 18ff may not be in chronological order. It could be further argued that the following (non-chronological) sequence of events were emphasized: Hezekiah's stirring victory over the Assyrians (18:13–19:37); Hezekiah's triumph over a life-threatening illness (20:1–11); but then, Hezekiah's short-sighted pride in the presence of the Babylonian embassy (20:12–19). Then, the last thing we are meant to contemplate concerning King Hezekiah is his short-sighted pride (no matter that that event probably took place well before the Sennacherib invasion of 701). Even the great king, who successfully challenged the greatest political and military power of his day, did not think about (or even care about) the future beyond his own lifespan, it would seem. The final image we have of this godly king is the ungodly refrain, "The [ultimately harshly judgmental] word of Yahweh is good" (20:19), since there would still be peace and security in his lifetime. Success against Assyria, brought a miraculous extension of life and health for a season, but it also predicted Babylonian disaster—such is the present rhythm of Hezekiah's kingship, and such was the ultimate experience of the Judahite believers. So it is to the second, still positive, episode that we now turn.*

20:1. Isaiah's announcement. By now we need no introduction to the prophet Isaiah (let the reader

2513.123		5621.521	881, 6686	420, 7306	6663.721	420, 3176
v Qal impf 2ms	**2.**	cj, v Hiphil impf 3ms	do, n mp, ps 3ms	prep, art, n ms	cj, v Hithpael impf 3ms	prep, pn
תִחְיֶה		וַיַּסֵּב	אֶת־פָּנָיו	אֶל־הַקִּיר	וַיִּתְפַּלֵּל	אֶל־יְהוָה
thichāyeh		wayyassēv	'eth-pānâv	'el-haqqîr	wayyithpallēl	'el-yehwāh
you will live		and he turned	his face	to the wall	and he prayed	to Yahweh

3937, 569.141		590	3176	2226.131, 5167	881	866	2050.715
prep, v Qal inf con	**3.**	intrg	pn	v Qal impv 2ms, part	do	rel part	v Hithpael pf 1cs
לֵאמֹר		אָנָּה	יְהוָה	זְכָר־נָא	אֵת	אֲשֶׁר	הִתְהַלַּכְתִּי
lē'mōr		'ānnāh	yehwāh	zekhār-nā'	'ēth	'ăsher	hithhallakhtî
saying		where	O Yahweh	remember please		that	I walked continually

3937, 6686	904, 583	904, 3949	8400	3008	904, 6084
prep, n mp, ps 2ms	prep, n fs	cj, prep, n ms	adj	cj, art, n ms	prep, n fd, ps 2ms
לְפָנֶיךָ	בֶּאֱמֶת	וּבְלֵבָב	שָׁלֵם	וְהַטּוֹב	בְּעֵינֶיךָ
lephānêkhā	be'ĕmeth	ûvelēvāv	shālēm	wehattôv	be'ênêkhā
before You	with faithfulness	and with a heart	complete	and what is good	in your eyes

6449.115	1098.121	2488	1104	1448		2030.121	3591	3940
v Qal pf 1cs	cj, v Qal impf 3ms	pn	n ms	adj	**4.**	cj, v Qal impf 3ms	pn	neg part
עָשִׂיתִי	וַיֵּבְךְּ	חִזְקִיָּהוּ	בְּכִי	גָּדוֹל		וַיְהִי	יְשַׁעְיָהוּ	לֹא
'āsîthî	wayyēvke	chizqîyāhû	bekhî	ghādhôl		wayhî	yesha'ăyāhû	lō'
I did	and he wept	Hezekiah	a weeping	great		and it was	Isaiah	not

3428.111	6111	8814	1745, 3176	2030.111	420
v Qal pf 3ms	art, n fs	art, adj	cj, *n ms*, pn	v Qal pf 3ms	prep, ps 3ms
יָצָא	הָעִיר	הַתִּיכֹנָה	וּדְבַר־יְהוָה	הָיָה	אֵלָיו
yātsā'	hā'îr	hattîkhōnāh	ûdhevar-yehwāh	hāyāh	'ēlâv
he had gone out of	the city	the middle	and the word of Yahweh	it was	to him

3937, 569.141		8178.131	569.113	420, 2488	5233, 6194
prep, v Qal inf con	**5.**	v Qal impv 2ms	cj, v Qal pf 2ms	prep, pn	*n ms*, n ms, ps 1cs
לֵאמֹר		שׁוּב	וְאָמַרְתָּ	אֶל־חִזְקִיָּהוּ	נְגִיד־עַמִּי
lē'mōr		shûv	we'āmartā	'el-chizqîyāhû	neghîdh-'ammî
saying		go back	and you will say	to Hezekiah	the leader of my people

3662, 569.111	3176	435	1784	1	8471.115	881, 8940
adv, v Qal pf 3ms	pn	*n mp*	pn	n ms, ps 2ms	v Qal pf 1cs	do, n fs, ps 2ms
כֹּה־אָמַר	יְהוָה	אֱלֹהֵי	דָּוִד	אָבִיךָ	שָׁמַעְתִּי	אֶת־תְּפִלָּתֶךָ
kōh-'āmar	yehwāh	'ĕlōhê	dāwidh	'āvîkhā	shāma'ttî	'eth-tephillāthekhā
thus He has said	Yahweh	the God of	David	your ancestor	I have heard	your prayer

7495.115	881, 1893	2079	7784.151	3937	904, 3219	8389
v Qal pf 1cs	do, n fs, ps 2ms	intrj, ps 1cs	v Qal act ptc ms	prep, ps 2ms	prep, art, n ms	art, num
רָאִיתִי	אֶת־דִּמְעָתֶךָ	הִנְנִי	רֹפֵא	לָךְ	בַּיּוֹם	הַשְּׁלִישִׁי
rā'îthî	'eth-dim'āthekhā	hinenî	rōphe'	lākh	bayyôm	hashshelîshî
I have seen	your tears	behold I	healing	you	on the day	the third

6148.123	1041	3176		3362.515	6142, 3219	2675	6462
v Qal impf 2ms	*n ms*	pn	**6.**	cj, v Hiphil pf 1cs	prep, n mp, ps 2ms	num	num
תַּעֲלֶה	בֵּית	יְהוָה		וְהֹסַפְתִּי	עַל־יָמֶיךָ	חֲמֵשׁ	עֶשְׂרֵה
ta'ăleh	bêth	yehwāh		wehōsaphtî	'al-yāmêkhā	chămēsh	'esrēh
you will go up to	the temple of	Yahweh		and I will add	onto your days	five	ten

8523	4623, 3834	4567, 831	5522.525	881	6111	2148
n fs	cj, prep, *n fs*	*n ms*, pn	v Hiphil impf 1cs, ps 2ms	cj, do	art, n fs	art, dem pron
שָׁנָה	וּמִכַּף	מֶלֶךְ־אַשּׁוּר	אַצִּילְךָ	וְאֵת	הָעִיר	הַזֹּאת
shānāh	ûmikkaph	melekh-'ashshûr	'atstsîlekhā	we'ēth	hā'îr	hazzō'th
years	and from the palm of	the king of Assyria	I will rescue you	and	the city	the this

him, Thus saith the LORD, Set thine house in order; for thou shalt die, and not live: ... Give your last instructions to your household, for you are dying; you will not recover, *REB* ... Set your affairs in order, for you are going to die. You will not recover from this illness, *NLT* ... you will die and not get well, *Beck*.

2. Then he turned his face to the wall, and prayed unto the LORD, saying: ... and addressed this prayer to Yahweh, *JB* ... turned toward the wall, *NCV* ... offered this prayer, *NEB* ... besought the Lord, *Tyndale*.

3. I beseech thee, O LORD, remember now how I have walked before thee in truth and with a perfect heart, and have done that which is good in thy sight: ... have walked before thee in faithfulness and with a whole heart, *RSV* ... remember how I served you faithfully and loyally, and did what was pleasing to you, *Anchor* ... in truth and sincerity of heart, *Goodspeed* ... and have done what is good in your eyes, *BB*.

And Hezekiah wept sore: ... wept bitterly, *RSV* ... began to cry bitterly, *Good News* ... wept profusely, *Goodspeed* ... shed many tears, *JB*.

4. And it came to pass, afore Isaiah was gone out into the middle court, that the word of the LORD came to him, saying: ... before Isaiah was gone, *KJVII* ... middle of the courtyard, *Knox* ... inner court of the city, *MAST* ... central courtyard, *NAB*.

5. Turn again, and tell Hezekiah the captain of my people, Thus saith the LORD, the God of David thy father, I have heard thy prayer, I have seen thy tears: ... ruler of my people, *Anchor* ... prince of my people, *ASV* ... the God of your ancestor David, *NRSV* ... Your prayer has come to my ears, and I have seen your weeping, *BB*.

behold, I will heal thee: on the third day thou shalt go up unto the house of the LORD: ... I will make you well, *BB* ... The day after tomorrow you will go, *Beck* ... I will cure you, *Fenton* ... I have granted thee recovery, *Knox*.

6. And I will add unto thy days fifteen years; and I will deliver thee and this city out of the hand of the king of Assyria: ... will add fifteen years to your life, *NIV* ... will lengthen thy days, *Tyndale* ... will rescue you and this city, *NAB* ... shall save you and this city, *JB*.

and I will defend this city for mine own sake, and for my servant David's sake: ... will protect this city, *Fenton* ... for the sake of my own honor and because of the promise I made to my servant David, *Good News* ... will keep this town safe, for my honour, and for the honour of my servant, *BB*.

---

note that this prophet played a prominent role in each of the three major episodes of Hezekiah's life recorded in 2 Kings). But, after the amazing end of the previous chapter, with death and destruction the hallmark of the enemy, we are little prepared for Isaiah's stern pronouncement of: get ready, Hezekiah, for you are going to die. Yes, Hezekiah is said to be ill (v. 1), but we would surely expect another word of life, not a word of death, from the prophet at this point. Nonetheless, we do know that "Surely the Lord God will do nothing, but he revealeth his secret unto his servants the prophets" (Amos 3:7), and, accordingly, Yahweh did Hezekiah the courtesy to declare to him the future. Perhaps God expected the king to do what He expects us to do—pray, intercede, repent if necessary (cf. the familiar message about the potter and the clay in Jer. 18:1–12, where the "clay" is expected to respond to the potter's intentions, even to the point of changing them entirely). In any case, God was not disappointed.

20:2–3. Hezekiah's response: fervent, heartfelt prayer, with tears. We have already noticed how Hezekiah was "incomparable," particularly in the area of prayer (cf. introductory comments on 19:14–34). Hezekiah's fervent, heartfelt prayers brought results—and such is exactly the case here, once again. Hobbs (WBC, 290), however, sees the king here as sulking ("turned to face the wall"), and too self-serving, too concerned for his own piety ("remember ... how I have walked before thee in truth and with a perfect heart, and have done that which is good in thy sight"). But surely Hobbs is being too harsh here. Hezekiah had truly been faithful, and who among us would not have been as self-concerned, especially after being blindsided with such an unexpected (and seemingly undeserved) message of judgment? It was Yahweh Who had a change of heart in the very next verse.

20:4–6. Yahweh's immediate change of heart. Yahweh seems to change his mind, or relent, rather often in Scripture (cf. the aforementioned Jer. 18:1–12, especially vv. 7–10; also Gen. 6:5–8, and its contrast in 8:21f; Exo. 32:7–10, and its contrast in vv. 31–35; 1 Sam. 15:11, 35, contrasted with v. 29; etc.). We hardly follow a God Who seeks our destruction, but much rather our repentance, and then our love and devotion ("not willing that any should perish, but that all should come to repentance" [2 Pet. 3:9]).

Yahweh's change of heart seems virtually immediate. He addressed Isaiah while he was still on his

1639.115	6142, 6111	2148	3937, 4775	3937, 4775	1784
cj, v Qal pf 1cs	prep, art, n fs	art, dem pron	prep, prep, ps 1cs	cj, prep, prep	pn
וְגַנּוֹתִי	עַל־הָעִיר	הַזֹּאת	לְמַעֲנִי	וּלְמַעַן	דָּוִד
weghannôthî	'al-hā'îr	hazzō'th	lema'ănî	ûlăma'an	dāwidh
and I will defend	concerning the city	the this	for my sake	and for the sake of	David

5860		569.121	3591	4089.133	1737	8711	4089.126
n ms, ps 1cs	**7.**	cj, v Qal impf 3ms	pn	v Qal impv 2mp	*n fs*	n fp	cj, v Qal impf 3mp
עַבְדִּי		וַיֹּאמֶר	יְשַׁעְיָהוּ	קְחוּ	דְּבֶלֶת	תְּאֵנִים	וַיִּקְחוּ
'avdî		wayyō'mer	yesha'āyāhû	qōchû	develeth	te'ēnîm	wayyiqōchû
my servant		and he said	Isaiah	take	a cake of	figs	and they took

7947.126	6142, 8253	2513.121		569.121	2488	420, 3591	4242
cj, v Qal impf 3mp	prep, art, n ms	cj, v Qal impf 3ms	**8.**	cj, v Qal impf 3ms	pn	prep, pn	intrg
וַיָּשִׂימוּ	עַל־הַשְּׁחִין	וַיֶּחִי		וַיֹּאמֶר	חִזְקִיָּהוּ	אֶל־יְשַׁעְיָהוּ	מָה
wayyāsîmû	'al-hashshechîn	wayyechî		wayyō'mer	chizqîyāhû	'el-yesha'āyāhû	māh
and they put	on the boil	and he lived		and he said	Hezekiah	to Isaiah	what

225	3706, 7784.121	3176	3937	6148.115	904, 3219	8389
n ms	cj, v Qal impf 3ms	pn	prep, ps 1cs	cj, v Qal pf 1cs	prep, art, n ms	art, num
אוֹת	כִּי־יִרְפָּא	יְהוָה	לִי	וְעָלִיתִי	בַּיּוֹם	הַשְּׁלִישִׁי
'ôth	kî-yirpā'	yehwāh	lî	we'ālîthî	bayyôm	hashshelîshî
a sign	that He will heal	Yahweh	me	that I will go up to	on the day	the third

1041	3176		569.121	3591	2172, 3937	225	4623, 881
n ms	pn	**9.**	cj, v Qal impf 3ms	pn	dem pron, prep, ps 2ms	art, n ms	prep, do
בֵּית	יְהוָה		וַיֹּאמֶר	יְשַׁעְיָהוּ	זֶה־לְּךָ	הָאוֹת	מֵאֵת
bêth	yehwāh		wayyō'mer	yesha'āyāhû	zeh-lekhā	hā'ôth	mē'ēth
the temple of	Yahweh		and he said	Isaiah	this to you	the sign	from

3176	3706	6449.121	3176	881, 1745	866	1744.311	2050.111
pn	cj	v Qal impf 3ms	pn	do, art, n ms	rel part	v Piel pf 3ms	v Qal pf 3ms
יְהוָה	כִּי	יַעֲשֶׂה	יְהוָה	אֶת־הַדָּבָר	אֲשֶׁר	דִּבֵּר	הָלַךְ
yehwāh	kî	ya'ăseh	yehwāh	'eth-haddāvār	'ăsher	dibbēr	hālakh
Yahweh	because	He will do	Yahweh	the word	which	He spoke	it will proceed

7009	6460	4766	524, 8178	6460	4766		569.121	2488
art, n ms	num	n fp	cj, v Qal impf 3ms	num	n fp	**10.**	cj, v Qal impf 3ms	pn
הַצֵּל	עֶשֶׂר	מַעֲלוֹת	אִם־יָשׁוּב	עֶשֶׂר	מַעֲלוֹת		וַיֹּאמֶר	יְחִזְקִיָּהוּ
hatstsēl	'eser	ma'ălôth	'im-yāshûv	'eser	ma'ălôth		wayyō'mer	yechizqîyāhû
the shadow	ten	steps	or it will go back	ten	steps		and he said	Hezekiah

7327.211	3937, 7009	3937, 5371.141	6460	4766	3940	3706	8178.121
v Niphal pf 3ms	prep, art, n ms	prep, v Qal inf con	num	n fp	neg part	cj	v Qal juss 3ms
נָקֵל	לַצֵּל	לִנְטוֹת	עֶשֶׂר	מַעֲלוֹת	לֹא	כִּי	יָשׁוּב
nāqēl	latstsēl	lintôth	'eser	ma'ălôth	lō'	khî	yāshûv
it is small	for the shadow	to lengthen	ten	steps	no	rather	let it return

7009	323	6460	4766		7410.121	3591	5204	420, 3176
art, n ms	adv	num	n fp	**11.**	cj, v Qal impf 3ms	pn	art, n ms	prep, pn
הַצֵּל	אֲחֹרַנִּית	עֶשֶׂר	מַעֲלוֹת		וַיִּקְרָא	יְשַׁעְיָהוּ	הַנָּבִיא	אֶל־יְהוָה
hatstsēl	'ăchōranîth	'eser	ma'ălôth		wayyiqōrā'	yesha'āyāhû	hannāvî'	'el-yehwāh
the shadow	backward	ten	steps		and he called	Isaiah	the prophet	to Yahweh

8178.521	881, 7009	4766	866	3495.112	904, 4766	271
cj, v Hiphil impf 3ms	do, art, n ms	prep, art, n fp	rel part	v Qal pf 3fs	prep, art, *n fp*	pn
וַיָּשֶׁב	אֶת־הַצֵּל	בַּמַּעֲלוֹת	אֲשֶׁר	יָרְדָה	בְּמַעֲלוֹת	אָחָז
wayyāshev	'eth-hatstsēl	bamma'ălôth	'ăsher	yāredhāh	bema'ălôth	'āchāz
and He caused to return	the shadow	on the steps	which	it had gone down	on the sundial	Ahaz

7. And Isaiah said, Take a lump of figs: ... cake of figs, *MRB* ... lump of figs, *Douay* ... a fig poultice, *JB* ... apply a fig-plaster, *NEB* ... Make an ointment from figs, *NLT*.

And they took and laid it on the boil, and he recovered: ... they brought one, applied it to the ulcer, and the king recovered, *JB* ... when it was made and applied to the inflammation, Hezekiah recovered, *REB* ... they brought and put it on the sore, *Tyndale,* ... he was healed, *Douay*.

8. And Hezekiah said unto Isaiah, What shall be the sign that the LORD will heal me, and that I shall go up into the house of the LORD the third day?: ... He asked Isaiah what proof there was that the LORD would cure him and that he would go up to the house of the LORD, *REB* ... that the Lord will make me well, and that I will go up, *BB* ... go up to the LORD's temple the day after tomorrow?, *Beck* ... What evidence is there that the EVER-LIVING will cure me, *Fenton*.

9. And Isaiah said, This sign shalt thou have of the LORD, that the LORD will do the thing that he hath spoken: shall the shadow go forward ten degrees, or go back ten degrees?: ... will do the thing that he has promised, *Goodspeed* ... Here is thy proof that the Lord will keep his promise, *Knox* ... Shall the shadow go forward ten steps, or go back ten steps?, *KJVII* ... shadow go forward ten lines, or that it go back so many degrees?, *Douay*.

10. And Hezekiah answered, It is a light thing for the shadow to go down ten degrees: nay, but let the shadow return backward ten degrees: ... It's easy for the shadow to go forward ten steps. Instead, let it go back ten steps, *NCV* ... It is a simple matter for the shadow to go forward ten steps, *NIV* ... The shadow always moves forward, Hezekiah replied. Make it go backward instead, *NLT* ... It is normal for the shadow to lengthen ten intervals; rather let the shadow retreat ten intervals, *NRSV*.

11. And Isaiah the prophet cried unto the LORD: and he brought the shadow ten degrees backward, by which it had gone down in the dial of Ahaz: ... Isaiah the prophet called to the Lord, *Tyndale* ... made prayer to the Lord, *BB* ... the LORD made the shadow go back ten steps on the stairway set up by King Ahaz, *Good News* ... made the shadow retreat the ten steps it had descended on the staircase to the terrace of Ahaz, *NAB*.

---

way out of the palace (before he had left "the middle court," presumably of the palace [v. 4]). "Go back," he was told—for Yahweh had heard Hezekiah's prayer and had seen his tears. He would be healed, and as a sign of this, he would be able to go up to the Temple in three days. In fact, the king would have fifteen more years added to his life, and, curiously, he was reassured that Yahweh would defend the city of Jerusalem "for mine own sake, and for my servant David's sake" (v. 6; the phraseology is virtually identical to 19:34). Of course, this healing represents God's grace, not some sort of earned reward on Hezekiah's part, yet the prayer and the tears of the godly king did make a difference: "Ye have not, because ye ask not" (Jam. 4:2). Hobbs (WBC, 291) is surely correct to see the parallel references to "my servant David" here and in 19:34 as a link between these two sections.

20:7–11. Isaiah's healing poultice and confirmatory short-term prediction. The ordering of the present narrative differs significantly from the Isaiah parallel (Isa. 38), with vv. 7f of the present Kings text (Isa. 38:21f) placed after vv. 9ff (Isa. 38:7f), and separated by a lengthy addition (entitled "a writing of Hezekiah, king of Judah" [Isa. 38:9–20]); thus placing the sign of the backward-moving shadow before the healing poultice of figs. The order in Kings, here, is probably earlier, even with v. 7 indicating recovery of the king before the sign of the shadow is even mentioned (so Cogan and Tadmor, AB, 256f). In any case, the poultice applied by Isaiah, acting in the place of the LORD, brought about the healing. Whatever the precise nature of Hezekiah's illness (presumably some sort of skin disorder, "boils" or the like), the treatment prescribed finds many parallels in the ancient Mediterranean world. Probably then, the cure should be categorized more in the realm of folk medicine than as a totally supernatural and unexplainable act (rather akin to many of our own contemporary miracles of healing, which often include the realm of medicine, traditional and/or folk, as well as the providence and supernatural power of God—there is certainly no need for a sharp either/or distinction here).

The confirmatory "short-term prediction" of the backward-moving shadow (vv. 8–11) is well-known in Christian circles, rather akin to the "long day" of Joshua. What really counts—whether or not the results are congenial to modern schools of thought—is what the text meant to its original audience. And here, rather clearly, the meaning appears to be that the shadow moved backward to a significant degree, seemingly indicating the likewise movement of the sun backwards as well. Once again, as in the Joshua miracle, the ancients, with their flat earth perspective,

323	6460	4766		904, 6496	2026	8365.111	1283	1283
adv	num	n fp		prep, art, n fs	art, dem pron	v Qal pf 3ms	pn	pn
אֲחֹרַנִּית	עֶשֶׂר	מַעֲלוֹת	**12.**	בָּעֵת	הַהִיא	שָׁלַח	בְּרֹאדַךְ	בַּלְאֲדָן
'ăchōranîth	'eser	ma'ălôth		bā'ēth	hahî'	shālach	bᵉrō'dhakh	bal'ădhān
backward	ten	steps		at the time	the that	he sent out	Berodak	Baladan

1158, 1121	4567, 928	5809	4647	420, 2488	3706	8471.111
n ms, pn	*n ms*, pn	n mp	cj, n fs	prep, pn	cj	v Qal pf 3ms
בֶּן־בַּלְאֲדָן	מֶלֶךְ־בָּבֶל	סְפָרִים	וּמִנְחָה	אֶל־חִזְקִיָּהוּ	כִּי	שָׁמַע
ben-bal'ădhān	melekh-bāvel	sᵉphārîm	ûminchāh	'el-chizqîyāhû	kî	shāma'
the son of Baladan	the king of Babylon	documents	and a gift	to Hezekiah	because	he heard

3706	2571.111	2488		8471.121	6142	2488	7495.521
cj	v Qal pf 3ms	pn		cj, v Qal impf 3ms	prep, ps 3mp	pn	cj, v Hiphil impf 3ms, ps 3mp
כִּי	חָלָה	חִזְקִיָּהוּ	**13.**	וַיִּשְׁמַע	עֲלֵיהֶם	חִזְקִיָּהוּ	וַיַּרְאֵם
kî	chālāh	chizqîyāhû		wayyishma'	'ălêhem	chizqîyāhû	wayyar'ēm
that	he was sick	Hezekiah		and he heard	about them	Hezekiah	and he showed them

881, 3725, 1041	5426	881, 3826B	881, 2174	881, 1337	881	8467
do, *adj*, *n ms*	n fs, ps 3ms	do, art, n ms	cj, do, art, n ms	cj, do, art, n mp	cj, do	n ms
אֶת־כָּל־בֵּית	נְכֹתֹה	אֶת־הַכֶּסֶף	וְאֶת־הַזָּהָב	וְאֵת־הַבְּשָׂמִים	וְאֵת	שֶׁמֶן
'eth-kol-bêth	nᵉkhōthōh	'eth-hakkeseph	wᵉ'eth-hazzāhāv	wᵉ'eth-habbᵉsāmîm	wᵉ'ēth	shemen
all the house of	his treasury	the silver	and the gold	and the balsam oils	and	olive oil

3005	881	1041	3747	881	3725, 866	4834.255	904, 212
art, adj	cj, do	*n ms*	n mp, ps 3ms	cj, do	*adj*, rel part	v Niphal ptc ms	prep, n mp, ps 3ms
הַטּוֹב	וְאֵת	בֵּית	כֵּלָיו	וְאֵת	כָּל־אֲשֶׁר	נִמְצָא	בְּאוֹצְרֹתָיו
hattôv	wᵉ'ēth	bêth	kēlâv	wᵉ'ēth	kol-'ăsher	nimtsā'	bᵉ'ôtsrōthâv
the virgin	and	the house of	his weapons	and	all that	it is found	in his storehouses

3940, 2030.111	1745	866	3940, 7495.511	2488	904, 1041
neg part, v Qal pf 3ms	n ms	rel part	neg part, v Hiphil pf 3ms, ps 3mp	pn	prep, n ms, ps 3ms
לֹא־הָיָה	דָבָר	אֲשֶׁר	לֹא־הֶרְאָם	חִזְקִיָּהוּ	בְּבֵיתוֹ
lō'-hāyāh	dhāvār	'ăsher	lō'-her'ām	chizqîyāhû	bᵉvêthô
there was not	a thing	which	he did not show them	Hezekiah	in his house

904, 3725, 4617		971.121	3591	5204	420, 4567	2488
cj, prep, *adj*, n fs, ps 3ms		cj, v Qal impf 3ms	pn	art, n ms	prep, art, n ms	pn
וּבְכָל־מֶמְשַׁלְתּוֹ	**14.**	וַיָּבֹא	יְשַׁעְיָהוּ	הַנָּבִיא	אֶל־הַמֶּלֶךְ	חִזְקִיָּהוּ
ûvᵉkhol-memshaltô		wayyāvō'	yᵉsha'ăyāhû	hannāvî'	'el-hammelekh	chizqîyāhû
or in all his dominion		then he went	Isaiah	the prophet	to the king	Hezekiah

569.121	420	4242	569.116	596	431	4623, 376
cj, v Qal impf 3ms	prep, ps 3ms	intrg	v Qal pf 3cp	art, n mp	art, dem pron	cj, prep, intrg
וַיֹּאמֶר	אֵלָיו	מָה	אָמְרוּ	הָאֲנָשִׁים	הָאֵלֶּה	וּמֵאַיִן
wayyō'mer	'ēlâv	māh	'āmᵉrû	hā'ănāshîm	hā'ēlleh	ûmē'ayin
and he said	to him	what	did they say	the men	the these	and from where

971.126	420	569.121	2488	4623, 800	7632	971.116
v Qal impf 3mp	prep, ps 2ms	cj, v Qal impf 3ms	pn	prep, n fs	adj	v Qal pf 3cp
יָבֹאוּ	אֵלֶיךָ	וַיֹּאמֶר	חִזְקִיָּהוּ	מֵאֶרֶץ	רְחוֹקָה	בָּאוּ
yāvō'û	'ēlêkhā	wayyō'mer	chizqîyāhû	mē'erets	rᵉchôqāh	bā'û
did they come	to you	and he said	Hezekiah	from a land	far away	they came

4623, 928		569.121	4242	7495.116	904, 1041	569.121
prep, pn		cj, v Qal impf 3ms	intrg	v Qal pf 3cp	prep, n ms, ps 2ms	cj, v Qal impf 3ms
מִבָּבֶל	**15.**	וַיֹּאמֶר	מָה	רָאוּ	בְּבֵיתֶךָ	וַיֹּאמֶר
mibbāvel		wayyō'mer	māh	rā'û	bᵉvêthekhā	wayyō'mer
from Babylon		and he said	what	have they seen	in your house	and he said

12. At that time Berodach-baladan, the son of Baladan, king of Babylon, sent letters and a present unto Hezekiah: for he had heard that Hezekiah had been sick: ... heard that he had been ill, *REB* ... heard of Hezekiah's illness, *NIV* ... had heard of his illness and his recovery, *JB* ... had taken ill, *Anchor.*

13. And Hezekiah hearkened unto them, and showed them all the house of his precious things, the silver, and the gold, and the spices, and the precious ointment, and all the house of his armour, and all that was found in his treasures: ... Hezekiah was so delighted with them he showed them his whole house of treasures, *Beck* ... was pleased with them, *Goodspeed* ... rejoiced at their coming, *Douay* ... received them and showed them all his treasure house, the silver, the gold, the spices, the aromatic oil, his armory, and everything deposited in his treasuries, *Berkeley.*

there was nothing in his house, nor in all his dominion, that Hezekiah showed them not: ... There wasn't a thing in his palace or anywhere else under his control that Hezekiah didn't show them, *Beck* ... there was nothing in his house and in all his realm that Hezekiah did not show them, *NEB* ... nothing in his palace or in all his kingdom, *NIV* ... not a thing in his residence or in his realm, *Anchor.*

14. Then came Isaiah the prophet unto king Hezekiah, and said unto him, What said these men? and from whence came they unto thee? And Hezekiah said, They are come from a far country, even from Babylon: ... What have these men said, and where have they come from?, *JB* ... where did they come to you from?, *KJVII* ... They came from a distant land, *NAB* ... from a far-off country, *NEB.*

15. And he said, What have they seen in thine house? And Hezekiah answered, All the things that are in mine house have they seen: there is nothing among my treasures that I have not showed them: ... What did they see in your residence?, *Anchor* ... in your Palace, *Fenton* ... there is nothing among my stores which I did not let them see, *BB* ... I showed them all my wealth, *NCV.*

---

would have had less trouble explaining this than we would—but even they, clearly, recognized the incongruity of the sign: "It is a light thing for the shadow to go down ten degrees: ... but let the shadow return backward ten degrees" (v. 10). Presumably, the "steps" are part of some sort of "sundial" or such—the indication of time is what is in view, after all. Whatever the specifics, the overall import is clear—Hezekiah asked for, and Isaiah was pleased to give, a "short-term prediction" (once again, the typical means of confirmation of the prophet's authenticity; cf. comments on 1:3f). In sharp contrast to his father Ahaz (cf. on 15:27–31), Hezekiah was neither reluctant to seek such a sign, nor to believe its testimony (also cf. comments on Isaiah's other short-term prediction for Hezekiah in 19:1–8). Hezekiah's prayers have once again changed history and brought about supernatural events.

20:12–19. *Shortsighted pride in connection with Merodach-Baladan, king of Babylon. Alas, here we see Hezekiah in more of a negative light. As already discussed (see introductory comments on 20:1–11), the treatment of Hezekiah in Kings seems purposely to be arranged to accentuate the negative, i.e., his short-sighted pride evidenced both by the display of his treasures to the Babylonian embassy, as well as his final comment in the passage: "Yahweh's word is good" (since Yahweh's coming judgment would take place only after his death). This perspective ironically anticipates a similar perspective of the other "incomparable" king of Judah, namely Josiah, whose foolhardy opposition to Pharaoh Neco (see comments on 23:26–30) would lead directly not only to his own untimely death, but also to the eventual death of the entire Davidic dynasty (at least as kings over an independent state of Judah) and, indeed, to the destruction of the Solomonic temple and the devastation of the city of Jerusalem.*

20:12–15. Hezekiah's prideful display. As Prov. 16:18 reminds us: "Pride goeth before destruction, and an haughty spirit before a fall." Hezekiah by now had two remarkable victories: over Assyria, and, as it were, over death. He had reason to feel "on top of the world," so to speak. And now came a delegation from Merodach-Baladan, "king of Babylon" (v. 12). A word of explanation concerning this Merodach-Baladan is in order here, for one would normally assume that no such king could exist during this powerful period of Assyrian domination. But, as we soon shall see, Merodach-Baladan was no ordinary person.

Already in the waning years of Tiglath-Pileser III, Merodach-Baladan was a prominent chieftain from the Yakin tribe in southern Babylon. By the death of Shalmaneser V in 722, he had consolidated his rule over the whole of Babylonia. Indeed, in that year he assumed kingship in the city of Babylon, and he was not ousted from that position until 710, when Sargon II finally took over the city.

2488	881	3725, 866	904, 1041	7495.116	3940, 2030.111	1745	866
pn	do	*adj*, rel part	prep, n ms, ps 1cs	v Qal pf 3cp	neg part, v Qal pf 3ms	n ms	rel part
חִזְקִיָּהוּ	אֵת	כָּל־אֲשֶׁר	בְּבֵיתִי	רָאוּ	לֹא־הָיָה	דָבָר	אֲשֶׁר
chizqîyāhû	'ēth	kol-'āsher	bevêthî	rā'û	lō'-hāyāh	dhāvār	'āsher
Hezekiah		all that	in my house	they saw	there was not	a thing	which

3940, 7495.515	904, 212		569.121	3591	420, 2488
neg part, v Hiphil pf 1cs, ps 3mp	prep, n mp, ps 1cs		cj, v Qal impf 3ms	pn	prep, pn
לֹא־הִרְאִיתִם	בְּאֹצְרֹתָי	**16.**	וַיֹּאמֶר	יְשַׁעְיָהוּ	אֶל־חִזְקִיָּהוּ
lō'-hir'îthim	be'ōtserōthāy		wayyō'mer	yesha'ăyāhû	'el-chizqîyāhû
I did not show them	in my storehouses		and he said	Isaiah	to Hezekiah

8471.131	1745, 3176		2079	3219	971.152	5558.255
v Qal impv 2ms	*n ms*, pn		intrj	n mp	v Qal act ptc mp	cj, v Niphal ptc ms
שְׁמַע	דְּבַר־יְהוָה	**17.**	הִנֵּה	יָמִים	בָּאִים	וְנִשָּׂא
shema'	devar-yehwāh		hinnēh	yāmîm	bā'îm	wenissā'
hear	the word of Yahweh		behold	days	coming	when being carried away

3725, 866	904, 1041	866	709.116	1	5912, 3219	2172
adj, rel part	prep, n ms, ps 2ms	cj, rel part	v Qal pf 3cp	n mp, ps 2ms	adv, art, n ms	art, dem pron
כָּל־אֲשֶׁר	בְּבֵיתֶךָ	וַאֲשֶׁר	אָצְרוּ	אֲבֹתֶיךָ	עַד־הַיּוֹם	הַזֶּה
kol-'āsher	bevêthekhā	wa'āsher	'ātserû	'ăvōthêkhā	'adh-hayyôm	hazzeh
all that	in your house	and that	they stored up	your fathers	until the day	the this

928	3940, 3613.221	1745	569.111	3176		4623, 1158	866
pn	neg part, v Niphal impf 3ms	n ms	v Qal pf 3ms	pn		cj, prep, n mp, ps 2ms	rel pron
בָּבֶלָה	לֹא־יִוָּתֵר	דָּבָר	אָמַר	יְהוָה	**18.**	וּמִבָּנֶיךָ	אֲשֶׁר
bāvelāh	lō'-yiwwāthēr	dāvār	'āmar	yehwāh		ûmibbānêkhā	'āsher
to Babylon	it will not be left	a thing	He said	Yahweh		and from your sons	who

3428.126	4623	866	3314.523	4089.126	2030.116
v Qal impf 3mp	prep, ps 2ms	rel pron	v Hiphil impf 2ms	v Qal impf 3ms	cj, v Qal pf 3cp
יֵצְאוּ	מִמְּךָ	אֲשֶׁר	תּוֹלִיד	יִקָּח	וְהָיוּ
yētse'û	mimmekhā	'āsher	tôlîdh	yiqqāch	wehāyû
they will go out	from you	whom	you will father	they will be taken	and they will be

5835	904, 2033	4567	928		569.121	2488	420, 3591
n mp	prep, *n ms*	*n ms*	pn		cj, v Qal impf 3ms	pn	prep, pn
סָרִיסִים	בְּהֵיכַל	מֶלֶךְ	בָּבֶל	**19.**	וַיֹּאמֶר	חִזְקִיָּהוּ	אֶל־יְשַׁעְיָהוּ
s̱ārîsîm	behêkhal	melekh	bāvel		wayyō'mer	chizqîyāhû	'el-yesha'ăyāhû
eunuchs	in the palace of	the king of	Babylon		and he said	Hezekiah	to Isaiah

3005	1745, 3176	866	1744.313	569.121	1950B, 3940	524, 8361
adj	*n ms*, pn	rel part	v Piel pf 2ms	cj, v Qal impf 3ms	intrg part, neg part	cj, n ms
טוֹב	דְּבַר־יְהוָה	אֲשֶׁר	דִּבַּרְתָּ	וַיֹּאמֶר	הֲלוֹא	אִם־שָׁלוֹם
ṯôv	devar-yehwāh	'āsher	dibbartā	wayyō'mer	hălô'	'im-shālôm
good	the word of Yahweh	which	you have spoken	and he said	is it not	if peace

16. And Isaiah said unto Hezekiah, Hear the word of the Lord: … Listen to what the LORD says, *Beck* … I have a message for thy hearing from the Lord, *Knox* … Listen to this message from the Lord, *NLT*.

17. Behold, the days come, that all that is in thine house, and that which thy fathers have laid up in store unto this day, shall be carried into Babylon: nothing shall be left, saith the Lord: … and what your fathers have accumulated until this day, shall be carried, *NKJV* … that which your ancestors have stored up until this day, *NRSV* … everything in your palace, and all that your forefathers have amassed till the present day, *REB* … everything in your residence and that which your ancestors have amassed, *Anchor.*

18. And of thy sons that shall issue from thee, which thou shalt beget, shall they take away; and they shall be eunuchs in the palace of the king of Babylon: … your sons, the offspring of your body, they will take away to be unsexed servants, *BB* ... your sons who proceed from you, whom you have produced, will be seized and made eunuchs, *Fenton* ... Some of your own direct descendants will be taken away, *Good News* ... Sons sprung from you, sons fathered by you, will be abducted, *JB*.

19. Then said Hezekiah unto Isaiah, Good is the word of the LORD which thou hast spoken. And he said, Is it not good, if peace and truth be in my days?: ... welcome be the word the Lord has spoken through thee!, *Knox* ... The word of the LORD which you have spoken is favorable, *NAB* ... For he thought, Will there not be peace and security in my lifetime?, *NIV* ... For he said, Will there not be peace and truth at least in my days?, *NKJV*.

20. And the rest of the acts of Hezekiah, and all his might, and how he made a pool, and a conduit, and brought water into the city, are they not written in the book of the chronicles of the kings of Judah?: ... The other events of Hezekiah's reign, his exploits, and how he made the pool and the conduit and brought water into the city, are recorded, *REB* ... The remnant of the deeds of Hezekiah and all his power, *Tyndale* ... written in the Book of the Annals of the Kings of Judah?, *NRSV* ... The rest of the history of Hezekiah and all his exploits, and how he constructed

---

The wounded Merodach-Baladan, however, eluded their capture, and the old tribal chieftain collected his forces in the south at his old tribal capital of Dur-Yakin. Sargon controlled the city of Babylon until his death in 705. Soon after his son Sennacherib ascended the throne, however, Merodach-Baladan reappeared as king of Babylon (for nine months, according to the Babylonian King List A), and the new Assyrian king directed his "first campaign" against this familiar Assyrian nemesis. Sennacherib claimed victory, and the ever resilient Merodach-Baladan once again fled to the southern swamps. Sennacherib's campaign of the year 700 was directed against his homeland. This is the last we hear about Merodach-Baladan, as he yet again eluded Assyrian efforts at capture.

Thus, such an embassy as we read about in the present passage could have taken place around 713, a time of Palestinian revolt against Assyria (so Cogan and Tadmor, AB, 261), or later, around 701 (so Brinkman; also Wiseman, TOTC, 288). Some opt for the earlier period (as Cogan and Tadmor point out, there is hardly time for such a state visit in the later, brief period of rule), although one should not be overly dogmatic about this matter. Not so incidental, however, is the issue of the "fourteenth year" synchronism in 18:13 (again, cf. on 18:13–16)—it would fit so nicely the present setting to date Merodach-Baladan's embassy to the year 713, which would indeed have been Hezekiah's fourteenth year of reign (Cogan and Tadmor).

The present embassy is represented as a state visit to congratulate Hezekiah on recovery from his illness (the chronicler, in passing [2 Chr. 32:31], also connects this visit with the "sign" which had just taken place), but many have seen hidden motives behind this ostensible good will. Possibly, coordination of rebellion against Assyria was of major interest, or at least the maintenance of diplomatic good will with Assyria's strongest western vassal (Cogan and Tadmor, AB, 262, compare the visit of the Queen of Sheba in the days of Solomon [1 Ki. 10:1–13]). Hezekiah spared his visitors no sight; he showed them everything (v. 13). Surely his motive was pride (cf. 2 Chr. 32:25f), shortsighted pride at that. As Isaiah questioned the king about the visit, Hezekiah proudly disclosed that he showed the visitors "everything" (v. 15); "there is nothing among my treasures that I have not shown them." That proved to be shortsighted indeed.

20:16–18. Isaiah's condemnatory prophecy. Isaiah was far from pleased with Hezekiah's answer. The king showed the Babylonians "everything"; well, "everything" would some day be carried off to Babylon—nothing would be left in palace or kingdom. Indeed, some of Hezekiah's own descendants would also be carried off to that distant place. Isaiah prophetically declared the inevitability of the Babylonian exile in response to Hezekiah's boast that he showed the emissaries everything in his palace. But (at least in the eyes of the writer of Kings), the very act of viewing all this royal property on the part of the Babylonians may have indicated some sort of legal transfer as well. Following a proposal first made by David Daube that in the case of the sale of something unable physically to be handed over (e.g., a house or land), a formal viewing of the property would be scheduled, at which time the exchange is deemed to have taken place. Daube notes that such a viewing must be accompanied by the intention of the owner to hand over the property in question.

20:19. Hezekiah's shortsighted response. Hezekiah had no such desire to "ensure" the eventual exile taking place. But his comments here were surely indefensible. They were shortsighted indeed

583	2030.121	904, 3219		3615	1745	2488
cj, n fs	v Qal impf 3ms	prep, n mp, ps 1cs	20.	cj, *n ms*	*n mp*	pn
וֶאֱמֶת	יִהְיֶה	בְיָמָי		וְיֶתֶר	דִּבְרֵי	חִזְקִיָּהוּ
we'ĕmeth	yihyeh	vᵉyāmāy		wᵉyether	divrê	chizqîyāhû
and reliability	it will be	in my days		and the remainder of	the events of	Hezekiah

3725, 1400	866	6449.111	881, 1320	881, 8916	971.521
cj, *adj*, n fs, ps 3ms	cj, rel part	v Qal pf 3ms	do, art, n fs	cj, do, art, n fs	cj, Hiphil impf 3ms
וְכָל־גְּבוּרָתוֹ	וַאֲשֶׁר	עָשָׂה	אֶת־הַבְּרֵכָה	וְאֶת־הַתְּעָלָה	וַיָּבֵא
wᵉkhol-gᵉvûrāthô	wa'ăsher	'āsāh	'eth-habbᵉrēkhāh	wᵉ'eth-hattᵉ'ālāh	wayyāvē'
and all his strength	and how	he made	the pool	and the conduit	and he brought

881, 4448	6111	1950B, 3940, 2062	3918.156	6142, 5809	1745
do, art, n md	art, n fs	intrg part, neg part, pers pron	v Qal pass ptc mp	prep, *n ms*	*n mp*
אֶת־הַמַּיִם	הָעִירָה	הֲלֹא־הֵם	כְּתוּבִים	עַל־סֵפֶר	דִּבְרֵי
'eth-hammayim	hā'îrāh	hălō'-hēm	kᵉthûvîm	'al-sēpher	divrê
the water	to the city	are they not	things written	on the scroll of	the events of

3219	3937, 4567	3171		8311.121	2488	6196, 1
art, n mp	prep, *n mp*	pn	21.	cj, v Qal impf 3ms	pn	prep, n mp, ps 3ms
הַיָּמִים	לְמַלְכֵי	יְהוּדָה		וַיִּשְׁכַּב	חִזְקִיָּהוּ	עִם־אֲבֹתָיו
hayyāmîm	lᵉmalkhê	yᵉhûdhāh		wayyishkav	chizqîyāhû	'im-'ăvōthâv
the days	of the kings of	Judah		and he lay	Hezekiah	with his ancestors

4566.121	4667	1158	8809		1158, 8692	6462	8523
cj, v Qal impf 3ms	pn	n ms, ps 3ms	prep, ps 3ms	21:1	*n ms*, num	num	n fs
וַיִּמְלֹךְ	מְנַשֶּׁה	בְּנוֹ	תַּחְתָּיו		בֶּן־שְׁתֵּים	עֶשְׂרֵה	שָׁנָה
wayyimlōkh	mᵉnashsheh	vᵉnô	tachtâv		ben-shᵉttêm	'esrēh	shānāh
and he reigned	Manasseh	his son	instead of him		a son of two	ten	years

4667	904, 4566.141	2675	2675	8523	4566.111	904, 3503
pn	prep, v Qal inf con, ps 3ms	cj, num	cj, num	n fs	v Qal pf 3ms	prep, pn
מְנַשֶּׁה	בְמָלְכוֹ	וַחֲמִשִּׁים	וְחָמֵשׁ	שָׁנָה	מָלַךְ	בִּירוּשָׁלָם
mᵉnashsheh	vᵉmālᵉkhô	wachmishshîm	wᵉchāmēsh	shānāh	mālakh	bîrûshālām
Manasseh	when his reigning	and fifty	and five	years	he reigned	in Jerusalem

8428	525	2762		6449.121	7737	904, 6084	3176
cj, *n ms*	n fs, ps 3ms	pn	2.	cj, v Qal impf 3ms	art, adj	prep, *n fd*	pn
וְשֵׁם	אִמּוֹ	חֶפְצִי־בָהּ		וַיַּעַשׂ	הָרַע	בְּעֵינֵי	יְהוָה
wᵉshēm	'immô	chephtsî-vāhh		wayya'as	hāra'	bᵉ'ênê	yᵉhwāh
and the name of	his mother	Hephzibah		and he did	what is evil	in the eyes of	Yahweh

3626, 8774	1504	866	3542.511	3176	4623, 6686	1158
prep, *n fp*	art, n mp	rel pron	v Hiphil pf 3ms	pn	prep, *n mp*	*n mp*
כְּתוֹעֲבֹת	הַגּוֹיִם	אֲשֶׁר	הוֹרִישׁ	יְהוָה	מִפְּנֵי	בְּנֵי
kᵉthô'ăvōth	haggôyim	'ăsher	hôrîsh	yᵉhwāh	mippᵉnê	bᵉnê
like the detestable things of	the nations	whom	He dispossessed	Yahweh	from before	the sons of

3547		8178.121	1161.121	881, 1154	866	6.311
pn	3.	cj, v Qal impf 3ms	cj, v Qal impf 3ms	do, art, n fp	rel part	v Piel pf 3ms
יִשְׂרָאֵל		וַיָּשָׁב	וַיִּבֶן	אֶת־הַבָּמוֹת	אֲשֶׁר	אִבַּד
yisrā'ēl		wayyāshāv	wayyiven	'eth-habbāmôth	'ăsher	'ibbadh
Israel		and he returned	and he built	the high places	which	he had demolished

2488	1	7251.521	4326	3937, 1197	6449.121	867
pn	n ms, ps 3ms	cj, v Hiphil impf 3ms	n mp	prep, art, n ms	cj, v Qal impf 3ms	pn
חִזְקִיָּהוּ	אָבִיו	וַיָּקֶם	מִזְבְּחֹת	לַבַּעַל	וַיַּעַשׂ	אֲשֵׁרָה
chizqîyāhû	'āvîw	wayyāqem	mizbᵉchōth	labba'al	wayya'as	'ăshērāh
Hezekiah	his father	and he erected	altars	for the Baal	and he made	Asherah

the pool and the conduit to bring water into the city, are indeed recorded, *Anchor.*

21. And Hezekiah slept with his fathers: and Manasseh his son reigned in his stead: ... rested with his forefathers, *NEB* ... became king in his stead, *Goodspeed* ... reigned after him, *Fenton* ... the throne passed to his son, *Knox* ... became king in his place, *NASB.*

21:1. Manasseh was twelve years old when he began to reign, and reigned fifty and five years in Jerusalem. And his mother's name was Hephzibah: ... when he became king, *Anchor* ... at his coronation, *Fenton* ... for fifty-five years he was ruling in Jerusalem, *BB* ... he continued to reign at Jerusalem for fifty-five years, *Berkeley.*

2. And he did that which was evil in the sight of the LORD, after the abominations of the heathen, whom the LORD cast out before the children of Israel: ... He did what was wrong before the LORD, *Beck* ... He did what is displeasing to Yahweh, copying the disgusting practices of the nations whom Yahweh had dispossessed for the Israelites, *JB* ... Manasseh defied the Lord's will, by courting the false gods of those nations which the Lord destroyed to make room for the sons of Israel, *Knox* ... did evil in the sight of the Lord, according to the idols of the nations which the Lord destroyed from before the face of, *Douay.*

3. For he built up again the high places which Hezekiah his father had destroyed: ... He rebuilt the hill-shrines, *NEB* ... built the hill altars again, *Tyndale* ... rebuilt the

---

(how much more so in such a communal society as that of ancient Judah, with its concern for clan solidarity). Maybe it was a poorly thought out wisecrack, or the like, but it is surely meant to leave a bad taste in our mouths. The godly king, incomparable in prayer, can say only this? As Hobbs (WBC, 295), declares in regard to the present verse, "The clay feet of Hezekiah are now apparent" (cf., also, Cogan and Tadmor [AB, 259f], who note that the parallel in Isaiah [Isa. 39:8] makes Hezekiah's self-concern all the more evident: "For there shall be peace and truth in my days"). Let us, in our pragmatic age, never be so tempted to look at the short-term repercussions of our behavior only, for we are to recognize that our actions and inactions will have eternal consequences.

20:20–21. Conclusion to King Hezekiah's reign. Only the briefest of notes bring the discussion of this most remarkable (if flawed) king to a close: a relatively lengthy "further reference" notice in v. 20, and the briefest of Judahite burial notices in v. 21 (curiously, no burial location is given for this important king; cf. comments on 8:23f).

Surely, the most famous archaeological feature of Hezekiah's reign is his great tunnel cut in the limestone below Jerusalem's "City of David" as a water conduit from the Gihon Spring (sometimes known as the "Virgin's Fountain") to the Pool of Siloam. Rather circuitous in route, and measuring some 1900 feet [580 meters] long, it represents a remarkable feat of engineering and can still be traversed today. Presumably cut in anticipation of the Assyrian invasion of 701, it originally included an inscription which now resides in the Istanbul Archaeological Museum. The inscription describes how the stone cutters started at both ends of the tunnel and met roughly in the middle, hearing each other's voices while three cubits (a cubit is about eighteen inches, or half a meter) yet remained to be cut through. By all accounts, it is a remarkable feat of engineering and serves well to bring the present discussion of King Hezekiah to a close. Hezekiah was a king definitely to be reckoned with—a brave reformer, a fervent prayer-warrior, but, alas, on one occasion too filled with shortsighted and self-seeking pride to lament the eventual fall of his, and his ancestor David's, kingdom. May we be ever inspired by his fervent and effectual godliness, as well as admonished by his momentary lapse into shortsighted self-concern.

21:1–18. Manasseh, king of Judah: A wicked and ungodly ruler. Not a single good thing is said about King Manasseh, who, not so incidentally, reigned longer than any other king of either kingdom. As we shall see below, the chronicler had a more nuanced view of King Manasseh, certainly not denying his great wickedness, but nonetheless pointing to his repentance as a proper example to emulate. But in the Kings, Manasseh is nothing less than the evil King Ahab of the land of Judah. It is to the story of this king, who made the Babylonian exile apparently inevitable (cf. 24:3f), that we now turn.

A typical Judahite accession formula (v. 1) and a devastating judgment notice (v. 2) lead into a lengthy oration concerning the numerous cultic sins of this monarch (vv. 3–9); then an anonymous prophetic indictment of his reign (vv. 10–15), again entirely negative; and finally a concluding note concerning Manasseh's shedding of much blood (v. 16; cf. 24:4); followed by the "further reference" notice (v. 17) and the burial formula (v. 18). (For references to prior discussions of these various formulas and notices, see the introduction to ch. 15.)

3626, 866	6449.111	255	4567	3547	8246.721	3937, 3725, 6893
prep, rel part	v Qal pf 3ms	pn	*n ms*	pn	cj, v Hithpael impf 3ms	prep, *adj*, *n ms*
כַּאֲשֶׁר	עָשָׂה	אַחְאָב	מֶלֶךְ	יִשְׂרָאֵל	וַיִּשְׁתַּחוּ	לְכָל־צְבָא
ka'ăsher	‘āsāh	'ach'āv	melekh	yisrā'ēl	wayyishtachû	lekhol-tsevā'
just as	he had made	Ahab	the king of	Israel	and he bowed down	to all the host of

8452	5856.121	881		1161.111	4326	904, 1041	3176
art, n md	cj, v Qal impf 3ms	do, ps 3mp	**4.**	cj, v Qal pf 3ms	n mp	prep, *n ms*	pn
הַשָּׁמַיִם	וַיַּעֲבֹד	אֹתָם		וּבָנָה	מִזְבְּחֹת	בְּבֵית	יְהוָה
hashshāmayim	wayya‘ăvōdh	'ōthām		ûvānāh	mizbechōth	bevêth	yehwāh
the heavens	and he served	them		and he built	altars	in the temple of	Yahweh

866	569.111	3176	904, 3503	7947.125	881, 8428		1161.121
rel part	v Qal pf 3ms	pn	prep, pn	v Qal impf 1cs	do, n ms, ps 1cs	**5.**	cj, v Qal impf 3ms
אֲשֶׁר	אָמַר	יְהוָה	בִּירוּשָׁלַםִ	אָשִׂים	אֶת־שְׁמִי		וַיִּבֶן
'ăsher	'āmar	yehwāh	bîrûshālam	'āsîm	'eth-shemî		wayyiven
which	He had said	Yahweh	in Jerusalem	I will put	my name		and he built

4326	3937, 3725, 6893	8452	904, 8692	2793	1041, 3176
n mp	prep, *adj*, *n ms*	art, n md	prep, num	*n fp*	*n ms*, pn
מִזְבְּחוֹת	לְכָל־צְבָא	הַשָּׁמָיִם	בִּשְׁתֵּי	חַצְרוֹת	בֵּית־יְהוָה
mizbechôth	lekhol-tsevā'	hashshāmāyim	bishtê	chatsrôth	bêth-yehwāh
altars	to all the host of	the heavens	in the two of	the courtyards of	the temple of Yahweh

	5882.511	881, 1158	904, 813	6280.311
6.	cj, v Hiphil pf 3ms	do, n ms, ps 3ms	prep, art, n fs	cj, v Poel pf 3ms
	וְהֶעֱבִיר	אֶת־בְּנוֹ	בָּאֵשׁ	וְעוֹנֵן
	wehe‘ĕvîr	'eth-benô	bā'ēsh	we‘ônēn
	and He caused to pass through	his son	in the fire	and he practiced soothsaying

5355.311	6449.111	177	3160	7528.511	3937, 6449.141
cj, v Piel pf 3ms	cj, v Qal pf 3ms	n ms	cj, n mp	v Hiphil pf 3ms	prep, v Qal inf con
וְנִחֵשׁ	וְעָשָׂה	אוֹב	וְיִדְּעֹנִים	הִרְבָּה	לַעֲשׂוֹת
wenichēsh	we‘āsāh	'ôv	weyidde‘ōnîm	hirbāh	la‘ăsôth
and he was a warlock	and he practiced	necromancy	and channelers	he multiplied	to do

7737	904, 6084	3176	3937, 3832.541		7947.121	881, 6705
art, adj	prep, *n fd*	pn	prep, v Hiphil inf con	**7.**	cj, v Qal impf 3ms	do, *n ms*
הָרַע	בְּעֵינֵי	יְהוָה	לְהַכְעִיס		וַיָּשֶׂם	אֶת־פֶּסֶל
hāra‘	be‘ênê	yehwāh	lehakh‘îs		wayyāsem	'eth-pesel
what is evil	in the eyes of	Yahweh	to provoke to anger		and he erected	the idol of

867	866	6449.111	904, 1041	866	569.111	3176	420, 1784
art, pn	rel part	v Qal pf 3ms	prep, art, n ms	rel part	v Qal pf 3ms	pn	prep, pn
הָאֲשֵׁרָה	אֲשֶׁר	עָשָׂה	בַּבַּיִת	אֲשֶׁר	אָמַר	יְהוָה	אֶל־דָּוִד
hā'ăshērāh	'ăsher	‘āsāh	babbayith	'ăsher	'āmar	yehwāh	'el-dāwidh
the Asherah	which	he made	in the Temple	which	He had said	Yahweh	to David

420, 8406	1158	904, 1041	2172	904, 3503	866	1013.115
cj, prep, pn	n ms, ps 3ms	prep, art, n ms	art, dem pron	cj, prep, pn	rel part	v Qal pf 1cs
וְאֶל־שְׁלֹמֹה	בְּנוֹ	בַּבַּיִת	הַזֶּה	וּבִירוּשָׁלַםִ	אֲשֶׁר	בָּחַרְתִּי
we'el-shelōmōh	venô	babbayith	hazzeh	ûvîrûshālam	'ăsher	bācharttî
and to Solomon	his son	in the Temple	the this	and in Jerusalem	which	I have chosen

4623, 3725	8101	3547	7947.125	881, 8428	3937, 5986		3940
prep, *n ms*	*n mp*	pn	v Qal impf 1cs	do, n ms, ps 1cs	prep, n ms	**8.**	cj, neg part
מִכֹּל	שִׁבְטֵי	יִשְׂרָאֵל	אָשִׂים	אֶת־שְׁמִי	לְעוֹלָם		וְלֹא
mikkōl	shivtê	yisrā'ēl	'āsîm	'eth-shemî	le‘ôlām		welō'
from all	the tribes of	Israel	I have put	my name	unto eternity		and not

pagan shrines, *NLT* ... He put up again the high places which had been pulled down by Hezekiah, *BB*.

and he reared up altars for Baal, and made a grove, as did Ahab king of Israel: ... he erected altars to the Baal and made a sacred pole as Ahab king of Israel had done, *NEB* ... raised up altars for Baal, and made a wooden image, *NKJV* ... constructed altars for Baal and set up an Asherah pole, *NLT* ... he built altars for Baal; he made a shame image, *Berkeley*.

and worshipped all the host of heaven, and served them: ... prostrated himself before all the host of heaven and worshipped them, *NEB* ... He bowed down to all the starry hosts and worshiped, *NIV* ... bowed before all the forces of heaven and worshiped, *NLT* ... he vowed himself unto all the host of heaven and served them, *Tyndale*.

4. And he built altars in the house of the LORD, of which the LORD said, In Jerusalem will I put my name: ... He built pagan altars in the Temple, the place that the LORD had said was where he should be worshiped, *Good News* ... though the Eternal had said, I will fix my Presence here for all time, in Jerusalem, *Moffatt* ... I will establish my name in Jerusalem, *NAB* ... Jerusalem shall receive my Name, *NEB*.

5. And he built altars for all the host of heaven in the two courts of the house of the LORD: ... in the two courtyards, *Anchor* ... put up altars for all the stars of heaven in the two outer squares of the house, *BB* ... built altars to all the Host of the Skies, *Fenton* ... built altars to the whole array of heaven, *JB* ... In both courts of the temple of the LORD, he built altars to all the starry hosts, *NIV*.

6. And he made his son pass through the fire, and observed times, and used enchantments, and dealt with familiar spirits and wizards: ... burned his son as an offering, *RSV* ... practiced soothsaying, used witchcraft, and consulted spiritists and mediums, *NKJV* ... used witchcraft and maintained workers with spirits, and tellers of fortunes, *Tyndale* ... practiced soothsaying and augury, *NRSV* ... practiced sorcery and divination, and he consulted with mediums and psychics, *NLT*.

he wrought much wickedness in the sight of the LORD, to provoke him to anger: ... did much evil in the sight of, *NKJV* ... did much wrong in the eyes of, *REB* ... greatly displeasing Yahweh to his anger, *Anchor* ... arousing his anger, *NLT*.

7. And he set a graven image of the grove that he had made in the house, of which the LORD said to David, and to Solomon his son, In this house, and in Jerusalem, which I have chosen out of all tribes of Israel, will I put my name for ever: ... the image of Asherah he made he set up in the temple, *Beck* ... He even fixed the Image of Fortune that he had made in the House, *Fenton* ... He put the graven image of the shame goddess he had made into the very house, *Berkeley* ... He placed the symbol of the goddess Asherah in the Temple, *Good News*.

8. Neither will I make the feet of Israel move any more out of the land which I gave their fathers: ... Nor shall I ever again set Israel's foot-

---

The name "Manasseh" (m^e^nashsheh, HED #4667) probably means "one who causes to forget [some misfortune]," or the like (cf. Gen. 41:51), and the name of the present Judahite king is attested in the Assyrian records of both Esarhaddon (681–669) and Ashurbanipal (669–627; cf. Cogan and Tadmor, AB, 265). The age at accession cited for King Manasseh is the young age of twelve (v. 1), giving rise to much speculation that (since it is highly unlikely that Manasseh was Hezekiah's firstborn—assuming the accuracy of all the relevant ages at accession, Hezekiah would have been forty-two when he brought forth Manasseh as coregent), perhaps all the previous heirs had already died, or else, they were passed over for reasons unknown (cf. Cogan and Tadmor, AB, 266). Some (e.g., Thiele) posit a ten-year co-regency for Manasseh and his father Hezekiah (perhaps in light of the latter's illness [cf. 20:1–11]). Albright, however, preferred emending Manasseh's regnal total from fifty-five down to forty-five years (both Thiele and Albright dated Hezekiah's accession to 715; hence, they had about ten "extra" years to work with). Cogan and Tadmor, on the other hand, with their earlier 727 date for Hezekiah's accession, have no trouble placing Manasseh on the throne in 698 (both Thiele and Albright preferred 686 or 687, respectively).

In any case, the beginning of the seventh century was a time of remarkable Assyrian strength (indeed, by 671 Esarhaddon had defeated the Egyptian Pharaoh Tirhakah in his homeland [concerning Tirhakah, cf., on 19:9–13], and even occupied briefly his capital Memphis); so perhaps it is not surprising that we read here virtually nothing about Manasseh's military adventures (since, presumably they were few and far between [but cf. 2 Chr. 33:11, 14]) or, for that matter, much else about his long and presumably prosperous reign. Rather, all that we encounter here in 2 Kings is a lengthy listing of his sins, mostly cultic but also social (v. 16). Hobbs (WBC, 303), who well characterizes

3362.525	3937, 5290.541	7559	3547	4623, 124	866
v Hiphil impf 1cs	prep, v Hiphil inf con	*n fs*	pn	prep, art, n fs	rel part
אוֹסִיף	לְהָנִיד	רֶגֶל	יִשְׂרָאֵל	מִן־הָאֲדָמָה	אֲשֶׁר
'ôsîph	lehānîdh	reghel	yisrā'ēl	min-hā'ădhāmāh	'ăsher
I will cause to continue	to shake	the foot of	Israel	from the land	which

5598.115	3937, 1	7828	524, 8490.126	3937, 6449.141	3626, 3725
v Qal pf 1cs	prep, n mp, ps 3mp	adv	cj, v Qal impf 3mp	prep, v Qal inf con	prep, n ms
נָתַתִּי	לַאֲבוֹתָם	רַק	אִם־יִשְׁמְרוּ	לַעֲשׂוֹת	כְּכֹל
nāthattî	la'ăvôthām	raq	'im-yishmerû	la'ăsôth	kekhōl
I have given	to their ancestors	only	if they are careful	to do	according to everything

866	6943.315	3937, 3725, 8784	866, 6943.311	881	5860
rel part	v Piel pf 1cs, ps 3mp	cj, prep, *adj*, art, n fs	rel part, v Piel pf 3ms	do, ps 3mp	n ms, ps 1cs
אֲשֶׁר	צִוִּיתִים	וּלְכָל־הַתּוֹרָה	אֲשֶׁר־צִוָּה	אֹתָם	עַבְדִּי
'ăsher	tsiwwîthîm	ûlăkhol-hattôrāh	'ăsher-tsiwwāh	'ōthām	'avdî
that	I have commanded them	and of all the Law	that he had commanded	them	my servant

5057		3940	8471.116	8912.521	4667	3937, 6449.141	881, 7737
pn	**9.**	cj, neg part	v Qal pf 3cp	cj, v Hiphil impf 3ms, ps 3mp	pn	prep, v Qal inf con	do, art, n ms
מֹשֶׁה		וְלֹא	שָׁמְעוּ	וַיַּתְעֵם	מְנַשֶּׁה	לַעֲשׂוֹת	אֶת־הָרָע
mōsheh		welō'	shāmē'û	wayyath'ēm	menashsheh	la'ăsôth	'eth-hārā'
Moses		but not	they listened	and he led them astray	Manasseh	to do	what is evil

4623, 1504	866	8436.511	3176	4623, 6686	1158	3547
prep, art, n mp	rel pron	v Hiphil pf 3ms	pn	prep, *n mp*	*n mp*	pn
מִן־הַגּוֹיִם	אֲשֶׁר	הִשְׁמִיד	יְהוָה	מִפְּנֵי	בְּנֵי	יִשְׂרָאֵל
min-haggôyim	'ăsher	hishmîdh	yehwāh	mippenê	benê	yisrā'ēl
from the nations	whom	He had destroyed	Yahweh	from before	the sons of	Israel

	1744.321	3176	904, 3135, 5860	5204	3937, 569.141
10.	cj, v Piel impf 3ms	pn	prep, *n fs*, n mp, ps 3ms	art, n mp	prep, v Qal inf con
	וַיְדַבֵּר	יְהוָה	בְּיַד־עֲבָדָיו	הַנְּבִיאִים	לֵאמֹר
	waydhabbēr	yehwāh	beyadh-'ăvādhâv	hannevî'îm	lē'mōr
	and He spoke	Yahweh	by the hand of his servants	the prophets	saying

	3391	866	6449.111	4667	4567, 3171	8774	431
11.	cj	rel part	v Qal pf 3ms	pn	*n ms*, pn	art, n fp	art, dem pron
	יַעַן	אֲשֶׁר	עָשָׂה	מְנַשֶּׁה	מֶלֶךְ־יְהוּדָה	הַתֹּעֵבוֹת	הָאֵלֶּה
	ya'an	'ăsher	'āsāh	menashsheh	melekh-yehûdhāh	hattō'ēvôth	hā'ēlleh
	because	that	he has done	Manasseh	the king of Judah	the detestable things	the these

7778.511	4623, 3725	866, 6449.116	578	866	3937, 6686
v Hiphil pf 3ms	prep, n ms	rel part, v Qal pf 3cp	art, pn	rel pron	prep, n mp, ps 3ms
הֵרַע	מִכֹּל	אֲשֶׁר־עָשׂוּ	הָאֱמֹרִי	אֲשֶׁר	לְפָנָיו
hēra'	mikkōl	'ăsher-'āsû	hā'ĕmōrî	'ăsher	lephānâv
he caused to be more evil	than everything	which they did	the Amorites	who	before him

2490.521	1612, 881, 3171	904, 1585		3937, 3772	3662, 569.111	3176
cj, v Hiphil impf 3ms	cj, do, pn	prep, n mp, ps 3ms	**12.**	prep, adv	adv, v Qal pf 3ms	pn
וַיַּחֲטִא	גַּם־אֶת־יְהוּדָה	בְּגִלּוּלָיו		לָכֵן	כֹּה־אָמַר	יְהוָה
wayyachti'	gham-'eth-yehûdhāh	beghillûlâv		lākhēn	kōh-'āmar	yehwāh
and he caused to sin	also Judah	with his idols		therefore	thus He said	Yahweh

435	3547	2079	971.551	7750	6142, 3503	3171	866
n mp	pn	intrj, ps 1cs	v Hiphil ptc ms	n fs	prep, pn	cj, pn	rel part
אֱלֹהֵי	יִשְׂרָאֵל	הִנְנִי	מֵבִיא	רָעָה	עַל־יְרוּשָׁלַםִ	וִיהוּדָה	אֲשֶׁר
'ĕlōhê	yisrā'ēl	hinenî	mēvî'	rā'āh	'al-yerûshālam	wîhûdhāh	'ăsher
the God of	Israel	behold I	bringing	a disaster	upon Jerusalem	and Judah	which

steps wandering outside the country which I gave to their ancestors, *JB* ... Nevermore will I let the sons of Israel be dislodged from the land I gave their fathers, *Knox* ... never will I send Israel wandering out of the land I have given to their fathers, *Moffatt* ... I will not again make Israel outcasts from the land which I gave to their forefathers, *NEB*.

only if they will observe to do according to all that I have commanded them, and according to all the law that my servant Moses commanded them: ... if only they will be careful to do just as I have commanded them, *Goodspeed* ... if only they will be true to all the observances I have enjoined, all the commands which my servant Moses taught them, *Knox* ... if only they will be mindful to obey exactly all my commands and all the laws laid down for them, *Moffatt* ... so that they will be diligent to do all I have commanded them, *Tyndale*.

9. But they hearkened not: ... they did not listen, *Anchor* ... did not give ear, *BB* ... did not obey the LORD, *Good News* ... That warning went unheeded, *Knox*.

and Manasseh seduced them to do more evil than did the nations whom the LORD destroyed before the children of Israel: ... Manasseh misled them to do evil, *Anchor* ... led them astray to do more evil, *Darby* ... Manasheh thus apostatized to practise sin with the heathen whom the EVER-LIVING swept from before the children of, *Fenton* ... led them to commit even greater sins than those committed by the nations whom the LORD had driven out of the land as his people advanced, *Good News*.

10. And the LORD spake by his servants the prophets, saying: ... declared by his servants, *Moffatt* ... spoke through his servants, *NAB* ... spoke in the hand of his servants, *Douay* ... said through his servants, *NIV*.

11. Because Manasseh king of Judah hath done these abominations, and hath done wickedly above all that the Amorites did, which were before him, and hath made Judah also to sin with his idols: ... King Manasseh of Judah has done many detestable things, *NLT* ... (he has acted more wickedly than all the Amorites who were before him, and has also made Judah sin with his idols), *NKJV* ... worse than anything the Amorites before him did, *Anchor* ... has led Judah into sin with his idols, *REB*.

12. Therefore thus saith the LORD God of Israel, Behold, I am bringing such evil upon Jerusalem and Judah, that whosoever heareth of it, both his ears shall tingle: ... I will send such evil on Jerusalem and Judah that the ears of all to whom the news comes will be burning, *BB* ... I'm going to bring such a disaster on Jerusalem and Judah that the ears of everyone who hears about it will ring, *Beck* ... everyone who hears

---

the present passage as "an overt theological interpretation of history," delineates it further as follows: (1) the sins of Manasseh are said to be worse than those even of the nations Yahweh had driven out before the Israelites (vv. 2, 9, 11; cf. the similar categorization of Ahaz in 16:3); (2) they were indeed as bad as the sins of Ahab (vv. 3, 13); (3) they thus provoked Yahweh to "anger" (vv. 6, 15); and, finally, (4) like Samaria, Jerusalem and its Temple would be destroyed (vv. 4, 7f, 13). Also, as Hobbs points out, the theme of "reversals" (concerning this characteristic activity of Yahweh, cf. on 3:13–19, above) well represents the present handling both of the traditional theme of Yahweh's settlement of Israel (vv. 7f, 14f), as well as the theme of Jerusalem/Zion bearing Yahweh's "name" (vv. 4, 7; the "name," or reputation of Yahweh, connected with the city of Jerusalem is one of the favorite themes; cf. Deut. 12:5, 11, 21; 14:23f; 16:2, 6, 11; etc.; 2 Sam. 7:13; 1 Ki. 3:2; 5:3, 5; 8:16–20; etc.; also 2 Ki. 23:27).

Nonetheless, despite these theological overtones, several specific sins of Manasseh stand out. First of all, the high places were rebuilt (v. 3). As we have already seen, this is a particularly heinous offense (cf. comments on 17:7–23). The familiar litany continues in v. 3—erecting altars to Baal, making an Asherah pole (cf., also, v. 7; and concerning this object, cf. comments on 17:7–23), and finally (cf., also v. 5), bowing down and worshiping all the "starry hosts" (just as the northern kingdom of Israel did, cf. 17:16). Cogan and Tadmor (AB, 266) would not see any particular Mesopotamian influence in these astral cults; rather, the typical reverence for the sun, moon and stars found in Syria-Palestine already in the second millennium B.C. (cf. Deut. 4:19; also note the antiquity of the Canaanite city of Jericho [8000 B.C., or earlier] and the fact that it was named in honor of the moon god). In short, the traditional scholarly suggestions that King Manasseh introduced these heterodox cults largely to please his Assyrian masters must now be firmly rejected. Assyrian cults are not mentioned in this passage.

Sadly, Manasseh also emulated Ahaz his grandfather in another area: he too "sacrificed his own son in the fire" (v. 6; cf. 16:3; the exact meaning of this phrase remains unclear). In light of this hideous reality, the words of the prophet Micah become particularly haunting: "Wherewith shall I

3725, 8471.152	7019.127	8692	238		5371.115
adj, v Qal act ptc mp, ps 3ms	v Qal impf 3fp	num	n fd, ps 3ms	**13.**	cj, v Qal pf 1cs
כָּל־שֹׁמְעָיו	תִּצַּלְנָה	שְׁתֵּי	אָזְנָיו		וְנָטִיתִי
kol-shōmᵉʻâv	titstsalnāh	shᵉttê	ʼāzᵉnâv		wᵉnāṭîthî
all those hearing about it	they will ring	the two of	their ears		and I will stretch out

6142, 3503	881	7241	8497	881, 5130	1041	255
prep, pn	do	*n ms*	pn	cj, do, *n fs*	*n ms*	pn
עַל־יְרוּשָׁלַם	אֵת	קָו	שֹׁמְרוֹן	וְאֶת־מִשְׁקֹלֶת	בֵּית	אַחְאָב
ʻal-yᵉrûshālam	ʼēth	qāw	shōmᵉrôn	wᵉʼeth-mishqōleth	bêth	ʼachʼāv
upon Jerusalem		the measuring line of	Samaria	and the level of	the household of	Ahab

4364.115	881, 3503	3626, 866, 4364.121	881, 7017	4364.111
cj, v Qal pf 1cs	do, pn	prep, rel part, v Qal impf 3ms	do, art, n fs	v Qal pf 3ms
וּמָחִיתִי	אֶת־יְרוּשָׁלַם	כַּאֲשֶׁר־יִמְחֶה	אֶת־הַצַּלַּחַת	מָחָה
ûmāchîthî	ʼeth-yᵉrûshālam	kaʼăsher-yimcheh	ʼeth-hatstsallachath	māchāh
and I will wipe	Jerusalem	just as someone wipes	the dish	he will wipe

2089.111	6142, 6686		5389.115	881	8086	5338
cj, v Qal pf 3ms	prep, n mp, ps 3fs	**14.**	cj, v Qal pf 1cs	do	*n fs*	n fs, ps 1cs
וְהָפַךְ	עַל־פָּנֶיהָ		וְנָטַשְׁתִּי	אֵת	שְׁאֵרִית	נַחֲלָתִי
wᵉhāphakh	ʻal-pānêāh		wᵉnāṭashtî	ʼēth	shᵉʼērîth	nachlāthî
and he will turn	on its face		and I will leave		the remainder of	my inheritance

5598.115	904, 3135	342.152	2030.116	3937, 993
cj, v Qal pf 1cs, ps 3mp	prep, *n fs*	v Qal act ptc mp, ps 3mp	cj, v Qal pf 3cp	prep, n ms
וּנְתַתִּים	בְּיַד	אֹיְבֵיהֶם	וְהָיוּ	לְבַז
ûnᵉthattîm	bᵉyadh	ʼōyᵉvêhem	wᵉhāyû	lᵉvaz
and I will give them	into the hand of	their enemies	and they will be	for plunder

3937, 5113	3937, 3725, 342.152		3391	866	6449.116	881, 7737
cj, prep, n fs	prep, *adj*, v Qal act ptc mp, ps 3mp	**15.**	cj	rel part	v Qal pf 3cp	do, art, n ms
וְלִמְשִׁסָּה	לְכָל־אֹיְבֵיהֶם		יַעַן	אֲשֶׁר	עָשׂוּ	אֶת־הָרַע
wᵉlimshissāh	lᵉkhol-ʼōyᵉvêhem		yaʻan	ʼăsher	ʻāsû	ʼeth-hāraʻ
and for booty	to all their enemies		because	which	they did	what is evil

904, 6084	2030.126	3832.552	881	4623, 3219	866
prep, n fd, ps 1cs	cj, v Qal impf 3mp	v Hiphil ptc mp	do, ps 1cs	prep, art, n ms	rel part
בְּעֵינַי	וַיִּהְיוּ	מַכְעִסִים	אֹתִי	מִן־הַיּוֹם	אֲשֶׁר
bᵉʻênay	wayyihyû	makhʻisîm	ʼōthî	min-hayyôm	ʼăsher
in my eyes	and they became	ones who provoke to anger	Me	since the day	which

3428.116	1	4623, 4875	5912	3219	2172		1612	1879
v Qal pf 3cp	n mp, ps 3mp	prep, pn	cj, adv	art, n ms	art, dem pron	**16.**	cj, cj	n ms
יָצְאוּ	אֲבוֹתָם	מִמִּצְרַיִם	וְעַד	הַיּוֹם	הַזֶּה		וְגַם	דָּם
yātsᵉʼû	ʼăvôthām	mimmitsrayim	wᵉʻadh	hayyôm	hazzeh		wᵉgham	dām
they went out	their ancestors	from Egypt	even until	the day	the this		and also	blood

5538	8581.111	4667	7528.542	4108	5912	866, 4527.311	881, 3503
adj	v Qal pf 3ms	pn	v Hiphil inf abs	adv	adv	rel part, v Piel pf 3ms	do, pn
נָקִי	שָׁפַךְ	מְנַשֶּׁה	הַרְבֵּה	מְאֹד	עַד	אֲשֶׁר־מִלֵּא	אֶת־יְרוּשָׁלַם
nāqî	shāphakh	mᵉnashsheh	harbēh	mᵉʼōdh	ʻadh	ʼăsher-millēʼ	ʼeth-yᵉrûshālam
innocent	he shed	Manasseh	making abundant	very	until	that he filled	Jerusalem

6552	3937, 6552	3937, 940	4623, 2496	866	2490.511	881, 3171
n ms	prep, art, n ms	prep, n ms	prep, n fs, ps 3ms	rel part	v Hiphil pf 3ms	do, pn
פֶּה	לָפֶה	לְבַד	מֵחַטָּאתוֹ	אֲשֶׁר	הֶחֱטִיא	אֶת־יְהוּדָה
peh	lāpheh	lᵉvadh	mēchattāʼthô	ʼăsher	hechĕṭîʼ	ʼeth-yᵉhûdhāh
a mouth	to the mouth	besides	of his sins	which	he caused to sin	Judah

about it will be stunned, *Good News* ... I mean to bring such calamity ... as shall ring in the ears of all who hear it, *Knox*.

13. And I will stretch over Jerusalem the line of Samaria, and the plummet of the house of Ahab: and I will wipe Jerusalem as a man wipeth a dish, wiping it, and turning it upside down: ... I will measure Jerusalem for destruction like Samaria, like the dynasty of Ahab, and I will wipe Jerusalem empty as a man wipes a dish, *Moffatt* ... I will wipe Jerusalem clean as one wipes a dish, wiping it inside and out, *NAB* ... I will mark down every stone of Jerusalem with the plumbline of Samaria and the plummet of the house of, *NEB* ... I will stretch over Jerusalem the squaring line of Samaria, *Tyndale*.

14. And I will forsake the remnant of mine inheritance, and deliver them into the hand of their enemies; and they shall become a prey and a spoil to all their enemies: ... will abandon the remnant, *Anchor* ... cast off the remnant, *ASV* ... handing them over to their enemies; they shall be plunder and prey for their enemies, *Berkeley* ... they shall become a contempt and scorn to all their enemies, *Fenton*.

15. Because they have done that which was evil in my sight, and have provoked me to anger, since the day their fathers came forth out of Egypt, even unto this day: ... they have done what is displeasing to me and have provoked my anger, *JB* ... have aroused me to anger, *Goodspeed* ... they have never ceased defying me and provoking my anger, *Knox* ... and have stirred up my anger from the time their ancestors came out of Egypt, *Good News*.

16. Moreover Manasseh shed innocent blood very much, till he had filled Jerusalem from one end to another: ... Manasseh also sacrificed many innocent people, till he filled Jerusalem with murders from end to end, *Moffatt* ... shedding so much innocent blood as to fill the length and breadth of Jerusalem, *NAB* ... shed innocent blood exceeding abundantly, insomuch that he replenished Jerusalem in all corners, *Tyndale* ... took the lives of upright men, till Jerusalem from one end to the other was full of blood, *BB* ... he filled Jerusalem full to the brim, *NEB*.

beside his sin wherewith he made Judah to sin, in doing that which was evil in the sight of the Lord: ... This was besides the sin he led Judah to do; he led Judah to do what the Lord said was wrong, *NCV* ... This was in addition to the sin that he caused the people of Judah to commit, leading them to do evil in the Lord's sight, *NLT* ... apart from causing Judah to sin by displeasing Yahweh, *Anchor* ... beside the sin he led Judah into by his own wrong doing before the LORD, *Beck*.

---

come before the Lord, and bow myself before the high God? ... shall I give my firstborn for my transgression, the fruit of my body for the sin of my soul? He hath shown thee, O man what is good; and what doth the Lord require of thee, but to do justly and to love mercy and to walk humbly with thy God?" (Mic. 6:6ff). Apparently, alas, child sacrifice was a harsh reality, not merely a rhetorical reference, both in Assyria, as well as in Syria-Palestine.

Mention has already been made to the anonymous prophetic pronouncement found in vv. 10–15. As many have pointed out, we lack any clear reference to known prophetic figures during Manasseh's reign. (Isaiah and Micah probably had ceased their public activities before the death of Hezekiah, and Jeremiah and Zephaniah would not begin theirs until the reign of Josiah.) Yet, as the later prophetic reference in Jer. 15:1–4 illustrates quite clearly, "what Manasseh did in Jerusalem" was well-remembered even in the later period. Thus, what the writer states here repeatedly in the present passage, as well as once again later on (24:3f), namely that Manasseh's sins were the major cause of the Judahite exile, he was surely not representing a minority, still less, an idiosyncratic opinion.

This brings up the relevant parallels in the chronicler's discussion on Manasseh. As already noted, in clear contrast to the material just reviewed, 2 Chr. 33:1–20 indicates that King Manasseh, though as wicked as ever, was brought by Yahweh to a time of deep and heartfelt repentance (vv.12f), as the result of being dragged off to Babylon by the king of Assyria (v. 11; for the essential historicity of this event, cf. Japhet, OTL, 1002ff). As the result of such repentance (cf. the reference in 2 Chr. 7:14, a major theme of the Books of Chronicles), Yahweh "listened to his plea" and "brought him back to Jerusalem and to his kingdom," and then "Manasseh knew that the Lord he was God" (33:13). Manasseh then removed all the pagan altars he had built on and around Jerusalem (vv. 15ff). A further favorable comment is given about his prayer. God's response is found in v. 19 (whence the apocryphal "Prayer of Manasseh," a moving entreaty) within the chronicler's summary of Manasseh's reign. Yet again, Manasseh's humbling of himself is mentioned once again in 2 Chr. 33:23, in the chronicler's discussion of his son Amon.

Finally, the sordid reference to Manasseh's social sins (he also "shed so much innocent blood that he

3937, 6449.141	7737	904, 6084	3176	17.	3615	1745
prep, v Qal inf con	art, adj	prep, *n fd*	pn		cj, *n ms*	*n mp*
לַעֲשׂוֹת	הָרַע	בְּעֵינֵי	יְהוָה		וְיֶתֶר	דִּבְרֵי
la'ăsôth	hāra'	be'ênê	yehwāh		weyether	divrê
to do	what is evil	in the eyes of	Yahweh		and the remainder of	the events of

4667	3725, 866	6449.111	2496	866	2490.111	1950B, 3940, 2062
pn	cj, *adj*, rel part	v Qal pf 3ms	cj, n fs, ps 3ms	rel part	v Qal pf 3ms	intrg part, neg part, pers pron
מְנַשֶּׁה	וְכָל־אֲשֶׁר	עָשָׂה	וְחַטָּאתוֹ	אֲשֶׁר	חָטָא	הֲלֹא־הֵם
menashsheh	wekhol-'ăsher	'āsāh	wechattā'thô	'ăsher	chātā'	hălō'-hēm
Manasseh	and all which	he did	and his sins	which	he sinned	are they not

3918.156	6142, 5809	1745	3219	3937, 4567	3171
v Qal pass ptc mp	prep, *n ms*	*n mp*	art, n mp	prep, *n mp*	pn
כְּתוּבִים	עַל־סֵפֶר	דִּבְרֵי	הַיָּמִים	לְמַלְכֵי	יְהוּדָה
kethûvîm	'al-sēpher	divrê	hayyāmîm	lemalkhê	yehûdhāh
things written	on the scroll of	the events of	the days	of the kings of	Judah

18.	8311.121	4667	6196, 1	7196.221	904, 1629, 1041
	cj, v Qal impf 3ms	pn	prep, n mp, ps 3ms	cj, v Niphil impf 3ms	prep, *n ms*, n ms, ps 3ms
	וַיִּשְׁכַּב	מְנַשֶּׁה	עִם־אֲבֹתָיו	וַיִּקָּבֵר	בְּגַן־בֵּיתוֹ
	wayyishkav	menashsheh	'im-'ăvōthâv	wayyiqqāvēr	beghan-bêthô
	and he lay	Manasseh	with his ancestors	and he was buried	in the garden of his house

904, 1629, 6011	4566.121	534	1158	8809	19.	1158, 6465
prep, *n ms*, pn	cj, v Qal impf 3ms	pn	n ms, ps 3ms	prep, ps 3ms		*n ms*, num
בְּגַן־עֻזָּא	וַיִּמְלֹךְ	אָמוֹן	בְּנוֹ	תַּחְתָּיו		בֶּן־עֶשְׂרִים
beghan-'uzzā'	wayyimlōkh	'āmôn	benô	tachtâv		ben-'esrîm
in the garden of Uzza	and he reigned	Amon	his son	instead of him		a son of twenty

8692	8523	534	904, 4566.141	8692	8523	4566.111	904, 3503
cj, num	n fs	pn	prep, v Qal inf con, ps 3ms	cj, num	n fp	v Qal pf 3ms	prep, pn
וּשְׁתַּיִם	שָׁנָה	אָמוֹן	בְּמָלְכוֹ	וּשְׁתַּיִם	שָׁנִים	מָלַךְ	בִּירוּשָׁלָם
ûshettayim	shānāh	'āmôn	bemālekhô	ûshettayim	shānîm	mālakh	bîrûshālām
and two	years	Amon	when his reigning	and two	years	he reigned	in Jerusalem

8428	525	5102	1351, 2846	4623, 3298
cj, *n ms*	n fs, ps 3ms	pn	*n fs*, pn	prep, pn
וְשֵׁם	אִמּוֹ	מְשֻׁלֶּמֶת	בַּת־חָרוּץ	מִן־יָטְבָה
weshēm	'immô	meshullemeth	bath-chārûts	min-yātevāh
and the name of	his mother	Meshullemeth	the daughter of Haruz	from Jotbah

20.	6449.121	7737	904, 6084	3176	3626, 866	6449.111	4667
	cj, v Qal impf 3ms	art, adj	prep, *n fd*	pn	prep, rel part	v Qal pf 3ms	pn
	וַיַּעַשׂ	הָרַע	בְּעֵינֵי	יְהוָה	כַּאֲשֶׁר	עָשָׂה	מְנַשֶּׁה
	wayya'as	hāra'	be'ênê	yehwāh	ka'ăsher	'āsāh	menashsheh
	and he did	what is evil	in the eyes of	Yahweh	just as	he did	Manasseh

1	21.	2050.121	904, 3725, 1932	866, 2050.111	1	5856.121
n ms, ps 3ms		cj, v Qal impf 3ms	prep, *adj*, art, n ms	rel part, v Qal pf 3ms	n ms, ps 3ms	cj, v Qal impf 3ms
אָבִיו		וַיֵּלֶךְ	בְּכָל־הַדֶּרֶךְ	אֲשֶׁר־הָלַךְ	אָבִיו	וַיַּעֲבֹד
'āvîw		wayyēlekh	bekhol-hadderekh	'ăsher-hālakh	'āvîw	wayya'ăvōdh
his father		and he walked	in all the ways	that he walked	his father	and he served

881, 1585	866	5856.111	1	8246.721	3937
do, art, n mp	rel part	v Qal pf 3ms	n ms, ps 3ms	cj, v Hithpael impf 3ms	prep, ps 3mp
אֶת־הַגִּלֻּלִים	אֲשֶׁר	עָבַד	אָבִיו	וַיִּשְׁתַּחוּ	לָהֶם
'eth-haggillulîm	'ăsher	'āvadh	'āvîw	wayyishtachû	lāhem
the idols	which	he served	his father	and he bowed down	to them

22.	6013.121 cj, v Qal impf 3ms וַיַּעֲזֹב wayya'ăzōv and he abandoned	881, 3176 do, pn אֶת־יְהוָה 'eth-yehwāh Yahweh	435 *n mp* אֱלֹהֵי 'ĕlōhê the God of	1 n mp, ps 3ms אֲבֹתָיו 'ăvōthâv his ancestors	3940 cj, neg part וְלֹא welō' and not	2050.111 v Qal pf 3ms הָלַךְ hālakh he walked	904, 1932 prep, *n ms* בְּדֶרֶךְ bedherekh in the way of

3176 pn יְהוָה yehwāh Yahweh	**23.**	7489.126 cj, v Qal impf 3mp וַיִּקְשְׁרוּ wayyiqōshrû and they conspired	5866, 534 *n mp*, pn עַבְדֵי־אָמוֹן 'avdhê-'āmôn the servants of Amon	6142 prep, ps 3ms עָלָיו 'ālâv against him	4322.526 cj, v Hiphil impf 3mp וַיָּמִיתוּ wayyāmîthû and they executed

17. Now the rest of the acts of Manasseh, and all that he did, and his sin that he sinned, are they not written in the book of the chronicles of the kings of Judah?: ... and the sin he committed, are they not told in the book of, *Berkeley* ... As to the other affairs of Manasheh, and all that he did and the sins that he sinned, they are related in the history of events during the period of the kings of Judah, *Fenton* ... The rest of the history of Manasseh, his entire career, the sins he committed, is this not recorded, *JB* ... What else Manasses did, his history, and the record of his crimes, is to be found in the Annals, *Knox*.

18. And Manasseh slept with his fathers, and was buried in the garden of his own house, in the garden of Uzza: and Amon his son reigned in his stead: ... Manasseh rested with his ancestors, *NAB* ... rested with his forefathers and was buried in the garden-tomb of his family, *NEB* ... Amon his son became king in his place, *NASB* ... succeeded him as king, *NIV*.

19. Amon was twenty and two years old when he began to reign, and he reigned two years in Jerusalem. And his mother's name was Meshullemeth, the daughter of Haruz of Jotbah: ... twenty-two years old when he became king, *NKJV* ... when he started to rule, *Beck* ... when he came to the throne, *REB* ... ruling in Jerusalem for two years, *BB*.

20. And he did that which was evil in the sight of the LORD, as his father Manasseh did: ... did wrong in the sight of the EVER-LIVING, *Fenton* ... He did what is displeasing to Yahweh, as Manasseh his father had done, *JB* ... He disobeyed the Lord's will, like his father, *Knox* ... Like his father Manasseh, he sinned against the LORD, *Good News*.

21. And he walked in all the way that his father walked in, and served the idols that his father served, and worshipped them: ... He followed exactly the path his father had trod, serving and worshiping the idols his father had served, *NAB* ... served the abominations, *Douay* ... Following in his father's footsteps he served the idols ... and prostrated himself before them, *REB* ... and bowed himself to them, *Tyndale*.

22. And he forsook the LORD God of his fathers, and walked not in the way of the LORD: ... He abandoned Yahweh, the God of his fathers, and did not follow Yahweh's way, *Anchor* ... Turning away from the Lord ... and not walking in his ways, *BB* ... and did not walk in the paths of the EVER-LIVING, *Fenton* ... He deserted the LORD, the God of his fathers, and did not live in the LORD's way, *Beck*.

23. And the servants of Amon conspired against him, and slew the king in his own house: ... At length the servants of Amon conspired, *Goodspeed* ... Amon's retinue plot-

filled Jerusalem from end to end" [v. 16; cf. 24:4]), must not be ignored. This brief note probably represents largely the oppression of the poor and the underprivileged (so Cogan and Tadmor, AB, 269; cf. Jer. 7:6; 22:3, 17; Ezek. 22:6ff, 25ff); Jewish tradition, however, has linked this statement with the "dramatic silence" of the prophets during the time of Manasseh, and, more specifically the death of the prophet Isaiah (cf. the references in Cogan and Tadmor; also Hobbs, WBC, 308f). In any case, the sinfulness of his reign seemingly knew no bounds. Even the "further reference" notice in v. 17 once again makes specific mention of "the sin he committed." What a dismal epitaph for such a long-lived king!

21:19–26. Amon King of Judah. Only the briefest of references are to be found to this son of Manasseh, for Amon walked in the wicked ways of his father seemingly without exception (except that the chronicler notably contrasts his lack of repentance with his father's eventual humbling of himself before Yahweh; cf. 2 Chr. 33:23). Even though his reign was for a total of only two years, his evident wickedness may have been sufficient to lead to his own assassination (v. 23 in the present passage), with the result that "the people of the land" placed his eight-year-old son Josiah on the throne in his place.

The standard Judahite accession formula (v. 19) leads to the judgment formula (v. 20), with

881, 4567	904, 1041		5409.521	6194, 800	881
do, art, n ms	prep, n ms, ps 3ms	24.	cj, v Hiphil impf 3ms	*n ms*, art, n fs	do
אֶת־הַמֶּ֫לֶךְ	בְּבֵיתוֹ		וַיַּךְ	עַם־הָאָרֶץ	אֵת
'eth-hammelekh	bevêthô		wayyakh	'am-hā'ārets	'ēth
the king	in his house		and they struck down	the people of the land	

3725, 7489.152	6142, 4567	534	4566.526	6194, 800
adj, art, v Qal act ptc mp	prep, art, n ms	pn	cj, v Hiphil impf 3mp	*n ms*, art, n fs
כָּל־הַקֹּשְׁרִים	עַל־הַמֶּלֶךְ	אָמוֹן	וַיַּמְלִיכוּ	עַם־הָאָרֶץ
kol-haqqōsherîm	'al-hammelekh	'āmôn	wayyamlîkhû	'am-hā'ārets
all those conspiring	against the king	Amon	and they caused to rule	the people of the land

881, 3086	1158	8809		3615	1745	534	866
do, pn	n ms, ps 3ms	prep, ps 3ms	25.	cj, *n ms*	*n mp*	pn	rel part
אֶת־יֹאשִׁיָּהוּ	בְּנוֹ	תַּחְתָּיו		וְיֶתֶר	דִּבְרֵי	אָמוֹן	אֲשֶׁר
'eth-yō'shîyāhû	venô	tachtâv		weyether	divrê	'āmôn	'ăsher
Josiah	his son	instead of him		and the remainder of	the events of	Amon	which

6449.111	1950B, 3940, 2062	3918.156	6142, 5809	1745	3219
v Qal pf 3ms	intrg part, neg part, pers pron	v Qal pass ptc mp	prep, *n ms*	*n mp*	art, n mp
עָשָׂה	הֲלֹא־הֵם	כְּתוּבִים	עַל־סֵפֶר	דִּבְרֵי	הַיָּמִים
'āsāh	hălō'-hēm	kethûvîm	'al-s̱ēpher	divrê	hayyāmîm
he did	are they not	things written	on the scroll of	the events of	the days

3937, 4567	3171		7196.121	881	904, 7197	904, 1629, 6011
prep, *n mp*	pn	26.	cj, v Qal impf 3ms	do, ps 3ms	prep, n fs, ps 3ms	prep, *n ms*, pn
לְמַלְכֵי	יְהוּדָה		וַיִּקְבֹּר	אֹתוֹ	בִּקְבֻרָתוֹ	בְּגַן־עֻזָּא
lemalkhê	yehûdhāh		wayyiqŏbber	'ōthô	biqŏvurāthô	beghan-'uzzā'
of the kings of	Judah		and someone buried	him	in his tomb	in the garden of Uzza

4566.121	3086	1158	8809		1158, 8470	8523	3086
cj, v Qal impf 3ms	pn	n ms, ps 3ms	prep, ps 3ms	22:1	*n ms*, num	n fs	pn
וַיִּמְלֹךְ	יֹאשִׁיָּהוּ	בְּנוֹ	תַּחְתָּיו		בֶּן־שְׁמֹנֶה	שָׁנָה	יֹאשִׁיָּהוּ
wayyimlōkh	yō'shîyāhû	venô	tachtâv		ben-shemōneh	shānāh	yō'shîyāhû
and he reigned	Josiah	his son	instead of him		a son of eight	years	Josiah

904, 4566.141	8421	259	8523	4566.111	904, 3503	8428
prep, v Qal inf con, ps 3ms	cj, num	cj, num	n fs	v Qal pf 3ms	prep, pn	cj, *n ms*
בְּמָלְכוֹ	וּשְׁלֹשִׁים	וְאַחַת	שָׁנָה	מָלַךְ	בִּירוּשָׁלִָם	וְשֵׁם
vemālekhô	ûshelōshîm	we'achath	shānāh	mālakh	bîrûshālām	weshēm
when his reigning	and thirty	and one	years	he reigned	in Jerusalem	and the name of

525	3149	1351, 5930	4623, 1244		6449.121	3596
n fs, ps 3ms	pn	*n fs*, pn	prep, pn	2.	cj, v Qal impf 3ms	art, adj
אִמּוֹ	יְדִידָה	בַּת־עֲדָיָה	מִבָּצְקַת		וַיַּעַשׂ	הַיָּשָׁר
'immô	yedhîdhāh	vath-'ădhāyāh	mibbotsqath		wayya'as	hayyāshār
his mother	Jedidah	the daughter of Adaiah	from Bozkath		and he did	what is right

904, 6084	3176	2050.121	904, 3725, 1932	1784	1
prep, *n fd*	pn	cj, v Qal impf 3ms	prep, *adj*, *n ms*	pn	n ms, ps 3ms
בְּעֵינֵי	יְהוָה	וַיֵּלֶךְ	בְּכָל־דֶּרֶךְ	דָּוִד	אָבִיו
be'ênê	yehwāh	wayyēlekh	bekhol-derekh	dāwidh	'āvîw
in the eyes of	Yahweh	and he walked	in all the ways of	David	his ancestor

3940, 5681.111	3332	7972		2030.121	904, 8470	6462	8523
cj, neg part, v Qal pf 3ms	n fs	cj, n fs	3.	cj, v Qal impf 3ms	prep, num	num	n fs
וְלֹא־סָר	יָמִין	וּשְׂמֹאול		וַיְהִי	בִּשְׁמֹנֶה	עֶשְׂרֵה	שָׁנָה
welō'-s̱ār	yāmîn	ûsemō'wl		wayhî	bishmōneh	'esrēh	shānāh
and he did not turn aside to	the right	nor the left		and it was	in eight	ten	years

ted against the king and killed him in his own palace, *JB* ... there was a conspiracy among the courtiers, and the king was slain in his own palace, *Knox* ... put the king to death in his own house, *MAST.*

24. And the people of the land slew all them that had conspired against king Amon; and the people of the land made Josiah his son king in his stead: ... the nation killed all the conspirators and elected Amon's son Josiah to reign instead of him, *Moffatt* ... the people of the land killed all who had plotted against King Amon, *NIV* ... executed all those who had conspired against King Amon, *NKJV* ... made Josiah his son king in his place, *NASB.*

25. Now the rest of the acts of Amon which he did, are they not written in the book of the chronicles of the kings of Judah?: ... The other events of Amon's reign are recorded in the annals of the kings, *REB* ... The rest of the history of Amon (and) what he did are indeed recorded, *Anchor* ... things that Amon did, aren't they recorded, *Beck* ... are they not told in the book of the chronicles of, *Berkeley.*

26. And he was buried in his sepulchre in the garden of Uzza: and Josiah his son reigned in his stead: ... they buried him in his own tomb in the Park of Aza, and his son Joshiah reigned after him, *Fenton* ... buried him in the grave of his father, *Goodspeed* ... in the tomb he had made for himself, *Knox* ... son Josiah reigned instead of him, *Moffatt* ... succeeded him as king, *Good News.*

22:1. Josiah was eight years old when he began to reign, and he reigned thirty and one years in Jerusalem. And his mother's name was Jedidah, the daughter of Adaiah of Boscath: ... when he became king, *Anchor* ... when he started to rule, *Beck* ... at his coronation, *Fenton* ... he was ruling in Jerusalem for thirty-one years, *BB.*

2. And he did that which was right in the sight of the LORD, and walked in all the way of David his father, and turned not aside to the right hand or to the left: ... He was obedient to the Lord's will, and fol-

---

generic corroborating statements concerning cultic sin (vv. 21f) akin to those found previously for Manasseh. Immediately after this, we read of his assassination (v. 23). Then the subsequent punishment of the perpetrators (who were said to be his own "officials" [v. 24]) by the "people of the land." Cogan and Tadmor AB, 276 suggest the possibility that his own brothers, who had been bypassed in the line of succession, may have given impetus for the assassination. The second occasion we read of this stabilizing element in Judahite society is in connection with dynastic succession; cf. 11:18ff. The present passage closes with the standard "further reference" notice (v. 25) and the Judahite burial notice (v. 26). Like his father two years previously, Amon was buried "in the Garden of Uzza" (possibly Uzziah). These are the only two kings whose burial sites were specified as being thus located.

Amon's name ('āmôn, HED #534) may reflect the common Hebrew root 'āman (HED #548) "to confirm," "to have confidence in," which, for example, underlies the familiar English word "amen." Alternatively, the name may be a reflection of the Egyptian god Amon, said to be the king of the Egyptian gods and usually coupled in this period with the sun god Re. The former option is the more likely, and this would then provide an ironic name ("faithful one") for this forgettable king.

22:1–23:30. *Josiah king of Judah: A righteous religious reformer who meets a tragic fate. In many respects, the Books of Kings have been leading up to this passage, for finally we have a king who recognizes the pressing need for religious reform in Judah and who moved vigorously to alleviate this need. Finally, we hear about the pagan cult objects and sanctuaries, as well as the so-called high places decisively, permanently destroyed. A number of archaeological discoveries seem to confirm most strikingly these radical reform measures of King Josiah. Yet, finally as well, as even Josiah succumbed to the allure of international prestige and power, we must mourn his untimely death "with all Judah and Jerusalem" (cf. 2 Chr. 35:24). It is to this memorable story of the king who was without peer in cult reform (concerning this "incomparability" of King Josiah, see below), the last, best hope of pre-exilic Judah, that we now turn.*

22:1–20. Discovery of the Book of the Law. The familiar Judahite accession formula in v. 1 is followed by the glowing judgment formula in v. 2: "He did that which was right ... and walked in all the way of David his father." These terms are reminiscent of King Hezekiah in 18:5. Both Hezekiah and Josiah are compared to King David, with Asa being the only other king out of a total of twenty Judahite monarchs to be so spoken of (cf. 1 Ki. 15:11; also cf. comments on 18:1–4). The "incomparability" of Hezekiah and Josiah (i.e., that each of them is described in such terms as there was "no one else like him" among all the kings of Judah, either before or after [cf. 18:5 for Hezekiah, and

3937, 4567	3086	8365.111	4567	881, 8597	1158, 706
prep, art, n ms	pn	v Qal pf 3ms	art, n ms	do, pn	*n ms*, pn
לַמֶּלֶךְ	יֹאשִׁיָּהוּ	שָׁלַח	הַמֶּלֶךְ	אֶת־שָׁפָן	בֶּן־אֲצַלְיָהוּ
lammelekh	yō'shîyāhû	shālach	hammelekh	'eth-shāphān	ben-'ătsalyāhû
to the king	Josiah	he sent out	the king	Shaphan	the son of Azaliah

1158, 5098	5810	1041	3176	3937, 569.141		6148.131
n ms, pn	art, n ms	*n ms*	pn	prep, v Qal inf con	**4.**	v Qal impv 2ms
בֶּן־מְשֻׁלָּם	הַסֹּפֵר	בֵּית	יְהוָה	לֵאמֹר		עֲלֵה
ven-meshullām	hassōphēr	bêth	yehwāh	lē'mōr		'ălēh
the son of Meshullam	the secretary	the temple of	Yahweh	saying		go up

420, 2619	3669	1448	8882.521	881, 3826B	971.655
prep, pn	art, n ms	art, adj	cj, v Hiphil juss 3ms	do, art, n ms	art, v Hophal ptc ms
אֶל־חִלְקִיָּהוּ	הַכֹּהֵן	הַגָּדוֹל	וְיַתֵּם	אֶת־הַכֶּסֶף	הַמּוּבָא
'iel-chilqîyāhû	hakkōhēn	haggādhôl	weyattēm	'eth-hakkeseph	hammûvā'
to Hilkiah	the priest	the great	that he may reckon	the silver	what was brought into

1041	3176	866	636.116	8490.152	5790	4623, 882	6194
n ms	pn	rel part	v Qal pf 3cp	*v Qal act ptc mp*	art, n ms	prep, prep	art, n ms
בֵּית	יְהוָה	אֲשֶׁר	אָסְפוּ	שֹׁמְרֵי	הַסַּף	מֵאֵת	הָעָם
bêth	yehwāh	'ăsher	'āsephû	shōmerê	hassaph	mē'ēth	hā'ām
the temple of	Yahweh	which	they gathered	the keepers of	the threshold	from with	the people

	5598.121	6142, 3135	6449.152	4536	6734.656
5.	cj, v Qal juss 3ms, ps 3ms	prep, *n fs*	*v Qal act ptc mp*	art, n fs	art, v Hophal ptc mp
	וְיִתְּנֹה	עַל־יַד	עֹשֵׂי	הַמְּלָאכָה	הַמֻּפְקָדִים
	weyittenōh	'al-yadh	'ōsê	hammelā'khāh	hammuphqādhîm
	and let him give it	onto the hand of	the ones doing	the duties	those appointed

904, 1041	3176	5598.126	881	3937, 6449.152	4536
prep, *n ms*	pn	cj, v Qal juss 3mp	do, ps 3ms	prep, *v Qal act ptc mp*	art, n fs
בְּבֵית	יְהוָה	וְיִתְּנוּ	אֹתוֹ	לְעֹשֵׂי	הַמְּלָאכָה
bevêth	yehwāh	weyittenû	'ōthô	le'ōsê	hammelā'khāh
over the temple of	Yahweh	and let them give	it	to the ones doing	the duties

866	904, 1041	3176	3937, 2480.341	955	1041		3937, 2900
rel pron	prep, *n ms*	pn	prep, v Piel inf con	*n ms*	art, n ms	**6.**	prep, art, n mp
אֲשֶׁר	בְּבֵית	יְהוָה	לְחַזֵּק	בֶּדֶק	הַבָּיִת		לֶחָרָשִׁים
'ăsher	bevêth	yehwāh	lechazzēq	bedheq	habbāyith		lechārāshîm
who	in the temple of	Yahweh	to make strong	the breaches of	the Temple		for the engravers

3937, 1161.152	3937, 1473.152	3937, 7353.141	6320	63
cj, prep, art, v Qal act ptc mp	cj, prep, art, v Qal act ptc mp	cj, prep, v Qal inf con	n mp	cj, *n fp*
וְלַבֹּנִים	וְלַגֹּדְרִים	וְלִקְנוֹת	עֵצִים	וְאַבְנֵי
welabbōnîm	welaggōdherîm	weliqnôth	'ētsîm	we'avnê
and for the builders	and for the masons	and to buy	wood	and stones of

4412	3937, 2480.341	881, 1041		395	3940, 2913.221	882	3826B
n ms	prep, v Piel inf con	do, art, n ms	**7.**	adv	neg part, v Niphal impf 3ms	prep, ps 3mp	art, n ms
מַחְצֵב	לְחַזֵּק	אֶת־הַבָּיִת		אַךְ	לֹא־יֵחָשֵׁב	אִתָּם	הַכֶּסֶף
machtsēv	lechazzēq	'eth-habbāyith		'akh	lō'-yēchāshēv	'ittām	hakkeseph
squared stone	to make strong	the temple		only	it was not reckoned	with them	the silver

5598.255	6142, 3135	3706	904, 536	2062	6449.152
art, v Niphal ptc ms	prep, n fs, ps 3mp	cj	prep, n fs	pers pron	v Qal act ptc mp
הַנִּתָּן	עַל־יָדָם	כִּי	בֶאֱמוּנָה	הֵם	עֹשִׂים
hanittān	'al-yādhām	kî	ve'ĕmûnāh	hēm	'ōsîm
what was given	onto their hand	because	with faithfulness	they	doing

lowed in all things the example of his ancestor, *Knox* ... he followed closely in the footsteps of his forefather David, *NEB* ... did what was pleasing to the LORD; he followed the example of his ancestor King David, *Good News* ... not deviating from it to right or left, *JB*.

3. And it came to pass in the eighteenth year of king Josiah, that the king sent Shaphan the son of Azaliah, the son of Meshullam, the scribe, to the house of the LORD, saying: ... sent the secretary, Shaphan, *NIV* ... court secretary, *NLT* ... Josias had an errand for the controller of the temple, Saphan, *Knox*.

4. Go up to Hilkiah the high priest, that he may sum the silver which is brought into the house of the LORD, which the keepers of the door have gathered of the people: ... to weigh out all the money brought into the temple, *Moffatt* ... which those on duty at the entrance have received from the people, *NEB* ... have him get ready the money that has been brought, *NIV* ... that he may count the money, *NKJV*.

5. And let them deliver it into the hand of the doers of the work, that have the oversight of the house of the LORD: ... deliver it to the workmen in charge, *Anchor* ... He is to hand it over to the masters of works attached to the Temple, *JB* ... have it handed over to the foremen in charge, *Moffatt* ... Have them entrust it to the men appointed to supervise the work, *NIV* ... They were to be consigned to the master workmen in the temple of the LORD, *NAB*.

and let them give it to the doers of the work which is in the house of the LORD, to repair the breaches of the house: ... and they will pay it to the workmen of the House of Yahweh, *Anchor* ... to repair the temple, *Beck* ... the damage of the house, *Berkeley* ... the breaks of, *KJVII* ... the decayed places, *Tyndale* ... the dilapidations, *Moffatt*.

6. Unto carpenters, and builders, and masons, and to buy timber and hewn stone to repair the house: ... that timber may be bought, and stones out of the quarries, to repair the temple, *Douay* ... purchase timber and dressed stone, *NIV* ... cut stone, *NLT* ... quarried stone, *NRSV*.

7. Howbeit there was no reckoning made with them of the money that was delivered into their hand, because they dealt faithfully: ... They are not to be asked to account for the money that has been given them; they are acting on trust, *REB* ... for they deal honestly, *RSV* ... the silver delivered to them is not to be audited, *Anchor* ... you can trust them in their work, *Beck*.

23:25 for Josiah]) is probably best understood as applying to the areas of prayer for Hezekiah and cult reform for Josiah.

But impetus for this radical "cult reform" for the present king came from a chance discovery in the Temple, it would seem, occurring as the result of routine temple repair in Josiah's eighteenth year (by this late period in Judahite history, virtually every chronographer dated Josiah's eighteenth year closely to the year 622, apparently precisely, or nearly precisely, a century after the fall of Samaria to the Assyrians). As the discovery of the "Book of the Law" (better translated as "the Scroll of the Torah," or "the Scroll of the Teachings," or the like, HED #5809, 8784), was made, entirely inadvertently as it would seem (v. 8), King Josiah was reminded, afresh and anew, of Yahweh's very present "anger" (cf. vv. 13, 17) against his people and against his land, largely due to their laxity and to their syncretistic religious tendencies. This was the reason for Josiah's thoroughgoing reforms, which were so intricately delineated in the next chapter. Just as Hezekiah was called upon to face unprecedented crisis after crisis in his reign, and thus developed a powerful prayer presence, so Josiah, as the result of seeming chance discovery was compelled to confront the cultic corruptions in the lives of his people, and in so many locations throughout his kingdom.

For centuries, it would seem, the kings of Judah were oblivious to the offense to Yahweh represented by the syncretistic worship at the "high places," against which the writer has railed, time and time again. Even the actions of the godly King Hezekiah to remove such worship (18:4), were apparently totally reversed by his son and successor, King Manasseh (21:3; in both cases the issue of the "high places" comes first in the discussion of these kings' reigns). Therefore, it is significant that, in 23:8, we are told that King Josiah's first action, apart from cult reform in Jerusalem itself (vv. 4–7), was to "desecrate" (ṯāmmē', HED #3041, "to defile, make unfit for use") the high places (cf. also v. 5, where "pagan" worship is mentioned), thus rendering them irreversibly unfit in the future for religious purposes (in addition, he removed their priests, who had mixed false relgions with the worship of Yahweh; cf. v. 9; from those locations, and resettled them in Jerusalem, at the "place where Yahweh would choose to put his name"). Finally, the worship of Yahweh was effectively concentrated in one basic location, as envisioned, for example, in ch. 12 of Deuteronomy, and it was effectually purified from its previously syncretistic tendencies. This, proba-

8. 569.121	2619	3669	1448	6142, 8597	5810	5809
cj, v Qal impf 3ms	pn	art, n ms	art, adj	prep, pn	art, n ms	*n ms*
וַיֹּאמֶר	חִלְקִיָּהוּ	הַכֹּהֵן	הַגָּדוֹל	עַל־שָׁפָן	הַסֹּפֵר	סֵפֶר
wayyō’mer	chilqîyāhû	hakkōhēn	haggādhôl	‘al-shāphān	hassōphēr	sēpher
and he said	Hilkiah	the priest	the great	upon Shaphan	the secretary	the scroll of

8784	4834.115	904, 1041	3176	5598.121	2619	881, 5809
art, n fs	v Qal pf 1cs	prep, *n ms*	pn	cj, v Qal impf 3ms	pn	do, art, n ms
הַתּוֹרָה	מָצָאתִי	בְּבֵית	יְהוָה	וַיִּתֵּן	חִלְקִיָּה	אֶת־הַסֵּפֶר
hattôrāh	mātsā’thî	bevêth	yehwāh	wayyittēn	chilqîyāh	’eth-hassēpher
the Law	I have found	in the temple of	Yahweh	and he gave	Hilkiah	the scroll

420, 8597	7410.121	**9.** 971.121	8597	5810	420, 4567
prep, pn	cj, v Qal impf 3ms, ps 3ms	cj, v Qal impf 3ms	pn	art, n ms	prep, art, n ms
אֶל־שָׁפָן	וַיִּקְרָאֵהוּ	וַיָּבֹא	שָׁפָן	הַסֹּפֵר	אֶל־הַמֶּלֶךְ
’el-shāphān	wayyiqōrā’ēhû	wayyāvō’	shāphān	hassōphēr	’el-hammelekh
to Shaphan	and he read it	and he came	Shaphan	the secretary	to the king

8178.521	881, 4567	1745	569.121	5597.516	5860
cj, v Hiphil impf 3ms	do, art, n ms	n ms	cj, v Qal impf 3ms	v Hiphil pf 3cp	n mp, ps 2ms
וַיָּשֶׁב	אֶת־הַמֶּלֶךְ	דָּבָר	וַיֹּאמֶר	הִתִּיכוּ	עֲבָדֶיךָ
wayyāshev	’eth-hammelekh	dāvār	wayyō’mer	hittîkhû	‘ăvādhêkhā
and he brought back to	the king	a word	and he said	they have poured out	your servants

881, 3826B	4838.255	904, 1041	5598.126	6142, 3135
do, art, n ms	art, v Niphal ptc ms	prep, art, n ms	cj, v Qal impf 3mp, ps 3ms	prep, *n fs*
אֶת־הַכֶּסֶף	הַנִּמְצָא	בַּבַּיִת	וַיִּתְּנֻהוּ	עַל־יַד
’eth-hakkeseph	hanimtsā’	vabbayith	wayyittenuhû	‘al-yadh
the silver	what was found	in the Temple	and they gave it	onto the hand of

6449.152	4536	6734.656	1041	3176	**10.** 5222.521
v Qal act ptc mp	art, n fs	art, v Hophal ptc mp	*n ms*	pn	cj, v Hiphil impf 3ms
עֹשֵׂי	הַמְּלָאכָה	הַמֻּפְקָדִים	בֵּית	יְהוָה	וַיַּגֵּד
‘ōsê	hammelā’khāh	hammuphqādhîm	bêth	yehwāh	wayyaggēdh
the ones doing	the duties	those appointed	the temple of	Yahweh	and he reported

8597	5810	3937, 4567	3937, 569.141	5809	5598.111	3937	2619
pn	art, n ms	prep, art, n ms	prep, v Qal inf con	n ms	v Qal pf 3ms	prep, ps 1cs	pn
שָׁפָן	הַסֹּפֵר	לַמֶּלֶךְ	לֵאמֹר	סֵפֶר	נָתַן	לִי	חִלְקִיָּה
shāphān	hassōphēr	lammelekh	lē’mōr	sēpher	nāthan	lî	chilqîyāh
Shaphan	the secretary	to the king	saying	a scroll	he has given	to me	Hilkiah

3669	7410.121	8597	3937, 6686	4567	**11.** 2030.121
art, n ms	cj, v Qal impf 3ms, ps 3ms	pn	prep, *n mp*	art, n ms	cj, v Qal impf 3ms
הַכֹּהֵן	וַיִּקְרָאֵהוּ	שָׁפָן	לִפְנֵי	הַמֶּלֶךְ	וַיְהִי
hakkōhēn	wayyiqōrā’ēhû	shāphān	liphnê	hammelekh	wayhî
the priest	and he read it	Shaphan	before	the king	and it was

3626, 8471.141	4567	881, 1745	5809	8784	7458	881, 933
prep, v Qal inf con	art, n ms	do, *n mp*	*n ms*	art, n fs	cj, v Qal impf 3ms	do, n mp, ps 3ms
כִּשְׁמֹעַ	הַמֶּלֶךְ	אֶת־דִּבְרֵי	סֵפֶר	הַתּוֹרָה	וַיִּקְרַע	אֶת־בְּגָדָיו
kishmōa‘	hammelekh	’eth-divrê	sēpher	hattôrāh	wayyiqōra‘	’eth-beghādhâv
when hearing	the king	the words of	the scroll of	the Law	then he tore	his clothes

12. 6943.321	4567	881, 2619	3669	881, 297	1158, 8597
cj, v Piel impf 3ms	art, n ms	do, pn	art, n ms	cj, do, pn	*n ms*, pn
וַיְצַו	הַמֶּלֶךְ	אֶת־חִלְקִיָּה	הַכֹּהֵן	וְאֶת־אֲחִיקָם	בֶּן־שָׁפָן
waytsaw	hammelekh	’eth-chilqîyāh	hakkōhēn	we’eth-’ăchîqām	ben-shāphān
and he commanded	the king	Hilkiah	the priest	and Ahikam	the son of Shaphan

8. And Hilkiah the high priest said unto Shaphan the scribe, I have found the book of the law in the house of the Lord. And Hilkiah gave the book to Shaphan, and he read it: ... Hilkiah said to Shaphan the secretary, *JB* ... a copy of the law, which he gave him to read, *Knox* ... I have found a law-book in the temple, *Moffatt* ... found the Book of the Teachings in the Temple, *NCV.*

9. And Shaphan the scribe came to the king, and brought the king word again: ... came to report to the king, *NEB* ... going back to the king with news of his errand, *Knox.*

and said, Thy servants have gathered the money that was found in the house: ... told him that his servants had melted down the silver in the house of the Lord, *NEB* ... Your officials have paid out the money that was in the temple, *NIV* ... to report that the temple offerings had been reckoned up, *Knox.*

and have delivered it into the hand of them that do the work, that have the oversight of the house of the Lord: ... and handed it over to the foremen there, *NEB* ... have entrusted it to the workers and supervisors at the temple, *NIV* ... paid over to the temple overseers, for distribution to the workmen, *Knox.*

10. And Shaphan the scribe showed the king, saying, Hilkiah the priest hath delivered me a book. And Shaphan read it before the king: ... has given me a book, *NIV* ... read out to the king, *Moffatt* ... read it aloud to, *NAB* ... read it in the presence of, *NASB.*

11. And it came to pass, when the king had heard the words of the book of the law, that he rent his clothes: ... tore his clothes, *NKJV* ... rent his garments, *Anchor* ... took his robe in his hands, violently parting it as a sign of his grief, *BB* ... tore his robes, *Fenton.*

12. And the king commanded Hilkiah the priest, and Ahikam the son of Shaphan, and Achbor the son of Michaiah, and Shaphan the scribe, and Asahiah a servant of the king's, saying: ... gave the following order to Hilkiah, *Good News* ... he gave his orders to Helcias, *Knox* ... ordered the priest Hilkiah, *NEB.*

---

bly above all else, was the major reform activity of King Josiah most lauded by the writer (besides the verses already cited, cf. 23:13, 15, 19f).

The name "Josiah" may mean "May Yahweh give" or the like, or else "May Yahweh bring forth" or even, "May Yahweh heal"; cf. *Anchor Bible Dictionary*, 3:1015. As already noted, by this time the Judahite kings may be closely dated; both Albright and Thiele dated Josiah's accession to the year 640 (actually 641/640 for Thiele; 639, is preferable for this important king).

Hobbs (WBC, 319) nicely delineates the present chapter as follows: introductory formulas (vv. 1f; cf. comments); narrative about the redistribution of the temple collection to facilitate temple repairs (vv. 3–7; cf. Joash's similar repairs in ch. 12, and especially the parallels between the supervisors who need no accounting of their expenses "because they are acting faithfully," both here in v. 7 and also in 12:15); and, finally, the king's energetic reaction to the finding of the Torah scroll (vv. 8–20; Hobbs also includes the covenant renewal ceremony in 23:1ff in this section as well). As Hobbs (WBC, 319–20) further notes, "in an extremely clever way the writer maintains an air of mystery about the contents of the [Torah] book until late in the story." The first mention of the Torah scroll is in v. 8, when Hilkiah the high priest gives it to Shaphan the secretary to read. In v. 10, Shaphan reads from it to the king—but still no contents of it are disclosed to us. In v. 11, the king's reaction, namely, tearing his robes, hints at the serious nature of the still undisclosed book; and in v. 13, the king's advice to seek out Huldah the prophetess, for "great is Yahweh's anger that burns against us because our fathers have not obeyed the words of this book" hints even more strongly that something very serious is about to be disclosed, but we do not hear about its contents or its implications until v. 16. There we read about the serious judgments impending against "this place and its people" in accordance with "everything written in the book the king of Judah has read." "Because they have forsaken me, and have burned incense unto other gods, that they might provoke me to anger with all the works of their hands" (v. 17). As Hobbs points out, this delay in disclosure is truly an insightful way to arrest and to keep the reader's close attention.

A further note on the king's command to seek out the prophet (in this case, the prophetess) is in order. The king must seek the oracle of Yahweh through the prophet. Josiah, therefore, not only did the right thing in seeking her out (indeed, he did the only thing he could do, in order to obtain a message from God). But not only is this to obtain God's message for the hour, for once again, the protagonist here refuses to accept the revealed word of destruction passively; rather he actively seeks to mollify Yahweh's righteous anger, if at all possible.

881, 6129	1158, 4460	881	8597	5810	881	6454
cj, do, pn	*n ms*, pn	cj, do	pn	art, n ms	cj, do	pn
וְאֶת־עַכְבּוֹר	בֶּן־מִיכָיָה	וְאֵת	שָׁפָן	הַסֹּפֵר	וְאֵת	עֲשָׂיָה
we’eth-‘akhbôr	ben-mîkhāyāh	we’ēth	shāphān	hassōphēr	we’ēth	‘ăsāyāh
and Achbor	the son of Micaiah	and	Shaphan	the secretary	and	Asaiah

5860, 4567	3937, 569.141	**13.** 2050.133	1938.133	881, 3176	1185
n ms, art, n ms	prep, v Qal inf con	v Qal impv 2mp	v Qal impv 2mp	do, pn	prep, ps 1cs
עֶבֶד־הַמֶּלֶךְ	לֵאמֹר	לְכוּ	דִרְשׁוּ	אֶת־יְהוָה	בַּעֲדִי
‘evedh-hammelekh	lē’mōr	lekhû	dhirshû	’eth-yehwāh	ba‘ădhî
the servant of the king	saying	go	seek	Yahweh	for me

1185, 6194	1185	3725, 3171	6142, 1745	5809	4838.255
cj, prep, art, n ms	cj, prep	*adj*, pn	prep, *n mp*	art, n ms	art, v Niphal ptc ms
וּבְעַד־הָעָם	וּבְעַד	כָּל־יְהוּדָה	עַל־דִּבְרֵי	הַסֵּפֶר	הַנִּמְצָא
ûve‘adh-hā‘ām	ûve‘adh	kol-yehûdhāh	‘al-divrê	hassēpher	hanimtsā’
and for the people	and for	all Judah	concerning the words of	the scroll	the found one

2172	3706, 1448	2635	3176	866, 2026	3448.212	904
art, dem pron	cj, adj	*n fs*	pn	rel part, pers pron	v Niphal pf 3fs	prep, ps 1cp
הַזֶּה	כִּי־גְדוֹלָה	חֲמַת	יְהוָה	אֲשֶׁר־הִיא	נִצְּתָה	בָּנוּ
hazzeh	kî-ghedhôlāh	chămath	yehwāh	’ăsher-hî’	nitstsethāh	vānû
the this	because great	the wrath of	Yahweh	which it	it has been kindled	against us

6142	866	3940, 8471.116	1	6142, 1745	5809
prep	cj	neg part, v Qal pf 3cp	n mp, ps 1cp	prep, *n mp*	art, n ms
עַל	אֲשֶׁר	לֹא־שָׁמְעוּ	אֲבֹתֵינוּ	עַל־דִּבְרֵי	הַסֵּפֶר
‘al	’ăsher	lō’-shāme‘û	’ăvōthênû	‘al-divrê	hassēpher
on account of	because	they did not listen	our ancestors	concerning the words of	the scroll

2172	3937, 6449.141	3626, 3725, 3918.155	6142	**14.** 2050.121
art, dem pron	prep, v Qal inf con	prep, *adj*, art, v Qal pass ptc ms	prep, ps 1cp	cj, v Qal impf 3ms
הַזֶּה	לַעֲשׂוֹת	כְּכָל־הַכָּתוּב	עָלֵינוּ	וַיֵּלֶךְ
hazzeh	la‘ăsôth	kekhol-hakkāthûv	‘ālênû	wayyēlekh
the this	to do	according to all which was written	concerning us	and he went

2619	3669	297	6129	8597	6454	420, 2569
pn	art, n ms	cj, pn	cj, pn	cj, pn	cj, pn	prep, pn
חִלְקִיָּהוּ	הַכֹּהֵן	וַאֲחִיקָם	וְעַכְבּוֹר	וְשָׁפָן	וַעֲשָׂיָה	אֶל־חֻלְדָּה
chilqîyāhû	hakkōhēn	wa’ăchîqām	we‘akhbôr	weshāphān	wa‘ăsāyāh	’el-chuldāh
Hilkiah	the priest	and Ahikam	and Achbor	and Shaphan	and Asaiah	to Huldah

5206	828	8362	1158, 8952	1158, 2848	8490.151
art, n fs	*n fs*	pn	*n ms*, pn	*n ms*, pn	*v Qal act ptc ms*
הַנְּבִיאָה	אֵשֶׁת	שַׁלֻּם	בֶּן־תִּקְוָה	בֶּן־חַרְחַס	שֹׁמֵר
hannevî’āh	’ēsheth	shallum	ben-tiqōwāh	ben-charchas	shōmēr
the prophetess	the wife of	Shallum	the son of Tikvah	the son of Harhas	the keeper of

933	2026	3553.153	904, 3503	904, 5112	1744.326	420
art, n mp	cj, pers pron	v Qal act ptc fs	prep, pn	prep, art, n ms	cj, v Piel impf 3mp	prep, ps 3fs
הַבְּגָדִים	וְהִיא	יֹשֶׁבֶת	בִּירוּשָׁלַם	בַּמִּשְׁנֶה	וַיְדַבְּרוּ	אֵלֶיהָ
habbeghādhîm	wehî’	yōsheveth	bîrûshālam	bammishneh	waydhabberû	’ēleāh
the garments	and she	dwelling	in Jerusalem	in the second part	and they spoke	to her

15. 569.122	420	3662, 569.111	3176	435	3547	569.133
cj, v Qal impf 3fs	prep, ps 3mp	adv, v Qal pf 3ms	pn	*n mp*	pn	v Qal impv 2mp
וַתֹּאמֶר	אֲלֵיהֶם	כֹּה־אָמַר	יְהוָה	אֱלֹהֵי	יִשְׂרָאֵל	אִמְרוּ
wattō’mer	’ălêhem	kōh-’āmar	yehwāh	’ĕlōhê	yisrā’ēl	’imrû
and she said	to them	thus He has said	Yahweh	the God of	Israel	say

13. Go ye, inquire of the LORD for me, and for the people, and for all Judah, concerning the words of this book that is found: ... Go, ask the LORD for me ... in regard to what this book that was found says, *Beck* ... consult the Lord, he told them, in my name, and in the name of this whole people of Juda, about this new-found copy of the law, *Knox* ... go and seek guidance of the LORD, *NEB* ... speak to the LORD for me, *NLT.*

for great is the wrath of the LORD that is kindled against us, because our fathers have not hearkened unto the words of this book: ... the wrath of the Lord which is burning against us ... have not given ear to, *BB* ... great is the LORD's indignation stirred up against us ... did not listen, *Berkeley* ... Fiercely the Lord's anger burns against us, that the words of this book should have fallen on deaf ears, *Knox* ... great is the wrath ... that is aroused against us, *NKJV* ... for a blaze of anger from the Eternal flames against us ... have not obeyed the words of this book, *Moffatt.*

to do according unto all that which is written concerning us: ... to do all that is prescribed for us, *Anchor* ... to conform to all that is written in it concerning us, *Goodspeed* ... to carry out all its injunctions, *Moffatt* ... they have not acted in accordance with all that is written there concerning us, *NIV.*

14. So Hilkiah the priest, and Ahikam, and Achbor, and Shaphan, and Asahiah, went unto Huldah the prophetess, the wife of Shallum the son of Tikvah, the son of Harhas, keeper of the wardrobe: ... keeper of the robes, *Tyndale* ... who was in charge of the wardrobe, *Beck* ... in charge of the Temple robes, *Good News* ... kept the royal wardrobe, *Knox.*

(now she dwelt in Jerusalem in the college;): ... she resided in Jerusalem in the Second Quarter, ... in the second part of the town, *BB* ... in the Second Rank of the Levites, *Fenton* ... a prophet who lived in the newer part of Jerusalem, *Good News.*

and they communed with her: ... consulted her, *NRSV* ... spoke with her, *Darby* ... conferred with her, *Berkeley* ... talked with her, *RSV.*

15. And she said unto them, Thus saith the LORD God of Israel, Tell the man that sent you to me: ... she gave them this message from the Eternal the God of Israel, *Moffatt* ... Say to the man that sent you, *NEB* ... This is what the LORD, the God of Israel, says, *NIV* ... The LORD, the God of Israel, has spoken!, *NLT.*

Once again, we are reminded that we are not to see ourselves as passive puppets in some divine drama—rather we are to approach our God boldly, and to seek his favor actively. We are to repent, if necessary—the mistake the audience makes in Jer. 18:1–12 (the so-called "potter's house sermon"; cf. comments on 20:1) is their very passivity—they will do nothing to alter their prophetically revealed faith ("There is no hope: but we will walk after our own devices, and we will every one do the imagination of his evil heart" [Jer. 18:12]). It is quite evident by now as we approach the end of 2 Kings: we are not to accept our fate passively. Rather we are to mourn and weep, if necessary; and of course, to repent of our sins. The sins of the parents are largely the reason for their present occasions of distress, but there still is hope. There nearly always is hope. Our God is a merciful God; He may still relent. This possibility Josiah seems to recognize instinctively. The king tore his robes in grief and despair, and he immediately sought out Yahweh's oracle from the prophetess. Not surprisingly, Yahweh was pleased by the king's response to the judgmental message of the newly-discovered "Scroll of the Torah," and so he responded to the king's evident distress by acknowledging it: "Because thine heart was tender, and thou hast humbled thyself before the LORD ... and hast rent thy clothes and wept before me; I also have heard thee" (v. 19). And to hear is often to relent: "Behold therefore, I will gather thee unto thy fathers, and thou shalt be gathered unto thy grave in peace; and thine eyes shall not see all the evil which I will bring upon this place" (v. 20; the comparison with Hezekiah's reprieve in 20:16–19 is uncanny; both Hezekiah, and now Josiah, were spared a first-hand experience of the seemingly unavoidable and eventual judgment of Yahweh upon the nation of Judah).

Two more brief notes, before looking at the "second movement" of the Josiah narrative. First of all, the immediate impetus for the temple refurbishing in vv. 3–7 was probably not that of the waning of Assyrian hegemony, as sometimes alleged, but rather that of the continuation of the policy for financing temple projects initiated by King Joash in 2 Ki. 12 (cf. Hobbs, WBC, 323f). Nonetheless, it is certainly the case that throughout this period of time Assyrian power continued to suffer irreversible decline, and by the time of the death of Ashurbanipal in 627, Assyria was only a shadow of her former self (cf. Cogan and Tadmor, AB, 291f). Indeed, by 626, Babylon had achieved final independence under Nabopolassar, a prince of Chaldean descent (his well-known son, Nebuchadnezzar, eventually besieged and destroyed the city of Jerusalem in 586); and, as Cogan and Tadmor (AB, 293) argue,

3937, 382	866, 8365.111	881	420		3662	569.111	3176	2079
prep, art, n ms	rel pron, v Qal pf 3ms	do, ps 2mp	prep, ps 1cs	**16.**	adv	v Qal pf 3ms	pn	intrj, ps 1cs
לָאִישׁ	אֲשֶׁר־שָׁלַח	אֶתְכֶם	אֵלָי		כֹּה	אָמַר	יְהוָה	הִנְנִי
lā'îsh	'ăsher-shālach	'ethkhem	'ēlāy		kōh	'āmar	yᵉhwāh	hinᵉnî
to the man	who he sent	you	to me		thus	He has said	Yahweh	behold I

971.551	7750	420, 4887	2172	6142, 3553.152	881
v Hiphil ptc ms	n fs	prep, art, n ms	art, dem pron	cj, prep, v Qal act ptc mp, ps 3ms	do
מֵבִיא	רָעָה	אֶל־הַמָּקוֹם	הַזֶּה	וְעַל־יֹשְׁבָיו	אֵת
mēvî'	rā'āh	'el-hammāqôm	hazzeh	wᵉ'al-yōshᵉvâv	'ēth
bringing	a disaster	to the place	the this	and on its dwellers	

3725, 1745	5809	866	7410.111	4567	3171		8809	866
adj, n mp	art, n ms	rel part	v Qal pf 3ms	*n ms*	pn	**17.**	cj	rel part
כָּל־דִּבְרֵי	הַסֵּפֶר	אֲשֶׁר	קָרָא	מֶלֶךְ	יְהוּדָה		תַּחַת	אֲשֶׁר
kol-divrê	hassēpher	'ăsher	qārā'	melekh	yᵉhûdhāh		tachath	'ăsher
all the words of	the scroll	which	he read	the king of	Judah		because	that

6013.116	7281.326	3937, 435	311	3937, 4775
v Qal pf 3cp, ps 1cs	cj, v Piel impf 3mp	prep, n mp	adj	prep, prep
עֲזָבוּנִי	וַיְקַטְּרוּ	לֵאלֹהִים	אֲחֵרִים	לְמַעַן
'ăzāvûnî	wayqattᵉrû	lē'lōhîm	'ăchērîm	lᵉma'an
they have abandoned Me	and they burned incense	to gods	others	so that

3832.541	904, 3725	4801	3135	3448.212	2635
v Hiphil inf con, ps 1cs	prep, *n ms*	*n ms*	n fd, ps 3mp	cj, v Niphal pf 3fs	n fs, ps 1cs
הַכְעִיסֵנִי	בְּכֹל	מַעֲשֵׂה	יְדֵיהֶם	וְנִצְּתָה	חֲמָתִי
hakh'îsēnî	bᵉkhōl	ma'ăsēh	yᵉdhêhem	wᵉnitstsᵉthāh	chămāthî
to provoke Me to anger	with the entirety of	the work of	their hands	it will be kindled	my wrath

904, 4887	2172	3940	3637.122		420, 4567	3171
prep, art, n ms	art, dem pron	cj, neg part	v Qal impf 3fs	**18.**	cj, prep, *n ms*	pn
בַּמָּקוֹם	הַזֶּה	וְלֹא	תִכְבֶּה		וְאֶל־מֶלֶךְ	יְהוּדָה
bammāqôm	hazzeh	wᵉlō'	thikhbeh		wᵉ'el-melekh	yᵉhûdhāh
in the place	the this	and not	it will be extinguished		and to the king of	Judah

8365.151	881	3937, 1938.141	881, 3176	3662	569.128	420
art, v Qal act ptc ms	do, ps 2mp	prep, v Qal inf con	do, pn	adv	v Qal impf 2mp	prep, ps 3ms
הַשֹּׁלֵחַ	אֶתְכֶם	לִדְרֹשׁ	אֶת־יְהוָה	כֹּה	תֹאמְרוּ	אֵלָיו
hashshōlēach	'ethkhem	lidhrōsh	'eth-yᵉhwāh	kōh	thō'mᵉrû	'ēlâv
the one sending	you	to inquire from	Yahweh	thus	you will say	to him

3662, 569.111	3176	435	3547	1745	866	8471.113		3391
adv, v Qal pf 3ms	pn	*n mp*	pn	art, n mp	rel part	v Qal pf 2ms	**19.**	cj
כֹּה־אָמַר	יְהוָה	אֱלֹהֵי	יִשְׂרָאֵל	הַדְּבָרִים	אֲשֶׁר	שָׁמָעְתָּ		יַעַן
kōh-'āmar	yᵉhwāh	'ĕlōhê	yisrā'ēl	haddᵉvārîm	'ăsher	shāmā'ăttā		ya'an
thus He has said	Yahweh	the God of	Israel	the things	which	you have heard		because

7690.111, 3949	3789.223	4623, 6686	3176	904, 8471.141
v Qal pf 3ms, n ms, ps 2ms	cj, v Niphal impf 2ms	prep, *n mp*	pn	prep, v Qal inf con, ps 2ms
רַךְ־לְבָבְךָ	וַתִּכָּנַע	מִפְּנֵי	יְהוָה	בְּשָׁמְעֲךָ
rakh-lᵉvāvᵉkhā	wattikkāna'	mippᵉnê	yᵉhwāh	bᵉshāmᵉ'ăkhā
your heart was tender	and you humbled yourself	from before	Yahweh	when your hearing

866	1744.315	6142, 4887	2172	6142, 3553.152	3937, 2030.141
rel part	v Piel pf 1cs	prep, art, n ms	art, dem pron	cj, prep, v Qal act ptc mp, ps 3ms	prep, v Qal inf con
אֲשֶׁר	דִּבַּרְתִּי	עַל־הַמָּקוֹם	הַזֶּה	וְעַל־יֹשְׁבָיו	לִהְיוֹת
'ăsher	dibbartî	'al-hammāqôm	hazzeh	wᵉ'al-yōshᵉvâv	lihyôth
what	I spoke	against the place	the this	and against its dwellers	to be

3937, 8439	3937, 7329	7458.123	881, 933	1098.123	3937, 6686
prep, n fs	cj, prep, n fs	cj, v Qal impf 2ms	do, n mp, ps 2ms	cj, v Qal impf 2ms	prep, n mp, ps 1cs
לְשַׁמָּה	וְלִקְלָלָה	וַתִּקְרַע	אֶת־בְּגָדֶיךָ	וַתִּבְכֶּה	לְפָנָי
leshammāh	weliqǒlālāh	wattiqǒra‘	'eth-beghādhêkhā	wattivkeh	lephānāy
unto destruction	and unto a curse	and you tore	your clothes	and you wept	before Me

1612	609	8471.115	5177, 3176		3937, 3772	2079
cj, cj	pers pron	v Qal pf 1cs	*n ms*, pn	20.	prep, adv	intrj, ps 1cs
וְגַם	אָנֹכִי	שָׁמַעְתִּי	נְאֻם־יְהוָה		לָכֵן	הִנְנִי
wegham	'ānōkhî	shāma‘ättî	ne'um-yehwāh		lākhēn	hinenî
and also	I	I have heard	the declaration of Yahweh		therefore	behold I

16. Thus saith the Lord, Behold, I will bring evil upon this place, and upon the inhabitants thereof, even all the words of the book which the king of Judah hath read: ... I am about to bring disaster on this place, *Anchor* ... and the people living here and everything threatened in the book, *Beck* ... I will bring misery upon this place, *Fenton* ... For this city and its citizens I have punishments in store, *Knox*.

17. Because they have forsaken me, and have burned incense unto other gods: ... the people have abandoned me, *Moffatt* ... given me up, *BB* ... deserted Me, *Berkeley* ... have sacrificed to strange gods, *Douay* ... have made offerings to other gods, *NRSV*.

that they might provoke me to anger with all the works of their hands: ... to vex me with all their evil practices, *Moffatt* ... They have made me angry by all that they have done, *NCV* ... provoking my anger with all the idols they have made with their own hands, *NEB* ... to insult Me by all their practices, *Fenton*.

therefore my wrath shall be kindled against this place, and shall not be quenched: ... wrath shall blaze, *Moffatt* ... shall be aroused against this place, *NKJV* ... My fury will blaze against this place never to be put out, *Beck* ... and it cannot be extinguished, *NAB*.

18. But to the king of Judah which sent you to inquire of the Lord, thus shall ye say to him, Thus saith the Lord God of Israel, As touching the words which thou hast heard: ... As for the king of Judah who sent you to consult Yahweh, *JB* ... who sent you to seek guidance of the Lord, *NEB* ... Regarding the words which you have heard, *Goodspeed* ... As for the threats, *NAB*.

19. Because thine heart was tender, and thou hast humbled thyself before the Lord, when thou heardest what I spake against this place, and against the inhabitants thereof: ... your heart was responsive, *NIV* ... was penitent, *NRSV* ... shown a willing heart and humbled yourself, *REB* ... was soft, and you made yourself low before me, *BB*.

that they should become a desolation and a curse, and hast rent thy clothes, and wept before me; I also have heard thee, saith the Lord: ... shall become desolate, and despised, *Fenton* ... will become an object of horror and cursing, *JB* ... would become accursed and laid waist, and because you tore your robes and wept in my presence, *NIV* ... you gave signs of grief, weeping before me: truly, I have given ear to you, *BB*.

20. Behold therefore, I will gather thee unto thy fathers, and thou shalt be gathered into thy grave in peace: ... gather you to your ancestors, *NAB* ... forefathers, *NEB* ...

"Viewed on the political level, Judah's resurgence under Josiah, including his activity in Samaria (cf. 23:15–18), must have coincided with and resulted from the retreat of Assyria from Judah's borders and the termination of the former's century-long sovereignty over that region." Therefore, there was general political and religious independence from Assyria during this period of Josiah's reign. But there was probably not specific impetus for the refurbishing of the Jerusalem temple.

Second, the novelty of Huldah as the only woman prophet acknowledged by name during the period of the Israelite monarchy deserves further discussion. Perhaps the distraught Josiah consulted a woman prophet, as the later rabbis have suggested, since women tend to be more merciful than men, and Huldah would have been expected to have delivered a more lenient oracle (cf. the rabbinic sources cited by Cogan and Tadmor); or else, as R. R. Wilson has suggested, Huldah represented the north Israelite/Ephraimite priestly circles who were instrumental in fostering Josiah's reforms in the first place (again, cf. Cogan and Tadmor). In any case, Huldah was undoubtedly the "court prophet on duty," so to speak, during this time, thus the one who would have been most naturally consulted by the king. Once again, even the Davidic king of Judah, himself, was compelled to repair to the prophet of Yahweh to receive the authentic word of the Lord.

636.151	6142, 1	636.213	420, 7197	904, 8361
v Qal act ptc ms, ps 2ms	prep, n mp, ps 2ms	cj, v Niphal pf 2ms	prep, n mp, ps 2ms	prep, n ms
אֹסִפְךָ	עַל־אֲבֹתֶיךָ	וְנֶאֱסַפְתָּ	אֶל־קִבְרֹתֶיךָ	בְּשָׁלוֹם
'ōsiphkhā	'al-'ăvōthêkhā	wene'ĕsaphtā	'el-qivrōthêkhā	beshālôm
One Who gathers you	beside your ancestors	and you will be gathered	to your tomb	in peace

3940, 7495.127	6084	904, 3725	7750	866, 603	971.551
cj, neg part, v Qal impf 3fp	n fd, ps 2ms	prep, *n ms*	art, n fs	rel part, pers pron	v Hiphil ptc ms
וְלֹא־תִרְאֶינָה	עֵינֶיךָ	בְּכֹל	הָרָעָה	אֲשֶׁר־אֲנִי	מֵבִיא
welō'-thir'ênāh	'ênêkhā	bekhōl	hārā'āh	'ăsher-'ănî	mēvî'
and they will not look	your eyes	on the entirety of	the disaster	which I	bringing

6142, 4887	2172	8178.526	881, 4567	1745	**23:1** 8365.121
prep, art, n ms	art, dem pron	cj, v Hiphil impf 3mp	do, art, n ms	n ms	cj, v Qal impf 3ms
עַל־הַמָּקוֹם	הַזֶּה	וַיָּשִׁבוּ	אֶת־הַמֶּלֶךְ	דָּבָר	וַיִּשְׁלַח
'al-hammāqôm	hazzeh	wayyāshivû	'eth-hammelekh	dāvār	wayyishlach
on the place	the this	and they brought back to	the king	a word	and he sent out

4567	636.126	420	3725, 2292	3171	3503
art, n ms	cj, v Qal impf 3mp	prep, ps 3ms	*adj, n mp*	pn	cj, pn
הַמֶּלֶךְ	וַיַּאַסְפוּ	אֵלָיו	כָּל־זִקְנֵי	יְהוּדָה	וִירוּשָׁלָם
hammelekh	wayya'asphû	'ēlâv	kol-ziqnê	yehûdhāh	wîrûshālām
the king	and they were gathered	to him	all the elders of	Judah	and Jerusalem

2. 6148.121	4567	1041, 3176	3725, 382	3171
cj, v Qal impf 3ms	art, n ms	*n ms*, pn	cj, *adj, n ms*	pn
וַיַּעַל	הַמֶּלֶךְ	בֵּית־יְהוָה	וְכָל־אִישׁ	יְהוּדָה
wayya'al	hammelekh	bêth-yehwāh	wekhol-'îsh	yehûdhāh
and he went up	the king	the temple of Yahweh	and all the men of	Judah

3725, 3553.152	3503	882	3669	5204	3725, 6194
cj, *adj, v Qal act ptc mp*	pn	prep, ps 3ms	cj, art, n mp	cj, art, n mp	cj, *adj*, art, n ms
וְכָל־יֹשְׁבֵי	יְרוּשָׁלַם	אִתּוֹ	וְהַכֹּהֲנִים	וְהַנְּבִיאִים	וְכָל־הָעָם
wekhol-yōshevê	yerûshālam	'ittô	wehakkōhenîm	wehannevî'îm	wekhol-hā'ām
and all the dwellers of	Jerusalem	with him	and the priests	and the prophets	and all the people

3937, 4623, 7275	5912, 1448	7410.121	904, 238	881, 3725, 1745	5809
prep, prep, adj	cj, prep, adj	cj, v Qal impf 3ms	prep, n fd, ps 3mp	do, *adj, n mp*	*n ms*
לְמִקָּטֹן	וְעַד־גָּדוֹל	וַיִּקְרָא	בְאָזְנֵיהֶם	אֶת־כָּל־דִּבְרֵי	סֵפֶר
lemiqqātōn	we'adh-gādhôl	wayyiqrā'	ve'āzenêhem	'eth-kol-divrê	sēpher
from insignificant	even unto great	and he called	in their ears	all the words of	the scroll of

1311	4838.255	904, 1041	3176	**3.** 6198.121	4567
art, n fs	art, v Niphal ptc ms	prep, *n ms*	pn	cj, v Qal impf 3ms	art, n ms
הַבְּרִית	הַנִּמְצָא	בְּבֵית	יְהוָה	וַיַּעֲמֹד	הַמֶּלֶךְ
habberîth	hanimtsā'	bevêth	yehwāh	wayya'ămōdh	hammelekh
the Covenant	what was found	in the temple of	Yahweh	and he stood	the king

6142, 6204	3901.121	881, 1311	3937, 6686	3176	3937, 2050.141	313
prep, art, n ms	cj, v Qal impf 3ms	do, art, n fs	prep, *n mp*	pn	prep, v Qal inf con	prep
עַל־הָעַמּוּד	וַיִּכְרֹת	אֶת־הַבְּרִית	לִפְנֵי	יְהוָה	לָלֶכֶת	אַחַר
'al-hā'ammûdh	wayyikhrōth	'eth-habberîth	liphnê	yehwāh	lālekheth	'achar
beside the pillar	and he cut	the covenant	before	Yahweh	to walk	after

3176	3937, 8490.141	4851	881, 5925	881, 2807
pn	cj, prep, v Qal inf con	n fp, ps 3ms	cj, do, n fp, ps 3ms	cj, do, n fp, ps 3ms
יְהוָה	וְלִשְׁמֹר	מִצְוֹתָיו	וְאֶת־עֵדְוֹתָיו	וְאֶת־חֻקֹּתָיו
yehwāh	welishmōr	mitswōthâv	we'eth-'ēdhewōthâv	we'eth-chuqqōthâv
Yahweh	and to observe	his commandments	and his testimonies	and his statutes

will be buried in peace, *NIV* ... shalt be gathered to thy sepulchre in peace, *Douay*.

and thine eyes shall not see all the evil which I will bring upon this place. And they brought the king word again: ... your eyes shall not see all the disaster I am bringing, *Moffatt* ... your eyes shall not see all the calamity which I will bring, *NKJV* ... You will not behold all the disasters which I am bringing, *Anchor* ... they took her answer back to the king, *NIV*.

23:1. And the king sent, and they gathered unto him all the elders of Judah and of Jerusalem: ... king called for all the elders, *Beck* ... called together all the elders, *NIV* ... summoned for himself, *Berkeley* ... the responsible men of Judah, *BB*.

2. And the king went up into the house of the LORD, and all the men of Judah and all the inhabitants of Jerusalem with him, and the priests, and the prophets, and all the people, both small and great: ... all the people, young and old, *Moffatt* ... the entire population, high and low, *REB* ... from the lowest to the highest, *Fenton* ... all the people from the least to the greatest, *NLT*.

and he read in their ears all the words of the book of the covenant which was found in the house of the LORD: ... he read out to them the whole scroll of the covenant which had been discovered in the house, *REB* ... Before them all the king read aloud the whole book, *Good News* ... he read out the terms of the law from the book they had found, *Knox* ... read in their hearing all the contents of the Book of Laws, *Fenton*.

3. And the king stood by a pillar: ... stood upon the step, *Douay* ... standing on the dais, *JB* ... standing on the platform, *Moffatt* ... Standing by the column, *NAB*.

and made a covenant before the LORD, to walk after the LORD, and to keep his commandments and his testimonies and his statutes with all their heart and all their soul: ... made an agreement before the Lord, *BB* ... bound himself by the covenant, *JB* ... made a promise, there in the Lord's presence, *Knox* ... renewed the covenant in the presence of, *NIV*.

to perform the words of this covenant that were written in this book: ... to uphold the terms of this covenant, *Anchor* ... to keep the words of the agreement recorded in the book, *BB* ... carry out the words, *NASB* ... thus reviving the terms of the covenant, *NAB*.

And all the people stood to the covenant: ... people committed themselves to the covenant, *Anchor* ... gave their word to keep the agreement, *BB* ... confirmed the covenant, *Goodspeed* ... pledged their allegiance, *JB*.

23:1–25. Religious reform and celebration. The present section represents, as it were, "the second movement" in the Josiah story. And what a movement it was, verse after verse detailing vigorous religious reform, whether in the capital city of Jerusalem, or in the Judahite countryside, or even in the northern territories of what used to be Samaria (vv. 15–20). Finally, we hear about the fulfillment of the stirring prophecy given in 1 Ki. 13:1ff by an unnamed Judahite prophet at the Bethel altar in the hearing of Jeroboam I, the first king of the newly-separated northern nation of Israel, as well as the greatest Passover celebration since the days of the judges. Indeed, King Josiah truly is to be reckoned as absolutely "incomparable" in the area of religious reform (v. 25; cf. comments at the beginning of 22:1–20).

The present passage starts off with covenant renewal (vv. 1ff), once again alluding to the newly-discovered "Scroll of the Torah" (cf. 22:8), but this time called "the Scroll of the Covenant" (v. 2). As Hobbs (WBC, 332) notes, the king now takes "center stage" in the narrative, with the ever widening circle of participants now including "all the people from the least to the greatest." Yet another comparison with King Joash of old is to be found in the present passage—namely the reference in v. 3 to the king standing "by the pillar" (cf. above, on 11:13–16). Once again, some sort of column, podium or platform was probably in view (Wiseman [TOTC, 299–300] suggests "a standing place"; cf. the parallel in 2 Chr. 34:31). But what really should be emphasized in these verses—indeed, what may well be one of the most important topics in OT theology—is the renewal of the Covenant. For it is the Covenant (b^e^rîth, HED #1311) which is at the heart of the present passage, not to mention much of the rest of the OT. To simplify greatly a complex and crucial topic, the "Covenant" in Israelite thought represented a legally binding agreement between Yahweh and his people Israel—with obligatory stipulations (i.e., rules and regulations) for both parties. Not to keep the Covenant faithfully would lead to the most terrible of consequences (cf. the covenant curses of Deut. 28; also Jer. 34:18ff; etc.). It should be noted, even in passing, that the great OT theologian Walther Eichrodt made the concept of covenant the crucial center of his influential two-volume *Theology of the Old Testament* (OTL, 1961, 1967). Few since have followed him completely in this area (most would see the issue of the "center" of OT

904, 3725, 3949	904, 3725, 5497	3937, 7251.541	881, 1745	1311	2148
prep, *adj*, n ms	cj, prep, *adj*, n fs	prep, v Hiphil inf con	do, *n mp*	art, n fs	art, dem pron
בְּכָל־לֵב	וּבְכָל־נֶפֶשׁ	לְהָקִים	אֶת־דִּבְרֵי	הַבְּרִית	הַזֹּאת
bekhol-lēv	ûvekhol-nephesh	lehāqîm	'eth-divrê	habberîth	hazzō'th
with all the heart	and with all the soul	to establish	the words of	the Covenant	the this

3918.156	6142, 5809	2172	6198.121	3725, 6194	904, 1311
art, v Qal pass ptc mp	prep, art, n ms	art, dem pron	cj, v Qal impf 3ms	*adj*, art, n ms	prep, art, n fs
הַכְּתֻבִים	עַל־הַסֵּפֶר	הַזֶּה	וַיַּעֲמֹד	כָּל־הָעָם	בַּבְּרִית
hakkethuvîm	'al-hassēpher	hazzeh	wayya'ămōdh	kol-hā'ām	babberîth
the things written	on the scroll	the this	and they stood	all the people	with the Covenant

4.	6943.321	4567	881, 2619	3669	1448	881, 3669
	cj, v Piel impf 3ms	art, n ms	do, pn	art, n ms	art, adj	cj, do, *n mp*
	וַיְצַו	הַמֶּלֶךְ	אֶת־חִלְקִיָּהוּ	הַכֹּהֵן	הַגָּדוֹל	וְאֶת־כֹּהֲנֵי
	waytsaw	hammelekh	'eth-chilqîyāhû	hakkōhēn	haggādhôl	we'eth-kōhenê
	and he commanded	the king	Hilkiah	the priest	the great	and the priests of

5112	881, 8490.152	5790	3937, 3428.541	4623, 2033
art, n ms	cj, do, *v Qal act ptc mp*	art, n ms	prep, v Hiphil inf con	prep, *n ms*
הַמִּשְׁנֶה	וְאֶת־שֹׁמְרֵי	הַסַּף	לְהוֹצִיא	מֵהֵיכַל
hammishneh	we'eth-shōmerê	hassaph	lehôtsî'	mēhêkhal
the second part	and the keepers of	the threshold	to bring out	from the temple of

3176	881	3725, 3747	6449.156	3937, 1197	3937, 867
pn	do	*adj*, art, n mp	art, v Qal pass ptc mp	prep, art, n ms	cj, prep, n fs
יְהוָה	אֵת	כָּל־הַכֵּלִים	הָעֲשׂוּיִם	לַבַּעַל	וְלָאֲשֵׁרָה
yehwāh	'ēth	kol-hakkēlîm	hā'ăsûyim	labba'al	welā'ăshērāh
Yahweh		all the vessels	those made	for the Baal	and for Asherah

3937, 3725	6893	8452	8041.121	4623, 2445	3937, 3503
cj, prep, *n ms*	*n ms*	art, n md	cj, v Qal impf 3ms, ps 3mp	prep, n ms	prep, pn
וּלְכֹל	צְבָא	הַשָּׁמָיִם	וַיִּשְׂרְפֵם	מִחוּץ	לִירוּשָׁלַם
ûlăkhōl	tsevā'	hashshāmāyim	wayyisrephēm	michûts	lîrûshālam
and for the entirety of	the host of	the heavens	and he burned them	from outside	to Jerusalem

904, 8166	7224	5558.111	881, 6312	1044	5.	8139.511
prep, *n fp*	pn	cj, v Qal pf 3ms	do, n ms, ps 3mp	pn		cj, v Hiphil pf 3ms
בְּשַׁדְמוֹת	קִדְרוֹן	וְנָשָׂא	אֶת־עֲפָרָם	בֵּית־אֵל		וְהִשְׁבִּית
beshadhmôth	qidhrôn	wenāsā'	'eth-'ăphārām	bêth-'ēl		wehishbîth
in the fields of	Kidron	and he carried	their ashes	Bethel		and he brought to a stop

881, 3771	866	5598.116	4567	3171	7281.321
do, art, n mp	rel pron	v Qal pf 3cp	*n mp*	pn	cj, v Piel impf 3ms
אֶת־הַכְּמָרִים	אֲשֶׁר	נָתְנוּ	מַלְכֵי	יְהוּדָה	וַיְקַטֵּר
'eth-hakkemārîm	'ăsher	nāthenû	malkhê	yehûdhāh	wayqattēr
the cultic priests	whom	they had put	the kings of	Judah	and they burned incense

904, 1154	904, 6111	3171	4673	3503
prep, art, n fp	prep, *n fp*	pn	cj, *n mp*	pn
בַּבָּמוֹת	בְּעָרֵי	יְהוּדָה	וּמְסִבֵּי	יְרוּשָׁלָם
babbāmôth	be'ārê	yehûdhāh	ûmesibbê	yerûshālām
on the high places	in the cities of	Judah	and the surrounding areas of	Jerusalem

881, 7281.356	3937, 1197	3937, 8507	3937, 3507	3937, 4342
cj, do, art, v Piel ptc mp	prep, art, n ms	prep, art, n fs	cj, prep, art, n ms	cj, prep, art, n fp
וְאֶת־הַמְקַטְּרִים	לַבַּעַל	לַשֶּׁמֶשׁ	וְלַיָּרֵחַ	וְלַמַּזָּלוֹת
we'eth-hamqatterîm	labba'al	lashshemesh	welayyārēach	welammazzālôth
and those burning incense	to the Baal	to the sun	and to the moon	and to the constellations

4. And the king commanded Hilkiah the high priest, and the priests of the second order: ... his vicar, *NAB* ... the priests under him, *Beck* ... priests of the second rank, *Berkeley* ... priests of lesser rank, *Knox*.

and the keepers of the door: ... doorkeepers, *Beck* ... keepers of the threshold, *Goodspeed* ... gatekeepers, *NCV* ... guardians of the threshold, *JB*.

to bring forth out of the temple of the Lord all the vessels that were made for Baal, and for the grove, and for all the host of heaven: ... all the utensils made for Baal and Asherah, and for all the army of heaven, *Beck* ... containers made for Baal, for the shame images, and for all the host, *Berkeley* ... Host of the Skies, *Fenton* ... remove all the cult objects which had been made for Baal, Asherah and the whole array of heaven, *JB*.

and he burned them without Jerusalem in the fields of Kidron, and carried the ashes of them unto Beth-el: ... burned them outside Jerusalem, *Beck* ... in the limekilns by the Kidron, *Goodspeed* ... valley of Cedron, *Knox* ... slopes of Kidron, *NAB*.

5. And he put down the idolatrous priests: ... suppressed the heathen priests, *NEB* ... did away with the pagan priests, *NIV* ... put an end to, *Anchor* ... false priests, *BB* ... idol-worshiping priests, *KJVII*.

whom the kings of Judah had ordained to burn incense in the high places in the cities of Judah: ... kings of Judah had appointed to burn sacrifices at the hill-shrines, *NEB* ... who had been installed ... to offer sacrifices, *Anchor* ... who had been put in their positions by the kings of Judah to see to the burning of offerings, *BB* ... townships of Judah, *Moffatt*.

and in the places round about Jerusalem: ... neighbourhood of Jerusalem, *JB* ... environs of, *Anchor* ... outskirts of, *BB* ... in the sanctuaries around, *Goodspeed*.

them also that burned incense unto Baal, to the sun, and to the moon, and to the planets, and to all the hosts of heaven: ... burnt sacrifices to Baal, *NEB* ... made offerings to Baal, *BB* ... sun, the moon, and the constellations, and all the host of, *Goodspeed* ... whole array of heaven, *JB*.

6. And he brought out the grove from the house of the Lord: ... removed the sacred pole, *NAB* ...

---

theology as more complicated than any one topic), but most still would concede that the idea of covenant is clearly one of the most crucial concepts in the entire Bible.

After the present occasion of covenant renewal (vv. 1ff), reform began in earnest (vv. 4–20). Once again, the reform measures were thorough and far-reaching. In the very Temple of Yahweh in Jerusalem, the high priest Hilkiah was to remove trappings of Baal worship, as well as that of Asherah and of all the "starry hosts" (v. 4; concerning the god Baal [Hadad], see above, on 1:2; on the worship of the goddess Asherah, cf. comments on 17:7–23; and concerning the "starry host," cf. above, on 21:1–18). In all three cases Canaanite, not Assyrian deities seem to be in view. The "pagan priests" of v. 5 seem to be largely Canaanite as well; the Hebrew term kemarîm (only used here in 2 Kings) is probably to be linked with the Aramaic *kumra'*, the common term for priest (Cogan and Tadmor [AB, 285]; they specifically reject once again any reference here to indigenous Assyrian religion, but rather to the "religious amalgam" of the western Assyrian empire of that time). All these pagan shrines and cult objects were systematically destroyed—"burned" (vv. 4, 6); "ground to powder" (v. 6); "torn down" (v. 7); "defiled" (v. 8); "broken down" (v. 8); "removed" (v. 11); "pulled down" (v. 12); etc. Some less familiar pagan practices are mentioned here as well. The "male shrine prostitutes" of v. 7, NIV (cf. 1 Ki. 14:24), are believed by some to be shrine prostitutes of both genders (cf. NLT), inasmuch as fertility worship (i.e., heterosexual, not homosexual activity) is most likely in view (cf. Simon J. De Vries, *1 Kings*, WBC, 185; also Jones, NCBC, 277, 619). Whatever the case, the imagery here shows how debased and perverse worship even in and near the Temple of Yahweh had become. (Concerning the reference to the "high places" in v. 8, also to the resettling of the Yahwistic priests mentioned in that verse, cf. comments on 22:1–20.)

Another unfamiliar reference in the present passage is to the "Topheth" in the Ben Hinnom Valley (v. 10) where worship of the god Molech took place. This valley, south and southwest of the City of David (the southern part of Jerusalem), is also mentioned repeatedly by the prophet Jeremiah (cf. Jer. 7:31f; 19:2, 6; 32:35); it also underlies the repeated NT references (e.g., Matt. 5:22, 29f; 18:9; 23:33; Mark 9:45, 47; etc.) to "Gehenna" or "hell" ("Gehenna" is derived from the Hebrew word for "valley of," gê, HED #1547, plus the name "Hinnom"). The "Tophet" was the cultic institution where children were sacrificed to Molech (Cogan and Tadmor, AB, 287f; the term itself probably

3937, 3725	6893	8452		3428.521	881, 867
cj, prep, *n ms*	*n ms*	art, n md	**6.**	cj, v Hiphil impf 3ms	do, art, pn
וּלְכֹל	צְבָא	הַשָּׁמָיִם		וַיֹּצֵא	אֶת־הָאֲשֵׁרָה
ûlăkhōl	tsevā'	hashshāmāyim		wayyōtsē'	'eth-hā'ăshērāh
and to the entirety of	the host of	the heavens		and he caused to go out	the Asherah

4623, 1041	3176	4623, 2445	3937, 3503	420, 5337	7224	8041.121
prep, *n ms*	pn	prep, n ms	prep, pn	prep, n ms	pn	cj, v Qal impf 3ms
מִבֵּית	יְהוָה	מִחוּץ	לִירוּשָׁלַם	אֶל־נַחַל	קִדְרוֹן	וַיִּשְׂרֹף
mibbêth	yehwāh	michûts	lîrûshālam	'el-nachal	qidhrôn	wayyisrōph
from the temple of	Yahweh	from outside	to Jerusalem	to Wadi	Kidron	and he burned

881	904, 5336	7224	1914.521	3937, 6312	8390.521	881, 6312
do, ps 3fs	prep, *n ms*	pn	cj, v Hiphil impf 3ms	prep, n ms	cj, v Hiphil impf 3ms	do, n ms, ps 3fs
אֹתָהּ	בְּנַחַל	קִדְרוֹן	וַיָּדֶק	לְעָפָר	וַיַּשְׁלֵךְ	אֶת־עֲפָרָהּ
'ōthāhh	benachal	qidhrôn	wayyādheq	le'āphār	wayyashlēkh	'eth-'ăphārāhh
it	by the Wadi	Kidron	and he pulverized	into dust	and he threw	its dust

6142, 7197	1158	6194		5606.121	881, 1041	7228
prep, *n ms*	*n mp*	art, n ms	**7.**	cj, v Qal impf 3ms	do, *n mp*	art, n mp
עַל־קֶבֶר	בְּנֵי	הָעָם		וַיִּתֹּץ	אֶת־בָּתֵּי	הַקְּדֵשִׁים
'al-qever	benê	hā'ām		wayyittōts	'eth-bāttê	haqqedhēshîm
on the tombs of	the children of	the people		and he razed	the temples of	the male cult prostitutes

866	904, 1041	3176	866	5571	730.154	8427	1041	3937, 867
rel pron	prep, *n ms*	pn	rel part	art, n fp	v Qal act ptc fp	adv	n mp	prep, art, pn
אֲשֶׁר	בְּבֵית	יְהוָה	אֲשֶׁר	הַנָּשִׁים	אֹרְגוֹת	שָׁם	בָּתִּים	לָאֲשֵׁרָה
'ăsher	bevêth	yehwāh	'ăsher	hannāshîm	'ōreghôth	shām	bāttîm	lā'ăshērāh
who	in the Temple of	Yahweh	where	the women	weaving	there	temples	for the Asherah

	971.521	881, 3725, 3669	4623, 6111	3171	3041.321	881, 1154
8.	cj, Hiphil impf 3ms	do, *adj*, art, n mp	prep, *n fp*	pn	cj, v Piel impf 3ms	do, art, n fp
	וַיָּבֵא	אֶת־כָּל־הַכֹּהֲנִים	מֵעָרֵי	יְהוּדָה	וַיְטַמֵּא	אֶת־הַבָּמוֹת
	wayyāvē'	'eth-kol-hakkōhenîm	mē'ārê	yehûdhāh	waytammē'	'eth-habbāmôth
	and he brought	all the priests	from the cities of	Judah	and he defiled	the high places

866	7281.316, 8427	3669	4623, 1419	5912, 916	916	5606.111
rel part	v Piel pf 3cp, adv	art, n mp	prep, pn	prep, pn	pn	cj, v Qal pf 3ms
אֲשֶׁר	קִטְּרוּ־שָׁמָּה	הַכֹּהֲנִים	מִגֶּבַע	עַד־בְּאֵר	שָׁבַע	וְנָתַץ
'ăsher	qitterû-shāmmāh	hakkōhenîm	miggeva'	'adh-be'ēr	shāva'	wenāthats
which	they had burned incense there	the priests	from Geba	unto Beer	Sheba	and he razed

881, 1154	8554	866, 6860	8554	3193	8015, 6111
do, *n fp*	art, n mp	rel part, *n ms*	*n ms*	pn	*n ms*, art, n fs
אֶת־בָּמוֹת	הַשְּׁעָרִים	אֲשֶׁר־פֶּתַח	שַׁעַר	יְהוֹשֻׁעַ	שַׂר־הָעִיר
'eth-bāmôth	hashshe'ārîm	'ăsher-pethach	sha'ar	yehôshua'	sar-hā'îr
the high places of	the gates	which the entrance of	the gate of	Joshua	the official of the city

866, 6142, 7972	382	904, 8554	6111		395	3940	6148.126	3669
rel part, prep, *n ms*	n ms	prep, *n ms*	art, n fs	**9.**	adv	neg part	v Qal impf 3mp	*n mp*
אֲשֶׁר־עַל־שְׂמֹאול	אִישׁ	בְּשַׁעַר	הָעִיר		אַךְ	לֹא	יַעֲלוּ	כֹּהֲנֵי
'ăsher-'al-semō'wl	'îsh	besha'ar	hā'îr		'akh	lō'	ya'ălû	kōhenê
which on the left of	a man	in the gate of	the city		only	not	they went up	the priests of

1154	420, 4326	3176	904, 3503	3706	524, 404.116	4843
art, n fp	prep, *n ms*	pn	prep, pn	cj	cj, v Qal pf 3cp	n fp
הַבָּמוֹת	אֶל־מִזְבַּח	יְהוָה	בִּירוּשָׁלָם	כִּי	אִם־אָכְלוּ	מַצּוֹת
habbāmôth	'el-mizbach	yehwāh	bîrûshālām	kî	'im-'ākhelû	matstsôth
the high places	to the altar of	Yahweh	in Jerusalem	but	rather they ate	unleavened bread

took the symbol of Asherah, *NEB* ... brought out the wooden image, *NKJV* ... removed the shame image, *Berkeley*.

without Jerusalem, unto the brook Kidron, and burned it at the brook Kidron: ... outside Jerusalem, *NAB* ... to the valley of the Kidron, *Berkeley* ... away from Jerusalem, *Knox*.

and stamped it small to powder: ... had it ... beaten to dust, *NAB* ... ground it to powder, *NIV* ... ground it to ashes, *NKJV* ... reduced it to dust, *Douay* ... pounded it to dust, *NEB*.

and cast the powder thereof upon the graves of the children of the people: ... scattered over the common graveyard, *NAB* ... scattered over the common burial-ground, *NEB* ... threw its ashes on the graves of the common people, *NKJV* ... threw the dust in the public cemetery, *NLT*.

7. And he brake down the houses of the sodomites, that were by the house of the LORD, where the women wove hangings for the grove: ... tore down the houses of the sacred males, *Anchor* ... tore down the huts of the male prostitutes, *Beck* ... where women were making robes for the Asherah, *BB* ... women wove tunics for the Asherah, *Goodspeed*.

8. And he brought all the priests out of the cities of Judah, and defiled the high places where the priests had burned incense, from Geba to Beer-sheba: ... rendered unsanctified the high places, *JB* ... desecrated the hill-shrines, *NEB* ... where the priests had made offerings, *NRSV* ... burnt sacrifices, *REB*.

and brake down the high places of the gates that were in the entering in of the gate of Joshua the governor of the city, which were on a man's left hand at the gate of the city: ... pulled down the High Place of the Gates, which stood at the gate of Joshua, *JB* ... pulled down, too, the wayside altars at the approach to the gate of Josue, *Knox* ... to the left as one enters the city gate, *NAB* ... which were to the left of the city gate, *NKJV*.

9. Nevertheless the priests of the high places came not up to the altar of the LORD in Jerusalem, but they did eat of the unleavened bread among their brethren: ... sweet bread, *Tyndale* ... bread without yeast among their people, *Beck* ... biscuits, *Fenton* ... unleavened cakes, *Goodspeed*.

---

referred either to the stand over the fire upon which the child was placed, or to the hearth as a whole). This abhorrent rite is mentioned also in Jer. 32:35, where the god "Molech" is also to be found; another reference to "Molech" may be found in 1 Ki. 11:7 (but some commentators prefer reading "Milcom" there, instead of "Molech"; cf. 1 Ki. 11:5; 23; also v. 13 of the present chapter). However vocalized, the term "Molech/Milcom" clearly is related to the familiar Semitic root mālakh, meaning "king" or "royalty." Thus, some have likened this most grisly offering to a "royal" sacrifice or the like—King Mesha's sacrifice of his eldest son in 3:27 (cf. comments on 3:26f, above) immediately comes to mind (although it should be noted that no actual term from the root mālakh is to be found there; HED #4566).

The final obscure rite to be discussed here is the intriguing reference to the "horses dedicated to the sun" found in v. 11 of the present passage. Here, for once, the image seems to be Assyrian, not Canaanite (Cogan and Tadmor, AB, 288). Shamash, the sun god (cf. the Hebrew term for the sun, shemesh, HED #8507), that is, the emblem of the god, would be carried about in a horse-drawn chariot on festal days (as would be those of other Mesopotamian deities). Hobbs (WBC, 334f) cites the archaeological discoveries of small figurines of horses with disks on their heads by Kathleen Kenyon in her City of David excavations, but whether these should be related to the present text remains uncertain (cf., also, Wiseman, TOTC, 302f). Once again, rank paganism, including syncretistic worship from Canaanite, and now Assyrian, practice, is amply illustrated here. But Josiah worked long and hard to rid the city of all such images and objects.

Not only pagan practices, but worship of pagan gods and goddesses is also described in vv. 12ff of the present text. The goddess "Ashtoreth" (not to be confused with "Asherah" in v. 4) was the consort of Baal-Hadad; she is better known as "Astarte," the goddess of love and fertility, and is probably related to the Mesopotamian goddess "Ishtar" (cf. Wiseman, TOTC, 135; John Day, *Anchor Bible Dictionary*, 1:491–94). She is also mentioned back in 1 Ki. 11 (cf. vv. 5, 33), and may well be the "Queen of Heaven" mentioned by Jeremiah several times in his Book (cf. Jer. 7:18; 44:17–25). Although parallels with Mesopotamia and even Egypt are attested, probably a local Canaanite cult is in view in the Jeremiah texts. Likewise, here, the reference is clearly to that of the goddess of the "Sidonians," a Phoenician (north Canaanite) location. (In regard to the reference to the Moabite god Chemosh in v. 13, cf. comments on 3:26f.)

In light of the strong emphasis on the "altar at Bethel" in 1 Ki. 13:1ff, it is not surprising that

904, 8761	250	10.	3041.311	881, 8947	866	904, 1549	1549
prep, *n ms*	n mp, ps 3mp		cj, v Piel pf 3ms	do, art, pn	rel part	prep, pn	pn
בְּתוֹךְ	אֲחֵיהֶם		וְטִמֵּא	אֶת־הַתֹּפֶת	אֲשֶׁר	בְּגֵי	בְנֵי
bethôkh	'ăchêhem		wetimmē'	'eth-hattōpheth	'ăsher	beghê	venê
in the midst of	their brothers		and he defiled	the Topheth	which	in the Valley of	Ben

1549	3937, 1153	3937, 5882.541	382	881, 1158	881, 1351	904, 813
pn	prep, neg part	prep, v Hiphil inf con	n ms	do, n ms, ps 3ms	cj, do, n fs, ps 3ms	prep, art, n fs
הִנֹּם	לְבִלְתִּי	לְהַעֲבִיר	אִישׁ	אֶת־בְּנוֹ	וְאֶת־בִּתּוֹ	בָּאֵשׁ
hinnlm	leviltî	leha'ăvîr	'îsh	'eth-benô	we'eth-bittô	bā'ēsh
Hinnom	that not	to cause to pass through	a man	his son	or his daughter	in the fire

3937, 4571	11.	8139.521	881, 5670	866	5598.116	4567	3171
prep, pn		cj, v Hiphil impf 3ms	do, art, n mp	rel part	v Qal pf 3cp	*n mp*	pn
לַמֹּלֶךְ		וַיַּשְׁבֵּת	אֶת־הַסּוּסִים	אֲשֶׁר	נָתְנוּ	מַלְכֵי	יְהוּדָה
lammōlekh		wayyashbēth	'eth-hassûsîm	'ăsher	nāthenû	malkhê	yehûdhāh
to Molech		and he brought to a stop	the horses	which	they put	the kings of	Judah

3937, 8507	4623, 971.141	1041, 3176	420, 4099	5603	5835
prep, art, n fs	prep, v Qal inf con	*n ms*, pn	prep, *n fs*	pn	art, n ms
לַשֶּׁמֶשׁ	מִבֹּא	בֵּית־יְהוָה	אֶל־לִשְׁכַּת	נְתַן־מֶלֶךְ	הַסָּרִיס
lashshemesh	mibbō'	vêth-yehwāh	'el-lishkath	nethan-melekh	hassārîs
to the sun	from entering	the temple of Yahweh	to the chamber of	Nathan-Melech	the eunuch

866	904, 6767	881, 4980	8507	8041.111	904, 813
rel pron	prep, art, n mp	cj, do, *n fp*	art, n ms	v Qal pf 3ms	prep, art, n fs
אֲשֶׁר	בַּפַּרְוָרִים	וְאֶת־מַרְכְּבוֹת	הַשֶּׁמֶשׁ	שָׂרַף	בָּאֵשׁ
'ăsher	bapparwārîm	we'eth-markevôth	hashshemesh	sāraph	bā'ēsh
who	in the outer courtyards	and the chariots of	the sun	he burned	with the fire

12.	881, 4326	866	6142, 1437	6168	271	866, 6449.116
	cj, do, art, n mp	rel part	prep, art, n ms	*n fs*	pn	rel part, v Qal pf 3cp
	וְאֶת־הַמִּזְבְּחוֹת	אֲשֶׁר	עַל־הַגָּג	עֲלִיַּת	אָחָז	אֲשֶׁר־עָשׂוּ
	we'eth-hammizbechôth	'ăsher	'al-haggāgh	'ălîyath	'āchāz	'ăsher-'āsû
	and the altars	which	on the roof	the upper room of	Ahaz	that they had done

4567	3171	881, 4326	866, 6449.111	4667	904, 8692
n mp	pn	cj, do, art, n mp	rel part, v Qal pf 3ms	pn	prep, num
מַלְכֵי	יְהוּדָה	וְאֶת־הַמִּזְבְּחוֹת	אֲשֶׁר־עָשָׂה	מְנַשֶּׁה	בִּשְׁתֵּי
malkhê	yehûdhāh	we'eth-hammizbechôth	'ăsher-'āsāh	menashsheh	bishtê
the kings of	Judah	and the altars	which he had made	Manasseh	in the two of

2793	1041, 3176	5606.121	4567	7608.121	4623, 8427
n fp	*n ms*, pn	v Qal impf 3ms	art, n ms	cj, v Qal impf 3ms	prep, adv
חַצְרוֹת	בֵּית־יְהוָה	נָתַץ	הַמֶּלֶךְ	וַיָּרָץ	מִשָּׁם
chatsrôth	bêth-yehwāh	nāthats	hammelekh	wayyārāts	mishshām
the courtyards of	the temple of Yahweh	he demolished	the king	and he ran	from there

8390.511	881, 6312	420, 5337	7224	13.	881, 1154	866	6142, 6686
cj, v Hiphil pf 3ms	do, n ms, ps 3mp	prep, n ms	pn		cj, do, art, n fp	rel part	prep, *n mp*
וְהִשְׁלִיךְ	אֶת־עֲפָרָם	אֶל־נַחַל	קִדְרוֹן		וְאֶת־הַבָּמוֹת	אֲשֶׁר	עַל־פְּנֵי
wehishlîkh	'eth-'ăphārām	'el-nachal	qidhrôn		we'eth-habbāmôth	'ăsher	'al-penê
and he threw	their dust	to Wadi	Kidron		and the high places	which	opposite

3503	866	4623, 3332	3937, 2098, 5072	866	1161.111
pn	rel part	prep, n fs	prep, *n ms*, art, n ms	rel part	v Qal pf 3ms
יְרוּשָׁלַם	אֲשֶׁר	מִימִין	לְהַר־הַמַּשְׁחִית	אֲשֶׁר	בָּנָה
yerûshālam	'ăsher	mîmîn	lehar-hammashchîth	'ăsher	bānāh
Jerusalem	which	from the south	to the mountain of the demonic religion	which	he had built

10. And he defiled Topheth, which is in the valley of the children of Hinnom, that no man might make his son or his daughter to pass through the fire to Molech: ... through the fire of sacrifice, *JB* ... no one might burn his son or daughter, *Moffatt* ... there would no longer be an immolation of sons or daughters by fire, *NAB* ... pass through fire as an offering to Molech, *NRSV.*

11. And he took away the horses that the kings of Judah had given to the sun, at the entering in of the house of the LORD: ... he rid the temple of those horses, *Knox* ... had dedicated to the worship of the sun, *Good News* ... kings of Judah had set up in honour of the sun, *NEB* ... at the entrance to the House, *Anchor.*

by the chamber of Nathan-melech the chamberlain: ... near the room of the eunuch Nathan-melech, *Beck* ... by the cell of, *Berkeley* ... near the apartment of, *JB* ... beside the room of, *NEB.*

which was in the suburbs: ... in the precincts, *Berkeley* ... among the summer houses, *Goodspeed* ... in the large building, *NAB* ... in the colonnade, *NEB.*

and burned the chariots of the sun with fire: ... he burned the chariots used in this worship, *Good News* ... burned the solar chariot, *JB* ... chariots of the sun he burned to ashes, *Knox.*

12. And the altars that were on the top of the upper chamber of Ahaz, which the kings of Judah had made, and the altars which Manasseh had made in the two courts of the house of the LORD: ... altars that were on the roof, *NKJV* ... in the two outer squares, *BB.*

did the king beat down: ... he pulled down from there, *NRSV* ... hastily removed them from there, *Anchor* ... king broke down, *NASB* ... demolished, *Goodspeed.*

and brake them down from thence: ... broke in pieces, *NRSV* ... crushed to bits, *BB* ... smashed them there, *NASB* ... powdered them, *Fenton.*

and cast the dust of them into the brook Kidron: ... threw the rubble into the Wadi Kidron, *NRSV* ... into the stream Kidron, *BB* ... dumped their rubble in the Kidron Valley, *Beck.*

13. And the high places that were before Jerusalem, which were on the right hand of the mount of corruption: ... Mount of the Destroyer, *Anchor* ... mount of destruction, *Berkeley* ... Hill of Shame, *Knox* ... Mount of Misconduct, *NAB.*

which Solomon the king of Israel had builded for Ashtoreth the abomination of the Zidonians, and for Chemosh the abomination of the Moabites, and for Milcom the abomination of the children of Ammon, did the king defile: ... the king destroyed, *Fenton* ... king made unclean, *BB.*

---

vv. 15–18 of the present passage singles out King Josiah's destruction of that altar for special mention. In the most remarkable "long-term prediction" in this literature, an unnamed Judahite prophet denounces the Bethel altar erected by Jeroboam I, the first king of the newly-separated Northern Kingdom, and he specifically predicts that a "son named Josiah will be born to the house of David" and that upon that very same altar, "he will sacrifice the priests of the high places who now make offerings here, and human bones will be burned on you [the altar]" (and the prophet also gives the characteristic "short-term" prediction of ashes being poured out of the altar at that time; cf. 1 Ki. 13:3, 5). Therefore, it is not surprising that the present text takes great pains, not only to record the precise fulfillment of the anonymous prophet's prediction (vv. 15f), but also King Josiah's care not to disturb the tomb of the prophet himself (vv.17f), nor that of the prophet from Samaria who was also mentioned in 1 Ki. 13 (and who, indeed, by his duplicity led the Judahite prophet to an early death; cf. vv. 11–32 of that chapter).

Finally, as already noted, Josiah's cult reforms clearly involved much of the original kingdom of Samaria (vv. 19f). Indeed, as earlier described in v. 8 of the present chapter, Josiah's kingdom stretched "from Geba to Beersheba."

This brings up the important issue of archaeological corroboration of the Josianic cult reform activities. The excavations at Arad (about 40 miles [60 kilometers] south of Jerusalem), in particular, give evidence of major change around the time of Josiah: a temple which had existed since the tenth century had been abandoned and destroyed (in Stratum VII), with part of a casemate wall cut through it. The destruction could be dated possibly to the time of Manasseh, but, more probably to the time of Josiah (cf. *Anchor Bible Dictionary*, 1:334; also cf. Bright, *History of Israel*, 319, n. 26, who notes that the high place at Beersheba may also have been destroyed at this time as well). Both Hobbs (WBC, 339) and Wiseman (TOTC, 304) also note the important information provided by the Mesad Hashavyahu archaeological excavation, including the famous fourteen-line Hebrew ostracon (inscribed potsherd) found there, detailing confiscation of an agricultural worker's garment (for unspecified reasons), and asking for its return. The

8406	4567, 3547	3937, 6492	8617	6992	3937, 3767
pn	*n ms*, pn	prep, pn	*n ms*	pn	cj, prep, pn
שְׁלֹמֹה	מֶלֶךְ־יִשְׂרָאֵל	לְעַשְׁתֹּרֶת	שִׁקֻּץ	צִידֹנִים	וְלִכְמוֹשׁ
shelōmōh	melekh-yisrā'ēl	le'ashtōreth	shiqquts	tsîdhōnîm	welikhmôsh
Solomon	the king of Israel	for Ashteroth	the detestable thing of	Sidonians	and to Chemosh

8617	4262	3937, 4585	8774	1158, 6205
n ms	pn	cj, prep, pn	*n fs*	*n mp*, pn
שִׁקֻּץ	מוֹאָב	וּלְמִלְכֹּם	תּוֹעֲבַת	בְּנֵי־עַמּוֹן
shiqquts	mô'āv	ûlămilkōm	tô'ăvath	benê-'ammôn
the detestable thing of	Moab	and to Milcom	the abomination of	the sons of Ammon

3041.311	4567		8132.311	881, 4851	3901.121
v Piel pf 3ms	art, n ms	**14.**	cj, v Piel pf 3ms	do, art, n fp	cj, v Qal impf 3ms
טִמֵּא	הַמֶּלֶךְ		וְשִׁבַּר	אֶת־הַמַּצֵּבוֹת	וַיִּכְרֹת
ṯimmē'	hammelekh		weshibbar	'eth-hammatstsēvôth	wayyikhrōth
he defiled	the king		and he broke in pieces	the memorials	and he cut down

881, 867	4527.321	881, 4887	6344	119		1612
do, art, pn	cj, v Piel impf 3ms	do, n ms, ps 3mp	*n fp*	n ms	**15.**	cj, cj
אֶת־הָאֲשֵׁרִים	וַיְמַלֵּא	אֶת־מְקוֹמָם	עַצְמוֹת	אָדָם		וְגַם
'eth-hā'ăshērîm	waymallē'	'eth-meqômām	'atsmôth	'ādhām		wegham
the Asherah poles	and he filled with	their place	the bones of	men		and also

881, 4326	866	904, 1044	1154	866	6449.111	3493
do, art, n ms	rel part	prep, pn	art, n fs	rel part	v Qal pf 3ms	pn
אֶת־הַמִּזְבֵּחַ	אֲשֶׁר	בְּבֵית־אֵל	הַבָּמָה	אֲשֶׁר	עָשָׂה	יָרָבְעָם
'eth-hammizbēach	'ăsher	bevêth-'ēl	habbāmāh	'ăsher	'āsāh	yārov'ām
the altar	which	in Bethel	the high place	which	he had made	Jeroboam

1158, 5203	866	2490.511	881, 3547	1612	881, 4326	2000
n ms, pn	rel part	v Hiphil pf 3ms	do, pn	cj	do, art, n ms	art, dem pron
בֶּן־נְבָט	אֲשֶׁר	הֶחֱטִיא	אֶת־יִשְׂרָאֵל	גַּם	אֶת־הַמִּזְבֵּחַ	הַהוּא
ben-nevāṯ	'ăsher	hechĕṯî'	'eth-yisrā'ēl	gam	'eth-hammizbēach	hahû'
the son of Nebat	which	he caused to sin	Israel	also	the altar	the that

881, 1154	5606.111	8041.121	881, 1154	1914.511	3937, 6312
cj, do, art, n fs	v Qal pf 3ms	cj, v Qal impf 3ms	do, art, n fs	v Hiphil pf 3ms	prep, n ms
וְאֶת־הַבָּמָה	נָתָץ	וַיִּשְׂרֹף	אֶת־הַבָּמָה	הֵדַק	לְעָפָר
we'eth-habbāmāh	nāthāts	wayyisrōph	'eth-habbāmāh	hēdhaq	le'āphār
and the high place	he demolished	then he burned	the high place	he pulverized	into dust

8041.111	867		6680.121	3086	7495.121	881, 7197
cj, v Qal pf 3ms	pn	**16.**	cj, v Qal impf 3ms	pn	cj, v Qal impf 3ms	do, art, n mp
וְשָׂרַף	אֲשֵׁרָה		וַיִּפֶן	יֹאשִׁיָּהוּ	וַיַּרְא	אֶת־הַקְּבָרִים
wesāraph	'ăshērāh		wayyiphen	yō'shîyāhû	wayyare'	'eth-haqqevārîm
and he burned	the Asherah		and he turned	Josiah	and he saw	the tombs

866, 8427	904, 2098	8365.121	4089.121	881, 6344	4623, 7197
rel part, adv	prep, art, n ms	cj, v Qal impf 3ms	cj, v Qal impf 3ms	do, art, n fp	prep, art, n mp
אֲשֶׁר־שָׁם	בָּהָר	וַיִּשְׁלַח	וַיִּקַּח	אֶת־הָעֲצָמוֹת	מִן־הַקְּבָרִים
'ăsher-shām	bāhār	wayyishlach	wayyiqqach	'eth-hā'ătsāmôth	min-haqqevārîm
which there	on the mountain	and he sent out	and he took	the bones	from the tombs

8041.121	6142, 4326	3041.321	3626, 1745	3176	866
cj, v Qal impf 3ms	prep, art, n ms	cj, v Piel impf 3ms, ps 3ms	prep, *n ms*	pn	rel part
וַיִּשְׂרֹף	עַל־הַמִּזְבֵּחַ	וַיְטַמְּאֵהוּ	כִּדְבַר	יְהוָה	אֲשֶׁר
wayyisrōph	'al-hammizbēach	waytamme'ēhû	kidhvar	yehwāh	'ăsher
and he burned	on the altar	and he defiled it	according to the word of	Yahweh	which

7410.111	382	435	866	7410.111	881, 1745	431
v Qal pf 3ms	*n ms*	art, n mp	rel pron	v Qal pf 3ms	do, art, n mp	art, dem pron
קָרָא	אִישׁ	הָאֱלֹהִים	אֲשֶׁר	קָרָא	אֶת־הַדְּבָרִים	הָאֵלֶּה
qārā'	'îsh	hā'ĕlōhîm	'ăsher	qārā'	'eth-hadd^{e}vārîm	hā'ēlleh
he had proclaimed	the man of	God	who	he had proclaimed	the words	the these

17.

569.121	4242	6994	2044	866	603	7495.151	569.126
cj, v Qal impf 3ms	intrg	art, n ms	dem pron	rel part	pers pron	v Qal act ptc ms	cj, v Qal impf 3mp
וַיֹּאמֶר	מָה	הַצִּיּוּן	הַלָּז	אֲשֶׁר	אֲנִי	רֹאֶה	וַיֹּאמְרוּ
wayyō'mer	māh	hatstsîyûn	hallāz	'ăsher	'ănî	rō'eh	wayyō'm^{e}rû
and he said	what	the landmark	this one	which	I	seeing	and they said

14. And he brake in pieces the images: ... smashed the sacred pillars, *JB* ... broke in pieces the statues, *Douay* ... broke the stone pillars to pieces, *Good News*.

and cut down the groves: ... cut down the sacred poles, *JB* ... sacred trees, *Knox* ... Asherim, *NASB* ... wooden images, *NKJV* ... symbols of the goddess, *Good News*.

and filled their places with the bones of men: ... filled up the ruins with the bones, *Knox* ... filled up their site with dead men's bones, *Moffatt* ... the ground where they had stood he covered with human bones, *Good News* ... Then he desecrated these places by scattering human bones over them, *NLT*.

15. Moreover the altar that was at Beth-el, and the high place which Jeroboam the son of Nebat, who made Israel to sin, had made, both that altar and the high place he brake down, and burned the high place: ... He also tore down the altar at Bethel, the high place, *Berkeley* ... both that Altar, and the Columns, he threw down, *Fenton* ... he demolished and shattered its stones, *Goodspeed* ... breaking up its stones, *JB*.

and stamped it small to powder: ... stamping it to dust, *Berkeley* ... fine dust, *Fenton* ... grinding them to powder, *Goodspeed* ... reducing them to powder, *JB*.

and burned the grove: ... burning the shame images, *Berkeley* ... Shrines, *Fenton* ... sacred pole, *Goodspeed* ... sacred trees, *Knox*.

16. And as Josiah turned himself, he spied the sepulchres that were there in the mount: ... turned and saw the graves there on the mountainside, *NAB* ... Josiah set eyes on the graves which were there on the hill, *NEB* ... looked around, and when he saw the tombs that were there on the hillside, *NIV*.

and sent, and took the bones out of the sepulchres, and burned them upon the altar: ... he ordered the bones taken from the graves, *NAB* ... he had the bones removed, *NIV* ... ordered that the bones be brought out, *NLT*.

and polluted it, according to the word of the LORD which the man of God proclaimed, who proclaimed these words: ... and defiled it according to the word, *NASB* ... desecrate it, *NEB* ... who had foretold these things, *Douay* ... who had predicted these things, *NLT*.

17. Then he said, What title is that that I see?: ... What is that monument that I see?, *NRSV* ... gravestone, *Tyndale* ... this marker, *Anchor* ... headstone, *BB*.

And the men of the city told him, It is the sepulchre of the man of God, which came from Judah, and proclaimed these things that thou hast done against the altar of Beth-el: ...

ostracon was found inside one of the guard rooms of the ancient fort (this fortress, just south of Yavneh-Yam along the Mediterranean seacoast, only existed for a short time in the late pre-exilic period; cf. *Anchor Bible Dictionary*, 4:706). We therefore seem to have clear attestation of Josiah's assertion of power to the west, as well as to the north (Geba, possibly also Megiddo) and to the south (Arad, En-Gedi).

Now, we must turn to a brief discussion of Josiah's Passover, as described in vv. 21ff of the present passage. As already noted, this was said to be the greatest Passover celebration since the days of the judges (v. 22). Assuming Saul's accession to kingship in ca. 1020 (actually, probably a decade or so earlier), this would be, at a minimum, a period of some 400 years. Indeed, the only other notable Passover was the well-known Passover of Joshua, described as taking place at Gilgal "on the plains of Jericho" in Josh. 5:10f. Apparently, the biblical writer wishes us to see an important inclusio (concerning this literary term, cf. comments on 7:1–20) here between Joshua and Josiah—the first and the last great leaders in the Books of Joshua through 2 Kings. Just like Joshua in earlier days, King Josiah was also a mighty man of the Law, using it to lead his people effectively and decisively. So, just like Joshua, Josiah also offered a great Passover as

420	596	6111	7197	382, 435	866, 971.111	4623, 3171
prep, ps 3ms	*n mp*	art, n fs	art, *n ms*	*n ms*, art, n mp	rel pron, v Qal pf 3ms	prep, pn
אֵלָיו	אַנְשֵׁי	הָעִיר	הַקֶּבֶר	אִישׁ־הָאֱלֹהִים	אֲשֶׁר־בָּא	מִיהוּדָה
'ēlâv	'anshê	hā'îr	haqqever	'îsh-hā'ĕlōhîm	'ăsher-bā'	mîhûdhāh
to him	the men of	the city	the tomb of	the man of God	who he came	from Judah

7410.121	881, 1745	431	866	6449.113	6142	4326
cj, v Qal impf 3ms	do, art, n mp	art, dem pron	rel part	v Qal pf 2ms	prep	art, *n ms*
וַיִּקְרָא	אֶת־הַדְּבָרִים	הָאֵלֶּה	אֲשֶׁר	עָשִׂיתָ	עַל	הַמִּזְבַּח
wayyiqŏrā'	'eth-haddevārîm	hā'ēlleh	'ăsher	'āsîthā	'al	hammizbach
and he proclaimed	the words	the these	which	you have done	against	the altar of

1044		569.121	5299.533	3937	382	414, 5309.121	6344
pn	18.	cj, v Qal impf 3ms	v Hiphil impv 2mp	prep, ps 3ms	n ms	adv, v Qal juss 3ms	n fp, ps 3ms
בֵּית־אֵל		וַיֹּאמֶר	הַנִּיחוּ	לוֹ	אִישׁ	אַל־יָנַע	עַצְמֹתָיו
bêth-'ēl		wayyō'mer	hanîchû	lô	'îsh	'al-yāna'	'atsmōthâv
Bethel		and he said	let rest	him	a man	do not disturb	his bones

4561.326	6344	881	6344	5204	866, 971.111	4623, 8497
cj, v Piel impf 3mp	n fp, ps 3ms	do	*n fp*	art, n ms	rel pron, v Qal pf 3ms	prep, pn
וַיְמַלְּטוּ	עַצְמֹתָיו	אֵת	עַצְמוֹת	הַנָּבִיא	אֲשֶׁר־בָּא	מִשֹּׁמְרוֹן
waymalletû	'atsmōthâv	'ēth	'atsmôth	hannāvî'	'ăsher-bā'	mishshōmerôn
so they left unscathed	his bones		the bones of	the prophet	who he came	from Samaria

	1612	881, 3725, 1041	1154	866	904, 6111	8497	866
19.	cj, cj	do, *adj*, *n mp*	art, n fp	rel part	prep, *n fp*	pn	rel part
	וְגַם	אֶת־כָּל־בָּתֵּי	הַבָּמוֹת	אֲשֶׁר	בְּעָרֵי	שֹׁמְרוֹן	אֲשֶׁר
	wegham	'eth-kol-bāttê	habbāmôth	'ăsher	be'ārê	shōmerôn	'ăsher
	and also	all the temples of	the high places	which	in the cities of	Samaria	which

6449.116	4567	3547	3937, 3832.541	5681.511	3086
v Qal pf 3cp	*n mp*	pn	prep, v Hiphil inf con	v Hiphil pf 3ms	pn
עָשׂוּ	מַלְכֵי	יִשְׂרָאֵל	לְהַכְעִיס	הֵסִיר	יֹאשִׁיָּהוּ
'āsû	malkhê	yisrā'ēl	lehakh'îs	hēsîr	yō'shîyāhû
they had made	the kings of	Israel	to provoke to anger	he removed	Josiah

6449.121	3937	3626, 3725, 4801	866	6449.111	904, 1044
cj, v Qal impf 3ms	prep, ps 3mp	prep, *adj*, art, n mp	rel part	v Qal pf 3ms	prep, pn
וַיַּעַשׂ	לָהֶם	כְּכָל־הַמַּעֲשִׂים	אֲשֶׁר	עָשָׂה	בְּבֵית־אֵל
wayya'as	lāhem	kekhol-hamma'ăsîm	'ăsher	'āsāh	bevêth-'ēl
and he did	to them	like all the deeds	that	he had done	in Bethel

	2159.121	881, 3725, 3669	1154	866, 8427	6142, 4326
20.	cj, v Qal impf 3ms	do, *adj*, *n mp*	art, n fp	rel pron, adv	prep, art, n mp
	וַיִּזְבַּח	אֶת־כָּל־כֹּהֲנֵי	הַבָּמוֹת	אֲשֶׁר־שָׁם	עַל־הַמִּזְבְּחוֹת
	wayyizbach	'eth-kol-kōhenê	habbāmôth	'ăsher-shām	'al-hammizbechôth
	and he slaughtered	all the priests of	the high places	who there	on the altars

8041.121	881, 6344	119	6142	8178.121	3503
cj, v Qal impf 3ms	do, *n fp*	n ms	prep, ps 3mp	cj, v Qal impf 3ms	pn
וַיִּשְׂרֹף	אֶת־עַצְמוֹת	אָדָם	עֲלֵיהֶם	וַיָּשָׁב	יְרוּשָׁלִָם
wayyisrōph	'eth-'atsmôth	'ādhām	'ălêhem	wayyāshāv	yerûshālām
then he burned	the bones of	a man	on them	then he returned to	Jerusalem

	6943.321	4567	881, 3725, 6194	3937, 569.141	6449.133	6699
21.	cj, v Piel impf 3ms	art, n ms	do, *adj*, art, n ms	prep, v Qal inf con	v Qal impv 2mp	n ms
	וַיְצַו	הַמֶּלֶךְ	אֶת־כָּל־הָעָם	לֵאמֹר	עֲשׂוּ	פֶּסַח
	waytsaw	hammelekh	'eth-kol-hā'ām	lē'mōr	'ăsû	phesach
	and he commanded	the king	all the people	saying	perform	the Passover

3937, 3176	435	3626, 3918.155	6142	5809	1311	2172
prep, pn	n mp, ps 2mp	prep, art, v Qal pass ptc ms	prep	*n ms*	art, n fs	art, dem pron
לַיהוָה	אֱלֹהֵיכֶם	כַּכָּתוּב	עַל	סֵפֶר	הַבְּרִית	הַזֶּה
layhwāh	'ĕlōhêkhem	kakkāthûv	'al	sēpher	habbᵉrîth	hazzeh
to Yahweh	your God	like what was written	on	the scroll of	the Covenant	the this

22.	3706	3940	6449.211	3626, 6699	2172	4623, 3219
	cj	neg part	v Niphal pf 3ms	prep, art, n ms	art, dem pron	prep, *n mp*
	כִּי	לֹא	נַעֲשָׂה	כַּפֶּסַח	הַזֶּה	מִימֵי
	kî	lō'	na'ăsāh	kappesach	hazzeh	mîmê
	because	not	it has been performed	like the Passover	the this	since the days of

It is the tomb of the man of God who came from Judah, *NRSV* ... grave of the man of God, *REB* ... resting-place of the man, *BB* ... and predicted these things which you have done, *RSV*.

18. And he said, Let him alone; let no man move his bones: ... Nobody should move his bones, *Beck* ... Let him be; let no one disturb his bones, *Berkeley* ... Let his bones rest! No one shall touch his bones!, *Fenton* ... Leave it as it is, Josiah ordered. His bones are not to be moved, *Good News*.

So they let his bones alone, with the bones of the prophet that came out of Samaria: ... left his bones alone, *Berkeley* ... preserved his bones,—the bones of the Preacher who came, *Fenton* ... his bones rescued the bones of the prophet, *Goodspeed* ... his bones were not moved, neither were those of the prophet, *Good News*.

19. And all the houses also of the high places that were in the cities of Samaria, which the kings of Israel had made to provoke the LORD to anger, Josiah took away: ... Josiah also destroyed, *JB* ... abolished, *Knox* ... removed, *Moffatt* ... moving the Lord to wrath, *BB*.

and did to them according to all the acts that he had done in Beth-el: ... he treated these places exactly as he had treated the one at Bethel, *JB* ... treating them as he had treated the shrine, *Knox* ... he did to them according to all the deeds he had done in Bethel, *NKJV* ... He did to them everything he had done at, *Beck*.

20. And he slew all the priests of the high places that were there upon the altars, and burned men's bones upon them, and returned to Jerusalem: ... slaughtered ... the priests, *NAB* ... burned human bones, *NASB* ... killed all the priests, *NCV* ... went back to Jerusalem, *NEB*.

21. And the king commanded all the people, saying, Keep the passover unto the LORD your God, as it is written in the book of this covenant: ... king issued an order to all his people: Celebrate the Passover, *Anchor* ... as it says in this book of the law, *BB* ... Make a Passover, *Fenton* ... in honor of the LORD their God, *Good News*.

22. Surely there was not holden such a passover from the days of the judges that judged Israel, nor in all the days of the kings of Israel, nor of the kings of Judah: ... No Passover like this had ever been celebrated, *JB* ... had any such Passover been observed, *NIV* ... had never been held, *NKJV* ... had not been kept, *Goodspeed*.

both celebration and culmination of his radical political leadership (whether crossing the Jordan River miraculously on dry ground, and performing the ancient rite of circumcision for the first time since the people had left the land of Egypt nearly forty years previously [Josh.3:1–5:8]; or discovering the "Scroll of Torah" serendipitously in the Temple, and inaugurating the radical era of religious reform the land of Judah had ever known [2 Ki. 22:11–23:20]). Just like Joshua, the immediate successor of Moses the servant of Yahweh; so also Josiah, "who turned to Yahweh ... with all his heart and with all his soul and with all his strength, in accordance with all the Torah of Moses" (v. 25). Once again, "neither before nor after Josiah was there a king like him who turned to Yahweh as he did." Truly incomparable was he in the more than half-millennium history of Judahite and Ephraimite political power. (Commentators who note the great Passover of Hezekiah, as described in 2 Chr. 30 [but nowhere mentioned in 2 Kings], often cite Josiah's Passover as the first since the days of Joshua which took place entirely as a national festival, and following closely the procedure found in Deut. 16:5f [cf. Cogan and Tadmor, AB, 290; Hobbs, WBC, 337; Wiseman, TOTC, 304; also cf. 2 Chr. 35:1–19]—certainly there were many other Passovers besides that of Hezekiah celebrated in the intervening years between Joshua and King Josiah.)

The last two verses of this section (vv. 24f) summarize, both in some detail (v. 24), as well as in the most general of terms (v. 25), the extent of Josiah's religious reforms. They were more far-reaching than ever been seen before. The "medi-

8570.152	866	8570.116	881, 3547	3725	3219	4567
art, v Qal act ptc mp	rel pron	v Qal pf 3cp	do, pn	cj, *n ms*	*n mp*	*n mp*
הַשֹּׁפְטִים	אֲשֶׁר	שָׁפְטוּ	אֶת־יִשְׂרָאֵל	וְכֹל	יְמֵי	מַלְכֵי
hashshōpheṭîm	'ăsher	shāpheṭû	'eth-yisrā'ēl	wekhōl	yemê	malkhê
the judges	who	they judged	Israel	nor the entirety of	the days of	the kings of

3547	4567	3171		3706	524, 904, 8470	6462	8523	3937, 4567
pn	cj, *n mp*	pn	**23.**	cj	cj, prep, num	num	n fs	prep, art, n ms
יִשְׂרָאֵל	וּמַלְכֵי	יְהוּדָה		כִּי	אִם־בִּשְׁמֹנֶה	עֶשְׂרֵה	שָׁנָה	לַמֶּלֶךְ
yisrā'ēl	ûmalkhê	yehûdhāh		kî	'im-bishmōneh	'esrēh	shānāh	lammelekh
Israel	and the kings of	Judah		except	only in the eight	ten	year	of the king

3086	6449.211	6699	2172	3937, 3176	904, 3503		1612
pn	v Niphal pf 3ms	art, n ms	art, dem pron	prep, pn	prep, pn	**24.**	cj, cj
יֹאשִׁיָּהוּ	נַעֲשָׂה	הַפֶּסַח	הַזֶּה	לַיהוָה	בִּירוּשָׁלִַם		וְגַם
yō'shîyāhû	na'ăsāh	happesach	hazzeh	layhwāh	bîrûshālām		wegham
Josiah	it was performed	the Passover	the this	to Yahweh	in Jerusalem		and also

881, 177	881, 3160	881, 8994	881, 1585	881
do, art, n mp	cj, do, art, n mp	cj, do, art, n mp	cj, do, art, n mp	cj, do
אֶת־הָאֹבוֹת	וְאֶת־הַיִּדְּעֹנִים	וְאֶת־הַתְּרָפִים	וְאֶת־הַגִּלֻּלִים	וְאֵת
'eth-hā'ōvôth	we'eth-hayyidde'ōnîm	we'eth-hatterāphîm	we'eth-haggillulîm	we'ēth
the necromancers	and the channelers	and the teraphim	and the idols	and

3725, 8629	866	7495.216	904, 800	3171	904, 3503
adj, art, n mp	rel part	v Niphal pf 3cp	prep, *n fs*	pn	cj, prep, pn
כָּל־הַשִּׁקֻּצִים	אֲשֶׁר	נִרְאוּ	בְּאֶרֶץ	יְהוּדָה	וּבִירוּשָׁלִַם
kol-hashshiqqutsîm	'ăsher	nir'û	be'erets	yehûdhāh	ûvîrûshālam
all the detestable things	that	they were seen	in the land of	Judah	and in Jerusalem

1220.311	3086	3937, 4775	7251.541	881, 1745	8784	3918.156
v Piel pf 3ms	pn	prep, prep	v Hiphil inf con	do, *n mp*	art, n fs	art, v Qal pass ptc mp
בִּעֵר	יֹאשִׁיָּהוּ	לְמַעַן	הָקִים	אֶת־דִּבְרֵי	הַתּוֹרָה	הַכְּתֻבִים
bi'ēr	yō'shîyāhû	lema'an	hāqîm	'eth-divrê	hattôrāh	hakkethuvîm
he burned	Josiah	so that	to establish	the words of	the Law	those written

6142, 5809	866	4834.111	2619	3669	1041	3176		3765
prep, art, n ms	rel part	v Qal pf 3ms	pn	art, n ms	*n ms*	pn	**25.**	cj, prep, ps 3ms
עַל־הַסֵּפֶר	אֲשֶׁר	מָצָא	חִלְקִיָּהוּ	הַכֹּהֵן	בֵּית	יְהוָה		וְכָמֹהוּ
'al-hassēpher	'ăsher	mātsā'	chilqîyāhû	hakkōhēn	bêth	yehwāh		wekhāmōhû
on the scroll	which	he found	Hilkiah	the priest	the temple of	Yahweh		and like him

3940, 2030.111	3937, 6686	4567	866, 8178.111	420, 3176	904, 3725, 3949
neg part, v Qal pf 3ms	prep, n mp, ps 3ms	n ms	rel pron, v Qal pf 3ms	prep, pn	prep, *adj*, n ms, ps 3ms
לֹא־הָיָה	לְפָנָיו	מֶלֶךְ	אֲשֶׁר־שָׁב	אֶל־יְהוָה	בְּכָל־לְבָבוֹ
lō'-hāyāh	lephānâv	melekh	'ăsher-shāv	'el-yehwāh	bekhol-levāvô
he was not	before him	a king	who he returned	to Yahweh	with all his heart

904, 3725, 5497	904, 3725, 4108	3626, 3725	8784	5057
cj, prep, *adj*, n fs, ps 3ms	cj, prep, *adj*, n ms, ps 3ms	prep, *n ms*	*n fs*	pn
וּבְכָל־נַפְשׁוֹ	וּבְכָל־מְאֹדוֹ	כְּכֹל	תּוֹרַת	מֹשֶׁה
ûvekhol-naphshô	ûvekhol-me'ōdhô	kekhōl	tôrath	mōsheh
and with all his soul	and with all his strength	according to the entirety of	the Law of	Moses

313	3940, 7251.111	3765		395	3940, 8178.111	3176
cj, prep, ps 3ms	neg part, v Qal pf 3ms	prep, ps 3ms	**26.**	adv	neg part, v Qal pf 3ms	pn
וְאַחֲרָיו	לֹא־קָם	כָּמֹהוּ		אַךְ	לֹא־שָׁב	יְהוָה
we'achrâv	lō'-qām	kāmōhû		'akh	lō'-shāv	yehwāh
and after him	not he rose	like him		only	He did not turn back	Yahweh

23. But in the eighteenth year of king Josiah, wherein this passover was holden to the LORD in Jerusalem: ... passover was held in honour of the Eternal, *Moffatt* ... kept to the LORD, *MAST* ... was celebrated to the LORD, *NLT* ... held to the LORD, *KJVII*.

24. Moreover the workers with familiar spirits: ... mediums, *Moffatt* ... diviners by spirits, *Douay* ... all those who had control of spirits, *BB* ... those who talked to ghosts, *Beck*.

and the wizards: ... spiritists, *NASB* ... soothsayers, *Tyndale* ... fortune-tellers, *NCV* ... wonder-workers, *BB*.

and the images: ... terraphim, *NASB* ... figures of idols, *Douay* ... household gods, *NEB* ... images of witchcraft, *Tyndale*.

and the idols: ... uncleannesses, *Douay* ... false gods, *BB* ... family idols, *Beck* ... disgusting idols, *Berkeley*.

and all the abominations that were spied in the land of Judah and in Jerusalem, did Josiah put away: ... and any detestable idols, *Moffatt* ... and all the other horrors to be seen in the land, *NAB* ... all the loathsome objects seen, *NEB* ... Josias took away, *Douay*.

that he might perform the words of the law which were written in the book that Hilkiah the priest found in the house of the LORD: ... he might establish the words, *Goodspeed* ... to give effect to the words, *JB* ... he might carry out the terms of the law, *Moffatt* ... carry out the stipulations, *NAB*.

25. And like unto him was there no king before him, that turned to the LORD with all his heart, and with all his soul, and with all his might, according to all the law of Moses: ... with all his soul and with all his strength, *NIV* ... and with all his power, *BB* ... before him there was no king like him, *NKJV* ... No king before him had turned to the LORD as he did, with all his heart, *REB*.

neither after him arose there any like him: ... nor after him did any arise like him, *NKJV* ... there has never been a king like him since, *NLT* ... nor did any king like him appear again, *REB* ... after him there was no king like him, *BB*.

26. Notwithstanding the LORD turned not from the fierceness of his great wrath, wherewith his anger was kindled against Judah: ... the LORD didn't turn from the fury of His great anger blazing against Judah, *Beck* ... Yahweh did not renounce the heat of his great anger, *JB* ... which had flamed up against Judah, *Anchor* ... which had been aroused, *Berkeley*.

because of all the provocations that Manasseh had provoked him withal: ... Manasseh angered him, *Anchor* ... on account of all the insults with which Manasseh had insulted him, *Fenton* ... because of all Manasseh had done to make him angry, *NCV* ... the provocation which Manasseh had given him, *NEB*.

27. And the LORD said, I will remove Judah also out of my sight,

---

ums and spiritists" in Judah (cf. 21:5, above) had violated the plain teaching of Deut. 18:9–12; they represented blatant attempts to ascertain, thus to control the future. As for Josiah's incredible "incomparability," as attested in v. 25, cf. the comments on 19:14–34, and 22:1–20, above.

23:26–30. A foolhardy errand, and a tragic death. Just at the high point of Josiah's narrative, however, we come across this negative note. As Huldah had intimated earlier (22:16f, 20), "disaster" against Judah seemed to be inevitable. Even the great King Josiah could not put off permanently the future catastrophe facing the nation. In any case, King Josiah himself soon faced untimely disaster; after the characteristic "further reference" notice of v. 28, the laconic comment appears that Josiah marched out to meet Pharaoh Neco "in battle," and the Pharaoh fatally wounded the Judahite king at Megiddo. (Again, the chronology is firm—this death may be closely dated to the year 609.) The notice of Josiah's burial "in his own tomb" in Jerusalem, plus the accession of Jehoahaz (who was not Josiah's eldest son, as will be evident below) as king by the "people of the land" (v. 30; concerning the stabilizing influence of the "people of the land," cf. on 21:19–26, above) concludes the unit.

But this laconic notice concerning this tragic demise of this godly king deserves further scrutiny. Thankfully, the Chronicles parallel (2 Chr. 35:20–27) helps out considerably. (The terse note here in 2 Kings may well represent embarrassment concerning the disreputable demise of the writer's hero, or at least extreme reluctance to moralize concerning this tragic turn of events.) In 2 Chronicles, Pharaoh Neco (Necho II, king of Egypt [610–595], who had just succeeded his father Psammetichus I, founder of the Twenty-sixth Dynasty, to the throne the previous summer, continued his predecessor's policy of assisting the rapidly weakening Assyrians (Nineveh, the Assyrian capital, had already fallen to the Babylonians in 612), by marching to confront the Babylonians at Carchemish on the Euphrates (35:20). Thus Neco was marching against the new

4623, 2841	653	1448	866, 2835.111	653	904, 3171	6142
prep, *n ms*	n ms, ps 3ms	art, adj	rel pron, v Qal pf 3ms	n ms, ps 3ms	prep, pn	prep
מֵחֲרוֹן	אַפּוֹ	הַגָּדוֹל	אֲשֶׁר־חָרָה	אַפּוֹ	בִּיהוּדָה	עַל
mēchărôn	'appô	haggādhôl	'ăsher-chārāh	'appô	bîhûdhāh	'al
from the heat of	his nose	the great	which it was kindled	his nose	against Judah	because

3725, 3833	866	3832.511	4667		569.121	3176
adj, art, n mp	rel part	v Hiphil pf 3ms, ps 3ms	pn		cj, v Qal impf 3ms	pn
כָּל־הַכְּעָסִים	אֲשֶׁר	הִכְעִיסוֹ	מְנַשֶּׁה	**27.**	וַיֹּאמֶר	יְהוָה
kol-hakke'āsîm	'ăsher	hikh'îsô	menashsheh		wayyō'mer	yehwāh
all the provocations	which	he provoked Him to anger	Manasseh		and He said	Yahweh

1612	881, 3171	5681.525	4623, 6142	6686	3626, 866	5681.515
cj	do, pn	v Hiphil impf 1cs	prep, prep	n mp, ps 1cs	prep, rel part	v Hiphil pf 1cs
גַּם	אֶת־יְהוּדָה	אָסִיר	מֵעַל	פָּנַי	כַּאֲשֶׁר	הֲסִרֹתִי
gam	'eth-yehûdhāh	'āsîr	mē'al	pānay	ka'ăsher	hesirōthî
also	Judah	I will remove	from beside	my presence	just as	I removed

881, 3547	4128.115	881, 6111	2148	866, 1013.115	881, 3503
do, pn	cj, v Qal pf 1cs	do, art, n fs	art, dem pron	rel part, v Qal pf 1cs	do, pn
אֶת־יִשְׂרָאֵל	וּמָאַסְתִּי	אֶת־הָעִיר	הַזֹּאת	אֲשֶׁר־בָּחַרְתִּי	אֶת־יְרוּשָׁלַם
'eth-yisrā'ēl	ûmā'astî	'eth-hā'îr	hazzō'th	'ăsher-bācharti	'eth-yerûshālam
Israel	I have rejected	the city	the this	which I had chosen	Jerusalem

881, 1041	866	569.115	2030.121	8428	8427		3615
cj, do, art, n ms	rel part	v Qal pf 1cs	v Qal impf 3ms	n ms, ps 1cs	adv		cj, *n ms*
וְאֶת־הַבַּיִת	אֲשֶׁר	אָמַרְתִּי	יִהְיֶה	שְׁמִי	שָׁם	**28.**	וְיֶתֶר
we'eth-habbayith	'ăsher	'āmartî	yihyeh	shemî	shām		weyether
and the Temple	which	I said	it will be	my name	there		and the remainder of

1745	3086	3725, 866	6449.111	1950B, 3940, 2062	3918.156
n mp	pn	cj, *adj*, rel part	v Qal pf 3ms	intrg part, neg part, pers pron	v Qal pass ptc mp
דִּבְרֵי	יֹאשִׁיָּהוּ	וְכָל־אֲשֶׁר	עָשָׂה	הֲלֹא־הֵם	כְּתוּבִים
divrê	yō'shîyāhû	wekhol-'ăsher	'āsāh	hălō'-hēm	kethûvîm
the events of	Josiah	and all which	he did	are they not	things written

6142, 5809	1745	3219	3937, 4567	3171		904, 3219	6148.111
prep, *n ms*	*n mp*	art, n mp	prep, *n mp*	pn		prep, n mp, ps 3ms	v Qal pf 3ms
עַל־סֵפֶר	דִּבְרֵי	הַיָּמִים	לְמַלְכֵי	יְהוּדָה	**29.**	בְּיָמָיו	עָלָה
'al-sēpher	divrê	hayyāmîm	lemalkhê	yehûdhāh		beyāmâv	'ālāh
on the scroll of	the events of	the days	of the kings of	Judah		in his days	he went up

6799	5412	4567, 4875	6142, 4567	831	6142, 5282, 6828
pn	pn	*n ms*, pn	prep, *n ms*	pn	prep, *n ms*, pn
פַּרְעֹה	נְכֹה	מֶלֶךְ־מִצְרַיִם	עַל־מֶלֶךְ	אַשּׁוּר	עַל־נְהַר־פְּרָת
phar'ōh	nekhōh	melekh-mitsrayim	'al-melekh	'ashshûr	'al-nehar-perāth
Pharaoh	Neco	the king of Egypt	against the king of	Assyria	unto the river Euphrates

2050.121	4567	3086	3937, 7410.141	4322.521	904, 4163
cj, v Qal impf 3ms	art, n ms	pn	prep, v Qal inf con, ps 3ms	cj, v Hiphil impf 3ms, ps 3ms	prep, pn
וַיֵּלֶךְ	הַמֶּלֶךְ	יֹאשִׁיָּהוּ	לִקְרָאתוֹ	וַיְמִיתֵהוּ	בִּמְגִדּוֹ
wayyēlekh	hammelekh	yō'shîyāhû	liqŏrā'thô	waymîthēhû	bimghiddô
and he went	the king	Josiah	to meet him	and he executed him	at Megiddo

3626, 7495.141	881		7680.526	5860	4322.151
prep, v Qal inf con, ps 3ms	do, ps 3ms		cj, v Hiphil impf 3mp, ps 3ms	n mp, ps 3ms	v Qal act ptc ms
כִּרְאֹתוֹ	אֹתוֹ	**30.**	וַיַּרְכִּבֻהוּ	עֲבָדָיו	מֵת
kir'ōthô	'ōthô		wayyarkivuhû	'ăvādhâv	mēth
when his seeing	him		and they caused him to ride	his servants	the dead one

as I have removed Israel: ... remove Judah also from my presence, *NIV* ... Judah also I shall banish from my presence ... as I banished Israel, *REB* ... will send Judah away from before my face, as I have sent Israel, *BB* ... destroy Judah just as I have destroyed Israel, *NLT*.

and will cast off this city Jerusalem which I have chosen: ... reject Jerusalem, *NIV* ... will have nothing more to do with this town, which I had made mine, even Jerusalem, *BB* ... reject my chosen city, *NLT*.

and the house of which I said, My name shall be there: ... the house where I promised that my name should be, *REB* ... the holy house of which I said, My name will be there, *BB* ... the place I said was where I should be worshiped, *Good News* ... the Temple where my name was to be honored, *NLT*.

28. Now the rest of the acts of Josiah, and all that he did, are they not written in the book of the chronicles of the kings of Judah?: ... The rest of the history of Josiah, his entire career, is this not recorded, *JB* ... is to be found in the Annals of the kings, *Knox* ... are they not described in the book, *Moffatt* ... The other events and acts of Josiah's reign are recorded in, *NEB*.

29. In his days Pharaoh-nechoh king of Egypt went up against the king of Assyria to the river Euphrates: and king Josiah went against him: ... went up to the king of Assyria, *NASB* ... King Josiah confronted him, *Anchor* ... went to meet him, *Beck* ... Josias, going out to offer resistance, *Knox*.

and he slew him at Megiddo, when he had seen him: ... put him to death at Megiddo, *Anchor* ... killed him, *Beck* ... when he saw him, *Berkeley* ... as soon as he saw him, *Fenton*.

30. And his servants carried him in a chariot dead from Megiddo, and brought him to Jerusalem: ... His attendants conveyed his body in a chariot from Megiddo to Jerusalem, *NEB* ... took his body in a carriage from Megiddo, *BB* ... servants transported his dead body in a chariot, *Goodspeed*.

and buried him in his own sepulchre: ... own grave, *NCV* ... burial place, *NEB* ... tomb, *NIV* ... tomb he had made for himself, *Knox* ... put him into the earth there, *BB*.

And the people of the land took Jehoahaz the son of Josiah, and anointed him, and made him king in his father's stead: ... anointed him king in place of his father, *NEB* ... in his father's place, *NKJV* ... made him king to succeed his father, *Anchor* ... poured olive oil on him to make him king in his father's place, *NCV*.

Mesopotamian power, Babylonia, who, it appears, had just taken the city of Haran from the Assyrian king Ashur-Uballit II. Whether King Josiah was marching against the Egyptian advance and attempting to cut it off at the mountain pass at Megiddo (so most commentators; cf., e.g., Hobbs, WBC, 339f; Wiseman, TOTC, 305; concerning the strategic location of the site of Megiddo, cf. concluding comments on 9:14–29), or whether he merely was summoned to a meeting (something like a "court-martial") by the Egyptian Pharaoh there, King Josiah apparently received his mortal wound at this apocalyptic location (2 Chr. 35:24 has him badly wounded at Megiddo but ultimately dying in Jerusalem). The theological lesson is clear. Godly King Josiah died entirely out of the will of God. (It should be noted, however, that a number of the added details in the chronicler's account here accord closely with the Ahab battle account; cf. the discussion in Japhet, OTL, 1042ff.) For, as the chronicler indeed intimates, "Josiah would not listen to what Neco had said at God's command but went to fight him on the plain of Megiddo" (2 Chr. 35:22). But this then brings up the question of motive—why would such a godly king perform such an ungodly action? Why would he oppose the revealed will of God? It is difficult, of course, to be dogmatic when so little is known, but I have a strong suspicion that the words of the prophetess Huldah are an important factor in all this. These words—at least the words concerning Josiah dying in peace (cf. 2 Ki. 22:20; 2 Chr. 34:28)—"remain a striking example of unfulfilled prophecy" (Cogan and Tadmore, AB, 295). Not, of course, indicating that Huldah somehow "missed God," but rather that Josiah himself misunderstood the import of Huldah's prophecy. Perhaps, Josiah thought he had a magic promise, as it were, to do whatever he wished. After all God had promised that he himself would die in peace. Why else would Josiah defy both reason and revelation in acting as he did? But, whatever the reason, the results were, once again, entirely tragic, and apparently entirely unnecessary. For the kingdom of Judah went quickly downhill after the year 609, and indeed we cannot speak of any future measure of independence for this part of Palestine until near the middle of the second century B.C., the time of the Maccabees, some 450 years later. All this, due to foolish pride, and misunderstanding, willful or otherwise, of the nature of divine prophecy. For God wishes only the best for us—and often promises that very thing in the

4623, 4163	971.526	3503	7196.126	904, 7185
prep, pn	cj, v Hiphil impf 3mp, ps 3ms	pn	cj, v Qal impf 3mp, ps 3ms	prep, n fs, ps 3ms
מִמְּגִדּוֹ	וַיְבִאֻהוּ	יְרוּשָׁלַם	וַיִּקְבְּרֻהוּ	בִּקְבֻרָתוֹ
mimmeghiddô	wayvi'uhû	yerûshālam	wayyiqōbberuhû	biqōvurāthô
from Megiddo	and they brought him to	Jerusalem	and they buried him	in his tomb

4089.121	6194, 800	881, 3168	1158, 3086	5066.126
cj, v Qal impf 3ms	*n ms*, art, n fs	do, pn	*n ms*, pn	cj, v Qal impf 3mp
וַיִּקַּח	עַם־הָאָרֶץ	אֶת־יְהוֹאָחָז	בֶּן־יֹאשִׁיָּהוּ	וַיִּמְשְׁחוּ
wayyiqqach	'am-hā'ārets	'eth-yehô'āchāz	ben-yō'shîyāhû	wayyimshechû
and they took	the people of the land	Jehoahaz	the son of Josiah	and they anointed

881	4566.526	881	8809	1		1158, 6465	8421
do, ps 3ms	cj, v Hiphil impf 3mp	do, ps 3ms	prep	n ms, ps 3ms	**31.**	*n ms*, num	cj, num
אֹתוֹ	וַיַּמְלִיכוּ	אֹתוֹ	תַּחַת	אָבִיו		בֶּן־עֶשְׂרִים	וְשָׁלֹשׁ
'ōthô	wayyamlîkhû	'ōthô	tachath	'āvîw		ben-'esrîm	weshālōsh
him	and they caused to rule	him	instead of	his father		a son of twenty	and three

8523	3168	904, 4566.141	8421	2414	4566.111	904, 3503
n fs	pn	prep, v Qal inf con, ps 3ms	cj, num	n mp	v Qal pf 3ms	prep, pn
שָׁנָה	יְהוֹאָחָז	בְּמָלְכוֹ	וּשְׁלֹשָׁה	חֳדָשִׁים	מָלַךְ	בִּירוּשָׁלָם
shānāh	yehô'āchāz	bemālekhô	ûshelōshāh	chădhāshîm	mālakh	bîrûshālām
year	Jehoahaz	when his reigning	and three	months	he reigned	in Jerusalem

8428	525	2638	1351, 3532	4623, 3975		6449.121
cj, *n ms*	n fs, ps 3ms	pn	*n fs*, pn	prep, pn	**32.**	cj, v Qal impf 3ms
וְשֵׁם	אִמּוֹ	חֲמוּטַל	בַּת־יִרְמְיָהוּ	מִלִּבְנָה		וַיַּעַשׂ
weshēm	'immô	chămûtal	bath-yirmeyāhû	millivnāh		wayya'as
and the name of	his mother	Hamutal	the daughter of Jeremiah	from Libnah		and he did

7737	904, 6084	3176	3626, 3725	866, 6449.116	1
art, adj	prep, *n fd*	pn	prep, n ms	rel part, v Qal pf 3cp	n mp, ps 3ms
הָרַע	בְּעֵינֵי	יְהוָה	כְּכֹל	אֲשֶׁר־עָשׂוּ	אֲבֹתָיו
hāra'	be'ênê	yehwāh	kekhōl	'ăsher-'āsû	'ăvōthâv
what is evil	in the eyes of	Yahweh	according to everything	that they had done	his fathers

	646.121	6799	5412	904, 7540	904, 800	2679	904, 4566.141
33.	cj, v Qal impf 3ms, ps 3ms	pn	pn	prep, pn	prep, *n fs*	pn	prep, v Qal inf con
	וַיַּאַסְרֵהוּ	פַּרְעֹה	נְכֹה	בְרִבְלָה	בְּאֶרֶץ	חֲמָת	בִּמְלֹךְ
	wayya'asrēhû	phar'ōh	nekhōh	verivlāh	be'erets	chemāth	bimlōkh
	and he bound him	Pharaoh	Neco	in Riblah	in the land of	Hamath	when reigning

904, 3503	5598.121, 6296	6142, 800	4109	3724, 3826B	3724	2174
prep, pn	cj, v Qal impf 3ms, n ms	prep, art, n fs	num	*n fs*, n ms	cj, *n fs*	n ms
בִּירוּשָׁלָם	וַיִּתֶּן־עֹנֶשׁ	עַל־הָאָרֶץ	מֵאָה	כִּכַּר־כֶּסֶף	וְכִכַּר	זָהָב
bîrûshālām	wayyitten-'ōnesh	'al-hā'ārets	mē'āh	khikkar-keseph	wekhikkar	zāhāv
in Jerusalem	and he put a fine	on the land	one hundred	talents of silver	and a talent of	gold

	4566.521	6799	5412	881, 476	1158, 3086	8809	3086
34.	cj, v Hiphil impf 3ms	pn	pn	do, pn	*n ms*, pn	prep	pn
	וַיַּמְלֵךְ	פַּרְעֹה	נְכֹה	אֶת־אֶלְיָקִים	בֶּן־יֹאשִׁיָּהוּ	תַּחַת	יֹאשִׁיָּהוּ
	wayyamlēkh	par'ōh	nekhōh	'eth-'elyāqîm	ben-yō'shîyāhû	tachath	yō'shîyāhû
	and he caused to reign	Pharaoh	Neco	Eliakim	the son of Josiah	instead of	Josiah

1	5621.521	881, 8428	3181	881, 3168	4089.111
n ms, ps 3ms	cj, v Hiphil impf 3ms	do, n ms, ps 3ms	pn	cj, do, pn	v Qal pf 3ms
אָבִיו	וַיַּסֵּב	אֶת־שְׁמוֹ	יְהוֹיָקִים	וְאֶת־יְהוֹאָחָז	לָקָח
'āvîw	wayyassēv	'eth-shemô	yehôyāqîm	we'eth-yehô'āchāz	lāqāch
his father	and he caused to turn around	his name	Jehoiakim	and Jehoahaz	he took

971.121	4875	4322.121	8427		3826B	2174	5598.111
cj, v Qal impf 3ms	pn	cj, v Qal impf 3ms	adv	**35.**	cj, art, n ms	cj, art, n ms	v Qal pf 3ms
וַיָּבֹא	מִצְרַיִם	וַיָּמָת	שָׁם		וְהַכֶּסֶף	וְהַזָּהָב	נָתַן
wayyāvō'	mitsrayim	wayyāmāth	shām		wehakkeseph	wehazzāhāv	nāthan
and he came to	Egypt	and he died	there		and the silver	and the gold	he gave

3181	3937, 6799	395	6424.511	881, 800	3937, 5598.141	881, 3826B
pn	prep, pn	adv	v Hiphil pf 3ms	do, art, n fs	prep, v Qal inf con	do, art, n ms
יְהוֹיָקִים	לְפַרְעֹה	אַךְ	הֶעֱרִיךְ	אֶת־הָאָרֶץ	לָתֵת	אֶת־הַכֶּסֶף
yehôyāqîm	lephar'ōh	'akh	he'ĕrîkh	'eth-hā'ārets	lāthēth	'eth-hakkeseph
Jehoiakim	to Pharaoh	only	he assessed	the land	to give	the silver

31. Jehoahaz was twenty and three years old when he began to reign; and he reigned three months in Jerusalem. And his mother's name was Hamutal, the daughter of Jeremiah of Libnah: ... when he became king, *NIV* ... at his consecration, *Fenton* ... when he came to the throne, *JB* ... when he started to rule, *Beck*.

32. And he did that which was evil in the sight of the LORD, according to all that his fathers had done: ... he did wrong in the sight of, *Fenton* ... Jehoahaz disobeyed the Lord's will, after the fashion of his ancestors, *Knox* ... He did what was wrong in the eyes of the LORD, as his forefathers had done, *NEB* ... Following the example of his ancestors, he sinned against the LORD, *Good News*.

33. And Pharaoh-nechoh put him in bands at Riblah in the land of Hamath, that he might not reign in Jerusalem: ... put him in chains, *NIV* ... put him in prison, *NKJV* ... to prevent him from ruling, *NLT* ... removed him from the throne, *REB*.

and put the land to a tribute of an hundred talents of silver, and a talent of gold: ... he imposed on Judah a levy, *NIV* ... imposed on the land an indemnity, *REB* ... laid upon the land a tribute of, *RSV* ... took from the land a tax, *BB*.

34. And Pharaoh-nechoh made Eliakim the son of Josiah king in the room of Josiah his father, and turned his name to Johoiakim: ... to succeed his father and changed his name to, *Beck* ... in place of his father, *Berkeley* ... Pharaoh Neco appointed Eliakim, son of Josiah, king, *NAB*.

and took Jehoahaz away: and he came to Egypt, and died there: ... Joachaz was carried off to Egypt, where he died, *Knox* ... took Jehoahaz and went to Egypt, *NKJV* ... brought him to Egypt, where he died, *Anchor*.

35. And Jehoiakim gave the silver and the gold to Pharaoh; but he taxed the land to give the money according to the commandment of Pharaoh: ... taxed the country to give the silver Pharaoh demanded, *Beck* ... He assessed the land to pay the money in accordance with the demand of Pharaoh, *Berkeley* ... assessed the land so as to pay the amount set, *Anchor* ... he had to lay a forced levy on the land in order to give the money according to the demand, *Goodspeed*.

he exacted the silver and the gold of the people of the land, of every one according to his taxation, to give it unto Pharaoh-nechoh: ... By taxing everyone he got the silver and the gold from the people of the country to give it to Pharaoh Necho, *Beck* ... from each one according to his assessment, *Berkeley* ... From each according to his ability, *Goodspeed* ... he levied the silver and gold to be paid over to Pharaoh Necho from each according to his means, *JB*.

Bible—but we immediately recognize that all such gracious promises of divine provision and protection are entirely dependent on our own faithfulness and our own future submission to God's will. All promises (and seemingly all threats, except for the Great Tribulation) are, in the end, conditional. God is the potter and we are the clay, yes, but we have much to say through obedience about our future (cf., once again, Jeremiah's potter's house sermon, as presented in Jer. 18:1–12; cf. comments on 20:1). Let us never forget this painful and powerful lesson from the life and the death of King Josiah of Judah.

23:31–35. Jehoahaz's evil reign. As just noted, Jehoahaz was a younger son of Josiah. Jehoahaz's given name was probably "Shallum" (cf. Jer. 22:10ff), with the present name "Jehoahaz" being his throne name (once again, Albright preferred naming the present king "Jehoahaz II," with King Ahaz reckoned as "Jehoahaz I"; cf. comments on 16:1–4 [for the meaning of the name "Jehoahaz," cf. discussion of the name "Ahaz" above; both names undoubtedly come from the same Hebrew root, and mean "Yahweh has overcome," or the like]).

For the balance of the Book of 2 Kings, the final four kings of Judah will merit only brief discussions, mostly consisting of formulaic notices akin to those found in ch. 15. (These brief, formulaic notices are

881, 3826B	5241.111	3626, 6425	382	6799	6142, 6552
do, art, n ms	v Qal pf 3ms	prep, n ms, ps 3ms	n ms	pn	prep, *n ms*
אֶת־הַכֶּסֶף	נָגַשׂ	כְּעֶרְכּוֹ	אִישׁ	פַּרְעֹה	עַל־פִּי
'eth-hakkeseph	nāghas	ke'erkô	'îsh	phar'ōh	'al-pî
the silver	he levied	according to his assessment	each	Pharaoh	because of the mouth of

1158, 6465		5412	3937, 6799	3937, 5598.141	800	881, 6194	881, 2174
n ms, num	**36.**	pn	prep, pn	prep, v Qal inf con	art, n fs	do, *n ms*	cj, do, art, n ms
בֶּן־עֶשְׂרִים		נְכֹה	לְפַרְעֹה	לָתֵת	הָאָרֶץ	אֶת־עַם	וְאֶת־הַזָּהָב
ben-'esrîm		nekhōh	lephar'ōh	lāthēth	hā'ārets	'eth-'am	we'eth-hazzāhāv
a son of twenty		Neco	to Pharoah	to give	the land	the people of	and the gold

4566.111	8523	6462	259	904, 4566.141	3181	8523	2675
v Qal pf 3ms	n fs	num	cj, num	prep, v Qal inf con, ps 3ms	pn	n fs	cj, num
מָלַךְ	שָׁנָה	עֶשְׂרֵה	וְאַחַת	בְּמָלְכוֹ	יְהוֹיָקִים	שָׁנָה	וְחָמֵשׁ
mālakh	shānāh	'esrēh	we'achath	bemālekhô	yehôyāqîm	shānāh	wechāmēsh
he reigned	years	ten	and one	when his reigning	Jehoiakim	years	and five

4623, 7602	1351, 6546	2163	525	8428	904, 3503
prep, pn	*n fs*, pn	pn	n fs, ps 3ms	cj, *n ms*	prep, pn
מִן־רוּמָה	בַּת־פְּדָיָה	זְבִידָה	אִמּוֹ	וְשֵׁם	בִּירוּשָׁלָם
min-rûmāh	vath-pedhāyāh	zevîdhāh	'immô	weshēm	bîrûshālām
from Rumah	the daughter of Pedaiah	Zebudah	his mother	and the name of	in Jerusalem

3626, 3725	3176	904, 6084	7737	6449.121	
prep, n ms	pn	prep, *n fd*	art, adj	cj, v Qal impf 3ms	**37.**
כְּכֹל	יְהוָה	בְּעֵינֵי	הָרַע	וַיַּעַשׂ	
kekhōl	yehwāh	be'ênê	hāra'	wayya'as	
according to everything	Yahweh	in the eyes of	what is evil	and he did	

4567	5194	6148.111	904, 3219		1	866, 6449.116
n ms	pn	v Qal pf 3ms	prep, n mp, ps 3ms	**24:1**	n mp, ps 3ms	rel part, v Qal pf 3cp
מֶלֶךְ	נְבֻכַדְנֶאצַּר	עָלָה	בְּיָמָיו		אֲבֹתָיו	אֲשֶׁר־עָשׂוּ
melekh	nevukhadhne'tstsar	'ālāh	beyāmâv		'ăvōthâv	'ăsher-'āsû
the king of	Nebuchadnezzar	he went up	in his days		his fathers	that they had done

8178.121	8523	8421	5860	3181	2030.121, 3937	928
cj, v Qal impf 3ms	n fp	num	n ms	pn	cj, v Qal impf 3ms, prep, ps 3ms	pn
וַיָּשָׁב	שָׁנִים	שָׁלֹשׁ	עֶבֶד	יְהוֹיָקִים	וַיְהִי־לוֹ	בָּבֶל
wayyāshāv	shānîm	shālōsh	'evedh	yehôyāqîm	wayhî-lô	bāvel
then he turned back	years	three	a servant	Jehoiakim	and he was to him	Babylon

3908	881, 1447	904	3176	8365.321		4937.121, 904
pn	do, *n mp*	prep, ps 3ms	pn	cj, v Piel impf 3ms	**2.**	cj, v Qal impf 3ms, prep, ps 3ms
כַּשְׂדִּים	אֶת־גְּדוּדֵי	בּוֹ	יְהוָה	וַיְשַׁלַּח		וַיִּמְרָד־בּוֹ
khasdîm	'eth-gedhûdhê	bô	yehwāh	wayshallach		wayyimrādh-bô
the Chaldeans	the raiders of	against him	Yahweh	and He sent		and he rebelled against him

1158, 6205	1447	881	4262	1447	881	782	881, 1447
n mp, pn	*n mp*	cj, do	pn	*n mp*	cj, do	pn	cj, do, *n mp*
בְּנֵי־עַמּוֹן	גְּדוּדֵי	וְאֵת	מוֹאָב	גְּדוּדֵי	וְאֵת	אֲרָם	וְאֶת־גְּדוּדֵי
venê-'ammôn	gedhûdhê	we'ēth	mô'āv	gedhûdhê	we'ēth	'ărām	we'eth-gedhûdhê
the sons of Ammon	the raiders of	and	Moab	the raiders of	and	Aram	and the raiders of

3176	3626, 1745	3937, 6.541	904, 3171	8365.321
pn	prep, *n ms*	prep, v Hiphil inf con, ps 3ms	prep, pn	cj, v Piel impf 3ms, ps 3mp
יְהוָה	כִּדְבַר	לְהַאֲבִידוֹ	בִּיהוּדָה	וַיְשַׁלְּחֵם
yehwāh	kidhvar	leha'ăvîdhô	bîhûdhāh	wayshallechēm
Yahweh	according to the word of	to destroy it	against Judah	and He sent them out

36. Jehoiakim was twenty and five years old when he began to reign; and he reigned eleven years in Jerusalem. And his mother's name was Zebudah, the daughter of Pedaiah of Rumah: ... when he came to the throne, *NEB* ... when he became king, *NIV* ... at his coronation, *Fenton* ... he was ruling in Jerusalem for eleven years, *BB*.

37. And he did that which was evil in the sight of the LORD, according to all that his fathers had done: ... did what is displeasing to Yahweh, just as his ancestors had done, *JB* ... He, too, disobeyed the Lord's will, after the fashion of his ancestors, *Knox* ... He did what was wrong in the eyes of the LORD, *NEB* ... Following the example of his ancestors, Jehoiakim sinned against the LORD, *Good News*.

24:1. In his days Nebuchadnezzar king of Babylon came up, and Jehoiakim became his servant three years: ... king of Babylon marched forth, *Anchor* ... moved against him, *NAB* ... took the field, *NEB* ... invaded the land, *NIV.*

then he turned and rebelled against him: ... rebelled from him, *Fenton* ... he broke with him and revolted, *REB* ... then he changed his mind and rebelled, *NIV.*

2. And the LORD sent against him bands of the Chaldees, and bands of the Syrians, and bands of the Moabites, and bands of the children of Ammon, and sent them against Judah to destroy it, according to the word of the LORD, which he spake by his servants the prophets: ... sent upon him men of war out of Caldeye, out of Siria, out of the Moabites, and from the children of Ammon, *Tyndale* ... sent against him the troops of, *Fenton* ... sending them against Judah for its destruction, *BB* ... as the LORD had predicted by His servants, *Beck*.

---

even more evident in the parallel sections in the Book of 2 Chronicles.) And, as already noted, the destiny for the land of Judah was steadily and inevitably downhill, as she no longer enjoyed even relative independence from the major powers of the day. First Egypt (cf. v. 33 of the present passage), then Babylon (cf. 24:1, 10–17, and especially 24:7, "the king of Egypt came not again any more out of his land: for the king of Babylon had taken from the river of Egypt unto the River Euphrates") exercises dominion over this entire area—until the final demise of Jerusalem in the year 586, when King Nebuchadnezzar of Babylon finally destroyed the Temple completely. What a melancholy final few passages lie before us!

For the present King Jehoahaz, who reigned only some three months, we have the characteristic Judahite accession formula (v. 31; the "Jeremiah" mentioned there was almost certainly not the great prophet by that name, even though he was very active during this time; cf. *Anchor Bible Dictionary*, 3:684); then the customary judgment notice (v. 32; note that the judgment notices for these final Judahite kings are quite stereotypical, each mentioning the "evil in the eyes of Yahweh, just as his father[s] had done" [23:32, 37; 24:9; cf. v. 19, "just as Jehoiakim had done"; cf., also, comments on 8:18f]); and then a brief archival-style notice of his imprisonment by Pharaoh Neco (vv. 33f; we will hear much more about "Riblah in the land of Hamath" below, in connection with King Zedekiah [25:6, 21]). Pharaoh Neco placed his elder brother Jehoiakim on the throne, after changing his name from "Eliakim," and he carried off the deposed Jehoahaz into Egyptian exile, where the latter died. The present passage ends with the notice concerning the new king paying the tribute demanded by the Pharaoh—assessing the people of the land to raise the necessary funds ("a hundred talents of silver and a talent of gold"; concerning the size of the Hebrew talent, cf. on 5:19–25; also on 15:17–22, and 18:13–16). Once again, what a dreary account of Yahweh's seeming indifference to his now-doomed people! The time of Jehoahaz's brief reign is usually dated quite closely to the year 609. (Concerning the change of Jehoiakim's name, see immediately below.)

23:36–24:7. Jehoiakim, king of Judah. As just noted, Jehoiakim was an elder brother of the deposed King Jehoahaz. Even though Pharaoh Neco placed Jehoiakim on the throne as a puppet king, he did survive some eleven tumultuous years, indeed nearly outlasting Pharaoh Neco himself. (Jehoiakim's death is usually dated to the year 598, and Neco's death to 595.) A typical Judahite accession formula (23:36) leads into the familiar judgment formula for these late Judahite kings (v. 37; cf. on v. 32), with material comprising the first four verses of the next chapter, mostly involving various enemies of Judah which "Yahweh sent to destroy Judah" (24:2) "to remove them out of [Yahweh's] sight, for the sins of Manasseh, according to all that he did; and also for the innocent blood that he shed" (24:3f). A brief "further reference" notice (v. 5), burial notice (v. 6) and archival comment concerning the non-involvement of the king of Egypt (v. 7) bring the present passage to a close.

Once again, little is actually said here about this rather important and influential king (cf. Bright,

866	1744.311	904, 3135	5860	5204		395	6142, 6552
rel part	v Piel pf 3ms	prep, *n fs*	n mp, ps 3ms	art, n mp	**3.**	adv	prep, *n ms*
אֲשֶׁר	דִּבֶּר	בְּיַד	עֲבָדָיו	הַנְּבִיאִים		אַךְ	עַל־פִּי
'ăsher	dibber	beyadh	'ăvādhâv	hannevî'îm		'akh	'al-pî
which	He spoke	by the hand of	his servants	the prophets		surely	because of the mouth of

3176	2030.112	904, 3171	3937, 5681.541	4623, 6142	6686	904, 2496
pn	v Qal pf 3fs	prep, pn	prep, v Hiphil inf con	prep, prep	n mp, ps 3ms	prep, *n fp*
יְהוָה	הָיְתָה	בִּיהוּדָה	לְהָסִיר	מֵעַל	פָּנָיו	בְּחַטֹּאת
yehwāh	hāyethāh	bîhûdhāh	lehāsîr	mē'al	pānâv	bechattō'th
Yahweh	it was	on Judah	to remove	from beside	his presence	because of the sins of

4667	3626, 3725	866	6449.111		1612	1879, 5538
pn	prep, n ms	rel part	v Qal pf 3ms	**4.**	cj, cj	*n ms*, art, adj
מְנַשֶּׁה	כְּכֹל	אֲשֶׁר	עָשָׂה		וְגַם	דַּם־הַנָּקִי
menashsheh	kekhōl	'ăsher	'āsāh		wegham	dam-hannāqî
Manasseh	according to everything	that	he did		and also	the blood of the innocent

866	8581.111	4527.321	881, 3503	1879	5538	3940, 13.111
rel part	v Qal pf 3ms	cj, v Piel impf 3ms	do, pn	n ms	adj	cj, neg part, v Qal pf 3ms
אֲשֶׁר	שָׁפָךְ	וַיְמַלֵּא	אֶת־יְרוּשָׁלַם	דָּם	נָקִי	וְלֹא־אָבָה
'ăsher	shāphākh	waymallē'	'eth-yerûshālam	dām	nāqî	welō'-'āvāh
which	he shed	and he filled with	Jerusalem	blood	innocent	and He was not willing

3176	3937, 5739.141		3615	1745	3181	3725, 866
pn	prep, v Qal inf con	**5.**	cj, *n ms*	*n mp*	pn	cj, *adj*, rel part
יְהוָה	לִסְלֹחַ		וְיֶתֶר	דִּבְרֵי	יְהוֹיָקִים	וְכָל־אֲשֶׁר
yehwāh	lislōach		weyether	divrê	yehôyāqîm	wekhol-'ăsher
Yahweh	to forgive		and the remainder of	the events of	Jehoiakim	and all which

6449.111	1950B, 3940, 2062	3918.156	6142, 5809	1745	3219
v Qal pf 3ms	intrg part, neg part, pers pron	v Qal pass ptc mp	prep, *n ms*	*n mp*	art, n mp
עָשָׂה	הֲלֹא־הֵם	כְּתוּבִים	עַל־סֵפֶר	דִּבְרֵי	הַיָּמִים
'āsāh	hălō'-hēm	kethûvîm	'al-sēpher	divrê	hayyāmîm
he did	are they not	things written	on the scroll of	the events of	the days

3937, 4567	3171		8311.121	3181	6196, 1	4566.121
prep, *n mp*	pn	**6.**	cj, v Qal impf 3ms	pn	prep, n mp, ps 3ms	cj, v Qal impf 3ms
לְמַלְכֵי	יְהוּדָה		וַיִּשְׁכַּב	יְהוֹיָקִים	עִם־אֲבֹתָיו	וַיִּמְלֹךְ
lemalkhê	yehûdhāh		wayyishkav	yehôyāqîm	'im-'ăvōthâv	wayyimlōkh
of the kings of	Judah		and he lay	Jehoiakim	with his ancestors	and he reigned

3180	1158	8809		3940, 3362.511	5968	4567	4875
pn	n ms, ps 3ms	prep, ps 3ms	**7.**	cj, neg part, v Hiphil pf 3ms	adv	*n ms*	pn
יְהוֹיָכִין	בְּנוֹ	תַּחְתָּיו		וְלֹא־הֹסִיף	עוֹד	מֶלֶךְ	מִצְרַיִם
yehôyākhîn	benô	tachtâv		welō'-hôsiph	'ôdh	melekh	mitsrayim
Jehoiachin	his son	instead of him		and he did not do again	anymore	the king of	Egypt

3937, 3428.141	4623, 800	3706, 4089.111	4567	928	4623, 5337
prep, v Qal inf con	prep, n fs, ps 3ms	cj, v Qal pf 3ms	*n ms*	pn	prep, *n ms*
לָצֵאת	מֵאַרְצוֹ	כִּי־לָקַח	מֶלֶךְ	בָּבֶל	מִנַּחַל
lātsē'th	mē'artsô	kî-lāqach	melekh	bāvel	minnachal
to go out	from his land	because he had taken	the king of	Babylon	from the river of

4875	5912, 5282, 6828	3725	866	2030.112	3937, 4567	4875
pn	prep, *n ms*, pn	n ms	rel part	v Qal pf 3fs	prep, *n ms*	pn
מִצְרַיִם	עַד־נְהַר־פְּרָת	כֹּל	אֲשֶׁר	הָיְתָה	לְמֶלֶךְ	מִצְרָיִם
mitsrayim	'adh-nehar-perāth	kōl	'ăsher	hāyethāh	lemelekh	mitsrāyim
Egypt	unto the River Euphrates	everything	that	it was	to the king of	Egypt

3. Surely at the commandment of the LORD came this upon Judah, to remove them out of his sight, for the sins of Manasseh, according to all that he did: ... It was by the Lord's own decree that this befell; he would banish Juda from his presence, in return for all Manasses' sins, *Knox* ... for all the sinful practices of Manasseh, *Moffatt* ... All this happened to Judah in fulfilment of the LORD's purpose to banish them from his presence, *NEB* ... These disasters happened to Judah according to the LORD's command, *NLT*.

4. And also for the innocent blood that he shed: for he filled Jerusalem with innocent blood; which the LORD would not pardon: ... LORD was not willing to pardon, *NRSV* ... would not forgive, *NAB* ... he had flooded Jerusalem with innocent blood, and the LORD would not forgive him, *REB* ... especially because of all the innocent people he had killed, *Good News*.

5. Now the rest of the acts of Jehoiakim, and all that he did, are they not written in the book of the chronicles of the kings of Judah?: ... rest of the history of Jehoiakim, *Anchor* ... everything he did, isn't it written in the annals of Judah's kings?, *Beck* ... are they not told in the book of the chronicles, *Berkeley* ... As regards to the other affairs of Jehoiakim ... they are written in the history of events during the times of the kings, *Fenton*.

6. So Jehoiakim slept with his fathers: ... fell asleep with his ancestors, *JB* ... died, *Good News* ... rested with his ancestors, *NAB* ... with his forefathers, *NEB*.

and Jehoiachin his son reigned in his stead: ... succeeded him as king, *Good News* ... became king in his stead, *Goodspeed* ... the throne passed to his son, *Knox* ... reigned instead of him, *Moffatt*.

7. And the king of Egypt came not again any more out of his land: ... did not march out from his own country again, *NIV* ... did not come out of his land anymore, *NKJV* ... didn't again leave his country on a campaign, *Beck* ... never returned after that, *NLT*.

for the king of Babylon had taken from the river of Egypt unto the river Euphrates all that pertained to the king of Egypt: ... king of Babylon had taken all his territory, from the Wadi of Egypt to the Euphrates River, *NIV* ... had taken all that belonged to the king of Egypt from the Brook of Egypt, *NKJV* ... had stripped him of all he possessed from the wadi of Egypt to, *REB* ... occupied the entire area formerly claimed by Egypt, *NLT*.

History of Israel, 325f, who labels him "a petty tyrant unfit to rule"; cf. below). It seems the basic concern of the writer, after the death of Josiah, is to move directly to the exile, while noting in passing various reasons for Yahweh's abandonment of his own people (indeed, some reasons for Yahweh actively and repeatedly sending enemy "raiders" [24:2; gedhûdhê, HED #1447, used some four times in the verse] against his own people). Once again, of course, the sins of King Manasseh were emphasized. Because of that heinous king, the exile was both inevitable and entirely justifiable.

As already noted, Pharaoh Neco, who had set King Jehoiakim on the Judahite throne in the first place, also changed his name from "Eliakim" to "Jehoiakim." As Hobbs (WBC, 341) points out, presumably this Eliakim was willing to "toe the line" concerning Egyptian influence more than his younger brother Jehoahaz had been. In any case, the name "Eliakim" is particularly ironic, for it means "God raises up" or "May God establish" or the like. The name "Jehoiakim" also is derived from the same Hebrew verb "to establish" (qûm, HED #7251), but with the theophoric (divine name) element "Yahweh"; hence, "May Yahweh establish," or the like. In any case, Jehoiakim vacillated between loyalty to Egypt, then loyalty to Babylon (now under the control of Nebuchadnezzar, who is mentioned here for the first time in 2 Kings), then, seemingly, loyalty to neither (24:1; these vacillations seem to correspond quite closely to the waxing and waning of Babylonian power during this time).

The prophet Jeremiah had much to say about King Jehoiakim, none of it good. Certainly by now, any vestiges of Josiah's reform activity in 622 had disappeared completely. Surely Josiah's own untimely and embarrassing death, along with the dynastic instability which resulted in three kings on the throne in the single year 609 (Josiah, Jehoahaz and now Jehoiakim) contributed greatly to its demise. In any case, as the prophet Jeremiah amply attested, pagan practices soon reasserted themselves (cf. Jer. 7:16ff; 11:9–13; Ezek. 8). Jeremiah held up Jehoiakim for special censure when the king, early in his reign, apparently dissatisfied with his father's palace, built a new and finer one, wasting money and utilizing the hated corvée (i.e., forced labor of the Israelites, as found, e.g., in the days of King Solomon) to do it (Jer. 22:13–19; cf. Bright, *History of Israel*, 325f; also 222, concerning the despised institution of the corvée in Solomon's time). As the prophet Jeremiah concluded (Jer. 22:18f), "They shall not

8.	1158, 8470	6462	8523	3180	904, 4566.141	8421	2414
	n ms, num	num	n fs	pn	prep, v Qal inf con, ps 3ms	cj, num	n mp
	בֶּן־שְׁמֹנֶה	עֶשְׂרֵה	שָׁנָה	יְהוֹיָכִין	בְּמָלְכוֹ	וּשְׁלֹשָׁה	חֳדָשִׁים
	ben-shᵉmōneh	‘esrēh	shānāh	yᵉhôyākhîn	bᵉmālᵉkhô	ûshᵉlōshāh	chădhāshîm
	a son of eight	ten	years	Jehoiachin	when his reigning	and three	months

4566.111	904, 3503	8428	525	5363	1351, 501
v Qal pf 3ms	prep, pn	cj, *n ms*	n fs, ps 3ms	pn	*n fs*, pn
מָלַךְ	בִּירוּשָׁלָם	וְשֵׁם	אִמּוֹ	נְחֻשְׁתָּא	בַּת־אֶלְנָתָן
mālakh	bîrûshālām	wᵉshēm	’immô	nᵉchushtā’	vath-’elnāthān
he reigned	in Jerusalem	and the name of	his mother	Nehushta	the daughter of Elnathan

4623, 3503	9.	6449.121	7737	904, 6084	3176	3626, 3725
prep, pn		cj, v Qal impf 3ms	art, adj	prep, *n fd*	pn	prep, n ms
מִירוּשָׁלָם		וַיַּעַשׂ	הָרַע	בְּעֵינֵי	יְהוָה	כְּכֹל
mîrûshālām		wayya‘as	hāra‘	bᵉ‘ênê	yᵉhwāh	kᵉkhōl
from Jerusalem		and he did	what is evil	in the eyes of	Yahweh	according to everything

866, 6449.111	1	10.	904, 6496	2026	6148.111	5860
rel part, v Qal pf 3ms	n ms, ps 3ms		prep, art, n fs	art, dem pron	v Qal pf 3ms	*n mp*
אֲשֶׁר־עָשָׂה	אָבִיו		בָּעֵת	הַהִיא	עָלָה	עַבְדֵי
’āsher-‘āsāh	’āvîw		bā‘ēth	hahî’	‘ālāh	‘avdhê
that he had done	his father		at the time	the that	they went up to	the servants of

5194	4567, 928	3503	971.122	6111	904, 4857
pn	*n ms*, pn	pn	cj, v Qal impf 3fs	art, n fs	prep, art, n ms
נְבֻכַדְנֶאצַּר	מֶלֶךְ־בָּבֶל	יְרוּשָׁלָם	וַתָּבֹא	הָעִיר	בַּמָּצוֹר
nᵉvukhadhne’tstsar	melekh-bāvel	yᵉrûshālām	wattāvō’	hā‘îr	bammātsôr
Nebuchadnezzar	the king of Babylon	Jerusalem	and it entered	the city	into the siege

11.	971.121	5194	4567, 928	6142, 6111	5860
	cj, v Qal impf 3ms	pn	*n ms*, pn	prep, art, n fs	cj, n mp, ps 3ms
	וַיָּבֹא	נְבוּכַדְנֶאצַּר	מֶלֶךְ־בָּבֶל	עַל־הָעִיר	וַעֲבָדָיו
	wayyāvō’	nᵉvûkhadhne’tstsar	melekh-bāvel	‘al-hā‘îr	wa‘ăvādhâv
	and he came	Nebuchadnezzar	the king of Babylon	against the city	and his servants

6961.152	6142	12.	3428.121	3180	4567, 3171	6142, 4567
v Qal act ptc mp	prep, ps 3fs		cj, v Qal impf 3ms	pn	*n ms*, pn	prep, *n ms*
צָרִים	עָלֶיהָ		וַיֵּצֵא	יְהוֹיָכִין	מֶלֶךְ־יְהוּדָה	עַל־מֶלֶךְ
tsārîm	‘ālêāh		wayyētsē’	yᵉhôyākhîn	melekh-yᵉhûdhāh	‘al-melekh
laying siege	against it		and he went out	Jehoiachin	the king of Judah	against the king of

928	2000	525	5860	8015	5835
pn	pers pron	cj, n fs, ps 3ms	cj, n mp, ps 3ms	cj, n mp, ps 3ms	cj, n mp, ps 3ms
בָּבֶל	הוּא	וְאִמּוֹ	וַעֲבָדָיו	וְשָׂרָיו	וְסָרִיסָיו
bāvel	hû’	wᵉ’immô	wa‘ăvādhâv	wᵉsārâv	wᵉsārîsâv
Babylon	he	and his mother	and his servants	and his commanders	and his eunuchs

4089.121	881	4567	928	904, 8523	8470	3937, 4566.141
cj, v Qal impf 3ms	do, ps 3ms	*n ms*	pn	prep, *n fs*	num	prep, v Qal inf con, ps 3ms
וַיִּקַּח	אֹתוֹ	מֶלֶךְ	בָּבֶל	בִּשְׁנַת	שְׁמֹנֶה	לְמָלְכוֹ
wayyiqqach	’ōthô	melekh	bāvel	bishnath	shᵉmōneh	lᵉmālᵉkhô
and he took	him	the king of	Babylon	in the year of	eight	of his reigning

13.	3428.521	4623, 8427	881, 3725, 212	1041	3176
	cj, v Hiphil impf 3ms	prep, adv	do, *adj*, *n mp*	*n ms*	pn
	וַיּוֹצֵא	מִשָּׁם	אֶת־כָּל־אוֹצְרוֹת	בֵּית	יְהוָה
	wayyôtsē’	mishshām	’eth-kol-’ôtsrôth	bêth	yᵉhwāh
	and he caused to go out	from there	all the treasures of	the temple of	Yahweh

8. Jehoiachin was eighteen years old when he began to reign, and he reigned in Jerusalem three months. And his mother's name was Nehushta, the daughter of Elnathan of Jerusalem: ... when he became king, *Berkeley* ... at his coronation, *Fenton* ... when he came to the throne, *JB* ... started to rule, *Beck.*

9. And he did that which was evil in the sight of the LORD, according to all that his father had done: ... did wrong in the sight of, *Fenton* ... disobeyed the Lord's will no less than his father before him, *Knox* ... exactly as his father had done, *Moffatt* ... did what the LORD said was wrong, *NCV.*

10. At that time the servants of Nebuchadnezzar king of Babylon came up against Jerusalem, and the city was besieged: ... the troops of Nebuchadnezzar king of Babylon advanced on Jerusalem and besieged the city, *NEB* ... city came under siege, *Anchor* ... armies of Nebuchadnezzar came up to Jerusalem and the town was shut in on every side, *BB* ... attacked Jerusalem, *NAB.*

11. And Nebuchadnezzar king of Babylon came against the city, and his servants did besiege it: ... laid siege to it, *KJVII* ... came to the city, *NASB* ... came up to the city, *NIV* ... with his servants to assault it, *Douay.*

12. And Jehoiachin the king of Judah went out to the king of Babylon, he, and his mother, and his servants, and his princes, and his officers: ... surrendered to the king, *REB* ... gave himself up, *NRSV.*

and the king of Babylon took him in the eighth year of his reign: ... took him prisoner, *NKJV* ... captured him, *Fenton* ... took him captive, *Goodspeed* ... year of his rule, *Beck.*

13. And he carried out thence all the treasures of the house of the LORD, and the treasures of the king's house: ... carried off from there, *Anchor* ... took away all the stored wealth, *BB* ... All the treasures of temple and palace he took away, *Knox* ... carried off all the treasures of the temple of the Eternal and the treasures of the royal palace, *Moffatt.*

and cut in pieces all the vessels of gold which Solomon king of Israel had made in the temple of the LORD, as the LORD had said: ... he broke up all the gold objects, *Anchor* ... gold utensils, *Good News* ... golden furnishings, *JB* ... golden ornaments, *Knox.*

---

lament for him, ... He [Jehoiakim] shall be buried with the burial of an ass, drawn and cast forth beyond the gates of Jerusalem" (cf., also, Jer. 36:30). (Concerning Jehoiakim's reciprocal contempt for Jeremiah, cf. Jer. 36:1–26, where the king systematically and repeatedly casts Jeremiah's written words into the fire.) In fact, we do not know much about the actual circumstances surrounding Jehoiakim's death, only that it was, in a way, quite timely inasmuch as it corresponded with what is usually termed the "first" exile of the Judahites to Babylon in 598 or early 597.

24:8–17. Jehoiachin, king of Judah. In brief fashion, analogous to the previous passage concerning his father Jehoiakim, King Jehoiachin is introduced with the by-now familiar formulas, and then, after only a three-month reign, we find discussion of his surrender and subsequent exile under Nebuchadnezzar. Once again, an accession formula (v. 8) leads into the stereotypical judgment formula for these last several kings of Judah (v. 9; cf. on 23:32). Archival material concerning King Jehoiachin's surrender and the "first" exile of the Judahites then takes up essentially all of the rest of the present passage (vv. 10–17). We have no burial formula for this king since he remained alive and well (although still very much in exile) at the end of the present Book (cf. 25:27–30). Jeremiah 52:34, however, reminds us that King Jehoiachin did die in exile, far away from his native land. He was gone, but he was certainly not forgotten. The chronological framework of the Book of Ezekiel uniformly cites the particular "year of exile" of King Jehoiachin in its dating of Ezekiel's oracles (cf. Ezek. 1:2; 8:1; 20:1, 24:1; 26:1; etc.). Also, Zerubbabel, the Davidic leader of the early post-exilic Judahite community was apparently Jehoiachin's grandson (cf. 1 Chr. 3:17ff). As Hag. 2:23 reminds us, the Davidic hope lived on in Zerubbabel (note that the "signet ring" image there represented a conscious and glorious reversal of Jeremiah's prophecy against Jehoiachin in Jer. 22:24–30, especially v. 24).

The name "Jehoiachin" is spelled differently in Jeremiah and in 1 Chronicles: "Coniah" in Jer. 22:24, 28; etc.; and "Jeconiah" in 1 Chr. 3:16f; Jer. 24:1; 28:4; etc. But all these variants reflect the same theophoric element (some form of the name Yahweh), plus the Hebrew root kûn, HED #3679, "to be established," "to be firm," or the like. Hence, the name probably means "May Yahweh be enduring," or "May Yahweh confirm," a prayer which was not answered literally in regard to a lengthy reign for this king, but was indeed answered indirectly in his descendants surviving the exile. In cuneiform documents dating

212	1041	4567	7401.321	881, 3725, 3747	2174
cj, *n mp*	*n ms*	art, n ms	cj, v Piel impf 3ms	do, *adj*, *n mp*	art, n ms
וְאוֹצְרוֹת	בֵּית	הַמֶּלֶךְ	וַיְקַצֵּץ	אֶת־כָּל־כְּלֵי	הַזָּהָב
we'ôtsrôth	bêth	hammelekh	wayqatstsēts	'eth-kol-kelê	hazzāhāv
and the treasures of	the household of	the king	and he cut into pieces	all the vessels of	the gold

866	6449.111	8406	4567, 3547	904, 2033	3176	3626, 866
rel part	v Qal pf 3ms	pn	*n ms*, pn	prep, *n ms*	pn	prep, rel part
אֲשֶׁר	עָשָׂה	שְׁלֹמֹה	מֶלֶךְ־יִשְׂרָאֵל	בְּהֵיכַל	יְהוָה	כַּאֲשֶׁר
'ăsher	'āsāh	shelōmōh	melekh-yisrā'ēl	behêkhal	yehwāh	ka'ăsher
which	he had made	Solomon	the king of Israel	in the temple of	Yahweh	just as

1744.311	3176	**14.** 1580.511	881, 3725, 3503	881, 3725, 8015	881
v Piel pf 3ms	pn	cj, v Hiphil pf 3ms	do, *adj*, pn	cj, do, *adj*, art, n mp	cj, do
דִּבֶּר	יְהוָה	וְהִגְלָה	אֶת־כָּל־יְרוּשָׁלַםִ	וְאֶת־כָּל־הַשָּׂרִים	וְאֵת
dibber	yehwāh	wehighlāh	'eth-kol-yerûshālam	we'eth-kol-hassārîm	we'ēth
He had spoken	Yahweh	and he deported	all Jerusalem	and all the commanders	and

3725, 1399	2524	6463	512	1580.151	3725, 2900
adj, *n mp*	art, n ms	num	num	v Qal act ptc ms	cj, *adj*, art, n ms
כָּל־גִּבּוֹרֵי	הַחַיִל	עֲשָׂרָה	אֲלָפִים	גּוֹלֶה	וְכָל־הֶחָרָשׁ
kol-gibbôrê	hachayil	'ăsārāh	'ălāphîm	gôleh	wekhol-hechārāsh
all the warriors of	the army	ten	thousands	going into exile	and all the craftsmen

4674	3940	8080.211	2190	1864	6194, 800
cj, art, n ms	neg part	v Niphal pf 3ms	prep	*n fs*	*n ms*, art, n fs
וְהַמַּסְגֵּר	לֹא	נִשְׁאַר	זוּלַת	דַּלַּת	עַם־הָאָרֶץ
wehammasgēr	lō'	nish'ar	zûlath	dallath	'am-hā'ārets
and all the smiths	not	he was left	except	the poor of	the people of the land

15. 1580.521	881, 2180	928	881, 525	4567	881, 5571
cj, v Hiphil impf 3ms	do, pn	pn	cj, do, *n fs*	art, n ms	cj, do, *n fp*
וַיֶּגֶל	אֶת־יְהוֹיָכִין	בָּבֶלָה	וְאֶת־אֵם	הַמֶּלֶךְ	וְאֶת־נְשֵׁי
wayyeghel	'eth-yehôyākhîn	bāvelāh	we'eth-'ēm	hammelekh	we'eth-neshê
and he deported	Jehoiachin	to Babylon	and the mother of	the king	and the wives of

4567	881, 5835	881	191	800	2050.511	1506
art, n ms	cj, do, n mp, ps 3ms	cj, do	*n mp*	art, n fs	v Hiphil pf 3ms	n fs
הַמֶּלֶךְ	וְאֶת־סָרִיסָיו	וְאֵת	אוּלֵי	הָאָרֶץ	הוֹלִיךְ	גּוֹלָה
hammelekh	we'eth-sārîsâv	we'ēth	'ûlê	hā'ārets	hôlîkh	gôlāh
the king	and his eunuchs	and	the prominent men of	the land	he caused to go	exile

4623, 3503	928	**16.** 881	3725, 596	2524	8124	512
prep, pn	pn	cj, do	*adj*, *n mp*	art, n ms	num	num
מִירוּשָׁלַםִ	בָּבֶלָה	וְאֵת	כָּל־אַנְשֵׁי	הַחַיִל	שִׁבְעַת	אֲלָפִים
mîrûshālam	bāvelāh	we'ēth	kol-'anshê	hachayil	shiv'ath	'ălāphîm
from Jerusalem	into Babylon	and	all the men of	the army	seven	thousands

2900	4674	512	3725	1399	6449.152
cj, art, n ms	cj, art, n ms	num	art, *n ms*	adj	*v Qal act ptc mp*
וְהֶחָרָשׁ	וְהַמַּסְגֵּר	אֶלֶף	הַכֹּל	גִּבּוֹרִים	עֹשֵׂי
wehechārāsh	wehammasgēr	'eleph	hakkōl	gibbôrîm	'ōsê
and the craftsmen	and the smiths	one thousand	the entirety of	the mighty	the makers of

4560	971.521	4567, 928	1506	928
n fs	cj, v Hiphil impf 3ms, ps 3mp	*n ms*, pn	n fs	pn
מִלְחָמָה	וַיְבִיאֵם	מֶלֶךְ־בָּבֶל	גּוֹלָה	בָּבֶלָה
milchāmāh	wayvî'ēm	melekh-bāvel	gôlāh	bāvelāh
war	and he brought them	the king of Babylon	exile	to Babylon

14. And he carried away all Jerusalem: ... deported all Jerusalem, *NAB* ... carried the people of Jerusalem into exile, *NEB* ... carried into captivity, *NKJV* ... took away all the people, *BB*.

and all the princes, and all the mighty men of valour: ... officers and men of the army, *NAB* ... all the valiant men of the army, *Douay* ... officers and the fighting men, *NEB* ... captains and all the mighty men, *NKJV*.

even ten thousand captives, and all the craftsmen and smiths: ... ten thousand in number, *NAB* ... ten thousand prisoners, *BB* ... craftsmen and artisans, *NIV* ... craftsmen and joiners, *Tyndale*.

none remained, save the poorest sort of the people of the land: ... None were left among the people of the land except the poor, *NAB* ... only the weakest class of people were left, *NEB* ... Only the poorest people of the land were left, *NIV* ... He left none except the lower class of the country, *Fenton*.

15. And he carried away Jehoiachin to Babylon, and the king's mother, and the king's wives, and his officers, and the mighty of the land: ... He deported Jehoiachin, *JB* ... led Jehoiachin away into exile to Babylon, *NASB* ... leading men of the land, *Berkeley* ... chief men, *Goodspeed* ... the elite of the land, *NRSV*.

those carried he into captivity from Jerusalem to Babylon: ... he caused to go into captivity, *Goodspeed* ... he made them all leave Jerusalem for exile in Babylon, *JB* ... he led away into exile from Jerusalem to Babylon, *NASB*.

16. And all the men of might, even seven thousand, and craftsmen and smiths a thousand: ... all the warriors, seven thousand, *Anchor* ... all the men of war, *BB* ... men of valor, *Berkeley* ... mighty men, *KJVII*.

all that were strong and apt for war: ... all brave men, trained soldiers, *Anchor* ... all of them strong and able to take up arms, *BB* ... all mighty men trained to fight, *Berkeley* ... all of them able-bodied men fit for military duty, *Good News*.

even them the king of Babylon brought captive to Babylon: ... brought them as exiles to Babylon, *Anchor* ... took away as prisoners into Babylon, *BB* ... carried into captivity from Jerusalem to Babylon, *KJVII* ... led them captives into Babylon, *Douay*.

---

to the year 592, the thirteenth year of Nebuchadnezzar, the exiled king Jehoiachin and his five sons are included as recipients of food rations in Babylon. There his name seems to be spelled "Yahu-kîn," probably the Aramaic equivalent to "Jehoiachin" (so R. Zadok, as cited in Cogan and Tadmor).

Although the length of Nebuchadnezzar's siege is unknown, we do know that he captured Jerusalem in the second of Adar in year seven of his reign (equivalent to March 15/16, 597, according to Wiseman, TOTC, 309; also cf. Cogan and Tadmor). But it was probably some months later that the exiles actually left the city of Jerusalem for Babylon, hence the "eighth year" of v. 12 (Cogan and Tadmor; they note that such a dating in terms of the regnal year of a foreign ruler is unusual and probably reflects a writer familiar with the official practice of the conquering Babylonians, perhaps one even in their employ [cf., also, Hobbs, WBC, 352]). Most of the precious vessels in Temple and palace were removed at this time as spoils of war (v. 13). Jeremiah 27:19–22, however, indicates that some of the temple furnishings and vessels remained, inasmuch as "Nebuchadrezzar clearly made provision for the continuation of the economic and political life of Judah after the first deportation, albeit in a much reduced form, by the appointment of Zedekiah as king" (Hobbs).

Many of the privileged classes were carried off into exile as well (vv. 14ff). Among those, was the prophet Ezekiel (cf., e.g., Ezek. 1:1f). Indeed, many of Ezekiel's prophecies focused on the interplay of exiles versus non-exiles, as so many of the Judahites languished in a foreign land, while others were privileged to take their place back in Jerusalem. ("This city is a cooking pot, and we are the meat," the non-exiles boast in Ezek. 11:3, but Yahweh reminds them in v. 11 of that same chapter, "This city will not be a pot for you, nor will you be the meat in it; I will execute judgment on you at the borders of Israel.")

The present passage closes with the notice that Jehoiachin's "uncle" (thus another son of Josiah), one "Mattaniah" was put on the throne by Nebuchadnezzar and renamed "Zedekiah" (see below). Although he was apparently never recognized as legitimate king by the prophet Ezekiel, for example (Ezekiel, who never even mentions Zedekiah by name, also never refers to him as "king," but only "prince"; cf. Ezek. 12:10, 12; also 21:25); however, here he is recognized as king, and the reader is apprised of his dubious distinction of being the last king of the Davidic line to sit on the throne in David's city, Jerusalem. It is to this final king of Judah that we now must turn.

17.	4566.521	4567, 928	881, 5157	1782	8809
	cj, v Hiphil impf 3ms	*n ms*, pn	do, pn	n ms, ps 3ms	prep, ps 3ms
	וַיַּמְלֵךְ	מֶלֶךְ־בָּבֶל	אֶת־מַתַּנְיָה	דֹּדוֹ	תַּחְתָּיו
	wayyamlēkh	melekh-bāvel	'eth-mattanyāh	dhōdhô	tachtâv
	and he caused to rule	the king of Babylon	Mattaniah	his uncle	instead of him

5621.521	881, 8428	6931	18.	1158, 6465	259	8523
cj, v Hiphil impf 3ms	do, n ms, ps 3ms	pn		*n ms*, num	cj, num	n fs
וַיַּסֵּב	אֶת־שְׁמוֹ	צִדְקִיָּהוּ		בֶּן־עֶשְׂרִים	וְאַחַת	שָׁנָה
wayyassēv	'eth-shemô	tsidhqîyāhû		ben-'esrîm	we'achath	shānāh
and he caused to turn around	his name	Zedekiah		a son of twenty	and one	years

6931	904, 4566.141	259	6462	8523	4566.111	904, 3503
pn	prep, v Qal inf con, ps 3ms	cj, num	num	n fs	v Qal pf 3ms	prep, pn
צִדְקִיָּהוּ	בְּמָלְכוֹ	וְאַחַת	עֶשְׂרֵה	שָׁנָה	מָלַךְ	בִּירוּשָׁלָם
tsidhqîyāhû	vemālekhô	we'achath	'esrēh	shānāh	mālakh	bîrûshālām
Zedekiah	when his reigning	and one	ten	years	he reigned	in Jerusalem

8428	525	2638	1351, 3532	4623, 3975	19.	6449.121
cj, *n ms*	n fs, ps 3ms	pn	*n fs*, pn	prep, pn		cj, v Qal impf 3ms
וְשֵׁם	אִמּוֹ	חֲמִיטַל	בַּת־יִרְמְיָהוּ	מִלִּבְנָה		וַיַּעַשׂ
weshēm	'immô	chămîṭal	bath-yirmeyāhû	millivnāh		wayya'as
and the name of	his mother	Hamutal	the daughter from Jeremiah	from Libnah		and he did

7737	904, 6084	3176	3626, 3725	866, 6449.111	3181
art, adj	prep, *n fd*	pn	prep, n ms	rel part, v Qal pf 3ms	pn
הָרַע	בְּעֵינֵי	יְהוָה	כְּכֹל	אֲשֶׁר־עָשָׂה	יְהוֹיָקִים
hāra'	be'ênê	yehwāh	kekhōl	'ăsher-'āsāh	yehôyāqîm
what is evil	in the eyes of	Yahweh	according to everything	that he had done	Jehoiakim

20.	3706	6142, 653	3176	2030.112	904, 3503	904, 3171
	cj	prep, *n ms*	pn	v Qal pf 3fs	prep, pn	cj, prep, pn
	כִּי	עַל־אַף	יְהוָה	הָיְתָה	בִּירוּשָׁלַם	וּבִיהוּדָה
	kî	'al-'aph	yehwāh	hāyethāh	vîrûshālam	ûvîhûdhāh
	because	on account of the anger of	Yahweh	it was	in Jerusalem	and in Judah

5912, 8390.541	881	4623, 6142	6686	4937.121	6931
adv, v Hiphil inf con, ps 3ms	do, ps 3mp	prep, prep	n mp, ps 3ms	cj, v Qal impf 3ms	pn
עַד־הִשְׁלִכוֹ	אֹתָם	מֵעַל	פָּנָיו	וַיִּמְרֹד	צִדְקִיָּהוּ
'adh-hishlikhô	'ōthām	mē'al	pānâv	wayyimrōdh	tsidhqîyāhû
until his throwing them out	them	from beside	his presence	and he rebelled	Zedekiah

904, 4567	928	25:1	2030.121	904, 8523	9012
prep, *n ms*	pn		cj, v Qal impf 3ms	prep, *n fs*	art, num
בְּמֶלֶךְ	בָּבֶל		וַיְהִי	בִּשְׁנַת	הַתְּשִׁיעִית
bemelekh	bāvel		wayhî	vishnath	hatteshî'îth
against the king of	Babylon		and it was	in the year of	the ninth

3937, 4566.141	904, 2414	6455	904, 6452	3937, 2414	971.111
prep, v Qal inf con, ps 3ms	prep, art, n ms	art, num	prep, art, num	prep, art, n ms	v Qal pf 3ms
לְמָלְכוֹ	בַּחֹדֶשׁ	הָעֲשִׂירִי	בֶּעָשׂוֹר	לַחֹדֶשׁ	בָּא
lemālekhô	bachōdhesh	hā'ăsîrî	be'āsôr	lachōdhesh	bā'
of his reigning	in the month	the tenth	on the tenth	of the month	he came

5194	4567, 928	2000	3725, 2524	6142, 3503
pn	*n ms*, pn	pers pron	cj, *adj*, n ms, ps 3ms	prep, pn
נְבֻכַדְנֶאצַּר	מֶלֶךְ־בָּבֶל	הוּא	וְכָל־חֵילוֹ	עַל־יְרוּשָׁלַם
nevukhadhne'tstsar	melekh-bāvel	hû'	wekhol-chêlô	'al-yerûshālam
Nebuchadnezzar	the king of Babylon	he	and all his army	against Jerusalem

17. And the king of Babylon made Mattaniah his father's brother king in his stead, and changed his name to Zedekiah: ... king in his place, *NKJV* ... king instead of him, *Moffatt* ... made the king's uncle Mattaniah the king to succeed him, *Beck* ... king of Babylon deposed Jehoiachin in favour of his paternal uncle Mattaniah, whose name he changed, *JB*.

18. Zedekiah was twenty and one years old when he began to reign, and he reigned eleven years in Jerusalem. And his mother's name was Hamutal, the daughter of Jeremiah of Libnah: ... twenty-one years old when he became king, *NAB* ... he came to the throne, *REB* ... he started to rule, *Beck* ... at his coronation, *Fenton*.

19. And he did that which was evil in the sight of the LORD, according to all that Jehoiakim had done: ... He disobeyed the Lord's will, as Joakim had, *Knox* ... did what was wrong in the eyes of the LORD, *NEB* ... exactly as Jehoiakim had done, *Moffatt* ... King Zedekiah sinned against the LORD, just as King Jehoiakim had done, *Good News*.

20. For through the anger of the LORD it came to pass in Jerusalem and Judah, until he had cast them out from his presence, that Zedekiah rebelled against the king of Babylon: ... Because of Yahweh's wrath did these things happen to Jerusalem and Judah, until he rid himself of them, *Anchor* ... till he had sent them all away from before him: and Zedekiah took up arms against the king of Babylon, *BB* ... Zedekiah happened to rebel against the king of Babylon in Jerusalem and in Judah, until God had put them out of His presence, *KJVII* ... the Lord was angry against Jerusalem and against Juda, till he cast them out from his face, *Douay*.

25:1. And it came to pass in the ninth year of his reign, in the tenth month, in the tenth day of the month, that Nebuchadnezzar king of Babylon came, he, and all his host, against Jerusalem: ... came to Jerusalem with his whole army, *Beck* ... attacked Jerusalem, *Good News* ... advanced on Jerusalem with his entire army, *JB*.

and pitched against it: ... camped against it, *Beck* ... pitched camp in front of the city, *JB* ... set up against it, *KJVII* ... invested it, *NEB* ... surrounded it, *Knox*.

and they built forts against it round about: ... built a surrounding wall against it, *Fenton* ... built siege walls all around it, *Beck* ... constructed a siege-wall, *Berkeley* ... erected watch-towers against it on every side, *NEB* ... threw up earthworks round it, *JB*.

24:18–25:21. *Zedekiah and the fall of Jerusalem. Once again, we move pell-mell to the end, with only the shortest of regnal summaries to detain us. The accession formula of 24:18, with its somewhat awkward age at accession (i.e., in connection with the listing of the brothers in 1 Chr. 3:15; cf. Japhet, OTL, 97f), leads into the final Judahite judgment formula of 24:19 (cf. on 23:32). Virtually no details of the eleven-year reign of this last king are to be found here except for the vague note concerning his "rebellion" against the king of Babylon (24:20) and its gruesome results (25:1–7). Lengthier summaries of the aftermath of Nebuchadnezzar's devastating victory take up the rest of the present passage (25:8–21), which ends with the bleak summary, "So Judah went into captivity, away from her land" (25:21b). From Solomon to the exile—this phrase encompasses the Books of 1–2 Kings in a nutshell. (Much of the material in this section to the end of the present Book is paralleled in the Book of Jeremiah, as the following correspondences will indicate: 2 Ki. 24:18ff; Jer. 52:1ff; 2 Ki. 25:1–12; Jer. 39:1–10; 52:4–16; 2 Ki. 25:13–21; Jer. 52:17–27; 2 Ki. 25:22–26; Jer. 40:5–9; 41:1ff; 2 Ki. 25:27–30; Jer. 52:31–34 [in both cases, the conclusion of the Book].*

24:18–20a. Zedekiah's reign and God's anger. The name "Zedekiah" (tsidhqiyāhû, HED #6931) means, incongruously, "Yahweh is my righteousness," or the like. As already noted, it was the throne name of the son of Josiah originally named "Mattaniah" (itself meaning "gift of Yahweh"; cf. the name of "Mattan" priest of Baal in the days of Joash, as noted above, on 11:17–21).

24:20b–25:7. Defeat of Jerusalem and judgment on Zedekiah. After a brief notice concerning King Zedekiah's rebellion against Babylon, we immediately move into the final bleak days of Zedekiah's reign. Additional material in the Book of Jeremiah helps fill in the setting considerably. It appears that Zedekiah once again sought help from Egypt, even though he was a sworn vassal of Babylon and was indeed placed on the throne by Nebuchadnezzar. As this evidence indicates, Zedekiah seemed to oscillate between continued subservience to Babylon and open revolt against her. "The picture that emerges is that of a weakling king, who sought the prophet Jeremiah's guidance, yet was drawn into rebellion against his overlord at the urging of his court. It should be noted that these extremists were part of the new leadership which had replaced the veteran nobility, exiled together with Jehoiachin in 597. The experience of that earlier revolt did not result in a moderate policy on the part of Zedekiah and Judah's leaders" (Cogan and Tadmor, AB, 322). As already noted, Egypt

2684.121	6142	1161.126	6142	1842	5623		971.122
cj, v Qal impf 3ms	prep, ps 3fs	cj, v Qal impf 3mp	prep, ps 3fs	n ms	adv	**2.**	cj, v Qal impf 3fs
וַיִּחַן	עָלֶיהָ	וַיִּבְנוּ	עָלֶיהָ	דָּיֵק	סָבִיב		וַתָּבֹא
wayyichan	'ālêāh	wayyivnû	'ālêāh	dāyēq	sāvîv		wattāvō'
and he encamped	beside it	and they built	beside it	siegeworks	all around		and it entered

6111	904, 4857	5912	6490	6462	8523	3937, 4567	6931		904, 9013
art, n fs	prep, art, n ms	adv	num	num	n fs	prep, art, n ms	pn	**3.**	prep, num
הָעִיר	בַּמָּצוֹר	עַד	עַשְׁתֵּי	עֶשְׂרֵה	שָׁנָה	לַמֶּלֶךְ	צִדְקִיָּהוּ		בְּתִשְׁעָה
hā'îr	bammātsôr	'adh	'ashtê	'esrēh	shānāh	lammelekh	tsidhqîyāhû		bethish'āh
the city	into the siege	until	eleventh	ten	year	of the king	Zedekiah		on nine

3937, 2414	2480.121	7743	904, 6111	3940, 2030.111	4035
prep, art, n ms	cj, v Qal impf 3ms	art, n ms	prep, art, n fs	cj, neg part, v Qal pf 3ms	n ms
לַחֹדֶשׁ	וַיֶּחֱזַק	הָרָעָב	בָּעִיר	וְלֹא־הָיָה	לֶחֶם
lachōdhesh	wayyechĕzaq	hārā'āv	bā'îr	welō'-hāyāh	lechem
of the month	and it was severe	the famine	in the city	and there was not	food

3937, 6194	800		1260.222	6111	3725, 596	4560
prep, *n ms*	art, n fs	**4.**	cj, v Niphal impf 3fs	art, n fs	cj, *adj*, *n mp*	art, n fs
לְעַם	הָאָרֶץ		וַתִּבָּקַע	הָעִיר	וְכָל־אַנְשֵׁי	הַמִּלְחָמָה
le'am	hā'ārets		wattibbāqa'	hā'îr	wekhol-'anshê	hammilchāmāh
for the people of	the land		and it was broken into	the city	and all the men of	the war

4050	1932	8554	1033	2440	866	6142, 1629	4567
art, n ms	*n ms*	n ms	prep	art, n fd	rel part	prep, *n ms*	art, n ms
הַלַּיְלָה	דֶּרֶךְ	שַׁעַר	בֵּין	הַחֹמֹתַיִם	אֲשֶׁר	עַל־גַּן	הַמֶּלֶךְ
hallaylāh	derekh	sha'ar	bên	hachōmōthayim	'ăsher	'al-gan	hammelekh
at night	the way of	the gate	between	the two walls	which	beside the garden of	the king

3908	6142, 6111	5623	2050.121	1932	6400
cj, pn	prep, art, n fs	adv	cj, v Qal impf 3ms	*n ms*	art, n ms
וְכַשְׂדִּים	עַל־הָעִיר	סָבִיב	וַיֵּלֶךְ	דֶּרֶךְ	הָעֲרָבָה
wekhasdîm	'al-hā'îr	sāvîv	wayyēlekh	derekh	hā'ărāvāh
and the Chaldeans	opposite the city	all around	and they went	the way of	the Arabah

	7579.126	2524, 3908	313	4567	5560.526	881
5.	cj, v Qal impf 3mp	*n ms*, pn	prep	art, n ms	cj, v Hiphil impf 3mp	do, ps 3ms
	וַיִּרְדְּפוּ	חֵיל־כַּשְׂדִּים	אַחַר	הַמֶּלֶךְ	וַיַּשִּׂגוּ	אֹתוֹ
	wayyirdephû	chêl-kasdîm	'achar	hammelekh	wayyassighû	'ōthô
	and they pursued	the army of the Chaldeans	after	the king	and they overtook	him

904, 6400	3509	3725, 2524	5492.216	4623, 6142
prep, *n fp*	pn	cj, *adj*, n ms, ps 3ms	v Niphal pf 3cp	prep, prep, ps 3ms
בְּעַרְבוֹת	יְרֵחוֹ	וְכָל־חֵילוֹ	נָפֹצוּ	מֵעָלָיו
be'arvôth	yerēchô	wekhol-chêlô	nāphōtsû	mē'ālâv
on the plains of	Jericho	and all his army	they were scattered	from beside him

	8945.126	881, 4567	6148.526	881	420, 4567	928
6.	cj, v Qal impf 3mp	do, art, n ms	cj, v Hiphil impf 3mp	do, ps 3ms	prep, *n ms*	pn
	וַיִּתְפְּשׂוּ	אֶת־הַמֶּלֶךְ	וַיַּעֲלוּ	אֹתוֹ	אֶל־מֶלֶךְ	בָּבֶל
	wayyithpesû	'eth-hammelekh	wayya'ălû	'ōthô	'el-melekh	bāvel
	and they captured	the king	and they brought up	him	to the king of	Babylon

7540	1744.326	882	5122		881, 1158	6931	8250.116
pn	cj, v Piel impf 3mp	prep, ps 3ms	n ms	**7.**	cj, do, *n mp*	pn	v Qal pf 3cp
רִבְלָתָה	וַיְדַבְּרוּ	אִתּוֹ	מִשְׁפָּט		וְאֶת־בְּנֵי	צִדְקִיָּהוּ	שָׁחֲטוּ
rivlāthāh	waydhabberû	'ittô	mishpāṭ		we'eth-benê	tsidhqîyāhû	shāchăṭû
to Riblah	and they spoke	with him	a judgment		and the sons of	Zedekiah	they slaughtered

2. And the city was besieged unto the eleventh year of king Zedekiah: ... The siege of the city continued until the eleventh year, *NAB* ... city was shut up and besieged, *Douay* ... kept under siege, *NIV* ... the town was shut in by their forces till, *BB*.

3. And on the ninth day of the fourth month the famine prevailed in the city, and there was no bread for the people of the land: ... the hunger became severe in the city, *Anchor* ... there was no food for the common people, *Beck* ... famine was sore in the city, *MAST* ... famine was so bad that the people had nothing left to eat, *Good News*.

4. And the city was broken up, and all the men of war fled by night by the way of the gate between two walls, which is by the king's garden: ... a breach was made in the walls of the city, *Moffatt* ... city was broken into, *NASB* ... city wall was broken through, *NIV* ... a section of the city wall was broken down, *NLT*.

(now the Chaldees were against the city round about:): ... Chaldaeans had invested the city on all sides, *Moffatt* ... besieged the city round about, *Douay* ... were all around, *NASB* ... surrounding, *NIV*.

and the king went the way toward the plain: ... fled by the way that leadeth to the plains of the wilderness, *Douay* ... They fled toward the Arabah, *NIV* ... king went by way of the plain, *NKJV* ... went straight toward the desert, *Tyndale*.

5. And the army of the Chaldees pursued after the king, and overtook him in the plains of Jericho: and all his army were scattered from him: ... overtook him in the lowlands of Jericho, *REB* ... his army was scattered, deserting him, *NRSV* ... all his troops dispersed, *Anchor* ... his army went in flight from him in every direction, *BB*.

6. So they took the king, and brought him up to the king of Babylon to Riblah; and they gave judgment upon him: ... they had captured the king, *Beck* ... seized the king, *Fenton* ... The king was arrested and brought, *NAB* ... pronounced sentence upon him, *Berkeley*.

7. And they slew the sons of Zedekiah before his eyes, and put out the eyes of Zedekiah, and bound him with fetters of brass, and carried him to Babylon: ... slaughtered the sons of Zedekiah, *NASB* ... sons were slain, *NEB* ... before his face, *Douay* ... bound

---

seemed to play an important part here. Until the year 605, she exercised considerable control over Syria-Palestine; and the more recent Babylonian presence in the area was something new, seemingly only a passing phenomenon. (Nebuchadnezzar's failure to invade Egypt in 601 only served to underscore that impression all the more.) By the year 592, the "triumphal progress" of Psammetichus II (595–589), successor to Neco, to Palestine, although mostly peaceful in nature, nevertheless was intended "to broadcast his military success in the Sudan, and to galvanize his allies and subjects in hither Asia by his presence against the Babylonian menace" (K. S. Freedy and D. B. Redford, as cited by Cogan and Tadmor, AB, 323). In any case, we are starkly apprised in our present passage (24:20), "Now Zedekiah rebelled against the king of Babylon."

Nebuchadnezzar's counter-move seemed to be slow in coming. Not until January 587 (in Zedekiah's ninth year; cf. 25:1 of the present text), did he move against Jerusalem, but at that time he besieged her, and for the next eighteen months, with the exception of a short respite occasioned by the arrival of some Egyptian forces (cf. Jer. 37:5, 11), the city stood against the Babylonian invaders. But Jerusalem was finally subdued by hunger, "perhaps the most effective factor in siege operations employed by the great empires" (Cogan and Tadmor; cf. 25:3 of the present passage; also cf. comments on 6:24f and 6:26–31, above). In July 586, the city wall was breached (25:4), and, though Zedekiah was able to escape by night, he was captured "on the plains of Jericho" east of that city (25:5; that location is a particularly exposed area, mostly devoid of vegetation [Hobbs, WBC, 363]), taken to Riblah (concerning the significance and location of this town, see below) to face King Nebuchadnezzar, was tried and convicted of violation of covenant (25:6), and was cruelly punished. He was forced to observe the execution of his sons, and then he was blinded (cf. Ezek. 12:13), bound in bronze shackles and taken to Babylon (25:7). Such is the public fate of captured covenant violators—a dire warning to any others contemplating the same.

Riblah, in northern Syria, some 70 miles (110 kilometers) north of Damascus "in the land of Hamath" (23:33), where Nebuchadnezzar had placed his military headquarters for his western campaign, and where Zedekiah's sons had met their death before their father's very eyes, had already been mentioned as well in regard to the prior exile of King Jehoahaz (cf. 23:31–35, above). Situated on the east bank of the Orontes River, the city was located in a wide plain suitable for a large military campsite (Riblah had presumably also been used for this purpose also by Pharaoh Neco in his march

3937, 6084	881, 6084	6931	5996.311	646.121
prep, n fp, ps 3ms	cj, do, *n fd*	pn	v Piel pf 3ms	cj, v Qal impf 3ms, ps 3ms
לְעֵינָיו	וְאֶת־עֵינֵי	צִדְקִיָּהוּ	עִוֵּר	וַיַּאַסְרֵהוּ
le‘ênâv	we’eth-‘ênê	tsidhqîyāhû	‘iwwēr	wayya’asrēhû
before his eyes	and the eyes of	Zedekiah	they gouged out	and they bound him

904, 5333	971.521	928		904, 2414	2653
prep, art, n md	cj, v Hiphil impf 3ms, ps 3ms	pn	**8.**	cj, prep, art, n ms	art, num
בַּנְחֻשְׁתַּיִם	וַיְבִאֵהוּ	בָּבֶל		וּבַחֹדֶשׁ	הַחֲמִישִׁי
vanchushtayim	wayvi’ēhû	bāvel		ûvachōdhesh	hachmîshî
with the two bronze fetters	and they brought him to	Babylon		and in the month	the fifth

904, 8124	3937, 2414	2026	8523	9013, 6462	8523	3937, 4567	5194
prep, num	prep, art, n ms	pers pron	*n fs*	num, num	n fs	prep, art, n ms	pn
בְּשִׁבְעָה	לַחֹדֶשׁ	הִיא	שְׁנַת	תְּשַׁע־עֶשְׂרֵה	שָׁנָה	לַמֶּלֶךְ	נְבֻכַדְנֶאצַּר
beshiv‘āh	lachōdhesh	hî’	shenath	tesha‘-‘esrēh	shānāh	lammelekh	nevukhadhne’tstsar
on seven	of the month	it	the year of	nineteen	years	to the king	Nebuchadnezzar

4567, 928	971.111	5193	7521, 2986	5860
n ms, pn	v Qal pf 3ms	pn	*n ms*, n mp	*n ms*
מֶלֶךְ־בָּבֶל	בָּא	נְבוּזַרְאֲדָן	רַב־טַבָּחִים	עֶבֶד
melekh-bāvel	bā’	nevûzar’ădhān	rav-tabbāchîm	‘evedh
the king of Babylon	he came to	Nebuzaradan	the chief of the executioners	the servant of

4567, 928	3503		8041.121	881, 1041, 3176	881, 1041
n ms, pn	pn	**9.**	cj, v Qal impf 3ms	do, *n ms*, pn	cj, do, *n ms*
מֶלֶךְ־בָּבֶל	יְרוּשָׁלָם		וַיִּשְׂרֹף	אֶת־בֵּית־יְהוָה	וְאֶת־בֵּית
melekh-bāvel	yerûshālām		wayyisrōph	’eth-bêth-yehwāh	we’eth-bêth
the king of Babylon	Jerusalem		and he burned	the temple of Yahweh	and the household of

4567	881	3725, 1041	3503	881, 3725, 1041	1448	8041.111	904, 813
art, n ms	cj, do	*adj*, *n mp*	pn	cj, do, *adj*, n ms	adj	v Qal pf 3ms	prep, art, n fs
הַמֶּלֶךְ	וְאֵת	כָּל־בָּתֵּי	יְרוּשָׁלַם	וְאֶת־כָּל־בֵּית	גָּדוֹל	שָׂרַף	בָּאֵשׁ
hammelekh	we’ēth	kol-bāttê	yerûshālam	we’eth-kol-bêth	gādhôl	sāraph	bā’ēsh
the king	and	all the houses of	Jerusalem	and all houses	great	he burned	with the fire

	881, 2440	3503	5623	5606.116	3725, 2524	3908	866
10.	cj, do, *n fp*	pn	adv	v Qal pf 3cp	*adj*, *n ms*	pn	rel pron
	וְאֶת־חוֹמֹת	יְרוּשָׁלַם	סָבִיב	נָתְצוּ	כָּל־חֵיל	כַּשְׂדִּים	אֲשֶׁר
	we’eth-chômōth	yerûshālam	sāvîv	nāthetsû	kol-chêl	kasdîm	’ăsher
	and the walls of	Jerusalem	all around	they tore down	all the army of	the Chaldeans	who

7521, 2986		881	3615	6194	8080.256	904, 6111
n ms, n mp	**11.**	cj, do	*adj*	art, n ms	art, v Niphal ptc mp	prep, art, n fs
רַב־טַבָּחִים		וְאֵת	יֶתֶר	הָעָם	הַנִּשְׁאָרִים	בָּעִיר
rav-tabbāchîm		we’ēth	yether	hā‘ām	hanish’ārîm	bā‘îr
the chief of the executioners		and	the remainder of	the people	those remaining	in the city

881, 5489.152	866	5489.116	6142, 4567	928	881
cj, do, art, v Qal act ptc mp	rel pron	v Qal pf 3cp	prep, art, *n ms*	pn	cj, do
וְאֶת־הַנֹּפְלִים	אֲשֶׁר	נָפְלוּ	עַל־הַמֶּלֶךְ	בָּבֶל	וְאֵת
we’eth-hannōphelîm	’āsher	nāphelû	‘al-hammelekh	bāvel	we’ēth
and those falling away	who	they fell away	beside the king of	Babylon	and

3615	2066	1580.511	5193	7521, 2986
adj	art, n ms	v Hiphil pf 3ms	pn	*n ms*, n mp
יֶתֶר	הֶהָמוֹן	הֶגְלָה	נְבוּזַרְאֲדָן	רַב־טַבָּחִים
yether	hehāmôn	heghlāh	nevûzar’ădhān	rav-tabbāchîm
the remainder of	the multitude	he deported	Nebuzaradan	the chief of the executioners

him with bronze shackles and took him to Babylon, *NIV.*

8. And in the fifth month, on the seventh day of the month, which is the nineteenth year of king Nebuchadnezzar king of Babylon, came Nebuzar-adan, captain of the guard, a servant of the king of Babylon, unto Jerusalem: ... Nebuzaradan, captain of the guard, an official of the Babylonian king, arrived in Jerusalem, *NLT* ... captain of the king of Babylon's bodyguard, came, *REB* ... servant of the king of Babilon and chief marshal, *Tyndale* ... chief cook, *Anchor.*

9. And he burnt the house of the LORD, and the king's house, and all the houses of Jerusalem, and every great man's house burnt he with fire: ... he burned every important house, *Beck* ... every important building, *Berkeley* ... every mansion, *Fenton* ... houses of all the important people, *Good News.*

10. And all the army of the Chaldees, that were with the captain of the guard, brake down the walls of Jerusalem round about: ... with the commander of the guard, *Goodspeed* ... demolished the walls surrounding Jerusalem, *JB* ... broke down, *KJVII* ... tore down the walls, *NAB.*

11. Now the rest of the people that were left in the city, and the fugitives that fell away to the king of Babylon: ... and those who had deserted to the king of Babylon, *Anchor* ... the rest of the people who were still in the town, and all those who had given themselves up to the king, *BB* ... the residue of the people, *MAST* ... Nebuzaradan, captain of the guard, led into exile the last of the people remaining in the city, *NAB.*

with the remnant of the multitude, did Nebuzar-adan the captain of the guard carry away: ... the rest of the masses, *Anchor* ... the rest of the great crowd, *Fenton* ... the common folk, *Knox* ... captain of the armed men, took away as prisoners, *BB.*

---

north against the Babylonians, in 609, on which occasion Josiah met his death at Megiddo [cf. above, on 23:26–30], and his son and successor, Jehoahaz, was, as just noted, deported to Egypt [cf. *Anchor Bible Dictionary*, 5:721]).

The present work reminds us by means of a melancholy inclusio that "the plains of Jericho" were both the location of the glorious entrance of the Israelite leader Joshua and his nation in the days of Moses (cf. Josh. 3–6), as well as the ignominious exit of Judah's last king Zedekiah (here, in 25:5). What a sad and inauspicious ending to what was intended to be such a glorious (and, indeed, for so many years truly was a glorious) example of the "kingdom of God" here on earth! It would be another 600 years before another deliverer, Jesus, stood on "the plain of Jericho," indeed within the river itself, to be baptized by a man named John (cf. Matt. 3:1–17, etc.). To the glory of God, this NT inauguration of the kingdom of God will know no end.

25:8–21. The Temple ransacked, and the Judahites sent off into exile. But we must move back once again into the early sixth century B.C., indeed to the somber events of the summer of 586. After taking the town of Jerusalem in July, Nebuchadnezzar ordered the Temple razed in mid-August (seventh of Ab [v. 8]; cf. Cogan and Tadmor, AB, 323). "Conquest and looting were insufficient punishment for the capital city that had proven itself recalcitrant so many times; the city's destruction establishes that there were no plans to reconstitute Judah around a Babylonian provincial center in Jerusalem" (Cogan and Tadmor, AB, 323f, citing the work of E. J. Bickerman). To this day, the "Tisha b'Av" ("ninth of Ab") is commemorated in Judaism as a day of mourning for the destruction of both the first and the second temples (the latter destroyed by the Romans in A.D. 70) in the city of Jerusalem.

Reasons for the destruction of the Temple and the razing of the city walls have already been cited. Nebuchadnezzar wished, in brief, to punish the city, not occupy it. One "Nebuzaradan commander of the imperial guard" came to effect this wish (cf. Cogan and Tadmor, AB, 318f; Nebuzaradan is also mentioned in a cuneiform list of Nebuchadnezzar's courtiers). He burned down "every important building" (v. 9); "the first task of this official was to destroy all the important symbolic centers in the city" (Hobbs, WBC, 364). His second task was no less destructive: to break down the city walls which could be used to fend off future attack (v. 10; commonly these walls are seen as destroyed until the time of Nehemiah, some 140 years later [cf. Neh. 1–7], but most scholars see the walls rebuilt many years prior to that time [ca. 445], and then again breached in Ezra's time due to some new rebellion; this would explain both Nehemiah's obvious surprise and intense dismay, when he first heard the news about the walls being broken down and the gates burned with fire [cf. Neh. 1:1–2:9]). Exile of most of the city's inhabitants then commenced (often called the "second" exile); only the

12.	4623, 1878	800	8080.511	7521, 2986	3937, 3885.152
	cj, prep, *n fs*	art, n fs	v Hiphil pf 3ms	*n ms*, n mp	prep, v Qal act ptc mp
	וּמִדַּלַּת	הָאָרֶץ	הִשְׁאִיר	רַב־טַבָּחִים	לְכֹרְמִים
	ûmiddallath	hā'ārets	hish'îr	rav-ṯabbāchîm	lekhōremîm
	but among the poor of	the land	he left	the chief of the executioners	for husbandmen

3937, 3118.152	13.	881, 6204	5361	866	1041, 3176
cj, prep, v Qal act ptc mp		cj, do, *n mp*	art, n fs	rel part	*n ms*, pn
וּלַיֹּגְבִים		וְאֶת־עַמּוּדֵי	הַנְּחֹשֶׁת	אֲשֶׁר	בֵּית־יְהוָה
ûlāyōghevîm		we'eth-'ammûdhê	hannechōsheth	'ăsher	bêth-yehwāh
and for farmers		and the pillars of	the bronze	which	the temple of Yahweh

881, 4488	881, 3328	5361	866	904, 1041, 3176	8132.316
cj, do, art, n fp	cj, do, n ms	art, n fs	rel part	prep, *n ms*, pn	v Piel pf 3cp
וְאֶת־הַמְּכֹנוֹת	וְאֶת־יָם	הַנְּחֹשֶׁת	אֲשֶׁר	בְּבֵית־יְהוָה	שִׁבְּרוּ
we'eth-hammekhōnôth	we'eth-yām	hannechōsheth	'ăsher	bevêth-yehwāh	shibberû
and the bases	and the sea	the bronze	which	in the temple of Yahweh	they broke in pieces

3908	5558.126	881, 5361	928	14.	881, 5707	881, 3381
pn	cj, v Qal impf 3mp	do, n fs, ps 3mp	pn		cj, do, art, n fp	cj, do, art, n mp
כַשְׂדִּים	וַיִּשְׂאוּ	אֶת־נְחֻשְׁתָּם	בָּבֶלָה		וְאֶת־הַסִּירֹת	וְאֶת־הַיָּעִים
khasdîm	wayyis'û	'eth-nechushtām	bāvelāh		we'eth-hassîrōth	we'eth-hayyā'îm
the Chaldeans	and they carried	their bronze	to Babylon		and the pots	and the shovels

881, 4345	881, 3834	881	3725, 3747	5361	866
cj, do, art, n fp	cj, do, art, n fp	cj, do	*adj*, *n mp*	art, n fs	rel part
וְאֶת־הַמְזַמְּרוֹת	וְאֶת־הַכַּפּוֹת	וְאֵת	כָּל־כְּלֵי	הַנְּחֹשֶׁת	אֲשֶׁר
we'eth-hamzammerôth	we'eth-hakkappôth	we'ēth	kol-kelê	hannechōsheth	'ăsher
and the hooks	and the ladles	and	all the vessels of	the bronze	which

8664.326, 904	4089.116	15.	881, 4426	881, 4353	866	2174
v Piel impf 3mp, prep, ps 3mp	v Qal pf 3cp		cj ,do, art, n fp	cj, do, art, n mp	rel part	n ms
יְשָׁרְתוּ־בָם	לָקָחוּ		וְאֶת־הַמַּחְתּוֹת	וְאֶת־הַמִּזְרָקוֹת	אֲשֶׁר	זָהָב
yeshārethû-vām	lāqāchû		we'eth-hammachtôth	we'eth-hammizrāqôth	'ăsher	zāhāv
they ministered with them	they took		and the censers	and the basins	which	gold

2174	866, 3826B	3826B	4089.111	7521, 2986	16.	6204
n ms	cj, rel part, n ms	n ms	v Qal pf 3ms	*n ms*, n mp		art, n mp
זָהָב	וַאֲשֶׁר־כֶּסֶף	כֶּסֶף	לָקַח	רַב־טַבָּחִים		הָעַמּוּדִים
zāhāv	wa'ăsher-keseph	kāseph	lāqach	rav-ṯabbāchîm		hā'ammûdhîm
gold	and which silver	silver	he took	the chief of the executioners		the pillars

8530	3328	259	4488	866, 6449.111	8406	3937, 1041
num	art, n ms	art, num	cj, art, n fp	rel part, v Qal pf 3ms	pn	prep, *n ms*
שְׁנַיִם	הַיָּם	הָאֶחָד	וְהַמְּכֹנוֹת	אֲשֶׁר־עָשָׂה	שְׁלֹמֹה	לְבֵית
shenayim	hayyām	hā'echādh	wehammekhōnôth	'ăsher-'āsāh	shelōmōh	levêth
two	the sea	the one	and the bases	which he had made	Solomon	for the temple of

3176	3940, 2030.111	5129	3937, 5361	3725, 3747	431	17.	8470
pn	neg part, v Qal pf 3ms	n ms	prep, *n fs*	*adj*, art, n mp	art, dem pron		num
יְהוָה	לֹא־הָיָה	מִשְׁקָל	לִנְחֹשֶׁת	כָּל־הַכֵּלִים	הָאֵלֶּה		שְׁמֹנֶה
yehwāh	lō'-hāyāh	mishqāl	linchōsheth	kol-hakkēlîm	hā'ēlleh		shemōneh
Yahweh	it was not	a weight	to the bronze of	all the vessels	the these		eight

6462	527	7253	6204	259	3934	6142	5361
num	n fs	*n fs*	art, n ms	art, num	cj, n fs	prep, ps 3ms	n fs
עֶשְׂרֵה	אַמָּה	קוֹמַת	הָעַמּוּד	הָאֶחָד	וְכֹתֶרֶת	עָלָיו	נְחֹשֶׁת
'esrēh	'ammāh	qômath	hā'ammûdh	hā'echādh	wekhōthereth	'ālâv	nechōsheth
ten	cubits	the height of	the pillar	the one	and the capital	on it	bronze

12. But the captain of the guard left of the poor of the land to be vinedressers and husbandmen: ... vinedressers and plowmen, *NASB* ... left only the weakest class of people to be vine-dressers and labourers, *NEB* ... to work the vineyards and fields, *NIV* ... dress the vines and to till the ground, *Tyndale*.

13. And the pillars of brass that were in the house of the LORD, and the bases, and the brasen sea that was in the house of the LORD, did the Chaldees break in pieces, and carried the brass of them to Babylon: ... Babylonians broke in pieces the bronze columns and the carts that were in the Temple, together with the large bronze tank, *Good News* ... bronze pool at the LORD's temple, *Beck* ... took the metal to Babylon, *REB* ... carried their bronze to, *NKJV*.

14. And the pots, and the shovels, and the snuffers, and the spoons, and all the vessels of brass wherewith they ministered, took they away: ... with which the service was conducted, they took, *Goodspeed* ... all the bronze furnishings used in worship, *JB* ... all the appurtenances of worship, *Knox* ... any bronze article used in the temple service, *Moffatt*.

15. And the firepans, and the bowls, and such things as were of gold, in gold, and of silver, in silver, the captain of the guard took away: ... carried off, *NAB* ... censers, and the bowls, *Douay* ... firepans and the basins, *NASB* ... sprinkling bowls, *Anchor*.

16. The two pillars, one sea, and the bases which Solomon had made for the house of the LORD; the brass of all these vessels was without weight: ... two pillars, the great water-vessel and the wheeled bases, which Solomon had made, *BB* ... all these things couldn't be weighed, *Beck* ... The bronze of all these vessels was beyond weighing, *KJVII* ... was never calculated, *NAB*.

17. The height of the one pillar was eighteen cubits, and the chapiter upon it was brass: and the height of the chapiter three cubits: ... Each pillar was twenty-seven feet high. The bronze capital on top of one pillar was four and a half feet high, *NIV* ... and a bronze capital was on it, *NASB* ... with a crown of brass on it, *BB* ... and the head thereon was brass, *Tyndale*.

and the wreathen work, and pomegranates upon the chapiter round about, all of brass: ... a decoration of network and pomegranates ran all round it, wholly of bronze, *NEB* ... and was decorated with a network of bronze pomegranates all the way around, *NLT* ... latticework and pomegranates, all of bronze, were on the capital, *NRSV* ... a meshwork with pomegranates, all of bronze, *Anchor*.

and like unto these had the second pillar with wreathen work: ... the second pillar had the like adorning, *Douay* ... was exactly like it, *NEB* ... was similar, *NIV* ... was the same, with a network, *NKJV* ... with the latticework, *NRSV*.

"poorest people of the land" were left behind. Ezekiel's prophecy about the "pot" and the "meat" (as cited above, on 24:8–17) had certainly come true with a vengeance.

The following verses return to an inventory of the loot taken from the Temple (vv. 13–17); even though the description here has somewhat of a "pedantic" flavor, it serves as a fitting, if somber, counterpoint to the similar description of many of these same objects and furnishings found back in 1 Ki. 6ff. Thus, once again, a major concern of the writer is stressed—the centrality of the Solomonic temple (cf. earlier concerns over the Ark of the Covenant, in Joshua, Judges, and 1–2 Samuel). All that is probably necessary further to do here is to cite the earlier descriptions in 1 Kings for the convenience of the present reader: the bronze pillars (1 Ki. 7:15–22); the "moveable stands" (vv. 27–37); the bronze Sea (vv. 23–26); the pots (v. 45), shovels (v. 40), and "wick trimmers" (v. 50, originally made of gold, but probably replaced by bronze at a later date; cf. the "dishes" mentioned here as well). The "censers and sprinkling bowls" of v. 15 find their counterpart in 1 Ki. 7:50 as well. As far as the twelve bronze bulls, which had originally supported the bronze Sea, they had been sent by King Ahaz in payment to Tiglath-Pileser in 16:17—that is probably why they are not mentioned here (cf. Cogan and Tadmor, AB, 320).

The third action of Nebuchadnezzar (for this enumeration, cf. Hobbs, WBC, 365) was to eliminate certain key figures who did not fit into the future plans of the Babylonians (vv. 18–21). Both religious (v. 18), as well as civil and military (v. 19) officials were taken into custody; they were dragged off to the Babylonian king's headquarters at Riblah (v. 20; cf. above on 24:20–25:7), and summarily executed. "Their elimination effectively robs Judah of any firm leadership" (Hobbs). In connection with "Seraiah the chief priest," the notice in 1 Chr. 6:15 indicates that his son Jehozadak was led off into exile in Babylon (he became the father of Joshua, the well-known post-exilic high priest during the time of Zerubbabel; cf. Ezra 3:2; Hag. 1:1; Zech. 3:1; etc.). What a sobering reminder of the full extent of the sinfulness of the people of Yahweh

7253	3934	8421	527	7877	7705	6142, 3934
cj, *n fs*	art, n fs	num	n fs	cj, n fs	cj, n mp	prep, art, n fs
וְקוֹמַת	הַכֹּתֶרֶת	שָׁלֹשׁ	אַמָּה	וּשְׂבָכָה	וְרִמֹּנִים	עַל־הַכֹּתֶרֶת
weqômath	hakkōthereth	shālōsh	'ammāh	ûsevākhāh	werimmōnîm	'al-hakkōthereth
and the height of	the capital	three	cubits	and a netting	and pomegranate	on the capital

5623	3725	5361	3626, 431	3937, 6204	8529	6142, 7877
adv	art, n ms	n fs	cj, prep, dem pron	prep, art, n ms	art, num	prep, art, n fs
סָבִיב	הַכֹּל	נְחֹשֶׁת	וְכָאֵלֶּה	לַעַמּוּד	הַשֵּׁנִי	עַל־הַשְּׂבָכָה
sāvîv	hakkōl	nechōsheth	wekhā'ēlleh	la'ammûdh	hashshēnî	'al-hassevākhāh
all around	everything	bronze	and like these	the pillar	the second	on the netting

18.	4089.121	7521, 2986	881, 8034	3669	7513
	cj, v Qal impf 3ms	*n ms*, n mp	do, pn	n ms	art, adj
	וַיִּקַּח	רַב־טַבָּחִים	אֶת־שְׂרָיָה	כֹּהֵן	הָרֹאשׁ
	wayyiqqach	rav-tabbāchîm	'eth-serāyāh	kōhēn	hārō'sh
	and he took	the chief of the executioners	Seraiah	the priest	the chief

881, 7122	3669	5112	881, 8421	8490.152	5790
cj, do, pn	n ms	n ms	cj, do, num	*v Qal act ptc mp*	art, n ms
וְאֶת־צְפַנְיָהוּ	כֹּהֵן	מִשְׁנֶה	וְאֶת־שְׁלֹשֶׁת	שֹׁמְרֵי	הַסַּף
we'eth-tsephanyāhû	kōhēn	mishneh	we'eth-shelōsheth	shōmerê	hassaph
and Zephaniah	the priest	a second one	and the three of	the keepers of	the threshold

19.	4623, 6111	4089.111	5835	259	866, 2000	6746
	cj, prep, art, n fs	v Qal pf 3ms	n ms	num	rel pron, pers pron	n ms
	וּמִן־הָעִיר	לָקַח	סָרִיס	אֶחָד	אֲשֶׁר־הוּא	פָּקִיד
	ûmin-hā'îr	lāqach	sārîs	'echādh	'ăsher-hû'	phāqîdh
	and from the city	he took	a eunuch	one	who he	a commissioned officer

6142, 596	4560	2675	596	4623, 7495.152	6686, 4567
prep, *n mp*	art, n fs	cj, num	n mp	prep, *v Qal act ptc mp*	*n mp*, art, n ms
עַל־אַנְשֵׁי	הַמִּלְחָמָה	וַחֲמִשָּׁה	אֲנָשִׁים	מֵרֹאֵי	פְּנֵי־הַמֶּלֶךְ
'al-'anshê	hammilchāmāh	wachmishshāh	'ănāshîm	mērō'ê	phenê-hammelekh
over the men of	the war	and five	men	of those seeing	the face of the king

866	4834.216	904, 6111	881	5810	8015	6893
rel pron	v Niphal pf 3cp	prep, art, n fs	cj, do	art, n ms	*n ms*	art, n ms
אֲשֶׁר	נִמְצְאוּ	בָעִיר	וְאֵת	הַסֹּפֵר	שַׂר	הַצָּבָא
'ăsher	nimtse'û	vā'îr	we'ēth	hassōphēr	sar	hatstsāvā'
who	they were found	in the city	and	the secretary	the commander of	the army

6892.551	881, 6194	800	8666	382	4623, 6194	800
art, v Hiphil ptc ms	do, *n ms*	art, n fs	cj, num	n ms	prep, *n ms*	art, n fs
הַמַּצְבִּא	אֶת־עַם	הָאָרֶץ	וְשִׁשִּׁים	אִישׁ	מֵעַם	הָאָרֶץ
hammatsbi'	'eth-'am	hā'ārets	weshishshîm	'îsh	mē'am	hā'ārets
those conscripted	the people of	the land	and sixty	men	from the people of	the land

4834.256	904, 6111	20.	4089.121	881	5193
art, v Niphal ptc mp	prep, art, n fs		cj, v Qal impf 3ms	do, ps 3mp	pn
הַנִּמְצְאִים	בָּעִיר		וַיִּקַּח	אֹתָם	נְבוּזַרְאֲדָן
hanimtse'îm	bā'îr		wayyiqqach	'ōthām	nevûzar'ădhān
those found	in the city		and he took	them	Nebuzaradan

7521, 2986	2050.521	881	6142, 4567	928	7540
n ms, n mp	cj, v Hiphil impf 3ms	do, ps 3mp	prep, *n ms*	pn	pn
רַב־טַבָּחִים	וַיֹּלֶךְ	אֹתָם	עַל־מֶלֶךְ	בָּבֶל	רִבְלָתָה
rav-tabbāchîm	wayyōlekh	'ōthām	'al-melekh	bāvel	rivlāthāh
the chief of the executioners	and he brought	them	near the king of	Babylon	to Riblah

21.	5409.521 cj, v Hiphil impf 3ms וַיַּךְ wayyakh and he struck down	881 do, ps 3mp אֹתָם 'ōthām them	4567 *n ms* מֶלֶךְ melekh the king of	928 pn בָּבֶל bāvel Babylon	4322.521 cj, v Hiphil impf 3ms, ps 3mp וַיְמִיתֵם waymîthēm and he executed them	904, 7540 prep, pn בְּרִבְלָה b^{e}rivlāh in Riblah

904, 800 prep, *n fs* בְּאֶרֶץ b^{e}'erets in the land of	2679 pn חֲמָת ch^{e}māth Hamath	1580.121 cj, v Qal impf 3ms וַיִּגֶל wayyighel and it was deported	3171 pn יְהוּדָה y^{e}hûdhāh Judah	4623, 6142 prep, prep מֵעַל mē'al from on	124 n fs, ps 3ms אַדְמָתוֹ 'adhmāthô its land	22.	6194 cj, art, n ms וְהָעָם w^{e}hā'ām and the people

18. And the captain of the guard took Seraiah the chief priest, and Zephaniah the second priest, and the three keepers of the door: ... The chief officer took Seraiah, *Berkeley* ... and the three other important Temple officials, *Good News* ... three keepers of the threshold, *Goodspeed* ... guardians of the threshold, *JB*.

19. And out of the city he took an officer that was set over the men of war: ... took from the civilians a eunuch in charge of the army, *Moffatt* ... took one courtier, a commander of soldiers, *NAB* ... took one official who was overseer of the men of war, *NASB* ... a eunuch who was in charge of the fighting men, *NEB*.

and five men of them that were in the king's presence, which were found in the city: ... five royal advisers, *NIV* ... five ... that saw the king's face, *MAST* ... five men in the personal service of the king, *NAB* ... five ... that had stood before the king, *Douay* ... five of those with right of access to the king, *NEB*.

and the principal scribe of the host, which mustered the people of the land: ... the chief scribe of the army, who called the people of the land together, *KJVII* ... the secretary of the commander, who kept the army registers, *Moffatt* ... the adjutant-general whose duty was to muster the people for war, *NEB* ... secretary who was chief officer in charge of conscripting the people of the land, *NIV*.

and threescore men of the people of the land that were found in the city: ... sixty men of the people of the land, *KJVII* ... countryfolk who were found inside the city, *Moffatt* ... sixty of his men who were found in, *NIV*.

20. And Nebuzar-adan captain of the guard took these, and brought them to the king of Babylon to Riblah: ... captain of the armed men, *BB* ... the chief officer, *Berkeley* ... took these and conducted them to the king, *Fenton* ... commander of the guard, *JB*.

21. And the king of Babylon smote them, and slew them at Riblah in the land of Hamath: ... had them struck down and put to death, *Anchor* ... and killed them, *Beck* ... king had them beaten and put to death, *Good News* ... had them flogged and put to death, *NEB* ... had them executed, *NIV*.

So Judah was carried away out of their land: ... Judah was exiled from its land, *Anchor* ... left its land to go into captivity, *Beck* ... was carried from its own country into exile, *Moffatt* ... went into captivity, away from her land, *NIV*.

22. And as for the people that remained in the land of Judah,

and of the extreme lengths our Jealous God will go to address it (as is well-known, the entire Book of Lamentations is written in light of the destruction of Jerusalem and the exile of her people; yet we read even there [Lam. 3:22f], "For his compassions never fail; they are new every morning—great is your faithfulness." Even harsh judgments from our God represent his never-failing love for us.)

25:22–26. Gedaliah the Judahite appointed and assassinated. In what may be a sort of appendix to the Book, we read briefly about the appointment of a native Judahite as "governor" over the people left behind in Judah. Akin to the message of the prophet Jeremiah, the new leader reassures the people: "Do not be afraid of the Babylonian officials" (v. 24); as Cogan and Tadmor (AB, 326) point out, this probably was meant to reassure the army officers who had just fought the Babylonians that they would not be further punished. More information concerning all this is found in Jer. 40:7–41:18; cf. introductory comments on 24:18–25:21.

Gedaliah was from a prominent Jerusalem family; his grandfather Shaphan was the scribe (NIV, "secretary") in the days of King Josiah (cf. 22:3, above), and his father Ahikam was also a member of the group of officials sent to consult Huldah the prophetess at that time (cf. 22:12). A seal impression reading "Belonging to Gedaliah, the Royal Steward" was found at Lachish; it dates to the late seventh century, and may well have come from a seal belonging to the present official

8080.255	904, 800	3171	866	8080.511	5194	4567
art, v Niphal ptc ms	prep, *n fs*	pn	rel pron	v Hiphil pf 3ms	pn	*n ms*
הַנִּשְׁאָר	בְּאֶרֶץ	יְהוּדָה	אֲשֶׁר	הִשְׁאִיר	נְבוּכַדְנֶאצַּר	מֶלֶךְ
hanish'ār	be'erets	yehûdhāh	'ăsher	hish'îr	nevûkhadhne'tstsar	melekh
those remaining	in the land of	Judah	whom	he left	Nebuchadnezzar	the king of

928	6734.521	6142	881, 1466	1158, 297	1158, 8597
pn	cj, v Hiphil impf 3ms	prep, ps 3mp	do, pn	*n ms*, pn	*n ms*, pn
בָּבֶל	וַיַּפְקֵד	עֲלֵיהֶם	אֶת־גְּדַלְיָהוּ	בֶּן־אֲחִיקָם	בֶּן־שָׁפָן
bāvel	wayyaphqēdh	'ălêhem	'eth-gedhalyāhû	ben-'ăchîqām	ben-shāphān
Babylon	and he appointed	over them	Gedaliah	the son of Ahikam	the son of Shaphan

23.	8471.126	3725, 8015	2524	2065	596
	cj, v Qal impf 3mp	*adj, n mp*	art, n mp	pers pron	cj, art, n mp
	וַיִּשְׁמְעוּ	כָּל־שָׂרֵי	הַחֲיָלִים	הֵמָּה	וְהָאֲנָשִׁים
	wayyishme'û	khol-sārê	hachyālîm	hēmmāh	wehā'ănāshîm
	and they heard	all the commanders of	the soldiers	they	and the men

3706, 6734.511	4567, 928	881, 1466	971.126	420, 1466
cj, v Hiphil pf 3ms	*n ms*, pn	do, pn	cj, v Qal impf 3mp	prep, pn
כִּי־הִפְקִיד	מֶלֶךְ־בָּבֶל	אֶת־גְּדַלְיָהוּ	וַיָּבֹאוּ	אֶל־גְּדַלְיָהוּ
kî-hiphqîdh	melekh-bāvel	'eth-gedhalyāhû	wayyāvō'û	'el-gedhalyāhû
that he had appointed	the king of Babylon	Gedaliah	and they came	to Gedaliah

4870	3579	1158, 5602	3212	1158, 7431	8034
art, pn	cj, pn	*n ms*, pn	cj, pn	*n ms*, pn	cj, pn
הַמִּצְפָּה	וְיִשְׁמָעֵאל	בֶּן־נְתַנְיָה	וְיוֹחָנָן	בֶּן־קָרֵחַ	וּשְׂרָיָה
hammitspāh	weyishmā'ē'l	ben-nethanyāh	weyôchānān	ben-qārēach	ûserāyāh
the Mizpah	and Ishmael	the son of Nethaniah	and Johanan	the son of Kareah	and Seraiah

1158, 8905	5372	3080	1158, 4759	2065
n ms, pn	art, pn	cj, pn	*n ms*, art, pn	pers pron
בֶּן־תַּנְחֻמֶת	הַנְּטֹפָתִי	וְיַאֲזַנְיָהוּ	בֶּן־הַמַּעֲכָתִי	הֵמָּה
ven-tanchumeth	hannetōphāthî	weya'ăzanyāhû	ben-hamma'ăkhāthî	hēmmāh
the son of Tanhumeth	the Netophathite	and Jaazaniah	the son of the Maacathite	they

596	24.	8123.221	3937	1466	3937, 596	569.121
cj, n mp, ps 3mp		cj, v Niphal impf 3ms	prep, ps 3mp	pn	cj, prep, n mp, ps 3mp	cj, v Qal impf 3ms
וְאַנְשֵׁיהֶם		וַיִּשָּׁבַע	לָהֶם	גְּדַלְיָהוּ	וּלְאַנְשֵׁיהֶם	וַיֹּאמֶר
we'anshêhem		wayyishshāva'	lāhem	gedhalyāhû	ûlă'anshêhem	wayyō'mer
and their men		and he swore	to them	Gedaliah	and to their men	and he said

3937	414, 3486.128	4623, 5860	3908	3553.133	904, 800
prep, ps 3mp	adv, v Qal juss 2mp	prep, *n mp*	art, pn	v Qal impv 2mp	prep, art, n fs
לָהֶם	אַל־תִּירְאוּ	מֵעַבְדֵי	הַכַּשְׂדִּים	שְׁבוּ	בָּאָרֶץ
lāhem	'al-tîre'û	mē'avdhê	hakkasdîm	shevû	vā'ārets
to them	do not be afraid	of the servants of	the Chaldeans	dwell	in the land

5856.133	881, 4567	928	3296.121	3937	25.	2030.121
cj, v Qal impv 2mp	do, *n ms*	pn	cj, v Qal juss 3ms	prep, ps 2mp		cj, v Qal impf 3ms
וְעִבְדוּ	אֶת־מֶלֶךְ	בָּבֶל	וְיִטַב	לָכֶם		וַיְהִי
we'ivdhû	'eth-melekh	bāvel	weyitav	lākhem		wayhî
and serve	the king of	Babylon	that it may be good	for you		and it was

904, 2414	8113	971.111	3579	1158, 5602	1158, 481
prep, art, n ms	art, num	v Qal pf 3ms	pn	*n ms*, pn	*n ms*, pn
בַּחֹדֶשׁ	הַשְּׁבִיעִי	בָּא	יִשְׁמָעֵאל	בֶּן־נְתַנְיָה	בֶּן־אֱלִישָׁמָע
bachōdhesh	hashshevî'î	bā'	yishmā'ē'l	ben-nethanyāh	ben-'ĕlîshāmā'
in the month	the seventh	he came	Ishmael	the son of Nethaniah	the son of Elishama

whom Nebuchadnezzar king of Babylon had left, even over them he made Gedaliah the son of Ahikam, the son of Shaphan, ruler: ... governor, *NKJV* ... in charge, *Knox* ... those whom Nebuchadnezzar king of Babylon left behind, he appointed Gedaliah son of Ahikam son of Shaphan over them, *Anchor* ... whom Nebuchadnezzar ... did not take away, *BB*.

23. And when all the captains of the armies, they and their men, heard that the king of Babylon had made Gedaliah governor, there came to Gedaliah to Mizpah, even Ishmael the son of Nethaniah, and Johanan the son of Careah, and Seraiah the son of Tanhumeth the Netophathite, and Jaazaniah the son of a Maachathite, they and their men: ... captains of the armed bands and their men heard, *REB* ... captains of the men of war and the men, *Tyndale* ... they came with their men, *NRSV* ... all their men, *NLT*.

24. And Gedaliah sware to them, and to their men, and said unto them: ... Gedaliah gave them and their men this assurance, *NEB* ... took an oath to reassure them, *NIV* ... assured them and their men with an oath, *Moffatt* ... swore to them, *Douay*.

Fear not to be the servants of the Chaldees: ... Do not be afraid to serve the Chaldeans, *Anchor* ... Do not fear to be the servants, *KJVII* ... They need have no fear of living under Chaldaean rule, *Knox* ... of the Chaldean officials, *NAB*.

dwell in the land, and serve the king of Babylon; and it shall be well with you: ... Stay in the land, *Anchor* ... go on living in the land under the rule of the king of Babylon, and all will be well, *BB* ... you will get along well, *Beck* ... settle in the land, *Goodspeed*.

25. But it came to pass in the seventh month, that Ishmael the son of Nethaniah, the son of Elishama, of the seed royal, came: ... who was a member of the royal house, *NEB* ... who was of royal blood, *NIV* ... of the royal family, *NKJV* ... royal line, *Anchor* ... of the king's blood, *Tyndale*.

and ten men with him, and smote Gedaliah, that he died, and the Jews and the Chaldees that were with him at Mizpah: ... murdered Gedaliah, *NEB* ... assassinated, *NIV* ... struck and killed, *NKJV* ... attacked and killed, *RSV*.

(cf. Cogan and Tadmor, AB, 325; also cf. Wiseman [TOTC, 315f], who note the apparent pro-Babylonian proclivities of his father Ahikam, who was a supporter of the prophet of Jeremiah [even rescuing him from death at one point], as evidenced in Jer. 26:24). The name "Gedaliah" probably means "Yahweh is great," and it was a common name (Hobbs, WBC, 366).

25:22–24. Gedaliah appointed as governor. Unfortunately, we do not know much about the precise office to which Gedaliah was appointed (the Hebrew in vv. 22f simply means "to appoint over the people" [hiphqîdh]). Cogan and Tadmor (AB, 327) characterize his appointment as an "administrator of local affairs"; they go on to point out, "His official title is unknown, which does not help to determine the exact status of Judah at this juncture. Was Judah a province of which Gedaliah was governor? Or had some sort of interim status with minimal Babylonian supervision been imposed?" In view of our lack of any Babylonian administrative records to clarify the situation, we remain uncertain. (Assyrian practice was not to appoint a local noble to such an office, with the possible exception of local Delta princes in Egypt under Esarhaddon and Ashurbanipal.) Later Persian parallels include the later appointment of the Davidic descendant, Zerubbabel (cf. Ezra 3:2; 4:1–5; 6:7; also comment on 24:8–17, above); also the cupbearer Nehemiah (cf. Neh. 1:11). In any case, this appointment clearly angered a significant Judahite faction who opposed collaboration with Babylon, and they assassinated Gedaliah seemingly within two months or so of his first taking office. Jeremiah commentators, however, seem to prefer a longer period of time; in light of the more abundant details in that Book (cf. comments in the next section, below), some tend to posit a five-year governorship, possibly corresponding to the so-called third exile in ca. 582 by Nebuchadnezzar (cf. Jer. 52:30) as direct retaliation for the deed; also cf. the numerous events that seemed to have taken place during the time leading up to the assassination (cf., e.g., Gerald L. Keown, Pamela J. Scalise, and Thomas G. Smothers, Jeremiah 26–52, WBC, 241).

25:25–26. Gedaliah assassinated; the Judahites flee to Egypt. As just noted, not all agreed with the pro-Babylonian stance of Gedaliah. One "Ishmael son of Nethaniah, the son of Elishama, who was of royal blood," came with ten accomplices to assassinate the new governor, along with a number of his supporters, both Judahite and Babylonian, at Mizpah (v. 25; the site is some eight miles [13 kilometers] north of Jerusalem). More information concerning this incident can be found in Jer. 40:10–41:15, includ-

4623, 2320	4548	6463	596	882	5409.526
prep, *n ms*	art, n fs	cj, num	n mp	prep, ps 3ms	cj, v Hiphil impf 3mp
מִזֶּרַע	הַמְּלוּכָה	וַעֲשָׂרָה	אֲנָשִׁים	אִתּוֹ	וַיַּכּוּ
mizzera‘	hammelûkhāh	wa‘ăsārāh	'ănāshîm	'ittô	wayyakkû
from the descendants of	the kingdom	and ten	men	with him	and they struck down

881, 1466	4322.121	881, 3173	881, 3908	866, 2030.116	882
do, pn	cj, v Qal impf 3ms	cj, do, art, pn	cj, do, art, pn	rel pron, v Qal pf 3cp	prep, ps 3ms
אֶת־גְּדַלְיָהוּ	וַיָּמֹת	וְאֶת־הַיְּהוּדִים	וְאֶת־הַכַּשְׂדִּים	אֲשֶׁר־הָיוּ	אִתּוֹ
'eth-gedhalyāhû	wayyāmōth	we'eth-hayyehûdhîm	we'eth-hakkasdîm	'ăsher-hāyû	'ittô
Gedaliah	and he died	and the Jews	and the Chaldeans	who they were	with him

904, 4870		7251.126	3725, 6194	4623, 7277	5912, 1448
prep, art, pn	**26.**	cj, v Qal impf 3mp	*adj*, art, n ms	prep, adj	cj, prep, adj
בַּמִּצְפָּה		וַיָּקֻמוּ	כָל־הָעָם	מִקָּטֹן	וְעַד־גָּדוֹל
bammitspāh		wayyāqumû	khol-hā‘ām	miqqātōn	we‘adh-gādhôl
at the Mizpah		and they arose	all the people	from insignificant	even unto great

8015	2524	971.126	4875	3706	3486.116	4623, 6686
cj, *n mp*	art, n mp	cj, v Qal impf 3mp	pn	cj	v Qal pf 3cp	prep, *n mp*
וְשָׂרֵי	הַחֲיָלִים	וַיָּבֹאוּ	מִצְרָיִם	כִּי	יָרְאוּ	מִפְּנֵי
wesārê	hachyālîm	wayyāvō'û	mitsrāyim	kî	yāre'û	mippenê
and the commanders of	the soldiers	and they went to	Egypt	because	they were afraid	from before

3908		2030.121	904, 8421	8124	8523	3937, 1588	3180
pn	**27.**	cj, v Qal impf 3ms	prep, num	cj, num	n fs	prep, *n fs*	pn
כַשְׂדִּים		וַיְהִי	בִשְׁלֹשִׁים	וָשֶׁבַע	שָׁנָה	לְגָלוּת	יְהוֹיָכִין
khasdîm		wayhî	vishlōshîm	wāsheva‘	shānāh	leghālûth	yehôyākhîn
the Chaldeans		and it was	in thirty	and seven	year	of the exile of	Jehoiachin

4567, 3171	904, 8530	6461	2414	904, 6465	8124	3937, 2414	5558.111
n ms, pn	prep, num	num	n ms	prep, num	cj, num	prep, art, n ms	v Qal pf 3ms
מֶלֶךְ־יְהוּדָה	בִּשְׁנֵים	עָשָׂר	חֹדֶשׁ	בְּעֶשְׂרִים	וְשִׁבְעָה	לַחֹדֶשׁ	נָשָׂא
melekh-yehûdhāh	bishnêm	‘āsār	chōdhesh	be‘esrîm	weshiv‘āh	lachōdhesh	nāsā'
the king of Judah	in two	ten	month	on twenty	and seven	of the month	he lifted up

189	189	4567	928	904, 8523	4566.141	881, 7513
pn	pn	*n ms*	pn	prep, *n fs*	v Qal inf con, ps 3ms	do, *n ms*
אֱוִיל	מְרֹדַךְ	מֶלֶךְ	בָּבֶל	בִּשְׁנַת	מָלְכוֹ	אֶת־רֹאשׁ
'ĕwîl	merōdhakh	melekh	bāvel	bishnath	mālekhô	'eth-rō'sh
Evil	Merodach	the king of	Babylon	in the year of	his reigning	the head of

3180	4567, 3171	4623, 1041	3728		1744.321
pn	*n ms*, pn	prep, *n ms*	n ms	**28.**	cj, v Piel impf 3ms
יְהוֹיָכִין	מֶלֶךְ־יְהוּדָה	מִבֵּית	כֶּלֶא		וַיְדַבֵּר
yehôyākhîn	melekh-yehûdhāh	mibbêth	kele'		waydhabbēr
Jehoiachin	the king of Judah	from the house of	the prison		and he spoke

882	3008	5598.121	881, 3802	4623, 6142	3802	4567
prep, ps 3ms	n fp	cj, v Qal impf 3ms	do, n ms, ps 3ms	prep, prep	*n ms*	art, n mp
אִתּוֹ	טֹבוֹת	וַיִּתֵּן	אֶת־כִּסְאוֹ	מֵעַל	כִּסֵּא	הַמְּלָכִים
'ittô	tôvôth	wayyittēn	'eth-kis'ô	mē‘al	kissē'	hammelākhîm
with him	good things	and he gave	his seat	from above	the seats of	the kings

866	882	904, 928		8521.311	881	933	3728
rel pron	prep, ps 3ms	prep, pn	**29.**	cj, v Piel pf 3ms	do	*n mp*	n ms, ps 3ms
אֲשֶׁר	אִתּוֹ	בְּבָבֶל		וְשִׁנָּא	אֵת	בִּגְדֵי	כִלְאוֹ
'ăsher	'ittô	bevāvel		weshinnā'	'ēth	bighdhê	khil'ô
who	with him	in Babylon		and he changed		the clothes of	his prison

26. And all the people, both small and great: ... people of all classes, *Beck* ... high and low, *JB* ... from the least to the greatest, *Fenton* ... rich and poor alike, *Good News*.

and the captains of the armies, arose, and came to Egypt: for they were afraid of the Chaldees: ... captains of the armed bands took off for Egypt, *Beck* ... officers of the army arose and went to Egypt, *Berkeley* ... officers of the forces, *Fenton* ... with the military leaders, *JB*.

27. And it came to pass in the seven and thirtieth year of the captivity of Jehoiachin king of Judah, in the twelfth month, on the seven and twentieth day of the month, that Evil-merodach king of Babylon in the year that he began to reign did lift up the head of Jehoiachin king of Judah out of prison: ... he was released from prison, *Knox* ... in the inaugural year of his own reign, raised up Jehoiachin ... from prison, *NAB* ... in his accession year, pardoned Jehoiachin ... and released him, *Anchor* ... summoned Jehoiachin, *Goodspeed*.

28. And he spake kindly to him, and set his throne above the throne of the kings that were with him in Babylon: ... put his seat higher than the seats of the other kings who were with him, *BB* ... set his seat above the seat of the kings, *Darby* ... spoke kindly, *MAST* ... he was civil to Jehoiakin and treated him better than his fellow-monarchs in captivity at Babylon, *Moffatt*.

---

ing a prior warning to Gedaliah about Ishmael's evil intentions, as well as the fact that Ishmael killed him while they ate together. All in all, the nobility of Gedaliah (also, possibly his seeming naiveté) versus the perfidy of his assassin are dramatically contrasted in the Jeremiah account. Whether the reference to Ishmael being of "royal blood" is meant to imply his being a legitimate heir to the throne is also unclear (Hobbs, "his pedigree provides no hint"); the Jeremiah account seems to put the blame for the assassination at least partly on foreigners, who still seem bent on rebellion against Babylon (cf. the reference to "Baalis king of the Ammonites" in Jer. 40:14). In any case, the Kings account is not interested in such details, only the sharp contrast between lack of order, stability, and optimism in Judah, and the presence of these three qualities in, of all places, Babylon (cf. the next, and indeed, the final passage in the present Book). The present passage ends with the perpetrators fleeing ignominiously to Egypt (for further details, cf. Jer. 41:16–44:30; it will be recalled that Jeremiah himself was compelled to accompany them back to this ancient land symbolic of bondage and death).

25:27–30. Conclusion to the Books of Kings: Jehoiachin released from prison. As just noted, surely the contrast between the instability and pessimism resident in Judah after the fall of Jerusalem in 586 is being distinguished, with the relative stability and optimism in the land of Babylon (cf. Jer. 29:4–7). Let the reader be reminded of the great Jewish community which flourished in the land of Babylonia until well into the Christian era (e.g., Ezra the scribe brought the Torah back from Babylon to Judah in ca. 458 [cf. Ezra 7:1–10; Neh. 7:73–8:8]; and the great "Babylonian Talmud" [possibly sixth century A.D.] remains the centerpiece of Orthodox Judaism to the present day). So it is entirely appropriate that the great Book of 2 Kings ends with a positive, if muted, note concerning the Jews in Babylon, especially the Davidic king Jehoiachin—he has spent some thirty-seven years in exile, to be sure, but he is welcomed by the new Babylonian monarch Evil-Merodach (Amel-Marduk), and given a place of honor at his table. The Davidic hope still lives on. Our God is ever faithful.

Amel-Marduk (562–560) was the son and successor to Nebuchadnezzar. Alas, virtually nothing certain is known about his reign apart from the present text (and its parallel in Jer. 52:31), plus some mostly legendary stories related by later Jewish and Christian commentators (cf. Ronald H. Sack, *Anchor Bible Dictionary,* 2:679). His brief reign apparently ended in assassination (by his successor Neriglissar, said to be his brother-in-law). Cogan and Tadmor (AB, 329) comment that King Jehoiachin presumably had previously fallen into disfavor with the Babylonian authorities, whence his being thrown into prison, where he languished until the act of amnesty announced in the present passage took place (this is their understanding of the phrase "he spoke kindly to him" in v. 28). Whatever the case, this new policy is presented as representing the magnanimous actions of a new king on the throne; and its sharp contrast with the previous Babylonian treatment of King Zedekiah (in 25:6f) is surely deliberate (cf. Hobbs, WBC, 367–68). Previously noted was the extant Babylonian documentation of food rations given to Jehoiachin and his five sons in 592 (cf. above, on 24:8–17)—presumably something significantly greater is in

404.111	4035	8878	3937, 6686	3725, 3219	2522
cj, v Qal pf 3ms	n ms	adv	prep, n mp, ps 3ms	*adj, n mp*	n mp, ps 3ms
וְאָכַל	לֶחֶם	תָּמִיד	לְפָנָיו	כָּל־יְמֵי	חַיָּיו
we'ākhal	lechem	tāmîdh	lephānâv	kol-yemê	chayyâv
and he ate	food	continually	before him	all the days of	his life

	760	760	8878	5598.212, 3937	4623, 881
30.	cj, n fs, ps 3ms	*n fs*	adv	v Niphal pf 3fs, prep, ps 3ms	prep, do
	וַאֲרֻחָתוֹ	אֲרֻחַת	תָּמִיד	נִתְּנָה־לּוֹ	מֵאֵת
	wa'ăruchāthô	'ăruchath	tāmîdh	nittenāh-lô	mē'ēth
	and his provision	a provision of	continually	it was given to him	from

4567	1745, 3219	904, 3219	3725	3219	2508
art, n ms	*n ms*, n ms	prep, n ms, ps 3ms	*n ms*	*n mp*	n mp, ps 3ms
הַמֶּלֶךְ	דְּבַר־יוֹם	בְּיוֹמוֹ	כֹּל	יְמֵי	חַיָּו
hammelekh	devar-yôm	beyômô	kōl	yemê	chayyaw
the king	the matter of a day	in its day	the entirety of	the days of	his life

29. And changed his prison garments: ... took off his prison garb, *NAB* ... discarded his prison clothes, *NEB* ... put aside his prison clothes, *NIV* ... exchanged, *Berkeley.*

and he did eat bread continually before him all the days of his life: ... ate at the king's table as long as he lived, *NAB* ... for the rest of his life ate regularly at the king's table, *NIV* ... dined regularly in the king's presence, *NRSV* ... ate food continually before the king as long as he lived, *Beck.*

30. And his allowance was a continual allowance given him of the king, a daily rate for every day, all the days of his life: ... his upkeep was permanently ensured by the king, day after day, for the rest of his life, *JB* ... his allowance was a regular allowance given him from the king, a daily ration for every day, *KJVII* ... Each day, for as long as he lived, he was given a regular allowance for his needs, *Good News* ... An allowance was made for him daily by the king, to maintain him, as long as he lived, *Moffatt.*

view here, especially in reference to the "seat of honor higher than those of the other kings who were with him in Babylon" (v. 28). Yet, the second Book of the Kings with its patient, careful analysis and its honest, searching criticisms of the status quo, still speaks anew and afresh more than 2500 years later—advising what not to do, spiritually and politically, to be sure, in order not to repeat the mistakes of the past; but even more so, reminding time and again of the faithfulness and the patience of our God, whose name is Jealous, but whose essential nature offers covenant love.

1 KINGS OVERVIEW

Background

Outline

Summary

Overview

BACKGROUND

The Hebrew canon includes Joshua, Judges, Samuel and Kings among the Prophets, that is, Books they considered written by prophets. Because they precede the Books of the great writing prophets, Isaiah, Jeremiah, Ezekiel and the Twelve Minor Prophets, they are called the former prophets. Together they continue the history of the Books of Moses and carry it from the death of Moses to the Babylonian Exile, a period of over 800 years from about 1400 B.C. to 586 B.C.

The Septuagint translators divided the Books of Samuel and Kings in half, probably to make the scrolls easier to handle. They also named them the First, Second, Third and Fourth Books of Kingdoms (Basileôn). The Latin Vulgate followed this by calling them First, Second, Third and Fourth Kings (Regnorum). Not until A.D. 1448 were Samuel and Kings divided in the Hebrew Bible.

First Kings covers a period of about 120 years, from the accession of Solomon to the beginning of the reigns of Jehoram in Judah and Ahaziah in Northern Israel. The record of Ahaziah's reign continues in Second Kings, as does the account of Elijah and Elisha, showing that the division of the Book of Kings was somewhat arbitrary.

The author of the Book shows concern that the reader understand the causes of both the glory and the decline of the kingdom. He puts great emphasis on God's dealings with the people and shows the effects of backsliding and unbelief. Less emphasis is put on the political situation of the day. For example, King Omri of Israel built the city of Samaria and made it the capital, brought Moab under his control and became a powerful political figure. Even after his death, the Assyrians continued to call Northern Israel the "Land of Omri" and gave political recognition to the reign of Jehu (who wiped out the descendants of Omri) by calling him the son of Omri. The Bible summarizes his reign in only six verses (16:23–28). It gives far more attention to the time of Ahab and Jezebel because of the crisis where Jezebel attempted to destroy the worship of the LORD (YHWH) and substitute the worship of the Baal of Tyre. Even more attention is given to Elijah and Elisha, whom God raised up to combat Baal worship. Thus, the history of the Book of Kings is told from God's point of view, rather than from a mere political point of view.

After the death of Solomon and the division of the kingdom, the kings of Judah and Israel form the framework of the Book of Kings. Each of them is introduced by a formula, and the reign is concluded by a formula. But the prophets appear suddenly without any such introductory formula. It is as if the framework of the history of the kings is pulled apart, and the prophets are injected into that history. The prophets are the real heroes of the Book. The kings, even though there were revivals in Judah under Asa, Jehoshaphat, Hezekiah and Josiah, show a steady decline. All the kings of Northern Israel "did evil in the sight of the LORD." But the prophets laid a foundation for the future and gave hope that God would carry out His plan. They show an ever-expanding knowledge of God's will and God's purpose for Israel and for the world.

Date and Author

The Book names no author. The author used contemporary sources that he identifies as (1) The Book of the Annals of Solomon (1 Ki. 11:41), (2) The Book of the Annals of the Kings of Judah (1 Ki. 14:29;15:7) and (3) The Book of the Annals of the Kings of Israel (1 Ki. 14:19). These "annals" were probably the daily court records of the kings (cf. 2 Sam. 8:16, which mentions a recorder [Hebrew mazkîr; HED #4339], and Est. 6:1ff). At the time the Book of Kings was written, people could still go to these records for further information. The phrase "unto this day" ("they are still there today," NIV) indicates that the city of Jerusalem and the Temple were still in existence at the time when the writing of the Book began.

Edwin R. Thiele in *The Mysterious Numbers of the Hebrew Kings* points out that the writer of Kings must have taken the notations for the lengths of the reigns from those court records. He shows that Jeroboam changed the system of counting the years of the reigns of the kings to an accession years system, instead of the non-accession year system used in Judah. Thus, he is able to show how the reigns of the kings of Israel and Judah related to each other and to provide the dates of the kings. He also points out that some of the reigns overlapped, though he does not go far enough in dealing with the kings in Isaiah's time. The probable dates for the accession of the kings have been added to the following outline.

OUTLINE

I. The Reign of Solomon (971–931 B.C.) 1 Ki. 1–11
- A. David's Old Age and Death 1:1–2:12
  - 1. Abishag Ministers to David 1:1–4
  - 2. Adonijah Plans to Be King 1:5–10
    - a. He Exalts Himself 1:5–6
    - b. He Calls Joab and Selected People to a Sacrifice 1:7–10
  - 3. Nathan and Bath-Sheba Plead for Solomon 1:11–27
    - a. Nathan Persuades Bath-Sheba to Go to David 1:11–21
    - b. Nathan Comes in to David 1:22–27
  - 4. Solomon Anointed King 1:28–40
    - a. David Assures Bath-Sheba that Solomon Will Be King 1:28–31
    - b. Solomon Rides David's Mule and Is Anointed King 1:32–40
  - 5. Adonijah Bows to Solomon 1:41–53
    - a. Adonijah Fears 1:41–52
    - b. Solomon Releases Adonijah 1:53
  - 6. David's Final Instructions to Solomon 2:1–9
    - a. How to Prosper 2:1–4
    - b. Judgment for Joab 2:5–6
    - c. Kindness for Barzillai 2:7
    - d. Judgment for Shimei 2:8–9
  - 7. David's Death and Solomon's Rule Established 2:10–12
- B. Solomon's Early Reign 2:13–3:3
  - 1. Adonijah Killed 2:13–25
    - a. Adonijah Persuades Bath-Sheba to Ask Solomon to Let Him Marry Abishag 2:13–21
    - b. Solomon Has Adonijah Put to Death 2:22–25
  - 2. Abiathar Removed from the Priesthood 2:26–27
  - 3. Joab Slain 2:28–35
    - a. Joab Deserved Death 2:28–33
    - b. Benaiah Kills Joab and Buries Him 2:34
    - c. Benaiah Takes Joab's Place; Zadok Takes Abiathar's Place 2:35
  - 4. Shimei's Disobedience and Death 2:36–46
  - 5. Solomon's Treaty with Pharaoh Sealed by Marriage of Pharaoh's Daughter 3:1–3
- C. Solomon's Wisdom 3:4–4:34
  - 1. God Appears to Solomon in a Dream 3:4–15
  - 2. Solomon's Wisdom Tested 3:16–28
  - 3. Solomon Organizes His Kingdom 4:1–19
  - 4. Israel's Prosperity 4:20–28
  - 5. Solomon's Wisdom Excels and Is Recognized 4:29–34
- D. Solomon Builds the Temple and His Palace 5:1–8:66
  - 1. Preparations for Building the Temple 5:1–18
    - a. Hiram of Tyre Supplies Lumber 5:1–12
    - b. Forced Labor 5:13–16
    - c. Stones and Lumber Prepared 5:17–18
  - 2. The Temple Built in Seven Years 6:1–38
  - 3. Solomon's Palace Buildings 7:1–12
  - 4. Furnishings Prepared for the Temple 7:13–51
  - 5. The Ark Brought into the Temple 8:1–11

6. The Temple Dedicated 8:12–66
E. Solomon's Continuing Reign 9:1–10:29
1. God Appears to Him a Second Time 9:1–9
2. Solomon Gives Hiram Twenty Cities 9:10–14
3. Further Building Projects 9:15–24
4. Offerings to the Lord 9:25
5. Solomon's Navy 9:26–28
6. The Queen of Sheba Visits 10:1–13
7. Solomon's Riches and Wisdom 10:14–29
F. Solomon's Downfall and Death 11:1–43
1. Foreign Wives Lead Him to Idolatry 11:1–8
2. God Will Divide the Kingdom 11:9–13
3. God Raises Adversaries 11:14–25
a. Hadad 11:14–22
b. Rezon 11:23–25
4. Ten Tribes Promised to Jeroboam 11:26–40
5. Solomon's Death 11:41–43
II. The Divided Monarchy to Ahaziah 1 Ki. 12–22
A. The Division of the Kingdom 12:1–24
1. Rehoboam Takes Bad Advice 12:1–15
2. Israel Rebels 12:16–20
3. God Warns Rehoboam Not to Resist 12:21–24
B. Jeroboam's Evil Reign (931/30–910/9 B.C.) 12:25–14:20
1. Sinful Worship 12:25–13:34
a. Golden Calves Placed in Bethel and Dan 12:25–29
b. Changes in the Worship 12:30–33
c. A Prophet from Judah Speaks Against Jeroboam's Altar 13:1–32
d. Jeroboam Continues False Worship 13:33–34
2. Jeroboam's Son Abijah Falls Sick and Dies 14:1–18
3. Jeroboam Dies and Nadab Succeeds Him 14:19–20
C. Rehoboam's Evil Reign (931/30–913 B.C.) 14:21–31
1. Rehoboam's Sins 14:21–24
2. Shishak of Egypt Defeats and Robs Jerusalem 14:25–28
3. Rehoboam Dies and Abijam Succeeds Him 14:29–31
D. Abijam's Evil Reign (913–910 B.C.) 15:1–8
E. Asa's Good Reign (910–869 B.C.) 15:9–24
1. Restored Worship 15:9–15
2. War with Baasha of Israel 15:16–22
3. Asa's Disease and Death 15:23–24
F. Nadab's Evil Reign and Murder (910–909 B.C.) 15:25–32
G. Baasha's Evil Reign (909–886 B.C.) 15:33–16:7
H. Elah's Evil Reign and Murder (886–885 B.C.) 16:8–14
I. Zimri's Evil Reign and Suicide (885 B.C.) 16:15–20
J. Omri's Evil Reign and His Building of Samaria (Omri and Tibni 885–880; Omri's Sole Reign 880–874 B.C.) 16:21–28
K. Ahab's Evil Reign (874–853 B.C.) 16:29–22:40
1. Ahab Marries Jezebel and Worships Baal 16:29–33
2. Hiel Rebuilds Jericho 16:34
3. Elijah's Contest with Baal 17:1–18:46

a. A Drought Prophesied 17:1
b. Ravens Feed Elijah 17:2–7
c. A Widow's Food Multiplied 17:8–15
d. The Widow's Son Raised 17:16–24
e. Fire From Heaven Consumes Elijah's Sacrifice 18:1–40
f. Rain Returns 18:41–46
4. Elijah Flees from Jezebel 19:1–18
5. Elisha Follows Elijah 19:19–21
6. War with Ben-Hadad 20:1–43
7. Ahab Takes Naboth's Vineyard 21:1–29
8. Micaiah's Prophecy and Ahab's Death 22:1–40
L. Jehoshaphat's Good Reign (872–869 as Co-regent; 869–848, Full Reign) 22:41–50
M. Ahaziah's Evil Reign (853–852 B.C.) 22:51–53

Overview

SUMMARY

The first eleven chapters of First Kings describe Solomon's reign. The Book begins by describing David's old age and his need of a concubine to warm and comfort him. His son, Adonijah, recognizing David's weakness, attempts to declare himself king. However, Nathan and Bath-sheba remind David of his promise to make Solomon king. So David commands that Solomon be brought out at the Spring Gihon and anointed king.

David lived about seven more years and continued to gather materials for the Temple. Then, as his death approached, he gave final instructions to Solomon, encouraging him to obey God and the Law of Moses and warning him about Joab and Shimei. Solomon was crowned a second time (as full king; 1 Chr. 29:22). After David's death, Adonijah's action brought his execution. Joab was also executed, and Zadok was made the high priest. Shimei was also executed. Thus Solomon removed all threats to his throne. He also sealed a treaty with Egypt by marrying the daughter of Pharaoh.

While Solomon was worshiping at Gibeon, God gave Solomon a dream, offering him whatever he might ask for. Solomon's request for wisdom pleased the LORD. As an example of this wisdom and the justice it brought, Solomon settled the claim of two prostitutes to a baby. His wisdom was further seen in the way he organized the kingdom in the three thousand proverbs he spoke.

In the fourth year of his full reign (about 959 B.C.), Solomon, with the help of workmen and materials supplied by Hiram, king of Tyre, began building the Temple. He finished in seven years. His own palace took eleven years, probably overlapping with the building of the Temple.

After preparing the furnishings for the Temple, Solomon collected the elders of the people together, and the priests took the Ark of the Covenant into the Temple. Solomon then prayed a prayer of dedication that recognized God's greatness and called the people to worship Him. The LORD then appeared to Solomon, encouraging him to continue to serve Him.

The report of Solomon's wisdom spread in all directions. The Queen of Sheba's visit is an example of how others recognized his wisdom and appreciated it. However, Solomon was not wise in the way he accumulated wealth, wives and concubines. This led to his downfall. God allowed adversaries to trouble him. The prophet Ahijah told Jeroboam God would give him rulership over the northern ten tribes.

After Solomon's death, the northern tribes rebelled against Solomon's son, Rehoboam. Jeroboam became king of the northern ten tribes, which took the name of Israel, while the southern kingdom became known as Judah. Jeroboam made Shechem his capital at first, and soon moved it to Tirzah. He was afraid that if the people went to Jerusalem's temple to worship, they might be won over by Rehoboam. So he widened the gap between the two kingdoms by setting up golden calves in shrines at Bethel and Dan. These were intended as aids to the worship of Yahweh. However, a prophet warned that the altar at Bethel would be destroyed. Then, because the prophet disobeyed God's instruction, a lion killed him. This was a warning to future prophets to obey the LORD.

In the sequence of kings that followed, all the kings of Northern Israel continued to worship the golden calves, did evil in the sight of the LORD and allowed a mixed worship, where many Israelites worshiped the Canaanite Baals, while still considering the LORD as their chief God. Judgment did fall on the Northern Kingdom again and again. After Jeroboam's son, Nadab, reigned less than two years (parts of years were counted as years), Jeroboam's dynasty came to an end. Nineteen kings reigned in Northern Israel. Seven reigned less than two years. Eight of the kings were killed or committed suicide, and in each case, another family took the throne.

In the southern kingdom of Judah, however, the people remained loyal to David's line. Its territory included that of the tribe of Judah and most of Benjamin. There was war between Judah and Israel from time to time until Ahab and Jehoshaphat made peace and made both a political and family alliance. Pharaoh Shishak of Egypt plundered Jerusalem in the fifth year of Rehoboam's reign.

Asa and Jehoshaphat were good kings, worshiping the LORD. Both had long reigns. However, Asa, at the end of his life, became diseased in the feet and sought help from physicians, refusing to seek help from the LORD. Most of the other kings of Judah in this period allowed mixed worship and "did evil in the sight of the LORD."

Chapter 17 begins the account of the ministries of Elijah and Elisha that runs to 2 Ki. 13:21. King Ahab of Israel married Jezebel, the daughter of the king of Sidon. She persuaded Ahab to build a temple for Baal in Samaria and to worship at its altar. Her purpose was to root out the worship of the LORD, kill off his prophets and make Baal the national god of Israel. Elijah began the contest with her and Baal by prophesying that it would not rain until he said. God encouraged Elijah's faith by sending ravens to feed him while he hid by the Brook Cherith. Then God sent him to a widow in Zarephath (in Jezebel's home territory) whose flour and oil miraculously multiplied to feed Elijah, the widow and her son. When the son died, Elijah prayed and the boy was restored to life.

In the third year of the drought, God sent Elijah to Ahab for a contest with the prophets of Baal, which took place on Mount Carmel. The prophets of Baal were unable to call down fire from heaven on their sacrifice. But Elijah's simple prayer brought the fire and his continued prayer brought the rain. The people responded, recognizing that the LORD is God and that Baal is no god at all. Elijah apparently hoped that this would convince even Jezebel. Instead, the wicked queen threatened to kill Elijah. Elijah fled, and in the strength of two supernatural meals went to Horeb, where God spoke to him, gave him work to do and told him to anoint Jehu to be king and Elisha to be the prophet who would carry on his ministry.

This was followed by war with Ben-Hadad of Syria. Later, Ahab tried to obtain Naboth's vineyard. When Naboth refused, Jezebel arranged for his death, so Ahab could have the vineyard. Elijah rebuked him for this, and he humbled himself before the LORD. But when Israel and Judah tried to retake Ramoth-Gilead from Syria, Micaiah prophesied Ahab's death. Ahab was killed in battle by a random arrow. The Book ends with a summary of Jehoshaphat's good reign and the accession of Jehoram in Judah and Ahaziah in Israel.

2 KINGS OVERVIEW

Background

Outline

Summary

Overview

BACKGROUND

Since Second Kings was originally a continuing part of the Book of Kings. See the background section of the First Kings overview for the general background of the Book.

The Book is very much concerned with showing the reasons for the decline and fall of both Israel and Judah. It draws attention to the worship of Baal and Asherah as well as to the influence of heathen high places and the religion of Damascus and Assyria. Attention is also given to the way kings broke their covenants and oppressed the people. But again, the kings are the framework of the Book, and even though there were some good kings in Judah, all of the kings of Israel continued to worship at the shrine of the golden calves, and many of the kings of both Judah and Israel worshiped the Canaanite Baals. Thus, the prophets are the key people and the real heroes. They continued to lay a foundation for the future in spite of the failures of the kings.

Hezekiah did have a revival at the beginning of his full reign, but he broke the treaty with Assyria and depended on Egypt in spite of Isaiah's warnings. But after his repentant prayer, the fifteen added years of life God gave him were a time of peace and blessing (where Isaiah was able to give the new messages of Isaiah 40–66; see the commentary on Isaiah).

Josiah was another who gave attention to the Law and saw revival. But by his time, the nation was already on the skids leading to destruction, and though the revival had a deep affect on some, it did not last and the kingdom came to an end.

Date and Author

Since Second Kings ends with the release of King Jehoiachin from prison in Babylon about 560 B.C., the writer must have continued to depend on earlier records for the facts he recorded. The fact that chapters 18–20 are almost identical with chapters 36–39 of Isaiah has caused many to believe that the writer of Kings used not only Isaiah but the writings of other prophets (most of which were not preserved elsewhere) as well as the court records of Israel and Judah (which were not preserved).

OUTLINE

I. Ahaziah to the Northern Exile 2 Ki. 1–17
- A. Divine Judgment on King Ahaziah and His Army 2 Ki. 1:1–18
  1. Moab Rebels Against Israel 1:1
  2. Ahaziah's Illness; and His Seeking Baal-Zebub 1:2–4
  3. The King's Messengers Meet Yahweh's Messenger 1:5–8
  4. Threefold Military Encounter with Elijah 1:9–15
  5. Death for the Faithless King (952 B.C.) 1:16–18
- B. Elijah Taken Up Into Heaven; Elisha Takes His Place 2:1–18
  1. Elisha Insists on Accompanying Elijah to the Jordan 2:1–6
  2. Elijah's Moses-like Miracle 2:7–8
  3. Elisha's Joshua-like Desire 2:9–10
  4. Elijah's Moses-like (and Enoch-like) Departure 2:11–12
  5. Elisha's Joshua-like Miracle 2:13–14
  6. Sons of the Prophets Ask to Search for Elijah 2:15–18
- C. Healing the Waters of Jericho 2:19–22
- D. Cursing of the Youths of Bethel 2:23–25
- E. The Revolt of Moab and Its Aftermath 3:1–27
  1. Jehoram's Evil Reign over Israel (852–841 B.C.) 3:1–3
  2. Revolt of Moab: Mobilization of Israel and Judah 3:4–8
  3. Impending Disaster for the Israelite Coalition 3:9–12
  4. Elisha's Response 3:13–19
  5. Prophetic Fulfillment 3:20–25
  6. Mesha's Desperate Sacrifice; Utter Defeat Averted 3:26–27
- F. An Israelite Widow's Debts Are Paid 4:1–7
- G. The Shunammite Woman and Her Son: A Miracle of Birth and Rebirth 4:8–37
  1. The Shunammite's Hospitality 4:8–10
  2. Birth of the Shunammite's Son 4:11–17
  3. Sudden Death for the Shunammite's Son 4:18–21
  4. The Shunammite Takes Charge 4:22–30
  5. The Shunammite's Son Brought Back to Life 4:31–37
- H. Purifying Poisonous Food 4:38–41
- I. Food Multiplied for a Hundred People 4:42–44
- J. Naaman the Foreigner Healed; Gehazi the Servant Stricken Instead 5:1–27
  1. A Great Man Stricken with Leprosy 5:1
  2. Letter to the King of Israel, Seeking the Prophet of God 5:2–7
  3. Elisha's Message to the King and Naaman 5:8–10
  4. Naaman's Servants Give Him Sage Advice 5:11–14
  5. Naaman's Praise for Israel's God and His Prophet 5:15–19a
  6. Greedy Gehazi's Deceitful Appeal 5:19b–25a
  7. Prophetic Pronouncement of Eternal Judgment on Dishonest Gehazi 5:25b–27
- K. A Borrowed Axhead Made to Float 6:1–7
- L. Elisha Opens and Closes the Eyes of Friends and Foes 6:8–23
  1. Elisha "Sees" the Enemy Plans 6:8–10
  2. The Enemy King of Syria Seeks Out Elisha 6:11–14
  3. Elisha Causes His Servant to See Heavenly Armies 6:15–17
  4. The Syrians Blinded, Captured, and Their Sight Restored 6:18–20
  5. Elisha "Sees to It"—Celebration, Not Slaughter; Leading to Cessation of Enemy Oppression 6:21–23

Overview

M. Siege in Samaria and Its Aftermath 6:24–7:20
  1. Israel's King Powerless to Break the Famine 6:24–33
    a. Famine as a Result of the Syrian Siege 6:24–25
    b. The King Unable to Help a Desperate Woman 6:26–33
  2. Elisha Predicts an Immediate End to the Famine 7:1–20
    a. Elisha Prophesies an Amazing Supply of Food 7:1–2
    b. Two Lepers Discover that Syrians Deserted Their Camp 7:3–11
    c. The King's Officers Corroborate the Leper's Discovery 7:12–16
    d. Elisha's Prophecy Confirmed to the Last Detail 7:17–20
N. Conclusion of the Story of the Shunammite Woman: Famine and Restoration 8:1–6
O. Elisha's International Ministry and Its Ramifications 8:7–15
  1. Ill Ben-Hadad of Syria Inquires of Yahweh 8:7–8
  2. Hazael's Inquiry and Elisha's Response 8:9–10
  3. Elisha's Further Revelation to and about Hazael 8:11–13
  4. Hazael Kills His Master and Succeeds Him as King 8:14–15
P. Jehoram of Judah's Evil Reign (848–841) 8:16–24
Q. Ahaziah of Judah's Evil Reign (841) 8:25–29
R. Jehu Anointed and Acclaimed as King over Israel; Judgment on the House of Omri and on the Worshipers of Baal 9:1–10:36
  1. Elisha Has Jehu Anointed King over Israel 9:1–13
  2. Jehu Kills Kings Joram of Israel and Ahaziah of Judah 9:14–29
  3. Jezebel the Queen Mother Killed 9:30–37
  4. Children of the House of Ahab and Relatives of Ahaziah Killed 10:1–17
  5. Priests and Worshipers of Baal Killed 10:18–27
  6. Conclusion of Jehu's Reign (Reigned 841–814 B.C.) 10:28–36
S. Athaliah the Queen Mother Versus Jehoiada the High Priest: Contending for the Kingship, the Life of Joash and the Future of the Davidic Dynasty 11:1–21
  1. Athaliah Takes over as Queen; Jehosheba Hides Joash 11:1–3
  2. Jehoiada Prepares for Joash's Coronation 11:4–12
  3. Athaliah Seized and Put to Death 11:13–16
  4. Covenant with Yahweh; Peace in the Land 11:17–21
T. Joash Commissions Repair of the Temple 12:1–21
  1. Joash's Reign (835–796) 12:1–3
  2. The Temple Repaired 12:4–16
  3. Hazael of Syria Takes Gath and Threatens Jerusalem 12:17–18
  4. Joash Killed 12:19–21
U. Jehoahaz of Israel's Evil Reign (814–798 B.C.) 13:1–9
V. Jehoash of Israel's Evil Reign (798–782 B.C.) 13:10–13
W. Elisha's Sickness and Death 13:14–21
  1. Sick Elisha Prophesies Limited Victory for Joash of Israel 13:14–19
  2. Elisha Dies and a Dead Israelite Thrown into His Tomb Lives 13:20–21
X. Concluding Notes on Kings Hazael and Ben–Hadad of Syria and on King Jehoash of Israel: Further Evidence of Yahweh's Graciousness to Israel 13:22–25
Y. Amaziah's Reign Over Judah (796–767 B.C.) 14:1–22
  1. His Good Reign 14:1–4
  2. Early Successes 14:5–7
  3. Defeated by Israel 14:8–14
  4. Jehoash of Israel Dies, Amaziah Assassinated; Azariah Made King 14:15–22
Z. Jeroboam II of Israel's Evil Reign (794–782 as Co-regent; 782–753 B.C. Sole Reign)14:23–29

AA. Azariah (or Uzziah) of Judah's Good Reign (791–767 as Co-regent; 767–750 Sole Reign; 750–739 as a Leper) 15:1–7
BB. Zechariah of Israel's Evil Reign (753) 15:8–12
CC. Shallum of Israel's Evil Reign (752) 15:13–16
DD. Menahem of Israel's Evil Reign (752–742 B.C.) 15:17–22
EE. Pekahiah of Israel's Evil Reign (742–740) 15:23–26
FF. Pekah of Israel's Evil Reign (752–740 East of Jordan; 740–732 over All Israel) 15:27–31
GG. Jotham of Judah's Good Reign (750–738) 15:32–38
HH. Ahaz of Judah's Evil Reign (744–731 as Co-regent; 731–715 Full Reign) 16:1–20
  1. His Evil Reign and Evil Sacrifices 16:1–4
  2. The Syro-Ephraimite War 16:5–9
  3. His Visit to Damascus; Resulting Modifications to Temple Worship 16:10–18
  4. His Death 16:19–20
II. Hoshea the Last King of Israel (732–722 B.C.) 17:1–6
JJ. Why North Israel Fell to Assyria 17:7–41
  1. Reasons for Israel's Fall: Idolatry and Disobedience 17:7–23
  2. Results of Israel's Fall: Syncretism and Disobedience 17:24–41

II. THE SOUTHERN KINGDOM OF JUDAH UP TO THE BABYLONIAN EXILE 2 Ki. 18–25
A. Hezekiah: A Man of Faith and Prayer (728–686 B.C.) 18:1–20:21
  1. Hezekiah's Early Reign as Co-regent (728–715) 18:1–12
  2. Sennacherib's Siege of Jerusalem 18:13–19:37
    a. Sennacherib Takes the Cities of Judah in 701 B.C. and Hezekiah Sends Tribute 18:13–16
    b. The Assyrian Rab-shakeh Warns Jerusalem Not to Listen to Hezekiah 18:17–37
    c. Hezekiah Prays and Isaiah Prophesies Deliverance 19:1–8
    d. Sennacherib's Letter: No God Ever Delivered out of His Hand 19:9–13
    e. Hezekiah Prays and Isaiah Prophesies Deliverance 19:14–34
    f. The Death Angel Kills 185,000 Assyrians; Sennacherib Assassinated 19:35–37
  3. Hezekiah's Sickness (701 B.C.) 20:1–11
    a. Isaiah Announces Hezekiah Will Die 20:1
    b. Hezekiah Prays 20:2–3
    c. Yahweh's Change of Heart and Assurance of Deliverance from Assyria 20:4–6
    d. Isaiah's Healing Poultice and Miraculous Confirmation 20:7–11
  4. Visit by Emissaries of Merodach-Baladan, King of Babylon 20:12–19
    a. Hezekiah's Prideful Display 20:12–15
    b. Isaiah's Condemnatory Prophecy 20:16–18
    c. Hezekiah's Shortsighted Response 20:19
  5. Conclusion to Hezekiah's Reign 20:20–21
B. Manasseh's Most Wicked Reign (696–686 as Co-regent; 686–641 Sole Reign) 21:1–18
C. Amon's Evil Reign (641–640) 21:19–26
D. Josiah's Righteous Reign (640–609) 22:1–23:30
  1. Book of the Law Discovered 22:1–20
  2. Reform and Religious Celebration 23:1–25
  3. Tragic Death 23:26–30
E. Jehoahaz's Evil Reign (609 B.C.) 23:31–35
F. Jehoiakim's Evil Reign (609–598 B.C.) 23:36–24:7
G. Jehoiachin's Evil Reign (597 B.C.) 24:8–17
H. Zedekiah's Evil Reign (597–586 B.C.) and Jerusalem's Fall 24:18–25:21
  1. Zedekiah's Reign and God's Anger 24:18–20:a

Overview

2. Defeat of Jerusalem and Judgment on Zedekiah 24:20b–25:7
3. The Temple Ransacked and Judahites Sent into Exile 25:8–21

I. Governorship of Gedaliah of Judah 25:22–26

1. Nebuchadnezzar Appoints Gedaliah as Governor 25:22–24
2. Gedaliah Assassinated; Judahites Flee to Egypt 25:25–26

J. Evil Merodach Releases Jehoiachin from Prison (c. 560 B.C.) 25:27–30

SUMMARY

Second Kings continues the account of Elijah and Elisha. It begins with the illness of King Ahaziah of Israel and Elijah's encounter with the king's messengers who were on their way to the shrine of Baal-Zebub the god of Ekron. Elijah told them the king would die, and sent the messengers back. Three times the king sent a captain with fifty men to bring Elijah to him. At Elijah's word, fire from heaven consumed the first two companies and their captains. The third time Elijah went to the king but did not change his message, and the king died.

At Gilgal, Elijah knew it was time for God to take him to heaven. He told Elisha to stay there, but Elisha refused to leave him and accompanied him to the Jordan River. While sons (students) of the prophets watched, Elijah rolled up his cloak, struck the waters, and they divided so that Elijah and Elisha crossed the river on dry ground. Elijah asked what he could do for Elisha before he was taken from him. Elisha asked for a double portion of Elijah's spirit (the portion of the heir) to be on him. A chariot and horses of fire then swept between them and a whirlwind carried Elijah into heaven. Elisha then rolled up Elijah's cloak and hit the waters of the Jordan. They divided and he crossed over.

This miracle caused the sons of the prophets to recognize that the spirit of Elijah rested on Elisha. However, they could not believe Elijah was taken into heaven, and they pictured Elijah dropped on some mountain or valley and insisted that they look for him. But after three days of searching, they did not find him.

Elisha continued to be the central figure in the history until his death (13:20). His miracles were outstanding. Twice as many as Elijah's are recorded (including the miracle of a dead man restored to life when his body touched Elisha's bones). God used him to teach the people and conserve the results of Elijah's ministry. Elijah had been like an evangelist, bringing the people to decisions for the LORD and against Baal. Elisha traveled around a circuit teaching the people. He was also responsible for Hazael becoming king of Syria and Jehu becoming king of Israel. Jehu went too far (cf. Hos. 1:4) and wiped out all the descendants of Omri including Ahaziah, king of Judah. This caused Athaliah, the daughter of Jezebel and the mother of Ahaziah, to usurp the throne of Judah and attempt to kill off all of the descendants of David's royal line, which would have broken God's covenant to David. But Jehosheba, who was probably the half-sister of King Ahaziah, hid his son Joash or Jehoash (whose mother was Zibiah, 12:1) in one of the side rooms of the Temple for six years. Then the priest Jehoiada had Athaliah slain and Baal's temple with its altars and priest destroyed. Thus Joash continued David's line and repaired the temple of the LORD, but after a forty-year reign was assassinated and his son Amaziah reigned.

Jehoahaz and then Jehoash continued the line of Jehu reigning over Israel. Elisha became sick, but before he died, he tried to encourage Jehoash of Israel to show an active trust in the LORD for victory over Syria. Amaziah then declared war on Israel, but Jehoash defeated him, broke down Jerusalem's wall and robbed the temple and palace of everything made of gold and silver.

The next kings, Jeroboam II of Israel and Azariah (also called Uzziah), had long and prosperous reigns. But after the time of Jeroboam, the Northern Kingdom had a rapid downfall with a series of assassinations and takeovers. Zechariah reigned only six months, Shallum reigned only one month. Menahem reigned ten years, but only over part of the land. Pul (the Babylonian name of Tiglath-pileser III) of Assyria reestablished the Assyrian Empire and demanded tribute from Menahem. Jotham and Ahaz followed Uzziah in Judah. But when Syria and Israel sought to force Judah to help them stop Assyria, Ahaz sought Assyria's aid and met Tiglath-Pileser at Damascus. After his return, he made an altar like one he saw in Damascus. After that, Shalmaneser V of Assyria made the last king of Israel, Hoshea, a tributary, but when Hoshea rebelled, Shalmaneser came, and after a three year siege, took Samaria and made Northern Israel a province of the Assyrian Empire.

In Judah, Hezekiah, the son of Ahaz, restored the worship but rebelled against Sennacherib of Assyria. Sennacherib came down in 701 B.C. and destroyed all the fortified cities of Judah except Jerusalem. Hezekiah paid heavy tribute to get him to bypass Jerusalem. God sent Isaiah to tell him he would die, but Hezekiah repented and prayed, and God relented, promising him fifteen added years of life and assuring him of deliverance from the Assyrians. This news caused Sennacherib to send his chief officer with an army to Jerusalem to demand its surrender. But the people took a stand for the LORD, and Sennacherib left without taking Jerusalem. Later, after Sennacherib destroyed Babylon in 689 B.C., he again turned westward and threatened Jerusalem by letter, where he made himself more important than any god or God. In fulfillment of Isaiah's prophecy, the death angel killed 185,000 of Sennacherib's troops, and he returned to Nineveh with the remnants of his army, never to make another military campaign. He was assassinated by his own sons in 681 B.C. (See the commentary on Isaiah for more details of this period.)

Hezekiah's son Manasseh became a very wicked king, filling Jerusalem from end to end with the innocent blood of martyrs who stood true to the LORD. His son Amon was just as bad. But the next king, Josiah, was one of the best of Judah's kings. He restored the Temple where they found the Book of the Law, made a covenant before the LORD to keep the Law and got rid of false worship. But he was killed in an attempt to stop Pharaoh Necho. The people put Jehoahaz, son of Josiah, on the throne, but the Pharaoh deposed him and made his brother Jehoiakim king. Egypt did not retain control, for Nebuchadnezzar defeated him at the battle of Carchemish (605 B.C.), one of the important turning points of ancient history. Then Nebuchadnezzar established the Babylonian Empire and took control of Judah, making Jehoiakim his vassal. Jehoiakim's son Jehoiachin rebelled against Babylon, and Nebuchadnezzar came and besieged the city. Jehoiachin surrendered (March 15/16, 597 B.C.), and was taken to Babylon along with 10,000 of the best people of Judah (including Ezekiel). Nebuchadnezzar then made Jehoiachin's uncle, Zedekiah, king. But Zedekiah rebelled, and in 586 B.C. Nebuchadnezzar destroyed the city and the temple of the LORD, slew Zedekiah's sons, blinded Zedekiah and took him with all but the poorest of the land to Babylon. He left Gedaliah as governor, but a prince, Ishmael, killed him, and the people who were left fled to Egypt (carrying Jeremiah; see commentary on Jeremiah). The Book of Kings then ends on a note telling how Evil-Merodach about 560 B.C. released Jehoiachin out of prison, honored him and gave him a pension, which he enjoyed for the rest of his life.

APPENDICES

Explanation of Grammar

Translations of the Various Versions

Books of the Old and New Testaments and the Apocrypha

How the Old Testament Came to Us

Manuscripts

Appendices

APPENDIX A

Explanation of Grammar

Explanation of Verb Stems

There are basically seven verb stems in the Hebrew language. Verbs are either active or passive, and they deal with past, present or future actions or conditions. The mood of the verb relates the general meaning, but context—the relationships of words within the literary unit—always determines the final meaning.

This volume uses a verb numbering system formatted to give (1) the word number; (2) the mood; (3) the tense; and (4) the person, gender and number. The first number is to the left of the decimal point, and the last three numbers are to the right of the decimal point. Following is a brief explanation of the numbers that occur to the right of the decimal point.

Mood (first position)

1. *Qal*—simple active verb stem. The Qal mood accounts for most of the verbs in the Old Testament. Qal usually indicates an action of the subject (*he told*). It can also indicate the state of the subject (*he was old*).

2. *Niphal*—the simple passive or reflexive counterpart of the Qal stem. Used passively, Niphal means the action of the verb is received by the subject (*he was told,* or, *it was told*). Although rare, Niphal is sometimes used reflexively, meaning that the subject performs the action of the verb upon himself or herself (*he realized*). The reflexive meaning is usually expressed using the Hithpael.

3. *Piel*—the intensive active or causative stem. The most common use of the Piel is as intensification of the action of the verb (*he often told,* or, *he fully explained*). It sometimes, however, is used in a causative sense like the Hiphil (*he caused to learn/he taught*).

4. *Pual*—the intensive passive counterpart of the Piel stem (*he was often told,* or, *he was completely informed,*or, *it was fully explained*).

5. *Hiphil*—the causative active counterpart of the Qal stem (*he caused to tell*). Sometimes it is used in a declarative sense (*he declared guilty*). Some Hiphil verbs are closer to the meaning of the simple active use of the Qal stem (*he destroyed*). Finally, some Hiphil verbs do not fit any of these categories, and they must be understood by their context.

6. *Hophal*—the causative passive counterpart of the Hiphil stem (*he was caused to tell*).

7. *Hithpael*—reflexive action (*he realized*). However, some Hithpael verbs are translated in a simple active sense like the Qal stem (*he prayed*), since the one performing the action is not transferring that action to anyone or anything else.

Tense (second position)

1. *Perfect.* The Hebrew perfect may be translated as a simple completed action (*he walked* to the store). It may also be translated as a *past perfect*, which is an action completed prior to a point of reference in past time (she gave money as *she had promised*). The perfect is translated in the present tense when the verb concerns the subject's attitude, experience, perception or

state of being (*you are old*, or, *I love you*). It may also represent action that is viewed as completed as soon as it was mentioned (*I anoint you* as king over Israel, 2 Ki. 9:3).

When this tense is used in promises, prophecies and threats, it commonly means that the action of the verb is certain and imminent (A star *will come* out of Jacob, Num. 24:17). Since this use is common in the prophetic writings, it is usually called the *prophetic perfect*. It is usually translated into English as either a present or future tense verb.

Finally, when the perfect occurs with the vav conjunctive prefixed, it is usually translated in the future tense (*I will lie down* with my fathers, Gen. 47:30).

2. *Imperfect*. This tense indicates an incomplete action or state. Perhaps the most common use of the imperfect is to describe a simple action in future time (*he will reign* over you). The imperfect is also used to express habitual or customary actions in the past, present or future (And so *he did* year by year, 1 Sam. 1:7; A son *honors* his father, Mal. 1:6; The LORD *will reign* forever and ever, Exo. 15:18). The imperfect frequently expresses contingency, and English modal auxiliaries such as *may, can, shall, might, could, should, would* and *perhaps* are used with the verb (Who is the LORD that I *should obey* his voice?, Exo. 5:2).

The modal use of the imperfect is common after the particles אֵיךְ (how) and אוּלַי (perhaps), and the interrogatives מָה (what), מִי (who) and לָמָּה (why). Two other uses of the imperfect are the *jussive* and *cohortative*.

The jussive expresses a desire for action from a third person subject (I pray *let* the king *remember* the LORD your God, 2 Sam. 14:11; *May* the LORD *lift up* his countenance unto you, Num. 6:26). The cohortative expresses the speaker's desire or intention to act, so it occurs only in the first person singular and plural (*let me pass* through the roadblock, *let us draw near* to God).

3. *Imperative*. This tense occurs only in the second person singular and plural. The main use of the imperative is in direct commands (*Separate yourself* from me, Gen. 13:9). The imperative can also grant permission (*Go up*, and *bury* your father, according as he made you swear, Gen. 50:6). It may also disclose a request (*Give* them, I pray, a talent of silver, 2 Ki. 5:22).

Imperatives may convey a wish (*May you be* the mother of thousands of millions, Gen. 24:60).

Imperatives are even used sarcastically (Come to Bethel and *transgress*, Amos 4:4).

Some uses of the imperative, however, do not carry the ordinary force of meaning. Sometimes it emphatically and vividly communicates a promise or prediction (And in the third year *sow* and *reap*, *plant* vineyards and *eat* the fruits thereof, 2 Ki. 19:29).

4. *Infinitive*. The infinitive occurs in either the absolute or the construct state. Infinitives express the idea of a verb, but they are not limited by person, gender and number.

The infinitive absolute is used in several ways. It most often stands before a finite verb of the same root to intensify the certainty or force of the verbal idea (You shall *surely* die, Gen. 2:17). It also functions as a verbal noun (*slaying* cattle and *killing* sheep, Isa. 22:13; It is not good *to eat* much honey, Prov. 25:27).

The infinitive absolute sometimes occurs after an imperative (Kill me *at once*, Num. 11:15; Listen *diligently* to me, Isa. 55:2). It may also occur after a verb to show continuance or repetition (*Keep on* hearing but do not understand, Isa. 6:9; and it went *here and there*, Gen. 8:7). Frequently, it is used in place of an imperative (*Remember[ing]* the Sabbath day, Exo. 20:8). Sometimes it is used in place of a finite verb (and he *made* him ruler over all the land of Egypt, Gen. 41:43).

The infinitive construct also has several uses. It may function as the object or subject of a sentence (I know not how *to go out* or *come in*, 1 Ki. 3:7; *to obey* is better than sacrifice, 1 Sam. 15:22). However, it most often occurs after the subject to express purpose (he turned aside *to see*, Exo. 3:4). The infinitive construct may also occur after a finite verb to express a gerundial meaning (The people sin against the LORD *by eating* blood, 1 Sam. 14:33). Moreover, it is frequently used in temporal clauses (*When you eat* from it, you shall surely die, Gen. 2:17).

5. *Participle*. This tense in the Hebrew does not indicate person, but it does indicate gender and number. It may be either masculine or feminine, and either singular or plural. Participles may also occur in either the active or passive voice. However, only the Qal stem has both active and passive participles. Verbal tense is not indicated by the Hebrew participle, so it must be inferred from the context, whether it is *past*, *present* or *future* tense. Uses of the participle include the following.

Since it is a verbal noun, a participle may indicate a continuous activity or state (I saw also the LORD *sitting* upon a throne, Isa. 6:1). Participles may also be used as attributive or predicative adjectives. As an attributive adjective, it follows the noun it modifies, and it agrees with the noun in gender, number and definiteness (blessed is *he who comes* in the name of the LORD, Ps. 118:26; the glory of the LORD was like a *devouring* fire, Exo. 24:17).

As a predicative adjective, the participle follows the noun it modifies and agrees with the noun in gender and number, but it never has the definite article (the man is *standing*, the women are *standing*). When the noun is indefinite, the participle may be attributive or predicative, so context must determine the correct translation. Participles are also used as substantives (one who climbs, *climber*; one who works, *worker*; one who loves, *lover*).

Person, Gender, and Number (third position)

Person—whether the verb is *first person* (I, we), *second person* (you) or *third person* (he, she, it, they).

Gender—whether the verb is *masculine, feminine* or *common*.

Number—whether the verb is *singular* or *plural* (Infinitives are only indicated as construct or absolute. Participles are indicated as active or passive, masculine or feminine and singular or plural).

Verb Identification Chart

Following is the verb identification chart used in this volume, for the three digits following the decimal of every verb. This pattern follows the usual verb chart found in Hebrew grammars.

First numeral after decimal:

1. Qal
2. Niphal
3. Piel
4. Pual
5. Hiphil
6. Hophal
7. Hithpael

Second numeral after decimal:

1. Perfect
2. Imperfect
3. Imperative
4. Infinitive
5. Participle

Third numeral after decimal:

Perfect	*Imperfect*	*Imperative*	*Infinitive*	*Participle*
1. 3ms	3ms	2ms	construct	active ms
2. 3fs	3fs	2fs	absolute	active mp
3. 2ms	2ms	2mp		active fs
4. 2fs	2fs	2fp		active fp
5. 1cs	1cs			passive ms
6. 3cp	3mp			passive mp
7. 2mp	3fp			passive fs
8. 2fp	2mp			passive fp
9. 1cp	2fp			
0.	1cp			

Grammatical Abbreviations*:

abs=absolute; act=active; adj=adjective; adv=adverb; art=article; c=common (neither masculine, nor feminine); cj=conjunction; con=construct (genitival); dem pron=demonstrative pronoun; do=direct object; f=feminine; impf=imperfect; impv=imperative; inf=infinitive; intrg=interrogative; intrg part=interrogative particle; intrj=interjection; juss=jussive (optative); m=masculine; n=noun; neg part=negative particle; num=number; p=plural; part=particle; pass=passive; pers pron=personal pronoun; pf=perfect; pn=proper noun; prep=preposition; ps=pronominal suffix; ptc=participle; rel part=relative particle; rel pron=relative pronoun; s=singular; sub=substantive; v=verb; 1=1st person; 2=2nd person; 3=3rd person.

*construct relationships are shown by italicizing.

APPENDIX B

Translations of the Various Versions

In order to provide the reader with a sample representation of many versions of the Old Testament, the following versions are compared with the King James Version. These versions are used as much as needed to illustrate various shades of meaning and main differences among the translations. All of the material could not be included. Rather, the best representation of the thirty-seven versions listed below has been used.

Abbreviation:	**Translation:**
Anchor	Anchor Bible Commentaries
ASV	American Standard Version
BB	Dutton's Basic Bible
Beck	An American Translation
Berkeley	Berkeley's Version in Modern English
CEV	Contemporary English Version
Darby	Darby's The Holy Scripture
Douay	The Douay Version
Fenton	Fenton's Holy Bible
Geneva	Geneva Bible
Good News	Good News, The Bible in Today's English
Goodspeed	The Bible, An American Translation by Edgar Goodspeed
GW	God's Word
JB	The Jerusalem Bible
KJVII	King James Version II
Knox	The Holy Bible
LIVB	Living Bible
MAST	The Holy Scriptures According to the Masoretic Text
MLB	Modern Language Bible
Moffatt	A New Translation of the Bible
MRB	The Modern Readers Bible
NAB	New American Bible
NASB	New American Standard Bible
NCV	New Century Version
NEB	New English Bible
NIV	New International Version
NKJV	New King James Version
NLT	The New Living Translation
NRSV	New Revised Standard Version
Phillips	The Old Testament in Modern English
REB	Revised English Bible
Rotherham	Rotherham's Emphasized Bible
RSV	Revised Standard Version
Torah	A New Translation of the Holy Scriptures According to the Traditional Hebrew Text
Tyndale	Tyndale's Old Testament
WEB	Young's Literal Translation
Young	Young's Literal Translation

APPENDIX C

Books of the Old and New Testaments and the Apocrypha

Old Testament

Genesis
Exodus
Leviticus
Numbers
Deuteronomy
Joshua
Judges
Ruth
1 Samuel
2 Samuel
1 Kings
2 Kings
1 Chronicles
2 Chronicles
Ezra
Nehemiah
Esther
Job
Psalms
Proverbs
Ecclesiastes
Song of Songs
Isaiah
Jeremiah
Lamentations
Ezekiel
Daniel
Hosea
Joel
Amos
Obadiah
Jonah
Micah
Nahum
Habakkuk
Zephaniah
Haggai
Zechariah
Malachi

New Testament

Matthew
Mark
Luke
John
Acts
Romans
1 Corinthians
2 Corinthians
Galatians
Ephesians
Philippians
Colossians
1 Thessalonians
2 Thessalonians
1 Timothy
2 Timothy
Titus
Philemon
Hebrews
James
1 Peter
2 Peter
1 John
2 John
3 John
Jude
Revelation

Books of the Apocrypha

1 & 2 Esdras
Tobit
Judith
Additions to Esther
Wisdom of Solomon
Ecclesiasticus of the Wisdom of Jesus Son of Sirach
Baruch
Prayer of Azariah and the Song of the Three Holy Children
Susanna
Bel and the Dragon
The Prayer of Manasses
Maccabees 1–4

APPENDIX D

How the Old Testament Came to Us

The Hebrew canon was written over a period of about 1000 years (1450–400 B.C.). These books were considered inspired and therefore canonical from the time they were written. The word *canon* means a "straight edge," "rod" or "ruler." It came to mean "the rule" or "the standard" of divine inspiration and authority. The only true test of canonicity is the testimony of God regarding the authority of his own Word.

Protestants and Jews have always agreed to a standard 39 books of the Old Testament as canonical, although the Jews have divided them differently to form 22, 24 or 36 books. The Roman Catholic Church, since the Council of Trent in A.D. 1546, also accepts seven books of the Apocrypha (Tobit, Judith, Wisdom, Ecclesiasticus, Baruch, 1 and 2 Maccabees, and some additions to the books of Esther and Daniel) as canonical.

We no longer have access to the infallible original manuscripts (called "the autographs") of the Hebrew Scriptures. The earliest manuscripts in some cases are a thousand years removed from the original writing. However, they constitute our primary authority as to the inspired Word of God, and all copies and orthodox translations are dependent upon the best and earliest Hebrew and Aramaic manuscripts. We must review all written evidence upon which our modern editions of the Hebrew Bible are based and have some knowledge of the wide range of evidence with which Old Testament textual criticism deals. Hebrew texts take priority in value, since God's revelation came first to Israel in the Hebrew tongue. Moreover, in the instances where very early manuscripts have been found, divine guidance is evident in the extreme accuracy of the copies.

Liberal scholars consider only the human side of the equation, thereby rejecting inspiration. From a nearly spiritually dead European church came the school of theology which developed a theory on the development of the Biblical text known as Documentary Hypothesis. Due, in particular, to the development of deistic philosophy and evolutionary science, the stage was set for literary and redaction criticism of the Bible and the rejection of the supernatural.

As a precursor, however, the humanistic philosophies developed during the Age of Enlightenment made their way into the churches of Europe, sadly producing a spiritual deadness. Consequently, every area of academics was affected, producing an antireligious stupefaction upon the milieu of the scholarly world.

With regard to the Pentateuch, the most famous of these theories is known as JEDP. Julius Wellhausen is perhaps the most famous proponent of this theory publishing his version in the 1800s.

The Documentary Hypothesis method of document analysis was used on the works of Homer, Horace and Shakespeare, as well as on works purported to have been written by them. However, it was eventually used only to attack the validity and reliability of the Bible. The "J" document is titled as such because of the use of *Yahweh* (sometimes called Jehovah), and the "E" document is titled as such because of the use of *Elohim* for God. Whether God's name or title is used, it is speculated, determines whether that section of the first Books of the Pentateuch is from the "J" or the "E" document. It is theorized that if the entire Pentateuch were written by one person, only one name would be used for God. The dozens of etymological unifying elements threaded throughout the Pentateuch are simply ignored. The "D" document is considered a *deuteronomic work*, and the "P" document is considered primarily a *priestly editorial*. Dates of these documents are set at 950 B.C. for J, 850 B.C. for E, 625 B.C. for D and 450 B.C. for P. The first five Books of the Bible, known for millennia as the Books of Moses, are viewed by JEDP theorists as four documents written over hundreds of years instead of one document written by Moses, as the Bible itself claims.

The major assumptions of the Documentary Hypothesis are (1) the guideline of divine names (Yahweh and Elohim) as evidence of diverse authorship; (2) the origin of J, E and P as separate documents, written at different periods of time; (3) the separate origin of E as distinct from J and compared prior to J; and (4) the origin of D in the reign of Josiah (621 B.C.). As referred to above, the essential purpose of the JEDP theory was to discount the miraculous and the prophetical. However, with the discovery of the Dead Sea Scrolls, this theory has been thoroughly disproven to the point that no Bible scholar who understands the Bible to be inspired can possibly subscribe to such a theory.

With regard to Isaiah, two or three separate writers are usually proposed; but theories range all the way up to nine. Once again, the so-called stylistic differences noted are merely a pretext for discounting the miraculous and the prophetical.

The Dead Sea Scrolls have clearly pointed to the unity of the Old Testament, particularly with regard to the Pentateuch and Isaiah. Moreover, the unity of each Book defends the miracles and prophecies of the Bible as genuine and thoroughly accurate.

APPENDIX E

Manuscripts

The Masoretic Text

The Masoretic Text (MT) was developed A.D. 500–950, and it gave the final form to the Old Testament. It preserved in writing the oral tradition (*masorah*) concerning correct vowels and accents, and the number of occurrences of rare words of unusual spellings.

Vowel Pointing of YHWH

Due to Jewish fears of bringing upon themselves possible retribution for breaking the third commandment, they began refusing to pronounce the divine name. This began in Nehemiah's time. It became the normal practice to substitute the title "Lord" (*adonai*) for the name Yahweh when reading aloud. The Masoretes, to indicate this replacement, inserted the vowels from *Adonai* under the consonants of YaHWeH, resulting in the word YeHoWaH, which came to be pronounced as *Jehovah*. Scholars of the Renaissance period misunderstood the purpose of this vowel pointing and began pronouncing the name as *Jehovah*, rather than pronouncing the name *Yahweh* or the title *Adonai*. This erroneous pronunciation became so common that many are still generally unwilling to accept the more correct pronunciation, Yahweh.

Qere Kethib

The terms are used to refer to textual variants that are understood, though not written. The word *qere* means "what is read," and the word *kethib* means "what is written." (Hence, "read for what is written.") One classic example of a *qere kethib* is mentioned in the preceding paragraph. Although the text has *written* Yahweh, Adonai is *read*, the hearers understanding what was meant by the reader. *Qere kethibs* were marginal notes written to the side of the manuscript.

The Masoretes

The Masoretes deserve much credit for their painstaking care in preserving the consonantal text that was entrusted to them. They devoted greater attention to accurately preserving the Hebrew Scriptures than has ever been given to any ancient literature in human history. They left the consonantal text exactly as it was given to them, refusing to make even the most obvious corrections. The work of the Masoretes has preserved for us a text which essentially duplicates the text considered authoritative at the time of Christ. Moreover, the Qumran evidence is that we have a Hebrew text with a true record of God's revelation.

The Major Codices

1. British Museum Oriental 4445—a copy of the Pentateuch consonantal text (A.D. 850), vowel points added one century later, most of Genesis and Deuteronomy missing.

2. Codex Cairensus (C)—former prophets and latter prophets, copied by Aaron ben Asher (A.D. 895).

3. Leningrad MS—latter prophets (A.D. 916).

4. Leningrad MS B-19A—entire Old Testament, contains Ben Asher Masoretic Text (A.D. 1010), faithful copy of A.D. 980 MS (since lost), basis for Kittel's *Biblia Hebraica* (3rd edition and subsequent editions).

5. Samaritan Pentateuch—earliest MSS of this version is still in Nablus, withheld by Samaritan sectarians from publication, about 6,000 variants from MT (mostly spelling differences), contains biased sectarian insertions, no MS of the Samaritan Pentateuch known to be older than tenth century A.D.

6. Bologna Edition of the Psalter—A.D. 1477.

7. Soncino Edition of the Old Testament—(vowel-pointed) A.D. 1488.

8. Second Bomberg Edition of the Old Testament—(A.D. 1525–26) printed under the patronage of Daniel Bomberg, became basis for all modern editions up to 1929; contains text of Jacob ben Chayim, with Masorah and Rabbinical notes.

The Qumran Manuscripts

The Qumran manuscripts, or Dead Sea Scrolls, were discovered in a series of caves near the canyon of Wadi Qumran, along the northwest coast of the Dead Sea.

Technical identification of these documents consists of: (1) a number specifying which of the caves was the scene of the discovery of the document, (2) an abbreviation of the name of the book itself and (3) a superscript letter indicating the order in which the manuscript came to light, as opposed to other copies of the same book.

Thus, the famous Dead Sea Scroll of Isaiah is labeled 1 QIsa, meaning that it was the first discovered, or most important, manuscript of Isaiah found in Cave 1 at Wadi Qumran. This particular discovery severely damaged any theories of multiple authorship. The following is a list of the most important finds at Wadi Qumran.

1. Dead Sea Scroll of Isaiah (1QIsa)—(150-100 B.C.) entire sixty-six chapters, same family of MS as MT.

2. Habakkuk Commentary (1QpHb)—(100-50 B.C.) chapters one and two only, with commentary notes between verses; commentary is usually concerned with how each verse is fulfilled in recent (Hasmonean) history and current events.

3. Hebrew University Isaiah Scroll (1QIsb)—(copied ca. 50 B.C.) substantial portions of chapters 41–66, closer to MT than 1QIsa is.

4. 1Q Leviticus fragments—(fourth or second century B.C.) a few verses each of chapters 19–22, written in paleo-Hebrew script.

5. 4Q Deuteronomy-B—32:41–43, written in hemistichs as poetry, not as prose, no date suggested.

6. 4Q Samuel-A—1 Samuel 1, 2, twenty-seven fragments (first century B.C.).

7. 4Q Samuel-B—1 Samuel 16, 19, 21, 23 (225 B.C. or earlier).

8. 4Q Jeremiah-A (no date suggested).

9. 4Q XII-A (XII signifies a MS of the minor prophets)—(third century B.C.) cursive script.

10. 4Q Qoha—(second century B.C.) cursive text of Ecclesiastes, derived from a source that is at least third century B.C. or earlier.

11. 4Q Exodus—a fragment of chapter 1.

12. 4Q Exodus—portions of chapters 7, 29, 30, 32 (and perhaps others), written in paleo-Hebrew script.

13. 4Q Numbers—written in square Hebrew with Samaritan type expansions (after 27:33 there is an insert derived from Deuteronomy 3:21).

14. 4Q Deuteronomy-A—chapter 32 (Song of Moses).

15. 11Q Psalms—a manuscript of Psalms from cave 11, copied in formal bookhand style of the Herodian period, the bottom third of each page has been lost, thirty-three Psalms are preserved with fragments containing portions of four others, Psalms represented are 93, 101–103, 105, 109, 118, 119, 121–130, 132–146, 148–150, and 151 from the LXX.

16. Nash Papyrus—(100–50 B.C.) contains the Decalogue and the Shema (Exo. 20:1–17 and Deut. 6:4–9), purchased by W. L. Nash from an Egyptian antique dealer.

The Aramaic Targums

The word Targum means "interpretation," and these documents became necessary because the Hebrew people lost touch with their ancestral Hebrew during the Babylonian exile and Persian empire period. First there was a need for an interpreter in the synagogue services, and later the interpretations were written down. However, there is no evidence of a written Targum until about A.D. 200. Because their primary purpose was for interpretation, they have limited value for textual criticism. Following is a list of several targums:

1. The Targum of Onkelos on the Torah—(ca. third century A.D.) produced by Jewish scholars in Babylon. Traditionally assigned to a certain Onkelos, supposedly a native of Pontus. It is not quoted by extant Palestinian sources earlier than A.D. 1000.

2. The Targum of Jonathan ben Uzziel on the Prophets section (i.e., Joshua–Kings, Isaiah–Malachi)—(fourth century A.D.) composed in Babylonian circles. Far more free in its rendering of the Hebrew text than in Onkelos.

3. The Targum of Pseudo-Jonathan on the Torah—(ca. A.D. 650) a mixture of Onkelos and Midrashic materials.

4. The Jerusalem Targum on the Torah—(ca. A.D. 700).

The Septuagint (LXX)

This is the Greek translation of the Hebrew Old Testament. It was translated for Greek-speaking Jews who knew no Hebrew. It is called the LXX because it was said to have been translated by seventy, or more accurately seventy-two, Jewish scholars. This was the common Bible of New Testament times, and it is quoted frequently in the New Testament. However, Matthew and the author of Hebrews follow a text that is closer to the MT. We must remember that the Septuagint is a translation of inspired Scripture, not the original or even a copy of the original. As such, it is subject to error as is any other translation.

It should also be noted, however, that the translators of the Septuagint were highly skilled to translate an accurate Greek Old Testament that could be depended upon by the New Testament writers for quotations and by early Christians for use. When all of the Greek manuscripts are compared with the Hebrew manuscripts, a rather high degree of textual certainty exists in spite of some difficulties.

Bibliography

Aharoni, Yohanan. *The Archeology of the Land of Israel: From the Pre-historic Beginnings to the End of the First Temple Period*. translated by Anson F. Rainey. Philadelphia: The Westminster Press, 1982.

Aharoni, Yohanan. *The Land of the Bible: A Historical Geography*, rev. Philadelphia: The Westminster Press, 1979.

Aharoni, Yohanan, Michael Avi-yonah, Anson F. Rainey, and Ze'ev Safrai. *The Macmillan Bible Atlas*, rev. 3rd ed. New York: Macmillan Publishing Co., 1993.

Albright, W. F. "Chronology," Bulletin of the American Schools of Oriental Research, 100 [1945], 16–22.

Allis, Oswald T. *The Old Testament: Its Claims and its Critics*. Philadelphia: Presbyterian and Reformed Publishing Company, 1972.

Amerding, Carl E. *The Old Testament and Criticism*. Grand Rapids, MI: William B. Eerdmans Publishing Company, 1984.

Archer, Gleason L. *Encyclopedia of Bible Difficulties*. Grand Rapids, MI: Zondervan Publishing House, 1982.

Archer, Gleason L. *A Survey of Old Testament Introduction*, rev. ed. Chicago: Moody Press, 1974.

Barker, Kenneth, gen. ed. *The NIV Study Bible: New International Version*. Grand Rapids, MI: Zondervan Bible Publishers, 1985.

Beitzel, Barry J. *The Moody Atlas of Bible Lands*. Chicago: Moody Press, 1985.

Blaiklock, Edward M. and R. H. Harrison, eds. *The New International Dictionary of Biblical Archeology*. Grand Rapids, MI: Zondervan Publishing House, 1983.

Bromiley, Geoffrey W. ed. *The International Standard Bible Encyclopedia,* 4 vols. Grand Rapids, MI: William B. Eerdmans Publishing Company, 1979.

Brown, Francis, S.R. Driver, Charles A. Briggs. *The New Brown-Driver-Briggs-Gesenius Hebrew and English Lexicon*. Peabody, MA: Hendrickson Publishers, 1979.

Craigie, Peter C. *Ugarit and the Old Testament*. Grand Rapids, MI: William B. Eerdmans Publishing Company, 1985.

Davis, John D. *The Westminster Dictionary of the Bible*, rev. by Henry Snyder Gehman. Philadelphia: The Westminster Press, 1944.

Douglas, J. D., ed. *New Bible Dictionary*. Wheaton, IL: Tyndale House Publishers, Inc., 1962.

Eissfedlt, Otto. *The Old Testament, an Introduction*. Translated by Ackroyd. New York: Harper, 1965.

Even-Shoshan, Abraham, ed. *A New Concordance of the Old Testament Using the Hebrew and Aramaic Text*. Grand Rapids, MI: Baker Book House, 1990.

Finegan, Jack. *Light from the Ancient Past: The Archaeological Background of Judaism and Christianity*, 2nd ed. Princeton: Princeton University Press, 1959.

Freedman, David N. *Pottery, Poetry, and Prophecy*. Winona Lake, IN: Eisenbrauns, 1980.

Freedman, Noel David, ed. *The Anchor Bible Dictionary*, 6 vols. New York: Doubleday, 1992.

Gaebelein, Frank E., ed. *The Expositor's Bible Commentary*, 12 vols., John H. Sailhamer, Walter C. Kaiser, Jr., R. Laird Harris, Ronald B. Allen. Grand Rapids, MI: Zondervan Publishing House, 1990.

Gottwald, Norman K. *The Hebrew Bible—a Socio-Literary Introduction*. Philadelphia: Fortress Press, 1985.

Harris, R. Laird. *Inspiration and Canonicity of the Bible*. Grand Rapids, MI: Zondervan Publishing House, 1957.

Harris, R. Laird, Gleason L. Archer, Jr. and Bruce K. Waltke, eds. *Theological Wordbook of the Old Testament*, 2 Vols. Chicago: Moody Press, 1980.

Harrison, R. K., B. K. Waltke, D. Guthrie, G. D. Fee. *Biblical Criticism: Historical, Literary and Textual*. Grand Rapids, MI: Zondervan Publishing House, 1980.

Harrison, R. K. *Old Testament Times*. Grand Rapids, MI: William B. Eerdmans Publishing Company, 1970.

Holladay, William L. *A Concise Hebrew and Aramaic Lexicon of the Old Testament*. Grand Rapids, MI: William B. Eerdmans Publishing Company, 1971.

Horton, Stanley M., ed. *Systematic Theology*. Springfield, MO: Logion Press, 1994.

Humphreys, W. Lee. *Crisis and Story: An Introduction to the Old Testament*. Mountain View, CA: Mayfield Publishing Co., 1990.

Jennings, F. C. *Studies in Isaiah*. Neptune, NJ: Loizeaux Brothers, 1935, 1970.

Johns, Alger F. *A Short Grammar of Biblical Aramaic*. Berrien Springs, MI: Andrews University Press, 1963.

Kaiser, Walter C., Jr. *Toward an Old Testament Theology*. Grand Rapids, MI: Acadamie Books, 1978.

Kautzch, E. and A. E. Cowley, eds. *Gesenius' Hebrew Grammar*. Oxford: Clarendon Press, 1910.

Keil, C. F. and F. Delitzsch. *Commentary on the Old Testament*. translated by James Martin. Peabody, MA: Hendrickson Publishers, 1989.

Bibliography

Keller, Werner. *The Bible as History*, 2nd rev. ed. translated by William Neil and B. H. Rasmussen. New York: Bantam Books, 1982.

Kelley, Page H. *Biblical Hebrew: An Introductory Grammar*. Grand Rapids, MI: William B. Eerdmans Publishing Company, 1992.

Kitchen, K. A. *The Bible in its World: The Bible and Archaeology Today*. Exeter: Paternoster Press, 1977.

Koehler, Ludwig and Walter Baumgartner. *The Hebrew and Aramaic Lexicon of the Old Testament*, 4 vols. Leiden, Netherlands: E. J. Brill, 1994.

Lasor, William Sanford, David Allan Hubbard, Frederic William Bush. *Old Testament Survey: The Message, Form, and Background of The Old Testament*. Grand Rapids, MI: William B. Eerdmans Publishing Company, 1992.

LaSor, William, David Allan Hubbard, and Frederic William Bush. *Old Testament Survey: The Message, Form, and Background of The Old Testament*. 2nd ed. Grand Rapids, MI: William B. Eerdmans Publishing Co., 1996.

Leupold, H. C. *Exposition of The Psalms*. Grand Rapids, MI: Baker Book House, 1969.

Lewis, C. S. *Reflections on the Psalms*. London: Geoffrey Bles, 1958.

Luckenbill, D. D. *Ancient Records of Assyria and Babylonia*, 2 vols. Chicago: The University of Chicago Press, 1926-1927.

MacLaren, Alexander. The Expositor's Bible: Psalms. New York: A. C. Armstrong & Son, 1890. [Adapted for the Psalms Commentary.]

Martens, Elmer A. *God's Design: A Focus on Old Testament Theology*. Grand Rapids, MI: Baker Book House, 1986.

Mays, James L. *Psalms*. (Interpretation). Louisville: John Knox Press, 1994.

Merrill, Eugene H. *An Historical Survey of the Old Testament*. Nutley, NJ: The Craig Press, 1966.

Miller, J. Maxwell and John H. Hayes. *A History of Ancient Israel and Judah*. Philadelphia: The Westminster Press, 1986.

New Interpreter's Bible. Nashville, TN: Abingdon Press, 1994.

Owens, John Joseph. *Analytical Key to the Old Testament*, 4 vols. Grand Rapids, MI: Baker Book House, 1990.

Payne, J. Barton. *The Theology of the Older Testament*. Grand Rapids, MI: Academie Books, 1962.

Petersen, David L., Kent Harold Richards. *Interpreting Hebrew Poetry*. Minneapolis: Fortress Press, 1992.

Pfeiffer, Charles F., ed. *Baker's Bible Atlas*. Grand Rapids, MI: Baker Book House, 1961.

Pfeiffer, Charles F. *Old Testament History*. Grand Rapids, MI: Baker Book House, 1987.

Pfeiffer, Charles F., Howard F. Vos, John Rea, eds. *Wycliffe Bible Encyclopedia*, 2 Vols. Chicago: Moody Press, 1975.

Pritchard, James B., ed. *The Ancient Near East: An Anthology of Texts and Pictures*, vol. 1. Princeton: Princeton University Press, 1973.

Purkiser, W. T., ed. *Exploring the Old Testament*. Kansas City, MO: Beacon Hill Press, 1955.

Rahlfs, Alfred, ed. *Septuaginta*. Stuttgart, Germany: Deutsche Bibelgesellschaft Stuttgart, 1935.

Rogerson, John and Philip Davies. *The Old Testament World*. Englewood Cliffs, NJ: Prentice-Hall, 1989.

Schoville, Keith N. *Biblical Archaeology in Focus*. Grand Rapids, MI: Baker Book House, 1982.

Schultz, Samuel J. *The Old Testament Speaks*. New York: Harper & Brothers, Publishers, 1960.

Seow, Choon Leong. *A Grammar for Biblical Hebrew*. Nashville, TN: Abingdon Press, 1987.

Shanks, Hershel, ed. Ancient Israel: *A Short History from Abraham to the Roman Destruction of the Temple*. Englewood Cliffs, NJ: Prentice-Hall, 1988.

Smith, George Adam. *The Historical Geography of the Holy Land*. London: Hodder and Stoughton, 1931.

Soulen, Richard N. *Handbook of Biblical Criticism*. Atlanta: John Knox Press, 1978.

Stuart, Douglas K. *Studies in early Hebrew meter*. Missoula, MT: Scholars Press, 1976.

Tyndale Old Testament Commentary, Downers Grove, IL: Inter-Varsity, 1925–.

Van Der Woude, A. S., ed., *The World of the Old Testament*. translated by Sierd Woudstra. Grand Rapids, MI: William B. Eerdmans Publishing Company, 1989.

Waltke, Bruce K. and M. O'Connor. *An Introduction to Biblical Hebrew Syntax*. Winona Lake, IN: Eisenbrauns, 1990.

Watts, John D.W. *The Word Biblical Commentary on the Old Testament*, 34 vols. Waco, TX: Word Books, 1987.

Watts, J. Wash. *Old Testament Teaching*. Nashville, TN: Broadman Press, 1967.

White, Wilbert Webster. *Studies in Old Testament Characters*. New York: The Biblical Seminary in New York, 1931.